MW01231764

THE
FOREIGN CORRUPT
PRACTICES ACT
HANDBOOK

A Practical Guide for
Multinational General Counsel,
Transactional Lawyers and
White Collar Criminal Practitioners

Robert W. Tarun

FOURTH EDITION

AMERICAN BAR ASSOCIATION
Defending Liberty
Pursuing Justice

Praise for THE FOREIGN CORRUPT PRACTICES ACT HANDBOOK: A PRACTICAL GUIDE FOR MULTINATIONAL GENERAL COUNSEL, TRANSACTIONAL LAWYERS AND WHITE COLLAR CRIMINAL PRACTITIONERS from New York, Silicon Valley, Washington, D.C., London, Chicago, Birmingham, Boston, Houston, Indianapolis, San Francisco, Toronto, and Shanghai.

"This is a must read for any lawyer handling FCPA matters. It is a comprehensive and well written book by one of the country's outstanding white-collar criminal lawyers." —**Robert S. Bennett, Partner, Hogan Lovells LLP, Washington, D.C.**

"In order to operate successfully, international companies must be alert to and effectively manage a number of key risk areas including the Foreign Corrupt Practices Act and the UK Bribery Act. To assist these companies in meeting their ethical and legal responsibilities, Bob Tarun, one of the most accomplished white-collar criminal lawyers in the United States, has now updated and expanded his supremely valuable *Foreign Corrupt Practices Act Handbook*, which was first published in 2010. I found Mr. Tarun's new *Handbook*, which is over 1,100 pages in length, to be even better than his original. This *Handbook* is very well organized, comprehensive, scholarly, well written, and surprisingly easy to navigate. In addition to setting forth in the *Handbook* all the relevant legal requirements and potential liabilities in the anti-corruption area, Mr. Tarun also gives the reader dozens of valuable observations, insights, and practical compliance suggestions. Every attorney at any level of experience who works in the international arena will benefit tremendously by having a copy of Mr, Tarun's *Handbook* within arms length of their desk."—**Jay G. Martin, Vice President, Chief Compliance Officer, and Senior Deputy General Counsel, Baker Hughes, Houston**

"Bob Tarun first taught me about the FCPA 14 years ago, when I was a student in his *White Collar Criminal Practice* course at the University of Chicago Law School—a truly exceptional course that inspired me to become an anti-corruption attorney. Mr. Tarun continues to share his deep knowledge of the FCPA and related anti-corruption laws in the third edition of *The Foreign Corrupt Practices Act Handbook*, which contains over 1,100 pages of practical guidance that is grounded in reality and easy to understand. *The Foreign Corrupt Practices Act Handbook* provides solutions across the full spectrum of anti-corruption issues and, as my dog-eared copies of the prior editions attest, is a must-have tool for any anti-corruption attorney. The fourth edition is an invaluable anti-corruption resource that will stay on your desk, not in your bookcase."—**Trent J. Sandifur, FCPA and International Anti-Corruption Practice Area Leader, Taft Stettinius & Hollister LLP, Indianapolis**

"Bob Tarun's book is both a highly accessible and deeply authoritative treatment of the FCPA. It has been invaluable to me, as a practitioner, on several occasions. UK and European lawyers will especially appreciate the way in which the main concepts behind the legislation are explained early, in a thoughtful and comprehensive 'overview' section. The key issue of jurisdiction is also explained straightforwardly and from first principles. As well as detailed legal analysis, the book contains a multitude of practical advice on 'real world' issues and is complemented by very useful appendices containing source material."—**Eoin O'Shea, Lawrence Graham, London**

"No one knows the Foreign Corrupt Practice Act better than Bob Tarun. Bob's book is a valuable reference guide for all FCPA practitioners and is a must read for all."—**Lori-Ann Beausoleil, Forensic Partner, PwC Canada and Steven Henderson, Forensic Partner, PwC Canada, Toronto**

"One of the most experienced practitioners in the field, Bob Tarun delivers exactly what his title promises: a practical guide to the FCPA. This is the best FCPA book in my library, and I have them all." —**Peter B. Clark, Partner, Cadwalader, Wickersham & Taft LLP, Former Deputy Chief, Fraud Section, U.S. Department of Justice 1977–2005, Washington, D.C.**

"We have found Bob Tarun to be an invaluable resource in our assisting both corporate and private equity clients in evaluating the complexities of the FCPA and related compliance issues for portfolio companies and transactions throughout Asia. Having worked in various interim management, restructuring and investigative matters throughout Asia, Bob's book has served as an excellent reference source as it captures his specific, hands on experience across multiple issues and countries in Asia."—**Michael Murphy and Brent Carlson, AlixPartners, Asia**

"The fourth edition of *The Foreign Corrupt Practices Act Handbook* is the ultimate security blanket for any practitioner who needs to understand how this important federal criminal statute works and the practical measures needed to assist a client. Its well-organized format provides ready access to the major issues and questions that often require quick responses. Bob Tarun's immense investigative and trial experience on behalf of numerous clients faced with FCPA and international corruption issues permeates the real-world strategies and solutions provided in the 1,100-page fourth edition. Both seasoned practitioners and novices should turn to the newly revised *Foreign Corrupt Practices Act Handbook* as the first place to look when such issues need to be addressed."—**Vincent J. Connelly, Co-Chair White Collar Criminal Practice, Mayer Brown LLP, Chicago**

"An exceptional resource for the forensic accounting professional, Bob Tarun's book is an essential for any professional seeking to better understand the FCPA in real world applications. Whether evaluating potential violations, considering practical compliance measures or gaining an appreciation of the evolving issues in FCPA enforcement, Bob provides thoughtful insights and practical suggestions evident of his significant experience with all aspects of the FCPA. This book should be required reading for any professional working in FCPA matters."—**John LaBella, Director, AlixPartners LLC, San Francisco**

"With its comprehensive analysis of potential FCPA liabilities and sound practical suggestions as to how to deal with them, this book is a very valuable asset for both unseasoned and seasoned FCPA practitioners." —**Robert B. Fiske, Jr., Senior Partner, Davis Polk & Wardwell LLP, New York**

"Increasingly aggressive enforcement of the Foreign Corrupt Practices Act during the past 10 years has spawned an entire industry of counselors and investigators—many with limited experience and a few with broad and deep experience, possessing insights founded in experience and practice. There have also been many articles and books written on compliance with the FCPA, most looking the same in addressing the requirements and interpretation of the Act, but lacking the sound, thorough practical advice that corporate counsel need to address both general and specific strategic issues—whether in the early stages of investigation triage or in final negotiations with prosecutors and regulators.

"In this industry, Bob Tarun stands out—he has a firm grasp of the practical application of the FCPA based upon his hands-on experience as an investigator of alleged misconduct in over 50 countries, a federal prosecutor, a nationally recognized white-collar criminal defense lawyer, and most recently, an independent corporate monitor in Asia. He truly understands how companies operate and what will—and won't—work in different business environments. The first edition of the *FCPA Handbook* was the first book to provide a comprehensive investigative and reference text for not only practitioners but also their audience—companies struggling with proactive and reactive compliance with the Act and challenging investigations. The fourth edition expands the advice and coverage of the prior two and further succeeds in crossing the chasm between a technical reference text and a highly practical FCPA investigative and defense guide. The 1,100-page fourth edition is a must-have book that should be on the desk of anyone wishing to understand today's application of the Foreign Corrupt Practices Act as well as the direction prosecutors and regulators are moving in international anticorruption enforcement."—**Joe Zier, retired Partner and Silicon Valley FCPA Practice Chair, Deloitte Financial Advisory Services LLP, Silicon Valley**

"Bob Tarun brings a wealth of experience and common sense to a challenging area of the law. His sensible advice addresses all aspects of FCPA and corruption practice and is applicable throughout the globe. Drawing upon his substantial international experience, Tarun identifies the critical issues about which all lawyers and investigators covering this field should be aware. His deep understanding of the relevant issues enables him to explain complicated technical concepts and procedures in a way that is understandable and compelling. In this fourth edition, Tarun analyzes the most recent cases and identifies trends currently adopted by prosecutors and regulators. Armed with Tarun's insights and suggested approaches, investigators and lawyers can manage cases in this highly charged area with confidence. Failing to take advantage of this resource would be a mistake." —**Lisa Kate Osofsky, Regulatory Advisor, European Chair, Exiger Limited, London, and former Deputy General Counsel, Federal Bureau of Investigation, Washington, D.C.**

"An indispensable guide for FCPA practitioners. Bob Tarun achieves a distinctive blend of scholarly analysis with sage practical advice in one invaluable package."
—**Bruce Singal, Donoghue Barrett & Singal, Boston**

"Whether used to refresh basic concepts, guide compliance program enhancements, plot a course for interfacing with enforcement agencies, or to better understand the contours of the broad range of anti-corruption issues, *The Foreign Corrupt Practices Act Handbook* is a critical component to formulating and dispensing practical advice to clients. Bob Taurn's mastery of the subject matter and wealth of real-world experience shines through in every chapter of this invaluable resource. You can be an FCPA lawyer without a dog-eared copy of his book in your library, but you'll be a much better one with it."—**Bill Athanas, Waller Lansden Dortch & Davis, LLP, Birmingham, Alabama**

Cover by ABA Publishing.

The materials contained herein represent the opinions of the authors and editors, and should not be construed to be the views or opinions of the law firms or companies with whom such persons are in partnership with, associated with, or employed by, nor of the American Bar Association or the ABA Publishing Section unless adopted pursuant to the bylaws of the Association.

Nothing contained in this book is to be considered as the rendering of legal advice for specific cases, and readers are responsible for obtaining such advice from their own legal counsel. This book is intended for educational and informational purposes only.

Printed in the United States of America.

19 18 17 16 15   5 4 3 2 1

Library of Congress Cataloging-in-Publication Data

Tarun, Robert W., 1949- author.
    [Foreign Corrupt Practices Act]
    The Foreign Corrupt Practices Act handbook : a practical guide for multinational general counsel, transactional lawyers, and white collar criminal practitioners / authored by Robert W. Tarun.—Fourth Edition.
        pages cm
Includes bibliographical references and index.
    ISBN 978-1-63425-155-6 (print : alk. paper)
    1. Corporations—Corrupt practices—United States. 2. United States. Foreign Corrupt Practices Act of 1977. 3. Bribery—United States. 4. International business enterprises—Law and legislation—United States—Criminal provisions. 5. Great Britain. Bribery Act 2010. I. Title.
    KF9351.T37 2015
    345.73'02323—dc23

                                                                                2015014075

Discounts are available for books ordered in bulk. Special consideration is given to state bars, CLE programs, and other bar-related organizations. Inquire at ABA Publishing, American Bar Association, 321 North Clark Street, Chicago, Illinois 60654-7598.

www.ShopABA.org

This book is dedicated to my children
Abigail, Aimee, Parker, and Tyler

Contents

Preface

Enforcement of the Foreign Corrupt Practices Act (FCPA) in the past decade has increased dramatically. The United States Department of Justice (DOJ) and the Securities and Exchange Commission (SEC) are reportedly conducting over 150 investigations of U.S. and foreign companies,[1] their joint ventures, employees, and third-party contractors for alleged improper payments around the world. There is no reason to believe this trend will subside here in the United States or elsewhere. Indeed, there is now clear momentum and a clear incentive among foreign governments to investigate bribery and related conduct under various international conventions.

The era of mysterious "one man" consultancies, extravagant behind-the-curtain gifts to foreign officials, minimal due diligence of foreign agents, and willful blindness to the conduct of joint venture partners has been coming to a close. Corporate directors and officers can no longer ignore or rationalize unusually large foreign sales budgets, lucrative consultancies, or extravagant entertainment with shadowy or unknown figures with the words, "This is the way business is done in that part of the world." While there remain some lax foreign states that knowingly permit their citizens to engage in corrupt practices in distant countries, they are a minority, their world is shrinking, and they will likely have to reform if they wish to remain members of an increasingly transparent international business community. Transparency has become the governing watchword in multinational mergers, acquisitions, joint ventures, and corporate transactions.

Increased FCPA and anticorruption enforcement means increased responsibilities for boards of directors, general counsel, and transactional lawyers—and new and uncharted waters for white-collar criminal prosecutors and defense lawyers. "Preventative law" in the form of proactive counseling and director, officer, and employee training is the smart way for corporations to manage risk in an area where missteps can be very costly. Quality antibribery and record-keeping training along with regular monitoring and recorded due diligence on the front end of mergers, acquisitions, joint ventures, and third-party contracts can minimize criminal liability and avoid lengthy investigations, serious fines and disgorgement, substantial legal fees, and damage to corporate and executive reputations. There is no substitute for live antibribery training of senior officers and employees responsible for foreign sales, finance, and accounting. As important, thorough preacquisition due diligence may be the most compelling defense and route to avoid costly successor criminal liability.

Over five years ago, Professor Julie R. O'Sullivan of Georgetown Law Center observed:

> FCPA work is a vital area of white-collar criminal practice because lawyers are consulted not just when a potentially corrupt payment is uncovered by the government, but also at every stage leading up to that point. Thus, FCPA practitioners consult with companies, among

other things: on how to put in place systems to prevent such violations; on companies' potential exposure under the FCPA were they to engage in proposed mergers, acquisitions, joint ventures, contracts, consulting arrangements, and the like; on structuring transactions and contracts to avoid FCPA problems; on whether and how to conduct a corporate investigation of allegations of wrongdoing; on how to avoid an enforcement action by the SEC or a criminal prosecution by the Justice Department; and on how to settle or litigate such cases if they are brought.

The challenge of [an] FCPA practice lies in part in the fact that there is little in the way of public precedents on the subject, and the FCPA itself is complex and, in many areas, vague. Much of this practice is conducted under the legal waterline: "success" means that counsel has put in place an effective system to avoid FCPA problems or, if such problems arise, has dealt with the matter in such a way as to avoid any governmental interest or enforcement. Thus, FCPA practitioners' expertise depends more on experience in similar cases and consultations among lawyers who do FCPA work than on reading law reports. The practice is also extremely challenging for many of the reasons that white-collar practice in general is challenging, including the potential that a client will be facing potential liability on a number of fronts simultaneously (civil enforcement action, criminal prosecution, private or shareholder litigation, etc.).[2]

The Foreign Corrupt Practices Act Handbook is based on 30 years' experience of working with and representing multinational companies in sensitive payment investigations, as well as sharing best practices and compliance ideas with corporate counselors and white-collar criminal lawyers. Its guidance stems from investigating and prosecuting white-collar crimes for a decade and defending the often misunderstood in the same vineyard for thrice as long. This book is intended, above all, to be a *practical* resource for three audiences—general counsel, transactional lawyers, and white-collar criminal lawyers—not a treatise detailing legislative history or domestic bribery precedent nor a definitive compilation of every FCPA investigation, prosecution, or enforcement action ever brought. This handbook is also not intended to serve as a substitute for corporate counsel regularly consulting FCPA experts or retaining experienced criminal defense counsel to assist or represent their companies in significant anticorruption investigations. Because there are few cases directly interpreting the FCPA and because the statute is complex, this handbook necessarily offers interpretation of the FCPA's unique, broad, and often undefined terms and the 150-plus DOJ plea agreements and SEC settlements with companies and individuals in the past decade.

Chapter 1 covers the elements and defenses under the FCPA's antibribery regime and its accounting provisions—record-keeping and internal controls—that also subject companies and individuals to criminal liability. The chapter also addresses conspiracy and other offenses often charged in FCPA prosecutions as well as the potential penalties, fines, and other sanctions. It discusses the five-year statute of limitations and the three-year suspension available to the DOJ to secure foreign evidence, FCPA opinion releases, and the collateral litigation that may follow FCPA investigations and prosecutions.

Chapters 2 and 3 examine the expansive jurisdiction of the FCPA and other antibribery conventions, including the increasingly important 1997 Organization for Economic and Cooperative Development (OECD) Anti-Bribery Convention. Chapter 4 reviews the important responsibilities of boards of directors and how compliance programs of multinational companies can be tailored to FCPA and related issues. It also examines the Avon Products corporate governance issues. Live FCPA training of multinational officers and key employees in high-risk countries is arguably the most important component of an effective compliance program. Chapter 5 covers the frequent transactional third-party issues that have resulted in many FCPA prosecutions and enforcement actions involving agents, consultants, subcontractors, distributors, and joint venture partners. It also addresses the importance of conducting risk assessments for foreign acquisitions, identifies 15 key FCPA risks, lists documents necessary for a quality review, and emphasizes that a thorough acquisition due diligence record is the best defense to successor liability. Chapter 6 addresses gift, travel, lodging, and entertainment issues and the importance of securing quality written legal opinions from experienced FCPA counsel. Chapter 7 discusses and offers practical advice on the potentially thorny issues of foreign charitable donations and political contributions.

Chapter 8 is dedicated to conducting FCPA investigations and discusses disclosure and cooperation options, reflecting the fact that today many management teams, boards, or audit committees elect to conduct thorough bribery investigations, implement constructive remedial measures, and voluntarily disclose and cooperate with the hope of obtaining substantial credit from the DOJ and SEC. While managements may elect in the wake of misconduct to promptly discipline employees, institute reforms, and improve internal controls, the imposition of mammoth, crippling fines on cooperative public companies, particularly during a global recession, too often punishes innocent shareholders and jeopardizes the jobs of tens of thousands of decent employees. Chapter 8 recommends a five-step investigative process first outlined over 20 years ago in WEBB, TARUN, AND MOLO, CORPORATE INTERNAL INVESTIGATIONS (Law Journal Press 1993–2015). The template has in large part stood the test of time and sensitive investigations in over 55 countries. This chapter includes a revised sample working chronology and interview outline for a hypothetical FCPA scenario to illustrate and record key components of the investigation process.

Chapter 9 focuses on the defense of companies and individuals that are the subjects and targets of DOJ investigations. It covers the DOJ and SEC charging criteria and lists 30 potential defenses to FCPA charges. The chronology and type of interview outline discussed in Chapter 8 are equally applicable and important to coordinating an aggressive defense of corporations or their officers.

Chapter 10 summarizes over 155 significant DOJ and SEC foreign bribery and FCPA accounting provision cases—a list certain to grow in the coming decade—and highlights a variety of effective remedial measures to combat improper payment schemes. Because there is little FCPA case law, practitioners are guided by the challenging statutory language and legislative history, but also by the DOJ and FCPA resolutions and FCPA opinions issued in the past decade. This chapter gives counsel practical advice on how to interpret FCPA settlements and strategize the legal and factual challenges of an FCPA investigation.

Chapter 11 is devoted to explaining three important sections of the United Kingdom Bribery Act 2010: the foreign official bribery section; the failure of a corporation to prevent bribery by an employee, agent, or subsidiary—a strict liability offense; and the "adequate procedures" defense available to corporations. It addresses each of the six principles that inform "adequate procedures." In addition, this chapter addresses corporate criminal liability as well as voluntary disclosure, corporate prosecution guidance, bribery sentencing guidance, the new deferred prosecution agreement statute, and Transparency International U.K.'s antibribery transaction due diligence. Many of the fourth edition's chapters contain insights from the 2012 DOJ-SEC *Resource Guide to the U.S. Foreign Corrupt Practices Act.*

I am grateful for the insights of my Baker & McKenzie partners and especially my colleagues John F. McKenzie of San Francisco, whose knowledge of the U.S. export laws and the Foreign Corrupt Practices Act is encyclopedic; William Joseph Linklater of Chicago, whose prismatic issue analysis is always keen; Peter P. Tomczak of Chicago, a most talented litigator whose corporate background and governance insights make an invaluable contribution to corporate internal investigations; and Henry Garfield of London, whose insights into the U.K. Bribery Act and corporate criminal law were extremely helpful in organizing and revising Chapter 11. I also wish to thank Jay G. Martin, Vice President, Chief Compliance Officer, and Senior Deputy General Counsel, Baker Hughes, Inc., of Houston, whose experience with and study of FCPA compliance is second to none, for his most generous review of and comments on the first edition's manuscript. I am also grateful to our paralegal in San Francisco Nada Hitti for tracking anticorruption cases for me. Finally, and above all, I wish to acknowledge and thank Linda Braggs of Oakland for her tireless patience, professionalism, and attention to detail in helping me bring this fourth edition of the handbook to fruition.

Robert W. Tarun
San Francisco
April 1, 2015

NOTES

1. Dionne Searcey, *U.S. Cracks Down on Corporate Bribes*, WALL ST. J., May 26, 2009, at A1.

2. DAVID LUBAN, JULIE O'SULLIVAN & DAVID STEWART, *Corruption*, ch. 14 in INTERNATIONAL AND TRANSNATIONAL CRIMINAL LAW (Aspen 2009).

Introduction to the Fourth Edition

Since the original publication of *The Foreign Corrupt Practices Act Handbook* in 2010, there have been major developments in anti-corruption enforcement and as a result in this Handbook. In November 2012 the U.S. Department of Justice (DOJ) and the U.S. Securities and Exchange Commission (SEC) released the long-awaited *Resource Guide to the U.S. Foreign Corrupt Practices Act*. The DOJ–SEC 120-page *Resource Guide* is largely a compendium of past FCPA resolutions and represents a vast improvement over the outdated six-page DOJ *Lay-Person's Guide to FCPA*, replacing the latter as Appendix 4. It provides in-house counsel, compliance officers, and FCPA practitioners with the DOJ and SEC's interpretation of the FCPA and the two agencies' enforcement investigative and prosecutorial approach and priorities. The *Resource Guide* does not represent the law, does not quantify how much credit companies that disclose and cooperate will receive, and does not cover the critical subjects of conducting and defending FCPA investigations[1] (Chapters 8 and 9). And of course, in 2010 the United Kingdom enacted the Bribery Act, which is expected to bear fruit in the coming years. The Fourth Edition discusses and appends the United Kingdom's recent Deferred Prosecution Agreements Code of Practice. Ironically, in early 2015, the DOJ began to reconsider the merits of DPAs. (See Chapter 9, XIII.C.)

The Fourth Edition addresses and analyzes the DOJ–SEC *Resource Guide*'s four main chapters: the FCPA Anti-Bribery Provisions; the FCPA Accounting Provisions; Guiding Principles of FCPA Enforcement; and FCPA Penalties, Sanctions, and Remedies. It also discusses the increasing number of FCPA resolution options utilized by U.S. authorities. The DOJ and SEC rarely publicize matters they decline to prosecute or bring an enforcement action, but the 2012 *Resource Guide* shared select details of six FCPA anonymized declinations involving five public companies and one privately held company. This Handbook analyzes those six examples. For companies considering voluntary disclosure but that are wary that disclosure will result in a prosecution or enforcement action, Chapter 9 of the Fourth Edition discusses what these declinations mean and do not mean for potential targets and subjects.

The Fourth Edition of *The Foreign Corrupt Practices Act Handbook* addresses much more than the *Resource Guide*. Over 75 percent of the sections of the Third Edition have been updated or replaced in the Fourth Edition. In addition to discussion of 35 new FCPA resolutions (through December 31, 2014) and two new FCPA Opinion Releases, the Handbook also delves further into the issues that investigation counsel, outside auditors, and forensic accountants routinely face in complex FCPA investigations.

Among other topics in the Fourth Edition are import and export risks impli- cated by the FCPA and royal family member issues (Chapter 1); the in personam jurisdiction decisions in *SEC v. Straub* and *SEC v. Steffen* (Chapter 2); recent anti- bribery developments and prosecutions in Canada (Chapter 3); effective compliance programs and internal audit departments including a summary of the November 2014 DOJ Criminal Division's ten hallmarks of effective compliance programs (Chapter 4); emerging distributorship issues (Chapter 5); a much updated discus- sion of gifts, travel, and entertainment (Chapter 6); charitable donation and politi- cal contribution advice (Chapter 7); enforcement trends, including imposition of self-assessments in lieu of corporate monitorships and aggressive disgorgement positions (Chapter 9); and a discussion of 35 new FCPA matters and new brib- ery schemes and increased focus on health-care and life science companies (Chap- ter 10). Finally, Chapter 11 addresses the United Kingdom Bribery Act 2010 and reviews U.K. principles of corporate criminal liability and corporate prosecution guidance; Deferred Prosecution Agreements; U.K. definitive sentencing guidance on bribery offenses; the U.K. Serious Fraud Office's list of 19 corruption indica- tions; Transparency International U.K.'s 2012 finalized analysis of merger and acquisition due diligence titled *Anti-Bribery Due Diligence for Transactions* (provided in Appendix 16); and the October 2012 SFO revised policies on facilitation pay- ments, business expenditure (hospitality), and self-reporting.

I continue to invite and welcome the comments and suggestions of other anti- corruption practitioners, corporate counsel, and scholars for future editions.

Robert W. Tarun
San Francisco
April 15, 2015

NOTES

1. *See, e.g.*, Mike Koehler, *Grading the Foreign Corrupt Practices Act Guidance*, 7 WHITE COLLAR CRIME REPORT 871 (Nov. 16, 2012).

2. David Barstow, *Vast Mexico Bribery Case Hushed Up by Wal-Mart After Top- Level Struggle*, N.Y. TIMES, Apr. 14, 2012, at A1, http://www.nytimes.com/interactive /business/walmart-bribery-abroad-series.html?_r=0.

CHAPTER 1

Foreign Corrupt Practices Act Overview

The Foreign Corrupt Practices Act (FCPA)[1] contains two types of provisions: anti-bribery provisions, which prohibit corrupt payments to foreign officials, foreign political parties or party officials, or candidates for foreign political office to influence the official in the exercise of his or her official duties to assist in obtaining or retaining business or securing any improper advantage; and record-keeping and internal controls provisions, which impose certain obligations on all companies whose securities are registered in the United States or that are required to file reports with the Securities and Exchange Commission (SEC), regardless of whether the companies have foreign operations.

I. ANTIBRIBERY

A. Application

The FCPA's antibribery provisions apply to three categories of persons: (1) "issuers"[2] (or an agent thereof); (2) "domestic concerns"[3] (or an agent thereof); and (3) foreign nationals or businesses[4] (or an agent or national thereof) who take any action in furtherance of a corrupt payment while within the territory of the United States. "Issuer" means any company whose securities are registered in the United States or that is required to file periodic reports with the SEC.[5] "Domestic concern" and "any officer, director, employee or agent of such domestic concern or any stockholder thereof acting on behalf of such domestic concern" mean any individual who is a citizen, national, or resident of the United States and any corporation, partnership, association, joint-stock company, business trust, unincorporated organization, or sole proprietorship that has its principal place of business in the United States, or that is organized under the laws of a state of the United States, or a territory, possession, or commonwealth of the United States.[6] Issuers and domestic concerns, along with their officers, directors, employees, agents, and shareholders, are prohibited from using "the mails or any other instrumentality of interstate commerce corruptly in furtherance of" an offer or an actual payment to any foreign official.[7] "Interstate commerce" has been expansively interpreted to mean phone calls, e-mails, and text messages.

The third category significantly increases the exposure of non-U.S. companies and their employees or agents, regardless of whether the person is a resident or does business in the United States.[8] The FCPA now covers foreign persons who, while in the territory of the United States, corruptly make use of instrumentalities of interstate commerce or do "any act in furtherance of an illegal payment to a foreign official."[9] The legislative history is clear that Congress intended that "the territorial basis for jurisdiction . . . be interpreted broadly so that an extensive physical connection to the bribery act is not required."[10] In *United States v. Syncor Taiwan*, the Department of Justice (DOJ) alleged that the mere e-mailing of budgets to the parent company in the United States containing line items for corrupt payments was sufficient to establish jurisdiction.[11]

Issuers and domestic concerns may be held liable for violating the antibribery provisions of the FCPA whether or not they took any action in the United States in furtherance of the corrupt foreign payment. Prior to the 1998 FCPA amendments, only issuers and domestic concerns could be held liable, and only if they used the U.S. mails or instrumentalities of interstate commerce in furtherance of the illicit foreign payment. The FCPA defines "interstate commerce" as "trade, commerce, transportation, or communication among the several States, or between any foreign country and any State or between any State and any place or ship outside thereof."[12] The term also includes the *intrastate* use of a telephone or any interstate means of communication, or any other interstate instrumentality. The DOJ–SEC *Resource Guide to the U.S. Foreign Corrupt Practices Act* (*Resource Guide*) offers the following illustrations of interstate commerce:

> Placing a telephone call or sending an e-mail, text message, or fax from, to, or through the United States involves interstate commerce—as does sending a wire transfer from or to a U.S. bank or otherwise using the U.S. banking system, or traveling across state borders or internationally to or from the United States.[13]

The 1998 amendments expanded the FCPA's jurisdiction to cover corrupt foreign payments outside the United States by U.S. persons without any link to interstate commerce; the FCPA amendments make it illegal for any United States person to violate the FCPA "irrespective of whether such United States person makes use of the mails or any means or instrumentality of interstate commerce in furtherance of [the illegal foreign activity]."[14] Thus, a U.S. company or issuer can be liable for the conduct of overseas employees or agents, even if no money was transferred from the United States and no U.S. person participated in any way in the foreign bribery. The DOJ–SEC *Resource Guide* offers the following examples:

> Thus, for example, a foreign national who attends a meeting in the United States that furthers a foreign bribery scheme may be subject to prosecution, as may any co-conspirators, even if they did not themselves attend the meeting. A foreign national or company may also be liable under the FCPA if it aids and abets, conspires with, or acts as an agent of an issuer or domestic concern, regardless of whether the foreign national or company itself takes any action in the United States.[15]

Until 1998, foreign persons were not subject to the FCPA's antibribery provisions unless they were issuers or domestic concerns. The amendments, however, expanded the statute to allow for the prosecution of any (foreign) person who takes any act in furtherance of a corrupt payment while in the territory of the United States.[16] Thus, for example, a foreign subsidiary that causes directly, or through agents, an act in furtherance of a bribe to take place within the United States is liable under the FCPA. The 1998 amendments were passed to implement the 1997 Organization for Economic and Cooperative Development (OECD) Convention on Combating Bribery of Foreign Officials in International Business Transactions (the OECD Convention).

B. Elements

A violation of the antibribery prohibition by a person as defined above consists of five elements:

1. A payment, offer, authorization, or promise to pay money or anything of value, directly or through a third party;
2. To (a) any foreign official, (b) any foreign political party or party official, (c) any candidate for foreign political office, (d) any official of a public international organization, or (e) any other person while "knowing" that the payment or promise to pay will be passed on to one of the above;
3. Using an instrumentality of interstate commerce (such as telephone, telex, e-mail, or the mail) by any person (whether U.S. or foreign) or an act outside the United States by a domestic concern or U.S. person, or an act in the United States by a foreign person in furtherance of the offer, payment, or promise to pay;
4. For the corrupt purpose of (a) influencing an official act or decision of that person, (b) inducing that person to do or omit doing any act in violation of his or her lawful duty, (c) securing an improper advantage, or (d) inducing that person to use his influence with a foreign government to affect or influence any government act or decision;
5. In order to assist the company in obtaining or retaining business for or with any person or directing business to any person.[17]

C. Key Concepts

1. *Offers, Payments, Promises to Pay, or Authorizations of Payments*

A company or person can be liable under the FCPA not only for making improper payments, but also for an offer, promise, or authorization of a corrupt payment, even if the employees or agents do not ultimately make a payment. In other words, a bribe need not actually be paid, and a corrupt act need not succeed in its purpose.

2. *Recipients*

The FCPA prohibition extends only to corrupt payments (or offers, promises to pay, or authorizations of payment) to a foreign official, foreign political party, party official, or a candidate for foreign political office, and any other person while the payer "knows" that the payment or promise to pay will be passed on to one of the above.

a.   Foreign Official

The term "foreign official" is defined under the FCPA as "any officer or employee of a foreign government or any department, agency or instrumentality thereof, or of a public international organization, or any person acting in an official capacity or on behalf of any such government, department, agency or instrumentality or for, or on behalf of, any such public international organization."[18] The *Resource Guide* asserts that the term covers low-ranking employees as well as high-ranking officials of governments.[19] This broad definition is normally considered to encompass executive branch employees, elected legislators or parliamentarians and their family members, and, in the clear view of the DOJ and the SEC, employees of state-owned or state-controlled enterprises and officials of quasi-governmental entities. For example, the U.S. government charged Dow Chemical with making payments to a key member of a committee in India that determined when certain chemical products would receive government registrations;[20] it charged Monsanto with improper payments to 140 current and former Indonesian government officials and their families under a bogus product registration scheme in Indonesia;[21] and it charged Schnitzer Steel with making payments to a scrap metal manager of a state-owned enterprise in Asia.[22]

State-owned or state-controlled enterprises are prevalent in emerging economies. As the *Resource Guide* points out, many foreign governments operate through state-owned or state-controlled entities, especially in industries like aerospace and defense manufacturing, banking and finance, healthcare and life sciences, energy and extractive industries, telecommunications, and transportation.[23] Employees of the state-owned electrical utility in Mexico and the state-owned telecommunications company of Haiti have been charged as *foreign officials* in FCPA cases. (See summaries of *United States v. Aguilar* and *United States v. Esquenazi* in chapters 8 and 10.) The government need not prove the identity of a foreign official in its pleadings.[24]

Finally, the FCPA bribery provision only prohibits the payment for giving of things of value to foreign officials, not to foreign governments.[25] Thus, in the numerous UN Oil-for-Food program prosecutions involving kickbacks to the Iraqi government by publicly traded companies, the DOJ charged books-and-records violations and not bribery conduct. (See chapter 10.)

b.   Public International Organization Officials

The 1998 amendments added "public international organization officials" to the definition of "foreign official." A "public international organization" is defined as "(1) an organization that is designated by Executive Order pursuant to section 288 of title 22; or (2) any other international organization that is designated by the President by Executive Order for the purposes of this section."[26] Examples include the World Bank, the International Monetary Fund, the World Trade Organization, the Organization for Economic Cooperation and Development, the Organization of American States (OAS), the Red Cross, and the African Union.[27] The FCPA has long been interpreted to preclude prosecution of foreign officials, party officials, or candidates who are recipients of bribes.[28]

c.   Royal Family Members

Royal Family members can present challenging facts and determinations of whether they constitute foreign officials for purposes of the FCPA; the problems often arise when they are asked to serve as local sponsors. In some countries and situations, royal family members wield enormous influence over government contracts and awards. In other countries and cases, royal family members are members only through custom and tradition, and have no real privileges, benefits, or influence. Royal Family member "foreign official" and local sponsorship analyses tend to be very fact intensive and, typically, no single factor is dispositive.

In 2012, the DOJ received an FCPA opinion request relating to a consultancy that had three partners, one of whom was a royal family member in an unidentified foreign country. The requestor, a partnership engaged in lobbying activities, sought guidance as to whether, under the facts presented, the consultancy's partner qualified as a foreign official under the FCPA.[29] The requestor wished to represent the Embassy of the foreign country (the "Foreign Country") to the United States and the Foreign Country's Foreign Ministry (collectively, the "Foreign Country Embassy") in its lobbying activities in the United States. To facilitate this representation, the requestor further wished to contract with a third-party consulting company ("Consultancy") to introduce the requestor to the Foreign Country Embassy, to advise on cultural awareness issues in dealing with the foreign country's officials and businesses, to act as a local sponsor in the Foreign Country, to help establish an office in the Foreign Country, and to identify additional business opportunities in the Foreign Country.

Some of the facts critical to the opinion were that the requestor represented that the royal family member partner held no title or position in the government, had no governmental duties or responsibilities, was a member of the royal family through custom and tradition rather than blood relation, and had no benefits or privileges because of his status. The royal family member had held only one governmental position in the Foreign Country—overseeing a governmental construction project—for less than a year in the late 1990s. Other than this position, the royal family member had never acted in any capacity for, or on behalf of, the Foreign Country, or any department, agency, or instrumentality of the Foreign Country, or in any public organization. The Foreign Country at issue required by law that any private-sector company opening an office or operating a business have a local sponsor—a requirement not uncommon in the Middle East. The royal family member here had previously sponsored numerous foreign companies doing business in his country and interacted in his personal capacity (i.e., not on behalf of the royal family) with government officials there who were not themselves members of the royal family.

In this engagement, the requestor assured the DOJ it would monitor actions taken by the U.S. Congress and the U.S. Administration that could impact the Foreign Country, present analyses of those activities, recommend courses of action, and engage in lobbying services for the Foreign Country related to U.S. governmental activity. The requestor would also introduce Foreign Country officials to members of Congress and administration officials who might be able to take appropriate actions to help improve the Foreign Country's economic and business relationship with the United States. The requestor and the consultancy would create culturally appropriate promotional materials to complement a strategic plan of raising the Foreign Country's visibility in the United States. The proposed agreement between the requestor and the consultancy included the latter's representation that "none of its members, or principals are 'foreign officials' as that term is defined in the FCPA." The consultancy further represented that its principals and members here were familiar with, and agreed to abide by, the FCPA and all U.S. and Foreign Country antibribery and anticorruption laws.[30]

In finding that the proffered facts did not qualify the royal family member as a "foreign official" under the FCPA, DOJ FCPA Opinion Release 12-2 observed:

> A person's mere membership in the royal family of the Foreign Country, by itself, does not automatically qualify that person as a "foreign official." Rather, the question requires a fact-intensive, case-by-case determination that will turn on, among other things, the structure and distribution of power within a country's government; a royal family's current and historical legal status and powers; the individual's position within the royal family; an individual's present and past positions within the government; the mechanisms by which an individual could come to hold a position with governmental authority or responsibilities (such as, for example, royal succession); the likelihood that an individual would come to hold such a position; an individual's ability, directly or indirectly, to affect governmental decision-making; and numerous other factors.[31]

In declining to take enforcement action, the DOJ also considered the careful steps that the requestor and the consultancy took to comply with the FCPA and other antibribery laws. This opinion and its prophylactic measures should be considered by multinational companies wishing to engage royal family members as local sponsors—along with a thorough analysis of the royal family member's actual power, benefits, and privileges; the transparency of the relationship; and the particular compensation arrangement.

d.   Foreign Political Party, Political Party Official, or Candidate for Foreign Office

The FCPA prohibits an illicit offer and payment not only to a foreign official but also to a foreign political party, an official of a foreign political party, or a candidate for foreign office.[32] A potential problem can arise where a U.S. person's foreign agent or partner makes political campaign contributions to persons in the country where a multinational company (MNC) is doing business. The MNC should consider instituting a policy that prohibits its foreign agents, partners, or consultants from making any political contributions whatsoever for or on behalf of their venture or relating in any way to a venture. Absent a blanket corporate prohibition, proposed foreign political contributions by an agent, consultant, or employee should be reviewed in advance on a formal, case-by-case basis by a company's legal department or outside counsel.

3.   *Money or Anything of Value*

The FCPA prohibits paying, offering, or promising to pay (or authorizing to pay or offer) money or making a gift of anything of value.[33] Although neither has the statute defined nor has any FCPA decision addressed the concept of a "thing of value," it certainly includes cash equivalents and other forms of valuable inducements such as travel and travel-related expenses, jewelry, housing expenses, country club memberships, cars, entertainment, shopping excursions, and the hiring of relatives. Federal courts addressing similar domestic bribery statutes have construed the term broadly to include tangible and intangible property such as "information,"[34] the testimony of a witness,[35] loans,[36] promises of future employment,[37] a college scholarship,[38] medical expenses,[39] and sports equipment.[40] In *United States v. King,* the Eighth Circuit found that the planned payment of a $1 million "kiss payment" or "closing cost" to senior Costa Rican officials and political parties to obtain land concessions on which a port development was to be built satisfied the "thing of value" requirement.[41] Improper payments have frequently been disguised as consultancy payments for which no services or expertise is really needed or present, or no services are in fact provided. While the FCPA contains no de minimis exception, the *Resource Guide* indicates that the DOJ and SEC will not pursue items of nominal value and have "focused on small gifts and payments only when they comprise part of a systemic or longstanding course of conduct that evidences a scheme to corruptly pay for foreign officials to obtain or retain business."[42]

4. *Corrupt Intent*

a. Corruptly

To violate the FCPA's antibribery provisions, a payment, offer, or promise to pay or making of a gift must be made corruptly.[43] Unlike with willfulness, *infra,* the government must prove corrupt intent as to both individuals and corporations.[44] Although the FCPA does not define "corruptly," the legislative history indicates there must be an "evil motive" or purpose or intent to wrongfully influence the recipient to "misuse his official position" in order to wrongfully direct, obtain, or retain business.[45] The history indicates that the motive or purpose is the same as that required under 18 U.S.C. § 201(b), which prohibits domestic bribery.[46]

In *United States v. Liebo,*[47] the Eighth Circuit affirmed the following jury instruction definition of the term "corruptly":

> [T]he offer, promise to pay, payment or authorization of payment, must be intended to induce the recipient to misuse his official position or to influence someone else to do so. . . . [A]n act is "corruptly" done if done voluntarily [a]nd intentionally, and with a bad purpose of accomplishing either an unlawful end or result, or a lawful end or result by some unlawful method or means.[48]

In 2007 the Fifth Circuit upheld the *Liebo* jury instruction definition in *United States v. Kay (Kay III)* and further held that the prosecution must prove both that the defendant knew he was doing something generally "unlawful" and that his misconduct was willful.[49] Willfulness, however, does not require a defendant to have known that he was violating the specific provisions of the law, that is, the FCPA.[50]

In 2009 in *United States v. Bourke,* the Southern District of New York court gave the following "corruptly and willfully" instruction as part of the jury charge for a conspiracy to violate the FCPA and the Travel Act:

The third element of a violation of the FCPA is that the person intended to act "corruptly" and "willfully."

A person acts "corruptly" if he acts voluntarily and intentionally, with an improper motive of accomplishing either an unlawful result, or a lawful result by some unlawful method or means. The term "corruptly" is intended to connote that the offer, payment, and promise was intended to influence an official to misuse his official position.

A person acts "willfully" if he acts deliberately and with the intent to do something that the law forbids, that is, with a bad purpose to disobey or disregard the law. The person need not be aware of the specific law and rule that his conduct may be violating, but he must act with the intent to do something that the law forbids.[51]

Bourke unsuccessfully appealed his one-count conviction, principally contending a "conscious avoidance" instruction was error.[52]

b.   Willfully

While the term "willfully" is not defined in the FCPA, the government must prove an individual acted purposefully and with knowledge he was doing a "bad act" under the general rules of law.[53] The government must prove an individual acted willfully to be held criminally liable.[54] However, proof of willfulness is not required to establish corporate criminal or civil liability.[55]

c.   Factual Considerations

Prosecutors look at potential bribery allegations to both see whether a government official recipient has personally benefited or whether a target or subject has personally benefited. While there is no such requirement under the FCPA antibribery section, the DOJ understands there is less jury appeal when a defendant has not personally benefited. In at least one FCPA opinion release the DOJ has declined to take enforcement action where a recipient has not personally benefited. Still, as to a businessperson paying foreign officials or authorizing a payment, travel, or gift, the DOJ routinely maintains that a subject or target maintained his employment, earning a good salary or a bonus, and thus personally benefited. The lack of any personal benefit to the government official recipient rather than to the businessperson is usually a more successful defense argument.[56]

Although officers and employees routinely reject any suggestion that they acted corruptly or with an evil motive in offering or giving money or things of value to foreign government officials or employees, a review of the facts, circumstances, transparency, and motivations surrounding payments or gifts to foreign officials or employees can prove troublesome. For example, a multinational employee will have difficulty explaining or justifying a substantial cash voucher and payment or gift to a mid-level foreign government official whom he has met only once or twice in his life. Similarly, a pharmaceutical company's payment of a luxurious conference trip for a state-employed physician and his spouse requires very careful and thorough examination. That said, there are many gift, travel, lodging, and entertainment investigations involving undisputed isolated conduct and relatively small amounts of cash or gifts where lack of a corrupt intent is the most viable defense to otherwise indisputable periodic gifts or small cash payments to local officials.

5. *Business Purpose Test*

The FCPA prohibits payments, offers, or promises to pay made in order to assist a company in obtaining or retaining business for or with, or directing business to, any person. Business to be obtained or retained does not need to be with a foreign government or foreign government instrumentality. As a result of the 1998 amendments, the FCPA now prohibits payments to foreign officials for the purpose of securing "any improper advantage" in obtaining or retaining business. Although it remains unclear what conduct falls within the scope of this language, it certainly can include payments to foreign customs and tax officials.

The leading FCPA business purpose decision is *United States v. Kay*[57] (*Kay II*), in which the Fifth Circuit reversed a district court dismissal of an indictment that charged a businessman with bribing a Haitian official to understate customs duties and sales taxes on rice shipped to Haiti, to assist American Rice, Inc., in obtaining or retaining business. The district court ruled that as a matter of law, illicit payments to foreign officials to avoid portions of customs duties and sales taxes were not the type of bribes that the FCPA criminalizes. On appeal, the Fifth Circuit found that such bribes could (but do not necessarily) come within the ambit of the FCPA, but "[i]t still must be shown that the bribery was intended to produce an effect—here, through tax savings—that would assist in obtaining or retaining business."[58] In other words, bribes need not, in order to obtain or retain business, be direct payments to government officials to win contracts.[59] Local bribes to tax or customs officials that enable companies to compete with other companies can satisfy the "retain business" language of the FCPA and similarly run afoul of the books-and-records provisions for public companies.

a. Government Contract Cases

Most multinational companies and their general counsel are well aware of the Siemens, Daimler, and KBR FCPA prosecutions involving multimillion-dollar bribes to secure foreign government or state-owned enterprise (SOE) contracts. Some multinational legal and compliance departments mistakenly assume that the FCPA essentially applies to bribes of foreign officials to procure foreign government or SOE contracts. To be sure, many FCPA prosecutions and enforcement actions do involve substantial bribes to obtain government goods and services contracts, for example, *United States v. Marubeni* (bribes to obtain multibillion-dollar engineering, procurement, and construction contracts in Nigeria); *In re Allianz SE* (bribes to obtain insurance contracts related to large government projects in Indonesia); and *United States v. Orthofix International N.V.* (bribes to foreign officials to purchase products for state-owned hospitals in Mexico). But nongovernment contract cases have made MNCs and their employees equally liable under the FCPA.

b. Nongovernment or Contract Retain Business Cases

Many multinationals fail to focus on *Kay's* broad business purpose test and do not evaluate their risks in direct noncontract scenarios. The *Resource Guide's* examples of improper actions taken to obtain or retain business include overlooking rules for importation of products; gaining access to nonpublic tender business information; evading taxes or penalties; influencing the adjudication of lawsuits or enforcement actions; obtaining exceptions to regulations; and avoiding contract termination.[60] Numerous and perhaps less sensational FCPA matters have involved improper payments to foreign officials for noncontract securing purposes. The statutory language expressly prohibits payments to foreign officials for the payment of (1) influencing an act or decision by that official; (2) inducing that foreign official to do or omit to do any act in violation of his or her lawful duty; (3) securing any improper advantage; or (4) inducing the foreign official to use his or her influence to assist the payor in obtaining or retaining business, or directing business to another purpose. This language has been used to prosecute corporations and individuals who have paid foreign officials to keep food inspectors from disrupting operations of a meat-production facility (*United States v. Tyson Foods Inc.*); to influence approval and registration of products (*United States v. Pfizer H.C.P. Corp.*); to avoid tax investigations (*United States v. Alliance One International Inc.*); and to improve product placement (*In re Diageo plc*).

c.   Import-Export Operations

Perhaps no area is more rife for improper payment and false books-and-records abuses but less carefully monitored for such risks than multinational import and export operations. International trade expert John F. McKenzie has thoughtfully identified seven areas where FCPA compliance risk and problems are most likely to be encountered in connection with import/export operations:

1. Avoidance of customs duties and import taxes—especially in a number of emerging countries that impose high customs duties and import taxes on imported merchandise;
2. Underinvoicing schemes whereby foreign customers ask United States suppliers to understate a declared value for local customs purposes;
3. Avoidance of import regulatory requirements and restrictions including import licensing requirements, product certification and detailed technical data filing requirements, and product testing and inspection requirements;
4. Offshore payments to third-party intermediaries including customs brokers, import/export agents, and trade consultants who may provide bona fide services, or be a vehicle to avoid dealing directly with wayward local officials;
5. Hospitality and gifts for foreign customs and import regulatory officials;
6. Export compliance with respect to the export of defense articles under the International Traffic in Arms Regulations (ITAR); and
7. Merger and acquisition transactions and the failure to engage international trade professionals in the FCPA compliance pre- and post-acquisition due diligence.[61]

As McKenzie warns, each of these areas presents not only potential bribery challenges but false books-and-records issues for issuers and their officers, employees, and agents.

The *Resource Guide* confirms multinational risks with customs officials by citing the Panalpina investigation where oil services companies bribed customs officials in more than ten countries for benefits including

- evading customs duties on imported goods;
- improperly expediting the importation of goods and services;
- extending drilling contracts and lowering tax assessments;
- obtaining false documentation related to temporary import permits for drilling rigs; and
- enabling the release of drilling rigs and other equipment from customs officials.[62]

Multinational companies are wise to thoroughly and regularly examine their direct or indirect foreign government touchpoints in the import/export area.

6.   *Constructive Knowledge*

The FCPA does not require proof of actual knowledge that a payment to or promise to pay an intermediary will be passed on to a foreign official. A person may be liable on the basis of constructive knowledge. In addressing the knowledge requirement, the FCPA states:

> (2)(A) A person's state of mind is "knowing" with respect to conduct, a circumstance, or a result if—
> (i)   such person is aware that such person is engaging in such conduct, that such circumstance exists, or that such result is substantially certain to occur; or
> (ii) such person has a firm belief that such circumstance exists or that such result is substantially certain to occur.[63]

When knowledge of the existence of a particular circumstance is required for an offense, such knowledge is established if a person is aware of a high probability of the existence of such circumstance, unless the person actually believes that such circumstance does not exist.[64] The statute does not require the government to prove the defendant knew of the FCPA or that he knew his conduct violated the FCPA.[65] Two civil cases have held that a defendant utilizing an intermediary need not know the identity of the foreign official involved.[66]

The FCPA's legislative history speaks of "willful blindness," "deliberate ignorance," and taking a "head in the sand" attitude as constituting knowledge under the statute. The DOJ–SEC *Resource Guide* cited the following legislative history in addressing this statute's unique knowledge standard:

> [T]he so-called "head-in-the-sand" problem—variously described in the pertinent authorities as "conscious disregard," "willful blindness" or "deliberate ignorance"—should be covered so that management officials could not take refuge from the Act's prohibitions by their unwarranted obliviousness to any action (or inaction), language or other "signaling device" that should reasonable alert them of the "high probability" of an FCPA violation.[67]

Individuals or corporations who consciously disregard or deliberately ignore known circumstances that should have put them on notice of an improper payment may be prosecuted for knowing that a payment would be passed on to a foreign official. The requisite state of mind in light of the legislative history requires either direct or actual knowledge, or a "conscious purpose to avoid learning the truth."[68]

7. Use of Third Parties

A company may be liable for a payment by an agent or third party if the company authorized such payment or if it "knew" the improper payment would be made. Many companies regularly employ or contract with third parties, such as sales or marketing agents, consultants, joint venture partners, consortium partners, freight forwarders, customs agents, law firms, accountants, distributors, and resellers. These relationships can greatly increase FCPA risks, which usually arise in one of two ways: (1) a third party makes improper payments to government officials, or (2) a third party is owned by or affiliated with a government official.[69]

A company is deemed to have knowledge of an offer, promise to pay, or payment if it is aware of a "high probability" that such an offer, promise, or payment will be made.[70] This risk of vicarious liability means that companies and employees subject to the FCPA must undertake significant steps to minimize the risk of becoming liable due to actions by agents or other third parties. Third-party misconduct represents the most common violation of the FCPA.

8. Instrumentalities

The FCPA defines a foreign official as "any officer or employee of a foreign government or any department, agency or instrumentality thereof."[71] It further prohibits payments to foreign officials to induce them to use their influence with a foreign government or instrumentality thereof to affect or influence any act or decision of such government or instrumentality.[72] Nowhere does the statute define "instrumentality" or provide guidance about what types of partially state-owned or state-controlled entities are foreign government "instrumentalities" such that their officers or employees are foreign officials.

a.   State-Owned or State-Controlled Entity as an Instrumentality

Multinational companies often deal with foreign government partners, for example, joint ventures doing business with SOEs including oil, steel, telecommunication, and transportation companies.[73] For example, it is currently estimated that 75 percent of all oil and gas reserves in the world are owned in whole or in part by state-owned entities. Further, some foreign governments have invested in minority interests in foreign ventures, muddling the instrumentality issue, while other governments are investing in second- or third-tier state-owned subsidiaries. Two California district courts addressed the state-owned or state-controlled instrumentality issue in 2011. In 2014, the 11th Circuit affirmed a broad definition of "instrumentality" and upheld the longest sentence—15 years—ever imposed in an FCPA case.

i.   United States v. Esquenazi[74]

In *United States v. Esquenazi*, the 11th Circuit reviewed the definition of "instrumentality," which the appellants argued was overbroad in the district court's jury instruction. Appellants Esquenazi and Rodriguez co-owned Terra Communications

Comp (Terra), a Florida reseller that purchased phone time from foreign vendors and resold the minutes to customers in the United States. Telecommunications D'Haiti S.A.M. (Teleco) was a major vendor of Terra and was owned by the Haitian government.

Teleco was given a government monopoly on telecommunications services at the time of its formation in 1968. It became 97 percent owned by the National Bank of Haiti in the 1970s. The country's president appointed all of its board members. A 2001 Haitian anticorruption law listed Teleco as a public administration of the government. During the Internal Revenue Service's investigations of the case, Esquenazi admitted he bribed Teleco's director of international relations and other Teleco officials.

In determining whether an entity is an "instrumentality" under the FCPA, the 11th Circuit provided a nonexhaustive list of nine factors to consider.

First, in determining whether the government "controls" the entity, courts and juries should look at the following five factors:

1. The foreign government's formal designation of that entity;
2. Whether the foreign government has a majority interest in the entity;
3. The foreign government's ability to hire and fire the entity's principals;
4. The extent to which the government profits from or subsidizes the entity; and
5. The length of time that these indicia have existed.

Second, courts and juries should assess whether "the entity performs a function the government treats as its own" by examining the following four factors:

1. Whether the entity has a monopoly over the function it exists to carry out;
2. Whether the government subsidizes the costs associated with the entity providing services;
3. Whether the entity provides services to the public at large; and
4. Whether the public and government generally perceive the entity to be performing a governmental function.

The 11th Circuit observed that "it will be relatively easy to decide what functions a government treats as its own" by considering objective factors, including control, exclusivity, governmental authority to hire and fire, subsidization, and whether an entity's finances are treated as part of the public [fisc].

The appellate court concluded that Teleco was an "instrumentality" of Haiti, noting that throughout the years that the defendants were involved with Teleco, it was 97 percent owned by the government; the company's director general was chosen by the Haitian president with the consent of the prime minister and the ministers of public works and finance; and the Haitian president appointed all of its board members.

Esquenazi is the first appellate decision to interpret "instrumentality" under the FCPA and essentially buttressed California's jurisprudence, broadly interpreting "instrumentality." An instrumentality owned by a government with 50 percent or less interest and involving less government oversight and control will likely present a more challenging legal test and perhaps lead to a different result.

ii.   United States v. Aguilar (Lindsey Manufacturing)

In April 2011, a Central District of California court addressed in *United States v. Aguilar* the issue of whether an officer or employee of a state-owned corporation could be "a foreign official" for purposes of the FCPA liability.[75] Defendants argued that under no circumstances could a state-owned corporation be a department, agency, or instrumentality of a foreign government and highlighted the fact that despite an amendment in 1998, Congress did not define foreign officials to include persons of state-owned or state-controlled entities. In *Aguilar* the quasi-government entity at issue was the Comisión Federal de Electricidad (CFE), an electric utility company wholly owned by the Mexican government. Judge Matz denied the defendants' motion to dismiss, finding that a state-owned corporation having the attributes of the CFE can be an "instrumentality" of a foreign government within the meaning of the FCPA, and officers of such a state-owned corporation may therefore be "foreign officials" within the meaning of the statute.[76]

Recognizing that "instrumentality" is not defined in the FCPA, Judge Matz pointed out five characteristics of government agencies and departments that fall within the following common dictionary definitions of "instrumentality":

> [T]he ordinary meaning of instrumentality is "the quality or state of being instrumental," which, in turn, means "serving as a means or agency: implemental," or "of, relating to, or done with an instrument or tool." *Webster's II New College Dictionary* (*Webster's II*) 589 (3d ed. 2005). *See also American Heritage Dictionary* 908 (4th ed. 2000) (defining instrumentality as "[a] means; an agency," or "[a] subsidiary branch, as of a government, by means of which functions or policies are carried out"); *Black's Law Dictionary* 870 (9th ed. 2009) (defining instrumentality as "[a] thing used to achieve an end or purpose," or "[a] means or agency through which a function of another entity is accomplished, such as a branch of a governing body").[77]

The nonexhaustive list of five characteristics the district court found that support a quasi-government entity being an "instrumentality" are

1. The entity provides a service to the citizens—indeed, in many cases to all the inhabitants—of the jurisdiction;
2. The primary officers and directors of the entity are government officials, or are appointed by them;
3. The entity is financed, at least in large measure, through governmental appropriations or through revenues obtained as a result of government-mandated taxes, licenses, fees, or royalties, such as entrance fees to a national park;
4. The entity is vested with and exercises exclusive or controlling power to administer its designated functions; and
5. The entity is widely perceived and understood to be performing official (i.e., governmental) functions.

The district court in *Aguilar* found that CFE possessed all these characteristics and added that the Mexican Constitution recognizes that the supply of electric power is "exclusively a [function] of the general nation."[78] Still, it held that the FCPA legislative history on "instrumentality" is inconclusive in that it does not demonstrate that Congress intended to include or exclude all state-owned corporations within the ambit of the FCPA.[79] The facts in *Aguilar* surrounding the nexus of the state-owned utility to the Mexican government as well as the unique constitutional language were compelling. FCPA prosecutions alleging as instrumentalities other state-owned or state-controlled entities with a less clear connection to their governments may prove more susceptible to challenge.

iii. *United States v. Carson (Control Components, Inc.)*

Another Central District of California court addressed the "instrumentality" issue in *United States v. Carson*, when in May 2011 Judge Selna ruled that "the question of whether state-owned companies qualify as instrumentalities under the FCPA is a question of fact."[80] Acknowledging that "a mere monetary investment in a business entity by the government may not be sufficient to transform that entity into a governmental instrumentality," the district court nonetheless held that "when a monetary investment is combined with additional factors that objectively indicate the entity is being used as an instrument to carry out governmental objectives, that business entity would qualify as a governmental instrumentality." Judge Selna stated that several factors "bear on the question of whether a business entity constitutes a government instrumentality," including

- the foreign state's characterization of the entity and its employees;
- the foreign state's degree of control over the entity;
- the purpose of the entity's activities;
- the entity's obligations and privileges under the foreign state's law, including whether the entity exercises exclusive or controlling power to administer its designated functions;
- the circumstances surrounding the entity's creation; and
- the foreign state's extent of ownership of the entity, including the level of financial support by the state (e.g., subsidies, special tax treatment, and loans).[81]

The district court in *Carson* stated that "[s]uch factors are not exclusive, and no single factor is dispositive," explaining that the "chief utility" of the factors "is simply to point out that several types of evidence are relevant when determining whether a state-owned company constitutes an 'instrumentality' under the FCPA, with state-ownership only one of several considerations."[82]

iv. *Resource Guide Instrumentality Factors*

The *Resource Guide* cites the factors outlined in *Aguilar* and *Carson* and the DOJ and SEC add that they have long used an analysis of ownership, control, status, and function to determine whether a particular entity is an agency or instrumentality of a foreign government.[83] The guide does clarify that "as a practical matter, an entity is unlikely to qualify as an instrumentality if a government does not own[84] or control a majority of its shares. Citing the example of *Alcatel-Lucent*, the *Resource Guide* cautions that under certain minority shareholder (43 percent) circumstances, for example, veto power over all major expenditures, "special shareholder" status, and continued control of operational decisions, the DOJ and SEC may still bring an action.[85]

b.   Foreign Sovereign Immunities Act Precedent

Another foreign conduct-directed statute and the U.S. antiboycott regulations give some guidance on the likely breadth of the term "instrumentality." First, the Foreign Sovereign Immunities Act of 1976,[86] enacted one year before the FCPA, defines "an agency or instrumentality of a foreign state" as an entity that is "a separate legal person or otherwise," and "which is an organ of a foreign state or political subdivision thereof, or a majority of whose shares or other ownership interest is owned by a foreign or political subdivision thereof."[87]

Second, under the U.S. antiboycott regulations, an SOE will be presumed governmental if:

- The foreign government entity owns or controls, directly or indirectly, more than 50 percent of the voting rights;
- The foreign government owns or controls 25 percent or more of the voting securities, and no other entity or person owns or controls an equal or larger percentage;
- A majority of members of the board are also members of the governing body of the government department;
- The foreign government has the authority to appoint the majority of the members of the board; or
- The foreign government has the authority to appoint the chief operating officer.

An entity majority-owned or controlled by a foreign government will very likely be considered an "instrumentality" for FCPA purposes.[88] The most relevant factor in determining whether a company, partnership, or joint venture is an instrumentality remains whether a foreign government exercises "effective control" over it.[89]

c.   Sovereign Wealth Funds

A sovereign wealth fund (SWF) is a state-owned investment fund composed of financial assets such as stocks, bonds, property, precious metals, or other financial instruments. The original SWF is the Kuwait Investment Fund, an entity created in 1953 from vast oil revenues. SWFs are typically created for governments with surpluses and little or no international debt. Major SWFs include the Abu Dhabi Investment Authority, Government Pension Fund of Norway, Government of Singapore Investment Corporation, Kuwait Investment Authority, China Investment Corporation, Singapore's Temasek Holdings, and Qatar Investment Authority. For FCPA purposes, investment goals, internal checks and balances, due diligence of placement agents, and disclosure of relationships raise issues for SWFs.

The SEC has reportedly looked into whether financial institutions, including banks, private equity firms, and hedge funds that have sought investments from partnerships with SWFs, have violated the FCPA. Possible issues include whether these financial institutions have "made (or promised) payments or conferred other benefits, including travel or entertainment, in connection with efforts to transact business with SWFs or foreign, state-owned pension funds."[90] The DOJ and SEC no doubt broadly view the latter as government "instrumentalities" and their employees as "foreign officials" for purposes of the FCPA. Payments or in-kind benefits, such as travel and lodging not directly related to the promotion of products or services or the execution of contracts, to SWF or pension fund employees are prohibited. Equally important, payments to placement agents, consultants, or third parties, while knowing or disregarding that the payee will pass monies to a foreign official to secure access to benefits such as an investment or asset purchase for the SWF, are prohibited.[91] Finally, allowing a state-owned entity's employee or related party to co-invest could be considered an illicit benefit to the employee.[92]

9. *Authorization*

The FCPA prohibits the "authorization of the payment of any money, or offer, gift, promise to give, or authorization of the giving of anything of value"[93] to foreign officials for improper purposes. This language applies to issuers, domestic concerns and individuals, and foreign firms or individuals who engage in acts in furtherance of improper payments while in the territory of the United States. The statute does not define "authorization," but the legislative history makes clear that authorization can be either implicit or explicit. Authorization issues frequently arise when U.S. companies fund overseas operations, approve budgets, and take similar actions with respect to foreign subsidiaries or joint ventures. In suspicious circumstances, U.S. directors and managers should disavow any possible improper payments and take affirmative steps to avoid even the appearance of acquiescence.[94]

10. *Permissible Payments and Affirmative Defenses*

a.   Facilitating-Payment Exception for Routine Governmental Actions

As a result of the 1998 amendments, the FCPA provides an exception for so-called "facilitating," "expediting," or "grease" payments to low-level foreign officials who perform "routine governmental actions."[95] The purpose of this exception is to avoid FCPA liability where small sums are paid to facilitate certain routine, non-discretionary government functions such as the processing of permits, licenses, visas, work orders, or other official documents; providing police protection, power and water supply, cargo handling, or protection of perishable products; and scheduling inspections associated with contract performance or transit of goods across the country.[96] "Routine governmental actions" do not include decisions by foreign officials to award new business or to continue business with a particular party.[97]

The *Resource Guide* points out that a routine government action does not include acts that are within an official's discretion or that would constitute misuse of an office—offering as an example that paying an official a small amount to have the power turned on at a factory is a facilitating payment while paying an inspector to allow a company without a permit to operate is not.[98] The DOJ–SEC Guidance cautions that this exception focuses on the *purpose* of a payment rather than its *value*, but concedes that the size of a payment can be telling as "a large payment is more suggestive of corrupt intent to influence a non-governmental action."[99] The *Resource Guide* also warns that "labeling a bribe as a 'facilitating payment'" in a company's books and records does not make it so.[100]

While the FCPA may exempt facilitating payments, the bribery laws of many foreign countries do not; for example, the United Kingdom, and some multinational companies have decided as a matter of policy to ban all facilitating payments, for example, BHP Billiton. To the extent country laws conflict, it is generally wiser for a multinational company to adopt the more demanding standard.

b.   Affirmative Defenses

The 1998 FCPA amendments incorporated two affirmative defenses to the antibribery provisions. First, the FCPA provides an affirmative defense where the payment, gift, offer, or promise of anything of value at issue was permitted by the written laws of the foreign official's or political candidate's country.[101] Second, an affirmative defense exists where a payment, gift, offer, or promise of anything of value was for "reasonable and bona fide" expenditures related to the execution or performance of a contract with a foreign government or agency thereof, or the promotion, demonstration, or explanation of products or services.[102] For each of these affirmative defenses, the company or its officers or employees bears the burden of establishing in the first instance facts underlying the defense.

i.   *Written Laws of Foreign Country*

A person or entity charged with an antibribery violation may assert as an affirmative defense that the payment was lawful under the written laws and regulations of the foreign country. Expatriates frequently assert that bribery is permitted and recognized in the host or work country. However, a country's laws rarely, if ever, expressly permit bribery, and absent a written law or regulation, this affirmative defense fails. Further, in legislating this defense in 1988, Congress sought "to make clear that the absence of written law in a foreign officials country would not by itself be sufficient to satisfy this defense."[103]

The issue of what constitutes a payment permissible under the laws of a country to a commercial agent or government official can, in select circumstances, be a matter of significant debate. Although no country has "written laws" permitting bribery, it can be far less clear whether a payment to a government official who can, under local law, undertake commercial activities constitutes a permissible payment under the FCPA. Similarly, a significant political contribution that is legal under foreign law may make a payment to a foreign political party candidate or official permissible. However, if an individual makes a foreign political contribution with a corrupt intent, for example, to obtain or retain business, the mere fact that a sizable political contribution is lawful in the foreign country will not negate an offense under U.S. law. In *United States v. Kozeny*, the defense argued that an exception under Azeri law that permitted voluntary disclosure absolved bribe payors who voluntarily reported bribe payments; the district court rejected the argument that this narrow exception somehow made the underlying bribery legal in Azerbaijan.[104] The transparent nature of a particular transaction or payment will in many cases determine whether the DOJ prosecutes or the SEC files an enforcement action.

ii.   *Reasonable and Bona Fide Expenditures*

An affirmative defense to an antibribery violation also exists where a payment, offer, or promise of anything of value was a reasonable and bona fide expenditure, such as travel and lodging expenses incurred by or on behalf of a foreign official, party official, or candidate, and was directly related to the promotion, demonstration, or explanation of products or services; or the execution or performance of a contract with a foreign government or agency. Thus, a company may pay the reasonable, necessary, and bona fide expenses of government officials who are transported to a corporate location to inspect equipment or facilities in connection with a potential sale of the equipment or facilities. Similarly, a company may cover the reasonable expenditures involved in bringing foreign officials to review and/or approve contractual work (e.g., fabrication of equipment at other locations). A side trip to a luxury resort en route to a corporate location, or payment for the travel of a foreign official's spouse, will generally not be found reasonable, necessary, or bona fide.

The reasonable expenses affirmative defense does not give companies carte blanche to pay travel expenses for government officials. In a 1999 civil enforcement action, the DOJ took the position that a U.S. company, Metcalf & Eddy, Inc., violated the FCPA by providing an Egyptian official and his family with first-class air travel to the United States and with food, lodging, and other expenses because the purpose of the visit allegedly was to influence the official to use his authority to help direct a U.S. Agency for International Development contract award to Metcalf & Eddy. The DOJ alleged, among other things, that the Egyptian official received 150 percent of the estimated per diem expenses in a lump-sum payment and then was not required to pay for any of his expenses while in the United States. Metcalf & Eddy settled the case with a consent decree, without admitting or denying culpability, and agreed to pay a $400,000 civil fine as well as $50,000 to reimburse the U.S. government for the cost of the investigation.[105]

Counsel for companies considering the payment of travel expenses for foreign government officials should scrutinize the proposed travel carefully to ensure that it falls within the confines of this affirmative defense, for example, it is directly related to the explanation, promotion, and demonstration of a product or service, and is not a disguised attempt to provide compensation for help in securing business. Some companies compare the proposed government travel expense to their own employee travel reimbursement policies and approve only foreign government official travel expenses that are consistent with employee travel reimbursement policies.

The *Resource Guide* states perhaps the obvious: the analysis of whether a particular payment is a bona fide expenditure is fact-specific.[106] It offers the following list of safeguards that are helpful in evaluating whether a particular expense is appropriate or more likely problematic under this statute. The *Resource Guide* summarizes that where certain expenditures are more likely to raise red flags, they will not give rise to prosecution if they are

1. reasonable,
2. bona fide, and
3. directly related to
4. the promotion, demonstration, or explanation of products or services or the execution or performance of a contract.[107]

Gifts, travel, lodging and entertainment risks, scenarios, and precautions are covered in detail in chapter 6.

D. Parent Subsidiary Liability

The *Resource Guide* offers two ways a parent company may be liable for bribes paid by a subsidiary: (1) direct liability arising out of sufficient parent activity in the bribery activity; and (2) agency liability where under circumstances of sufficient control, a subsidiary's action and knowledge are imputed to the parent.[108] Under direct liability, a parent company whose officers knowingly funded bribery payments for a subsidiary can be held criminally liable. The *Resource Guide* points out as to agency, its fundamental characteristic is control[109] and that the DOJ and SEC will "evaluate the parent's control—including the parent's knowledge and direction of the subsidiary's actions, both generally and in the context of the specific transaction, when evaluating whether a subsidiary is an agent of the parent."[110]

E. Commercial Bribery

The FCPA antibribery provisions do not govern or prohibit bribes paid to officers or employees of wholly private, nongovernmental entities. These provisions apply only to improper payments made, directly or indirectly, to a foreign official, foreign political party or official thereof, or foreign political candidate in order to obtain or retain business or to direct business to any business or to secure an improper advantage.[111] However, commercial bribery payments that are mischaracterized or undercharacterized on the books and records of a public company may constitute FCPA books-and-records or internal controls violations. In addition, the DOJ has charged private improper payments or kickbacks along with public official bribes in FCPA cases[112] under the general conspiracy statute[113] and the Travel Act.[114] It has also required in some deferred prosecution agreements that the company not engage in acts of commercial bribery. Other countries such as the United Kingdom have enacted legislation that prohibits both public- and private-sector bribery.[115]

II. RECORD-KEEPING AND INTERNAL CONTROLS

In addition to the antibribery provisions, the FCPA imposes record-keeping and internal controls requirements on issuers (not on domestic concerns or other persons). Essentially, these requirements mandate that publicly traded companies keep accurate books and records and sound systems of internal controls. Neither the record-keeping nor the internal controls provisions limit themselves to transactions above a certain amount or impose a materiality requirement. The FCPA accounting provisions are primarily enforced by the SEC,[116] but the DOJ can bring criminal charges of knowing circumvention of internal controls as well as knowing falsification of books, records, and accounts.[117] As with the antibribery provisions, individuals are subject to criminal liability only for willful accounting violations.[118] The accounting provisions are frequently used when the DOJ and SEC cannot sustain all the elements of bribery against a public company.[119]

The SEC can bring civil accounting provision enforcement actions where the burden of proof is only preponderance of the evidence and there is no scienter requirement. While the DOJ has exclusive jurisdiction to prosecute criminal violations of the FCPA, both the DOJ and the SEC may obtain injunctive relief to prevent bribery and record-keeping violations of the Act.[120]

The rationale behind the books-and-records and internal controls provisions being complementary to the antibribery provisions was explained by Stanley Sporkin, the former federal judge and SEC general counsel who played a major role in drafting the FCPA legislation in the late 1970s. According to Judge Sporkin, the SEC proposed the record-keeping and financial control provisions because investigations had revealed that multinational companies that paid bribes overseas never accurately recorded the illicit transactions on their books. Instead, he had found companies had concealed the bribes by falsely describing the payments as other transactions. Judge Sporkin theorized that "requiring the disclosure of all bribes paid would, in effect, foreclose that activity."[121]

A. Application

The record-keeping and internal controls provisions of the FCPA apply to issuers, those companies whose securities are registered with the SEC, or those who are required to file reports with the SEC, pursuant to the Securities Exchange Act of 1934, regardless of whether they have any foreign operations.[122]

B. Record-Keeping Provisions

1. *"Records"*

The FCPA requires every issuer to "make and keep books, records, and accounts which, in reasonable detail, accurately and fairly reflect the transactions and dispositions of the assets."[123] The Act broadly defines "records" to include "accounts, correspondence, memorandums, tapes, discs, papers, books, and other documents or transcribed information of any type."[124] "Reasonable detail" means such level of detail as would satisfy prudent officials in the conduct of their own affairs.[125] Congress noted when it adopted this version that "the concept of reasonableness of necessity contemplates the weighing of a number of factors, including the costs of compliance."[126] There is no materiality requirement for a books-and-records violation.[127] An individual or entity may be criminally liable if he knowingly falsifies a book, record, or account.[128] However, inadvertent mistakes will not give rise to enforcement actions or prosecutions.[129]

In *United States v. Jensen*,[130] the Northern District of California rejected a defendant's argument that the "books and records" statute was too vague and did not give a person of ordinary intelligence fair notice of what is proscribed. The defendant, a corporate human-resources director, had falsified minutes of a committee meeting during which stock option grants had been discussed. In dismissing the "void for vagueness" argument as applied to these facts, the district court ruled that "helping to create false committee meeting minutes that have the effect of understating corporate expenses constitutes the falsification of a record that 'reflects the transactions and dispositions of the assets of the issuer.'"[131]

Record-keeping violations normally involve three types of offenses:

1. Records that simply fail to record improper transactions at all, for example, off-the-books transactions such as bribes and kickbacks;
2. Records that are falsified to disguise aspects of improper transactions otherwise recorded correctly; and

3. Records that correctly set forth the quantitative aspects of transactions but fail to record the qualitative aspects of the transactions that would reveal their illegality or impropriety, such as the true purpose of particular payments to agents, distributors, or customers.[132]

To establish an FCPA violation, it is not necessary that the inaccurately recorded transactions in question be material under federal securities laws.

2. *Examples of Transactions That Accounting Records May Fail to Adequately or Accurately Record or Disclose*

Certain transactions have been found to be inaccurately or inadequately recorded on company books and records:

- Substantial payments to mid- or high-level foreign government officials,
- "Facilitating payments" to low-level foreign government officials,
- Commercial bribes or kickbacks,
- Political contributions,
- Charitable donations,
- Smuggling activities,
- Income tax violations,
- Customs or currency violations, and
- Extraordinary or lavish gifts.

3. *Bribe Mischaracterizations in Books and Records*

The DOJ–SEC *Resource Guide* lists 14 examples of how bribes have been mischaracterized on books and records:

- Commissions on royalties,
- Consulting fees,
- Sales and marketing expenses,
- Scientific incentives or studies,
- Travel and entertainment expenses,
- Rebates or discounts,
- After sales service fees,
- Miscellaneous expenses,
- Petty cash withdrawals,
- Free goods,
- Intercompany accounts,
- Supplier vendor payments,
- Write-offs, and
- "Customs intervention" payments.[133]

General counsel often ask whether a mischaracterization of one or two entries in a company's books and records will lead to a criminal or civil charge. For both the DOJ and SEC, the decision will frequently depend on whether there was "misreporting of large bribery payments or widespread inaccurate recording of smaller payments made as part of a systemic pattern of bribery."[134]

4.   Foreign Subsidiaries

The *Resource Guide* makes clear that responsibility for the FCPA's accounting provisions extend to foreign subsidiaries and joint ventures under an issuer's control.[135] Thus, an issuer can violate the books-and-records provisions if a majority-owned foreign subsidiary creates false records to conceal an illicit payment, and the issuer parent then incorporates the subsidiary's information into its books and records. For example, in 2000 the SEC brought a books-and-records action against IBM Corp. related to "presumed illicit payments" to foreign officials by one of IBM's wholly owned subsidiaries. The SEC alleged that IBM-Argentina paid money to a subcontractor, which payment in turn was given to certain foreign officials. The SEC charged that IBM-Argentina's then-senior management overrode IBM's procurement and contracting procedures and fabricated documentation to conceal the details of the subcontract. IBM-Argentina allegedly recorded the payments to the subcontractor as third-party subcontractor expenses, and IBM incorporated this information into the Form 10-K it filed with the SEC in 1994. Without admitting or denying the SEC's allegations, IBM consented to the entry of a cease-and-desist order and agreed to pay a $300,000 civil penalty.[136] The IBM settlement with the SEC was unusual in that it did not include an internal controls violation.

In 2010, the DOJ and SEC brought enforcement actions against RAE Systems, a California company, for violating the FCPA's accounting provisions when two Chinese joint ventures in which RAE Systems was a partner paid over $400,000 in bribes for it to obtain business in China.[137] Chinese employees of the joint venture made improper payments from "cash advances" to state-owned entity officials who recorded the payments on the books as "business fees" or "travel and entertainment" expenses. The SEC alleged that the public company failed to have adequate internal controls and failed to act on red flags indicating that its affiliates were engaged in bribery.[138] RAE Systems was required to disgorge $1.15 million and to pay $4.7 million in penalties.

The accounting provisions of the FCPA do not normally apply when the issuer holds 50 percent or less interest in the foreign entity.[139] However, when an issuer holds 50 percent or less interest, it must "proceed in good faith to use its influence to the extent reasonable under the circumstances to cause [the affiliate] to devise and maintain a system of internal controls"[140] consistent with the accounting and record-keeping provisions. Where an issuer demonstrates good-faith efforts to influence the internal controls system of the affiliate, it enjoys a conclusive presumption that it has complied with the books-and-records accounting provisions of the statute.[141]

C.   Internal Controls

The FCPA's internal controls provisions codify existing auditing standards[142] and require issuers to devise and maintain a system of internal accounting controls sufficient to provide reasonable assurances that

1.   transactions are executed in accordance with management's general or specific authorization;

2. transactions are recorded as necessary:
   a. to permit preparation of financial statements in conformity with generally accepted accounting principles or any other criteria applicable to such statements; and
   b. to maintain accountability for assets;
3. access to assets is permitted only in accordance with management's general or specific authorization; and
4. the recorded accountability for assets is compared with the existing assets at reasonable intervals and appropriate action is taken with respect to any differences.[143]

"Reasonable assurances" means such a degree of assurance as would satisfy prudent officials in the conduct of their own affairs.[144]

Signally, the FCPA does not mandate "any particular kind of internal controls systems."[145] Rather, the test for compliance is "whether a system, taken as a whole, reasonably meets the statute's specified objectives."[146] Because there are no specific standards by which to evaluate the sufficiency of controls, any evaluation is a highly subjective process.[147] Still, in conducting an FCPA controls assessment, one should evaluate (1) the industry(ies) the company is in; (2) the countries where the company does business and their corruption reputations; (3) whether customers in those countries are government or state-owned or state-controlled entities; and (4) the company's business model.[148]

The *Resource Guide* stresses that an effective compliance program is a critical component of an issuer's internal controls:

> Fundamentally, the design of a company's internal controls must take into account the operational realities and risks attendant to the company's business, such as: the nature of its products or services; how the products or services get to market; the nature of its workforce; the degree of regulation; the extent of its government interaction; and the degree to which it has operations in countries with a high risk of corruption. A company's compliance program should be tailored to these differences. Businesses whose operations expose them to a high risk of corruption will necessarily devise and employ different internal controls than businesses that have a lesser exposure to corruption, just as a financial services company would be expected to devise and employ different internal controls than a manufacturer.[149]

The *Resource Guide* used the *Daimler* case to illustrate an internal controls failure:

> [T]he company used dozens of ledger accounts, known internally as "internal third party accounts," to maintain credit balances for the benefit of government officials. The accounts were funded through several bogus pricing mechanisms, such as "price surcharges," "price inclusions," or excessive commissions. The company also used artificial discounts or rebates on sales contracts to generate the

money to pay the bribes. The bribes also were made through phony sales intermediaries and corrupt business partners, as well as through the use of cash desks. Sales executives would obtain cash from the company in amounts as high as hundreds of thousands of collars, enabling the company to obscure the purpose and recipients of the money paid to government officials.[150]

Daimler was charged with bribery and books-and-records and internal controls violations (see chapter 10 summary of *United States v. Daimler*).

A person or entity that knowingly circumvents or knowingly fails to implement an internal accounting controls system may be criminally liable.[151] No criminal liability, however, is imposed for insignificant or technical accounting errors.[152] One well-respected FCPA commentator, Stuart H. Deming, has observed that the internal controls provisions will always be applied in hindsight, where the DOJ or SEC rarely finds them to be adequate.[153] Where an issuer holds 50 percent or less of the voting power with respect to a foreign or domestic firm, the FCPA requires only that the issuer proceed in good faith to cause the affiliate to devise and maintain a system of internal accounting controls to the extent reasonable under the circumstances.[154]

Certain industries, such as the energy, pharmaceutical/healthcare, and chemicals industries, have presented widely known bribery challenges. However, recent DOJ and SEC enforcement actions make clear that no industry is immune from FCPA investigation or prosecution. Importantly, multinational companies must examine not only their own industry, but also the nature of the logistics services they require and the companies that provide such services, as there is a risk that multinationals may knowingly use vendors and service providers to handle more problematic local government tasks.

Companies that conduct business in geographic locales where corruption risks are high require a stronger set of internal controls for those operations. The Transparency International Corruption Perception Index (CPI) ranks each of 176 countries from 1 (highly corrupt) to 100 (very clean) (see chapter 5), and multinationals must consider the countries or regions where corruption risk profiles are substantial. Controls for countries or regions with high-risk profiles require greater oversight of accounting and purchasing functions. Internal audits and, in particular, FCPA audits should be undertaken with greater frequency in high-risk jurisdictions.

Many multinational companies, including energy and pharmaceutical companies, find foreign governments and agencies their largest customers or partners in developing regions or economies. Where potential customers or partners are state-owned or state-controlled entities, companies must be careful not only in the direct procurement process, but also with travel, lodging, and entertainment related to customer product or service demonstrations. Controls should be established to identify all government-related customers, to identify customers' expenses, and to ensure appropriate advance authorizations and proper record-keeping.

A particular business model may necessitate additional internal controls. For example, if a company employs a limited sales force and relies largely on distributors and resellers, it will have to address the distributor and reseller risks and evaluate their background, to draft contracts with FCPA warranties and representations,

and to monitor their activities on an ongoing basis. If a company uses consultants or marketing personnel as "agents" to help develop business, that business
model significantly increases FCPA risks. Policies and procedures for conducting
thorough due diligence and the retention of consultants, agents, and distributors
should be developed and implemented. A due diligence file should be created to
ensure a strong record of the background of the agent, contractor, distributor, or
vendor engaged to represent the company. Ongoing due diligence is also an important internal control. For example, documentation of payments to agents (such as
banking and payee details and changes) should be compiled during contracting
and compared to payment instructions received with invoices from the third party
over time to ensure that discrepancies do not exist or unexpectedly occur.

If a company's business model involves substantial customer travel and entertainment, such budgets and related policies must be carefully reviewed and monitored
(see chapter 4). Other practices occasionally unique to certain industries, such as charitable donations or political contributions, should consider prior approval requirements and regular monitoring of related general ledger accounts (see chapter 7).

If a company operates in a highly regulated industry, for example, pharmaceuticals or state-owned telecommunications, specific internal controls should be
implemented regarding licenses, permits, and other approvals. Companies that
engage in merger and acquisition activity must implement detailed due diligence
practices and preserve a record of the same (see chapter 5). Day One compliance
plans should be organized well in advance for any new acquisitions or joint venture
operations—and adhered to.

The senior management of companies committed to compliance regularly analyze their particular risks and their industry's risks, implement controls to reduce
the same, consider the "best practice" internal controls of others in the industry(ies),
constantly reassess their control environment, and establish due diligence and Day
One compliance controls for mergers and acquisitions.

III.   CONSPIRACY AND OTHER FEDERAL STATUTES USED BY THE FRAUD SECTION OF THE CRIMINAL DIVISION IN FCPA ENFORCEMENT

A.   General Conspiracy Statute: 18 U.S.C. § 371

The DOJ's Fraud Section frequently includes a conspiracy count in FCPA prosecutions under the federal general conspiracy statute (18 U.S.C. § 371). The statute
provides:

> If two or more persons conspire either to commit any offense against
> the United States, or to defraud the United States, or any agency thereof
> in any manner or for any purpose, and one or more of such persons do
> not act to effect the object of the conspiracy, each shall be fined under
> this title or imprisoned not more than five years, or both. If, however,
> the offense, the commission of which is the object of the conspiracy,
> is a misdemeanor only, the punishment for such conspiracy shall not
> exceed the maximum punishment for such misdemeanor.[155]

This statute addresses two types of conspiracies: (1) conspiracies to commit violations of specific federal statutes (the "offense clause") and (2) conspiracies to defraud the United States (the "defraud clause"). In the FCPA area, the United States typically charges the "offense clause" conspiracy and, specifically, a conspiracy to violate the antibribery section of the FCPA. On occasion, the United States will charge a conspiracy to violate the FCPA and another statute, such as the wire fraud statute.[156]

1. *Elements*

The four elements of the general conspiracy statute are

    a. An agreement by two or more persons,
    b. To commit the unlawful object of the conspiracy,
    c. With knowledge of the conspiracy and with actual participation in the conspiracy, and
    d. At least one coconspirator committed one overt act in furtherance of the conspiracy.[157]

To sustain a conviction, the United States must prove beyond a reasonable doubt that a defendant knew of the conspiracy and its essential objective(s). The essence of the crime of conspiracy is the agreement and not the commission of an objective substantive crime.[158] The government need not prove that the victim of the conspiracy lost money or that the defendant intended that the victim lose money.[159]

2. *Agreement*

The essence of a conspiracy is an agreement to commit an unlawful act.[160] The offense of conspiracy necessarily involves an agreement by at least two persons.[161] The courts are split over whether a corporation may conspire with its officers and employees.[162] A corporation may be indicted as a coconspirator,[163] but the acquittal of a corporation's employee of conspiracy does not require acquittal of the corporation.[164] Proof of conspiratorial conduct is frequently established by circumstantial evidence.[165]

3. *Overt Act*

The crime of general conspiracy is not complete until an overt act has been committed.[166] The overt act need not be a crime.[167] For example, it may consist of merely purchasing office supplies, opening a bank account, or transmitting an e-mail as long as that act is in furtherance of the conspiracy.

4. *Government Advantages in Charging the General Conspiracy Statute*

The government gains considerable advantage by including a conspiracy count in a criminal case. First, the ongoing nature of conspiracy lends itself to expansive drafting, particularly in temporal terms. Conspiracies frequently are alleged to have continued for years and occasionally decades. Second, the breadth and vagueness of a conspiracy count allow the admission of much proof that might otherwise be inadmissible. Third, a conspiracy count enables the government to broadly join persons and allegations. A conspiracy can allege an agreement to defraud multiple entities, individuals, and companies or both the government (e.g., the SEC) and private entities and individuals. Fourth, evidentiary rules with respect to coconspirator declarations enlarge the admissibility of often-damaging statements in conspiracy trials.[168] Fifth, because conspiracy is a continuing crime, its five-year statute of limitations does not begin to run until either the conspiracy's objectives are met,[169] the conspiracy is abandoned,[170] its members affirmatively withdraw,[171] or the last overt act committed in furtherance of the conspiracy occurs.[172]

B. Other Federal Statutes Used by the Fraud Section of the Criminal Division in FCPA Enforcement

The DOJ Fraud Section not only charges the FCPA and the federal conspiracy statute,[173] but has also used the false statements,[174] money laundering,[175] mail fraud,[176] and wire fraud[177] statutes in FCPA prosecutions. In addition, the Fraud Section increasingly collaborates with the Antitrust Division to investigate price-fixing or bid-rigging violations[178] and also pursues tax[179] and export[180] violations. The conspiracy statute in particular enables the government to charge relevant conduct five or more years old.

IV. PENALTIES, FINES, AND OTHER SANCTIONS

A. Criminal Penalties

The FCPA is a criminal statute for which sentences of individuals and corporations are considered in the context of the U.S. Sentencing Guidelines.[181] Individuals who commit willful violations of the FCPA antibribery provisions may be punished by up to $100,000 in fines and/or five years of imprisonment.[182] Individuals who violate the FCPA accounting provisions may be fined up to $5 million and imprisoned for up to 20 years.[183] Corporations may be fined up to $25 million per violation of the FCPA accounting provisions[184] and $2 million per violation of the FCPA antibribery provisions.[185] Moreover, under the Alternative Fines Act, fines for both individuals and corporations can be much higher: the fine may be up to twice the amount of loss to the victim or of the benefit the defendant obtained or sought to obtain by making the corrupt payment.[186] In practice, Alternative Fines Act fines often exceed the statutory maximum fine in significant FCPA cases and enable the DOJ to secure megafines.

The 1998 amendments eliminated a disparity in penalties between U.S. nationals who are employees or agents of issuers or domestic concerns and foreign nationals who are employees or agents of issuers or domestic concerns. Previously, foreign nationals were subject only to FCPA civil penalties. Now, both U.S. and foreign persons may be prosecuted and face criminal penalties.[187]

Any property, real or personal, "which constitutes or is derived from proceeds traceable to a violation of the FCPA, or a conspiracy to violate the FCPA," may be forfeited.[188] Fines imposed on individuals may not be paid by their employer or principal.[189] An unlawful payment under the FCPA is not deductible under U.S. tax laws as a business expense.[190]

B. Civil Penalties

The FCPA also allows a civil penalty of up to $10,000 against any company that violates the antibribery provisions of the FCPA, and against any officer, director, employee, or agent of a company who willfully violates the antibribery provisions of the Act.[191] The SEC may bring an enforcement action seeking an additional fine, depending on the circumstances, of up to $500,000 on the gain obtained as a result of the violation.[192]

C. Disgorgement of Profits and Prejudgment Interest

Beginning in mid-2004, the SEC began seeking disgorgement of profits and prejudgment interest in FCPA cases. The government first obtained this type of relief in an FCPA proceeding in *SEC v. ABB Ltd.*,[193] where a Swiss-based global provider of power and automation technologies agreed to pay $5.9 million in disgorgement of profits. Since 2004, the SEC has regularly sought this relief from issuers based in the United States and issuers that trade in the United States through American depositary receipts (ADRs). Approximately 1,600 foreign companies trade ADRs or on U.S. securities exchanges, thereby submitting themselves to FCPA jurisdiction.

D. Government Suspension and Debarment Sanctions

1. *United States*

Public procurement projects are a substantial revenue source for many multinational companies. A company found in violation of the FCPA may be suspended or barred from federal programs such as Defense Department procurement programs, the Commodity Futures Trading Commission, and the Overseas Private Investment Corporation.[194] A suspension by one U.S. government agency generally has government-wide effect.[195] Indictment alone can lead to the suspension of the right to do business with the U.S. government. Other potential collateral consequences for FCPA violations include ineligibility to receive export licenses, and SEC suspension and debarment from the securities industry.[196]

2. *European Union—Article 45*

In 2004, the European Union implemented mandatory debarment provisions under its Public Procurement Directive.[197] Specifically, Article 45 provides that "any candidate or tenderer who has been the subject of conviction by final judgment of which the contracting authority is aware . . . shall be excluded from participation in a public contract."[198] It is widely believed that the record-setting Siemens $1.6 billion settlement with the U.S. and German governments was carefully designed to avoid a bribery conviction of the parent company and pleas by any European Community subsidiaries to the same in order to avoid a corruption conviction and mandatory debarment under Article 45 of the EU Directive.[199]

V. STATUTE OF LIMITATIONS

A. General Five-Year Statute

The statute of limitations begins to run when a crime is complete.[200] The criminal statute of limitations for most noncapital federal offenses,[201] including mail and wire fraud,[202] securities fraud,[203] and violations of the FCPA, is five years.[204] General conspiracy charges[205] have a five-year limitation unless the alleged conspiracy involves a substantive offense that has a different limitation provision period.[206] A charge of conspiracy to commit a substantive offense cannot have a longer statute of limitations from that provided for the substantive offense itself.[207]

B. Conspiracy

The important "continuing offense doctrine" exception involves conspiracy prosecutions. FCPA indictments typically include a conspiracy count.[208] A conspiracy ends when the central criminal purpose of the conspiracy has been attained.[209] The Supreme Court has held that in conspiracy prosecutions, "the period of limitation must be computed from the dates of the overt act rather than the formation of the conspiracy . . . where, during the existence of the conspiracy, there are successive acts, the period of limitation must be computed from the last of them."[210] The fact that the conspiracy began outside the limitations period will not prevent prosecution as long as at least one overt act in furtherance of the conspiracy occurred within five years of the indictment.[211]

Acts of concealment, without more, will generally not "extend the life of the conspiracy after its main objective has been obtained."[212] In addressing statute of limitations challenges, many courts, particularly in Sherman Act prosecutions, have focused on and upheld conspiracies through the point of receipt of economic benefits.[213] For example, in *United States v. Kozeny*, Judge Scheindlin found that the alleged conspiracy did not end until a return had been made on the bribe.[214] Courts have attempted to distinguish between overt acts in furtherance of a conspiracy and the result of a conspiracy.[215] To escape continuing liability for a conspiracy, a coconspirator must unequivocally and affirmatively withdraw.[216] Mere cessation of participation is not enough to constitute withdrawal.[217] The burden of proof is generally on a defendant to establish withdrawal.[218]

C. Potential Three-Year Suspension of Limitations to Obtain Foreign Evidence

If in an FCPA criminal investigation the DOJ seeks evidence located in a foreign country, the running of the statute of limitations may be suspended for a period of up to three years.[219] The United States may, before the return of an indictment, apply to the grand jury supervisory court to suspend the running of the statute of limitations. To suspend the statute, the district court must find by a preponderance of the evidence that an official request has been made for evidence located in a foreign country and that it reasonably appears, or reasonably appeared at the time the request was made, that such evidence is, or was, in a foreign country.[220]

The period of suspension begins when the official request is made and ends when the foreign court or authority takes final action on the request. In no event may the suspension exceed three years, or extend the period within which a criminal case must be initiated for more than six months if all foreign authorities take final action on the request before the period would expire.[221] "Official request" as used in this context means a letter rogatory, a request under a treaty or convention, or any other request for evidence made by a court of the United States or an authority of the United States having criminal law enforcement responsibility, to a court or other authority of a foreign country.[222]

D. Extensions of the Statute of Limitations

Near the eve of the expiration of the criminal statute of limitations, federal pros-ecutors often will advise defense counsel that in the absence of a written waiver of the statute of limitations and tolling agreement, the United States will file a criminal complaint or return an indictment against the client in order to keep the case within the statute of limitations. Under such threat, counsel must evaluate all facts and circumstances of the investigation and the prosecutor's intentions and decide whether a waiver or tolling agreement is appropriate. If a company is gener-ally cooperating with the DOJ, it will be difficult for it to refuse an extension of the statute of limitations, as often the DOJ will have sufficient evidence to return a charge against the company based on the conduct of one or more employees or agents. For this reason, companies usually accede to a government request for a limited or reasonable extension of the statute.

However, if counsel concludes that the DOJ has not conducted anywhere near an adequate investigation and is unlikely to file charges despite the threat, an individual client may decide to refuse to enter into a tolling agreement. If counsel concludes that the DOJ remains truly undecided about whether to file criminal charges, the client may be wise to consent to an extension. By agreeing to a limited waiver, a target or subject may establish goodwill with the government and pave the way for a noncriminal disposition of a case.

From an evidentiary point of view, an extension often will not disadvantage a client, since the passage of time generally favors the defense.[223] If a client agrees to execute a limited waiver or extension of the statute of limitations, it should not agree to any waiver of defenses that may exist as of the date of execution of the tolling agreement.

E. Books-and-Records and Internal Controls Violations

The government can argue that books-and-records and internal controls violations are "continuing offenses." In *SEC v. Jackson*, the government charged the defendant with aiding and abetting, and asserted that the statute of limitations did not bar prosecution of these two violations because the violations will "inherently be con-tinuing in nature."[224] The district court in this civil action agreed, observing that these violations "inflict significant harm on the investing public" and Congress did not intend for "wrongdoers [to] continue to reap the benefit of their continuing violations with no threat of punitive enforcement actions."[225] The Southern District of Texas court language speaks of "enforcement actions"; whether such a court in a criminal case would apply the "continuing offense" principle to books-and-records and internal controls violations remains unclear.

F. Civil Statute of Limitations

28 U.S.C. § 2462 provides for a five-year limitation on any "suit or proceeding for the enforcement of any civil find, penalty or forfeiture. This five-year period, which applies to SEC actions, begins to run when the claim first accrued." In cases against individuals who are not residents of the United States, the statute of limitations

may be tolled for any period when the defendants are not "found within the United States in order that proper service may be made thereon."[226]

VI. DOJ FCPA OPINION LETTERS

In 1980, the Department of Justice instituted an FCPA review or opinion procedure,[227] and in 1992 it published a final rule[228] that enables public companies and all domestic concerns to obtain an enforcement opinion of the attorney general as to whether prospective conduct conforms with the DOJ's enforcement policy regarding the antibribery provisions of the FCPA. Under this procedure, a request must relate to an actual transaction and not a hypothetical one. It also must be prospective, that is, made prior to the requestor's commitment to proceed with a transaction. The request must be specific and furnish all relevant and material information bearing on the conduct, including any supporting materials.[229]

A favorable opinion from the DOJ creates a rebuttable presumption, applicable in any subsequent enforcement action, that the conduct described in the request conformed with the FCPA. In considering the presumption, a court will weigh all relevant factors, including whether the submission to the attorney general was accurate and complete and whether the actual conduct diverged from that described in the request. An FCPA opinion provides a safe harbor only to the requestor and affords no protection to any party that did not join in the request.

While many of the early FCPA opinions involved minor gifts or payments, a number of the opinions have addressed issues that multinational corporations routinely encounter, including marketing representative agreements with foreign SOEs,[230] payments to foreign officials during a leave of absence,[231] joint ventures with a foreign company that has numerous agent agreements,[232] and a foreign official as a shareholder and chairman or consortium member.[233] The opinions can provide guidance to companies entertaining mergers, acquisitions, or divestitures.[234] While the opinions provide protection only to specific requestors, many contain terms, language, and principles useful to contemplated contractual relationships with third parties.

Since 1980 the DOJ has released 61 opinions pursuant to this review procedure. The reluctance of corporations to use the FCPA opinion procedure has been attributed to the risk of the loss of confidentiality, the possibility of negative results, government delays in issuing opinions, and the risk of instigating further government investigation.[235] Although one might anticipate that the 1998 amendments would have spawned greater use of the FCPA opinion procedure as businesses sought clarification of the new provisions, there were, in fact, no opinions released in 1999 or 2005 and only 17 opinions issued from 2000 through 2008. The DOJ issued only one opinion in 2009; three opinions in 2010; one opinion in 2011; two opinions in 2012; one opinion in 2013; and two opinions in 2014.[236] The prompt turnaround time on several recent opinion requests makes clear that the DOJ has recognized past criticism that it has been slow to respond to opinion requests.

VII. DODD-FRANK WHISTLEBLOWER PROTECTION LAW AND RULES

Section 922 of the Dodd-Frank Wall Street Reform and Consumer Protection Act required the SEC to promulgate whistleblower protection rules.[237] On May 25, 2011, the SEC issued its final rules implementing the Dodd-Frank whistleblower provisions. The rules in conjunction with the Act provide whistleblowers with (1) a substantial monetary incentive to report wrongdoing under the federal securities laws to the SEC and (2) increased protection against retaliation for whistleblowing. Since the FCPA is a federal securities law, it is expected that there will be a significant increase in FCPA whistleblowers alleging foreign bribery serious enough to result in an SEC sanction of greater than $1 million.

A. Basic Elements

A whistleblower is an individual who, alone or with others, provides information to the SEC that relates to the possible violation of the federal securities laws (including any rules or regulations thereunder) that has occurred, is going on, or is about to occur. The bounty program applies only to individuals who provide information of securities laws violations that results in sanctions of greater than $1 million. For reporting leads to such successful enforcement actions, a whistleblower is eligible to receive 10 percent to 30 percent of the amount collected.[238]

To recover an award, a whistleblower must:

1. voluntarily provide the Commission
2. with original information
3. that leads to a successful enforcement action by the Commission in a federal court or administrative action, and
4. in which the Commission obtains monetary sanctions totaling more than $1 million.[239]

While the clear focus of most companies has been on potential employee whistleblowers, anyone—a counterparty in a transaction, a customer, a vendor, an adversary in litigation,[240] a journalist, or an academician—can "blow the whistle" under these rules.

B. Discussion of Key Elements

1. *Voluntary*

The first element requires a voluntary submission of information to the SEC.[241] A whistleblower must "voluntarily provide" information before a related request, inquiry, or demand is directed to him by the SEC, the Public Company Accounting Oversight Board (PCAOB), any self-regulating organization, Congress, any other federal authority, or any state attorney general or securities regulatory authority. A whistleblower may provide information after he or she becomes aware of the existence of an investigation so long as no request has been directed to the whistleblower personally.

2. *Original Information*

All information must be original. The new provision defines "original information" to mean information that is

1. derived from one's independent knowledge or independent analysis;
2. not already known to the Commission from any other source unless the whistleblower is the original source of the information;
3. not exclusively derived from an allegation made in a judicial or administrative hearing, a governmental report, hearing, audit, or investigation from the news or media, unless the whistleblower is a source of the information; and
4. provided to the Commission for the first time after July 21, 2010 (the date of the enactment of the Dodd-Frank Act).[242]

The Original Information provisions require that the whistleblower have "independent knowledge" not derived from publicly available sources, but from his or her experiences, communications, and observations in business or social situations. The Original Information provisions further require "independent analysis," meaning one's own analyses, which vary whether done alone or in combination with others. Analysis means examination and analysis of information that may be publicly available, but that reveals information that is not greatly known or available to the public. Whistleblowers are incentivized to first provide original information through an internal compliance program.[243] Internal reporting first is viewed as a positive factor in settling the amount of the bounty.[244] Whistleblowers are expected to provide such information to the SEC within 120 days of providing it internally. The SEC states that in appropriate cases it may notify a company of its receipt of whistleblower information and give the company an opportunity to investigate and report back to the SEC.

3. *Leads to a Successful Enforcement Action*

Rule 21F-4(c) addresses the third award requirement of under what circumstances Original Information provided by a whistleblower can lead to a successful enforcement action by the SEC. The final rules define "information that leads to a successful enforcement action" as information that is (1) "sufficiently specific, credible and timely to cause the staff to commence an examination and open an investigation"; or (2) to "reopen an investigation or to inquire concerning different conduct," and "significantly contributes to the success of the investigation." The SEC must thereafter bring "a successful judicial or administrative action based in whole or in part on conduct that was the subject" of the information.

4. *$1 Million in Monetary Sanctions*

Monetary sanctions means "any money, including penalties, disgorgement, and interest, ordered to be paid and any money deposited into a disgorgement fund or other fund . . . as a result of a Commission action or a related action."[245] Several proceedings brought by the SEC, if arising from the "same nucleus of operative facts," may be treated together, for purposes of making an award.[246]

C. Exclusions

The final rules exclude certain individuals from eligibility for award: (1) persons associable with regulatory and law enforcement authorities; (2) foreign government officials; (3) persons convicted of criminal violations that are related to the SEC action or a related action; (4) persons who obtain original information through the performance of an audit of a company's financial statements; and (5) persons who knowingly and willfully make false, fictitious, or fraudulent statements or representations in their whistleblower submissions to the SEC.[247]

D. Conformance with Form TCR (Tip, Complaint, or Referral)

Absent a showing of extraordinary circumstances, a whistleblower must give the SEC information in the form and manner that it requires. The procedure for submitting original information to the SEC is quite clear and can be accomplished in one of two ways: (1) through the SEC's web-based interactive database for the submission of tips, complaints, and referrals; and (2) by completing Form TCR (Tip, Complaint, or Referral) and mailing or faxing the form to SEC headquarters in Washington, D.C. Specifically, the whistleblower must file and certify a six-page Form TCR,[248] which addresses information about the whistleblower and his counsel; information about the individual or entity that is the subject of the complaint; details about the complaint including its nature and date of occurrence; whether the whistleblower has first reported any potential violation to his supervisor, compliance officer, whistleblower hotline, and so on; how the whistleblower obtained any information; supporting materials with particularity; eligibility requirements; and the whistleblower's declaration and counsel's certification.[249]

E. Award Criteria

The award criteria create positive and negative factors for determining the appropriate award percentage (10 percent to 30 percent) of assessed monetary sanctions that the SEC and other authorities are able to collect exceeding $1 million.[250] Subject to this requirement, the amount of any bounty award is within the discretion of the SEC.[251]

The rules cite four factors that can increase the amount of a whistleblower's award:[252]

1. The significance of the information provided by the whistleblower;
2. Assistance provided by the whistleblower;
3. Law enforcement interests; and
4. Participation in internal compliance systems, which shall include
   a. whether, and the extent to which, a whistleblower reported the possible securities violations through internal whistleblower, legal or compliance procedures before or at the same time as reporting them to the SEC; and
   b. whether, and the extent to which, a whistleblower assisted any internal investigation[253] or inquiry concerning the reported securities violation.

Conversely, the rules cite three factors the SEC will consider in determining whether to decrease an award:[254]

1. Culpability, including the whistleblower's role in the securities violation; the whistleblower's education, training, experience, and position of responsibility at the time the violations occurred; the whistleblower's scienter, both generally and in relation to others who participated in the violations; his or her personal financial benefit from violations; whether the whistleblower is a recidivist; the egregiousness of the underlying fraud committed by the whistleblower; and whether the whistleblower knowingly interfered with the SEC's investigation;
2. Unreasonable reporting delay, including whether there was a legitimate reason for the whistleblower to delay reporting violations;
3. Whether the whistleblower undermined the integrity of internal compliance or reporting systems.

F.   Confidentiality

In general, the SEC will not disclose information that reasonably could be expected to reveal the identity of the whistleblower.[255] The rules provide for anonymous submission of information but in such circumstances a whistleblower must have an attorney represent him or her in connection with both the submission of information and claim for an award. The attorney's contact information must be provided at the time a whistleblower submits information to the SEC.

G.   SEC Whistleblower Report to Congress (2014)[256]

On November 18, 2014, the SEC published its 2014 Annual Report to Congress on the Dodd-Frank Whistleblower Program. The highlights from the report included:

- A majority of the award recipients were not represented by counsel when they submitted their tip or complaint to the Commission. However, a majority of the recipients were represented by counsel when they applied for an award.
- In fiscal year 2014 the SEC authorized rewards to nine whistleblowers, out of a total of 14 since the program's inception in August 2011.
- Of the award recipients who were current or former employees, over 80 percent raised their concerns initially to their supervisors or compliance personnel before reporting the information to the Commission.
- On August 14, 2014, a Final Order of the Commission was issued denying an individual's claims for awards in 143 different Notices of Covered Action (NoCA).[258] The SEC had already found the individual ineligible for an award in 53 other matters. It found that individual ineligible for an award in the 196 matters or in any future covered or related action.
- On August 29, 2014, the Office of the Whistleblower announced a whistleblower award of $300,000 to a company employee with audit and compliance responsibilities who reported a securities violation internally and then

reported the violation to the SEC after the company failed to take appropriate, timely action in response to the information.

- On June 13, 2014, the Commission awarded $875,000 to be divided equally by two whistleblowers who acted in concert to voluntarily furnish information and assistance to the SEC that resulted in a successful enforcement action.
- On June 16, 2014, the SEC brought its first enforcement action under the antiretaliation provisions of the Dodd-Frank Act. The head trader of Paradigm Capital Management reported to the SEC that his company had engaged in prohibited principal transactions. After learning the trader had reported the potential misconduct, Paradigm changed the whistleblower's job function, stripping him of supervisory responsibilities and otherwise marginalizing his role. The SEC ordered the firm to pay $2.2 million to settle the retaliation and other charges.[257]
- On July 22, 2014, the Commission awarded three whistleblowers collectively 30 percent of the recoveries in an SEC action. Based on the level of assistance each whistleblower provided to the SEC staff, one whistleblower received 15 percent, another 10 percent, and the third received 5 percent
- On July 31, 2014, a whistleblower aggressively worked internally to bring a securities law violation to the attention of company personnel. Only after the company failed to take action did the individual bring the matter to the SEC's attention and receive a $400,000 reward.
- On September 22, 2014, the Commission authorized an award of more than $30 million—the largest to date—to a whistleblower who provided key original information that led to a successful enforcement action.
- The number of whistleblower tips annually has increased since the program's inception with 334 in FY 2011 (a partial year), 3001 in FY 2012, 3,238 in FY 2013, and 3620 in FY 2014. Over 150 FCPA tips were filed in 2014; California, Florida, New York, and Texas were the top states for whistleblower tips in 2014.
- The SEC has given awards to four whistleblowers living in foreign countries. In the Commission's view, there is sufficient U.S. territorial nexus whenever a claimant's information leads to the successful enforcement of a covered action brought in the United States, concerning violations of the U.S. securities laws, by the Commission.
- The SEC's very first award recipient has seen his whistleblower award grow from an initial payout of nearly $50,000 to over $385,000, or over seven times the amount of the original payout.
- To date, over 40 percent of the individuals who received rewards were current or former employees. An additional 20 percent of the award recipients were consultants, contractors, or were solicited to act as consultants for the company committing the securities violation. The remaining award recipients obtained their information because they were investors who were victims of the fraud, or were professionals working in the same or similar industry or had a personal relationship with one of the defendants.

H. Practical Whistleblower Advice for Multinational Companies and Counsel

The final whistleblower rules can have a significant effect on various aspects of a company's business and operations. Consequently, companies should carefully review their compliance programs and policies and determine whether revisions need be made in view of the Dodd-Frank Act and its whistleblower rules. In particular, companies and counsel should review the following three critical components of an effective and robust compliance program and sound protocol for whistleblower complaints: (1) the compliance culture; (2) internal reporting procedures; and (3) internal investigation practices. Below are *25 whistleblower-related* recommendations—broken into the three categories of culture, internal reporting procedures, and internal investigation practices—representing the views of various law firms and counsel that have considered the Dodd-Frank Wall Street Reform and Consumer Protection Act and its final whistleblower protection rules.

1. Positive Compliance Culture

Smart whistleblower management begins with a genuine, ethical "tone at the top." As prominent labor lawyers Eugene Scalia, Jason Schwartz, and Thomas M. Johnson Jr. counseled in the wake of the implementation of the SEC's final whistleblower rules:

> A culture of compliance is important to prevent wrongdoing and misconduct from occurring and encouraging employees to report possible violations internally when they do occur. Creating an atmosphere in which employees understand that they are to rigorously adhere to the law, follow company rules and procedures, and report potential misconduct when they first become aware of it will significantly alleviate many of the issues raised by the Whistleblower Rules. In the event of an enforcement investigation, the company's compliance culture and the efficacy of its compliance programs are also important determinants in whether a firm will be sanctioned and the nature of any sanction imposed.[259]

There are 25 measures (each italicized) that can foster a culture of compliance. *Review codes of conduct, employee training, and policies for anonymous reporting, hotlines, and whistleblower reporting.*[260] Companies should examine their codes of conduct to see whether any changes are appropriate, particularly with respect to encouraging communications and the avenues provided for such communications. Compliance is an ongoing process. Companies should also update ethics training to make sure it reflects the federal whistleblower law and rules; as always, they should maintain copies of training materials and attendance lists. Finally, companies should review their anonymous reporting, hotline, and whistleblower procedures. Many whistleblowers complain that hotlines are not anonymous or confidential but instead are designed to identify whistleblowers and intimidate them. Companies should analyze the above policies and materials from the perspective of an employee, regulator, or prosecutor to determine how these audiences would respectively view the language.

Encourage compliance throughout the organization.[261] Companies with a strong compliance culture embrace compliance from top to bottom, and multinational companies make a special effort to transmit this core value in particular to foreign operations. Companies should encourage employees to talk to their supervisors or use other internal reporting procedures when they first become aware of any possible misconduct. If nothing else, early detection raises the likelihood that the matter will not reach the Dodd-Frank whistleblower million-dollar monetary sanction threshold. Early bad information is usually preferable to and less costly than delayed or late bad information. Companies can send out the strong compliance culture message in employee newsletters, at annual regional or country manager meetings, or in "town hall" compliance meetings.

Incorporate compliance as an element of job performance.[262] Companies routinely evaluate and reward employees in annual performance evaluations for meeting financial goals and contributing to team efforts, but not very often for proven commitment to compliance. Job performance evaluations can include a component for managerial and employee demonstrated commitment to compliance, for example, attendance at ethics training, managerial success in having all employees undertake ethical training, two-hour anticorruption sessions annually for international sales managers, organizing "town hall" compliance meetings, and so on. A company that includes compliance commitment as part of an officer or employee performance matrix will very likely distinguish itself from other companies that come before the SEC or DOJ under whistleblower circumstances.

Require employees to report possible violations.[263] Companies should require employees to promptly report all possible violations of the code of conduct and any laws and regularly remind employees of the requirement. Annual certifications can include employee acknowledgments that they are not aware of any potential violations of the code of conduct, including any federal securities laws, that have not already been reported to the company.

Emphasize—and mean—that the company's management will not tolerate any retaliation against whistleblowers who report legitimate concerns of potential misconduct. This recommendation applies to officers, supervisors, and coworkers and requires the company to follow through with disciplinary actions against any employees, supervisors, or officers who engage in retaliatory conduct.

Report periodically to the board of directors or the audit or compliance committee on whistleblower allegations, investigations, conclusions, and decisions. The DOJ and SEC expect meaningful board oversight in the compliance area to include receiving reports on matters as important as ones arising under the Dodd-Frank whistleblower law and rules. Many companies provide their boards or audit committee on a quarterly basis a summary of all compliance matters, however resolved, to confirm the existence and importance of a quality compliance program and to assess the effectiveness and timeliness of the whistleblower reporting protocol. (See the first item under Internal Investigation Practices, below.)

2.   Internal Reporting Procedures

Make sure the company's code of conduct, ethics materials, and new-hire employment forms provide clear guidance on internal reporting procedures. Companies should explain in writing to new hires as well as to current employees the internal reporting procedures. In the event of a later problem, the company will be able to establish that on the very first day the whistleblower joined the company, the importance of reporting any possible misconduct and how to do so was made clear to the new employee.

Develop programs designed to encourage employees to report internally and highlight benefits to whistleblowers of first reporting to the company.[264] Companies should consider offering employees incentives for appropriate internal reporting of potential violations.[265]

Repeat internal reporting procedures as a part of online or live ethics training. Companies should take the opportunity to remind employees of internal reporting procedures whenever possible. One or two training slides as part of an annual ethics or anticorruption slide deck can easily accomplish this recommendation.

Make internal reporting easy and accessible.[266] Any hotline should be available 24/7, and related procedures posted appropriately within all workplaces. Reporting guidance should also be provided in all appropriate languages. Many whistleblower reports of foreign official corruption are naturally expected to come from overseas; if foreign nationals report that internal reporting procedures were not made known or available in their respective languages, a company can assume the SEC will consider the absence of translated whistleblower policies a negative factor.

Include a compliance component in exit interviews that solicits information about any compliance issues.[267] Many companies dedicated to strong compliance conduct thorough exit interviews. If a departing employee discloses questionable conduct, the company should review and address it. If the employee fails to disclose such conduct and later raises it as whistleblower information, that inconsistency may affect the SEC's view of his or her credibility. The person conducting the exit interview should ask about compliance issues in a manner designed to elicit information and record any responses including that the employee has or perceives no compliance issues. The interviewer should ask an employee who provides problematic information in an exit interview whether he or she has any supporting materials for the information and request copies of the same or their location.

3.   *Internal Investigation Practices*

Have a global whistleblower response protocol for human resources, security, compliance, and/or legal personnel in place to timely and thoroughly respond to whistleblslower reports. A company should have a clear global protocol for expeditiously intaking, reviewing, and resolving whistleblower information or complaints. Brad Preber and Trent Gazzaway in *The Anti-Corruption Handbook*[268] offer a protocol to handle whistleblower reports in connection with accounting, internal controls over financial reporting, and auditing matters. Called the Model Accounting Complaint-Handling Process or MACH Process, this protocol has six steps:

1.   Receive the complaint;
2.   Analyze the complaint;
3.   Investigate the complaint;
4.   Resolve the compliant;
5.   Report the resolution of the complaint; and
6.   Retain the necessary documentation.

The "MACH" terminology is intended to convey that this process is to be effective and done as quickly as possible.[269]

Many companies under the direction of the compliance or legal department employ a timetable or deadline for each step of the whistleblower reporting process or protocol to ensure the review is expeditious. The second step—analysis of the complaint—should include a prompt determination of who within or outside the company should investigate the complaint or information. Depending on its nature (complex accounting, theft, etc.), the location of the alleged misconduct (local or distant), and its seriousness (potential dollar value, high-level managers, multiple countries, high-level government officials, etc.), the investigation may be assigned to HR, security, or internal audit personnel or in-house or outside counsel. For serious whistleblower complaints, the audit committee or its chair should be promptly notified of a whistleblower report.

As few people as possible should be provided with the name of any whistleblower who wishes to report confidentially. A company should respect an employee who in good faith provides confidential whistleblower information and should take steps to protect the employee's identity to the maximum extent possible.[270] The fewer people who know the whistleblower's identity, the more forthcoming he or she likely will be with the company or its counsel and the fewer people there are to disseminate misinformation or to engage in retaliatory conduct. Of course, those who are part of a whistleblower response team—HR, compliance, internal audit, legal—must be coordinated and not working at cross-purposes.

Do not dismiss or treat anonymous whistleblower allegations lightly. Some managers dismiss anonymous allegations as difficult to evaluate or less worthy than allegations where the whistleblower readily identifies himself or herself. An anonymous whistleblower may be genuinely concerned about retaliation and reluctant to directly report his concerns or information. A failure to pursue a sufficiently detailed anonymous allegation may prove costly to a company and lead to it being blindsided and its entire compliance commitment and program second-guessed by the SEC. Companies should review detailed anonymous reports to determine whether they reveal enough information to conduct a credible, responsible investigation, and because such reports may have been carefully drafted by an employee represented by counsel who may hope the company does nothing and thereby compounds and adds to the financial value of any misdeeds.

Absent exceptional circumstances, interviews of whistleblower employees in potentially serious anticorruption investigations should be conducted by counsel. Counsel will best understand the applicable anticorruption statutes, their legal elements, and defenses along with the factors—both positive and negative—that the SEC will consider in evaluating a whistleblower's information, conduct, damages, and cooperation with the SEC and the company.

Ask the whistleblower to relate in detail all facts pertinent to the allegations and whether he or she believes the acts described constitute a violation of any laws, for example, the federal securities laws. This recommendation largely incorporates and tracks the SEC's Form TCR Box D at 6 but does not assume the employee believes there is a violation of the laws or direct the employee's attention to federal securities laws. A whistleblower reporting information to the SEC or another government agency should describe the same misconduct and detail to his employer.

Ask the whistleblower to describe all the supporting materials in his or her possession and the availability and location of any additional supporting materials. This recommendation also incorporates and tracks the SEC's Form TCR. Again, in an interview a company should seek to confirm what, if any, supplemental information a whistleblower has or does not have and ask where other relevant information can be located and record any responses.

Avoid multiple employee/witness interviews and disclosing information from the interviews. Often there will be widespread speculation within a company as to who is the potential whistleblower. Not infrequently the speculation is wrong. Multiple interviews and disclosure of any details from other interviews can create misinformation and lead to retaliatory action against presumed or actual whistleblowers as well as create distractions in an investigation and within the company. Interviewees should also be instructed to not share the nature or substance of their interview with other employees.

Consider offering an employee the option to obtain counsel. General counsel can reasonably differ on this recommendation that some labor lawyers and/or FCPA practitioners favor. Sometimes employees have grandiose ideas of what constitutes wrongdoing or what award may result, and counsel can make them more realistic. In any event, companies should not affirmatively discourage employees from retaining counsel if they so desire. Company counsel might do well to assume that whistleblowing employees already have counsel.

Instruct whistleblowers to report immediately to a designated person at the company if they are subject to or perceive any retaliatory conduct. Once a whistleblower has identified himself or herself and provided the company with information in good faith, the company must ensure that no retaliatory action is taken against the employee and must convey to the employee its interest in making sure that no retaliation does take place. An employee's perception of postdisclosure retaliatory behavior by colleagues or supervisors may be incorrect, but a company is wise to understand his or her contemporaneous perception(s) and to promptly address and remedy any valid concerns.

Keep whistleblowers advised of the general status of the investigation.[271] Whistleblowers should be kept apprised of the general status of the investigation. This does not mean that they should receive a list of interviewees or updates of interviews or other investigative efforts; what it does mean is that the whistleblower should be kept informed that the company is taking the allegations seriously and is proceeding with an appropriate timely review. Otherwise, there is a risk that the employee will assume the worst: that the company does not care and has done nothing, that the company is going to make the whistleblower a scapegoat, that the company is going to fire the employee, or that the company is going to cover up or whitewash the incident(s). All of these misperceptions are bad for the company. If whistleblower allegations are proven in whole or in part, the company may wish to share with the whistleblower what remedial measures it plans to undertake.

Institute remedial actions and at a minimum have a written timetable to implement remaining ones in place within 30 days of any whistleblower report. The timetable to investigate whistleblower information and to remediate, as appropriate, is now accelerated due to the whistleblower rules' requirement that an employee report information to the SEC within 120 days of first providing a company with information. If he or she approaches the SEC earlier with valid information, a company will be best served by having a contemporaneous record of the action plan it had in place for the SEC and DOJ.

Make sure disciplinary action is taken with respect to any wrongdoing and with respect to all appropriate wrongdoers. In the wake of highly problematic conduct, some companies impose light disciplinary actions, fail to take any actions against supervisors, or avoid discipline altogether in hope the issue will fade away. If major disciplinary action or discipline of supervisors is appropriate, it is wise to impose it sooner rather than later.

Document decisions regarding whistleblowers.[272] Counsel should carefully document all decisions regarding whistleblowers, describing exactly what the whistleblower alleged, what investigation was conducted, whether the complaint was founded in whole or in part, and how the allegation was resolved, including any remedial actions or legitimate reasons for taking adverse employment action.[273]

Consider carefully what investigation report and work product to share with the SEC.[274] In the event a whistleblower has reported information to the SEC, the Commission will no doubt want to evaluate the company's response to the information, learn what investigation it conducted, and understand its findings or conclusion. Counsel will need to evaluate what, if any, privileged materials it will waive and share with the SEC or DOJ. Counsel will likely want to design for the government a PowerPoint different from what has been furnished under privilege to management, a board, or a committee.

VIII. *RESOURCE GUIDE TO THE U.S. FOREIGN CORRUPT PRACTICES ACT* (2012)

In November 2012 the Criminal Division of the U.S. Department of Justice and the Enforcement Division of the U.S. Securities and Exchange Commission released the long-awaited *Resource Guide to the U.S. Foreign Corrupt Practices Act* (reprinted as appendix 4).[275] This guidance replaces and represents a vast improvement over the outdated *Laypersons Guide to the Foreign Corrupt Practices Act*. The 120-page publication covers a wide variety of FCPA topics, including who and what is covered by the FCPA's antibribery provisions; who is covered by the accounting provisions; the definition of a foreign official; what constitute proper and improper gifts, travel, and entertainment expenses; the nature of facilitating payments; how successor liability applies in the mergers and acquisitions context; the hallmarks of an effective corporate compliance program; and the different types of civil and criminal resolutions available in the FCPA context.

Notwithstanding its welcome coverage of these important topics, the *Resource Guide* is expressly "non-binding, informal, and summary in nature and the information contained therein does not constitute rules and regulations. As such, it is not intended to, does not and may not be relied upon to create any rights, substantive or procedural, that are enforceable at law by any party, any criminal, civil or administrative matter."[276] Nevertheless, counsel representing companies and individuals will carefully study the *Resource Guide* to understand how the DOJ and SEC view and analyze various improper payment situations and how other companies have fared with these agencies in resolving substantial corruption matters. The *Resource*

Guide represents the joint guidance of the DOJ and SEC and is not a statement of the FCPA law but is for the most part the U.S. government's interpretation of a statute that has led to comparatively little case law since its enactment over three decades ago. It is valuable in educating boards, management, compliance officers, and outside counsel about the corruption risks in conducting international business and how the DOJ and SEC interpret and enforce a very broad statute. The examples found in the *Resource Guide* are certain to be included in multinational anticorruption training programs.

IX. COLLATERAL LITIGATION

The FCPA does not expressly provide for a private cause of action, and most federal courts have held that the FCPA does not imply a private cause of action. However, in the wake of a public company's disclosure of an FCPA investigation or the filing of a criminal or enforcement action, follow-on collateral litigation has been common. Derivative lawsuits or class-action suits have been filed, and plaintiffs in collateral litigation have included shareholders, competitors, employees, sovereigns, and pension plans. Specifically, three types of civil actions are typically filed: (1) securities class actions against companies and directors alleging inaccurate disclosures in violation of section 10(b) and Rule 10b-5 thereunder and section 20(a) of the Exchange Act; (2) shareholder derivative actions brought on behalf of companies against directors and officers for breach of fiduciary duties; and (3) class actions under section 502 of the Employee Retirement Income Security Act (ERISA) on behalf of participants in and beneficiaries of a qualified ERISA plan against the company and its directors for breach of fiduciary duties. Although collateral litigation is beyond the scope of this handbook, counsel must advise clients who are considering voluntary disclosure or who will be charged by government authorities with FCPA violations that follow-on civil litigation is likely.

X. ADDITIONAL RESOURCES

- Lowell Brown, *Parent Subsidiary Liability under the Foreign Corrupt Practices Act*, 50 Baylor L. Rev. 1 (1998).
- Peter B. Clark & Jennifer A. Suprenant, Siemens—Potential Interplay of FCPA Charges and Mandatory Debarment under the Public Procurement Directive of the European Union, ABA National Institute on White Collar Crime (San Francisco, Mar. 5–6, 2009).
- Donald Cruwer, Complying with the Foreign Corrupt Practices Act (ABA, 2d ed. 1999).
- Stuart Deming, The Foreign Corrupt Practices Act and the New International Norms (ABA 2005).
- Stuart Deming, *The Potent and Broad-Ranging Implications of the Accounting and Record-Keeping Provisions of the Foreign Corrupt Practices Act*, 96 J. Crim. L. & Criminology 465 (2006).
- Gibson Dunn, U.S. SEC Adopts Final Rules Implementing Whistleblower Provisions of Dodd-Frank (May 31, 2001), http://www.gibsondunn.com /publications/pages/SECFinal Rules-DoddFrankWhistleblowerProvisions.aspx.

- Gibson Dunn, 2012 Year End FCPA Update, http://www.gibsondunn.com /publications/ pages/2012YearEndFCPAUpdate.aspx.
- Richard W. Grime & Alison Fischer, Obvious and Not-So-Obvious Consequences from the Rise of FCPA Enforcement, ABA National Institute on White Collar Crime (Mar. 2008).
- Richard W. Grime & Stephanie Rogers, Why the Accounting Provisions of the Foreign Corrupt Practices Act Should Concern You, ABA National Institute on White Collar Crime (Mar. 2009).
- Richard W. Grime, et al., Potential Defenses in FCPA Enforcement Actions: Key Issues and Open Questions, ABA National Institute on White Collar Crime (Mar. 2013).
- Jones Day, SEC's Final Whistleblower Rules Provide Important Incentives for Effective Corporation Compliance Program (July 2011), http://jonesday .com/sec_final_whistleblower_rules/.
- Latham & Watkins, *The SEC's Whistleblower Program: Meeting the Challenges, Minimizing the Risks*, Corporate Governance Newsl., June 2011, http://www .lw.com.
- David Luban, Julie O'Sullivan & David Stewart, *Corruption*, ch. 14 *in* International and Transnational Criminal Law (Aspen 2009).
- Jay G. Martin, Compliance with the Foreign Corrupt Practices Act and the Developing International Anti-Corruption Environment (unpublished manuscript, on file at Baker Hughes, Inc.).
- Gary A. Naftalis, *The Foreign Corrupt Practices Act*, 11(8) White-Collar Crime Rep. 6 (Sept. 1997).
- O'Melveny & Myers, Foreign Corrupt Practices Act: An O'Melveny Handbook (6th ed. 2009).
- *PBS/Frontline World: The Business of Bribes* (Feb. 2009), http://www.pbs.org /frontlineworld/stories/bribe.
- John Savarese, *The New Dodd-Frank Whistleblower Rules: Hype and Reality*, Harv. L. Sch. Forum on Corp. Governance & Fin. Regulation, July 5, 2011, http://blogs.law.harvard.edu/corpgov/2011/07/28/hype-and-reality-in -the-dodd-frank-whistleblower-rules/.
- Eugene Scalia, Jason Schwartz & Thomas Johnson, *Whistleblower Protection under the SEC's New Dodd-Frank Regulations: A Practical Guide for Employers*, Daily L. Rep. (BNA) no. 117, at DLR1-1 (June 17, 2011).
- Schiff Hardin, The SEC's Final Rules Establishing Its Whistleblower Program (June 2011), http://www.schiffhardin.com.
- Shearman & Sterling, FCPA Digest (Mar. 2011) (comprehensive listing of every FCPA case since 1977), http://www.shearman.com.
- Skadden, Arps, SEC Finalizes Rules Implementing Whistleblower Bounty Programs (June 14, 2011), http://www.skadden.com.
- Robert W. Tarun, *A Baker's Dozen: Practical Foreign Corrupt Practices Act Advice for Multinational Executives, General Counsel, Boards of Directors and Audit Committees*, Ethisphere (Quarter 1, 2011).
- Philip Urofsky, *Recent Trends and Patterns in the Enforcement of the Foreign Corrupt Practices Act*, Shearman & Sterling LLP (2012), http://www.shearman.com.
- Crim. Div., U.S. Dep't of Justice & Enforcement Div., U.S. Sec. & Exch.

COMM., FCPA: A RESOURCE GUIDE TO THE U.S. FOREIGN CORRUPT PRACTICES ACT (2012), http://www.justice.gov/criminal/fraud/fcpa/guide/ or http://www.sec.gov/spotlight/fcpa.shtml (reprinted as appendix 4).

- DEP'T OF JUSTICE, U.S. ATTORNEYS' MANUAL, http://www.usdoj.gov.
- SEC. & EXCH. COMM'N, DIV. OF ENFORCEMENT, ENFORCEMENT MANUAL, http://www.sec.gov/divisions/enforce/enforcementmanual.pdf.
- DAN K. WEBB, ROBERT W. TARUN & STEVEN F. MOLO, CORPORATE INTERNAL INVESTIGATIONS (1993–2013).
- ROGER WITTEN & KIMBERLY PARKER, COMPLYING WITH THE FOREIGN CORRUPT PRACTICES ACT (7th ed. 2012).
- Roger M. Witten, Kimberly A. Parker & Thomas J. Koffer, Navigating the Increased Anti-Corruption Environment in the United States and Abroad, paper presented at the 20th Annual ACI Conference on the Foreign Corrupt Practices Act (Washington, D.C., Nov. 18, 2008).
- DON ZARIN, DOING BUSINESS UNDER THE FOREIGN CORRUPT PRACTICES ACT (PLI 2007).

NOTES

1. Foreign Corrupt Practices Act of 1977, Pub. L. No. 95-213, 91 Stat. 1494 (codified as amended at 15 U.S.C. §§ 78m, 78dd-1 to -3, 78ff (1999)) [hereinafter FCPA]. The text of the Act is appended hereto as appendix 1.

2. 15 U.S.C. § 78dd-1(a)(3) (for issuers).

3. 15 U.S.C. § 78dd-2(a)(3) (for domestic concerns).

4. 15 U.S.C. § 78dd-3(a)(3) (for "any person").

5. 15 U.S.C. § 78dd-1(a).

6. 15 U.S.C. § 78dd-2(h).

7. 15 U.S.C. § 78dd-1(a), -2(a).

8. 15 U.S.C. §§ 78dd-1(a), -2(a), -3(a).

9. 15 U.S.C. § 78dd-3(a).

10. S. REP. NO. 105-277, at 6 (1998) (quoting Commentaries on the Convention on Combating Bribery of Foreign Public Officials in International Business Transactions (OECD Commentary re: Article 41)).

11. Information ¶ 17, United States v. Syncor Taiwan, Inc., MO CR-02-12441 (C.D. Cal. 2002). *See* chapter 10.

12. 15 U.S.C. § 78dd-2(h)(5).

13. CRIM. DIV., U.S. DEP'T OF JUSTICE & ENFORCEMENT DIV., U.S. SEC. & EXCH. COMM., FCPA: A RESOURCE GUIDE TO THE U.S. FOREIGN CORRUPT PRACTICES ACT (2012), http://www.justice.gov/criminal/fraud/fcpa/guidance/orhttp://www.sec.gov/spotlight/fcpa.shtml [hereinafter RESOURCE GUIDE] (reprinted as appendix 4).

14. 15 U.S.C. § 78dd-2(i)(1). *See also* 15 U.S.C. § 78dd-1(g) (setting forth the same rule for "Issuers").

15. RESOURCE GUIDE, *supra* note 13, at 12; *see, e.g.*, Criminal Information, United States v. JGC Corp., No. 11-CR-260 (S.D. Tex. Apr. 5, 2011).

16. 15 U.S.C. § 78dd-3(a).

17. 15 U.S.C. §§ 78dd-1(a), -2(a), -3(a).

18. 15 U.S.C. §§ 78dd-1(f)(1)(A), -2(h)(2)(A), -3(f)(2)(A).

19. Resource Guide, *supra* note 13, at 20.

20. *See* SEC v. Dow Chem. Co., No. 07-336 (D.D.C. Feb. 12, 2007).

21. *See, e.g.*, United States v. Monsanto Co., No. 05-008 (D.D.C. Jan. 6, 2005); SEC v. Monsanto Co., No. 05-014 (D.D.C. Jan 6, 2005).

22. SEC Admin. Proceeding File No. 2-17456 (Oct. 16, 2006). *See In re* Schnitzer Steel Indus., Inc., Order Imposing and Instituting Cease-and-Desist Proceedings, Exchange Act Release No. 54,606, 89 SEC Docket 302 (Oct. 16, 2006).

23. Resource Guide, *supra* note 13, at 20.

24. SEC v. Jackson, No. H-12-0563 (KPE), 2012 WL 6137551 (S.D. Tex. Dec. 11, 2012) (Ellison, J.).

25. Resource Guide, *supra* note 13, at 20.

26. 15 U.S.C. §§ 78dd-1(f)(1)(B), -2(h)(2)(B), -3(f)(2)(B).

27. *See* 22 U.S.C. § 288 for a comprehensive list of organizations as "public international organizations."

28. *See, e.g.*, United States v. Castle, 925 F.2d 831, 834 (5th Cir. 1999) (noting the "overwhelming evidence of a Congressional intent to exempt foreign officials from prosecution for receiving bribes").

29. Opinion Procedure Release No. 2012-02 (Oct. 18, 2012).

30. *Id.*

31. *Id.*

32. 15 U.S.C. §§ 78dd-1(a), -1(g), -2(a), -2(i), -3(a) (1998).

33. 15 U.S.C. §§ 78dd-1(a)(2), -2(a)(2), -3(a)(2) (1998).

34. United States v. Sheker, 618 F.2d 607, 609 (9th Cir. 1980).

35. United States v. Zouras, 497 F.2d 1115, 1121 (7th Cir. 1974).

36. United States v. Crozier, 987 F.2d 893, 901 (2d Cir. 1993); United States v. Hare, 618 F.2d 1085 (4th Cir. 1980).

37. United States v. Gorman, 807 F.2d 1299 (6th Cir. 1987).

38. United States v. McDade, 827 F. Supp. 1153 (E.D. Pa. 1993).

39. Indictment, para. 23, United States v. Kozeny, No. 05-cr-00518 (S.D.N.Y. 2008).

40. *Id.*

41. United States v. King, 351 F.3d 859, 863 (8th Cir. 2003).

42. Resource Guide, *supra* note 13, at 15.

43. 15 U.S.C. §§ 78dd-1(a); -1(g); -2(a); -2(i); -3(a) (1998).

44. 15 U.S.C. §§ 78dd-1(a), -2(a), -3(a).

45. S. Rep. No. 95-114, at 10 (1977).

46. H.R. Rep. No. 95-650, at 18 (1977); chapter 4 of Don Zarin, Doing Business under the FCPA (PLI 2007), has thorough coverage of domestic bribery cases that provide precedent for the Department of Justice in the FCPA area.

47. 923 F.2d 1308 (8th Cir. 1991).

48. *Id.* at 1312.

49. 513 F.3d 461, 464 (5th Cir. 2007), *aff'g* 359 F.3d 738 (5th Cir. 2004), *cert. denied*, 129 S. Ct. 42 (Oct. 6, 2008).

50. 513 F.3d at 465.

51. Jury Charge, S2 05 CR 518 (SAS) (S.D.N.Y. July 1, 2009).

52. United States v. Frederic Bourke, No. 09-4704-cr (L) 2011 WL 6184494 (Dec. 14, 2011).

53. United States v. Kay, 513 F.3d 432, 448 (5th Cir. 2009).

54. *See* 15 U.S.C. §§ 78dd-1(c)(2)(A), -2(g)(2)(A), -3(3)(2)(A).

55. *Compare* 15 U.S.C. § 78ff(c)(1)(A) (corporate criminal liability under issuer provision) *with* § 78ff(c)(2)(A) (individual criminal liability under issuer provision); *compare* 15 U.S.C. § 78dd-2(g)(1)(A) (corporate provision) *with* § 78dd-2(g)(2)(A) (individual criminal liability under issuer provision); *compare* 15 U.S.C. § 78dd-3(e)(1)(A) (corporate criminal liability for territorial provision) *with* § 78dd-2(e)(2)(A) (individual criminal liability for territorial provision).

56. FCPA Opinion Procedure Release No. 82-03 (Apr. 22, 1982) (no expectation that any individual will personally benefit from the proposed agency relationship).

57. 359 F.3d 738 (5th Cir. 2004).

58. *Id.* at 756.

59. In remanding the *Kay* case, the Fifth Circuit indicated that the prosecution would have to prove that the defendant intended for the foreign official's anticipated conduct in consideration of a bribe (the "quid pro quo") to produce an anticipated result, in this case a diminution of customs duties or sales taxes that would assist in obtaining or retaining business. 359 F.3d at 740.

60. RESOURCE GUIDE, *supra* note 13, at 13.

61. John F. McKenzie, Foreign Corrupt Practices Act Compliance Issues for Import/Export Operations at 11–22 (Jan. 2013) (unpublished manuscript).

62. RESOURCE GUIDE, *supra* note 13, at 13.

63. 15 U.S.C. § 78dd-1(f)(2)(A).

64. 15 U.S.C. §§ 78dd-1(f)(2), -2(h)(3), -3(f)(3).

65. United States v. Kay, 513 F.3d 432, 447–48 (5th Cir. 2007).

66. SEC v. Jackson, No. H-12-0563 (KPE), 2012 WL 6137551, at *11 (S.D. Tex. Dec. 11, 2012); Mem. and Order, SEC v. Straub, No. 11 Civ. 9645 (RJS) (S.D.N.Y. Feb. 8, 2013).

67. RESOURCE GUIDE, *supra* note 13, at 22.

68. H.R. CONF. REP. No. 576, 100th Cong., 2d Sess. (1988) 919–20 (citing United States v. Jacobs, 475 F.2d 270, 277–88 (2d Cir. 1973)).

69. Roger M. Witten, Kimberly A. Parker & Thomas J. Koffer, Navigating the Increased Anti-Corruption Environment in the United States and Abroad, 20th Annual ACI Conference on the Foreign Corrupt Practices Act, Nov. 18, 2008, Wash., D.C.

70. 15 U.S.C. §§ 78dd-1(f)(2)(B), -2(h)(3)(B), -3(f)(3(B).

71. 15 U.S.C. §§ 78dd-1(a), -2(a), -3(a).

72. 15 U.S.C. §§ 78dd-1(a)(2)(B), -2(a)(2)(B), -3(a)(2(B).

73. *See* chapter 5.

74. United States v. Esquenazi, No. 11-15331, 2014 U.S. App. LEXIS 9096 (11th Cir. May 16, 2014), *cert. denied*, No. 14-189 (Oct. 6, 2014).

75. United States v. Aguilar, Case No. 2:10-cr-01031-AHM (C.D. Cal. Apr. 20, 2011).

76. *Id.*, Opinion at 2–3.

77. *Id.* at 9.

78. *Id.* at 10.

79. *Id.* at 14.

80. Order Denying Defendant's Motions to Dismiss Counts 1 through 10 of the Indictment at 5, United States v. Carson, Case No. SA CR 09-00077-JVS (C.D. Cal. May 18, 2011).

81. *Id.*

82. *Id.*

83. RESOURCE GUIDE, *supra* note 13, at 20.

84. *Id.* at 21.

85. *Id.*

86. 28 U.S.C. §§ 1602–1611.

87. 28 U.S.C. § 1603(b)(2).

88. For a thoughtful discussion of "instrumentality" case law, see ZARIN, *supra* note 46, at 4:4:2.

89. Philip Urofsky, *Recent Trends & Patterns in Enforcement of the U.S. Foreign Corrupt Practices Act*, 2011 Shearman & Sterling LLP, PLI # 29082 (2011).

90. Paul Berger & Sean Hecker, *Doing Business with Sovereign Wealth Funds*, LAW 360 (July 8, 2011), http://www.law360.com/internationaltrade/articles/256492?htm.

91. *Id.*

92. *Id.*

93. 15 U.S.C. §§ 78dd-1(a), -2(a), -3(a).

94. *See* H.R. REP. No. 95-640, at 18 (1977) (Conf. Rep.).

95. 15 U.S.C. §§ 78dd-1(b), -2(b), -3(b).

96. 15 U.S.C. §§ 78dd-1(f)(3), -2(h)(4), -3(f)(4).

97. *Id.*

98. RESOURCE GUIDE, *supra* note 13, at 25.

99. *Id.*

100. *Id.*

101. 15 U.S.C. §§ 78dd-1(c)(1), -2(c)(1), -3(c)(1).

102. *Id.* §§ 78dd-1(c)(2), -2(c)(2), -3(c)(2).

103. H.R. REP. No. 100-576, at 920 (1988); RESOURCE GUIDE, *supra* note 13, at 23.

104. 582 F. Supp. 2d 535, 537–40 (S.D.N.Y. 2008).

105. United States v. Metcalf & Eddy, Inc., No. 99 Civ. 12566 NG (D. Mass. 1999).

106. RESOURCE GUIDE, *supra* note 13, at 24.

107. *Id.*

108. *Id.* at 27 (citing Pacific Can Co. v. Hewes, 95 F.2d 42, 46 (9th Cir. 1938); United States v. Nynex Corp., 788 F. Supp. 16, 18 n.3 (D.D.C. 1992)).

109. *Id.*

110. *Id.*

111. 15 U.S.C. §§ 78dd-1(a), -2(a).

112. *See, e.g.*, Press Release, U.S. Dep't of Justice, Schnitzer Steel Industries Inc.'s Subsidiary Pleads Guilty to Foreign Bribes and Agrees to Pay a $7.5 Million Criminal Fine (Oct. 16, 2006) (SSI Korea admitted that it violated the FCPA and the conspiracy and wire fraud statutes in connection with more than $1.8 million in corrupt payments paid over a five-year period to officers and employees of nearly all Schnitzer Steel's government-owned customers in China and private customers in China and South Korea to induce them to purchase scrap material from Schnitzer Steel.).

113. 18 U.S.C. § 371.

114. 18 U.S.C. § 1952.

115. U.K. Bribery Act, 2010, ch. 23. The text of the U.K. Bribery Act is appended hereto as appendix 3.

116. 15 U.S.C. § 78m(a) (1994).

117. *See, e.g.*, United States v. Rothrock, 4 FCPA Rep. 699.818801 (W.D. Tex. 2001) (plea to knowingly and willfully falsifying and causing to be falsified certain books, records, and accounts in violations of FCPA); United States v. UNC/Leah Servs., 2 FCPA Rep. 600.050 (W.D. Ky.) (recording $140,000 payments to a subcontractor falsely as engineering fees).

118. 15 U.S.C. § 78ff(a); *see also* RESOURCE GUIDE, *supra* note 13, at 44.

119. RESOURCE GUIDE, *supra* note 13, at 39.

120. 15 U.S.C. §§ 78dd-2(d)(l), -3(d)(l).

121. Stanley Sporkin, *The Worldwide Banning of Schmiergeld: A Look at the Foreign Corrupt Practices Act on Its Twentieth Birthday*, 18 Nw. J. INT'L. L. BUS. 269, 274 (1998).

122. 15 U.S.C. § 78(m)(a).

123. Reasonableness, rather than materiality, is the threshold standard. Criminal liability under the accounting provisions requires that a person "knowingly" falsify its books and records and "knowingly" circumvent a system of internal accounting records. 15 U.S.C. §§ 78m(b)(4)–(5).

124. 15 U.S.C. § 78c(a)(37).

125. 15 U.S.C. § 78m(b)(7).

126. H.R. REP. No. 100-576, at 917 (1988); *see also* Harold Williams, Chairman, Sec. & Exch. Comm'n, Address to the SEC Developments Conference of AICPA (Jan. 13, 1981), Exchange Act Release No. 17,500 (Jan. 29, 1981).

127. RESOURCE GUIDE, *supra* note 13, at 39.

128. *Id.* at 44.

129. *See* Williams, *supra* note 126, at 16.

130. 532 F. Supp. 2d 1187 (N.D. Cal. 2008).

131. *Id.* at 1196–97.

132. DONALD CRUWER, COMPLYING WITH THE FOREIGN CORRUPT PRACTICES ACT (ABA, 2d ed. 1999).

133. RESOURCE GUIDE, *supra* note 13, at 39–40.

134. *Id.*

135. *Id.* at 43.

136. *See* SEC v. Int'l Bus. Machs. Corp., SEC Litig. Release No. 16,839 (Dec. 21, 2000).

137. *See, e.g.*, Complaint, SEC v. RAE Sys., Inc., No. 10-CV-2093 (D.D.C. Dec. 10, 2010); ECF No. 1 Non-Probs. Agreement, *In re* RAE Sys., Inc. (Dec. 10, 2010).

138. *Id. See* chapter 10 discussion of *RAE Systems Inc.*

139. 15 U.S.C. § 78m(b)(6).

140. *Id.*

141. *Id.*

142. Am. Inst. of Certified Pub. Acct., Statement on Auditing Standard No. 1,320.28 (1973) (*cited in* Report of the Securities and Exchange Commission on Questionable and Illegal Corporate Payments and Practices, May 12, 1976, at 12, *reprinted in* Sec. Reg. & L. Rep. (BNA), No. 353, Special Supp. (May 19, 1976)).

143. 15 U.S.C. § 78m(b)(2).

144. 15 U.S.C. § 78m(b)(7).

145. Williams, *supra* note 126, at 22.

146. *Id.*

147. SEC v. World-Wide Coin Inv., Ltd., 567 F. Supp. 724, 751 (N.D. Ga. 1983).

148. Kelly Gentenaur & William Olsen, *"Controlling" FCPA Risk: Assessing Internal Controls to Ensure Risk Is Mitigated*, Corp. Compliance Insights, Aug. 10, 2009, http:// http://www.corporatecomplianceinsights.com/controlling-fcpa-risk-assessing-internal-controls/.

149. Resource Guide, *supra* note 13, at 40.

150. *Id.* at 41.

151. 15 U.S.C. §§ 78m(b)(4)–(5).

152. 15 U.S.C. § 78m(b)(4) (1994).

153. Stuart H. Deming, *The Potent and Broad-Ranging Implications of the Accounting and Record-Keeping Provisions of the Foreign Corrupt Practices Act*, 96 J. Crim. L. & Criminology 465, 500 (2006).

154. 15 U.S.C. § 78m(b)(6).

155. 18 U.S.C. § 371.

156. 18 U.S.C. § 1343.

157. *See generally* First Circuit: United States v. Brandon, 17 F.3d 409 (1st Cir.), *cert. denied sub nom.* Granoff v. United States, 513 U.S. 820 (1994); Second Circuit: United States v. Svoboda, 374 F.3d 471, 476 (2d Cir. 2003); United States v. Ferrarini, 219 F.3d 145, 155 (2d Cir. 2000); Fifth Circuit: United States v. Parks, 68 F.3d 860, 866 (5th Cir. 1995); United States v. Williams, 12 F.3d 452, 458 (5th Cir. 1994); United States v. Medrano, 836 F.2d 861, 863 (5th Cir.), *cert. denied*, 488 U.S. 818 (1988); Sixth Circuit: United States v. Dolt, 27 F.3d 235, 238 (6th Cir. 1994); United States v. Reifsteck, 841 F.2d 701, 704 (6th Cir. 1988); Seventh Circuit: United States v. Jones, 317 F.3d 363, 366 (7th Cir. 2004); United States v. Gee, 226 F.3d 885, 893 (7th Cir. 2000); United States v. Knox, 68 F.3d 990 (7th Cir. 1995); United States v. Brown, 31 F.3d 484, 488 (7th Cir. 1994); United States v. Sophie, 900 F.2d 1064, 1080 (7th Cir.), *cert. denied sub nom.* Duque v. United States, 498 U.S. 843 (1990); Eighth Circuit: United States v. Powell, 853 F.2d 601, 604 (8th Cir. 1988); Ninth Circuit: United States v. Chong, 419 F.3d 1076 (9th Cir. 2005); United States v. Wright, 215 F.3d 1020, 1028 (9th Cir. 2000); United States v. Indelicato, 800 F.2d 1482, 1484 (9th Cir. 1986); Tenth Circuit: United States v. Daily, 921 F.2d 994, 999 (10th Cir. 1991); Nelson v. United States, 406 F.2d 1136, 1137 (10th Cir. 1969); 11th Circuit: United States v. Cure, 804 F.2d 625, 628 (11th Cir. 1986); United States v. Kammer, 1 F.3d 1161, 1164 (11th Cir. 1993).

158. United States v. Rabinowich, 238 U.S. 78, 87–89 (1915).

159. United States v. Easton, 54 F. App'x 242 (8th Cir. 2002).

160. Supreme Court: Ianelli v. United States, 420 U.S. 770, 777 (1975); Second Circuit: United States v. Savarese, 404 F.3d 651 (2d Cir. 2005); United States v. Mittelstaedt, 31 F.3d 1208, 1218 (2d Cir. 1994); United States v. Beech-Nut Nutrition Corp., 871 F.2d 1181, 1191 (2d Cir. 1989); Third Circuit: United States v. Applewhaite, 195 F.3d 679, 684 (3d Cir. 1999); Fifth Circuit: United States v. Bright, 630 F.3d 804 (5th Cir. 1980); Seventh Circuit: United States v. Hooks, 848 F.2d 785, 792 (7th Cir. 1988); Tenth Circuit: United States v. Arutunoff, 1 F.3d 1112, 1116 (10th Cir. 1993); 11th Circuit: United States v. Chandler, 376 F.3d 1303, 1314 (11th Cir. 2004); United States v. Toler, 144 F.3d 1423, 1425 (11th Cir. 1998); D.C. Circuit: United States v. Lam Kwong-Wah, 924 F.2d 298, 303 (D.C. Cir. 1991).

161. Morrison v. California, 291 U.S. 82, 92 (1934).

162. Several courts have held that a corporation can conspire with its officers and employees. *See* Fifth Circuit: Alamo Fence Co. v. United States, 240 F.2d 179, 181 (5th Cir. 1957); Sixth Circuit: United States v. Ames Sintering Co., 916 F.2d 713 (6th Cir. 1990); United States v. S & Vee Cartage, 704 F.2d 914, 920 (6th Cir.), *cert. denied*, 464 U.S. 935 (1983); 11th Circuit: McAndrew v. Lockheed Martin Corp., 206 F.3d 1031 (11th Cir. 2000). On the other hand, the Seventh Circuit, in Pearson v. Youngstown Sheet & Tube Co., 332 F.2d 439, 442 (7th Cir. 1964), held that a corporation is not capable of conspiring with its own officers and employees.

163. Joplin Mercantile Co. v. United States, 213 F. 926, 936 (8th Cir. 1914), *aff'd*, 236 U.S. 531 (1915).

164. United States v. Hughes Aircraft Co., 1994 U.S. App. LEXIS 12526 (9th Cir., Mar. 28, 1994).

165. *See, e.g.*, Supreme Court: Glasser v. United States, 315 U.S. 60, 80 (1942); Second Circuit: United States v. Svoboda, 374 F.3d 471, 476 (2d Cir. 2003); United States v. Samaria, 239 F.3d 228, 234 (2d Cir. 2001); Third Circuit: United States v. Helbling, 209 F.3d 226, 238 (3d Cir. 2000); United States v. Carr, 25 F.3d 1194 (3d Cir. 1994); Fourth Circuit: United States v. Wilson, 135 F.3d 291, 306 (4th Cir. 1998); United States v. Whittington, 26 F.3d 456, 465 (4th Cir. 1994); Sixth Circuit: United States v. Salgado, 250 F.3d 438, 447 (6th Cir. 2001); United States v. Mullins, 22 F.3d 1365, 1368 (6th Cir. 1994); Seventh Circuit: United States v. Miller, 405 F.3d 551 (7th Cir. 2005); United States v. Viezca, 265 F.3d 597 (7th Cir. 2001); United States v. Redwine, 715 F.2d 315 (7th Cir. 1973); Eighth Circuit: United States v. Fletcher, 322 F.3d 508 (8th Cir. 2003); United States v. Hermes, 847 F.2d 493, 495 (8th Cir. 1988); Ninth Circuit: United States v. Daychild, 357 F.3d 1082, 1097 (9th Cir. 2004); Tenth Circuit: King v. United States, 402 F.2d 289, 292 (10th Cir. 1968).

166. Compare RICO conspiracy (18 U.S.C. § 1962(d)), which has been interpreted by some courts as not requiring an overt act. *See, e.g.*, United States v. Barton, 647 F.2d 224 (2d Cir.), *cert. denied*, 454 U.S. 857 (1981).

167. Supreme Court: Yates v. United States, 354 U.S. 298, 334 (1957); First Circuit: United States v. Hurley, 957 F.2d 1, 3 (1st Cir. 1992); United States v. Tarvers, 833 F.2d 1068, 1075 (1st Cir. 1987); United States v. Medina, 761 F.2d 12, 15 (1st Cir. 1985); Second Circuit: United States v. Montour, 944 F.2d 1019, 1026 (2d Cir. 1991); Sixth Circuit: United States v. Reifsteck, 841 F.2d 701, 704 (6th Cir. 1988); Seventh Circuit: United States v. Crabtree, 979 F.2d 1261, 1267 (7th Cir. 1992), *cert. denied*, 510 U.S. 878 (1993); Eighth Circuit: United States v. Fletcher, 322 F.3d 508 (8th Cir. 2003); United States v. Hermes, 847 F.2d 493, 496 (8th Cir. 1988).

168. *See* OTTO G. OBERMAIER & ROBERT G. MORVILLO, WHITE COLLAR CRIME: BUSINESS AND REGULATORY OFFENSES § 4.01 (1989); *see also* Bourjaily v. United States, 483 U.S. 171, 179-80 (1987); FED. R. EVID. 801(d)(2)(E).

169. Second Circuit: United States v. Roshko, 969 F.2d 9, 12 (2d Cir. 1992).

170. Fiswick v. United States, 329 U.S. 211 (1946).

171. Second Circuit: United States v. Diaz, 176 F.3d 52, 98 (2d Cir. 1999); United States v. Cruz, 797 F.2d 90, 96-97 (2d Cir. 1986); Fifth Circuit: United States v. Mann, 161 F.3d 840, 859-60 (5th Cir. 1998); Sixth Circuit: United States v. Rogers, 118 F.3d 466, 473-74 (6th Cir. 1997); Seventh Circuit: United States v. Febus, 218 F.3d 784, 796

(7th Cir. 2000); United States v. Read, 658 F.2d 1225, 1232 (7th Cir. 1981); 11th Circuit: United States v. LaQuire, 943 F.2d 1554, 1563 (11th Cir. 1991); *cert. denied*, 505 U.S. 1223 (1992).

172. Second Circuit: United States v. Guerro, 694 F.2d 898, 903 (2d Cir. 1982); Eighth Circuit: United States v. Perry, 152 F.3d 900, 904 (8th Cir. 1998); Ninth Circuit: United States v. Koonin, 361 F.3d 1250, 1254–55 (9th Cir. 2004), *vacated on other grounds*, 544 U.S. 945 (2005); 11th Circuit: United States v. Anderson, 326 F.3d 1319 (11th Cir.), *cert. denied*, 540 U.S. 825 (2003); United States v. Butler, 792 F.2d 1528, 1532 (11th Cir. 1986).

173. 18 U.S.C. § 371.

174. 18 U.S.C. § 1001.

175. 18 U.S.C. §§ 1956, 1957.

176. 18 U.S.C. § 1341.

177. 18 U.S.C. § 1343.

178. 15 U.S.C. § 1.

179. 26 U.S.C. §§ 7201 *et seq.*

180. 50 U.S.C. app. §§ 1701–1706 (2000).

181. Sentencing for individuals who violate FCPA accounting provisions is considered under § 2B1.1. Sentencing for individuals who violate FCPA bribery provisions is determined under § 2B4.1. *See* U.S. SENTENCING GUIDELINES MANUAL (2004). In United States v. Booker, 543 U.S. 220 (2005), the Supreme Court held that the guidelines were supervisory and not mandatory.

182. 15 U.S.C. §§ 78dd-2(g)(2)(A), -3(e)(2)(A), 78ff(c)(2)(A).

183. 15 U.S.C. § 78ff(a).

184. 15 U.S.C. §§ 78dd-2(g), -3(e).

185. 15 U.S.C. § 78ff(a) (accounting); 15 U.S.C. § 78dd-2(g)(1)(A) (bribery).

186. 18 U.S.C. § 3571(d).

187. *See* 15 U.S.C. §§ 78ff(c), 78dd-2(a), 78dd-3(a), 77d-1(a).

188. U.S. ATTORNEYS' MANUAL, tit. 9, Criminal Resource Manual § 1019 [hereinafter USAM]; *see* 18 U.S.C. §§ 981(a)(i)(c), 1956(c)(7).

189. *See* 15 U.S.C. §§ 78dd-2(g)(3), 78dd-3(e)(3), 78ff(c)(3).

190. 26 U.S.C. § 162(c).

191. 15 U.S.C. §§ 78dd-2(g)(1)(B), 78dd-3(e)(1)(B), 78ff(c)(2)(C).

192. 15 U.S.C. § 78u(d)(3).

193. No. 1.04 CV 1141 [RBW] (D.D.C.).

194. 48 C.F.R. § 9.406-2(a)(3).

195. *See* Exec. Order No. 12,549, 51 Fed. Reg. 6,370 (Feb. 18, 1986).

196. USAM, *supra* note 188, at § 1019.

197. Directive 2004/18/EC of the European Parliament of the Council of 31 March 2004 and coordination of procedures for the award of public work contracts, public supply contracts, and public service contracts. Recital 1, O.J. (L 134), 114–20.

198. *Id.*

199. Peter B. Clark & Jennifer A. Suprenant, Siemens—Potential Interplay of FCPA Charges and Mandatory Debarment under the Public Procurement Directive of the European Union, 2009 ABA National Institute on White Collar Crime (San Francisco, Mar. 5–6, 2009).

200. For a thorough discussion of federal statute of limitation issues, see J. Anthony Chavez, *Federal Criminal Statutes of Limitations: Shifting the Balance toward Punishment*, 1994 Complex Crimes J. 1.

201. United States v. Eckhardt, 843 F.2d 989, 993 (7th Cir.), *cert. denied*, 488 U.S. 839 (1988).

202. Second Circuit: United States v. Scop, 846 F.2d 135, 138 (2d Cir.), *modified in part on other grounds on reh'g*, 856 F.2d 5, 7 (1988); Fourth Circuit: United States v. United Med. & Surgical Supply Corp., 989 F.2d 1390 (4th Cir. 1993); Tenth Circuit: United States v. Jensen, 608 F.2d 1349, 1355 (10th Cir. 1979).

203. 18 U.S.C. § 3282.

204. 18 U.S.C. § 371.

205. For example, the six-year statute of limitations provided in 26 U.S.C. § 6351(1) applies to conspiracies to commit tax fraud. United States v. Fletcher, 928 F.2d 495, 498 (2d Cir.), *cert. denied*, 502 U.S. 815 (1991).

206. *Id.*

207. Bridges v. United States, 346 U.S. 209, 223 (1952).

208. 18 U.S.C. § 371.

209. Supreme Court: Grunewald v. United States, 353 U.S. 391, 402–03 (1957); Seventh Circuit: United States v. McKinney, 954 F.2d 471, 475 (7th Cir.), *cert. denied*, 506 U.S. 1023 (1992).

210. United States v. Elliott, 225 U.S. 392, 401 (1912); *see also* Fiswick v. United States, 329 U.S. 211, 216 (1946).

211. Second Circuit: United States v. Scop, 846 F.2d 135, 139 (2d Cir.), *modified in part on reh'g on other grounds*, 856 F.2d 5, 7 (1988); Fourth Circuit: United States v. Head, 641 F.2d 174, 177 (4th Cir. 1981); Eighth Circuit: United States v. Andreas, 458 F.2d 491 (8th Cir.), *cert. denied*, 409 U.S. 848 (1972).

212. *Grunewald*, 353 U.S. at 405–06 (1957); *see also* Second Circuit: United States v. Crozier, 987 F.2d 893, 898 (2d Cir.), *cert. denied*, 510 U.S. 880 (1993); Seventh Circuit: United States v. Eisen, 974 F.2d 1362, 1368 (7th Cir.), *cert. denied*, 507 U.S. 1029 (1993); *but see* United States v. Masters, 924 F.2d 1362, 1368 (7th Cir.), *cert. denied*, 500 U.S. 919 (1991).

213. Supreme Court: United States v. Lane, 474 U.S. 438, 451–53 (1986); Second Circuit: United States v. Mennuti, 679 F.2d 1032, 1035 (2d Cir. 1982); Fourth Circuit: United States v. A-A-A Elec. Co., 788 F.2d 242, 244 (4th Cir. 1986); Fifth Circuit: United States v. Girard, 744 F.2d 1170, 1172 (5th Cir. 1984); Seventh Circuit: United States v. Dick, 744 F.2d 546, 552 (7th Cir. 1984); Eighth Circuit: United States v. N. Improvement Co., 814 F.2d 540 (8th Cir.), *cert. denied*, 484 U.S. 846 (1987); Ninth Circuit: United States v. Walker, 653 F.2d 1343, 1350 (9th Cir. 1981), *cert. denied*, 484 U.S. 846 (1987); United States v. Inryco, Inc., 642 F.2d 290, 293–94 (9th Cir. 1981), *cert. dismissed*, 454 U.S. 1167 (1982); 11th Circuit: United States v. Helmich, 704 F.2d 547, 549 (11th Cir.), *cert. denied*, 464 U.S. 939 (1983).

214. United States v. Kozeny, 638 F. Supp. 2d 348, 354 (S.D.N.Y. 2009).

215. Second Circuit: United States v. Borelli, 336 F.2d 376, 388 (2d Cir. 1964), *cert. denied*, 379 U.S. 960 (1965); Fifth Circuit: United States v. Bradsby, 628 F.2d 901, 905 (5th Cir. 1980); 11th Circuit: United States v. Roper, 874 F.2d 782, 787 (11th Cir.), *cert. denied*, 493 U.S. 867 (1989).

216. 18 U.S.C. § 3292.

217. 18 U.S.C. § 3292(a)(1).

218. 18 U.S.C. § 3292(c).

219. 18 U.S.C. § 3292(d).

220. 18 U.S.C. § 3292(a)(1).

221. 18 U.S.C. § 3292(c).

222. 18 U.S.C. § 3292(d).

223. Dan K. Webb, Robert W. Tarun & Steven F. Molo, Corporate Internal Investigations § 15.09(1) (1993–2014).

224. SEC v. Jackson, No. H-12-0563, 2012 U.S. Dist. LEXIS 17494, at *101–02 (S.D. Tex. Dec. 11, 2012).

225. *Id.* at *105; *see also* Richard W. Grime et al., Potential Defenses in FCPA Enforcement Actions: Key Issues and Open Questions, ABA National Institute on White Collar Crime (Mar. 2013).

226. 28 U.S.C. § 2462.

227. USAM, *supra* note 188, at § 1016.

228. 28 C.F.R. § 80.6.

229. *See* appendix 14 for details of what a whistleblower and counsel should provide to the SEC in order to perfect and qualify for whistleblower relief.

230. FCPA Opinion Procedure Release No. 96-2 (Nov. 25, 1996).

231. FCPA Opinion Procedure Release No. 2000-1 (Mar. 29, 2000).

232. FCPA Opinion Procedure Release No. 2001-01 (May 24, 2001).

233. FCPA Opinion Procedure Release No. 2001-02 (July 18, 2001).

234. FCPA Opinion Procedure Release Nos. 2003-01 (Jan. 15, 2003), 2004-02 (July 12, 2004).

235. Gary P. Naftalis, *The Foreign Corrupt Practices Act*, 11(8) White-Collar Crime Rep. 6 (Sept. 1997) ("In connection with any request for an FCPA Opinion, the Department of Justice may conduct whatever independent investigation it believes appropriate.").

236. FCPA Opinion Procedure Releases, http://www.usdoj.gov/criminal/fraud /fcpa/opinion (last visited May 20, 2013).

237. 15 U.S.C. § 78u-7.

238. 15 U.S.C. § 78u-6(b)(1).

239. 15 U.S.C. § 78u-6(a)(3); *see also* Rule 21F-3, 17 C.F.R. § 240.21F-3.

240. Schiff Hardin, *The SEC's Final Rule Establishing Its Whistleblower Program* (June 2011), http://www.schiffhardin.com/publications.

241. 17 C.F.R. § 240.21F-4(a).

242. 15 U.S.C. § 78u-6(a)(3).

243. *See* Exchange Act Rule 21 F, 17 C.F.R. § 240.21F.

244. 17 C.F.R. § 240.21F-6(a)(b)(4).

245. 17 C.F.R. § 240.21F-4(e).

246. 17 C.F.R. § 240.21F-3.

247. 17 C.F.R. § 240.21F-8(c)(1)–(7).

248. Section F in Form TCR has a Whistleblower Declaration, which the complainant is required to sign under penalty of perjury. Section G in the form is a Counsel Qualification, which also emphasizes the importance of providing and responsibility to provide accurate information. (See appendix 14.)

249. *Id.*

250. 15 U.S.C. § 78u-6(a)(1).

251. 17 C.F.R. § 240.21F-5(a).

252. 17 C.F.R. § 240.21F-6(a).

253. 17 C.F.R. § 240.21F-6(a)(4).

254. 17 C.F.R. § 240.21F-6(b).

255. 17 C.F.R. § 240.21F-7.

256. U.S. Sec. & Exch. Comm., Annual Report to Congress on the Dodd-Frank Whistleblower Program (Nov. 17, 2014), http://www.sec.gov/about/offices/owb/annual-report-2014.pdf.

257. *See Paradigm Capital Mgmt., Inc.*, SEC Release No. 72393, File No. 3-15930 (June 16, 2014).

258. The Office of the Whistleblower posts a Notice of Covered Action (NoCa) on its website for every Commission action that results in monetary sanctions over $1 million.

259. Eugene Scalia, Jason Schwartz & Thomas Johnson, *Whistleblower Protection under the SEC's New Dodd-Frank Regulations: A Practical Guide for Employers*, Daily L. Rep. (BNA) no. 117, at DLR1-1 (June 17, 2011).

260. *Id. See also* Gibson Dunn, *U.S. SEC Adopts Final Rules Implementing Whistleblower Provisions of Dodd-Frank* (May 31, 2001), http://www.gibsondunn.com/publications/pages/SECFinalRules-DoddFrankWhistleblowerProvisions.aspx.

261. *Id.*

262. John Savarese, *The New Dodd-Frank Whistleblower Rules: Hype and Reality*, Harv. L. Sch. Forum on Corp. Governance & Fin. Regulation, July 5, 2011, http://blogs.law.harvard.edu/corpgov/2011/07/28/hype-and-reality-in-the-dodd-frank-whistleblower-rules/.

263. Dunn, *supra* note 260.

264. *Id.*

265. Latham & Watkins, *The SEC's Whistleblower Program: Meeting the Challenges, Minimizing the Risks*, Corporate Governance Newsl., June 2011, http://www.lw.com.

266. *Id.*

267. Savarese, *supra* note 262.

268. Brad Preber & Trent Gazzaway, *Whistle-Blower Programs*, ch. 10 *in* William Olsen, The Anti-Corruption Handbook (2010).

269. *Id.* at 63.

270. Jones Day, *SEC's Final Whistleblower Rules Provide Important Incentives for Effective Corporation Compliance Program* (July 2011), at 35, http://www.jonesday.com/SEC_Final_Whistleblower_Rules/.

271. Gibson Dunn, *U.S. SEC Adopts Final Rules Implementing Whistleblower Provisions of Dodd-Frank* (May 31, 2001), http://www.gibsondunn.com/publications/pages/SECFinalRules-DoddFrankWhistleblowerProvisions.aspx.

272. *Id.*

273. *Id.*

274. *Id.*

275. Resource Guide, *supra* note 13.

276. *Id.* at 2.

CHAPTER 2

The FCPA's Expansive Jurisdiction

I. ORIGINAL AND EXPANDED JURISDICTION

In enacting the Foreign Corrupt Practices Act in 1977, Congress originally limited its jurisdictional scope to U.S. companies and individuals.[1] The 1998 amendments expanded the Act's jurisdiction to include foreign individuals and corporations. In particular, Congress amended the FCPA to implement the provisions of the Convention on Combating Bribery of Foreign Officials in International Business Transactions adopted by the Organization for Economic Cooperation and Development (OECD) on December 17, 1997 (the OECD Convention). The OECD Convention, which the U.S. Senate ratified on July 31, 1998, required signatories to conform their laws to its terms. The United States did so with the International Anti-Bribery and Fair Competition Act of 1998, which President William J. Clinton signed on November 10, 1998.[2] Among its provisions, the OECD Convention called on signatories to make it a criminal offense for "any person" to bribe a foreign public official[3] and required them "to take such measures as may be necessary to establish its jurisdiction over the bribery of a foreign public official when the offense is committed in whole or in part in its territory."[4] As a result, the FCPA was amended in 1998 to conform to the 1997 OECD Convention by extending its antibribery provisions to cover any bribery committed by any person (not just issuers or domestic concerns) who commits an offense, in whole or in part, in U.S. territory.

II. ENTITIES AND PERSONS COVERED BY THE ANTIBRIBERY PROVISIONS

The following persons and entities are now covered by the FCPA's antibribery provisions:

1. Issuers of securities—essentially, publicly traded companies: any corporation (domestic or foreign) that has registered a class of securities with the Securities and Exchange Commission or is required to file reports with the Securities and Exchange Commission (SEC), for example, any corporation with its stocks, bonds, or American depositary receipts traded on a U.S. securities exchange;[5]
2. Domestic concerns—any individual who is a citizen, national, or resident of the United States and any corporation, partnership, association, joint-stock company, business trust, unincorporated organization, or sole

proprietorship that has its principal place of business in the United States, or that is organized under the laws of a state of the United States or a territory, possession, or commonwealth of the United States;[6]

3. Persons—a national of the United States (as defined in section 101 of the Immigration and Nationality Act)[7] or any corporation, partnership, association, joint-stock company, business trust, unincorporated organization, or sole proprietorship organized under the laws of the United States or any state, territory, possession, or commonwealth of the United States, or any political subdivision thereof, who commits an act outside the United States in furtherance of a prohibited payment;[8]

4. Foreign nationals and entities (whether or not they are issuers) that commit any act in United States territory in furtherance of a prohibited payment;[9] and

5. Any officers, directors, employees, or agents of the entities or persons described in 1 through 4 above.[10]

III.   TERRITORIAL AND NATIONALITY JURISDICTION BASES

The traditional federal jurisdictional basis over U.S. companies and individuals has been territorial, that is, "the use of the mails or any means of instrumentality of interstate commerce in furtherance of 'an improper payment.'"[11] The interstate commerce element, which has long been broadly interpreted under the mail and wire fraud statutes,[12] is easily satisfied through the use of the U.S. mails, e-mails, computer transmissions, and telephone calls.

The 1998 amendments to the FCPA created an alternative jurisdictional basis of nationality. Issuers and domestic concerns may now be held liable under either territorial or nationality bases. Under the nationality principle, improper payments made by U.S. citizens and U.S. companies that take place wholly outside the United States may be prosecuted under the FCPA without any interstate commerce requirement.[13] Nationality jurisdiction has not been challenged under the FCPA, and a successful challenge is doubtful in view of the broadly interpreted interstate commerce jurisprudence.

The 1998 amendments and recent Department of Justice prosecutions confirm that non-U.S. individuals and companies can and will be the subject of U.S. FCPA charges. Both non-U.S. and foreign persons should keep in mind the due process limitation on personal jurisdiction of U.S. courts. Even where a defendant falls within the broad subject matter jurisdiction of the amended FCPA, the due process clause may be a bar to U.S. courts exercising personal jurisdiction over a defendant in either civil or criminal FCPA actions.

A.   Civil Cases

The due process clause of the Constitution was interpreted in the 1945 landmark Supreme Court decision of *International Shoe v. Washington* to provide that a U.S. court may exercise personal jurisdiction only over persons who have sufficient "minimum contacts" with the jurisdiction.[14] The exercise of such jurisdiction must also be "reasonable" and not "offend 'traditional notions of fair play and substantial justice.'"[15] A defendant must have had sufficient activities in the forum jurisdiction to reasonably anticipate being brought into the forum court.[16] In an action brought under a federal statute, the due process inquiry generally turns on a defendant's contacts with the United States as a whole—not simply the state or forum where the federal district court is located.[17]

Defense counsel should consider a due process challenge to personal jurisdiction over a foreign person in an FCPA case where the defendant has little or no contact with the United States. Extraterritorial conduct that causes a substantial effect in the United States can create personal jurisdiction over a defendant who personally had little or no contact with the United States. A person committing such conduct should reasonably anticipate being brought into court in this country.[18] For example, U.S. authorities have asserted that telephone calls, e-mails, and even bank transfers briefly passing through the United States permit the U.S. Department of Justice (DOJ) and SEC to assert jurisdiction over foreign nationals and entities.[19]

De minimis consequences do not, however, suffice to create personal jurisdiction. For example, in the securities context, the Second Circuit has held that "not every causal connection between action abroad and ultimate injury to American investors will suffice. . . . ('[E]ven assuming . . . some causal relation . . . the test for *in personam* jurisdiction is somewhat more demanding')"[20] but found that a foreign person who defrauds U.S. investors through illicit insider trading of the securities of a U.S. company traded exclusively in a U.S. stock exchange was plainly subject to U.S. jurisdiction.[21] The issue is much less clear in the case of a foreign person who pays a bribe to a foreign official, by money transfer from the United States, in circumstances that do not affect any U.S. investor or company. When a defendant has little or no contact with the United States, the strength of his personal jurisdiction argument will turn largely on the materiality (or lack thereof) of the U.S. consequences resulting from the foreign conduct.

In February 2013, two SEC FCPA enforcement actions filed in the Southern District of New York resulted in *in personam* jurisdiction decisions with opposite outcomes:

1. SEC v. Straub

SEC v. Straub,[22] an SEC enforcement action against executives of the Hungarian telecommunications company Magyar Telekom, Plc., arose from an alleged scheme of Magyar in March 2005 to bribe public officials from both political parties in Macedonia's coalition government in connection with legislation that would increase frequency fees, impose regulatory burdens, and authorize the licensing of a third competitor. At that time both Magyar's and Deutsche Telekom's (which had a controlling interest in Magyar) securities were publicly traded through American depositary receipts (ADRs) on the New York Stock Exchange. Magyar executive Straub signed management representation letters to Magyar's auditors stating that he was unaware of any irregularities (such as sham consulting and marketing contracts, which were falsely recorded in the company's books and records). The auditors in turn provided unqualified audit opinions that accompanied Magyar's annual filings with the SEC. The executive defendants in this case had no other connections to the United States such as participation in negotiations or meetings in furtherance of a scheme, payment of a bribe through the U.S. banking system, or travel to the United States in furtherance of the alleged scheme.

In defendant Straub's motion to dismiss, Judge Sullivan of the Southern District of New York observed that due process for personal jurisdiction purposes has two related components: a "minimum contacts" inquiry and a "reasonableness" inquiry. Judge Sullivan stated a defendant may not be haled into a jurisdiction as a result of "random, fortuitous or attenuated contacts. . . . Jurisdiction is proper . . . where the contacts proximately result from actions by the defendant *himself* that create a 'substantial connection with the forum,'"[23] and a defendant's physical absence from a forum is insufficient to defeat personal jurisdiction. Notwithstanding the absence of entry into or meetings or banking in the United States with respect to the alleged scheme, Judge Sullivan found that the SEC had adequately alleged that Magyar executive defendants engaged in conduct designed to violate U.S. securities regulations and thus necessarily directed toward the United States, even if not principally directed from inside the United States. Further, he found that the SEC had adequately alleged that defendants knew or had reason to know that any false or misleading financial reports would be given to prospective American purchasers of the securities.

With respect to the second inquiry focusing on reasonableness, Judge Sullivan ruled that where the "minimum contacts" are satisfied, the jurisdiction still needs to comport with "fair play and substantial justice."[24] He found that "the reasonableness inquiry is largely academic in non-diversity cases [such as in the instant case] brought under a federal law . . . because of the strong federal interests involved."[25] Judge Sullivan also wrote that the SEC rightly noted that there is no alternative forum available for the U.S. government.

2.   SEC v. Steffen

In February 2013, Judge Scheindlin of the Southern District of New York granted German citizen Herbert Steffen's motion to dismiss for lack of personal jurisdiction.[26] In this SEC case alleging a bribery scheme by Siemens executives to pay millions of dollars to top government officials in Argentina from 1996 to 2007 in connection with a billion-dollar national identity card project, defendant Steffen held the positions of CEO of Siemens SA Argentina from 1983 to 1989 and again in 1991, and group president of Siemens Transportation Systems from 1996 until his retirement in 2003. In 2010 the German conglomerate settled corruption charges with the U.S. DOJ and SEC and Munich law enforcement authorities for $1.6 billion.

With respect to the "minimum contacts" test, Steffen had encouraged and "pressured" Siemens Business Services Chief Financial Officer Bernd Regendatz to authorize bribes from Siemens Business Services to Argentine officials. However, Judge Scheindlin found that "once the Argentine CFO agreed to make bribes—following receipt of instructions from Siemens' management rather than Steffen, Steffen's role was tangential at best. Steffen did not actually authorize the bribes." The court wrote that the SEC did not allege that Steffen directed, ordered, or even had awareness of the cover-ups, much less that he had any involvement in the falsification of SEC filings in furtherance of a cover-up. Nor was it alleged that his position as group president of Siemens Transportation Systems would make him aware of false filings.

Judge Scheindlin distinguished the conduct of Steffen from Straub, *supra*, noting that as part of the bribery, Straub had signed off on misleading management representations to the company's auditors and signed false SEC filings. In outlining the need for a limiting jurisdiction principle, Judge Scheindlin stated:

> If this Court were to hold that Steffen's support for the bribery scheme satisfied the minimum contacts analysis, even though he neither authorized the bribe, nor directed the cover up, much less played any role in the falsified filings, minimum contacts would be groundless. Illegal corporate action almost always requires cover up, which to be successful must be reflected in financial statements. Thus, under the SEC's theory *every* participant in illegal actions taken by a foreign company subject to U.S. securities laws would be subject to the jurisdiction of US courts no matter how attenuated their connection with falsified financial statements. This would be akin to a tort-like foreseeability requirement, which has long been held to be insufficient.[27]

In analyzing the second due process component—the "reasonableness" test—Judge Scheindlin found that Steffen's lack of geographic ties to the United States, his age (74), his poor proficiency in English, and the forum's diminished interest in adjudicating the matter all weighed against personal jurisdiction. Further, the court stated that the DOJ and SEC had already obtained comprehensive remedies against Siemens, and Germany had resolved an action against Steffen individually. Under these circumstances, Judge Scheindlin concluded that the SEC's interest in ensuring that this type of conduct not go unpunished would not be furthered by continuing a suit against the defendant. The court found that absent a cover-up role, let alone a false financial statement role, an exercise of jurisdiction here exceeded due process limits.

While two judges in the Southern District of New York reached opposite results within 11 days, the in personam jurisdiction decisions seem to suggest that the "minimum contacts" test will likely be satisfied where a foreign defendant (1) knowingly signs false certifications to auditors that will be rolled up into SEC filings; and (2) participates in a cover-up.

Once the "minimum contacts" test is satisfied, courts will look to assess the "reasonableness" of a defendant being haled into U.S. courts and may consider such factors as the defendant's age, last active participation in the misconduct, geographic ties to the United States, English-speaking ability, prior imposition of fines by another government, and the U.S. forum's continuing interest in pursuing the defendant.

B.   Criminal Cases

For a criminal trial of an individual, the defendant must be actually present—at least at the beginning of the trial.[28] For a corporate defendant the presence of corporate counsel in court is sufficient to confer personal jurisdiction.[29] A district court has personal jurisdiction over a party who appears before it regardless of how the party's appearance was obtained.[30] In essence, once the defendant is before the court in actuality, the defendant is before the court for personal jurisdiction purposes.[31]

The best-known criminal case upholding personal jurisdiction over a foreign citizen is *United States v. Nippon Paper Industries Co.*, a price-fixing indictment charging a Japanese corporation in Massachusetts even though the corporation had no appreciable contacts with Massachusetts. There, Judge Gertner first observed that in providing for nationwide service of process, companies defined the territorial jurisdiction of the federal courts as encompassing the entire country and as a result, the due process clause does not require that a defendant have sufficient contacts with the state. The court then analyzed the corporation's national contacts, as opposed to Massachusetts contacts, and found them substantial—U.S. bank accounts, two offices in Seattle with eight employees, and millions of dollars of commerce in the United States.[32]

The best-known FCPA criminal case to address jurisdiction over a foreign citizen is *United States v. Bodmer*.[33] In 2004 Judge Scheindlin considered a motion to dismiss of Swiss lawyer Bodmer, who was charged with conspiracy to violate the FCPA and money laundering. Bodmer had served as counsel to entities including U.S. affiliates seeking to invest in a Azerbaijan state-owned oil company that was in the process of privatization. He had allegedly paid cash bribes to senior Azeri officials, arranged to have additional shares issued to pay bribes, and opened bank accounts to launder money in furtherance of the bribery scheme. In August 2003 Bodmer was arrested while traveling in South Korea two weeks after a sealed indictment was returned against him in the United States. While he was incarcerated in South Korea for five months and not permitted to consult with U.S. counsel, Bodmer ultimately consented to extradition to the United States.

In *Bodmer*, Judge Scheindlin addressed the question of whether prior to the 1998 FCPA amendments, foreign nationals who were agents of domestic concerns and who were not residents of the United States could be criminally prosecuted under the FCPA. The district court noted that Federal Rule of Criminal Procedure 12(b)(2) includes the defense of "lack of jurisdiction over the person" and the law requires that a civil defendant have "minimum contacts" with the forum. In contrast, Rule 12(b)(3) does not address jurisdiction over a person but only the court's jurisdiction, that is, subject matter jurisdiction. In analyzing the personal jurisdiction differences between civil and criminal cases, Judge Scheindlin wrote:

> But the issue of "minimum contacts" does not arise in criminal cases. If a defendant appears in court to defend charges, the court may inquire into whether venue is proper. This is because the Constitution provides that "the Trial of all Crimes . . . shall be held in the State where the said Crimes shall have been committed," U.S. Const. art. III, § 2, cl. 3, and "the accused shall enjoy the right to a speedy and public trial, by an impartial jury of the State and district wherein the crime shall have been committed." U.S. Const. amend. VI. *See also United States v. Rodriguez-Moreno*, 526 U.S. 275, 278, 143 L. Ed. 2d 388, 119 S. Ct. 1239 (1999); *United States v. Geibel*, 369 F.3d 682,

696 (2d Cir. 2004) ("Where a federal statute defining an offense does not explicitly indicate where a criminal act is deemed to have been committed, the site of a charged offense must be determined from the nature of the crime alleged and the location of the act or acts constituting it." (quotation marks and citations omitted)). If venue is proper, the court does not inquire into whether it has jurisdiction over the defendant, or the extent of the defendant's contacts with the forum state. Jurisdiction is presumed by virtue of the defendant's presence. *See Ker v. Illinois*, 119 U.S. 436, 440–43, 30 L. Ed. 421, 7 S. Ct. 225 (1886); *United States v. Rosenberg*, 195 F.2d 583, 602 (2d Cir. 1952) ("The court in a criminal case, unlike a civil case, would still have jurisdiction over [a criminal defendant's] person, as long as he was physically present at the trial." (citing cases)).

With this in mind, the criminal penalty provision of the FCPA of 1977 appears to implicate the concept of personal jurisdiction as articulated in Ker and Rosenberg. *See Morissette v. United States*, 342 U.S. 246, 263, 96 L. Ed. 288, 72 S. Ct. 240 (1952) ("Where Congress borrows terms of art in which are accumulated the legal tradition and meaning of centuries of practice, it presumably knows and adopts the cluster of ideas that were attached to each borrowed word in the body of learning from which it was taken."); *Buckhannon Bd. and Care Home, Inc. v. West Virginia Dep't of Health and Human Res.*, 532 U.S. 598, 615, 149 L. Ed. 2d 855, 121 S. Ct. 1835 (2001) ("Words that have acquired a specialized meaning in the legal context must be accorded their legal meaning."). I therefore conclude that in 1977, Congress likely intended that the FCPA's criminal sanctions applied to non-resident foreign nationals who properly appeared in United States courts; personal jurisdiction over the defendant derived from the defendant's (1) arrest in the United States, (2) voluntary appearance in court, or (3) lawful extradition.[34]

Judge Scheindlin dismissed the FCPA conspiracy count against Bodmer after expressing serious doubts about the defendant's consensual appearance and extradition in light of his arrest and incarceration in South Korea and extradition to the United States. The court found that Bodmer was subject to jurisdiction under the money laundering offense since that statute (18 U.S.C. § 1956) expressly provides for extraterritorial jurisdiction over a non-U.S. person where the conduct occurs in part in the United States and the transaction(s) involve funds or monetary instruments having a value exceeding $10,000. Bodmer subsequently pled guilty in 2004 and was sentenced in March 2013 to time already served in the South Korean jail.

No doubt, lawyers representing foreign defendants for which the United States seeks extradition will argue that the U.S. "minimum contacts" and "reasonableness" test factors such as those addressed in *Steffen* should be considered by foreign governments or courts before they permit extradition of their citizens to the United States.

IV. CORPORATE CRIMINAL LIABILITY

In addition to the expansive geographic reach of the FCPA, parent companies not only face the traditionally broad principles of corporate criminal liability for the acts of their agents and employees but also various theories of criminal liability for the conduct of foreign subsidiaries, agents, and employees.

A. Corporate Criminal Liability Principles

In general, a corporation can be held criminally liable for any criminal act carried out by one of its agents or employees if that act occurs within the scope of the employment for the benefit of the corporation.[35] Low-level employees acting contrary to expressed directions may create criminal liability for a corporation.[36] Liability may also be imposed on a corporation even if the individual employees involved in the criminal conduct are not indicted.[37] Only two requirements must be met to impute criminal liability of an agent or employee to the corporation. First, the conduct must occur within the scope of the agent or employee's employment. Second, the conduct must in some way be undertaken for the benefit of the corporation.

1. Scope of Authority

The "scope of authority" requirement means that the agent or employee was exercising the duties and authority conferred upon him by his employment position. It does not mean that the corporation must actually have authorized the agent or employee to commit illegal acts. Indeed, often an agent's acts will have been ultra vires and contrary to express authority. Rather, "within the agent's scope of authority" means that the agent or employee must have committed the acts in the course of his ordinary duties. For example, an international salesman agreeing to bribe a foreign official in order to obtain or retain business will be deemed to be acting within the scope of his authority. The focus is on the function delegated to the agent or employee and whether the conduct falls within that general function.[38] So long as an agent or employee's acts are consistent with his general employment function, his employer may be held liable for those acts, even if they were contrary to express corporate policy.[39]

2. Benefit of the Corporation

The "for the benefit of the corporation" requirement means an agent or employee's acts must be intended to benefit the corporation in some way.[40] The benefit to the corporation need not have been the sole reason for the agent or employee's acts nor must the corporation have received some actual benefit.[41] The corporate agent or employee committing the act almost always will receive some direct or indirect personal benefit. For example, increased sales may entitle an executive to a commission, or better performance ratings may entitle him to a bonus or raise. However, corporate liability will not be avoided merely because the primary motivation may have been the personal benefit to an agent or employee. So long as the motive includes a direct or ancillary benefit to the corporation—either realized or unrealized—a corporation will be accountable for an agent or employee's acts.[42]

B. Foreign Subsidiaries

1. *Bribery Conduct*

While the legislative history and one case indicate that foreign subsidiaries of U.S. companies acting on their own and not as agents of a U.S. parent are not subject to the antibribery provisions,[43] the *Resource Guide to the U.S. Foreign Corrupt Practices Act* states that a parent company can be liable in two ways for bribes paid by a subsidiary:

> First, a parent may have participated sufficiently in the activity to be directly liable for the conduct—as, for example when it directed its subsidiary's misconduct or otherwise directly participated in the bribe scheme. Second, a parent may be held liable for its subsidiary's conduct under traditional agency principles.[44]

Noting that the fundamental characteristic of agency is control,[45] the *Resource Guide* makes clear that both the formal relationship between the parent and the subsidiary and the practical realities of how the two interface are important.[46]

The FCPA does not specifically address foreign subsidiaries, and no court has directly addressed the Act's coverage of foreign subsidiaries. Still, FCPA investigations have regularly resulted in charges against parent companies and/or foreign subsidiaries. There are at least five statutory and common law theories under which a U.S. parent company may be liable for the misconduct of a foreign subsidiary. First, a U.S. company may be liable for bribery under agency principles if it had knowledge of or was willfully blind to the misconduct of its subsidiary. Second, a U.S. parent corporation that authorizes, directs, or controls the wayward acts of a foreign subsidiary may be liable. Third, a U.S. company may be held liable under principles of respondeat superior where its corporate veil can be pierced. Fourth, a U.S. company that takes actions abroad in furtherance of a bribery scheme may be found liable under the Act's 1998 alternative theory of nationality jurisdiction. Fifth, foreign subsidiaries may be liable if any act in furtherance of an illegal bribe took place in the U.S. territory.[47]

2. *Accounting Misconduct*

The DOJ may charge a publicly traded parent company with FCPA accounting violations by a foreign subsidiary when the books and records of the parent and subsidiary are consolidated in SEC filings. Specifically, a parent may be criminally liable where it knowingly fails to keep accurate books and records or maintain internal controls sufficient to provide "reasonable assurances" that transactions are executed in a proper manner.[48] Companies may also be liable for books-and-records misconduct by the employees of foreign subsidiaries if the parent owns or controls more than 50 percent of a subsidiary's voting securities.[49]

V. ADDITIONAL RESOURCES

- ABA SECTION OF ANTITRUST LAW, CRIMINAL ANTITRUST LITIGATION HANDBOOK (2d ed. 2006).
- H. Lowell Brown, *Parent Subsidiary Liability under the Foreign Corrupt Practices Act*, 50 BAYLOR L. REV. 1 (1998).
- Richard Grime & Anne Savage, *Expanding Boundaries: FCPA Jurisdiction over Foreign Entities and Individuals: The Trend of Increasingly Aggressive Enforcement*, 9(1) CRIM. LITIG. (Fall 2008).
- David Luban, Julie O'Sullivan & David Stewart, *Corruption*, ch. 14 *in* INTERNATIONAL AND TRANSNATIONAL CRIMINAL LAW (Aspen 2009).
- RICHARD C. SMITH, *Combating FCPA Charges: Is Resistance Futile?*, 54 VA. J. INT'L L. 157 (2013).
- Lawrence A. Sullivan & Warren S. Grimes, *Antitrust in Global Markets: The Extra Territorial Reach of Unilateral Rules; Comparative Antitrust; and Conflicting National Requirements and Bilateral and Multilateral Efforts to Resolve Them*, ch. XVIII in THE LAW OF ANTITRUST: AN INTEGRATED HANDBOOK (2d ed. 2006).

NOTES

1. Foreign Corrupt Practices Act of 19077, Pub. L. No. 95-213, 91 Stat. 1494 (codified as amended at 15 U.S.C. §§ 78m, 78dd-1 to -3, 78ff (1999)) [hereinafter FCPA]. The full text of the FCPA is appended hereto as appendix 1.

2. Pub. L. No. 105-366.

3. OECD Convention, art. 1.

4. OECD Convention, art. 4.

5. *See* 15 U.S.C. § 78dd-1(a).

6. *See* 15 U.S.C. § 78dd-2(a).

7. 8 U.S.C. § 1101.

8. *See* 15 U.S.C. § 78dd-1(g).

9. 15 U.S.C. § 78dd-3.

10. 15 U.S.C. §§ 78dd-1(a), -2(a), -3(a).

11. 15 U.S.C. §§ 78dd-1(a), -2(a).

12. *See, e.g.*, Schmuck v. United States, 489 U.S. 705 (1989).

13. International Anti-Bribery and Fair Competition Act of 1998, Pub. L. No. 105-366, § 4, 112 Stat. 3302, 3306 (1998) (codified at 15 U.S.C. §§ 78dd-1(g), -2(i)).

14. Int'l Shoe Co. v. Washington, 326 U.S. 310, 316 (1945).

15. *Id.* (quoting Miliken v. Meyer, 311 U.S. 457, 463 (1940)).

16. World-Wide Volkswagen Corp. v. Woodson, 444 U.S. 286, 297 (1980).

17. *See, e.g.*, Cent. States v. Reimer, 230 F.3d 934, 946 (7th Cir. 2000); United States v. Int'l Bhd. of Teamsters, 945 F. Supp. 609, 620 (S.D.N.Y. 1996).

18. SEC v. Unifund Sal, 910 F.2d 1028, 1033 (2d Cir. 1990). Commentators and other countries have criticized the exercise of jurisdiction over foreign nationals based solely on the U.S. Effects of overseas conduct. *See, e.g.*, H. Lowell Brown, *Extraterritorial Jurisdiction under the 1998 Amendments to the Foreign Corrupt Practices Act: Does the Government's Reach Now Exceed Its Grasp?*, 26 N.C. J. INT'L LAW & COM. REG. 239, 335 (Spring 2001) (discussing criticism).

19. *See, e.g.*, United States v. SSI Int'l Far E. Ltd., No. 06-398 (D. Or. Oct. 10, 2006) (changing foreign subsidiary based on international wire transfers originating from the United States).

20. *Unifund Sal*, 910 F.2d at 1033 (quoting Bersch v. Drexel Firestone, Inc., 519 F.2d 974, 1000 (2d Cir. 1975).

21. *Id.*

22. SEC v. Straub, No. 11 CV 09645, 921 F. Supp. 2d 244 (S.D.N.Y. Feb. 8, 2013) (Sullivan, J.).

23. Burger King v. Rudzewicz, 471 U.S. 462, 475 (1985).

24. *Id.* at 476.

25. *Straub*, No. 11 CV 09645, at 12 (citing SEC v. Syndicated Food Servs. Int'l, Inc., No. 04 Civ. 1303 (NGG) (ALC), 2010 WL 3528406, at *3 (E.D.N.Y. Sept. 3, 2010)).

26. SEC v. Sharef, 924 F. Supp. 2d 539 No. 11 CIV. 9073 (SAS) (S.D.N.Y. Feb. 19, 2013) (No. 11 CIV 9073) (Scheindlin, J.).

27. *Id.* at 18–19.

28. FED. R. CRIM. P. 43(a).

29. FED. R. CRIM. P. 43(b).

30. First Circuit: United States v. Lussier, 929 F.2d 25, 27 (1st Cir. 1991).

31. ABA SECTION OF ANTITRUST LAW, CRIMINAL ANTITRUST LITIGATION HANDBOOK (2d ed. 2006).

32. 944 F. Supp. 55 (D. Mass. 1996), *rev'd on other grounds*, 109 F.3d 1 (1st Cir. 1997).

33. 342 F. Supp. 2d 176 (S.D.N.Y. 2004).

34. 342 F. Supp. 2d at 188 (footnotes omitted).

35. Supreme Court: United States v. Wise, 370 U.S. 405 (1962); N.Y. Cent. & Hudson River R.R. v. United States, 212 U.S. 481, 493 (1909); First Circuit: United States v. Potter, 463 F.3d 9 (1st Cir. 2006); United States v. Cincotta, 689 F.2d 238 (1st Cir. 1982); Second Circuit: United States v. Koppers Co., 652 F.2d 290, 298 (2d Cir.), *cert. denied*, 454 U.S. 1083 (1981); Granite Partners, L.P. v. Bear, Stearns & Co., 17 F. Supp. 2d 275, 296 (S.D.N.Y. 1998); Third Circuit: Mininshon v. United States, 101 F.2d 477 (3d Cir. 1939); Seventh Circuit: United States v. Empire Packing Co., 174 F.2d 16 (7th Cir. 1949); Ninth Circuit: United States v. Hilton Hotels Corp., 467 F.2d 1000 (9th Cir. 1972), *cert. denied sub nom.* W. Int'l Hotels Co. v. United States, 409 U.S. 1125 (1973). *See generally* 1 KATHLEEN BRICKEY, CORPORATE CRIMINAL LIABILITY, ch. 3 (2d ed. 1991).

36. See cases holding that low-level employees may bind a corporation for purposes of imposing criminal liability, *e.g.* Supreme Court: United States v. Ill. Cent. R.R., 303 U.S. 239 (1938) (manual laborers; employee whose duty was unloading cattle for carrier); First Circuit: St. Johnsbury Trucking Co. v. United States, 220 F.2d 393 (1st Cir. 1955) (rating clerk); Second Circuit: United States v. George F. Fish, Inc., 154 F.2d 798 (2d Cir.), *cert. denied*, 328 U.S. 869 (1946) (salesman); Fourth Circuit: United States v. E. Brooke Matlack, Inc., 149 F. Supp. 814 (D. Md. 1957) (truck drivers); Fifth Circuit: Steere Tank Lines, Inc. v. United States, 330 F.2d 719 (5th Cir. 1963) (truck driver); Seventh Circuit: Zito v. United States, 64 F.2d 772, 775 (7th Cir. 1933) (sales agent); Eighth Circuit: Riss & Co. v. United States, 262 F.2d 245 (8th Cir. 1958) (terminal log clerk); Ninth Circuit: Dollar S.S. Co. v. United States, 101 F.2d 638 (9th Cir. 1939) (manual laborers; crew member emptying garbage); United States v. Wilson, 59 F.2d 97 (W.D.

Wash. 1932) (sales manager); Tenth Circuit: United States v. Harry L. Young & Sons, Inc., 464 F.2d 1295 (10th Cir. 1972) (truck driver); Tex.-Okla. Express, Inc. v. United States, 429 F.2d 100 (10th Cir. 1970) (truck drivers). *See also* United States v. Dye Constr. Co., 510 F.2d 78, 82 (10th Cir. 1975) (pipe-laying crew consisting of supervisor, foreman, and backhoe operator). *But see* State v. Black on Black Crime, Inc., 136 Ohio App. 3d 436, 444, 736 N.E.2d 962, 968 (2000) (business entity is guilty of criminal act only if it was approved, recommended, or implemented by high managerial personnel who make basic corporate policies).

37. *Id.*

38. *See* K. Brickey, *Corporate Criminal Liability: A Primer for Corporate Counsel*, 40 Bus. Law. 129, 131 (1984). *See also* C.J.T. Corp. v. United States, 150 F.2d 85, 89 (9th Cir. 1945).

39. *See, e.g.*, United States v. Portac, Inc., 869 F.2d 1288, 1293 (9th Cir. 1989); United States v. Hilton Hotels Corp., 467 F.2d 1000 (9th Cir. 1972), *cert. denied sub nom.* W. Int'l Hotels Co. v. United States, 409 U.S. 1125 (1973).

40. *See generally* Supreme Court: N.Y. Cent. & Hudson River R.R. v. United States, 212 U.S. 481, 493 (1909); First Circuit: United States v. Cincotta, 689 F.2d 238, 241–242 (1st Cir. 1982); Second Circuit: United States v. Georgopoulos, 149 F.3d 169, 171 (2d Cir. 1998), *cert. denied*, 525 U.S. 1139 (1999); United States v. Jacques Dessange, Inc., 103 F. Supp. 2d 701, 706 (S.D.N.Y. 2000), *aff'd*, 4 F. App'x 59 (2d Cir. 2001); Third Circuit: United States v. Am. Standard Radiator & Standard Sanitary Corp., 433 F.2d 174 (3d Cir. 1970); Fifth Circuit: United States v. Ridglea State Bank, 357 F.2d 495 (5th Cir. 1966); Steere Tank Lines, Inc. v. United States, 330 F.2d 719 (5th Cir. 1963); Standard Oil Co. of Tex. v. United States, 307 F.2d 120, 128 (5th Cir. 1962); Sixth Circuit: Trollinger v. Tyson Foods, Inc., 2007 WL 1091217 (E.D. Tenn. Apr. 10, 2007); United States v. Carter, 311 F.2d 934, 941–942 (6th Cir.), *cert. denied*, 373 U.S. 915 (1963); Seventh Circuit: United States v. One Parcel of Land, 965 F.2d 311, 316 (7th Cir. 1992); United States v. One 1997 E35 Ford Van, 50 F. Supp. 2d 789, 796 (N.D. Ill. 1999); Eighth Circuit: Egan v. United States, 137 F.2d 369, 380 (8th Cir.), *cert. denied*, 320 U.S. 788 (1943); Ninth Circuit: Magnolia Motor & Logging Co. v. United States, 264 F.2d 950 (9th Cir.), *cert. denied*, 361 U.S. 815 (1959); United States v. Banco Internacional/Bital, 110 F. Supp. 2d 1272 (C.D. Cal. 2000); Tenth Circuit: United States v. Harry L. Young & Sons, Inc., 464 F.2d 1295 (10th Cir. 1972); D.C. Circuit: United States v. Sun-Diamond Growers of Cal., 138 F.3d 961 (D.C. Cir 1998), *aff'd on other grounds*, 526 U.S. 398 (1999). *See also* Brickey, *supra* note 35, § 4.02.

41. Fourth Circuit: Old Monastery Co. v. United States, 147 F.2d 905 (4th Cir.), *cert. denied*, 326 U.S. 734 (1945); Sixth Circuit: United States v. NHML, Inc., 225 F.3d 660 (6th Cir. 2000); United States v. Rhoad, 36 F. Supp. 2d 792, 792 (S.D. Ohio 1998); Ninth Circuit: United States v. Beusch, 596 F.2d 871, 877–878 (9th Cir. 1979); Eleventh Circuit: United States v. Gold, 743 F.2d 800, 823 (11th Cir. 1984), *cert. denied*, 469 U.S. 1217 (1985). *See, e.g.*, United States v. Sun-Diamond Growers of Cal., 138 F.3d 961, 970 (D.C. Cir. 1998), *aff'd on other grounds*, 526 U.S. 398 (1999) (finding corporate liability even though the employee's scheme "came at some cost to [the corporation]" because it "also promised some benefit."). *See also* Brickey, *supra* note 35, § 4.02; Burgess & Stein, *Carrots, Sticks and Criminal Penalties*, Ariz. Att'y, Feb. 2001, at 32.

42. United States v. Automated Med. Labs., 770 F.2d 399 (4th Cir. 1985).

43. H.R. Conf. Rep. No. 95-831, at 15; J. Dooley v. United Techs. Corp., 803 F. Supp. 428, 439 (D.D.C. 1992).

44. Crim. Div., U.S. Dep't of Justice & Enforcement Div., U.S. Sec. & Exch. Comm., FCPA: A Resource Guide to the U.S. Foreign Corrupt Practices Act 27 (2012), http://www.justice.gov/criminal/fraud/fcpa/guidance/ or http://www.sec.gov /spotlight/fcpa.shtml (appended as appendix 4).

45. *Id.* (citing Pacific Can Co. v. Hewes, 95 F.2d 42, 46 (9th Cir. 1938); United States v. Nynex Corp., 788 F. Supp. 16, 18 n.3 (D.D.C. 1992)).

46. *Id.*

47. This discussion reflects the analysis of Professor Julie O'Sullivan of Georgetown Law Center in David Luban, Julie O'Sullivan & David Stewart, *Corruption*, ch. 14 *in* International and Transnational Criminal Law (Aspen 2009).

48. 15 U.S.C. § 78m(b)(4).

49. *See generally* H. Lowell Brown, *Parent Subsidiary Liability under the Foreign Corrupt Practices Act*, 50 Baylor L. Rev. 1–29 (1998).

CHAPTER 3

Antibribery Conventions and Global Law Enforcement Efforts

Multinational companies should take notice of the increasing global focus on prosecuting bribery of foreign government officials. This focus is evident from a number of major international treaties directed against these practices; legislation in the signatory nations implementing these pacts, and 2011 and 2013 foreign bribery prosecutions by law enforcement authorities in Australia and Canada, as well as in France, Germany, Switzerland, the United Kingdom, and the United States in 2010. The U.K. Bribery Act 2010, which became effective July 1, 2011, in particular has drawn major attention from companies that carry on business in whole or in part in the United Kingdom and are thereby now subject to a very expansive law. It draws in significant part upon the language of the Organization for Economic and Cooperative Development (OECD) Convention on Combating Bribery of Foreign Officials in International Business Transactions. The increased presence of multijurisdictional government investigations will require multinational companies to increasingly engage counsel to handle the often conflicting interests, privacy laws, local anticorruption laws, and demands of U.S. and foreign law enforcement authorities.

I. THE ORGANIZATION FOR ECONOMIC AND COOPERATIVE DEVELOPMENT CONVENTION

A. Background

The OECD was formed in 1961. The OECD Convention on Combating Bribery of Foreign Officials in International Business Transactions (the OECD Convention) was signed on December 17, 1997.[1] This treaty requires all signatories to take steps to criminalize the payment of bribes to foreign public officials and to establish appropriate sanctions on firms and individuals guilty of violating these provisions. The OECD Convention does not eliminate the tax deductibility of bribes permitted by some countries and does not generally apply to bribes made to political parties. The U.S. State Department has described the OECD Convention as "one of the most rigorous anti-corruption conventions and [one that] continues to serve as a model for new initiatives."[2]

B. The OECD Convention and Domestic Legislation

The OECD Convention is the narrowest of the multilateral treaties and, like the U.S. Foreign Corrupt Practices Act, focuses only on transnational active bribery.[3] There are 40 parties to the Anti-Bribery Convention: 35 member country signatories and five non-OECD member countries (Argentina, Brazil, Bulgaria, the Russian Federation, and South Africa).[4] In the United States, the International Anti-Bribery and Fair Competition Act of 1998 amended the FCPA to implement the 1997 OECD Convention.[5] Other countries have similarly adopted legislation, which varies widely on many significant points. As a result, corporations conducting international business must carefully scrutinize the law in each OECD country where they do business.

The OECD Convention has not yet achieved the goal of leveling the playing field between U.S. persons subject to the FCPA and their foreign competitors. In 2004 a U.S. State Department report found many deficiencies in the implementing legislation of the signatories, including, among others, France, Japan, and the United Kingdom.[6] The report noted, however, that many of the deficient countries are in the process of considering, or implementing, amendments to their legislation that may put more teeth in their enforcement programs.[7] In the wake of the enactment of the U.K. Bribery Act of 2010, the United Kingdom has finally put teeth in its antibribery enforcement program. Persons engaged in international commerce and their counsel are wise to stay abreast of new foreign bribery legislation and related developments.

C. The Main Provisions of the OECD Convention

In general, the OECD Convention requires signatory nations to adopt "effective, proportionate, and dissuasive criminal sanctions" to those persons who bribe foreign public officials.[8] It calls for each nation to exercise its full jurisdictional powers to punish foreign bribery where the offense is committed in whole or in part on its soil, or is committed by its nationals abroad.[9] Like the FCPA, the OECD Convention contains both antibribery and record-keeping provisions. Other significant points of the OECD Convention include the following:

1. Active Bribery Only

The OECD Convention criminalizes only "active bribery," which involves offering or giving a bribe. "Passive bribery," or the act of soliciting a bribe, is not addressed on the basis that it is presumably already a criminal offense in most countries.

2. Definition of Bribery

"Active bribery" is defined as a bribe offered or given "in order to obtain or retain business or other improper advantage in the conduct of international business." As with the FCPA, small facilitation payments made with the intention of expediting or securing the performance of a routine governmental action are excluded from the definition of improper payments under the OECD Convention. By referring to "other improper advantage," the OECD Convention intends to address situations where a payment is made to obtain something to which the company is clearly not entitled (e.g., an operating permit for a factory that failed to meet local health and safety standards).[10] The convention also requires signatories to prohibit the use of off-the-book accounts and other practices used to conceal bribes made to public officials.

3. Public Officials

The OECD Convention defines "public official" as "any person holding a legislative, administrative or judicial office of a foreign country, whether appointed or elected; any person exercising a public function or involved in a public agency or public enterprise; and any official or agent of a public international organization." A "public function" includes any activity in the public interest delegated by a foreign country, such as the performance of a task delegated by it in connection with public procurement.[11] A "public enterprise" is any enterprise, regardless of its legal form, over which a government or governments may, directly or indirectly, exercise a dominant influence. This is deemed the case when the government or governments hold the majority of the enterprise's subscribed capital, control the majority of the enterprise's subscribed capital, control the majority of votes attaching to shares issued by the enterprise, or can appoint a majority of the members of the enterprise's administrative or managerial body or supervisory board.[12]

An official of a public enterprise shall be deemed to perform a public function unless the enterprise operates on a normal commercial basis in the relevant market, that is, on a basis that is substantially equivalent to that of a private enterprise, without preferential subsidies or other privileges.[13] According to an OECD report of the negotiating conference, the term "public official" does not encompass political parties, persons on the verge of being elected or appointed to public office, or private-sector corruption.[14]

4. Civil Liability if Not Criminal

The OECD Convention recognizes that in countries like Brazil, Japan, and Germany, legal entities (e.g., corporations) generally cannot be criminally responsible under domestic law. However, Article 2 of the convention requires all signatories to hold legal entities liable for the bribery of foreign public officials without specifying whether such liability is to be criminal or civil. Article 3.2 further requires that in countries that do not impose criminal liability on legal entities, "effective, proportionate, and dissuasive noncriminal sanctions, including monetary sanctions" should be imposed.

5. Reliance on Domestic Laws

The OECD Convention seeks to impose general standards rather than detailed prohibitions. Though it provides a definition of the offense it seeks to criminalize, the convention also relies on the fact that its signatories' domestic laws regarding the issue of internal bribery or their rules pertaining to criminal law will be extended so as to address the bribery of foreign public officials.

6. Confiscations

The term "confiscation" includes forfeiture where applicable and means the permanent deprivation of property by order of a court or other competent authority.[15] This term is the equivalent of disgorgement in the United States.

7. *Mutual Legal Assistance*

The OECD Convention recognized that to combat bribery in international business transactions, cooperation among law enforcement agencies is essential. In particular, parties agreed that, upon request, they should facilitate or encourage the presence or availability of persons, including persons in custody, who consent to assist in investigations or participate in proceedings; that parties should take measures to be able, in appropriate cases, to transfer temporarily such a person in custody to a party requesting it, and to credit time in custody in the requesting party to the transferred person's sentence in the requested party; and that parties wishing to use this mechanism should also take measures to be able, as a requesting party, to keep a transferred person in custody and return this person without necessity of extradition proceedings.[16] Signally, a party shall not decline to render mutual assistance on the ground of bank secrecy.[17]

8. *Extradition*

Article 10 of the 1997 Convention provides that bribery of a foreign public official shall be deemed an extraditable offense under the laws of the parties and the extradition treaties between them.

D.   OECD Working Group on Bribery

Established in 1994, the OECD Working Group on Bribery is responsible for monitoring the OECD Convention, the 2009 Recommendation on Further Combating Bribery of Foreign Officials in International Business Transactions, and related instruments. The Working Group meets four times a year in Paris and publishes all of its country reports online.[18] Country reports, which take place in three phases, contain recommendations from rigorous peer review examinations of each country. Phase 1 evaluates the adequacy of a country's legislation to implement the OECD Convention. Phase 2 assesses whether a country is applying this legislation effectively. Phase 3 focuses on the enforcement of the OECD Convention, the 2009 Anti-Bribery Recommendations, and outstanding recommendations from Phase 2.

E.   OECD's Good Practice Guidance in Internal Controls, Ethics, and Compliance

On February 18, 2010, the OECD issued its Good Practice Guidance on Internal Controls, Ethics, and Compliance (Guidance). This Guidance offers a dozen good practices:

1. "Strong, explicit and visible support and commitment from senior management" for a company's compliance objectives;
2. "A clearly articulated and visible corporate policy prohibiting foreign bribery";
3. Shared responsibility for compliance among all individuals at all levels of the company;
4. Oversight of the compliance program by senior corporate officers, with adequate resources, autonomy from management, and authority, including

the authority to report matters directly to independent monitoring bodies such as internal audit committees of boards of directors or of supervisory boards;

5. A compliance program covering the following areas: "(i) gifts; (ii) hospitality, entertainment and expenses; (iii) customer travel; (iv) political contributions; (v) charitable donations and sponsorships; (vi) facilitation payments; and (vii) solicitation and extortion";

6. Safeguards to ensure compliance by third parties, including properly documented due diligence, proper oversight of business partners, advising third parties of the company's commitment to compliance, and seeking a reciprocal commitment from business partners;

7. A system of financial and accounting procedures, including internal controls, reasonably designed to ensure the maintenance of fair and accurate books, records, and accounts;

8. Communication and training for all levels of the company, and for subsidiaries, on the company's compliance program;

9. Appropriate measures to encourage and provide positive support for the observance of the compliance program at all levels of the company;

10. Appropriate disciplinary procedures to address violations of the compliance program;

11. Effective measures regarding guidance to employees on how to comply with the program, including when they need urgent advice on difficult situations in foreign jurisdictions; internal reporting of violations; and taking appropriate action based upon such reports; and

12. Periodic reviews of the compliance program to measure effectiveness and ensure that the program is state of the art.

In the past few years many FCPA resolutions have incorporated the above practices for effective compliance programs as part of the required settled terms. The OECD good practice list is also helpful for companies wishing to make their codes of conduct and compliance programs more global and less U.S.-centric.

F. 2014 OECD Analysis of the Cost of Bribery and Corruption

In December 2014, the OECD published *Analysis of the Cost of Foreign Bribery and Corruption*.[21] The report analyzed more than 400 cases worldwide over a 15-year period (February 1999 to June 2014), involving companies or individuals from the 41 signatory countries to the OECD Anti-Bribery Convention.[22] It found that almost two-thirds of the cases have arisen in four industries:

- Extractive (19 percent),
- Construction (15 percent),
- Transportation and storage (15 percent), and
- Information and communication (10 percent).

These four industries were followed by manufacturing (8 percent); public health (8 percent); electricity and gas (6 percent); public administration and defense

(5 percent); agriculture, forestry, and fishing (4 percent); wholesale and retail trade (4 percent); and water supply (3 percent); with the remaining categories 1 percent or less.

In most cases bribes were made to obtain public procurement contracts (57 percent), followed by clearance of customs procedures (12 percent) and bribes paid to obtain preferential tax treatment (6 percent). Other interesting findings include

- In 41 percent of the 400-plus cases, management-level employees paid or authorized the bribe, and CEOs were involved in 12 percent of cases.[23]
- Three-fourths of the cases involved intermediaries, with 41 percent involving agents (local sales and marketing agents), brokers, and distributors; another 35 percent involved corporate vehicles, such as subsidiaries, local consulting firms, companies located in offshore financial centers or tax havens, or companies established under the beneficial ownership of the public official who received the bribe.
- Almost half of the cases involved bribes of public officials from countries with high (22 percent) to very high (21 percent) levels of human development (UN Human Development Index).
- One-third of the cases came from self-reporting.
- Approximately one-seventh of the cases came from investigations initiated by law enforcement authorities, and another one-seventh came to light in the context of formal or informal mutual legal assistance treaties between countries.
- Bribes were paid, offered, or given most frequently to employees of state-owned or state-controlled enterprises (27 percent), followed by customs officials (11 percent), health officials (7 percent) and defense officials (6 percent).
- Companies that self-reported became aware of bribery in international operations primarily from internal audits (31 percent) and merger and acquisition due diligence procedures (28 percent).
- Eighty individuals were imprisoned after bribery conviction. Another 38 individuals received suspended sentences, suggesting a convicted individual's chances of going to jail were two in three.

While the report found that whistleblowers accounted for only 2 percent of the cases, the data covers a period for which the Dodd-Frank Whistleblower Act was not in force (Dodd-Frank became effective in 2011).

G. Transparency International Tenth Annual Assessment of Enforcement of the OECD Convention on Combating Foreign Exporting Corruption [24]

Based on reports by Transparency International experts, Transparency International arrived at the following October 2014 classification of foreign bribery enforcement in OECD Anti-Bribery Convention countries (listed in order of their share of world exports):

Active enforcement. Four countries with 23.1 percent of world exports: United States, Germany, United Kingdom, and Switzerland.
Moderate enforcement. Five countries with 8.3 percent of world exports: Italy, Canada, Australia, Austria, and Finland.

> *Limited enforcement.* Eight countries with 7.6 percent of world exports: France, Sweden, Norway, Hungary, South Africa, Argentina, Portugal, and New Zealand.
>
> *Little or no enforcement.* Twenty-two countries with 27 percent of world exports: Japan, Netherlands, Korea (South), Russia, Spain, Belgium, Mexico, Brazil, Ireland, Poland, Turkey, Denmark, Czech Republic, Luxembourg, Chile, Israel, Slovak Republic, Colombia, Greece, Slovenia, Bulgaria, and Estonia.

The above represents the tenth annual independent progress report on OECD Anti-Bribery Convention enforcement by Transparency International, the global coalition against corruption. Fifteen years after the Convention entered into force, there are still 22 countries with little or no enforcement and eight countries with only limited enforcement. The OECD Working Group on Bribery, which represents the 41 parties to the Convention, conducts a follow-up monitoring program under which nine to ten countries are reviewed each year.

H. OECD: Country Sanction Efforts

In December 2014 the OECD published in its Analysis of the Cost of Foreign Bribery the number of foreign bribery schemes (often involving multiple individual and corporate defendants) sanctioned per country since 1999. The results are shown in the following table.

Country	Number of Foreign Bribery Schemes Sanctioned per Country
United States	128
Germany	26
South Korea	11
Italy	6
Switzerland	6
United Kingdom	6
France	5
Norway	5
Canada	4
Japan	3
Belgium	1
Bulgaria	1
Hungary	1
Luxembourg	1
Netherlands	1
Poland	1
Sweden	1

Thus, the United States has brought 61 percent and Germany 12 percent of the total sanctions.

II. UNITED NATIONS CONVENTION AGAINST CORRUPTION

On December 14, 2005, the United Nations Convention against Corruption (UNCAC) entered into force. UNCAC currently has 140 signatories and 165 parties.[25] UNCAC is the broadest and most comprehensive of all the multilateral corruption conventions. The purpose of the UNCAC is threefold:

1. To promote and strengthen measures to prevent and combat corruption more efficiently and effectively;
2. To promote, facilitate, and support international cooperation and technical assistance in the prevention of and fight against corruption, including in asset recovery; and
3. To promote integrity, accountability, and proper management of public affairs and property.

The UNCAC is built upon five pillars: prevention; criminalization and law enforcement; internal cooperation; asset recovery; and technical assistance and information exchange. It does not explicitly exclude facilitating agents, but its definition of "bribe" is thought to exclude such payments.[26] The UNCAC covers commercial bribery and not simply bribes of government officials. It also addresses embezzlement, money laundering, obstruction of justice, corporate record-keeping, extradition, and international law enforcement cooperation. The United States ratified the UNCAC on October 30, 2006.

III. REGIONAL CONVENTIONS

A. The Organization of American States Inter-American Convention against Corruption

The Organization of American States (OAS) Inter-American Convention against Corruption (IACAC), which entered into force on March 6, 1997, was the first multilateral treaty to address corruption.[27] Thirty-four countries have signed the IACAC,[28] which is considered a model for laws on jurisdiction, extradition, legal assistance cooperation, bank secrecy, and tax deductibility of international bribes.[29] Similar to the FCPA, the convention requires parties to criminalize the bribery of foreign officials.[30] To serve its purpose of preventing, detecting, punishing, and eradicating corruption, the IACAC calls for cooperation among countries in the fight against domestic and transnational corruption in the Western Hemisphere.[31] The convention requires that member states afford one another the "widest measure of mutual assistance" in the criminal investigation and prosecution of such acts.[32] As a result, parties must extradite individuals who violate another country's anticorruption laws.[33] Moreover, member states cannot invoke bank secrecy as a basis for refusing to assist another state.[34]

Parties are also required to update their domestic legislation to criminalize corrupt acts, such as transnational bribery, to prevent any national from bribing an official of another state, and illicit enrichment, to prohibit inexplicable increases in assets of government officials.[35] The United States, however, ratified the IACAC in September 2000 with the understanding that the United States would not establish a new criminal offense of illicit enrichment because it is constitutionally problematic.[36]

B. The Council of Europe Convention

The Council of Europe (CoE), founded in 1949, consists of 46 member countries whose aims include a solution to organized crime and corruption. The CoE Criminal Law Convention on Corruption is more comprehensive than the OECD Convention or the IACAC, as it seeks to criminalize active and passive bribery of domestic public officials (articles 2 and 3); foreign public officials (article 5); domestic public assemblies (article 4); foreign public assemblies (article 6); international or company officials (article 9); members of international parliamentary assemblies (article 10); judges and officials of international courts (article 11); and those in the private sector (articles 7 and 8).[37] Article 2 defines bribery as giving "any undue advantage" for an official "to act or refrain from acting in the exercise of his or her functions." The CoE Convention makes no explicit exception for facilitating payments. The Group of States against Corruption (GRECO), which is an enlarged partial agreement, was established in 1999 by the CoE to monitor states' compliance with the organization's anticorrupt standards. Currently, GRECO has 46 member states (45 European states and the United States).[38] The convention criminalizes a wide range of corrupt practices in both the public and private sectors, such as bribery of domestic and foreign public officials, active and passive bribery in the private sector, and money laundering of proceeds from corruption offenses.[39] Similar to the IACAC, the CoE Convention calls for states to afford one another the "widest measure of mutual assistance" in investigating or prosecuting such acts.[40] Likewise, the CoE Convention deems corrupt acts outlined in the convention as extraditable offenses.[41]

IV. UNITED KINGDOM ANTICORRUPTION DEVELOPMENTS

A. U.K. Bribery Act, 2010

The United Kingdom Bribery Act 2010 (c.23) became effective July 1, 2011.[42] The long-awaited enactment of this legislation may prove a watershed development for the global anticorruption movement. The Bribery Act addresses only bribery, which is generally defined as giving someone a financial or other advantage to perform their functions or activities improperly or to reward that person for already having done so. The Act repeals all previous statutory and common law provisions in relation to bribery, instead replacing them with four bribery offenses: (1) offering a bribe; (2) receiving a bribe; (3) the bribery of a foreign public official; and (4) the failure of a commercial organization (corporation or partnership) to prevent bribery on its behalf. All four offenses can be committed by individuals or corporations.

On March 30, 2011, the Serious Fraud Office (SFO) and the director of Public Prosecutions issued Joint Prosecution Guidance (Guidance) about "adequate procedures" that companies can put into place to prevent persons associated with them from bribing.[43] "Adequate procedures" will establish a full defense to the strict liability corporations face for failure to prevent bribery by an employee, agent, or subsidiary. The SFO is the leading U.K. agency for investigating and prosecuting cases of overseas corruption. The Guidance addresses, inter alia, jurisdiction over foreign companies; "associated persons" including joint ventures; corporate hospitality; facilitation payments; mandatory debarment; and the six guiding principles that companies can put in place to establish "adequate procedures"—the statutory

defense available to corporations facing section 7 strict liability for failing to prevent bribery by an associated person. The U.K. Bribery Act's bribery of foreign public officials and failure of an organization to prevent bribery offenses along with
the adequate procedures defense and related Guidance are discussed in detail in
chapter 11.

B.   Major U.K. Antibribery Enforcement Actions

In fall 2008, United Kingdom authorities filed two separate corruption enforcement actions signaling a clear commitment to enforce foreign bribery laws. First,
the Overseas Anti-Corruption Unit of the London Police Department charged a
U.K. consulting firm managing director and a Ugandan official with bribery in a
scheme under which the managing director's security firm paid the foreign official for a contract with the Ugandan Presidential Guard. Both pled guilty, and the
Ugandan official was sentenced to a year in jail.[44] Second, the United Kingdom's
Serious Fraud Office announced a $3.9 million civil settlement with the major
construction firm Balfour Beatty PLC for unlawful accounting in connection with
payment irregularities.[45] While these two cases do not begin to approach the magnitude of U.S. anticorruption civil and criminal actions or fines, they signaled a
start by a country that has been criticized for lax corruption enforcement and highlight the conviction of a foreign government official—something unavailable to
U.S. prosecutors under the FCPA. Since 2008 the United Kingdom has filed seven
other foreign bribery cases against companies (see chapter 11).

In February 2010, the SFO along with the U.S. Department of Justice announced
a settlement with BAE Systems plc, in a ground-breaking global agreement. The
DOJ agreement involves BAE's business dealings in a number of countries, while
the SFO agreement concentrates on the company's operations in Tanzania. Under
the agreement, BAE Systems agreed to plead guilty in the Crown Court to an
offense under section 221 of the Companies Act of 1985 for failing to keep reasonably accurate accounting records in relation to its activities in Tanzania. The company agreed to pay £30 million comprising a financial order that was approved by
a Crown Court judge with the balance paid as an ex gratia payment for the benefit
of the people of Tanzania. In conjunction with this agreement, the SFO took into
account BAE's implementation of substantial ethical and compliance reforms and
the company's agreement with the DOJ, and has determined that no further prosecutions would be brought against BAE Systems in relation to the matters that had
been under SFO investigation.[46]

In March 2010, Innospec Inc., a manufacturer and seller of specialty chemicals, pleaded guilty in the United States to bribery charges while its U.K. subsidiary, Innospec Ltd., pleaded guilty in the Southwark Crown Court in London in
connection with corrupt payments to Indonesian officials. In connection with the
U.K. charges, Innospec Ltd. agreed to pay a criminal penalty of $12.7 million. The
SFO's case was developed as a result of a DOJ referral in October 2007. Parentheti-
cally, the Crown Court was troubled by the Innospec three-party plea agreement
(among the United Kingdom, United States, and Innospec) and warned the SFO

not to bring such a de facto agreement before it again. In June 2014, a Southwark Crown Court jury convicted Dennis Kerrison, a former CEO of the predecessor to Innospec, and Dr. Miltiades Papachristos, former regional sales director for the Asia-Pacific region, of conspiracy to commit corruption. Kerrison was ultimately sentenced to three years in jail and Papachristos to 18 months.[47]

In July 2014, the SFO commenced criminal proceedings against Alstom Network UK Ltd., formerly called Alstom International Ltd., alleging corruption contrary to section 1 of the Prevention of Corruption Act 1906, as well as three offenses of conspiracy contrary to section 1 of Criminal Law Act 1997. Alstom, the parent, is a French industrial conglomerate. The alleged corruption took place between June 2000 and November 2006 on transport projects in India, Poland, and Tunisia.[48]

In December 2014 Smith and Ouzman Ltd., a printing company, and two employees were convicted of corruptly agreeing to make payments to secure business contracts in Kenya and Mauritania, in violation of the Prevention of Corruption Act of 1906. The corrupt payments totaled £ 395,074. This was the SFO's first conviction, after trial, of a corporation for an offense involving bribery of a foreign public official.[49]

The United Kingdom and the United States will need to iron out certain enforcement issues for multinational corporations seeking global resolutions and increase their coordination and dialogue with the U.K. courts. The mutual interests of the anticorruption agencies will in time overcome such early hurdles. Soon the SFO is expected to prosecute foreign official corruption using the Bribery Act of 2010.

C. Money Laundering

Bribery routinely generates significant financial gain. As such it serves as a logical and compelling predicate offense for the three U.K. money laundering offenses.[50] Each money laundering offense in the United Kingdom carries a maximum sentence of 14 years. Moreover, the mere failure to report knowledge or suspicion to a financial investigation unit alone carries a maximum sentence of five years in the U.K.

D. Extradition

In March 2009 the London Metropolitan Police arrested Jeffrey Tesler for his alleged role in the efforts of an engineering and construction consortium, TKSJ, to bribe Nigerian officials in order to obtain engineering, procurement, and construction contracts. (See chapter 10 discussion of Technip, KBR, Snamprogetti, and JGC.) Tesler commenced legal efforts in London to avoid extradition, but in February 2011, he abandoned his extradition fight. In March 2011, Tesler flew to the United States, pled guilty to two FCPA counts in the Southern District of Texas, and agreed to forfeit $148,964,568, the largest ever FCPA forfeiture order against an individual. Tesler was sentenced in February 2012 to 21 months in prison. The DOJ's pursuit of Tesler is not an encouraging development for FCPA defendants resident in other developed countries who believe they can avoid extradition to and foreign bribery trials in the United States.

V. OTHER NOTABLE ANTIBRIBERY PROSECUTIONS

A. Australia

In July 2011, the Australian Federal Police (AFP) charged Securency International Pty Ltd. (Securency), its sister company Note Printing Australia Limited (NPA), and six Victoria, Australia, individuals with bribery of foreign public officials in connection with alleged bribes paid to public officials in Indonesia, Malaysia, and Vietnam between 1999 and 2005.[51] The AFP alleged that senior managers for the two companies utilized international sales agents to bribe foreign officials to obtain banknote contracts. In Vietnam the bribe was in the form of a university scholarship—again to secure a banknote contract.

The AFP began the investigation in 2009 upon a referral from the chairman of Securency and focused on the actions of Securency and NPA senior managers who allegedly represented the "mind and will" of the companies. The AFP charges allege that the money paid in bribes originated from the companies, which in turn received the resulting benefit of banknote contracts.[52] The AFP, which acknowledged significant cooperation by the Serious Fraud Office, Malaysian Anticorruption Commission, a Malaysian Attorney General's Chambers, and the Indonesian National Police, brought further charges in this investigation in March 2013.[53] The Securency case is the first prosecution brought under Australia's foreign bribery legislation that was introduced in 1999.

B. Brazil

In January 2014, Brazil's antibribery law,[54] commonly referred to as the Clean Company Act, became effective on January 29, 2014. The Clean Company Act applies to:

1. Business organizations in Brazil (whether incorporated or not);
2. Any Brazilian foundations or associations; and
3. Foreign companies with any presence in Brazil (even if temporary).

The Act provides for civil and administrative liability but not corporate criminal liability. The Act is enforced by the office of the Federal Comptroller General.

Under the Clean Company Act, companies can be strictly liable for prohibited acts committed in their interest or for their benefit (whether exclusively or not). To establish a strict liability violation, Brazilian authorities need only demonstrate that a prohibited act occurred; they need not prove the intent (or knowledge) of the company, or that of any individual officer.[55]

The Act applies to both bribery of foreign and local officials. It does not apply to commercial or private briberies. The Act is broader than the FCPA or U.K. Bribery Act in that it specifically addresses public tenders and prohibits the following conduct.

Brazil's Clean Company Act applies only to companies and, therefore, cannot be brought against individuals. Nevertheless, individuals involved in related wrongdoing can be subject to sanctions set forth in Brazil's Criminal Code and other Brazilian laws (e.g., the Public Tender Law and the Improbity Law).

Under the Clean Company Act, the following conduct is prohibited:

a. To promise, offer, or give, directly or indirectly, an undue advantage to a public agent or a related third person;

b. To finance, pay, sponsor or, in any way, subsidize the performance of a prohibited act;

c. To make use of any individual or legal entity to conceal or disguise its real interests or the identity of the beneficiaries of acts performed;

d. Regarding public tenders and contracts:

    i. To thwart or disturb the competitive character of a public tender procedure;

    ii. To prevent, disturb, or defraud the performance of any act of a public tender procedure;

    iii. To remove or try to remove a bidder by fraudulent means or by the offering of any type of advantage;

    iv. To defraud a public tender or a contract arising therefrom;

    v. To create, in a fraudulent or irregular manner, a legal entity to participate in a public tender or enter into an administrative contract;

    vi. To gain an undue advantage or benefit, in a fraudulent way, from modifications or extensions to contracts entered into with the public administration;

e. To manipulate or defraud the economic and financial terms of the contracts entered into with the public administration;

f. To hinder an investigation or audit by a public agency, or to otherwise interfere with this work.[56]

The Clean Company Act includes an alternative resolution mechanism for companies seeking to more efficiently resolve bribery-related matters with public authorities—so-called leniency agreements. Under the law's enforcement regime, companies can be given credit for self-disclosure and cooperation. While the Clean Company Act does not obligate companies to self-report violations, those that cooperate with investigations in this manner will receive credit in the ultimate calculation of sanctions. Moreover, companies that cooperate, enter into leniency agreements, and fulfill the related legal requirements (which include admissions of wrongdoing) can have their fines reduced by up to two-thirds of the total, and will be exempt from certain judicial and administrative sanctions, whether to self-disclose or include a calculation of whether other laws may apply to the facts of the case that might not, for example, include leniency provisions. Finally, while a leniency agreement might settle charges for companies, individuals can still be liable for the relevant illegal acts under other Brazilian statutes. The Clean Company Act provides for successor liability in the event of amendments to the articles of incorporation, transformation, restructuring, merger, acquisition, or spin-off of a company.

In 2014, the Petrobras General filed charges against 22 executives and 13 others involving a kickback scheme by Petroleo Brasileiro SA (Petrobras), the $52 billion state-owned oil company, to pay political officers. The executives have been accused of forming a "club" to rotate contracts with Petrobras and to pay politicians.[57] Six of the country's largest construction and engineering companies have been implicated to date.

C. Canada

In June 2011, the Royal Canadian Mounted Police (RCMP) International Anti-Corruption Unit concluded a six-year bribery investigation of Niko Resources Ltd., a Calgary-based oil and gas company.[58] Specifically, the company was charged with bribery under section 3(1)(b) of the Corruption of Foreign Public Officials Act (CFPOA), 1999, for conduct during the period February 1 to June 30, 2005. The RCMP alleged that in May 2005, Niko Resources, through its subsidiary Niko Bangladesh, provided the use of a vehicle that cost C$190,984 to the former Bangladesh State Minister for Energy and Mineral Resources in order to influence the Minister in dealings with Niko Bangladesh. In June 2005 the parent company paid travel and lodging expenses for the same minister to travel from Bangladesh to attend the GO EXPO oil and gas exposition. Niko is alleged to have improperly paid approximately $5,000 for nonbusiness travel to New York and Chicago so the Minister could visit his family.

Justice Brooker of the Court of Queens Bench accepted the Crown's recommendation of a fine of C$8.2 million and the victim surcharge for a total of nearly C$9.5 million. Niko is subject to the court's supervision for a period of three years pursuant to a probation order to ensure that audits are completed to examine Niko's compliance with the CFPOA. The RCMP acknowledged the cooperation of the Bangladesh Anticorruption Commission, the DOJ Fraud Section, and the FBI International Corruption Unit, along with law enforcement agencies in Switzerland, Japan, the United Kingdom, and Barbados.[59] The Niko Resources case was the first foreign bribery prosecution brought by Canada under the CFPOA.

In January 2013, Griffiths Energy International Inc. (GEI), another Calgary-based energy company, pleaded guilty to CFPOA charges and agreed to pay a C$10.35 million penalty.[60] GEI's chairman and cofounder, Brad Griffith, and a business partner, Naeem Tyab, spent six months in 2008 pursuing opportunities to acquire blocks in Chad. After a Canadian advised the pair against making payments to Chad's Ambassador to Canada, GEI paid a $2 million consulting fee to a company owned by the Ambassador's wife. Following Griffith's death in a boating accident in July 2011, new management learned of the payments, conducted an investigation, and voluntarily disclosed the results of the investigation to the RCMP. Notwithstanding its "full and extensive"[61] cooperation and the first Canadian bribery voluntary disclosure, the privately held company had to plead guilty to a felony and agreed to pay the largest CFPOA fine ever.[62]

In August 2013, an Ontario Superior Court convicted Nazir Karigar of conspiring in 2005 and 2006 to bribe Air India officials and an Indian Minister of Aviation in order to land a government contract for a facial recognition security system. Karigar, a Canadian, became the first person convicted under the CFPOA. [63] In May 2014 Judge Hackland sentenced Karigar to three years in jail. [64]

D. People's Republic of China

In early 2013 the People's Republic of China (PRC) Ministry of Public Security (MPS) began investigating suspicious activity involving a Shanghai travel agency and potential money laundering to funnel bribes to doctors, hospitals, medical associations, foundations, and government officials. According to Chinese investigators, the payoffs led to drug sales and allowed British pharmaceutical giant GlaxoSmithKline to sell its products for higher prices in the PRC.[65]

In July 2013 Beijing authorities accused Glaxo's China operations of "organizing fictitious conferences, overbilling for training sessions, and in various other ways filing sham expenses for which the cooperating travel agencies would issue bogus receipts."[66] This practice allegedly allowed GSK executives to be reimbursed while travel agencies took some of the monies for themselves. The Chinese government detained four GSK executives following a raid of the company's offices in China in late June. In July 2013, GSK issued a conciliatory statement that said, "Certain senior executives of GSK China who know our systems well appear to have acted outside of our processes and controls, which breaches Chinese law. We have zero tolerance for any behavior of this nature."[67] Glaxo vowed to continue to cooperate with the MPS and stated that the scandal involved only a few rogue Chinese-born employees.

In September 2014, after a one-day trial held in secrecy, the Changsha Intermediate People's Court in Hunan Province found that Glaxo's Chinese subsidiary had, according to Chinese law, offered money or property to nongovernment personnel in order to obtain commercial gain and had been found guilty of bribing nongovernment personnel.[68] In an unusual practice, Chinese authorities prosecuted the foreign-born former GSK country manager Mark Reilly and four other company managers who faced potential prison terms of two to four years. All five were given reprieves,[69] and Reilly is expected to be deported. The bribes reportedly led to illegal revenues of more than $150 million. In imposing the biggest fine ever by a Chinese court, the People's Court said, "[The firm] bribed, in various forms, people working in medical institutions across the country, and the amount of money involved was huge. Five senior executives actively organized, push forwarded and implemented sales with bribery."[70]

In addition to publishing a statement of apology to the Chinese government, Glaxo stated that it had taken comprehensive steps to rectify the issue, including fundamentally changing the incentive program for its sales forces (decoupling sales targets from compensation); significantly reducing and changing engagement activities with healthcare professionals, and expanding processes for review and monitoring of invoicing and payments.[71]

E. Mexico

In June 2012 Mexico enacted a Federal Law against Corruption in Public Procurement (Ley Federal Anticorrupción en Contrataciones Públicas or the Anticorruption Law) (FCPA). The Anticorruption Law holds individuals and companies accountable for offering money or gifts to obtain or maintain a business advantage in the procurement of public contracts with the Mexican government.[72] Violators are subject to administrative sanctions, including the imposition of monetary fines that are roughly $5,000 to $250,000 for individuals and $50,000 to $10 million for companies, and corporations are subject to suspension or debarment from federal procurement contracts for up to ten years. Signally, fines may be reduced by up to 70 percent for offenders who self-report violations to Mexican authorities.

The law applies to Mexican and non-Mexican companies and individuals engaged in federal government contracting, including bidders, participants in tenders, request for proposal recipients, suppliers, contractors, permit holders, concessionaires and their shareholders, and agents. The acts and omissions prohibited by the Anticorruption Law include, but are not limited to, the following:

- Promising, offering, or delivering money or gifts to a public official or a third party—regardless of whether the money or gift is accepted—so that the public official will either act or refrain from acting in his or her official capacity, in order to obtain or maintain an advantage in procuring public contracts;
- Engaging in acts or omissions with the purpose or effect of participating in federal public contracting when prohibited from participating under the law or relevant regulations; and
- Engaging in acts or omissions with the purpose or effect of evading the rules or requirements established in federal contracting procedures.

The Anticorruption Law also criminalizes bribery of non-Mexican government officials.[73]

F. Norway

In January 2014, Okokrim, the Norwegian National Authority for Investigation and Prosecution of Economic and Environmental Crime, settled a corruption investigation with Yara International ASA, a Norwegian fertilizer producer, which admitted it had agreed to pay approximately $12 million in bribes to government officials in India or Libya and Russian suppliers between 2004 and 2009. Yara agreed to pay a fine of $48 million, the largest corporate fine in Norwegian history.[74]

G. Russia

In January 2013 Russia's first comprehensive anticorruption law, Federal Law No. 273 on Combating Corruption, was amended to require companies to have compliance officers and programs. Specifically, Article 13.3 requires all organizations to develop and implement measures to prevent bribery, including (1) designating departments and structural units and officers who will be responsible for the prevention of bribery and related offenses; (2) cooperating with law enforcement authorities; (3) developing and implementing standards and procedures designed to ensure ethical business conduct; (4) adopting a code of ethics and professional conduct for all employees; (5) means for identifying, preventing, and resolving conflicts of interest; and (6) preventing the creating and use of false and altered documents.

Before Article 13.3 became an amendment, Russian law provided that organizations could be held liable for "failing to take all measures within their powers" to prevent bribery. Thus, an organization could point to its compliance program as evidence of its efforts to take measures to prevent bribery. However, there was no affirmative duty to create a compliance program or any legislative guidance as to what such a system should contain.[75]

Article 13.3 now requires companies to create a compliance program that meet its standards, and failure to do so will be evidence of noncompliance with established Russian laws. Further, retaining agents and third parties that lack compliance programs within their organizations may be viewed as failure to take all possible measures to prevent corruption.

In light of Article 13.3, companies doing business in Russia should

1. assess their existing compliance programs to determine whether they satisfy the standards of Article 13.3;
2. supplement existing programs to ensure compliance with Article 13.3;
3. ensure that they have
   a. designated compliance personnel and functions;
   b. procedures for conducting internal investigations;
   c. procedures for cooperating with law enforcement in the event that a serious violation is discovered;
   d. a code of corporate compliance and ethics that clearly addresses conflict of interest;
   e. a system for conducting regular risk assessments both within the company itself and among its business partners and third-party agents;
   f. regular training for employees on anticorruption compliance, business ethics, and conflict of interest; and
4. make sure that their counterparties are aware and comply with this requirement.[76]

Under Russian law, only individuals are subject to criminal liability. Companies are subject to administrative liability for bribery conduct and can be fined up to 100 times the value of the bribe and forfeiture of the money, securities, or the assets constituting the bribe.[77]

VI. ADDITIONAL RESOURCES

- David Luban, Julie O'Sullivan & David Stewart, *Corruption*, ch. 14 *in* INTERNATIONAL AND TRANSNATIONAL CRIMINAL LAW (Aspen 2009).
- EOIN O'SHEA, THE BRIBERY ACT 2010: A PRACTICAL GUIDE (Jordan 2011).
- PHILIP MONTAGUE RAPHAEL, BLACKSTONE'S GUIDE TO THE BRIBERY ACT 2010 (Oxford Univ. Press 2010).
- OECD FOREIGN BRIBERY REPORT (Dec. 2014), http://www.oecd.org/daf/anti -bribery/scale-of-international-bribery-laid-bare-by-new-OECD-report.htm.
- U.K. Bribery Act, 2010, ch. 23 & Explanatory Notes (appendix 3).
- Roger Witten, Kimberly Parker & Thomas Koffer, Navigating the Increased Anti-Corruption Environment in the United States and Abroad, paper presented at the ABA National Institute on White Collar Crime (San Francisco, Mar. 5–6, 2009).
- DON ZARIN, DOING BUSINESS UNDER THE FOREIGN CORRUPT PRACTICES ACT, ch. 13 (PLI 2007).

NOTES

1. The original signatories of the OECD Convention are Argentina, Australia, Austria, Belgium, Brazil, Bulgaria, Canada, Chile, the Czech Republic, Denmark, Finland, France, Germany, Greece, Hungary, Iceland, Ireland, Italy, Japan, Korea, Luxembourg, Mexico, the Netherlands, New Zealand, Norway, Poland, Portugal, the Slovak Republic, Slovenia, Spain, Sweden, Switzerland, Turkey, the United Kingdom, and the United States. Since 1998 Colombia, Israel, Russia, and South Africa have signed the Organization for Economic Cooperation and Development Convention on Combating Bribery of Foreign Officials in International Business Transactions, Dec. 18, 1997, OECD document DAFFE/IME/BR (97) 20, 37 I.L.M. 1 (1998). The Convention is appended hereto as appendix 2.

2. U.S. Dep't of State Bureau of Economic & Bus. Affairs, Battling International Bribery (2004), http://www.state.gov/documents/organization/36667.pdf.

3. *See* OECD Convention Members and Partners, art. 1 (appendix 2).

4. Press Release, OECD, Israel Joins OECD Working Group on Bribery (Sept. 12, 2008), http://www.oecd.org/israel/israeljoinsoecdworkinggrouponbribery.htm.

5. International Anti-Bribery and Fair Competition Act of 1998, Pub. L. No. 105-366, 112 Stat. 3302 (1998) (codified at 15 U.S.C. §§ 78dd-1 to -3, 78ff), amending the Foreign Corrupt Practices Act of 1977, Pub. L. No. 95-213, 91 Stat. 1494 (codified as amended at 15 U.S.C. §§ 78m, 78dd-1 to 78dd-2, 78ff (1994)) [hereinafter FCPA].

6. Battling International Bribery, *supra* note 2, at 12.

7. *Id*. at 14.

8. OECD Convention, art. 3.

9. OECD Convention, art. 4.

10. OECD, Convention on Combating Bribery of Foreign Public Officials in International Business Transactions and Related Documents: Commentaries on the Convention, Adopted on November 21, 1997, at 14, para. 5, http://www.oecd.org/investment/anti-bribery/anti-briberyconvention/38028044.pdf. (OECD Commentaries).

11. *Id*. ¶ 12.

12. *Id*. ¶ 14.

13. *Id*. ¶ 15.

14. However, under the laws of some countries, bribes promised or given to a person expecting to become a foreign public official may qualify under the convention. *See* Battling International Bribery, *supra* note 2, at B-6. Furthermore, there are some countries where certain individuals (such as political party officials in single-party states) are not formally recognized as public officials, but because of their de facto performance of a public function, they may be considered public officials under the legal principles of those states. *See id*. at B-7.

15. OECD Commentaries ¶ 22.

16. *Id*. ¶ 31.

17. OECD Convention, art. 9, ¶ 3.

18. OECD, Country Monitoring of the OECD Anti-Bribery Convention, http://www.oecd.org/daf/anti-bribery/countrymonitoringoftheoecdanti-briberyconvention.html.

19. Transparency Int'l, Progress Report 2014: Enforcement of the OECD Bribery Convention 12, http://www.transparency.org/whatwedo/pub/progress_report_2014_enforcement_of_the_oecd_anti_bribery_convention.

20. Press Release, Transparency Int'l, Efforts to Curb Foreign Bribery Remain Inadequate (July 28, 2010), http://www.transparency.org/news/pressrelease/20100728 _efforts_curb_foreign_bribery_remain_inadequate.

21. OECD, Bribery in International Business Scale of International Bribery Laid Bare by New OECD Report (Dec. 2, 2014). http://www.oecd.org/daf/anti-bribery/scale -of-international-bribery-laid-bare-by-new-OECD-report.htm.

22. *Id.*

23. *Id.*

24. Transparency Int'l, Progress Report 2014: Assessing Enforcement of the OECD Convention on Combating Foreign Bribery, http://www.transparency.org /exporting_corruption.

25. *See* U.N. Office on Drugs & Crime, UNCAC Signatories and Ratification Status as of 24 December 2012, http://www.unodc.org/unodc/en/treaties/CAC /signatories.html.

26. David Luban, Julie O'Sullivan & David Stewart, *Corruption*, ch. 14 *in* INTERNATIONAL AND TRANSNATIONAL CRIMINAL LAW (Aspen 2009).

27. Alejandro Posadas, *Combating Corruption under International Law*, 10 DUKE J. COMP. & INT'L L. 345, 384 (2000).

28. *See* Inter-American Convention against Corruption, Signatory Countries, http://www.oas.org/juridico/english/Sigs/b-58.html.

29. Nora M. Rubin, *A Convergence of 1996 and 1997 Global Efforts to Curb Corruption and Bribery in International Business Transactions: The Legal Implications of OECD Recommendations and Convention for the United States, Germany, and Switzerland*, 14 AM. U. INT'L L. REV. 257, 261–63 (1998).

30. *See* U.S. Dep't of State Fact Sheet, OAS Inter-American Convention against Corruption (May 27, 1997).

31. *See* Inter-American Convention against Corruption, Mar. 29, 1996, 35 I.L.M. 724, art. II.

32. *See id.* art. XIV.

33. *See id.* art. XIII.

34. *See id.* art. XVI.

35. *See id.* arts. VII–IX.

36. See U.S. Dep't of State, First Annual Report to Congress on the Inter-American Convention against Corruption (Apr. 2001).

37. Luban, O'Sullivan & Stewart, *supra* note 26, at 47.

38. Council of Europe, Group of States against Corruption (GRECO), http:// www.coe.int/t/dghl/monitoring/greco/general/3.%20what%20is%20greco_EN.asp.

39. *See* Criminal Law Convention on Corruption, ch. II. (July 1, 2002) CETS No 173.

40. *See id.* ch. IV, art. 26.

41. *See id.* art. 27.

42. The U.K. Bribery Act 2010 is reprinted in appendix 3.

43. Section 9 of the Act required the Secretary of State for Justice to publish guidance on the interpretation of the section 7 offense. On March 30, 2011, the Secretary of State published a 43-page guidance on the interpretation and use of the Act. (appendix 15).

44. Press Release, City of London Police, Government Official Guilty of Corruption (Sept. 22, 2008).

45. Press Release, U.K. Serious Fraud Office, Serious Fraud Office Successfully Obtains First Ever Civil Recovery Order Involving Major PLC (Oct. 6, 2008), http://www.sfo.gov.uk/press-room/press-release-archive/press-releases-2008/balfour-beatty-plc.aspx.

46. Press Release, U.K. Serious Fraud Office, BAE Systems plc (Feb. 5, 2010), http://www.sfo.gov.uk/press-room/press-release-archive/press-releases-2010/bae-systems-plc.aspx.

47. Press Release, U.K. Serious Fraud Office, Four Sentenced for Role in Innospec Corruption (Aug. 4, 2014), http://www.sfo.gov.uk/press-room/latest-press-releases/press-releases-2014/four-sentenced-for-role-in-innospec-corruption.aspx.

48. Press Release, U.K. Serious Fraud Office, Criminal Charges against Alstom in the UK (Jul. 24, 2014), http://www.sfo.gov.uk/press-room/latest-press-releases/press-releases-2014/criminal-charges-against-alstom-in-the-uk.aspx.

49. Press Release, U.K. Serious Fraud Office, UK Printing Company and Two Men Found Guilty in Corruption Trial (Dec. 22, 2014), http://www.sfo.gov.uk/press-room/latest-press-releases/press-releases-2014/uk-printing-company-and-two-men-found-guilty-in-corruption-trial.aspx.

50. Proceeds of Crime Act, 2002 (§§ 327–329). *See* Monty Raphael, Blackstone's Guide to the Bribery Act 2010, at 10.11 (Oxford Univ. Press 2010).

51. Press Release, Australia Fed. Police, Foreign Bribery Charges Laid in Australia (July 1, 2011), http://www.afp.gov.au/media-centre/news/afp/2011/july/foreign-bribery-charges-laid-in-australia.aspx.

52. *Id.*

53. *Id.* and Press Release, Australia Fed. Police, Further Charges Laid in Foreign Bribery Investigation (Mar. 14, 2013), http://www.afp.gov.au/media-centre/news/afp/2013/march/furth-charges-laid-in-foreign-bribery-investigation.aspx.

54. Law no. 12.846/2013.

55. Baker & McKenzie Alert, http://www.bakermckenzie.com/files/Publication/fcdc0ffb-eb39-4650-8b39-44fe871b6a64/Presentation/PublicationAttachment/17886ae8-ec84-46f1-821f-6a4a1ba585a4/AL_Global_CorruptionRiskWorldCup_Jul14.pdf .

56. *Id.*

57. *Brazil Company Executives Charged in Petrobras Scandal*, BBC News, Dec. 11, 2014, http://www.bbc.com/news/world-latin-america-30442790.

58. Press Release, Royal Canadian Mounted Police, Corruption Charges Laid against Niko Resources (June 24, 2011), http://www.rcmp-grc.gc.ca/ab/news-nouvelles/2011/110624-niko-eng.htm.

59. *Id.*

60. Carrie Tait, *Griffith to Pay Millions in African Bribery Case*, Globe & Mail, Jan. 22, 2013, http://www.theglobeandmail.com/report-on-business/industry-news/energy-and-resources/griffiths-to-pay-millions-in-african-bribery-case/article7622364/.

61. Her Majesty the Queen and Griffiths Energy International Inc. Agreed Statement of Facts (Jan. 14, 2003) Queen's Bench of Alberta, Judicial District of Calgary ¶¶ 15m 21–22,38, 42–45.

62. *Id.*

63. Megan Gillis, *Hi-Tech Executive Nazir Karigar Guilty of Trying to Bribe Air India Officials*, Ottawa Sun, Aug. 15, 2013, http://www.ottawasun.com/2013/08/15/high-tech-exec-nazir-karigar-guilty-of-trying-to-bribe-air-india-officials.

64. Dave Seglins, *Nazir Karigar, Air India Bribe Plotter, Sentenced to Three Years in Prison*, CBC NEWS, May 23, 2014, http://www.cbc.ca/news/air-india-bribe-plotter-nazir-karigar-gets-3-year-sentence-1.2649737.

65. David Barboza, *Glaxo Used Travel Firms for Bribery, China Says*, N.Y. TIMES, July 15, 2013, http://www.nytimes.com/2013/07/16/business/global/glaxo-used-travel-firms-in-bribery-china-says.html?pagewanted=all&_r=0.

66. *Id.*

67. Press Release, GSK Statement regarding Recent Meeting with Chinese Authorities (July 22, 2013), http://www.gsk.com/en-gb/media/press-releases/2013/gsk-statement-regarding-recent-meeting-with-chinese-authorities/.

68. Press Release, GSK China Investigation Outcome (Sept. 19, 2014), http://www.gsk.com/en-gb/media/press-releases/2014/gsk-china-investigation-outcome/.

69. Keith Bradsher & Chris Buckley, *China Fines GlaxoSmithKline Nearly $500 Million in Bribery Case*, N.Y. TIMES, Sept. 19, 2014, http://www.nytimes.com/2014/09/20/business/international/gsk-china-fines.html.

70. *GSK China Hit with Record Fine*, XINHUA NEWS (Sept. 19, 2014), http://news.xinhuanet.com/english/china/2014-09/19/c_133656449.htm.

71. GSK press release, *supra* note 67.

72. Morgan Lewis Bockius, Mexico Enacts Anti-Corruption Law for Federal Government Contracting (Oct. 12, 2012),http://www.morganlewis.com/pubs/FCPA_LF_MexicoCracksDownOnCorruptionInGovtContracting_12oct12.

73. *Id.*

74. *Norwegian Fertilizer Firm Yara International Fined for 3 Corruption Cases*, FINLAND TIMES, Jan. 16, 2014, http://www.finlandtimes.fi/europe/2014/01/16/4242/Norwegian-fertilizer-firm-Yara-International-fined-for-3-corruption-cases.

75. Baker & McKenzie Legal Alert, Russian Law Amended to Require Compliance Programs (Feb. 2013). http://www.bakermckenzie.com/files/Publication/201fa799-1bcf-454a-a8be-3a50cfab50a0/Presentation/PublicationAttachment/0a96121b-8ea8-4b73-86d9-4ffd76b204c7/al_moscow_russianlawamended_feb13.pdf.

76. *Id.*

77. Article 19.28 of the Administrative Offenses Act.

CHAPTER 4

Board of Directors and Management Responsibilities

I. BOARD OF DIRECTORS RESPONSIBILITIES

A board of directors has a duty of care to the company that requires it to be informed of developments in the company's business and of possible liabilities. Certain categories of Securities and Exchange Commission (SEC) investigations (including those raising issues of improper payments, false books and records, and circumvention of internal controls) may require directors to inform themselves of the underlying facts and risks. This is especially true where senior management is alleged to have personally engaged in improper conduct.[1] A responsible multinational board of directors must focus on antibribery risks, issues, policies, and compliance.

II. *IN RE* CAREMARK, ITS PROGENY, AND DIRECTOR OF CORPORATE GOVERNANCE RESPONSIBILITIES

In 1996 the Delaware Chancery Court in *In re Caremark International Inc. Derivative Litigation* issued a landmark opinion holding that the failure of a board of directors to ensure that its company has adequate corporate compliance information and reporting systems in place could "render a director liable for losses caused by noncompliance with the applicable standards."[2] The *Caremark* decision clearly struck fear in directors as it warned that, in the wake of misconduct, they could be held personally liable for corporate control system failures. Since this seminal corporate governance decision almost two decades ago, three other Delaware cases have addressed fiduciary duties. In 2010 the Delaware Chancery Court addressed director duties in a Foreign Corrupt Practices Act (FCPA) or foreign bribery allegation context in *In re Dow Chemical Company Derivative Litigation*.[3]

A. *In re* Caremark

In holding that directors may be personally liable for failing to ensure that adequate corporate compliance information and reporting systems are in place, the Delaware Chancery Court stated that elements of an adequate compliance program include

1. the appointment of the company's chief financial officer as "compliance officer";
2. a periodically updated code of business conduct for employees;
3. an ongoing ethics and compliance training program for employees;
4. an internal audit system designed to ensure compliance with ethics and compliance policies; and
5. the formation of a board audit and ethics committee that is regularly advised of the company's "efforts to assure compliance with the law."

Additional steps approved by the court included

1. establishment of a board committee to meet at least quarterly to monitor compliance and to report to the full board on compliance issues;
2. appointment of compliance officers at each of the company's business units to report regularly to the board committee on compliance issues;
3. consideration by the full board of the impact of significant changes in applicable legal and regulatory standards on the company's business and compliance responsibilities; and
4. modification of the company policies and procedures that led to the likelihood of violations.

This guidance led many companies to adopt these measures.

In *Caremark*, Chancellor Allen discussed the need for companies to have adequate corporate compliance programs in order to avoid potential director liability. Commenting on the 1991 enactment of the Organization Sentencing guidelines, he emphasized: "Any rational person attempting in good faith to meet an organizational governance responsibility would be bound to take into account this development and the enhanced penalties and the opportunities for reduced sanctions that it offers."[4] The court also noted that "[t]he Guidelines offer powerful incentives for corporations today to have in place compliance programs to detect violations of law, to promptly report violations to appropriate public officials when discovered, and to take prompt, voluntary remedial efforts."[5] A company's compliance program should be "reasonably designed to provide to senior management and to the board itself timely, accurate information sufficient to allow management and the board, each within its scope, to reach informed judgments concerning both the corporation's compliance with the law and its business performance."[6]

The *Caremark* decision concluded that "a director's obligation includes a duty to attempt in good faith to assure that a corporate information and reporting system, which the board concludes is adequate, exists, and that the failure to do so under some circumstances may, in theory at least, render a director liable for losses caused by noncompliance with applicable legal standards."[7] A decade later, the first of three major Delaware cases would revisit *Caremark* and give directors comfort that they would not simply be held liable whenever substantial losses occurred at companies for which they had director oversight roles.

B. *Stone v. Ritter* Derivative Litigation

In 2006, the Delaware Chancery Court reviewed in *Stone v. Ritter* a derivative complaint against present and former directors of AmSouth Bancorporation

(AmSouth) arising out of the failure of bank employees to file "suspicious activity reports" (SARs) as required by the Bank Secrecy Act (BSA) and various anti-money laundering (AML) regulations.[8] Two years earlier, AmSouth and its subsidiary AmSouth Bank had paid $40 million in fines and $10 million in civil penalties to resolve related government and regulatory investigations. The government investigations arose originally from an unlawful Ponzi scheme operated by a registered investment advisor and a licensed attorney who arranged for custodial trust accounts to be created for "investors" in the construction of medical clinics overseas. After convicting the registered representative on money laundering charges, authorities examined AmSouth's compliance with BSA reporting obligations.

In 2005 AmSouth entered into a deferred prosecution agreement (DPA) with the U.S. Department of Justice (DOJ). The supporting statement of facts asserted that AmSouth failed to file SARs in a timely manner but it did not ascribe any blame to the board or to any individual director. The Financial Crimes Enforcement Network, a bureau of the U.S. Department of the Treasury known as FinCen, determined that "AmSouth's [AML compliance] program lacked adequate board and management oversight," which determination AmSouth neither admitted nor denied.[9]

In upholding the lower court's dismissal of a derivative complaint, the Delaware Supreme Court cited the *Caremark* standard of care for assessing the liability of directors where directors are unaware of employee misconduct that results in the corporation being held liable:

> Generally where a claim of directorial liability for corporate loss is predicated upon ignorance of liability creating activities within the corporation, as in *Graham* or in this case, . . . only a sustained or systematic failure of the board to exercise oversight—such as an utter failure to attempt to assure a reasonable information and reporting system exists—will establish the lack of good faith that is a necessary condition to liability.[10]

In connection with a Federal Reserve Bank cease-and-desist order, KPMG Forensic Services was retained as an independent consultant to AmSouth, and it issued a report that reflected that AmSouth's board had dedicated considerable resources to the BSA/AML compliance program and put into place numerous procedures and systems to attempt to ensure compliance.

The plaintiff's complaint expressly incorporated by reference the KPMG report, repeating the assertion that the directors "never took the necessary steps to ensure that a reasonable BSA compliance and reporting system existed." The Delaware Supreme Court rejected the pleading, finding that the KPMG report established that the directors had in fact performed their fiduciary duty, and added:

> With the benefit of hindsight, the plaintiffs' complaint seeks to equate a bad outcome with bad faith. The lacuna in the plaintiff's argument is a failure to recognize that the directors' good faith exercise of oversight responsibility may not invariably prevent employees from violating criminal laws, or from causing the corporation to incur in *Graham*, *Caremark* and this very case. In the absence of red flags, good

faith in the context of oversight must be measured by the directors'
actions "to assure a reasonable information and reporting system
exists" and not by second-guessing after the occurrence of employee
conduct that results in an unintended adverse outcome. Accordingly,
we hold that the Court of Chancery properly applied *Caremark* and
dismissed the plaintiffs' derivative complaint for failure to excuse
demand by alleging particularized facts that created reason to doubt
whether the directors had acted in good faith in exercising their
oversight responsibilities.[11]

C. *In re* Citigroup Inc. Shareholder Derivative Litigation[12]

As a result of the financial crisis sweeping the globe in 2008 to 2009, a raft of
shareholder suits were filed against directors alleging breach of fiduciary duty
in overseeing the business affairs of troubled companies. In February 2009 the
Delaware Chancery Court reviewed such a complaint against Citigroup directors,
alleging (1) the failure to adequately oversee and manage the global financial service company's exposure to problems in the subprime market; and (2) the failure
to ensure that the group's financial repository and other disclosures were thorough and accurate. In essence, the Citigroup complaint represented a twist of the
traditional *Caremark* claim and argued that the defendants failed to monitor the
company's business risk.

Chancellor Chandler, in distinguishing the Caremark scenario of directors failing to oversee fraudulent or criminal conduct and the Citigroup situation of directors failing to recognize the extent of business risk, wrote:

> Directors should, indeed must under Delaware law, ensure that
> reasonable information and reporting systems exist that would
> put them on notice of fraudulent or criminal conduct within the
> Company. Such oversight programs allow directors to intervene
> and prevent frauds or other wrongdoing that could expose the
> company to risk of loss as a result of such conduct. While it may be
> tempting to say that directors have the same duties to monitor and
> oversee business risk, imposing Caremark-type duties on directors
> to monitor business risk is fundamentally different. Citigroup was
> in the business of taking on and managing investment and other
> business risks. To impose oversight liability on directors for failure to
> monitor "excessive" risk would involve courts in conducting hindsight
> evaluations of decisions at the heart of the business judgment of
> directors. Oversight duties under Delaware law are not designed to
> subject directors, even expert directors, to personal liability for failure
> to predict the future and to properly evaluate business risk.[13]

The Citigroup plaintiffs' alleged red flags consisted of general statements from
public documents that reflected worsening conditions in the financial markets

and in particular the subprime and credit markets. The Delaware Chancery Court found that the alleged red flags, which amounted to nothing more than indications of worsening economic conditions, did not support a reasonable inference that the director defendants approved or disseminated the financial disclosures knowingly or in bad faith.

Chancellor Chandler's conclusion can only give corporate directors solace and comfort in times of extraordinary financial crisis:

> Citigroup has suffered staggering losses, in part, as a result of the recent problems in the United States economy, particularly those in the subprime mortgage market. It is understandable that investors, and others, want to find someone to hold responsible for these losses, and it is often difficult to distinguish between a desire to blame someone and a desire to force those responsible to account for their wrongdoing. Our law, fortunately, provides guidance for precisely these situations in the form of doctrines governing the duties owed by officers and directors of Delaware corporations. This law has been refined over hundreds of years, which no doubt included many crises, and we must not let our desire to blame someone for our losses make us lose sight of the purpose of our law. Ultimately, the discretion granted directors and managers allows them to maximize shareholder value in the long term by taking risks without the debilitating fear that they will be held personally liable if the company experiences losses. This doctrine also means, however, that when the company suffers losses, shareholders may not be able to hold the directors personally liable.[14]

Still, where a complaint offers "well-pled allegations of pervasive, diverse and substantial financial fraud, involving managers at the highest levels,"[15] that pleading will survive a motion to dismiss as it adequately alleges a failure to exercise reasonable oversight over pervasive fraudulent and criminal conduct.[16]

D. *In re* Dow Chemical Company Derivative Litigation[17]

In July 2010 the Delaware Chancery Court had occasion to review FCPA-type allegations relating to a Kuwait joint venture of Dow Chemical Company (Dow) and a Kuwaiti petrochemical concern as Dow was about to enter into a large strategic merger in the United States. The factual background is as follows: In December 2007, the Dow board of directors approved a memorandum of understanding relating to a 50/50 joint venture (the K-Dow deal) with Kuwait's Petrochemicals Industries Company, which Dow expected to close in late 2008. In July 2008, following an intense auction, Dow entered into an $18.8 billion strategic merger agreement with Rohm & Haas Company. In November 2008 the Supreme Petroleum Council of Kuwait approved the K-Dow deal but shortly thereafter rescinded its approval, without explanation—amid Kuwaiti press reports of "external interference" and "politicizing" of the country's vital oil industry. Dow thereafter refused to close the merger with Rohm & Haas, citing concern for the economy and for the viability of the combined entity. In late January 2009 Rohm & Haas filed suit against Dow for specific performance.

In early February 2009 a shareholder derivative action was filed on behalf of Dow alleging inter alia that the joint venture fell apart because certain Dow officers bribed senior Kuwaiti officials, also citing Kuwaiti press releases and news articles. Asserting that Dow directors knew or should have known of the officers' alleged bribery and failed to do anything, plaintiffs contended that the director defendants breached their fiduciary oversight duties under *Caremark* and, more specifically, alleged that because bribery may have occurred in the past (Dow paid a fine to the SEC in 2007 to resolve charges of improper payments to pesticide regulators in India), the board should have suspected similar conduct by different members of management in a different country in an unrelated transaction. Finding this argument too attenuated to support a *Caremark* claim, the Delaware Chancery Court held that without knowledge of bribery or reason to suspect such conduct, the defendant directors could not consciously disregard their duty to supervise against bribery.[18] Thus, Dow represents a significant decision favorable to directors facing a *Caremark* breach of fiduciary duty claim in an FCPA context.

E. Proactive Multinational Director Actions

Directors of multinational companies can take proactive actions to both protect the company against corruption risks and reduce corporate fines and other sanctions and protect themselves against personal liability. Among the steps multinational directors should consider are

1. to receive and require live biennial anticorruption training of senior management, the board of directors, and all officers and employees who directly interface with and touch foreign governments;
2. to ask senior management to describe annually what efforts it has taken to convey an appropriate "tone at the top" and to make a clear record of the same;
3. to require an annual report on ethics and anticorruption training by the company and its subsidiaries, including the names of officers and employees who have not taken required training;
4. to hold an annual/quarterly meeting with the company's chief compliance officer in order to regularly assess the prior reporting period, issues that have arisen, a timetable to resolve same, and current priorities, and to consider additional resources that may be necessary;
5. to require of outside auditors anticorruption audits as a component of their regular audits, their assessment of the company's current corruption risks and the internal controls in place (financial and accounting), and their efforts to address any potential internal control weaknesses or deficiencies;
6. to require of the internal audit department its assessment of the company's corruption risks, internal controls, periodic testing of the company's code of conduct and systems designed to evaluate effectiveness in detecting and reducing violations of anticorruption laws, and its plan to address any potential weaknesses or deficiencies;

7. to ensure thorough due diligence procedures and reports with respect to the retention, oversight, and continuing due diligence of third parties, including agents, consultants, joint venture partners, and other business partners;

8. to inquire of the legal department whether contracts with third parties have all appropriate anticorruption warranties and representations, rights to conduct audits (wherever possible), and terms that enable the company to investigate parties or terminate contracts; and to require the legal department or outside counsel to report annually to the board on anticorruption cases and developments in the United States and countries of operation;

9. to require annual certifications by all directors, senior management, foreign country managers, and major business partner officers, for example, agents or distributors, stating that they have been trained in the past two years on anticorruption and are unaware of any violations of corruption laws;

10. to require senior management to conduct an annual risk assessment of the company's operations, joint ventures, business partners, current and changing business models, and growth plans, and to report on the same to the board;

11. to insist on an advance report of any potential merger or acquisition target's corruption risks, including countries of operations, business models, "tone at the top" commitment, compliance programs, agents, consultants, distributors, business partners, and joint ventures; and past corruption allegations, investigations, and outcomes;

12. to ensure that the company maintains an independent reporting mechanism, that is, a hotline or help line for employees and others to report, tracks and reports to the board or a committee on help line or hotline allegations and the review, investigation or resolution of same; and

13. to inquire of senior management and human resources how the company factors compliance commitment, performance, and contributions in the annual performance evaluations and compensation of management.

Some directors may consider the above steps to be solely within the province of management. However, if management is involved in potential or gray misconduct, has other pressing business matters, or is reluctant to elevate sensitive issues to the board, directors may have missed an opportunity to avoid very risky and costly corporate conduct and to avoid personal liability. In all cases care toward establishing a thoughtful record of such steps should be taken.

F. The Lessons of Avon Products

Avon Products highlights the perils of the lack of communication or poor communication between an internal audit department, a legal department and an audit committee, compliance committee or full board of directors. Avon's corruption saga in China is worth detailing as an instructive corporate governance lesson to all.[19]

1. Background

Avon Products China began operations in the People's Republic of China in 1989 as part of a joint venture that manufactured its products and used a direct selling model. However, in 1998 the Chinese government outlawed all direct selling in China for a number of years; Avon then marketed its products in independently owned retail operations. In 2001, the Chinese government agreed to allow direct selling within three years. Avon wanted to influence the legislation and regulations governing the reimplementation of direct selling in China. Avon also wanted to be the first company to implement direct selling if, and when, the new regulations became effective.

In the years leading up to 2003, Avon Products China had expanded its government relations department to liaise with the Ministry of Commerce (MOFCOM) and the State Administration for Industry and Commerce (AIC), the government agencies responsible for the implementation of direct selling regulation. In April 1999, an Avon Asia-Pacific subsidiary hired an executive to, as stated in his employment agreement, "bring [Avon] to the attention of relevant organizations and help open doors and develop the required 'Guanxi' to successfully conduct business." ("Guanxi" is a Chinese term that roughly translates as "goodwill.") Employees in his Corporate Affairs department provided gifts, entertainment, and travel to government officials in these agencies for the purpose of influencing the direct selling laws and to position Avon Products China as one of the companies to be selected to test direct selling when the new regulations were implemented.

In April 2004, when the form of the direct selling regulations was being negotiated within the Chinese government agencies, Avon continued to receive informal communications that Avon Products China would be the first company allowed to test the new regulations. After these communications, Avon Products China continued to provide travel, meals, and entertainment and began to meet more frequently with provincial and local MOFCOM and AIC officials. Avon Products China also retained the services of a third-party consultant (Consulting Company 1) to manage public-relations-related affairs with the government and external parties and to handle media matters in provinces and localities where the subsidiary did not maintain an office. Avon Products China did not contractually bind Consulting Company 1 to comply with the FCPA.

The Chinese government decided to issue one company a temporary license to conduct direct sales to test the planned regulations. In April 2005, MOFCOM and AIC officially approved Avon Products China as the first company to receive test approval to conduct direct selling in Beijing, Tianjin, and Guangdong Province.

2.   *Internal Audit Opening of a Compliance Case in 2005*

In April 2005, based on interviews and preliminary procedures it had conducted in China, Avon's global internal audit flagged gifts to government officials and inadequacies in related record-keeping as an area of concern.[20] Then, in a limited review conducted in May 2005 , Avon's internal audit personnel observed that Avon Products China employees had incurred meals and entertainment expenses with government officials, but had failed to record the names of the government officials or the business purpose of the expenses. As a result, Avon's Vice President of Internal Audit opened an internal compliance case and noted that a further review of discretionary payments would be made in an upcoming limited scope internal audit.

Rejection of FCPA Training in 2005 Due to Budgetary Restraints. During the spring and summer of 2005, Avon's global internal audit department considered the need to provide training on the provisions of the FCPA in the Asia-Pacific region, including China. However, ultimately, Avon determined that its budget for that year would not allow it to provide stand-alone FCPA training in the region.

Improper Record-keeping of Sensitive Entertainment for Government Officials. On June 2, 2005, a senior audit manager in Avon's internal audit group reported to Avon's Compliance Committee, which was composed of several senior Avon executives, that Avon China executives and employees were not maintaining proper records of entertainment for government officials and that Avon China Executive 2 had explained that the practice was intentional because information regarding that entertainment was "quite sensitive."

Subsidiary's Objection to 2005 Draft Audit Report and Potential Chilling Effect with Officials. In September 2005, an Avon internal audit team conducted field work for the limited scope audit, including looking at discretionary payments at the Corporate Affairs department in China. In late September, the team generated a draft audit report prominently noting that it was a common business practice for Avon Products China to offer gifts and meals to various government officials and that the majority of the government-related activities at Avon Products China were not adequately documented. The draft audit report also noted that the gifts and meals might be construed as the company's intent to expedite licenses from the government or to avoid unfavorable rulings against the company, therefore potentially violating the provisions of the FCPA. The day before the audit closing meeting, the senior management of Avon Products China told the internal audit team that recording the name of the government official and the purpose of the meeting would have a chilling effect with the officials. The internal audit team and the senior management of Avon Products China brought the draft audit report to the attention of the Vice President of Internal Audit, who headed Avon's global internal audit department. The V.P. Internal Audit in turn brought the draft audit report and its language to the attention of Avon's General Counsel.

3. Legal Department

Avon's Legal Department took the position that conclusions about potential FCPA violations fell within the purview of Legal, and not Internal Audit. The V.P. Internal Audit directed the internal audit team to have the FCPA conclusions removed from the draft, pending further study of the issues. After the V.P. Internal Audit conferred with the Vice President of Finance, Asia-Pacific, the internal audit team was directed to redraft the report, recall and destroy all hard copies, and delete any e-mail to which the draft was attached.[21]

2005 Cessation of Outside Law Firm Consultation. Avon's General Counsel discussed the issues raised in the report with Avon's Vice President, Legal & Government Affairs, and Avon's Regional Counsel, Asia-Pacific. They determined to follow-up on the information with the internal audit team and to consult outside counsel. Avon's V.P. Legal & Government Affairs contacted a major law firm to consult about potential FCPA issues. In early November 2005, Avon's General Counsel, V.P. Internal Audit, V.P. Legal & Government Affairs, and V.P. Finance, Asia-Pacific, directed the internal audit team to return to Avon Products China and to expand to the beginning of 2005 the time frame of their review of the expenses of the Corporate Affairs department. The internal audit team was told not to create any electronic documents, not to send any e-mails regarding the follow-up review, and not to use the term "FCPA" in any written document. The internal audit team completed the field work and created several handwritten spreadsheets that confirmed the concerns the team had reported in their draft audit report. Avon's V.P. Finance, Asia-Pacific then hand-carried the spreadsheets on a flight from Hong Kong to New York.

In mid-November 2005, after Avon's V.P. Legal & Government Affairs received the spreadsheets, he consulted the outside law firm and sent the spreadsheets to the firm. After two subsequent telephone conferences with the law firm, Avon's V.P. Legal & Government Affairs, in mid-December 2005, sent the law firm a short e-mail stating that the company had "moved on" from the issues and asking for an estimate of the fees incurred.

In December 2005, China's new direct selling regulations came into effect, lifting the ban on direct selling and allowing companies to apply for licenses to conduct direct selling. Under the direct selling regulations, a company was required to obtain a national direct selling license and a direct selling license from each province and municipality in which it sought to make direct sales. For a company to obtain a license, it was required to satisfy a number of conditions, including having "a good business reputation" and a record of no serious illegal operations for the previous five years.

The direct selling regulations also banned the recruitment of certain types of persons as direct sales staff, including persons under the age of 18, full-time students, foreigners, teachers, medical personnel, civil servants, active service members of the armed forces, and any person who was prohibited from taking any part-time job under applicable laws and regulations.

Failure to Implement Remedial Measures at China Subsidiary in 2005 and 2006. In late December 2005 and January 2006, Avon's General Counsel, Avon's V.P. Legal & Government Affairs, and Avon's Regional Counsel, Asia-Pacific decided to implement certain remedial measures at Avon Products China, including the creation of a log listing the government officials entertained or provided with gifts, and to require representations and warranties in Avon Products China's contracts with third parties, including Consulting Company 1, that interacted with government officials and government agencies on behalf of Avon Products China.

The ordered remedial measures did not require a description of the business purpose of any meeting with government officials. Moreover, Avon Products China was allowed to keep the log off-premises. In fact, none of the responsive measures were implemented. Moreover, there was no instruction to the employees at Avon Products China to otherwise change the practice of providing things of value to Chinese government officials or to change internal controls or to ensure the accuracy of Avon China's books and records.

In March 2006, the Chinese government did grant Avon Products China the first national direct selling business license. (Avon competitors did not receive test or permanent licenses until, or after, December 2006.) In the time between Avon Products China's receiving the test direct selling license, in April 2005, and the time when it received the permanent direct selling business license, the company provided over $100,000 in cash or things of value to government officials.[22]

Continuation of Providing Improper Things of Value to Government Media to Prevent Negative News Articles. Between March 2006 and July 2006, Avon Products China obtained all sought provincial and municipal approvals to conduct direct selling. After March 2006 , Avon Products China continued providing things of value to Chinese government officials at the national, provincial, and local levels to ensure that Avon had a clean corporate image in China. Avon Products China's General Manager and its Vice President of Corporate Affairs implemented a "zero penalty policy." Under the zero penalty policy, Avon Products China and Consulting Company I provided cash and things of value to Chinese government officials and government media to reduce or eliminate potential fines against the company and to prevent negative news articles from appearing in the media.

4. *Appointment of New Internal Audit Head and Termination of Corporate Affairs Officer for False Expense Reporting*

In December 2006, an Avon Products China executive informed an Avon Asia-Pacific executive and Avon's new head of internal audit by e-mail that Avon Products China's Associate Director of Corporate Affairs had been terminated because he had submitted false expense reports seeking reimbursement for gifts and entertainment provided to government officials.[23] Avon's General Counsel was provided with a copy of the e-mail.

5. *2007 False Reporting to Compliance Committee That Potential FCPA Violations in China Were "Unsubstantiated"*

In January 2007 an Avon executive reported to Avon's Compliance Committee that the matter regarding potential FCPA violations by Avon China executives and employees had been closed as "unsubstantiated" even though he and other Avon executives, attorneys, and employees knew of Avon China's payments and continuing practice of giving things of value to government officials.[24]

6. *Continued False Management Representation Letters to Outside Auditor from 2004 to 2008*

After consultation with the General Counsel, a new head of internal audit at Avon asked two members of the audit team that had conducted the 2005 Avon Products China internal audit to do follow-up work looking into expenses at the China Corporate Affairs group and to confirm that the remedial measures had been implemented. Based on their review, the two internal auditors advised the new head of internal audit that they had concluded that problematic payments and inadequate record-keeping continued at Avon Products China and that the measures had not been implemented. No remedial measures were implemented in response to the review. From 2004 to 2008 Avon China executives signed false management representation letters to Avon China's external auditor stating that Avon China's books and records were fair and accurate.

7. *May 2008 Terminated Subsidiary Executive Letter to Avon Parent CEO*

In May 2008, the Avon Products China Corporate Affairs executive who had been terminated wrote to Avon's Chief Executive Officer alleging improper payments to

Chinese government officials over several years in the form of meals, entertainment, travel, sponsorship of cultural events, gifts of art, and cash. The letter was forwarded to Avon's Legal Department and, in turn, to the audit committee of Avon's board of directors. The audit committee commenced an internal investigation into the allegations and, in October 2008, Avon informed the SEC and the DOJ.

8.   *Lessons from Avon*

The DOJ and SEC pleadings and correspondence for the Avon resolution portray a subsidiary allowed to operate without accountability to the parent company. At critical junctures parent company executives misled the board about delivery of improper payments, gifts, travel, and entertainment in China so that Avon could secure a direct sales foothold in a market of 1.3 billion people. As evidenced in detailed DOJ and SEC pleadings, executives, internal auditors, and lawyers bear responsibility for not only the underlying misconduct but the concealment of the same from board or its committees. Among the major control failures and judgment lapses were

- the ability of Avon and Avon China management to override and presumably silence the internal audit staff including removing details of widespread improper payments to Chinese government officials;
- a culture that permitted Avon and Avon China executives to order the destruction of sensitive draft internal audit reports;
- inadequate internal audit funding, staffing and resources for a country with massive market potential and a poor Transparency International Corruption Perception Index;
- a culture that permitted Avon lawyers to take the position that conclusions about potential FCPA violations fall within the purview of the Legal department but not the Internal Audit department—and then did nothing to address and stop the violations and remediate;
- the lack of periodic risk assessments in China, the country with the most DOJ–SEC FCPA enforcement actions to date;
- the lack of proper oversight of gifts, travel and entertainment in a country where gift giving and Guanxi have long raised potential FCPA issues;
- the lack of a thoughtful parent company compliance program;
- a Compliance Committee that heard from Internal Audit in 2005 that an Avon China executive had not maintained proper records of entertainment of government officials because the information was quite sensitive and then accepted two years later a statement that the allegation was "unsubstantiated";
- a parent company executive terminating a major law firm's engagement in 2005 because Avon had "moved on" from the (compliance) issues;
- no specific anticorruption policy and no stand-alone FCPA training;
- the failure of the Internal Audit department to elevate the continuation of improper payments in China to the Audit Committee or Compliance Committee in 2006; and
- the failure to conduct due diligence of consultants.

There was one final, painful lesson for Avon: a terminated executive departed with the ultimate revenge—dropping the bomb of widespread China corruption allegations on the desk of the CEO. Avon ignored two cardinal rules when a company has credible allegations of misconduct: (1) promptly and thoroughly investigate misconduct and (2) take all necessary steps to stop the misconduct. A cover-up only compounds a foreign corruption problem and invariably increases the DOJ and/or SEC fine.

Audit committees, compliance committees, and board members need to schedule regular meetings with the Legal and Audit departments and engage them on risk assessments, challenging foreign operations, best compliance practices, and necessary resources and benchmark the company against others in the industry or of similar-sized revenues and footprint.

III. SARBANES-OXLEY CERTIFICATIONS BY PUBLIC COMPANY OFFICERS

Under the Sarbanes-Oxley Act of 2002, chief executive officers and chief financial officers of public companies must certify the accuracy of periodic filings with the SEC.[25] A CEO or CFO must certify that he has reviewed the report, that to his knowledge the report does not contain any material misstatements or omissions, and that the financial statements and other information contained in the report fairly represent in all material respects the company's financial condition and results of operations of the issuer for the periods presented in the reports.[26]

The CEO and CFO must also certify in each quarterly or annual report that they are responsible for establishing and maintaining internal controls[27] and have designed such internal controls to ensure that material information relating to the company and its consolidated subsidiaries is made known to such officers by others within those entities;[28] that they have evaluated the effectiveness of the company's internal controls within the past 90 days;[29] that they have presented in the report their conclusions about the effectiveness of their controls;[30] and that they have disclosed to the company's auditors and the audit committee all significant deficiencies in the design or operation of internal controls that could adversely affect the company's ability to record, process, summarize, and report financial data, and have identified for the auditors any material weaknesses in internal controls and any fraud, whether material or not, that involves management or other employees who have a significant role in the issuer's internal controls.[31]

Whoever certifies one of the above statements knowing that the periodic report does not comport with all the requirements can be fined up to $1 million and imprisoned up to ten years.[32] Whoever willfully certifies such a statement knowing it does not comport with the statute's requirements can be fined up to $5 million and imprisoned up to 20 years.[33] FCPA investigations frequently trigger reporting or disclosure responsibilities and certification issues for publicly held companies and their CEOs and CFOs.

IV. REASONS TO AUTHORIZE AND CONDUCT AN INTERNAL INVESTIGATION

Boards of directors and senior management, confronted with potentially serious allegations, will often ask why an internal investigation is necessary or appropriate. There are usually compelling legal, practical, and tactical reasons to conduct an internal investigation in the wake of potentially serious corruption allegations. They include

- to fulfill the legal duties of directors and management;
- to address any misconduct, adopt remedial measures, modify the compliance program, and take appropriate disciplinary actions so as to minimize the recurrence of improper acts or the risk of future prosecution;[34]
- to marshal the facts and prepare for the defense of a potential investigation by the DOJ, SEC, or foreign authorities, or litigation with shareholders and others;
- to review, reconsider, and revise accounting procedures and internal controls to make sure that adequate systems are in place;
- to assist the board of directors and company in determining whether the company has disclosure obligations or has made accurate disclosures;
- to respond to a section 10(a) of the Exchange Act inquiry by external auditors;
- to respond to a shareholder demand in the nature of an actual or threatened derivative action;
- to persuade governmental agencies in the U.S. or elsewhere to forgo a separate or broader, more costly investigation;
- to obtain the benefit of prosecutorial discretion (e.g., declination, DPA, non-prosecution agreement, reduced fines) by demonstrating that upon discovering misconduct, the company was proactive, investigated the matter, took appropriate disciplinary action, instituted remedial measures, or voluntarily disclosed to one or more governments;
- to give a company conducting a credible investigation some opportunity to control the nature and scope of any government investigation;
- to reduce potential corporate sentencing exposure under the Organizational Guidelines (chapter 8 of the U.S. Sentencing Guidelines); and
- to make recommendations and provide legal advice to management, the audit committee, or the board of directors, consistent with the above objectives.

V. SELECTION OF OUTSIDE FCPA INVESTIGATION OR DEFENSE COUNSEL

To highlight perhaps the obvious, management personnel should not conduct an internal investigation, as they usually do not have investigative experience, they may be perceived as trying to minimize their role or involvement, and an investigation by management is not protected by any privilege.[35] For a variety of reasons, companies often turn to outside counsel to conduct internal investigations or to defend DOJ investigations involving FCPA allegations. These include the following:

- Outside counsel often have substantial FCPA investigation experience, DOJ and/or SEC backgrounds, and resources that inside counsel may not.
- Outside counsel generally enjoy at least a partial presumption of independence from management. Many companies find it prudent to retain or consult a law firm other than their regular primary outside corporate or litigation counsel to secure FCPA expertise, to demonstrate greater independence, or to avoid

potential conflicts where the role or advice of regular outside counsel may be an issue. The DOJ and SEC can be expected to closely examine the relationship between the company and outside counsel chosen to investigate FCPA allegations. The DOJ and SEC expect sufficient independence to assure a reasonable and logical scope of investigation and a full and rigorous investigation.

- Outside counsel may have more experience in designing and reviewing corporate compliance programs, policies and procedures and internal controls, including antibribery and anticorruption policies and procedures, and internal controls.
- An investigation by outside counsel will receive greater privilege protection from discovery by the DOJ, SEC, and in certain foreign jurisdictions, including attorney work product and attorney-client communication privileges, than one conducted by in-house counsel.[36]
- Outside FCPA or anticorruption counsel sometimes have more experience and established contacts with forensic accounting firms trained in bribery investigations as well as related books-and-records and internal control issues. Forensic accounting personnel should similarly be committed to opining on the quality of improved internal controls and traveling to and conducting appropriate investigations with outside counsel in any country at issue.
- Outside counsel may have offices in foreign jurisdictions that are also focusing on alleged misconduct, and such counsel may be able to advise the company on potential foreign criminal offenses, legal privileges, and data privacy laws.

For FCPA or other corruption matters, it is usually wise and cost effective to retain outside counsel with a substantial improper payment investigation background and overseas experience. A company, board of directors, or audit committee has the right to expect FCPA investigation or defense counsel to travel to and conduct appropriate investigations in risky countries.

VI. COMPLIANCE PROGRAMS

Perhaps no other federal law enforcement area places a greater premium or penalty on compliance programs than the FCPA enforcement area. If a multinational company has a quality compliance program in place, identifies a problem, takes the steps to stop it (company-wide), and implements substantial remedial measures, the efforts will generally be recognized and rewarded. Conversely, if a company has no compliance program in place, understaffs compliance, allows poor internal controls to continue, and does not address allegations in a timely and responsible manner, it can expect to be seriously punished when misconduct is discovered by U.S. prosecutors and regulators.

The hallmarks of a quality corporate compliance program are a clear statement of the company's code of conduct or ethics policy (a written confirmation of the "tone at the top"), strong managers and compliance officers, clear written compliance materials, periodic live training, thorough and ongoing third-party due diligence, and periodic audits and monitoring of specific work programs and transactions. Mere "paper" compliance programs will earn no credit for companies undergoing FCPA investigations by the SEC or the DOJ. Further, both the DOJ and SEC can be expected to look at how many employees are dedicated to the compliance function. The DOJ–SEC *Resource Guide* as well as Fraud Section person-nel have stated that paper compliance programs are readily identifiable and will not be given credit. The Fraud Section and the SEC Enforcement Division examine hundreds of compliance programs annually and can quickly separate the quality customized programs from cut-and-paste or canned programs.

A.   Effective Compliance and Ethics Programs

1.   *United States Sentencing Guidelines*

Corporations must bear in mind the relevant compliance program language in and commentary to the organization or corporate chapter of the U.S. Sentencing Guidelines (chapter 8 of the USSG).[37] Although the Guidelines were designed to determine the appropriate punishment for convicted persons and corporations, chapter 8 criteria have become the benchmark for U.S. corporations seeking to both satisfy corporate governance standards and to minimize sentencing exposure in the event of prosecution and conviction.

The organizational guidelines highlight seven minimum standards for an effec-tive corporate compliance and ethics program. The original commentary to the guidelines in essence provided that an organization must:

1.   Establish "compliance standards and procedures . . . capable of reducing . . . criminal conduct";
2.   Assign "high-level personnel" to "oversee compliance with such standards and procedures";
3.   Not delegate "substantial discretionary authority" to personnel with "a pro-pensity to engage in illegal activities";
4.   "[C]ommunicate effectively its standards and procedures to all employees and other agents";
5.   Take "reasonable steps to achieve compliance with its standards";
6.   "[C]onsistently enforce[ ]" its compliance standards; and
7.   "[R]espond appropriately to" a legal violation and take steps "to prevent fur-ther similar" violations.[38]

In addition to following the seven original minimum steps, company counsel should keep abreast of SEC enforcement actions and DOJ resolutions in the FCPA area, as they can offer valuable guidance on compliance programs and evolving compliance standards. The U.K. Ministry of Justice has issued "adequate proce-dures" guidance—similar to the USSG guidance—that enables companies carrying on business in the United Kingdom to avoid charges altogether (see chapter 11).

2.   *The DOJ Criminal Division on Ten Hallmarks of Good Compliance Programs*

In October 2014, Assistant Attorney General for the Criminal Division Leslie R. Caldwell spoke at the Annual Ethics and Compliance Conference and identified ten hallmarks of good compliance programs:[39]

1.   **High-level commitment.** A company must ensure that its directors and senior management provide strong, explicit, and visible commitment to its corporate compliance policy. Stated differently, and again, "tone from the top."

2. **Written Policies.** A company should have a clearly articulated and visible corporate compliance policy memorialized in a written compliance code. Again, employees need to know what to do—or not do—when faced with a tough judgment call involving business ethics. Companies need to make that as easy as possible for their employees.

3. **Periodic Risk-Based Review.** A company should periodically evaluate these compliance codes on the basis of a risk assessment addressing the individual circumstances of the company. Companies change over time through natural growth, mergers, and acquisitions.

4. **Proper Oversight and Independence.** A company should assign responsibility to senior executives for the implementation and oversight of the compliance program.

5. **Training and Guidance.** A company should implement mechanisms designed to ensure that its compliance code is effectively communicated to all directors, officers, employees. This means repeated communication, frequent and effective training, and an ability to provide guidance when issues arise.

6. **Internal Reporting.** A company should have an effective system for confidential, internal reporting of compliance violations. Many companies have multiple mechanisms, which is good.

7. **Investigation.** A company should establish an effective process with sufficient resources for responding to, investigating, and documenting allegations of violations. What this means on the ground will depend on the company. A sophisticated multi-national corporation obviously will be expected to have more resources devoted to compliance than a small regional company.

8. **Enforcement and Discipline.** A company should implement mechanisms designed to enforce its compliance code, including appropriately incentivizing compliance and disciplining violations.

9. **Third-Party Relationships.** A company should institute compliance requirements pertaining to the oversight of all agents and business partners.

10. **Monitoring and Testing.** A company should conduct periodic reviews and testing of its compliance code to improve its effectiveness in preventing and detecting violations. Kick the tires regularly. Compliance programs must evolve with changes in the law, business practices, technology and culture.

Corporate counsel and defense counsel should be mindful of these ten hallmarks in designing, revising, and updating compliance programs.

3. Alstom Compliance Program Elements

The DOJ often requires companies to comply with certain minimum criteria for a compliance program, and each iteration improves upon the last iteration. The Alstom S.A. FCPA DPA resolution of 2014 contained 18 elements of what that company's compliance program should include at a minimum.

High-Level Commitment

1. The Company will ensure that its directors and senior management provide strong, explicit, and visible support and commitment to its corporate policy against violations of the anti-corruption laws and its compliance code.

Policies and Procedures

2. The Company will develop and promulgate a clearly articulated and visible corporate policy against violations of the FCPA and other applicable foreign law counterparts (collectively, the "anti-corruption laws,"), which policy is and shall continue to be memorialized in a written compliance code.

3. The Company will develop and promulgate compliance policies and procedures designed to reduce the prospect of violations of the anti-corruption laws and the Company's compliance code, and the Company will take appropriate measures to encourage and support the observance of ethics and compliance policies and procedures against violation of the anti-corruption laws by personnel at all levels of the Company. These anti-corruption policies and procedures shall apply to all directors, officers, and employees and, where necessary and appropriate, outside parties acting on behalf of the Company in a foreign jurisdiction, including but not limited to, agents and intermediaries, consultants, representatives, distributors, teaming partners, contractors and suppliers, consortia, and joint venture partners (collectively, "agents and business partners"). The Company shall notify all employees that compliance with the policies and procedures is the duty of individuals at all levels of the company. Such policies and procedures shall address:
    a. gifts;
    b. hospitality, entertainment, and expenses;
    c. customer travel;
    d. political contributions;
    e. charitable donations and sponsorships;
    f. facilitation payments; and
    g. solicitation and extortion.

4. The Company will ensure that it has a system of financial and accounting procedures, including a system of internal controls, reasonably designed to ensure the maintenance of fair and accurate books, records, and accounts. This system should be designed to provide reasonable assurances that:
    a. transactions are executed in accordance with management's general or specific;
    b. transactions are recorded as necessary to permit preparation of financial statements in conformity with generally accepted accounting principles or any other criteria applicable to such statements, and to maintain accountability for assets;
    c. access to assets is permitted only in accordance with management's general or specific authorization; and
    d. the recorded accountability for assets is compared with the existing assets at reasonable intervals and appropriate action is taken with respect to any differences.

Periodic Risk-Based Review

5. The Company will develop these compliance policies and procedures on the basis of a periodic risk assessment addressing the individual circumstances of the Company, in particular the foreign bribery risks facing the Company, including, but not limited to, its geographical organization, interactions with various types and levels of government officials, industrial sectors of operation, involvement in joint venture arrangements, importance of licenses and permits in the Company's operations, degree of governmental oversight and inspection, and volume and importance of goods and personnel clearing through customs and immigration.

6. The Company shall review its anti-corruption compliance policies and procedures no less than annually and update them as appropriate to ensure their continued effectiveness, taking into account relevant developments in the field and evolving international and industry standards.

Proper Oversight and Independence

7. The Company will assign responsibility to one or more senior corporate executives of the Company for the implementation and oversight of the Company's anti-corruption compliance code, policies, and procedures. Such corporate official(s) shall have the authority to report directly to independent monitoring bodies, including internal audit, the Company's Board of Directors, or any appropriate committee of the Board of Directors, and shall have an adequate level of autonomy from management as well as sufficient resources and authority to maintain such autonomy.

Training and Guidance

8. The Company will implement mechanisms designed to ensure that its anti-corruption compliance code, policies, and procedures are effectively communicated to all directors, officers, employees, and, where necessary and appropriate, agents and business partners. These mechanisms shall include: (a) periodic training for all directors and officers, all employees in positions of leadership or trust, positions that require such training (e.g., internal audit, sales, legal, compliance, finance), or positions that otherwise pose a corruption risk to the Company, and, where necessary and appropriate, agents and business partners; and (b) corresponding certifications by all such directors, officers, employees, agents, and business partners, certifying compliance with the training requirements.

9. The Company will maintain, or where necessary establish, an effective system for providing guidance and advice to directors, officers, employees, and, where necessary and appropriate, agents and business partners, on complying with the Company's

anti-corruption compliance code, policies, and procedures, including when they need advice on an urgent basis or in any foreign jurisdiction in which the Company operates.

Internal Reporting and Investigation

10. The Company will maintain, or where necessary establish, an effective system for internal and, where possible, confidential reporting by, and protection of, directors, officers, employees, and, where appropriate, agents and business partners concerning violations of the anti-corruption laws or the Company's anti-corruption compliance code, policies, and procedures.

11. The Company will maintain, or where necessary establish, an effective and reliable 10 process with sufficient resources for responding to, investigating, and documenting allegations of violations of the anti-corruption laws or the Company's anti-corruption compliance code, policies, and procedures.

Enforcement and Discipline

12. The Company will implement mechanisms designed to effectively enforce its compliance code, policies, and procedures, including appropriately incentivizing compliance and disciplining violations.

13. The Company will institute appropriate disciplinary procedures to address, among other things, violations of the anti-corruption laws and the Company's anti-corruption compliance code, policies, and procedures by the Company's directors, officers, and employees. Such procedures should be applied consistently and fairly, regardless of the position held by, or perceived importance of, the director, officer, or employee. The Company shall maintain, or where necessary establish, procedures to ensure that where misconduct is discovered, reasonable steps are taken to remedy the harm resulting from such misconduct, and to ensure that appropriate steps are taken to prevent further similar misconduct, including assessing the internal controls, compliance code, policies, and procedures and making modifications necessary to ensure the overall anti-corruption compliance program is effective.

Third-Party Relationships

14. The Company will institute appropriate risk-based due diligence and compliance requirements pertaining to the retention and oversight of all agents and business partners, including:
    a. properly documented due diligence pertaining to the hiring and appropriate and regular oversight of agents and business partners;
    b. informing agents and business partners of the Company's commitment to abiding by anti-corruption laws, and of the

      Company's anti-corruption compliance code, policies, and procedures; and

  c. seeking a reciprocal commitment from agents and business partners.

15. Where necessary and appropriate, the Company will include standard provisions in agreements, contracts, and renewals thereof with all agents and business partners that are reasonably calculated to prevent violations of the anti-corruption laws, which may, depending upon the circumstances, include: (a) anti-corruption representations and undertakings relating to compliance with the anti-corruption laws; (b) rights to conduct audits of the books and records of the agent or business partner to ensure compliance with the foregoing; and (c) rights to terminate an agent or business partner as a result of any breach of the anti-corruption laws, the Company's compliance code, policies, or procedures, or the representations and undertakings related to such matters.

Mergers and Acquisitions

16. The Company will develop and implement policies and procedures for mergers and acquisitions requiring that the Company conduct appropriate risk-based due diligence on potential new business entities, including appropriate FCPA and anti-corruption due diligence by legal, accounting, and compliance personnel.

17. The Company will ensure that the Company's compliance code, policies, and procedures regarding the anti-corruption laws apply as quickly as is practicable to newly acquired businesses or entities merged with the Company and will promptly:

  a. train the directors, officers, employees, agents, and business partners consistent with Paragraph 8 above on the anti-corruption laws and the Company's compliance code, policies, and procedures regarding anti-corruption laws; and

  b. where warranted, conduct an FCPA-,specific audit of all newly acquired or merged businesses as quickly as practicable.

Monitoring and Testing

18. The Company will conduct periodic reviews and testing of its anti-corruption compliance code, policies, and procedures designed to evaluate and improve their effectiveness in preventing and detecting violations of anti-corruption laws and the Company's anti-corruption code, policies, and procedures, taking into account relevant developments in the field and evolving international and industry standards.

FCPA counsel should review the most current corporate compliance program template from DOJ and SEC FCPA resolutions to see if any new requirements or language have been added or apply to the particular client or company. As important, counsel should implement those requirements or terms whenever possible before a corruption allegation or problem arises and certainly promptly during a government investigation. Proactive and regular updating of compliance materials and documentation can help companies under investigation avoid charges in some cases, large fines in other cases, and monitorships in most cases.

B.   Risk Assessments

Many multinational companies that have not experienced a government antibribery or FCPA investigation all too often presume that they have no corruption or compliance program shortcomings and that their existing compliance programs would fare well if the companies were to become the subject or target of an antibribery or FCPA investigation.

Corporate counsel should annually conduct a risk assessment of their companies and subsidiaries. Regular risk assessment is fundamental to developing a quality compliance program and is a factor the DOJ and SEC evaluate when assessing a company's compliance program and compliance commitment.[40] Such assessments can help companies decide whether they meet industry or recommended compliance measures in place and how they would fare with an initial request by the DOJ and/or SEC for overall compliance program materials and antibribery/FCPA oversight documentation, such as board of director and/or audit committee records and antibribery/FCPA training documentation. In addition to focusing on any underlying allegation, for example, an alleged payment to a tax official in the Indonesian federal tax office, both the DOJ and SEC routinely make a general request for or subpoena compliance program, document retention, training, and internal audit materials. In many of the FCPA prosecutions to date, charged companies have had weak compliance programs and often little or no anticorruption training. The more quality and contemporaneous compliance and FCPA-oriented materials a company can produce early in an investigation, the greater the likelihood it will fare in avoiding a felony prosecution or serious enforcement action.

A risk assessment is inter alia designed to evaluate the compliance roles and activities of the board of directors, the chief executive officer, chief financial officer, general counsel, and the internal audit staff and the company as a whole; to review international operations and contracts, anticorruption training, and due diligence in hiring and mergers or acquisitions; and to then weigh the multinational company's country risks, regional and/or in-country management weaknesses, and prior enforcement history issues. The March 2011 U.K. Bribery Act Guidance, in addressing risk assessment as the third principle among six that can establish a defense to strict corporate liability for the failure to prevent a bribe, discusses five external and five internal factors that present common risks.[41] The five external risks are country risk, sectoral risk, transaction risk, business opportunity risk, and business partnership risk. The five common internal factors are deficiencies in employee training, a bonus culture that rewards excessive risk-taking, unclear corporate policies on issues such as hospitality and promotional expenditures, lack of clear financial controls, and no clear antibribery message from top management.[42] (See chapter 11.) A risk assessment should address these ten factors at a minimum.

C. DOJ–SEC *Resource Guide*: "One Size Does Not Fit All"

In 2012 the DOJ and SEC published a joint *Resource Guide to the U.S. Foreign Corrupt Practices Act* that devotes substantial attention to compliance programs and makes clear that compliance begins with the board of directors and senior management setting the proper tone.[43] It warns that paper programs or ones that simply employ a "check the box" format may be ineffective.[44] The DOJ and SEC recognize that the reporting structure will depend on the size and structure of a company.[45] In assessing whether a company has reasonable controls, both will examine whether a company has devoted adequate staffing and resources to its compliance program given its size, structure and business risk profile.

In addressing the frequent concern of mid-size and small companies that they cannot pay for and match the compliance programs and staffing of large corporations, the *Resource Guide* states:

> One-size-fits-all compliance programs are generally ill-conceived and ineffective because resources inevitably are spread too thin, with too much focus on low-risk markets and transactions to the detriment of high-risk areas. Devoting a disproportionate amount of time policing modest entertainment and gift-giving instead of focusing on large government bids, questionable payments to third-party consultants, or excessive discounts to resellers and distributors may indicate that a company's compliance program is ineffective. A $50 million contract with a government agency in a high-risk country warrants greater scrutiny than modest and routine gifts and entertainment. Similarly, performing identical due diligence on all third-party agents, irrespective of risk factors, is often counter-productive, diverting attention and resources away from those third parties that pose the most significant risks. DOJ and SEC will give meaningful credit to a company that implements in good faith a comprehensive, risk-based compliance program, even if that program does not prevent an infraction in a low risk area because greater attention and resources had been devoted to a higher risk area. Conversely, a company that fails to prevent an FCPA violation on an economically significant, high-risk transaction because it failed to perform a level of due diligence commensurate with the size and risk of the transaction is likely to receive reduced credit based on the quality and effectiveness of its compliance programs.[46]

Companies should design custom risk-based compliance programs that consider the particular risks presented by: the country and risk sector; the business opportunity; potential business partners; level of involvement with governments, amount of government regulation and oversight, and exposure to customs and immigration authorities in conducting business affairs.[47]

D. Tone at the Top

The mantra of many experienced general counsel, compliance officers, and corporate governance experts is that a good corporate citizen must have a proactive, ethical "tone at the top." In the United Kingdom, this quality is most often referred to by Serious Fraud Office authorities as "top level commitment."[48] Senior executives who adopt this key value regularly emphasize it in annual reports, in employee newsletters, on intranets, and at management conferences, retreats, and large employee gatherings. As important, they take firm, decisive action when employees or colleagues blur or cross ethical lines. Of course, they must hold themselves accountable to the same high ethical standards.

Many public company CEOs and CFOs claim that they embrace "tone at the top." In FCPA investigations, seasoned prosecutors, enforcement attorneys, and law enforcement agents are not hesitant to explore that commitment in interviews of senior officers, to examine employee perceptions of the actual "tone at the top," or to dissect the company's existing compliance program and personnel and budgetary commitment. Prudent multinational companies can demonstrate a strong "tone at the top" by conducting FCPA training for the boards of directors and annually reviewing how often and effectively the company and its senior executives and country managers have communicated the importance of compliance to employees and other important constituents such as third parties. They can also demonstrate "tone at the top" by having active antibribery and anticorruption oversight by a board committee such as an audit, compliance or ethics committee; establishing related management committees, for example, a compliance group that meets quarterly; employing one or more full-time compliance officers; and having an engaged internal audit staff or program that is committed to an antibribery and anticorruption component and has direct access to an audit or other board committee. It is important to memorialize and maintain all records of "tone at the top" such as board and committee minutes reflecting compliance oversight, board PowerPoint training slides, and third-party certifications.

E. Codes of Conduct

Effective codes of conduct both will provide an organizational compliance structure and will inform employees, officers, and directors of proscribed antibribery conduct in plain terms. An introductory message from the chief executive officer or chief compliance officer can convey the company's commitment to ethical values and the importance of adherence to the code of conduct by all employees, and thereby establish a correct "tone at the top" and promote values and leadership among managers.

Some codes are formal, adopting statutory language, while others are conversational. The best codes of conduct are custom-made for the company and its business and recognize the particular challenges that officers, employers, and business units face in the industries, countries, and regions where the company conducts business. They invariably address conflicts of interest, related-party interests, reporting of unusual activity, safety, accuracy of books and records, and disciplinary consequences. For multinational companies, antibribery law and export and import violations should be covered. Organizations can offer employees examples of problematic situations and appropriate guidance through short case studies or frequently asked questions.

Codes of conduct should provide a clear reporting mechanism and guidance to employees on how to seek advice. They should be made available and distributed to all employees, officers, and directors, and be translated into the languages of the countries where the company has significant operations. Most public companies require an annual certification that each employee has read and understands the code and is unaware of any violations in the past year.[49] Many require such certifications by major third parties such as distributors, large resellers, and foreign agents.

While broad and wide-ranging codes of conduct have become salutary and commonplace for U.S. companies, they can create risks for multinational companies in other jurisdictions. Global employment law expert Cynthia L. Jackson has cautioned that in order to mitigate against foreign legal liabilities, U.S. multinationals should:

- Draft non–U.S.-centric codes of conduct and related policies and procedures.
- Distinguish legally mandated from voluntary provisions in a Code of Conduct. If the company determines that voluntary policies are critical to its stakeholders, it should commit sufficient time and money to monitor, train, and ensure compliance.
- Understand and monitor for compliance with local legal requirements (e.g., wage and hour and other employment regulations, bribery, environmental, import-export, data privacy, and other local laws).
- Observe all local employment and privacy procedural prerequisites before rolling out a Code of Conduct.
- Not assume that "cause" to discipline in the United States will constitute "cause" in a local jurisdiction.
- Recognize that some countries, particularly within the European Union, restrict the types of violations that can be reported to the United States to, for instance, accounting, internal accounting controls, auditing matters, government bribery, banking, and financial matters.
- Recognize that most European Union countries permit, but discourage, anonymity. Some countries, such as Spain, prohibit anonymous hotlines.
- Consider deleting voluntary "feel good" policies, unless they are truly core to the company's culture and ingrained into corporate practice. In some jurisdictions, such as China, merely requiring compliance with local law may require "raising the bar" significantly and constant training and reinforcement.
- Review the Code of Conduct with the same precision as a proxy statement. Better to underpromise and overdeliver than the opposite.[50]

F. Anticorruption Policies

Companies that operate in foreign jurisdictions, or employ a significant number of foreign nationals, or conduct business in countries perceived to be corrupt usually conclude that a detailed stand-alone anticorruption policy is necessary both to emphasize the importance of compliance and to give employees more detailed operational guidance.

Practical anticorruption policies will consider and address the countries or regions in which a company operates, the nature of a company's foreign government interface, and the risks of the particular industry. If a company operates in countries with a Transparency International Corruption Perception Index score of less than 50 and its employees have regular interface with foreign government officials or employees with discretion to impact its business, it should likely institute a stand-alone anticorruption policy.

Many multinationals require all officers and heads of business units to certify compliance with the FCPA and the company's anticorruption policies annually. As with corporate codes of conduct, anticorruption policies should be written in plain terms and be available to all appropriate employees in languages relevant to the company's operations. Posting anticorruption policies on a company intranet is another way to convey to a workforce the importance of and commitment to rooting out corruption. Well-managed companies and legal departments will have a specific protocol for handlisng corruption allegations or whistleblower complaints that is at least generally outlined in the policies. (See whistleblower advice and discussion at VII. H of chapter 1.)

G.   Antibribery and Anticorruption Training

Multinational companies should conduct periodic live antibribery and anticorruption and ethics training for senior management, country general managers, compliance officers, and sales, legal, financial, accounting, and audit personnel. Custom anticorruption training will address, inter alia, the company's greatest risks, for example, hospitality practices in China or petty cash practices in Nigeria, and particular functions, for example financial review of contracts, payment instructions, and invoices from consultants; and cover recent FCPA prosecution and enforcement actions.

While numerous companies provide online anticorruption and ethics training packages to employees, most compliance experts consider live training essential to the thorough understanding of the statute's antibribery and accounting provisions for officers, directors, and senior employees who operate in the international business sectors. Live training permits interaction as well as the sharing of the most up-to-date FCPA and other anticorruption developments. Online training may be sufficient for employees who have minimal authority or interface with foreign government officials, but it is no substitute for live training in the case of key employees and officers who regularly deal with foreign government officials or have international contract and purchasing authority. Some companies have multitier training: general ethics awareness training for low-level employees, advanced antibribery and anticorruption training for international managers, and comprehensive antibribery workshops for those senior managers who most interface with foreign government officials. Companies should keep and maintain records of antibribery and anticorruption and ethics training attendance and copies of all related presentations.

A quality anticorruption and ethics training program will review fundamental antibribery provision elements, facilitating-payment exceptions, reasonable and bona fide expenditure and written law affirmative defenses, common myths (e.g., "it's a legal defense that everyone, including competitors, makes substantial payments to foreign officials in the country in question"), red flags, the types of corruption scenarios most likely to confront managers in particular countries or regions, and discuss relevant factual scenarios from recent FCPA cases. Solid training will also offer hypothetical scenarios—often borrowed from the examples in the DOJ–SEC

Resource Guide.[51] A training program should cover books-and-records issues and offer best record-keeping and internal control practices. It should also address local logistics, risks, and government touchpoints such as customs, taxes, visas, and freight-forwarding contractors. Anticorruption and ethics training should be mandatory for key international managers, including sales, accounting, financial, and human resource personnel, and it should be periodically refreshed. Companies that have indirect sales models and employ agents, consultants, and distributors should consider antibribery and anticorruption training for these third parties.

H. Antibribery and Anticorruption Audits

Multinational companies are stepping up antibribery and anticorruption audits of foreign operations, using attorneys and either internal audit staff or regular outside auditors. If possible, attorneys should conduct interviews to best preserve applicable legal privileges and supervise or handle audit report drafting. A company must ensure that its internal auditors have a clear audit plan and have received antibribery and anticorruption training before they begin to conduct bribery audits. Audits can focus on third-party due diligence, financial controls, consulting contracts, petty cash practices, travel and entertainment, joint ventures, charitable donations, campaign contributions, distributors, foreign government disputes, sales, commissions, agency relationships, gift practices, parastatals, and relationships with foreign government officials. Audits will customarily track or analyze the money flow and involve sample testing. A multinational may decide to prioritize its bribery audits based on prior company or audit issues; industry-wide investigations; books-and-records and internal controls issues; recent problems of other multinational companies in the industry, work countries, or regions; and the Transparency International CPI ratings. Audits of large operations in high-risk countries can last four weeks or more, but with the benefit of prior audits, experienced attorneys can often complete the required interviews in a week or so.

In planning an antibribery audit, many experienced attorneys and auditors find it helpful to conduct a thorough risk assessment based on the input of a variety of international managers who have regular visibility to corruption risks. Models can serve to identify points of potential vulnerability in a sales organization and to better focus a bribery audit. Tests of controls will commonly address the adequacy of policies and procedures; anticorruption training; agent, consultant, representative, and distributor agreements, payments and record-keeping; payments to government employees and foreign officials; foreign entity financial statements; foreign bank account reconciliations; travel and entertainment expenses; accounts payable; and petty cash disbursements. An audit will review foreign government touchpoints, for example, customs, taxes, permits, sales licenses, and zoning.

To understand the DOJ's current view of anticorruption audits, counsel should review recent FCPA resolutions and examine compliance program guidance. For example, the 2011 Johnson & Johnson resolution detailed in two paragraphs what was necessary for that company in terms of risk assessments as audits:

1. J&J will conduct risk assessments of markets where J&J has government customers and/or other anticorruption compliance

risks on a staggered, periodic basis. Such risk assessments shall
occur at reasonable intervals and include a review of trends in
interactions with government officials, including health care
providers, to identify new risk areas. On the basis of those assessments, as needed, J&J will modify compliance implementation to
minimize risks observed through the risk assessment process.

2. J&J will conduct periodic audits specific to the detection of vio-
    lations of anticorruption laws and regulations (FCPA Audits).
    Specifically, J&J will identify no less than five operating com-
    panies that are high risk for corruption because of their sector
    and location and will conduct FCPA Audits of those operating
    companies at least once every three years. High-risk operating
    companies shall be identified based on J&J's risk assessment
    process in consultation with the chief compliance officer, sec-
    tor compliance leaders, corporate internal audit, and the Law
    Department, taking into account multiple risk factors includ-
    ing, but not limited to: a high degree of interaction with gov-
    ernment officials; the existence of internal reports of potential
    corruption risk; a high corruption risk based on certain corrup-
    tion indexes; and financial audit results. The list of high-risk
    operating companies shall be reviewed annually and updated as
    necessary. FCPA Audits of other operating companies that pose
    corruption risk shall occur no less than once every five years.
    Each FCPA audit shall include
    a. On-site visits by an audit team composed of qualified audi-
        tors who have received FCPA and anticorruption training;
    b. Where appropriate, participation in the on-site visits by per-
        sonnel from the compliance and legal functions;
    c. Review of a statistically representative sample appropriately
        adjusted for the risks of the market, of contracts with and
        payments to individual health care providers;
    d. Creation of action plans resulting from issues identified
        during audits; these action plans will be shared with appro-
        priate senior management, including the chief compliance
        officer, and will contain mandatory undertakings designed
        to enhance anticorruption compliance, repair process weak-
        nesses, and deter violations; and
    e. Where appropriate, feasible, and permissible under local law,
        review of the books and records of distributors that, in the
        view of the audit team, may present corruption risk.[52]

I.   Periodic Risk Assessments, or "Audit Lites"

As the *Resource Guide* points out, a good compliance program should constantly
evolve and be refreshed:

A company's business changes over time, as do the environments in which it operates, the nature of its customers, the laws that govern its actions, and the standards of its industry. In addition, compliance programs that do not just exist on paper but are followed in practice will inevitably uncover compliance weaknesses and require enhancements. Consequently, DOJ and SEC evaluate whether companies regularly review and improve their compliance programs and now allow them to become stale.[53]

Some multinational companies annually conduct one-week corruption risk assessments or "audit lites" in a rotating, limited number of foreign countries. The nature and frequency of periodic testing and program evaluation will vary depending on the nature and size of a company.[54] There are clear advantages to having outside anticorruption legal experts conduct mini audits, as they can frequently identify percolating issues and present a set of fresh eyes that others who perform the regular audits may not. If mini or limited audits lead to improvements in the entire compliance program, they can save the company enormous costs and business disruption. The goals behind periodic, proactive internal evaluations are continuous improvement and sustainability.[55]

J.   FCPA Opinion Release Procedure 2004-02 (July 12, 2004)

In July 2004, two subsidiaries of the Swiss company ABB Ltd.—ABB Vetco Gray, Inc., a U.S. subsidiary, and ABB Vetco Gray U.K., Ltd.—pled guilty to FCPA violations relating to commissions and referral payments made to officials in Angola, Nigeria, and Kazakhstan. Prior to the announcement of the criminal charges, investment groups seeking to acquire certain companies and assets from ABB relating to ABB's oil, gas, and petrochemical business requested an opinion on the acquisition, filed a copy of their ABB Preliminary Agreement with the DOJ, and agreed to conduct a thorough investigation through separately engaged counsel. As part of the compliance, the successor companies agreed to adopt a rigorous anticorruption compliance code designed to detect and deter violations of the FCPA and foreign anticorruption laws.[56]

The newly acquired companies' antibribery compliance code, which is detailed in FCPA Opinion Release Procedure 2004-02 (July 12, 2004), consisted of the following elements:

- A clearly articulated corporate policy against violations of the FCPA and foreign antibribery laws and the establishment of compliance standards and procedures to be followed by all directors, officers, employees, and all business partners, including, but not limited to, agents, consultants, representatives, and joint venture partners and teaming partners involved in business transactions, representation, or business development or retention in a foreign jurisdiction (respectively, "agents" and "business partners") that are reasonably capable of reducing the prospect that the FCPA or any applicable foreign anticorruption law of the new company ("Newco") compliance code will be violated;

- The assignment to one or more independent senior Newco corporate officials, who shall report directly to the compliance committee of the audit committee of the board of directors, of responsibility for the implementation and oversight of compliance with policies, standards, and procedures established in accordance with Newco's compliance code;
- The effective communication to all shareholders' representatives directly involved in the oversight of Newco and to all directors, officers, employees, agents, and business partners of corporate and compliance policies, standards, and procedures regarding the FCPA and applicable foreign anticorruption laws, by requiring (1) regular training concerning the requirements of the FCPA and applicable anticorruption laws on a periodic basis to all shareholders, directors, officers, employees, agents, and business partners and (2) annual certifications by all shareholders, directors, officers, employees, including the head of each Newco business or division, agents, and business partners certifying compliance therewith;
- A reporting system, including a "helpline" for directors, officers, employees, agents, and business partners to report suspected violations of the compliance code or suspected criminal conduct;
- Appropriate disciplinary procedure to address matters involving violations or suspected violations of the FCPA, foreign anticorruption laws, or the compliance code;
- Clearly articulated corporate procedures designed to assure that all necessary and prudent precautions are taken to cause Newco to form business relationships with reputable and qualified business partners;
- Extensive preretention due diligence requirements pertaining to, as well as postretention oversight of, all agents and business partners, including the maintenance of complete due diligence records at Newco;
- Clearly articulated corporate procedures designed to ensure that Newco exercises due care to assure that substantial discretionary authority is not delegated to individuals whom Newco knows, or should know through the exercise of due diligence, to have a propensity to engage in illegal or improper activities;
- A committee consisting of senior Newco corporate officials to review and to record, in writing, actions relating to (1) the retention of any agent or subagents thereof, and (2) all contracts and payments related thereto;
- The inclusion in all agreements, contracts, and renewals thereof with all agents and business partners of provisions: (1) setting forth anticorruption representations and undertakings; (2) relating to compliance with foreign anticorruption laws and other relevant laws; (3) allowing for internal and independent audits of the books and records of the agent or business partner to ensure compliance with the foregoing; and (4) providing for termination of the agent or business partner as a result of any breach of applicable anticorruption laws and regulations or representations and undertakings related thereto;
- Financial and accounting procedures designed to ensure that Newco maintains a system of internal accounting controls and makes and keeps accurate books, records, and accounts; and

- Independent audits by outside counsel and auditors, at no longer than three-year intervals, to ensure that the compliance code, including its anticorruption provisions, are implemented in an effective manner.

Although the DOJ did not expressly endorse the above measures, it conceded that these measures constituted "significant precautions" against future violations. The compliance code and procedures are likely the new minimum standard for a company seeking to persuade the DOJ and SEC that it has a solid compliance program and procedures.

K. Siemens AG Corporate Compliance Program

In the wake of the largest corporate internal investigation ever undertaken and the uncovering of bribery conduct across the globe, Siemens AG agreed as a condition of its December 2008 plea agreement with the DOJ to appoint an independent monitor for a four-year term and to implement a compliance program with the following elements:

- A compliance code with a clearly articulated corporate policy against violations of the FCPA, including its antibribery, books-and-records, and internal controls provisions, and other applicable counterparts (collectively, the "anticorruption laws").
- A system of financial and accounting procedures, including a system of internal accounting controls, designed to ensure the maintenance of fair and accurate books, records, and accounts.
- Promulgation of compliance standards and procedures designed to reduce the prospect of violations of the anticorruption laws and Siemens AG's compliance code. These standards and procedures shall apply to all directors, officers, and employees and, where necessary and appropriate, outside parties acting on behalf of Siemens in foreign jurisdictions, including agents, consultants, representatives, distributors, teaming partners, and joint venture partners (collectively referred to as "agents and business partners").
- The assignment of responsibilities to one or more senior corporate officials of Siemens AG for the implementation and oversight of compliance with policies, standards, and procedures regarding the anticorruption laws. Such corporate official(s) shall have the authority to report matters directly to the audit or compliance committee of Siemens AG's supervisory board.
- Mechanisms designed to ensure that the policies, standards, and procedures of Siemens regarding the anticorruption laws are effectively communicated to all directors, officers, employees, and, where necessary and appropriate, agents and business partners. These mechanisms shall include (1) periodic training for all such directors, officers, employees, and, where necessary and appropriate, agents and business partners; and (2) annual certifications by all such directors, officers, employees, and, where necessary and appropriate, agents and business partners, certifying compliance with the training requirements.
- An effective system for reporting suspected criminal conduct and/or violations of the compliance policies, standards, and procedures regarding the

anticorruption laws for directors, officers, and, as necessary and appropriate, agents and business partners.

- Appropriate disciplinary procedures to address, among other things, violations of the anticorruption laws of Siemens's compliance code by directors, officers, and employees.
- Appropriate due diligence requirements pertaining to the retention and oversight of agents and business partners.
- Standard provisions in agreements, contracts, and renewals with all agents and business partners that are designed to prevent violations of the FCPA and other applicable anticorruption laws, which provisions may, depending upon the circumstances, include (1) anticorruption representations and undertakings related to compliance with the anticorruption laws; (2) rights to conduct audits of the books and records of the agent or business partner to ensure compliance with the foregoing; and (3) rights to terminate an agent or business partner as a result of any breach of anticorruption laws, and regulations or representations and undertakings related to such matters.
- Periodic testing of the compliance code and standards and procedures designed to evaluate Siemens's effectiveness in detecting and reducing violations of the anticorruption laws and its internal controls system and compliance code.[57]

These elements are not, of course, required or expected of all multinational companies, but general counsel, outside counsel, and compliance officers are wise to review and consider what elements or parts of the Siemens compliance program can help their clients or companies.

L.   Common Compliance Program Failures

Failures of compliance programs can significantly damage a corporate program's overall effectiveness and deprive the company of salutary benefits under the Organizational Sentencing Guidelines. Multinational companies can:

- Fail to adopt and distribute a clear, written code of conduct or ethics policy, and more particularly, written anticorruption policies prohibiting proscribed conduct and policies establishing a methodology for the identification, selection, approval, and retention of foreign agents, consultants, distributors, or other third-party contractors in connection with foreign government procurement or other projects; and clear gift, travel, and entertainment policies for non–U.S. government officials.
- Fail to adequately undertake and document due diligence efforts in evaluating and approving potential agents, consultants, distributors, joint venture partners, resellers, and other third parties. Decisions to decline or reject a potential agent or consultant relationship should be memorialized in some fashion, as they can establish that the company takes the FCPA, anticorruption laws, and related due diligence seriously.
- Fail to appoint company or regional compliance officers.
- Overload a compliance officer with other responsibilities.
- Fail to vet officers or key employees who are to be assigned or promoted to key positions of interface with government officials in high-risk countries;

vetting should include a thorough personnel file review, interviews by the legal department, and an overall assessment of such candidates.

- Delegate compliance to officers or employees who have no real understanding or training in FCPA or anticorruption requirements and issues. Similarly, companies mistakenly delegate compliance activities to persons who have an inherent conflict of interest, for example, having the sales, marketing, or project proponent undertake due diligence of proposed agents.
- Fail to make compliance a priority, with the result that, due to the press of other business matters, compliance efforts, training, and appropriate due diligence become a secondary priority.
- Fail to implement hotlines or other proper reporting mechanisms that minimize or offer little likelihood of retaliation.
- Take a "head in the sand" approach with agents, consultants, distributors, and business partners. For example, sales personnel often erroneously assume that if they conduct no due diligence of agents, consultants, and partners or if they disregard facts that should prompt them to make further inquiries, they will not face any personal liability.
- Take a laissez-faire attitude about foreign corruption with senior managers or sales personnel, rationalizing that other U.S. or foreign competitors regularly engage in corrupt conduct, for example, an "everybody does it" mentality.
- Fail to require senior management or newly hired senior managers to undertake periodic ethics and anticorruption training.
- Fail to conduct anticorruption training using legal or compliance FCPA experts.
- Fail to rotate in-country senior management and financial and accounting personnel out of high-risk countries.
- Fail to work closely with their outside auditors to evaluate anticorruption efforts annually and to modify audit work programs, policies, and training.
- Lack experienced internal auditors who understand, are trained in, and regularly focus on antibribery and anticorruption issues.
- Fail to implement internal administrative and financial controls that reduce risks of improper payments (e.g., check issuance, wire transfers, petty cash controls).
- Fail to adequately monitor the activities of foreign subsidiaries, distributors, or joint venture partners.
- Ignore their compliance rules and policies due to business deadlines and time constraints, permitting senior managers or sales personnel to engage in questionable practices without advance compliance clearance or legal advice.
- Fail to translate into appropriate foreign languages their compliance codes, anticorruption and ethics policies, forms, and questionnaires.
- Hire or appoint foreign nationals to run overseas operations without thoroughly training them on the specific requirements and prohibitions of the FCPA and other anticorruption laws such as the U.K. Bribery Act of 2010. Many foreign nationals erroneously assume they are not subject to FCPA or comparable criminal liability.
- Fail to employ standard-form baseline contracts for foreign agents, joint ventures, sales representatives, consultants, and other contractors, or to enforce model uniform covenant, warranty, representation, and audit clauses.

Random departures of the subsidiary from a parent company's standard-form foreign agent, consultant, or representative agreements can raise questions about a company's actual commitment and true adherence to compliance and internal controls.

- Fail to conduct due diligence of agents, consultants, distributors, and other third parties through the life of the contract.
- Fail in due diligence efforts to address local law issues that may be relevant to agency or consultant agreements, partnerships, distributorships, joint venture agreements, or employment relationships.
- Fail to monitor the public disclosures of competitors that can reveal a broadening industry investigation.
- Fail to take appropriate or sufficient disciplinary actions in the wake of FCPA or corrupt misconduct.
- Fail to apprise and involve boards of directors or audit committees in a timely manner of sensitive payment allegations in fulfillment of their oversight roles and obligations.
- Fail to design and undertake anticorruption audit plans.
- Fail to periodically refresh ethics and anticorruption compliance programs. In particular, in-house legal departments can fail to regularly review, reevaluate, and modify compliance programs along with agent, consultant, third-party, and joint venture agreements for FCPA- or anticorruption-related issues, developments, and new best practices.
- Fail to make a compliance program sustainable. Many compliance programs arise due to a significant problems and management usually responds forcefully for the near or mid-term. A quality, compliance program must be sustainable.

Finally, even though the USSG's original seventh and final step to an effective compliance program is to take steps to prevent further violations (section VI.A, *supra*), it is remarkable how often, after the completion of a thorough FCPA or other corruption investigation and the identification and punishment of wrongdoers, well-intentioned companies will not take adequate steps to prevent the recurrence of violations. This lapse is usually not willful, but a result of investigation fatigue and the press of new matters or business priorities. A company should maintain and adhere to a postinvestigation action plan with objectives, action steps, responsible persons, and commitment dates. Otherwise, the original problems are likely to recur. Above all, a compliance program must be sustainable.

VII.   WRITTEN LEGAL OPINIONS

Corporate managers and in-house counsel often request "quick advice on a simple hospitality issue" (or a small distributor or agent issue) from outside FCPA counsel. In some cases the answer will be simple and straightforward; in other more complex or risky situations, the correct answer will be less immediately clear and it will be wise for both in-house and outside counsel to carefully gather and address relevant facts and issue(s) and for outside counsel to provide a written legal opinion to the client. The latter will save the client substantial costs in later reconstructing the relevant facts, analyzing the then current law and applicable anticorruption guidance, and defending any arguably wayward conduct in any U.S. government inquiry. By securing a contemporaneous, written legal opinion after obtaining all relevant facts, the company can in many circumstances establish a credible good-faith, advice-of-counsel defense.

A quality written legal opinion will state the issue, summarize the relevant known facts, and address the purpose of the contemplated activity and advise the client of the legality of its proposed conduct and any key conditions or limitations. As with any legal opinion and advice-of-counsel defense, the client must furnish all relevant facts to counsel. For example, if a multinational company seeks permission to sponsor trips to the United States for Chinese employees of a state-owned enterprise, a legal opinion will recite the essential facts and will address the identity and titles of Chinese employees, their likely status as government officials, the purpose of the trip (e.g., to learn about U.S. products and to visit manufacturing facilities), the trip agenda and content, the estimated length and costs of the trip, the potential authority of the visiting Chinese employees to award business, and the relationship of the Chinese employees to any government officials. In approving the travel and lodging expenses, FCPA counsel will provide a written opinion that contains cautionary guidance, including that payment for airline tickets should be made directly to the airline; that no side trips, for example, to Disneyland or Las Vegas, should be taken or paid for by the company; that attendance sheets should be kept; that per diem coverage should be made to the recipient's employer rather than directly to the recipient; that private and government customers will be treated or lodged equally, that no cash distributions should be permitted; and that foreign expenses should be consistent with the parent company's domestic travel and lodging expense policies.

An FCPA opinion for a public company addressing a potential bribery situation will typically review books-and-records and internal control practices. Even if a payment or thing of value is made or given lawfully to a foreign official, the person making the payment or giving the gift or thing of value may still be criminally liable if he fails to accurately record in reasonable detail a transaction in a public company's books or records. The opinion should further examine what the legal consequences of potential FCPA improper payments are under local law. In addition to reviewing local bribery laws, an inquiry could examine potential local tax consequences. For example, payments made to hospital personnel to assist in promoting products in the People's Republic of China could implicate two types of Chinese turnover taxes: (1) value-added taxes levied on the sale and importation of goods and the provision of processing services and repair and replacement services, and (2) business taxes levied on the provision of taxable services, the transfer of intangible assets, and the sale of improvable property. While not directly related to bribery, informal payments can create potential corporate liability for the client in the foreign country in a host of other areas. Therefore, an opinion should not be narrowly confined to the FCPA's antibribery and accounting provisions; it should also consider foreign law implications and exposure. The cost of securing and memorializing a quality written legal opinion can later save a client enormous investigative and defense costs and also establish a credible good-faith defense.

VIII. INTERNAL AUDIT

Internal auditing is an independent, objective assurance and consulting activity designed to add value and improve a company's operations. Public companies typically have an internal audit department led by a chief audit executive who reports to the audit committee of the board of directors with administrative reporting to the chief executive officer or the chief financial officer. Since enactment of the Sarbanes-Oxley Act of 2002 (SOX), internal auditors have taken on an increasingly important role in public companies. In the United States, internal auditors may also assist management with SOX compliance.

A. Audit Reports

Internal auditors typically issue reports at the conclusion of audits that summarize findings, recommendations and any responses or action plans from management. Each audit finding within the body of a report may contain five elements sometimes called the 5 Cs:

1. *Condition:* What is the particular problem identified?
2. *Criteria:* What is the standard that was not met? The standard may be a company policy or other benchmark.
3. *Cause:* Why did the problem occur?
4. *Consequence:* What is the risk or negative outcome (or opportunity forgone) because of the finding?
5. *Corrective action:* What should management do about the finding? What have they agreed to do and by when?

The five Cs can present problems for multinational companies when their internal audit departments receive corruption allegations and do not pursue them in logical order and take corrective action, or have staff that are inadequately trained in identifying and addressing foreign corruption issues such as gifts, travel and entertainment, charitable contributions, and political donations.

B. *SEC v. Eli Lilly & Co.*[57]

In certain cases multinational internal audit departments have condoned superficial paperwork in connection with distant, emerging market operations. In December 2012 the SEC filed a complaint against Eli Lilly and Company alleging FCPA violations that led to a consent decree and combined penalties of $29,395,734. The complaint highlighted anticorruption shortcomings of the company's audit department in regard to operations in Brazil, China, Poland, and Russia.[58] Specifically the SEC, in charging that Lilly failed to devise and maintain an adequate system of internal accounting, alleged that

> Lilly did not adequately verify that intermediaries with which the company was doing government-related business would not provide a benefit to a government official on Lilly's behalf in order to obtain or retain business. Lilly and its subsidiaries primarily relied on assurances and information provided in the paperwork by

these intermediaries or by Lilly personnel rather than engaging in adequate verification and analyzing the surrounding circumstances of the transaction. Lilly and its subsidiaries considered and offered benefits to government officials at the same time they were asking those government officials to assist with the reimbursement or purchase of Lilly's products with inadequate safeguards to ensure that its employees were not offering items of value to a government official with the purpose to assist Lilly in retaining or obtaining business. *Moreover, despite an understanding that certain emerging markets were most vulnerable to FCPA violations, Lilly's audit department, based out of Indianapolis, had no procedures specifically designed to assess the FCPA or bribery risk of sales and purchases. Accordingly, transactions with offshore entities or with government affiliated entities did not receive specialized or closer review for possible FCPA violations. In assessing these transactions, the auditors relied upon the standard accounting controls which primarily assured the soundness of the paperwork. There was little done to assess whether, despite the existence of facially acceptable paperwork, the surrounding circumstances or terms of the transaction suggested the possibility of an FCPA violation or bribery.*[59]

Lilly illustrates that even audit departments of large global companies can fail to investigate relationships or transactions at issue, a practice that can, in turn, be particularly risky and costly in emerging market countries. Public companies should assume that in government FCPA investigations, the DOJ and SEC, especially with its accounting staff, will examine the role, depth, training, and quality of internal audit departments and, in particular, their antibribery audit components and expertise. As Avon demonstrates, II. F., *supra*, the DOJ and SEC may also carefully review what funding and resources a company committed or did not commit to compliance.

IX. ADDITIONAL RESOURCES

- Dennis Block, Nancy Barton & Stephen Radin, The Business Judgment Rule: Fiduciary Duties of Corporate Directors (Aspen 1998).
- Leslie E. Caldwell, Remarks by Assistant Attorney General for the Criminal Division at the 22nd Annual Ethics and Compliance Conference, Oct. 1, 2014, Atlanta, GA. http://www.justice.gov/opa/speech/remarks-assistant-attorney-general-criminaldivision-leslie-r-caldwell-22nd-annual-ethics.
- Richard Dean, *The Necessity of an Effective Anti-Corruption Compliance Policy*, in The Foreign Corrupt Practices Act 2008: Coping with Heightened Enforcement Risks (PLI 2008).
- Sheila Finnegan, *Briefly Speaking . . . The First 72 Hours of a Government Investigation*, 11(2) Nat'l Legal Ctr., Feb. 2007.
- James Hamilton & Ted Trautmann, Sarbanes-Oxley Act of 2002 (CCH 2002).
- William Knepper & Dan Bailey, Liability of Corporate Officers and Directors (8th ed. 2013).
- Stewart Landefeld, Andrew Moore & Jens M. Fischer (Perkins Coie LLP), The Public Company Handbook (4th ed. 2011).

- Henry Klehm III & Joshua S. Roseman, *Ten Questions Every Director Should Ask about FCPA Compliance*, JONES DAY (Sept. 2010), http://www.jonesday.com/ten_questions/.
- Jay Martin & Robert W. Tarun, FCPA Compliance and Risk Assessment, 2014 ABA National Institute on White Collar Crime (Miami, Mar. 6-7, 2014).
- Mark D. Pollack & Erin R. Schrantz, *Conducting Internal Investigations after Sarbanes-Oxley: Best Practices*, SH083 ALI-ABA 8791 (2003).
- Robert W. Tarun, *A Baker's Dozen: Practical Foreign Corrupt Practices Act Advice for Multinational Executives, General Counsel, Boards of Directors and Audit Committees*, ETHISPHERE (Quarter 1, 2011).
- Robert W. Tarun, *Tarun's Ten Commandments for Conducting Internal Investigations, in* INTERNAL INVESTIGATIONS 2009 (PLI Course Handbook No. B-1745, 2009), *reprinted in* ETHISPHERE, Q3 2009, at 12.
- Robert W. Tarun, *Ten Tips for Handling Sensitive Corporate Investigations: Practical Advice in the Sarbanes-Oxley Era*, 10 BUS. CRIMES BULL. 10 (Nov. 2003).
- Dan K. Webb, Robert W. Tarun & Steven F. Molo, *Persuading the Government Not to Indict*, ch. 16 *in* CORPORATE INTERNAL INVESTIGATIONS (1993-2014).
- FRANK BURKE, DAN GUY & KAY TATUM, AUDIT COMMITTEES: A GUIDE FOR DIRECTORS, MANAGEMENT, AND CONSULTANTS (CCH 2008).
- CRIM. DIV., U.S. DEP'T OF JUSTICE & ENFORCEMENT DIV., U.S. SEC. & EXCH. COMM., FCPA: A RESOURCE GUIDE TO THE U.S. FOREIGN CORRUPT PRACTICES ACT 57 (2012), http://www.justice.gov/criminal/fraud/fcpa/guidance/ or http://www.sec.gov/spotlight/fcpa.shtml [hereinafter RESOURCE GUIDE] (appendix 4).
- U.K. Bribery Act, 2010 Guidance, http://www.justice.gov.uk/guidance/bribery.htm (appendix 17).

NOTES

1. *See* Report of Investigation in the Matter of the Cooper Companies, Inc. as It Relates to the Conduct of Cooper's Board of Directors, Exchange Act Release No. 34-35082, 1994 SEC Lexis 3975, at *18-20 (Dec. 12, 1994).

2. *In re* Caremark Int'l Inc. Derivative Litig., 698 A.2d 959 (Del. Ch. 1996).

3. *In re* Dow Chem. Co. Derivative Litig., 2010 Del. Ch. LEXIS 2 (July 11, 2010).

4. *In re* Caremark Int'l Inc. Derivative Litig., 698 A.2d 959 (Del. Ch. 1996).

5. *Id.*

6. *Id.*

7. *Id.*

8. Stone v. Ritter, 911 A.2d 362 (Del. 2006).

9. U.S. Dep't of Treasury Financial Crimes Enforcement Network, Assessment of Civil Money Penalty, in the Matter of Amsouth Bank, No. 2004-02, at 2 (Oct. 12, 2004), http://www.fincen.gov/news_room/ea/files/amsouthassessmentcivilmoney.pdf.

10. *Stone*, 911 A.2d at 373 (citing *In re* Caremark, 698 a.2d at 971).

11. *Id.*

12. *In re* Citigroup Inc., S'holder Derivative Litig., 964 A.2d 106, 111 (Del. Ch. 2009).

13. *Id.* at 131.

14. *Id.* at 139.

15. *See* Am. Int'l Group, Inc. Consol. Derivative Litig., 2009 WL 366613 (Del. Ch. Feb. 10, 2009).

16. *Id.* at *23.

17. 2010 Del. Ch. Lexis 2 (Jan. 11, 2010).

18. *Id.* at *49.

19. The section is directly taken in substantial part from the December 2014 Complaint of SEC v. Avon Products Inc., 14 CV 9956, USDC SDNY (Dec. 17, 2014). *See* ¶¶ 14–18.

20. *Id.* Complaint ¶¶ 19–21.

21. *Id.* Complaint ¶¶ 22–23.

22. Altogether, Avon Products China provided approximately $8 million in cash and things of value to Chinese government officials during the period from 2004 through the third quarter 2008. The following are examples: During the period, Avon Products China employees made approximately 9,000 payments totaling $1.65 million for meals and entertainment involving government officials. The majority of these payments were for meals and entertainment expenses under $200 per occurrence, without indication as to who attended the meal/entertainment or the business purpose of the expense. One expense report submitted by a Corporate Affairs associate in May 2007 listed $8,100 for entertainment of government officials in a two-month period during the time that Avon Products China was negotiating a certification of apparel for sale in China. Another expense of $4,147 in April 2007 paid for a Pear River cruise for 200 State and Regional AIC officials during a conference of officials with responsibility for the oversight of Avon Products China's direct selling business license. During the cruise, Avon Products China also placed free products in each official's hotel room. In January 2008, an expense of $4,808 was incurred to "accompany government officials" in Guangdong Province during a period in which Avon management met with the governor of that Province.

23. *Id.* Complaint ¶¶ 34–37.

24. ¶ 69 of Avon DPA Statement of Facts.

25. 15 U.S.C. § 7241.

26. 15 U.S.C. § 7241(a)(1)–(3).

27. 15 U.S.C. § 7241(a)(4)(a).

28. 15 U.S.C. § 7241(a)(4)(b).

29. 15 U.S.C. § 7241(a)(4)(c).

30. 15 U.S.C. § 7241(a)(4)(d).

31. 15 U.S.C. § 7241(a)(5).

32. 18 U.S.C. § 1350(c)(1).

33. 18 U.S.C. § 1350(c)(2).

34. *See* Dan K. Webb, Robert W. Tarun & Steven F. Molo, *Persuading the Government Not to Indict*, ch. 16 in CORPORATE INTERNAL INVESTIGATIONS (1993–2014).

35. *In re* Grand Jury Subpoena, 599 F.2d 504, 510 (2d Cir. 1979).

36. *But see In re* Steinhardt Partners, L.P., 9 F.2d 230, 235–39 (2d Cir. 1993) (voluntary submission of report to SEC is disclosure to an adversary, waiving work-product protection).

37. U.S. SENTENCING GUIDELINES MANUAL ch. 8. The Guidelines' Effective Compliance and Ethics Program Commentary is appended hereto as appendix 11.

38. *See* appendix 11 for the U.S. Sentencing Guidelines' discussion of effective compliance programs.

39. Remarks of Assistant Attorney General Leslie R. Caldwell, 22nd Annual Ethics and Compliance Conference, Atlanta, GA (Oct. 1, 2014) http://www.justice.gov/opa/speech/remarks-assistant-attorney-general-criminal-division-leslie-r-caldwell-22nd-annual-ethics.

40. CRIM. DIV., U.S. DEP'T OF JUSTICE & ENFORCEMENT DIV., U.S. SEC. & EXCH. COMM., FCPA: A RESOURCE GUIDE TO THE U.S. FOREIGN CORRUPT PRACTICES ACT 57 (2012), http://www.justice.gov/criminal/fraud/fcpa/guidance/ or http://www.sec.gov/spotlight/fcpa.shtml [hereinafter RESOURCE GUIDE] (appendix 4).

41. *See* U.K. Bribery Act Guidance 25–26, http://www.justice.gov/uk/guidance/docs/bribery-act-2010-guidance.pdf (appendix 15).

42. *Id.*

43. RESOURCE GUIDE, *supra* note 39, at 57.

44. *Id.*

45. *Id.*

46. *Id.* at 60.

47. *Id.* at 59.

48. *See* Principle 2 of Adequate Procedures and Discussion in chapter 11.

49. The Ethisphere Institute, an organization dedicated to business ethics, has identified eight critical components to benchmarking codes of conduct. *See* 50 Codes of Conduct Benchmarked, http://www.ethisphere.com.

50. Cynthia L. Jackson, *Overreacting Global Codes of Conduct Can Violate the Law*, L.A. & S.F. DAILY J., June 7, 2006.

51. *See* appendix 4.

52. Complaint, SEC v. Johnson & Johnson, No. 11-CV-00686 (D.D.C. filed Apr. 8, 2011). The Agreement defined "operating company" in paragraph (2) as "a pharmaceutical, medical device, or consumer company located in a single country that may include multiple J&J franchises." with regard to FCPA audits, the agreement stated that "[f]or those operating companies that are determined not to pose corruption risk, J&J will conduct periodic FCPA audits, or will incorporate FCPA components into financial audits." *Id.*

53. RESOURCE GUIDE, *supra* note 39, at 62.

54. *Id.*

55. *Id.*

56. FCPA Opinion Procedure Release No. 2004-02 (July 12, 2004), http://www.justice.gov/criminal/fraud/fcpa/opinion/2004/0402.pdf.

57. SEC v. Eli Lilly & Co., 1:12-CV-02045 (D.D.C. Dec. 20, 2012).

58. 1:12-cv-02045 (D.D.C. filed Dec. 30, 2012).

59. *Id.* Complaint ¶¶ 45–46, SEC v. Eli Lilly & Co., 1:12-CV-02045 (D.D.C. filed Dec. 20, 2012).

60. *Id.* (emphasis added).

CHAPTER 5

Transaction Issues
and Considerations

I. OVERVIEW

Persons transacting business internationally must always consider possible issues arising under the Foreign Corrupt Practices Act (FCPA).[1] While these issues are particularly relevant in the contractual context of the sale of goods or services to foreign governments and their instrumentalities, FCPA issues can arise as well in the context of purely private-sector transactions. For example, an improper payment to a foreign government official to obtain a license to commence or continue a business activity, such as a telecommunications license, may equally present an FCPA violation. General counsel and transaction counsel must be sensitive to FCPA issues in all international transactions, regardless of the direct or indirect role of or existence of a contract with a governmental entity.[2]

A second significant issue is that some transaction counsel mistakenly consider FCPA potential exposure only in situations of "intermediaries" (e.g., agents, commission sales representatives, or consultants) who could be possible conduits or payors of an improper payment. Multinational companies must undertake appropriate review and due diligence in connection with potential mergers, acquisitions, and joint ventures (JVs) as well.

The March 2005 DOJ–SEC case against Titan Corporation demonstrated how a shrewd suitor can protect itself through careful due diligence in connection with a merger (discussed in chapter 10).[3] Similarly, Monsanto's acquisition of Delta & Pine demonstrated how an acquirer protected itself from successor criminal liability when it discovered improper payments by the target to Turkish Ministry of Agriculture officials.[4] In contrast, Pfizer acquired Wyeth in 2009 and there was significant improper payment conduct[5] that Pfizer had to investigate and eventually disclose. FCPA issues arise in transactions involving foreign investments or acquisitions, JVs, licensing arrangements, infrastructure projects, offset and countertrade agreements, and mergers. Also, a company may face FCPA liability for the actions of a JV partner or a subcontractor and its employees and agents. Increasingly, acquirers have urged, if not required, targets to voluntarily disclose problematic payments to the Department of Justice and the Securities and Exchange Commission before a transaction closes.

Companies operating internationally should implement procedures and steps to assure that FCPA and related antibribery compliance considerations are taken into account in every overseas transaction. General counsel and transactional counsel must ensure that the following elements are systematically included in reviewing and implementing all overseas transactions:

- *Selection criteria.* Agents, consultants, customs clearing brokers, sales representatives, partners, distributors, professionals (attorneys and accountants), or other third-party contractors (collectively "third-party representatives") must be identified and selected on the basis of objective and written evaluation criteria; for example, a partner is selected on the basis of identifiable commercial and technical competence and not because he or she is the relative of an important government official.

- *Reasonableness of price or compensation.* In reviewing an acquisition or other transaction, counsel should review the economics of the contemplated transaction or agency; for example, is the agency fee reasonable given the contemplated services? Unsupported general statements or folklore that "10 percent finder's fees are common in the industry or region" should be viewed with skepticism.

- *Target of joint venturer's business with foreign governments.* In considering a target or JV partner, one should consider the volume and percentage of the acquiree's business derived from foreign government contracts as well as its countries of operation (see Transparency International's Corruption Perception Index at section III.A).

- *Due diligence and reputation check.* Third-party representatives should be objectively evaluated and due diligence undertaken into their contracts, business reputation, qualifications, ownership, and integrity. Depending upon the scope of the contemplated relationship and other factors, due diligence may include (1) obtaining an independent background report that identifies red flags; (2) reviewing the preliminary background report and any identified red flags; (3) reviewing company questionnaires completed by the representative; (4) reviewing the representative's government contracts; (5) reviewing the representative's foreign government touchpoints, for example, customs, permits, and licenses; (6) checking other sources of information (Internet, public databases); (7) checking business references provided by the potential third-party representative; (8) interviewing third-party representatives face to face whenever possible; (9) obtaining information from U.S. government sources (Department of Commerce business liaison and State Department desk office inquiries); and (10) obtaining information from institutions (banks, accounting firms, lawyers) in the third-party representative's country of operations. Due diligence efforts should be memorialized.

- *Contract provisions.* Written agreements with third-party representatives must be within the norm for and consistent with standard arrangements in the industry or geographic sector. The agreements should specify duties or services to be provided by agents, consultants, or contractors. The agreements must contain standard anticorruption representations, warranties, covenants, and the like. The agreements should also provide for audit rights, annual or periodic FCPA certifications, and termination for breach of any representations, warranties, covenants, or other FCPA-related requirements.

- *Related and unrelated agreements.* Transactional counsel must consider the big picture to assure that a third-party representative is not possibly structuring the transaction and related or unrelated agreements so as to generate funds, with or without the company's explicit knowledge, and utilizing the funds to make improper payments. Particular business arrangements and structures may not make economic sense and should heighten concerns about funds being delivered to third-party representatives to facilitate improper payments. For example, SEC enforcement attorneys have evaluated unrelated offshore or third-country investment projects, offset and counter trade arrangements, inflated subcontracts, and contracts for "advisory" or other vaguely defined services.

- *Relationship of directors, officers, or employees to foreign government officials.* Transactional counsel will want to determine whether employees, officers, or directors of a target company, JV, partner, or agent are relatives or close associates of foreign government officials.
- *Subject of law enforcement investigations.* Transactional counsel will want to explore directly with the third-party representative and through other sources whether the third party or its owners, directors, officers, or employees has been the subject of any DOJ, SEC, Interpol, or in-country law enforcement investigation or the recipient of any subpoena or correspondence from any of these law enforcement agencies.
- *Red flags.* There are certain "signaling devices" or "red flags" that should put transactional counsel on notice to review a transaction carefully, since such signs are possible indications that improper payments may be intended by third-party representatives.

II. EXAMPLES OF AGENT, CONSULTANT, AND OTHER THIRD-PARTY REPRESENTATIVE RED FLAGS

Certain signs or the lack of transparency in accounting records may suggest that improper payment activity has occurred or may be occurring. Standing alone, these red flags certainly do not prove the existence of illicit or improper activity. However, they may suggest the need for further inquiry and economic justification for certain business arrangements as well as greater vigilance and increased audit activity.

Twenty-five third-party warning signs that can portend FCPA problems are listed next. Although these red flags focus on agents and consultants, they apply equally to joint venturers, contractors, distributors, and other business partners.

1. The agent or consultant resides outside the country in which the services are to be rendered.
2. The commission payments to the agent or consultant are required to be made outside the country and/or to a country linked to money laundering activity.
3. Company wire transfers do not disclose the identity of the sender or recipient.
4. The agent or consultant demands an unusually high commission without a corresponding level of services or risk (e.g., an agent who bears financial risks on delivery of goods or performs substantial pre- or postsales services may be entitled to greater compensation than a pure commission agent/broker).
5. The agent or consultant refuses to disclose its complete ownership, ownership structure, or other reasonable requested information.

6. The agent or consultant does not have the organizational resources or staff to undertake the scope of work required under the agreement (e.g., preaward technical activities or logistical assistance, and postaward activities such as assistance with customs, permits, financing, and licenses).
7. The agent or consultant has a close family connection with or other personal or professional affiliation with the foreign government or official.
8. An agent or consultant's family members or relatives are senior officials in the foreign government or ruling political party.
9. The agent or consultant has been recommended to the company by a foreign official of the potential government customer.
10. The agent or consultant has undisclosed subagents or subcontractors who assist in his or her work.
11. The agent or consultant's commissions are greater than the range that is customary or typical within the industry and region.
12. The agent or consultant refuses to sign representations, warranties, and covenants stating that he or she has not violated and will not violate the requirements of the FCPA.
13. The agent or consultant requests or requires payment in cash.
14. The agent or consultant requests that payments be made to a bank located in a foreign country unrelated to the transaction, or be made to undisclosed third parties.
15. The agency or consultancy is headquartered in a country with a reputation for corruption.
16. The agent or consultant requests a substantial up-front payment or fee.
17. The agent or consultant insists on the involvement of third parties who bring no apparent value.
18. The agent or consultant intends to or reserves the right to assign its rights or obligations to a third party.
19. The agency or consultancy is incorporated in a tax haven.
20. The agent or consultant requests that false invoices or other documents be prepared in connection with a transaction.
21. The transaction involves or takes place in a country with a general reputation for bribery and corruption.
22. There is a lack of transparency in expenses and/or accounting records.
23. A party to a contract requests that a cash or undisclosed campaign contribution be made to a foreign party candidate.
24. The agent or consultant has no established track record.
25. There is a rumor that the agent or consultant has a silent partner.

III. TRANSPARENCY INTERNATIONAL 2014 CORRUPTION PERCEPTION INDEX

In 2014, Berlin-based Transparency International (TI) released its 20th Corruption Perception Index (CPI) survey, ranking 175 countries according to their perceived level of public sector corruption, based on expert opinion and international surveys.[6] In the most recent TI survey, CPI scores ranged from 8 (the most corrupt) to 90 (the least corrupt). A CPI score below 50 indicates a serious level of perceived corruption; almost three-quarters of the 174 countries have a CPI score below 50. North Korea and Somalia (8) ranked the worst, followed by Sudan (11), Afghanistan (12), South Sudan (15) and Iraq (16). Denmark (92), New Zealand (91), and Finland (89) were perceived as the least corrupt, followed by Sweden (87), Norway (86), and Switzerland (86). The United States ranked 17th in the 2014 survey with a CPI score of 74.

These rankings, while subjective at some level, can highlight business environment risks for multinationals and provide guidance on compliance programs and annual risk assessments. U.S. prosecutors and regulators are well aware of the TI CPI surveys and expect multinational companies to adopt global compliance measures, consistent with increased perceived corruption risks. Because law enforcement authorities may evaluate a company's controls environment, especially in countries with well-known corruption issues and correspondingly low CPI scores, in deciding which companies or individuals to prosecute, resolve civilly, or decline altogether, multinationals should monitor and analyze these surveys in the context of their ongoing foreign operations, acquisition targets, special international projects, and potential merger partners.

Historically, the harshest DOJ and SEC FCPA resolutions have involved multinationals that have had poor or little compliance programs and few or no internal controls. In order to be able to prove a current quality compliance and audit program, a multinational should keep and maintain memos and minutes of compliance meetings and related improvements. Then, if a federal grand jury convenes, the company can prove through its records a robust compliance program and argue that it should not be prosecuted for the wayward conduct of a few when good controls were in place and quality training had been implemented.

The TI rankings are especially important to any contemplated international merger or acquisition and an evaluation of the corruption risks of a partner or target's foreign operations. Absent thorough due diligence, an acquirer risks both successor criminal liability and a risk that a target's corrupt obligations and payments may be ongoing. In a close case, the DOJ may consider a weak due diligence effort that ignores TI-type CPI rankings in deciding whether to prosecute a company that acquires a company that has engaged in, or, far worse, continues to engage in, improper payments. The DOJ may also evaluate how quickly the acquirer implemented a new company-wide robust compliance program that reflects the parent company's values. For these reasons, a legal department in conjunction with the chief compliance officer or internal audit staff should annually consider the TI survey rankings in light of the operations of any foreign subsidiaries, foreign-acquired companies or JV partners, and planned mergers and acquisitions activity.

A. 2014 Transparency International Scores and Country Rankings

The 2014 TI rankings from least corrupt to most corrupt and CPI scores are as follows:

Rank	Country/Territory	CPI 2014 Score
1	Denmark	92
2	New Zealand	91
3	Finland	89
4	Sweden	87
5	Norway	86
5	Switzerland	86
7	Singapore	84
8	Netherlands	83
9	Luxembourg	82
10	Canada	81
11	Australia	80
12	Germany	79
12	Iceland	79
14	United Kingdom	78
15	Belgium	76
15	Japan	76
17	Barbados	74
17	Hong Kong	74
17	Ireland	74
17	United States	74
21	Chile	73
21	Uruguay	73
23	Austria	72
24	Bahamas	71
25	United Arab Emirates	70
26	Estonia	69
26	France	69
26	Qatar	69
29	Saint Vincent and the Grenadines	67
30	Bhutan	65
31	Botswana	63
31	Cyprus	63
31	Portugal	63
31	Puerto Rico	63
35	Poland	61
35	Taiwan	61
37	Israel	60
37	Spain	60
39	Dominica	58

Rank	Country/Territory	CPI 2014 Score
39	Lithuania	58
39	Slovenia	58
42	Cape Verde	57
43	Korea (South)	55
43	Latvia	55
43	Malta	55
43	Seychelles	55
47	Costa Rica	54
47	Hungary	54
47	Mauritius	54
50	Georgia	52
50	Malaysia	52
50	Samoa	52
53	Czech Republic	51
54	Slovakia	50
55	Bahrain	49
55	Jordan	49
55	Lesotho	49
55	Namibia	49
55	Rwanda	49
55	Saudi Arabia	49
61	Croatia	48
61	Ghana	48
63	Cuba	46
64	Oman	45
64	The FYR of Macedonia	45
64	Turkey	45
67	Kuwait	44
67	South Africa	44
69	Brazil	43
69	Bulgaria	43
69	Greece	43
69	Italy	43
69	Romania	43
69	Senegal	43
69	Swaziland	43
76	Montenegro	42
76	Sao Tome and Principe	42
78	Serbia	41

Rank	Country/Territory	CPI 2014 Score
79	Tunisia	40
80	Benin	39
80	Bosnia and Herzegovina	39
80	El Salvador	39
80	Mongolia	39
80	Morocco	39
85	Burkina Faso	38
85	India	38
85	Jamaica	38
85	Peru	38
85	Philippines	38
85	Sri Lanka	38
85	Thailand	38
85	Trinidad and Tobago	38
85	Zambia	38
94	Armenia	37
94	Colombia	37
94	Egypt	37
94	Gabon	37
94	Liberia	37
94	Panama	37
100	Algeria	36
100	China	36
100	Suriname	36
103	Bolivia	35
103	Mexico	35
103	Moldova	35
103	Niger	35
107	Argentina	34
107	Djibouti	34
107	Indonesia	34
110	Albania	33
110	Ecuador	33
110	Ethiopia	33
110	Kosovo	33
110	Malawi	33
115	Cote d'Ivoire	32
115	Dominican Republic	32
115	Guatemala	32

Rank	Country/Territory	CPI 2014 Score
115	Mali	32
119	Belarus	31
119	Mozambique	31
119	Sierra Leone	31
119	Tanzania	31
119	Vietnam	31
124	Guyana	30
124	Mauritania	30
126	Azerbaijan	29
126	Gambia	29
126	Honduras	29
126	Kazakhstan	29
126	Nepal	29
126	Pakistan	29
126	Togo	29
133	Madagascar	28
133	Nicaragua	28
133	Timor-Leste	28
136	Cameroon	27
136	Iran	27
136	Kyrgyzstan	27
136	Lebanon	27
136	Nigeria	27
136	Russia	27
142	Comoros	26
142	Uganda	26
142	Ukraine	26
145	Bangladesh	25
145	Guinea	25
145	Kenya	25
145	Laos	25
145	Papua New Guinea	25
150	Central African Republic	24
150	Paraguay	24
152	Congo Republic	23
152	Tajikistan	23
154	Chad	22
154	Democratic Republic of the Congo	22
156	Cambodia	21

Rank	Country/Territory	CPI 2014 Score
156	Myanmar	21
156	Zimbabwe	21
159	Burundi	20
159	Syria	20
161	Angola	19
161	Guinea-Bissau	19
161	Haiti	19
161	Venezuela	19
161	Yemen	19
166	Eritrea	18
166	Libya	18
166	Uzbekistan	18
169	Turkmenistan	17
170	Iraq	16
171	South Sudan	15
172	Afghanistan	12
173	Sudan	11
174	Korea (North)	8
174	Somalia	8

Transparency International 1994–2014.

Naturally, there are clear differences of opinion about any characterization of these (or any) countries as "most corrupt," insofar as the bribery reputation of a particular foreign country is a red flag. However, the TI CPI and similar lists from other organizations may be useful to counsel in evaluating the potential risks of a proposed foreign transaction, handling an internal investigation, defending a government investigation, or prioritizing FCPA audits of foreign operations. At the same time, such surveys inform enforcement authorities' views of what countries' multinational companies should have known or been alert to in preventing potential corruption problems.

B. Regional Corruption Perceptions

The 2014 CPI broke down the survey data by regions:

Region	Percentage of Countries with Score below 50 out of 100
Americas	68%
Asia-Pacific	64%
Eastern Europe and Central Asia	95%

Region	Percentage of Countries with Score below 50 out of 100
EU and Western Europe	16%
Middle East and North Africa	84%
Subsaharan Africa	92%

Regional and country compliance officers should be mindful of this data.

C. The Three Most Vulnerable Sectors: Energy, Healthcare and Pharmaceuticals, and Information Technology

For different reasons, three major industries in particular seem vulnerable to FCPA issues, investigations, and prosecutions for the mid if not long term: energy, healthcare and pharmaceuticals, and information technology.

1. Energy

Given global oil production demand and opportunities in high-risk business environments, large production-sharing agreements (PSAs) with foreign governments, and the proliferation of state-owned oil companies, the energy sector and related industries have been the most fertile area for FCPA enforcement action in the past decade. See, for example, Aibel Group, Baker Hughes, BJ Services, Chevron, Flowserv, Halliburton, KBR, Paradigm, B.V., Statoil ASA, Vetco Gray, and Willbros and numerous UN Oil-for-Food program cases. Leading oil producers China (36), Russia (27), Saudi Arabia (49), Iran (27), Kuwait (44), Mexico (35), Nigeria (27), and Venezuela (19) all rank low in the TI CPI scores,[7] and oil is the dominant export in those countries. The global demand for oil and natural gas is not likely to subside in the next decade, nor is the DOJ Fraud Section's interest in the sector.

2. Healthcare and Pharmaceuticals

In November 2009, then Assistant Attorney General of the Criminal Division, Lanny A. Breuer, announced that health care would be a major FCPA investigative priority under the Obama administration.[8] The medical device and pharmaceutical industries represent a ripe area for FCPA abuses, and the aging population worldwide makes health care an expanding sector. It is especially vulnerable to public corruption, as foreign governments typically regulate, operate, and finance their countries' health systems and state-owned hospitals, which are "instrumentalities" under the FCPA. Close to $100 billion of pharmaceutical sales are generated outside the United States, and many of those sales involve foreign government customers.[9] Due to heavy regulation in many countries, nearly every aspect of the approval, manufacture, import, export, pricing, sale, and marketing can involve a "foreign official" in the broad meaning of the FCPA.[10] Notable FCPA enforcement actions in the medical device and pharmaceutical sector have involved AGA Medical, DPC-Tianjin, Eli Lilly, Johnson & Johnson, Micrus, Orthofix, Pfizer-Wyeth, and Schering-Plough.

3. Information Technology

Information technology is a dominant U.S. industry that outsources manufacturing and, of course, sells software as well as hardware worldwide. The Fraud Section has made it clear that Silicon Valley is in need of strong FCPA compliance programs and is subject to potential corruption abuses as a result of its channel sales distribution model. The sector also presents complex export issues that can become intertwined with FCPA issues. As the leader in the global innovation index, the United States will continue to offer computer hardware and software worldwide, with an increasing emphasis on untapped emerging markets. This still young sector is ripe for FCPA investigations and prosecutions.

4. Other Risky Sectors

Four other sectors have historically presented substantial bribery problems: telecom (see, for example, Alcatel, Bell South, Congressman William Jefferson, Latin Node, and Lucent Technologies); aerospace and defense (e.g., BAE Systems, Nexus Technologies); insurance (Allianz SE and Aon); and infrastructure (Siemens), and none is likely to experience a decline in corruption issues soon. Given that many financial institutions are now owned in part by foreign governments as a result of national efforts to stimulate the worldwide recession, the financial services industry also finds itself subject to increased FCPA exposure and scrutiny. Government-led stimulus efforts are likely to result in more FCPA investigations, as large infrastructure projects have historically spawned corruption. Finally, there is substantial DOJ interest in private equity firms and sovereign wealth funds, any underlying due diligence and the entertainment of or offer of personal investment opportunities to managers and employees of state-owned enterprises.

D. BRIC Countries and Beyond

1. Macro View

The four BRIC countries—Brazil, Russia, India, and China—offer large, expanding markets that are marked by problematic TI CPI scores:

Country	GDP per Head	Population	Annual GDP Growth Rate	2014 CPI Score
Brazil	$12,670	196.5 m	4.2%	43
Russia	$14,570	142.5 m	3.9%	27
India	$1,770	1.24 bn	6.5%	38
China	$6,890	1.34 bn	8.6%	36

Economist, The World in 2013, at 109–17 (2013 ed.); *see also* Transparency Int'l, Corruption Perceptions Index 2014, http://cpi.transparency.org/cpi2014/results/-.

The BRIC markets collectively represent close to 3 billion consumers and far outpace the growth of the remaining 11 of the top 15 economies save Turkey. Examination of the remaining 11 of the 15 largest economies in terms of GDP per head and GDP growth rate reveals many low CPI scores:

Country	GDP per Head	Population	Annual GDP Growth Rate	2014 CPI Score
United States	$51,525	317 m	2.1%	74
Japan	$45,680	125.7 m	1.2%	76
Germany	$41,660	81.3 m	0.6%	79
United Kingdom	$33,850	63.6 m	0.5%	78
France	$40,930	64.0 m	0.4%	69
Italy	$32,770	61.1 m	−0.3%	43
Mexico	$10,420	116.2 m	3.7%	35
Spain	$29,260	46.5 m	−1.2%	60
South Korea	$24,590	49.9 m	3.7%	55
Canada	$53,160	35 m	1.9%	81
Turkey	$11,840	75.4 m	4.1%	45

Economist, The World in 2013, at 109–17 (2013 ed.); *see also* Transparency Int'l, Corruption Perceptions Index 2014, http://cpi.transparency.org/cpi2014/results/-; 15 U.S.C. §§ 78dd-l(f)(2), -2(h)(3), -3(f)(3).

Thus, almost half of the 15 largest economies have CPI scores below 50 indicating a serious likelihood of corruption, and many multinationals are moving to significant emerging markets if they are not already in them. Of the nearly 4 billion citizens in the 15 largest economy countries, 80 percent live in countries with CPI scores under 50.

2. *Micro View*

The macro analysis of course does not address the business challenges and goals of particular multinational companies. For example, an oil field services company will likely encounter serious bribery issues in petroleum-rich Eastern Europe and West Africa. Most multinational companies are focusing on emerging markets, which usually means greater corruption risks (low CPI scores) and higher rewards—and greater compliance challenges.

Also, a successful and safe marketing model in one large country may not work for another country of similar size. While Canada and China are remarkably close in terms of large land mass and thus confound parent companies managing business in those countries in determining the optimum sales model (i.e., direct or channel), China has 14 cities with over 3.3 million people while Canada has only two cities with over 3.3 million people. China has 41 times as many people; Canada has the highest CPI score (81, ranking tenth in the world) of any country with a population of 30 million or more, while the most-populated country, China (1.34 billion), has a low CPI score of 36, ranking 100th in the world. Multinationals have to know and vet their sales agents, consultants, and distributors (see, for example, Oracle, Johnson & Johnson, Data Systems and Solutions) and evaluate the risks of their sales, business models, and countries of operations.

For these reasons, each multinational should carefully design an antibribery compliance program that on a micro level is geared to its particular products, markets, countries, and special projects (e.g., Olympic sponsorship) and that also recognizes the macro data utilized by international law enforcement authorities to identify and measure corruption risk. Well-managed companies and legal departments annually reevaluate both macro and micro risks, utilizing TI scores and rankings in connection with both their current business model and operations and long-term business plans and markets.

IV. AGENTS, CONSULTANTS, AND OTHER THIRD-PARTY INTERMEDIARIES

A. Liability

The "knowing" standard under the FCPA means that a company is equally liable whether an improper payment is made directly by the company's employees or through third parties, such as agents, consultants, distributors, resellers, or subcontractors. As a result of stronger codes of conduct and ethics policies at multinational companies, it is more likely that an agent, consultant, or other intermediary will make an improper payment than that a company officer or employee directly will. A company can be held responsible for the actions of an agent or other third party if it (1) authorizes an agent or third party to make improper payments to foreign officials or (2) makes payments to an agent or third party, knowing that all or a portion of the money will be paid directly or indirectly to foreign officials. The FCPA clarifies that proof of actual knowledge is not required. Knowledge is satisfied when a person is aware of a high probability of the existence of a particular circumstance.[11] In short, companies and their employees may not consciously disregard or deliberately ignore suspicious facts before entering into a third-party contract, or while engaged in one.

B. Business Partner and Third-Party Due Diligence

The following are practical due diligence steps companies should consider and conduct with respect to agents, consultants, distributors, and resellers (hereafter "third party"):

- Obtain the full legal name of the third party, including any trade names.
- Obtain its principal business street address (a post office box may be a red flag).
- Obtain the names and websites of any entities sharing the same business address, facilities, or employees as the third party and state the nature of the business of such entities.
- Determine the ownership of the third party or at a minimum any person or entity owning more from a 10 percent ownership interest.
- Determine whether the third party has current or former government officials serving as directors, officers, or employees, and evaluate such relationships.
- Determine whether a reseller or distributor receives a financial benefit, for example, a discount or marketing development fund, and conduct appropriate due diligence and where such benefits flow.
- Determine whether the third party has a compliance infrastructure and policies that are consistent with and complementary to the client's compliance standards and needs.
- Determine the number of years the third party has been in business using the above legal name or other names.

- Obtain the full names (first, middle, and last) of the third party's five most senior officers and the third party's three principal business contacts with the client.
- List the proposed countries in which the third party intends to represent the client and consult their most current TI CPI scores.
- Determine the country under which the third party was incorporated and the third party's legal form, for example, sole proprietorship, JV partnership, or limited liability company. If the company is incorporated in a country from where its principal place of business is, understand why and memorialize the relevant facts.
- List all shareholders or owners of 10 percent or more of the outstanding shares of the third party.
- Identify the names and websites of other businesses owned or controlled by the 10 percent-plus shareholders (of the third party) and their family members and review the same.
- Identify any shareholders or family members of the third party who are or have been foreign government officials, political party officials, or political party candidates, and describe their financial interests, management role, or control in the business.
- Determine whether the third party has had anticorruption or FCPA training and, if so, the format, for example, live or online. Obtain a copy of the training materials.
- Obtain three business references from the third party (other than the client), contact and interview them, and make a memorandum to a file incorporating the substance of the references and any interviews.
- Determine whether the third party intends to use subcontractors, agents, subagents, or other third parties and ensure that appropriate due diligence of the same is performed.
- Have someone other than the sponsor or proposer of the third party conduct the due diligence, evaluate red flags and risks, and approve the third party.
- Determine whether any officers or employees of the third party have been known or found by a court or government agency to have violated any laws prohibiting fraud, bribery, or other corruption in the past ten years.
- When furnishing a due diligence questionnaire to a third party, direct the third-party applicant to attest to the accuracy of its answer(s) to all relevant areas of inquiry.
- Be sure to fully review and read all responses for completeness.
- Obtain a local background check of the third party and conduct an Internet search of the third party, its five most senior officers, and three principal business contacts. Place a copy of all responsive downloaded information—positive and negative—into a permanent, separate due diligence file, including any About, Management, Customers, Countries of Operation, Investor Relations, and annual report links.
- Review and download a copy of the third party's website. Place a copy of all relevant downloaded information into a permanent due diligence file.
- Review the following U.S. government-published lists for the third party and its directors or five most senior officers: Denied Persons List, Unverified List,

Entity List, Specifically Designated Nationals List, Debarred List, Nonprolif-eration Sanctions, and the World Bank List of Ineligible Firms.

- Prepare and maintain a separate, permanent written file memorializing and reflecting all due diligence efforts undertaken with respect to each third-party applicant—successful or otherwise. Analyze the collected data for current and future risk and prepare a memorandum analyzing the risks.
- Schedule firm *ongoing due diligence* deadlines and revisit past information and in particular, any ownership, management, business model and/or increased government contacts.

Due diligence for major distributors will be more intensive than due diligence for second-tier distributors or resellers. However, principal factors in deciding what amount of due diligence is necessary remains what financial benefits the client intends to extend to the third party, such as a distributor or reseller, the anticipated revenues from the particular third party and the corruption risks if the countries in which the third party will represent the company and the amount of government interface.

C.   Agent, Consultant, and Other Third-Party Contracts

Many multinational companies routinely enter into arrangements with local agents, sales representatives, distributors, resellers or consultants that assist in procuring foreign, private, or government business. While each company has its own particular approach to these contractual relationships, it is prudent for the multinational to provide clear direction to the local third party concerning FCPA-proscribed behavior and to obtain the local third party's written acknowledgment of these standards.[12] Typically, this direction and affirmation is and should be confirmed in written agree-ments. Counsel drafting agency, consulting, or other third-party agreements should consider the following principles, subjects, and terms.

1.   *Description of Duties and Services*

An agreement should specify as much as is practical the duties and services that will be undertaken and provided by the agent or consultant, as the more general the duties and description, the more questionable the role of or need for the agent or consultant. Further, the agreement should customarily limit the duties and ser-vices to a particular project or contract. Some agent and consultant contracts set forth limitations on duties, for example, the agent or consultant shall not obtain or procure information where procurement of such information is unauthorized, illegal, or unethical.

2.   *Time Frames*

Most agency or consulting agreements should be for a year or two, or the duration of a particular project or contract. Evergreen agency or consulting contracts should be cancelable with 90 days' notice, and they should be reevaluated annually.

3.   *Representations and Warranties*

Agreements should include the following representations and warranties:

- A representation about the identity of all shareholders, directors, officers, and other "stakeholders" of the agent or consultant.
- A representation that no shareholder, director, officer, or employee of an agent or consultant is a foreign official or is related to a foreign official (as broadly defined in the FCPA).
- A representation that the agent or consultant has read and understands the company's code of conduct and that he or she will do nothing to violate the company's code of conduct.
- A representation that in respect of any business for which it provides or may have provided consulting services to the company, the agent or consultant has not paid, offered, or agreed to pay any political contributions or charitable donations. Alternatively, a representation that the agent or consultant will disclose in writing and has no objection to the disclosure of all political contributions or charitable donations to the U.S. and/or foreign governments.
- A representation that the agent or consultant has no undisclosed subagents, subcontractors, or third parties who have any role in the agency or consultancy.
- A representation that the agent or consultant has not been convicted of or pled guilty to an offense involving fraud, corruption, or moral turpitude, and that it is not now listed by any U.S. or foreign government agency as debarred, suspended, proposed for suspension or disbarment, or otherwise ineligible for government procurement programs.
- A representation that the agent or consultant will not make and has not made directly or indirectly any payments or given anything of value to any foreign official, foreign political party, or foreign party candidate in connection with the company's activities or in obtaining or retaining business from any governmental agency or instrumentality (e.g., a parastatal).

4. *Covenants*

An agreement should include covenants that all of the listed representations and warranties will remain true, accurate, and complete at all relevant times and that the agent or consultant will promptly notify the company in writing if any of them change (e.g., a shareholder becomes a foreign official).

5. *Annual Certifications re: FCPA Compliance and Understanding*

The agent or consultant should agree to provide annual certifications to the company relating to its understanding of and compliance with the FCPA or other anticorruption laws. The agent or consultant should also acknowledge that he or she has read and understands the FCPA.[13] This guide can be appended to an agreement so that the agent or consultant cannot later claim that he or she did not understand the U.S. law, had never read the law, or had never received any clear explanation of the law.

6. *Audit Rights*

The agent or consultant should permit the company, or an independent accountant, to audit its books and records annually to assure compliance with the FCPA.

A provision permitting direct access to an agent or consultant's books and records is sometimes difficult to negotiate. Often, a third-party audit right conducted by an internationally recognized accounting firm is a reasonable compromise. An audit right that is never exercised can be a problem. Companies should consider exercising audit rights based on risk assessments, for example, volume of business, transparency, international ranking of countries in question.

7. *Payments*

The company should make payments only upon receipt of an invoice from the agent or consultant that includes a clear description of services rendered, and only to an established bank account in the country where the business activities are taking place (payments in another offshore location should be limited to special cases that can be justified). Under no circumstances should significant payments be made in cash or to unknown third parties.

8. *Assignment*

The agent or consultant should not assign, transfer, or subcontract any of its rights or duties under the contract without the prior written approval of the company.

9. *Compliance with Applicable Laws*

The agent or consultant should certify that it is in compliance with all applicable laws relating to (1) its status as a legal entity; (2) its role as an agent for the company; (3) its scope of work for the company, including its appearance before governmental agencies and instrumentalities; and (4) its receipt of funds as set forth in the agreement.

10. *Termination*

A company should specify the grounds for agent or consultant termination. Grounds for cause shall include but not be limited to:

- Any material breach of the contract;
- Any false or misleading information provided by consultant or agent;
- Any failure to comply with the representations and warranties;
- Any failure to timely provide annual certifications;
- Any refusal to timely comply with the company's annual audit right;
- Any failure to comply with applicable U.S. and foreign laws;
- Any failure by the agent or consultant to notify the company within 30 days of a material change in a representation or warranty or any event that renders or materially alters a prior representation or warranty;
- Any failure to cooperate in an investigation of alleged FCPA or related corruption misconduct;
- Termination clauses are particularly important even though sometimes awkward to negotiate at the outset of a relationship. As Don Zarin, a highly respected FCPA expert, has aptly pointed out, without clear and appropriate contract language, a company will be in a difficult position to ascertain the facts and be able to terminate a relationship.[14] For these reasons, transaction

counsel must give considerable thought to the cause provisions and the rights to investigate and terminate in agency, consultant, JV, distributor, and other third-party agreements. It is wise to draft an agreement that enables the client to obtain relevant facts of an FCPA issue or allegation or risk and to terminate the third party for misconduct or failure to fully cooperate in an internal inquiry or government investigation.

11. Choice of Law

U.S. companies will typically insist that an agency or consultant agreement be governed by, subject to, and interpreted under the laws of a U.S. state (e.g., Delaware or the company's principal state of business).

12. Disputes

In some circumstances, the parties may agree to international arbitration to resolve disputes. A condition that the arbitrator(s) be trained in U.S. law is preferable in an FCPA agent or consultant agreement.

D. Severance Agreements

When terminating agents or third parties for reasons relating to potential misconduct, counsel should be careful to steer free of muzzling as a prosecutor or regulator could interpret clauses that prohibit third parties from speaking to agent including law enforcement as obstruction of justice.

V. DISTRIBUTORS AND RESELLERS

A. Models

A distributor is usually a wholesaler who buys goods in bulk quantities for its own account from a manufacturer at a discount and independently resells the goods at a higher price to other dealers or retailers. Distributor models and contracts vary greatly. Some companies have substantial control over and knowledge of their distributors' activities. For example, they know their distributors' customers and resale policies and have contractual and supervisory control over the activities of the distributors. Other companies have little control or relationship with their distributors once the goods are shipped. Some companies, including telecommunications and technology companies, have two-tier distribution models under which they have a very strong relationship and structure with Tier 1 distributors and a much less formal relationship with Tier 2 distributors—often resellers. For other companies the distributor occupies largely a warehousing function and the reseller assumes a closer relationship with government end users and has more touchpoints with government authorities. In these scenarios the resellers present greater corruption risks than distributors.

A reseller is a company or individual that purchases goods or services with the intention of reselling them rather than consuming or using them. Resellers often buy goods from distributors. In some industries, there are multiple tiers of distributors, resellers, subcontractors, and agents, and a manufacturer must know the transaction flow. It is helpful to diagram the parties to a sale and to understand what benefits each received as a channel partner. For example, a channel indirect sales model in the software industry might have the following transaction flow:

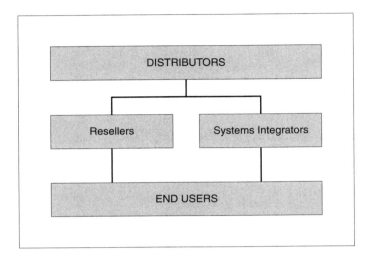

If the distributors, resellers, subcontractors, or agents receive a discount or a marketing development fund from the manufacturer, as is often common, then some level of due diligence is appropriate, including inquiry into the ownership structure, compensation, government, anticipated invoice detail, and audit rights. Too often, the principal inquiry is the financial condition and wherewithal of the third party and not its integrity.

B. Liability

Because of distributors' general independence and the customary transfer of title of goods from the manufacturer to the distributor, many companies mistakenly assume that distributors pose little or no risk to them under the FCPA. The fact is that the FCPA prohibits the use of an agent to violate the statute.[15] A distributor can itself be an "agent" of the manufacturer or supplier and thus subject the company to criminal liability if the company corruptly gives the distributor anything of value, for example, goods or a price discount, knowing that all or some of the things of value will be offered, given, or promised, directly or indirectly, to a foreign official to obtain or retain business.

If a distributor receives a substantial discount and the controlling company or supplier knows with a "high probability" that an improper payment may take place or has taken place, the latter may be held criminally liable. Under such circumstances, the independence of the distributor or the passage of title from the company to the distributor are irrelevant.[16] However, where a distributor makes payments to a foreign official to obtain or retain business, the DOJ will face a substantial burden to prove a "high probability of knowledge" on the part of the manufacturer. Similarly, a significant reseller can create FCPA liability for a manufacturer under select circumstances.

C. Risk Reduction

To minimize FCPA exposure, many multinational companies recite and incorporate relevant FCPA or antibribery language in their distributor and reseller agreements. Others require mandatory FCPA training for Tier 1 parties such as distributors or large resellers. Some also impose audit rights whereby independent auditors may annually examine the distributor's or reseller's books and records in whole or in part.

   Counsel should review the traditional red flags for third parties to determine whether they prove or corroborate the requisite high standard of knowledge that establishes a violation in the distributor context. Recent DOJ or SEC FCPA distributor cases have included AGA Medical Corporation, DPC (Tianjin) Co. Ltd., Fiat, and Johnson & Johnson (see chapter 10).

D. Subagents, Subcontractors, and Subdistributors

Many companies perform adequate due diligence for direct agents, contractors, and distributors. However, problems can arise when vetted and approved agents, contractors, and distributors engage and contract with subagents, subcontractors, and subdistributors unbeknownst to the client. These subparties can create liability for a multinational client. For this reason, agent, contractor, and distributor contracts must be explicit about agent, contractor, and distributor vetting and approval obligations with respect to any subdistributors and subagents.

E. Business Partner Compliance Risk

Recent FCPA resolutions portend increased responsibility and liability for third-party conduct. As a result, professional firms are designing compliance systems for companies that gather information from business partners; evaluate the risks with which deep risk analytics lead to modification of audit plans, processes, and controls; and instituting increased oversight. The best programs[17] gather and analyze not just FCPA data, but third-party background, ethical, and export compliance infrastructures and employ embedded risk ranking by question and between questions. Business partners will increasingly be asked to absorb compliance program costs; those who decline are likely not profitable or compliance-oriented business partners.

VI. MERGER, ACQUISITION, AND INVESTMENT DUE DILIGENCE

A. Reasons to Conduct Merger, Acquisition, and Investment Due Diligence

A company contemplating an acquisition, merger, or investment should promptly conduct sufficient due diligence to assure itself that the target's employees or agents have not engaged in making and/or do not intend to make improper payments to government officials in the performance of company business. A "check the box" approach or broad target representation that the company is unaware of any bribery-type conduct is simply no longer adequate. Justifications for thorough due diligence include good corporate citizenship; prosecution of the acquiring entity under successor liability principles; enforcement action against the acquiring entity for improper internal controls; prosecution of the acquired entity or its executives; avoidance of ongoing obligations by the successor entity to make improper payments; overpayment of assets such as contracts that were obtained through foreign bribes; accounting and disclosure issues that can arise if there are material contracts or licenses obtained through bribery that may be void or voidable; damage to reputation from the investigation; and follow-on civil litigation.[18]

B.   Transparency International UK's Ten Good Principles for Antibribery Due Diligence in Mergers, Acquisitions, and Investments

In May 2012, Transparency International UK published its final *Anti-Bribery Due Diligence for Transactions: Guidance for Anti-Bribery Due Diligence in Mergers, Acquisitions and Investments*. This very helpful 32-page transaction guidance is appended in its entirety at appendix 16. At the outset, it lays out ten sound principles for antibribery due diligence in mergers, acquisition, and investments:

Internal Policies and Procedures

1.   The purchaser (or investor) has a public antibribery policy.

Comment: This will provide a reference point for the due diligence approach and also specific protection for the due diligence process—for example, in helping to ensure that no bribe should be made to obtain information or speed up the transaction, either directly or through a third party.

2.   The purchaser ensures it has an adequate antibribery program that is compatible with the Business Principles for Countering Bribery or an equivalent international code or standard.

Due Diligence—Preacquisition

3.   Antibribery due diligence is considered on a proportionate basis for all investments.

Comment: This includes M&A transactions, acquisitions of businesses, private equity investments and other forms of investment.

4.   The level of antibribery due diligence for the transaction is commensurate with the bribery risks.

Comment: The level of bribery risk should be determined at the start of the process. This will be to ensure that the due diligence is conducted with sufficient depth and resources to be undertaken effectively.

5.   Antibribery due diligence starts sufficiently early in the due diligence process to allow adequate due diligence to be carried out and for the findings to influence the outcome of the negotiations or stimulate further review if necessary.

6.   The partners or board provide commitment and oversight to the due diligence reviews.

Comment: The findings of antibribery due diligence should be properly examined and understood at the highest level of decision-making during the transaction, for example, at the level of the board or investment committee.

7. Information gained during the antibribery due diligence is passed on efficiently and effectively to the company's management once the investment has been made.

Comment: For example, information about the adequacy of the anticorruption procedures in the target company should be used to initiate remedial action.

Due Diligence—Postacquisition

8. The purchaser starts to conduct due diligence on a proportionate basis immediately after purchase to determine if there is any current bribery and if so, takes immediate remedial action.

Comment: Gathering sufficiently detailed information is one of the challenges of antibribery due diligence. Where this has not been possible preclosure, a full due diligence should be carried out within a set time period postcompletion.

9. The purchaser ensures that the target has or adopts an adequate antibribery program equivalent to its own.
10. Bribery detected through due diligence is reported to the authorities.

Comment: This principle is based on the presumption that bribery discovered during due diligence should be reported to the authorities. Purchasers may use their discretion, bearing in mind factors such as proportionality in reporting, the deal timetable, and their own legal obligations, but it is in their interest to report to authorities as in this way they can discuss the issue and establish how the bribery could affect the deal.

C. Successor Criminal Liability

In general, when a company acquires or merges with another company, it assumes the predecessor company's liabilities.[19] The DOJ–SEC 2012 *Resource Guide to the U.S. Foreign Corrupt Practices Act* warns that successor liability applies to all kinds of civil and criminal liabilities[20] and that FCPA violations are no exception. While no court has reviewed successor criminal liability in an FCPA context, there is little question that a district court would enforce this long established principle to prevent successor companies avoiding liability.

There is no question that U.S. prosecutors and regulators intend to utilize successor liability principles against companies that acquire entities with prior bribery activity. In July 2010 the SEC charged General Electric Company with books-and-records and internal controls violations of the FCPA in connection with the UN Oil-for-Food program for Iraq. In 2004 and 2005 respectively, GE acquired the liabilities of Amersham plc of the United Kingdom and Ionics Inc. of Italy along with their assets.[21] Between 2000 and 2002, Ionics' Italba S.R.L. and Amersham's Norway-based subsidiary Nycomed Imaging AS had made approximately $1.55 million in cash kickback payments to obtain contracts under the UN Oil-for-Food program. The SEC charged GE along with Ionics and Amersham[22] with failing to keep accurate books and records through their subsidiaries[23] and failing to ensure that the subsidiaries devised and maintained adequate systems of internal accounting controls.[24] As a result of the $1.55 million in bribes paid by these two acquired entities and bribes totaling $2.04 million paid by two other GE subsidiaries in Europe, GE agreed to pay the SEC over $23.4 million in disgorgement, interest, and penalties.[25]

Perhaps the two most compelling reasons to conduct thorough due diligence of a foreign acquisition today are (1) to determine whether the acquisition is worth the business risk; and (2) to build a full legal record so that if an improper payment scheme does surface, the acquirer can demonstrate to the DOJ or SEC that it conducted comprehensive due diligence that did not disclose the problem and thus it should not be criminally or civilly charged for misconduct by its predecessor.[26]

1.   *United States v. Alliance One International Inc.–Department of Justice Agreement*

The FCPA resolution of Alliance One International illustrates the risk of successor criminal liability. In August 2010, Alliance One International AG (AOIAG), a Swiss subsidiary of Alliance One International Inc. (Alliance One), a global tobacco leaf merchant headquartered in Morrisville, N.C., pleaded guilty to a three-count FCPA criminal information.[27] The charges related to bribes paid to Thai government officials to secure contracts with the Thailand Tobacco Monopoly, a Thai government agency, for the sale of tobacco leaf. Alliance One Tobacco Osh LLC (AOI-Kyrgyzstan), a Kyrgyzstan corporation, also pleaded guilty to a separate three-count criminal information charging it with conspiracy to violate the FCPA, violations of the antibribery provisions of the FCPA, and violations of the books-and-records provisions of the FCPA relating to bribes paid to Kyrgyzstan government officials in connection with its purchase of Kyrgyz tobacco.[28]

The DOJ and Alliance One entered into a nonprosecution agreement in which the U.S. parent company agreed to cooperate with the ongoing investigation and to retain an independent compliance monitor for a minimum of three years to oversee the implementation of an antibribery and anticorruption compliance program and to report periodically to the DOJ.

The parent, Alliance One, was formed in 2005 as the result of a merger of Dimon Incorporated and Standard Commercial Corporation, both of which were wholesale leaf tobacco merchants. The guilty pleas related to conduct that was committed by employees and agents of foreign subsidiaries of both Dimon and Standard prior to the merger. As part of the plea agreements, AOIAG agreed to pay a fine of $5.25 million and AOI-Kyrgyzstan agreed to pay a fine of $4.2 million, for a total of $9.45 million in criminal fines. The parent company agreed in a separate SEC proceeding to disgorge $10 million in profits. The SEC alleged that "despite . . . extensive international operations" the company "had failed to establish a program to monitor compliance with the FCPA by its employees, agents and subsidiaries." The Alliance case remains a classic illustration of successor liability, and the DOJ may have felt compelled to impose it due to the fact that employees and agents of subsidiaries of *both* companies to the merger had engaged in prior bribery conduct.

2.   *FCPA Opinion No. 14-02*

In November 2014, the DOJ issued Opinion Procedure Release 14-02, which addressed potential successor liability in the context of an acquisition by a U.S. multinational company that in the course of its preacquisition due diligence of a target, identified a number of likely improper payments—none of which had a discernible jurisdictional nexus to the United States—by the target to government officials of the foreign country, as well as substantial weaknesses in accounting and record-keeping.[29] In light of the bribery and other concerns identified in the due diligence process, the requestor set forth a plan that included remedial preacquisition measures and detailed postacquisition integration steps.[30]

In preparing for the acquisition, the requestor undertook due diligence aimed at identifying, among other things, potential legal and compliance concerns at the target. The requestor retained an experienced forensic accounting firm to carry out the due diligence review. This review brought to light evidence of apparent improper payments, as well as substantial accounting weaknesses and poor record-keeping. On the basis of a risk profile analysis of the target, the forensic accounting firm reviewed approximately 1,300 transactions with a total value of approximately $12.9 million. The forensic accounting firm identified over $100,000 in transactions that raised compliance issues. The vast majority of these transactions involved payments to government officials related to obtaining permits and licenses. Other transactions involved gifts and cash donations to government officials, charitable contributions and sponsorships, and payments to members of the state-controlled media to minimize negative publicity. Signally, none of the payments, gifts, donations, contributions, or sponsorships occurred in the United States, and none was made by or through a U.S. person or issuer.

The due diligence showed that the target had significant record-keeping deficiencies. The vast majority of the cash payments and gifts to government officials and the charitable contributions were not supported by documentary records. Expenses were improperly and inaccurately classified in the target's books. In fact, the target's accounting records were so disorganized that the forensic accounting firm was unable to physically locate or identify many of the underlying records for the tested transactions. Finally, the target had not developed or implemented a written code of conduct or other compliance policies and procedures, nor have the target's employees shown adequate understanding or awareness of antibribery laws and regulations. In light of the target's clear compliance, accounting, and record-keeping deficiencies, the requestor took several preclosing steps to begin to remediate the target's weaknesses prior to the planned closing in 2015.

The requestor anticipated completing the full integration of the target into the requestor's compliance and reporting structure within one year of the 2015 closing. It set forth an integration schedule of the target that encompassed risk mitigation, dissemination and training with regard to compliance procedures and policies, standardization of business relationships with third parties, and formalization of the target's accounting and record-keeping.

The DOJ opined that it did not intend to take any enforcement action with respect to preacquisition bribery the seller or the target may have committed and observed:

It is a basic principle of corporate law that a company assumes certain liabilities when merging with or acquiring another company. In a situation such as this, where a purchaser acquires the stock of a seller and integrates the target into its operations, successor liability may be conferred upon the purchaser for the acquired entity's pre-existing criminal and civil liabilities, including, for example, for FCPA violations of the target.

"Successor liability does not, however, create liability where none existed before. For example, if an issuer were to acquire a foreign company that was not previously subject to the FCPA's jurisdiction, the mere acquisition of that foreign company would not retroactively create FCPA liability for the acquiring issuer." FCPA—A Resource Guide to the U.S. Foreign Corrupt Practices Act, at 28 ("FCPA Guide"). This principle, illustrated by hypothetical successor liability "Scenario 1" in the FCPA Guide, squarely addresses the situation at hand. See FCPA Guide, at 31 ("Although DOJ and SEC have jurisdiction over Company A because it is an issuer, neither could pursue Company A for conduct that occurred prior to the acquisition of Foreign Company. As Foreign Company was neither an issuer nor a domestic concern and was not subject to U.S. territorial jurisdiction, DOJ and SEC have no jurisdiction over its pre-acquisition misconduct.").

Because none of the potentially improper preacquisition payments by the seller or the target was subject to the jurisdiction of the United States, for example, none of the payments occurred in the United States, no U.S. person or issuer had participated in the payments and contracts or other assets were determined to have been acquired through bribery from which the requestor would derive financial benefit following the acquisition, the DOJ opined it would lack jurisdiction under the FCPA to prosecute the requestor (or for that matter, seller or the target) for improper payments made by seller or the target prior to the acquisition.[31]

In conclusion, the DOJ commented that acquirors in the M&A context should

1. Conduct thorough risk-based FCPA and anticorruption due diligence;
2. Implement the acquiring company's code of conduct and anticorruption policies as quickly as practicable;
3. Conduct FCPA and other relevant training for the acquired entity's directors and employees, as well as third-party agents and partners;
4. Conduct an FCPA-specific audit of the acquired entity as quickly as practicable; and
5. Disclose to the Department any corrupt payments discovered during the due diligence process.[32]

Finally, the DOJ opined that adherence to the above elements by the requestor might later, among several other factors, determine whether and how it would seek to impose postacquisition successor liability in case of a putative violation.

D. DOJ–SEC Successor Liability Guidance and Practical Tips to Reduce FCPA Risk in Mergers and Acquisitions

The *Resource Guide* states that when a company merges or acquires another company, the successor company acquires the predecessor's liabilities.[33] The DOJ and SEC state that they have

> declined to take action against companies that voluntarily disclosed and remediated conduct in the merger and acquisition context and the DOJ and SEC have only taken action against successor companies in limited circumstances, generally in cases involving egregious and sustained violations or where the company directly participated in the violations or failed to stop the misconduct from continuing after the acquisition.[34]

The *Resource Guide* then offers two practical tips to reduce FCPA risk in mergers and acquisitions:

1. *M&A Opinion Procedure Release Requests:* One option is to seek an opinion from DOJ in anticipation of a potential acquisition, such as occurred with Opinion Release 08-02. That case involved special circumstances, namely, severely limited pre-acquisition due diligence available to the potential acquiring company, and, because it was an opinion release (i.e., providing certain assurances by DOJ concerning prospective conduct), it necessarily imposed demanding standards and prescriptive timeframes in return for specific assurances from DOJ, which SEC, as a matter of discretion, also honors Thus, obtaining an opinion from DOJ can be a good way to address specific due diligence challenges, but, because of the nature of such an opinion, it will likely contain more stringent requirements than may be necessary in all circumstances.

2. *M&A Risk-Based FCPA Due Diligence and Disclosure:* As a practical matter, most acquisitions will typically not require the type of prospective assurances contained in an opinion from the DOJ. The DOJ and SEC encourage companies engaging in mergers and acquisitions to: (1) conduct thorough risk-based FCPA and anti-corruption due diligence on potential new business acquisitions; (2) ensure that the acquiring company's code of conduct and compliance policies and procedures regarding the FCPA and other anti-corruption laws apply as quickly as is practicable to newly acquired businesses or merged entities; (3) train the directors, officers, and employees of newly acquired businesses or merged entities, and when appropriate, train agents and business partners, on the FCPA and other relevant anti-corruption laws and the company's code of conduct and compliance policies and procedures; (4) conduct an FCPA-specific audit of all newly acquired or merged businesses

as quickly as practicable; and (5) disclose any corrupt payments discovered as part of its due diligence of newly acquired entities or merged entities DOJ and SEC will give meaningful credit to companies who undertake these actions, and, in appropriate circumstances, DOJ and SEC may consequently decline to bring enforcement actions.[35]

Opinion Release 08-02 is addressed in section VI.L of this chapter. Like all opinion releases, it carries the risk that the DOJ can use disclosed information to prosecute the submitter, however unlikely. Similarly, the second tip does not ensure a declination but only "meaningful credit" to companies that self-disclose corrupt payments, ensure the acquiring company's code of conduct and compliance policies apply to the target as quickly as practicable, train the target's directors, officers and employees, and conduct an FCPA audit of the newly acquired company.

E.   FCPA Risk Assessment—15 Key Risk Factors

Certain foreign acquisition risk factors should cause an acquirer to conduct extra-careful, heightened due diligence or even reconsider the acquisition. There are 15 key risk factors for targets:

1. A presence in a BRIC (Brazil, Russia, India, and China) country and other countries where corruption risk is high, for example, the country has a TI CPI rating of 50 or less;
2. An industry that has been the subject of recent antibribery or FCPA investigations, for example, the oil and energy, telecommunications, and pharmaceuticals sectors;
3. Significant use of third-party agents, for example, sales representatives, consultants, distributors, subcontractors, or logistics personnel (customs, visas, freight forwarders);
4. Significant contracts with a foreign government or instrumentality;
5. Substantial revenue from a foreign government or instrumentality;
6. Substantial projected revenue growth in the foreign country;
7. High amount or frequency of claimed discounts, rebates, or refunds in the foreign country;
8. Substantial system of regulatory approval, for example, for licenses and permits, in the foreign country;
9. History of prior government antibribery or FCPA investigations or prosecutions;
10. Poor or no antibribery or FCPA training;
11. Weak corporate compliance program and culture, in particular from legal, sales, and finance perspectives at the parent level or in foreign country operations;
12. Significant issues in past FCPA audits, for example, excessive undocumented entertainment of government officials;
13. The degree of competition in the foreign country;
14. Weak internal controls at the parent or in foreign country operations; and
15. In-country managers who appear indifferent or uncommitted to U.S. laws, the FCPA, and/or antibribery laws.

Prudent legal departments will weigh risk factors relevant to their business operations and models and combine the individual rankings and arrive at low-, middle-, and high-risk ranges. Composite or individual rankings can lead potential acquirers to pull out of a deal, step up the due diligence, or plan and enact a comprehensive "Day One" compliance program (see section VI.K.2, *infra*).

F.   Due Diligence Questionnaire

An acquirer should submit a thoughtful, custom due diligence questionnaire to a target. Sample questions: Have you ever been advised orally or in writing of a government inquiry into any of your operations, including foreign subsidiaries, regarding potential acts of bribery? Who are the shareholders of your Nigerian affiliate holding 48.2 percent of the stock? How often have you conducted anti-bribery training of your Middle Eastern sales team and who conducted the training? Do you require anticorruption training and annual certifications of any third parties with whom you do business?

As important, persons trained in compliance must analyze answers to the questionnaire for completeness and for red flags that need to still be addressed. The due diligence questionnaire and follow-up will be tailored to the operations, foreign government touchpoints, and particular risks of the target.

G.   Document Review

An acquiring company should consider reviewing the following materials during its due diligence:

- Ownership records and interests of merger partners or acquisition candidates;
- Contracts with foreign governments;
- Local registration and other local public records;
- All consulting and agency agreements;
- All foreign commission agreements and books and records;
- Websites for contractors, subcontractors, and vendors;
- Due diligence files for foreign business and/or JV partners;
- Due diligence files for agents and consultants;
- Due diligence files for distributors;
- Due diligence files for significant local vendors, for example, freight forwarders and customs agents;
- Leases and any related party interests or connections to government officials or family members;
- Protective contract language (audit rights, FCPA warranties, etc.);
- Manager compliance certification requirements;
- Contributions to foreign political candidates or parties;
- Employee and officer rotation policies;
- Internal controls;
- Overseas compliance training programs, including FCPA training;
- All audits, particularly prior FCPA audits;
- Petty cash accounts;
- Charitable donations, activities, and gifts;

- Travel and entertainment records;
- In-country purchase records;
- In-country court files where the target is a party;
- The most recent TI CPI of the countries in which the target company or its subsidiaries operate; and
- U.S. government–published lists: Denied Persons List, Unverified List, Entity List, Specifically Designated Nationals List, Debarred List, Nonproliferation Sanctions, and the World Bank List of Ineligible Firms.

The company should keep and maintain copies of all relevant and responsive document review materials. Some multinationals ask FCPA experts to spend a set number of hours in a data room to search for problematic relationships, contracts, or transactions.

H. On-Site Visits and Interviews

Due diligence should include on-site visits to the target's business operations and sales offices. It will often include interviews of the target's foreign sales, accounting, financial, compliance, and legal personnel, and third parties. Interviews will be appropriate when the target has operations in countries with low TI CPIs (e.g., below 50); when it competes in an industry known for corruption or abuses (e.g., oil, healthcare and pharmaceuticals, telecommunications); when it has weak compliance, poor books and records, and few or inconsistent internal controls; or when it utilizes third-party intermediaries. Memoranda summarizing the interviews should be prepared.

I. Overall Assessment of Target's Operations and Books and Records

Due diligence should include a review of the target's books and records. In this separate component, the acquirer should assess the general quality of the target's books and records. Reasonable inquiries include the following:

- Are they readily accessible and organized?
- Has the target demonstrated a commitment to financial transparency?
- Does the target have entertainment and travel and expense reports that describe employees' activities in reasonable and sufficient detail?
- Is any training of foreign customer personnel directly related to the performance of a contract?
- Are there questionable side trips of foreign officials visiting the United States to inspect plant operations?
- Have all third-party contracts been kept and secured in one place?
- Do foreign books and records generally comply with generally accepted accounting principles (GAAP)?
- Is backup documentation complete?
- Are consulting or agency contracts signed and annual certifications current?
- Do they contain clear antibribery language?
- Are cash vouchers reasonable and appropriate under the circumstances?
- Are the record-keeping practices of U.S. and foreign operations consistent?
- Have relevant books-and-records policies been translated into the appropriate foreign languages?

If the acquirer proceeds with the transaction, a "Day One" compliance program should address any areas where the target's books and records fall short.

J.   Example of Acquirer-Honed Due Diligence Request

Prominent international trade lawyer Harry Clark has recommended that after an acquirer obtains basic information about a target's international markets and typical sales values, it proceed with narrow requests utilizing value thresholds and sampling. He offers as an example of a common and useful due diligence request:

> . . . the target company produce sales, payment and shipping documentation for transactions that satisfy parameters such as the following: The transaction involved a sales agent or other intermediary; the end user was located in one of a group of identified corruption-sensitive countries; the end user was a government or was government-controlled; the sales value was at least $100,000; and the transaction occurred within the past five years. The acquirer would evaluate whether, for example, commission payments or discounts to buyer-resellers were unusually or inexplicably high.[36]

After written questions and interviews, a follow-up inquiry—potentially including in-depth forensic auditing—is merited if produced information and documents raise compliance issues. If indications of a violation emerge, it might be advisable for the acquirer to insist on disclosure to, and resolution with, enforcement authorities before the transaction can go forward.[37]

If a violation is not detected during this type of due diligence but later surfaces, the acquirer will be in an optimal position to argue that it conducted thorough due diligence and that it should not be penalized given its good-faith effort.

K.   Proceeding to Acquire a Target with Confirmed FCPA Issues

Upon discovering FCPA problems, an acquirer must weigh the legal and business risks. Several acquirers have strongly encouraged targets to voluntarily disclose and resolve FCPA matters before closing, such as GE, Syncor International, ABB Vetco Gray (2004), and Paradigm. Others have stumbled at the altar, for example, Lockheed-Titan, with the result that target shareholders lost substantial value. Still others have conducted inadequate merger and acquisition due diligence and paid substantial sums later, for example, Delta & Pine Land Co., Baker Hughes, and Latin Node. FCPA expert Lucinda Low cautions that in certain scenarios an acquisition may be a violation itself: for example, where it is known that a portion of the purchase price will be used to make an improper payment, such as to secure government approvals; or where a company provides benefits to shareholders who are foreign government officials in return for discretionary action.[38]

1.   *Four Critical Acquirer Steps*

If a company elects to pursue an acquisition in the face of some red flags, well-respected FCPA expert Margaret Ayres recommends that the acquirer take the following four steps:

1. Obtain appropriate representations, warranties, and indemnifications in the purchase agreement coupled with the possible disclosure to the DOJ and SEC;

2. Develop and implement a comprehensive plan to terminate the FCPA-related misconduct;

3. Develop and implement an effective compliance program for the target, which will commence immediately upon closing; and

4. In the case of an "issuer," correct any inaccurate books and records (bribes and facilitating payments) of the target before the close of its fiscal year.[39]

Ayres further cautions the acquirer to preserve any evidence or books and records relating to illegal bribes and facilitating payments.[40] If a company makes facilitating or expediting payments consistent with the "routine governmental action" exemption, it must ensure that these payments are accurately recorded in reasonable detail.

2. "Day One" Compliance

FCPA due diligence expert Gary DiBianco has written of "Day One" compliance, recommending a postclosing compliance framework that includes (1) written policies that address governing anticorruption laws; (2) revised reporting procedures; (3) compliance resources for sales personnel and other relevant employees; (4) training; and (5) an audit function to review compliance.[41] A postclosing compliance program should have a short, firm deadline, and remedial steps should be addressed as early as the signing of a letter of intent.[42]

L. FCPA Opinion Procedure Release 2008-02 (June 13, 2008): Safe Harbor for Acquirers

In June 2008, the DOJ responded to a three-part request from Halliburton and its controlled subsidiaries. Halliburton, a U.S. issuer, was considering making a bid for a United Kingdom target that operates internationally in the upstream oil and gas industry. A competitor was also bidding to acquire the target.

Halliburton asked the DOJ whether (1) the acquisition would violate the FCPA; (2) Halliburton would "inherit" FCPA liability for any unlawful preacquisition conduct by the target; and (3) Halliburton would be held criminally liable for any postacquisition conduct by the target prior to Halliburton's completion of its FCPA and anticorruption due diligence, when such conduct was identified and disclosed to the DOJ within 180 days of closing. Halliburton effectively argued that a competing foreign bidder could underbid Halliburton's negotiation by not imposing any FCPA contingency term or by ignoring any antibribery due diligence. Halliburton also detailed the legal reasons why it did not have sufficient time to conduct due diligence before closing, and proposed a postclosing action plan of investigations and disclosures in order to avoid any potential FCPA violations.[43]

Specifically, within ten days of closing, Halliburton agreed to provide a comprehensive, risk-based FCPA and anticorruption work plan that would address

- relationships with distributors, sales agents, consultants, and other third parties who could be used to facilitate improper payments;

- commercial dealings with state-owned customers;
- JV, teaming, or consortium arrangements;
- customs and immigration issues;
- tax issues; and
- government licenses and permits.

As the target does business in Africa, Asia, the Middle East, South America, and the former Soviet Union, the risk profile of this acquisition was substantial.

The DOJ indicated in Opinion Release 08-02 that it did not presently intend to take any enforcement action against Halliburton based on the three points Halliburton described in its request. The DOJ was careful to note that its opinion took the particular circumstances into account, and it reserved the right to take enforcement actions against Halliburton for violations beyond the scope of the three questions.[44]

This opinion is significant because it affords acquirers some measure of safe harbor as they compete to acquire a target under challenging due diligence deadlines and with competitors that are less interested in FCPA compliance. At the same time the opinion placed multiple restrictions upon Halliburton as the requestor to comply with numerous disclosure obligations and due diligence milestones. Still, under the FCPA opinion procedure the DOJ can use disclosed information in a prosecution of a target.

M. Due Diligence Analysis Memoranda

Where there is due diligence of a major business partner or a project (or for even minor business partners or projects) or the presence of a risky country environment or industry, it is prudent for counsel (1) to review all gathered materials, such as completed questionnaires, background checks, interview memoranda, business partner policies, organizational charts, and training materials, in a data room or virtual data room; (2) to prepare a memorandum acknowledging the specific risks and analyzing the same, including such factors as the applicable TI country rankings, industry risk, and proposed partner risks such as a brief operating history, inadequate training, and poor controls; and (3) to propose prophylactic measures, such as special contractual provisions ensuring compliance, anticorruption training of the JV personnel, and imposition of audit rights. A simple background check for all but the most minor business partners is usually inadequate; a final written analysis is usually necessary to close out and memorialize the due diligence effort and analysis. Where clear red flags arise or major country, transactional, or sector risks are present, interviews of the target management or a third party are recommended. An FCPA due diligence analysis memorandum that does not address specific risks and speaks only positively of the business partner and opportunity is often not realistic or credible.

In a routine final written analysis of all due diligence materials, one person should take ownership of compiling the materials and analyzing the risks of the proposed business partner or project. This person should ideally be a lawyer and not a proponent of the business partner or project, as the latter may minimize the corruption risks to ensure the deal or relationship goes forward. The situation to be avoided is one where one or more red flags are raised in the process, but no one takes ownership of reviewing and analyzing the final materials, resulting in the partnership or project proceeding with red flags unaddressed. A memorandum should also recommend any necessary follow-up due diligence, such as remaining key manager interviews, ownership clarification, court record checks, and explanation of incomplete or vague questionnaire answers, and it should direct someone to gather the remaining materials.

N. DOJ FCPA Opinion Releases

When significant FCPA concerns arise during due diligence, an acquirer may wish to consider seeking an FCPA opinion from the DOJ in order to avoid the risk of successor criminal liability. An index of all the DOJ FCPA opinions issued to date is found in appendix 5. The turnaround time of the DOJ on such opinions has historically been slow and can be impractical in a fast-moving transaction context. However, the DOJ has more recently responded to such criticisms by issuing opinions more quickly. For example, Opinion Release 08-03 relating to approval of journalist travel expenses in China was released just four days after it was requested.

O. Practical Acquisition Due Diligence Advice

Multinational corporations should carefully plan out acquisition due diligence and prioritize those portions likely to require follow-up. Below are suggestions for how to make the executive team more understanding of the importance of the exercise and protocol steps:

- Explain to the executive team the risks and costs of a failed due diligence effort of a wayward target or partner (e.g., damage to reputation, lengthy government investigations of the company and its officers, disclosure obligations, decrease in share value, and substantial legal and accounting fees). Describe the problematic and costly acquisition cases of Titan, InVision, and Latin Node (see chapter 10).
- Consider the present value of an acquisition if it were discovered that the price was based in significant part on contracts procured by bribes or improper payments to local customs, tax officials, or other regulators who may soon enforce and investigate potential regulatory infractions.
- Visit the target's foreign business offices and facilities, including sales offices and major agents, consultants, or distributors, and examine whether other businesses in the same buildings appear to be related in business or to employ some of the target's employees.
- Conduct a criminal records search and review all prior U.S. and foreign government investigations of the target and its executives, key managers, and owners.
- Review the local public records of the target and conduct a thorough Internet search of the target, its executives, and its key managers and employees.
- Secure warranties and representations, indemnification agreements, and closing conditions that protect the acquisition.
- Review all government contracts, relationships, or touchpoints (e.g., with customs, taxes, visas, licenses, permits).
- Review all third-party contracts (e.g., with agents, consultants, distributors, JV partners, freight forwarders, and customs brokers).

- Review the target's historic due diligence files for third parties (e.g., agents, consultants, distributors, JV partners, freight forwarders, and customs brokers).
- Assess the quality of the target's books and records, internal controls and compliance codes, policies, and culture.
- Review potential red flags and resolve them before signing any agreement.
- Draft a memorandum that analyzes the due diligence data room review, background check, business partner corporate history and documentation, memorandum of understanding regarding a project or JV, and any interviews, and that outlines the potential risks and prophylactic measures to reduce the risks of corruption.
- Keep track of remedial measures and all Day One compliance efforts.

It is critical that an acquisition due diligence file be kept.

Resolution may include disclosing potential FCPA violations to the DOJ and SEC before closing or securing an agreement with the DOJ to further timely disclose after closing and a plan to immediately stop any improper practices and, in the case of issuers, correct any inaccurate books and records before the end of the target's fiscal year.

A sample FCPA Acquisition Due Diligence Checklist is provided in appendix 6. Further, the Transparency International UK *Anti-Corruption Due Diligence in Transactions* is discussed in chapter 11 and reprinted in appendix 16.

VII. JOINT VENTURES

A. Form

A joint venture is a business agreement to carry on a business with other parties in which the parties agree to develop, usually for a finite period or a specific project, a new entity and new assets typically by contributing equity. The unrelated parties pool, exchange, or integrate some of their reserves with a view to mutual gain, while at the same time remaining independent.[45] The form of a JV can be a jointly owned corporation or group of corporations, a partnership (either general or limited), a limited liability corporation, or a contractual one. A contractual or nonequity JV can be a co-ownership model or simply a contract where the parties retain all their own assets and agree as to their separate rights and obligations. Most "partnering" arrangements, strategic alliances, and outsourcing services agreements fall into contractual or nonequity JVs.

B. Foreign Joint Ventures

FCPA issues often arise in foreign JV transactions. U.S. companies seeking to sell goods or services in other countries will frequently enter into JVs for various commercial, legal, or financial reasons. In many countries it is a legal requirement that foreign parties have a local partner to undertake certain projects. In other cases it will be essential, as a matter of operational necessity, that a foreign company have a local partner in order to access local labor, equipment, financing, and other resources. In large infrastructure projects, the requirements of different forms of input (construction, equipment, labor), level of financing, and risk allocation may require the formation of a JV company to undertake such projects.

A foreign JV can be as simple as a contractual agreement relating to a particular project, with each party agreeing to undertake certain activities and receive certain benefits and compensation in return. More typically, a JV will consist of the formation of a new legal entity under the laws of the country in question, with its equity ownership, board of directors, steering committee, and day-to-day management shared between the partners. In considering a potential foreign JV, a partner will consider whether it wishes to take an active or passive role. An active role will give a partner greater influence on compliance and finance and controller functions. Voting rights—unanimous, supermajority, or majority—as well as blocking rights are very important considerations. Whatever the form, the foreign joint venture partner should adopt the same due diligence procedures and methodology for its JV partners that were outlined earlier in this chapter for mergers and acquisitions to minimize the risk of past or future FCPA antibribery violations.

C. Common Foreign Joint Venture Scenarios

There are two common JV scenarios whereby issuers or persons face potential FCPA criminal risk for antibribery conduct. The first involves a JV partnership with a state-owned entity, under which the issuer or subsidiary has a substantial operation in the foreign state and customarily half of the directors are foreign government officials. The second involves a JV partnership of a U.S. issuer or person, such as a manufacturer, and a privately owned foreign entity whereby the latter manufactures under license the product for the often U.S.–based issuer or its foreign subsidiary. Each scenario presents substantial and unique commercial and FCPA risks.

1. Joint Venture with a State-Owned Entity

FCPA exposure frequently arises in JVs between companies subject to the FCPA and foreign state-owned entities. The first priority is to confirm that the structure and relationship are legal under the local laws. Many foreign countries encourage, if not require, joint ventures, and in certain industries use of a joint venture agreement (JVA) is common. For example, in the energy sector it is common for the petroleum or natural resource government authority to enter into a JVA and a production-sharing agreement (PSA) whereby a resource extraction company and the foreign government contract over how much of the resource (e.g., oil) extracted from the country each will receive. The private company typically provides management and technical services while the foreign government provides natural resources. In the oil and gas industry the extraction company is customarily allowed to recover capital and operational expenses, known as "cost oil," first. The remaining money is known as "profit oil" and is split between the company and the government—usually 20 percent to 80 percent.

To the extent the directors of the JV knowingly authorize improper payments to foreign government officials, they, as well as the venture itself and the U.S. shareholder, may be found criminally liable. A potential major FCPA issue is the payment of directors' fees, as the state-owned entity's directors[46] not only can award business but also can influence other government entities, for example, customs and taxes, that can otherwise impede the JV's business. To avoid potential improper "influence" accusations, it is better for each partner to pay its own directors, to cover travel and lodging for its respective directors, and to handle similar expenses whenever possible. Transparency and disclosure of all foreign government approvals, agency relationships, and transactions are essential where state-owned entities partner with issuers and U.S. companies and subject their managing employees and directors to the jurisdiction of the FCPA.

2. *Joint Venture with a Foreign Private Entity*

As indicated above, many U.S. companies enter into JVAs with foreign private companies to secure lower manufacturing and labor costs in foreign countries. As with foreign distributors, U.S. companies often mistakenly assume that faraway JVs pose little FCPA risk absent direct payments by an in-country U.S. manager to local officials. Issuers, directors, and the JV face FCPA criminal liability under various provisions of the Act.[47] Where the foreign partner has the operating responsibilities and employs only foreign nationals, it is oftentimes more difficult for the U.S. partner and its directors to know the in-country activities and, in particular, any improper activities there. Still, any authorization of improper payments and acts while in the territory of the United States can put the U.S. partner and directors in peril. The traditional red flags that apply to agents and consultants should be considered with JV partners. Multiple red flags may establish the highly likely knowledge of the improper payments standard necessary for a criminal prosecution. JV partners cannot bury their heads in the sand and are wise to require FCPA/antibribery training of their staffs, to conduct regular audits, and to enforce a strong "tone at the top."

D. Issuer, Director, and Joint Venture Liability

1. *Issuer*

There are usually two scenarios under which an issuer faces FCPA antibribery liability for a foreign JV. First, it is unlawful for any issuer or any stockholder thereof acting on behalf of the issuer, that is, a JV, to make use of the mails or any means or instrumentality of interstate commerce corruptly in furtherance of an offer, payment, promise to pay, or authorization of the payment of any money, offer, gift, promise to give, or authorization of the giving of anything of value to any foreign official for purposes of influencing any act or decision of such foreign official in his or her official capacity or inducing such foreign official to do or omit to do any act in violation of the lawful duty of such official.[48] Second, it is unlawful for any stockholder acting on behalf of a foreign firm while in the territory of the United States corruptly to make use of the mails or any means or instrumentality of interstate commerce or to do any other act in furtherance of any offer, payment, promise to pay, or authorization of the payment of any money, offer, or gift for the aforementioned purposes.[49]

2. Directors

U.S. directors often compose half of a JV's board and can be subject to FCPA criminal liability under all three substantive antibribery provisions—15 U.S.C. § 78dd-1, 78dd-2, and 78dd-3. First, directors can be liable as employees or agents of an issuer if they make use of the mails or interstate commerce corruptly in furtherance of an offer, payment, promise to pay, or authorization of the payment of any money, or offer, gift, promise to give, or authorization of the giving of anything of value to foreign officials for the aforementioned purposes.[50] Second, they can be liable either as a domestic concern (any individual who is a citizen, national, or resident of the United States), or as employees of a corporation with its principal place of business in the United States if they make use of the mails or any means of instrumentality corruptly in furtherance of any offer, payment, promise to pay, or authorization of the payment of any money, offer, gift, or promise to give for the above-mentioned purposes.[51] Third, directors can be directors or agents of a foreign firm while in the territory of the United States corruptly to make use of the mails or do any other act in furtherance of an offer, payment, promise to pay, or authorization of the giving of anything of value to any foreign official for the above-mentioned purposes.[52] U.S. directors of JVs invariably engage in many acts while in U.S. territory, but whether any of their acts are in furtherance of an improper offer, promise to pay, or gift becomes an issue in some investigations.

3. Joint Venture

A JV itself may be liable if it as a foreign firm has a stockholder or agent on its behalf while in the territory of the United States corruptly make use of the mails or do any other act in furtherance of an offer, payment, promise to pay, or authorization of the payment of any money, offer, gift, promise to give, or authorization of the giving of anything of value to a foreign official.[53] The United States generally takes a very expansive view of "acts in furtherance" of improper payments, for example, wiring funds or e-mailing authorizations. The DOJ or SEC will also look closely at the circumstances surrounding any authorization of expenses and any relevant red flags at the time of the improper payments or giving of things of value. The DOJ has to date preferred to charge the U.S. JV partner—as opposed to the JV itself.[54]

E. Internal Controls

Under the FCPA, an issuer that holds 50 percent or less of the voting power with respect to a foreign firm is required only to proceed in good faith to use its influence to the extent reasonable under the issuer's circumstances to cause such foreign firm to devise and maintain a system of internal controls that satisfies the Act's internal control standards.[55] Such circumstances shall include the relative degree of the issuer's ownership of the foreign firm and the laws and practices governing the business operations of the country in which the firm is located. An issuer that demonstrates good-faith efforts to use such influence shall be conclusively presumed to have complied with the FCPA's internal controls provisions.[56]

F. Joint Venture Risk Assessment and Due Diligence

1. *Practical Joint Venture Risk and Due Diligence Advice*

JVs are common in international business transactions, and in some countries they are required by law. Too often, multinational companies, in assessing foreign JV liability or risk, simply look at their respective equity contributions. Many wishfully conclude that if they do not have a majority interest, they are not at FCPA risk. *United States v. Kellogg, Brown & Root* makes clear that a 25 percent or less JV interest can put a partner at criminal risk. Instead, multinational corporations should consider governance structure and the management vehicle; the management board (management committee or board of directors); the meetings of the co-venturers and which decisions require majority approval or unanimity; day-to-day management (general manager, CEO, CFO, etc.); auditor appointment and authority; reporting and access to information; actions requiring consent; business plan and budgets; distributions; financing sources; ID or technology; share transfer restrictions and related programs; and termination rights.[57]

Before entering into an international joint venture, a multinational company should look well beyond its equity interest or contribution and conduct due diligence into the qualifications of the proposed JV partner(s):

- The ownership of the proposed JV partner;
- The prior business experience of the proposed JV partner;
- The presence of any owners, managers, directors, officers, or their family members, who are foreign government officials;
- Its corporate compliance programs;
- Its familiarity, policies, and training in FCPA, OECD, and related antibribery conventions;
- Any prior criminal record, litigation, and local administrative history of the proposed JV partner;
- Any audit opinions and history;
- The transparency of its financial statements;
- The qualifications and experience of its senior management; and
- Review of U.S. government lists as described in section VI.G., *supra*.

It is also important to examine any underlying agency or consulting relationships; the payment procedure and history; the due diligence conducted with respect to current and past agents and consultants; and the compensation structure for agents and consultants (e.g., success fee, hourly fee).

Upon confirming that there are no ongoing FCPA issues or irresolvable red flags, counsel will want to focus on securing strong warranties and representations and indemnification rights for the final JVA and insert antibribery controls and inspection rights in the venture's governing documents.[58]

2.   FCPA Opinion Procedure Release 2001-01 (May 24, 2001): Preexisting Contract Due Diligence and Liability

U.S. companies forming JVs with other foreign companies under which each party will contribute preexisting contracts to the venture should be aware of potential FCPA issues relating to the contracts procured by the foreign company prior to formation of the venture. In May 2001, the DOJ addressed this subject through its opinion release procedure when a U.S. company sought guidance concerning its plans to enter into a JV with a French company.[59] Both companies planned to contribute preexisting contracts to the venture, including contracts procured by the French company before the effective date of the new French Law No. 2000-595 against Corrupt Practices. In indicating that it would not take any enforcement action under the facts and circumstances there presented, the DOJ raised several important issues.

The U.S. company requesting the opinion letter informed the DOJ that the French company had represented that none of the contracts and transactions to be contributed by the French company were procured in violation of applicable anti-bribery or other laws. In response, the DOJ noted that it specifically interpreted this representation to mean that all the contracts the French company was bringing to the JV were obtained in compliance with all applicable antibribery law—not just French law. The DOJ then stated that if the French company's representation was "limited to violation of then-applicable French law, the Requestor, as an American company, may face liability under the FCPA if it or the joint venture knowingly takes any act in furtherance of a payment to a foreign official with respect to previously existing contracts irrespective of whether the agreement to make such payments was lawful under French law when the contract was entered into."[60] Thus, a U.S. company can be held liable if it takes any act in furtherance of a payment (e.g., payment of a commission due an agent who had previously assisted in obtaining a contract for the foreign partner) to a foreign official in violation of the antibribery provisions of any country.

FCPA Opinion Release 2001-01 also allowed the DOJ to state its view concerning the appropriate termination provision for the JV. The JVA provided that the U.S. company could opt out of the venture or terminate its obligations if "(i) the French company is convicted of violating the FCPA; (ii) the French company enters into a settlement with an admission of liability under the FCPA; or (iii) the Requestor learns of evidence that the French company violated antibribery laws and that violation, even without a conviction or settlement, has a material adverse effect upon the joint venture."[61] The DOJ objected to the "material adverse effect" standard, which it called "unduly restrictive," and warned, "Should the Requestor's inability to extricate itself result in the Requestor taking, in the future, acts in furtherance of original acts of bribery by the French company, the Requestor may face liability under the FCPA."[62] As a result, the DOJ specifically declined to endorse the "materially adverse effect" standard. This opinion highlights for transaction counsel the importance of structuring JVs and acquisitions so that "FCPA-tainted" assets or contracts will not result in liability for the U.S. party.

3.   *FCPA Opinion Procedure Release No. 2009-01 (August 3, 2009):*
Product Samples and Foreign Government Procurement Processes

Foreign governments are very often major customers of multinational companies. In tenders for government purchases, it is not uncommon for foreign government officials to request samples as part of technical performance evaluations. FCPA issues can arise when there is a request for samples in connection with a product that has both commercial and personal uses and when an official requests or is offered manufacturer samples of personal products that are not part of the proposed tender. Providing samples for the personal use or benefit of a government official or family members presents clear risks.

In August 2009, the DOJ issued FCPA Opinion Procedure Release 2009-01,[63] which reviewed the request of a U.S. domestic concern that manufactured a specific type of medical device and sought approval to provide sample devices to foreign government health centers for evaluation of its technology, measured outcomes, and feedback from the top physicians. A senior official had explained that the foreign government was not familiar with its products, that it would endorse only products that it had technically evaluated with favorable results, and that it had already found competitors qualified. The foreign government and the requestor jointly determined that the optimal sample size for an evaluation study was 100 units distributed among ten experienced health centers, each receiving ten devices at $19,000 per device, or $1.9 million for all 100 units.

Both the manufacturer and its potential government customer undertook a series of steps to make the provision of expensive samples to government health centers fair and transparent. The 100 recipients were to be selected from a list of candidates provided by the participating medical centers and were to be culled from long lists of candidates based on certain objective criteria outlined in a letter of request. All candidates were required to present a certificate of economic difficulty from the relevant local government authority establishing the candidates' inability to pay. The recipients were to be selected from the list of candidates by a working group of healthcare professionals familiar with the type of medical device and the requestor's country manager who had received FCPA training.

The names of the 100 recipients were to be published on the government agency's website for two weeks. Close family members of government officials were ineligible, unless (1) the government-employed relatives of such recipient held low-level positions and were not in positions to influence either the selection or the testing process; (2) the government-employed relatives of such recipient clearly met the requisite economic criteria; and (3) the recipient was determined to be a more suitable candidate than candidates who were not selected based on technical criteria. Further, the requestor's country manager was to review the selection of any immediate family members of any other government official (e.g., those unaffiliated with the medical device project or the government agency) to make certain that the criteria were properly and fairly applied and would report his determination to requestor's legal counsel. A favorable evaluation under this process would only make the requestor's products eligible for the government's subsidized medical device program and not necessarily result in the award of business.

The evaluation of the donated medical devices was to be based on objective criteria that are standard for this type of medical device and that were provided to the DOJ. The results of the evaluation were to be collected by the country manager, who would enlist the help of two other medical experts to review the results and provide an overall report, as well as individual objective results, to a senior health official in the foreign country who would share his assessment with the government agency. The government agency was to then evaluate the results of the evaluation and the report by the country manager, along with the senior health official's assessments, to determine the suitability of the requestor's technology for the medical device program. If the results of the evaluation were favorable, the requestor's devices would be identified by the government agency as eligible for the subsidized medical device program, along with the devices of the requestor's competitors, which had already been declared eligible. The foreign government advised the requestor that none of the company's devices would be promoted by the foreign government above any of the other qualified devices.

The requestor represented that more than 30 government health centers throughout the country would receive the evaluation results, which would in large part determine whether those centers would purchase the requestor's products as part of the government's medical device program. As a result of the anticipated success of the proposed evaluation, the requestor expected that its products would meet all technical criteria for this program and that its opportunities for participation in the program would be greater as a result of the awareness among government physicians of the performance of the requestor's devices. Finally, the requestor represented to the DOJ that it had no reason to believe that the senior official who suggested providing the medical devices to the government would personally benefit from the donation of the devices and related items and services.

The DOJ approval of this opinion request rested largely on the fact that the proposed provision of 100 medical devices fell outside the scope of the FCPA in that the donated products were to be provided to the government—and not to government officials—for ultimate use by patient recipients. While the decision is not surprising in light of the absence of anything of value being given to a government official, Opinion Procedure Release No. 2009-01 nonetheless provides very useful guidance on the detailed and lengthy prophylactic measures a company can and should take when it considers offering samples to potential government customers.

VIII. ONGOING AGENCY, CONSULTANCY, OR JOINT VENTURE DUE DILIGENCE

Multinational companies must not only conduct due diligence prior to entering into an agency, consultancy or JV, but also review and document the agent, consultant, or partner's performance of its duties during the life of the contract or relationship. To that end, companies should require such third parties to detail the nature of goods or services in invoices and explain any charges for goods or such services that raise questions. They should require third parties to disclose all subdistributors, subagents, and subcontractors. Finally, they should be prepared to cancel any contracts with third parties that unreasonably refuse to provide documentation of ongoing goods and services to disclose subdistributor, subcontractor, and subagent relationships and conduct adequate due diligence or to submit to an audit.

IX. ADDITIONAL RESOURCES

- Margaret Ayres & Bethany K. Hipp, *M&A and Third-Party Transactions under the FCPA, in* THE FOREIGN CORRUPT PRACTICES ACT: COPING WITH HEIGHTENED ENFORCEMENT RISK (PLI Course Handbook 2008).
- Margaret Ayres, Carlos M. Pelayo & Bethany K. Hipp, *FCPA Considerations in Mergers and Acquisitions, in* THE FOREIGN CORRUPT PRACTICES ACT 2007: COPING WITH HEIGHTENED ENFORCEMENT RISK (PLI Course Handbook No. B-1619, 2007).
- Sharie A. Brown, *Steps to an Effective Foreign Corrupt Practices Act Compliance Program*, 20 COMM. CORP. COUNS. NEWSL. (Summer 2006).
- Harry L. Clark & Nicholas Hartigan, *Given Recent FCPA Cases, M&A Risk Management Is Key*, NAT'L L.J. (June 6, 2011).
- Gary DiBianco, Due Diligence of Business Partners and Agents, paper presented at ACI FCPA Boot Camp (San Francisco, June 4–5, 2007).
- Gary DiBianco & Wendy E. Pearson, *Anti-Corruption Due Diligence in Corporate Transactions: One Size Does Not Fit All*, Feb. 2009, http://www.skadden.com.
- Jeffrey T. Harfenist & Saul Pilchen, *Anti-Corruption Risk Assessments: A Primer for General Counsels, Internal Auditors, and Other Compliance Personnel*, 2 FIN. FRAUD L. REP. 9 (Oct. 2010).
- Peter M. Kriendler, Ellen S. Friedenberg, Alan G. Kashdan, James B. Kobak Jr. & Daniel H. Weiner, *Joint Ventures*, ch. 50 *in* SUCCESSFUL PARTNERING BETWEEN INSIDE AND OUTSIDE COUNSEL (Haig ed., West Group 2008).
- Lucinda Low & Thomas Best, *Addressing FCPA Risk in Mergers and Acquisitions: At What Price Safety?, in* THE FOREIGN CORRUPT PRACTICES ACT 2009: COPING WITH HEIGHTENED ENFORCEMENT RISKS (PLI Course Handbook No. B-1737, 2009).
- Susan Muck, Catherine D. Kevane, Cathleen Donohue & J. Carlos Orellana, *Avoiding FCPA Risk in Dealing with Agents, Consultants and Other Third Parties, in* THE FOREIGN CORRUPT PRACTICES ACT 2009: COPING WITH HEIGHTENED ENFORCEMENT RISKS (PLI Course Handbook No. B-1737, 2009).
- Claudius Sokenu, *DOJ Again Clarifies FCPA Due Diligence Expected in Business Combinations*, 40(34) SEC. REG. & LAW REP. (Aug. 25, 2008).
- Transparency International, http://www.transparency.org.
- Dale Turza, *The Foreign Corrupt Practices Act: Elements, Due Diligence and Affirmative Defenses—A Practical Guide, in* ABA FOREIGN CORRUPT PRACTICES ACT 2006 (ABA 2006).
- DON ZARIN, DOING BUSINESS UNDER THE FOREIGN CORRUPT PRACTICES ACT, ch. 9 (PLI 2007).

NOTES

1. Foreign Corrupt Practices Act of 1977, Pub. L. No. 95-213, 91 Stat. 1494 (codified as amended at 15 U.S.C. §§ 78m, 78dd-1 to -3, 78ff (1999)) [hereinafter FCPA].

2. In investigating FCPA issues, counsel must often master international transaction agreements and practices, including joint venture agreements, shareholder agreements, merger and acquisition agreements, operating and management agreements, transfer of technology and license agreements, production-sharing agreements (PSAs), and joint operation agreements (JOAs), as well as commercial agency agreements, distribution agreements, commission sales representation agreements, consulting contracts, and so forth.

3. United States v. Titan Corp., No. 05 CR 0314 BEN (S.D. Cal. Mar. 1, 2005); SEC v. Titan Corp., Civil Action No. 05-0411 (D.D.C.) (JR) (filed Mar. 1, 2005).

4. *In re* Delta & Pine Land Co. & Turk Deltapine Inc., SEC Release No. 56,138, Admin. Proceeding File No. 3-12712 (July 26, 2007).

5. *See* discussion of United States v. Pfizer H.C.P. Corp. and SEC v. Pfizer Inc., *infra* chapter 10.

6. Transparency Int'l, Corruption Perceptions Index 2012, http://cpi.transparency .org/cpi2012/results/-.

7. *See id.*

8. Assistant Att'y Gen. Lanny A. Breuer, U.S. Dep't of Justice, Keynote Address at the 10th Annual Pharmaceutical Regulatory and Compliance Congress and Best Practices Forum (Nov. 12, 2009), http://www.justice.gov/criminal/pr/speeches-testimony /documents/11-12-09breuer-pharmaspeech.pdf.

9. *Id.*

10. *Id.*

11. *See* DON ZARIN, DOING BUSINESS UNDER THE FCPA (PLI 2007), ch. 9.

12. The FCPA is reproduced in appendix 1.

13. *See* ZARIN, *supra* note 11, at ch. 6, § 6.2.2.

14. 15 U.S.C. §§ 78dd-1(a), -2(a), -3(a).

15. ZARIN, *supra* note 11, § 6.2.2.

16. *See* Deloitte Financial Advisory Services LLP's Business Party Survey, a web-based self-representation survey, http://www.deloitte.com.

17. Margaret M. Ayres & Bethany K. Hipp, *Third-Party Transactions under the FCPA*, *in* THE FOREIGN CORRUPT PRACTICES ACT 2008: COPING WITH HEIGHTENED ENFORCEMENT RISKS 163 (PLI 2008).

18. CRIM. DIV., U.S. DEP'T OF JUSTICE & ENFORCEMENT DIV., U.S. SEC. & EXCH. COMM., FCPA: A RESOURCE GUIDE TO THE U.S. FOREIGN CORRUPT PRACTICES ACT (2012), http:// www.justice.gov/criminal/fraud/fcpa/guidance/ or http://www.sec.gov/spotlight/fcpa .shtml [hereinafter RESOURCE GUIDE] (reprinted in appendix 4).

19. *Id.* at 28 (citing, *e.g.*, Melrose Distillers, Inc. v. United States, 359 U.S. 271, 274 (1959) (affirming criminal successor liability for antitrust violations); United States v. Alamo Bank of Tex., 880 F.2d 828, 830 (5th Cir. 1989) (affirming criminal successor liability for bank secrecy violations); United States v. Polizzi, 500 F.2d 856, 907 (9th Cir. 1974) (affirming criminal successor liability for conspiracy and Travel Act violations); United States v. Shields Rubber Corp., 732 F. Supp. 569, 571–72 (W.D. Pa. 1989)).

20. Press Release, SEC, SEC Charges General Electric and Two Subsidiaries with FCPA Violations (July 27, 2010), http://www.sec.gov/news/press/2010/2010-133.htm.

21. Sec. & Exch. Comm'n v. Gen. Elec. Co., Ionics Inc. & Amersham plc, Case No. 1:10-cv-01258 (D.D.C. (July 27, 2010).

22. 15 U.S.C. § 78m(b)(2)(A).

23. 15 U.S.C. § 78u(d)(3).

24. SEC News Digest, SEC Files Settled Books and Records and Internal Controls Charges against General Electric Company and Two Subsidiaries for Improper Payments to Iraqi Ministries under the UN Oil for Food Program, GE Agrees to Pay Over $23.4 Million in Disgorgement, Interest and Penalties (July 27, 2010, http://www.sec.gov/news/digest/2010/dig072710.htm; see also case discussion *infra* chapter 10.

25. *See* Gary DiBianco & Wendy E. Pearson, *Anti-Corruption Due Diligence: One Size Does Not Fit All*, SKADDEN, ARPS (Feb. 2009), http://www.skadden.com.

26. Press Release, U.S. Dep't of Justice, Alliance One International Inc. and Universal Corporation Resolve FCPA Matters Involving Bribes Paid to Foreign Government Officials (Aug. 6, 2010), http://www.justice.gov/opa/pr/2010/August/10-crm-903.html.

27. No. 10-CV-01319 (D.D.C. filed Aug. 6, 2010).

28. RESOURCE GUIDE, *supra* note 18.

29. FCPA Opinion Procedure Release No. 14-02 (Nov. 7, 2014).

30. The DOJ expressed no view as to the adequacy or reasonableness of the proposed integration plan for the target by the requestor.

31. *See* 15 U.S.C. §§ 78dd-1, et seq. (setting forth statutory jurisdictional bases for anti-bribery provisions).

32. *See* RESOURCE GUIDE, *supra* note 18, at 29.

33. *Id.* at 28.

34. *Id.* at 29.

35. Harry L. Clark & Nicholas J. Hartigan, *Given Recent FCPA Cases, M&A Risk Management Is Key*, NAT'L L.J., at 12 (June 6, 2011).

36. *Id.*

37. Lucinda Low & Thomas R.L. Best, *Addressing FCPA Risk in Mergers and Acquisitions: At What Price Safety?*, *in* THE FOREIGN CORRUPT PRACTICES ACT 2009: COPING WITH HEIGHTENED ENFORCEMENT RISKS (PLI Course Handbook No. B-1737, 2009).

38. Margaret M. Ayres & Bethany K. Hipp, *FCPA Considerations in Mergers and Acquisitions*, *in* THE FOREIGN CORRUPT PRACTICES ACT: COPING WITH HEIGHTENED ENFORCEMENT 17–18 (PLI Course Handbook No. B-1619, 2007).

39. *Id.* at 19.

40. *See* DiBianco & Pearson, *supra* note 25.

41. *Id.*

42. *See* FCPA Opinion Procedure Release No. 2008-02 (June 13, 2008).

43. *Id.*

44. Model Joint Venture Checklist Introduction, http://apps.americanbar.org/buslaw/newsletter/0049/materials/book.pdf.

45. *See* FCPA Opinion Procedure Release No. 93-01 (Apr. 20, 1993).

46. Ellen S. Friedenberg et al., Joint Ventures, in SUCCESSFUL PARTNERING BETWEEN INSIDE AND OUTSIDE COUNSEL (Robert Haig ed., 2008).

47. 15 U.S.C. § 78dd-1(a).

48. 15 U.S.C. § 78dd-3(a).

49. 15 U.S.C. § 78dd-1(a).

50. 15 U.S.C. § 78dd-2(a).

51. 15 U.S.C. § 78dd-3(a).

52. 15 U.S.C. § 78dd-3.

53. *See*, e.g., Information, United States v. Kellogg Brown & Root, No. 09-CR-00071 (S.D. Tex.—Hous. filed Feb 6, 2009); *see* case discussion *infra* chapter 10.

54. 15 U.S.C. § 78m(b)(2).

55. 15 U.S.C. § 78m(b)(6).

56. *Id.*

57. Roger M. Witten, Kimberly A. Partner & Thomas J. Koffer, Navigating the Increased Anti-Corruption Environment in the United States and Abroad, paper presented at the 20th Annual ACI Conference on the Foreign Corrupt Practices Act, Washington, D.C. (Nov. 18, 2008).

58. *See* FCPA Opinion Procedure Release No. 2001-01 (May 24, 2001).

59. *Id.*

60. *Id.*

61. *Id.*

62. *See* FCPA Opinion Procedure Release No. 09-01 (Aug. 3, 2009).

63. Mark Mendelsohn, Acting Chief, Fraud Section, Criminal Div., U.S. Dep't of Justice, Remarks at the ABA National Institute on White Collar Crime (San Francisco, Mar. 5, 2009).

CHAPTER 6

Gifts, Travel, Lodging, and Entertainment

I. INTRODUCTION

Gifts, travel, lodging, and entertainment for non–U.S. government officials present common and frequent Foreign Corrupt Practices Act[1] issues for multinational companies and their counsel. If a company has clear written policies and procedures for such requests, most of the issues will resolve themselves without any substantial risk. Thoughtful, customized written policies and internal controls can greatly reduce the risk of FCPA antibribery, books-and-records, and internal controls violations; establish sound guidance for managers; and deter many potential wrongdoers. The *Resource Guide to U.S. Foreign Corrupt Practices Act*[2] confirms that the Department of Justice (DOJ) and the Securities and Exchange Commission (SEC) do not intend to pursue modest gift, travel, lodging, and entertainment expenditures.

Some multinational companies (MNCs) prohibit all forms of gifts, hospitality, or entertainment, but they are clearly a minority. Many rely largely on a two- or three-paragraph summary of the FCPA or anticorruption laws in their code of company conduct to guide employees. Still others that operate in challenging countries provide specific written FCPA guidance to employees utilizing a reasonableness and proportionality standard—often tied to the value or size of the gift, travel, or entertainment—and have automated gift-giving or entertainment clearance processes. Because the FCPA has no de minimis exclusion for gifts, travel, lodging, or entertainment expenditures, the analysis routinely reverts to the Act's use of the word "corruptly" (see chapter 1 at I.C.4). Most well-managed multinational companies conduct regular FCPA or anticorruption training—live or, at least, online—that addresses gifts, travel, lodging, and entertainment, among other topics. MNCs that sponsor special sporting events like the Olympics or the World Cup prepare and train their employees, temporary employees, and agents on the specific corruption, risks, and scenarios they are likely to encounter in such sponsorships. Adverse publicity from an arrest or an investigation can completely defeat the goodwill intended by a major sponsorship.

For many gift, travel, lodging, and entertainment issues, it is often helpful to, in addition to considering the value of the gift or related thing of value, consider the simple question: How would the host officer or employee feel about being pictured with the donee or beneficiary in the local newspaper, and the gift, travel, or entertainment and supporting invoice(s) were next featured in a front-page story of *The New York Times*? In essence, one must ascertain whether under the particular travel, lodging, and entertainment facts and circumstances, there is a quid pro quo. Thoughtful, stand-alone written company travel and entertainment policies with examples are more likely to provide a safe haven for a company and its employees alike. In such policies, "reasonableness" (borrowing from the FCPA's travel and entertainment language relating to certain marketing and contracting activities) or "reasonable and proportionate" (borrowing from the U.K. Bribery Act Guidance[3]) should be the governing standard and is best met and assured under policies where prior written approval is required.

Because the FCPA expressly affords protection for certain types of travel and lodging, but does not directly address gifts anywhere, the topics are next addressed separately.[4]

II. GIFTS

Most business gifts are simply that: gifts designed to promote products or services and thus business and business relationships. Under the FCPA, the term "corruptly" connotes an evil motive or purpose, and only a gift with an intent to wrongfully influence the recipient in awarding or retaining business or gaining an improper business advantage should provide the basis for an FCPA bribery charge. The FCPA does not state a minimum dollar threshold for corrupt gifts. A gift or entertainment that is provided to create a favorable business climate with only a generalized hope or expectation of ultimate benefit to the donor lacks the benefit of a quid pro quo for the award of business.[5]

A. The Gift Spectrum and the *Resource Guide*

Gifts can range from modest to extravagant, and the more extravagant the gift, the more likely it was given with an improper purpose. The DOJ and SEC *Resource Guide* recognizes that a small gift or token of esteem or gratitude is an appropriate way to display respect in a business setting. Accordingly, reasonable meals and entertainment expenses or company promotional items (free pens, hats, T-shirts) are unlikely to draw FCPA enforcement action.[6] On the other hand, the *Resource Guide* points out that gifts of sports cars and fur coats as well as widespread gifts of smaller items as part of a pattern of bribes cross the line.[7] The *Resource Guide* highlights several extravagant gifts, for example, sports cars, as improper and conversely offers multinationals comfort with respect to small gifts of nominal value; it, however, leaves a wide spectrum uncertain in the middle. The guidance below is intended to address that gulf. Not surprisingly, side trips, discussed *infra*, to tourist attractions such as Las Vegas, Disney World, Universal Studios, Napa, and the Grand Canyon can be very risky.

The following value questions may be relevant:

- Is the gift extravagant (e.g., sports car, fur coat, and other luxury items) and likely to be interpreted as able to influence the recipient?

- Is the value of the gift consistent or at odds with the donor company's domestic gift policy?
- Is the value of the gift substantial when compared to the annual income of the recipient or the annual per capita income of the country of the recipient?

In addition to its value, whether an item in the middle of the spectrum presents risk will frequently turn on the nature and transparency of the gift.

B. Nature of the Gift

In general, the nature of a gift to a non–U.S. government official can determine whether the gift is *corruptly* motivated. The following questions and factors should be considered in determining whether a gift is proper under the FCPA:

- Is the gift business-appropriate?
- Would a donor be at all embarrassed if the fact of the gift were to be publicly disclosed?
- Is the gift something a donor would be comfortable accurately describing on an expense voucher?
- Is the gift a memento of a business occasion, for example, a bowl with an engraved corporate logo to commemorate a joint venture opening?
- Is the gift cash or one involving something not appropriate for a business, for example, adult entertainment?
- Is the gift a one-time event to a recipient, or has the recipient received repeated gifts over time? That is, is there a widespread pattern of gifts?
- Does the recipient or a close friend or relative of the recipient have any decision-making authority with respect to the donor's business, bid, award, or contract?

C. Transparency of the Gift

Transparency questions include the following:

- Will the gift be given openly to the intended recipient, for example, presented to the intended recipient at a group setting rather than one-on-one?
- Is the gift to be presented directly to the intended recipient?
- Has the intended recipient requested the gift?
- What is the intended recipient's role in any current or upcoming business or contract award or approval process?
- Has the donor provided multiple gifts of value to one recipient for that recipient to distribute to other recipients?
- Is the gift reciprocal (e.g., has a visiting group presented a gift to the host, and is it a custom and practice in the country in question for the host to reciprocate and present a similar gift)?
- Does the recipient's government, company, or organization have any written policies governing or prohibiting gifts, and does the gift in question conform to or violate that policy?

- Has the donor consulted his or her supervisor and obtained advance approval to give the gift?
- Has the donee consulted his or her supervisor and obtained advance approval to receive the gift?
- Is the gift legal under local law?

D. FCPA Opinion Procedure Release 13-1 (December 19, 2013)

In 2013, the DOJ reviewed the Foreign Corrupt Practices Act (FCPA) opinion procedure request of a partner with a U.S. law firm (the requestor) regarding whether he could pay for medical expenses costing between approximately $13,500 and $20,500 for a foreign official's daughter who suffered from a severe medical condition. The foreign official works for his country's Office of the Attorney General (OAG) and the U.S. law firm received legal fees of nearly $1 million a year from the foreign country for handling international arbitrations.

The requestor presently represents the foreign country in two international arbitrations for which the law firm receives payment. In the past 18 months, the law firm has billed fees to the foreign country of over $2 million, and the requestor anticipates that in 2014, the fees on matters for the foreign country will exceed $2 million.

Over the past several years of these representations, the requestor became a personal friend of the foreign official. The OAG is responsible for selecting and contracting with international counsel on behalf of the foreign country. According to the requestor, however, the foreign official had not had and would not have in the future any role in the selection of the requestor or the law firm as counsel for the foreign country. The requestor is not the law firm's "primary relationship attorney," "originating attorney," or "lead attorney" for the OAG or the government of the foreign country, but has participated in the selection or pitch processes for new business with OAG and/or the government of the foreign country, and would expect to do so with regard to future business from these clients.

The requestor proposes to pay the medical expenses of the foreign official's daughter, who suffers from a severe medical condition that cannot effectively be treated in the foreign country or anywhere in the region. The physicians treating the foreign official's daughter had recommended that she receive inpatient care at a specialized facility located in another country. The requestor reported that the treatment would cost between approximately $13,500 and $20,500 and that the foreign official lacks financial means to pay for this treatment for his daughter.

In addition, to the above representations, the requestor further represented that, among other things:

- The requestor's intention in paying for the medical treatment of the foreign official's daughter is purely humanitarian, with no intent to influence the decision of any foreign official with regard to engaging the services of the law firm, the requestor, or any third person.
- The funds used to pay for the medical treatment will be the requestor's own personal funds. The requestor will neither seek nor receive reimbursement from the law firm for such payments.

- The requestor will make all payments directly to the facility where the foreign official's daughter will receive treatment. The official will pay for the costs of his daughter's related travel.
- The foreign country is expected to retain the law firm to work on one new matter in the near future. The requestor is presently unaware of any additional, potential matters as to which the foreign country might retain the law firm. However, if such a matter develops, the requestor anticipates that the foreign country would likely retain the law firm given its successful track record and their strong relationship.
- Under the law of the foreign country, any government agency such as OAG that hires an outside law firm must publicly publish a reasoned decision justifying the engagement. It is a crime punishable by imprisonment under the penal code of the foreign country for any civil servant or public employee to engage in corrupt behavior in connection with public contracting.

In addition, the foreign official and the requestor discussed this matter transparently with their respective employers. The government of the foreign country and the leadership of the law firm expressly indicated that they have no objection to the proposed payment of medical expenses. The requestor provided a certified letter from the attorney general of the foreign country that represented the following:

- The requestor's decision to pay for or not to pay for this medical treatment will have no impact on any current or future decisions of the OAG in deciding on the hiring of international legal counsel.
- In the opinion of the attorney general, the payment of medical expenses for the foreign official's daughter under these circumstances would not violate any provision of the foreign country's laws.

The attorney general further confirmed that while the foreign official handles aspects of the cases on which the law firm and the requestor work, the foreign official had not taken part in any decisions regarding the law firm's retention for any matter, nor would the foreign official have such a role in any possible future decision regarding contracting outside counsel, as such decisions are outside of the foreign official's responsibilities. Finally, the foreign official represented and warranted in writing that he has not had, does not have, and will not have any influence in the contacting of international lawyers to represent the foreign country; he will not attempt to assist the requestor or the law firm in the award of future work; and he would not get involved in any decision that the OAG might make in the future in this regard.

Based upon all of the facts and circumstances, the DOJ responded it did not intend to take any enforcement action with respect to the proposed payment of approximately $13,500 to $20,500 described in the request. The facts overall suggested an absence of corrupt intent and adequate assurances that the proposed benefit to the foreign official's daughter would have no impact on the requestor's or his law firm's present or future business with the foreign country. The foreign official does not and will not play any role in the decision to award his country's legal business to the requestor's law firm. The requestor and the foreign official had informed their respective employers of the proposed gift and neither had objected. Indeed, the attorney general of the foreign country had expressly stated that the proposed gift will not affect the decision to award work to the requestor's law firm and, under the circumstances presented, is not illegal under the foreign country's laws. This is further reinforced by the foreign country's public contracting laws, which require transparent reasoning in contracting for legal work and criminally punish corrupt behavior. Finally, the requestor represented he intended to reimburse the medical provider directly, ensuring that the payments will not be improperly diverted to the foreign official.

The unique medical circumstances of this opinion release made the corrupt intent element difficult for the DOJ to establish. Further, the full disclosure of the relevant facts to the foreign country's OAG, the lack of influence of the foreign official in the award of any legal work, and the opinion of the OAG that the proposed payment was not a violation of the foreign country's laws weighed heavily in the DOJ's decision. To approve this type of humanitarian medical payment, the opinion release highlights the importance of transparency and compliance with local laws.

E.   Practical Gift Advice

The following rules of thumb or policies can minimize the risk that a gift to a non–U.S. government official may be corruptly construed:

- The nature, value, and transparency of any gift to a government official should be considered, and extravagant gifts should be avoided.
- No gifts of cash or cash equivalents such as gift cards should be given.
- No direct per diem payments to the recipient should be permitted—that is, per diem payments should be made by check to the intended recipient's employer, which may then reimburse the employee.
- No gift should be offered or given to a foreign official that violates the local written laws and regulations of the country.
- No gift should be offered or given that violates written policies of the donor company or the donee agency, department, or state-owned or state-controlled entity.
- No gift other than a modest public gift (e.g., of a value of $50 or less) should be made to a foreign official unless there is advance written disclosure of the nature, the amount, or the value and purpose of the gift to the foreign official's immediate supervisor and a clear understanding that the gift will be accurately recorded.
- Any gift to a foreign official of other than nominal value should require at least one supervisory prior approval by the donor company.
- Any gift to a foreign official should not exceed the maximum amount permitted by the company in a comparable domestic setting involving a comparable U.S. national, state, or local government official.
- Any gift to a foreign official should be accurately described in the company's books and records including the name and title of the recipient, the amount or value, the purpose, and the date of the gift.

- Gifts should be infrequent and should not establish a widespread pattern of smaller items.
- Multiple gifts should not be permitted to one recipient in a one-year period without approval of the legal department. Alternatively, a maximum combined annual limit for any recipient should be established.
- Determination of the value of the gift should be from the recipient's point of view (e.g., a $1,000 gift to a recipient who has a $9,000 annual salary).
- If returning a gift would offend the giver, have a plan or policy in place to either donate the item to charity, or to distribute it or raffle it to a large group of employees. A record of this type of disposition should be made.

The *Resource Guide* concludes with respect to gift-giving: "The FCPA does not prohibit gift-giving. Rather, just like its domestic counterparts, the FCPA prohibits the payments of bribes, including those disguised as gifts."[8]

III. TRAVEL, LODGING, AND ENTERTAINMENT

A. Affirmative Defenses

The FCPA permits companies to provide certain types of entertainment or travel to non–U.S. government officials, to the extent that the travel or entertainment expenses are (1) reasonable and bona fide, and directly related to certain marketing and contracting activities; and (2) lawful under applicable written local law. Both of these are affirmative defenses.

A company may pay for reasonable travel and lodging expenses for a foreign official that directly relate to the promotion, demonstration, or explanation of products or services, or to the execution or performance of a contract with a foreign government or agency.[9] A travel or entertainment expenditure that is lawful under the written laws and regulations of a foreign official's country similarly provides an affirmative defense under the FCPA because no written laws condone bribery; this is a rare defense but there are exceptions where it can arise. For example, foreign campaign contribution laws may permit substantial campaign contributions to a local political party or candidate and thus create a defense to an otherwise improper payment. As to the propriety of other travel and entertainment expenses not expressly covered by the FCPA, the issue is invariably whether things of value were provided to a foreign official for a corrupt purpose and to obtain or retain business or gain an improper advantage.

B. Side Trips

In connection with bona fide business trips, foreign officials often request side trips; once these are granted, it is difficult or awkward to charge or seek reimbursement from a valued customer. The *Resource Guide* offers the UTStarcom[10] example, in which a California company paid for an all-expenses-paid (side) trip with spouses to Las Vegas, where the company had no facilities.[11] In indicating that this trip is extravagant and designed to curry favor with foreign government officials, the *Resource Guide* points out that if this side trip were booked as a legitimate business expense—such as the provision of training at its facilities—the company would be in violation of the FCPA's accounting provisions, and the conduct also indicates deficiencies in the company's internal controls.[12]

C. FCPA Opinion Releases

1.   *FCPA Opinion Procedure Release 2008-03 (July 11, 2008)*

In 2008 the DOJ responded to a request submitted by Trace International, Inc., an Annapolis, Maryland–based antibribery organization. Trace had submitted a request just four days earlier, on July 7, proposing to pay for expenses (transportation, lodging, and incidentals) for 20 journalists employed by the People's Republic of China (PRC) media outlets, so that the journalists could attend a Trace Shanghai press conference. The press conference was scheduled to coincide with an international anticorruption conference at the same hotel. The journalists were "foreign officials" under the FCPA because the media outlets were owned by the PRC.

Trace requested a determination of the DOJ's present intent to bring an enforcement action against such conduct, and the department responded that it had no such intent.[13] The DOJ concluded that the stipend and expenses, as detailed by Trace, fell within the FCPA's promotional expenses affirmative defense.[14] As is customary, the DOJ limited this opinion to Trace and stated that it has no binding application on other parties. However, this opinion does afford some guidance to multinational companies doing business in China, where generous hospitality has long been a tradition, and it confirms the breadth of the DOJ's interpretation of the term "foreign official."

2.   *FCPA Opinion Procedure Release 2011-01 (June 30, 2011)*

In 2011 the DOJ reviewed an FCPA opinion procedure request of a U.S. adoption service provider that proposed to pay certain expenses for a trip to the United States by one official from each of two foreign government agencies to learn more about the requestor's adoption services. The two officials were to be selected by their agencies, without the involvement of the requestor, to travel to the United States. The sponsored program was to last for approximately two days (not including travel time). The requestor proposed to pay for economy class airfare, domestic lodging, local transport, and meals. The requestor represented, among other things, that

- It had no nonroutine business (e.g., licensing or accreditation) under consideration by the relevant foreign government agencies.
- Its routine business before the relevant foreign government agencies consisted primarily of seeking approval of pending adoptions. Such routine business is guided by international treaty and administrative rules with identified standards.
- It would not select the particular officials who would travel. That decision would be made solely by the foreign government agencies.
- It would host only the designated officials, and not their spouses or family members.
- It intended to pay all costs directly to the providers and no cash would be provided directly to the officials.

- Any souvenirs that the requestor would give the visiting officials would reflect the requestor's business and/or logo and would be of nominal value.
- Apart from the expenses identified above, the requestor would not compensate the foreign government agencies or the officials for their visit, nor would it fund, organize, or host any other entertainment, side trips, or leisure activities for the officials, or provide the officials with any stipend or spending money.
- The visit would be for a two-day period (exclusive of travel time), and costs and expenses would be only those necessary and reasonable to educate the visiting officials about the operations and services of U.S. adoption service providers.
- The requestor had invited another adoption service provider to participate in the visit.

Based upon all of the facts and circumstances, as represented by the requestor, and consistent with these prior opinions, the DOJ opined that the expenses contemplated were reasonable under the circumstances and directly related to "the promotion, demonstration, or explanation of [the requestor's] products or services"[15] and that it did not presently intend to take any enforcement action.

Especially noteworthy in this opinion release are the facts that the foreign agencies—not the foreign officials—would select who would travel; the requestor would not host spouses or family members; no cash would be provided to the officials; no side trips would be hosted; and no nonroutine business was pending. The last factor is always important but especially when the visiting foreign official is someone who can influence the award of a contract. On the other hand, if the visiting foreign official travels to observe and inspect, for example, plant facilities or R&D facilities, and to ensure that the host can perform under the contract, the trip, so long as it is reasonable in terms of expenditures and primarily confined to business, will be appropriate.

IV. TEN LEADING FCPA GIFT, TRAVEL, LODGING, AND ENTERTAINMENT CASES

Since 1977 numerous FCPA settlements have included gift, travel, and entertainment misconduct, but eight have addressed questionable gift, travel, and entertainment practices in significant detail. In 2009 the DOJ and SEC settled with UTStarcom for misconduct that primarily involved travel and entertainment abuses in connection with purported foreign government customer training in the United States. In 2010 the SEC settled with Veraz Networks alleging inter alia an improper gift of flowers to the wife of an executive. In 2011 the SEC charged IBM with inter alia improper travel and entertainment to government officials in South Korea and China. In 2014, the SEC brought two major travel and entertainment abuse cases: Timms & Ramahi and Bruker Corp., *infra*. Signally, five of the eight leading gift, travel, lodging, and entertainment cases involve China, where gift-giving has a long cultural tradition. China is also a country with a relatively large number of persons who are political party officials and persons who work for state-owned and state-controlled entities, making the conduct of their officers more subject to FCPA investigation. Finally, three of the eight leading cases involved lavish side trips.

A. *United States v. Metcalf & Eddy*[16]

In December 1999, Metcalf & Eddy, Inc., of Wakefield, Massachusetts, as successor to Metcalf & Eddy, International, Inc., agreed to a civil judgment as a result
of the payment of excessive travel and entertainment expenses for an Egyptian
government official and his family. Metcalf & Eddy had promised to pay travel,
lodging, and entertainment expenses to the chairman of the Alexandria General
Organization for Sanitary Drainage (AGOSD). In exchange the chairman, an official of the Egyptian government, would use his influence to have AGOSD support contracts between the U.S. Agency for International Development (USAID)
and Metcalf & Eddy. AGOSD was the beneficiary of these contracts. The AGOSD
chairman did not directly participate in the selection of bidders, but the contract
to operate and maintain wastewater treatment facilities managed by AGOSD was
ultimately awarded to Metcalf & Eddy. The chairman, along with his wife and two
children, traveled to the United States twice as guests of Metcalf & Eddy. The first
trip included visits to Boston, Washington, D.C., Chicago, and Disney World. The
second trip took the AGOSD chairman and his family to Paris, Boston, and San
Diego. The chairman was paid 150 percent of his estimated per diem expenses and
his airline tickets were upgraded to first class by Metcalf & Eddy. The civil judgment permanently enjoined Metcalf & Eddy from further violations of the FCPA,
and the company agreed to pay a $400,000 civil fine; no criminal charges were filed.
Further, as part of the settlement, the DOJ required Metcalf & Eddy to adopt an
11-point compliance and ethics program (detailed in chapter 10).[17]

B. U.S. DOJ–Lucent Technologies Inc. Agreement;[18]
    SEC v. Lucent Technologies Inc.[19]

In a two-year nonprosecution agreement also significant for its travel and entertainment guidance, Lucent Technologies Inc. agreed in 2007 to pay the DOJ a $1 mil-
lion fine to resolve allegations of bribery violations of the FCPA and a $1.5 million
civil penalty to the SEC. In 2002 and 2003 alone, Lucent paid for 24 presale trips for
Chinese government customers. Of these trips, at least 12 were primarily for sightseeing. Lucent spent over $1.3 million on at least 65 presale visits between 2000 and
2003. Significantly, these "business trips" were actually for entertainment purposes,
including the destinations of Disneyland and the Grand Canyon. In addition to the
fines, Lucent was required to adopt new or modify existing internal controls, policies,
and procedures with the objective of ensuring that Lucent makes and keeps true and
accurate books, records, and accounts, as well as rigorous anticorruption compliance
code standards and procedures designed to detect and deter FCPA violations and
other applicable anticorruption laws.

C. U.S. DOJ–UTStarcom Inc. Agreement; *SEC v. UTStarcom*

In December 2009 UTStarcom Inc. (UTSI) entered into a nonprosecution agreement with the DOJ (*United States v. UTStarcom, Inc.*),[20] agreeing to pay a $1.5 mil-
lion fine for violations of the FCPA by providing travel and other things of value
to foreign officials, specifically employees at state-owned telecommunications

companies in the PRC. The same day, the SEC obtained a $1.5 million penalty and permanent injunctive relief (*SEC v. UTStarcom*).[21] UTSI, a publicly traded Delaware-based corporation headquartered in California, is a global telecommunications company that designs, manufactures, and sells network equipment and handsets and has historically done most of its business in China with government-controlled municipal and provincial telecommunications companies through its wholly owned subsidiary UTStarcom China, Co. Ltd. (UTS-China). Most of the alleged misconduct specifically involved travel and entertainment abuses.

The SEC alleged that UTStarcom's wholly owned subsidiary in China paid nearly $7 million between 2002 and 2007 for hundreds of overseas trips by employees of Chinese government-controlled telecommunications companies that were customers of UTStarcom, purportedly to provide customer training. It is part of UTS-China's standard practice to include as part of its internal sales contracts for wireless networks a provision for UTS-China to pay for some of the customer's employees to attend the purported training overseas after installation of the network. In reality, the trips were entirely or primarily for sightseeing at popular tourist destinations in the United States, including Hawaii, Las Vegas, and New York City. Most trips lasted two weeks and cost $5,000 per customer employee. Further, the trips were supposed to be for training at UTSI training facilities when UTSI had no training facilities at the purported training locations and conducted no training.

The SEC also alleged that on at least seven occasions between 2002 and 2004, UTSI paid for executive training programs at U.S. universities that were attended by managers and other employees of government customers in China. The programs covered general management topics and were not specifically related to UTSI's products or business. UTSI paid for all expenses associated with the program, which totaled more than $4 million and included travel, tuition, room and board, field trips to tourist destinations, and a cash allowance of between $800 and $3,000 per person. UTSI accounted for the cost of the programs as "marketing expenses." The company's senior management believed that the executive training programs helped it obtain or retain business.

As part of the travel and entertainment abuses, the SEC alleged that in 2004, UTSI submitted a bid for a sales contract to a government-controlled telecommunications company in Thailand. While its bid was under consideration, UTSI's general manager in Thailand spent nearly $10,000 on French wine as a gift to agents of the government, including rare bottles that cost more than $600 each. The manager also spent $13,000 for entertainment expenses to secure the same contract. UTSI's then chief executive officer and executive vice president of UTS-China approved the payments. UTSI reimbursed the expenditures and accounted for them as marketing expenses.

The UTStarcom case highlights the not uncommon travel and entertainment expenses associated with service contracts, product inspection, and training where foreign customers of state-owned or state-controlled entities visit U.S. manufacturers or service companies and request or are offered side trips, car allowances, and sometimes expensive entertainment. In some cases the visits become annual excursions or junkets that not only result in improper payments or the improper provision of things of value to obtain and retain business, but lead to voluminous false books-and-records violations. The purposes of these trips must be consistent with the limited exceptions permitted under the FCPA (e.g., directly related to the promotion, demonstration, or explanation of products or services or the execution or performance of a contract), and books-and-records entities for such trips must be scrupulously accurate.

D. *SEC v. Veraz Networks, Inc.*[22]

In June 2010 the SEC settled with San Jose, California–based telecommunications company Veraz Networks, Inc., for alleged violations of FCPA books-and-records and internal controls provisions. The alleged violations stemmed from improper payments and gifts made by Veraz to foreign officials in China and Vietnam after the company went public in 2007. Veraz was ordered to pay a penalty of $300,000 and consented to an order granting injunctive relief.

The SEC alleged that Veraz engaged a consultant in China who in 2007 and 2008 gave gifts and offered improper payments together valued at approximately $40,000 to officials at a government-controlled telecommunications company in China in an attempt to win business for Veraz. A Veraz supervisor who approved the gifts described them in an internal Veraz e-mail as the "gift scheme." Specifically, in late 2007, Veraz's consultant in China provided approximately $4,500 worth of gifts to officials at a telecommunications company in an attempt to secure a business deal for Veraz. The consultant requested that his Veraz supervisor approve the funding for those gifts via e-mail. The supervisor approved the gift scheme in an e-mail.

In January 2008, the consultant offered a separate improper payment to officials at the same telecommunications company to secure a deal valued at $233,000. The fee was described as a "consultant fee" and was set at approximately $35,000. The telecommunications company awarded the contract to Veraz, even though Veraz's bid was higher than other bids. Veraz discovered the improper offer of payment prior to receiving any money from the transaction and canceled the sale.

The SEC alleged that in 2007 and 2008, a Veraz employee made improper payments to the CEO of a government-controlled telecommunications company in Vietnam through a Singapore reseller in order to win business for Veraz. Veraz approved and reimbursed its employee for questionable expenses related to the telecom, including gifts and entertainment for telecom employees and flowers for the wife of the CEO. The Veraz gift allegations—down to the detail of giving flowers for an executive's wife—represent an extreme SEC charging example and would not by themselves have likely resulted in an enforcement action. Still, the case demonstrates that the SEC will charge even minor gift abuses if they are part of a scheme.

E. *SEC v. IBM Corp.*[23]

In March 2011, the SEC charged IBM with violating the books-and-records and internal controls provisions of the FCPA as a result of the provision of improper cash payments, gifts, and travel and entertainment to government officials in South Korea and China. IBM agreed to pay disgorgement of $5.3 million, $2.7 million in prejudgment interest, and a $2 million civil penalty. The amount of business IBM obtained as a result of improper payments, the fact that there were reports in the South Korean press of much larger improper payments, and the fact that the company had been the subject of an SEC FCPA enforcement action in 2000 for bribes in Argentina likely led to the substantial combined fine of $10 million.

While the South Korean improper payments and gifts were fairly typical (e.g., cash, free cameras, computers, and computer equipment), the Chinese improper travel and entertainment allegations address less classic issues that multinationals frequently face. The SEC complaint alleges that from at least 2004 to early 2009, employees of IBM (China) Investment Company Limited and IBM Global Services (China) Co., Ltd. (collectively, IBM-China), both wholly owned IBM subsidiaries, engaged in a widespread practice of providing overseas trips, entertainment, and improper gifts to Chinese government officials.

IBM-China entered into contractual agreements with government-owned or -controlled customers in China for hardware, software, and other services. The contracts contained provisions requiring IBM-China to provide training to customer employees. In some cases, IBM held this training off site and required the customers to travel. In advance of training, IBM-China employees were required to submit a delegation trip request (DTR). IBM-China's policies required customers to pay for side trips and stopovers unrelated to training and for IBM-China managers to approve all DTRs.

The SEC alleged that over a six-year period IBM's internal controls failed to detect at least 114 instances in which (1) IBM employees and its local travel agency worked together to create fake invoices to match approved DTRs; (2) trips were not connected to any DTRs; (3) trips involved unapproved sightseeing itineraries for Chinese government employees; (4) trips had little or no business content; (5) trips involved one or more deviations from the approved DTR; and (6) trips were per diem payments and were provided to Chinese government officials.

IBM-China also used its official travel agency in China to funnel money that was approved for legitimate business trips to fund unapproved trips. IBM-China personnel utilized the company's procurement process to designate its preferred travel agents as "authorized training providers." IBM-China personnel then submitted fraudulent purchase requests for "training services" from those "authorized training providers" and caused IBM-China to pay these vendors. The money paid to these vendors was used to pay for unapproved trips by Chinese government employees.

The IBM enforcement action confirms that the SEC will look closely at customer travel and entertainment protocols, subsidiaries, customer training, funding and content, and related audits. Counsel may wish to consider the following advice:

- Companies must have and follow a clear protocol for approving customer travel to avail themselves of the FCPA's affirmative defense of a payment or thing of value that was a reasonable and bona fide expenditure, such as travel and lodging expenses, incurred by or on behalf of a foreign official that was directly related to the promotion, demonstration, or explanation of products or services.
- Companies have to make sure in advance that any customer training or product or service promotion, demonstration, and explanation events have real content.

- Companies need to vet and examine the relationship and possibly the disbursements of their preferred travel agencies (at a minimum, they should insist upon itemized statements from the travel agencies).
- Companies should, in contractual agreements or correspondence, share their ethics and compliance values and commitments with preferred travel providers.
- Customer trips should not vary from the planned itineraries unless there are prepayments of the same by customers.
- Per diem payments present clear opportunities for abuse and should be avoided whenever possible.
- Sightseeing trips, if any, should be modest.
- Foreign managers should be provided, as part of regular anticorruption training, the IBM customer training and entertainment scenarios described above so they understand the very real risks and costs of missteps.
- Foreign managers should be randomly interviewed about their customer travel practices and policies as the SEC and DOJ plainly view this as a ripe enforcement area.
- Internal audit departments should periodically review customer travel expenses, including adherence to protocols, requisite approvals, side trip policies or reimbursement, extravagant entertainment, and travel agency relationships.

F. *United States v. Diebold;*[24] *SEC v. Diebold*[25]

In October 2013, Diebold, an Ohio-based provider of integrated self-service delivery and security systems, including automated teller machines (ATMs), agreed to pay a $25.2 million annual penalty to resolve DOJ allegations that it violated the FCPA by bribing government officials in China and Indonesia and falsifying records in Russia in order to obtain and retain contracts to provide ATMs to state-owned and private banks in those countries. The company also agreed to pay the SEC $22.97 million in disgorgement and prejudgment interest for the same notations.

With respect to China and Indonesia, the court documents alleged that from 2005 to 2010, in order to secure and retain business with bank customers, including state-owned and -controlled banks, Diebold repeatedly provided things of value, including payments, gifts, and nonbusiness travel for employees of the banks, totaling approximately $1.75 million. Diebold's subsidiary in China provided government officials with annual [company] gifts ranging from less than $100 to more than $600. Officials also were treated to European vacations. For example, eight officials at a government-owned bank in China enjoyed a two-week trip at Diebold's expense that included stays in Paris, Brussels, Amsterdam, Cologne, Frankfurt, Munich, Salzburg, Vienna, Klagenfurt, Venice, Florence, and Rome. Destinations of leisure trips for other officials included Australia, Bali, and New Zealand. In total, Diebold spent approximately $1.6 million to bribe government-owned bank officials in China, and more than $147,000 to bribe officials at government banks in Indonesia. Among the tourist destinations of U.S. trips were the Grand Canyon, Napa Valley, Disneyland, and Universal Studios, as well as Las Vegas, New York City, Chicago, and Washington, D.C. Diebold attempted to disguise the payments and benefits through various means, including by making payments through third parties designated by the banks and by inaccurately recording leisure trips for bank employees as "training." Diebold is a textbook example of improper lavish entertainment of state-owned entities.

G. *In re* Timms & Ramahi[26]

In November 2014, the SEC settled FCPA travel and entertainment charges with Stephen Timms and Yasser Ramahi, two former managers of FLIR Systems Inc., a publicly traded Oregon-based defense contractor. Timms and Ramahi had worked in sales in the Dubai office of FLIR, the world's largest commercial company specializing in the design and production of thermal imaging, night vision, and infrared camera and sensor systems. They violated the FCPA by taking government officials in Saudi Arabia on a "world tour" to help secure business for the company. The two employees later falsified records in an attempt to hide their misconduct. Timms and Ramahi agreed to settle the SEC's charges and pay financial penalties.

According to the SEC's order instituting a settled administrative proceeding, FLIR entered into a multimillion-dollar contract to provide thermal binoculars to the Saudi government in November 2008. Timms and Ramahi were the primary sales employees responsible for the contract, and also were involved in negotiations to sell FLIR's security cameras to the same government officials. At the time, Timms was the head of FLIR's Middle East office in Dubai and Ramahi reported to him. The SEC's order found that Timms and Ramahi traveled to Saudi Arabia in March 2009 and provided five officials with luxury watches during meetings to discuss several business opportunities. Timms and Ramahi believed these officials were important to sales of both the binoculars and the security cameras. A few months later, they arranged for key officials, including two who received watches, to embark on what Timms referred to as a "world tour" of personal travel before and after they visited FLIR's Boston facilities for a factory equipment inspection that was a key condition to fulfillment of the contract. The officials traveled for 20 nights with stops in Casablanca, Paris, Dubai, Beirut, and New York City. There was no business purpose for the stops outside of Boston, and the airfare and hotel accommodations were paid for by FLIR. Prior to providing the gifts and travel to the Saudi Arabian officials, Ramahi and Timms each had taken FCPA training at the company that specifically identified luxury watches and side trips as prohibited gifts.

When FLIR's finance department flagged the expense reimbursement request for the watches during an unrelated review of expenses in the Dubai office and questioned the $7,000 cost, Timms and Ramahi obtained a second, fabricated invoice showing a cost of 7,000 Saudi riyal (approximately $1,900) instead of the true cost of $7,000. They directed FLIR's local third-party agent to provide false information to the company to back up their story that the original submission was merely a mistake. Ramahi and Timms also falsely claimed that FLIR's payment for the world tour had been a billing mistake by FLIR's travel agent, and again used false documentation and FLIR's third-party agent to bolster their cover-up efforts.

Timms and Ramahi are U.S. citizens who reside in Thailand and the United Arab Emirates, respectively. The SEC's order found that they violated the antibribery provisions of section 30A of the Securities Exchange Act of 1934 and the internal controls and false records provisions of section 13(b)(5) and rule 13b2-1 of the Exchange Act. The SEC's order further found that Timms and Ramahi caused

FLIR's violations of the books-and-records provisions of section 13(b)(2)(A) of the Exchange Act. Timms and Ramahi consented to the entry of the order and agreed to pay financial penalties of $50,000 and $20,000 respectively.

H.   *In re* Bruker Corp.[27]

In December 2014, the SEC charged Bruker Corporation, a global manufacturer of scientific instruments, with violating the FCPA by providing non-business-related travel and improper payments to various Chinese government officials in an effort to win business. The SEC investigation found that the company lacked sufficient internal controls to prevent and detect approximately $230,000 in improper payments out of its China-based offices that falsely recorded them in books and records as legitimate business and marketing expenses.[28] (See fuller discussion in chapter 10.)

Improper payments involved *inter alia* reimbursements to Chinese government officials for leisure travel to Austria, Czech Republic, Italy, Norway, Sweden, France, Germany, Switzerland, and the United States. These officials often were responsible for authorizing the purchase of Bruker products, and the leisure trips typically followed business-related travel for the officials funded by the company. For example, Bruker paid for the purported training expenses of a Chinese government official who signed the sales contract on behalf of a state-owned entity, but the payment actually was reimbursement for sightseeing, tour tickets, shopping, and other leisure activities in Frankfurt and Paris. Bruker also funded some trips for Chinese government officials that had no legitimate business component. For example, two Chinese government officials received paid travel to New York despite the lack of any Bruker facilities there, and also to Los Angeles where they engaged in sightseeing activities.[29]

The SEC found that Bruker failed to adequately monitor and supervise the senior executives at its China Offices to ensure that they enforced anticorruption policies or kept accurate records concerning payments to Chinese government officials. The Bruker China Offices had no independent compliance staff or an internal audit function that had authority to intervene into management decisions and, if appropriate, take remedial actions. Bruker also failed to tailor its preapproval processes for conditions in China, instead allowing the Bruker China Offices approval over items such as nonemployee travel and changes to contracts. As a result, senior employees of the Bruker China Offices had unsupervised control over the compliance process; these employees in turn abused their privileges, approving suspect payments to Chinese government officials for non-business-related travel and for purported collaboration agreements.[30] Bruker highlights the clear dangers of side trips that often start as modest in plan but grow quickly into very expensive junkets. To the extent foreign officials—either traditional government officials or officers of state-owned entities—travel to corporate headquarters or plants for product or services demonstrations or inspections, companies should be clear and insist at the outset that their visitors fully pay for side trips and sightseeing.

I.   *United States v. Avon Products, Inc.*[31]

In December 2014, Avon Products (China) Co. Ltd., a wholly owned Chinese subsidiary of issuer Avon Products, Inc., pled guilty to conspiring to violate the FCPA's accounting provisions to conceal $8 million in gifts, cash, and nonbusiness travel and entertainment it gave to Chinese government officials. Because the Avon misconduct was so widespread and the People's Republic of China has increasingly presented FCPA gifts, cash, and travel and entertainment challenges, we now detail portions of the FCPA allegations to highlight potential minefields.[32]

From 2004 through September 2008, Avon China, acting through certain executives and employees, disguised on its books and records over $8 million in things of value, including gifts, cash, and nonbusiness travel, meals, and entertainment, which it gave to Chinese government officials in order to obtain and retain business benefits for Avon China. During this period Avon China executives and employees falsely described the nature and purpose of numerous transactions on Avon China's books and records, in part because they believed that Chinese government officials did not want a paper trail reflecting their acceptance of money, gifts, travel, entertainment, and other things of value from Avon China executives and employees. The executives and employees also knew that, contrary to how the expenses were being described in Avon China's books and records, the expenses were not incurred for legitimate business purposes.

To conceal its executives' and employees' practice of giving things of value to Chinese government officials, Avon China executives and employees intentionally falsified transactions on the subsidiary's books and records by, among other things, falsely describing expenses related to government officials as employee-related or falsely describing the nature or purpose of, or participants associated with, such expenses in order to conceal that the expenses related to government officials or that there were expectations of benefits from government officials. Additionally, the subsidiary's executives and employees intentionally falsified the books and records by falsely recording payments to a consulting company as payments for legitimate services, notwithstanding the fact that an Avon China executive knew the consulting company's invoices were often false and that no Avon China executives or employees knew of any legitimate services being provided by the consulting company.

High-level executives, attorneys, and internal auditors at the parent company learned that executives and employees of Avon China had in the past routinely provided things of value to Chinese government officials and failed to properly document it. Instead of ensuring the practice was halted, disciplining culpable individuals, and implementing appropriate controls at Avon and Avon China, parent company executives and employees, in conjunction with Avon China executives and employees, concealed significant concerns raised about the accuracy of the subsidiary's books and records and its practice of giving things of value to government officials. These Avon and Avon China executives and employees, knowing that the subsidiary's books and records would continue to be inaccurate if steps were not taken to correct improper conduct at the subsidiary, failed to take steps to correct such actions, despite knowing that Avon China's books and records were consolidated into the parent company's books and records.

1. Gifts for Government Officials

Avon China executives and employees intentionally falsified the books and records related to gifts given to Chinese government officials, including products and personal luxury items such as designer wallets, bags, and watches, to obtain benefits from government officials, such as obtaining and retaining the direct selling license and requisite provincial and local approvals, avoiding fines, avoiding negative media reports, obtaining favorable judicial treatment, and obtaining government approval to sell nutritional supplements and healthcare apparel products, via direct selling, that did not meet or had yet to meet government standards. At various times, the China subsidiary's executives and employees concealed in its books and records the actual purposes of the gifts, the identity of the recipients, or the price per gift. Also, they, at various times, falsely described the gifts, including describing them as employee travel and entertainment, "samples," or "public relations business entertainment." They did so in order to conceal that gifts were given to government officials with an expectation of receiving a business benefit. For example, Avon China employees falsely or misleadingly described gifts as follows:

- In 2006, Avon China employees falsely described approximately $890 of "gifts" for government officials as an "entertainment" expense, and omitted from the records the recipient of the gifts and the purpose of the gifts.
- In March 2008, Avon China employees inaccurately described an approximately $960 gift purchased from Louis Vuitton for a government official as a "public relations entertainment" expense, and omitted from the records the recipient of the gift and the purpose of the gift.
- In July 2008, Avon China employees falsely described an approximately $800 Gucci bag given to a government official as a "business entertainment" expense, and omitted from the records the recipient of the bag and the purpose of the gift.
- In July 2008, Avon China employees falsely described an approximately $460 gift from Louis Vuitton for a government official as a "public relation business entertainment" expense, and omitted from the records the recipient of the gift and the purpose of the gift.

2. Meals and Entertainment

Beginning in August 2005, two Avon China executives created a "Direct Selling Special Task Force," which was composed primarily of employees from the Corporate Affairs Group, whose task was to obtain local and provincial direct selling approvals for Avon China through "relations," which was a term the subsidiary's personnel used to refer to things of value provided to government officials or goodwill that had been obtained by giving such things, including nonbusiness meals and entertainment.

Members of the Direct Selling Special Task Force and other Avon China executives and employees intentionally concealed improper meal and entertainment expenses in Avon China's books and records by (1) intentionally omitting reference to the participation of government officials in order to conceal their participation, using descriptions like "business entertainment," "public relation entertainment," or no description at all; or (2) revealing the participation of government officials but intentionally describing the event inaccurately by omitting the identity or number of officials, the cost of the event, or the true purpose of the event.

As a result, meal and entertainment expenses for government officials were falsely or misleadingly described on Avon China's books, including the following expenses:

- In 2006, Avon China employees falsely described as "sales-business entertainment" approximately $8,100 an Avon China executive spent on meals and entertainment provided to government officials in order to obtain government approval to sell a healthcare apparel product that did not meet government standards.
- In January 2008, Avon China employees falsely described as "business entertainment" and employee "accommodation" approximately $3,206 spent on meals, entertainment, and lodging for government officials.

3. *Travel* for *Government Officials*

Avon China executives and employees caused Avon China to pay for travel expenses for government officials, and sometimes their families, in order to obtain improper business benefits. To conceal the true nature of these expenses, these executives and employees intentionally omitted from or concealed in Avon China's records the names of the government officials, the fact that the travelers were government officials or relatives of government officials, and, at times, the number of travelers.

Avon China executives and employees also intentionally falsified in Avon China's books and records the purpose of the travel, which often was for personal, not legitimate business, purposes. For example, Avon China employees described personal trips for government officials (and occasionally their spouses and children) as "study trips" or "site visits" when the officials were instead sightseeing or taking a beach vacation.

As a result, nonbusiness travel expenses for government officials were falsely or misleadingly described on the books of Avon China, including the following expenses:

- In December 2005, Corporate Affairs Group employees sought approval to take six officials from the Guangdong Food and Drug Administration with responsibility for approving Avon China's healthcare products for sale, to the United States, purportedly for a "site visit/study visit" to Avon's headquarters in New York City and its research and development facility in upstate New York.
- In September 2006, Avon China employees falsely described the approximately $90,000 Avon China spent on a trip for four of those officials in Avon China's books and records as a business-related site visit and study trip for Chinese government officials, notwithstanding the fact that the officials never visited Avon's headquarters, spent only one morning at Avon's research and development facility, and spent the rest of the 18-day trip sightseeing and being entertained by an Avon China employee in New York, Vancouver, Montreal, Ottawa, Toronto, Philadelphia, Seattle, Las Vegas, Los Angeles, Hawaii, and Washington, D.C.

- In January 2008, Avon China employees falsely described in Avon China's books and records as a "site visit to Guangzhou" for "3 AIC [Administration for Industry and Commerce] officials" approximately $1,200 worth of expenses associated with a personal trip Avon China provided to a government official and the official's spouse and child to Guangzhou and Macau. The same month, Avon China employees falsely described in Avon China's books and records as "site visit/inspection" expenses approximately $15,400 Avon China paid for government officials to travel to Guangzhou, Shenzhen, and Sanya notwithstanding the fact that the underlying records include charges for a tour guide, sightseeing van, and items purchased at the beach.
- In February 2008, Avon China employees falsely described in Avon China's books and records as "business entertainment" approximately $11,000 Avon China paid for separate trips for two government officials who oversaw Avon China's activities in the Shaanxi Province (and no Avon China employees) to take personal trips to celebrate the Chinese New Year—one a nine-day personal trip to Hainan Island and the other a 12-day personal trip that included stays in Hong Kong and Macau.

4. *Cash for Government Officials*

Avon China executives and employees also gave cash to government officials and falsified Avon China's records to conceal the true recipient of and purpose for the money. In large part, these employees accomplished this by submitting for reimbursement meal or entertainment receipts given to them by government officials and falsely claiming that the receipts reflected employee business expenses. In truth, the employees had no such expenses, and the receipts were used to obtain cash to make payments to government officials. On occasion, employees would falsely submit receipts for multiple meals on the same date, none of which the employees had actually attended.

In other instances, Avon Corporate Affairs Group employees and other Avon China executives and employees gave cash to government officials in order to obtain business benefits for Avon China and falsely reported the payments as fine payments. Avon China executives and employees also made payments to organizations designated by government officials in order to obtain business benefits for Avon China and intentionally omitted from Avon China's records the true purpose of the payments.

Due to these practices, from in or around 2004 through in or around September 2008, cash given to government officials was falsely or misleadingly described on the books and records of Avon China.

For example, Avon China employees falsely or misleadingly described the following cash payments to government officials:

a.   Cash to Avoid a Fine

On August 16, 2006, an Avon China executive approved a request from a Corporate Affairs Group employee to send RMB 100,000 (approximately $12,000) to a government official's bank account to avoid a fine for violating China's direct selling regulations. The same day, to support the request for a RMB 100,000 payment to a government official, the requesting Corporate Affairs Group employee submitted a handwritten certificate, purportedly from a Chinese government agency, falsely stating that the official would give the funds to the government bureau. The next day, an Avon China employee caused RMB 100,000 to be wired in three separate wires to the government official's personal bank account. In the month of August 2006, an Avon China finance employee sent an e-mail to an Avon China employee, who forwarded it to the above-mentioned Avon China executive, stating that "the company paid RMB 100,000 to [the Chinese government official] as compensation payment and now we need to enter it into the book." In late August, notwithstanding that the Avon China finance employees knew the payment to the government official was "compensation," they recorded the payment in the "management expenses—government relations expenses" account as a legitimate payment related to "issue of AIC [Administration for Industry and Commerce] in [] county of [] province."

b.   Sponsorship to Avoid a Negative Media Article

In December 2006 an Avon China executive expressed concern to the Corporate Affairs Group that an article that a leading government-owned newspaper intended to run about Avon China improperly recruiting sales associates could cause Avon China to lose a direct selling license. To convince the newspaper not to run the article, a Corporate Affairs Group employee caused Avon China to pay approximately RMB 620,000 (approximately $77,500) to become a "sponsor" of the paper at the request of a government official at the paper who was in charge of determining whether the potential article would run and who may have received a commission on monies received from sponsors. A Corporate Affairs Group employee circulated an internal e-mail regarding the potential newspaper article, noting that the "the story alerted us to re-consider to invest more time and efforts on building key medium's relationship. [The paper] is the one with responsibility to submit confidential memo to the State Counsel and release media story to public as well."

While Avon represents an alarming array of company travel and entertainment abuses in China, counsel should not dismiss it outright as an extreme example. Each of the above factual scenarios can arise for multinationals doing business in China.

J.   Other FCPA Gift, Travel, Lodging, and Entertainment Cases

While the above ten cases have a particular focus on gift, travel, lodging, and entertainment abuses, there are other significant FCPA cases, including Siemens AG, Daimler AG, Avery Dennison Corp., Paradigm, Schnitzer Steel, and Johnson & Johnson, that alleged other serious misconduct but also bear reading and study for gift, travel, lodging, and entertainment abuses and guidance. (See chapter 10.)

In 2014, the People's Republic of China charged British pharmaceutical giant GlaxoSmithKline with wide-scale bribery to allow the company to sell its products for higher prices, and imposed a $497 million fine—the largest ever in the PRC. Central to the scheme was the use of travel agencies to launder money and funnel bribes to doctors, hospitals, and medical associations.[33] (See chapter 3, section V.D.) Travel agencies in China have long been viewed as potential money laundering vehicles.

V. BOOKS AND RECORDS AND INTERNAL CONTROLS

All gifts, travel, lodging, and entertainment for foreign officials must be accurately and timely recorded in the books and records of the company. Expense vouchers should accurately relate the date, event, amount, recipient, title, and attendees and should be no less rigorously enforced than for vouchers submitted in the company's domestic operations. If an officer or employee who intends to make a gift or host a foreign official is reluctant to accurately record the event or transaction in a company's or subsidiary's books and records, that may be an indication that the gift or entertainment is problematic. The more thoughtful and custom-made the FCPA policies and procedures for companies operating in challenging countries are, the better such companies are able to withstand a "failure to maintain adequate internal controls" investigation by the SEC or DOJ.

VI. EFFECTIVE GIFT, TRAVEL, LODGING, AND ENTERTAINMENT COMPLIANCE PROGRAMS

A. General

There are "no formulaic requirements regarding compliance programs."[34] In drafting FCPA or anticorruption policies, a company should consider the corruption reputation of the countries in which it does business; the customs and practices of the countries where it operates; the local laws of the countries; and the likely gift, travel, lodging, and entertainment situations that its employees face abroad in order to ensure that policies provide employees practical real-world guidance. For example, if a company is in an industry that offers customers substantial entertainment (e.g., golf, hunting trips, sporting events), conducts business in countries where there are widespread gift traditions (e.g., red packets in China), or has operations in countries where there are substantial cash economies (e.g., Nigeria), the FCPA policies should be tailored to address these practices and issues in a forthright, practical fashion. Prudent companies will retain experienced FCPA counsel to vet FCPA policies, practices, and gift, travel, lodging, and entertainment issues and in some instances to conduct live training of international managers with examples of gift, travel, and entertainment violations from DOJ and SEC FCPA resolutions.

A multinational compliance program that is simply left to the "good judgment" or "common sense" of employees from different cultures or local companies is in most circumstances not adequate. Custom FCPA policies offer the additional benefit of giving foreign-based employees and foreign nationals who face awkward circumstances an "out"—something in writing that explains to potential "donees" why a gift or donation is not appropriate and cannot be made under a clear company policy. Under no circumstances should in-house counsel simply "cut and paste" other companies' FCPA policies, procedures, or forms.

B. Sensitivity to Red Flags

In all gift, travel, lodging, and entertainment situations, a company, its officers, and its employees must remain mindful of traditional FCPA red flags, including the following:

- The country in which the gift or hospitality taking place has a reputation for significant corruption under the Transparency International Index (or ranking of a similar organization) and/or has seen its corruption ranking worsen, for example, PRC in 2014.
- A foreign bank account or foreign bank is involved in any way.
- A relative of the intended recipient is a foreign government official, foreign political party representative, or foreign political candidate.
- There has been suspicious conversation or behavior (e.g., "The Minister will need an advance in the amount of $15,000, and his staff will handle travel details and payments"; "A $25,000 diamond necklace is insignificant in value compared to His Excellency's fortune/net worth/annual income"; "There are no direct commercial flights available from Dubai to Miami").
- An intended recipient has requested inappropriate things of value in connection with this event or in the past (e.g., "Our chief of state has customarily been given a Rolex by business visitors and his office would be demeaned if your good company does not recognize his Office and high position with an appropriate goodwill gesture"; "The Deputy always has her family and staff travel with her, and they will all of course require an advance per diem").
- An intended recipient is unwilling or unable to obtain prior written approval for a gift, travel, or entertainment from his or her government or agency.
- A proposed trip "directly related to the promotion, demonstration, or explanation of products or services" is dominated by sightseeing and other side trips.

C. Gifts, Hospitality, and Travel Compliance Guidance

In April 2011, the DOJ, as part of a deferred prosecution agreement (DPA) with Johnson & Johnson, required enhanced gifts, hospitality, and travel guidance; the company agreed to institute gift, hospitality, and travel policies in each jurisdiction that were appropriately designed to prevent violations of the anticorruption laws and regulations. At a minimum, said the DOJ, these policies must contain the following restrictions regarding government officials:

- Gifts must be modest in value, appropriate under the circumstances, and given in accordance with anticorruption laws and regulations, including those of the government official's home country.
- Hospitality shall be limited to reasonably priced meals, accommodations, and incidental expenses that are part of product education and training programs, professional training, and conferences or board meetings.

The Johnson & Johnson DPA is especially important reading and guidance for companies in the pharmaceutical and medical products industry.

D. Emergency Circumstances

There are invariably short-notice or emergency circumstances where a host officer or employee is unable to secure the requisite prior written approval of a gift, travel, or entertainment expense under company policies. These situations are best addressed by policies that require the donor officer or employee to notify the legal department in writing within a certain time (e.g., 72 hours) of the offer of any gift, travel, lodging, or entertainment or face serious disciplinary action for failure to do so.

E. Tiered Authorizations

Many multinational companies employ a multitiered authorization system for approving gifts, travel, lodging, and entertainment. For example, a one-time gift with a value of $100 or less to a nongovernment official requires no approval; gifts with a value of $100 to $400 may require one supervisory authorization; gifts exceeding $400 in value require two supervisory authorizations; and gifts above $1,000 in value require prior legal department approval. Some companies have separate policies for government officials. Tiered authorization systems for gifts, travel, lodging, or entertainment purposes should require advance written approval for any significant levels.

F. Request Forms and Questionnaires

A request for a travel or entertainment expenditure will routinely require the names, titles, and employers of those attending or traveling to an event; the destination(s) and starting and ending dates of the events or travel; and the anticipated expenditures in detail (flights, rental cars, hotels, and entertainment costs).

The *Avon* resolution lists in detail how expense reports were inadequate and violative of the FCPA. State-of-the-art compliance programs will in addition list questions that make the requestor consider antibribery compliance and issues. For example, Baker Hughes's guidelines for travel and entertainment of a non–U.S. government official contain the following questions:

- Why was the particular venue or destination chosen?
- Is there a contract with a government entity that requires the proposed expenditure?
- Is the purpose of the proposed expenditure for training?
- Please explain in detail the purpose and business justification for this proposed expenditure.
- Have any of the proposed guests or travelers been entertained or traveled at the company's expense before? If so, please provide the details below.
- Is there any additional relevant information relating to the proposed expenditures that has not been discussed in this form?
- Are there any stopovers en route (other than stopovers of less than one day necessary to make an airline or other transportation connections) or indirect routing of transportation?
- Signature and details of person requesting expenditures.
- Approval signatures.

This type of request-form procedure will often discourage requests for travel or entertainment that are problematic under the FCPA.

G. No-Reimbursement Policy

Some companies employ firm expense account policies whereby employee reimbursement claims for which advance approval or detailed information was required but not provided are rejected and the employee is required to personally pay all expenses. It is remarkable how a multinational company with a firm policy of no reimbursement for inadequately detailed or non-preapproved expenses will find that sales employees and others soon begin to follow expense account requirements.

H. Training

Annual FCPA training is recommended for appropriate personnel (e.g., sales personnel, controllers, regional country managers, financial officers, internal audit staff, and accounting personnel) of a company that does business regularly with foreign governments, has joint ventures with foreign governments, or employs expatriate personnel who regularly interface with foreign government employees (e.g., immigration, environmental, customs, tax)—in short, multinational companies that have foreign sales or manufacturing operations. Live, quality training of sales personnel in particular can educate them before problematic promises or offers are made and have to be reversed. FCPA training is particularly critical for foreign employees who are not U.S. citizens, who speak a language other than English, or who are not familiar with U.S. laws. Annual FCPA training will address gifts, travel, lodging, and entertainment and include any recent FCPA opinions or relevant DOJ or SEC enforcement actions or policy statements. All ethics and FCPA training must emphasize the importance of accurate books and records and timely notification of appropriate personnel of suspicious conduct or transactions.

In its April 2011 DPA with Johnson & Johnson, the DOJ required enhanced training obligations, to wit:

- Annual training on anticorruption laws and regulations to directors, officers, executives, and employees who could present corruption risk to J&J;
- Enhanced and in-depth FCPA training for all internal audit, financial, and legal personnel involved in FCPA audits, due diligence reviews, and acquisition of new businesses; and
- Training as necessary based on risk profiles to relevant third parties acting on the company's behalf that may interact with government officials at least once every three years.

Training remains a critical compliance component for the DOJ and represents a fairly easy way for a company to demonstrate its anticorruption commitment and arguably avoid a corporate enforcement proceeding. The 2014 SEC enforcement action against two wayward FLIR salesmen, Stephen Timms and Yasser Rahami, as opposed to FLIR Systems itself, may have been the result of the company having trained the salesmen twice before their transgressions and having had a code of conduct in place that prohibited their misconduct.

VII. PRACTICAL TRAVEL, LODGING, AND ENTERTAINMENT ADVICE

Rules of thumb or policies for travel, lodging, and entertainment of non–U.S. government officials may include the following:

- All travel, lodging, and entertainment expenses must be accurately reported.
- All travel, lodging, and entertainment expenses must be "reasonable and necessary"—and not lavish or extravagant.
- All lodging should be in economy or business-class hotels and not in first-class hotels.
- No general advancement of travel, lodging, and entertainment expenses should be permitted (e.g., the company should provide a nonexchangeable transportation ticket to the foreign government and not a cash advance to a government official).
- No travel, lodging, or entertainment expenses should exceed the amounts under the donor company's corresponding written domestic travel, lodging, and entertainment policy for customers (e.g., the donor company should not host guests in a manner more lavish than it hosts comparable personnel at the parent company).
- No travel, lodging, or entertainment should be extended to a foreign government official in a position to award or influence an award without legal department written preapproval.
- No travel, lodging, or entertainment should be extended for events that are not completely or substantially business-related.
- To avail itself of the affirmative defense of reasonable travel and lodging expenses directly related to the promotion, demonstration, and explanation of products or services, a company should require and maintain records of agendas, PowerPoint training or demonstrations, technical or explanatory papers, and attendance sheets.
- No travel, lodging, or entertainment should be offered or provided that violates the local laws of the foreign country or the internal policies and regulations of the recipient's employer.
- No travel, lodging, or entertainment should be provided to a foreign government official recipient's spouse, significant other, or family members that is not promptly and accurately reimbursed.
- Daily incidental expenses should be supported with receipts.
- No travel, lodging, or entertainment should be offered for a trip whose purpose could be equally accomplished in the official's own country.
- No side travel, lodging, or entertainment for the foreign official to another city, resort, or entertainment venue (e.g., Paris, Las Vegas, Disney World) should be allowed or permitted absent appropriate and timely reimbursement. In fact, prepayment of all side travel is highly recommended.
- The value of the travel, lodging, and entertainment should be determined from the recipient's point of view (e.g., is a trip to Disney World an expensive, once-in-a-lifetime event for the recipient and guest?).

- Overnight side trips should be avoided and addressed in a company policy.
- Sightseeing trips, if any, should be modest.
- Per diem advances, if necessary, should be made to the guest's employer—department or agency—for distribution to the employee.
- It is usually preferable to have the foreign government department or agency select any travel and lodging for guests rather than for the host company to do so.
- Companies should carefully examine the relationships, invoices, other documentation, and potential money laundering role of travel service providers (e.g., GlaxoSmithKline scenario in the People's Republic of China).
- Multinational companies should, in contractual agreements or correspondence, share their ethics and compliance values, commitments, and applicable policies with travel service providers.
- Multinational companies in particular should conduct internal audits that regularly focus on travel and entertainment expenses, especially at operations in foreign countries with poor Transparency International corruption perception indices, for example, under 50, or with substantial travel and entertainment budgets.
- Multinational companies should conduct regular training of international sales employees using detailed travel and entertainment scenarios from FCPA matters like Lucent, Timms and Ramahi, and Avon.
- Multinational corporations that host or sponsor special events such as the Olympics or World Cup should prepare in advance a live training program to educate employees, temporary employees, agents, and any other intermediaries about the corruption risks they will likely encounter and how representatives of state-owned or state-controlled organizations may be foreign government officials for purposes of the FCPA.
- Counsel should of course consider the foreign official bribery laws and policies of other countries. The U.K. Bribery Act, for example, does not have an affirmative defense or exception for hospitality and travel.

VIII. SPECIAL SPORTING EVENTS AND ANTIBRIBERY TRAINING AND PRECAUTIONS

Many large MNCs sponsor major or special sporting events such as the FIFA World Cup and the Olympics. Other companies sponsor annual off-site trade shows with customer product or services demonstrations that often involve government officials with significant purchasing power. FIFA official partners have included Adidas, Budweiser, Coca-Cola, Emirates Airlines, Sony, Toyota, and Visa. Issues of rights protection, licensing, travel, and hospitality are common in sponsorships. Travel and hospitality for government officials of course presents potential anticorruption risks, and counsel need to carefully determine whether certain organizations are state-owned or state-controlled entities and whether their managers are therefore government officials under the FCPA (see chapter 1). Further, officers, employees, and agents need to understand and adhere to the local laws of the host country. All contracts related to special events should contain appropriate anti-bribery warranties and representations.

In underwriting these events, companies should consider what specific assets and marketing elements present corruption risks and, of course, review the Transparency International or similar corruption perception indices of the host countries. Problematic areas include the following:

- Excessive distribution of logoed athletic gear to national teams and team officials;
- Distribution of expensive event tickets to government officials and customers;
- Requests for company products from government officials and customers;
- Requests by government officials for payment for travel to and lodging at special events;
- Lavish and/or improper entertainment of government officials;
- Payments or things of value to and for broadcasting spots and special locations from state-owned telecommunication companies;
- Local licenses and permits;
- Use of agents, consultants, and other third-party representatives; and
- Visa processing.

Multinational corporations should consider all the potential event "touches" in the host country with both government agencies and state-owned and state-controlled entities and provide written guidelines to officers, employees, temporary employees, contractors, subcontractors, subvendors, and agents for these major events. Guidance should include concrete examples of problematic situations and types of government or quasi-government officials or overtures they may encounter. In addition, multinational corporations must be mindful of requests from charitable organizations and for political donations from persons in the host country when the requests are linked to improper business advantages.

A number of well-managed multinational companies require preapproval of a government official's travel and lodging at special sporting events. John Lewis Jr., senior managing and global antibribery counsel of the Coca-Cola Company, explains that his company requires officers and employees who propose to host government officials to (1) complete a questionnaire explaining the purpose of the proposed trip, the historical relationship with the official, and any pending business with the official; and (2) draft a written invitation to the foreign government office or agency with a request that the office or agency designate an employee or official to attend with copies to his or her supervisors.[35] Some companies require a detailed proposed itinerary outlining travel dates, travel and lodging accommodations, visits to company plants or facilities, and estimated costs.

Companies should also consider devoting advance anticorruption planning and training for staff for special sporting events in order to (1) reemphasize a company's anticorruption values and commitment; (2) remind employees and temporary employees of sensitive issues involving travel, lodging, hospitality, and entertainment of government officials that arise in connection with these events; (3) identify state-owned or state-controlled entities whose government affiliation may not be apparent to all permanent and temporary employees; (4) identify and explain relevant local laws; and (5) create a strong record that the multinational corporation acted in good faith to minimize corrupt conduct and activities.

IX. ADDITIONAL RESOURCES

- CRIM. DIV., U.S. DEP'T OF JUSTICE & ENFORCEMENT DIV., U.S. SEC. & EXCH. COMM., FCPA: A RESOURCE GUIDE TO THE U.S. FOREIGN CORRUPT PRACTICES ACT (2012), http://www.justice.gov/criminal/fraud/fcpa/guide/ or http://www .sec.gov/spotlight/fcpa.shtml (reprinted as appendix 4).

NOTES

1. Foreign Corrupt Practices Act of 1977, Pub. L. No. 95-213, 91 Stat. 1494 (codified as amended at 15 U.S.C. §§ 78m, 78dd-1 to -3, 78ff (1999)) [hereinafter FCPA]. The FCPA is appended hereto as appendix 1.

2. CRIM. DIV., U.S. DEP'T OF JUSTICE & ENFORCEMENT DIV., U.S. SEC. & EXCH. COMM., FCPA: A RESOURCE GUIDE TO THE U.S. FOREIGN CORRUPT PRACTICES ACT (2012), http:// www.justice.gov/criminal/fraud/fcpa/guidance/ or http://www.sec.gov/spotlight/fcpa .shtml [hereinafter RESOURCE GUIDE] (appended hereto as appendix 4).

3. *See* U.K. Bribery Act Guidance, http://www.justice.gov.uk/guidance/bribery .com (appended hereto as appendix 15).

4. Facilitating payments that may be interpreted as gifts are not addressed in this section. Facilitating payments should be only for nondiscretionary actions and should always be modest. They must always be accurately recorded in the books and records of the company.

5. DON ZARIN, DOING BUSINESS UNDER THE FOREIGN CORRUPT PRACTICES ACT 6–7 (PLI 2007).

6. RESOURCE GUIDE, *supra* note 2, at 15.

7. *Id.*

8. *Id.* at 16.

9. U.S.C. §§ 78dd-1(c)(1), (2), 78dd-2(c)(1), (2), 78dd-3 (c)(1), (2).

10. Complaint, SEC v. UTStarcom Inc., No. 09-cv-6094 (N.D. Cal. Dec. 31, 2009), ECF No. 1.

11. RESOURCE GUIDE, *supra* note 2, at 15.

12. *Id.* at 18.

13. FCPA Opinion Procedure Release No. 2008-03 (July 11, 2008), http://www .justice.gov/criminal/fraud/fcpa/opinion/2008/0803pdf.

14. *See* 15 U.S.C. § 78dd-2(c)(2)(A).

15. 15 U.S.C. § 78dd-2(c)(2)(A).

16. United States v. Metcalf & Eddy, Inc., No. 99 Civ. 12566 (D. Mass. Dec. 14, 1999).

17. Consent and Undertaking of Metcalf & Eddy, Inc., No. 99 Civ. 12566-NG (D. Mass. filed Dec. 14, 1999).

18. Press Release, U.S. Dep't of Justice, Lucent Technologies, Inc. Agrees to Pay $1 Million Fine to Resolve FCPA Allegations (Dec. 21, 2007), http://www.justice.gov /opa/pr/2007/December/07_crm_1028.html.

19. No. 07-CV-02301 (D.D.C. 2007).

20. Press Release, U.S. Dep't of Justice, UTStarcom Inc. Agrees to Pay $1.5 Million Penalty for Acts of Foreign Bribery in China (Dec. 31, 2009), http://www.justice.gov /opa/pr/2009/December/09-crm-1390.html.

21. SEC v. UTStarcom Inc., Case No. CV/09 6094 (JSW) (N.D. Cal. Dec. 31, 2009), Litig. Release No. 21357, http://www.sec.gov/litigation/litreleases/2009/lr21357.htm.

22. SEC v. Veraz Networks, Inc., CV 10-2849 DVT (N.D. Cal. filed June 29, 2010).

23. Complaint, SEC v. Int'l Bus. Machs. Corp., 1:11-cv-00563 (D.D.C. filed Mar. 18, 2011)

24. Press Release, U.S. Dep't of Justice, Diebold Incorporated Resolves Foreign Corrupt Practices Act Investigation and Agrees to Pay $25.2 Million Criminal Penalty (Oct. 22, 2013), http://www.justice.gov/opa/pr/2013/October/13-crm-1118.html.

25. Press Release, U.S. Sec. & Exch. Comm'n, SEC Charges Diebold with FCPA Violations (Oct. 22, 2013), http://www.sec.gov/News/PressRelease/1370539977273

26. RELEASE NO. 73616 (Nov. 17, 2014), ADMIN. PROCEEDING FILE NO. 3-16281.

27. RELEASE NO. 78835 (DEC. 15, 2014), ADMIN. PROCEEDING FILE NO. 3-16314.

28. Press Release, U.S. Sec. Exch. Comm'n, SEC Charges Massachusetts-Based Scientific Instruments Manufacturer with FCPA Violations (Dec. 15, 2014), http://www .sec.gov/News/PressRelease/Detail/PressRelease/1370543708934.

29. Admin. Proceeding Order, In the Matter of Bruker Corp., Exchange Act Release No. 73835 (Dec. 15, 2014), *available at* http://www.sec.gov/litigation /admin/2014/34-73835.pdf.

30. *Id.*

31. S1 14 Cr. 828-GBD (S.D.N.Y. 2014).

32. *See* Dec. 15, 2014, letter of William J. Stellmach to Evan R. Chesler and Benjamin Gruenstein, Cravath, Swaine & Moore Ltd. DPA Statement of Facts (¶¶ 33–50).

33. DAVID BARBOZA, *Glaxo Uses Travel Firms for Bribery, China Says*, N.Y. TIMES, July 15, 2013, http://www.nytimes.com/2013/07/16/business/global/glaxo-used-travel -firms-in-bribery-china-says.html?pagewanted=all&_r=0.

34. RESOURCE GUIDE, *supra* note 2, at 56.

35. John Lewis Jr., Senior Managing Compliance & Global Anti-Bribery Counsel, Coca-Cola Co., Remarks at Gifts & Hospitality Panel Discussion of ACI FCPA Boot Camp, Chicago, Ill. (June 27, 2011).

CHAPTER 7

Charitable Donations and Political Contributions

I. INTRODUCTION

Charitable donation and political contribution corruption issues arise not infrequently for brand-name multinational companies because many engage in legitimate social outreach and publicize their corporate generosity and good citizenship; because they operate in challenging countries where charitable needs are many; and to some degree, because they are perceived as having deep pockets. The U.S. Department of Justice (DOJ) and the Securities and Exchange Commission's (SEC) *Resource Guide to the U.S. Foreign Corrupt Practices Act* makes clear that the "FCPA does not prohibit charitable contributions or prevent corporations from acting as good corporate citizens. Companies, however, cannot use the pretense of charitable contributions as a way to funnel bribes to government officials."[1] With respect to charitable donations, the *Resource Guide* further identifies five questions multinational companies should consider when making charitable payments in a foreign country, discussed *infra*.[2] The DOJ–SEC *Resource Guide* does not provide specific advice with respect to political contributions.

Potential charitable and political payment risks are best minimized by means of clear global corporate policies that govern local charitable and political campaign activities, proper due diligence and funding controls, and a clear message to foreign country and financial managers that the company's global policies relating to charitable contributions and political donations will be strictly enforced. Many companies benefit by requiring that all political donations and campaign contributions above a certain threshold (e.g., $250) have advance written approval from the parent compliance or law departments. With the notable exceptions of *In re* Schering-Plough and *United States v. Titan*, discussed *infra*, the DOJ and SEC have brought few FCPA charitable donation and political contribution cases. There have also been few FCPA opinion releases in this area.

II. GLOBAL CORPORATE POLICIES AND LOCAL LAWS

In-country managers of foreign operations or subsidiaries are frequently approached to make local charitable donations and political contributions. The first consideration is whether the parent company has global charitable donation and political contribution policies that govern such requests. Sometimes, foreign subsidiaries are not familiar with a parent's global policies; other times, their personnel see U.S.-centric language, for example, "political action committee" (PAC), and interpret such policies as applying only to U.S. operations. The second consideration is whether local laws permit, prohibit, or cap charitable donations or political contributions. With regard to this second consideration, the inquiry is not what local practice or custom is, but what the written local law is. Assuming that a proposed donation or contribution is permitted by both corporate policy and written local law, the third and most critical consideration is whether the contemplated donation or contribution could be interpreted as having a corrupt motive. Obviously, a modest annual contribution to a local youth football organization team will not pose an FCPA problem. However, a sizable charitable donation urged by a local government official to his favorite charity may portend a serious FCPA issue.

What constitutes a risky charitable donation or political contribution will depend on a number of factors including the size of the request or funding; pending or current business, bids, or awards; the transparency of the request and donation or contribution; and the particular relationship of any requestor to the company and its management. While the two types of funding requests present similar risks, are not mutually exclusive, and can overlap, it is best to at least initially separate charitable donations and political contributions and address their respective risks separately.

III. CORRUPT MOTIVES

A. Charitable Donations

In evaluating the possible corrupt motive surrounding a proposed or completed charitable donation, counsel will want to consider:

- The amount or value of the charitable donation;
- The reputation and history of the charitable organization;
- The relationship and purpose of the charitable organization to the donor company, that is, whether the purpose or mission of the charity is logically associated with or related to the company's principal business—for example, a pharmaceutical company contributing to a local children's hospital versus a pharmaceutical company contributing to a local castle restoration foundation;
- The relationship of the officers or employees of the charitable organization to foreign government officials, foreign party officials, or foreign party candidates;
- The authority or ability of the recipient or a relative to award business to the company or to influence local licenses, taxes, customs duties, or other regulatory approvals;
- The transparency or public record of the contribution, for example, whether there is a local filing requirement by the candidate or party, or the candidate or party objects to disclosure;

- The deductibility of the charitable contribution, for example, whether the charitable donation is deductible under local law, and whether the company will exercise the deductibility;
- Evidence of receipt—whether the charitable organization is reluctant to issue a receipt that fully and accurately describes the donation and to ensure that funds are transferred to a valid bank account;
- Certification by the donee or recipient that it is complying with the FCPA and local laws; and
- Ongoing monitoring of the efficacy of the charitable program.

Under no circumstances should a company endorse or approve cash charitable donations. Sometimes, employees or officers view donations in kind, for example, use of a corporate jet, computers, office space, or business facilities, as less problematic or less likely to require review. That is not the case, and significantly, neither the DOJ nor the SEC shares that view.

B. Political Contributions

In evaluating a possible corrupt motive surrounding a proposed or completed campaign contribution, counsel will want to consider:

- The amount or value of the political contribution;
- The nature of the political contribution, for example, a check, use of a company facility, office equipment, a plane or other vehicle, or hosting a reception on corporate premises;
- The authority or ability, official or practical, of the recipient/candidate to award business to the company, retain business for the company, or to influence local licenses, taxes, customs duties, or other regulatory approvals;
- The timing of the contribution, for example, whether it coincides with the award of a bid opening or contract;
- The entity receiving the contribution, that is, whether it is clear that the actual recipient is a foreign candidate or foreign political party as opposed to an individual or shell organization not implicitly tied to a campaign or candidate; and whether there will be a local public record of the contribution, for example, whether the donor, candidate's name, and size of the contribution will be on file locally;
- Whether the requestor—a candidate, a member of a campaign staff, or a government official—is connected directly or indirectly to a pending bid, business opportunity, or regulatory approval application;
- Requests by the political party or candidate to limit or conceal the political contribution, or otherwise involve suspicious circumstances; and
- The overall propriety of the contribution, for example, whether the company's contributor would be embarrassed to be pictured with the political candidate in a local newspaper.

Under no circumstances should a company endorse or approve cash contributions to a foreign political candidate or foreign political party.

IV. CONTRACTS CONTAINING CHARITABLE DONATION BEQUESTS

In some countries a bid will request a contribution to a worthy local cause, for example, construction of a clinic, school, firehouse, or police station. In this circumstance, counsel should confirm that this condition or term is uniform and applicable to all bidders and is contained in the local bid documents available to the public. Further, any contractual donation should be made payable to a governmental body—as opposed to an individual—and earmarked for the intended purpose or should expressly restrict the use of funds. Ideally, payments for a construction funding should be periodic to ensure the project is built and details of the project should be reflected in the company records. The more public, detailed, and transparent the donation, the better and the safer for the donor. For example, a pharmaceutical company might be wise to require a plaque on a children's hospital facility that reads, "Premier Pharmaceutical Prenatal Care Center. This Facility Is Made Possible through a Donation of Premier Pharmaceutical, September 15, 2012." Of course, contracts should contain the standard FCPA warranties and representations. Finally, a requirement that the donee provide audited financial statements is a worthwhile contractual term and goal.

V. TRANSPARENCY OF CHARITABLE DONATIONS AND POLITICAL CONTRIBUTIONS

As with all transactions implicated by the FCPA, transparency is the cornerstone. If the donor or donee is hesitant about the company's recording of or the eventual or potential disclosure to the public of the donation or contribution, counsel and management will want to inquire about and understand the reasons. As with all books-and-records entries, the description of the donation or contribution should be in reasonable detail, that is, such level of detail that would satisfy prudent officers in the conduct of their own affairs. Companies that have formal internal controls and approval procedures and forms in place for both domestic and foreign political contributions or charitable donations substantially reduce the risk of corrupt or improper payments. Some multinational corporations have clear U.S. political contribution policies but leave foreign contributions unattended, creating an internal control problem.

VI. RESOURCE GUIDE'S FIVE CHARITABLE PAYMENT QUESTIONS

The DOJ–SEC FCPA *Resource Guide* raises five questions to consider when making charitable payments in a foreign country:[3]

1. What is the purpose of the payment?
2. Is the payment consistent with the company's internal guidelines on charitable giving?
3. Is the payment at the request of a foreign official?

4. Is a foreign official associated with the charity and if so, can the foreign official make decisions regarding your business in that country?
5. Is the payment conditioned upon receiving business or other benefits?

The *Resource Guide* states that "Proper due diligence and controls are critical for charitable giving. In general, the adequacy of measures taken to prevent misuse of charitable donations will depend on a risk-based analysis and the specific facts at hand."[4] One prudent internal control is to have a written analysis of the aforementioned five questions and written approval before authorizing or permitting a charitable payment. U.S. authorities will appreciate a control that incorporates their *Resource Guide* advice.

VII. LEADING FCPA CHARITABLE DONATION AND POLITICAL CONTRIBUTION CASES

A. Overview

FCPA charitable donation and political contribution cases generally fall into two categories: (1) those where a foreign government official requests or directs a company to make a charitable donation to an actual charitable organization or political contribution to the foreign government official, political party, or political party candidate in order for the company to obtain or retain business; and (2) those where a company disguises an improper payment or thing of value as a charitable donation when in some instances there is no charitable organization or expense.

B. Actual Charitable Organization, Political Party Official, Political Party, or Political Party Candidate

1. *In re* Schering-Plough[5]

In June 2004, Schering-Plough Corporation, headquartered in New Jersey, settled an SEC complaint alleging improper payments made by Schering-Plough Poland (S-P Poland), a branch office of a wholly owned subsidiary of the company's Swiss division, to a charitable organization called the Chudow Castle Foundation.[6] The parent company agreed to pay a civil penalty of $500,000 for violations of the FCPA's books-and-records and internal controls provisions[7] and to retain an independent consultant to review its internal controls and financial reporting policies and procedures.

The Foundation, which was dedicated to the restoration of castles, was headed by an individual who was also director of the Silesian Health Fund, a Polish governmental body that, among other things, provided money for the purchase of pharmaceutical products and influenced the purchase of those products by other entities such as hospitals. The complaint alleged that S-P Poland paid $76,000 to the Foundation over a three-year period to induce its director to influence the health fund's purchase of S-P Poland pharmaceutical products. The complaint alleged that S-P Poland paid more money to the Foundation than any other recipient of promotional donations.

Signally, the SEC complaint did not allege that the parent company or anyone in the United States knew of the improper payments. Indeed, according to the complaint, the payments were structured at or below the local Schering-Plough manager's approval limit so that the parent would not detect or discover the true nature of the payments, which were recorded on the books and records as "medical donations."

The SEC asserted that the parent company should have been alerted to FCPA issues by the following:

1. The fact that the Foundation was not a healthcare–related entity;
2. The magnitude of the payments to the Foundation in relation to the company's budget for such donations;
3. The structuring of certain charitable payments by the manager, which allowed him to exceed his authorized limits; and
4. The fact that the chairman of the Foundation was also a regional government official with the ability to influence formulary payments.

The DOJ did not file criminal charges against Schering-Plough or any officers or employees.

2.   United States v. Titan[8]

In March 2005, Titan Corporation, a San Diego, California, defense contractor, pled guilty to three FCPA criminal violations: one count of violating the anti-bribery provision; one count of falsifying the books-and-records provision; and one felony tax count. Titan also agreed to pay a then-record FCPA criminal fine of $13 million.[9] Combined with its agreement with the SEC to pay $15.5 million in disgorgement and prejudgment interest,[10] Titan paid over $28.5 million to resolve the FCPA investigation. The company was further required to retain a consultant to review the company's FCPA compliance and procedures and to adopt and implement the consultant's recommendations.

The military intelligence and communications company did not contest that from 1999 to 2001 it paid $3.5 million to its agent in the West African country of Benin and that the agent was then known by Titan to be the president of Benin's business advisor. The complaint alleged that Titan failed to conduct any meaningful due diligence into the background of this agent. Much of the money funneled to the agent went to the election campaign of Benin's then-incumbent president. The complaint alleged that some of these funds were used to reimburse Titan's agent for the purchase of T-shirts adorned with the president's picture and instructions to vote for him in the upcoming election. A former senior Titan officer also directed that payments be falsely invoiced as consulting services and that actual payment of the money be spread over time and into smaller increments.[11]

3.   In re Stryker Corp.[12]

In 2013, the SEC settled FCPA allegations with Stryker Corporation, a medical device and products manufacturer and distributor. A Stryker Greek subsidiary was alleged to have made an atypical donation of $197,500 to a public university to fund a laboratory that was being established by a foreign official who served as a prominent professor at the Greek university. The donation was made pursuant to a Greek research arrangement in return for public hospital business with which the official was affiliated. Stryker improperly booked the donation as a legitimate marketing expense in an account titled "Donation and Grants."

4.   United States v. Alstom S.A.[13]

In 2014, Alstom S.A., a French power industry conglomerate, pled guilty to FCPA violations. It admitted that it "paid bribes directly to foreign officials by providing gifts and petty cash, by hiring their family members, and, in one instance, by paying over $2 million to a charity associated with a foreign official, all in exchange for those foreign officials' assistance in obtaining or retaining business in connection with projects for Alstom and its subsidiaries."[14] As with consultant payments, Alstom knowingly and falsely recorded these payments in its books and records as consultant expenses, as "donations" or other purportedly legitimate expenses.

C. Fictitious Charity or Charitable Donation

The other abuse in this area is the scenario where a company makes an improper payment or gives a thing of value to a government official, but falsely describes and records it as a charitable donation in the company's books or records. For example, in 2013, Archer Daniels Midland (ADM), a global agricultural commodity processor, settled with the DOJ with respect to *inter alia* improper practices at subsidiaries in Germany and the Ukraine.[15] E-mails discussed "contractors [who] usually ask for donations" and that "donations could be up to 20% of the VAT receivable."[16] During the period in question, the ADM subsidiaries made no charitable donations and paid amounts to vendors for the purpose of passing nearly all of the money to pay bribes to government officials to obtain VAT refunds.[17]

VIII. DOJ FCPA OPINION RELEASES

Few of the DOJ FCPA opinion releases have dealt with charitable donations or political campaign contributions. The four opinions below represent the major FCPA opinion guidance in the area.

A. FCPA Opinion Procedure Release No. 95-01 (January 11, 1995): Charitable Donation for Substantial Medical Facility[18]

In 1995 the DOJ reviewed the FCPA opinion request by a U.S.–based energy company that planned to acquire and operate a plant in a country in South Asia that lacked modern medical facilities in the region where the plant was located. The requestor addressed the situation where a formal contract contemplated a very large charitable contribution for a medical facility, and the DOJ approved the prospective donation relying on the following facts.

A modern medical complex was presently under construction near the requestor's future plant. Costs for the medical facility were projected to run to hundreds of millions of dollars. If the acquisition of the plant was completed, the requestor planned to donate $10 million in a public ceremony to the medical facility for construction and equipment costs. The donation was to be made through a charitable organization incorporated in the United States and through a public limited liability company located in the South Asian nation. Because the medical facility was to be open to the public, the requestor's employees and affiliates would be allowed to use the facility when completed.

The requestor represented that, before releasing any funds, it would require certifications from all officers of the U.S. charitable organization and the foreign limited liability company that none of the funds would be used, promised, or offered in violation of the FCPA. The requestor further represented that none of the persons employed by or acting on behalf of the charitable organization or the limited liability company were affiliated with the foreign government. The requestor also represented that it would require audited financial reports from the U.S. charitable organization, accurately detailing the disposition of the donated funds.[19]

Based on all the facts and circumstances, as represented by the requestor, the DOJ indicated it did not intend to take any enforcement action with respect to this prospective donation for the construction and equipment of the medical facility.[20]

B. FCPA Opinion Procedure Release No. 97-02 (November 5, 1997): Charitable Donation for Elementary School[21]

In 1997 a requestor sought permission to donate $100,000 to a proposed elementary school construction project, and the DOJ indicated that under the submitted facts and circumstances it would not take any enforcement action. The DOJ reviewed the FCPA opinion request by a U.S.-based utility company. The requestor had commenced construction of a plant in a country in Asia that lacks adequate primary-level educational facilities in the region where the plant is under construction.

An elementary school construction project had been proposed near the location of the requestor's plant. Construction and supply costs of the elementary school were to exceed $100,000. The requestor planned to donate $100,000 to the proposed school construction project. The donation would be made by the company directly to the government entity responsible for the construction and supply of the proposed elementary school.

The requestor represented that, before releasing any funds, it would require a written agreement from the government entity that the funds would be used solely to construct and supply the elementary school. The written agreement would set forth other conditions to be met by the government entity, including guaranteeing the availability of land, teachers, and administrative personnel for the school; guaranteeing timely additional funding of the school project in the event of any financial shortfall; and guaranteeing provision of all funds necessary for the daily operation of the school.

As the requestor's donation would be made directly to a government entity—and not to any foreign government official[22]—the DOJ found that the provisions of the FCPA did not appear to apply to this prospective transaction. Based on all the facts and circumstances, as represented by the requestor, the DOJ indicated it did not intend to take any enforcement action with respect to the proposed transaction.

C. FCPA Opinion Procedure Release No. 06-01 (October 16, 2006): $25,000 Contribution to Improve Local Law Enforcement[23]

In 2006 the DOJ reviewed the FCPA opinion procedure request of a Delaware corporation with headquarters in Switzerland. The requestor sought to contribute $25,000 to a regional customs department or the Ministry of Finance (collectively, the counterparty) in an African country as part of a pilot project to improve local enforcement of anticounterfeiting laws. The requestor sought to make the monetary contribution to the counterparty in order for the agency to fund incentive awards to local customs officials to improve local enforcement relating to seizures of counterfeit products bearing the trademarks of the requestor and its competitors.

The letter of request stated that counterfeiting had become "a serious issue" for manufacturers such as the requestor and that the issue "is often not a major priority for Customs authorities (particularly in developing countries)." According to the requestor, the African country selected for this "anticounterfeiting coalition" serves as a major transit point for illicit trade in counterfeit products, including the products of the requestor and its competitors. The requestor stated that a transit tax was collected on all goods transiting the country, even those that were contraband or counterfeit. The requestor noted that the salaries of local customs officials included a small percentage of any transit tax they collected, whether on authentic or counterfeit products. Thus, there was a financial disincentive for thorough inspection by local customs officials of goods for counterfeit products. The requestor asked for a determination of the DOJ's present enforcement intention under the FCPA with respect to the proposed $25,000 contribution.

The requestor represented, among other things, that in connection with its proposed $25,000 contribution, it would execute a formal memorandum of understanding (MOU) with the counterparty in the African country to:

- Encourage the mutual exchange of information related to the trade of counterfeit products bearing the trademarks of the requestor and its competitors;
- Establish procedures for an incentive compensation fund for the payment of awards to local customs officials who detain, seize, and destroy counterfeit products ("award candidates");
- Establish eligibility criteria for the calculation of awards and the methods and frequency of distribution; and
- Provide that the awards be given to award candidates directly by the counterparty or be given to local customs offices to distribute to their qualified award candidates.

The requestor further represented that it would establish "a number of procedural safeguards designed to assure that the funds made available by the [requestor's] contribution were, in fact, going to provide incentives to local customs officials for the purposes intended." The requestor was required to ensure that the Ministry of Justice in the African country was aware of the pilot program and that all aspects of the program were consistent with local laws, including but not limited to the following procedural safeguards:

- First, the requestor would make its contribution to the incentive compensation fund by electronic transfer to an official government bank account in the African country controlled by and in the name of the counterparty, and would require written confirmation that the account was a valid government account, subject to periodic internal audit by the relevant government authorities.
- Second, the requestor would be notified upon a seizure of suspected counterfeit items by local customs officials, and would examine the suspect

goods to confirm they were in fact counterfeit. The requestor further represented that payments to award candidates would not be distributed unless
and until destruction of the counterfeit goods was confirmed by delivery of
a destruction certificate to the counterparty (a copy of which would be sent
to the requestor).

- Third, the requestor would have no part in choosing the award candidates,
and the counterparty would have sole control over, and full responsibility for,
the appropriate distribution of funds. The requestor, however, would require
written evidence that its entire contribution would be used only to pay identified award candidates and that the awards would be based upon a predeter-
mined award eligibility criteria and calculation method.

- Fourth, the requestor would monitor the efficacy of the incentive program
and discuss with the counterparty during periodic reviews whether changes
or refinements were necessary. As part of its monitoring effort, the requestor
would monitor the number of notices received from local customs officials
relating to relevant seizures during each six-month period and follow the pro-
gression of such seizures.

- Fifth, the requestor would require as part of its MOU with the counterparty
that the counterparty would retain for five years the records of the distribution
and receipt of funds, and permit inspection of such records by the requestor
upon request during the life of the pilot project and for three years thereafter.

The requestor stated in its letter of request that its pending business activities
in the African country were relatively small and "entirely unrelated to the current
request for an advisory opinion." The requestor further stated that its future business in the country was not dependent upon the existence of the proposed incentive program, and that the program was not intended to influence any foreign
official to obtain or retain business. Finally, the requestor stated that if the program were successful, the requestor would continue to fund the central account on
an as-needed basis to ensure that there would be no interruption in merited awards
to local customs officials, and that the requestor would seek, both initially and over
time, to encourage its competitors to contribute funds to the effort as well.[24]

Based upon all of the facts and circumstances, as represented by the requestor,
the DOJ indicated it did not intend to take any enforcement action with respect to
the proposed $25,000 payment. This opinion, however, was subject to the follow-
ing two important caveats, as stated in the opinion procedure release:

> The Department's Opinion should not be deemed to endorse the
> proposed language of the MOU or the methodology for selection of
> the proposed Award Candidates and distribution of funds, as neither
> the language of the MOU nor any proposed methodology were
> submitted to the Department. This Opinion likewise should not be
> deemed to address any possible expansion of the program within
> or outside the African country. Rather, this Opinion is limited to
> consideration of the $25,000 contribution to the particular African
> country set forth in the letter of request.

This Opinion does not apply to any monetary payments made by the Requestor for purposes other than those expressed in the letter of request; nor does it apply to any individuals involved in authorizing or distributing the monetary awards to the Award Candidates.[25]

Finally, pursuant to standard DOJ opinion release procedures, this FCPA opinion letter and this release had no binding application to any party that did not join in the request, and could be relied upon by the requestor only to the extent that the disclosure of facts and circumstances in its request was accurate and complete and would remain accurate and complete.

D. FCPA Opinion Procedure Release No. 10-02 (July 16, 2010): Microfinance Institution Grant[26]

In 2010 a requestor, a nonprofit U.S.-based microfinance institution (MFI), whose mission was to provide loans and other basic financial services to the world's lowest-income entrepreneurs, was in the process of converting all of its local operations to licensed commercial financial entities in order to permit them to attract capital and expand their services. In this matter a Eurasia-based subsidiary of the MFI was asked by an agency of a foreign government to make a grant to a local MFI as a prerequisite to the subsidiary's transformation to bank status. The subsidiary proposed a $1.42 million contribution to a local MFI to satisfy the request. The subsidiary undertook extensive three-stage due diligence to select the proposed grantee and imposed significant controls on the proposed grant, including

- staggered payment of grant funds;
- ongoing independent monitoring and auditing;
- earmarked funds for capacity building (toward organizational infrastructure);
- prohibitions on compensating board members; and
- anticorruption compliance measures.

Noting the above FCPA opinion releases (95-01, 97-02, and 06-01), the DOJ approved the requestor-proposed grant of donation, based on due diligence and controls such as

- certifications by the recipient regarding compliance with the FCPA;
- due diligence to confirm that none of the recipient's officers were affiliated with the foreign government at issue;
- a requirement that the recipient provide audited financial statements;
- a written agreement with the requirement restricting the use of funds;
- steps to ensure that the funds were transferred to a valid bank account;
- confirmation that the charity commitments were met before funds were disbursed; and
- ongoing monitoring of the efficacy of the program.

Each of the above requests was very fact specific. The DOJ assurance that it would take no enforcement action under the FCPA opinion procedure was predicated upon any disclosure and request being complete and accurate.

IX. PRACTICAL CHARITABLE DONATION AND POLITICAL CONTRIBUTION ADVICE

A. Charitable Donations

- Make clear in the company's code of conduct and/or charitable donation policy that all foreign charitable donations must be approved in advance, in writing, by the parent company's legal or compliance department.
- Conduct a risk-based analysis for charitable giving and always consider the specific facts at hand.
- Determine what, if any, local laws govern or limit foreign charitable donations. Even if local laws permit or are silent about charitable contributions by a foreign company, subsidiary, or officer, a charitable donation may still have a corrupt motive and violate the FCPA.
- Consider whether the company's charitable donation policy should confine the type of charities the company will consider for significant contributions to those directly related to the company's principal business, for example, a pharmaceutical company's donation might be limited to oncology care or related research and development.
- Determine whether the foreign operation or subsidiary's charitable donation policies and written procedures are consistent with the parent company's written policies and procedures for charitable donations. Absent unique circumstances, the two should be the same or very similar in their objectives, limits, eligibility, and approvals.
- Ask what the in-country manager or requesting officer or employee specifically knows about the charitable organization and request brochures, local registration, and other materials describing the charity's goals and activities.
- Ask the requesting officer or employee why he or she wishes to support the particular charitable organization and what the exact purpose of the charitable donation is.
- Ask the requesting officer or employee whether there is any pending or forthcoming contract or award that the charitable organization or its officers might directly or indirectly influence.
- Determine whether the charitable organization's officers, employees, or agents are affiliated with the foreign government at issue or are connected in any way to the company's obtaining, retaining, or being awarded business.
- Question what assurance there is that the charitable donation will go to a specific end, for example, bricks and mortar as opposed to a general administrative fund, and seek to ensure that the specific purpose is memorialized in advance in writing.
- Question any pattern of repeat donations to one charitable organization and insist that any request for a donation address cumulative charitable donations to the entity.
- Obtain a legitimate, contemporaneous receipt for any charitable donation.
- Consider publicizing the charitable donation to promote and confirm transparency.
- Make sure all charitable donations are recorded accurately and in sufficient detail in the company's or subsidiary's books and records.

- Direct internal audit to review (1) whether purported "charitable donations" are tied to a request or direction of a foreign government official; and (2) whether the alleged charitable organization in fact exists.
- Review the *Resource Guide*'s five questions to consider when making any significant charitable donation, and prepare a legal memorandum analyzing the facts and circumstances of the request and proposed funding, confirming the logic and propriety of any significant charitable donation and appending all documents verifying the legitimacy and purpose of the charitable organization.
- Require that the charitable organization provide audited financial statements through the period of the donations or use of the funds.
- Confirm that the charitable organization's commitments are met before any funds are disbursed.
- Monitor the ongoing efficacy of the charitable program and charitable organization.

B. Political Contributions

- Make clear in the company's code of conduct and/or political contribution policy that either no foreign political contributions may be made or all foreign political contributions must be approved in advance and in writing by the parent company's legal or compliance department.
- Determine what, if any, local laws govern or limit foreign political party or candidate contributions. Even if local laws permit campaign contributions by a foreign company, subsidiary, affiliate, or officer, a political contribution may still carry a corrupt motive and violate the FCPA.
- Determine whether the foreign operation or subsidiary's political contribution policies and written procedures are consistent with the parent company's written policies and procedures for political contributions. Absent unique circumstances, the two should be the same or very similar in their objectives, limits, eligibility, and control and approval procedures.
- Ascertain what the in-country manager or requesting officer or employee specifically knows about the particular foreign candidate or campaign and the circumstances surrounding any requests for a contribution.
- Ascertain why the requesting officer or employee wishes to support the particular foreign candidate or campaign and what the purpose of the political contribution is.
- Determine from the requesting in-country manager officer or employee whether there is a pending or upcoming contract or award that the foreign candidate or political party might directly or indirectly influence.
- Question any pattern of repeat contributions to one foreign candidate, political party, or campaign.
- Consider whether the company is better off with a simple ban of all foreign political contributions—or at least a maximum or cap on contributions to any one foreign candidate or party in a given year.
- Make sure the company's code of conduct or political contribution policy does not adopt solely U.S. terminology, for example, "Congress" or "PAC," if

the company intends the code or policy to be global or universal. Otherwise, foreign employees or expats may misinterpret the policy as applying only to U.S. political candidates, political parties, campaigns, or activities and incorrectly assume, absent other guidance, that they are allowed to exercise their business judgment with respect to foreign political contributions.

- Determine whether the contemplated foreign political contribution will be fully transparent in both the host country and the parent country, and if not, why not.
- Obtain a legitimate contemporaneous receipt for any political contribution.
- Make sure all political contributions are recorded accurately and in sufficient detail in the company's or subsidiary's books and records.
- Prepare a legal memorandum analyzing the facts and circumstances and confirming the propriety of any significant political contribution.

X. ADDITIONAL RESOURCES

- CRIM. DIV., U.S. DEP'T OF JUSTICE & ENFORCEMENT DIV., U.S. SEC. & EXCH. COMM., FCPA: A RESOURCE GUIDE TO THE U.S. FOREIGN CORRUPT PRACTICES ACT (2012), http://www.justice.gov/criminal/fraud/fcpa/guidance/ or http://www.sec.gov/spotlight/fcpa.shtml (appendix 4).
- Claudius Sokenu, *Government Tackles the Thorny Issue of Travel and Entertainment under the FCPA*, *in* THE FOREIGN CORRUPT PRACTICES ACT 2008: COPING WITH HEIGHTENED ENFORCEMENT RISKS (PLI 2008).
- Roger Witten, Kimberly Parker & Thomas Koffer, Navigating the Increased Anti-Corruption Environment in the United States and Abroad, paper presented at the National Institute on White Collar Crime 2009 (San Francisco, Mar. 5–6, 2009).

NOTES

1. CRIM. DIV., U.S. DEP'T OF JUSTICE & ENFORCEMENT DIV., U.S. SEC. & EXCH. COMM., FCPA: A RESOURCE GUIDE TO THE U.S. FOREIGN CORRUPT PRACTICES ACT (2012), http://www.justice.gov/criminal/fraud/fcpa/guidance/orhttp://www.sec.gov/spotlight/fcpa.shtml [hereinafter RESOURCE GUIDE] (appendix 4).

2. *Id.* at 16.

3. *Id.* at 19.

4. *Id.* at 19.

5. Complaint, *In re* Schering-Plough Corp., Exchange Act Release No. 49,838, 82 S.E.C. Docket 3644, Litig. Release No. 18,740 (June 9, 2004).

6. *In re* Schering-Plough, Exchange Act Release No. 49,838, 82 SEC Docket 3644 (June 9, 2004). (This example is addressed in the RESOURCE GUIDE, *supra* note 1, at 16–17.)

7. 15 U.S.C. §§ 78m (b)(2)(a), (b) (1999).

8. Criminal Information, United States v. Titan Corp., No. 05-CR-0314-BEN (S.D. Cal. filed Mar. 1, 2005).

9. United States v. Titan Corp., cr No. 05 314 (S.D. Cal. 2005).

10. SEC Litig. Release No. 19,107 (Mar. 1, 2005).

11. *Id.*

12. Press Release, U.S. Sec. & Exch. Comm'n, SEC Charges Stryker Corporation with FCPA Violations (Oct. 24, 2013), http://www.sec.gov/News/PressRelease/Detail PressRelease/1370540044262.

13. United States v. Alstom, S.A., 3:14-cr-00246-JBA (D. Conn. Dec. 22, 2014).

14. *Id.*

15. Press Release, U.S. Dep't of Justice, ADM Subsidiary Pleads Guilty to Conspiracy to Violate the Foreign Corrupt Practices Act (Dec. 20, 2013), http://www.justice.gov /opa/pr/adm-subsidiary-pleads-guilty-conspiracy-violate-foreign-corrupt-practices-act.

16. NPA Agreement, ¶ 16.

17. *Id.* ¶ 28.

18. FCPA Opinion Procedure Release No. 95-01 (Jan. 11, 1995), http://www .justice.gov/criminal/fraud/fcpa/opinion/1995/9501.pdf.

19. *Id.*

20. *Id.*

21. FCPA Opinion Procedure Release No. 97-02 (Nov. 5, 1997), http://www .justice.gov/criminal/fraud/fcpa/opinion/1997/9702.pdf.

22. *Id.*

23. FCPA Opinion Procedure Release No. 06-01 (Oct. 16, 2006), http://www .justice.gov/criminal/fraud/fcpa/opinion/2006/0601.pdf.

24. *Id.*

25. *Id.*

26. FCPA Opinion Procedure Release No. 10-02 (July 16, 2010), http://www .justice.gov/criminal/fraud/fcpa/opinion/2010/1002.pdf.

CHAPTER 8

Conducting a Foreign Corrupt Practices Act Investigation

The basic steps and best practices of conducting an internal investigation are largely the same whether for the board of directors, the audit committee, a special committee, or senior management. Today, the emphasis on corporate governance means that the board or a committee is more likely to engage special counsel to perform a Foreign Corrupt Practices Act investigation and report the results to the entire board or the audit committee, especially where the conduct of senior management is at issue.

I. BASIC STEPS OF AN FCPA INTERNAL INVESTIGATION AND RELATED ACTIONS

A. Five Basic Steps and Logical Lines of Inquiry

The five basic steps of an FCPA internal investigation[1] are as follows:

1. Determine the nature of the allegation(s) (e.g., bribery payments through business advisors to a foreign official in Brazil; substantial payments to a consultant whose pricey services coincide with an oil concession in Qatar; the hiring of a relative of a French government official who approved a government tender; corporate sponsorship of lavish U.S. visits of Chinese governmental officials; payment to an Indonesian tax official to reduce a local tax assessment) and establish a preliminary and credible scope of the investigation of allegation(s).
2. Develop the facts through U.S. and foreign electronic and hard document reviews and thorough interviews—preparing a working chronology and retaining experts as necessary, including forensic accountants for evaluating books-and-records and internal controls practices and making control recommendations; potential liability experts to address, for example, tender, product, or market issues not obvious to Department of Justice or Securities and Exchange Commission staff; and economists or accountants to analyze ill-gotten gains to address disgorgement claims.
3. Analyze the jurisdictional and legal elements for each bribery, books-and-records, or internal controls offense, and any permissible payments and affirmative defenses of the Foreign Corrupt Practices Act. Common legal issues include corrupt intent, knowledge, nationality and territorial jurisdiction issues, foreign official status, and relevant local laws.

4. Report to the company, board, or committee consistent with the client's objectives, for example, to defend the company in a grand jury FCPA investigation; to provide legal advice to a board of directors, audit committee, special committee, or management as part of an internal investigation, including recommendations on compliance programs, disciplinary actions, internal controls and corporate policies; to voluntarily disclose to and cooperate with the U.S. Department of Justice (DOJ) and SEC in order to obtain leniency (e.g., nonprosecution agreement, deferred prosecution agreement), to minimize civil and criminal penalties; to avoid a monitorship; and so on.

5. Prepare and recommend appropriate quality remedial measures and implement the same as soon as practicable.

In determining what questions to logically pursue in interviews and what documents to review as a result of an FCPA bribery allegation, counsel will, in addition to being mindful of the elements of the antibribery, books-and-records, and internal controls provisions outlined in chapter 1, want to review the red flag and due diligence steps and issues discussed in other chapters. For example, if an agent is alleged to have made improper payments through a relative employed by a foreign government, the investigation will focus in part on the relative's government official position, authority, and access to decision makers; third-party due diligence, anticorruption training, and anticorruption warranties and representations in any third-party agreements; Internet searches of the agent and relative business references; descriptions of agency services on agency invoices; and of course, all hard and electronic correspondence between the agent and the company. Answers to the interview questions or telltale e-mails may establish the requisite knowledge on the part of the company or a strong defense.

In some cases the record of payments, gifts, or travel will be beyond dispute, and criminal liability will turn on corrupt intent—an "evil motive" or purpose or intent to wrongfully influence the recipient to "misuse his official position" in order to wrongfully direct, obtain, or retain business.[2] In other cases, the issue may be whether a government official ever received anything of value; such cases may still be prosecuted on a books-and-records theory but are much less damaging to a company's business reputation or attractive to a jury. For example, in the numerous UN Oil-for-Food program cases, the Iraqi government, not Iraqi government officials, received kickbacks, and the DOJ elected to proceed with only books-and-records violations, not bribery charges. Still, in other cases a U.S. company's conduct can appear to be driven more by the negligence or incompetence of employees than by a corrupt motive, thereby negating the requisite criminal knowledge standard. Yet, in other cases, there will be an examination of the jurisdictional nexus with the United States.

Whatever the improper payment allegation, counsel will want to examine not only the basic bribery elements and permissible payments and affirmative defenses, but also the red flags and due diligence factors outlined in earlier chapters as they can frequently bear on ultimate issues of corrupt intent, knowledge, and authorization and will be factors that U.S. law enforcement agencies will likely examine if the matter is disclosed to them or they otherwise learn of and investigate alleged violations. Counsel in some cases may have the opportunity to examine the broad jurisdictional reach of the FCPA or another anticorruption statute, for example, the U.K. Bribery

Act of 2010. Counsel will want to implement appropriate remedial measures, usually in conjunction with forensic accountants expert in internal controls.

B. Scoping

Often, the general counsel, business unit manager, or regional counsel will have the best overall understanding of the nature of the allegation(s) and will be able to identify those employees likely to have relevant knowledge. The scope of the investigation should focus on the time period and geography and remain flexible, depending on what is uncovered. For example, if a regional manager is responsible for Countries A, B, and C, and is found to have authorized a series of bribes in Country A in Years 1, 2, and 3, his conduct in Countries B and C should be examined for Years 1, 2, and 3. Because the federal statute of limitations is five years, it may well be prudent to institute a litigation hold of five years or longer. Government agencies including the DOJ and SEC as well as regular outside auditors will be skeptical of a corporate internal investigation that unduly limits the scope of the engagement or does not pursue logical paths of inquiry. For example, if an allegation relating to payments by an agent in Country A is corroborated, the government agencies and outside auditors will want some assurance that such payments are not occurring with other agents in other countries. It may be advisable to screen all third parties or agents receiving payments in excess of $50,000 in one year for suspicious payments, due diligence checks, and certifications. It is prudent for all involved—client and counsel—to think carefully about the language used in an engagement letter, a board of directors resolution, or an audit committee resolution, or minutes, as DOJ and SEC lawyers may later review them and insert expansion language if circumstances and investigations so warrant. At some point, the U.S. government may seek to determine whether the company, the board, or a committee truly committed to discovering the truth in an investigation.

C. Document Review, Forensic Teams, Witness Interviews, and Working Chronology Overview

Document review and witness interviews will often be conducted both in the United States and in foreign countries. Promptly identifying relevant custodians and securing and preserving electronic data is essential to a thorough internal investigation—and to establishing credibility with both the Department of Justice and the Securities and Exchange Commission. Investigation counsel, while being mindful of applicable data privacy laws, should take steps to promptly secure electronic storage facilities such as hard drives, network backup tapes, and flash drives. The DOJ and SEC, when evaluating a company's cooperation, will look to see how quickly and thoroughly management moved to secure both documentary and electronic evidence. Of course, the responsibility of preserving such evidence is even greater when responding to a formal government subpoena.

Forensic accounting firms and investigators often assist investigation counsel in sensitive payment investigations. They can gather and secure electronic evidence, deal with encrypted data, assist in identifying robust search terms, conduct searches for sensitive terms (e.g., *bribe, sunshine money, kickback, gift, tea, oil, grease, comisión confidencial, caisse noire*), identify books-and-records and internal controls issues, and assist in recommending and formulating improved internal controls and other remedial measures. These forensic specialists should normally be independent and not the company's regular outside accounting or auditing firm. The retention of qualified forensic accountants under the direction of investigation counsel can provide regular outside auditors an increased level of comfort about the thoroughness of the investigation, the forensic component, and the status of internal controls.

Since there is no federal accountant-client privilege, investigation counsel—not the client—should retain the forensic accounting firm under a clearly defined scope of work set forth in an engagement letter. Investigation counsel should carefully monitor the scope of the accountant or investigation engagement, the work plan, interviews, and progress. Whenever nonlawyers are assigned responsibilities, they should perform under the direction of and report to counsel in order to maintain the attorney-client privilege and work-product protection.[3] Counsel should determine early on what types of memoranda forensic accountants or investigations will prepare and if they will remain in draft form.

E-mails are the primary form of internal and external communications for many multinational corporations (MNCs) in almost all industries today and frequently provide the DNA in white-collar criminal investigations. Indeed, some lawyers contend the "e" in e-mail stands for evidence. As a result, thorough e-mail searches are standard and a must for virtually any significant internal investigation to be credible. Sometimes companies resist conducting detailed electronic searches by internal auditors, inside counsel, or outside investigation counsel, considering them too expensive, invasive, and time-consuming. E-mail searches have proven very telltale in anticorruption investigations, and the discovery of highly relevant e-mails has led the DOJ and SEC to benefit from and expect, if not insist upon, thorough e-mail searches in any credible internal investigation. Oftentimes, a company's outside auditor will shadow an internal investigation because the audit firm wants to know how deep and wide any potential problems may be and, in particular, to know if past financial statements are accurate and whether it can rely on the representations of the company's senior management. For these reasons, it is common to share planned search terms with shadow auditors and to provide an overview of the investigation work plan. (See also section II.E.)

The following employee e-mail, which was uncovered in Tenaris, S.A.'s FCPA investigation into payments to an Uzbekistan agent to influence the bidding process with a state-controlled oil company, illustrates the potential minefield from electronic searches:

> So dirty game is when . . . [p]eople from the [OAO, a wholly owned subsidiary of the state holding company of Uzbekistan's oil and gas industry] tender department . . . [c]an carefully open required bids and check the prices and deliveries of competitors and advise for where you need to be lower and where you need to be higher. . . . And if you decide to revise your prices & delivery, it can be done and physically your commercial offer will be replaced by a revised offer and envelope

will be sealed again. But this is very risky for them also, because if people get caught while doing this they will go automatically to jail. So as [OAO] agent said, that's why this dirty service is expensive.[4]

There are numerous forensic software programs and narrowing techniques available to investigation counsel and forensic accountants that can substantially reduce the number of e-mails that need to be searched. This in turn substantially reduces attorney and investigator review time, which usually constitutes the bulk of the expense of electronic searches.

Focused interviews, preferably in the country in question, are the sine qua non of any corporate internal investigation and are particularly challenging in an FCPA investigation given the typical cultural and language challenges. It is useful for counsel to have all relevant documents, including e-mails, and to prepare and update a comprehensive working chronology that not only tracks and analyzes key underlying conduct and meetings but identifies key players (and their counsel), questionable payments, hot electronic and hard documents, false books and records, potential red flag issues, due diligence steps, disciplinary actions, disclosure to one or more agencies, cooperation efforts, internal controls issues, remedial measures, and other important events or mitigating factors. Without a continuously updated chronology, it is usually difficult to recall and understand the relationships and timing of key events and documents in a lengthy or complex multicountry investigation. Chronologies can be particularly helpful in tracking the activities of employees or agents in several countries, regions, ventures, or operations. Finally, they are helpful in recalling key documents, preparing for important interviews, and drafting internal reports, position papers, Wells submissions, PowerPoint presentations, and remedial recommendations for companies, boards of directors, and government authorities.

Legal issue development will obviously focus on the statutory provisions, the legislative history, the FCPA case law, FCPA national or territorial jurisdiction over a company and individuals, FCPA criminal prosecutions, SEC enforcement actions,[5] deferred prosecution agreements (DPAs), nonprosecution agreements (NPAs), foreign or local law, and any relevant FCPA opinions issued by the DOJ. It can include a review of analogous statutes such as domestic bribery statutes, applicable conventions (as implemented), and related case law.

D. Investigations Likely to Be Disclosed to and Shared with U.S. Government Law Enforcement Authorities and SEC Criticism of Investigative Tactics

Increasingly, companies, boards of directors, or audit committees authorize internal investigations, knowing there is a reasonable likelihood that any report or results may be shared in some fashion with the DOJ or SEC. This practice is especially common where the client seeks voluntary disclosure and cooperation credit. Whether counsel actually shares the contents of a PowerPoint presentation or a report with the government as part of disclosure or cooperation, there is a strong probability that government attorneys will examine the thoroughness and investigation plan of counsel conducting the investigation and seeking cooperation credit for a client.

Government attorneys will review the scope of the engagement, the e-mail and hard document collection and search protocols, the number of interviews, the seniority of the interviewees, and any logical investigation avenues. Oftentimes, the DOJ or SEC will ask counsel to expand the scope of an investigation, add search terms, and conduct additional interviews or work. Perhaps, as important, the DOJ or SEC staff may come to question the ethical practices of lawyers conducting corporate internal investigations. On June 1, 2011, then Director Robert S. Khuzami of the SEC Division of Enforcement offered in a speech in New York City[6] four questionable investigative tactics the SEC has observed in internal investigations:

1. Interviewing multiple witnesses at once;
2. Aggressively promoting exculpatory evidence while dismissing clear and identifiable red flags;
3. Scapegoating lower-level employees and/or protecting senior management who have long-standing relationships with the counsel in question; and
4. Failing to acknowledge the constraints placed on the scope of the inquiry.

These tactics can undermine the goal of voluntary disclosure following an often expensive investigation: to obtain meaningful credit for the client. Investigation counsel should be mindful of these criticisms in conducting an investigation where the client will likely disclose and cooperate or at least intends to preserve that option.

II. PRELIMINARY INVESTIGATION ISSUES AND PRACTICES

A. Identification of the Client

An important early question to decide is: Who is the client—the corporation, the board of directors, the audit committee, or a special committee? The answer will in part be determined by the company's structure and whether the investigation involves alleged wrongdoing by any members of senior management.[7] Retainer letters and agreements with outside counsel should specify who counsel represents.[8]

B. Use of In-House or Outside Counsel and the Role of Independence

At the outset, a company or its general counsel will decide whether an FCPA allegation should be handled internally by the legal department. It is wise to insist at a minimum that internal audit staff, security personnel, or nonlawyers review any significant credible FCPA allegations with the oversight of counsel so that legal privilege will attach. Sometimes an FCPA allegation can be ably handled by in-house attorneys. Other times, due to limited corporate legal department resources, the scope of the allegation(s), in-house counsel's advice or participation in the transaction at issue, the awkwardness of interviewing senior management or one's colleagues, or in-house counsel's lack of DOJ or SEC experience, a company or a board will retain independent outside counsel.

If an allegation is credible and indicates any pattern of improper payments and/or approval by senior management and there is likely a disclosure obligation by a public company, it is usually wise to retain a law firm expert in FCPA and white-collar criminal defense matters. If the matter has a potential to become substantial and disclosure is likely, the DOJ and SEC will want to be sure credible and experienced independent counsel are conducting the investigation. In the current and foreseeable regulatory environment, independent counsel—without a substantial inside or regular outside counsel company role—are more likely to be credited by prosecutors, regulators, private counsel and courts (e.g., when justifying settlement of a class or derivative lawsuit).[9]

C. Legal Representation

Issues of legal representation can arise, especially in dealing with officers and employees.

- In representing the company, the board, or an audit committee, investigative counsel will come into contact with many mid- and low-level employees. These individuals may assume that outside counsel represents them personally and offer self-incriminating information. ABA Model Rule 1.13(D) requires an attorney who represents only a company, board, or committee to ensure that employees understand at the outset of interviews that only the company or committee is the client—not the employees—and that the employees may wish to seek separate counsel.
- Counsel should also advise employees that the interview is privileged, that the privilege belongs to the company or committee, which alone retains the right to waive it, and that the company or committee may decide to share the results of the interview with government agencies such as the DOJ or SEC.[10] If the company or committee is highly likely to waive the privilege, employees should be so advised.
- Employees may be warned that the company may take disciplinary action against them later based on the information learned in the interview.
- Counsel should control who attends interviews of employees. The presence of a nonattorney at an interview can result in a waiver of the attorney-client privilege.[11]
- Counsel should avoid tape-recording or transcribing verbatim interviews. Tape-recorded interviews are less likely to enjoy the protection of opinion work product since they do not reflect counsel's mental processes. Also, unless counsel is prepared to tape-record every interview, the decision to record some interviews but not others will be questioned.
- Counsel and the client should consider whether "pool counsel" for a group of nonconflicted mid- and low-level employees is appropriate.

D. Legal Privileges

Oftentimes, a company will opt for the least expensive review without first considering the privilege implications. Unless the attorney-client and attorney work-product privileges are carefully protected, a written report or PowerPoint presentation and/or underlying work product may become discoverable.[12] Also, the work product of an internal audit department, accounting firm, or a forensic firm is going to receive far less privilege protection than the work product of a law firm.

E. Communications with Outside Auditors

A company conducting an internal investigation will need to decide when and whether to disclose the nature and findings of an FCPA investigation to its regular outside auditor. The latter will be concerned inter alia about the accuracy of prior public financial statements, the adequacy of internal controls, and the integrity of management representation letters. Inasmuch as the regular outside auditor has a vested interest in the accuracy and integrity of past and future public filings, the quality of an FCPA internal investigation is critically important to it. Investigation counsel's retention of a quality forensic accounting firm can provide the regular outside auditor with comfort about search protocols, internal central analyses, and appropriate remedial measures.

The regular outside auditor will want to review any hot documents; understand who will be or has been interviewed, particularly any members of senior management who made representations; what search terms are to be employed; whether hard and soft data/documents have been preserved; and what type of report findings will be forthcoming. Informal exchange of necessary information can usually be negotiated by responsible professionals. While the regular outside auditor should not guide an independent FCPA investigation, it is usually wise to have early and ongoing communication with its personnel so that its engagement partner, national office, and risk group have trust in the integrity and thoroughness of the investigation and continued confidence in senior management. What an outside auditor neither wants nor needs is notification of a completed internal investigation on the eve of a public filing.

Any disclosure to an auditor raises waiver risks, and the courts are split on whether the disclosure of investigation results to a company's outside auditor waives work-product protection. In *Medinol Ltd. v. Boston Scientific Corp.*,[13] Medinol provided internal investigation information to its outside auditors in connection with their audit of the company's litigation exposure. A Southern District of New York court found that the disclosure of meeting minutes of the Special Litigation Committee to Ernst & Young (E&Y) waived the protection of the work-product doctrine. The court found that, as an outside auditor, E&Y's interests were not necessarily united with those of Boston Scientific and that the disclosure served a litigation purpose.

In *Merrill Lynch & Co., Inc. v. Allegheny Energy Inc.*,[14] a Southern District of New York court in 2004 reviewed the disclosure of the internal investigation reports (conducted by and under the supervision of in-house and outside counsel) to outside auditors Deloitte & Touche. Allegheny Energy sought to obtain the reports, contending that the disclosure to outside auditors constituted a waiver of any applicable privilege. The district court found that Merrill Lynch and Deloitte & Touche were not adversaries as contemplated by the work-product doctrine. Specifically, any business between an auditor and a corporation that arises from an auditor's need to scrutinize and investigate a corporation's records and bookkeeping practices simply is not the equivalent of the adversarial relationship contemplated by the doctrine.

The Merrill Lynch district court observed that a business and its auditor can and should be aligned insofar as they both seek to prevent, detect, and root out corporate fraud. Without access to information regarding internal controls that directly relate to the reliability of financial information and legality of corporate behavior, auditors would likely fail in the fulfillment of their important public trust. The district court concluded that to construe a company's auditor as an adversary and to find a blanket rule of waiver of the applicable work-product privilege could and would discourage companies from conducting critical self-analysis and addressing the fruits of such inquiries with appropriate actions. Other courts have since adopted the Merrill Lynch rationale, and now the majority view is that disclosure to independent auditors does not waive work-product protection.[15]

III. AMERICAN COLLEGE OF TRIAL LAWYERS' RECOMMENDED PRACTICES FOR INTERNAL INVESTIGATIONS

In February 2008, the American College of Trial Lawyers published a best internal investigation practices report titled *Recommended Practices for Companies and Their Counsel in Conducting Internal Investigations* (appendix 8). The report addresses factors to consider when evaluating whether to commence an internal investigation, the role of the board and management in conducting and overseeing an investigation, the need for independent outside counsel, and the appropriate scope of the inquiry. It also covers the mechanics of a litigation hold, document collection and review, and witness interviews. This "best practices" report is recommended reading for both the general counsel and investigation counsel of companies undertaking FCPA internal investigations as well as counsel representing officers or employees in these investigations.

IV. DOCUMENTS

A. Nondestruction Memoranda or Litigation Hold Memoranda

As soon as counsel and a client determine there is a credible FCPA allegation and a possible violation, a company should take prompt steps to ensure that relevant documents—hard and electronic—are preserved. This invariably means issuance of a timely, formal nondestruction memorandum or a litigation hold memorandum to all relevant officers and employees, including domestic and foreign information technology personnel. If the matter becomes public or investigated by U.S. prosecutors or regulators, one of their first questions will concern what the company did to secure and preserve all relevant documents. How well a company answers this question can determine its credibility with the board, audit committee, prosecutors, and regulators. Companies and counsel should take precautions to make sure that persons whose conduct may be the subject of the investigation are not responsible for gathering, organizing, and preserving documents. Often, counsel, forensic accountants, or paralegals can perform this function.

B.   Security of Documents and Databases[16]

Corporate internal investigations present challenging security implications because investigations often deal with information that is very sensitive and may never become public. This is particularly true of FCPA investigations where different security issues may arise by virtue of the documents' location on foreign soil, including issues raised by foreign data privacy laws.

Counsel should implement proper security issues at the outset of any document-gathering process for several reasons. First, the documents may contain sensitive business information. Second, although the documents may not be sensitive on their face, their designation as "relevant to the investigation" can make them de facto sensitive. Third, proper security can enhance the efficiency of storage, organization, and retrieval. Fourth, proper security will decrease the chance of loss or destruction of critical documents and lessen the likelihood of the company being party to an obstruction of justice investigation.

Whether the documents consist of hard copies stored in boxes, or computer data stored electronically, or both, care must be taken to prevent unauthorized persons from having access to them. Counsel should limit access to investigative documents on a "need to know" basis. Whether the documents are stored in a locked drawer in counsel's office or in a warehouse off site, the premises should be kept secure, knowledge about the storage of the data should be limited, and access should be restricted. Depending upon the nature of the investigation, the number of documents, and the site of storage, counsel may implement sign-in or key-card procedures to limit and track access.

Although automated data support systems can be advantageous to investigating counsel, they can also make it possible for unauthorized third parties to quietly access large volumes of records, possibly off-site. Confidential passwords for system access and data encryption during any electronic transmission are easily available and usually inexpensive. Encryption generally renders the data useless to persons gaining unauthorized access.[17] How much or how little metadata to transmit will depend on the mandate of the investigation. If data is being stored electronically, counsel should also take appropriate measures to reduce the chances of electronic or system problems that can cause the loss of data. Antivirus programs and other preventive measures will lessen the chance of a computer virus creating havoc with the data.[18] Quality surge protectors and an uninterruptible power supply will minimize the risk of problems caused by electric surges, lightning strikes, and short circuits.[19]

Document security can take different forms. Object-based security systems in electronic review platforms allow for restrictions on the objects (tags, folders, etc.) and metadata elements that reviewers can see. Since many of the objects used in a document review reflect privileged attorney work product, restricting certain reviewers from access to work product is often appropriate. Document-based security systems limit reviewers' access to specific sets of documents. Feature-based security systems can be used to restrict users from using certain features, for example, restricted download or redaction features. Most electronic document review vendors can provide review groups with different levels of security.

C. Foreign Document Preservation and Review

Because FCPA investigations extend beyond the borders of the United States, counsel should pay particular attention to foreign laws and treaties governing access to documents relevant to investigation. In some countries, the code law is inconsistent with unwritten local custom and practice. Close collaboration with local counsel and personnel is usually essential to the success of an FCPA investigation. If the company intends to cooperate with U.S. authorities, the DOJ or SEC will want and expect the company or its investigative counsel to preserve appropriate chains of custody for evidence.

D. Data Protection or Data Privacy Laws

"Data protection" or "data privacy" laws govern the use of personal information relating to an identified or identifiable individual and have been adopted internationally in often haphazard fashion. There is significant variance among countries in the scope of personal information that qualifies for legal protection, the necessity for the individual's consent for the review of such information, the nature of actions that legally can be performed with the information, and the rights and remedies afforded to both the individual and the investigating counsel. Other countries—notably, the United States—do not have a comprehensive data protection regime.

The best-known data protection regime is that adopted by nations of the European Union, set forth in Directive 95/46/EC of the European Parliament and of the Council on the Protection of Individuals with Regard to the Processing of Personal Data and on the Free Movement of Such Data. Many other regions also have data protection regimes. Some regional regimes are formalized, such as the Asia Pacific Economic Cooperation (APEC) area's common data principles for Asia.[20] Others are informal, consisting of similarities between the data protection laws of the countries within the region. Still others are specific to individual countries and are not common at all to a region. The regional variations of data protection regimes necessarily influence the practical mechanics of integrating data protection considerations into data collection, processing, and review.

1. *Elements of Data Protection Regimes*

Data protection regimes have two key elements: (1) the definition of data subject to protection and (2) the definition of circumstances under which certain actions with respect to such data are permissible.

a. Definition of Personal Data

Generally, data subject to protection includes any information relating to an identified or identifiable natural person.[21] Most regimes have an extraordinarily broad approach to defining personal data, with many regimes—for example, the European Union countries—even expressly including the individual's name within the scope of personal data.[22] Moreover, certain individual data is deemed even more worthy of special protection, such as data relating to the custodian's race or ethnic background, sexual and criminal history, and political, philosophical, religious, and trade union affiliations, and may be subject to even more stringent regulations—including, in some circumstances, a complete bar on the processing of such data even with the custodian's consent. For that reason, investigating counsel must take data protection law into account with almost any collection or interview undertaken in a data protection jurisdiction.

b.   Data Processing Restrictions

The second element of data protection is the restriction on certain types of data processing under certain circumstances. "Data processing" is generally defined—equally broadly—as any action taken with respect to personal data, including its collection, review, replication, transmission, export, modification, or deletion. The key difference between data protection regimes lies in the precise actions that can be performed with personal data, and the circumstances under which they are permissible. For instance, many data protection regimes, including Europe's, prohibit the export of personal data to countries that do not assure a similar level of data protection.[23] That prohibition certainly includes the United States, which has no comprehensive data privacy regime. (Note, however, that a limited exception to that prohibition exists pursuant to the safe harbor self-certification program between the EU and the United States, which allows export to companies that participate in the program.)[24]

Other restrictions may include those on transferring personal data to "third parties," which may or may not include the company's outside counsel, auditors, and consultants, and which may even encompass other legal entities within the company's corporate group. In the case of a multinational corporation, the company's parent organization may thus be precluded from reviewing its employees' personal data. Investigating counsel must be mindful of such restrictions and take them into account when planning the international portion of the investigation.

2.   Consent of Data Subject

The most challenging aspect of data protection law compliance, from the standpoint of conducting a foreign investigation, is the necessity to obtain consent of the affected individual (data subject) before processing the data. Most data protection regimes generally require the consent of the data subject before any data processing begins.[25] The need to obtain a data subject's consent, if not handled correctly, can pose a problem to the investigating counsel; particularly where the data subject's documents may contain information damaging to the data subject, as is often the case in an internal investigation, the data subject will have every incentive to withhold consent. Moreover, the company may be precluded from disciplining or threatening to discipline the data subject on these grounds: many regimes provide that consent must be "freely given," and some expressly prohibit termination on such grounds.[26] Although data protection regimes sometimes provide exceptions to the consent requirement, such exceptions may be insufficient for the performance of a proper investigation. Accordingly, investigating counsel must design the investigation in such a manner as to either maximize the likelihood of obtaining consent, or find an exception to the consent requirement.

a. Consent as a Condition of Employment

The best approach is prevention—in this case, of the need to secure an uncooperative data subject's consent, or an exception to the consent requirement, in the middle of the investigation. Such consent is best obtained at the time the data subject becomes an employee of the company, when the data subject may be required to provide it as a condition of employment, and, not yet having done anything improper, is unlikely to have a vested interest in withholding it. An advance consent must be both specific enough to comply with the consent specificity requirements and broad enough to encompass any data relating to the data subject, whether maintained by the company or by the data subject himself or herself, that might become relevant in an investigation.

Relatively few companies have an advance consent provision in place when the need for an FCPA investigation arises. Some companies may have a consent requirement that is insufficiently broad; others may have one that is legally questionable. In some cases, investigating counsel, in coordination with the company, may offer the data subject "immunity," or guarantee that no adverse action will result from the investigation, in exchange for the data subject's cooperation in the investigation. This tactic may be useful in an internal investigation targeting higher-level misconduct, particularly where it is likely that the data subject may have relevant information, and where the review of such information would not violate the rights of others. In cases where this is not possible, investigating counsel must devise a strategy to proceed with the investigation, without obtaining the data subject's consent, but in compliance with the local data privacy law.

b. Use of In-House Personnel

One strategy is to make substantial use of in-house company personnel or contract lawyers in executing the review, at least in the initial stages. While investigating counsel may be prohibited from engaging in any data processing due to lack of consent, the company itself may not be. The company's in-house legal, compliance, or control personnel can be key in performing functions that require access to the data subject's personal data. For example, they may be tasked with performing the first-level review of the unconsenting data subject's files. They can then communicate their findings, or even specific documents, to the investigating counsel, provided that personal data is redacted. Specific data subjects and other individuals may be assigned code names or numbers, and investigating counsel may use such code names and numbers to keep track of documents, request additional information, and designate specific individuals for further action (such as an additional collection or an interview).

In circumstances where in-house personnel entrusted with this responsibility are not available (e.g., in a multinational corporation's small subsidiary lacking its own legal or compliance function, or where such personnel may have been compromised), local laws may permit an arrangement whereby outside personnel or lawyers may be seconded to the company to temporarily work as the company's own employees. Under such circumstances, the seconded personnel (which can come from the investigating counsel's firm, a consulting firm, or elsewhere) will act just like in-house personnel with respect to preventing the investigating counsel from seeing anything that may be deemed "personal data."

E.   Document Preservation Mechanics in FCPA Investigations

1.   *Physical Presence*

Since data may be governed both by the law of the jurisdiction in which the original data controller is located and the law of the jurisdiction to which the data is to be exported, the physical scope of the data collection is relevant to the choice of data collection and processing vendor. Under the European Directive, for example, data export to a country without "adequate" data protection laws may be prohibited. As a practical matter, counsel should consider not only the formal data protection safeguards a vendor has in place, but also whether the vendor has sufficient reach to collect the data in all of the relevant locations, or good relationships with qualified local subvendors who can do so. Subvendors may be desirable in some locations because they may have experience with obscure hardware and local operating systems, as well as with local data archival practices, and they may be helpful in planning the scope of the collection effort. A vendor should provide technical specifications for the types of load files it needs to process the data. If documents are to be collected from several locations, it may be useful to collect, process, and review samples of data from each location to ensure that the process is working correctly before fully committing to it.

2.   *Server Location and Cross-Border Data Flows*

Counsel should also consider the physical location of the server that will host the data to be collected and reviewed. A client may feel safer if counsel hosts its data within the company itself (which is often unfeasible without compromising the investigation) or within outside counsel's firm, especially if the law firm is certified as a safe harbor, rather than with an outside vendor. In other circumstances, it may be advantageous to physically store the data within the jurisdiction of collection, in order to obviate cross-border data transfer issues in jurisdictions that impose such restrictions.

3.   *Data Transfer Agreements and Data Subject Consent*

Even where the law does not require a data transfer agreement or data subject consent, counsel may consider obtaining them anyway, to the extent that it can be done without compromising the investigation. It is not always easy to determine at the beginning of an FCPA investigation all of the countries to which the data might need to be exported or that might host a portion of the data subject's data. Obtaining consent early in an investigation can avoid delay.[27]

4.   *Foreign Language Documents*

Documents and data located in foreign countries are often in languages other than English. Sometimes even a single document may contain several languages (e.g., an e-mail where a data subject corresponds with a colleague in Spanish and another person replies with history in English, or a contract prepared in multiple languages simultaneously). The languages involved in an investigation will affect the selection of the vendor or vendors to process the data and the system used to store and review the data. Many U.S.–based electronic data vendors and review systems use only the American Standard Code for Information Interchange (ASCII). These vendors cannot process special characters used in other languages. The best format for supporting a multilingual review is Unicode, as it will process diacritical marks (such as accents, umlauts, diereses, and cedillas) and special characters in Latin alphabets (such as eszett (ß) and ethel (œ)), as well as characters from languages not written in the Latin alphabet, for example, Chinese and Arabic. Additionally, language recognition systems vary across vendors. Accordingly, counsel should also consider language issues when selecting a vendor.

5. *Search Terms for Foreign Language Documents*

Search terms play an essential role in data processing by trimming the amount of data to export, host, and review, and therefore limiting expense and data export issues. Counsel and client will want to use search terms that are relevant and appropriate for the country in question, for example, "red packets" and "UDPs" (under the desk payments) in China. Search terms will be more successful if they address language-specific characters and modifications (e.g., in German, writing terms with "ss" in addition to "ß" or "ue" in addition to "ü") and account for various word forms, such as conjugation and cases, through the use of wildcards. Often, the most sensitive e-mails in a corruption investigation will be in a foreign language. Local company personnel and vendors may be able to provide information on these common issues; however, investigating counsel should take care to ensure that the vendor offers the ability to arrange the search terms accordingly.

6. *Multilingual Data Reviewers*

Depending on the scope of an FCPA investigation, it may be necessary to employ contract attorneys who read foreign languages. Many countries lack markets for contract attorneys; therefore, somewhat counterintuitively, investigating counsel may have an easier time finding contract attorneys with specific language skills in major international centers than in the "home country." Lead investigation counsel should conduct overview presentations for contract attorneys in order to introduce them to the hot topics and alert them to the categories of hot documents.

F. Electronic Evidence

Electronic evidence may be divided into two broad categories: (1) structured electronically stored information (ESI) and (2) unstructured ESI. Structured ESI is contained in databases, such as financial or accounting databases (e.g., general ledger, accounts payable, and payroll). Unstructured ESI includes e-mails and other resources (e.g., Word and Excel documents, instant messaging logs, and voicemail). Too often internal investigations focus on structured data at the expense of unstructured data and, in particular, e-mails, which can be the source of evidence that bears heavily on search for intent.

Data mining is an analytic technique that involves searching through large amounts of data to identify relevant information, patterns, trends, and differences indicative of fraud. Electronic evidence experts Ben Hawksworth and Jennifer Had-sell have observed:

> Typically, 80% of data collected during an investigation is e-mail and other unstructured data. Investigators should consider the use of alternative search methods, such as concept clustering, social network analysis, and thread analysis, in order to facilitate the discovery of important evidence. Concept clustering groups data into sets with similar scenes. Social network analysis captures the pattern and frequency of communications between custodians, and thread analysis groups together e-mails that are part of a chain so that the investigator can more easily understand the entire conversation.[28]

Clients often understandably question the cost of collection and analysis of large volumes of electronic data. However, to the extent that the government, an outside auditor, or other third parties will review an internal investigation and be expected to credit and rely on its work, an investigation that does not substantially review and analyze relevant unstructured data is likely to be given little weight.

V. SOURCES OF IN-COUNTRY INFORMATION

In conducting an internal investigation of a foreign operation, there are many sources of information that can help determine whether it is more likely than not that a certain event occurred or that it was a factor in a questionable transaction. Many sources are the same that transactional lawyers use in conducting the due diligence for a foreign transaction. Helpful foreign sources and records include

1. In-country records
   a. Consulting contracts and agency agreements
   b. Joint venture documentation
      i. Agreement outlining rights and responsibilities
      ii. Articles of association
      iii. Partner shareholders
      iv. Partner director, officer, and key employee backgrounds
      v. Government touchpoints and interface
      vi. Business contracts with governments and others
         a. Anticorruption warranties and representations
         b. Books-and-records warranties and representations
      vii. Minutes
      viii. Anticorruption training programs for directors, managers, and employees
      ix. Audits
   c. Electronic databases
   d. General ledgers
   e. Local bank account statements
   f. Subcontracts

      g. Vendor lists and aging accounts
      h. Expense reports (e.g., travel and entertainment)
      i. Correspondence files
      j. Petty cash accounts
      k. Purchase records
      l. Professional service fees and expenses
          i. Attorneys
          ii. Accountants
      m. Off-the-books records
      n. Charitable contributions
      o. Gift lists
      p. Cash vouchers
      q. Leases
      r. Court records
          i. Federal
          ii. State

2. In-country employees
      a. General managers or managing directors
      b. Financial officers
      c. Sales and marketing personnel
      d. Accounting and bookkeeping personnel
      e. Operations personnel
      f. Legal personnel
      g. Information technology personnel
      h. Purchasing department personnel
      i. Project managers, superintendents, and engineers
      j. Project estimators
      k. Security personnel

3. Former employees
4. Subcontractors
5. Agents
6. Periodicals and publications
      a. Transparency International reports and surveys
      b. International company profiles (ICPs) of the U.S. Commerce Department
      c. Local and regional business and trade journals
      d. Dun & Bradstreet reports
      e. Local government publications, circulars, or gazettes

7. Local law firms
8. Local accounting firms
9. American Local Chambers of Commerce[29]
10. Banking references
11. Local industry associations
12. U.S. embassies or consulates (Commercial Attaché)
13. Internet sites of vendors, consultants, agents, and others
14. State Department and Commerce Department desk officers
15. Trace International reports

16. Local registrations
17. Private investigators

None of these sources will likely be dispositive in itself, but a combination can help one draw inferences or conclusions.

VI. INTERVIEWS

FCPA investigations are the most challenging of all corporate investigations because the potential misconduct is serious, many countries in which misconduct may have occurred are distant and tolerant of corruption, interviewees are frequently hostile and indifferent to U.S. laws, and, in limited cases, there is personal risk to investigating counsel. A first-rate FCPA investigation requires a comprehensive chronology, *infra*, that covers witness backgrounds, legal issues, factual issues, hot documents, and key events and meetings. Counsel should have strong interview skills, a command of the FCPA, and a knowledge of the local laws and practices—as well as patience, persistence, and discretion. The goal should be to conduct fair, firm, and focused interviews where persons are able to provide their best and most accurate recollections and express opinions. The object of the investigation is to obtain as much accurate and reliable information from knowledgeable witnesses as quickly and efficiently as possible.

A. Hot Documents

To conduct quality interviews, counsel should secure key hot documents in advance and, where appropriate, have documents translated. Most often, interviews are conducted by subject and/or in chronological order. Counsel (in coordination with forensic teams) will often conduct extensive electronic searches in order to best capture relevant documents among databases containing hundreds of thousands (or more) of documents. Concurrent with the review of documents to determine whether improper payments occurred will be a review of a company's or subsidiary's books and records for false entries. Where numerous false books and records are uncovered, there may be an internal controls weakness. It is recommended, where practical, that witnesses be provided key documents in advance, including e-mails, invoices, and other company books and records.[30]

Because of the particular countries and distances often involved in multinational operations, e-mail is routinely used by employees and frequently critical to the investigation, prosecution, and defense of FCPA cases and, in particular, the corrupt intent element the DOJ must prove beyond a reasonable doubt. Counsel will want to conduct exhaustive searches of a client's electronic database to determine whether employees authored or received sensitive e-mails; were copied on such e-mails; approved, authorized, or ratified payments or excessive travel and entertainment; utilized intermediaries; and, of course, had direct or indirect contact with any foreign government officials. One should assume that the DOJ Fraud Section and SEC Enforcement Division are conducting thorough searches of the company's computers and databases in their investigations. E-mail trails may establish that a broad or narrow group of company officers, employees, or third-party intermediaries were privy to questionable transactions or that counsel approved a payment. Contemporaneous e-mail patterns can negate or establish good faith. In order to conduct effective interviews, counsel should first collect and catalogue all hot e-mail and hard documents.

B. In-Country

With few exceptions, FCPA investigations and interviews should be conducted in the countries where the employees or witnesses worked during the alleged conduct in question. This usually enables counsel to interview a number of knowledgeable persons at once in-country and to be able to easily gather original additional documents that may have not been secured, produced, or even contemplated initially. Employees or witnesses often prefer an off-site interview location (e.g., local law office, hotel conference room) where there are fewer employment distractions and others may not be able to observe the interview(s). Another advantage of in-country interviews is that bilingual lawyers, investigators, or translators may be more accessible and less expensive; the former may also be able to properly opine on local written laws and language idioms. Where interviewees do not speak or understand English well, professional translators will be necessary. Counsel will usually want to have a colleague present since a second lawyer can take more careful notes, help clarify unclear statements, prepare memoranda of interviews, and be able to confirm the essence of the interview, if necessary later. It may be helpful for counsel to first review a country profile by *The Economist* or a thorough country or regional analysis by an organization such as Control Risks.

C. Third-Party Interviews

Investigation counsel will usually have the authority to require current employees to submit to interviews or face termination. Former employees and third parties present a different challenge as there is often no control or leverage to make them submit to interviews. In some instances, cooperation clauses in agency or consulting agreements may compel agents or consultants to submit to interviews. Severance agreements may also require former employees to cooperate. Some third parties and former employees who have joined or advise competitors may use knowledge of the investigation or information gleaned during an interview to their or their new employer's business advantage. Counsel will in such situations have to weigh the potential benefits and costs of third-party interviews to the client and act in its best interest.

D. *Upjohn* Warning

At the outset, counsel should give an interviewee an *Upjohn* warning[31] and make clear whom he represents, the purpose of the interview, and that the interview is privileged. If the interviewing lawyer represents a corporation, a board of directors, an audit committee, or a special committee and is interviewing an employee, he or she should make clear the identity of the company or entity he or she represents and equally clarify that he or she does not represent the employee. Often, employees or officers mistakenly assume company counsel also represents them. Counsel should further explain that the client controls the privilege and confidentiality of the communication, and that only the corporate client may elect to waive and disclose the communication to others. If a company is in fact cooperating with the U.S. government or a foreign government, the employee should be apprised of that fact and told that waiver of the privilege is probable, likely, or certain. The employee or witness should be asked if he or she has any questions and be directed not to discuss the substance of the interview with other employees.

E. Order and Methodology

FCPA investigation interviews may not be as orderly as desired due to employees being engaged in assignments elsewhere, being on vacation, or having schedule and travel conflicts. Usually, there is a company lawyer or manager who can give an overview of the operation in question and sensitive issues. This person may have valuable insight into not only the issues, but the likely biases, candor, cooperation, and reliability of employees to be interviewed. The overview person may also provide valuable input into the most effective order of interviews, including who may have the most firsthand knowledge, who may be the most forthright, or who may try to intimidate or influence other employees or witnesses. Ordinarily, managers should not be present for interviews of subordinates since their presence may lessen the candor or cooperation of the employee and, as important, vitiate privileges.

Absent unique circumstances, each witness should be interviewed separately. Further, each witness should be instructed not to discuss the substance of the interview with anyone else (other than counsel). Otherwise, there is a risk others will claim that the company or counsel gathered key employees or other witnesses to get their story straight. In many cases, it is advantageous to interview lower-level employees first and to work up to senior personnel. Sometimes, schedules do not permit investigating counsel to interview in this order, and flexibility or adaptability by all is necessary.

F. Clarification and Omnibus Questions

Before the conclusion of an interview, investigation counsel can ask the employee or witness if he or she wishes to add or clarify any topic and pose an omnibus question that covers the central subject(s), for example, "Are you aware of any (other) improper payments, gifts, or vacations, paid for by Alpha, directly or indirectly, to government officials or employees in Angola?" To the extent the company is cooperating with U.S. authorities who may conduct later interviews, the omnibus question can be expected to be asked by prosecutors or SEC staff. It is better for the company and its counsel to know the answer to any omnibus questions in advance. With some long-time employees or senior managers, it can also be instructive at the end of the interview to ask if they have any remedial suggestions or ideas as to who else should be interviewed. Their answers may form what remedial measures or new controls may be practical or helpful.

G. Memoranda of Interviews

Ordinarily, memoranda of interviews should be prepared or at least drafted by investigation counsel within 72 hours of the interview(s). Lawyers will best remember the substance of the interview if a memorandum is promptly dictated or written shortly after the interview. This practice reduces the risk of mischaracterizing a witness statement or confusing a witness with another interviewee near the same time. The memorandum should contain mental impressions of its author and address legal theories, thereby preserving the work-product privilege. The memorandum should identify, if not append for easy convenience, any key records or hot documents covered in the interview. It is usually best for one person to conduct the questioning and another to take notes and draft the memorandum of interview and another to conduct the interview. Above all, interview memoranda should be clear, fair, and accurate. There is an increased risk today that investigation counsel will be called as a witness in administrative, civil, or criminal litigation to summarize a witness's statement—usually for impeachment purposes. Therefore, counsel should take extra care to be sure the work product is clear, fair, and accurate.

In an investigation involving a dozen or more interviewees, it is often helpful to obtain photographs of the employees or witnesses so that months or years later, counsel can recall the identities of persons interviewed long ago. Employee photographs can often be obtained from human resources or personnel files.

H. Potential Remedial Action Lists

If problematic conduct is uncovered in an investigation, a running list of potential remedial actions will be helpful—for example, disciplinary actions, rotation of expats or other personnel, new anticorruption policies, new third-party due diligence, correction of false books and records, increased FCPA audits, and implementation of FCPA training for local managers, accounting, and finance staff. It is best to promptly record possible remedial actions during the investigation lest they be forgotten later. In some cases, counsel can test on location the in-country practicality or efficacy of potential remedial measures with employees or managers.

VII. HYPOTHETICAL FCPA WITNESS INTERVIEW OUTLINE

The interviews of each investigation will vary depending upon the sensitive issue(s), and each interview may differ depending upon the employee's possible connection to or knowledge of the alleged bribery, books-and-records, or internal controls issues. The nature of the interview of the persons at corporate headquarters may differ substantially from those at foreign operation locations. In-country topics for one employee may be irrelevant to the interview of an accounting manager at corporate headquarters in the United States. It can be helpful in an outline to italicize exhibits to be shown to the witness or areas for follow-up or corroboration. An abbreviated FCPA hypothetical interview outline in an investigation into alleged improper payments in Angola[32] follows. Note that this interview outline is a work of fiction. Names, characters, places, and incidents are products of the author's imagination or are used fictitiously. Any resemblance to actual events, locales, or persons living or dead is entirely coincidental.

Hypothetical FCPA Witness: Owen Officer

1. *Upjohn* **Warning**
   - Explanation of the nature of the inquiry or investigation
   - Representation of company and not any individuals
   - Privileged nature of the interview and sole right of company to waive the privilege
   - Importance of telling the truth and distinguishing between what you know and what you are speculating
   - Request that you do not discuss the substance of interview with other employees

2. **Background**
   - Age and birthplace
   - Nationality
   - Language proficiency (Rank English skills 1 to 10: _____)
   - Education
     - Apprenticeships or degrees and dates
     - Degrees and advance degrees and dates
     - Relevant continuing education and dates
   - Work history
     - Current Alpha-Angola position and dates and responsibilities
     - Supervisors—direct and dotted line
     - Subordinates
     - Interface with U.S. parent corporation or headquarters
     - Current organization chart
     - Prior titles/positions with Company (e.g., sales, finance, procurement)
       - 2010—
       - 2007—2010:
       - 2004—2007:
     - Original hiring and interviews in 2010
       - Employee personnel file
     - Relevant travel
       - To Luanda
       - To Cabinda
       - To Geneva
       - To U.S. Headquarters (Houston)
   - Prior employment history
     - Titles/positions/dates
     - Locations
     - Reporting chain/interfaces
     - Antibribery or FCPA training
   - Computer practices
     - Desktop
     - Laptop
     - Other
   - Licenses (e.g., CPA, CFA)

- Determine whether the company used a recruiter or conducted any due diligence and reference checks

3. **Alpha Compliance and Training**
   - "Tone at the Top" messages
   - Company code of business conduct
     ° Receipt of code of business conduct
   - Ethics training
   - Antibribery or FCPA training
     ° 3/11 Annual sales meeting
     ° 2/10 Madrid sales meeting
     ° Ascertain whether there is documentary proof, for example, a sign-in sheet, that interviewee attended FCPA or antibribery training
   - Conflicts of interest coverage
     ° Receipt
   - Related-party interests coverage

4. **Key Topics**
   - Alleged improper payments for offshore Cabinda, Block Zero, Area R
     ° Cash receipts
       - Detail
       - Internal controls
     ° Meetings at Cabinda
       - Personal calendars
       - Dates
       - Documents
       - Expense reports
     ° Contract bids and awards and dates
     ° Books-and-records entries
   - 7/21/12 Award of Cabinda, Block Zero Area A to Petroangola–China Oil JV
   - 7/27/13 Award to Alpha of Cabinda, Block Zero Area Q EPC Contract
     ° Confirm signatures on contract
   - Rumors re: Cabinda award
     ° Conversations with Bodkin
     ° Conversations with Flagler
     ° Phone records to Cabinda
     ° E-mails to Cabinda July 1–29, 2013
   - Gifts to Petroangola officials in Luanda
     ° Dollar value
       - Given as a group or to an individual
       - Government official status
       - Requisition forms to purchase gifts
       - Title, agency, government website check
       - Transparency of gifts in subsidiary books and records
       - Description
       - Dollar value
       - Recipients

- ° Authority of recipients to award or retain business (e.g., Block Zero Areas D and E contracts)
- ° Block Zero Area B
- ° Contract award date
  - Approval of gifts by Finance Dept.
- Cash payments to local police to guard expats' compound and provide transportation to and from work
  - ° U.S. Embassy's cash payments for protection services of embassy personnel (counterargument)
  - ° Cash economy in Angola (e.g., gasoline stations, hotels, restaurants)
- Consultant Conrad Flagler
  - ° CV and engineering background of Conrad Flagler
  - ° Warranties and representations of his London-based company, Conrad Flagler Ltd. (CFL)
  - ° Brochures of CFL
  - ° Letters of reference from Congo, Dubai, and Qatar government officials
  - ° Other businesses and entities
  - ° Knighthood in 2004
  - ° 2/03/12 *Financial Times* article, "Flagler's Growing Ex-Minister Network in Western Africa"
  - ° Familiarity with CFL
  - ° Due diligence on CFL
    - 4/13/13 Recommendation of Petroangola official that Alpha retain Flagler as consultant
    - Interview
    - Bank
    - Trace International
  - ° Due diligence files
    - Where?
    - Who is responsible for EMEA (Europe, Middle East, and Africa) files?
    - Legal department input?
  - ° Other consultants considered for this project
  - ° CFL reference checks
    - Tobias Freeman
    - Foreign Minister Miguel Ilanguo
  - ° CFL local representation
  - ° Other CFL projects/clients in Angola or West Africa
  - ° Offices and staff of CFL
    - Luanda office
    - London office
    - Experience in oil and gas
    - Other multinational CFL customers
    - Visits to CFL offices
  - ° Awareness of consulting contract
    - CFL "Success Fee"

- Discussions
- Negotiation
- 10 percent figure
- "Payable Immediately" term when contract is three years
  - ° Payments to Swiss bank accounts
    - Who approved?
    - Who at CFL requested?
  - ° Retention known only to select subsidiary officers
  - ° CFL industry or energy sector history
  - ° Meetings with Conrad Flagler and the employees of CFL before award of CFL consulting contract
  - ° Flagler contacts with Petroangola
- Due diligence of consulting services
  - ° Invoices
  - ° Witness any efforts/successes of CFL
  - ° Contract performance
  - ° Any regular record of Alpha ongoing due diligence
- Circumvention of consultant contract approval procedure
  - ° No approval signatures
  - ° No forwarding of consultant contract to legal department
    - No audit rights clause
  - ° Finance Department
    - Payment of services under a general contract
    - No copy of CFL contract in records dept. files
    - No audit rights
- Four hot documents
  - ° 7/22/13 Deletion of audit rights clause by CFL on consultants draft agreement
  - ° 7/26/13 Request for $250,000 political campaign contribution to MPLA (ruling Angola political party)
  - ° 7/29/13 Conrad Flagler e-mail from Cabinda re: need to approve consultancy agreement ASAP and for $1 million advance
  - ° 7/26/13 e-mail of Alpha-Angola CFO to Flagler re: authorization for "extra expenses"
- Acts in the United States and other U.S. contacts
  - ° Travel to and purpose
  - ° E-mails
  - ° Telephone calls
  - ° Wire transfers
- Electrical fire
  - ° Security of storage facility
  - ° First awareness of fire
  - ° 10/16/10 Internal Security Report

5. **Parent Company Audits**
   - Frequency
   - EMEA

- Angola—2009
  - ° Poor books-and-records finding
  - ° No petty cash controls
- Findings

6. **Related-Party Interests**
   - Angola Dive
   - Luanda Trucking Ltd.
   - Determine whether local registrations exist and who are listed as owners

7. **Clarification and Omnibus Questions**
   - Is there anything you wish to clarify about what we have discussed today with respect to Alpha-Angola?
   - Is there any other information or documents you have with respect to possible improper payments by Alpha-Angola that you can share with us?

8. **Potential Remedial Actions (Optional)**
   - Based on your experience in the EMEA region, how would you go about ensuring that no improper payments are made by Alpha, or reducing the risk of such payments?

An FCPA interview outline can cover a host of key topics, such as facilitating payments, corrupt intent, evidence of transparency, acts by foreign employees while in the United States, state-owned enterprises, tours of overseas plants, local laws, and the detail of books-and-record entries. While proof of bribery conduct may be lacking, proof of books-and-records and internal controls violations may still exist, and such evidence should be addressed in interviews as well. When the U.S. government lacks proof of bribery conduct, it often tries to establish and file books-and-records and internal controls violations.

VIII. THE WORKING CHRONOLOGY

A. Overview

A working chronology is, at its essence, a privileged detailed record of both the underlying events and the FCPA investigation (internal and/or government) as it unfolds.[33] This key memorandum will provide counsel with a comprehensive overview of the documentary and interview evidence gathered in an investigation. Counsel will continually refer to the chronology to check dates, relevant payments, key players, hot documents including e-mails, important meetings, travel and entertainment records, and descriptions of other events, and to compare new information from document reviews and interviews against facts discovered previously.

The working chronology is often customized for the specifics or needs of the investigation. It may begin with a section that identifies the corporate hierarchy, listing key officers and employees of particular foreign operations. It can identify and break down the central legal issues to be addressed. Many investigating counsel include separate sections headed Investigation Team Contacts, U.S. Government Attorneys (e.g., DOJ and SEC) and FBI Agents, SEC Accountants, Legal Theories, Foreign Government Attorneys and Law Enforcement Agents, Potential Remedial Measures, and a To-Do List. Sections addressing important consulting contracts, questionable vendors, due diligence files, prior internal audits, financial performance at the parent or subsidiary level, applicable data privacy laws, or other facts bearing on relevant FCPA issues can also be inserted in a working chronology for easy and quick reference.

The actual chronology section itself will begin with the earliest known date relevant to the underlying issues. Any significant event, meeting, communication, or document should be noted with a brief description following the date. Counsel may review and include memoranda of interviews, diaries, calendars, general correspondence, telephone records, regulatory filings, facsimile transmissions, financial records, audit data, travel records, expense reports, correspondence with foreign government agencies, and other documents to help develop a thorough and accurate time line. The source of each key document, event, or conversation should be noted (e.g., 2/12/10 Employment Contract of J.D. Bodkin [see Bonus Clause re: Cabinda Offshore, Block Zero, Areas E-H Contract Awards]; 10/15/10 Electrical Fire [source: Internal Security]). Counsel can employ an asterisk system in the left margin of the working chronology to weigh particular facts, events, red flags, or developments, for example, one asterisk to denote a significant event, four asterisks to identify a seminal event or action.

This time line of the working chronology consists of two sections and should not simply end with the last date relevant to the underlying events. Rather, it should continue with the dates and descriptions of key investigation events—for example, the dates on which document preservation memoranda were issued, specific witnesses were interviewed, DOJ or SEC subpoenas were served, documents were produced to law enforcement, meetings with prosecutors or regulators were held, and the like.

The working chronology will track the company's FCPA investigation as well as any parallel U.S. and foreign government investigations and usually do it all in one easy-to-view document. In complex investigations, counsel may draft separate chronologies to address topics, allegations, or countries. For example, there may be separate chronologies for Angola and for China, or separate chronologies for improper cash payments and for hospitality issues.

The working chronology will typically be distributed among counsel only. Otherwise, its privilege protection may be waived. It should contain a legend describing its purpose and limiting its circulation. Because the working chronology is a work-product memorandum, under no circumstances should it be shown to a client or potential witness, since the Federal Rules of Evidence[34] may require production and disclosure of any writing used to refresh a witness's memory.[35] Often, a working chronology in a simple investigation will be 30 pages or less. However, in complicated FCPA investigations, a working chronology can run 100 pages or longer.

B. Hypothetical FCPA Working Chronology

This is a simple, much abbreviated hypothetical working chronology for an audit committee investigation of alleged payments by a U.S. oil company's foreign subsidiary in Luanda, Angola, to local government officials. Note that it is a work of fiction. Names, characters, places, and incidents are products of the author's imagination or are used fictitiously. Any resemblance to actual events, locales, or persons living or dead is entirely coincidental.

Alpha Corp—Angola Working Chronology

This working chronology is the attorney work product of [Name of Outside Counsel] and is privileged and confidential investigative and trial preparation material. This composite summary of events, documents, transactions, and meetings relating to an internal investigation by ALPHA CORPORATION and a federal grand jury investigation of ALPHA CORPORATION in the Southern District of Texas and the District of Columbia, of alleged improper payments in Angola, contains mental impressions, conclusions, and legal theories of its author(s). **UNDER NO CIRCUMSTANCES SHOULD THIS WORKING CHRONOLOGY BE FURNISHED OR SHOWN TO A POTENTIAL WITNESS.** The distribution of this memorandum or revisions thereto is to be limited to the following persons:

Lead Outside Counsel (Firm name):   [Name]

General Counsel of Alpha Corporation: [Name]

Associate General Counsel: [Name]

Outside Counsel (Law Firm):   [Name]

Deputy General Counsel: [Name]

Chief Compliance Officer   [Name]

unless express permission is obtained from [Name]. The holders of this memorandum are requested to destroy earlier editions of this memorandum as revised editions are distributed.

1. Alpha Corporation

World Headquarters	Alpha Corporation, Inc. 1000 Oil Patch Way Houston, TX (714) 555-5555 www.alpha.corp
Angola Office:	Alpha-Angola SARL 123 Cabinda Way Luanda, Angola
Audit Committee: (Names and contact information)	1. AC Chair: 2. AC Committee Member: 3. AC Committee Member:
Alpha Management: (Houston, TX) (E-mail addresses, office phones, and cell phones)	Chair/CEO: Admin. Asst.: General Counsel: Admin. Asst.: Deputy General Counsel: Admin. Asst.: Chief Operating Officer: Chief Financial Officer: Director of Internal Audit:

Alpha EMEA	Managing Director: Legal Manager: Director of Worldwide Procurement: IT Director:
Alpha-Angola (Luanda): (E-mail addresses and mobile phone numbers)	Managing Director: Administrator: Controller: Local Shareholders: Finance Director: V.P. Sales: Admin. Asst.:

2. Preliminary Allegations and Issues

1. Whether consultant Conrad Flagler Ltd. (CFL) of Luanda and London was used in Angola to indirectly pay Angolan federal government officials to award contracts to Alpha-Angola.
2. Whether overstated expense accounts (e.g., fuel) were used by Alpha-Angola to generate funds to pay local officials in Cabinda.
3. Whether U.S. persons in Houston, Texas, approved, facilitated, or participated in improper payments by the West African subsidiary.
4. Whether dividends to local Angolan shareholders were used to make payments to government officials in Luanda to obtain or retain Alpha-Angola business.
5. Whether monthly cash payments to military police in Angola (FAA—Forças Armadas Angolans) for police protection in guarding Alpha-Angola personnel from separatist guerillas (FLEC-FAC) and transporting Alpha-Angola managers and employees to and from home in Cabinda constitute improper payments, that is, corrupt intent.
6. Whether Conrad Flagler or CFL made a $1 million political contribution to MPLA, the leading Angolan political party.
7. Whether local freight forwarder AEC made improper payments with Alpha-Angola's knowledge or authorization to reduce Angolan customs duties and speed up inspections.
8. Whether new country manager J.D. Bodkin had undisclosed party interests and a kickback relationship with local officials or vendors, making Alpha a victim of his conduct.
9. What Alpha due diligence and background check was conducted into the background of J.D. Bodkin prior to his hiring as Angola country manager.
10. Whether there are any false books-and-records entries.
11. Whether internal controls in Luanda are adequate or can be improved to (a) prevent improper payments or (b) vet local consultants or other vendors.
12. Whether Alpha has sufficient financial controls over Alpha-Angola and other EMEA operations.

3. Alpha Audit Committee Investigative Team
A. Law Firm
    [Names and contact information]
B. Forensic Accounting Firm
    [Names and contact information]
C. Contract Lawyers
    [Names and contact information]

4. U.S. Government Attorneys
Main Justice—Fraud Section
[Names]
Department of Justice—Fraud Section
1400 New York Ave., 9th Floor
Washington, D.C. 20005
(202) 514-7023
E-mail address:

U.S. Attorney—Southern District of Texas
AUSAs [Names]
U.S. Attorney's Office
P.O. Box 61129
Houston, TX 77208
(713) 567-9000

Securities and Exchange Commission
[Enforcement Division attorney names]
U.S. Securities and Exchange Commission
Fort Worth Regional Office
Burnett Plaza, Ste. 1900
801 Cherry Street, Unit 18
Fort Worth, TX 76102
(817) 978-3821

U.S. Securities and Exchange Commission Headquarters
100 F Street, NE
Washington, D.C. 20549
(202) 942-8088

Investigative Agencies
[Lead agent name]
FBI
Arlington, VA
(301) 555-5555

U.S. Embassy/Consulate
[Names]
U.S. Embassy
Rua Houari Boumedienne, 32-Miramar
Luanda, Angola

Telephone: 244 222 641 1222
Website: http://luanda.usembassy.gov

5. PDQ, LLP
500 Madison Avenue
New York, NY 10085
Partner: Montague
Regular Outside Auditor

6. Other
A. Petroangola: a national oil company of Angola
B. Alpha-Angola SARL: 50 percent-owned Subsidiary opened following cessation of 27-year Angolan civil war
C. The Republic of Angola: The West African country is widely viewed as one of the last major oil frontiers
D. MPLA: Party of the President of the Republic of Angola
E. AEC: Angola Expedited Customs Ltd. is a local freight forwarder in Luanda

7. Chronology

Date	Event
2012	
7/21/12 **a	Alpha-Angola SARL lost bid in award of Cabinda Block Zero, Area P to Petroangola-China Oil JV
2013	
2/12/13 **	J.K. Bodkin hired away from Chinese competitor to be Alpha-Angola's senior officer effective 4/1/10
4/1/13 **	J.K. Bodkin appointed Managing Director of Alpha EMEA Region/Priority: Previously beat Russian and Indian competition in Angola and Cabinda offshore blocks
4/3/13 ***	Alpha-Angola received "recommendation" from Petroangola to retain Conrad Flagler of London as Project Consultant: A. Doala 4/03/13 e-mail to J.K. Bodkin: "J.K., CFL awaits your call re: Area Q at Dorchester. Proceed now. Time of essence. A.D."
7/4/13 ****	U.S.–based Alpha CEO received very vague handwritten note about J.K. Bodkin, new Angola country manager, and villa in Cannes
7/27/13	Alpha-Angola awarded $258 million government contract for offshore Cabinda Block Zero, Area Q
7/30/13	CFL directed Alpha-Angola to wire $25.8 million success fee to a numbered account at UBS, Geneva
8/7/13	E-mail from S. Luango to J.K. Bodkin: "When can friends expect Swiss cheese?"
9/15/13	Special Dividend to two local shareholders, Reijos and Castillo, declared
10/1/13 ***	General Counsel of Alpha Corporation receives a detailed anonymous letter alleging (1) improper payments by a consultant in Angola to local government officials to obtain a contract; (2) improper payments funneled by the two local Angola shareholders to MPLA Party; (3) CFO contribution to MPLA on eve of Area Q award; (4) phony fuel bills; and (5) use of a local freight forwarder to make improper payments

Date	Event
10/15/13 ****	Electrical fire at Alpha-Angola records storage area
10/28/13 ***	Anonymous note re: $1 million wire to account of J.K. Bodkin, UBS, Zurich
11/24/13	Audit Committee engagement of outside law firm to conduct internal investigation (AC Resolution 11/21/11) • Review of FCPA statute • Discussion of scope of investigation and voluntary disclosure option
11/25/13 *	Nondestruction Memorandum and Imaging coordinated by IT Director J.D. Dork for Angola, and for management and accounting personnel in Houston
12/1/13	Memorandum re: Data Privacy Structure and Issues
12/2/13	Memorandum re: Angolan Bribery Laws. Republic of Angola Statute 666
12/2/13	Global retention of XYZ Forensic, Inc., NY, NY • Collection of ESI • Internal Controls Assessment Preliminary list of 112 search terms in English, Portuguese • Potential accounting issues • Potential tax issues • Sample audit of 500 transactions and analysis of same by 2/01/14 • Data hosting
12/7/13	Overview by Deputy GC of Operations and Personnel Initial Angola interview schedule • Ubjo—Cabinda • Bodkin—Luanda • Abubu—Cabinda • Soros—Luanda • Paralegal Document Review Teams assigned for Angola U.S. per 37 search terms
12/9/13 ***	J.K. Bodkin refused to be interviewed by outside counsel absent Alpha indemnification and release for all liability
12/10/13 **	Bodkin terminated per letter from Alpha General Counsel
12/11/13	Ubjo interviewed in Luanda and consulted a local lawyer to determine whether to make personal and bank records available to outside law firm
12/12/13 **	Termination of CFL consulting contract
12/12/13	Zurich counsel for Bodkin filed for International Arbitration re: Employment Contracts in London
12/12/13	Legal Issue Memorandum: Elements of 18 U.S.C. § 371; FCPA Bribery; Facilitating Payments; Recent FCPA Angola Enforcement Actions-U.S. DPA Trends; SEC Disgorgement Analysis
12/10/13	Alpha Audit Committee Status Report: Committee updated
12/10/13 ***	Interview of Alpha-Angola CFO Juan Soros • Bodkin told Soros he had disclosed his related-party interests to Alpha's General Counsel in February 2013 and stated, "The Chinese play the game."

Date	Event
2014	
2/22/14	Federal grand jury subpoena duces tecum served on Alpha Corp. returnable 3/22/11: 1. All consulting, contracts, memoranda, agreements, and correspondence relating to Conrad Flagler Ltd. Consulting (London) 2. All employment agreements, salary and bonus information, background and due diligence checks, severance agreements, stock options, and other remuneration relating to J.K. Bodkin 3. Any and all correspondence, findings, memoranda, and disciplinary actions relating to the company's Angolan investigation 4. All e-mails to or by management including but not limited to CEO, CFO, CAO, and Internal Audit from 2007 to present relating to CFL Consulting of Luanda 5. All Alpha FCPA audits or other internal audits for Angola, Brazil, Russia, and India
2/26/14	RWT contact of Fraud Section attorney Mark Miller and SEC enforcement attorney Laura Smith
2/28/14	Alpha and Audit Committee Telephonic Conference. Report on Angola Investigation and likely DOJ and SEC Investigations and U.S. interviews
3/2/14	Alpha Full board of directors meeting
3/10/14	RWT obtains extension of time to provide documents to FGJ until 5/30/14
3/15/14	RWT contact of SEC Fort Worth Regional Office; discussion of search terms
3/17/14	RWT meeting with DOJ Fraud Section attorney Mark Miller, Washington, D.C., re: FCPA FGJ/requests for hot documents by 4/15/14; discussion of search terms
3/30/14	10Q due to be filed by Alpha Corporation, Inc.
5/30/14	Extended Grand Jury return date for Alpha Corporation
7/12–15/14	Live Alpha FCPA HQ Training
8/18/14	Board Meeting: Status Report re DOJ-SEC/interviews/additional document reviews/remedial measures and third-party due diligence
9/1/14	SEC requests book accounts of Conrad Flagler
9/18/14	DOJ requests interviews of five Angolan employees
10/18/14	Board Meeting: Status Report re DOJ-SEC/interviews/additional document reviews/remedial measures and third-party due diligence/candidates for Chief Compliance officer position; propose DOJ-SEC negotiation/discussion meeting for May 2012
2015	
1/11/15	Board of Director and Audit Committee Update: Status of Remaining Interviews; DOJ and SEC requests; remedial measures
1/20/15	Conference call with PDQ, regular outside auditor

[a]Asterisks indicate relative weight of facts or events; for example, one asterisk denotes a significant event, four asterisks identify a seminal event or action.

8. **Alpha Remedial Measures**
   • Implemented live FCPA and Export Controls Training in APAC (Asia Pacific), EMEA (Europe, Middle East, Africa), and HQ (Houston) by 7/30/14.
   • Drafted Alpha Worldwide FCPA Policy (effective 1/02/14).
   • Moved all Alpha-Angola SARL records to secure location.
   • Eliminated direct reporting line from Alpha-Angola CFO to Alpha-Angola Managing Director and made local CFO report to Alpha CFO (Houston) (12/08/13).
   • Terminated J.K. Bodkin 12/10/13.
   • Terminated Alpha-Angola SARL-CFL Consultants of Luanda, Inc., Agreement (12/12/13).
   • Suspended Angolan CFO Juan Soros 12/15/13.
   • Translated Code of Conduct and new FCPA Policy into four foreign languages with Introduction by Alpha CEO (12/22/13), including Portuguese, effective 1/1/14.

9. **To Do**
   • Review Alpha-Angola Block Zero, Areas Q and R Budget Analyses.
   • Consider rotation policy for Alpha foreign subsidiary, country managers, and CFOs—every five years.
   • Determine what due diligence was conducted for CFL, what coordination there was with U.S. (Houston), and what due diligence has been conducted in EMEA for consultants.
   • XYZ Forensics to analyze internal controls, petty cash, and vendor due diligence procedures for Alpha-Angola.
   • Review anonymous note to CEO in context of phony fuel bills.
   • Organize Alpha Consultant and Agent Due Diligence procedures worldwide.
       ° High risk
       ° Medium risk
       ° Low risk
       ° Annual review of all high and medium risks
       ° Training of third parties
   • Reinterview CEO re: 4/3/13 and 7/4/13 CFL Consulting e-mails.
   • Interview freight forwarder and invoices.
   • Evaluate benefits of voluntary disclosure.
   • Consult with Alpha's securities disclosure counsel.
   • Confer with Alpha's outside auditors.
   • Institute annual FCPA audits in Angola, India, and China through 2017.
   • Draft new local Shareholder Agreements with antibribery warranty and representations and access to bank records provisions.
   • Alpha-Angola Investigation PowerPoint Presentation to DOJ 4/14.

IX. REPORTS AND RECOMMENDATIONS TO MANAGEMENT, BOARDS OF DIRECTORS, AUDIT COMMITTEES, OR SPECIAL COMMITTEES

A written report simplifies presentation to a board, audit committee, or management and memorializes counsel's work, conclusions, and recommendations. However, it also increases the danger of waiver and exposes the company to litigation over discovery of the report. The company may also run a risk of appearing noncooperative if it refuses to share a written report with the government.[36] Increasingly, Power-Point presentations to boards or committees are an effective and sound compromise between oral presentations and written reports.

Because the results of an internal investigation report or presentation may be disclosed at some point, careful draftsmanship is critical in either form. Counsel should draft a report bearing in mind the possibility of the broadest disclosure, that is, that the report will be read or misread by customers, vendors, employees, lenders, regulators, prosecutors, auditors, private litigants, competitors, shareholders, or the media. Inartful phrasing can mislead important constituents or even result in unintended allegations that give rise to libel claims.[37]

At the conclusion of an FCPA investigation into improper payments, problematic books and records, or inadequate internal controls, counsel will likely make recommendations to the client to correct problems, including modifying, updating, or creating new policies and procedures, hiring additional compliance and audit personnel, modifying audit work programs or priorities, instituting or increasing anticorruption training, disciplining wrongdoers, and conducting periodic anticorruption audits in foreign jurisdictions where the company does business, where there are substantial corruption perception indices, or where the company has encountered FCPA-type problems.

Recommendations must be constructive and reasoned: if they are minor, too rigid, too numerous, too vague, or overly burdensome, there is a risk that they will not ever be implemented. However, recommendations should not be rejected simply because they might embarrass management, prove burdensome, or increase expenses. The company will likely face more serious consequences if the DOJ or SEC later discovers problematic conduct and learns that the company previously declined to undertake remedial measures and institute better controls.

When making recommendations, it is useful to set reasonable, firm deadlines for implementation of specific recommendations and to assign specific responsibility to managers, lawyers, or compliance officers. If not, other business priorities can overtake or interfere, and the recommendations will not be implemented timely or ever. The board of directors, audit committee, shareholders, or prosecutors and regulators may then draw the harmful but possibly appropriate conclusion that compliance is not very important to management.

X. VOLUNTARY DISCLOSURE

A. Advantages

The benefits of voluntary disclosure and cooperation vary case by case and are rarely fully known at the time of a company's disclosure election. While the DOJ has encouraged and trumpeted the benefits of voluntary disclosure and cooperation, it has issued no comprehensive policy clarifying under what facts and circumstances such disclosure and cooperation will lead to nonprosecution, deferred prosecution, or other favorable treatment.[38] A review of DOJ–SEC FCPA resolutions involving voluntary disclosures can give counsel a range of possible outcomes and trends, but each case is fact-dependent. Voluntary disclosure cases include Watts Water Technologies Inc., Tyson Foods, Johnson & Johnson, BizJet, Morgan Stanley (Garth Peterson), Nordam, Pfizer, ITT Corp., Latin Node Inc., United Industrial Corp., Control Components Inc., Avery Dennison, Helmerich & Payne, Inc., Willbros Group, Inc., and Nature's Sunshine Products Inc. (see chapter 10 for a discussion of each).

The DOJ and SEC do need companies to voluntarily disclose and cooperate because government resources are limited. The purported government "carrot" is twofold: the ultimate DOJ criminal and/or SEC enforcement sanctions will be less severe, and the cooperative path to resolution is much less onerous, costly, and distracting to management. For public companies whose senior officers are now required to certify the accuracy of corporate financial statements and attest to the company's internal controls, the decision to voluntarily disclose may be one that accelerates what would be filed in a quarterly or annual filing. For a number of companies, prompt, voluntary disclosure to the DOJ has avoided indictment and debarment and resulted instead in a DPA or no charges at all.

B. Disadvantages

Voluntary disclosure has both legal and practical ramifications. On the legal side, there is a risk that counsel's disclosure will constitute a statement against interest or an admission.[39] As important, civil litigants may try to gain access to disclosure materials in parallel civil proceedings, including private or civil litigation by shareholders, competitors, and foreign governments. Also, disclosure can dilute defenses and enable the government to attack the defenses in any court proceedings.[40] In general, disclosure of an attorney-client privileged communication as to one entity, for example, a department or agency of a government, waives the privilege as to all. While the elements of the work-product doctrine are different and somewhat more protective of privilege,[41] counsel should carefully consider the implications of disclosure of privileged work product as well.

As for practical disadvantages, voluntary disclosure is never a simple or quick act of contrition. It usually is protracted, distracting, embarrassing, expensive, and, unfortunately, uncertain in benefits.[42] It can also lead to a foreign law enforcement investigation and expansion of the scope of the company's original investigation. Although many executives question the time, resources, and costs associated with voluntary disclosure and cooperation, the costs of defending an FCPA investigation initiated by the DOJ or SEC can be far greater. Before a company or a board elects to voluntarily disclose improper payments, counsel should carefully advise the client of the potential adverse legal and practical consequences.[43]

C. Disclosure Mechanics

Voluntary disclosure should be timely, informative, and continuing. There is no prescribed form of disclosure. Many companies elect to contact the Fraud Section through counsel, set up a meeting, and provide in person a detailed oral overview of the known facts to DOJ attorneys and, in some instances, FBI agents. If the company is publicly held, it usually makes sense to schedule a similar disclosure meeting with SEC enforcement attorneys assigned to the FCPA unit. Because the DOJ and SEC work closely on such matters, a joint meeting can frequently be arranged. It is best to stick to the facts, and not to leave copies of any presentations or privileged material with the government. Counsel will want to consider the benefits of simultaneously or closely in time voluntarily disclosing misconduct to relevant foreign governments. In making this decision, counsel will weigh the foreign government's anticorruption interest; the acts that took place in the foreign jurisdiction; whether local anticorruption laws apply to corporations, individuals, or both; whether the foreign government has a voluntary disclosure program; and the perceived relationship between the foreign government and U.S. authorities on corruption matters.

The DOJ and SEC will want to know who investigated the facts (inside counsel, outside counsel, the board of directors, a special committee), who the participants in the wrongdoing were, what the likely potential magnitude of the improper payments is, what and how promptly efforts have been made to secure and preserve both electronic evidence and hard copy records, what findings were reached, what disciplinary actions have been taken, and what remedial measures are under way. The DOJ and SEC are especially interested in the process the company, board, or audit committee employed once it learned of the allegations. The DOJ and SEC will invariably examine how independent, how thorough, and, in some cases, how ethical any internal investigation has been.

In general, the DOJ does not expect a company to report immediately an FCPA allegation. It understands that the board, the audit committee, or management and its counsel need a reasonable period of time to verify an allegation and to gather facts, particularly given that the alleged incidents or transactions have usually occurred in a foreign country. The DOJ does welcome disclosure early enough to allow it to employ covert investigative techniques if it chooses. In certain instances, the DOJ may prefer and even request that cooperating wrongdoers remain on a company payroll for a reasonable time. In contrast, the SEC generally does not become involved in a company's employment or termination decisions.

D. Selective Waiver of Attorney Work-Product Doctrine and Attorney-Client Privilege

Where a company or audit committee elects to cooperate with the DOJ and share information from its investigation with the DOJ, it may do so orally or provide access to reports, interview memoranda, and investigative working papers. While the DOJ is not bound by an agreement to treat such materials as permanently confidential, it does provide cooperating companies the following nonbinding assurance:

XXXX

Fraud Section, Criminal Division

U.S. Department of Justice

1400 New York Avenue, N.W.

Washington, D.C. 20005

Re: In the Matter of COMPANY Y

Dear XXXX:

The Audit Committee of COMPANY Y commenced an investigation into potential violations of the Foreign Corrupt Practices Act on or about [**date**]. The Audit Committee, through its retained representatives at LAW FIRM A, has identified relevant documents and prepared reports, interview memoranda, and investigative working papers in connection with this investigation. In light of the interest of the Department of Justice (the "Department") in determining whether there have been any violations of applicable law, and the Audit Committee's interests in investigating and analyzing the circumstances and people involved in the events at issue, the Audit Committee, through LAW FIRM A, will provide to the Department copies of or access to the reports, interview memoranda, and investigative working papers regarding its investigation, in addition to oral briefings regarding its investigation ("Protected Confidential Materials"). As part of its ongoing productions, the Audit Committee, through LAW FIRM A, will identify with specificity which productions to the Department are Protected Materials and which are not Protected Materials.

Please be advised that by producing the Protected Confidential Materials pursuant to this agreement, the Audit Committee does not intend to waive the protection of the attorney work-product doctrine, attorney-client privilege, or any other privilege applicable as to third parties. The Audit Committee believes that the Protected Confidential Materials are protected by, at a minimum, the attorney work-product doctrine and the attorney-client privilege. The Audit Committee believes that the Confidential Materials warrant protection from disclosure.

The Department will maintain the confidentiality of the Confidential Materials pursuant to this agreement and will not disclose them to any third party, except to the extent that the Department determines that disclosure is otherwise required by law or would be in furtherance of the Department's discharge of its duties and responsibilities.

Should it be necessary to litigate the question whether the Audit Committee's production of the Confidential Materials to the Department constitutes a waiver of the protection of the attorney work-product doctrine, the attorney-client privilege, or any other privilege applicable as to any third party, the Audit Committee understands that the Department will be bound by the broader views of the Department of Justice on questions of law, and that it cannot agree at this time to particular litigating positions.

The Department's agreement to the terms of this letter is signified by your signature on the line provided below.

Sincerely,

AGREED AND ACCEPTED:

United States Department of Justice

By:

Fraud Section, Criminal Division

Many federal courts have rejected the selective waiver doctrine,[44] and therefore the penultimate paragraph affords cooperating companies only limited protection. As a result, many companies cooperate but limit the amount of work product provided to the DOJ. Particularly in the wake of the August 2008 Filip Amendment to the Department of Justice Manual, the DOJ and SEC have become less insistent about requiring a waiver of the corporate attorney-client privilege as long as a company makes reasonable efforts to communicate essential facts and leads, and to advance the government investigation.

E. Follow-up

The DOJ and SEC will expect a disclosing company and its counsel to continue any necessary investigation, to secure and provide documents, to make cooperating employees available for interviews in the United States or elsewhere, and to keep the DOJ and/or SEC apprised in real time of any material developments. The DOJ and SEC often schedule conferences or telephone calls to understand and update events and transactions and to be kept informed of any company investigation progress. To the extent a company's investigation indicates or uncovers more misconduct elsewhere, the government expects the company, board of directors, or audit committee to expand the scope of its investigation.

Given their limited resources and the number of companies discovering and disclosing FCPA violations, the DOJ and SEC welcome and need companies to cooperate and to conduct investigations with law enforcement monitoring or oversight. Government attorneys, of course, retain the right to formalize an investigation, that is, to subpoena documents and witnesses, to execute search warrants, and so on, if they determine that a company's investigation and cooperation are inadequate or misleading.

F. Cooperation Log

The government may keep a cooperation log that records what documents and witnesses the company has provided or made available and any other requests that have been accommodated. It is useful for company counsel to maintain a similar detailed log, to record and quantify the company's cooperative efforts during an investigation, and to seek credit for these acts when negotiating a resolution.

G. Siemens's Exceptional Cooperation and Corporate Amnesty and Leniency Programs

In reaching a $1.6 billion settlement with Siemens in December 2008, the Department of Justice commended as exceptional "Siemens' wide-ranging cooperation efforts throughout this investigation, which included a sweeping internal investigation, the creation of innovative and effective amnesty and leniency programs, and exemplary efforts with respect to preservation, collection, testing, and analysis of evidence."[45]

1. *Manpower Commitment and Document Preservation*

The Siemens internal investigation involved over 1.5 million hours of billable time by its audit committee's outside law firm and forensic professionals. Their investigative work took place in 34 countries and included over 1,750 interviews and 800 informational meetings. Over 100 million documents were collected and preserved, many of which were searched or reviewed for evidence relevant to the investigation. Siemens, either directly or through its outside law firm, produced to the Department of Justice over 24,000 documents, amounting to over 100,000 pages. Siemens also established a Project Office at headquarters staffed by 16 full-time employees who facilitated interviews and document collection. To facilitate visits to regional companies by the investigation team, the Project Office communicated with regional management to explain and prepare them for the interviews and other investigative work.

2. *Corporate Amnesty and Leniency Programs*

In consultation with the DOJ, Siemens designed and implemented a unique company-wide amnesty program to facilitate the internal investigation. The four-month amnesty program provided that all but the most senior employees who voluntarily disclosed to the law firm truthful and complete information about possible violations of relevant anticorruption laws would be protected from unilateral employment termination and company claims for damages. The policy that implemented the amnesty program made clear that it was in no way binding on any prosecutors or regulators, including the DOJ and the SEC, but provided that Siemens would bring an employee's cooperation to the attention of such authorities if he or she were the subject of a government investigation.

For employees too senior to qualify for the amnesty program, as well as those employees who did not come forward during the amnesty program period, Siemens established a leniency program that provided for individualized leniency determinations for cooperating employees. The creation of these two programs was an effective way to further the investigation. Over 100 employees provided information in connection with the two programs, including numerous employees who previously provided incomplete or less than truthful information and employees who previously had not come forward.

Shortly after Siemens's amnesty program began, the DOJ and the SEC identified various individuals and projects for more extensive debriefings, referred to by the parties as "deep dives." The amnesty and leniency programs were essential to obtaining the types of detailed information needed for the deep dives. These deep dive sessions enabled the DOJ to evaluate the overall case, properly target its limited resources, and develop the evidence necessary to bring charges. Siemens represents the most thorough bribery investigation ever necessitated by serious compliance lapses and misconduct. Its global cooperation led to a lesser penalty and the avoidance of a bribery charge that could have debarred them from government business and contracts (Siemens pled guilty to books-and-records and internal controls violations). Large multinationals uncovering serious misconduct will need to consider the cooperative efforts of Siemens and its unique amnesty and leniency programs, which should be carefully vetted with DOJ in advance. Whether Siemens employees who cooperated under the internal amnesty or leniency programs are prosecuted by U.S. or foreign governments will determine whether that proves a wise and fair strategy for other companies and their officers.

XI. UNIQUE ASPECTS OF FCPA INVESTIGATIONS AND MULTINATIONAL OPERATIONS

A. In-Country Visits and Interviews

In-country interviews and investigation are essential to a full understanding of a company or an agent's, consultant's, or contractor's operations and procedures in a foreign country and related FCPA issues. They can strengthen the facts and arguments that a company's officers or employees did not have reason or a high probability to know that improper payments to foreign officials would or did occur. Conversely, they can dispel a claim that payments were for a charitable organization rather than a government official's spouse. To the extent a company elects to voluntarily disclose or otherwise cooperate with the U.S. authorities, foreign visits, on-site interviews, and document preservation at the locations of the alleged improper activity will enhance the credibility of an investigation and any final report. In many cases the U.S. government will not have the ability or resources to travel to the foreign country and will not have the advantage defense counsel has in evaluating firsthand the overseas business and legal practices and foreign witnesses.

As a rule, investigation counsel will seek to maintain a low profile when reviewing documents and interviewing company personnel and other witnesses in foreign locations.[46] Foreign nationals frequently question the authority of U.S. counsel or investigators to interview or look into local payments or books-and-records practices. They sometimes disclose the identity of or visit by FCPA investigation counsel to persons in the foreign countries whose conduct has been problematic or worse. Such disclosure can subject investigation counsel to personal risk. Finally, FCPA investigations may require translation of documents not in English and use of interpreters for witnesses who do not speak English.

B. Claims That the Payments or Practices in Question Are Common and Necessary

Employees, agents, and consultants, while sometimes conceding that payments or related practices have occurred, frequently contend that the corrupt payments were necessary to do business and customary in the country in question. The U.S.

government does not recognize this response as a defense; DOJ attorneys reply routinely that Congress was well aware of corrupt customs and practices in foreign countries when it enacted the FCPA in 1977 and criminalized such payments.

C. Foreign Data Privacy Laws

Many foreign jurisdictions have enacted privacy, data protection, wiretapping, state secrecy, bank secrecy, blocking, and other local laws or requirements that apply to data and documentation collection activities.[47] Violations of these laws can lead to private rights of action by the affected individuals, risk of foreign enforcement actions against companies by data protection authorities (and corresponding fines and injunctive relief), and potential foreign criminal liability for the company and corporate officers.[48]

Foreign privacy and data protection laws restrict the collection, handling, and transfer of any personally identifiable information about individuals. Perhaps the most important foreign privacy laws relevant to FCPA investigations were enacted in 1995 by the European Union on the Protection of Individuals with Respect to the Processing of Personal Data.[49] This EU directive is implemented through the national laws of each EU member country and often applies to FCPA investigations.

For example, the collection, use, and transfer of a document or e-mail that contains the name of a foreign subsidiary employee, personal financial information, data about payments made or received by the employee, and the name of the third-party payee or payor would implicate personal data concerning both the employee and the third party.[50] The collection, use, or transfer of this type of personal data could trigger a range of data protection requirements for the foreign subsidiary, including obligations to (1) ensure that there is a "legitimate" purpose to collect and use such data; (2) provide a sufficient privacy notice to the affected individuals; (3) obtain consent in certain cases; (4) maintain reasonable measures to protect the security and confidentiality of the personal data; (5) complete a filing with the foreign data protection authority describing the data collection and processing activities; and (6) confirm that any international transfers of the personal data to the United States or other non–EU locations are properly subject to "adequate protection."[51]

In some instances a parent company's global privacy policy and compliance program will have effectively addressed these issues. Depending on the country, it may be necessary to obtain employee consents to searches with the condition that the reviewing personnel not review personal data. A company or board of directors with counsel will in most cases have to evaluate the types of data at issue, company operations, potential penalties, and the company's risk tolerance at the outset of an investigation.[52] Other foreign statutes and laws that need to be considered in internal investigations include wiretapping and electronic communication, bank secrecy, and common law confidentiality and blocking statutes.

D. Local Labor Laws

In many countries, local labor laws greatly favor their citizens. Often it is very difficult to terminate a local officer or employee notwithstanding significant proof of misconduct. For example, a local executive's refusal to cooperate in an investigation may not be grounds for termination. Privacy laws may also affect the ability of a multinational company to secure and review electronic data. Local laws or a Worker's Council in Europe may impede a company's desire to take swift remedial measures, including disciplinary actions. Notwithstanding suspicious conduct, termination packages that favor local executives or employees may be necessary. If a company has voluntarily disclosed misconduct and is cooperating with U.S. authorities, it is usually wise to promptly advise the U.S. government of local labor law issues, termination or severance agreements, and related developments.

Investigative counsel can often benefit from the advice of experienced local partners or counsel, not only on local employment law, but also on local antibribery laws, local campaign laws, local due diligence resources, the reputation of local parties or consultants, and local self-reporting practices.

E.   Relevant Local Laws

In FCPA investigations, local laws can be highly relevant in at least three respects. First, the written local law may provide an affirmative defense. Second, it may not exempt certain practices, for example, facilitating or expediting payments, that are permitted by the FCPA, thereby creating a conflict with U.S. law. Third, the misconduct in question may well violate local antibribery laws and present local enforcement disclosure, cooperation, and prosecution issues. Often the law and legal systems in third-world countries are undeveloped, as legislative history, case precedent, and enforcement are scant. Compounding the undeveloped law scenario is that executive branch agencies in foreign countries often wield enormous administrative discretion and authority. Local counsel in FCPA investigations will commonly assist in analyzing local anticorruption, conflicts of interest, data privacy, and money laundering laws and in advising whether bribery in general or more specifically facilitating payments are lawful and enforced. Counsel may where available wish to review OECD Working Group monitoring reports of member countries to understand how much antibribery enforcement effort there has been.

F.   Separate Sets of U.S. and In-Country Books and Records

Multinational companies sometimes keep and maintain separate sets of financial records for U.S. and in-country operations. For example, overseas companies may have joint ventures with major competitors for which it would be inappropriate for a parent corporation or subsidiary to share all financial information. In these circumstances it can be appropriate or necessary to keep separate financial records. Internal controls of a foreign operation that do not include independent audits of consultants or third parties or that do not require keeping all copies of all consulting agreements only at the subsidiary will likely be viewed with skepticism by the DOJ and SEC.

G.   Access to Third-Party Foreign Bank Accounts

Absent an express contractual provision that a foreign agent, consultant, or partner must provide bank records to a company, its counsel, or an independent accountant, a company or its investigation counsel will normally have no access to third-party foreign bank records. This can limit the ability of a company to determine whether a joint venture partner, agent, consultant, or business partner has made improper payments to a foreign official. In very limited circumstances, local law may provide judicial remedies to obtain access to bank accounts and trace the disposition of funds from these accounts.

H. Pressure to Enter into an Overseas Commercial Agreement

Foreign governments vary a great deal in the manner and timing of offering investment opportunities and contract awards to international companies. Moreover, many overseas project opportunities are subject to local and foreign political pressures, including, in the case of developing countries, pressures from favored allies or ex-colonial powers, bilateral financing entities, and lending agencies. Unique procedural requirements and delays in project announcements and competitive bidding are not uncommon. Occasionally, foreign investment opportunities are substantially altered, restructured, or accelerated by the host governments for political and financial reasons. Accordingly, multinational companies, with layered levels of review approval, must often rush to meet a newly announced deadline, leading to a lack of a complete paper trail and inadequate due diligence compared to what might occur in a purely domestic transaction.

Large investments and ventures with foreign partners or contractors can also be informally documented in a manner contrary to the custom and practice of such companies and their counsel. Moreover, until such time as a company is assured of a project award, it may not wish to enter into full-blown, properly documented arrangements. In some cases, a company may never enter into such detailed documentation, due to the priority of other ongoing projects. Seemingly negligent failures to document significant projects need to be understood in context. Examples occur in small as well as large projects, including major resource exploitation, infrastructure, and privatization projects. The more thorough the due diligence record, the more likely a company that inherits a bribery problem can avoid the conclusion by U.S. authorities that it intentionally closed its eyes to facts that should have prompted inquiries.

I. Third-Party Motivations to Disparage a Multinational Company

From time to time, multinational companies receive FCPA allegations and quickly conclude that the allegations are the product of disgruntled employees, foreign competitors, subcontractors and agents, or foreign government officials or candidates who may have strong political and economic motivation to disrupt and disparage the operations. Notwithstanding questionable motives, many disgruntled employees or others with an incentive to harm companies have alleged corruption and been proven right. No allegation can be dismissed without some level of review, and it is reasonable to, whenever possible, locate and determine the source of the allegation to evaluate preliminarily its legitimacy before commencing a full-scale investigation. Regardless of the merits of the allegation, it is usually prudent for company counsel to memorialize the efforts undertaken to address even minor FCPA allegations, the facts learned, and any actions taken. Many companies as a matter of course also report even minor FCPA allegations to their audit committees and their review of same.

J. Forensic Accountants and Investigators

In substantial FCPA investigations, law firms typically engage qualified forensic accountants or investigators to retrieve, image, and recover computer and electronic evidence, to search electronic databases, and to assist in internal control analyses and recommendations. Forensic services are expected by the DOJ and SEC staff in both significant FCPA investigations and monitorships. Sometimes companies try to use internal information technology and audit staff for these purposes. Absent the availability of fully qualified in-house IT personnel and audit personnel, it is prudent for an investigative law firm to engage outside forensic investigators in substantial anticorruption investigations. Qualified, independent forensic accountants can also give increased confidence in an investigation to a company's regular outside auditors and offer constructive internal control improvements. Forensic firms should provide details of their work plans and meaningful budgets before engagement by investigation counsel and the client.

K. Books-and-Records and Internal Controls Issues

In most FCPA investigations, the primary focus is understandably on potential improper payments to foreign officials. Still, counsel must focus on the accounting provisions of the FCPA—the books-and-records and internal controls provisions. If a company is making lawful "facilitating payments" under the FCPA in a foreign country, these expenses should be identified and recorded as "facilitating payments," for example, "facilitating payments to Nigeria Electric Power Authority Utility Clerk in Port Harcourt." Otherwise, the company may have a false books-and-records violation.

L. Other Potential Criminal Violations

Investigation counsel must be mindful of other potential criminal violations including money laundering, false statements to the U.S. government, bid rigging, commercial bribery, false tax returns, export violations, and obstruction of justice.

XII. POTENTIAL REMEDIAL MEASURES

It is best for company counsel to plan and, where possible, to promptly implement appropriate remedial measures—certainly in advance of any voluntary disclosure. Law enforcement agencies have a strong interest in ensuring that wrongful acts or conduct do not recur and that management understands the seriousness of the misconduct and has taken and will take appropriate steps to reduce any possibility of recurrence.

FCPA remedial measures can include

- Appointment of an executive compliance committee to oversee compliance program;
- Disciplinary actions, including demotion, transfer, suspension, and termination of employees who engaged in wrongdoing or failed to adequately supervise those who engaged in wrongdoing;
- Standard third-party contract template including anticorruption claims and audit rights;
- Increased FCPA training—for employees, officers, and directors;
- FCPA audits and testing;
- Improved hotline and reporting procedures;
- Implementation of stand-alone FCPA policies;
- Appointment of new financial and accounting personnel;
- Data privacy consents by new employees;
- Improved financial controls;
- Standard employee offer including receipt and certification of adherence to company code of conduct;
- Revised reporting chains of command;
- Expatriate country rotation policies;
- Certifications of compliance (by employees, agents, business partners, and consultants);
- Translation of all anticorruption policies and procedures, and compliance program materials into all appropriate languages;
- New or revised travel and entertainment relating to the approval, review, and record-keeping of reimbursement policies and procedures;
- New or revised policies on charitable or educational contributions;
- New or revised consultant, partner, and local agent approval policies and procedures;
- New or revised gift-giving policies and procedures;
- Policies, procedures, and/or guidance related to petty cash and cash advances;
- Policies and procedures for authorizing and approving facilitation or expediting payments;
- Appointment of regional or in-country compliance and/or ethics officers;
- Heightened due diligence of agents and consultants including third-party vetting and web-based tools;
- Heightened due diligence requirements for joint venture partners and for mergers and acquisitions;
- Policies and procedures and internal control guidelines relating to payments to offshore banking location;
- Policies and procedures regarding the review and approval of intercompany transactions associated with third-party activities;
- E-mail certifications for reporting interactions with government officials;
- Policies or procedures relating to ongoing and periodic effectiveness of the company's anticorruption compliance program;
- Procedure for periodic risk assessment of business activity in high risk corruption company locations;

- Increased reporting to the audit committee and board of directors regarding compliance training and remedial efforts;
- Increased compliance oversight role responsibility of the board of directors;
- Annual work plan specifically describing responsibility of implementation and oversight of anticorruption policies, standards, and procedures;
- Coordination of corporate compliance in legal, internal audit, compliance, and finance departments;
- Reduction of the number of company bank accounts; and
- Change in the structure of bonuses to reflect executives' fulfillment of compliance standards and values.

Of course, some remedial measures will not be obvious or available at early stages. Others, such as the need for FCPA training, may be readily apparent and should be conducted promptly or concurrently with the investigation.

XIII. EFFECTIVE CORRUPTION DISCOVERY RESPONSES AND REMEDIATION

Two DOJ and SEC FCPA settlement resolutions have specially praised the responses of companies that have discovered bribery misconduct. Siemens AG, a German conglomerate, was the subject of dawn raids in Germany and promptly instituted a massive global investigation that, along with its remedial program, has been heralded as a model response for large multinational companies. Willbros, a Texas-based oil pipeline company, discovered wrongdoing by a senior officer, and its audit committee immediately authorized an internal investigation. Willbros then self-disclosed the problematic conduct to both the DOJ and SEC and promptly implemented a host of remedial actions. The responses and actions described below provide guidance for midsize and large companies discovering bribery conduct.

In order to understand the best practices of companies that have faced serious anticorruption investigations, it is useful to review the most recent compliance program elements imposed on companies that have resolved FCPA investigations. As of January 2015, counsel should review the required 18-element programs imposed on Avon Products and Alstom (see chapter 10).

A. Siemens Response to Munich Dawn Raids and Lessons Learned for Large Multinational Companies

In response to raids at multiple Siemens offices and the homes of Siemens employees in Munich, Germany, in November 2006, Siemens commenced, in the words of U.S. authorities, a "sweeping global investigation"[53] of possible bribery of foreign public officials and falsification of corporate books and records. This investigation uncovered what SEC Enforcement Director Linda Thomsen described as a "pattern of bribery unprecedented in scale and geographic reach." The company's follow-on cooperation was "exceptional and its reforms real."[54] While few multinational companies have 400,000 employees or operations in 191 countries, let alone uncover tens of millions of dollars in bribes, there are important compliance lessons from the Siemens resolution for large multinational companies.

As part of its remedial response, Siemens:

- Terminated members of senior management implicated in the misconduct.
- Reorganized the company to be more centralized from both a business and compliance perspective, with measures including the creation of a new position on the managing board with responsibility for legal and compliance matters.
- Overhauled and expanded its compliance organization, with more than 500 full-time compliance personnel worldwide.
- Vested control and accountability for all compliance matters in a chief compliance officer, who, in turn, reports directly to the general counsel and the chief executive officer.
- Reorganized its audit department, which is now headed by a chief audit officer, who reports to the company's audit committee.
- Requested that every member of its 450-person audit staff reapply for their jobs.
- Enacted a series of anticorruption compliance policies, including a new anticorruption handout, sophisticated web-based tools for due diligence and compliance matters, a confidential communications channel for employees to report irregular business practices, and a corporate disciplinary committee to impose appropriate disciplinary measures for substantial misconduct.
- Organized a working group devoted to fully implementing new compliance initiatives, consisting of eight employees from Siemens's finance and compliance departments and outside professionals from a major accounting firm. The working group developed a step-by-step guide on the new compliance program and improved financial controls known as the "Anti-Corruption Toolkit." The toolkit and its accompanying guide contain clear steps and timelier requirements on local management to ensure full implementation of the global anticorruption program and enhanced controls. Over 150 people, including outside accounting professionals, provided support in implementing the toolkit at 162 Siemens entities. Dedicated support teams spent six weeks on the ground at 56 of those entities deemed to be "higher risk," assisting management in those locations with all aspects of the implementation. The total external cost to Siemens for these remediation efforts has exceeded $150 million.
- Imposed a moratorium on entering into new business consulting agreements or making payments under existing business consulting agreements until a complete collection and review was undertaken of all such agreements. The company also initiated, and has nearly completed, a review of all third-party agents with whom it has agreements. This has resulted in a significant reduction in the number of business consultants used by Siemens.
- Enhanced its review and approval procedures for business consultants. The new state-of-the-art system requires any employee who wishes to engage a business consultant to enter detailed information into an interactive computer system, which assesses the risk of the engagement and directs the request to the appropriate supervisors for review and approval.
- Increased corporate-level control over company funds, centralizing and reducing the number of company bank accounts and outgoing payments to third parties.

The DOJ described Siemens's reorganization and remediation efforts as extraordinary and setting a "high standard for multinational companies to follow." Absent discovery of serious corruption problems, few multinational companies will be expected to hire or employ hundreds of full-time compliance personnel or enact most of these measures, but multinational companies in risky industries or regions will review the Siemens measures and adopt ideas or measures as appropriate.

B.   Model Willbros Group Inc. Response

In *United States v. Willbros Group Inc. & Willbros International Inc.*,[55] a pipeline company was able to obtain a DPA and avoid a felony as a result of prompt and exceptional cooperation and remedial measures notwithstanding egregious bribery conduct in three countries under the direction of a senior officer.

Upon discovering misconduct by a senior officer in Bolivia, Willbros undertook numerous remedial steps enabling it to obtain a DPA, including

- Commencing a thorough audit committee internal investigation within 24 hours of notice of allegations of corporate tax fraud committed by employees and purported consultants working on behalf of the Willbros Group's Bolivian subsidiary;
- Quickly expanding the scope of the internal investigation, which included extensive forensic analysis, into alleged misconduct in other international locations, primarily Nigeria and Ecuador, and promptly and voluntarily reporting the results of its investigation to the DOJ and the SEC;
- Severing its employment relationship with a senior international executive within 10 days of receiving allegations of his involvement in the Bolivian tax scheme, and seizing from him critical encrypted electronic evidence at the time of his severance;
- Taking prompt and appropriate disciplinary actions, without regard to rank, against 18 additional employees;
- Voluntarily agreeing, as to the DOJ only, to a limited waiver of attorney-client privilege with respect to certain specific subject matters important to the DOJ's understanding of the internal investigation;
- Promptly terminating commercial relationships with purported "consulting" companies based in Nigeria, which companies Willbros suspected of assisting in making improper payments to Nigerian government officials;
- Promptly reporting the misconduct of certain Willbros International employees who, along with others, made additional improper payments in Nigeria after Willbros Group Inc. and the government had begun investigations, which reporting was a substantial factor in causing the guilty pleas of two of the responsible individuals;
- Upon conclusion of the internal investigation, continuing to cooperate with the DOJ and SEC in their parallel investigations, which cooperation included making numerous current and former employees available for interviews and testimony in the United States and abroad, and responding promptly to requests for documentary evidence, much of which was located in remote international locations;

- Expanding, enhancing, and, where appropriate, centralizing its worldwide legal, accounting, and international audit functions;
- Issuing an enhanced, stand-alone FCPA policy and conducting worldwide training upon implementation of that policy;
- Retaining new senior management with substantial international experience and understanding of FCPA requirements;
- Acknowledging responsibility for the misconduct; and
- Delaying pursuit of civil remedies against certain former employees so as not to prejudice the DOJ's criminal investigation of the individuals.

The above cooperative and remedial steps were specifically recognized in the Willbros DPA and represented the most comprehensive list of remedial or cooperation steps to date by a midsize company discovering and promptly investigating FCPA misconduct. Likely because of its efforts to promptly disclose and cooperate fully with the DOJ, it obtained DPAs for the parent and subsidiary notwithstanding the delivery of a million dollars in cash by a country manager during the investigation. The Willbros resolution offers important guidance on how midsize companies uncovering serious misconduct by senior management can promptly institute strong remedial measures and manage to avoid a felony conviction for the parent company and subsidiaries.

Because FCPA settlements with the DOJ and the SEC have featured independent monitors for terms of three years—in the case of Siemens, four years—some companies under investigation have attempted to line up independent consultants to review and oversee their compliance reforms in advance and thereby avoid or at least influence the government's selection of a monitor in a DOJ or SEC settlement.[56]

XIV. LOGISTICAL ADVICE IN CONDUCTING FOREIGN INVESTIGATIONS[57]

There is no substitute for conducting FCPA interviews, if at all possible, in-country at the site of the alleged wrongful conduct. An interview of a foreign national tied to a gratuity to a foreign tax official or an informal meeting with U.S. Department of Commerce officers at a U.S. embassy can enable company counsel to obtain and paint a vivid picture and possibly persuade DOJ prosecutors or SEC regulators that an FCPA bribery charge is inappropriate.

The opportunity to interview (let alone reinterview) foreign witnesses is usually limited, and many foreign nationals, unaccustomed to the detailed nature of U.S. litigation or white-collar criminal investigations, will understandably seek to avoid a second meeting. When counsel is considerate of overseas witnesses and staff and well prepared in initial interviews, the likelihood of a productive follow-up meeting or telephone conference is greatly enhanced. As often as not, company counsel will have earlier and greater access to documents and witnesses than U.S. authorities will.

A. Logistics

In representing a corporate client and coordinating logistics, investigation counsel will want to work closely with the general counsel, an assistant general counsel, or his or her designate. Usually the client will have an in-country manager or regional counsel who can facilitate document preservation and imaging, and line up document reviews and interviews a week or two before the trip. This person often has helpful insights into the matters under review and the factual perspectives of certain practices and potential witnesses. He or she can often provide useful documents in advance, such as the local organization chart, accounts payable procedures, the audit plan, or the storage plan, and can also guide investigation counsel on what to wear at interviews or on a plant tour. An overseas contact can normally secure work space on company premises or another convenient location such as a law office or quality hotel conference room.

An unnecessarily broad request from American counsel to review every in-country file or transaction and interview dozens of employees can create a crisis atmosphere before counsel even arrives. While the company should take all appropriate steps to preserve all relevant documents—hard and electronic—at the outset, it usually helps to narrow initial interview and document requests and expand the requests after counsel has a better on-the-ground understanding of the value of witnesses and scope of relevant records. In planning meetings, counsel should be mindful of foreign holidays and travel schedules of interviewees. The order of the document review and witness interviews, as well as their location, can be important.

Foreign counsel can be very helpful in familiarizing U.S. counsel with local laws and customs. They also can advise where necessary on how to deal with third-party sources of information or local government officials and policies. Logistics will also customarily include visa procurement, transportation, lodging reservations, airport and customs assistance, copying and fax services, and arrangements for weekend and evening support services.

B. Documents

U.S. and foreign document reviews will normally precede in-country interviews. This process can often take weeks or even months depending on the volume or translation requirements. This review should search hot or key documents and sort them by witness and topic and incorporate them into each witness's interview outline. Important documents—particularly e-mails—are found through a quality electronic search with carefully thought-out search terms. Of course, any relevant U.S.-based documents should be addressed in the outline and interview, as well. Key domestic and foreign documents will usually be described and analyzed in a privileged working chronology, *supra*.

Many foreign-based corporate documents are in English. If there are key documents in foreign languages, counsel must plan ahead for translation services. Particularly where documents are sensitive, one should retain a trustworthy interpreter. Many multinational companies have experienced translators on call. If work product and copies of documents may be couriered back to the States, counsel should determine the legality of the transfer of documents outside the country, what overseas services are available, and the delivery schedules for time-sensitive documents. Counsel will want to consider whether there are compelling legal reasons—American or foreign—for not copying or removing documents from distant locations.

C. Interviews

Most foreign legal systems do not impose the intense discovery experience of U.S.-litigation-style interviews or depositions. How one treats foreign employees and witnesses will often determine the success of interviews and the overall FCPA investigation. The more senior the officer or employee, the more likely he or she will speak English. If not, an interpreter or a colleague who speaks the foreign language and understands the culture at issue can bridge many substantive and cultural gaps. Counsel should be prepared to be far more patient with foreign employees and witnesses than with U.S. employees and witnesses.

Counsel may wish at the outset to provide employees and witnesses a general overview or idea of what will be covered. Counsel should normally start with general noncontroversial topics such as background, that is, work history and schooling, and save more sensitive matters for later. Even when the foreign witness speaks English, counsel should allow almost twice as much time for the interview as for one with a person whose first language is English. Counsel should also schedule time overseas to review and supplement work product. A week or two later, one's recollection of five or more whirlwind interviews will usually be muddled.

Above all, counsel must try to appreciate the culture of the employees and witnesses and the likelihood that a detailed interview is a very different experience for them. Counsel should always bring an ample supply of business cards. In most countries it is customary to exchange professional cards at the outset of a meeting, and a formal presentation, as is the custom in Japan, can establish or advance the necessary initial professional rapport. Having carefully explained the privileged nature and purpose of the interview, counsel may be able to test important theories and the knowledge of these officers and employees about sensitive practices. Thoughtful foreign officers and expats often present relevant scenarios and business practices that American lawyers may not anticipate. They invariably appreciate a team approach and consideration of their experience and views.

Counsel frequently elect to conduct interviews away from the client's business offices. Some clients find interviews at their offices disruptive and attention drawing and will ask investigation counsel to use a conference room at a nearby hotel. Even that may not assure the desired confidentiality, as many hotels are reportedly bugged (e.g., in Middle Eastern and former Soviet Republic countries). Counsel may need to be creative in selecting safe interview locations.

If counsel foresees the need for sworn statements, he or she should predetermine what the particular countries' practices are, as they differ widely. Some countries require notaries to review each line of a declaration or affidavit with the affiant. Some countries require the local filing of official statements; counsel may conclude for confidentiality purposes that a less official statement will suffice. He or she may want to prearrange a notary (or the foreign equivalent overseas) as they may be scarce in foreign countries.

D. Forensic Accountants and Investigators

Forensic accountants can be most helpful to a financial fraud or accounting investigation. Most large accounting firms have forensic groups consisting of former law enforcement officers, certified public accountants, and certified fraud examiners. Experienced forensic investigators can assist not only in the gathering and imaging of and electronic searching for relevant evidence but also in the logical organization and presentation of complex transactions. As important and especially for public companies, the work of recognized forensic accountants can be most helpful in assessing internal controls, making appropriate control recommendations, and assuring regular outside auditors that the investigation is mindful of the books-and-records and internal controls provisions of the FCPA. The work of accountants and others under the direction of counsel must be protected by the applicable privilege(s) since U.S. federal law, for example, does not recognize an accountant-client privilege.

In large FCPA investigations, the number of countries or questionable transactions may make the cost of a review of all transactions prohibitive. In these cases, forensic teams can design an audit using a representative random sample whereby the investigation team reviews initially a limited number of files for either liability or fine purposes. For example, counsel and the forensic team may review 1,000 possibly improper payments, files, or accounting transactions out of a five-year universe of 20,000 or more. If the company is cooperating with the DOJ or SEC, it is wise to consult in advance U.S. authorities to define a representative sample and sampling criteria, for example, by country, by year, or by sensitive practices.

U.S. and foreign investigators can be most helpful and cost effective in FCPA investigations. Counsel will want to carefully oversee investigation planning, communications, and expectations. At the outset, counsel should discuss what types of memoranda, analyses, or work papers will be created, which particular team members will prepare them, and what kind of detail or commentary will be expected in any written product. Counsel will want to make sure that any retained investigators conduct investigations or interviews in a legally compliant and ethical way and understand the company's related policies and values.

E. Experts

Experts can be important to a full understanding of an alleged business crime scenario and can be especially important in FCPA investigations. They can tip the scales in close white-collar criminal investigations. For example, in-country lawyers can opine on whether certain conduct is legal under the written laws of the country. Counsel should anticipate the types of experts in the foreign locale who could assist the investigation and explore with the in-country counsel or contact possible sources of witnesses. An in-country expert conversant with English may be much more effective and credible in rendering an opinion on a business issue or practice in the native country than an American counterpart would be. He or she will also usually be less expensive. Counsel should explore with both lay employees and experts whether there are any helpful in-country or regional books, treatises, brochures, or articles. A credible foreign publication may bring a different and helpful perspective to an FCPA investigation.

In general, there are three categories of experts potentially useful for FCPA investigations: liability, damages, and internal controls.

1. Liability

Liability experts are case-specific and can, for example, rebut misunderstandings about tender procedures, products, markets, or an industry. In such cases, a pinpoint opinion or two on a key issue from an expert in the United States or elsewhere can undermine a critical assumption of government prosecutors or investigators. Often a client will believe there is expertise readily available on a particular point—only to learn that the envisioned expert does not really have the expertise, will not be permitted by his employer to be a litigation expert, is unwilling to assist in a foreign criminal investigation, or is leery of alienating local government authorities or competitors who may be customers. For these reasons, counsel should be careful not to assert that a certain expertise is available until an expert has been fully vetted and secured.

2. Damages

Damages in FCPA cases arise in the form of criminal and civil fines and disgorgement and can be staggering. They are often driven by DOJ attorneys utilizing U.S. Sentencing Guidelines to determine gains or losses and multiplying the same. Where the SEC is likely to seek disgorgement, retention of a qualified economist is recommended to analyze arguable ill-gotten-gains issues and potential fines by the DOJ and SEC. Retention for such purposes is recommended earlier rather than later and in some cases as soon as the government floats a mammoth fine or restitution figure.

Foreign economic experts frequently view themselves as consultants rather than as trial witnesses. They may view their role at most as providing an affidavit. Therefore, if counsel envisions a need for their testimony or presentation to U.S. authorities, near the outset he or she will want to obtain the expert's full commitment to travel and give live testimony or a presentation to the government when and where necessary. As with all court experts, these witnesses need to be thoroughly prepared for cross-examination—frequently a new and challenging experience for foreign nationals.

3. Internal Controls

Usually, the circumstances that lead to bribery or false books-and-records issues call out internal control problems. The DOJ and SEC place greater faith usually in accountants than lawyers to design and implement internal controls. If it is apparent that a client's internal controls were weak or lax, counsel should consider engaging a forensic or internal controls to redesign the control environment—and avoid the impression that the company does not understand the risk or, worse, needs a monitor.

F. Computers and Support Services

A laptop is essential for lengthy trips or distant investigation work. It is the most effective way to memorialize interviews quickly and communicate with clients, colleagues, and secretaries many time zones away. There is in certain countries a risk that a computer may be seized and imaged by local authorities at an airport. For this reason, it is often wise to take a loaner laptop that has limited and safe files for this matter and no other clients' documents.

An airplane adapter kit and extra battery pack also may be useful. It is wise to check out in advance if the overseas client, contact, or law office has a compatible word-processing system and to have a contingency plan. Counsel should keep a laptop not in use in a generic bag.

G. Cameras

There is hardly an FCPA investigation that cannot benefit from a digital 35-mm camera (with a modest zoom lens). Photos can capture a manufacturing operation in a dangerous country, a modest office building, or the grandiose headquarters of a tyrannical local bureaucrat. Investigation counsel will want to consult local counsel to see if there are any local or cultural issues with photographing persons or buildings. Quality photographs can portray a foreign business operation or client in a favorable light that an American jury or prosecutor might not otherwise draw.

H. Mobile Phones

In many foreign countries landlines have become extinct, and everyone uses mobile phones. Counsel have four choices overseas: (1) use an international credit card; (2) rent a mobile phone; (3) arrange for the client to lend you one; and (4) buy a mobile phone with worldwide calling capability. For both business and legal reasons, counsel should be circumspect or, at most, generally descriptive in overseas calls.

I. Security

The increased risks of foreign travel by U.S. counsel require thought. With relatively few exceptions, Americans enjoy a much higher standard of living than other citizens of the world, and that fact is well known to the less advantaged. In many countries, counsel should carefully think about what they say, what they wear, what they pull out of their pockets (e.g., a blue American passport), how and what time of day they venture out, and what they truly need to carry on their persons. Lawyers should be particularly cautious about mentioning in public the name of the client or witnesses they are meeting. In third-world countries, American counsel should normally wear comfortable, nondescript clothing and avoid jewelry. One should typically avoid wearing client-logo or USA-marked apparel. Counsel may also want to leave large document carriers or computer bags with a law firm's name and logo back home.

J. Travel, Lodging, Passport, Vaccinations, and Medicines

Counsel should ensure his or her passport is current and find out what visas are required and how long they last for the countries to be visited. Visa applications to select countries may take weeks to process, so the team should allow sufficient time for the relevant consulate to process visas. Some countries will not permit visitors whose passports expire in less than six months. One also needs to check on any recommended or required vaccinations before departure, mindful that some do not take effect for a week or more. Counsel should pack all necessary common and prescription medications for a trip.

Counsel should be on time for departures as many FCPA investigation destinations have limited flights. Airline clubs are helpful for at least three reasons. First, they are normally cleaner and quieter than the public areas of foreign (and American) airports. Second, they often have business facilities including conference rooms. Third, clubs at many international airports have shower facilities. Ideally, counsel will arrive at a distant destination a day in advance to adjust for the time change, meet the country manager, and be fully prepared and rested.

What matters most for hotel selection are safety, proximity to the client, quiet, and business services. A fitness center and a decent restaurant are welcome, but personal security should be foremost in a lodging choice. Hotels and multinational companies routinely have on staff reliable and knowledgeable drivers who can take one to destinations efficiently and ensure safety.

It is easy and wise to familiarize oneself with host countries, regions, or cities one is visiting. *The Economist* Pocket Series on the world and its regions includes Africa, Asia, Europe, Latin America and the Caribbean, and the Middle East and North Africa. It also publishes detailed county reports that feature political and economic analyses and forecasts and cross-country comparisons (www.eiu.com). The CIA and State Department have websites with country profiles and travel advisories (www.cia.gov and www.travel.state.gov). Counsel should also review the websites of applicable foreign governments.

Effective representation in sensitive international investigations requires thorough preparation, patience, persistence, and discretion. The most valuable lessons are often basic, but a misstep in one of them by a partner or associate can quickly derail the objectives of an investigation.

XV. TEN COMMANDMENTS FOR CONDUCTING INTERNAL INVESTIGATIONS OF PUBLIC COMPANIES[58]

The following are ten lessons learned in conducting internal investigations that apply equally to FCPA investigations.

One: Thou Shalt Fully Consider the Scope and Independence of the Client Engagement and Investigation, and Reevaluate as Necessary.
Two: Thou Shalt Take Immediate Steps to Secure and Preserve All Potentially Relevant Documents—Hard and Electronic—and to Make Sure All Appropriate Personnel Are Advised of the Importance of Not Destroying Potentially Relevant Documents.
Three: Thou Shalt Keep the Client Regularly Informed of the Law and the Likely Course, Progress, and Results of an Investigation.
Four: Thou Shalt Take Prompt and Effective Measures to Stop Illegal Conduct.
Five: Thou Shalt Advise Employees and Others of Whom Counsel Represents, to Whom the Attorney-Client Privilege Belongs, and Who May Waive It.

Six: Thou Shalt Be Firm and Fair in Conducting Witness Interviews.

Seven: Thou Shalt Review and Respect All Relevant Laws and Policies.

Eight: Thou Shalt in Representing the Client Remain Mindful of All Audiences and Constituents in Draft Presentations or Reports and Making Recommendations.

Nine: Thou Shalt Discipline Wrongdoers.

Ten: Thou Shalt Implement Effective Remedial Measures and Regularly Review the Progress of Their Implementation.

It can be helpful to revisit and examine these commandments throughout an internal investigation.

XVI. ADDITIONAL RESOURCES

- AMERICAN COLLEGE OF TRIAL LAWYERS, RECOMMENDED PRACTICES FOR COMPANIES AND THEIR COUNSEL IN CONDUCTING INTERNAL INVESTIGATIONS (Feb. 2008) (appendix 8).
- Dennis Block & Nancy Barton, *Implications of the Attorney-Client Privilege and Work Product Doctrine*, in INTERNAL INVESTIGATIONS (Brian & McNeil eds., ABA, 3d ed. 2007).
- CONTROL RISKS, RISKMAP REPORT 2014 (2013 Control Risks Group Ltd.) Control Risks, a global risk consultancy in political, integrity and security risks, publishes a very informative annual global risk analysis.
- THE ECONOMIST "Pocket" Series (2015) (economic and political profiles of regions of the world). THE ECONOMIST also publishes informative country profiles for over 100 countries that can be very helpful in understanding the local government, political, and economic conditions.
- ERNST & YOUNG, THE GUIDE TO INVESTIGATING BUSINESS FRAUD (AICPA 2009).
- Sheila Finnegan, *Briefly Speaking … The First 72 Hours of a Government Investigation*, 11(2) NAT'L LEGAL CTR. (Feb. 2007).
- Lawrence A. Gaydos, *Gathering and Organizing Relevant Documents: An Essential Task in Any Investigation*, in INTERNAL CORPORATE INVESTIGATIONS (Brian & McNeil eds., ABA, 3d ed. 2007).
- Brian Hengesbaugh & Michael Mensik, *Global Internal Investigations: How to Gather Data and Documents without Violating Privacy Laws*, 8(7) BNA WORLD DATA PROT. REP. (July 2008).
- INTERNAL CORPORATE INVESTIGATIONS (Brian & McNeil eds., ABA, 3d ed. 2007).
- Scott Muller & Klaus Moosmayer, Responding to a Multi-Jurisdictional Government Investigation: How to Deal with Enforcement Agencies, Minimize Cost and Management Distraction, presentation at the 20th Annual ACI Conference on the Foreign Corrupt Practices Act Conference, Washington, D.C. (Nov. 18, 2008).
- STEVEN SKALAK, THOMAS GOLDEN, MONA CLAYTON, & JESSICA PILL, A GUIDE TO FORENSIC ACCOUNTING INVESTIGATION (Wiley, 2d ed. 2011).
- Robert W. Tarun, A Baker's Dozen: *Practical FCPA Advice for Multinational Executives, General Counsel and Audit Committees*, ETHISPHERE (Quarter 1, 2011).

- Robert W. Tarun, *Tarun's Ten Commandments for Conducting Internal Investigations*, in INTERNAL INVESTIGATIONS 2009 (PLI Course Handbook No. B-1745, 2009).
- Robert W. Tarun, *Thirty Countries Later: Lessons of an International Business Crimes Lawyer*, BUS. CRIMES BULL. (Dec. 2001, Jan. 2002).
- Randall Turk, *The Interview Process*, in INTERNAL CORPORATE INVESTIGATIONS (Brian & McNeil eds., ABA 3d ed. 2007).
- Lawrence Urgenson, Voluntary Disclosures: Criteria to Determine When to Disclose or Not, presentation at the 20th Annual ACI Foreign Corrupt Practices Act Conference, Washington, D.C. (Nov. 19, 2008).
- DAN K. WEBB, ROBERT W. TARUN & STEVEN F. MOLO, CORPORATE INTERNAL INVESTIGATIONS (Law Journal Press 1993–2014).
- Martin Weinstein & Robert J. Meyer, *A Strategic Approach to the Disclosure of FCPA Violations*, in THE FOREIGN CORRUPT PRACTICES ACT 2011 (PLI 2011).
- Kenneth B. Winer, Brian S. Chilton & Rohan A. Virginkar, *International Investigations and the Foreign Corrupt Practices Act*, in THE FOREIGN CORRUPT PRACTICES ACT: COMPLYING WITH HEIGHTENED ENFORCEMENT RULES (PLI Course Handbook 2007).
- Douglas R. Young & Jessica K. Nall, *Considerations When Conducting an Internal Investigation*, in THE FOREIGN CORRUPT PRACTICES ACT 2008: COMPLYING WITH HEIGHTENED ENFORCEMENT RISKS (PLI Course Handbook B-1665, 2008).

NOTES

1. DAN K. WEBB, ROBERT W. TARUN & STEVEN F. MOLO, *Duties of Management* (ch. 3), *Developing and Implementing a Strategy* (ch. 4), *The Grand Jury* (ch. 12), and *Persuading the Government Not to Indict* (ch. 16), in CORPORATE INTERNAL INVESTIGATIONS (1993–2014).

2. H.R. REP. NO. 95-640, at 18 (1977); *see generally* DON ZARIN, DOING BUSINESS UNDER THE FCPA (PLI 2007), at ch. 4 (thorough coverage of domestic bribery cases that provide precedent for the Department of Justice in the FCPA area).

3. *See In re* John Doe Corp., 675 F.2d 482 (2d Cir. 1983) (investigation by accounting firm as part of its audit is not privileged); *In re* Grand Jury Subpoena, 599 F.2d 504, 510 (2d Cir. 1979) (investigation by management is not privileged).

4. *See* Letter from Jerrob Duffy, U.S. Dep't of Justice Criminal Div., to Robert J. Giuffra Jr., Sullivan & Cromwell NPA, app. A, Statement of Facts, at A2 (Mar. 14, 2011).

5. Peter Romatowski & Geoffrey Stewart, Basics of SEC Investigations: What Every Criminal Lawyer Should Know, presentation at the National Institute on White Collar Crime 1992, San Francisco (Mar. 2–3, 1992).

6. Robert S. Khuzami, Dir., Div. of Enforcement, Remarks to Criminal Law Group of the UJA-Federation of New York, New York City (June 1, 2011), http://www.sec.gov/news/speech/2011/spch060111rk.htm.

7. *See* WEBB, TARUN, & MOLO, *Ascertaining the Appropriate Client*, ch. 4 in CORPORATE INTERNAL INVESTIGATIONS, *supra* note 1, § 4.03(1)(a).

8. *See, e.g.,* SEC v. Gulf & W. Indus. Inc., 518 F. Supp. 675, 680–82 (D.D.C. 1981).

9. Am. Coll. of Trial Lawyers, Recommended Practices for Companies and Their Counsel in Conducting Internal Investigation (Feb. 2008) (appendix 8).

10. *See* Upjohn Co. v. United States, 449 U.S. 391, 394–95 (1981) (holding that communications between corporate counsel and lower-level employees for the purpose of seeking legal advice were protected as privileged attorney-client communications).

11. *In re* Six Grand Jury Witnesses, 979 F.2d 939 (2d Cir. 1992).

12. *See In re* Salomon Bros. Treasury Litig., Fed. Sec. L. Rep. (CCH) ¶ 97,254 at ¶ 95,146 (S.D.N.Y. 1992).

13. 214 F.R.D. 113 (S.D.N.Y. 2002).

14. 229 F.R.D. 441 (S.D.N.Y. 2004).

15. *See, e.g.*, Region Fin. Corp. & Subsidiaries v. United States, No. 06-00895, 2008 U.S. Dist. LEXIS 41,940 at §§ 27–28 (N.D. Ala. May 8, 2008); Lawrence E. Jaffe Pension Plan v. Household Int'l, Inc., 237 F.R.D. 176, 183 (N.D. Ill. 2006).

16. Substantial parts of this data protection law discussion come from the author's colleagues at Baker & McKenzie, Michael Mensik and Brian Hengesbaugh, who authored *Global Internal Investigations: How to Gather Data and Documents without Violating Privacy Laws*, 8 World Data Protection Rep. (BNA) No. 7 (July 2008), in THE FOREIGN CORRUPT PRACTICES ACT: COPING WITH HEIGHTENED ENFORCEMENT (PLI 2007 COURSE HANDBOOK No. B-1619).

17. RONALD W. STAUDT & J. KEANE, LITIGATION SUPPORT SYSTEMS § 6:53 (1992).

18. *Id.*

19. *Id.*

20. *See* APEC Privacy Network, *available at* http://www.apec.org.

21. Directive 95/46/EC § 1.2(a).

22. Russian Federation Law 152-FX, art. III, sec. 1 (July 27, 2006).

23. Directive 95/46/EC art. 25.

24. *See* 65 Fed. Reg. 45,666 (July 24, 2000).

25. *Id.* § 7(a).

26. *See, e.g.*, Russian Federation, Labor Code art. 81 (listing 14 statutorily permissible causes of termination, of which the refusal to grant consent to personal data processing is not one).

27. *See, e.g.*, European Comm'n, Model Contracts, http://ec.europa.eu/justice _home/fsj/privacy/ modelcontracts/index_en.htm; Protection of Personal Data, http:// ec.europa.eu/justice/data-protection/index_en.htm; and Model Contracts for the Transfer of Personal Data to Third Countries, http://ec.europa.eu/justice/data-protection /document/international-transfers/transfer/index_en.htm.

28. Ben Hawksworth & Jennifer Hadsell, *Electronic Evidence*, in ERNST & YOUNG, THE GUIDE TO INVESTIGATING BUSINESS FRAUD 160 (AICPA 2009).

29. Counsel must understand the customs and practices of the country in question. For example, a due diligence check with the in-country Chamber of Commerce might strike many Americans as of little value. Yet under the laws of Colombia, the Chamber of Commerce is recognized by statute as the official business registry of the country.

30. *See* appendix 8.

31. The *Upjohn* warning originates from Upjohn Co. v. United States, 449 U.S. 383 (1981).

32. A related hypothetical Working Chronology is at *section VIII.B* of this chapter.

33. WEBB, TARUN, & MOLO, *Ascertaining the Appropriate Client*, ch. 4 in CORPORATE INTERNAL INVESTIGATIONS, supra note 1, at § 4.05[3].

34. FED. R. EVID. 612.

35. See Redvanly v. Nynex Corp., 152 F.R.D. 460 (S.D.N.Y. 1993); Berkey Photo, Inc. v. Eastman Kodak Co., 74 F.R.D. 613, 616 (S.D.N.Y. 1977), *aff'd in part, rev'd in part*, 603 F.2d 263 (2d Cir. 1979), *cert. denied*, 444 U.S. 1093 (1980).

36. See, e.g., Lawrence Pedowitz, *Conducting and Protecting Internal Corporate Investigations*, BUS. CRIMES BULL.: COMPLIANCE & LITIG. 9 (Mar. 1994).

37. *Id.*

38. The Antitrust Division has issued corporate amnesty policy with clear incentives and rewards.

39. FED. R. EVID. 801(d)(2)(c).

40. Thomas E. Holliday & Charles J. Stevens, *Disclosure of Results of Internal Investigations to the Government or Third Parties*, in INTERNAL INVESTIGATIONS (Brian & McNeil eds., 2d ed. 2003).

41. *See, e.g., In re* Subpoena Duces Tecum (Fulbright & Jaworski), 738 F.2d 1367, 1369.

42. Lawrence Urgenson, Voluntary Disclosures: Criteria to Determine When to Disclose or Not, Remarks to the 20th Annual ACI Foreign Corrupt Practices Act Conference, Washington, D.C. (Nov. 19, 2008).

43. Id.

44. Selective Waiver Doctrine Rejection—Case Law CII. Majority view: *In re* Columbia/HCA Healthcare, 293 F.3d 289, 298–302 6th Cir. 2002), *cert. dismissed*, 539 U.S. 977 (2003). Minority view: Diversified Indus. v. Meredith, 572 F.2d 596 (8th Cir. 1977).

45. Press Release, U.S. Dep't of Justice, Siemens AGW Three Subsidiaries Plead Guilty to Foreign Corrupt Practices Act Violations and Agree to Pay $450 Million in Combined Criminal Fines (Dec. 15, 2008), http://www.usdoj.gov/opa/pr/2008/December/08-crm-1105.html.

46. See Robert W. Tarun, *Thirty Countries Later: Lessons of an International Business Crimes Lawyer*, BUS. CRIMES BULL. 1 (Dec. 2001–Jan. 2002).

47. Brian Hengesbaugh & Michael Mensik, *Global Internal Investigations: How to Gather Data and Documents without Violating Privacy Laws*, WORLD DATA PROT. REP. (BNA) No. 7 (July 2008).

48. *Id.*

49. Directive 95/46/EC.

50. Hengesbaugh & Mensik, *supra* note 47.

51. *Id.*

52. *Id.*

53. Press Release, U.S. Dep't of Justice, Transcript of Press Conference Announcing Siemens AG and Three Subsidiaries Plead Guilty to Foreign Corrupt Practices Act Violations (Dec. 15, 2008), http://www.usdoj.gov/opa/pr/2008/December/08-opa-1112.html.

54. Sentencing Memorandum, United States v. Siemens AG, 1:08-cr-00367-RJL (D.D.C. filed Dec. 12, 2008), http://www.justice.gov/opa/documents/siemens-sentencing-memo.pdf.

55. SEC v. Willbros Group Inc., Civil Action No. 4:08-CV-01494, (S.D. Tex.—Hous.), Litig. Release No. 20,571 (May 14, 2008); see Press Release, U.S. Dep't of Justice,

Willbros Group Inc. Enters Deferred Prosecution Agreement and Agrees to Pay $22 Million Penalty for FCPA Violations (May 14, 2008), http://www.justice.gov/opa /pr/2008/May/08-crm-417.html.

56. SEC v. Dow Chem. Co., Civil Action No. 07 CV 0033 (D.D.C.), Litig. Release No. 20,000 (Feb. 13, 2007).

57. Much of this advice was first published in a two-part article, Robert W. Tarun, *Thirty Countries Later: Lessons of an International Business Crimes Lawyer*, 8(11) BUS. CRIMES BULL. (Dec. 2001) and 9(1) BUS. CRIMES BULL. (Jan. 2002).

58. This section is reprinted with permission of the Practicing Law Institute. Robert W. Tarun, Tarun's *Ten Commandments for Conducting Internal Investigations*, in INTERNAL INVESTIGATIONS 2009 (PLI Course Handbook, Chicago and San Francisco, June 2009), and ETHISPHERE magazine, which printed a version of the same in its Q3/2009 Issue.

CHAPTER 9

Defending an FCPA Investigation

I. U.S. GOVERNMENT INVESTIGATIONS

The Department of Justice (DOJ) and the Securities and Exchange Commission (SEC) are jointly responsible for enforcing the Foreign Corrupt Practices Act (FCPA) and may jointly or separately initiate and conduct an investigation. The two increasingly conduct joint or parallel civil and criminal investigations of the same FCPA allegations and have substantially increased resources for enforcement of the statute: approximately 60 DOJ prosecutors and SEC enforcement attorneys are dedicated to FCPA matters. Not surprisingly, it has become common for the DOJ and SEC to announce settlements of FCPA investigations simultaneously or within a day or so of each other.

A. Department of Justice

The DOJ is solely responsible for the criminal enforcement of the FCPA. Allegations of FCPA criminal violations are generally investigated by the Federal Bureau of Investigation, but the Department of Homeland Security and the Internal Revenue Service—Criminal Investigation Division regularly investigate potential FCPA violations. The Fraud Section of the DOJ's Criminal Division in Washington, D.C., has FCPA expertise and frequently coordinates with the SEC on FCPA matters. The FBI is required by internal regulation to bring alleged FCPA violations to the Fraud Section of the Criminal Division of the DOJ. No prosecution of alleged FCPA violations may be instituted without the express permission of the DOJ Criminal Division in Washington, D.C.[1]

Grand juries have broad latitude and "can investigate merely on suspicion that the law is being violated."[2] Individual clients need to understand, particularly in weighing whether to testify before a grand jury, that decisions to charge a company or its officers and employees with a criminal FCPA violation will be made by the Fraud Section of the Criminal Division in Washington, D.C., not by a grand jury. Justice William O. Douglas most succinctly captured the reality of the grand jury when he observed: "Any experienced prosecutor will admit he can indict anybody at any time for almost anything before any grand jury."[3]

Grand jury investigations normally proceed first with the issuance of subpoenas duces tecum for records followed by subpoenas ad testificandum for the testimony of witnesses. However, if the government secures early cooperation from a company or individuals, it may ask cooperating companies to voluntarily provide documents and cooperating individuals to meet and record others covertly, and their cooperation may not be immediately public or known for a long time. Cooperating individuals can remain secret and provide the factual basis to secure a search warrant.

In criminal investigations it is the custom and practice of the DOJ to advise counsel whether a client is a subject or target. If an individual client is considered a subject or target, the conventional wisdom is that he or she should assert a Fifth Amendment privilege in a grand jury proceeding and also decline to be interviewed.[4] This privilege protects individuals and sole proprietorships but not corporations, partnerships, and other business entities. If subpoenaed, corporations will in most investigations have to produce a broad range of documents, subject to primarily the attorney-client privilege.

B.   Securities and Exchange Commission

The SEC is the primary regulator of the nation's securities markets.[5] Allegations of civil violations of the antibribery and accounting provisions (books and records and internal controls) are investigated by the SEC's Division of Enforcement. The SEC takes a strong interest in the accounting provisions that apply to public companies. In August 2009, the SEC Enforcement Division announced the creation of a specialized unit dedicated to FCPA enforcement. The specialized unit is headed by a unit chief and is staffed around the country by SEC enforcement attorneys, many of whom already have FCPA expertise as well as new hires who have FCPA experience from the private sector.[6]

The SEC has the authority to bring an action in federal court or before an administrative law judge when it concludes that an FCPA violation has occurred and that enforcement is appropriate. The Division and its staff employ attorneys, accountants, and analysts and may proceed on their own initiative to informally investigate without subpoena power, or with subpoena power through a "formal order of investigation" issued privately by the Commission. In 2008 the SEC published an enforcement manual, which is available on its website.[7]

In informal investigations, SEC enforcement staff ask companies and employees to provide information on a voluntary basis. Interviews can be in person or by telephone and on or off the record. Informal investigations can include extensive document production and sworn testimony. The Division staff may request compilation of data or counsel may elect to submit to the SEC a chronology or similar data. Counsel should understand that while the SEC staff have no authority to compel the production of such data, the voluntary submissions will likely be deemed admissible.[8]

Staff requests for orders for formal investigations are routinely granted by the Commission and are used whenever the staff needs subpoena authority to obtain the testimony of persons who are reluctant to appear or production of documents that cannot be obtained voluntarily, such as telephone and bank records. The formal order will describe the investigation in general terms and the suspected statutory violations.

The various federal securities laws grant broad authority to the Commission to conduct investigations.[9] A challenge to the SEC's right to investigate a public company has virtually no chance of success.[10] However, a challenge to the breadth of documents the SEC initially requests or subpoenas has some possibility of success. The scope of such requests is often negotiable with SEC staff. SEC civil enforcement matters may lead to a criminal referral to the Criminal Division.[11] Full access to SEC files is routinely granted to federal prosecutors by the SEC Director of the Division of Enforcement. A DOJ Fraud Section Attorney or a U.S. Attorney may independently request access to SEC files.[12]

SEC staff do not use the "subject" or "target" terminology common to federal prosecutors. Defense counsel should normally ask SEC attorneys whether prosecutors have been granted access to SEC files—unless there is a slim likelihood and a concern that merely raising the question could prompt the staff to refer the matter to the DOJ. Given the increase in parallel government proceedings, it is today prudent to assume a referral to the DOJ and to ask the question.

Unlike in grand jury proceedings, witnesses who testify in SEC investigative proceedings are entitled to copies of their transcripts upon payment of a fee.[13] Witnesses in SEC proceedings also have a right to assert attorney-client, attorney work-product, and Fifth Amendment privileges. However, the Commission may draw an adverse inference from an individual's assertion of the Fifth Amendment privilege, and such an assertion makes an enforcement action highly probable. Still, in most if not all cases, an SEC civil enforcement action is preferable to a DOJ criminal charge. However, when bribery is the subject or focus of an investigation, dual enforcement proceedings by the DOJ and SEC are far more common.

In considering whether to bring an enforcement action, the SEC will ask: "Did the company commit to learn the truth, fully and expeditiously? Did it do a thorough review of the nature, extent, origins, and consequences of the conduct and related behavior?" A public company conducting an internal investigation that is either cooperating with the SEC or intends to disclose the investigation to the SEC should be mindful of this standard.[14] In FCPA matters, the SEC intends to charge more individuals.[15]

II. SOURCES OF ALLEGATIONS AND INVESTIGATIONS

Potential sources of FCPA and, in particular, bribery allegations are many and include

- former or current employees, including whistleblowers,
- public filings,
- investigations of one FCPA matter that leads to discovery of another FCPA matter,
- competitors—often cooperating with one or more governments,
- computer hacking (e.g., Sony Corporation),
- agents,
- consultants,
- contractors,
- subcontractors,

- freight forwarders,
- distributors or resellers,
- foreign government officials or party representatives,
- joint venture partners,
- internal audits,
- independent auditors,
- federal agency audits (e.g., Department of Defense, Inspector General),
- worldwide media reports of "corruption" or "bribery" tracked through programmed Google searches,
- Internet surveillance,
- Department of State and Embassy staff, and
- merger or acquisition due diligence.

Occasionally, an FCPA investigation arises from the federal investigation of another offense, for example, antitrust or money laundering violations.[16]

III. FACTUAL AND LEGAL DEFENSES TO THE FCPA

A. The Statute

The FCPA is one of the most convoluted statutes in the federal criminal code and one that in three and a half decades has had comparatively little judicial interpretation. For this reason, there are more untested defense arguments for clients facing FCPA charges than with many other federal criminal statutes. Under the FCPA, defense counsel must pay particular attention to who is covered and in what circumstances such persons are covered.[17]

The defense strategy may well differ depending on whether counsel represents an issuer, a domestic concern, a foreign company or citizen, an officer, a director, a stockholder, an employee, or an agent. In representing an issuer, a U.S. corporation, or a foreign company before the DOJ, the broad principles of corporate criminal liability apply, meaning that a corporation is criminally responsible for the acts carried out by its agents within the scope of the agent's employment for the benefit of the corporation.[18] For nonissuers, the SEC will have no jurisdiction.

After identifying under what section(s) a client may face liability, counsel will turn to the particular facts and circumstances. Because the statute is complex, convoluted, and with little precedent, and turns on who is acting and the specific facts and circumstances, there remain a significant number of legal and factual defenses available to companies and individuals.

B. Beyond a Reasonable Doubt

In every criminal prosecution the government has the burden of proving each element of the alleged offense(s) beyond a reasonable doubt. If the defense can demonstrate that the government will likely fail to prove any single element beyond a reasonable doubt, it will in most instances be able to dissuade the DOJ from charging the client with that particular offense. Because most conduct in an FCPA investigation has taken place in a foreign country, and many relevant witnesses and documents are not in the United States, the DOJ's ability to secure reliable, admissible quality evidence before a U.S. grand or petit jury is sometimes difficult.

C. "The Search for Intent"

While defense counsel will attempt to challenge the DOJ's ability to prove every element of a contemplated charge, the element most important to the government in many FCPA cases, and the most overriding one if there is questionable or inconclusive evidence, is corrupt intent or evil motive. The venerable Washington, D.C., trial lawyer Robert S. Bennett has aptly described white-collar crime as a "search for intent."[19] In FCPA investigations and trials, it is a search for corrupt intent, and the search will frequently turn on the transparency of a payment or relationship, direct or indirect, with a foreign government official. While some transactions or relationships will be fully concealed and thus likely corroborative of a corrupt plan or scheme, others will reveal a confounding mixture of visibility and secrecy that can defeat a conclusion of evil motive beyond a reasonable doubt.

Related books-and-records entries will often be telltale: a willful mischaracterization of a payment or expense on the company's books can confirm or corroborate an improper payment scenario. Conversely, a fair or reasonable description of a payment on the company's books and records can belie a criminal motive by a payer or donor. In some investigations the DOJ and SEC cannot establish the payment of a bribe to a foreign official, but they can prove that a related or underlying expense in the books and records of the company was misleading, false, or did not occur, resulting in a "false books-and-records" charge and resolution. If defense counsel can undermine the corrupt intent proof, it will be a major step in avoiding an FCPA bribery prosecution and possibly result in less serious books-and-records and internal controls charges or in no charges at all.

D. Outline of FCPA Defenses

Defenses to the FCPA's three central antibribery provisions, its false books-and-records and internal controls provisions, and the federal conspiracy statute are outlined below.

1. *Defenses Available under 15 U.S.C. §§ 78dd-1 (Issuers), 78dd-2 (Domestic Concerns), and 78dd-3 (Persons Other than Issuers or Domestic Concerns)*
   - Lack of corrupt intent:[20]
     (1) Good faith;
     (2) Advice of counsel;[21]
     (3) Thorough due diligence of the company in contracting with a third party or acquiring a target;
   - Insufficient proof of "conscious purpose to avoid learning the truth";
   - Insufficient proof of a payment, gift, offer, or promise of anything of value to a foreign official, party, party official, or candidate;
   - Insufficient proof of a payment, gift, offer, or promise of anything of value to a foreign official, foreign political party, or foreign party candidate;

- Insufficient proof of a payment, gift, offer, or promise of anything of value to a foreign official, party, party official, or candidate for purposes of:
    (1) Influencing any act or decision of such foreign official in his official capacity; inducing such foreign official to do or omit to do any act in violation of the lawful duty of the foreign official; or securing any improper advantage; or
    (2) Inducing a foreign official to use his influence with a foreign government or instrumentality to affect or influence any act or decision of such government official, in order to assist such person in obtaining or retaining business for or with, or directing business to any person;
- Insufficient proof of a business nexus between the bribe and obtaining or retaining business;
- Insufficient proof that an intermediary in fact made a payment, gift, offer, or promise of anything of value to a foreign official;
- Insufficient proof of authorization of payment, gift, offer, or promise of anything of value;
- "Routine government action" exception (facilitating or expediting payments);
- Affirmative defense that the payment, gift, offer, or promise of anything of value that was made was lawful under the written laws and regulations of the foreign country;
- Affirmative defense that the payment, gift, offer, or promise of anything of value that was made was a reasonable and bona fide expenditure, such as travel and lodging expenses, incurred by or on behalf of a foreign official, party, party official, or candidate and was directly related to:
    (1) the promotion, demonstration, or explanation of products or services;
    (2) the execution or performance of a contract with a foreign government or agency thereof;
- Insufficient proof that an instrumentality of a foreign government is involved;
- Insufficient proof that a company officer or employee knew a payment would be passed on to a foreign official, foreign political party or party official, or candidate for foreign political office—that is, that a company officer or employee was aware that an intermediary was engaging in misconduct, that such circumstance exists or that such result is substantially certain to occur, or that such person has a firm belief that such circumstance exists or that such result is substantially certain to exist;[22]
- Extortion;[23] and
- "Rogue employee defense" (see *United States v. Peterson, SEC v. Peterson,* and the related declination of Morgan Stanley in chapter 10).

2. *Defenses Available under 15 U.S.C. § 78dd-3 (Persons Other than Issuers or Domestic Persons)*

- Insufficient proof of a person while in the territory of the United States corruptly using the mails or any means of instrumentality of interstate commerce or doing any other act in furtherance of an offer, payment, promise to pay, or authorization of the payment of money, or offer, gift, promise to give, or authorization of the giving of anything of value.

3. *Defenses Available under 15 U.S.C. § 78m(b)(2)(A)*
    (False Books and Records)

    - Insufficient proof that any book, record, or account was false;
    - Insufficient proof that a person knowingly falsified any book, record, or account;
    - The person merely committed a technical violation;
    - The books-and-record entries contained reasonable detail about the transactions or disposition of assets; and
    - Nonpublic company or issuer.

4. *Defenses Available under 15 U.S.C. § 78m(b)(2)(B) (Circumvention*
    or Failure to Implement Internal Controls)

    - Insufficient proof that a person knowingly circumvented a system of internal accounting controls;
    - Insufficient proof that a person knowingly failed to implement a system of internal accounting controls; and
    - Nonpublic company or issuer.

5. *Defenses Available under 18 U.S.C. § 371 (Conspiracy)*

    - Insufficient proof of an agreement by two or more persons to violate the FCPA;
    - Insufficient proof of an overt act in furtherance of a conspiracy;
    - Insufficient proof of a person's knowing joinder of a conspiracy; and
    - Withdrawal from a conspiracy.

6. *Statute of Limitations Defenses (All Offenses)*[24]

    - Failure to charge within five years; and
    - Failure to timely obtain a three-year extension of the statute of limitations to obtain foreign evidence.

Needless to say, the DOJ and SEC may proceed on a number of theories or causes of action, and the defense may counter with a combination of the above defenses.

IV. DISCOVERY OF U.S. GOVERNMENT INVESTIGATION

Companies learn of U.S. government investigations in a variety of ways. Occasionally, company officials will learn informally that an employee or officer has been contacted by FBI agents or an SEC staff attorney. Sometimes an internal audit or independent auditors will uncover a problem. Still other times a company can learn of an investigation through a whistleblower—a scenario likely to increase in the wake of section 922 of the Dodd-Frank Wall Street Reform and Consumer Protection Act (Dodd-Frank Act). Or the company may be served by law enforcement with a federal grand jury subpoena duces tecum or service of a search warrant. Or perhaps most startling, a company may learn that its employees have been arrested at a trade show as a part of an FBI sting operation. The SEC is more likely to phone or serve an informal request on the company, but in some instances the SEC staff will at the outset seek and obtain a formal order from the Commission to begin an investigation. Under any of these scenarios, prudent corporate counsel will respond promptly, preserve company records, gather facts in a privileged fashion so as to fully understand the risks, design a careful and thoughtful strategy, and, as appropriate, implement constructive remedial actions.

V. NOTIFICATION OF EMPLOYEES OF THEIR RIGHTS

Whether a company is voluntarily cooperating with the government or not, it is entitled to advise employees of the possibility of contact by government authorities. Specifically, it can apprise them of the possibility that federal agents may attempt to contact them at work or at home, that they can choose to speak to the agents or refuse to speak to the agents, that they may ask for counsel, that the company may provide them with individual counsel, and that if they choose to speak, they should tell the truth but also not speculate or guess. Most citizens have not had the experience of being approached or interviewed by federal law enforcement and are not aware of their rights. Therefore, it usually makes sense to advise officers and employees who are likely to be contacted by federal agents or attorneys of their rights.

VI. BASIC INTERNAL INVESTIGATION STEPS

The five basic steps that apply to a board, audit, or special committee internal investigation of an FCPA allegation (see chapter 8 at I.A) apply equally to the defense of a grand jury or SEC investigation. The DOJ or SEC can be expected to look into the legal elements and red flags and due diligence step issues discussed at the beginning of chapter 8. Defense counsel should review not only the same legal elements but also the permissible payments and affirmative defenses enumerated in this chapter. The working chronology described in chapter 8 is equally if not more helpful in defending a DOJ or SEC investigation. There may, in a defensive context, be a need to meet, coordinate, and consider sharing information with counsel for other officers and employees or entities that may be subjects, targets, or witnesses in a government investigation.[25] The sharing of information and possible strategies is protected under joint defense or common interest privilege case law, *infra*.[26]

The timetable for the planning and completion of the defense of a company is sometimes accelerated because the fallout of a public FCPA criminal charge or enforcement action can be very serious and the government may impose a short prosecution or deal deadline. The large volume of government FCPA investigations has made this a less urgent or common problem. Counsel for multinational companies are able in most instances to more quickly and successfully interview employees and foreign third parties and obtain relevant documents than U.S. government agencies. However, this traditional advantage has become less certain with the proliferation of treaties, increased informal cooperation between U.S. and foreign law enforcement agencies, and the incentives of whistleblowers and others to cooperate with U.S. or foreign governments.

VII. JOINT DEFENSE AGREEMENTS

It is wholly appropriate for a company and officers or employees of a company under an FCPA investigation by the DOJ or SEC to enter a joint defense or common interest agreement whereby they share information and work product in anticipation of litigation. Counsel for a company should, however, first determine whether there is in fact a common interest with other potential parties.

VIII. DOJ CHARGING POLICIES

The ultimate challenge and goal of defense counsel is to persuade the DOJ not to indict the client. To do so one must know the factors federal prosecutors weigh when determining whether to charge individuals and corporations. In 1980 the DOJ first published its *Principles of Federal Prosecution*, which provided uniform charging criteria to federal prosecutors who were considering charges against individuals. In the decade that followed, relatively few corporations were prosecuted. As a result of enhanced corporate criminal penalties and promulgation of the Organizational Sentencing Guidelines in 1990, federal prosecutors began to aggressively pursue corporate malefactors in the 1990s. In February 2000, the DOJ announced its first corporate charging criteria, *infra*, which proved problematic and controversial. Since then, corporate charging criteria have evolved as a result of both case law and congressional concerns over prosecutorial overreaching. In particular, DOJ corporate charging criteria have been controversial in two respects: invasion of the attorney-client privilege and government interference with the ability of corporate executives to defend themselves.

A. Principles of Federal Prosecution (Individuals) (1980)

In deciding whether to charge individuals, federal prosecutors have, since 1980, considered the sufficiency of the evidence; the likelihood of success at trial; the probable deterrent, rehabilitative, and other consequences of conviction; and the adequacy of noncriminal approaches.[27] These factors were first identified in the *Principles of Federal Prosecution*. Defense lawyers for individuals routinely address these criteria when seeking to avoid charges.

B. Evolution of the DOJ Corporate Prosecution Policy

In February 2000 the DOJ issued a Federal Prosecution of Corporations policy that outlined eight factors federal prosecutors should consider in deciding the proper treatment of corporate targets. In January 2003, it clarified its corporate prosecution policy under a revised policy titled "Federal Prosecution of Business Organizations"[28] with respect to (1) charging employees responsible for misconduct; (2) cooperation of the corporation; (3) alternatives to criminal prosecution; and (4) compliance programs. Having encountered criticism about its attempts to obtain waivers of privileged attorney-client communication, the DOJ has modified its corporate prosecution policies over time.

C. Amendments to *DOJ Manual* 9-28.000 (2008)

In August 2008, then Deputy Attorney General Mark R. Filip addressed criticisms of DOJ's attorney-client privilege waiver demands and interference with the right to and payment of counsel, and further refined prior DOJ corporate charging criteria by announcing future revisions.[29] The following nine current DOJ corporate charging criteria are formal amendments to the *DOJ Manual*:

1. The nature and seriousness of the offense, including the risk of harm to the public, and applicable policies and priorities, if any, governing the prosecution of corporations for particular categories of crime;
2. The pervasiveness of wrongdoing within the corporation, including the complicity in, or the condoning of, the wrongdoing by corporate management;
3. The corporation's history of similar misconduct, including prior criminal, civil, and regulatory enforcement actions against it;
4. The corporation's timely and voluntary disclosure of wrongdoing and its willingness to cooperate in the investigation of its agents;
5. The existence and effectiveness of the corporation's preexisting compliance program;
6. The corporation's remedial actions, including any efforts to implement an effective corporate compliance program or to improve an existing one, to replace responsible management, to discipline or terminate wrongdoers, to pay restitution, and to cooperate with the relevant government agencies;
7. Collateral consequences, including whether there is disproportionate harm to shareholders, pension holders, employees, and others not proven personally culpable, as well as influence on the public arising from the prosecution;
8. The adequacy of the prosecution of individuals responsible for the corporation's malfeasance; and
9. The adequacy of remedies such as civil or regulatory enforcement actions.[30]

D. Fine Calculations

1. *Sentencing Guidelines*

Whether a company and the government are considering a plea, a deferred prosecution agreement (DPA), or some other resolution, the customary starting point for the DOJ when calculating a possible corporate fine is chapter 8 of the U.S. Sentencing Guidelines (USSG). The Alternative Fines Act, in particular, can subject corporations to staggering nine-figure fines. Counsel must study the potential fines under the Guidelines and the Alternative Fines Act to evaluate maximum corporate exposure before any negotiations with the DOJ begin. For corporations, the Guidelines recommend a range of fines. The Office of the General Counsel of the U.S. Sentencing Commission has published the helpful *Chapter Eight Fine Primer: Determining the Appropriate Fine under the Organizational Guidelines*.[31] For individuals, the Guidelines recommend a range of an incarceration period defined in terms of months.[32] Although the Sentencing Guidelines were declared discretionary in 2005 by the Supreme Court in *United States v. Booker*, many district courts have not strayed far from guidelines that have been in place and long familiar to them and often impose sentences consistent with the Guidelines or those ultimately agreed to by the parties.

2.   Negotiations

If liability for antibribery books-and-records or internal controls violations is clear, there will typically be a criminal or civil penalty and, in the case of a public company, disgorgement of profit plus prejudgment interest. If the proof of misconduct in a certain country or region is less than clear, or the time frame in which misconduct occurred less than certain, counsel may be able to persuade the government to discount those factors and agree to a lesser fine or disgorgement. By any measure, fines, penalties, and disgorgement are rarely an exact science.

In egregious cases, the fine may be a substantial multiple of the company's improper payments or a figure within the middle or upper range of the sentencing guidelines. If a company accepts responsibility early and fully cooperates, the government may agree to a criminal fine well below the minimum guideline range.

In some cases economists, accountants, or financial experts will be retained to review and, as appropriate, rebut DOJ or SEC profit or loss calculations. In some cases, experts from both sides may meet and see if common ground is possible. It is not unusual for financial resolution negotiations to take months. For public companies, getting a matter on the Commission agenda for review and approval can take a half year or more. In addition to financial terms, negotiations will routinely address an acceptable statement of facts and appropriate credit for acts of mitigation and cooperation. Remedial measures, such as a monitor or self-reporting, are important not only in terms of potential costs to a client but may signal a positive or negative message to the business and financial communities.

3.   Avon Products Public Negotiation

Most negotiations between the Fraud Section and/or the SEC, on the one hand, and corporations under investigation, on the other, are conducted in private. An exception to this widespread practice occurred with Avon Products Inc., a global beauty products manufacturer that had serious FCPA problems in the People's Republic of China. Avon's internal audit learned of improper papers and gifts in China in 2005. Three years later, a whistleblower's complaint was sent to the parent company's chief executive officer and that resulted in a $300 million internal investigation. In time, the president, chief financial officer, and top government affairs officer of Avon's wholly owned subsidiary in China resigned along with the parent company's head of internal audit in New York. In 2014, Avon and its subsidiary conceded that improper payments and things of value exceeding $8 million had been paid, and continued in China despite an internal audit finding widespread cash, travel, and payment abuses. As important, the parent company's compliance committee had been affirmatively misled in 2005 about widespread bribes in China and told the allegations were "unfounded."

In August 2012, Avon first disclosed it had begun negotiations toward an FCPA resolution with the U.S. government. In 2013 Avon filed an SEC filing that stated "the Securities and Exchange Commission offered an FCPA settlement last month with monetary penalties that were significantly greater than the $12 million the company had offered. Monetary penalties at the level proposed by the SEC staff are not warranted."[33] In late 2014, Avon settled with the DOJ and SEC for $135 million—$67.6 million to the DOJ and $67.4 million to the SEC. Although this author was not privy to the negotiations or counteroffers, it would appear that publicizing the status of the financial negotiation and stand-off in a mid-2013 securities filing was not a successful ploy. A $12 million settle-ment position, in the wake of the widespread misconduct spanning eight years, exceeding $8 million, and including concealment of the crimes from the compli-ance committee, was wholly unrealistic. In any event, playing the negotiation out in public did not dampen the DOJ and SEC's resolve.

IX. SEC CHARGING POLICIES

A. 2001 SEC Statement on the Relationship of Cooperation to Agency Enforcement Decisions (Seaboard)

The SEC has similarly issued a charging policy that provides companies and their counsel a better understanding of its civil enforcement charging criteria. Specifi-cally, in October 2001, the SEC issued a Statement on the Relationship of Coopera-tion to Agency Enforcement Decisions, which set forth the civil law enforcement agency's policy for evaluating the impact of a company's cooperation in determin-ing whether to bring an enforcement action.[34] The policy, announced in a 21(a) report known as the Seaboard Report, applies to all matters within SEC jurisdic-tion, including the FCPA. Companies considering self-reporting any matter to the SEC should consider carefully the implications of this SEC policy. In the Seaboard opinion, the SEC identified 13 criteria it will consider in determining whether, and how much, to credit self-policing, self-reporting, remediation, and cooperation:

1. What is the nature of the misconduct involved? Did it result from inadver-tence, honest mistake, simple negligence, reckless or deliberate indifference to indicia of wrongful conduct, willful misconduct, or unadorned venality? Were the company's auditors misled?

2. How did the misconduct arise? Is it the result of pressure placed on employ-ees to achieve specific results, or a tone of lawlessness set by those in con-trol of the company? What compliance procedures were in place to prevent the misconduct now uncovered? Why did those procedures fail to stop or inhibit the wrongful conduct?

3. Where in the organization did the misconduct occur? How high up in the chain of command was knowledge of, or participation in, the misconduct? Did senior personnel participate in, or turn a blind eye toward, obvious indi-cia of misconduct? How systemic was the behavior? Is it symptomatic of the way the entity does business, or was it isolated?

4. How long did the misconduct last? Was it a one-quarter, or one-time, event, or did it last several years? In the case of a public company, did the miscon-duct occur before the company went public? Did it facilitate the company's ability to go public?

5. How much harm has the misconduct inflicted upon investors and other corporate constituencies? Did the share price of the company's stock drop significantly upon its discovery and disclosure?

6. How was the misconduct detected and who uncovered it?

7. How long after discovery of the misconduct did it take to implement an effective response?

8. What steps did the company take upon learning of the misconduct? Did the company immediately stop the misconduct? Are persons responsible for any misconduct still with the company? If so, are they still in the same positions? Did the company promptly, completely, and effectively disclose the existence of the misconduct to the public, to regulators, and to self-regulators? Did the company cooperate completely with appropriate regulatory and law enforcement bodies? Did the company identify what additional related misconduct is likely to have occurred? Did the company take steps to identify the extent of damage to investors and other corporate constituencies? Did the company appropriately recompense those adversely affected by the conduct?

9. What processes did the company follow to resolve many of these issues and ferret out necessary information? Were the audit committee and the board of directors fully informed? If so, when?

10. Did the company commit to learn the truth, fully and expeditiously? Did it do a thorough review of the nature, extent, origins, and consequences of the conduct and related behavior? Did management, the board, or committees consisting solely of outside directors oversee the review? Did company employees or outside persons perform the review? If outside persons, had they done other work for the company? Where the review was conducted by outside counsel, had management previously engaged such counsel? Were scope limitations placed on the review? If so, what were they?

11. Did the company promptly make available to our staff the results of its review and provide sufficient documentation reflecting its response to the situation? Did the company identify possible violative conduct and evidence with sufficient precision to facilitate prompt enforcement actions against those who violated the law? Did the company produce a thorough and probing written report detailing the findings of its review? Did the company voluntarily disclose information our staff did not directly request and otherwise might not have uncovered? Did the company ask its employees to cooperate with our staff and make all reasonable efforts to secure such cooperation?

12. What assurances are there that the conduct is unlikely to recur? Did the company adopt and ensure enforcement of new and more effective internal controls and procedures designed to prevent a recurrence of the misconduct? Did the company provide our staff with sufficient information for it to evaluate the company's measures to correct the situation and ensure that the conduct does not recur?

13. Is the company the same company in which the misconduct occurred, or has it changed through a merger or bankruptcy reorganization?[35]

These criteria are nonexhaustive or limiting on the SEC.[36] Moreover, the fact that a company has satisfied all of the criteria does not guarantee that the SEC will refrain from taking enforcement action. Instead, the SEC has stated, "there may be circumstances where conduct is so egregious and harm so great that no amount of cooperation or other mitigating conduct can justify a decision not to bring any enforcement action at all."[37] The Seaboard criteria will be used to determine how much credit to give a company for its cooperation "from the extraordinary step of taking no enforcement action to bringing reduced charges, seeking lighter sanctions, or including mitigating language in documents [used] to announce or resolve actions."[38]

As with the DOJ, one of the most sensitive issues related to the SEC's cooperation policy involves the potential waiver of the attorney-client and/or work-product privileges with respect to a company's internal investigation materials. Once a company crosses that threshold, it may be very difficult to limit the scope of the waiver. To illustrate, privileged materials turned over to the SEC will routinely be turned over to other law enforcement agencies, like the DOJ, and may be available to civil plaintiffs through discovery. The SEC has recognized this issue, and has gone so far as to advocate that disclosure of privileged information to the SEC does not constitute a waiver of privilege as to third parties.[39] Still, serious doubts remain as to whether federal courts will accept a limited waiver argument.

The SEC's Seaboard policy raises a number of important issues for companies that have discovered potential corporate misconduct. In each case, the decision to cooperate and voluntarily disclose sensitive information to the government requires careful and thorough analysis of the legal issues (including the potential criminal, enforcement, and private litigation exposure) and as complete an understanding of all relevant facts as possible. Because the benefits of cooperation can decrease in time, management and counsel must move quickly upon the discovery of potential misconduct to put themselves in a position to make fully informed disclosure and cooperation decisions.

B. January 2010 SEC Policy Statement Concerning Cooperation by Individuals in Its Investigations and Related Enforcement Actions[40]

1. Overview

In January 2010, the SEC announced a series of measures to strengthen its enforcement program by encouraging greater cooperation from individuals and companies in the agency's investigations and enforcement actions.[41] The SEC cooperation initiative clarifies incentives for individuals and companies to cooperate and assist with SEC investigations and enforcement actions and is intended to achieve early assistance in identifying the scope, participants, victims, and ill-gotten gains associated with fraudulent schemes.

To improve the quality, quantity, and timeliness of information and assistance it receives, the SEC approved several measures. First, the Division of Enforcement authorized its staff to use various tools to encourage individuals and companies to report violations and provide assistance to the agency. The tools are laid out in a revised version of the Division's enforcement manual[42] in a new section titled "Fostering Cooperation." The SEC acknowledges that similar cooperation tools have been used by the DOJ in investigations and prosecutions. The cooperation tools, not previously formally recognized or available in SEC enforcement matters, include

- *Cooperation agreements.* Formal written agreements in which the Enforcement Division agrees to recommend to the Commission that a cooperator receive credit for cooperating in investigations or related enforcement actions if the cooperator provides substantial assistance such as full and truthful information and testimony.[43]

- *Deferred prosecution agreements.* Formal written agreements in which the Commission agrees to forgo an enforcement action against a cooperator if the individual or company agrees, among other things, to cooperate fully and truthfully and to comply with express prohibitions and undertakings during a period of deferred prosecution.[44]
- *Nonprosecution agreements.* Formal written agreements, entered into under limited and appropriate circumstances, in which the Commission agrees not to pursue an enforcement action against a cooperator if the individual or company agrees, among other things, to cooperate fully and truthfully and comply with express undertakings.[45]

Second, the SEC streamlined the process for submitting witness immunity requests to the DOJ for witnesses who have the capacity to assist in its investigations and related enforcement actions. Specifically, the Commission has delegated authority to the Director of the Division of Enforcement to submit witness immunity order requests to the DOJ for witnesses who have provided or have the potential to provide substantial assistance in SEC investigations.

Third, the Commission explained, for the first time, the way in which it will evaluate whether, how much, and in what manner to credit cooperation by individuals to ensure that potential cooperation arrangements maximize the Commission's law enforcement interests. This pronouncement is similar to the Seaboard Report, *supra*, which was issued in 2001 and details the factors the SEC considers when evaluating cooperation by companies.

In the January 2010 policy statement, the SEC identified four general considerations:

1. The assistance provided by the cooperating individual;
2. The importance of the underlying matter in which the individual cooperated;
3. The societal interest in ensuring the individual is held accountable for his or her misconduct; and
4. The appropriateness of cooperation credit based upon the risk profile of the cooperating individual.

2. *Four Cooperation Credit Consideration Factors* [46]

The January 2010 SEC policy statement recognizes that there is an array of options available to the SEC to encourage, facilitate, and reward cooperation by individuals, ranging from taking no enforcement action to pursuing reduced charges and sanctions in connection with enforcement actions. Although the evaluation of cooperation requires a case-by-case analysis of the specific circumstances presented, the Commission announced that its general approach will be to determine whether, how much, and in what manner to credit cooperation by individuals by evaluating four considerations: (1) the assistance provided by the cooperating individual in the Commission's investigation or related enforcement actions (Investigation); (2) the importance of the underlying matter in which the individual cooperated; (3) the societal interest in ensuring that the cooperating individual is held accountable for his or her misconduct; and (4) the appropriateness of cooperation credit based upon the profile of the cooperating individual. The specific criteria to be utilized in evaluating these four considerations are:

1. *Assistance provided by the individual.* The Commission assesses the assistance provided by the cooperating individual in the investigation by considering, among other things:

   a. The value of the individual's cooperation to the investigation including, but not limited to:

      i. Whether the individual's cooperation resulted in substantial assistance to the investigation;

      ii. The timeliness of the individual's cooperation, including whether the individual was first to report the misconduct to the Commission or to offer his or her cooperation in the investigation, and whether the cooperation was provided before he or she had any knowledge of a pending investigation or related action;

      iii. Whether the investigation was initiated based on information or other cooperation provided by the individual;

      iv. The quality of cooperation provided by the individual, including whether the cooperation was truthful, complete, and reliable; and

      v. The time and resources conserved as a result of the individual's cooperation in the investigation.

   b. The nature of the individual's cooperation in the investigation including, but not limited to:

      i. Whether the individual's cooperation was voluntary or required by the terms of an agreement with another law enforcement or regulatory organization;

      ii. The types of assistance the individual provided to the Commission;

      iii. Whether the individual provided nonprivileged information, which was not requested by the staff or otherwise might not have been discovered;

      iv. Whether the individual encouraged or authorized others to assist the staff who might not have otherwise participated in the investigation; and

      v. Any unique circumstances in which the individual provided the cooperation.

2. *Importance of the underlying matter.* The Commission assesses the importance of the investigation in which the individual cooperated by considering, among other things:

   a. The character of the investigation including, but not limited to:

      i. Whether the subject matter of the investigation is a Commission priority;

      ii. The type of securities violations;

      iii. The age and duration of the misconduct;

      iv. The number of violations; and

      v. The isolated or repetitive nature of the violations.

    b. The dangers to investors or others presented by the underlying violations involved in the investigation including, but not limited to:

        i. The amount of harm or potential harm caused by the underlying violations;

        ii. The type of harm resulting from or threatened by the underlying violations; and

        iii. The number of individuals or entities harmed.[47]

3. *Interest in holding the individual accountable.* The Commission assesses the societal interest in holding the cooperating individual fully accountable for his or her misconduct by considering, among other things:

    a. The severity of the individual's misconduct assessed by the nature of the violations and in the context of the individual's knowledge, education, training, experience, and position of responsibility at the time the violations occurred;

    b. The culpability of the individual, including, but not limited to, whether the individual acted with scienter, both generally and in relation to others who participated in the misconduct;

    c. The degree to which the individual tolerated illegal activity including, but not limited to, whether he or she took steps to prevent the violations from occurring or continuing, such as notifying the Commission or other appropriate law enforcement agency of the misconduct or, in the case of a violation involving a business organization, by notifying members of management not involved in the misconduct, the board of directors or the equivalent body not involved in the misconduct, or the auditors of such business organization of the misconduct;

    d. The efforts undertaken by the individual to remediate the harm caused by the violations including, but not limited to, whether he or she paid or agreed to pay disgorgement to injured investors and other victims or assisted these victims and the authorities in the recovery of the fruits and instrumentalities of the violations; and

    e. The sanctions imposed on the individual by other federal or state authorities and industry organizations for the violations involved in the investigation.

4. *Profile of the individual.* The Commission assesses whether, how much, and in what manner it is in the public interest to award credit for cooperation, in part, based upon the cooperating individual's personal and professional profile by considering, among other things:

    a. The individual's history of lawfulness, including complying with securities laws or regulations;

    b. The degree to which the individual has demonstrated an acceptance of responsibility for his or her past misconduct; and

    c. The degree to which the individual will have an opportunity to commit future violations of the federal securities laws in light of his or her occupation—including, but not limited to, whether he or she serves as: a licensed individual, such as an attorney or accountant; an associated person of a regulated entity, such as a broker or dealer; a fiduciary for other individuals or entities regarding financial matters; an officer or director of public companies; or a member of senior management—together with any existing or proposed safeguards based upon the individual's particular circumstances.

3.   Five Cooperation Tools

The SEC policy statement recognizes five cooperation tools and discusses the basics, procedures, considerations, and related consideration for each of the five tools. Below are the SEC's basic definitions and considerations for each.

a.   Proffer Agreements

A proffer agreement[48] is a written agreement providing that any statements made by a person, on a specific date, may not be used against that individual in subsequent proceedings, except that the Commission may use statements made during the proffer session as a source of leads to discover additional evidence and for impeachment or rebuttal purpose if the person testifies or argues inconsistently in a subsequent proceeding. The Commission also may share the information provided by the proffering individual with appropriate authorities in a prosecution for perjury, making a false statement, or obstruction of justice. The policy statement expresses the following consideration with regard to proffer agreements:

- In most cases, the SEC staff will require a potential cooperating individual to make a detailed proffer before selecting and utilizing other cooperation tools.
- The Commission may use information provided at a proffer session to advance its investigation or to generate leads to new evidence that the staff might not have otherwise discovered.
- To avoid potential misunderstandings regarding the nature of proffer sessions, with few exceptions, proffer sessions will be conducted pursuant to written proffer agreements.
- The SEC staff uses a standard proffer agreement, and modifications to the standard agreement will normally be made only after consultations with staff in the Office of Chief Counsel or the Chief Litigation Counsel.
- If the SEC staff conducts a joint proffer session with the DOJ or other criminal authorities, the staff will address any potential substantive or procedural issues with his or her supervisors, as well as the Assistant U.S. Attorney or state prosecutor on the case, before the proffer begins. In cases where the SEC staff participates in a proffer with the criminal authorities and the cooperating individual has not asked for a proffer letter from the Commission, the staff is directed to remind the individual that the proffer agreement with the criminal authorities does not apply to the Commission.

The SEC Enforcement Manual contains a sample proffer agreement.[49]

b.   Cooperation Agreements

A cooperation agreement[50] is a written agreement between the Division of Enforcement and a potential cooperating individual or company prepared to provide substantial assistance to the Commission's investigation and related enforcement actions. Specifically, under a cooperation agreement, the Division agrees to recommend to the Commission that the individual or company receive credit for cooperating in its investigation and related enforcement actions and, under certain circumstances, to make specific enforcement recommendations if, among other things: (1) the Division concludes that the individual or company has provided or is likely to provide substantial assistance to the Commission; (2) the individual or company agrees to cooperate truthfully and fully in the Commission's investigation and related enforcement actions and waive the applicable statute of limitations; and (3) the individual or company satisfies his/her/its obligations under the agreement. If the agreement is violated, the SEC staff may recommend an enforcement action to the Commission against the individual or company without any limitation.

In addition to the standard cooperation analysis in the SEC Enforcement Manual, when assessing whether to recommend that the Division enter into a cooperation agreement with an individual or company, the staff is to consider:

- Whether other means of obtaining the desired cooperation are available and likely to be timely and effective; and
- Whether the individual or company has entered into or is likely to enter into a plea agreement with criminal prosecutors that will require the individual or company to cooperate in the Commission's investigation and related enforcement actions.

The staff advises potential cooperating individuals or companies that cooperation agreements entered into with the Division do not bind the Commission and that the Division cannot, and does not, make any promise or representation as to whether or how the Commission may act on enforcement recommendations made by the Division.

Cooperation agreements will generally include the following terms:

- The cooperating individual or company agrees to cooperate truthfully and fully, as directed by the Division's staff, in investigations and related enforcement proceedings, including, but not limited to, producing all potentially relevant nonprivileged documents and materials to the Commission, responding to all inquiries, appearing for interviews, and testifying at trials and other judicial proceedings as requested by the staff, and waiving the territorial limits on service contained in Rule 45 of the Federal Rules of Civil Procedure;
- The cooperating individual or company agrees to waive the applicable statute of limitations period;
- The cooperating individual or company agrees not to violate the securities laws;
- The cooperating individual or company acknowledges that the agreement does not constitute a final disposition of any potential enforcement action;
- The Division will bring the assistance provided by the cooperating individual or company to the attention of the Commission and other regulatory and law enforcement authorities requested by the cooperating individual or company; and
- The cooperating individual or company acknowledges that, although the Division has discretion to make enforcement recommendations, only the Commission has the authority to approve enforcement dispositions and accept settlement offers.

If the Division agrees to make a specific enforcement recommendation to the Commission, the staff is to consider the settlement terms of other similar cases to identify prior precedent involving similar alleged misconduct and include the following terms in the cooperation agreement:

- The federal securities laws alleged to have been violated;
- The cooperating individual or company agrees to resolve the matter without admitting or denying the alleged violations;
- The specific enforcement recommendation the Division expects to make if the cooperating individual or company satisfies the terms of the agreement; and
- Any agreement to make a specific enforcement recommendation to the Commission shall be conditioned upon the Division's assessment that the cooperating individual or company has rendered substantial assistance in a Commission investigation or related enforcement action.

The Division uses a standard form of cooperation agreement that is adapted to the specific circumstances of the investigation or related enforcement action.

c.   Deferred Prosecution Agreements

A DPA[51] is a written agreement between the Commission and a potential cooperating individual or company in which the Commission agrees to forgo an enforcement action against the individual or company if the individual or company agrees to, among other things: (1) cooperate truthfully and fully in the Commission's investigation and related enforcement actions; (2) enter into a long-term tolling agreement; (3) comply with express prohibitions and/or undertakings during a period of deferred prosecution; and (4) under certain circumstances, agree either to admit or not to contest underlying facts that the Commission could assert to establish a violation of the federal securities laws. If the agreement is violated during the period of deferred prosecution, the staff may recommend an enforcement action to the Commission against the individual or company without limitation for the original misconduct as well as any additional misconduct. Furthermore, if the Commission authorizes the enforcement action, the staff may use any factual admissions made by the cooperating individual or company to file a motion for summary judgment, while maintaining the ability to bring an enforcement action for any additional misconduct at a later date.

The SEC policy statement expresses the following considerations with respect to DPAs:

- To determine whether to recommend that the Commission enter into a DPA, the staff should use the standards cooperation analysis set forth in the SEC Enforcement Manual.
- An admission or an agreement not to contest the relevant facts underlying the alleged offenses generally is appropriate and should be carefully considered for the following:
  ° Licensed individuals, such as attorneys and accountants;
  ° Regulated individuals, such as registered brokers or dealers;
  ° Fiduciaries for other individuals or entities regarding financial matters;

  ° Officers and directors of public companies; and
  ° Individuals or companies with a prior history of violating the securities laws.

A DPA will generally include the following terms:

- The cooperating individual or company agrees to cooperate truthfully and fully, as directed by the Division's staff, in investigations and related enforcement proceedings including, but not limited to, producing all potentially relevant nonprivileged documents and materials to the Commission, responding to all inquiries, appearing for interviews, and testifying at trials and other judicial proceedings as requested by staff, and waiving the territorial limits on service contained in Rule 45 of the Federal Rules of Civil Procedure;
- The cooperating individual or company agrees to toll the applicable statute of limitations period;
- The cooperating individual or company agrees not to violate the securities laws;
- The cooperating individual or company shall make any agreed-upon disgorgement or penalty payments;
- If the cooperating individual or company satisfies the terms of the DPA during the term of the agreement, the Commission will not pursue any further enforcement action concerning the matter referenced in the agreement;
- If the individual or company violates the agreement during its term, the Division may recommend and the Commission may pursue an enforcement action against the individual or company without limitation;
- The cooperating individual or company agrees that the Commission may use statements, information, and materials provided pursuant to the agreement against him/her/it if the individual or company violates the terms of the agreement; and
- Additional prohibitions and undertakings designed to protect the investing public.

The term of a DPA will normally not exceed five years. In determining the appropriate term, the staff is to consider whether there is sufficient time to ensure that the undertakings in the agreement are fully implemented and the related prohibitions have adequately reduced the likelihood of future securities law violations.

In May 2011, the SEC entered into its first DPA with a company under investigation for FCPA misconduct.[52] The SEC credited Tenaris, S.A., a Luxembourg-based global manufacturer, with "extensive, thorough, real-time cooperation." In 2014, the United Kingdom's Serious Fraud Office, which prosecutes foreign official bribery, published deferred prosecution agreement guidance (see chapter 11 and appendix 6).

d. Nonprosecution Agreements

A nonprosecution agreement (NPA)[53] is a written agreement between the Commission and a potential cooperating individual or company, entered into in limited and appropriate circumstances, that provides that the Commission will not pursue an enforcement action against the individual or company if the individual or company agrees to, among other things, (1) cooperate truthfully and fully in the Commission's investigation and related enforcement actions and (2) comply, under certain circumstances, with express undertakings. If the agreement is violated, the staff retains its ability to recommend an enforcement action to the Commission against the individual or company without limitation.

The policy statement outlines the following considerations with respect to NPAs:

- In virtually all cases, for individuals who have previously violated the federal securities laws, NPAs will not be appropriate and other cooperation tools should be considered.
- NPAs should not be entered into in the early stages of an investigation when the role of the cooperating individuals or companies and the importance of their cooperation are unclear.
- In addition to the standard cooperation analysis set forth in the SEC Enforcement Manual, when attempting to determine whether to recommend that the Commission enter into an NPA, the staff should consider:
  ° Whether the individual or company has entered into or is likely to enter into a plea agreement with criminal prosecutors that will require them to cooperate in the Commission's investigation and related enforcement actions; and
  ° Whether other means of obtaining the desired cooperation are available and likely to be timely and effective.

An NPA will generally include the following terms:

- The cooperating individual or company agrees to cooperate truthfully and fully, as directed by the Division's staff, in investigations and related enforcement proceedings including, but not limited to, producing all potentially relevant nonprivileged documents and materials to the Commission, responding to all inquiries, appearing for interviews, and testifying at trials and other judicial proceedings as requested by the staff, and waiving the territorial limits on service contained in Rule 45 of the Federal Rules of Civil Procedure;
- The cooperating individual or company shall make any agreed-upon disgorgement or penalty payments;
- Additional undertakings designed to protect the investing public;
- If the individual or company violates the agreement, the Division may recommend and the Commission may pursue an enforcement action against the individual or company without limitation and not subject to the applicable statute of limitations; and
- The cooperating individual or company agrees that the Commission may use statements, information, and materials provided pursuant to the agreement against him/her/it if the individual or company violates the terms of the agreement.

e.   Immunity Requests

In many circumstances, individuals may not be willing to provide testimony or cooperate without receiving protection against criminal prosecution. Experienced defense counsel will seek this protection before a client makes a statement of cooperation. To obtain testimony and/or facilitate cooperation that will sub-stantially assist in the enforcement of the federal securities laws, the SEC staff may seek immunity orders or letters in order to obtain testimony and/or witness cooperation.[54]

When a witness asserts his or her Fifth Amendment privilege against self-incrimination in enforcement proceedings, the Commission may seek one of two types of immunity: statutory immunity or letter immunity. Statutory immunity permits the Commission, pursuant to 18 U.S.C. §§ 6001–6004, to seek a court order compelling the individual to give testimony or provide other information that may be necessary to the public interest, if the request is approved by the U.S. Attorney General. In contrast, letter immunity is conferred by agreement between the individual and a U.S. Attorney's Office. Both types of immunity prevent the use of statements or other information provided by the individual, directly or indi-rectly, against the individual in any criminal case, except for perjury, giving a false statement, or obstruction of justice. Neither an immunity order nor an immunity letter, however, prevents the Commission from using the testimony or other infor-mation provided by the individual in its enforcement actions, including actions against the individual for whom the immunity order or letter was issued. The staff are encouraged to seek a proffer from potential immunity candidates.

The policy statement provides the following considerations with respect to immunity:

- As a general rule, immunity orders or letters will not be requested in the early stages of an investigation when the role of the cooperating individuals and the benefits of their cooperation may be unclear.
- Pursuant to 18 U.S.C. §§ 6001–6004, an immunity order will be sought only if:
  - The testimony or other information from the witness may be necessary to the public interest; and
  - The witness has refused, or is likely to refuse, to testify or provide other information on the basis of his or her privilege against self-incrimination.
- When attempting to determine whether to recommend that an immunity order or letter be sought, the staff will conduct the standard analysis set forth in the SEC Enforcement Manual.
- Since the Supreme Court has interpreted the Fifth Amendment privilege against self-incrimination to include the act of producing business records by a sole proprietorship,[55] the Commission may request immunity for the limited purpose of obtaining such documents. However, the witness immu-nity request form submitted to the DOJ should expressly state the purpose of the application.

Both DPAs and NPAs must be approved by the Commission. The Commis-sion has again delegated responsibility for securing immunity from the DOJ to its Director of the Division of Enforcement.

f. Publicity

Under the January 2010 policy, the SEC staff are urged to provide sufficient infor-mation to the public about the nature of the Commission's cooperation program and its significant benefits. However, the staff retains discretion regarding whether and how to disclose the fact, manner, and extent of an individual or company's cooperation in documents filed or issued by the Commission in connection with an enforcement action.

4. *Conclusion*

The January 2010 SEC policy statement on cooperation defines and formalizes "tools" or incentives that have long been recognized and utilized in DOJ investigations of individuals. To the extent that many FCPA investigations of public companies are joint or parallel investigations of the DOJ and SEC, it is useful for both to have similar definitions of incentives they can offer counsel for companies and individuals. The SEC policy statement has also helped reduce situations where some SEC staff were uncomfortable discussing cooperation guidelines with company or individual counsel or terms such as proffer that were theretofore recognized as essentially criminal in context. The SEC policy statement is likely to reduce stalemates where SEC staff have been able to offer less assurance on policies than their DOJ counterparts to defense counsel representing individuals in joint proceedings. It will also expedite immunity requests where both DOJ prosecutors and SEC staff desire to offer individuals immunity. Finally, as with DOJ charging policies, this SEC policy gives defense counsel a clear set of criteria to address and satisfy in order to secure favorable treatment for clients, for example, an NPA or immunity.

X. JOINT DOJ–SEC FCPA GUIDANCE: *THE RESOURCE GUIDE TO THE U.S. FOREIGN CORRUPT PRACTICES ACT*

The long-awaited *Resource Guide to the U.S. Foreign Corrupt Practices Act*[56] was published in November 2012. The *Resource Guide* is more a compendium of FCPA resolutions of the past decade than a broad policy statement, and provides insight into how the DOJ and SEC analyze corruption cases and related books-and-records and internal control violations. It is an advocacy piece and does not in all instances represent a neutral interpretation of the statute. Chapter 7 of the *Resource Guide*, titled "Resolutions," addresses the different types of resolutions with the DOJ—criminal complaints, informations, and indictments; plea agreements; DPAs; NPAs; and declinations. It then addresses the different types of resolutions with the SEC—civil injunctive actions and remedies; civil administrative actions and remedies; DPAs; NPAs; and termination letters and declinations.

Chapter 7 provides six examples of past declinations by the DOJ and SEC—five involving public companies and a sixth involving a private company.[57] (*See* VIII.E. of chapter 7.) Declination examples are rare for the DOJ or SEC to discuss publicly and no doubt are intended to encourage companies to self-report and understand that there is a possibility that neither the DOJ nor SEC will file a prosecution or enforcement action. Unfortunately, the six examples of declinations do not disclose the dollar value of the anonymous bribes or attempted bribes and leave unclear whether, for example, a company discovering and facing a six-figure bribery scheme may avoid a prosecution or enforcement action through voluntary disclosure and full cooperation. It is also not clear whether the DOJ and SEC declined these matters in recognition of cooperation or because the evidence was insufficient.

The *Resource Guide* also covers criminal penalties under the U.S. Sentencing Guidelines; civil penalties; collateral consequences including debarment, cross-debarment by multilateral development banks, and loss of export privileges; and compliance monitors. It gives concrete examples of prior enforcement actions and insight into how the government and various companies and individuals under investigation have resolved select FCPA matters. It makes clear that robust compliance programs are essential to uncovering improper conduct and will be credited in DOJ and SEC resolutions. The 418 endnotes provide counsel in many instances the names of the companies and individuals, enabling counsel to cite in negotiations favorable prior FCPA resolutions. While the DOJ and SEC insist that the *Resource Guide* is not binding in any way,[58] the agencies will not deny counsel the opportunity to argue that clients similarly situated to examples cited in this *Resource Guide* should not receive similar treatment in resolving FCPA matters or interpreting key terms or provisions of the statute. For these reasons, counsel contemplating or negotiating an FCPA resolution and/or presenting a position paper to the DOJ and/or a Wells submission to the SEC should consult the *Resource Guide* not only for its summary of cases in a particular context, for example, third-party intermediaries or mergers, but also for, inter alia, key terms like "foreign official" or "instrumentality" under the antibribery statute; principles of corporate criminal liability; interpretation of the FCPA accounting provisions; an understanding of other related U.S. statutes (e.g., conspiracy, the Travel Act, money laundering, mail and wire fraud, certification and reporting violations, and tax violations); and guiding principles of enforcement as well as its discussion of possible resolutions with both the DOJ and SEC.

XI. WELLS SUBMISSIONS, POSITION PAPERS, AND POWERPOINT PRESENTATIONS

At the conclusion of a DOJ or SEC investigation, counsel for a company or its officers will often submit a position paper outlining why no prosecution or enforcement action is necessary or appropriate. This filing with the SEC is known as a Wells submission.[59] Within the DOJ and U.S. Attorney's offices, preindictment submissions are commonly called white papers or position papers. In complex criminal or enforcement matters, these submissions commonly exceed 50 pages. In such instances, three-to-five-page executive summaries are recommended.

A. Wells Submissions

The SEC rules provide that its enforcement staff may "advise [defendants] of the general nature of the investigation, including the indicated violations as they pertain to them, and the amount of time that may be available for preparing and submitting a statement prior to the presentation of a staff recommendation to the Commission for the commencement of an administrative or injunction proceeding."[60] The deadlines can be short. Unlike position papers with DOJ attorneys,

Wells submissions are made in a context different from offers of settlement and negotiations and may be used as evidence in a subsequent proceeding. The original Wells release in 1972 envisioned that the submissions would focus on questions of policy and occasionally questions of law,[61] because the Commission carefully considers the legal implications and messages to the securities marketplace that each enforcement action communicates. Still, the practice has become that many Wells submissions to the SEC address factual issues, credibility of witnesses, and evidentiary matters, as well as policy and legal implications. Counsel will customarily address in a Wells submission the nature of relief that the SEC is likely seeking and why it is inappropriate or too harsh.

B. Position Papers

Position papers can persuade federal prosecutors to decline criminal cases, bring less serious charges, or offer deferred prosecution or NPAs. DOJ attorneys typically agree that a written presentation will not waive applicable privileges and will not be used directly against a later defendant as an admission. While there are no specific DOJ guidelines on position papers, most defense counsel discuss in these papers the charging criteria addressed in the *Principles of Federal Prosecution*, the *DOJ Manual*, and now the *Resource Guide*, combining the most recent corporate charging criteria (appendix 9). Most responsible prosecutors are willing to share their legal theories and view of the government's evidence at the conclusion of an investigation and to give defense counsel an opportunity to make an oral or written presentation outlining why charges should not be brought or why more lenient charges are appropriate.

C. PowerPoint Presentations

Where a group of DOJ or SEC supervisors and staff attorneys are considering the prosecutorial or enforcement merits of a matter under investigation, counsel representing a company or an executive under investigation may wish to offer a PowerPoint presentation to the DOJ and/or SEC. A 20-to-30-slide presentation with charts or graphs can highlight key defense themes, factual weaknesses, problematic legal issues, and remedial measures already undertaken by the corporate client. A visual presentation often will better sustain the attention of a large government audience. As with all PowerPoint presentations, careful and accurate wording, thoughtful organization, and powerful graphics will improve the impact. A position paper or letter can follow and address issues orally raised by the DOJ or SEC during a PowerPoint presentation.

D. General Advice

Before submitting a Wells submission to the SEC or a position paper to the Fraud Section, or offering an FCPA PowerPoint or oral presentation, counsel for the company or executives must (1) determine what issues remain at the forefront for the prosecutors or regulators so as to address them and only them; and (2) again ascertain whether the government attorneys have an "open mind" about the issues and the merits of an enforcement action or prosecution. If they do not, there may be no advantage in detailing or foretelling the company's strategy or defense theory. If the underlying investigation has been thorough and focused, counsel for the company or individuals will normally have as great a mastery of key witnesses, documents, and in-country issues as the government attorneys. It is wise during a government investigation to outline or draft a Wells submission or position paper early since the DOJ and SEC may give the defense a short opportunity to submit views and arguments—and counsel should prepare for the possibility there may be only one opportunity to present or defend a client's position.

An effective presentation will usually marshal factual, legal, and policy arguments as to why a DOJ prosecution or an SEC enforcement action is inappropriate in a particular case.[62] In addressing the alleged FCPA transactions and activities at issue, the factual component will frequently focus on the knowledge element of the participants, that is, whether the company's employees knew with a high probability that a payment or offer would be made, whether there existed corrupt intent, and so on. The presentation may also discuss the transaction documentation, due diligence efforts, the absence of red flags, and the presence of an effective compliance program—all of which may defeat the "high probability of knowledge" threshold set forth in the FCPA.

E. Timing

The timing of a presentation to the Fraud Section or SEC is important. If it is too early, the government will say it is premature, and counsel may address matters not at issue or, worse yet, raise problems unknown to the government. If it is too late, it may fall on deaf ears. One has to carefully track the progress of the grand jury or SEC investigation and maintain communication with prosecutors in order to determine the optimal time to address the real remaining issues. Defense counsel should maintain a dialogue with Fraud Section attorneys in Washington, D.C., in order to understand what they consider the central factual and/or legal FCPA issues. Those key issues should be addressed in the defense presentation along with other legal and factual defenses the government may not have fully considered.

F. The "Bribery Is Accepted and Routine There" Defense

In FCPA investigations, in-country managers often assert that "the company conducted business in a foreign country where corrupt practices are routine and long established, and there was no other practical way to do business and compete." This argument simply will not succeed with either the DOJ or the SEC. The uniform government response is that Congress was fully aware of foreign customs and practices where bribery payments were the norm when it enacted the FCPA three and a half decades ago, and it sought to establish ethical business practices for U.S. companies doing business overseas. Foreign policy or national security considerations may in limited circumstances be relevant, persuasive, or mitigating, but as a rule, the argument that "bribery is pervasive in the countries in question" will be counterproductive and will be rejected outright.

G. Corporate Compliance Programs

A quality corporate compliance program decreases the likelihood that improper payments will occur. If improper conduct is discovered, a proactive company that has effective policies in place will be in a better position, when a government FCPA investigation arises, to dissuade prosecutors from bringing serious criminal charges or the SEC enforcement staff from bringing an enforcement action and seeking serious sanctions. (*See United States v. Peterson* and Morgan Stanley discussion at XIII.E.1.) Assessment of risk is critical and fundamental to developing a quality compliance program and is another factor the DOJ and SEC will evaluate when assessing a company's compliance program.[63]

Even if a company's compliance program was mediocre or worse at the time of the improper payments in question, counsel should make every effort to promptly improve and overhaul the compliance program and FCPA policies before negotiations with the SEC or DOJ begin. In many instances, government attorneys will credit quality compliance programs or enhanced policies; the *Resource Guide* makes clear what the DOJ and SEC value in compliance programs.[64] A belated but high-quality and thoughtful compliance program can help a company avoid a costly compliance monitor. In the wake of discovery of corrupt practices, experienced counsel promptly reassess and redesign a compliance program not only to prevent recurrence of bad acts and improve the program—often engaging a compliance expert—but to demonstrate to the authorities a company's genuine commitment to compliance. Too often multinational companies belatedly discover that DOJ and SEC attorneys are adept in evaluating corporate compliance programs and can readily identify paper programs or ones that have in fact few resources to support them.

H. Whistleblowers

As detailed in chapter 1, in May 2011 the SEC promulgated its Final Rules to implement the whistleblower award program of section 21F of the Securities Exchange Act of 1934, which was amended by section 922 of the Dodd-Frank Act (appendix 16). Whistleblowers are encouraged and incentivized to first report information about potential securities violations through corporate internal compliance programs. If whistleblowers in fact report the same information to the SEC, or others, U.S. law enforcement authorities will look back carefully at how companies responded to such information and how well their internal compliance programs worked, particularly upon the receipt of sensitive information. The SEC annually publishes a Whistleblower Report for Congress, and counsel should review that publication if at all uncertain about the origin of an investigation. (See chapter 1.)

Absent exceptional circumstances, a Wells submission, position paper, or PowerPoint presentation should address known whistleblower reporting events. Facts a company should consider addressing in these various presentations include when and how the company received the information; what steps it took to evaluate the credibility of the information; who conducted the investigation; who management shared the allegations and information with (e.g., the audit committee or full board); what steps the company took to make sure the whistleblower suffered no retaliation; how the company scoped its analysis of the information and pursued reasonable or logical avenues; whether it investigated the conduct of the alleged wrongdoers *and* appropriate supervisors; what evidence—electronic and hard copy—it sought to preserve; what conclusions the company or a special committee drew; and what, if any, remedial measures the company promptly implemented. A company will want whenever possible to demonstrate to the government that its internal compliance system ultimately worked.

XII.   PERSUADING THE DOJ NOT TO INDICT

The technical legal standard for indictment is, of course, whether the prosecutor has established probable cause to believe a crime has been committed.[65] Notwithstanding all the criteria and principles of prosecution that prosecutors are urged to consider, the principal standard for indictment, applied by line federal prosecutors and supervisors across the country, is whether the prosecution believes that the defendant(s) can be convicted on admissible evidence. Responsible prosecutors do not indict cases they do not believe they can win.

An overriding reason why many federal prosecutors decline to charge a company or its officers is that defense counsel persuade them that they are not likely to win their case for factual or legal reasons. Losing a case is a clear and understandable fear of the DOJ. Federal prosecutors, who have broad discretion in selecting whom and what to charge, are expected to win most of their cases. That expectation is even greater in high-profile business crime prosecutions. Because of the attendant publicity and often heightened expectations of conviction in major white-collar criminal cases, defeats or acquittals can be devastating to the government and affect the reputation of the offices or the prosecutors who bring the charges. Defense counsel must, above all, convey to the DOJ that the likelihood of prosecutorial success in the particular case is doubtful. If counsel believes that an indictment can truly be avoided, he or she should outline for the Fraud Section the factual, legal, and policy reasons why FCPA charges should not be brought and should present those arguments at an appropriate time.

While evidence supporting one or more of the factual or legal defenses outlined in section III of this chapter may alone not warrant a declination, a combination of these defenses along with prompt effective remedial measures may persuade the DOJ to decline prosecution. In this context, counsel will want to assure the government that the likelihood of a recurrence of the problem is minimal and that the client's management is seriously committed to a quality compliance program and has implemented remedial controls and measures. Policy reasons alone will normally not deter a prosecutor from instituting a case, but they can, in combination with significant factual or legal arguments and prompt, effective remedial measures, persuade a prosecutor not to indict and to resolve the matter in a civil enforcement action.

In deciding whether to attempt to persuade the DOJ not to indict, counsel must fully assess whether the "collective government audience" has an open mind. If it is clear that the DOJ or Fraud Section attorneys or supervisors have already reached a decision to return charges, there may well be no point in advancing legal or factual defense theories in a preindictment or precompliant context. An exception may be where counsel and the client conclude that a conviction or enforcement action is inevitable, and there is an opportunity to obtain a more favorable plea agreement or civil resolution by highlighting evidentiary or legal weaknesses along with recent remedial measures. In general, however, if the DOJ or SEC attorneys have a closed mind and the client intends to go to trial, it is better to save persuasive legal and factual arguments for a judge or jury.

If a company or individual intends to try to persuade the DOJ not to indict, the decision of whether to do so orally or in writing must be made. An oral presentation often has the advantage of allowing an exchange of issues and ideas, and allows the opportunity to follow up with a written position. On the other hand, the permanent nature of a detailed written submission makes it more likely that all arguments will be fully and carefully considered by supervisors or the ultimate decision makers.

XIII. FCPA PLEAS, DEFERRED PROSECUTION AGREEMENTS, NONPROSECUTION AGREEMENTS, CONSENT DECREE RESOLUTIONS, AND DECLINATIONS

A. General

In major FCPA investigations, public companies, officers, and employees frequently face separate but parallel investigations by the DOJ and SEC involving the same underlying allegations. The optimum outcome for the company or individuals is of course to avoid any criminal indictment or enforcement action and to receive a declination. Short of that outcome, corporate and officer targets will seek to avoid criminal charges; to obtain a DPA or NPA from the DOJ; to enter into civil SEC consent decrees whereby the parties neither admit nor deny any liability; and to minimize fines, disgorgement, and prejudgment interest and injunctive relief. An SEC books-and-records consent decree will in virtually all circumstances be preferable to a DOJ bribery indictment or an SEC bribery complaint.

Although they are not a prerequisite, DOJ position papers and SEC Wells submissions frequently lead to settlement discussions with the agencies. The vast majority of both SEC and DOJ FCPA matters are resolved short of trial and in advance of the filing of criminal or civil charges, and solid legal or equitable arguments in a Wells submission or position paper can result in an acceptable compromise.

In enforcement matters, the SEC routinely agrees to settle with the defendant or respondent neither admitting nor denying the Commission's allegations of wrongdoing. Federal Rule of Evidence 408 provides that a settlement or compromise "is not admissible to prove liability for or invalidity of the claim or its amount." Additional reasons to settle with the SEC include the time and expense of litigation; the potential effect of Enforcement Division litigation on a company's relations with other SEC divisions, for example, the Division of Corporate Finance; the impact of continuing negative publicity on a company during government litigation; the need of senior management to devote substantial time to litigation; the uncertainty of ongoing government litigation on a company's stock price;[66] and the need for a company to return its attention to its core businesses.

DOJ resolutions raise different issues. The burden of proof in a criminal case is beyond a reasonable doubt, and the collateral consequences of a felony plea as opposed to a consent decree are far greater. A corporate plea is generally admissible in subsequent civil and criminal matters, may lead to debarment and suspension of government contractors, and may also affect lending covenants and the ability to raise capital.

Prosecution difficulties in securing proof to meet the criminal burden of "beyond a reasonable doubt" may in certain cases lead the DOJ to not file criminal charges and to permit the company or individuals to accept responsibility through an SEC consent decree. Many of the factors listed above that favor settlement in SEC matters apply equally to resolution of criminal issues. If a settlement is the best possible resolution for the company and its officers, counsel will want to secure a global settlement that simultaneously concludes all DOJ and SEC matters.

B. Debarment and Suspension

An individual or a company that violates the FCPA or other criminal statutes may be barred from doing business with the U.S. government or foreign governments. Federal Acquisition Regulations (FAR) provide for the potential debarment or supervision of companies that contract with the U.S. government upon conviction of or civil judgment for bribery, such as the FCPA, or the "commission of any other offense indicating a lack of business integrity or business honesty that seriously and directly affects the present responsibility of a government contractor or sub-contractor."[67] Under FAR, a decision to debar or suspend a government contractor is discretionary. That decision is not made by the DOJ or SEC but instead by respective debarment authorities at each agency. The DOJ can, however, provide favorable information to contracting authorities about the underlying criminal conduct and remediation measures taken by the company.[68]

C. Deferred Prosecution Agreements

A deferred prosecution agreement[69] (DPA) is a negotiated agreement whereby the government files select criminal charges against a defendant, usually in the form of a criminal information; the prosecution is deferred for a set period, for example, three years; and the government agrees to seek dismissal of the charges at the end of the period if the defendant has complied with terms and provisions. The terms and conditions often include payment of a penalty; full and truthful cooperation; implementation of an effective corporate compliance program; appointment of a monitor or an independent compliance consultant; a provision that the statute of limitations is not time-barred and is tolled; and a provision that in the event of a breach, the Statement of Facts, which accompanies the DPA, will be admissible in evidence in all criminal proceedings.[70]

In the vast majority of DPAs, district courts acknowledge the agreements, keep the cases on their docket, and, unless the government moves to revoke the agreement due to a breach, or dismiss the complaint early, await dismissal of the information at the expiration of the agreed period. Two district courts in non-FCPA DPA cases have exercised significant supervisory authority over DPAs. In *United States v. HSBC Bank USA, N.A.,*[71] Judge Gleeson of the Eastern District of New York reviewed an Information charging HSBC Bank USA, N.A. with Bank Secrecy Act[72] violations, including willfully failing to maintain an effective anti-money laundering (AML) program and willfully facilitating financial transactions on behalf of sanctioned countries in violation of the International Emergency Economics Powers Act[73] and the Trading with the Enemy Act.[74] The district court advised the parties it had authority to accept or reject the DPA agreement under Fed. R. Crim. P. 11(c)(1)(A) and United States Sentencing Guideline § 6B1.2, and inquired whether the DPA reflected the seriousness of the offense behavior and why accepting the DPA would yield a result consistent with the goals of the federal sentencing scheme.

Both parties contended that the above provisions did not apply as the defendant did not intend to plead guilty or *nolo contendre* to a charged offense. The court in *HSBC Bank USA* concluded it had authority to approve or reject a DPA pursuant to its supervisory power citing *United States v. Paymer*, 447 U.S. 727, 735, n. 7, 100 S.Ct. 2439, 65 2.Ed.2d 48 (1980). "The Supervisory Power . . . permits federal courts to supervise "the administration of criminal justice among the parties before the bar." It found a primary purpose of the supervisory power is to protect the integrity of judicial proceedings. Nonetheless, it approved the DPA subject to continued monitoring of its execution and implementation.

In *United States v. Fokker Services B.V.*,[75] Judge Leon of the District of Columbia district court reviewed a one count information alleging against a Dutch aerospace services provider a conspiracy to unlawfully export U.S.-origin goods and services to Iran, Sudan, and Burma. The information was filed with a DPA, an attendant Factual Statement, and a Motion to Exclude Title under the Speedy Trial Act. The D.C. court concluded it, too, had authority to approve or reject a DPA pursuant to its supervisory authority.[76] The *Fokker* court found that the parties, in essence, had requested "the Court to lend its judicial imprimatur to their DPA."[77]

Noting that the five-year conspiracy to violate export laws for the benefit of Iran, one of the United States' worst enemies, the proposed $10.5 million fine and the absence of an independent monitor requirement, Judge Leon declined to approve the DPA in its then current form. In view of the increased judicial role in reviewing and approving DPAs, the DOJ has indicated it may return to a binary corporate charging calculus—charge or decline—and wholly avoid cases where district courts intervene and decide to rigorously approve or reject DPAs negotiated by the executive branch, i.e., the DOJ, and party defendants.

A DPA can avoid a formal guilty plea, but a defendant corporation will not be able to publicly assert its innocence or deny the filed charges. A DPA will signal corporate responsibility and a resolution of the matter to important audiences such as lenders, investors, and customers; nonetheless, a DPA can lead to an onerous and costly three-year monitor requirement and include substantial fines, *infra*.

In November 2010 the parties in *United States v. Pride International* agreed to a three-year DPA alleging FCPA violations. In November 2012, the DOJ moved to terminate the DPA a year early, noting that Pride had adhered to its compliance undertakings under the DPA by, among other things,

> (a) instituting and maintaining a compliance and ethics program that is designed to prevent and detect violations of the FCPA among other laws; (b) maintaining internal controls, policies and procedures to ensure that books, records and accounts are fairly and accurately made and kept; and (c) reducing its reliance on third-party business

partners to appropriate due diligence requirements pertaining to its retention and oversight of agents and business partners.[78]

This was the first early termination of an FCPA DPA. Ensco Plc.'s acquisition of Pride in 2011 and its agreement to be bound by the terms of the DPA may have been factors in the DOJ's decision to agree to an early termination of the DPA.

D. U.S. Sentencing Guidelines and Corporate Fine Calculations

Whether a company and the government are considering a guilty plea, a DPA, or an NPA resolution, the customary starting point for the DOJ when calculating an appropriate corporate fine is chapter 8 of the U.S. Sentencing Guidelines. The Alternative Fines Act, in particular, can subject corporations to staggering nine-figure fines.[79] Counsel must study the potential fines under the Guidelines and Alternative Fines Act to evaluate maximum corporate exposure before any negotiations with the DOJ begin. Although the sentencing guidelines were declared discretionary by the Supreme Court in *United States v. Booker*,[80] many district courts have since not strayed far from guidelines that have been in place and long familiar to them.

1. *Chapter 8 Overview*

Chapter 8 of the *U.S. Sentencing Guidelines Manual* sets forth the guidelines and policy statements that are applicable when the convicted defendant is an company and that provide the criteria by which companies convicted of federal criminal offenses will be punished. The term "organization" means a person other than an individual and includes corporations, partnerships, associations, and joint stock companies.[81] These guidelines, which were initially promulgated by the U.S. Sentencing Commission in 1991, were "designed so that the sanctions imposed upon companies and their agents, taken together, will provide just punishment, adequate deterrence, and incentives for companies to maintain internal mechanisms for preventing, detecting, and reporting criminal conduct."[82]

    The chapter 8 guidelines reflect a number of general principles relating to the sentencing of companies. First, when the convicted defendant is an company, the court must, whenever practicable, order the company to remedy any harm caused by the offense.[83] The harm caused by the offense may be remedied through a restitution order, a remedial order, an order of probation requiring restitution or community service, or an order of notice to victims.[84] Second, the court must determine the appropriate fine to be imposed on the company.[85] For corporations, other than those operated primarily for a criminal purpose or primarily by criminal means, the sentencing court should base the fine range on the seriousness of the offense and the culpability of the company.[86] Finally, the court may order probation for a corporate defendant when needed to ensure that another sanction will be fully implemented, or to ensure that steps will be taken within the company to reduce the likelihood of further criminal conduct.[87]

2. *Corporate Fine Calculations (§§ 8C2.1-8C2.10)*

The rules for calculating the fine range in §§ 8C2.2 through 8C2.9 of the guidelines are limited to specifically enumerated offenses for which pecuniary loss or harm

can be more readily quantified, including fraud (§ 2B1.1), which is the offense conduct that governs Foreign Corrupt Practices Act bribery context.

a.   Total Offense Level

The court first determines the total offense level by calculating the base offense level
and any applicable enhancements contained in the applicable chapter 2 guidelines.[88]
The most common § 2B1.1 (Fraud) enhancements for FCPA cases are (i) increased
values of resulting gain (b)(1); and (ii) substantial part of the scheme outside the
United States.

   § 2B.1 on the fraud guideline governs the FCPA fine provider base offense level
and specific offense characteristics as follows:

   § 2B1.1. Larceny, Embezzlement, and Other Forms of Theft; Offenses
   Involving Stolen Property; Property Damage or Destruction; Fraud and
   Deceit; Forgery; Offenses Involving Altered or Counterfeit Instruments
   Other than Counterfeit Bearer Obligations of the United States.

b.   Base Offense Level

   (1) **7**, if (A) the defendant was convicted of an offense referenced to this guide-
       line; and (B) that offense of conviction has a statutory maximum term of
       imprisonment of 20 years or more; or
   (2) **6**, otherwise.

c.   Specific Offense Characteristics

   (1) If the loss exceeded $5,000, increase the offense level as follows:

Loss (Apply the Greatest)		Increase in Level
(A)	$5,000 or less	no increase
(B)	More than $5,000	add **2**
(C)	More than $10,000	add **4**
(D)	More than $30,000	add **6**
(E)	More than $70,000	add **8**
(F)	More than $120,000	add **10**
(G)	More than $200,000	add **12**
(H)	More than $400,000	add **14**
(I)	More than $1,000,000	add **16**
(J)	More than $2,500,000	add **18**
(K)	More than $7,000,000	add **20**
(L)	More than $20,000,000	add **22**
(M)	More than $50,000,000	add **24**
(N)	More than $100,000,000	add **26**
(O)	More than $200,000,000	add **28**
(P)	More than $400,000,000	add **30**

Under this base fine section (§ 8C2.4), the court determines the base fine in one of three ways: (1) by using the fine amount from the table set forth at § 8C2.4(d) that corresponds to the offense level determined under § 8C2.3;[89] (2) by using the pecuniary gain to the company from the offense; or (3) by using the pecuniary loss caused by the company, to the extent that such loss was caused intentionally, knowingly, or recklessly.[90] Whichever method results in the greatest base fine amount is applied. In FCPA cases, the resulting pecuniary gain to the company typically results in the greatest base fine amount.

d. Culpability Score

After calculating the base fine, the sentencing court must determine the company's culpability score. The court starts with a culpability score of five points and thereafter adds or subtracts points for certain aggravating and mitigating factors.[91]

i. *High-Level or Substantial Authority*

The guideline lists four aggravating factors that increase the culpability score. The first aggravating factor concerns high-level or substantial authority personnel in companies of varying sizes that participate in, condone, or are willfully ignorant of criminal activity.[92] The company's culpability score is increased by between one and five points depending on the number of employees in the company or unit of the company and the involvement of individuals who are either within high-level personnel or substantial authority personnel.[93]

The commentary to the guidelines define the terms "high-level personnel" and "substantial authority personnel." "High-level personnel" means individuals who have substantial control over the company or who have a substantial role in the making of policy within the company, such as directors, executive officers, individuals in charge of sales, administration, or finance, and individuals with substantial ownership interests.[94] "Substantial authority personnel" means individuals who within the scope of their authority exercise a substantial measure of discretion in acting on behalf of an company, such as plant managers, sales managers, individuals with authority to negotiate or set price levels, or individuals authorized to negotiate or approve significant contracts.[95]

ii. *Prior History of Misconduct*

The second aggravating factor involves the company's prior history of misconduct.[96] The court adds one or two points to the company's culpability score if the company committed the instant offense within a specified time after a criminal adjudication based on similar misconduct or a civil or administrative adjudication based on two or more separate instances of similar misconduct.[97]

iii. *Violation of Judicial Order*

The third aggravating factor increases the culpability score by one or two points if the commission of the instant offense violated a judicial order or injunction, or the company violated a condition of probation.[98]

iv. *Obstruction of Justice*

The fourth aggravating factor concerns obstruction of justice. Under this provision, if the company willfully obstructed or impeded, attempted to obstruct or impede, or aided, abetted, or encouraged obstruction of justice during the inves-tigation, prosecution, or sentencing of the instant offense, the court adds three points to the company's culpability score.[99] This three-point enhancement is also applicable if the company knew of such obstruction or impedance or attempted obstruction or impedance and failed to take reasonable steps to prevent it.[100]

v.   Effective Compliance Programs

The guideline lists two mitigating factors that decrease the culpability score. The first allows the court to subtract three points from the company's culpability score if the company had an effective compliance and ethics program as defined in § 8B2.1 in place at the time of the offense.[101] This reduction should be denied, however, if the company unreasonably delayed reporting the offense to the appro-priate governmental authorities or under specified instances in which high-level or substantial authority personnel participated in, condoned, or were willfully igno-rant of the offense.[102] It should be noted, however, that the involvement of high-level or substantial authority personnel is not an absolute bar to this reduction.[103]

vi.   Self-Reporting

The second mitigating factor decreases the culpability score by five points if the company self-reported the offense to the appropriate governmental authorities, fully cooperated in the investigation, and clearly demonstrated recognition and affirma-tive acceptance of responsibility for its conduct.[104] If the company did not self-report, but fully cooperated in the investigation and accepted responsibility for its conduct, the culpability score is reduced by two points.[105] Finally, if the company did not self-report or cooperate, but clearly demonstrated recognition and affirmative acceptance of responsibility for its conduct, the culpability score is reduced by one point.[106]

e.   Minimum and Maximum Multipliers

Once the court has determined the culpability score, the court looks to the table set forth in § 8C2.6 to identify the minimum and maximum multipliers that cor-respond to that culpability score.[107] For instance, a culpability score of 10 or more results in a minimum multiplier of 2.00 and a maximum multiplier of 4.00, while a lower culpability score of 3 results in a minimum multiplier of 0.60 and a maxi-mum multiplier of 1.20.[108] The maximum and minimum multipliers are then used to calculate the guideline fine range under § 8C2.7.

The guideline fine range is then determined by multiplying the base fine cal-culated under § 8C2.4 by both the minimum multiplier calculated under § 8C2.6, which yields the minimum of the guideline fine range, and by the maximum mul-tiplier calculated under § 8C2.6, which yields the maximum of the guideline fine range.[109] For example, if the base fine is $85,000 and the culpability score is 5, the base fine is multiplied by 1.00 to determine the minimum fine and by 2.00 to deter-mine the maximum fine, resulting in a guideline fine range of $85,000 to $170,000.

f.   Other Factors

The policy statement at § 8C2.8(a) instructs the sentencing court that, in determin-ing the appropriate fine (§ 8C.2.2), the court must consider certain factors under 18 U.S.C. §§ 3553(a) and 3572(a), as well as additional factors that the Commission concluded may be relevant in determining the appropriate fine in a particular case, such as any nonpecuniary loss caused or threatened by the offense and whether the company failed to have an effective compliance and ethics program at the time of the offense.[110] In addition, § 8C2.8(b) allows a court to consider the relative importance of any factor used to determine the fine range, so that a court is able to differentiate between cases that have the same offense level but differ in seriousness or between two cases with the same aggravating factors but where the factors vary in their intensity.[111]

Once the court has determined the fine pursuant to § 8C2.8, it must add to that fine any gain that the company has made from the offense that has not and will not be paid as restitution or through any other remedial measure.[112] This section typically will apply in cases where, although the company received gain from the offense, the offense did not result in harm to identifiable victims.[113] Examples include money laundering, obscenity, and regulatory reporting offenses.[114]

Section 8C3.1 describes the interaction of the fine or fine range determined under the guidelines with the maximum fine allowed by statute and any minimum fine required by statute.[115] Where the minimum guideline fine is greater than the maximum fine authorized by statute, the sentencing court must impose the maximum fine authorized by statute.[116] Where the maximum guideline fine is less than a minimum fine required by statute, the sentencing court must import the minimum fine required by statute.[117] When an company is convicted of multiple counts, the maximum fine authorized may increase because the maximum fine for each count of conviction may be added together for an aggregated maximum authorized fine.[118]

3. *Departures from the Fine Range (§§ 8C4.1-8C4.11)*

Subpart 4 of part C of chapter 8 sets forth policy statements for both aggravating and mitigating factors that may not have been adequately taken into consideration in the guidelines for certain offenses.[119] These factors include

1. the company's substantial assistance to the authorities in the investigation or prosecution of crimes committed by individuals not directly affiliated with the company or by other individuals (§ 8C4.1);
2. the company, in connection with the offense, bribed or unlawfully gave gratuity to a public official, or attempted or conspired to do the same (§ 8C4.6);
3. the company is a public entity (§ 8C4.7);
4. the company has paid or has agreed to pay remedial costs that greatly exceed the gain the company received from the offense (§ 8C4.9);
5. the company's culpability score was reduced for having an effective compliance and ethics program, but it had implemented that program in response to a court order or administrative order, or the company was required to have such a program, but did not (§ 8C4.10); and
6. the company's culpability score is greater than 10 (§ 8C4.11).

4. *Avon Products FCPA Resolution USSG Calculation*

In order to apply the above chapter 8 framework, it is useful to look at an actual calculation of an FCPA fine for a corporate party. Below is the calculus used in the Avon Products resolution in December 2014.

a. The 2013 USSG are applicable to this matter.
b. Offense Level. Based upon the USSG, the total offense level is 22, calculated as follows:

> § 2B1.1(a)(2) Base Offense Level: 6
> § 2B1.1(b)(1) Value of resulting gain more than $50 million: +   24
> § 2B1.1(b)(1) Substantial Part of the Scheme Outside the United States: +   2
> TOTAL   32

c. Base Fine. Based upon USSG § 8C2.4(a)(2), the base fine is $52,850,000 (the resulting gain to the organization)
d. Culpability Score. Based upon the USSG § 8C2.5, the culpability score is 8, calculated as follows:

> (a) Base Culpability Score: 5
> (b)(1) the organization had 5,000 or more employees and an individual within high-level personnel of the organization participated in, condoned, or was willfully ignorant of the offense: +   5
> (g)(2) The organization fully cooperated in the investigation and clearly demonstrated recognition and affirmative acceptance of responsibility for its criminal conduct: –   2
> TOTAL   8
> Calculation of Fine Range:
> Base Fine: $52,850,000
> Multipliers: 1.6(min)/3.2(max)
> Fine Range: $84,560,000 to $169,120,000

Pursuant to an agreement with the DOJ, Avon Products paid a $67,648,000 monetary penalty to the United States Treasury or approximately midway between the base fine and the low end of the multiplier. Under the multiplier, Avon was penalized for the size of the organization (5,000+ employees), but received credit for its cooperation and acceptance of responsibility. It received no credit for an effective compliance program and only partial credit for its cooperation. As a result, Avon Products had an unusually high multiplier.

E. Declinations

1. Morgan Stanley

In April 2012, the DOJ charged Garth Peterson, a former managing director for Morgan Stanley's Real Estate Group in People's Republic of China, in the Eastern District of New York in a one-count criminal information with conspiring to evade internal accounting controls that Morgan Stanley was required to maintain under the FCPA. Morgan Stanley was not charged by either the DOJ or the SEC.[120]

According to court documents, Peterson conspired with others to circumvent Morgan Stanley's internal controls in order to transfer a multimillion-dollar owner-ship interest in a Shanghai building to himself and a Chinese public official with whom he had a personal friendship. The corruption scheme began when Peterson encouraged Morgan Stanley to sell an interest in a Shanghai real estate deal to Shang-hai Yongye Enterprise (Group) Co. Ltd., a state-owned and state-controlled entity through which Shanghai's Luwan District managed its own property and facilitated outside investment in the district. Peterson falsely represented to others within Morgan Stanley that Yongye was purchasing the real estate interest, when in fact Peterson knew the interest would be conveyed to a shell company controlled by him, a Chinese public official associated with Yongye, and a Canadian attorney. After Peterson and his coconspirators falsely represented to Morgan Stanley that Yongye owned the shell company, Morgan Stanley sold the real estate interest in 2006 to the shell company at a discount to the interest's actual 2006 market value. As a result, the conspirators realized an immediate paper profit of more than $2.5 million. After the sale, Peterson and his coconspirators continued to claim falsely that Yongye owned the shell company, which in reality they owned. In the years after Peterson and his coconspirators gained control of the real estate interest, they periodically accepted equity distributions and the real estate interest appreciated in value.

After considering all the available facts and circumstances, including that Morgan Stanley constructed and maintained a system of extensive internal controls that provided reasonable assurances that its employees were not bribing government officials, the DOJ declined to take any action against Morgan Stanley related to Peterson's conduct. The company had voluntarily disclosed this matter and cooperated throughout the DOJ's investigation. On the same day that the DOJ took no action, the SEC announced civil charges and a settlement with Peterson and that Morgan Stanley would not be sanctioned.[121]

The *Peterson* case is an example of awarding a declination to a company that has a strong compliance program in place. The case involved an officer who, notwithstanding repeated ethics training, secretly victimized his employer in a $1.8 million fraud. This matter signals that where a company is largely the victim of a rogue employee, has strong internal controls in place that were circumvented by an employee, and voluntarily discloses the misconduct and fully cooperates, the DOJ and SEC may elect to decline.[122] Indeed, the Morgan Stanley investigation and nonprosecution was the basis for a compliance program case study in the DOJ and SEC's *Resource Guide*.[123]

2.   Six Examples of DOJ and SEC Anonymized FCPA Declinations

The November 2012 DOJ–SEC *Resource Guide* listed six anonymized examples of matters they have declined to pursue:

a.   Example 1: Public Company Declination

DOJ and SEC declined to take enforcement action against a public U.S. company. Factors taken into consideration included the following:

- The company discovered that its employees had received competitor bid information from a third party with connections to the foreign government.
- The company began in internal investigation, withdrew its contract bid, terminated the employees involved, severed ties to the third-party agent, and voluntarily disclosed the conduct to DOJ's Antitrust Division, which also declined prosecution.
- During the internal investigation, the company uncovered various FCPA red flags, including prior concerns about the third-party agent, all of which the company voluntarily disclosed to DOJ and SEC.
- The company immediately took substantial steps to improve its compliance program.

b. Example 2: Public Company Declination

DOJ and SEC declined to take enforcement action against a public U.S. company. Factors taken into consideration included the following:

- With knowledge of employees of the company's subsidiary, a retained construction company paid relatively small bribes, which were wrongly approved by the company's local law firm, to foreign building code inspectors.
- When the company's compliance department learned of the bribes, it immediately ended the conduct, terminated its relationship with the construction company and law firm, and terminated or disciplined the employees involved.
- The company completed a thorough internal investigation and voluntarily disclosed to DOJ and SEC.
- The company reorganized its compliance department, appointed a new compliance officer dedicated to anticorruption, improved the training and compliance program, and undertook a review of all of the company's international third-party relationships.

c. Example 3: Public Company Declination

DOJ and SEC declined to take enforcement action against a U.S. publicly held industrial services company for bribes paid by a small foreign subsidiary. Factors taken into consideration included the following:

- The company self-reported the conduct to DOJ and SEC.
- The total amount of the improper payments was relatively small, and the activity appeared to be an isolated incident by a single employee at the subsidiary.
- The profits potentially obtained from the improper payments were very small.
- The payments were detected by the company's existing internal controls. The company's audit committee conducted a thorough independent internal investigation. The results of the investigation were provided to the government.
- The company cooperated fully with investigations by DOJ and SEC.
- The company implemented significant remedial actions and enhanced its internal control structure.

d. Example 4: Public Company Declination

DOJ and SEC declined to take enforcement action against a U.S. publicly held oil-and-gas services company for small bribes paid by a foreign subsidiary's customs agent. Factors taken into consideration included the following:

- The company's internal controls detected a potential bribe before a payment was made.
- When company management learned of the potential bribe, management immediately reported the issue to the company's general counsel and audit committee and prevented the payment from occurring.
- Within weeks of learning of the attempted bribe, the company provided in-person FCPA training to the employees of the subsidiary and undertook an extensive internal investigation to determine whether any of the company's subsidiaries in the same region had engaged in misconduct.

- The company self-reported the misconduct and the results of its internal investigation to DOJ and SEC.
- The company cooperated fully with investigations by DOJ and SEC.
- In addition to the immediate training at the relevant subsidiary, the company provided comprehensive FCPA training to all of its employees and conducted an extensive review of its anticorruption compliance program.
- The company enhanced its internal controls and record-keeping policies and procedures, including requiring periodic internal audits of customs payments.
- As part of its remediation, the company directed that local lawyers rather than customs agents be used to handle its permits, with instructions that "no matter what, we don't pay bribes"—a policy that resulted in a longer and costlier permit procedure.

e.   Example 5: Public Company Declination

DOJ and SEC declined to take enforcement action against a U.S. publicly held consumer products company in connection with its acquisition of a foreign company. Factors taken into consideration included the following:

- The company identified the potential improper payments to local government officials as part of its preacquisition due diligence.
- The company promptly self-reported the issues prior to acquisition and provided the results of its investigation to the government on a real-time basis.
- The acquiring company's existing internal controls and compliance program were robust.
- After the acquisition closed, the company implemented a comprehensive remedial plan, ensured that all improper payments stopped, provided extensive FCPA training to employees of the new subsidiary, and promptly incorporated the new subsidiary into the company's existing internal controls and compliance environment.

f.   Example 6: Private Company Declination

In 2011, DOJ declined to take prosecutorial action against a privately held U.S. company and its foreign subsidiary. Factors taken into consideration included the following:

- The company voluntarily disclosed bribes paid to social security officials in a foreign country.
- The total amount of the bribes was small.
- When discovered, the corrupt practices were immediately terminated.
- The conduct was thoroughly investigated, and the results of the investigation were promptly provided to DOJ.
- All individuals involved were either terminated or disciplined. The company also terminated its relationship with its foreign law firm.
- The company instituted improved training and compliance programs commensurate with its size and risk exposure.[124]

The *Resource Guide* asserts that the DOJ "in the past year alone . . . declined several cases against companies where potential violations were alleged."[125] Many of the six anonymous declinations share common characteristics: small or relatively small amounts of bribes (examples 2, 3 and 6); an internal investigation followed discovery of the problem (all 6); self-reporting or voluntary disclosure (all 6); and remedial action including discipline (1, 2 and 6). Still, many of these characteristics have long been present in FCPA prosecutions and DPAs.

Moreover, while it is plain that red flags with respect to a third party were present in Example 1, it remains unclear whether any improper payments were made. Example 3 does not address the jurisdictional nexus for misconduct at a foreign subsidiary. Perhaps, above all, it would have been more illuminating and disclosure-inducing if the *Resource Guide* had revealed whether the bribe payments involved here had been in the five- to six-figure range. Further, when the *Resource Guide* refers to potential improper payments, as with Example 4, it raises the question of whether the DOJ and SEC declined due to insufficient evidence or as a result of leniency.

Although the *Resource Guide* states that the DOJ and SEC place a "high premium on self-reporting,"[126] it avoids quantifying for boards of directors and management the actual credit companies can expect following self-disclosure, cooperation, and remediation. It leaves practitioners and general counsel still very unclear whether an expensive internal investigation, disclosure, and remediation program is likely to result in an expensive DOJ adjudication or an NPA. If a goal of the *Resource Guide* was to encourage more companies to self-disclose and cooperate, the six declination examples have left unanswered whether a company voluntarily disclosing a five- or six-figure improper payment problem can realistically avoid a felony or a DPA or whether the six declination examples provided involved lack of sufficient evidence to merit prosecution.

3.   *Declinations and Compliance Programs*

In February 2013, Jeffrey Knox, principal deputy chief of the DOJ's Fraud Section, told an Ethics Resource Center's policy summit that declinations are possible where companies facing an FCPA problem can demonstrate they had a strong compliance program in place that, "for no lack of trying, just didn't detect criminal conduct."[127] Knox added, "Many good compliance programs on paper fail to translate into the real world, whether due to shoddy processes or a lack of support from management."[128] Experienced prosecutors can quickly distinguish paper programs from fully functional compliance programs. Well-run multinationals are proactive in ensuring they have solid, robust compliance programs in place *before* problems arise.

4.   *Assistance to Foreign Governments*

In a little-noticed foreign corruption investigation, the Special Investigation Prosecution Team of Turks & Caicos acknowledged that a $12 million settlement payment by Jamaica-based Sandals Resorts to the Turks & Caicos government was the result of the "extraordinary and unique involvement" of U.S. authorities who voluntarily released evidence.[129] The resort company did not admit any liability in the continuing corruption investigation of the tiny Caribbean island by special British prosecutors. The Sandals disposition suggests that where a company assists a foreign government, the DOJ in special circumstances may decline in favor of the company's resolution with another government.

XIV. MULTIJURISDICTIONAL GOVERNMENT INVESTIGATIONS

As a result of more U.S. antibribery investigations and prosecutions, increased international cooperation between U.S. and foreign law enforcement authorities, and the risk of draconian FCPA corporate fines, the likelihood of a multijurisdictional government investigation is far greater today than in the past. Multijurisdictional government investigations have recently taken place at Siemens, Halliburton, Volvo AB, Statoil, BAE Systems plc, Panalpina, and Johnson & Johnson, and are likely to increase. Companies facing these investigations need experienced counsel to handle multijurisdictional government investigations.

Highly respected white-collar criminal lawyer Scott W. Muller has written that the challenges in cross-border or global government investigations include

- different data privacy laws;
- different labor laws;
- local law restrictions;
- different legal systems that may or may not impose corporate or individual criminal liability;
- different attorney-client privilege laws;
- different information technology infrastructure;
- different language and culture;
- different extradition principles and policies;
- different or lack of corporate cooperation incentives; and
- different or lack of reciprocity of mutual assistance between regulators, for example, Mutual Legal Assistance Treaties.[130]

The defense of a company facing multijurisdictional government investigations requires close client and counsel coordination and careful management of the often conflicting requirements of national and foreign law enforcement agencies.

XV. MONITORSHIPS

A. Trend

Independent monitors or consultants have been a staple in many FCPA settlements with the DOJ and/or SEC including Baker Hughes Services International, Biomet, Delta & Pine Land Company, DPC (Tianjin), Monsanto, Schnitzer Steel Industries Inc., Siemens, Syncor, Titan, Vetco, and Willbros Group Inc., discussed in chapter 10. The monitors usually have a mandate to review all remedial measures in addition to the problematic foreign operations of the companies. There has been a trend away from imposing three-year monitorships to lesser sanctions such as periodic reporting to the DOJ or SEC or the requirement of a corporate compliance consultant. The DOJ has agreed to independent corporate compliance consultants in several cases, for example, Marubeni Corporation and Smith & Nephew, discussed in chapter 10. The DOJ has required periodic reports on remediation and enhanced compliance efforts in some cases, for example, Armor Holdings Inc., Data Systems & Solutions, Johnson & Johnson, Orthofix, and Pfizer-Wyeth, also discussed in chapter 10. Prompt remedial actions can make a real difference in the postsettlement relief.

B. Typical Terms

Typically, monitors serve three-year appointments and submit two or three annual reports to the DOJ. In the Siemens case, a four-year monitorship was imposed, and the monitor is a German national.

C. Monitor Qualifications

In general, candidates for FCPA monitorships must meet the following four qualifications:

1. Demonstrated expertise with respect to the FCPA, including experience counseling on FCPA issues;
2. Experience designing and/or reviewing corporate compliance policies and procedures and internal controls, including FCPA-specific policies, procedures, and internal controls;
3. The ability to access and deploy resources as necessary to discharge the monitor's duties under the agreement with the DOJ; and
4. Sufficient independence from the company to ensure effective and impartial performance.

The DOJ customarily retains the discretion to accept or reject a monitor proposed by a settling company. Even where such misconduct has been continuous and substantial, a company may avoid a monitorship by implementing substantive remedial actions during an investigation. See Pride International, Panalpina, and Johnson & Johnson resolutions in chapter 10.

D. The Morford Memorandum

In March 2008, the DOJ issued a policy memorandum (the Morford Memorandum) titled "Selection and Use of Monitors in Deferred Prosecution Agreements with Corporations"[131] (appendix 10). In addition to requiring merit selection and addressing potential conflict issues, the policy sets forth six principles with respect to the scope of a monitor's duties:

1. A monitor is an independent third party, not an employee or agent of the corporation or of the government.
2. A monitor's primary responsibility should be to assess and monitor a corporation's compliance with those terms of the agreement that are specifically designed to address and reduce the risk of recurrence of the corporation's misconduct, including, in most cases, evaluating (and, where appropriate, proposing) internal controls and corporate ethics and compliance programs.
3. In carrying out his or her duties, a monitor will often need to understand the full scope of the corporation's misconduct covered by the agreement, but the monitor's responsibilities should be no broader than necessary to address and reduce the risk of recurrence of the corporation's misconduct.
4. Communication among the government, the corporation, and the monitor is in the interest of all the parties. Depending on the facts and circumstances, it may be appropriate for the monitor to make periodic written reports to both the government and the corporation.

5. If the corporation chooses not to adopt recommendations made by the monitor within a reasonable time, either the monitor or the corporation, or both, should report that fact to the government, along with the corporation's reasons. The government may consider this conduct when evaluating whether the corporation has fulfilled its obligations under the agreement.

6. The agreement should clearly identify any types of previously undisclosed or new misconduct that the monitor will be required to report directly to the government. The agreement should also provide that as to evidence of other such misconduct, the monitor will have the discretion to report this misconduct to the government or the corporation or both.

Companies that may be facing the appointment of a monitor should carefully review the entire DOJ policy memorandum on monitors and commentary. (See appendix 10.)

E. Selection and Work of a Monitor

The appointment of a monitor is an important and potentially costly event for a company that has likely endured a trying multiyear government investigation(s) and already implemented a host of remedial measures. In most cases, monitors have legal backgrounds and careers—frequently as former federal prosecutors or judges. A monitor should be independent, knowledgeable about the FCPA, committed to quality compliance, an effective communicator, and practical and mindful of the costs and shareholders' interests. Monitors are expected to be knowledgeable in the design and implementation of quality compliance programs. Experienced monitors will offer practical, constructive suggestions that add value and efficacy to the compliance program and controls of a company. Perhaps, above all, an independent monitor should be fair and willing to listen—to management and to the government.

A monitor should prepare a preliminary work plan that includes the work of any forensic accounting firm or other experts that will support the monitor. Forensic firms can be more expensive than the monitor and his staff. The work plan will include a de novo review of the issues that led to the prosecution or enforcement action but not involve a reinvestigation of the underlying matter. The work plan will include interviews of senior management, internal audit staff, the compliance officers, and any outside firm that conducted an investigation, and usually include periodic visits to the countries where the problems arose and possibly other jurisdictions that present a number of potential FCPA challenges. The monitor will typically issue two or three annual reports.

XVI. ADDITIONAL RESOURCES

- U.S. Attorneys' Manual tit. 9, Criminal Res. Manual, at 9-28.000 (appendix 9).
- 17 C.F.R. § 200.12 (appendix 14).
- Crim. Div., U.S. Dep't of Justice & Enforcement Div., U.S. Sec. & Exch. Comm., FCPA: A Resource Guide to the U.S. Foreign Corrupt Practices Act (2012), http://www.justice.gov/criminal/fraud/fcpa/guidance/ or http://www.sec.gov/spotlight/fcpa.shtml (appendix 4).

- DAVID LUBAN, JULIE O'SULLIVAN & DAVID STEWART, *Corruption*, ch. 14 in INTERNATIONAL AND TRANSNATIONAL CRIMINAL LAW (Aspen 2009).
- Colleen Mahoney et al., *The SEC Enforcement Process and Procedure in Handling an SEC Investigation after Sarbanes-Oxley*, 77-2nd C.P.S. (BNA).
- Memorandum from Craig S. Morford, Acting Deputy Att'y Gen., U.S. Dep't of Justice, to Heads of Department Components and United States Attorneys, Selection and Use of Monitors in Deferred Prosecution Agreements and Non-Prosecution Agreements with Corporations (Mar. 7, 2008), http://www .usdoj.gov/dag/morford-useofmonitorsmemo-03072008.pdf (appendix 10).
- RICHARD MORVILLO ET AL., SECURITIES INVESTIGATIONS: CRIMINAL, CIVIL AND ADMINISTRATIVE (PLI 2009).
- Scott Muller, Recent Developments in Corruption Cases: Multi-Jurisdictional Government Investigations, National Institute on White Collar Crime 2009 (ABA Mar. 5–6, 2009, San Francisco).
- Report of Investigation Pursuant to Section 21(a) of the Securities Exchange Act of 1934 and Commission Statement on the Relationship of Cooperation to Agency Enforcement Decisions (Exchange Act Release No. 44969, Accounting and Auditing Enforcement Release No. 1470, Oct. 23, 2001) (Seaboard Report) (appendix 11).
- Peter Romatowski & Geoffrey Stewart, Basics of SEC Investigations: What Every Criminal Lawyer Should Know, National Institute on White Collar Crime 1992 (ABA Mar. 2–3, 1992 San Francisco).
- United States Sentencing Commission Office of the General Counsel, ch. 8 Fine Primer: Determining the Appropriate Fine under the Organizational Guidelines (May 2014); http://www.ussc.gov/sites/default/files/pdf/training/annual-national-training-seminar/2011/011_Primer_Chapter_8_Appropriate_Fine.pdf (appendix 12).
- United States Sentencing Guidelines § 8b2.1, Effective Compliance and Ethics Program (appendix 13).
- DAN K. WEBB, ROBERT W. TARUN & STEVEN F. MOLO, CORPORATE INTERNAL INVESTIGATIONS, ch. 15, 16 (Law Journal Press 1993–2015).

NOTES

1. U.S. ATTORNEYS' MANUAL tit. 9, Criminal Res. Manual, at 9-47.110.

2. United States v. R. Enter., 498 U.S. 292 (1991).

3. United States v. Mara, 410 U.S. 19, 23 (1973).

4. DAN K. WEBB, ROBERT W. TARUN & STEVEN F. MOLO, CORPORATE INTERNAL INVESTIGATIONS (1993–2015).

5. For an excellent detailed review of the SEC enforcement process, *see* Colleen P. Mahoney, *The SEC Enforcement Process: Practice and Procedure in Handling an SEC Investigation after Sarbanes-Oxley*, 77-2nd C.P.S. (BNA).

6. Robert Khuzami, Director of Enforcement, SEC, Remarks before the New York City Bar: My First 100 Days as Director of Enforcement (Aug. 5, 2009), http:// www.sec.gov/news/speech/2009/spch080509rk.htm.

7. ENFORCEMENT DIV., SEC. & EXCH. COMM., ENFORCEMENT MANUAL (Jan. 13, 2010), http://www.sec.gov/divisions/enforce/enforcementmanual.pdf [hereinafter SEC ENFORCEMENT MANUAL].

8. *See* SEC v. First City Fin. Corp., 890 F.2d 1215, 1225 (D.C. Cir. 1989) (chronology submitted to SEC was admissible).

9. *See*, e.g., Securities Act of 1933 § 20(A), 15 U.S.C. § 77t(A); Securities Exchange Act of 1934 § 21(A)(1), 15 U.S.C. § 78u(A); SEC v. Jerry T. O'Brien, Inc., 467 U.S. 735 (1984).

10. *See*, e.g., SEC v. Arthur Young & Co., 584 F.2d 1018, 1022–28 & n.45 (D.C. Cir. 1978), *cert. denied*, 439 U.S. 1071 (1979) (*quoting* United States v. Morton Salt Co., 338 U.S. 632, 652 (1950)).

11. 15 U.S.C. § 78u(D)(1).

12. 17 C.F.R. § 202.5(B).

13. Commission Rule 6. But the Commission may, for good cause shown, deny a request.

14. Report of Investigation Pursuant to Section 21(a) of the Securities Exchange Act of 1934 and Commission Statement on the Relationship of Cooperation to Agency Enforcement Decisions, Exchange Act Release No. 44,969, Accounting and Auditing Enforcement Release No. 1470 (Oct. 23, 2001) [hereinafter Seaboard Report]. The SEC issued the Seaboard Report in the context of announcing that it was commencing and settling a cease-and-desist proceeding against the former controller of a public company's subsidiary for misstating financial information. The SEC stated that it was not taking any action against the parent company because of its extensive cooperation with the investigation, and, in the process, the SEC took the opportunity to state its general criteria for evaluating a company's cooperation (printed as appendix 11).

15. Yin Wilczek, *SEC to Unveil FCPA Actions against Individuals by Year's End*, BNA Corporate Counsel Weekly (Oct. 10, 2014), http://www.bna.com/sec-unveil-fcpa-n17179896476/.

16. *See* United States v. Misao Hioki, 4:08-Cr-00795 (S.D. Tex. 2008); *see* also Select DOJ Matters Discussion, infra.

17. *See* David Luban, Julie O'Sullivan & David Stewart, International and Transnational Criminal Law, ch. 14, at 4 (Aspen 2009).

18. United States v. N.Y. Cent. & Hudson River R.R. Co., 212 U.S. 481 (1909).

19. E-mail from Robert S. Bennett to author (Sept. 1, 2009).

20. 15 U.S.C. §§ 78dd-1(F)(2), 78dd-2(H)(3), 78dd-3(F)(3).

21. *See*, e.g., Stichting v. Schreiber, 327 F.3d 173 (2d Cir. 2003).

22. 15 U.S.C. §§ 78dd-1(F)(2), 78dd-2(H)(3), 78dd-3(F)(3).

23. *See* Philip Urofsky, *Extortionate Demands under the Foreign Corrupt Practices Act*, BNA White Collar Crime Rep., Dec. 19, 2008.

24. 18 U.S.C. §§ 3282, 3292.

25. *See* Webb, Tarun & Molo, supra note 4, at ch. 7, *Multiple Representation and Joint Defense Agreements*.

26. *See* Cont'l Oil v. United States, 330 F.2d 347 (9th Cir. 1964); United States v. McPartlin, 595 F.2d 1321 (7th Cir. 1978); Hunydee v. United States, 355 F.2d 183 (9th Cir. 1965).

27. *See* U.S. Attorneys' Manual 9-27.220.

28. This policy is printed in its entirety as appendix 9.

29. Memorandum from Mark R. Filip, Deputy Att'y Gen., U.S. Dep't of Justice, to Heads of Department Components and U.S. Attorneys, Principles of Federal Prosecution of Business Organizations (Aug. 28, 2008), http://www.justice.gov/opa/documents/corp-charging-guidelines.pdf.

30. U.S. Attorneys' Manual tit. 9, Criminal Res. Manual, at 9-28.300 (appendix 8 at 411–12).

31. Available at http://www.ussc.gov/sites/default/files/pdf/training/annual-national -training-seminar/2011/011_Primer_Chapter_8_Appropriate_Fine.pdf (May 2014).

32. If an individual substantially assists in an investigation and prosecution of another, the DOJ may agree to a 5K.1.1 departure under the Guidelines. In some cases this may be a free fall, allowing a court to impose probation. In other cases, the DOJ may agree to or recommend a specific departure, e.g., one-half off the low end of the Guidelines.

33. Thomas Fox, The Avon Settlement, pt. I (Dec. 22, 2014), https://twitter.com /tfoxlaw/status/546999612918075392.

34. Seaboard Report, *supra* note 14.

35. *Id.*

36. *Id.*

37. *Id.*

38. *Id.*

39. *Id.* at n.3 (citing Brief of SEC as Amicus Curiae, McKesson HBOC, Inc. No. 99-C-7980-3 (Ga. Ct. App. filed May 13, 2001)).

40. 17 C.F.R. § 202.12 (2010).

41. Press Release, U.S. Sec. & Exch. Comm., SEC Announces Initiative to Encourage Individuals and Companies to Cooperate and Assist in Investigations (Jan. 13, 2010) http://www.sec.gov/news/press/2010/2010-6.htm.

42. SEC Enforcement Manual, *supra* note 7, at 6.2.

43. *Id.* at 6.2.2, Cooperation Agreements.

44. *Id.* at 6.2.3, Deferred Prosecution Agreements.

45. *Id.* at 6.2.4, Non-Prosecution Agreements.

46. 17 C.F.R. § 202.12; SEC Release No. 34-61340.

47. The Commission noted that cooperation in investigations that involve priority matters or serious, ongoing, or widespread violations will be viewed most favorably.

48. *Id.*

49. *Id.* at 3.3.7, Proffer Agreements.

50. *Id.*

51. *Id.* at 6.2.3, Deferred Prosecution Agreements.

52. Press Release, U.S. Sec. & Exch. Comm., Tenaris to Pay $5.4 Million in SEC's First-Ever Deferred Prosecution Agreement (May 17, 2011), http://www.sec.gov/news /press/2011/2011-112.htm.

53. SEC Enforcement Manual, *supra* note 7, at 6.2.4, Non-Prosecution Agreements.

54. *Id.* at 6.2.5, Immunity Requests.

55. United States v. Doe, 456 U.S. 605 (1984).

56. Crim. Div., U.S. Dep't of Justice & Enforcement Div., U.S. Sec. & Exch. Comm., FCPA: A Resource Guide to the U.S. Foreign Corrupt Practices Act (2012), http:// www.justice.gov/criminal/fraud/fcpa/guidance/ or http://www.sec.gov/spotlight /fcpa.shtml [hereinafter Resource Guide]. The full text of the Resource Guide is reprinted as appendix 4.

57. *Id.*, ch. 7 at 77–79.

58. *Id.* at 2.

59. Securities Act Release No. 5310, Fed. Sec. L. Rep. (CCH) ¶ 79,010 (Sept. 27, 1972).

60. 17 C.F.R. § 202.5(C).

61. Securities Act Release No. 5310, Fed. Sec. L. Rep. (CCH) ¶ 79,010 (Sept. 27, 1972).

62. *See* Webb, Tarun & Molo, *supra* note 4, § 16.07.

63. Resource Guide, *supra* note 56, at 58.

64. *Id.* at 56–62.

65. *See* U.S. Attorneys' Manual tit. 9, Criminal Res. Manual, at 11.101.

66. Mahoney et al., *supra* note 5.

67. 48 C.F.R. §§ 9.406-2, 9.407-2.

68. *Id.*

69. For the SEC definition, *see* IX.B.3.c.

70. *See, e.g.*, United States v. Willbros Group Inc. and Willbros International, Inc., H-08-287, U.S.D.C. S.D. IX, Deferred Prosecution Agreement (May 14, 2008).

71. 2013 U.S. Dist. LEXIS 92438; 2013 WL 330616.

72. 31 U.S.C. § 5311, *et seq.*

73. 50 U.S.C. 50 §§ 1702, 1705.

74. 50 U.S.C. App. §§ 3, 5, 16.

75. 14-cr-121 (RJL) U.S.D.C. D.D.C. Memorandum Opinion (Feb. 5, 2015).

76. *Id.* at 8.

77. *Id.*

78. Matt Kelly, *A First: Department Ends DPA Early*, Compliance Wk., Nov. 9, 2012, http://www.complianceweek.com/a-first-justice-department-ends-dpa-early/article/267762/.

79. 18 U.S.C. § 3571(D).

80. 543 U.S. 220 (2005).

81. *See* U.S. Sentencing Guidelines Manual § 8.A1.1 cmt. (n.1) [hereinafter USSG].

82. *See* USSG, ch.8, intro. cmt.

83. *See* USSG, ch.8, intro. cmt.

84. *See* USSG, ch.8, pt. B, intro. cmt.

85. *See* USSG § 8A1.2(b).

86. *See* USSG, ch.8, intro. cmt.

87. *Id.*

88. *See* USSG § 8C2.3(a).

89. The offense level fine table at § 8C2.4(d) lays out the fine amount associated with each offense level, which, when combined with the multipliers derived from the culpability score in § 8C2.5, results in the applicable guideline fine range. *See* USSG §§ 8C2.4(d), 8C2.5, 8C2.6.

90. *See* USSG § 8C2.4(a)(1)–(3) cmt. (backg'd.).

91. *See* USSG § 8C2.5(a)–(g).

92. *See* USSG § 8C2.5(b)(1)–(5).

93. *Id.*

94. *See* USSG § 8A1.2, cmt. (n.3(B)).

95. *See* USSG § 8A1.2, cmt. (n.3(C)).

96. *See* USSG § 8C2.5(c).

97. *See* USSG § 8C2.5(c)(1)–(2).

98. *See* USSG § 8C2.5(d)(1)–(2).

99. *See* USSG § 8C2.5(e).

100. *Id.*

101. *See* USSG § 8C2.5(f)(1).

102. *See* USSG § 8C2.5(f)(2), (f)(3).

103. *See* USSG § 8C2.5(f)(3)(B)–(C).

104. *See* USSG § 8C2.5(g)(1).

105. *See* USSG § 8C2.5(g)(2).

106. *See* USSG § 8C2.5(g)(3).

107. *See* USSG § 8C2.6.

108. *Id.*

109. *See* USSG § 8C2.7(a), (b).

110. *See* USSG § 8C2.8(a)(1)–(11); *see also id.*, cmt. (backg'd.).

111. *See* USSG § 8C2.8(b); *see also id.*, cmt. (n.7).

112. *See* USSG § 8C2.9.

113. *See* USSG § 8C2.9, cmt. (n.1).

114. *Id.*

115. *See* USSG § 8C3.1, cmt. (backg'd.).

116. *See* USSG § 8C3.1(b).

117. *See* USSG § 8C3.1(c). In this regard, it is worth noting that the Supreme Court recently held that *Apprendi*'s prohibition against the use of judge-found facts to increase penalties for a crime beyond the statutory maximum (i.e., the maximum sentence a judge may impose solely on the basis of the facts reflected in the jury verdict or admitted by the defendant) applies to fines levied against a corporation. *See* Southern Union v. United States, 567 U.S. 160 (Jun. 21, 2012).

118. *See* USSG § 8C3.1, cmt. (backg'd).

119. *See* USSG ch.8, pt.4, intro. cmt.

120. Press Release, U.S. Dep't of Justice, Former Morgan Stanley Managing Director Pleads Guilty for Role in Evading Internal Controls Required by FCPA (Apr. 25, 2012), http://www.justice.gov/opa/pr/2012/april/12-crm-534.html.

121. SEC v. Peterson, No. Cv 12-2033 (E.D.N.Y.) (JBW) (filed Apr. 25, 2012), Litig. Release No. 22,346 (Apr. 25, 2012).

122. *See* discussion of full case *infra* chapter 10.

123. Resource Guide, *supra* note 56, at 61.

124. *Id.* at 77–79.

125. *Id.* at 75.

126. *Id.* at 54.

127. Erica Teichert, *Good FCPA Compliance Plans Can Halt Prosecutions: DOJ*, Law 360, Feb. 12, 2013, 6:54 p.m., http://www.law360.com/competition/articles/414972/good-fcpa-compliance-plans-can-halt-prosecutions-doj.

128. *Id.*

129. Jacqueline Charles, U.S. Helps Turks and Caicos Recoup Millions from Sandals Resort, Miami Herald, Jan. 23, 2013, http://www.miamiherald.com/2013/01/23/3197252/us-helps-turks-and-caicos-recoup.html.

130. *See* Scott Muller & Dr. Klaus Moosmayer, Responding to a Multi-Jurisdictional Government Investigation: How to Deal with Enforcement Agencies, Minimize Cost and Management Distraction, Presentation at the 20th Annual ACI Conference on the Foreign Corrupt Practices Act Conference, Washington, D.C. (Nov. 18, 2008).

131. Memorandum from Craig S. Morford, Acting Deputy Att'y Gen., U.S. Dep't of Justice, to Heads of Dep't Components & U.S. Attorneys, Selection and Use of Monitors in Deferred Prosecution Agreements and Non-Prosecution Agreements with Corporations (Mar. 7, 2008), http://www.justice.gov/dag/morford-useofmonitors memo-03072008.pdf. *See* appendix 10.

CHAPTER 10

SEC Enforcement Actions and DOJ Prosecutions

Foreign Corrupt Practices Act investigations, prosecutions, and enforcement actions have increased dramatically over the past decade. The increase is likely attributable to the Sarbanes-Oxley Act of 2002,[1] corporate governance reforms, increased international cooperation among law enforcement agencies, new foreign anticorruption legislation, pressure from the Organisation for Economic Co-operation and Development (OECD) to legislate and fight corruption, and a highly committed Fraud Section at the Department of Justice (DOJ) and FCPA Unit at the Securities and Exchange Commission (SEC) that together are responsible for and oversee FCPA enforcement nationwide. The Dodd-Frank whistleblower laws and rules of 2010[2] are no doubt contributing to more FCPA enforcement investigations and actions (see chapter 1). This chapter discusses several of the major trends that have emerged from FCPA U.S. DOJ prosecutions and SEC enforcement actions, reviews the factors DOJ and SEC attorneys weigh in prosecutorial and enforcement decisions, lists the stated or implied terms of FCPA resolutions, summarizes over 155 significant FCPA cases, and then offers practical guidance on how to interpret reported FCPA prosecution and SEC enforcement actions.

I. FCPA PROSECUTION AND ENFORCEMENT ACTION TRENDS AND RELATED DEVELOPMENTS

A. Continuing Large DOJ and SEC Corporate Penalties and Fines

The December 2008 Siemens $1.6 billion antibribery settlement best demonstrates how massive and serious criminal and civil anticorruption penalties can be. Shortly after that landmark resolution with the German and U.S. governments, the DOJ obtained in February 2009 a plea agreement from, and the SEC a consent decree with, Kellogg, Brown & Root LLC (KBR) that included penalties and disgorgement totaling $579 million. In calendar year 2010, the DOJ and SEC obtained record fines, penalties, and disgorgement of profits of approximately $1.8 billion, including six of the 15 largest FCPA monetary sanctions ever. In March 2010, BAE Systems plc pled guilty to FCPA-related violations and agreed to pay a DOJ fine of $400 million and a U.K. fine of $50 million.[3] In April 2010, Daimler AG and three subsidiaries agreed to pay combined fines of $185 million; Technip S.A. and Snamprogetti B.V., joint venture partners of KBR, agreed in June and July, respectively, to pay U.S. corruption-related fines of $365 million and $338 million, respectively; and, in November 2010, Panalpina, a global freight forwarder, agreed to pay corruption-related fines of $70.5 million to the DOJ and $11.3 million in disgorgement of profits to the SEC, while its oil and drilling customers—GlobalSantaFe Corporation, Noble Corporation, Pride International Inc., Royal Dutch Shell plc, Tidewater Marine International Inc., and Transocean Inc.—agreed to pay related fines and disgorgement amounts of over $155 million. In April 2011, JGC Corporation of Japan, the remaining joint venture partner of KBR not to have settled with the DOJ for the Bonny Island consortium bribes, and Johnson & Johnson agreed to pay FCPA fines of $218 million and $70 million, respectively. In 2012, Pfizer, a U.S.-based global pharmaceutical company, and Marubeni, a Japanese trading company charged with the Bonny Island bribes, entered into $60 million and $54.6 million FCPA settlements, respectively. In 2013, Total S.A., a French oil and gas company, resolved an FCPA investigation for $398.2 million.

In 2014, Alcoa, a U.S.-based global provider of aluminum and fabricated aluminum, resolved its FCPA investigation with combined penalties of $354 million. In 2014, Marubeni Corporation, a major Japanese trading company, became a second FCPA offender for bribes to high-ranking government officials in Indonesia and paid an $88 million DOJ fine. In 2014, Hewlett-Packard resolved FCPA allegations in Russia, Mexico, and Poland and agreed to pay DOJ and SEC fines exceeding $108 million. In December 2014, the DOJ and SEC resolved FCPA allegations with Avon Products, and the global beauty products company agreed to pay fines totaling $135 million. Finally, in December 2014, the DOJ filed charges against Alstom SA and three subsidiaries, and the global power industry conglomerate agreed to pay a $772 million fine. FCPA fines and penalties in 2014 exceeded $1.4 billion, surpassed only by the record year 2010, whose combined fines exceeded $1.5 billon.

In early December 2014, Assistant Attorney General Leslie R. Caldwell, at the launch of the OECD Foreign Bribery Report in Paris, reported that since 2009, the DOJ has resolved FCPA-related criminal cases against more than 50 companies with penalties and forfeitures of approximately $3 billion, and during the same period, the SEC resolved civil actions against more than 65 companies, resulting in total combined FCPA penalties and forfeitures by the DOJ and SEC of approximately $4.5 billion.[4] With the announcement of the Alstom FCPA charges in late December, 2014,[5] which resulted in a $772 million criminal penalty, the DOJ FCPA penalties now exceed $3.7 billion, and combined DOJ and SEC FCPA penalties exceed $5 billion.

The table depicts the 15 largest FCPA penalties by amount and year, demonstrating that FCPA enforcement remains strong and a clear DOJ and SEC priority.

Largest FCPA Penalties

Company	Year	Amount (millions)	Country
1. Siemens	2008	$800.0	Germany
2. Alstom	2014	$772.2	France
3. KBR	2009	$579.0	United States
4. BAE	2010	$400.0	United Kingdom
5. Total	2013	$398.2	France
6. Snamprogetti/ENI	2010	$365.0	Holland/Italy
7. Alcoa	2014	$384.0	United States
8. Technip	2010	$338.0	France
9. JGC	2011	$218.8	Japan
10. Daimler	2010	$185.0	Germany
11. Alcatel-Lucent	2010	$137.0	France
12. Avon	2014	$135.0	United States
13. Hewlett-Packard	2014	$108.0	United States
14. Magyar/Telekon	2011	$95.0	Hungary/Germany
15. Marubeni	2014	$85.0	Japan

Five of the 15 largest FCPA penalties ever were obtained in 2010, two in 2011, one in 2013, and five in 2014. Eleven of the top 15 have involved non-U.S. companies. In light of the above well-publicized megafines and the related investigative and defense costs, many boards of directors, general counsel, and FCPA counsel[6] question whether the benefits of voluntary disclosure and cooperation outweigh many of the negotiated criminal penalties that in many instances remain within the United States Sentencing Guidelines (USSG) range or are at least close to the USSG minimum fine. The DOJ has increasingly explained its USSG fine calculus in its FCPA resolution court filings and in 2012 along with the SEC published the helpful *Resource Guide to the U.S. Foreign Corrupt Practices Act.*[7] The DOJ and SEC have a wide variety of resolutions available, including plea agreements, deferred prosecution agreements (DPAs), nonprosecution agreements (NPAs), declinations, civil injunctive actions and remedies, and civil administrative actions and remedies.

The *Resource Guide* provides six anonymous examples of past declinations by the DOJ and SEC. Most of the declinations involved small bribe amounts or attempted bribes. Based on this recent guidance, it is unlikely that any public company discovering multicountry bribery conduct or a substantial bribery payment in one foreign country will obtain a declination.

B.   The SEC's Aggressive Pursuit of Disgorgement of Profits

For public companies, the SEC, especially through disgorgement of profits, can quickly eviscerate the credit the DOJ has extended to companies for voluntary disclosure and substantial cooperation in FCPA investigations. Since 2004, the SEC has increasingly used disgorgement as a remedy. The top 12 SEC FCPA disgorgement matters are

1.	Siemens	$350.0 million	2008
2.	KBR	$177.0 million	2009
3.	Alcoa	$161.0 million	2014
4.	Total	$153.0 million	2013
5.	Snamprogetti	$125.0 million	2010
6.	Technip	$98.0 million	2010
7.	Daimler	$91.4 million	2010
8.	Avon	$67.35 million	2014
9.	Johnson & Johnson	$48.6 million	2011
10.	Pfizer	$45.2 million	2012
11.	Alcatel-Lucent	$45.0 million	2012
12.	Bio-Rad	$40.7 million	2014

FCPA enforcement remains a major DOJ and SEC priority, and megasettlements of $100 million or more will continue.

C. Continued Prosecution of Foreign Corporations and Subsidiaries

The Fraud Section of the DOJ has aggressively pursued foreign corporations and their subsidiaries. Major FCPA resolutions with foreign entities include Aibel Group Ltd. (United Kingdom); Alcatel-Lucent S.A. (France); BAE Systems plc (United Kingdom); Daimler AG (Germany); Fiat S.p.A. (Italy); JGC Corporation (Japan); Magyar Telekom plc (Hungary/Germany); Marubeni Corporation (Japan); Panalpina (Switzerland); Siemens AG (Germany); Snamprogetti Netherlands B.V. (Holland/Italy); Technip S.A. (France); Total S.A. (France), and Alstom (France). Twelve of the top 15 FCPA penalties have involved companies headquartered outside the United States.

The jurisdictional bases for the foreign corporation and subsidiary prosecutions and enforcement actions vary. Approximately 1,500 foreign issuers, whose American depositary receipts (ADRs) are traded on U.S. securities exchanges, are issuers for purposes of the FCPA.[8] For example, the parent of Snamprogetti ENI had ADRs traded on the New York Stock Exchange. Similarly, Technip's ADRs were traded on the NYSE, thereby establishing "issuer" jurisdiction under the FCPA. In other cases, the conduct of foreign corporations or their employees or agents has extended into the territory of the United States, establishing FCPA territorial jurisdiction. Other jurisdictional theories, such as aiding and abetting U.S. issuers, conspiracy, and agency, remain in the DOJ and SEC arsenal.[9] Regardless of the jurisdictional nexus, the pattern is clear: The DOJ and SEC are aggressively pursuing bribery conduct by foreign corporations and subsidiaries.

D. Prosecution of Parent Company Where Failure to Timely Cooperate

The DOJ has, in the case of cooperative companies, often allowed the parent or holding company to avoid a plea of guilty in favor of a subsidiary pleading guilty and/or reserving a DPA or NPA for the parent company (e.g., Alcatel-Lucent SA, Alcoa, Archer Daniels Midland, Hewlett-Packard, Panalpina). Where companies have not been timely cooperative, the DOJ has insisted upon a guilty plea by the parent company (e.g., Alstom SA, Avon Products, and Marubeni (2014)).

E. SEC Increased Use of Administrative Proceedings

The SEC has increasingly filed FCPA matters as administrative proceedings rather than as civil complaints in federal district court. Gibson Dunn has reported that in 2012, the SEC filed 11 civil complaints as opposed to one administrative proceeding, while in 2014, SEC administrative proceedings for FCPA matters outnumbered civil complaints eight to one.[10] The SEC asserts that the administrative proceeding process is more streamlined, while private practitioners counter that administrative law judges are friendlier to the Commission.[11]

F. SEC Focus on Individuals and Small and Medium Sized Businesses

In October 2014, SEC Chief of the FCPA Unit Kara Brockmeyer outlined several SEC enforcement priorities, including increased focus on individuals and raising awareness among small and medium-sized companies on the need for effective compliance controls when they enter new markets, especially in risky jurisdictions. Brockmeyer cited Smith & Wesson Holding Corp. as an example of a smaller company that entered challenging markets without sufficient compliance controls.[12]

G. Monitoring Trends in FCPA Resolutions from Full-Blown Corporate Monitorships to Internal Self-Assessments

From 2000 to 2010, the DOJ and SEC frequently imposed an external or independent corporate monitor or consultant for a period of three years to oversee and monitor companies that had engaged in FCPA misconduct.[13] More recently, and especially in 2012, a DOJ–SEC trend of permitting corporate compliance self-assessment emerged. Under the latter, companies conduct self-assessments internally and periodically report their findings to the government after the FCPA resolution. For example, in six of 2012's 12 FCPA corporate resolutions, the DOJ and/or SEC permitted self-assessments: Biz Jet, Data Systems and Solutions, NORDAM Group, Orthofix, Pfizer/Wyeth, and Tyco. At the same time, independent or external corporate monitors were imposed on only four companies: Marubeni, Smith & Nephew, Biomet, and Eli Lilly. One company, Allianz SE, was no longer traded on a U.S. stock exchange, and another, Oracle, had implemented exceptional remedial measures. In 2014, the SEC permitted Layne Christensen, a global water management company, to self-report for two years on its remediation efforts. In 2014, the DOJ and SEC permitted Avon Products to self-report on its compliance efforts for 18 months following retention of an independent monitor for 18 months.

H. Joint DOJ–SEC Investigations and Global Resolutions

In FCPA investigations of public companies, the DOJ and SEC typically conduct parallel or joint investigations of public companies and file, where appropriate, simultaneous criminal charges, DPAs, civil complaints, and/or consent decrees. The pleadings are commonly detailed and accompanied by lengthy press releases and occasional press conferences. The filing of a criminal information, in contrast to the return of an indictment by a grand jury, is usually a clear signal that the charged company or individual is cooperating with the U.S. government. Moreover, the Siemens and Alcatel-Lucent prosecutions confirm that U.S. law enforcement authorities are willing to coordinate investigations and return criminal charges with foreign authorities. The Fraud Section of the DOJ, which has exclusive jurisdiction over all FCPA criminal matters, has increasingly enlisted assistant U.S. attorneys across the country to assist in FCPA investigations and prosecutions.

I. Deferred Prosecution Agreements, Nonprosecution Agreements, and Public Declinations

The Fraud Section has also made it clear that fulfillment of the voluntary disclosure and prompt remedial action criteria can in certain circumstances enable a corporation to secure an NPA and avoid criminal charges (e.g., Tyco International Ltd. and Aon Corporation) or to enter into a more formal court-filed DPA (e.g., *United States v. Monsanto*[14]) and avoid a trial or guilty plea. For companies that have provided valuable and prompt cooperation in FCPA investigations, the DPA holds out the promise that DOJ criminal charges may be held in abeyance and will not be admissible in civil matters. A recent trend has been to reward public companies that have provided exceptional cooperation with an NPA or a DPA for the parent or issuer and a felony plea by a subsidiary (e.g., Alcatel-Lucent, Baker Hughes Services International, Schnitzer Steel Industries Inc., Daimler AG, ABB, Pride International Inc., Panalpina World Transport (Holdings) Inc., and Weatherford International Ltd.). Moreover, in May 2008, despite improper payments by a senior executive in three countries for years and the payment of a million-dollar bribe by a country manager during the DOJ–SEC investigation, Willbros Group Inc. was able to obtain a DPA for itself and its international subsidiary because of what the DOJ described as "exemplary cooperation." In 2010, Noble Corporation, implicated in the broader Panalpina FCPA freight-forwarding investigation, received an NPA from the DOJ due to its voluntary disclosure and extensive remedial measures. In still other cases, the DOJ has taken no action while the SEC has filed an enforcement proceeding, leaving the entire matter resolved by a civil consent decree (e.g., *SEC v. Eli Lilly & Co.*).[15] In March 2015 Assistant Attorney General for the Criminal Division Leslie Caldwell indicated that the DOJ may return to a more binary charging system—indict or decline.[16] A change or decline in DPAs may be a response to the increased judicial scrutiny of DPAs. (See chapter 9 at XIII.C.)

A breach of a DPA can result in the government pursuing the original prosecution, a conviction, and substantial sentencing exposure. Moreover, the company, as part of the original agreement, must agree not to contest the underlying charges in the event of a breach, thus making a felony conviction a virtual certainty. The 2008 prosecution of Aibel Group Ltd. illustrates that the DOJ will revoke a DPA and heavily fine a corporate recidivist.[17] Conversely, however, in November 2012, the DOJ agreed to terminate early the three-year term of Pride International after two years—the first FCPA DPA to be terminated early. Thus, in special circumstances, the DOJ may reward exceptional compliance behavior during a DPA.

In select matters where improper payments usually total less than $1 million, voluntary disclosure is timely made and the cooperation and remedial measures are prompt and extensive, the DOJ may offer a company an NPA whereby if the company meets certain obligations for a prescribed period, for example, 18 to 24 months, and/or files annual compliance reports, the DOJ will not file any criminal charges. (See Micrus and Noble, *infra*.) *SEC v. Chevron* is an exception to the trend of fines being under $1 million. Chevron's UN Oil-for-Food program payments totaled $20 million and the combined disgorgement and fines against Chevron was $30 million. The UN Oil-for-Food program investigation resulted in a large number of FCPA false books-and-records and internal controls resolutions but not bribery resolutions—in large part because improper payments were made to the Iraqi government rather than to government officials, political parties, or party candidates as required under the FCPA's antibribery provisions.

The 2010 Noble NPA in the Panalpina freight-forwarding investigation signaled that the DOJ is listening to criticism that cooperating companies have not been sufficiently rewarded and that decisions not to file charges against companies that provide exemplary cooperation early may become more common. Still, despite its exceptional cooperation and improper payments totaling only $74,000, the SEC insisted Noble disgorge profits and pay prejudgment interest of $5.5 million—almost double the already considerable $2.59 million DOJ criminal penalty.

Usually, an NPA is publicized by the DOJ. Often, the fine is significant, a multiple—three to five times—of the improper payments. The voluntary disclosure necessary to warrant an NPA must be completely voluntary, that is, normally a matter the U.S. government would not otherwise have discovered, and the cooperation must be both exceptional and timely (e.g., InVision Agreement, U.S. DOJ–Paradigm B.V. Agreement, *SEC v. Chevron*, U.S. DOJ–Noble Corporation Agreement, U.S. DOJ–RAE Systems Inc., and Comverse Technology, *infra*).

In 2013, the SEC awarded its first NPA to Ralph Lauren Corporation arising from misconduct at an Argentine subsidiary. Ralph Lauren agreed to pay $734,846 in disgorgement and prejudgment interest. The company had undertaken a comprehensive new compliance program throughout its operation and had terminated employment and business arrangements with all persons involved in the wrongdoing. In conducting a global risk assessment, Ralph Lauren elected to close its operations in Argentina.

In April 2012, the DOJ and SEC charged Garth Peterson, a former Morgan Stanley managing director of real estate investment and advisory business in China, with conspiring to evade internal accounting controls that Morgan Stanley was required to maintain under the FCPA, but declined to file any fraud charges against his employer, Morgan Stanley.[18] The DOJ cited the strong Morgan Stanley compliance program and repeated training of Peterson as some of the reasons for a declination. This is the first public FCPA declination by the DOJ or SEC and may signal that both are willing to not file any charges in select circumstances where the company is a victim of a rogue employee.

J. U.K. Bribery Act 2010 and Global Antibribery Efforts

The long-awaited U.K. Bribery Act received Royal Assent on April 8, 2010, confirming that anticorruption enforcement has moved from largely the efforts of one superpower to a more coordinated multijurisdictional law enforcement commitment. Utilizing many of the same weapons as the DOJ and SEC and benefiting from the lessons learned in the United States, the U.K. Serious Fraud Office is enforcing the Bribery Act and may spearhead anticorruption enforcement in Europe and beyond—and achieve significant results and reforms far more quickly than the DOJ and SEC did three decades ago. It is likely there will be major prosecutions under the Bribery Act, which only came into effect in July 2011, in the coming years.

K. Merger and Acquisition Cases

FCPA cases have grown out of inadequate multinational acquisition due diligence. For example, the Titan case, which led to a $28.5 million fine and penalty, stemmed from merger and acquisition due diligence activity by Lockheed, the suitor of Titan. Lockheed abandoned the target when it uncovered improper overseas payments, and Titan responded slowly. When the deal collapsed, the DOJ and SEC proceeded to charge Titan and secured then-record penalties; in time, L3 Communications bought Titan at a significant discount.

In the General Electric/InVision matter, *infra*, General Electric, in conducting due diligence of target InVision, investigated and urged the target to disclose to the DOJ improper payments in China, the Philippines, and Thailand. The careful planning, disclosure, and comprehensive remedial measures implemented and overseen by General Electric resulted in the government not bringing any charges against the target or acquirer. Similarly, in the SEC's *In re* Delta & Pine Land Co. and Turk Deltapine, Inc., *infra*, improper payments in Turkey were discovered during the due diligence by acquirer Monsanto, and both avoided criminal charges through coordinated disclosure efforts. In the 2010 RAE Systems case,[19] *infra*, the DOJ and SEC reviewed $400,000 in improper payments to Chinese government officials that had been discovered during the preacquisition due diligence of a joint venture. In a second joint venture, RAE Systems failed to conduct any due diligence. As a result, the DOJ imposed a $1.7 million fine and the SEC obtained a consent decree disgorging $1.3 million in ill-gotten profits and prejudgment interest. It is clear that companies looking to acquire foreign operations but failing to conduct thorough due diligence can face both successor criminal and administrative liability.

Finally, in 2014, the DOJ issued FCPA Opinion Release No. 14-02, which illustrates the challenges and risks of international acquisitions and highlights successor liability principles. It further outlines recommended steps that acquirors should undertake to minimize postacquisition successor liability.

L. Industry-Wide Investigations

From time to time, the DOJ and SEC focus on an industry—often as a result of an investigation of one company leading to the discovery of problematic conduct by others in the same industry. Sometimes, an investigation of a company will spawn an investigation of a vendor or other third party that serves the industry. For example, the DOJ prosecution of Vetco Gray in Nigeria led to the investigation of almost a dozen companies in the oil and gas field services industry that used the same Swiss international freight-forwarding and customs clearance company, Panalpina.[20] In November 2010 the DOJ and SEC obtained fines and disgorgement of profits from seven companies in the oil and gas field services industry exceeding $236 million as a result of the freight-forwarding industry investigation. In 2014, the DOJ resolved an FCPA investigation of a third aircraft maintenance, repair, and overhaul provider, Dallas Airmotive Inc. This and the two earlier resolutions with BizJet International and the NORDAM Group make clear the DOJ will focus on smaller industries. This crossover trend suggests that in-house counsel should keep abreast of FCPA investigations not only in their industry but of third-party service suppliers to their clients and their industries.

M. Self-Reporting

The past decade witnessed an increase in self-reporting by public companies, and many FCPA investigations have been the result of self-reporting. While both the DOJ and SEC claim they credit early disclosure and substantial cooperation, many companies and their directors continue to question the costs and the benefits.[21] Numerous public companies elect not to self-report where possible.

N. Dodd-Frank Whistleblower Law and Rules

The Dodd-Frank Whistleblower Rules, which were promulgated May 25, 2011, and became effective August 12, 2011, create strong financial incentives for employees and others to report potential violations of securities laws such as the FCPA. The SEC anticipates a large increase in whistleblower reporting of foreign bribery by employees and by employers seeking to reduce their potential FCPA exposure, fines, and other sanctions (see chapter 1). The Dodd-Frank Whistleblower Rules make disclosure to the government arguably less voluntary than ever. The 2012 DOJ–SEC FCPA *Resource Guide* has a Whistleblowers Provisions and Protection chapter that contains very basic protection and contact information for SEC Office of the Whistleblower.[22] In 2014, the SEC Office of the Whistleblower released an annual report summarizing increased whistleblower activity and rewards. (See chapter 1 at VII.G.)

O. BRIC Countries Legislative Efforts and Successes

The four BRIC countries—Brazil, Russia, India, and China—have begun to focus more on anticorruption. In 2014, Brazil passed legislation addressing civil and administrative liability for corporations engaging in corrupt acts relating to the country's internal and foreign public administration. (See chapter 3, section V.) In May 2011 Russia enacted antibribery legislation that prohibits both public and private bribery and substantially increases criminal penalties; Russia nonetheless does not have corporate criminal liability. In 2013, Russia amended its bribery statute to require corporate compliance programs. (See chapter 3, section V.) In March 2011 India proposed a "Prevention of Bribery of Foreign Public Officials and Officials of Public International Organizations" bill to criminalize for the first time the conduct of "accepting or giving a bribe to secure a contract in India." Still, India has stalled in the past with anticorruption legislative efforts. In 2011, China amended the Criminal Law of the People's Republic of China to prohibit bribery of foreign officials. In 2014, the People's Republic of China prosecuted GlaxoSmithKline, a British pharmaceutical giant, for bribery conduct and secured a record China fine of $489 million.

P.   Leading U.S. Exports

Not surprisingly, FCPA cases arise from the leading U.S. export industries. The top ten exports of the United States in 2014 were:

1. Machines, engines: $219.5 billion (13.5 percent of total exports);
2. Electronic equipment: $171.9 billion (10.6 percent);
3. Oil: $157.2 billion (9.7 percent);
4. Vehicles: $135.7 billion (8.4 percent);
5. Aircraft, spacecraft: $124.8 billion (7.7 percent);
6. Medical, technical equipment: $84.8 billion (5.2 percent);
7. Mining and precious metals: $65.2 billion (4.0 percent);
8. Plastics $63 billion (3.9 percent);
9. Pharmaceuticals: $43.9 billion (2.7 percent); and
10. Organic chemicals: $42.2 billion (2.6 percent).

These industries combined represent 68.3 percent of all U.S. exports. The DOJ and the SEC have conducted investigations of multinationals in virtually all of these industries. There is no reason to believe that the U.S. government's interest in these industries will subside.

II. FACTORS THE DOJ AND SEC WEIGH IN PROSECUTORIAL AND REGULATORY DECISIONS

In determining whether to file civil or criminal FCPA charges, what types of charges to file (e.g., bribery versus a books-and-records violation), whether to impose substantial fines, and whether to require ongoing monitoring of a company, the DOJ and SEC consider various FCPA factors, including the following:

- The total amount of improper payments;
- The number of improper payments;
- The amount of business or revenue obtained as a result of the improper payments;
- The amount of profit to the company;
- The number of countries or geographic region(s) in which improper business payments occurred;
- The length of time over which improper payments occurred;
- The seniority of foreign government officials who received improper payments, for example, cabinet ministers;
- The seniority of corporate officers or employees who paid or authorized improper payments;
- The nature of the things of value, for example, travel and entertainment abuses versus cash payments to secure a large contract;

- The aggravating nature of any payments, for example, bribes of the judiciary or very senior officials of the executive branch;
- The pervasiveness of improper payments or related conduct within the company or in one or more subsidiaries, divisions, or business units;
- The number of false books-and-records entries;
- The role of the parent corporation or senior management in authorizing, approving, or sanctioning improper payments or misconduct;
- The company's overall perceived tolerance of improper payments;
- The nature of the transmission of payments (cash, wire transfer, cashier's check, bearer document, etc.);
- Red flags senior management saw or should have seen, for example, consultants who had no qualifications, agents recommended by government officials, vendor bank accounts in countries where the vendor has no business;
- The efforts of the company to conceal the nature of the payment (disguised records, elaborate bank transfers, foreign bank accounts, fictitious entities, and so on);
- The nature, quality, and extent of a company's compliance program and antibribery training at the time of the misconduct;
- The existence of a quality risk assessment that is periodic, informed, and documented;
- The presence or absence of adequate internal controls;
- Prior enforcement action and criminal history of the company;
- The length of time it took the company to respond to the improper payment or practices allegations;
- The quality and timeliness of the response by the board of directors and senior management to allegations of or the discovery of FCPA misconduct;
- The failure of senior management to fully remediate, truthfully, and timely report to an audit, compliance, or other committee, and to correct false books and records;
- Voluntary disclosure or self-reporting to the DOJ and/or SEC;
- Whether the company informed third parties of its compliance program and policies and sought assurances from third parties of their commitment to the same;
- The extent and promptness of corporate cooperation (providing the government with original documents, securing electronic databases and computer hardware, identifying wrongdoers, making domestic and foreign employees available as potential witnesses, providing privileged materials or the substance of same to the government, and so on);
- The quality and scope of the remedial efforts by the company, including prompt disciplinary action of wrongdoers, the breadth of the investigation, improved internal auditing and staffing, increased compliance training, and modifications to the corporate compliance program and internal controls; and
- The value of the company's cooperation in making cases against individual wrongdoers and/or other companies.

In addition to these factors, counsel should consult the DOJ's Principles of Federal Prosecution of Business Organizations (appendix 9) and the SEC's Seaboard factors (appendix 11), which govern that agency's enforcement charging criteria.

III. CORPORATE GOVERNANCE CHECKLIST

In resolving an FCPA problem, the DOJ and SEC want as much assurance as practicable that a public company will not repeat the misconduct at issue or engage in similar misconduct. To that end, counsel should examine various aspects of the company's corporate governance. PricewaterhouseCoopers has identified the following key elements of corporate governance:

- An independent board composed of a majority of directors who have no material relationship with the company;
- An independent chairperson of the board or an independent lead director;
- An audit committee that actively maintains relationships with internal and external auditors;
- An audit committee that includes at least one member who has financial expertise, with all members being financially literate;
- An audit committee that has the authority to retain its own advisors and launch investigations as it deems necessary;
- Nominating and compensation committees composed of independent directors;
- A compensation committee that understands whether it provides particularly lucrative incentives that may encourage improper financial reporting practices or other behavior that goes near or over the line;
- Board and committee meetings regularly held without management and the chief executive officer (CEO) present;
- Explicit ethical commitment ("walking the talk") and a tone at the top that reflects integrity in all respects;
- Prompt and appropriate investigation of alleged improprieties;
- Internally publicized enforcement of policies on a "no exception" or "zero tolerance" basis;
- The board and/or audit committee's reinforcement of the importance of consistent disciplinary action of individuals found to have committed fraud;
- Timely and balanced disclosure of material events concerning the company;
- A properly administered hotline or other reporting channels, independent of management;
- An internal audit function that reports directly to the audit committee without fear of being "edited" by management (CEO, chief financial officer (CFO), controller, et al.);
- Budgeting and forecasting controls;
- Clear and formal policies and procedures, updated in a timely manner as needed;
- Well-defined financial approval authorities and limits; and
- Timely and complete information flow to the board.[23]

Because the DOJ and SEC will examine the overall corporate governance culture and commitment of a company seeking credit or leniency in determining an appropriate resolution, the above is a useful checklist for counsel to consider prior to advancing settlement negotiations.

IV. STATED OR IMPLIED TERMS OF FCPA DOJ PLEAS, DEFERRED PROSECUTION AGREEMENTS, NONPROSECUTION AGREEMENTS, SEC CONSENT DECREES, AND DECLINATIONS

In DOJ pleas or other resolutions and SEC consent decrees, stated or implied terms include the following:

- Charging books-and-records and internal controls criminal violations in lieu of bribery charges;
- DPAs;
- NPAs;
- Charging a subsidiary rather than a parent corporation;
- Charging a business entity rather than employees or other individuals;
- Charging only an employee or officer and not the company when the individual is rogue;
- Disgorgement of ill-gotten gain plus prejudgment interest;
- Reduced fines due to voluntary disclosure, cooperation, and/or inability to pay;
- Periodic or reduced payments of fines for companies in poor financial condition;
- Periodic FCPA audits;
- Enhancements to compliance programs, including antibribery training, and monitoring and training of third parties such as agents, consultants, and subcontractors;
- The appointment of independent monitors, compliance experts, or consultants or the avoidance of the same due to exceptional remedial measures;
- Self-reporting in lieu of the imposition of a monitor;
- The length of a monitor's term, typically three years;
- No debarment or suspension from U.S. government business;
- Voluntary production of contemporaneous documents, records, or other tangible evidence;
- Access to outside accounting and legal consultant work product;
- Not asserting a claim of attorney-client or work-product privilege as to any memoranda of witness interviews (including exhibits thereto) and documents created contemporaneously with and related to the foreign transactions or events underlying the subject matter;
- Ongoing cooperation in the investigation and prosecution of employees and others; and
- Flexibility in issuing public statements.

Both the DOJ and SEC websites publish helpful press releases and copies of FCPA complaints, consent decrees, indictments, informations, DPAs, NPAs, plea agreements, and detailed statements of facts.[24] Shearman & Sterling has on its website the most comprehensive list of FCPA matters going back to the 1970s.[25] Founded by Danforth Newcomb, the *Shearman & Sterling FCPA Digest* lists all foreign bribery criminal prosecutions, foreign bribery civil actions instituted by the

DOJ under the FCPA, SEC actions relating to foreign bribery, DOJ FCPA Opinion Releases, and ongoing investigations involving FCPA allegations.

In sections V and VI of this chapter, significant SEC and DOJ actions are summarized in chronological order, and applicable countries, FCPA misconduct, and salient factors are highlighted with a summary of each case based on public information, such as DOJ and SEC press releases and pleadings. In some cases, descriptions are brief because public information about the actions is limited or because the resolution addressed one specific type of misconduct in a single jurisdiction or fairly predictable punishment. In other matters, the summaries are very detailed because the cases involve multijurisdictional misconduct or multiple types of improper payments, or because they offer insight into particular abuses (e.g., problematic distributor discounts). Signally, the vast majority of the 155-plus listed cases involve DOJ and/or SEC settlements in the past decade, and in some cases posit jurisdictional theories that have yet to be tested in court. Nonetheless, these resolutions give the reader guidance on what the DOJ and the SEC view as serious FCPA misconduct and have agreed upon as appropriate resolutions in various factual scenarios. Section VII offers practical pointers on how to read and interpret DOJ and SEC settlements. Emerging FCPA trends and policies are often discernible as much from what is not stated as from what is stated in public documents.

V. SELECT SEC ENFORCEMENT ACTIONS

A. *SEC v. IBM Corp.*[26]

▶ **Misconduct Category:**	False "third-party contractor" expenses (bribes)
▶ **Country:**	Argentina
▶ **Foreign Government Officials:**	Unclear
▶ **Improper Payment Dollar Value:**	$4.5 million
▶ **Combined Penalties:**	$300,000
▶ **Other:**	Foreign subsidiary's false records entries incorporated into parent's Form 10-K

In December 2000, the SEC settled with International Business Machines Corporation (IBM) for violations of the books-and-records provision,[27] relating to bribes paid by senior officers of its Argentine subsidiary. During 1994 and 1995, senior management of IBM-Argentina, S.A., a wholly owned subsidiary, entered into a subcontract with Capacitacion y Computacion Rural, S.A. (CCR). Money that IBM-Argentina paid to CCR was subsequently given to Argentine government officials. IBM's senior management did not follow procurement and contracting procedures when it provided false documentation and reasons why CCR had been hired. Payments to CCR were recorded by IBM-Argentina as "third-party subcontractor expenses" and were then incorporated into the parent corporation's 1994 Form 10-K. IBM agreed to an injunctive order prohibiting future violations of the books-and-records provision along with a $300,000 penalty.

B. *In re* Baker Hughes Inc.;[28] *SEC v. KPMG;*[29] *SEC v. Mattson & Harris*[30]

▶ **Misconduct Category:**	Use of accounting firm to make improper payments to tax official to reduce tax liability
▶ **Country:**	Indonesia
▶ **Foreign Government Official:**	Tax official
▶ **Improper Payment Dollar Value:**	$75,000
▶ **Combined Penalties:**	N/A
▶ **Other:**	First time that the DOJ and SEC filed a joint civil FCPA injunctive action

In September 2001, the SEC settled with Baker Hughes Inc., a Texas-headquartered oil field services company, with respect to a $75,000 improper payment to an Indonesian tax official. In March 1999, Baker Hughes's CFO, Eric Mattson, and controller, James Harris, authorized an illegal payment through its accounting firm agent, KPMG Indonesian firm Siddartha, Siddartha & Harsono, to the tax official despite warnings by both Baker Hughes's FCPA advisor and its general counsel that such a payment would violate the FCPA. KPMG created and sent a false invoice for $143,000 to PT Eastman Christiensen (PTEC), an Indonesian corporation controlled by Baker Hughes, and PTEC paid the invoice. Baker Hughes was aware that KPMG Indonesia intended to give all or part of the $143,000 to the official as a bribe to influence the official's decision to reduce Baker Hughes's tax liability. Senior managers at Baker Hughes had also authorized payments to agents in Brazil in 1995 and India in 1998, without making the proper inquiries to assure that the payments were not bribes. All three transactions were inaccurately recorded as routine business expenditures and thereby violated the books-and-records and internal controls provisions.

Upon learning that the Indonesian bribe had been authorized, Baker Hughes's general counsel and FCPA advisor attempted to stop the company's payment to the KPMG agent in Jakarta, and in turn that agent's payment to the tax official; they took steps to issue a true and accurate invoice; and they implemented new FCPA policies and procedures. No criminal charges were filed against Baker Hughes. The company was ordered to cease and desist from committing or causing future books-and-records violations by keeping books, records, or accounts with sufficient detail that truly represented the transactions and disposition of the assets. Baker Hughes agreed to an injunctive order prohibiting future internal controls violations by devising and maintaining a system of internal accounting controls that would provide reasonable assurances that transactions are executed with the approval of management and that the transactions are recorded to properly prepare financial statements in conformity with accepted accounting practices as well as to maintain accountability for assets. Mattson and Harris moved to dismiss the complaint on the grounds that the payments were extorted by the local tax official and they did not assist Baker Hughes in obtaining or retaining business. The district court agreed, but this argument was rejected by the Fifth Circuit in *United States v. Kay.*

In 2006, Baker Hughes uncovered improper payments exceeding $4 million to a Kazakh official, which led in 2007 to the then-largest monetary sanction—

$44 million—in FCPA enforcement history, discussed *infra*. The large fine was no doubt imposed in part because the U.S. government viewed Baker Hughes as a recidivist.

C. *In re* Chiquita Brands International, Inc.[31]

▶ **Misconduct Category:**	Payments for license renewal of port facility
▶ **Country:**	Colombia
▶ **Foreign Government Officials:**	Customs officials
▶ **Improper Payment Dollar Value:**	$30,000
▶ **Penalty:**	$100,000
▶ **Other:**	SEC enforcement action against parent Chiquita Brands International, Inc. for its wholly owned subsidiary's failure to adhere to FCPA accounting provisions. No criminal charges were filed.

In October 2001, the SEC settled charges of books-and-records and internal controls violations with Chiquita Brands International, Inc., of Cincinnati, Ohio. Employees of Banadex, Chiquita's Colombian subsidiary, authorized payments equaling $30,000 to local customs officials in exchange for a renewal license at Banadex's Turbo, Colombia, port facility. The internal audit staff at Chiquita found the two incorrectly identified installment payments and, after an internal investigation, took corrective measures, including terminating the responsible parties at Banadex. Chiquita agreed to an injunctive order prohibiting further violations of the books-and-records and internal controls provisions and to a $100,000 civil penalty. No criminal charges were filed against the company.

D. *SEC v. Bell South Corp.*;[32] *In re* Bellsouth Corp.[33]

▶ **Misconduct Category:**	Payment of lobbyist fees of $60,000 to spouse of legislator who chaired legislative committee with jurisdiction over foreign ownership restriction
▶ **Countries:**	Nicaragua and Venezuela
▶ **Foreign Government Official:**	Legislator who chaired telecommunications oversight
▶ **Improper Payment Dollar Value:**	$60,000
▶ **Penalty:**	$150,000
▶ **Other:**	Parent Bell South Corporation subject to FCPA civil liability for the actions of a Nicaraguan subsidiary in which it owned only a 49 percent interest, likely due to its eventual "operational control." The DOJ did not file criminal charges.

In January 2002, BellSouth Corporation settled with the SEC over the conduct of BellSouth International (BSI), an indirectly wholly owned subsidiary that in 1997 began to acquire majority ownership of Telcel, C.A., a Venezuelan corporation and the leading provider of wireless in that country, and Telefonia Celular de Nicaragua, S.A., a Nicaraguan corporation. Telcel senior management authorized payments totaling $10.8 million to six offshore companies between September 1997 and August 2000. The payments were recorded as "disbursements" based on fictitious invoices for professional, computer, and contracting services that were never provided. Telcel's internal controls failed to detect the unsubstantiated payments for at least two years. As an additional consequence of this control deficiency, Bell South was unable to reconstruct the circumstances or purpose of the Telcel payments, or determine the identity of the ultimate recipients of the payments. Telcel is Venezuela's leading wireless provider, contributing more revenue to BellSouth's Latin American Group segment than any other Latin American BellSouth operation.

The SEC complaint alleged that between October 1988 and June 1999, BellSouth's Nicaraguan subsidiary, Telefonia Celular de Nicaragua, improperly recorded payments to the wife of the Nicaraguan legislator who was the chairman of the Nicaraguan legislative committee with oversight of Nicaraguan telecommunications. In 1997, BellSouth owned a 49 percent share in Telefonia with an option to acquire an additional 40 percent. Nicaraguan law prohibited foreign companies from acquiring a majority interest in local telecommunications companies. BellSouth needed the Nicaraguan legislature to repeal the law in order to exercise their option.

In October 1998, Telefonia hired the wife of the Nicaraguan legislator in charge of telecommunications oversight to lobby their cause. The wife had prior telecommunications experience but did not have any legislative experience. Because the lobbyist's husband chaired the legislative committee with jurisdiction over the foreign ownership restriction, BSI, again an indirectly wholly owned subsidiary of BellSouth, knew that payments to the lobbyist could implicate the FCPA. Nevertheless, a BSI in-house attorney approved Telefonia's retention of the lobbyist. The SEC alleged that BSI officials knew or should have known that the attorney lacked sufficient experience or training to enable him properly to opine on the matter. Telefonia and the lobbyist agreed to a three-month trial period at a monthly salary of $6,500. The lobbyist worked primarily on the repeal of the Nicaraguan foreign ownership restriction.

The legislator-husband drafted the proposed repeal while his wife lobbied on behalf of Telefonia and, in April 1999, initiated hearings for the repeal. The lobbyist was terminated in May 1999, and the following month she received a payment of $60,000 for consulting services and severance. In December 1999, the Nicaraguan National Assembly voted to repeal the foreign ownership restriction, and BellSouth exercised its 40 percent option six months later. BSI acquired operational control of Telefonia and therefore was responsible for causing Telefonia's failure to comply with the FCPA by recording payments to the wife as consulting services.

BellSouth agreed to injunctive relief prohibiting future violations of the FCPA books-and-records and internal controls provisions. In reaching this resolution, the SEC recognized that BSI disciplined and terminated various employees involved in the case and also took steps to enhance its FCPA compliance program and internal auditing regime.[34] No criminal charges were filed against BellSouth.

E. *In re* BJ Services Co.[35]

▶ **Misconduct Category:**   Use of third-party agent to pay customs officials to release seized equipment and overlook import violations, and false amortization of fixed costs

▶ **Country:**   Argentina

▶ **Foreign Government Officials:**   Customs officials

▶ **Improper Payment Peso Value:**   75,000 Argentine pesos

▶ **Combined Penalties:**   None

▶ **Other:**   Voluntary disclosure to and full cooperation with the SEC, including retention of an independent forensic auditor, replacement of management in Latin America, and expansion of internal audit department. As a result of the full internal investigation and prompt remedial actions, no criminal charges were filed and no fines were imposed.

In March 2004, BJ Services Company, a Houston, Texas, provider of oil field services, products, and equipment, settled with the SEC after BJ Services, S.A. (BJSA), its wholly owned Argentinean subsidiary, made questionable payments of approximately 72,000 pesos to Argentinean customs officials in 2001. The controller of BJSA had learned that the equipment they were waiting for to begin work with a customer had been improperly imported under Argentinean customs laws. The Argentine customs official offered to release the equipment and overlook the import violation for 75,000 pesos. If he was not paid the money, the official would deport the equipment and BJSA would lose the 71,575 pesos that it had already paid in import taxes, pay a penalty of one to five times the cost of the equipment, and pay import taxes again when the equipment was properly imported. The controller contacted the BJ Services country manager, who contacted the regional manager. The country manager told BJ's Argentine controller that the payment had been approved and directed him to negotiate for a lower payment with the customs official. A third-party agent, previously used by BJSA to assist with customs matters, negotiated a 65,000-peso payment with the customs official. The amount was improperly characterized as amortization—fixed costs.

Also, in September 2001, BJSA's then treasury and purchasing manager authorized payments of 7,000 pesos to an Argentine customs official to overlook customs violations. The customs official drafted falsified documents to cover up the violation in exchange for the money. BJSA improperly recorded the payment as import duties paid to a third-party customs agent. The same BJSA employee approved a 10,994-peso payment in October 2000 to an official in Argentina's Department of

Industry and Commerce. The payment was made to expedite the approval process and was recorded as an importation cost.

In June 2002, BJ Services' senior management learned of the improper payments and began a full internal investigation, which revealed that 151,406 pesos in additional payments had been made from January 1998 through April 2002. BJ Services notified the SEC and fully cooperated with the agency's investigation. It also replaced management in Latin America, arranged for proper classification of the equipment, changed the account procedures for payments, and expanded the corporate internal audit department, placing a manager in Latin America who reported directly to the BJ Services internal audit director. Finally, BJ Services retained an independent forensic auditor for the books and records of the Argentinean subsidiary as well as expanded its FCPA education and prevention program. The SEC ordered BJ Services to cease and desist from committing or causing any future violations of the FCPA books-and-records and internal controls provisions. As a result of its full investigation and prompt remedial actions, BJ Services was not charged criminally.

F. *In re* Schering-Plough Corp.;[36] *SEC v. Schering-Plough Corp.*[37]

▶ **Misconduct Category:**	Payments to charitable castle restoration foundation, whose president purchased formulary for government-owned hospitals in Silesian region
▶ **Country:**	Poland
▶ **Foreign Government Official:**	Director of Silesian Health Fund, one of 16 regional health authorities in Poland
▶ **Improper Payment Dollar Value:**	$76,000
▶ **Penalty:**	$500,000
▶ **Other:**	Parent books-and-records and internal controls settlement, despite the fact that questionable payments were made without the knowledge or approval of any Schering-Plough officer or employee in the United States; structuring of donations to exceed local manager's authorization limit; leading FCPA charitable donation case; independent consultant requirement; query whether payments to a charitable organization constituted things of value to its chairman and founder
▶ **Related Matter:**	*SEC v. Eli Lilly & Co.* (2012) (similar Chudow Castle Foundation payments)

In June 2004, Schering-Plough Corporation, a pharmaceutical company headquartered in Kenilworth, New Jersey, settled a complaint with the SEC relating to improper payments totaling $76,000 made by a foreign subsidiary, Schering-Plough Poland (S-P Poland), over a three-year period to a charitable organization called the Chudow Castle Foundation to induce the foundation's chairman and founder to influence the purchase of Schering-Plough products in Poland. The head of the Chudow Castle Foundation was also director of the Silesian Health Fund, one of 16 regional governmental health authorities in Poland that, among other things, provided money for the purchase of pharmaceutical products and influenced the purchase of those products by other entities such as hospitals. None of the donations or payments to the charity were accurately reflected in Schering-Plough's books and records; instead, they were "dues" that were required to be paid for assistance by the director.

In February 1999, shortly after the Chudow Castle Foundation head assumed his director position with the Silesian Health Fund, S-P Poland made a $777 payment to the Chudow Castle Foundation. In early 2000 the director solicited S-P Poland's oncology unit manager to make additional payments. As a result, S-P Poland made four payments totaling $31,002 in 2000; seven payments totaling $49,183 in 2001; and one payment of $4,868 in 2002. The S-P Poland manager did not view the payments as charitable donations but as "dues" that were required for the assistance of the director. Many payments were structured to allow the S-P Poland manager to exceed his donation authorization limits. During 2000 and 2001 the payments to the Chudow Castle Foundation constituted approximately 40 percent and 20 percent, respectively, of S-P Poland's total promotional donations budget. During this period the sales of two Schering-Plough products increased disproportionately in Silesia compared with sales of those products in other areas of Poland. S-P Poland's internal policies provided that promotional donations generally were to be made to healthcare institutions and relate to the practice of medicine.

The books-and-records and internal controls settlement included a $500,000 civil penalty for the parent corporation; the retention of an independent consultant required to provide a written report to both the SEC and the company; and an injunctive order prohibiting future violations of the FCPA books-and-records and internal controls provision. The SEC complaint did not allege that any parent company employee knew of or was in any way involved in the approval or authorization of the payments by the Polish subsidiary to the Chudow Castle Foundation. It also did not charge the foundation founder and chairman with receiving a thing of value, leaving unsettled whether there was an actionable bribe to a government official under the FCPA. No criminal charges were filed against Schering-Plough.

G. *In re* Oil States International, Inc.[38]

▶ **Misconduct Category:**	Kickback payments by consultant through inflated invoices; use of subsidiary to make payments to employees of state-owned oil company who awarded service contracts
▶ **Country:**	Venezuela
▶ **Foreign Government Officials:**	State-owned oil company employees— Petroleos de Venezuela, SA (PdV)
▶ **Improper Payment Dollar Value:**	$348,000
▶ **Combined Penalties:**	None

▶ **Other:**   Cease-and-desist order: avoidance of
                                          bribery charge despite substantial
                                          payments due to effective remedial
                                          measures (restitution to victim,
                                          termination of consultant contract,
                                          correction of books and records) and
                                          voluntary disclosure

In April 2006 the SEC filed a cease-and-desist order against Oil States International Inc., a Houston-based oil and gas specialty provider, alleging FCPA books-and-records and internal controls violations arising from $348,350 in payments made through a subsidiary, Hydraulic Well Control Ltd. (HWC), to employees of state-owned Petroleos de Venezuela, S.A. (PdV). The payments were recorded as "ordinary business expenses" by the subsidiary and were consolidated onto the books and records of the parent company. The subsidiary HWC constituted approximately 1 percent of Oil States' consolidated revenues at the time.

HWC retained a Venezuelan consultant to provide translation services and to assist in invoice submissions but not to solicit business. Several PdV employees approached the consultant about a kickback scheme, and the consultant agreed to inflate bills for "lost rig time" and chemical costs in order to cover the kickbacks. As part of an annual budgeting process, HWC's senior management noticed narrower profit margins and brought the discrepancy to the attention of the parent's audit committee. The audit committee initiated an internal investigation and, as a result, terminated the contract with the Venezuelan consultant, disciplined the responsible employees, corrected the books and records, reimbursed the Venezuelan state-owned oil company for inflated billings, enhanced the company's controls, and voluntarily disclosed its findings to the DOJ and SEC.

Despite the substantial improper payment dollar value ($348,000), Oil States International was able to avoid SEC antibribery charges, a DOJ prosecution action, disgorgement of profit, and appointment of a monitor. This favorable cease-and-desist order outcome was likely the result of the parent's prompt remedial actions—an internal investigation, termination of the consultant, correction of the books and records, reimbursement of the victim, and voluntary disclosure to and full cooperation with U.S. authorities. The other two noticeable lessons of this case are that it confirms the U.S. government's position that state-owned oil company officers are "public officials" of an instrumentality under the FCPA and that a consultant need not pay anyone to "obtain business." Rather, the payments here were made to avoid work stoppage or delays by the state-owned oil company and, thus, "retain business."

H.   *SEC v. Tyco International Ltd.*[39]

▶ **Misconduct Category:**   Use of agents and lobbyists to pay
                                          ministers and military officials for the
                                          purpose of obtaining or retaining business

▶ **Countries:**   Brazil and South Korea

▶ **Foreign Government Officials:**   South Korean Minister of Construction and Finance and Military General

▶ **Improper Payment Dollar Value:**   Unspecified

▶ **Penalty:** $1 disgorgement and $50 million civil penalty (including for a wide variety of non-FCPA misconduct)

▶ **Other:**   Acquisition due diligence revealed that illicit payments to government officials were common and necessary in the foreign country (Brazil) that target Earth Tech conducted business; 60 percent of Earth Tech's total contracts involved some sort of payment to government officials; inadequate postacquisition training

▶ **Related Matters:**   U.S. DOJ–Tyco International Ltd. Agreement; *United States v. Tyco Valves & Controls Middle East*; *SEC v. Tyco International Ltd.* (all 2012)

In April 2006, the SEC filed a settled civil injunctive action in the U.S. District Court for the Southern District of New York against Tyco International Ltd. The SEC's complaint in that action alleged that from 1996 through 2002, Tyco violated the federal securities laws by, among other things, utilizing various improper accounting practices and a scheme involving transactions with no economic substance to overstate its reported financial results by at least $1 billion.[40]

Among many securities violations, the complaint alleged that Tyco violated the antibribery provisions of the Foreign Corrupt Practices Act when employees or agents of its Earth Tech Brasil Ltda. subsidiary made payments to Brazilian officials for the purpose of obtaining or retaining business for Tyco.

Specifically, the SEC alleged that from 1999 through 2002, Tyco acquired over 700 companies and that during that acquisition spree, Tyco employees or retained agents paid money or things of value to foreign officials to obtain or retain business for Tyco, that false entries were made to Tyco's books and records in an attempt to conceal these illicit payments, and that the misconduct was made possible by Tyco's failure to implement procedures sufficient to prevent and detect FCPA misconduct.

In 1998, Tyco acquired Multiservice Engenharia Ltda., a Brazilian engineering company, and renamed it Earth Tech Brasil Ltda. Tyco acquired Earth Tech Brasil notwithstanding that its due diligence for the acquisition revealed that illicit payments to government officials were common in Brazil and were portrayed as necessary in the industries in which Earth Tech Brasil conducted business. After its acquisition by Tyco, Earth Tech Brasil was extensively engaged in constructing and operating water, wastewater, sewage, and irrigation systems for various Brazilian government entities. Earth Tech Brasil reported to Tyco's Earth Tech corporate offices in Long Beach, California.

From 1999 through 2002, employees at Earth Tech Brasil repeatedly paid money to various Brazilian officials for the purpose of obtaining business, primarily in the construction and operation of municipal water and wastewater treatment systems. The payments to Brazilian officials were so widespread during this time that approximately 60 percent of Earth Tech Brasil's total contracts involved some form of payment to a government official. At times, the payments were made by lobbyists that Earth Tech Brasil retained with full knowledge that all or a portion of the money that Earth Tech Brasil paid to the lobbyists would be given to various Brazilian officials for the purpose of obtaining work for Earth Tech Brasil. Executives at Earth Tech's Long Beach corporate offices received e-mail communications, participated in telephone calls, and attended meetings where illicit payments to Brazilian officials for the purpose of obtaining or retaining business for Earth Tech Brasil were discussed.

False invoices from companies that were owned by various Earth Tech Brasil employees were typically submitted to obtain the funds for the illicit payments and to conceal these payments on Earth Tech Brasil's books and records. In some instances, lobbyists submitted inflated invoices to Earth Tech Brasil to obtain the funds needed to make the payments.

From 1999 through 2002, on at least one additional occasion, false entries were made to Tyco's books and records in an attempt to conceal illicit payments and entertainment that were provided to foreign officials by Tyco employees to obtain or retain business for Tyco. This misconduct was made possible by Tyco's failure to implement procedures sufficient to prevent and detect FCPA misconduct, despite knowledge and awareness within the company that corruption and illicit payments were common practices in the foreign country where the unlawful payments were made.

In 1999, Tyco acquired Dong Bang Industrial Co. Ltd., a South Korean fire protection services firm. Tyco's due diligence for the Dong Bang acquisition revealed that illicit payments to government officials were prevalent in the South Korean contracting business. From 1999 through 2002, certain executives at Dong Bang made cash payments and provided entertainment to various South Korean officials to assist Dong Bang in obtaining contracting work on various government-controlled projects. For example, during Tyco's fiscal year ended September 30, 2001, Dong Bang's then president spent $32,000 entertaining various South Korean officials for the purpose of obtaining business for Dong Bang. The president also regularly provided entertainment to the South Korean minister of construction and finance and a South Korean military general for the purpose of obtaining business for Dong Bang. In Tyco's fiscal year ended September 30, 2002, a Dong Bang executive paid $7,500 to an employee of the Wolsong Nuclear Power Plant, owned and operated by a South Korean governmental entity, to obtain contracting work for Dong Bang at the facility.

Dong Bang established fictitious employees on its books to finance some of the improper cash payments and entertainment that were provided to South Korean officials. Payroll disbursements for the fictitious employees were wired to Dong Bang executives, who subsequently used the funds to provide cash payments or entertainment to the various South Korean officials.

Prior to 2003, Tyco did not have a uniform, company-wide FCPA compliance program in place or a system of internal controls sufficient to detect and prevent

FCPA misconduct at its globally dispersed business units. Employees at Earth Tech Brasil and Dong Bang did not receive adequate instruction regarding compliance with the FCPA, despite Tyco's knowledge and awareness that illicit payments to government officials were a common practice in the Brazilian and South Korean construction and contracting industries.[41] The Tyco case highlights the importance of both preacquisition due diligence and postacquisition Day 1 compliance and training programs.

I.   SEC v. Pillor[42]

▶ **Misconduct Category:**	Improper payments or gifts to airport officials to obtain sales of explosive detection machines
▶ **Countries:**	China, Philippines, and Thailand
▶ **Foreign Government Officials:**	Airport
▶ **Improper Payment Dollar Value:**	Unclear
▶ **Penalty:**	$65,000
▶ **Other:**	Aiding and abetting employer's failure to establish adequate internal controls and indirectly causing the falsification of the company's books and records in connection with improper payments or gifts to airport officials to obtain sales of explosive detection machines. Failure to respond to or acknowledge e-mails was a critical factor in this SEC case. Use of distributors and sales agents.
▶ **Related Matter:**	InVision Technologies Inc.

In August 2006, the SEC announced charges against David M. Pillor, former senior vice president for sales and marketing and member of the board of directors of InVision Technologies, Inc., a manufacturer of explosive detection machines used in airports.[43] Pillor directed InVision's domestic and international sales and marketing efforts and hired regional sales managers, who reported to him, to oversee defined geographic markets.

The SEC's complaint, filed in the U.S. District Court for the Northern District of California, alleged that Pillor aided and abetted InVision's failure to establish adequate internal controls to prevent the company from violating the FCPA, and that he indirectly caused the falsification of the company's books and records. Simultaneous with the filing of the SEC's complaint, Pillor agreed to pay a $65,000 civil penalty and to entry of a permanent injunction against future FCPA violations, in settlement of the matter.

The SEC alleged that during the period from late 2001 through June 2004, InVision completed sales to airports in China, the Philippines, and Thailand. In the course of these transactions, Pillor received e-mail messages from his Asia regional sales manager that suggested that InVision's overseas sales agents and distributors intended to make improper payments or other gifts to foreign government officials, in violation of the FCPA. InVision subsequently paid invoices to its agents and distributors in China and the Philippines and improperly recorded the payments as legitimate business expenses. The things of value included cash and free trips.

Signally, the SEC complaint did not allege any knowledge on the part of Pillor in relation to the violations. Instead, it alleged that he acted "knowingly or with extreme recklessness."[44] For each of three country payments or things of value to foreign government officials in which an InVision regional manager sent Pillor e-mails alluding to the distributor or sales agent's bad intentions, the SEC alleged that "Pillor did not respond to the Regional Sales Manager's messages or acknowledge their receipt."[45] Whether this enforcement action was based on negligence rather than the statute's high knowledge standard or "extreme recklessness" remains debatable.[46]

InVision's FCPA violations occurred, in part, because it lacked adequate internal controls to detect and prevent such conduct. For example, InVision's sales department provided only informal training about the FCPA to its employees and foreign agents. Similarly, InVision's sales department failed to monitor its employees and foreign agents to ensure that they did not violate the requirements of the FCPA. As InVision's head of sales and a member of the company's board of directors, Pillor aided and abetted InVision's failure to establish adequate internal controls.

In February 2005, InVision settled related SEC charges by paying $1.1 million in disgorgement and penalties and agreeing to an SEC order to cease and desist from future FCPA violations. In December 2004, InVision paid $800,000 in penalties to settle similar charges brought by the DOJ. The conduct alleged by the SEC occurred prior to InVision's acquisition by General Electric Company in December 2004.

J. *SEC v. Dow Chemical Co.*;[47] *In re* Dow Chemical Co.[48]

▶ **Misconduct Category:**	Use of petty cash accounts, fictitious invoices, contractors, and "third-party" consultants to pay over $39,700 to a key official of an Indian federal agricultural regulatory board to influence regulatory actions, including product registrations; $87,400 in small amounts—well under $100 payments—to state-level agricultural officials; $11,800 to sales tax officials; $3,700 to excise tax officials; $1,500 to customs officials; and $37,600 for gifts, travel, entertainment, and other items
▶ **Country:**	India
▶ **Foreign Government Officials:**	Central Insecticides Board official; sales tax officials; excise tax officials; customs officials; and state-level agricultural inspectors
▶ **Improper Payment Dollar Value:**	$200,000
▶ **Penalty:**	$325,000

► **Other:**   Voluntary disclosure to the SEC,
                                       disciplinary actions, and training.
                                       Settlement provides for engagement of
                                       consultant to review compliance program
                                       rather than monitor; improper payments
                                       through a fifth-tier subsidiary; no DOJ
                                       prosecution.

In February 2007 the Dow Chemical Company of Midland, Michigan, settled a civil action alleging that DE-Nocil Crop Protection Ltd., a fifth-tier subsidiary headquartered in Mumbai, India, violated the books-and-records and internal controls provisions of the FCPA in connection with an estimated $200,000 in improper payments to various Indian government officials from 1996 to 2001. DE-Nocil was established in 1994 as a joint venture when a majority-owned Dow subsidiary, DowElanco, acquired a 51 percent ownership interest in the agro-chemicals business of a local India company owned by a prominent Indian family.

The SEC complaint alleged that the crop protection subsidiary made approximately $39,700 in corrupt payments to an official of India's Central Insecticides Board (CIB) to expedite the registration of three pesticide products; the CIB official had considerable influence within the Registration Committee and would determine whether and when a company's agricultural chemical products would be registered and in fact would refuse and delay registrations. Most of the payments were made through agreements with contractors, which added fictitious "incidental charges" on their bills or issued false invoices to the subsidiary. When needed, DE-Nocil contacted a contractor and asked it to disburse segregated funds, consisting of the "incidental charges," to third-party "consultants" who delivered the funds to the CIB official. DE-Nocil made approximately $20,000 in improper payments to the CIB official through this contractor. Using another complicit contractor, DE-Nocil accepted a false $12,000 invoice for "capital equipment" and paid that sum to the contractor, who in turn delivered it to the CIB official.

The SEC complaint further alleged that the DE-Nocil subsidiary made an estimated total of $87,400 in payments—usually well under $100 each—to state-level agriculture inspectors; $37,600 in gifts, travel, entertainment, and other items to Indian government officials; $19,000 to government business officials; $11,800 to sales tax officials; $3,700 to excise tax officials; and $1,500 to customs officials. In total, between 1996 and 2001, the Dow subsidiary distributed an estimated $200,000 through federal and state channels in India. None of these payments was accurately reflected on Dow's books and records, and the company's system of internal controls failed to prevent the payments.

The SEC issued a cease-and-desist order against findings that Dow violated the books-and-records and internal controls provisions of the Act in connection with the subsidiary's improper payments. Dow was fined $325,000. Dow voluntarily disclosed the payments to the SEC after an extensive internal investigation, in which it retained an independent auditor to conduct a forensic audit of the books-and-records and internal controls at DE-Nocil; took prompt disciplinary actions; trained relevant employees; and restructured its global compliance program. After it hired an independent consultant to review its FCPA compliance program, Dow was not required to have a three-year independent monitor appointed by the SEC. Dow's extensive internal investigation, voluntary disclosure, the age of the payments, the involvement of a fifth-tier subsidiary, and its remedial actions all likely helped to avoid any DOJ prosecution.

K. *In re* Delta & Pine Land Co. & Turk Deltapine, Inc.[49]

▶ **Misconduct Category:**	$43,000 in cash, air conditioners, computers, office furniture, refrigerators, and travel and hotel expenses in order to obtain governmental reports and certifications necessary to operate in-country
▶ **Country:**	Turkey
▶ **Foreign Government Officials:**	Ministry of Agricultural and Rural Affairs
▶ **Improper Payment Dollar Value:**	$43,000 over five years
▶ **Penalty:**	$300,000
▶ **Other:**	Low-dollar SEC threshold for FCPA enforcement action: $43,000 ($8,600/year) over five years; appointment of independent consultant; a seminal acquisition due diligence case; dubious prior internal investigation; voluntary disclosure

In July 2007, the SEC settled a civil action with Delta & Pine Land Company and its subsidiary Turk Deltapine, Inc., alleging that the two Scott, Mississippi, corporations violated the antibribery, internal controls, and books-and-records provisions with respect to improper payments to Turkish government officials. Delta & Pine was primarily engaged in the breeding, production, conditioning, and marketing of cotton planting seed. Turk Deltapine was a wholly owned subsidiary engaged in the production and sale of cottonseed in Turkey.

The two companies consented to an order that required them to cease and desist from committing violations of the antibribery, internal controls, and books-and-records provisions and to the appointment of an independent consultant to review and evaluate their internal controls, record-keeping, and financial reporting policies and procedures. The parent was required to provide the independent consultant with access to its files, books, records, and personnel as normally requested for the review. The SEC order found that:

* From 2001 to 2006, Turk Deltapine made payments valued at approximately $43,000 (including cash, travel and hotel expenses, air conditioners, computers, office furniture, and refrigerators) to officials of the Turkish Ministry of Agricultural and Rural Affairs (MOA). Turk Deltapine made the payments in order to obtain governmental reports and certifications that were necessary for Turk Deltapine to operate in Turkey.
* Prior to May 2004, payments to MOA officials were made in part using revenue generated from the sale of Turk Deltapine waste products and products

for waste allowance. The sales and payments were not recorded in the books, records, and accounts of the two companies. In the case of Turk Deltapine, some payments were recorded as "porter fees" paid to nonexistent persons.

- In May 2004, Delta & Pine officers in the United States learned that Turk Deltapine was making payments to MOA officials. Delta & Pine reviewed the circumstances but did not receive all facts concerning the payments from Turk Deltapine employees. Instead of halting the payments, Delta & Pine arranged going forward to have the payments made to MOA employees by a chemical company supplier to Turk Deltapine. The chemical company charged Turk Deltapine the improper payment sums plus a 10 percent handling fee. The post-May 2004 improper payments were similarly not recorded in the books, records, and accounts of Turk Deltapine or Delta & Pine. Moreover, an internal memorandum noted that there were "no effective controls to put in place to monitor this process."

- Turk Deltapine's payments to MOA officials did not cease until 2006, when the payments came to light in connection with due diligence being performed by Monsanto, a potential acquirer of Delta & Pine.

In addition, the SEC contemporaneously filed a complaint in the U.S. District Court for the District of Columbia charging the companies with antibribery and accounting violations and seeking a $300,000 civil penalty.[50] Delta & Pine and Turk Deltapine consented to the entry of a final judgment that required them to pay the penalty jointly and severally. Delta & Pine was acquired by Monsanto in June 2007.

L.   *SEC v. Textron, Inc.*[51]

▶ **Misconduct Category:**	Kickback payments as "after-sales service fees" to Iraqi government; bribes to officials of state-owned companies in Bangladesh, Egypt, India, Indonesia, and the United Arab Emirates
▶ **Countries:**	Bangladesh, Egypt, India, Indonesia, and the United Arab Emirates
▶ **Foreign Government Officials:**	Iraqi government and officials of state-owned companies in other countries
▶ **Improper Payment Dollar Value:**	$765,544 ($650,539 in Iraq and $114,995 in the other countries)
▶ **Combined Penalties:**	$4,685,040 ($1,150,000 DOJ fine; $2,284,579 in disgorgement of profits to SEC plus $450,561 in prejudgment interest; and $800,000 civil penalty)
▶ **Other:**	UN Oil-for-Food program; NPA

In August 2007, the SEC filed books-and-records and internal controls charges against Textron Inc., a Rhode Island–based industrial equipment company, in the U.S. District Court for the District of Columbia. The SEC's complaint alleged that from approximately 2001 through 2003, two of Textron's French subsidiaries authorized and made approximately $650,539 in kickback payments in connection with its sale of humanitarian goods to Iraq under the UN Oil-for-Food program. The kickbacks were made in the form of "after-sales services fees"; however, no bona fide services were actually rendered. The program was intended to provide humanitarian relief for the Iraqi population, which faced severe hardship under international trade sanctions. Iraq was allowed to purchase humanitarian goods through a UN escrow account. However, the SEC alleged that the kickbacks paid by Textron's subsidiaries bypassed the escrow account and were instead paid by third parties to Iraqi-controlled accounts. The contracts submitted to the United Nations did not disclose that the cost of the illicit payments was included in the inflated contract price. The SEC also alleged that Textron's subsidiaries made illicit payments of $114,995 to secure 36 contracts to officials of state-owned companies in Bangladesh, Egypt, India, Indonesia, and the United Arab Emirates from 2001 to 2005.

Textron agreed to a consent decree and order of disgorgement of $2,284,579 in profits, plus $450,461.68 in prejudgment interest and a civil penalty of $800,000. Textron was also required to pay a $1,150,000 fine pursuant to an NPA with the DOJ.

M. *In re* Bristow Group Inc.[52]

▶ **Misconduct Category:** Payments to tax officials to reduce local employee tax assessments

▶ **Country:** Nigeria

▶ **Foreign Government Officials:** State government officials including tax officials

▶ **Improper Payment Dollar Value:** $423,000

▶ **Combined Penalties:** None

▶ **Other:** Pay as You Earn (PAYE) payroll tax scheme

In September 2007, the SEC settled with Bristow Group Inc., a Houston-based and New York Stock Exchange–listed helicopter transportation services and oil and gas production facilities operation company, for violations of the FCPA. Bristow Group consented to an order that required it to cease and desist from committing violations of the FCPA antibribery, internal controls, and books-and-records provisions.

The SEC's order found that a Nigerian affiliate of Bristow Group made improper payments to a Nigerian state government official in return for the officials' reduction of the affiliate's employment taxes owed to the Nigerian state governments. The order also found that another Nigerian affiliate of Bristow Group underreported its expatriate payroll expenses in Nigeria. More specifically, the SEC order found that:

- Since at least 2003, and through approximately the end of 2004, Bristow Group's Nigerian affiliate Pan African Airlines Nigeria Ltd. (Paan) made improper payments totaling approximately $423,000 to employees of two Nigerian state governments to influence them to improperly reduce the amount of expatriate employment taxes payable by Paan to the respective Nigerian state governments.

- Paan was responsible for paying an annual expatriate "pay as you earn" (PAYE) tax to the Nigerian state governments in each state where Paan operated. At the end of each year, the government of each Nigerian state assessed a tax on the salaries of Paan employees in that state and sent Paan a demand letter. Paan then negotiated with the government tax officials to lower the amount assessed. In each instance, the PAYE tax demand amount was lowered and a separate cash payment amount for the tax officials was negotiated. Once Paan paid the state government and the tax officials, each state government provided Paan with a receipt reflecting only the amount payable to the state government.
- During the same time period, Bristow Group underreported Paan's and another Bristow Group Nigerian affiliate's payroll expenses to certain Nigerian state governments. As a result, Bristow Group's periodic reports filed with the SEC did not accurately reflect certain of the company's payroll-related expenses.

Additionally, the order found that during the same time period, Bristow Group lacked sufficient internal controls and had mischaracterized the improper payments as legitimate payroll expenses. Bristow Group cooperated with the SEC's investigation and took a number of remedial steps.

N. *SEC v. Srinivasan;*[53] *In re* Electronic Data Systems Corp.[54]

▶ **Misconduct Category:**	Bribes to retain contracts after senior employees of state-owned enterprise threatened to cancel contracts; fictitious invoices by outside accountant
▶ **Country:**	India
▶ **Foreign Government Officials:**	Senior employees of Indian state-owned enterprise
▶ **Improper Payment Dollar Value:**	$720,000
▶ **Combined Penalties:**	$560,902 (Srinivasan: $70,000 civil penalty; EDS: $358,800 in disgorgement of profits and $132,102 in prejudgment interest)
▶ **Other:**	Payments made in part to avoid cancelation of customer contracts, that is, to retain business

In September 2007, the SEC settled with Chandramowli Srinivasan, the president of A.T. Kearney India (ATKI), which at the time was a subsidiary of Electronic Data Systems (EDS), relating to his role in a bribery scheme. The SEC alleged that between early 2001 and September 2003, ATKI made at least $720,000 in illicit payments to senior employees of Indian state-owned enterprises to retain its business with those enterprises. ATKI made these payments at the direction of Srinivasan after the senior employees threatened to cancel the contracts with ATKI. Srinivasan consented to the entry of a final judgment enjoining him from violating the FCPA and ordering him to pay a $70,000 penalty.

In a separate but related action, the SEC instituted administrative proceedings against EDS for various violations of the issuer reporting and books-and-records provisions of the federal securities laws. The SEC order found that EDS engaged in the following misconduct:

- EDS failed to disclose the cost of certain derivatives contracts for the first and second quarters of 2002, and then selectively disclosed the cost and early settlement in the third quarter of 2002.
- EDS failed to adequately disclose in its Form 10-Q for the second quarter of 2002 an extraordinary transaction that comprised over 25 percent of EDS's operating cash flow in the first six months of 2002.
- EDS maintained inaccurate books and records by employing certain inaccurate assumptions in accounting models used to estimate revenues and expenses for the company's multibillion-dollar Navy/Marine Corps Intranet contract.
- The improper payments made by Srinivasan caused EDS to maintain inaccurate books and records.

EDS was also ordered to pay $358,800 in disgorgement and $132,102 in prejudgment interest.[55]

O. *SEC v. Chevron Corp.*[56]

▶ **Misconduct Category:**	Third-party contractors used to pay kickbacks and illegal surcharges
▶ **Country:**	Iraq
▶ **Foreign Government Officials:**	Iraqi government
▶ **Improper Payment Dollar Value:**	$20 million
▶ **Combined Penalties:**	$30 million, including disgorgement of $25 million in profits, a $ 3million civil penalty and a $2 million Office of Foreign Asset Controls penalty
▶ **Other:**	UN Oil-for-Food program; two-year NPA with the Southern District of New York U.S. Attorney's Office and the District Attorney of New York County

In November 2007, the SEC settled with Chevron Corporation, a global oil production company located in San Ramon, California, for $30 million regarding charges that third-party contractors of Chevron paid approximately $20 million in illegal kickbacks to Iraq in 2001–2002. These kickbacks were allegedly related to Chevron's purchases of oil under the UN Oil-for-Food program.

In 2000 the Iraqi government began requiring companies wishing to sell humanitarian goods to government ministries to pay a kickback, often mischaracterized as an "after-sales service fee," to the government in order to be granted a contract. The amount of that fee was usually 10 percent of the contract price. Such payments were not permitted under the UN Oil-for-Food program or other sanction regimes then in place.

The SEC alleged that

- Chevron knew or should have known that portions of the premiums it received from its oil purchases were being used by third parties to pay illegal surcharges to Iraq.
- Chevron failed to create and maintain an internal accounting controls system to detect and prevent illegal payments.
- Chevron's accounting for its Oil-for-Food program transactions did not accurately record its third-party payments.
- In January 2001, Chevron learned of surcharge demands by Iraq's State Oil Marketing Organization and adopted a company-wide policy prohibiting their payment. This policy required that traders obtain written approval before any Iraqi oil purchases, and it required that management review each proposed Iraqi oil deal.
- From April 17, 2001, to May 6, 2002, pursuant to 36 third-party contracts, Chevron purchased 78 million barrels of crude oil from Iraq. However, Chevron traders did not follow the policy, and Chevron's management did not enforce it.

Chevron consented to the entry of a final judgment permanently enjoining it from future books-and-records and internal controls violations and ordering it to disgorge $25 million in profits and pay a $3 million civil penalty. Chevron agreed to pay the U.S. Department of Treasury's Office of Foreign Asset Controls a $2 million penalty. Chevron also cooperated with both the DOJ and local district attorney investigations, ultimately entering into a two-year NPA with the U.S. Attorney's office for the Southern District of New York and the District Attorney of New York County, New York.

P.   *SEC v. Akzo Nobel, N.V.*;[57] U.S. DOJ–Akzo Nobel, N.V. Agreement[58]

▶ **Misconduct Category:**	Kickback payments disguised as "after-sales service fees"; United Nations Oil-for-Food programs
▶ **Country:**	Iraq
▶ **Foreign Government Officials:**	Iraqi government
▶ **Improper Payment Dollar Value:**	$279,491
▶ **Combined Penalties:**	$2,931,363 ($750,000 SEC civil penalty; $1,647,363 disgorgement of profits and $584,150 in prejudgment interest; and a Dutch government fine of $800,000)
▶ **Other:**	UN Oil-for-Food program; NPA; Dutch fine of $800,000

In December 2007, the SEC filed FCPA books-and-records and internal controls charges against Akzo Nobel N.V., a Netherlands-based pharmaceutical company, in the U.S. District Court for the District of Columbia. The SEC complaint alleged that from 2000 to 2003, two of Akzo Nobel's subsidiaries made $279,491 in kickback payments in connection with their sales of humanitarian goods to Iraq under the UN Oil-for-Food program. The kickbacks were characterized as "after-sales service fees" (ASSFs), but no bona fide services were performed. The program was intended to provide humanitarian relief for the Iraqi population, which faced severe hardship under international trade sanctions. It allowed the Iraqi government to purchase humanitarian goods through a U.S. escrow account. The kickbacks paid in connection with Akzo Nobel's subsidiaries' sales to Iraq bypassed the escrow account and were paid by third parties to Iraqi-controlled accounts in Lebanon and Jordan.

Akzo Nobel's subsidiary Intervet International B.V. entered into one program contract involving a kickback payment of $38,741. Akzo Nobel's subsidiary N.V. Organon entered into three contracts that involved the payment of $240,750 in ASSF payments. The SEC alleged the parent knew or was reckless in not knowing that illicit payments were either offered or paid in connection with all of these transactions. Akzo Nobel failed to maintain an adequate system of internal controls to detect and prevent the payments. Akzo Nobel's accounting for these transactions failed properly to record the nature of the company's payments and characterized the ASSFs as legitimate commission payments to the agent.

Akzo Nobel agreed to a consent decree and an order of disgorgement of profits of $1,647,363, $584,150 in prejudgment interest, and a civil penalty of $750,000. At the same time, Akzo Nobel entered into an NPA with the DOJ. Akzo Nobel's former subsidiary agreed to enter into a criminal disposition with the Dutch public prosecutor pursuant to which it agreed to pay an $800,000 fine.

Q. *SEC v. Con-Way Inc.*[59]

▶ **Misconduct Category:**	Hundreds of small payments to customs officials to reduce customs fines and shipping charges
▶ **Country:**	Philippines
▶ **Foreign Government Officials:**	Officials of 14 state-owned airlines; customs officials
▶ **Improper Payment Dollar Value:**	$417,000
▶ **Penalty:**	$300,000
▶ **Other:**	Cease-and-desist order; no criminal charges

In August 2008, Con-Way Inc., a San Mateo, California, international freight transportation company, paid a $300,000 civil penalty and accepted a cease-and-desist order to settle an FCPA enforcement action with the SEC. Con-Way violated the books-and-records and internal controls provisions of the FCPA through a Philippines-based subsidiary, Emery Transnational, which made hundreds of small payments to Philippines customs officials and to officials at 14 state-owned airlines. These payments were made between 2000 and 2003, and totaled at least $417,000. The

purpose and effect of these payments was to, inter alia, influence the foreign officials to violate customs regulations, settle customs disputes, and reduce or not
enforce otherwise legitimate fines for administrative violations. Con-Way failed to
record these payments accurately on its books and records and knowingly failed to
implement or maintain a system of effective internal accounting controls.

In early 2003, Con-Way discovered potential FCPA issues at Emery. Its subsidiary, Menlo Worldwide Forwarding, Inc., initiated steps to improve Emery's internal reporting requirements. After a broader review, Con-Way imposed heightened
financial reporting and compliance requirements upon Emery, Menlo terminated
a number of employees who had engaged in misconduct, and Con-Way provided
additional FCPA training and education to its employees and strengthened its regulatory compliance program.

R. SEC v. ITT Corp.[60]

▶ **Misconduct Category:** Improper payments through third-party agent or subsidiary employees to influence Chinese government purchasing decisions for large infrastructure projects; disguised commissions; improper use of Chinese design institutes

▶ **Country:** China

▶ **Foreign Government Officials:** Design institute officials and other state-owned-entity employees

▶ **Improper Payment Dollar Value:** $200,000

▶ **Combined Penalties:** $1,679,670 ($1,042,112 disgorgement of profits, $387,558 of prejudgment interest, and $250,000 civil penalty)

▶ **Other:** Voluntary disclosure and cooperation with the SEC and institution of remedial measures; allegation arose from anonymous complaint to corporate ombudsman. SEC alleged a violation of the books-and-records provision for "consolidat[ing] and includ[ing] in ITT's financial statements" the financial statements of a wholly owned Chinese subsidiary that made approximately $200,000 in illicit payments that it "improperly recorded . . . as commission payments."

In February 2009, the SEC settled with ITT Corporation, a New York City–based
global conglomerate, alleging FCPA violations in connection with improper payments to Chinese government officials by ITT's wholly owned Chinese subsidiary
Nanjing Goulds Pumps Ltd. (NGP) of the company's Fluid Technology Division.
This subsidiary distributed a variety of water pump products that were sold to
power plants, building developers, and general contractors throughout China. The

SEC complaint alleged that from 2001 through 2005, NGP, directly through certain employees or indirectly through third-party agents, made illicit payments totaling approximately $200,000 to state-owned entities (SOEs) to influence the purchase of NGP water pumps for large infrastructure projects in China. NGP made payments to employees of design institutes, some of which were SOEs, that assisted in the design of the projects to ensure that the design institutes recommended NGP water pumps to the project SOEs. The NGP payments were disguised as "commission payments" in NGP's books and records. The improper NGP entries were "consolidated and included in ITT's financial statements," which were part of SEC filings for the company's fiscal years 2001 through 2005.

ITT consented to entry of a final judgment permanently enjoining it from future violations of the books-and-records and internal controls provisions of the FCPA. The company agreed to pay disgorgement of profits of $1,042,112, prejudgment interest of $387,558, and a $250,000 civil penalty. In agreeing to this resolution, the SEC considered that ITT self-reported, cooperated with the investigation, and instituted subsequent remedial actions. The allegation arose from an anonymous complaint from wholly owned subsidiary NGP employees to ITT's corporate compliance ombudsman.

S.   *SEC v. Wurzel*;[61] *In re* United Industrial Corp.[62]

▶ **Misconduct Category:**	Use of agent to pay military officials to influence award of contracts
▶ **Country:**	Egypt
▶ **Foreign Government Officials:**	Egyptian Air Force officials
▶ **Improper Payment Dollar Value:**	In excess of $250,000
▶ **Combined Penalties:**	Wurzel: $35,000 civil penalty; UIC: $337,649 in disgorgement and prejudgment interest
▶ **Other:**	Payments to a retired Egyptian Air Force general continue after expiration of consulting agreement; before a new contract, agent e-mail stated, "it is very important to start giving motivation that we discussed"; improper marketing payments

In May 2009, the SEC filed an enforcement action in the U.S. District Court for the District of Columbia against Thomas Wurzel, formerly president of ACL Technologies, Inc., a subsidiary of United Industrial Corporation (UIC), which provided aerospace and defense systems to the U.S. Department of Defense and domestic and international customers.[63] The SEC complaint alleged that Wurzel authorized illicit payments to an Egypt-based agent while he knew or consciously disregarded the high probability that the agent would offer, provide, or promise at least a portion of such payments to Egyptian Air Force officials for the purpose of influencing these officials to award UIC business involving a military (F-16) aircraft depot in Cairo, Egypt. The SEC charged Wurzel with violations of the FCPA's antibribery, books-and-records, and internal controls provisions, and with aiding and abetting UIC's violations of the antibribery and books-and-records provisions of the FCPA.

The SEC's complaint further alleged that in late 2001 to 2002, Wurzel authorized three forms of illicit payments to the agent: (1) payments to the agent ostensibly for labor subcontracting work; (2) a $100,000 advance payment to the agent in June 2002 for "equipment and materials"; and (3) a $50,000 payment to the agent in November 2002 for "marketing services." Furthermore, Wurzel later directed his subordinates to create false invoices to conceal the fact that the $100,000 "advance payment" in June 2002 was never repaid. As a result, UIC, through ACL, was awarded a contract with gross revenues and net profits of approximately $5.3 million and $267,000, respectively. Wurzel agreed to pay the SEC a $35,000 civil penalty.

In a related action, the SEC initiated an administrative proceeding against UIC, the parent of ACL and a designer and manufacturer of defense, training, transportation, and energy systems for the U.S. Department of Defense and domestic and international customers. UIC agreed to an SEC order requiring it to cease and desist from committing or causing violations and any future FCPA violations and ordered UIC to pay $337,679.42 in disgorgement and prejudgment interest. In December 2007, UIC was acquired by an affiliate of Textron Inc.

T.   SEC v. Nature's Sunshine Products, Inc., Faggioli & Huff[64]

▶ **Misconduct Category:**	Brazilian subsidiary's payments to customs officials to import product into country and purchase of false documentation to conceal the nature of the payments
▶ **Country:**	Brazil
▶ **Foreign Government Officials:**	Customs officials
▶ **Improper Payment Dollar Value:**	Unknown
▶ **Penalty:**	$600,000
▶ **Other:**	First Section 20A of the Exchange Act "control person liability theory" against parent officers for misconduct at a foreign subsidiary in an FCPA case; voluntary disclosure by company; no criminal charges; no independent compliance monitor; parent officers disregarded numerous red flags at Brazilian subsidiary

In July 2009, Nature's Sunshine Products, Inc. (NSP), a Utah manufacturer of nutritional and personal care products, paid a $600,000 civil penalty and accepted a cease-and-desist order to settle an FCPA books-and-records and internal controls enforcement action with the SEC. The SEC complaint alleged that, faced with changes to Brazilian regulations that resulted in classifying many of NSP's products as medicines, NSP's Brazilian subsidiary made a series of cash payments to customs brokers, some of which were later paid to Brazilian customs officials to allow unregistered products to be imported into that country and then resold.

NSP purchased false documentation to conceal the nature of the payments. It also alleged that this conduct violated the FCPA, and, in particular, antifraud, issuer reporting, books-and-records, and internal controls provisions of the federal securities laws. It further alleged that NSP failed to disclose the payments to Brazilian customs agents in its filings with the SEC.

Signally, the SEC complaint alleged that NSP executives Douglas Faggioli and Craig D. Huff, in their capacities as control persons, violated the books-and-records and internal controls provisions of the securities laws in connection with the Brazilian cash payments. Specifically, the SEC invoked section 20A of the Exchange Act, which provides for control person liability under the theory that Faggioli, who was at the time COO (and later became CEO), had overall responsibility for the operations of the company and that Huff, the CEO at the time, had responsibility for internal controls and books and records. The SEC complaint suggested that there were red flags to the U.S. parent from the Brazil subsidiary, including substantial customer payments, that put Faggioli and Huff on notice, and such notice made the senior officers' conduct reckless. The purpose and effect of these payments was to inter alia influence the foreign officials to violate customs regulations, settle customs disputes, and reduce or not enforce otherwise legitimate fines for administrative violations. NSP also failed to record these payments accurately on its books and records and knowingly failed to implement or maintain a system of effective internal accounting controls. Approximately 80 cash payments on NSP Brazil's books had no supporting documentation.

U. *SEC v. Avery Dennison Corp.*[65]

▶ **Misconduct Category:**	Kickbacks using consulting fees to obtain sales contracts; excessive gifts; sightseeing trips; use of government official's relative; improper use of a distributor and customs broker; customs and tax official bribes; use of petty cash funds disguised as "travel" to pay monthly bribes; poor acquisition due diligence; and improper postacquisition payments in China, Indonesia, and Pakistan
▶ **Countries:**	China, Indonesia, and Pakistan
▶ **Foreign Government Officials:**	Ministry of Public Security—Traffic Management Research Institute (China); customs and tax officials (China, Indonesia, and Pakistan)
▶ **Improper Payment Dollar Value:**	$100,000+
▶ **Combined Penalties:**	$518,470 ($200,000 civil penalty; $273,213 in disgorgement of profits and $45,257 in prejudgment interest)
▶ **Other:**	Voluntary disclosure by the company; proactive 27-country global trade compliance review and ten-country comprehensive FCPA review; no independent monitor requirement

In July 2009, the SEC settled two enforcement proceedings against Avery Dennison Corporation, a Pasadena, California, label manufacturer, alleging FCPA violations in connection with improper payments and provisions to foreign officials by Avery's Chinese subsidiary and several entities Avery had acquired. The federal civil suit filed in the U.S. District Court for the Central District of California charged Avery with books-and-records and internal controls violations, and Avery agreed to pay a civil penalty of $200,000. The SEC administrative proceedings alleged the same violations and ordered the company to cease and desist from these violations and to disgorge $273,213 together with $45,257 in prejudgment interest.

Both SEC actions charged that from 2002 through 2008, the Reflectives Division of Avery (China) Co. Ltd. paid or authorized the payments of kickbacks, sightseeing trips, and gifts to officials of the Chinese Ministry of Public Security and, in particular, its Traffic Management Research Institute in Wuxi, Jiangu Province (Wuxi Institute). In January 2004, an Avery China sales manager gave Wuxi Institute Chinese officials each a pair of shoes worth a combined value of $500. Three months later, Avery China hired a former Wuxi Institute official as a sales manager because his wife was an official in charge of two projects that Avery China wished to pursue.

In August 2004, Avery China was awarded two government contracts through the Wuxi Institute to install new graphics on approximately 15,400 police cars for two Chinese government entities. The Reflectives China national manager obtained these contracts by agreeing to artificially increase the sales price and then refund that amount back to the Wuxi Institute as a "consulting fee." In doing so, he knew at least a portion of that refunded amount would be for the benefit of Wuxi Institute officials. The total sales under the two contracts were $677,494, and Avery China profited by approximately $363,953. However, Avery's Asia Pacific Group discovered the kickback scheme before any illegal payment was made, thereby avoiding illegal payments totaling approximately $41,138, or 6 percent of the total sales.

Further, in December 2002, another Reflectives Division salesman proposed, and the Reflectives China national manager approved, hosting a sightseeing trip for five government officials with a budget of about RMB 35,000 ($4,227). Two reimbursement requests were used to conceal the expenses for the trip. Also, in August 2004, the Reflectives China national manager approved a kickback payment to an official in Henan Luqiao, a state-owned enterprise, to secure a sales contract worth approximately $106,562, for which Avery China profited by $61,381. However, Avery China discovered the kickback arrangement and never made the promised $2,415 payment to the Henan Luqiao official.

From May to June 2005, an Avery Reflectives Division sales manager negotiated a sale to a state-owned end user. To secure the sale, the manager agreed to pay a commission to a project manager at the end user. He then asked a distributor to fill the order and fund the agreed-upon commission out of what ordinarily would have been the distributor's profit. The transaction was booked as a sale to the distributor, rather than to the end user. The distributor claimed to have paid the project manager approximately $24,752 out of its own profit margin. The total sales in the transaction were $466,162, and Avery China profited by $273,213.

In late 2005, during a sales conference that Avery China sponsored at a famous Chinese tourist destination, the successor to the Reflectives China national manager paid for sightseeing trips for at least four government officials. The national manager later attempted to cover up his role in planning the trip and the sightseeing during the conference. He altered the conference invoice by reallocating the sightseeing expenses to other expense categories and had the travel agency submit the changed invoice to Avery China for payment. The changed invoice did not contain any sightseeing expenses; rather, they were buried in expenses for rooms, meals, and transportation. The total cost from the 40-plus attendee conference was $15,000.

In 2005, Avery integrated the operations of an Indonesian contractor it had acquired. The contractor operated out of a bonded zone in Indonesia, and had a practice of paying approximately $100 each to three customs officials who regularly visited its warehouse to inspect goods. The contractor continued the practice postacquisition. To obtain cash for the payments, an employee of the acquired subsidiary obtained $10 petty cash on a daily basis for the $300 needed each month, and the accounting entry reflected $10 of travel expense each day for the employee.

In June 2007, Avery acquired Paxar Corporation, a NYSE-listed company. In September 2007, through a whistleblower, Avery discovered that the Paxar employees in Indonesia made illegal payments to customs and tax officials to obtain bonded zone licenses and to overlook bonded zone regulatory violations, and that the then-general manager of Paxar Indonesia directed employees to fabricate fake invoices to conceal illegal payments. An internal audit review also uncovered payments to customs officials in Pakistan made by Paxar Pakistan through its customs broker.

In April 2008, Avery commenced a global trade compliance review in 27 countries, which included an FCPA review. Three months later, it began a more comprehensive FCPA review in ten high-risk countries, including China. Beyond the illicit payments identified at Paxar Indonesia and Paxar Pakistan, the ten-country review also identified problematic payments in Paxar China. In all three locations, illicit payments were made both before and after the acquisition, with the latest illicit payment occurring in January 2008. The improper postacquisition payments amounted to $5,000, $30,000, and $16,000 at Paxar Indonesia, Paxar Pakistan, and Paxar China, respectively.

The Avery Dennison matter illustrates a host of common FCPA problems: kickbacks through improper consultation arrangements; misuse of a government official's relative; inadequate acquisition due diligence; improper payments through a distributor or customs broker; postacquisition improper payments; local tax and customs bribes; and travel and entertainment abuses. The SEC did not impose an independent monitor requirement; the SEC resolution suggests that, in the wake of problematic FCPA conduct in multiple countries, voluntary disclosure, a thorough global trade compliance review (27 countries), and a comprehensive FCPA review in high-risk countries (ten countries) may help a company avoid more severe sanctions. Avery Dennison also highlights the importance of promptly integrating a parent company's internal controls into the operations of acquired companies, particularly where the target's books and records are consolidated with the parent company's.

V.   SEC v. Benton[66]

▶ **Misconduct Category:**	Bribes to overlook customs violations and use of consultant to pay state-owned oil company official to obtain extensions of drilling contracts
▶ **Countries:**	Mexico and Venezuela
▶ **Foreign Government Officials:**	Customs officials and officials of Petroleos de Venezuela S.A. (state-owned oil company)
▶ **Improper Payment Dollar Value:**	$409,000
▶ **Penalty:**	$40,000
▶ **Other:**	Concealment of bribes from internal and external auditors through redaction of references to Venezuelan payments in an action plan responding to an internal audit report
▶ **Related Matters:**	*United States v. Pride International, Inc.*; *SEC v. Pride International, Inc.*

In December 2009, in the Southern District of Texas, the SEC charged Bobby Benton, Pride International, Inc.'s former vice president for operations, Western Hemisphere, with violations relating to bribes paid to foreign officials in Mexico and Venezuela. Pride International of Houston, Texas, is one of the world's largest offshore drilling companies.

The SEC complaint alleged that in December 2004, Benton authorized the payment of $10,000 to a third party, believing that all or a portion of the funds would go to a Mexican customs official in return for favorable treatment regarding customs deficiencies identified during an inspection of a Pride supply boat. The complaint further alleged that Benton had knowledge of a second bribe of $15,000 paid to a different Mexican customs official the same month to ensure that the export of a rig would not be delayed due to customs violations. It was also alleged that from approximately 2003 to 2005, a manager of a Pride subsidiary in Venezuela authorized payments totaling approximately $384,000 to third-party companies, knowing that all or a portion of the funds would be given to an official of Petroleos de Venezuela, S.A., Venezuela's state-owned oil company, in order to secure extensions of three drilling contracts. Benton, in an effort to conceal these payments, redacted references to bribery in an action plan responding to an internal audit report and signed two false certifications in connection with audits and reviews of Pride's financial statements, denying any knowledge of bribery. But for Benton's false statements, Pride's management and internal and external auditors would have discovered the bribery schemes and the corresponding false books-and-records entries. The SEC complaint sought a permanent injunction, a civil penalty, and the disgorgement of ill-gotten gains plus prejudgment interest.

W. *SEC v. NATCO Group Inc.*[67]

▶ **Misconduct Category:**	Improper payments to avoid expatriate deportation; false documentation to obtain visas
▶ **Country:**	Kazakhstan
▶ **Foreign Government Officials:**	Kazakh immigration prosecutors
▶ **Improper Payment Dollar Value:**	$125,000
▶ **Penalty:**	$65,000
▶ **Other:**	Extortionate threats of imprisonment and deportation of expatriate workers of a foreign subsidiary; very modest SEC fine; no DOJ charges

In January 2010, the SEC filed a settled civil action in the U.S. District Court for the Southern District of Texas charging Houston-based oil field services provider NATCO Group Inc. with violations of the books-and-records and internal controls provisions of the FCPA. According to the SEC complaint, TEST Automation & Controls, Inc., a wholly owned subsidiary of NATCO Group Inc., maintained a Kazakhstan branch office where it won a contract to provide instrumentation and electrical services. To perform the services, TEST Kazakhstan hired both expatriates and local Kazakh workers. Kazakhstan law requires companies to obtain immigration documentation before any expatriate worker enters the country; its immigration authorities periodically audit immigration documentation of companies operating in the country for compliance with local law.

In 2007, Kazakh immigration prosecutors conducted audits and claimed that TEST Kazakhstan's expatriate workers were working without proper immigration documentation. The prosecutors threatened to fine, jail, or deport the workers if TEST Kazakhstan did not pay cash fines. Believing the prosecutors' threats to be genuine, employees of the Kazakhstan subsidiary sought guidance from TEST's senior management in Louisiana, who authorized the payments. The TEST Kazakhstan employees used personal funds to pay the prosecutors $45,000 and then obtained reimbursement from TEST.

TEST Kazakhstan used consultants to assist it in obtaining immigration documentation for its expatriate employees. One of the consultants did not have a license to perform visa searches, but maintained close ties to an employee working at the Kazakh Ministry of Labor, the entity issuing the visas. The consultant requested cash from TEST Kazakhstan to help him obtain the visas. Kazakh law requires companies seeking to withdraw cash from commercial bank accounts to submit supporting invoices, and the subsidiary presented $80,000 worth of false invoices from the consultant to Kazakh banks to withdraw the requested cash.

TEST created and accepted false documents while paying extorted immigration fines and obtaining immigration visas in the Republic of Kazakhstan. NATCO's system of internal accounting controls failed to ensure that TEST recorded the true purpose of the payments, and NATCO's consolidated books and records did not accurately reflect these payments. Without admitting or denying the allegations in the SEC's complaint, NATCO agreed to pay a $65,000 civil penalty.

The NATCO case addresses the not-infrequent circumstance where foreign government officials threaten to fine or deport workers of a foreign subsidiary. The FCPA legislative history limits the duress defense to true extortion situations and offers as an example that a payment to a foreign official to keep an oil rig from being dynamited would negate the requisite corrupt intent.[68] It is telling that the DOJ chose not to file criminal charges under these unique extortionate facts and the SEC sought only a modest fine of $65,000.

X. SEC v. Veraz Networks, Inc.[69]

▶ **Misconduct Category:**	Gift scheme involving holiday gifts; consultant fee scheme to obtain contract aborted upon discovery by company
▶ **Countries:**	China and Vietnam
▶ **Foreign Government Officials:**	Government-controlled telecommunications company officials, including its CEO in Vietnam
▶ **Improper Payment Dollar Value:**	$40,000
▶ **Penalty:**	$300,000
▶ **Other:**	U.S. Department of Homeland Security assistance; holiday gifts totaling $4,500 form one basis for the SEC enforcement action; gift of flowers for wife of CEO alleged as improper; misuse of a reseller was part of one scheme

In June 2010, the SEC settled with San Jose, California–based telecommunications company Veraz Networks, Inc., in the Northern District of California for alleged violations of FCPA books-and-records and internal controls provisions. The alleged violations stemmed from improper payments made by Veraz to foreign officials in China and Vietnam after the company went public in 2007.

The SEC alleged that Veraz engaged a consultant in China who, in 2007 and 2008, gave gifts and offered improper payments together valued at approximately $40,000 to officials at a government-controlled telecommunications company in China in an attempt to win business for Veraz. A Veraz supervisor who approved the gifts described them in an internal Veraz e-mail as the "gift scheme." Specifically, in late 2007, Veraz's consultant in China provided approximately $4,500 worth of gifts to officials at a telecommunications company in an attempt to secure a business deal for Veraz. The consultant requested that his Veraz supervisor approve the funding for those gifts via e-mail. The supervisor approved the gift scheme in an e-mail.

In January 2008, the consultant offered a separate improper payment to officials at the same telecommunications company to secure a deal valued at $233,000. The fee was described as a "consultant fee" and was set at approximately $35,000. The telecommunications company awarded the contract to Veraz, even though Veraz's bid was higher than other bids. Veraz discovered the improper offer of payment prior to receiving any money from the transaction and canceled the sale.

The SEC also alleged that in 2007 and 2008, a Veraz employee made improper payments to the CEO of a government-controlled telecommunications company in Vietnam through a Singapore reseller in order to win business for Veraz. Veraz approved and reimbursed its employee for questionable expenses related to the telecom, including gifts and entertainment for telecom employees and flowers for the wife of the CEO.

The SEC complaint alleged that Veraz violated the books-and-records and internal controls provisions of the FCPA by failing to accurately record the improper payments on its books and records, and failing to devise and maintain a system of effective internal controls to prevent such payments. Veraz consented to the entry of a final judgment permanently enjoining it from future FCPA violations and an order to pay a $300,000 penalty.

Y. *SEC v. General Electric Co.*[70]

▶ **Misconduct Category:**	UN Oil-for-Food program: cash, computer equipment and freight supplied by GE subsidiary or subsidiaries later acquired by GE; kickback scheme with Iraqi government agencies to win contracts to supply medical equipment and water purification equipment
▶ **Countries:**	Germany, Iraq, Italy, and Norway
▶ **Foreign Government Officials:**	Iraqi Oil Ministry
▶ **Improper Payment Dollar Value:**	$3.6 million
▶ **Combined Penalties:**	$23.5 million ($18,397,949 in disgorgement of profits; $4,080,665 in prejudgment, interest, and $1 million civil penalty)
▶ **Other:**	Failure to ensure that European subsidiaries devised and maintained internal controls; successor liability for GE that acquired liabilities, along with assets, in the acquisitions; no DOJ criminal case was returned
▶ **Related Matters:**	See other UN Oil-for-Food program cases

In July 2010, the SEC charged General Electric Company in the U.S. District Court for the District of Columbia with violations of the FCPA for its involvement in a $3.6 million kickback scheme with Iraqi government agencies to win contracts to supply medical equipment and water purification equipment. The SEC alleged that two GE subsidiaries—along with two other subsidiaries of public companies that have since been acquired by GE—made illegal kickback payments in the form of cash, computer equipment, medical supplies, and services to the Iraqi Health Ministry or the Iraqi Oil Ministry in order to obtain valuable contracts under the UN Oil-for-Food program.

GE agreed to pay $23.4 million to settle the SEC's charges against the company as well as the two subsidiaries for which GE assumed liability upon acquiring: Ionics, Inc. and Amersham plc. The SEC charged GE, Ionics, and Amersham with violating the books-and-records and internal controls provisions of the FCPA. SEC enforcement actions against companies involved in Oil-for-Food program–related kickback schemes with Iraq have led to the recovery of more than $204 million.[71]

According to the SEC complaint, the kickback scheme occurred from approximately 2000 to 2003. GE subsidiaries Marquette-Hellige and OEC-Medical Systems (Europa) AG made approximately $2.04 million in kickback payments to the Iraqi government under the Oil-for-Food program. Ionics Italba S.R.L. (then a subsidiary of Ionics) and Nycomed Imaging AS (then a subsidiary of Amersham) made approximately $1.55 million in cash kickback payments. Since their acquisitions by GE, Amersham and Ionics are now known as GE Healthcare Ltd. and GE Ionics, Inc., respectively.

The SEC alleged that Germany-based Marquette paid or agreed to pay illegal kickbacks in the form of computer equipment, medical supplies, and services on three contracts worth $8.8 million. Through an Iraqi third-party agent, Marquette paid goods and services worth approximately $1.2 million to the Iraqi Health Ministry in order to obtain two of the contracts. The agent offered to make an additional in-kind kickback payment worth approximately $250,000 to obtain the third contract. The illegal kickbacks were made or offered with the knowledge and approval of Marquette officials.

The SEC further alleged that Switzerland-based OEC-Medical made an in-kind kickback payment of approximately $870,000 on one contract worth $2.1 million through the same third-party agent who handled the Marquette contracts. OEC-Medical and the agent entered into a fictitious "services provider agreement" identifying phony services the agent would perform in order to justify his increased commission and conceal the illegal kickback from UN inspectors.

According to the SEC's complaint, Norway-based Nycomed entered into nine contracts with Iraqi ministries involving the payment of approximately $750,000 in cash kickbacks between 2000 and 2002. As a result, Nycomed earned approximately $5 million in wrongful profits on the contracts. The contracts were all direct agreements between Nycomed and the Iraqi Ministry of Health for the provision of Omnipaque and Omniscan. Omnipaque is an injectable contrast agent used in conjunction with X-rays; Omniscan is a contrast agent used in conjunction with magnetic resonance imaging (MRI). Nycomed paid approximately $750,000 in kickbacks on the nine contracts and earned approximately $5 million in wrongful profits. The contracts were negotiated by Nycomed's Jordanian agent. The kickback payments were explicitly authorized by Nycomed's salesman in Cyprus. The Nycomed salesman increased the agent's commission from 17.5 percent to 27.5 percent of the contract price, and artificially increased the UN contract prices by

10 percent, all to cover the cost of the kickbacks. GE acquired Nycomed's parent company—Amersham—in 2004.

Italy-based Ionics Italba was a subsidiary of Ionics, Inc., which GE acquired in 2005. Between 2000 and 2002, Ionics Italba paid $795,000 in kickbacks and earned $2.3 million in wrongful profits on five program contracts to sell water treatment equipment to the Iraqi Oil Ministry. In the first of these contracts, the illegal kickback payment was concealed under a fictitious line item for "modification and adaptation at site of obsolete spare parts." When UN inspectors requested additional detail about the line item, officials at Ionics Italba passed the inquiry along to the Iraqi Oil Ministry. The ministry's proposed response, which described services neither party intended to be performed, was incorporated nearly verbatim in a letter that Ionics Italba provided to the UN. Four of the five contracts were negotiated with side letters documenting the commitment of Ionics Italba to make cash kickback payments. The side letters were concealed from UN inspectors in violation of a program requirement to provide all contract documentation for inspection and UN approval. On the majority of the Ionics Italba contracts, invoices provided by the sales agent included fictitious activities to justify the agent's inflated commission. GE acquired Ionic Italba's parent company, Ionics Inc., in 2005. GE was ordered to pay $18,397,949 in disgorgement of profits, $4,080,665 in prejudgment interest, and a penalty of $1 million. GE fully cooperated with the government investigation.

Z.   *SEC v. GlobalSantaFe Corp.*[72]

▶ **Misconduct Category:**	Bribes paid from freight-forwarder officials to circumvent customs regulations
▶ **Countries:**	Angola, Gabon, Equatorial Guinea, and Nigeria
▶ **Foreign Government Officials:**	Customs officials
▶ **Improper Payment Dollar Value:**	Unknown
▶ **Combined Penalties:**	$5.9 million ($2.1 million civil penalty; $2,694,405 in disgorgement of profits plus $1,063,760 in prejudgment interest)
▶ **Other:**	Payments to obtain preferential treatment described on invoices as "customs vacations," "customs escort," "costs extra police to obtain visa," "official duties," and "authorities fees." No criminal charges.
▶ **Related Matters:**	*United States v. Panalpina; United States v. Pride International; United States v. Shell Nigeria Exploration & Production Co.; United States v. Tidewater; United States v. Transocean Inc.; SEC v. Transocean Inc.;* Noble

In November 2010, the SEC charged GlobalSantaFe Corp. (GSF) (f/k/a Transocean Worldwide Inc.) in the U.S. District Court for the District of Columbia with bribery, record-keeping, and internal controls violations of the FCPA. The SEC complaint alleged that, from approximately January 2002 through July 2007, GSF made illegal payments to officials of the Nigerian Customs Service (NCS), through companies acting as customs brokers for GSF. In November 2007, GSF, an oil and gas drilling services company, merged with a subsidiary of Transocean Inc. In December 2008, the listed company became Transocean Ltd.

The SEC complaint further alleged that instead of moving its oil drilling rigs out of Nigerian waters as required by Nigerian law when GSF's permit to temporarily import the rigs into Nigeria expired, GSF, through its customs brokers, made illegal payments to NCS officials to secure documentation reflecting that the rigs had moved out of Nigerian waters, when in fact the rigs had not moved at all. GSF, through its customs brokers, made other suspicious payments, some characterized as "interventions," to Nigerian customs officials. In addition, GSF similarly made a number of suspicious payments to government officials in Gabon, Angola, and Equatorial Guinea. These payments were described on invoices as, for example, "customs vacation," "customs escort," "costs extra police to obtain visa," "official dues," and "authorities fees." None of the payments were accurately reflected in GSF's books and records, nor was GSF's system of internal accounting controls adequate at the time to detect and prevent these illegal payments.

GSF agreed to pay a total of approximately $5.9 million to settle the SEC's charges. Specifically, GSF also consented to the entry of a court order requiring GSF to pay disgorgement of $2,694,405, prejudgment interest of $1,063,760, and a civil penalty of $2.1 million.

AA.   SEC v. Jennings[73]

▶ **Misconduct Category:**	UN Oil-for-Food program fraud and improper payments to obtain chemical contracts
▶ **Countries:**	Indonesia and Iraq
▶ **Foreign Government Officials:**	Iraqi Ministry of Oil officials; Pertamina (Indonesian state-owned oil and gas company)
▶ **Improper Payment Dollar Value:**	$7.05 million
▶ **Combined Penalties:**	$229,037 ($116,092 disgorgement of profits, plus prejudgment interest of $12,945, and $100,000 penalty)
▶ **Other:**	Jennings, the former CEO of Innospec, Inc., cooperated with the SEC. E-mail stated that Innospec was "sharing most of its profits with Iraqi officials."
▶ **Related Matters:**	*United States v. Innospec Inc.*; *SEC v. Innospec*; *Regina v. Innospec Ltd.*; *United States v. Naaman*; *SEC v. Naaman & Turner*

In January 2011, the SEC charged Paul W. Jennings, a former CEO at Innospec, Inc., with violating the FCPA by approving bribes to government officials to obtain and retain business. The SEC alleged that Paul W. Jennings learned of the company's long-standing practice of paying bribes to win orders for sales of tetraethyl lead (TEL) in mid- to late 2004 while serving as the CFO. After becoming CEO in 2005, Jennings and others in Innospec's management approved bribery payments to officials at the Iraqi Ministry of Oil (MoO) in order to sell the fuel additive to Iraq refineries. Innospec used its third-party agent in Iraq to funnel payments to Iraqi officials.

According to the SEC complaint filed in the U.S. District Court for the District of Columbia, Jennings played a key role in Innospec's bribery activities in Iraq and Indonesia. Innospec, a manufacturer and distributor of fuel additives and other specialty chemicals, was charged in 2010 with making illicit payments of approximately $6.3 million and promised an additional $2.8 million in illicit payments to Iraqi ministries and government officials as well as Indonesian government officials in exchange for contracts worth approximately $176 million.

The SEC alleged that Innospec made payments totaling more than $1.5 million and promised an additional $884,480 to MoO officials. For example, in an October 2005 e-mail copying Jennings, the agent said that Iraqi officials were demanding a 2 percent kickback and that "[w]e are sharing most of our profits with Iraqi officials. Otherwise, our business will stop and we will lose the market. We have to change our strategy and do more compensation to get the rewards." The kickback and later payments were paid by increasing the agent's commission, which Jennings approved. The SEC complaint also alleges that Jennings was aware of the scheme to pay an official at the Trade Bank of Iraq in exchange for a favorable exchange rate on letters of credit. Another scheme involved a bribe to ensure the failure of a field test of a competitor product. A confidential MoO report for the field trial test was shared with Jennings. Bribes were offered to secure a 2008 long-term purchase agreement that would have caused approximately $850,000 to be shared with Iraqi officials. The agreement, however, did not go forward due to the investigation and ultimate discovery by U.S. regulators of widespread bribery by Innospec.

Innospec also paid bribes to Indonesian government officials from at least 2000 to 2005 in order to win contracts worth more than $48 million from state-owned oil and gas companies in Indonesia. Jennings became aware of and approved payments beginning in mid- to late 2004. Various euphemisms for the bribery were commonly used in e-mails and in discussions with Jennings and others at Innospec, including "the Indonesian Way," "the Lead Defense Fund," and "TEL optimization." Bribery discussions were held on a flight in the United States and even discussed at Jennings's performance review in 2005. In one bribery scheme with Pertamina, an Indonesian state-owned oil and gas company, Innospec agreed, with approval by Jennings, to a "one off payment" of $300,000 to their Indonesian agent with the understanding that it would be passed on to an Indonesian official.

The SEC complaint also alleged that from 2004 to February 2009, Jennings signed annual certifications that were provided to auditors where he falsely stated that he had complied with Innospec's Code of Ethics incorporating the company's FCPA policy. Jennings also signed annual and quarterly personal certifications pursuant to the Sarbanes-Oxley Act of 2002 in which he made false certifications concerning the company's books-and-records and internal controls.

Jennings consented, without admitting or denying the SEC's allegations, to the entry of a final judgment that permanently enjoins him from violating sections 30A and 13(b)(5) of the Securities Exchange Act of 1934 and Rules 13a-14, 13b2-1, and 13b2-2 thereunder, and from aiding and abetting Innospec's violations of Exchange Act sections 30A, 13(b)(2)(A), and 13(b)(2)(B). Jennings agreed to disgorge $116,092 plus prejudgment interest of $12,945, and to pay a penalty of $100,000 that took into consideration his cooperation in this matter.

AB.   *SEC v. IBM Corp.*[74]

► **Misconduct Category:**	Improper cash payments, gifts (cameras, computers, and computer equipment), and payments of travel and entertainment expenses government officials by IBM Korean subsidiaries and IBM joint venture in order to secure the sale of IBM products; use of joint venture partners to funnel bribes; absence of training program, expense accounts controls
► **Countries:**	China, South Korea
► **Foreign Government Officials:**	Officials of South Korean government entities and unspecified Chinese government officials
► **Improper Payment Dollar Value:**	$207,000
► **Combined Penalties:**	$10 million (disgorgement: $5.3 million; prejudgment interest: $2.7 million; and civil penalty of $2 million)
► **Other:**	Shopping bags of cash delivered to Korean government officials in parking lots; payments to the bank account of a "hostess in a drink shop"; joint venture liability: IBM had a 51 percent majority interest while LG Electronics Inc. had a 49 percent interest; widespread practice by over 100 employees of providing overseas trips, entertainment, and improper gifts to government officials; deficient internal controls allowed employees of IBM's subsidiaries and joint venture to use local business partners and travel agencies as conduits for bribes or other improper payments over ten-year period
► **Related Matter:**	*SEC v. IBM* (2000): IBM settled FCPA violations with the SEC that related to bribes by an Argentine subsidiary and was fined $300,000. The large fine of $10 million in 2011 likely reflects a recidivist factor. SDNY Judge Richard Leon insisted upon stringent court and SEC reporting requirements.

In March 2011, the SEC charged IBM with violating the books-and-records and internal controls provisions of the FCPA as a result of the provision of improper cash payments, gifts, and travel and entertainment to government officials in South Korea and China.

As alleged in the SEC's complaint in the Southern District of New York, from 1998 to 2003, employees of IBM Korea, Inc., an IBM subsidiary, and LG IBM PC Co., Ltd., a joint venture in which IBM held a 51 percent interest and LG Electronics of Korea held a 49 percent interest, paid cash bribes and provided improper gifts and payments of travel and entertainment expenses to various government officials in South Korea in order to secure the sale of IBM products. The foreign officials worked for 16 South Korean government entities. Payments were disguised as "payments for installation services" and "reimbursements." IBM's Korean joint venture partner provided free computers to key decision makers to entice them to purchase products or provide them information to assist in the bidding process. Entertainment payments included payments to the bank account of a "hostess in a drink shop."

It was further alleged that, from at least 2004 to early 2009, employees of IBM (China) Investment Company Limited and IBM Global Services (China) Co., Ltd. (collectively, IBM-China), both wholly owned IBM subsidiaries, engaged in a widespread practice of providing overseas trips, entertainment, and improper gifts to Chinese government officials. IBM-China entered into contractual agreements with government-owned or government-controlled customers in China for hardware, software, and other services. The contracts contained provisions requiring IBM-China to provide training to customer employees. In some cases, IBM held this training off-site and required the customers to travel. In advance of training, IBM-China employees were required to submit a delegation trip request (DTR). IBM-China's policies required customers to pay for side trips and stopovers unrelated to training and for IBM-China managers to approve all DTRs.

IBM's internal controls failed to detect over a six-year period at least 114 instances in which (1) IBM employees and its local travel agency worked together to create fake invoices to match approved DTRs; (2) trips were not connected to any DTRs; (3) trips involved unapproved sightseeing itineraries for Chinese government employees; (4) trips had little or no business content; (5) trips involved one or more deviations from the approved DTR; and (6) trips were per diem payments and were provided to Chinese government officials.

IBM-China also used its official travel agency in China to funnel money that was approved for legitimate business trips to fund unapproved trips. IBM-China personnel utilized the company's procurement process to designate its preferred travel agents as "authorized training providers." IBM-China personnel then submitted fraudulent purchase requests for "training services" from those "authorized training providers" and caused IBM-China to pay these vendors. The money paid to these vendors was used to pay for unapproved trips by Chinese government employees.

IBM consented to the entry of a final judgment that permanently enjoined the company from violating the FCPA's books-and-records and internal controls provisions. IBM also agreed to pay disgorgement of $5.3 million, $2.7 million in prejudgment interest, and a $2 million civil penalty. Judge Richard Leon, as part of his oversight responsibility, required IBM to submit to him and to the SEC annual reports regarding IBM's FCPA compliance efforts. Noting that IBM has a history of FCPA books-and-records violations, Judge Leon further insisted that IBM report to him and the SEC "immediately upon learning that it is reasonably likely" IBM violated the FCPA and to report within 60 days of learning that it is the subject of "any investigation or enforcement proceeding by any federal government agency, a party to any major civil litigation in the United States or the subject of any criminal investigation by the Department of Justice."[75] IBM has resisted these reporting requirements. The $10 million penalty imposed for $207,000 worth of improper payments likely reflects a recidivist factor that considers the FCPA misconduct of IBM in Argentina that IBM settled with the SEC in 2000.

AC.   *In re* Ball Corp.[76]

▶ **Misconduct Category:**	Improper payments to Argentine customs officials by customs agents to declare new equipment as being "used" and to reduce tariffs on the exportation of scrap copper
▶ **Country:**	Argentina
▶ **Foreign Government Officials:**	Argentina customs officials
▶ **Improper Payment Dollar Value:**	$106,479
▶ **Penalty:**	$300,000
▶ **Other:**	Postacquisition due diligence failure; bribes disguised on books and records as "customs advice," "professional fees," and "customs advisory services"; Ball accounts discovered improper payments postacquisition, yet payments continued for 18 months; voluntary disclosure and cooperation in a related investigation; no DOJ action and no SEC press release

In April 2011, the SEC charged that Ball Corporation, a Broomfield, Colorado, manufacturer of metal packaging for beverages, foods, and household products, paid through an Argentine subsidiary, Formametal, S.A., bribes totaling at least $106,749 to employees of the Argentine government to secure the importation of prohibited used machinery and the exportation of scrap copper at reduced tariffs. The SEC alleged that some of the payments and compliance failures occurred prior to Ball's March 2001 acquisition and that Ball failed to take adequate steps to ensure such activities did not recur at Ball-controlled Formametal. Soon after Ball acquired Formametal two (then) senior executives at the subsidiary authorized improper payments to Argentine officials. These payments and others were mischaracterized in Formametal's books and records as "customs assistance," "customs advisory services," "verification charge[s]," "fees," or "advice fees for temporary merchandise exported" and went undetected for more than a year. Even after being detected and reclassified, some improper payments were still inaccurately recorded as ordinary business "interest" or "miscellaneous" expenses in the books and records.

The SEC charged that Ball violated the FCPA's internal controls provision by failing to devise and maintain an effective system of internal controls. Such internal controls violations continued even after senior Ball officers were notified in mid-2006 that Formametal's employees had made questionable payments and caused other compliance issues. Ball failed to promptly terminate the responsible employees. Inadequate internal controls allowed, for example, equipment to be imported into Argentina without appropriate documentation and made it difficult to detect that Formametal paid bribes to facilitate the imports. Another internal controls failure occurred when key personnel responsible for dealing with customs officials remained at Formametal even though due diligence indicated Formametal had previously authorized questionable customs payments and Ball's executives were made aware of such issues as a result of the diligence. Ball agreed to pay a civil penalty of $300,000. The SEC recognized Ball's voluntary disclosure and cooperation in a related investigation.

AD.   *In re* Rockwell Automation, Inc.[77]

▶ **Misconduct Category:**	Bribes to influence purchase of products; travel and entertainment abuses, including sightseeing and other nonbusiness trips for employees of state-owned enterprises
▶ **Country:**	China
▶ **Foreign Government Officials:**	Employees of state-owned entities
▶ **Improper Payment Dollar Value:**	$1,065,000
▶ **Combined Penalties:**	$2,761,091 ($400,000 civil penalty, $1,771,000 disgorgement of profits and $590,091 prejudgment interest)
▶ **Other:**	Payments of $615,000 to employees of state-owned design institutes to influence the award of engineering contracts. Payment of $450,000 to fund sightseeing and other nonbusiness trips for state-owned company employees. Rockwell, unable to substantiate the specific services of the design institutes or the value of design institute services, was charged with a books-and-records violation. Civil penalties in SEC administrative proceeding.

In May 2011, Rockwell Automation, Inc., a global company engaged in the design and manufacture of industrial automation products and services, with principal executive offices in Milwaukee, Wisconsin, agreed to settle an administrative action involving FCPA books-and-records and internal controls charges by paying $2,761,098 to the SEC. Rockwell made improper payments over a four-year period through one of its subsidiaries in Shanghai, China, Rockwell Automation Power Systems (Shanghai) Ltd. (RAPS-China), which Rockwell later divested.

Specifically, the SEC alleged that from 2003 to 2006, certain employees of RAPS-China paid approximately $615,000 to design institutes, which are typically state-owned enterprises that provide design engineering and technical integration services and that can influence contract awards by end-user state-owned customers. The payments were made through third-party intermediaries at the request of design institute employees and at the direction of RAPS-China's marketing and sales director. RAPS-China's marketing and sales director intended that these funds be paid directly to the design institute employees, with the expectation that they would influence the ultimate state-owned customers to purchase RAPS products. While the design institutes did provide some bona fide engineering and other services in connection with RAPS-China's end-user contracts, RAPS-China could not substantiate the specific services rendered or the value of those services that were recorded as a "cost of sales." One lesson here is that companies must be able to contemporaneously substantiate the value of any services. Rockwell realized approximately $1.7 million in net profits on sales contracts with end-user Chinese government-owned companies that were associated with payments to the design institutes. Also during the same period, employees of RAPS-China paid approximately $450,000 to fund sightseeing and other nonbusiness trips for employees of design institutes and other state-owned companies.

In offering to settle, Rockwell agreed that it failed to accurately record the payments in its books and records, and failed to implement to or maintain a system of internal accounting controls sufficient to prevent and detect the payments. The company agreed to pay disgorgement of $1,771,000, prejudgment interest of $590,091, and a civil money penalty of $400,000. Rockwell acknowledged that because of its cooperation in the investigation, the SEC was not imposing a civil penalty in excess of $400,000. Pursuant to the recent Dodd-Frank amendments, the SEC here sought civil penalties in an administrative proceeding when, historically, penalties in administrative proceedings have been generally limited to broker-dealers and investment advisors.

AE.   Tenaris: SEC Deferred Prosecution Agreement[78] and DOJ Nonprosecution Agreement[79]

▶ **Misconduct Category:**   Bribes paid to sales agents to influence
                                         Uzbekistan state-owned agency
                                         procurement process

▶ **Country:**   Uzbekistan

▶ **Foreign Government Officials:**   Officials of a subsidiary of Uzbekneftegaz,
                                         the state-owned holding company of
                                         Uzbekistan's oil and gas industry

▶ **Improper Payment Dollar Value:**   Approximately $5 million

▶ **Combined Penalties:** $8.9 million (DOJ: $3.5 million
                                         criminal penalty; SEC: $5.4 million
                                         in disgorgement of profits and
                                         prejudgment interest)

▶ **Other:**   First SEC FCPA DPA; first FCPA case
                                against a Luxembourg company; two-
                                year DOJ NPA; Caspian Sea regional
                                sales represented only 1 percent of
                                parent's sales; Tenaris had no office in
                                Uzbekistan and paid an agent 3.5 percent
                                commission as part of a "dirty business."
                                Audit committee commended for prompt
                                retention of law firm to investigate
                                certain sales agent payments and prompt
                                reporting of same to the SEC.

In May 2011, the SEC entered into its first FCPA DPA with Tenaris, S.A., a Luxembourg-based global manufacturer and supplier of steel-type products and related services. The SEC alleged that in 2006 and 2007, Tenaris bribed Uzbekistan government officials during a bidding process to supply pipelines for transporting oil and natural gas. The company made almost $5 million in profits when it was awarded four contracts by Uzbekistan and agreed to pay $5.4 million in disgorgement of profits and prejudgment interest. In May 2011, Tenaris also agreed to pay a $3.5 million criminal penalty as part of a two-year DOJ NPA.

According to the Tenaris, S.A. NPA Statement of Facts,[80] Tenaris's operations included supplying steel pipe and related services in the Caspian Sea region, including Uzbekistan. Tenaris had no offices in Uzbekistan but rather operated from offices in Azerbaijan and Kazakhstan; and its Caspian Sea business represented only 1 percent of the company's total global sales between 2003 and 2008. Tenaris often used agents to assist in bidding on oil field service contracts solicited by state-owned companies or governmental agencies. From April 2006 to May 2007 Tenaris bid on a series of contracts with OJSC O'ztashqineftgaz (OAO), a wholly owned subsidiary of Uzbekneftegaz, the state holding company of Uzbekistan's oil and gas industry.

In December 2006, Tenaris was introduced to a potential agent who offered the company access to confidential bidding information of competitors obtained from officials in OAO's tender department who would allow Tenaris to submit revised bids after reviewing the confidential competitor bid information. Obviously, this arrangement increased the likelihood that Tenaris would and did win underlying contracts.

In a Christmas Day 2006 e-mail, a Tenaris employee described the services the company could obtain as follows:

> So dirty game is when . . . people from the [OAO] tender department . . . can carefully open required bids and check the prices and deliveries of competitors and advise for where you need to be lower and where you need to be higher . . . And if you decide to revise your prices & delivery, it can be done and physically your commercial offer will be replaced by a revised offer and envelope will be sealed again. But this is very risky for them also, because if people get caught while doing this they will go automatically to jail. So as [OAO agent] said, that's why this dirty service is expensive. . . .[81]

Beginning in January 2007, Tenaris retained this agent and agreed to pay a fee (3.5 percent of the successful bid) for such services. The Statement of Facts alleges that certain Tenaris employees were "aware or substantially certain that all or a portion of such money would be offered by the OAO agent to one or more OAO employees." Tenaris employees used the term "left handed" to refer to illegal activities of the agent. The company obtained four contracts worth $19.4 million utilizing this agency agreement.

Tenaris agreed to pay the DOJ a $3.5 million penalty as part of the NPA and to pay the SEC $5.4 million in disgorgement and interest as part of the DPA. In conferring its first FCPA DPA, the SEC stated that with respect to disclosure, Tenaris's audit committee promptly retained a law firm to investigate certain sales agent payments; the company filed and described, within 90 days and in a Form 27, a customer's allegation, the internal investigation, and its meeting with the Fraud Section. The internal investigation included a worldwide investigation of its business operations and controls, and the company provided "extensive, thorough, real-time cooperation" with the DOJ and SEC staffs. U.S. authorities also recognized that the Luxembourg-based company undertook steps to update and improve its compliance program, including adoption of a strengthened code of conduct, business conduct policy, and agent retention procedures to address anticorruption and compliance with the FCPA, and provided for enhanced due diligence procedures related to the retention of third-party agents and review of payments to third-party agents. It is unclear how the above cooperation differed from what other companies have provided in cooperating with the SEC and obtaining standard SEC consent decrees.

Tenaris paid collective DOJ and SEC penalties almost double the amount of the improper payments. While the DPA spared Tenaris an injunction and the attendant court supervision and does not bear the arguable additional adverse publicity of a formal SEC consent decree and proceeding, the collateral estoppel effects for Tenaris here remain uncertain. Pursuant to the SEC DPA, the company acknowledged a Statement of Facts whereas, under a standard consent decree, a company neither admits nor denies the underlying allegations. At the same time Tenaris with the DOJ, "acknowledged responsibility for the conduct of its employees, agencies and subsidiaries" set forth in a Statement of Facts. It remains to be seen how much better, if at all, an SEC DPA is than a consent decree, particularly in the situation where the DOJ does not bring a parallel action requiring an acknowledgement of facts.

AF.   *In re* Diageo plc[82]

▶ **Misconduct Category:** Pervasive practice of improper payments to various government officials, including customs, excise tax, and military officials, to obtain sales and tax benefits

▶ **Countries:** India, South Korea, and Thailand

▶ **Foreign Government Officials:**   Employees of Indian government, Korean customs and military officials, and senior Thai official

▶ **Improper Payment Dollar Value:** $2.7 million

▶ **Combined Penalties:** $16,373,820 ($11,306,081 disgorgement, $2,067,739 prejudgment interest, and $3 million civil penalty)

▶ **Other:**   Gifts, commissions, travel and entertainment, and lobbying abuses; side trips; ten years to improve compliance programs after major merger and acquisition activity beginning in 1997

In July 2011 the SEC issued a cease-and-desist order, finding that Diageo plc, through its wholly owned subsidiaries in India (DI), Thailand (DT), and South Korea (DK), made over $2.7 million in illicit payments to various government officials from 2003 to 2009 to obtain liquor sales and tax benefits. Diageo, a leading producer and/or distributor of premium branded spirits, beer, and wine headquartered in London, was formed in 1997 from the merger of Guinness plc and Grand Metropolitan plc. As a result of that merger, Diageo acquired its Indian subsidiary, DI, and an indirect majority economic interest in and operational control of its Thai joint venture, DT. The SEC alleged that at the time of its acquisitions, Diageo understood that its new subsidiaries had weak compliance policies, procedures, and controls and that Diageo's history of rapid multinational expansion through mergers and acquisitions contributed to defects in its FCPA compliance programs. Diageo's American depositary shares trade on the New York Stock Exchange. The SEC alleged that Diageo and its subsidiaries failed to account for the illicit payments in their books and records and failed to devise and maintain internal account controls sufficient to detect and prevent the payments.

The SEC alleged that from 2003 to 2009, DI paid $792,310 through third-party distributors to over 900 employees of Indian government liquor stores in or around Delhi to increase sales and improve product placement, as well as $185,299 in "cash service fees" to reimburse these distributors for payments made to government employees. The SEC further alleged that DI reimbursed $530,955, and made plans to reimburse an additional $79,364, to third-party sales promoters who made improper cash payments to Indian government employees of the military Canteen Stores Department to promote DI's products, obtain listings and registration for Diageo's brands, and secure the release of seized shipments. The SEC alleged that DI also paid $78,622 in commissions to reimburse distributors for payments to Indian excise officials to secure import permits and administrative approvals. DI allegedly failed to properly account for these payments and fees. The SEC described the practice of making illicit direct and indirect payments to governmental officials throughout India for liquor sales as "pervasive."

In Thailand, the SEC alleged that from April 2004 to July 2008, DT paid approximately $12,000 per month for 49 months, a total of $599,322, to a consulting firm, knowing this money was for the benefit of an active Thai government official who was a principal in the consulting firm. The Thai official was a broker of one of DT's senior officers at the time. The official lobbied on behalf of DT in customs and tax disputes between Diageo and the Thai government, and met with senior commerce, finance, and customs authorities, as well as the prime minister and members of the Thai parliament. DT allegedly improperly accounted for the monthly retainer paid to the Thai official.

According to the SEC's order, Diageo also made significant payments to tax and customs officials in South Korea. During negotiations on a difficult tax dispute, DK paid $109,253 in travel and entertainment costs to Korean customs and other government officials. After negotiations with South Korean officials on tax issues resulting in the grant of a rebate of approximately $50 million to DK, a DK manager allegedly paid the equivalent of $86,339 to a Korean Customs Service official by means of a kickback to a third-party customs broker. The SEC alleged that DK improperly and falsely accounted for this cash reward payment and for travel and entertainment expenses to other officials. The SEC also alleged that from 2002 to 2006, DK made payments of at least $229,415 in the form of holiday or business development gifts to South Korea military officials to obtain or maintain business and secure a competitive business advantage. DK allegedly failed to properly account for these gifts.

Diageo agreed to cease and desist from committing or causing any violations or any future violations of the accounting provisions of the Act. Diageo also agreed to pay disgorgement of $11,306,081, prejudgment interest of $2,067,739, and a civil penalty of $3 million.

AG. *In re* Watts Water Technologies, Inc. & Chang[83]

▶ **Misconduct Category:**	Improper payments by a wholly owned Chinese subsidiary to design institute employees to influence design institutes to recommend subsidiary products to project SOEs and to include specifications in their design proposals that would increase the likelihood that SOEs would select subsidiary products
▶ **Country:**	China
▶ **Foreign Government Officials:**	Employees of design institutes
▶ **Improper Payment Dollar Value:**	Unspecified
▶ **Combined Penalties:**	Watts: $3,776,606 ($2,755,815 disgorgement of profits; $820,791 prejudgment interest; and $200,000 civil penalty). Leesen Chang: $25,000 civil penalty.

▶ **Other:**   Payments to design institutes were
                                disguised as sales commissions. Vice
                                president of sales Chang took affirmative
                                steps to keep U.S. parent management
                                in the dark about improper payment
                                scheme. E-mail by Chang stated that
                                "involving U.S. parent management"
                                might cause Chinese subsidiary to "lose
                                many flexibility [sic] on working with
                                sale, sale agent and end buyer." Fourth
                                FCPA resolution involving abuse of
                                design institutes in China; strong legal
                                department response and remedial
                                measures in wake of FCPA training and
                                disclosure of problematic conduct; no
                                DOJ criminal charges.

In October 2011, Watts Water Technologies, Inc. (Watts), a Delaware designer, manufacturer, and seller of water valves and related products based in North Andover, Massachusetts, and Leesen Chang, a U.S. national and general manager of Watts's subsidiary in China, resolved FCPA allegations with the SEC and agreed to pay combined penalties of $3,796,606 and $25,000, respectively. The consent decree involved books-and-records and internal controls provisions of the FCPA. This is the fourth FCPA resolution involving improper payments to design institutes in China. (*See* ITT Corporation, Avery Dennison, and Rockwell Automation.) Because there was no evidence that the U.S. parent company was aware of the misconduct in China and the matter involves the potentially problematic design institute practice in China, a detailed review of the facts is appropriate.

Watts, an issuer listed on the New York Stock Exchange, designed, manufactured, and sold water valves and related products through its wholly owned subsidiary Watts Regulator Company, maintaining operations in North America, Europe, and China. It managed its Chinese subsidiaries through Watts (Shanghai) Management Co., Ltd. (Watts China), headquartered in Shanghai. Watts consolidated CWV's books and records into its financial statements, and CWV's revenues accounted for approximately 1 percent of Watts's gross revenues. Watts China is a Watts wholly owned foreign enterprise headquartered in Shanghai that managed the operations of Watts's manufacturing subsidiaries located in China, including CWV during the period of Watts's ownership. Although Watts had significant operations in China prior to CWV's purchase of Changsha Valve, CWV was Watts's first experience with a Chinese subsidiary that conducted business predominantly with SOEs. Watts's other Chinese subsidiaries are primarily engaged in the manufacture of products destined for sale or distribution to nongovernmental entities in China, the United States, and Europe.

The violations took place at Watts Valve Changsha Co., Ltd. (CWV), a wholly owned Chinese subsidiary and foreign enterprise that Watts established in November 2005 to purchase the assets and businesses of Changsha Valve Works (Changsha

Valve). CWV acquired Changsha Valve in April 2006 and Watts sold CWV in January 2010. CWV produced and supplied large valve products for infrastructure projects in China. Infrastructure projects in China are mostly developed, constructed, and owned by project SOEs. Project SOEs routinely retain state-owned design institutes to assist in the design and construction of their projects.

Employees of CWV made improper payments to employees of certain design institutes. The purpose and effect of those payments was to influence the design institutes to recommend CWV valve products to project SOEs and to create design specifications that favored CWV valve products. CWV's improper payments generated profits for Watts of more than $2.7 million. The payments were disguised as sales commissions in CWV's books and records, thereby causing Watts's books and records to be inaccurate. Watts failed to devise and maintain a system of internal accounting controls sufficient to prevent and detect the payments.

The SEC alleged that Chang, while serving as vice president of sales at Watts China between November 2008 and June 2009 and as interim general manager of CWV from April to November 2008, approved many of the payments to the design institutes and knew or should have known that the payments were improperly recorded on Watts's books as commissions. Chang maintained a residence in Los Angeles, California, but lived most of the year in China, where he was employed at the time of the October 2011 resolution.

As vice president of sales at Watts China and interim general manager of CWV, Chang was among those responsible for maintaining and enforcing Watts's policies and procedures, including the company's general prohibition against improper payments to SOEs. Nonetheless, Chang approved commission payments to CWV sales personnel that he knew included payments to design institutes. In fact, Chang signed commission payment approval requests that explicitly itemized payments of 3 percent to design institutes. Chang also knew that Watts's management in the United States was unaware of the CWV sales policy that facilitated the improper payments, and he resisted at least one attempt by several of his colleagues at Watts China to have the policy translated and submitted to Watts's senior management for approval. In an e-mail discussing this issue, Chang stated that "China sale policy should stay in control within China regional operation" because involving Watts's management in the United States might cause CWV to "lose many flexibility [sic] on working with sale, sale agent and end buyer." Accordingly, the SEC alleged Chang knew or should have known that, pursuant to the CWV sales policy, payments to design institutes were recorded in Watts's books and records as sales commissions. In addition, Chang's resistance to efforts to have the sales policy translated and submitted to Watts's management in the United States was a cause of Watts's internal controls violations, since it prevented the parent company from discovering the improper payments.

The SEC alleged that Watts failed to implement adequate internal controls to address the potential FCPA problems posed by its ownership of CWV—a subsidiary that sold its products almost exclusively to SOEs. In addition, although Watts implemented an FCPA policy in October 2006, Watts failed to conduct adequate FCPA training for its employees in China until July 2009. During the period of Watts's ownership, CWV sales personnel made payments to employees of certain design institutes to influence the design institutes to recommend CWV products to project SOEs and to include specifications in their design proposals that would increase the likelihood that project SOEs would select CWV products. The improper payments were facilitated by the CWV sales policy, an incentive policy that was created by Changsha Valve prior to its acquisition by CWV and adopted by CWV in December 2006. The CWV sales policy provided, among other things, that all sales-related expenses, including travel, meals, entertainment, and payment of "consulting fees" to design institutes, would be borne by the CWV sales employees out of their commissions, which were equal to 7 percent to 7.5 percent of the contract price, depending on the size of the contract. The CWV sales policy further provided that sales personnel at CWV could utilize their commissions to make payments to design institutes of up to 3 percent of the total contract amount. As a result, the payments to design institutes were improperly recorded in Watts's consolidated books and records as sales commissions. The CWV sales policy was never translated into English or submitted to Watts's management in the United States.

In March 2009, Watts's general counsel learned of an SEC enforcement action against another company[84] that involved unlawful payments to employees of Chinese design institutes. Because Watts's senior management in the United States knew that CWV's customers included project SOEs, Watts implemented anticorruption and FCPA training for its Chinese subsidiaries. This training took place starting in the spring of 2009. In July 2009, following FCPA training sessions for certain management of Watts China, Watts China's in-house corporate counsel became aware of potential FCPA violations at CWV through conversations with CWV sales personnel who were participating in the training. Shortly thereafter, the in-house lawyer notified Watts's management in the United States of the potential violations.

In July 2009, Watts retained outside counsel to conduct an internal investigation of CWV's sales practices. Watts's outside counsel subsequently retained forensic accountants to assist with the investigation. In August 2009, Watts self-reported its internal investigation to the SEC. As the internal investigation progressed, Watts shared the results of the investigation with its outside auditors and SEC staff through periodic reports, and undertook the remedial measures described below. Between the discovery of the conduct in July 2009 and the resolution in October 2011, Watts took the following remedial steps: At the start of its internal investigation, Watts directed all of its sales and finance employees at CWV and Watts China to stop all payments of any kind to SOEs. While the internal investigation was ongoing, Watts eliminated commission-based compensation at CWV to ensure that no further improper payments were made by CWV sales personnel and disclosed the internal investigation in its August 7, 2009, Form 10-Q. In addition, Watts retained additional outside counsel to draft and implement enhanced anticorruption policies and procedures, including an enhanced antibribery policy, a business courtesy policy designed to ensure that any payments made to customers comply with the FCPA, an enhanced travel and entertainment expense reimbursement policy for its Chinese subsidiaries, and enhanced intermediary due diligence procedures.

In conjunction with its internal investigation, Watts conducted a worldwide anticorruption audit. As part of its anticorruption audit, Watts conducted additional FCPA and anticorruption training for Watts China and the company's locations in Europe, conducted a risk assessment and anticorruption compliance review of Watts's international operations in Europe, China, and any U.S. location with international sales, and conducted anticorruption testing at seven international Watts sites, including each of the manufacturing and sales locations in China. In an effort to ensure FCPA compliance and training going forward, Watts contracted with an online global training organization to provide regular anticorruption training and hired a director of legal compliance, a new position that reports to Watts's general counsel regarding issues under the code of conduct and antibribery policy.

The SEC alleged that as evidenced by the extent and duration of the improper payments and the fact that Watts management was unaware of the CWV sales policy that facilitated the improper payments, Watts failed to devise and maintain a system of internal accounting controls sufficient to provide reasonable assurances that it maintained accountability for its assets, and that its transactions were executed in accordance with management's authorization and recorded as necessary to permit the preparation of financial statements in conformity with GAAP. Watts also failed to implement an FCPA compliance and training program commensurate with the extent of its international operations and its ownership of CWV, a subsidiary that sold its products almost exclusively to SOEs. Accordingly, Watts failed to implement an adequate system of internal controls.[85]

Under these facts and circumstances, the DOJ elected not to file any criminal charges against Watts or Chang. In determining to accept Watts's Offer of Settlement, and agreeing to a cease-and-desist order, the SEC considered remedial acts promptly undertaken by Watts and the cooperation afforded the SEC staff. Watts agreed to pay the U.S. Treasury disgorgement of $2,755,815, prejudgment interest of $820,791, and a civil money penalty of $200,000. Chang agreed to pay the U.S. Treasury a civil penalty of $25,000. The remedial steps of an appointment of a compliance director, an enhanced anticorruption policy, enhanced intermediary due diligence, and a new business courtesy policy are measures that multinational corporations, their counsel, and compliance officers should consider.

AH.   *SEC v. Jackson & Ruehlen;*[86] *SEC v. O'Rourke*[87]

▶ **Misconduct Category:**   Approval of payments to Nigerian customs agents to pass them on to Nigerian government officials in order to obtain temporary importation permits (TIPs) and TIP extensions for the employer's drilling rigs

▶ **Country:**   Nigeria

▶ **Foreign Government Officials:**   Customs officials

▶ **Improper Payment Dollar Value:**   Hundreds of thousands of dollars of bribes

▶ **Combined Penalties:**   Undetermined as to Jackson and Ruehlen; $35,000 as to O'Rourke

▶ **Other:**   Control person theory of liability against former CEO Jackson: charge and consent decree against former internal audit director; concealment of payments from outside auditors and audit committee

▶ **Related Matters:**   U.S. DOJ–Noble Corporation Agreement; *SEC v. Noble Corp.*

In February 2012, the SEC charged, as part of a sweep of the oil services industry, three Noble Corporation oil services executives in the Southern District of Texas with violating the FCPA by participating in a bribery scheme to obtain illicit permits for oil rigs in Nigeria in order to retain business under lucrative drilling contracts.[88] The SEC alleged that Noble CEO Mark A. Jackson, along with James J. Ruehlen, director and division manager of Noble's subsidiary in Nigeria, bribed customs officials to process false paperwork purporting to show the export and reimport of oil rigs, when in fact the rigs never moved. The scheme was designed to save Noble from losing business and incurring significant costs associated with exporting rigs from Nigeria and then reimporting them under new permits. The SEC alleged that bribes were paid through a customs agent for Noble's Nigerian subsidiary with Jackson and Ruehlen's approval.

The SEC separately charged Thomas F. O'Rourke, who was a controller and head of internal audit at Noble with helping approve the bribe payments and allowing the bribes to be booked improperly as legitimate operating expenses for the company. O'Rourke agreed to settle the SEC's charges and pay a $35,000 penalty. In November 2010, Noble was charged by the SEC with FCPA violations as part of a sweep of the oil services industry. The company, which entered into an NPA with the DOJ, cooperated with investigators and agreed to pay $8.1 million to the DOJ and SEC to settle both civil and criminal matters.

According to the SEC's complaint against Jackson and Ruehlen, the executives who perpetrated the scheme worked at Noble and its Nigerian subsidiary Noble Drilling (Nigeria) Ltd, whose rigs operated in Nigeria on the basis of temporary import permits granted by the Nigeria Customs Service (NCS). These temporary permits allowed the rigs to be in the country for a one-year period. NCS had the discretion to grant up to three extensions lasting six months each, after which the rigs were required to be exported and reimported under a new temporary permit or be permanently imported with the payment of sizeable duties. The SEC alleged that Jackson and Ruehlen had a role in arranging, facilitating, approving, making, or concealing the bribe payments to induce Nigerian customs officials to grant new temporary permits illegally and favorably exercise or abuse their discretion to grant permit extensions. Together, Jackson and Ruehlen allegedly participated in paying hundreds of thousands of dollars in bribes to obtain about 11 illicit permits and 29 permit extensions. According to the charges, Jackson approved the bribe payments and concealed the payments from Noble's audit committee and auditors. Ruehlen allegedly prepared false documents, sought approval for the bribes, and processed and paid the bribes.

The SEC's complaint against Jackson and Ruehlen alleged that the two directly violated the antibribery provisions as well as the internal controls and false records provisions. It alleged that they aided and abetted Noble's antibribery violations and the books-and-records and internal controls provisions. The complaint further alleged that Jackson as CEO directly violated Exchange Act Rule 13b2-2 by misleading auditors and Exchange Act Rule 13a-14 by signing false certifications of Noble's financial statements. Jackson also was potentially liable as a control person under section 20(a) of the Exchange Act for violations of the antibribery, books-and-records, and internal controls provisions by Noble, Ruehlen, and O'Rourke. On the eve of trial in July 2014, Jackson consented to an injunction for being a control person for Noble's books-and-records violations and Ruehlen consented to an injunction for aiding and abetting books-and-records violations. No civil penalty was imposed on either.[89]

In February 2013, the Supreme Court in *Gabelli v. SEC* held that the five-year statute of limitations under 28 U.S.C. § 2462 runs as applied to the government from when the fraud occurred, not when it is discovered. This opinion, which came down after the SEC had charged defendants in 2012 with conduct occurring between 2003 and 2007, likely was limited in its option in pursuing civil penalties against Jackson and Ruehlen.[90]

AI.   *SEC v. Oracle Corp.*[91]

▶ **Misconduct Category:**	Poor marketing and development fund (MDF) practices and controls; failure to accurately record side funds and to prevent improper use of company funds
▶ **Country:**	India
▶ **Foreign Government Officials:**	India's Ministry of Information Technology and Communications
▶ **Improper Payment Dollar Value:**	Unspecified
▶ **Penalty:**	$2 million
▶ **Other:**	Remedial measures related to MDFs, including firing Oracle India senior channel sales managers and other subsidiary employees; no evidence of improper payments, but false books and records at subsidiary and poor controls at the parent; offers useful distributor lessons especially for high-tech companies; exceptional remedial measures likely avoided on external monitor or consultant requirement

In August 2012, the SEC charged Oracle Corporation, the Redwood Shores, California–based enterprise software firm, with violating the FCPA by failing to prevent a subsidiary from secretly setting aside money off the company's books that was eventually used to make unauthorized payments to phony vendors in India.[92] At the relevant time, Oracle India's typical business model involved selling Oracle software licenses and services through local distributors who had written agreements with Oracle India. In the transactions at issue, Oracle India was heavily involved in identifying and working with the end-user customers in selling products and services to them and negotiating the final price. The purchase order, however, was placed by the customer with Oracle India's distributor. The distributor bought the licenses and services directly from Oracle, and then resold them to the customer at the higher price that had been negotiated by Oracle India. The difference between what the government end user paid the distributor and what the distributor paid

Oracle typically is referred to as "margin," which the distributor generally retained as payment for its services.[93]

The SEC alleged that certain employees of Oracle India Private Limited, an Indian subsidiary, structured transactions with India's government on more than a dozen occasions in a way that enabled Oracle India's distributors to hold approximately $2.2 million of the proceeds in unauthorized side funds. Those Oracle India employees then directed the distributors to make payments out of these side funds to purported local vendors, several of which were merely storefronts that did not provide any services to Oracle. Oracle's subsidiary documented certain payments with fake invoices.

According to the SEC's complaint filed in the U.S. District Court for the Northern District of California, the misconduct at Oracle's India subsidiary occurred from 2005 to 2007. In selling software licenses and services to India's government through local distributors, Oracle had the distributors "park" excess funds from the sales outside Oracle India's books and records. For example, according to the SEC's complaint, Oracle India secured a $3.9 million deal with India's Ministry of Information Technology and Communications in May 2006. As instructed by Oracle India's then sales director, only $2.1 million was sent to Oracle to record as revenue on the transaction, and the distributor kept $151,000 for services rendered. Certain other Oracle India employees further instructed the distributor to park the remaining $1.7 million for "marketing development purposes." Two months later, one of those same Oracle India employees created and provided to the distributor eight invoices for payments to purported third-party vendors ranging from $110,000 to $396,000. In fact, none of these storefront-only third parties provided any services or were included on Oracle's approved vendor list. The third-party payments created the risk that the funds could be used for illicit purposes such as bribery or embezzlement. The SEC's complaint alleged that Oracle violated the FCPA's books-and-records provisions and internal controls provisions by failing to accurately record the side funds that Oracle India maintained with its distributors. Oracle failed to devise and maintain a system of effective internal controls that would have prevented the improper use of company funds.

Oracle agreed to pay a $2 million penalty to settle the SEC's charges. The settlement took into account Oracle's voluntary disclosure of the conduct in India and its cooperation with the SEC's investigation, as well as remedial measures taken by the company, including firing the Oracle India senior channel sales managers and other employees involved in the misconduct and making significant enhancements to its FCPA compliance program. Among the other remedial measures taken to address FCPA risks and controls related to parked funds were conducting due diligence in its partner transactions in India so that Oracle had greater transparency into end-user pricing in government contracts; terminating its relationship with the distributor involved in the transaction at issue; directing its distributors not to allow the creation of side funds; requiring additional representations and warranties from distributors to include the fact that no side funds exist; and enhancing training for its partners and employees to address anticorruption policies.[94] The quality of Oracle's remedial measures may have avoided any independent monitor or an ongoing formal self-assessment requirement.

AJ.   *In re* Allianz SE[95]

▶ **Misconduct Category:**	"Off the books" account of subsidiary served as a slush fund for bribe payments to Indonesian government officials to procure or retain 295 insurance contracts related to large government projects in Indonesia; "overriding commissions" terminology concealing bribery payments; no bribery count filed
▶ **Country:**	Indonesia
▶ **Foreign Government Officials:**	Employees of state-owned entities
▶ **Improper Payment Dollar Value:**	$650,626
▶ **Combined Penalties:**	More than $12.3 million (disgorgement of $5,315,649, prejudgment interest of $1,765,125, and civil money penalty of $5,315,649)
▶ **Other:**	March 2005 complaint led to an internal investigation by special counsel but no reporting to the SEC staff of any misconduct and the misconduct continued. In April 2010 SEC received an anonymous complaint of possible FCPA violations. Case highlights costs of inadequate internal investigations that fail to stop misconduct. Civil money penalty equaled the disgorgement.

In December 2012 the SEC charged the Munich, Germany–based insurance and asset management company Allianz SE with violating the books-and-records and internal controls provisions of the FCPA following improper payments by a majority-owned subsidiary to government officials in Indonesia over a seven-year period.[96] The SEC's investigation uncovered 295 insurance contracts on large government projects that were obtained or retained by improper payments by Allianz's subsidiary in Indonesia to employees of SOEs. Allianz made more than $5.3 million in profits as a result of the improper payments. Allianz, which traded American depositary shares on the New York Stock Exchange through October 2009, agreed to pay more than $12.3 million to settle the SEC's charges.

Between 2001 and 2008 Allianz's majority-owned subsidiary PT Asurani Allianz Utama Indonesia (Utama) managers made improper payments to employees of SOEs in Indonesia in order to obtain and retain business. Utama, which was formed as a joint venture with a wholly owned subsidiary of Allianz and PT Asurani Jasa Indonesia (Jasindo), an SOE that offered general insurance products to individuals and corporate clients.

Allianz learned of the improper payments from two complaints made several years apart. The first complaint was submitted in 2005 alleging significant misconduct, including unsupported payments to agents. A subsequent audit of Utama's

accounting records uncovered that managers at Utama were using "special purpose accounts" to make illicit payments, many to government officials, in order to
secure business in Indonesia. The second complaint was lodged in 2009 to Allianz's
external auditors and alleged that Allianz created illicit off-the-books accounts. In
response, Allianz began an internal investigation. Upon receiving an anonymous
complaint of possible FCPA violations, the SEC opened an investigation in April
2010. The SEC investigation determined that from at least 2001 through December
2008, the Utama managers, with the assistance of others in the Indonesian office,
made payments to employees of SOEs in Indonesia to procure or retain insurance
contracts related to large government projects in Indonesia. As a result of improper
payments of approximately $650,626 to agents and employees of SOEs and oth-
ers, Allianz realized $5,315,649 in profits. The payments were improperly recorded
as legitimate transaction costs, thereby causing Allianz's books and records to be
inaccurate. Allianz failed to devise and maintain a system of internal controls sufficient to provide reasonable assurances to detect and prevent such payments. The
Allianz SE background is a worthwhile study of incomplete audits or investigations and the consequences of failing to stop misconduct.

In 1981, Allianz commenced its operations in Indonesia with a representative
office that provided financing and insurance for large government projects in Indonesia. Simultaneous with the opening of the office, Allianz opened a special purpose bank account with a local Indonesian broker. From 1981 to 1989, the account
was used to pay legitimate commissions to the local Indonesian broker for business it generated for Allianz. In 1989, Allianz established Utama and continued the
practice of using special purpose accounts for paying commissions to agents that
generated business for Allianz. However, in February 2001, an Indonesian agent for
Utama, Utama CEO 1, and Utama's CFO opened a separate, off-the-books account
in the agent's name. This special purpose account was used to make improper payments to employees of Indonesian SOEs and others for the purpose of obtaining
and retaining insurance contracts. In February 2001, the Indonesian agent and
Utama CEO 1 executed a paying agency agreement that set up the scheme to make
the payments to employees of SOEs. This agreement established the off-the-books
account that served as a slush fund to make bribe payments to foreign officials and
others as instructed by Utama.

During the period 2001 to 2005, Utama's marketing manager made payments
from the special purpose account to account introducers employed by SOEs to
secure insurance contracts on large government projects in Indonesia.[97] The marketing manager received approval from Utama management to use the special purpose
account for improper purposes. Utama CEO 2, the CEO from 2003 to 2006, was
aware of the special purpose account and the improper payments to foreign officials.

The improper payments made to foreign officials were disguised in the Utama
insurance contracts as "overriding commissions." Each insurance contract outlined two parts of the overall insurance premium: the technical premium (the
actual cost of the coverage), which was usually 75–95 percent of the premium, and
the nontechnical premium (the overriding commission), which was typically 5–25
percent of the premium. The overriding commission was the portion that was paid
to the foreign official as an inducement to purchase the Utama insurance product.

Once the entire premium was deposited in the Utama bank account and booked in Utama's internal accounting system, Utama's marketing manager would submit a "commission payment request" to the finance department. Once the request was approved the overriding commission portion was transferred to the special purpose account. The marketing manager would withdraw the commission in cash from the special purpose account and deliver the funds to the foreign official. Despite the fact that Allianz has a majority share of Utama and consolidated the subsidiary's accounts into its own books and records, Utama's accounting system was maintained in Indonesia and Allianz did not have effective controls over the accounting. Allianz did not have the ability to access Utama's accounting system and, therefore, did not detect the movement of funds to the special purpose account. In addition, the special purpose account was maintained in the name of the Indonesian agent to make it appear that all movement of funds to this account was for legitimate commission payments. Likewise, Allianz did not have effective controls over the commission payment request process, which allowed payments to go to the special purpose account without supporting documentation.

On December 1, 2005, a whistleblower complaint concerning the special purpose account was submitted to both the Allianz whistleblower hotline and Utama's joint venture partner Jasindo, and then forwarded to the head of Allianz Asia Pacific (AZAP). The complaint itemized a number of control weaknesses, most notably, the existence of the special purpose account and its lack of transparency. On December 8, 2005, Allianz Group Audit initiated an audit of the Indonesian office; however, the review was limited to embezzlement from the company. The audit identified the special purpose account as an account mainly used by the Utama marketing manager as a "vehicle to pay project development and overriding commissions to the special projects and clients for securing business with Utama." It also identified two internal accounts related to the Indonesian agent; one for the agent's normal commissions, and one for "various" purposes. However, no additional steps were taken to determine the nature and purpose of the accounts or to identify the recipients of payments from the accounts. On December 12, 2005, based on the audit findings, Allianz directed the Utama management to close the special purpose account. Although the Utama management agreed to close the account and to stop making the payments, it continued making improper payments to secure business for Allianz through 2008.

Despite the directive to close the account and to stop making payments, the Utama marketing manager continued to use the special purpose account to make improper payments to foreign officials from 2005 to 2008. In an e-mail dated May 20, 2006, the Utama chief technical officer e-mailed the Utama marketing manager and Utama CEO 2 that the finance department had detected that the special purpose account had been used to make payments in connection with two government insurance contracts. The marketing manager acknowledged that he used the special purpose account to make the payments because the account introducers expected to receive the promised improper payments on the government insurance contracts. Utama CEO 2 approved the continued use of the special purpose account to make payments on the two government insurance contracts at issue. Later, the marketing manager and his staff expanded the improper payments to numerous other foreign officials on government insurance contracts.

From 2005 to 2008, the Utama marketing manager employed various methods to make payments to foreign officials. In addition to booking payments through the special purpose account, the marketing manager made payments by either (1) booking commissions to an agent that was not associated with the account for the government insurance contract and then withdrawing the funds booked to the agent's account as cash to pay the foreign official; or (2) overstating the amount of a client's insurance premium, booking the excess amount to an unallocated account and then "reimbursing" the excess funds to the foreign officials, who were responsible for procuring the government insurance contracts.

As with the special purpose account, Allianz did not have effective controls over the Utama accounting system or the commission payment process, which allowed payments to be made to an agent's account without supporting documentation. Allianz did not have any controls over the use of the unallocated account that was maintained at Utama. As a result, the Utama marketing manager was able to take funds from Utama to pay foreign officials without detection. In March 2009, Allianz's outside auditor received an anonymous complaint alleging that an Allianz executive created or initiated slush funds during his tenure with AZAP. Between December 2005, when the Allianz executive vice president of the Asia-Pacific division directed Utama to close the special purpose account, and the March 2009 whistleblower complaint, Allianz took no steps to ensure that the special purpose account was closed and that similar improper payments were not being made.

In response to the March 2009 whistleblower complaint, Allianz convened a whistleblower committee to do an internal investigation and retained counsel to conduct the investigation of Utama's payment practices in Indonesia. Allianz did not report the conduct to the SEC staff. In April 2010, the SEC opened an investigation after receiving an anonymous complaint of possible FCPA violations (this whistleblower complaint preceded Dodd-Frank's passage on July 22, 2010). The staff contacted Allianz concerning the allegations. Allianz's cooperation in the staff's investigation and the timeliness of its response to the SEC's requests for documents and information improved over time. Allianz hired new counsel and took steps to further its cooperation and remedial efforts.

The SEC's investigation uncovered 295 government insurance contracts that were obtained or retained by improper payments of approximately $650,626 to Indonesian government officials and others from 2001 through 2008. In some instances the nature of the improper payments was disguised in invoices as an "overriding commission" or as a commission for an agent that was not associated with the government insurance contract. In other instances the improper payments were structured as an overpayment by the government insurance contract holder, who was later "reimbursed" for the overpayment. The excess funds were then paid to foreign officials, who were responsible for procuring the government insurance contracts.[98]

Allianz took various remedial measures, including employment action against several individuals who were involved in the conduct or failed to stop the conduct. Allianz issued new or enhanced FCPA compliance and internal accounting control policies and procedures, including mandating strict scrutiny of payments to third-party intermediaries. Allianz also updated the anticorruption clause in its third-party contracts to specifically refer to the FCPA. Allianz provided enhanced FCPA compliance training to its employees and improved its current global anticorruption compliance program. Allianz was not charged under the FCPA's antibribery provisions; it is not clear from the SEC order that Allianz used means of interstate commerce to effect any violations. Finally, as Allianz is no longer publicly traded in the United States, it was not subject to a consent decree or any monitor requirement.

AK.   *SEC v. Eli Lilly & Co.*[99]

▶ **Misconduct Category:**	Four types of bribery in four different countries: use of offshore "marketing agreements" to pay millions of dollars to third parties selected by government customers and distributors in Russia; widespread gift abuses in China; deep distribution discount and commission schemes in Brazil; and sponsorship lapses in Poland
▶ **Countries:**	Russia, China, Brazil, and Poland
▶ **Foreign Government Officials:**	Government-employed healthcare providers; person closely associated with a member of Russian parliament director of health authority
▶ **Improper Payment Dollar Value:**	In excess of $7.2 million; visits to bathhouses and karaoke bars
▶ **Combined Penalties:**	$29,398,734 ($13,955,196 disgorgement, prejudgment interest of $6,743,538, and penalty of $8.7 million). Independent compliance consultant requirement.
▶ **Other:**	Company had a "check the box" mentality with respect to third-party due diligence. Leading deep distributor discount and "marketing agreement" case. Nine-year DOJ investigation. E-mail: "I have given [the Health Fund director] a free hand as to managing the Lilly investment, emphasizing we are only doing this for him . . . and we don't need the publicity." Nine-year government investigation; independent compliance consultant; internal audit department criticism.
▶ **Related Matters:**	*In re* Schering-Plough Corp.; *SEC v. Schering-Plough Corp.* (2004)

In December 2012 the SEC charged Eli Lilly and Company in the U.S. District Court for the District of Columbia with violations of the FCPA for improper payments its subsidiaries made to foreign government officials beginning as early as 1994 to win millions of dollars of business in Russia, Brazil, China, and Poland. Outside of the United States, Lilly sells its products, both directly and through distributors and other intermediaries, to government-controlled entities, such as ministries of health and government-owned hospitals and clinics.[100] The SEC alleged that the Indianapolis-based pharmaceutical company's wholly owned subsidiary in Lilly-Vostok Russia used offshore "marketing agreements" to pay millions of dollars to third parties chosen by government customers or distributors, despite knowing little or nothing about the third parties beyond their offshore address and bank account information.[101] These offshore entities rarely provided any services and in some instances were used to funnel money to government officials in order to obtain business for the subsidiary. Transactions with offshore or government-affiliated entities did not receive specialized or closer review for possible FCPA violations. Paperwork was accepted at face value and little was done to assess whether the terms or circumstances surrounding a transaction suggested the possibility of foreign bribery.[102] The SEC further alleged that when the company became aware of possible FCPA violations in Russia, it did not curtail this subsidiary's use of the marketing agreements for more than five years. Lilly subsidiaries in Brazil, China, and Poland also made improper payments to government officials or third-party entities associated with government officials.[103]

Because the Lilly case provides valuable lessons and recurring fact patterns regarding "marketing agreement" abuses (Russia), widespread gift practices (China), a distributor discount scheme (Brazil), and sponsorships (Poland), we provide details near verbatim from the SEC complaint against the pharmaceutical company below.[104]

1. *Russia*[105]

From 1994 through 2005, Lilly-Vostok sold pharmaceutical products either directly to government entities in the former Soviet Union or through various distributors, often selected by the government, who would then resell the products to the government entities. Along with the underlying purchase contract with the government entity or distributor, Lilly-Vostok sometimes entered into another agreement with a third-party selected by a government official or by the government-chosen pharmaceutical distributor. Generally, these third parties, which had addresses and bank accounts located outside of Russia, were paid a flat fee or a percentage of the sale. These agreements were referred to as "marketing" or "service" agreements. In total, Lilly-Vostok entered into over 96 such agreements with over 42 third-party entities between 1994 and 2004.

Lilly-Vostok had little information about these third-party entities, beyond their addresses and bank accounts. Rarely did Lilly-Vostok know who owned them or whether the entities were actual businesses that could provide legitimate services. Senior management employees in Lilly-Vostok's Moscow branch assisted in the negotiation of these agreements. The contracts themselves were derived from a Lilly-Vostok-created template and enumerated various broadly defined services, such as ensuring "immediate customs clearance" or "immediate delivery" of the products; or assisting Lilly-Vostok in "obtaining payment for the sales transaction," "the promotion of the products," and "marketing research."

Contrary to what was recorded in the company's books and records, there was little evidence that any services were actually provided under any of these third-party agreements. In many instances, the "services" identified in the contract were already being provided by the distributor, a third-party handler (such as an international shipping handler) or Lilly itself. To the extent services such as expedited customs clearance or other services requiring interaction with government officials were provided, Lilly-Vostok did not know or inquire how the third party intended to perform their services.

Contemporaneous documents reflected that Lilly-Vostok employees viewed the payments as necessary to obtain the business from the distributor or government entity, and not as payment for legitimate services. For example, in November 1994, a senior manager at Lilly-Vostok e-mailed the commercial manager, the employee tasked with drafting and approving the language of the agreements, that the "standard Marketing Agreement [is] where the [service provider] delivers the service of getting this [purchase] contract for us. . . ." In August 1999, the commercial manager e-mailed senior managers that "if real services are provided the marketing agreement is not the appropriate form." In other documents, Lilly-Vostok employees described the payments as "discounts" or "commissions" to the distributor or government purchaser.

In 1997, Lilly conducted a business review of Lilly-Vostok to identify business risks and assess the subsidiary's policies and procedures, which resulted in a report. The report, which was sent to Lilly-Vostok offices in Geneva and to Lilly headquarters in Indianapolis, noted that "[b]usiness ethics [in Russia] are low" and that "[a] large base of opportunistic entrepreneurs, lacking national presence build the distribution network." The report concluded that "[t]he nature and complexity of customers require that 'consultants' be used to 'support' activities, leading to agreement signing." The report pointed out that the services provided by these consultants were broadly defined and duplicated activities usually performed by Lilly-Vostok's Russian staff, and that documentation of the services received was not available. The report recommended that Lilly-Vostok modify its internal controls to ensure that the services were documented and Lilly-Vostok was getting "value."

In 1999, Lilly again reviewed Lilly-Vostok's operations, including its use of marketing agreements, and concluded that they raised concerns. A second report, which was sent to Geneva and Indianapolis headquarters and distributed to, among others, Lilly's then-current CFO, president of Lilly International Operations, and general auditor, stated:

> Attention has been given to contain external unethical pressures through guidelines and training. The use of marketing agreements with third parties has been tightened; agreements substance and permanent education program continue to require effort and refinements.

Regarding the agreements, the second report concluded that the "[n]eed exists to call on third-parties to create sales potential." It recommended that Lilly-Vostok modify its internal controls to assure itself that the agreements accurately and fairly reflect the services to be provided.

Lilly did not curtail the use of marketing agreements by its subsidiary or make any meaningful efforts to ensure that the marketing agreements were not being used as a method to funnel money to government officials, despite recognition that the marketing agreements were being used to "create sales potential" or "to 'support' activities leading to agreement-signing" with government entities. During the 2000–2004 period—after the above reports, but before the company ended use of the agreements—Lilly-Vostok entered into the three most expensive of these arrangements.

For example, in 2002, the Russian Ministry of Health announced that it would engage in a "federal tender" in which it would purchase drugs for the treatment of diabetes to be provided free of charge to patients by the government. Under the tender terms, the ministry selected a large Russian pharmaceutical distributor from which to purchase the products, and this distributor, in turn, negotiated with Lilly-Vostok for the purchase of diabetes products for resale to the Ministry of Health.

The large Russian pharmaceutical distributor was owned and controlled by a wealthy and prominent Russian businessman. The Russian pharmaceutical distributor required Lilly-Vostok, as a condition of their agreement, to enter into a so-called storage and delivery agreement with an entity incorporated in Cyprus. In July 2002, Lilly-Vostok executed the purchase agreement with the distributor, which was signed on the distributor's behalf by its chairman, the prominent Russian businessman. At approximately the same time, Lilly-Vostok also entered into the storage and delivery agreement with the entity in Cyprus.

Lilly's due diligence regarding the entity in Cyprus was limited to ordering a Dun & Bradstreet report and conducting an Internet search of publicly available information. Neither the report nor the Internet search revealed the Cyprus entity's beneficial owner or anything about its business. Nonetheless, pursuant to the terms of its arrangement with the distributor, Lilly-Vostok paid the entity in Cyprus over $3.8 million in early 2003.

The Cyprus entity was, in fact, owned by the Russian businessman who was the owner of the distributor. There is no evidence of services provided to Lilly-Vostok by the Cyprus entity in consideration for Lilly-Vostok's $3.8 million in payments. Lilly's books and records improperly reflected these payments as payments for services.

In at least two instances, the arrangements involved foreign government officials. Between 2000 and 2005, Lilly-Vostok sold significant amounts of pharmaceutical products to a major Russian pharmaceutical distributor for resale to the Russian Ministry of Health. The pharmaceutical distributor was owned and controlled by an individual who, at the beginning of the distributor's relationship with Lilly-Vostok, was a close advisor to a member of Russia's parliament who exercised considerable influence over government decisions relating to the pharmaceutical industry in Russia.

As part of most of the sales arrangements with the distributor, the official demanded that Lilly-Vostok enter into separate "marketing" agreements with entities with addresses and bank accounts in Cyprus. Under the arrangement, Lilly-Vostok paid the Cypriot entities up to 30 percent of the sales price of the underlying sales contracts in return for the Cypriot entities entering into an agreement "to offer all assistance necessary" in various areas like storage, importation and payment.

In conjunction with outside counsel, Lilly-Vostok conducted limited due diligence on these third parties. However, the due diligence did not identify the beneficial owners of these third parties or determine whether the third parties were able to provide the contracted-for assistance. Nonetheless, Lilly-Vostok concluded that it could proceed with the transactions and paid the Cypriot entities over $5.2 million. In fact, the Cypriot entities were owned by an individual associated with the distributor and controlled by the member of Russia's parliament. The Cypriot entity transferred the payments from Lilly-Vostok to other offshore entities.

In connection with another series of contracts, from 2000 through 2004, Lilly-Vostok sold products to a distributor, headquartered in Moscow, which was wholly owned by a Russian government entity. The purchase agreements were signed on the government-owned distributor's behalf by its general director. As part of the arrangement, the government-owned distributor selected a third-party entity with an address in the British Virgin Islands (BVI) with which Lilly-Vostok entered into agreements for the broadly defined "services" enumerated in the Lilly-Vostok template (see above). Under the terms of the agreements between Lilly-Vostok and the BVI entity, Lilly-Vostok was to pay the BVI entity up to 15 percent of the price of the product purchased by the government-owned distributor. Accordingly, from 2000 through 2005, Lilly-Vostok made approximately 65 payments to the BVI entity totaling approximately $2 million.

There was no evidence that the BVI entity performed any of the services listed in its agreement with Lilly-Vostok. There was also no evidence that Lilly-Vostok performed any due diligence or inquiry as to whether the BVI entity was able or did perform the contracted-for services. Lastly, there was no evidence that Lilly-Vostok performed any due diligence or inquiry into the identity of the beneficial owner of the BVI entity. The beneficial owner of the BVI entity was the general director of the government-owned distributor, and he ultimately received the payments from the BVI entity. Lilly did not direct Lilly-Vostok to cease entering into these third-party agreements until 2004. However, Lilly permitted the subsidiary to continue making payments under already existing third-party contracts as late as 2005. From 2005 through 2008, Lilly-Vostok made various proposals to government officials in Russia regarding how Lilly-Vostok could donate to or otherwise support various initiatives that were affiliated with public or private institutions headed by the government officials or otherwise important to the government officials. Examples included their personal participation or the participation of people from their institutions in clinical trials and international and regional conferences and the support of charities and educational events associated with the institutes. At times, these proposals to government officials were made in a communication that also included a request for assistance in getting a product reimbursed or purchased by the government. Generally, Lilly-Vostok personnel believed these proposals were proper because of their relevance to public health issues and many of the proposals were reviewed by counsel. Nonetheless, Lilly-Vostok did not have in place internal controls through which such proposals were vetted to ascertain whether Lilly-Vostok was offering something of value to a government official for a purpose of influencing or inducing him or her to assist Lilly-Vostok in obtaining or retaining business.

2. *China*[106]

Lilly's wholly owned subsidiary through which it does business in China (Lilly-China) employed more than 1,000 sales representatives whose main focus was on marketing Lilly products to government-employed healthcare providers. The sales representatives worked from regional offices and traveled throughout China, interacting with the healthcare providers in order to convince them to prescribe Lilly products. The sales representatives were directly supervised by district sales managers who, in turn, were supervised by regional managers. Sales representatives paid out-of-pocket for their travel expenses and submitted receipts and other documentation to the company for reimbursement.

Between 2006 and 2009, various sales representatives and their supervisors abused the system by submitting, or instructing subordinates to submit, false expense reports. In some instances, Lilly-China personnel used reimbursements from those false reports to purchase gifts and entertainment for government-employed physicians in order to encourage the physicians to look favorably upon Lilly and prescribe Lilly products.

In one sales area, in 2006 and 2007, a district sales manager for Lilly's diabetes products instructed subordinates to submit false expenses reports and provide the reimbursement money to her. She then used the reimbursements to purchase gifts, such as wine, specialty foods, and a jade bracelet, for government-employed physicians. At least five sales representatives in the oncology sales group submitted false expense reports and then used those reimbursements to provide meals, visits to bathhouses, and card games to government-employed physicians.

Similarly, in three other provinces, three sales representatives submitted false expense reports and then used the reimbursements to provide government-employed physicians with visits to bathhouses and karaoke bars. In another city, five sales representatives submitted false reimbursements and then their regional manager used the money to provide door prizes and publication fees to government-employed physicians. In another city, seven sales representatives and the district sales manager for the diabetes sales team used reimbursements to buy meals and cosmetics for government-employed physicians.

Between 2008 and 2009, members of Lilly-China's "Access Group," which was responsible for expanding access to Lilly products in China by, among other things, convincing government officials to list Lilly products on government reimbursement lists, engaged in similar misconduct. At least six members of the 16-member group, including two associate access directors, falsified expense reports and used the proceeds to provide gifts and entertainment to government officials in China. The gifts included spa treatments, meals, and cigarettes. While the dollar value of each gift was generally small, the improper payments were widespread throughout the subsidiary.

3.   *Brazil*[107]

Between 2007 and 2009, Lilly-Brazil distributed drugs in Brazil through third-party distributors who then resold those products to both private and government entities. As a general rule, Lilly-Brazil sold the drugs to the distributors at a discount; the distributors then resold the drugs to the end users at a higher price and took the discount as their compensation. Lilly-Brazil negotiated the amount of the discount with the distributor based on the distributor's anticipated sale. The distributors discount in Brazil generally ranged between 6.5 percent and 15 percent, with most distributors receiving a 10 percent discount.

In early 2007, at the request of one of Lilly-Brazil's then sales and marketing managers, Lilly-Brazil granted a nationwide pharmaceutical distributor unusually large discounts of 17 percent and 19 percent for two of the distributor's purchases of a Lilly drug, which the distributor then sold to a Brazilian state's government. Lilly-Brazil's pricing committee approved the discounts without further inquiry. The policies and procedures in place to flag unusual distributor discounts were deficient. They relied on the representations of the sales and marketing manager without adequate verification and analysis of the surrounding circumstances of the transactions. In May 2007, Lilly sold 3,200 milligrams of the drug to the distributor for resale to this Brazilian state; in August 2007, Lilly-Brazil sold 13,500 milligrams of the drug to the distributor for resale to the Brazilian state, resulting in combined sales of approximately $1.2 million. The distributor used approximately 6 percent of the purchase price (approximately $70,000) to bribe government officials from the Brazilian state so that the state would purchase the Lilly product. The Lilly-Brazil sales and marketing manager who requested the discount knew of this arrangement.

4.   Poland[108]

During 2000 through 2003, Lilly's wholly owned subsidiary in Poland (Lilly-Poland) made eight payments totaling approximately $39,000 to the Chudow Castle Foundation (Chudow Foundation), a small charitable foundation in Poland that was founded and administered by the director of the Silesian Health Fund. The director established the Chudow Foundation in 1995 to restore the Chudow Castle and other historic sites in the Silesian region of Poland.

The Health Fund, one of 16 regional government health authorities in Poland, reimbursed hospitals and healthcare providers for the purchase of certain approved products. The Health Fund, through the allocation of public money, exercised considerable influence over which pharmaceutical products local hospitals and other healthcare providers in the region purchased.

Beginning in early 2000 and into 2002, Lilly-Poland was in negotiations with the Health Fund over, among other things, the Heath Fund's financing of the purchase of Gemzar, one of Lilly's cancer drugs, by public hospitals and other healthcare providers. Those negotiations occurred primarily between the Health Fund director and a team manager at Lilly-Poland; during these negotiations, the director asked that Lilly-Poland contribute to the Chudow Foundation. He made the initial request directly while subsequent requests came from the foundation.

The Lilly-Poland manager knew that the director had established the Chudow Foundation and that it was a project to which he was devoted and lent much effort. In requesting the approval of payments to the Chudow Foundation, the manager falsely described the first payment as being for the purchase of computers. The second Lilly-Poland payment request falsely characterized the proposed payment as "[t]o support foundation in its goal to develop activities in [Chudow Castle]." That request documentation also noted that the "value of the request" was "[i]ndirect support of educational efforts of foundation settled by Silesia [Health Fund]." The remaining payments were mischaracterized as monies paid by Lilly-Poland to secure the use of the Chudow Castle for postrenovation conferences that never took place.

Lilly-Poland eventually made a total of eight payments totaling approximately $39,000 to the Chudow Foundation, starting in June 2000 and ending in January 2003. The Lilly-Poland manager requested the approval of the payments to the Chudow Foundation with the intent of inducing the Health Fund director to allocate public monies to hospitals and other healthcare providers in the Health Fund for the purpose of purchasing Gemzar. For example, in February 2002, the Health Fund director, after a meeting with the Lilly-Poland manager, authorized financing a purchase of Gemzar. Two days later, the Chudow Foundation sent a letter to Lilly-Poland requesting a payment of 32,000 PLN. An internal record at Lilly-Poland (a spreadsheet titled "Expenses 2002") reflects that this payment to the Chudow Foundation was "for [the director]."

Two Lilly-Poland e-mails also reflect the improper purpose of the payments to the Chudow Foundation. Prior to the first payment, the manager told another Lilly-Poland employee in a May 31, 2000, e-mail that the Health Fund director needed more convincing about purchasing Gemzar. In that e-mail, under the heading "Sponsorships," the manager observed that Lilly-Poland was to pay

> 12,000 zlotys ($2,730) in two installments, not very far removed from each other, to the Chudow Castle Foundation, [the Health Fund director's] hobby, supposedly for the purchase of computers . . . For your information regarding the size of the budget for this year, I decided to invest 70–75% for Silesia. I have given [the Health Fund director] a free hand as to managing the Lilly investment, emphasizing the fact we are only doing this for him . . . and we don't need the publicity.

In a March 19, 2001 e-mail to a Lilly-Poland colleague, the manager noted that one of the tasks was Lilly-Poland's "[d]etermination of the amount of the rebate for the director in connection with the 'Castle' Foundation." In that e-mail, when describing the budget, the manager wrote: "the so-called rebate for the 'Castle' . . . will depend on the purchases of medicines." Accordingly, textual references in both e-mails—"supposedly for the purchase of computers" and "the so-called rebate for the 'Castle'"—underscore the manager's attempts to create a pretext and false justifications for the payments to the Chudow Foundation.

The final seven payments to the Chudow Foundation were approved by the Lilly-Poland medical grant committee (MGC), which included Lilly-Poland's managing director, finance director, and regulatory and medical director. The MGC approved the payments based largely on the justification and description in the submitted paperwork. The MGC procedures did not adequately analyze the circumstances outside the paperwork such as:

1. The Chudow Foundation was a project founded and administered by a high-level government health official who had significant authority over whether the Health Fund would pay for Lilly-Poland products in Silesia, one of Poland's most populous regions.
2. Lilly-Poland was in negotiations to persuade the Health Fund director to finance the purchase of one of Lilly's cancer products at the time of the requests from the Chudow Foundation for payments.

3. The justifications for the first two payments were different from each other and different from the justification given for the remaining six payments.

4. The request for one of the largest payments came two days after the director had met with the manager and agreed to authorize financing the purchase of a large quantity of Gemzar by the Health Fund.

5. The payments to the Chudow Foundation were the only payments by Lilly-Poland to an archeological and/or restoration project, despite the existence of numerous other such projects in Poland at the time.

5. *Internal Audit Department*

The SEC complaint alleged that despite an understanding that certain emerging markets were risky, the company's Indianapolis-based audit department had

> no procedures specifically designed to assess the FCPA or bribery risks of sales and purchases. Accordingly, transactions with offshore entities or with government-affiliated entities did not receive specialized or closer review for possible FCPA notation. In assessing these transactions, the auditors relied upon the standard accounting controls which primarily assumed the soundness of the paperwork. There was little done to assess whether, despite the existence of facially acceptable paperwork, the surrounding circumstances suggested the possibility of an FCPA violation or bribery.[109]

In announcing the settlement of the nine-year old SEC investigation, Kara Novaco Brockmeyer, chief of the SEC Enforcement Division's FCPA Unit, commented, "Eli Lilly and its subsidiaries possessed a 'check the box' mentality when it came to third party due diligence. Companies can't rely on paper-thin assurances by employees, distributors or customers. They need to look at the surrounding circumstances of any payment to adequately assess whether it could wind up in a government official's pocket."[110] Lilly made improvements to its global anticorruption compliance program, including enhancing anticorruption due diligence requirements for relationships with third parties; implementing compliance monitoring and corporate auditing specifically tailored to anticorruption; enhancing financial controls and governance; and expanding anticorruption training throughout the organization.

Lilly agreed to pay disgorgement of $13,955,196, prejudgment interest of $6,743,538, and a penalty of $8.7 million for a total payment of $29,398,734. Lilly consented to the entry of a final judgment permanently enjoining the company from violating the antibribery, books-and-records, and internal controls provisions of the FCPA. Finally, Lilly also agreed to retain an independent consultant to review and make recommendations about its foreign corruption policies and procedures. The Lilly SEC FCPA resolution supports the need for special attention by a multinational internal audit department in emerging markets.

AL.   *In re* Koninklijke Philips Electronics N.V.[111]

▶ **Misconduct Category:**	Improper payments by employees and third parties to secure favorable treatment on public tenders of medical equipment
▶ **Country:**	Poland
▶ **Foreign Government Officials:**	State healthcare officials
▶ **Improper Payment Dollar Value:**	Unspecified
▶ **Combined Penalties:**	$4,515,178 ($3.1 million disgorgement and $1.4 million in prejudgment interest)
▶ **Other:**	Bribes and kickbacks were 3 percent to 8 percent of contract amounts and recorded such percentages of the contracts' net value as commissions; employees kept a portion of the improper payments for themselves; internal audit led to self-reporting to the DOJ and SEC in 2010
▶ **Related Matters:**	In December 2009, the Prosecutor's Office in Poznan, Poland, indicted 16 individuals, including three former Philips Poland employees and 16 healthcare officials, for violating laws related to public tenders for the purchase of medical equipment

In April 2013, the SEC announced the issuance of an order instituting cease-and-desist proceedings pursuant to section 21C of the Securities Exchange Act of 1934 against Koninklijke Philips Electronics N.V. (Philips), a Netherlands-based parent of an affiliation of companies that manufacture and supply goods and services related to healthcare, consumer lifestyle, and lighting business sections. Philips New York Registry Shares are listed on the New York Stock Exchange, and the company files periodic reports pursuant to section 12 of the Exchange Act as a private issuer.

The order found that Philips failed to make and keep books, records, and accounts that, in reasonable detail, accurately and fairly reflected transactions and dispositions of its assets in violation of the books-and-records and internal controls provisions of the FCPA. The order found that Philips' violations took place through its operations in Poland from at least 1999 through 2007. The violations related to improper payments by employees of Philips' Polish subsidiary, Philips Polska sp. z o.o. (Philips Poland) to healthcare officials in Poland regarding public tenders proffered by Polish healthcare facilities to purchase medical equipment. The improper payments made by employees of Philips Poland to the Polish healthcare officials usually amounted to 3 percent to 8 percent of the contracts' net value as "commissions." At times, Philips Poland employees kept a portion of the improper payments and thereafter utilized a third-party agent to assist with the improper arrangements and payments to Polish healthcare officials.

Although Philips failed to implement a system of FCPA compliance and internal controls, upon becoming aware of the violations of Philips Poland in August 2007 the company conducted an internal audit, and in early 2010 self-reported the results of its investigation to the SEC staff and the DOJ. It also fired three employees and disciplined others. Philips cooperated with the SEC's investigation and also undertook numerous remedial measures, resulting in an administrative action. The order requires Philips to cease and desist from committing or causing any violations and future violations of section 12(b)(2)(A) and 13(b)(2)(B) of the Securities Exchange Act of 1934 and to pay disgorgement and prejudgment interest in the amount of $4,515,178.

AM.   *In re* Stryker Corp.[112]

▶ **Misconduct Category:**	Bribes to doctors and healthcare professionals; improper entertainment and excessive lodging of a director of a public hospital; purported "donation" of nearly $200,000 to a public university in Greece to fund a laboratory that was a pet project of a public hospital doctor
▶ **Countries:**	Argentina, Greece, Mexico, Poland, and Romania
▶ **Foreign Government Officials:**	Public hospital doctors
▶ **Improper Payment Dollar Value:**	$2.2 million
▶ **Combined Penalties:**	$13,283,823 ($7,502,635 disgorgement, $2,280,888 in prejudgment interest, and $3.5 million penalty)
▶ **Other:**	Use of a Mexican law firm that provided legal services to pay a $46,000 bribe and improper books-and-records reporting; travel and entertainment abuses included a six-night stay at a New York hotel, two Broadway shows, and a five-day trip to Aruba.

In October 2013, the SEC charged Stryker Corporation, a Michigan-based medical technology company, with violating the FCPA when subsidiaries in five different countries bribed doctors, healthcare professionals, and other government-employed officials in order to obtain or retain business. The SEC investigation found that Stryker Corporation's subsidiaries in Argentina, Greece, Mexico, Poland, and Romania made illicit payments totaling approximately $2.2 million that were incorrectly described as legitimate expenses in the company's books and records. Descriptions included charitable donation, consulting and service contracts, travel expenses, and commissions. Stryker made approximately $7.5 million in illicit profits as a result of the improper payments. Stryker agreed to pay more than $13.2 million to settle the SEC's charges.

The SEC's order instituting settled administrative proceedings details improper payments by employees of Stryker's subsidiaries as far back as 2003. They used third parties to make the payments in order to win or keep lucrative contracts for the sale of Stryker's medical technology products. For example, in January 2006, Stryker's subsidiary in Mexico directed a law firm to pay approximately $46,000 to a Mexican government employee in order to secure the winning bid on a contract. The result was $1.1 million in profits for Stryker. The subsidiary reimbursed the Mexico-based law firm for the bribe and booked the payment as a legitimate legal expense. However, no legal services were actually provided, and the law firm simply acted as a funnel to pay the bribe. According to the SEC's order, Stryker's subsidiary in Greece made a purported "donation" of nearly $200,000 in 2007 to a public university in Greece to fund a laboratory that was a pet project of a public hospital doctor. In exchange for the payment, the doctor agreed to provide business to Stryker.

The SEC's investigation also found that Stryker's subsidiaries bribed foreign officials by paying their expenses for trips that lacked any legitimate business purpose. For example, in exchange for the promise of future business from the director of a public hospital in Poland, Stryker paid travel costs for the director and her husband in May 2004. This included a six-night stay at a New York City hotel, attendance at two Broadway shows, and a five-day trip to Aruba.

The SEC's order required Stryker to pay disgorgement of $7,502,635, prejudgment interest of $2,280,888, and a penalty of $3.5 million. Without admitting or denying the allegations, Stryker agreed to cease and desist from committing or causing any violations and any future violations of sections 13(b)(2)(A) and 13(b)(2)(B) of the Securities Exchange Act of 1934.

AN.   *In re* Smith & Wesson Holding Corp.[113]

▶ **Misconduct Category:**	Use of third-party agents to pay bribes, including under the guise of firearm testing; bribes included $11,000 worth of guns as gifts to Pakistani police department officials
▶ **Countries:**	Pakistan, Indonesia, Turkey, Nepal, and Bangladesh
▶ **Foreign Government Officials:**	Pakistani police department
▶ **Improper Payment Dollar Value:**	In excess of $11,000
▶ **Combined Penalties:**	$2 million ($1.906 million penalty, $107,852 disgorgement, and $21,040 in prejudgment interest)

▶ **Other:**   Two-year reporting requirement to the SEC.
                                Company terminated its international sales
                                staff; a "wake-up call for small and medium
                                sized businesses" that want to expand
                                internationally; likely spawned by the DOJ
                                "SHOT Show" sting operation in 2010 (see
                                United States v. Alvirez)

In July 2014, the SEC charged Smith & Wesson Holding Corporation, a Springfield, Massachusetts–based firearms manufacturer, with violating the FCPA when employees and representatives of the U.S.-based parent company authorized and made improper payments to foreign officials while trying to win contracts to supply firearm products to military and law enforcement overseas.

Smith & Wesson, which profited by more than $100,000 from the one contract that was completed before the unlawful activity was identified, agreed to pay $2 million to settle the SEC's charges. The company must report to the SEC on its FCPA compliance efforts for a period of two years.

According to the SEC's order instituting a settled administrative proceeding, Smith & Wesson sought to break into new markets overseas starting in 2007 and continuing into early 2010. During that period, its international sales staff engaged in a pervasive effort to attract new business by offering, authorizing, or making illegal payments or providing gifts meant for government officials in Pakistan, Indonesia, and other foreign countries.

According to the SEC's order, Smith & Wesson retained a third-party agent in Pakistan in 2008 to help the company obtain a deal to sell firearms to a Pakistani police department. Smith & Wesson officials authorized the agent to provide more than $11,000 worth of guns to Pakistani police officials as gifts, and then make additional cash payments. Smith & Wesson ultimately won a contract to sell 548 pistols to the Pakistani police for a profit of $107,852.

The SEC's order found that Smith & Wesson employees made or authorized improper payments related to multiple other pending or contemplated international sales contracts. For example, in 2009, Smith & Wesson attempted to win a contract to sell firearms to an Indonesian police department by making improper payments to its third-party agent in Indonesia. The agent indicated he would provide a portion of that money to Indonesian officials under the guise of legitimate firearm lab testing costs. He said Indonesian police officials expected to be paid additional amounts above the actual cost of testing the guns. Smith & Wesson officials authorized and made the inflated payment, but a deal was never consummated.

The SEC's order found that Smith & Wesson also authorized improper payments to third-party agents who indicated that portions would be provided to foreign officials in Turkey, Nepal, and Bangladesh. The attempts to secure sales contracts in those countries were ultimately unsuccessful.

The SEC's order found that Smith & Wesson violated the antibribery, internal controls, and books-and-records provisions of the Securities Exchange Act of 1934. The company agreed to pay $107,852 in disgorgement, $21,040 in prejudgment interest, and a $1.906 million penalty. Kara Brockmeyer, chief of the SEC Enforcement Division's FCPA Unit, stated, "This is a wake-up call for small and medium-size businesses that want to enter into high-risk markets and expand their international sales. When a company makes the strategic decision to sell its products overseas, it must ensure that the right internal controls are in place and operating."[114] The SEC considered Smith & Wesson's cooperation with the investigation as well as the remedial acts taken after the conduct came to light. Smith & Wesson halted the impending international sales transactions before they went through, and implemented a series of significant measures to improve its internal controls and compliance process. The company also terminated its entire international sales staff. The DOJ declined a criminal prosecution of Smith & Wesson.

AO.   *In re* Layne Christensen Co.[115]

▶ **Misconduct Category:**	Bribes of over $800,000 to reduce tax liability, to avoid paying customs duties, and to obtain clear authority import and export its equipment; and $23,000 in cash to police, border patrol, immigration officials, and labor inspectors
▶ **Countries:**	Burkina Faso, Democratic Republic of the Congo, Guinea, and Tanzania
▶ **Foreign Government Officials:**	Tax officials, police, border patrol, immigration officials, and labor inspectors
▶ **Improper Payment Dollar Value:**	In excess of $823,000
▶ **Combined Penalties:**	$5,127,129 ($4.7 million in disgorgement and prejudgment interest and $375,000 penalty)
▶ **Other:**	Company to self-report on the status of its remediation for two years

In October 2014, the SEC charged Layne Christensen Company, a global water management, construction, and drilling company headquartered in Texas, with violating the FCPA by making improper payments to foreign officials in several African countries in order to obtain beneficial treatment and reduce its tax liability. After Layne Christensen Company self-reported its misconduct, an SEC investigation determined that the company received approximately $3.9 million in unlawful benefits during a five-year period as a result of bribes typically paid through its subsidiaries in Africa and Australia. Some payments were funded through cash transfers from Layne's U.S. bank accounts.

In addition to self-reporting the misconduct, Layne cooperated with the SEC's investigation by providing real-time reports of its investigative findings, producing English-language translations of documents, and making foreign witnesses available. The company also undertook an extensive remediation effort. Layne agreed to pay more than $5 million to settle the SEC's charges.

According to the SEC's order instituting settled administrative proceedings, Layne's misconduct occurred from 2005 to 2010. In addition to favorable tax treatment, the improper payments helped the company obtain customs clearance, work permits, and relief from inspections by immigration and labor officials in various African countries.

Among the findings in the SEC's order were:

- Layne paid nearly $800,000 to foreign officials in Mali, Guinea, and the Democratic Republic of the Congo (DRC) to reduce its tax liability and avoid associated penalties for delinquent payment. The bribes enabled Layne to realize more than $3.2 million in improper tax savings.
- Layne made improper payments to customs officials in Burkina Faso and the DRC to avoid paying customs duties and obtain clearance to import and export its equipment. The bribes were falsely recorded as legal fees and commissions in the company's books and records.
- Layne paid more than $23,000 in cash to police, border patrol, immigration officials, and labor inspectors in Burkina Faso, Guinea, Tanzania, and the DRC to obtain border entry for its equipment and employees. The bribes also helped secure work permits for its expatriate employees and avoid penalties for noncompliance with local immigration and labor regulations.

The SEC's order found that Layne violated the antibribery, books-and-records, and internal controls provisions of the Securities Exchange Act of 1934. Layne agreed to pay $3,893,472.42 in disgorgement plus $858,720 in prejudgment interest as well as a $375,000 penalty amount that reflects Layne's self-reporting, remediation, and significant cooperation with the SEC's investigation. For a period of two years, the settlement requires the company to report to the SEC on the status of its remediation and implementation of measures to comply with the FCPA.

AP.   *In re* Timms & Ramahi[116]

▶ **Misconduct Category:**	Improper 20-day "world tour" and provision of luxury watches to government officials
▶ **Country:**	Saudi Arabia
▶ **Foreign Government Officials:**	Ministry of Interior Officials
▶ **Improper Payment Dollar Value:**	Unspecified
▶ **Combined Penalties:**	$70,000 (Timms, $50,000; Ramahi, $20,000)
▶ **Other:**	Leading lavish business travel and entertainment case; officials traveled to Beirut, Casablanca, Dubai, New York City, and Paris with no business purpose; sales employees also falsified business records to conceal true value of gifts; company's provision of anticorruption training to salespeople likely helped company avoid FCPA sanctions

In November 2014, the SEC sanctioned two former employees, Stephen Timms and Yasser Ramahi, who worked in sales in the Dubai office of the Wilsonville, Oregon, FLIR Systems Inc., the world's largest commercial company specializing in the design and production of thermal imaging, night vision, and infrared camera and sensor systems, for violating the FCPA by allegedly taking government officials in Saudi Arabia on a "world tour" to help secure business for the company. The two employees later falsified records in an attempt to hide their misconduct. Timms and Ramahi agreed to settle the SEC's charges and pay financial penalties. The SEC's investigation is continuing.

According to the SEC's order instituting a settled administrative proceeding, FLIR entered into a multimillion-dollar contract to provide thermal binoculars to the Saudi government in November 2008. Timms and Ramahi were the primary sales employees responsible for the contract, and also were involved in negotiations to sell FLIR's security cameras to the same government officials. At the time, Timms was the head of FLIR's Middle East office in Dubai and Ramahi reported to him.

The SEC's order found that Timms and Ramahi traveled to Saudi Arabia in March 2009 and provided five officials with luxury watches during meetings to discuss several business opportunities. Timms and Ramahi believed these officials were important to sales of both the binoculars and the security cameras. A few months later, they arranged for key officials, including two who received watches, to embark on what Timms referred to as a "world tour" of personal travel before and after they visited FLIR's Boston facilities for a factory equipment inspection that was a key condition to fulfillment of the contract. The officials traveled for 20 nights with stops in Casablanca, Paris, Dubai, Beirut, and New York City. There was no business purpose for the stops outside of Boston, and the airfare and hotel accommodations were paid for by FLIR. Prior to providing the gifts and travel to the Saudi Arabian officials, Ramahi and Timms each had taken FCPA training at the company that specifically identified luxury watches and side trips as prohibited gifts. The FLIR Code of Conduct also clearly prohibited their misconduct.

According to the SEC's order, when FLIR's finance department flagged the expense reimbursement request for the watches during an unrelated review of expenses in the Dubai office and questioned the $7,000 cost, Timms and Ramahi obtained a second, fabricated invoice showing a cost of 7,000 Saudi Riyal (approximately $1,900) instead of the true cost of $7,000. They directed FLIR's local third-party agent to provide false information to the company to back up their story that the original submission was merely a mistake. Ramahi and Timms also falsely claimed that FLIR's payment for the world tour had been a billing mistake by FLIR's travel agent, and again used false documentation and FLIR's third-party agent to bolster their cover-up efforts.

Timms and Ramahi are U.S. citizens who reside in Thailand and the United Arab Emirates, respectively. The SEC's order found that they violated the anti-bribery provisions of section 30A of the Securities Exchange Act of 1934 and the internal controls and false records provisions of section 13(b)(5) and Rule 13b2-1 of the Exchange Act. The SEC's order further found that Timms and Ramahi caused

FLIR's violations of the books-and-records provisions of section 13(b)(2)(A) of the Exchange Act. Timms and Ramahi consented to the entry of the order and agreed to pay financial penalties of $50,000 and $20,000, respectively.

AQ.   *In re* Bruker Corp.[117]

▶ **Misconduct Category:**	Six-year scheme to give Chinese state-owned entity officials luxurious travel and entertainment in order to obtain or retain business
▶ **Country:**	China
▶ **Foreign Government Officials:**	Government officials of state-owned entities that were customers of Bruker
▶ **Improper Payment Dollar Value:**	$230,938
▶ **Combined Penalties:**	$2.4 million ($1,714,852 in disgorgement, $310,117 in prejudgment interest, and $375,000 penalty)
▶ **Other:**	Classic "side trip" abuse case: Chinese government officials received trips to Austria, Czech Republic, France, Germany, Italy, Norway, Sweden, Switzerland, and the United States. The leisure travel often followed business trips. Use of suspect "collaboration agreements." Weak internal controls that allowed senior employees of China offices to approve suspect payments to Chinese government officials for non-business-related travel and for purported "collaboration agreements." Following a board investigation, the company self-reported to the DOJ and SEC.

In December 2014, the SEC charged Bruker Corporation, a Billerica, Massachusetts–based global manufacturer of scientific instruments, with violating the FCPA by providing non-business-related travel and improper payments to various Chinese government officials in an effort to win business.[118] The SEC investigation found that the company lacked sufficient internal controls to prevent and detect approximately $230,000 in improper payments out of its China-based offices that falsely recorded them in books and records as legitimate business and marketing expenses. The payments enabled Bruker to realize approximately $1.7 million in profits from sales contracts with state-owned entities in China whose officials received the improper payments.

Bruker, which self-reported its misconduct and provided extensive cooperation during the SEC's investigation, agreed to pay approximately $2.4 million to settle the SEC's charges. According to the SEC's order instituting a settled administrative proceeding, a Bruker office in China paid more than $111,000 to Chinese government officials under 12 suspicious collaboration agreements contingent on state-owned entities providing research on Bruker products or using Bruker products in demonstration laboratories. The collaboration agreements did not specify the work product that the state-owned entities had to provide in order to be paid, and no work product was actually provided to the Bruker office by the state-owned entities. Certain collaboration agreements were executed directly with a Chinese government official rather than the state-owned entity itself, and in some cases Bruker's office paid the official directly.[119]

According to the SEC's order, the other improper payments involved reimbursements to Chinese government officials for leisure travel to the United States, Czech Republic, Norway, Sweden, France, Germany, Switzerland, and Italy. These officials often were responsible for authorizing the purchase of Bruker products, and the leisure trips typically followed business-related travel for the officials funded by the company. For example, Bruker paid for the purported training expenses of a Chinese government official who signed the sales contract on behalf of a state-owned entity, but the payment actually was reimbursement for sightseeing, tour tickets, shopping, and other leisure activities in Frankfurt and Paris. Bruker also funded some trips for Chinese government officials that had no legitimate business component. For example, two Chinese government officials received paid travel to New York despite the lack of any Bruker facilities there, and also to Los Angeles where they engaged in sightseeing activities.[120]

The SEC found that Bruker failed to adequately monitor and supervise the senior executives at its China offices to ensure that they enforced anticorruption policies or kept accurate records concerning payments to Chinese government officials. The Bruker China offices had no independent compliance staff or an internal audit function that had authority to intervene into management decisions and, if appropriate, take remedial actions. Bruker also failed to tailor its preapproval processes for conditions in China, instead allowing the Bruker China offices approval over items such as nonemployee travel and changes to contracts. As a result, senior employees of the Bruker China offices had unsupervised control over the compliance process; these employees in turn abused their privileges, approving suspect payments to Chinese government officials for non-business-related travel and for purported collaboration agreements.[121]

The SEC order found that Bruker violated the internal controls and books-and-records provisions of the Securities Exchange Act of 1934. The company agreed to pay $1,714,852 in disgorgement, $310,117 in prejudgment interest, and a $375,000 penalty.

VI. SELECT DOJ MATTERS

A. *United States v. Metcalf & Eddy*[122]

▶ **Misconduct Category:**	Travel, lodging, and entertainment abuses, including travel for family members and side trips to award sanitary district contracts
▶ **Country:**	Egypt

▶ **Foreign Government Officials:**   Alexandria General Organization for Sanitary Drainage (AGOSD)

▶ **Improper Payment Dollar Value:**   Unspecified

▶ **Combined Penalties:** $400,000

▶ **Other:**   Early FCPA Guidance re: Effective Compliance Programs

In December 1999, Metcalf & Eddy, Inc., of Wakefield, Massachusetts, as successor to Metcalf & Eddy, International, Inc., agreed to a civil judgment as a result of the payment of excessive travel and entertainment expenses for an Egyptian government official and his family. Metcalf & Eddy promised to pay travel, lodging, and entertainment expenses to the chairman of the Alexandria General Organization for Sanitary Drainage (AGOSD). In exchange the chairman, an official of the Egyptian government, would use his influence to have AGOSD support contracts between the United States Agency for International Development and Metcalf & Eddy. AGOSD was the beneficiary of these contracts. The AGOSD chairman did not directly participate in the selection of bidders, but the contract to operate and maintain wastewater treatment facilities managed by AGOSD was ultimately awarded to Metcalf & Eddy. The chairman along with his wife and two children traveled to the United States twice as guests of Metcalf & Eddy. The first trip included visits to Boston, Washington, D.C., Chicago, and Disney World. The second trip took the AGOSD chairman and his family to Paris, Boston, and San Diego. The chairman was paid 150 percent of his estimated per diem expenses, and his airline tickets were upgraded to first class by Metcalf & Eddy.

As part of the settlement, the DOJ required the defendant to adopt a compliance and ethics program for the purpose of preventing future FCPA violations.[123] The terms of the program set forth in the consent decree have been interpreted as signaling what the DOJ views as the components steps of an effective compliance program. These components include the following:

- A clearly articulated corporate policy prohibiting violations of the FCPA and the establishment of compliance standards and procedures to be followed by the company's employees, consultants, and agents that are reasonably capable of reducing the prospect of violations;
- The assignment to one or more senior corporate officials of the responsibility of overseeing the compliance program and the authority and responsibility to investigate criminal conduct of the company's employees and other agents, including the authority to retain outside counsel and auditors to conduct audits and investigations;
- Establishment of a committee to review and conduct due diligence on agents retained for business development in foreign jurisdictions as well as foreign joint venture partners;
- Corporate procedures to ensure that the company does not delegate substantial discretionary authority to individuals who the company knows, or should know, have a propensity to engage in illegal activities;

- Corporate procedures to ensure that the company forms business relationships with reputable agents, consultants, and representatives for purposes of business development in foreign jurisdictions;
- Regular training of officers, employees, agents, and consultants concerning the requirements of the FCPA and of other applicable foreign bribery laws;
- Implementation of an appropriate disciplinary mechanism for violations or failure to detect violations of the law or the company's compliance policies;
- Establishment of a system by which officers, employees, agents, and consultants can report suspected criminal conduct without fear of retribution or the need to go through an immediate supervisor;
- In all contracts with agents, consultants, and other representatives for purposes of business development in foreign jurisdictions, inclusion of warranties that no payments of money or anything of value will be offered, promised, or paid, directly or indirectly, to any foreign official public or political officer to induce such officials to use their influence with a foreign government or instrumentality to obtain an improper business advantage for the company;
- In all contracts with agents, consultants, and other representatives for purposes of business development in a foreign jurisdiction, inclusion of a warranty that the agent, consultant, or representative shall not retain any subagent or representative without the prior written consent of the company; and
- In all joint venture agreements where the work will be performed in a foreign jurisdiction, inclusion of similar contractual warranties regarding no payments to foreign officials and no hiring of subagents or representatives without prior written permission.[124]

The civil judgment permanently enjoined Metcalf & Eddy from further violations of the FCPA, and the company agreed to pay a $400,000 fine. No criminal charges were filed.

B. *United States v. Sengupta;*[125] *United States v. Basu*[126]

▶ **Misconduct Category:**	Consultant (Sweden) used to steer World Bank contracts
▶ **Country:**	Ethiopia and Kenya
▶ **Foreign Government Officials:**	Kenyan government official
▶ **Improper Payment Dollar Value:**	$177,000
▶ **Combined Penalties:**	Basu: 15 months in prison, two years' supervised release, and 50 hours of community service; Sengupta: two months in jail and $6,000 fine
▶ **Other:**	Swedish prosecution of consultants; unsuccessful attempt to withdraw a criminal guilty plea by Basu.

In November 2002, Ramendra Basu and Gautam Sengupta, World Bank task managers, were charged with steering World Bank contracts to consultants obtaining kickbacks in return, and with assisting a contractor in bribery of a foreign official in violation of the FCPA.[127] Basu admitted that he conspired with a Swedish consultant, among others, to steer World Bank contracts for business in Ethiopia and Kenya to certain Swedish companies, obtaining kickbacks in the amount of $127,000. Additionally, Basu assisted Swedish consultants in bribing a Kenyan government official, arranging for a $50,000 wire transfer to an account outside the United States for the government official's benefit. In December 2002, Basu pled guilty but later moved unsuccessfully to withdraw his guilty plea. In April 2008, Basu, an Indian national and permanent legal resident alien of the United States, was sentenced to 15 months in prison, two years' supervised release, and 50 hours of community service. Basu had previously cooperated with American and Swedish authorities, again pleading guilty in December 2002.[128]

Basu's coconspirator Sengupta pled guilty in 2002 to the same charges in a related case.[129] Sengupta was also a national of India and a permanent legal resident alien of the United States. He was sentenced in February 2006 to two months in jail and a fine of $6,000. The Swedish consultants were prosecuted and convicted by the Swedish government.

C. *United States v. Syncor Taiwan, Inc.;*[130] *SEC v. Syncor International Corp.;*[131] *SEC v. Fu*[132]

▶ **Misconduct Category:**	Cash commissions to doctors who made purchasing decisions of state-owned hospitals
▶ **Country:**	Taiwan
▶ **Foreign Government Officials:**	Hospital officials
▶ **Improper Payment Dollar Value:**	$344,110
▶ **Combined Penalties:**	$2.5 million ($2 million DOJ criminal penalty and $500,000 SEC civil penalty)
▶ **Other:**	Merger due diligence led to discovery of cash commissions; premerger disclosure by target to DOJ and internal investigation; independent consultant appointed; reorganization of internal controls for record-keeping

In November 2002, Syncor Taiwan, Inc., a Taiwanese subsidiary of Syncor International Corporation of Woodlands Hills, California, pled guilty to a one-count information alleging that over a four-year period the foreign subsidiary paid $344,110 in commissions to doctors who controlled the purchasing decisions for nuclear medicine departments, including hospitals owned by Taiwanese legal authorities, for the purpose of obtaining or retaining business. The cash payments were authorized by the chairman of the board of Syncor Taiwan while he was traveling in the United States. The payments were recorded as promotional and advertising expenses.

As part of its plea agreement, the Taiwanese subsidiary agreed to pay a $2 million criminal fine. In December 2002, Syncor settled with the SEC by consenting to a cease-and-desist order preventing future violations of the FCPA as well as a $500,000 civil penalty.[133] Syncor's board of directors was also required to appoint an independent consultant to review and reorganize Syncor's internal controls for record-keeping and financial reporting purposes.

While conducting due diligence for a merger, Cardinal Health, Inc., uncovered improper payments by Syncor Taiwan and brought the problem to the attention of Syncor. After being notified by Cardinal Health, Syncor promptly disclosed the improper payments to the DOJ and engaged outside counsel to conduct a thorough investigation.

In September 2007, Monty Fu, the founder of Syncor International, settled with the SEC under a consent decree by which he agreed to a permanent injunction against books-and-records violations and to pay a $75,000 civil penalty.[134] Fu was Syncor's chief executive officer from 1985 to 1989 and chairman of the board from 1985 to November 2002, when he went on paid leave. He resigned from Syncor in December 2002.[135]

D. *United States v. Giffen;*[136] *United States v. Williams*[137]

▶ **Misconduct Category:**	Payments through shell companies and use of Swiss bank accounts to influence government officials who could award oil and gas rights contracts
▶ **Country:**	Kazakhstan
▶ **Foreign Government Officials:**	Ministry of Oil officials
▶ **Improper Payment Dollar Value:**	$78 million
▶ **Combined Penalties:**	Civil forfeiture action. No jail for Giffen; 46 months' incarceration for Williams.
▶ **Other:**	FCPA, tax evasion, and money laundering charges; assertion of public authority (CIA) defense. Giffen's avoidance of a jail sentence may have been due to past service to U.S. intelligence agency(ies).
▶ **Related Matter:**	*United States v. Mercator Corp.*

In March 2003, James H. Giffen, the chairman and principal shareholder of Mercator, Inc., a small merchant bank with offices in New York and the Republic of Kazakhstan, was charged in the Southern District of New York with conspiracy to violate the FCPA in a scheme that awarded oil and gas rights contracts in Kazakhstan, and with money laundering. Mercator and the Kazakh Ministry of Oil and Gas Industries entered into an agreement to help develop a strategy for foreign investment in the oil and gas sector in 1994. The strategy included coordinating and negotiating several oil and gas transactions with foreign parties. Mercator would receive success fees only if the transactions closed. In 1995 the president of Kazakhstan named Giffen his counselor, a position that enabled him to influence matters of gas and oil transactions involving Mobil, Texaco, and Phillips Petroleum. Mercator received $67 million in success fees from 1995 to 2000. Giffen allegedly diverted $70 million of various oil companies' money to secret Swiss bank accounts that he controlled. From these two sources, the indictment charged, Giffen paid more than $78 million to two Kazakh government senior officials who had the power to determine whether Giffen and Mercator would retain their positions. The indictment further alleged that Giffen himself kept millions of dollars from the oil transactions to buy jewelry and a speedboat and to pay for a daughter's tuition. After five years of foreign discovery disputes and unsuccessful efforts to obtain classified CIA documents, in August 2010, Giffen pled guilty to one count of failing to disclose control of a Swiss bank account on his income tax return to resolve his criminal matters. In December 2010, he was not sentenced to jail—likely due to the fact that he had been a significant source of sensitive information for the U.S. government during the Cold War.

In April 2003, Williams, a former senior Mobil executive, was charged with conspiring to defraud the United States, tax evasion, and five counts of filing false tax returns. Williams negotiated Mobil's $1 billion purchase of a 25 percent interest in the Tengiz oil field in 1996. When the deal died, Mobil paid $41 million to a New York merchant bank that represented the Republic of Kazakhstan in the transaction. The merchant bank's president kicked back $2 million to Williams's Swiss bank accounts. Williams pled guilty to conspiracy and tax evasion and was sentenced to 46 months' incarceration.

E.   *United States v. Bodmer*[138]

▶ **Misconduct Category:**	Cash and wire transfers, percentage of profits from privatization of state-owned oil company, jewelry, and medical, travel, and gift expenses to be able to invest in an privatized oil company
▶ **Country:**	Azerbaijan
▶ **Foreign Government Officials:**	Officials of state-owned oil company
▶ **Improper Payment Dollar Value:**	Millions
▶ **Combined Penalties:**	Bodmer sentenced to time served (five months in a South Korean prison)
▶ **Other:**	Privatization of state-owned oil company; one coconspirator (Bourke) went to trial and was found guilty and another (Kozeny) remains a fugitive; money laundering charges
▶ **Related Matters:**	*United States v. Kozeny, Bourke & Pinkerton*

In August 2003, Hans Bodmer, a Swiss citizen and lawyer with the law firm von Meiss Blum & Partners, was charged in the Southern District of New York with conspiracy to violate the FCPA in connection with a plan to bribe Azerbaijani officials to be able to invest in the privatization of oil enterprises. Bodmer acted as an agent for Oily Rock Group, Ltd., a British Virgin Islands (BVI) corporation with its primary place of business in Baku, Azerbaijan; Minaret Group, Ltd., another BVI corporation based in Baku; Omega Advisors, Inc., a Delaware corporation with its principal place of business in New York; and various other members of the investment consortium. As an agent for the consortium, Bodmer paid bribes and authorized payments of bribes to Azeri officials in an attempt to convince the officials to allow the investment consortium to participate in the privatization auctions of the State Oil Company of the Azerbaijan Republic (SOCAR) and to acquire a controlling interest in SOCAR. In October 2004 Bodmer pled guilty to a money laundering conspiracy charge.[139] In the 2010 trial of Frederic Bourke, Bodmer testified for the prosecution. In March 2013 Judge Scheindlin sentenced Bodmer to time served (five months' incarceration in a South Korea prison). Kozeny remains a fugitive.

F.   *United States v. ABB Vetco Gray Inc. & ABB Vetco Gray U.K. Ltd.;*[140]
     SEC v. ABB Ltd.[141]

▶ **Misconduct Category:**	Cash payments, automobiles, shopping excursions, and country club memberships to secure contract awards
▶ **Countries:**	Angola, Kazakhstan, and Nigeria
▶ **Foreign Government Official:**	National Petroleum Investment Management Services officials
▶ **Improper Payment Dollar Value:**	$1.1 million
▶ **Combined Penalties:**	$16.4 million ($10.4 million criminal fines; $5.9 million in disgorgement of profits and prejudgment interest)
▶ **Other:**	First SEC-FCPA disgorgement of profits requirement case ($5.9 million); retention of independent consultant to review FCPA compliance policies and procedures; SEC jurisdiction under American depositary receipts
▶ **Related Matters:**	*United States v. Vetco Gray Controls Inc., Vetco Gray U.K. Ltd. & Vetco Gray Controls Ltd.*

In July 2004, ABB Vetco Gray Inc., a U.S. subsidiary of the Swiss company ABB Ltd., and ABB Vetco Gray U.K. Ltd., a U.K. subsidiary of the company, each pled guilty in the Southern District of Texas to a two-count information in connection with commissions and referral payments made to officials in Nigeria, Angola, and Kazakhstan. ABB Vetco Gray U.S. and ABB Vetco Gray U.K., from 1998 through 2001, paid bribes and authorized the payment of bribes to Nigerian officials in the government program known as National Petroleum Investment Management Services (NAPIMS). NAPIMS was responsible for reviewing and awarding bids to potential contractors for oil exploration projects in Nigeria. ABB Vetco Gray U.K. hired a Nigerian agent to perform consulting work related to marketing and goodwill.

ABB Vetco Gray U.K. used this agent to pay some of the bribes to NAPIMS officials. The bribes were in exchange for information regarding competitors' bids and to help secure contract awards. Six contract bids won by ABB had bribes attached to them, including automobiles, shopping excursions, country club memberships, and housing expenses, as well as cash payments. Pursuant to the plea agreement, each ABB subsidiary agreed to pay a criminal fine of $5,250,000.

In a separate action, the SEC, which had conducted a parallel investigation, filed a complaint against the Swiss parent company ABB Ltd., the stock of which is traded in the United States through American depositary receipts. Pursuant to a settlement, the SEC enjoined ABB Ltd. from future violations of the FCPA, and ABB Ltd. agreed to pay $5.9 million in disgorgement of profits and prejudgment interest and a $10.5 million civil penalty. The latter penalty was deemed satisfied by the payment of the ABB subsidiaries' criminal fines totaling the same amount. ABB Ltd. also agreed to retain an independent consultant to review its FCPA compliance policies and procedures.

G. United States v. Monsanto Co.;[142] SEC v. Monsanto Co.[143]

▶ **Misconduct Category:**	Bribe to repeal a government decree
▶ **Country:**	Indonesia
▶ **Foreign Government Officials:**	140 Ministry of Environment officials
▶ **Improper Payment Dollar Value:**	$700,000
▶ **Combined Penalties:**	$1.5 million ($1 million DOJ criminal penalty and $500,000 SEC civil penalty)
▶ **Other:**	DPA; discovery through international audit; voluntary disclosure to DOJ and SEC; appointment of independent consultant; likely avoidance of government suspension or debarment. SEC imposition of liability for Monsanto consolidation of inaccurate financial records from two of its affiliates into its own books.

In January 2005, Monsanto Company of St. Louis, Missouri, settled charges, under a DPA, with the Department of Justice in connection with improper payments to a senior Indonesian government environmental official. A senior Monsanto manager, based in the United States, had authorized payments to a senior Indonesian Ministry of Environment official in an attempt to influence the official to repeal a law that had an adverse effect on Monsanto. The bribes were made, but the law was not repealed. The senior Monsanto manager attempted to cover up the payments by creating false invoices that were submitted to Monsanto and approved for payment. From 1997 to 2002, Monsanto also made approximately $700,000 in improper payments to 140 current and former Indonesian government officials and their families under a bogus product registration scheme. The payments were inaccurately recorded or not recorded at all in Monsanto's books and records.

Under the DPA filed in the U.S. District Court for the District of Columbia, Monsanto accepted and acknowledged that it was responsible for the acts of employees set forth in a detailed Statement of Facts. In return, the DOJ Fraud Section agreed that prosecution of Monsanto under the filed false books-and-records information would be deferred for three years and that it would dismiss with prejudice the information if Monsanto complied with the terms of the agreement for three years. Monsanto agreed to pay a $1 million penalty, to retain an independent consultant to review its FCPA compliance policies and procedures, and to the entry of an injunction barring it from any future violations of the FCPA. There was no indication that Monsanto, under the DPA, would be suspended or barred from U.S. government contracts.

In a related proceeding, the SEC charged Monsanto with antibribery, books-and-records, and internal controls violations for the same FCPA misconduct. The SEC imposed liability for Monsanto's consolidation of inaccurate financial records from two of its affiliates into its own books.[144] Under the SEC settlement, Monsanto agreed to pay a $500,000 civil penalty.

H. *U.S. DOJ–InVision Technologies, Inc. Agreement;*[145] *SEC v. InVision Technologies, Inc.*[146]

▶ **Misconduct Category:** Use of sales agents and distributors

▶ **Countries:** China, Philippines, and Thailand

▶ **Foreign Government Officials:** Mid-level officials and political party members

▶ **Improper Payment Dollar Value:** Approximately $100,000

▶ **Combined Penalties:** $1.3 million ($800,000 monetary penalty plus disgorgement of profits of $589,000)

▶ **Other:** NPA; discovery of payments during acquisition due diligence; use of distributors to make improper payments

▶ **Related Matters:** *SEC v. Pillor* (2006)

In February 2005, the DOJ entered into an NPA with InVision Technologies, Inc., a Newark, California, public company that sold airport screening products, in connection with its sales or attempted sales of airport security explosive detection products to airports owned by the governments of China, the Philippines, and Thailand. InVision, through its employees and agents, authorized bribes to government officials in order to facilitate or retain business. In China and the Philippines, InVision employees paid sales agents who in turn gave the bribes to foreign officials. In Thailand, a manager and executive of InVision set up a company masked as an InVision distributor. The distributor used the price differential of the equipment to pay Thai government officials and political party members.

InVision voluntarily disclosed the conduct and related conduct to the Department of Justice and also prevented the improper payment in Thailand. InVision's cooperation and prompt disciplinary action and absence of prior FCPA-related charges led to the DOJ decision not to file criminal charges against the company, finding that InVision had accepted responsibility for the actions of its employees and their failure to maintain internal controls with respect to foreign transactions. InVision also agreed to pay a penalty of $800,000. At the time of the investigation InVision was merging with General Electric, which agreed to take the responsibility for assuring future compliance with FCPA policies and procedures. The agreement also required ongoing cooperation by General Electric and the retention of an independent consultant, and it allowed the DOJ to investigate and prosecute individuals and other entities.

In 2006 the SEC charged former InVision senior vice president David Pillor with aiding and abetting his employer's failure to establish adequate internal controls and indirectly causing the falsification of the company's books and records.[147] In alleging that Pillor did not respond to or acknowledge e-mail messages, the SEC complaint asserted he acted "knowingly, or with extreme recklessness."[148] Pillor agreed to a consent decree and payment of a $65,000 civil penalty.

I.   *United States v. Titan Corp.*;[149] **Report of Investigation Pursuant to Section 21(A) of the Securities Exchange Act of 1934 and Commission Statement on Potential Exchange Act Section 10(B) and Section 14(A) Liability;** *SEC v. Titan Corp.*;[150] *United States v. Head*[151]

▶ **Misconduct Category:**	Consultant; campaign contributions
▶ **Country:**	Benin
▶ **Foreign Government Official:**	President of Benin
▶ **Improper Payment Dollar Value:**	$13.5 million
▶ **Combined Penalties:**	$28.5 million ($13 million DOJ penalty; $15.5 million disgorgement of profits and prejudgment interest); Head sentenced only to six months in prison and three years' supervised release and fined $5,000, likely due to his substantial assistance and cooperation
▶ **Other:**	Campaign funding (president of Benin); discovery of improper payments by potential acquirer during due diligence; lack of internal controls; no due diligence files on 120 agents and consultants; SEC Guidance on disclosure to investors under section 21(a) report

In March 2005, Titan Corporation of San Diego, California, pled guilty in the Southern District of California to three FCPA criminal violations: one count of violating the antibribery provision, one count of falsifying the books-and-records provision, and one felony tax count; it also agreed to pay a record FCPA criminal fine of $13 million. The military intelligence and communications company did not contest that from 1999 to 2001 it paid $3.5 million to its agent in the West African country of Benin, who was then known by Titan to be the president of

Benin's business advisor. Much of the money funneled to Titan's African agent went to the election campaign of Benin's president. A senior Titan officer directed that payments be falsely invoiced as consulting services and that actual payment of the money be spread over time and into smaller increments.

Also in March 2005, the SEC brought an enforcement action against Titan that alleged violations of the antibribery, internal controls, and books-and-records provisions of the FCPA.[152] Under a consent decree, Titan agreed to pay the $13 million penalty to the Department of Justice; to pay approximately $15.5 million in disgorgement of profits and prejudgment interest; and to retain an independent consultant to review the company's FCPA compliance procedures and to adopt and implement the consultant's recommendations. The SEC stated that despite utilizing over 120 agents and consultants in over 60 countries, Titan never had a formal company-wide FCPA policy, had disregarded or circumvented the limited FCPA policies and procedures in effect, had failed to maintain sufficient due diligence files on its foreign agents, and had failed to have meaningful oversight over the foreign agents.

The background that led to the criminal and SEC enforcement case against Titan is as follows: In September 2003, Titan became a party to a merger agreement in which Lockheed-Martin agreed to acquire Titan pending certain contingencies. Titan affirmatively represented in that merger agreement that "to the knowledge of Titan, neither the Company nor any of its Subsidiaries, nor any director, officer, agent or employee of the Company or any of its Subsidiaries has . . . taken any action which would cause the Company or any of its Subsidiaries to be in violation of the FCPA."[153] This representation was publicly disclosed and disseminated by Titan. As a result of due diligence by Lockheed-Martin, the acquisition fell apart. In 2005, L-3 Communications acquired Titan in a separate buyout valued at $2.65 billion.

Titan's inclusion of the Lockheed merger agreement containing its affirmative FCPA representation in public disclosures, including a proxy statement filed with the SEC, also led the SEC to issue a section 21(a) report to provide guidance concerning potential liability under the antifraud and proxy provisions of the federal securities laws for publication of materially false or misleading disclosures in merger and other contractual agreements.[154]

In June 2006, former Titan Africa president Steven L. Head pled guilty to a single count of falsifying a false invoice for consulting services in Benin. While Head, who was assistant to Titan CEO Gene Ray before becoming president of Titan Africa, was subject to ten years in prison and a $1 million fine, his substantial assistance and cooperation resulted in a September 2007 sentence of six months in prison, three years' supervised release, and a $5,000 fine.[155]

J.   U.S. DOJ–Micrus Corp. Agreement

▶ **Misconduct Category:**   Payments to doctors disguised as false stock options, honoraria, and commissions in return for their public hospitals' purchase of medical products

▶ **Countries:**   France, Germany, Spain, and Turkey

▶ **Foreign Government Officials:**	Doctors of publicly owned hospitals
▶ **Improper Payment Dollar Value:**	$105,000
▶ **Penalty:**	$450,000
▶ **Other:**	Two-year NPA; voluntary disclosure and full cooperation; three-year independent compliance expert retention requirement

In March 2005, Micrus Corporation, a privately held company based in Sunnyvale, California, that develops and sells embolic coils, medical devices that allow minimally invasive treatment of neurovascular diseases, agreed to resolve its criminal liability associated with potential FCPA violations by paying $450,000 in penalties to the United States and cooperating fully with the DOJ investigation.

The investigation revealed that Micrus, through the conduct of certain officers, employees, agents, and salespeople, paid more than $105,000—disguised in Micrus's books and records as stock options, honoraria, and commissions—to doctors employed at publicly owned and operated hospitals in France, Turkey, Spain, and Germany in return for the hospitals' purchase of embolic coils from Micrus. Micrus had also made an additional $250,000 in payments for which the company did not obtain the necessary prior administrative or legal approval as required under the laws of the relevant foreign jurisdictions. The DOJ investigation followed the voluntary disclosure to the DOJ by Micrus of facts obtained in its internal investigation into the potential FCPA violations.

The term of the Micrus NPA with the government was two years. As a result of Micrus's cooperation commitment, its remedial actions, and voluntary disclosure of the wrongdoing, the DOJ agreed not to file criminal charges stemming from the investigation for the two-year period. Under the agreement, if Micrus failed to fully comply with the terms of the agreement during that two-year period, the DOJ would charge Micrus with FCPA violations.

In exchange for the DOJ's agreement not to prosecute Micrus for the conduct disclosed by Micrus to the department, Micrus agreed, among other things, to accept responsibility for its conduct; fully and affirmatively disclose to the DOJ activities that Micrus believes may violate the FCPA and continue to cooperate with the DOJ in its investigation; agree that a statement of facts summarizing the subject transactions was materially accurate and further agree not to contradict those facts; pay a monetary penalty to the United States of $450,000; adopt an FCPA compliance program, where previously it had none, as well as a set of internal controls designed to prevent violations in the future; and retain an independent compliance expert for a period of three years to ensure the company's compliance program and internal controls are effective.[156]

K.   *United States v. DPC (Tianjin) Co.;*[157] *In re* **Diagnostic Products Corp.**[158]

| ▶ **Misconduct Category:** | Illegal "commissions" (bribes) in order to obtain products and services contracts from state-owned hospitals |

▶ **Country:**   People's Republic of China

▶ **Foreign Government Officials:**   Physicians and laboratory personnel of
                                             government-owned hospitals

▶ **Improper Payment Dollar Value:** $1.6 million

▶ **Combined Penalties:** $4.8 million ($2 million DOJ criminal
                                             penalty and SEC $2.8 million
                                             disgorgement of profits plus prejudgment
                                             interest)

▶ **Other:**   Chinese subsidiary DOJ plea; SEC
                                             disgorgement of profits against parent
                                             company; independent compliance expert
                                             requirement

In May 2005, the United States charged DPC (Tianjin) Company, the Chinese subsidiary of Los Angeles–based Diagnostic Products Corporation (DPC) in the Central District of California, with violating the FCPA in connection with the payment of approximately $1.6 million in bribes in the form of illegal "commissions" to physicians and laboratory personnel employed by government-owned hospitals in the People's Republic of China. DPC, a producer and seller of diagnostic medical equipment, agreed to plead guilty to a single charge, adopt internal compliance measures, and cooperate with ongoing criminal and SEC civil investigations. An independent compliance expert was appointed to audit the company's compliance program and monitor its implementation of new internal policies and procedures. DPC Tianjin also agreed to pay a $2 million criminal penalty.

The bribes were allegedly paid from late 1991 through December 2002 for the purpose and with the effect of obtaining and retaining business with the Chinese hospitals. According to the criminal information and a statement of facts filed in court, DPC Tianjin made cash payments to laboratory personnel and physicians employed in certain hospitals in the People's Republic of China in exchange for agreements that the hospitals would obtain DPC Tianjin's products and services. This practice, authorized by DPC Tianjin's general manager, involved personnel who were employed by hospitals owned by the legal authorities in the People's Republic of China and, thus, "foreign officials" as defined under the FCPA.

In most cases, the bribes were paid in cash and hand-delivered by DPC Tianjin salespeople to the person who controlled purchasing decisions for the particular hospital department. DPC Tianjin recorded the payments on its books and records as "selling expenses." DPC Tianjin's general manager regularly prepared and submitted to DPC its financial statements, which contained sales expenses. The general manager also caused approval of the budgets for sales expenses of DPC Tianjin, including the amounts DPC Tianjin intended to pay to the officials of the hospitals in the following quarter or year. The "commissions," typically between 3 percent and 10 percent of sales, totaled approximately $1,623,326 from late 1991 through December 2002, and allowed DPC to earn approximately $2 million in profits from the sales.

Simultaneously with the criminal charge, the SEC filed an FCPA enforcement proceeding against DPC Tianjin's parent company, DPC. The SEC ordered the company to cease and desist from violating the antibribery, internal controls, and books-and-records provisions of the FCPA and to disgorge approximately $2.8 million in ill-gotten gains, representing its net profit in the People's Republic of China for the period of its misconduct plus prejudgment interest.[159]

L.   *United States v. Kozeny, Bourke & Pinkerton*[160]

► **Misconduct Category:**   Investment scheme: cash and wire transfers to Azeri officials and family members to share in profits from SOCAR privatization; profit and issuance of $300 million worth of Oily Rock shares; gifts totaling $600,000

► **Country:**   Azerbaijan

► **Foreign Government Officials:**   State-owned oil company officials and officials responsible for administering privatization program

► **Improper Payment Dollar Value:** $11 million plus

► **Combined Penalties:**   Bourke sentenced to a year and a day and a $1 million fine.

► **Other:**   Prosecution of Bourke, who largely had role of an investor; dismissal as to Pinkerton for government's failure to timely move for three-year extension of statute of limitations to obtain foreign evidence; jewelry, medical, travel, and gift expenses; government sought $100 million forfeiture; possible extortion defense pretrial opinion; "conscious avoidance" issues at trial; $1 million fine and one year and a day sentence for Bourke who went to trial but for whom the DOJ requested ten years in jail; Kozeny remains a fugitive

► **Related Matter:**   *United States v. Bodmer*

In October 2005, the United States charged, in a 27-count Southern District of New York indictment, Viktor Kozeny, Frederic A. Bourke, and David Pinkerton with, inter alia, participating in a conspiracy to bribe senior government officials in Azerbaijan to ensure that those officials would privatize the State Oil Company of the Azerbaijan Republic (SOCAR) and allow the three and others to share in the anticipated profits arising from that privatization and resale of its shares in the market. The Southern District of New York indictment charged that Kozeny, a Czech expatriate, Irish citizen, and resident of the Bahamas, on behalf of the codefendants and others made a series of corrupt payments to four Azeri officials. Payments allegedly included more than $11 million to the Azeri officials or their family members who sought $300 million worth of a controlled company's shares.

Pinkerton filed a successful motion to dismiss all FCPA counts on the basis that the government did not timely move to extend the statute of limitations to collect foreign evidence. Bourke filed a motion to dismiss all but the false statements charges on statute of limitations grounds. The district court granted the motion, and the Second Circuit affirmed the dismissal of select charges against Bourke.[161] Three others, Thomas Farrell, Clayton Lewis, and Hans Bodmer (*supra*), have in related cases pled guilty in connection with their participation in the bribery scheme.

Bourke, an investor for the most part, proceeded to trial in June 2009 and was convicted of a conspiracy to defraud the United States and making false statements, but was acquitted of money laundering charges, thereby avoiding a $100 million forfeiture. In November 2009 he was sentenced to a year and a day incarceration over the strong objection of the DOJ, which had sought a maximum incarceration term of ten years. Bourke was also fined $1 million. He unsuccessfully appealed his conviction on, among other grounds, a prejudicial conscious avoidance instruction.[162] Kozeny remains a fugitive.

M. *United States v. Sapsizian & Valverde*[163]

▶ **Misconduct Category:**	Use of consultant to bribe government officials to secure a telecommunications contract
▶ **Country:**	Costa Rica
▶ **Foreign Government Official:**	Board director of state-run telecommunications company
▶ **Improper Payment Dollar Value:**	$2.5 million
▶ **Combined Penalties:**	$261,500 forfeiture. Sapsizian, a French citizen, was sentenced to 30 months in jail and forfeiture of $261,500
▶ **Other:**	Valverde, a Costa Rican citizen and the former president of Alcatel's subsidiary in Costa Rica, remains a fugitive
▶ **Related Cases:**	*United States v. Alcatel-Lucent SA; United States v. Alcatel-Lucent France S.A., Alcatel-Lucent Trade International A.G. & Alcatel Centroamerica S.A.*

In December 2006, Christian Sapsizian, a former Alcatel CIT executive, and Edgar Valverde Acosta, a Costa Rican citizen who was Alcatel's senior country officer in Costa Rica, were charged in the Southern District of Florida with conspiracy with others between February 2000 and September 2004 to make more than $2.5 million in bribe payments to Costa Rican officials to obtain a telecommunications contract on behalf of Alcatel. According to information and plea documents, the payments were made to a board director for Instituto Costarricense de Electricidad (ICE), the state-run telecommunications authority in Costa Rica, which was responsible for awarding all telecommunications contracts. Sapsizian also admitted that the ICE official was an advisor to a senior Costa Rican government official and that the payments were shared with that senior official. The payments, funneled through one of Alcatel's Costa Rican consulting firms, were intended to cause the ICE official and the senior government official to exercise their influence to initiate a bid process that favored Alcatel's technology, Sapsizian admitted, and to vote to award Alcatel a mobile telephone contract. ICE awarded a mobile telephone contract to Alcatel in August 2001 valued at $149 million.

Sapsizian, a 62-year-old French citizen, pled guilty to two counts of violating the FCPA. As part of his plea, Sapsizian agreed to cooperate with U.S. and foreign law enforcement officials in the ongoing investigation. Until November 30, 2006, Sapsizian was employed by Alcatel, a French telecommunications company whose American depositary receipts were traded on the New York Stock Exchange.

In September 2008, Sapsizian was sentenced to 30 months in prison for engaging in an elaborate bribery scheme to obtain a mobile telephone contract from the state-owned telecommunications authority in Costa Rica by making more than $2.5 million in corrupt payments to Costa Rican officials. He was also ordered to forfeit $261,500, to serve three years of supervised release, and to pay a $200 special assessment. Valverde remains a fugitive. In December 2010, the DOJ and SEC resolved their FCPA investigation of the parent Alcatel-Lucent S.A. and three subsidiaries.

N.   *United States v. Statoil ASA*;[164] *In re* Statoil ASA[165]

► **Misconduct Category:**	Use of Turks and Caicos consultancy to funnel bribes to Iranian government official to obtain an oil field development contract
► **Country:**	Iran
► **Foreign Government Officials:**	Iranian Fuel Consumption Optimizing Organization (IFCOO), a subsidiary of the National Iranian Oil Company (NIOC); IFCOO was headed by an Iranian official who was a son of a former president of Iraq
► **Improper Payment Dollar Value:**	$5.2 million
► **Combined Penalties:**	$21 million ($10.5 million criminal penalty; $10.5 SEC disgorgement of profits and prejudgment interest)
► **Other:**	DPA; first FCPA enforcement action against a foreign company: jurisdiction based on American depositary receipts traded on NYSE; appointment of an independent compliance consultant requirement

In October 2006, the DOJ and SEC announced that Statoil ASA, an international oil exploration, development, and production company in Norway whose American depositary receipts are traded on the New York Stock Exchange, had agreed to pay a total of $21 million to settle criminal and administrative charges for violating the FCPA's antibribery and accounting provisions. According to the criminal information, in 2001 and 2002 Statoil sought to expand its business internationally, and focused specifically on Iran as a country in which to secure oil and gas development rights or "operatorships." At the time, Iran was awarding contracts for the development of the South Pars field, one of the largest natural gas fields in the world. In 2001, Statoil developed contacts with an Iranian government official who was believed to have influence over the award of oil and gas contracts in Iran. Following a series of negotiations with the Iranian official in 2001 and 2002, Statoil entered into a "consulting contract" with an offshore intermediary company to arrange payments to the Iranian official.

The Iranian official was the head of the Iranian Fuel Consumption Optimization Organization, a subsidiary of the National Iranian Oil Company. The purpose of that "consulting contract"—which called for the payment of more than $15 million over 11 years—was to induce the Iranian official to use his influence to assist Statoil in obtaining a contract to develop portions of the South Pars field and to open doors to additional Iranian oil and gas projects in the future. The Iranian official was the son of a former president of Iran. Two bribe payments, totaling more than $5 million, were actually made by wire transfer through a New York bank account, and Statoil was awarded a South Pars development contract that was expected to yield millions of dollars in profit.

Pursuant to the DPA filed in the Southern District of New York, Statoil agreed to a $10.5 million criminal penalty and the appointment of an independent compliance consultant to review and report on Statoil's FCPA compliance. In the parallel SEC administrative proceeding, Statoil consented to the entry of an administrative order requiring the company to cease and desist from committing any future FCPA violations, and to pay disgorgement of profits requesting an additional $10.5 million.

O. *United States v. SSI International Far East Ltd.*;[166] *In re* **Schnitzer Steel Industries, Inc.**;[167] **SEC v. Philip**[168]

▶ **Misconduct Category:**   Commissions, refunds, and gratuities to
                                    employees of both public and privately
                                    owned steel mills to induce purchase of
                                    scrap metal

▶ **Countries:**   China, Japan, and South Korea

▶ **Foreign Government Officials:** Government-owned steel mill

▶ **Improper Payment Dollar Value:** $1.8 million (only $200,000 to foreign
                                    officials)

▶ **Combined Penalties:** $15.2 million

▶ **Other:**   Commercial bribery or bribery of
                                    privately owned companies included
                                    in DOJ settlement; criminal plea by
                                    Korean subsidiary SSI Korea; DPA for
                                    U.S. parent; scrap metal manager at the
                                    Chinese companies wholly or partly
                                    owned by Chinese government alleged as
                                    "foreign official"; CEO charged by SEC
                                    with antibribery violations; independent
                                    compliance consultant requirement

In October 2006, the DOJ and SEC announced a plea and settlement with Schnitzer Steel Industries, Inc., based in Portland, Oregon, and its foreign subsidiary, SSI International Far East Ltd. (SSI Korea). In the plea documents, SSI Korea admitted that it violated the FCPA's antibribery provisions by making more than $1.8 million in corrupt payments over a five-year period to managers of a government-owned steel mill in China. SSI Korea made the payments to induce the steel mill managers to purchase scrap metal from Schnitzer Steel. The bribes, which took the form of commissions, refunds, and gratuities via off-book bank accounts, led to a substantial increase in business. In addition, the SEC alleged that Schnitzer Steel violated the FCPA's books-and-records and internal controls provisions.

To settle the criminal and administrative charges levied against it for violating the FCPA, Schnitzer Steel agreed to pay a total of $15.2 million. In the criminal proceeding, the company's wholly owned subsidiary, SSI Korea, pled guilty to violations of the FCPA's antibribery and books-and-records provisions. SSI Korea agreed to pay a $7.5 million criminal fine. A DPA was entered into with Schnitzer Steel, the parent corporation, in which Schnitzer Steel accepted responsibility for the conduct of its employees and agreed to enhance its internal compliance measures. The DPA also provided for the appointment of an independent compliance consultant to review Schnitzer Steel's compliance program and monitor the implementation of new internal controls related to the FCPA. In a parallel SEC administrative proceeding, the U.S. parent Schnitzer Steel consented to the entry of a cease-and-desist order and agreed to pay $7.7 million in disgorgement. The scrap metal manager at the Chinese companies wholly or partly owned by the Chinese government was alleged to be a "foreign official."

In December 2007, the SEC charged Robert W. Philip, the former chairman and CEO of Schnitzer Steel, with violating the FCPA antibribery provision by approving cash payments and other gifts to Chinese government officials of government-owned steel mills.[169] According to the SEC complaint, Philip authorized payments of more than $200,000 in cash bribes and other gifts to mill managers. Philip agreed to disgorge $169,863 in salary and bonuses he had received, to pay $16,536 in prejudgment interest, to pay a $75,000 civil penalty, and to enter into an order enjoining him from future FCPA violations.

P. *United States v. Vetco Gray Controls Inc., Vetco Gray U.K. Ltd. & Vetco Gray Controls Ltd.*[170]

▶ **Misconduct Category:**	Payments to secure preferential treatment in customs handling—"express courier services," "interventions," and "evacuations"
▶ **Country:**	Nigeria
▶ **Foreign Government Officials:**	Nigerian Customs Service officials
▶ **Improper Payment Dollar Value:**	$2 million
▶ **Combined Penalties:**	$26 million
▶ **Other:**	Recidivism a factor in large fine; independent monitor (see FCPA Opinion Release No. 04–02); use of major international freight forwarder as intermediary; any purchaser of company to be bound by the compliance and monitoring terms
▶ **Related Cases:**	Nobel, Panalpina, Pride International, Shell Nigeria Exploration and Production Company, Tidewater, Transocean, and GlobalSantaFeCorp

In February 2007, the United States charged Vetco Gray Controls Inc., Vetco Gray Controls Ltd., and Vetco Gray U.K. Ltd., wholly owned subsidiaries of Vetco International Ltd. of London, United Kingdom, in the Southern District of Texas with violating the antibribery provisions of the FCPA. Vetco International was acquired from ABB Ltd. in 2004 by private equity firms, but improper payments continued after the 2004 plea. The companies pled guilty to violations of the antibribery provisions of the FCPA, as well as conspiracy to violate the FCPA. Additionally, Aibel Group Ltd., another wholly owned subsidiary of Vetco International, simultaneously entered into a DPA with the Justice Department regarding the same underlying conduct. As part of the plea and DPAs, it was agreed that Vetco Gray Controls Inc., Vetco Gray Controls Ltd., and Vetco Gray U.K. Ltd. would pay criminal fines of $6 million, $8 million, and $12 million, respectively, for a total of $26 million.

Specifically, the United States charged that beginning in February 2001, Vetco Gray U.K. began providing engineering and procurement services and subsea construction equipment for Nigeria's first deepwater oil drilling project, the Bonga Project. Several Vetco Gray U.K. affiliates, including Aibel Group Ltd., Vetco Gray Controls Inc., and Vetco Gray Controls Ltd., supplied Vetco Gray U.K. with employees and manufacturing equipment for the project. From at least September 2002 to at least April 2005, each of the defendants engaged the services of a major international freight-forwarding and customs clearing company and, collectively, authorized that agent to make at least 378 corrupt payments totaling approximately $2.1 million to Nigerian Customs Service officials to induce those officials to provide the defendants with preferential treatment during the customs process.

This is the second time since July 2004 that Vetco Gray U.K. has pled guilty to violating the FCPA. On July 6, 2004, Vetco Gray U.K., then named ABB Vetco Gray U.K. Ltd., and an affiliated company pled guilty to violating the antibribery provision of the FCPA in connection with the payment of more than $1 million in bribes to officials of NAPIMS, a Nigerian government agency that evaluates and approves potential bidders for contract work on oil exploration projects. ABB Vetco Gray U.K. Ltd. was renamed Vetco Gray U.K. Ltd. after a group of private equity entities acquired the upstream oil and gas businesses and assets of its parent corporation, ABB Handels-und Verwaltungs AG (ABB). The July 12, 2004, acquisition included the sale of Vetco Gray U.K. and the predecessors to the two other Vetco International subsidiaries that pled guilty. In anticipation of the July 12, 2004, acquisition, the private equity acquirers requested and the DOJ issued an FCPA Opinion Release (No. 2004-02). The Opinion Release required the acquirers to effectively institute and implement a compliance system, internal controls, training, and other procedures sufficient to have deterred and detected violations of the FCPA, among other obligations. The corrupt payments underlying the guilty pleas continued unabated from the period prior to the acquisition until at least mid-2005, notwithstanding the acquirer's commitments to the DOJ under the Opinion Release.

The sale to new owners, the prior directives issued by the DOJ, and Vetco Gray U.K.'s prior FCPA conviction were all taken into account under the U.S. Sentencing Guidelines in calculating the $12 million criminal fine against Vetco Gray U.K. Ltd. The resolution of the criminal investigation of Vetco International and its subsidiaries resulted, in large part, from the actions of Vetco International in voluntarily disclosing the matter to the DOJ and Vetco International's subsidiaries' agreement to take significant remedial steps. In addition to the criminal fines, the plea agreements also required the defendants to (1) hire an independent monitor to oversee the creation and maintenance of a robust compliance program; (2) undertake and complete an investigation of the companies' conduct in various other countries as originally required under FCPA Opinion Release No. 2004-02; and (3) ensure that in the event any of the companies are sold, the sale shall bind any future purchaser to the monitoring and investigating obligations. The Vetco investigation spawned an investigation of Panalpina World Transport Holdings Inc., a global freight-forwarder company, and 11 of its customers in July 2007. These investigations were resolved with the DOJ in November 2010.

Q. *United States v. Baker Hughes Services International Inc.;*[171] *SEC v. Baker Hughes Inc. & Fearnley;*[172] *United States v. Baker Hughes Inc.*[173]

▶ **Misconduct Category:**   Consulting payments to consultants in Angola and on the Isle of Man to obtain project management services contract

▶ **Countries:**   Angola, Indonesia, Kazakhstan, Nigeria, and Russia

▶ **Foreign Government Officials:**   Government official; state-owned oil company official

▶ **Improper Payment Dollar Value:** $41 million

▶ **Combined Penalties:** $44 million ($11 million criminal fine; $10 million civil penalties; and $23 million in disgorgement of profits and prejudgment interest)

▶ **Other:**   Recidivist factor in large fine; plea by subsidiary, and DPA for parent company; disgorgement of profits and prejudgment interest ($23 million); largest FCPA fine at the time; Baker Hughes Incorporated now has a model compliance program

▶ **Related Matter:**   *In re* Baker Hughes (2001)

In April 2007, the United States charged Baker Hughes Services International Inc. (BHSI), a wholly owned subsidiary of Texas-headquartered Baker Hughes Inc., in the Southern District of Texas with violating the FCPA antibribery provisions, conspiracy to violate the FCPA, and aiding and abetting the falsification of the books and records of Baker Hughes Inc. in connection with improper payments to a Kazakh official. The parent company Baker Hughes Inc. simultaneously entered into a DPA with the DOJ regarding the same underlying conduct and accepted responsibility for the conduct of its employees. The subsidiary agreed to pay an $11 million criminal fine, serve a three-year probation, and adopt a comprehensive antibribery program.

In a related matter, Baker Hughes Inc., a global provider of comprehensive oil field services and products, reached a settlement with the SEC whereby it agreed to pay $10 million in civil penalties and more than $24 million in disgorgement of all profits it earned in connection with the Kazakh projects, including prejudgment interest. In the same civil complaint, the SEC charged Roy Fearnley, a former business development manager for Baker Hughes, with violating the FCPA and aiding and abetting his employer in doing so. A default judgment was entered against Fearnley in 2010.[174]

Subsidiary BHSI admitted that it paid approximately $4.1 million in bribes over two years to an intermediary whom the company understood and believed made the improper payments to an official of Kazakhoil, the state-owned oil company. The payments were made through an Isle of Man consulting firm that the parent retained as an agent in connection with a major oil field services contract. As the charging and plea documents reflect, the government of Kazakhstan and Kazakhoil entered into an agreement with a consortium of four international oil companies for the purpose of developing and operating a giant oil field known as Karachaganak in northwestern Kazakhstan. In February 2000, BHSI submitted a bid, on behalf of Baker Hughes, to perform comprehensive services such as project management, oil drilling, and support services in connection with the Karachaganak project.

Kazakhoil wielded considerable influence as Kazakhstan's national oil company, and the ultimate award of any contract by the consortium of international oil companies depended upon the favorable recommendation of Kazakhoil officials. After BHSI submitted its bid for the Karachaganak project and before the award was announced, Kazakhoil officials demanded that Baker Hughes pay a commission to a consulting firm located on the Isle of Man to act as its agent. Although the consulting firm had performed no services to assist Baker Hughes, in September 2000, BHSI agreed to pay a commission equal to 2 percent of the revenue earned on the Karachaganak project, and 3 percent on future projects in Kazakhstan. Baker Hughes was awarded the contract for Karachaganak in October 2000. From May 2001 through November 2003, Baker Hughes paid a total of $4.1 million in commissions to the consulting firm. The payments were made from the subsidiary's bank account in Houston to a London bank account in the consultant's name.

The then very large monetary sanction—$44 million[175]—and a DPA for the parent company likely balanced the fact that Baker Hughes Inc. had been subject to an FCPA cease-and-desist order in 2001 arising from improper payments to an Indonesian tax official and that it voluntarily disclosed to the DOJ the improper Kazakh payments of over $4.1 million, conducted an extensive and thorough internal investigation of its business practices in Kazakhstan and throughout its high-risk global operations, and implemented significant remedial steps and control enhancements.[176]

R.   *United States v. Jefferson, Jackson & Pfeffer*[177]

▶ **Misconduct Category:** Misuse of congressional office to obtain business delegations to Africa

▶ **Countries:** Nigeria, Ghana, Equatorial Guinea, Botswana, and the Congo

▶ **Foreign Government Officials:** Officials of NITEL, a Nigerian telecommunications service provider

▶ **Improper Payment Dollar Value:** Unknown

▶ **Combined Penalties:** 13 years' imprisonment

▶ **Other:** First prosecution of U.S. Congressman in an FCPA context; storage of $90,000 in cash in freezer

In June 2007, Congressman William J. Jefferson (D-La.) was charged in the Eastern District of Virginia with a conspiracy to commit bribery and wire fraud and to violate the FCPA, along with substantive bribery, fraud, and RICO counts. Two coconspirators, Vernon L. Jackson, a Louisville, Kentucky, businessman, and Brett M. Pfeffer, a former Jefferson congressional staff member, pled guilty before Jefferson's trial. Jackson was sentenced to 87 months in jail and Pfeffer to 96 months in prison.

In June 2009, Congressman Jefferson proceeded to trial where the DOJ proved *inter alia* that from 2000 to 2005, he performed a wide range of official acts in return for things of value, including leading official business delegations to Africa;

corresponding with U.S. and foreign government officials; and utilizing congressional staff meetings to promote businesses and businesspersons. The business ventures the Congressman promoted included telecommunications deals in Nigeria, Ghana, and elsewhere; oil concessions in Equatorial Guinea; satellite transmission contracts in Botswana, Equatorial Guinea, and the Republic of Congo; and development of different plants and facilities in Nigeria. In November 2009, Jefferson was sentenced to 13 years in jail.[178]

S. U.S. DOJ–Paradigm B.V. Agreement[179]

▶ **Misconduct Category:**	Commission payments and improper payments to "internal consultants" of state-owned entities (SOEs) in connection with the sale of software to the SOE subsidiary
▶ **Countries:**	China, Indonesia, Kazakhstan, Mexico, and Nigeria
▶ **Foreign Government Officials:**	Representatives of state-owned oil companies
▶ **Improper Payment Dollar Value:**	$100,000 to $222,250
▶ **Penalty:**	$1 million
▶ **Other:**	First FCPA enforcement action involving an initial public offering (IPO); no original consultant due diligence; due diligence in connection with the IPO uncovered FCPA problems and led to voluntary disclosure; NPA; retention of outside compliance counsel

In September 2007, the DOJ entered into an NPA with Houston-based Paradigm, B.V., involving improper payments to government officials in China, Indonesia, Kazakhstan, Mexico, and Nigeria. Paradigm identified misconduct in January 2007 in connection with its anticipated initial public offering and responded by conducting an investigation through outside counsel, voluntarily disclosing its findings to the DOJ, cooperating fully with the DOJ, and instituting extensive remedial compliance measures.

Paradigm, a private limited liability provider of enterprise software to the global oil and gas exploration and production industry, admitted to the payment of $22,250 into the Latvian bank account of a British West Indies company recommended as a consultant by an official of a KazMunaiGas, Kazakhstan's national oil company, to secure a tender for geological software. In connection with the consultant, Paradigm performed no due diligence on the British West Indies company, did not enter into any written agreement with the company, and did not appear to receive any services from the company. Paradigm also admitted using an agent in China to make commission payments to representatives of a subsidiary of the China National Offshore Oil Company (CNOOC) in connection with the sale of software to the CNOOC subsidiary. In addition, Paradigm directly retained and paid employees of Chinese national oil companies or state-owned entities as so-called internal consultants to evaluate Paradigm's software and to evaluate their employer's software and to influence their employer's procurement divisions to purchase Paradigm's products. Finally, Paradigm acknowledged similar conduct in dealings in Mexico, Indonesia, and Nigeria. The corrupt payments in Nigeria were between $100,000 and $200,000 and made through an agent to Nigerian politicians in order to obtain a contract to perform services and processing work for a subsidiary of the Nigerian National Petroleum Corporation.

As a result of Paradigm's thorough due diligence and investigation by outside counsel in the course of an IPO, voluntary disclosure before it sought to go public, full cooperation with the DOJ, and institution of extensive remedial compliance measures, the company would not be prosecuted if it satisfies obligations for 18 months, including ongoing cooperation, adoption of rigorous internal controls, retention of outside compliance counsel, and the payment of a $1 million penalty. Paradigm successfully completed the 18-month period.

T.   *United States v. Ingersoll-Rand Co., Ltd.*; *United States v. Ingersoll-Rand Italiana S.p.A.*;[180] *SEC v. Ingersoll-Rand Co.*[181]

▶ **Misconduct Category:**   Kickbacks recorded as "other commissions" or "sales deductions" paid to government of over $1.5 million to obtain contracts to provide road construction equipment and refrigerated trucks; side trips to Florence, Italy; $8,000 in "pocket money" to government officials in connection with visit to manufacturing facility

▶ **Country:**   Iraq

▶ **Foreign Government Officials:**   Iraqi government

▶ **Improper Payment Dollar Value:** $1,507,845

▶ **Combined Penalties:** $6.7 million ($2.5 million DOJ fine; $1.95 million SEC penalty and $1.7 million in disgorgement of profits and $560,000 in prejudgment interest)

▶ **Other:**   UN Oil-for-Food program; the parent company and Irish and Italian subsidiaries received DPAs; parent alleged to have known about or been reckless about kickbacks

In October 2007, the Ingersoll-Rand Company, Ltd. of Montvale, New Jersey, agreed, as part of a DPA filed in the U.S. District Court for the District of Columbia, to pay a $2.5 million fine. Charges had been brought against two subsidiaries of the company, Thermo King Ireland Limited and Ingersoll-Rand Italiana SpA, in connection with an ongoing investigation of the UN Oil-for-Food program. Ingersoll-Rand subsidiary Thermo King Ireland Limited was charged with conspiracy to commit wire fraud, and subsidiary Ingersoll-Rand Italiana SpA was charged with conspiracy to commit wire fraud and to violate the books-and-records provisions of the FCPA.[182]

The Justice Department agreed to defer prosecution of criminal charges against Ingersoll-Rand and its subsidiaries for three years, because Ingersoll-Rand had thoroughly reviewed the improper payments and implemented enhanced compliance policies. If Ingersoll-Rand abided by the terms of the DPA, the DOJ agreed to dismiss the charges. According to the DPA, Ingersoll-Rand acknowledged that its subsidiaries paid the Iraqi government kickbacks to obtain contracts to provide road construction equipment, air compressors and parts, and refrigerated trucks. The Iraqi government began requiring such illegal kickbacks in 2000, frequently portraying them incorrectly as "after-sales services fees." Between October 2000 and August 2003, employees of Ingersoll-Rand subsidiaries paid a total of approximately $600,000, and offered to pay an additional $250,000, in kickbacks to the Iraqi government by inflating the price of contracts by approximately 10 percent before submitting them to the United Nations for approval, and concealed from the United Nations the fact that the contract prices contained a kickback to the Iraqi government.

Simultaneously, Ingersoll-Rand reached a settlement with the SEC in a related complaint.[183] The SEC alleged that Ingersoll-Rand knew or was reckless in not knowing that kickbacks totaling $1.5 million were paid or agreed to. Initially, the company recorded the kickbacks as "other commissions" or "sales deductions." Ingersoll-Rand agreed to pay $1.95 million in civil penalties and approximately $2.27 million in disgorgement of all profits, including prejudgment interest. The two subsidiaries of Ingersoll-Rand generated these profits in connection with contracts for which they paid kickbacks to the Iraqi government.

U. *United States v. York International Corp.*[184]

▶ **Misconduct Category:**	Bribes and kickbacks to obtain government contract work
▶ **Countries:**	Bahrain, Egypt, India, Iraq, Turkey, and the United Arab Emirates
▶ **Foreign Government Officials:**	Iraqi government and others
▶ **Improper Payment Dollar Value:**	$647,000
▶ **Combined Penalties:**	$22 million (DOJ: $10 million penalty; SEC: $2 million civil penalties; $10 million in disgorgement of profits and prejudgment interest)
▶ **Other:**	UN Oil-for-Food program; DPA; three-year independent monitor review requirement

In October 2007, the DOJ agreed to defer the prosecution of York International Corporation of York, Pennsylvania, for three years. As part of this agreement filed in the U.S. District Court for the District of Columbia, York agreed to pay $10 million, to have its compliance program and procedures reviewed by an independent monitor, and to fully cooperate with the Justice Department's ongoing investigation of the UN Oil-for-Food program.

According to a criminal information filed October 1, 2007, York was charged with conspiracy to commit wire fraud and to violate the books-and-records provision of the FCPA.[185] York acknowledged that it was responsible for the actions of two subsidiaries, York Air Conditioning and Refrigeration, and York Air Conditioning and Refrigeration FZE. Employees and agents of these subsidiaries paid approximately $647,000 in kickbacks to the Iraqi government to obtain contracts with Iraqi ministries. They also paid kickbacks and bribes related to other government contract work in Bahrain, Egypt, India, Turkey, and the United Arab Emirates.

The Justice Department agreed to defer prosecution for three years, because York

- discovered the kickback payments early and reported them;
- thoroughly reviewed those payments;
- discovered and reviewed improper payments made in other countries;
- implemented enhanced compliance policies and procedures; and
- was willing to undergo a three-year review of its compliance policies and procedures by an independent monitor.

A settlement was also reached in a related SEC matter.[186] Under the terms of this settlement, York consented to the filing of a complaint and agreed to pay $2 million in civil penalties and approximately $10 million in disgorgement of profits, including prejudgment interest. Subsidiaries of York paid kickbacks to the Iraqi government and other governments in order to win the contracts that generated these profits.

V. *United States v. Steph;*[187] *United States v. Tillery & Novak*[188]

▶ **Misconduct Category:**	Consultants and cash payments to win a gas pipeline construction contract
▶ **Countries:**	Bolivia, Ecuador, and Nigeria
▶ **Foreign Government Officials:**	High-ranking executive-branch officials; tax officials; officials of state-owned oil company
▶ **Improper Payment Dollar Value:**	$6 million
▶ **Combined Penalties:**	Steph: 15 months in jail.
▶ **Other:**	Steph pled and cooperated with the DOJ; U.S. State Department cancellation of Novak's passport led to deportation from South Africa to the United States, where he pled guilty and is cooperating; Tillery is now a citizen of Nigeria from where the United States seeks to extradite him.
▶ **Related Matters:**	*United States v. Willbros Group Inc. & Willbros International Inc.*; *SEC v. Willbros Group Inc.*

In November 2007, Jason Edward Steph pled guilty in the Southern District of Texas to conspiracy to violate the FCPA by bribing Nigerian government officials with over $6 million. Steph was a Nigeria-based employee of Willbros International Inc., a subsidiary of Willbros Group Inc., a construction and engineering oil and gas services company. Steph was general manager of Willbros International Inc.'s onshore operations in Nigeria from 2002 to April 2005, and had been a Willbros employee since 1998.

Steph admitted that he agreed in late 2003 to make a series of corrupt payments totaling over $6 million to help to win a major gas pipeline construction contract in Nigeria. He made this agreement with a senior Willbros International Inc. executive, two of its "consultants," and certain Nigeria-based employees of a German engineering and construction firm. The $6 million in payments were offered to officials of the Nigerian state-owned oil company and its subsidiary, a Nigerian political party, and a senior employee in the executive branch of the Nigerian federal government. Steph also agreed that in furtherance of this conspiracy, he arranged for the payment of $1.8 million in cash to Nigerian government officials. He did this with former Willbros International Inc. executives. The maximum sentence for conspiring to violate the FCPA is five years in prison and a fine of $250,000. Steph is cooperating with an ongoing government investigation. In January 2010, he was sentenced to 15 months in jail.

In January 2008, J. Kenneth Tillery, a former Willbros executive vice president, and Paul Novak, a Willbros consultant, were charged in connection with a conspiracy to pay more than $6 million in bribes to government officials in Nigeria and Ecuador. The four-count indictment charged Tillery and Novak with one count of conspiracy to violate the FCPA, two FCPA violations for specific corrupt payments to officials in Nigeria, and one count of money laundering.

The indictment returned in January 2008 was sealed until December 2008, when Novak was arrested upon his arrival in Houston. He had returned to the United States from South Africa after his U.S. passport was revoked. In November 2009, Novak pled guilty to a conspiracy to violate the FCPA count and a substantive FCPA count and is cooperating with the government.[189] Tillery obtained Nigerian citizenship in 2009, and the United States has been unsuccessful in seeking to extradite him.[190] Tillery remains a fugitive.

W. U.S. DOJ–Lucent Technologies Inc. Agreement;[191] *SEC v. Lucent Technologies Inc.*[192]

▶ **Misconduct Category:**	Travel and entertainment for 315 trips of over 1,000 Chinese officials worth over $10 million to the United States, including Disneyland and Grand Canyon visits
▶ **Country:**	China
▶ **Foreign Government Officials:**	Employees of Chinese state-owned or state-controlled telecommunications enterprises
▶ **Improper Payment Dollar Value:**	Arguably several million dollars

| ▶ **Combined Penalties:** | $2.5 million ($1 million criminal penalty and $1.5 million civil penalty) |
| ▶ **Other:** | Leading China travel and entertainment guidance; NPA |

In December 2007, Lucent Technologies Inc., then a Murray Hill, New Jersey-based[193] global communications solutions provider, agreed under an NPA with the DOJ to pay a $1 million fine to resolve allegations of bribery violations of the FCPA.[194] From at least 2000 to 2003, Lucent paid millions of dollars for approximately 315 trips for Chinese government officials. While these trips were actually primarily for leisure, entertainment, and sightseeing, Lucent improperly recorded them in its books and records, in violation of the FCPA. Lucent typically characterized the trips as "factory inspections" or "training" even though, by 2001, Lucent no longer had any factories to tour as it had outsourced most of its manufacturing. In fact, the trips had little or no business content and were to destinations such as the Grand Canyon and Disneyland. Lucent's most senior Chinese officials requested and approved these trips, with support from Lucent employees in the United States, including Lucent's New Jersey headquarters. Lucent failed to provide internal controls to adequately monitor the provision to Chinese officials of travel and other things of value.

Lucent admitted to this conduct and agreed to pay a $1 million criminal fine. It also agreed to enhance its internal controls policies and procedures to ensure that Lucent keeps accurate books and records, develops a rigorous anticorruption compliance code, and implements standards and procedures designed to detect and deter violations of the FCPA and other anticorruption laws.

In a related matter and in connection with related conduct, the SEC filed a settled complaint against Lucent in December 2007.[195] The SEC's complaint asserted that Lucent spent $10 million on the trips discussed above, and that at least 1,000 Chinese government officials were involved. Lucent consented to the entry of a final judgment permanently enjoining it from future violations of books-and-records and internal controls provisions and agreed to pay a civil penalty of $1.5 million.

X. U.S. DOJ–Westinghouse Air Brake Technologies Corp. Agreement;[196] *SEC v. Westinghouse Air Brake Technologies Corp.*[197]

▶ **Misconduct Category:**	Payments to have bids for government business under tender process awarded or considered; monthly $31.50 facilitating payments to stop frequent governmental audits
▶ **Country:**	India
▶ **Foreign Government Officials:**	Indian Railway Board, 16 Zonal Railways, and Central Board of Excise and Customs officials

▶ **Improper Payment Dollar Value:**	$137,400
▶ **Combined Penalties:**	$677,000 ($300,000 criminal penalty; $288,000 in disgorgement of profits and prejudgment interest; and $89,000 civil penalty)
▶ **Other:**	NPA; disgorgement of profits; self-investigation, voluntary disclosure, full cooperation and remedial efforts; very low threshold for improper "facilitating payments"; SEC permits independent compliance consultant for 60-day review of compliance program; the Wabtech case is seen as an indication in the view of many of "the vanishing facilitating payment"

In February 2008, Westinghouse Air Brake Technologies Corporation (Wabtech) entered into an NPA with the Department of Justice regarding payments to Indian government officials, in violation of the FCPA. Wabtech's business includes the manufacture of brake subsystems for locomotives and transit vehicles. A fourth-tier, wholly owned subsidiary, Pioneer Friction Limited, based in Calcutta, India, made certain improper payments to Indian Railway Board (IRB) officials and other government entities in order to assist Pioneer in obtaining business during the IRB and Zonal Railway Contract tender process, scheduling preshipping product inspections, obtaining product delivery certificates, and curbing excise tax audits. The Indian government was Pioneer's largest customer. The NPA included monthly "facilitating payments" of $67 to Control Board of Excise and Customs personnel to stop the frequent audits. As a result, FCPA practitioners consider this case to represent the "vanishing facilitation payment" exception.

As part of its agreement with the DOJ, Wabtech agreed to pay a $300,000 penalty, implement rigorous internal controls, and cooperate fully with the DOJ. The agreement acknowledges Wabtech's voluntary disclosure of the conduct, its thorough self-investigation, full cooperation with the DOJ, and remedial efforts. These mitigating factors led the DOJ to agree not to prosecute Wabtech or Pioneer for making improper payments if Wabtech satisfied the obligations above for three years.

A settlement was reached in a related SEC matter.[198] In light of the business Pioneer obtained in exchange for unlawful payments to officials, Wabtech consented to the filing of an SEC complaint and agreed to pay approximately $288,000 in disgorgement of profits (including prejudgment interest) and approximately $89,000 in civil penalties. Instead of requiring an independent monitor, the SEC permitted Wabtech to retain an independent compliance consultant who was to issue a report and approve a compliance program within 60 days.

Y.   *United States v. Flowserve Corp.*;[199] *SEC v. Flowserve Corp.*[200]

▶ **Misconduct Category:**	Surcharges and kickbacks disguised as inflated "after-sales service fees"
▶ **Countries:**	France and Iraq
▶ **Foreign Government Officials:**	Iraqi government
▶ **Improper Payment Dollar Value:**	$646,488
▶ **Combined Penalties:**	$10.5 million ($4 million DOJ penalty; $3.5 million in disgorgement of profits and prejudgment interest and $3 million civil penalty)
▶ **Other:**	UN Oil-for-Food program; DPA

In February 2008, Flowserve Corporation (Flowserve), a Texas-based manufacturer of seals, valves, and pumps for the power, oil, gas, and chemical industries, agreed to pay a $4 million penalty as part of an agreement with the U.S. government regarding charges brought in connection with an ongoing investigation related to the UN Oil-for-Food program and the Iraqi government. The DOJ filed the DPA with Flowserve, as well as a criminal information against a French Flowserve subsidiary, Flowserve Pompes SAS (Flowserve Pompes), in the U.S. District Court for the District of Columbia. The criminal information charged that Flowserve Pompes engaged in a conspiracy to commit wire fraud and to violate the books-and-records provisions of the FCPA.[201]

Under the agreement, Flowserve acknowledged responsibility for the actions of its subsidiary, whose employees and agents paid kickbacks to the Iraqi government in order to obtain contracts for the sale of large-scale water pumps and spare parts for use in Iraqi oil refineries. Between July 2002 and February 2003, employees of Flowserve Pompes paid a total of approximately $604,651 and offered to pay an additional $173,758 in kickbacks to the Iraqi government by inflating the price of contracts by approximately 10 percent before submitting them to the UN for approval; and concealed from the UN the fact that the contract prices contained a kickback to the Iraqi government. In recognition of Flowserve's review of the improper payments and the company's implementation of enhanced compliance policies and procedures, the DOJ agreed to defer prosecution of Flowserve Pompes for three years. If Flowserve and Flowserve Pompes abided by the terms of the DPA, the DOJ would agree to dismiss the criminal information.

On the same date, Flowserve also reached a books-and-records and internal controls settlement with the SEC under which it agreed to pay a $3 million civil penalty and approximately $3.5 million in disgorgement of all profits, including prejudgment interest, in connection with contracts for which the subsidiaries—Flowserve Pompes (French) and Flowserve B.V. (Dutch)—paid kickbacks to the Iraqi government.[202] In total, Flowserve agreed to pay approximately $10.5 million in penalties and disgorgement of profits in the DOJ and SEC cases.

Z. *United States v. Volvo Construction Equipment AB;*[203] *United States v. Renault Trucks SAS;*[204] *SEC v. AB Volvo*[205]

► **Misconduct Category:**   Kickback payments disguised as "after-sales service fees"; UN Oil-for-Food program; use of agents and distributors

► **Countries:**   None

► **Foreign Government Officials:** Iraqi government

► **Improper Payment Dollar Value:** $6.3 million

► **Combined Penalties:** $19.6 million ($7 million DOJ penalty; $8.6 million in disgorgement of profits; and $4 million civil penalty)

► **Other:**   DPAs with parent and two subsidiaries (Renault and Volvo Construction AB); separate conspiracies to commit wire fraud and violate the books-and-records provisions of the FCPA filed against subsidiaries; UN Oil-for-Food program

In March 2008, AB Volvo and two subsidiaries entered into a DPA whereby it agreed to a $7 million fine to the DOJ, a $4 million civil penalty to the SEC, and approximately $8.6 million in disgorgement in connection with UN Oil-for-Food program contracts for which its subsidiaries paid kickbacks to the Iraqi government. The informations filed in the U.S. District Court for the District of Columbia charged that Renault Trucks and Volvo Construction Equipment AB (VCE) engaged in separate conspiracies to commit wire fraud and to violate the books-and-records provisions of the FCPA.

According to the letter agreement, AB Volvo acknowledged responsibility for the actions of its subsidiaries, whose employees, agents, and distributors paid kickbacks to the Iraqi government in order to obtain contracts for the sale of trucks and heavy commercial construction equipment. The DOJ alleged that between November 2000 and April 2003, employees and agents of Renault Trucks paid a total of approximately $5 million in kickbacks to the Iraqi government for a total of approximately 61 million euros' worth of contracts with various Iraqi ministries. To pay the kickbacks, Renault Trucks inflated the price of contracts by approximately 10 percent before submitting them to the UN for approval and concealed from the UN the fact that the contract prices contained a kickback to the Iraqi government. In some cases, Renault Trucks paid inflated prices to companies that outfitted the chassis and cabs produced by Renault Trucks. Those companies then used the excess funds to pay the kickbacks to the Iraqi government on behalf of Renault Trucks.

Further, between December 2000 and January 2003, Volvo Construction Equipment International AB (VCEI), the predecessor to VCE, and its distributors were awarded a total of approximately $13.8 million worth of contracts. During the same time period, employees, agents, and distributors of VCEI paid a total of approximately $1.3 million in kickbacks to the Iraqi government by inflating the price of contracts by approximately 10 percent before submitting them to the UN for approval and concealed from the UN the fact that the contract prices contained a kickback to the Iraqi government.

Beginning in 2000, the Iraqi government began requiring companies wishing to sell humanitarian goods to government ministries to pay a kickback, often mischaracterized as an "after-sales service fee," to the government in order to be granted a contract. The amount of that fee was usually 10 percent of the contract price. Such payments were not permitted under the Oil-for-Food program or other sanction regimes then in place.

In recognition of AB Volvo's thorough review of the improper payments and the company's implementation of enhanced compliance policies and procedures, the DOJ agreed to defer prosecution of Renault Trucks and VCE for three years. If AB Volvo, Renault Trucks, and VCE abided by the terms of the agreement, the DOJ agreed to dismiss the criminal informations.

In a related matter, AB Volvo reached a settlement with the SEC under which it agreed to pay a $4 million civil penalty and approximately $8.6 million in disgorgement of all profits, including prejudgment interest, in connection with contracts for which its subsidiaries paid kickbacks to the Iraqi government.

AA.   *United States v. Self* [206]

▶ **Misconduct Category:**	Sham marketing agreement with relative of a government official to obtain spare-parts contracts
▶ **Country:**	United Kingdom
▶ **Foreign Government Official:**	U.K. Ministry of Defence official
▶ **Improper Payment Dollar Value:**	$70,000
▶ **Combined Penalties:**	$20,000
▶ **Other:**	Eight months in jail and two years' probation; acquirer of employer referred the matter to the DOJ and fully cooperated in the government investigation

In May 2008, Martin Self, a former president of Pacific Consolidated Industries LP (PCI) of Santa Ana, California, pled guilty to charges related to the bribery of a U.K. Ministry of Defence (U.K.-MOD) official in order to obtain lucrative equipment contracts with the U.K. Royal Air Force. Self pled guilty to a two-count information in the U.S. District Court for the Central District of California, which charged him with violating the FCPA in connection with the illicit payment of more than $70,000 in bribes for the benefit of a U.K.-MOD official in exchange for obtaining and retaining lucrative contracts for PCI.

PCI was a private company that manufactured air separation units (ASUs) and other equipment for defense departments throughout the world. ASUs generate oxygen in remote, extreme, and confined locations for aircraft support and military hospitals. According to the plea agreement, in or about October 1999, Self as PCI's president and Leo Winston Smith,[207] PCI's then-executive vice president and director of sales and marketing, caused PCI to enter into a marketing agreement with a person Self understood to be a relative of the U.K.-MOD official. The official, as a result of his position within the U.K.-MOD, was able to influence the awarding of U.K.-MOD contracts for services and equipment.[208] Self admitted that he was not aware of any genuine services provided by the official's relative, and believed there was a high probability that the payments were being made to the official's relative in order to benefit the official in exchange for obtaining and retaining the ASU contracts. Despite these beliefs, Self initiated several improper wire transfers to the relative of the U.K.-MOD official and deliberately avoided learning the true facts relating to the nature and purpose of the payments.

Self was sentenced to a prison term of eight months. In late 2003, subsequent to the conduct alleged in the information, PCI was acquired by a group of investors and renamed Pacific Consolidated Industries, LLC. The acquirer referred the matter to the DOJ and fully cooperated in the government's investigation.

AB.   *United States v. Willbros Group Inc. & Willbros International Inc.;*[209] *SEC v. Willbros Group, Inc.*[210]

▶ **Misconduct Category:**	Consultant contracts used to generate cash bribes to obtain contracts and to avoid taxes
▶ **Countries:**	Bolivia, Ecuador, and Nigeria
▶ **Foreign Government Officials:**	Senior officials in executive branch; officials at Nigerian National Petroleum Corporation, the Nigerian state-owned oil company and Petroecuador, the Ecuadorian state-owned oil company
▶ **Improper Payment Dollar Value:**	$6.3 million
▶ **Combined Penalties:**	$32.3 million ($22 million criminal penalty and $10.3 million in disgorgement and prejudgment interest)
▶ **Other:**	Voluntary disclosure of ten-year scheme; termination of 15 officers or employees; $1 million improper payment during government investigation; corporate cooperation resulted in indictment of five individuals; DPAs for both parent and international subsidiary as a result of "exceptional cooperation"; $10.3 million in disgorgement of profits and prejudgment interest; fines to be paid over a three-year period; three-year monitorship requirement.
▶ **Related Matters:**	*United States v. Tillery & Novak*; *United States v. Steph*

In May 2008, Willbros Group, Inc. (WGI) and its wholly owned subsidiary Willbros International, Inc. (WII) entered into a DPA with the DOJ for violations of the Foreign Corrupt Practices Act in Nigeria, Bolivia, and Ecuador.[211] WGI and WII jointly and severally agreed to pay $32.3 million: a $22 million criminal penalty in four installments to the DOJ, and $10.3 million in disgorgement and prejudgment interest to the SEC. Willbros, which had incurred significant losses over the previous four years, was also allowed to pay its DOJ penalty over three years.

The DOJ filed a DPA and a criminal information against WGI and WII (collectively Willbros) in the U.S. District Court for the Southern District of Texas. This six-count criminal information included one count of conspiracy to bribe Nigerian and Ecuadorian officials; two counts of violating the FCPA by authorizing specific corrupt payments to Nigerian and Ecuadorian officials; and three counts of violating the FCPA by falsifying books and records relating to corrupt payments and a tax fraud scheme.

WGI is a provider of construction, engineering, and other services in the oil and gas industry. It conducted international operations through WII. Willbros conspired with others to make corrupt payments to government officials abroad to assist Willbros in obtaining and retaining business, to secure improper advantages, and to induce officials to provide preferential treatment to them. Moreover, Willbros conspired to falsify books, records, and accounts to make these payments appear legitimate when they were actually bribes.

Three subsidiaries of WII conducted most of Willbros's Nigerian business. From the 1990s through 2005, these subsidiaries performed work on joint venture and other Nigerian oil and gas projects. One Nigerian project for Willbros was the Eastern Gas Gathering System (EGGS) project, which aimed to construct a major natural gas pipeline system through remote, swampy terrain in the Niger Delta. Through certain consultants and others, Willbros made a series of corrupt payments totaling more than $6.3 million to assist in obtaining this $387 million project. These payments were made and authorized to be made to officials of the Nigerian National Petroleum Corporation (NNPC), the Nigerian state-owned oil company; NNPC's subsidiary, the National Petroleum Investment Management Services; a senior official in the executive branch of the Nigerian federal government; officials of a multinational oil company operating the EGGS joint venture; and a political party.

In Ecuador, through certain consultants and others, Willbros agreed to make approximately $300,000 in corrupt payments to Ecuadorian government officials of the state-owned oil company Petroecuador and its subsidiary PetroComercial, in order to assist in obtaining and retaining business. The business sought was a $3 million contract for the rehabilitation of approximately 16 kilometers of a gas pipeline, known as the Santo Domingo project.

In a related proceeding, the SEC filed a settled FCPA action in May 2008 against WGI and several former employees.[212] The complaint alleged that WGI engaged in multiple schemes to bribe foreign officials, including schemes to pay over $6 million to Nigerian government officials and employees to obtain contracts resulting in net profits of approximately $8.9 million; the aforementioned scheme to bribe Ecuadorian government officials to obtain a $3 million contract; and a scheme to avoid taxes fraudulently in Bolivia. In so doing, WGI violated the improper payment to foreign officials, books-and-records, internal controls, and false statement provisions. WGI agreed to entry of a judgment permanently enjoining it from future violations of these provisions. WGI also agreed to pay $8.9 million in disgorgement of profits, plus prejudgment interest of $1.4 million.

Aggravating facts against Willbros included the following. First, a payment was made to a senior official in the executive branch of the federal government of Nigeria. This was part of a series of corrupt payments that Willbros conspired to make and made through sham "consultancy agreements," and through the knowing payment of false invoices. Second, bribes were paid in three countries on two continents for ten years. Third, a million-dollar bribe by a Willbros country manager was paid during the government investigation.

Upon discovering officer misconduct in Bolivia, Willbros took numerous remedial steps enabling it to obtain a DPA, including

- Commencing a thorough audit committee internal investigation within 24 hours of notice of allegations of corporate tax fraud committed by employees and purported consultants working on behalf of the Willbros subsidiary's Bolivian subsidiary;
- Quickly expanding the scope of the internal investigation, which included extensive forensic analysis, into alleged misconduct in other international locations, primarily Nigeria and Ecuador, and promptly and voluntarily reporting the results of its investigation to the DOJ and the SEC;
- Severing its employment relationship with a senior international executive within ten days of receiving allegations of his involvement in the Bolivian tax scheme, and seizing from him critical encrypted electronic evidence at the time of his severance;
- Taking prompt and appropriate disciplinary actions, without regard to rank, against 18 additional employees;
- Voluntarily agreeing, as to the DOJ only, to a limited waiver of attorney-client privilege with respect to certain specific subject matters important to the DOJ's understanding of the internal investigation;
- Promptly terminating commercial relationships with purported "consulting" companies based in Nigeria, which companies Willbros suspected of assisting in making improper payments to Nigerian government officials;
- Promptly reporting the misconduct of certain WII employees who, along with others, made additional improper payments in Nigeria after WGI and the government had begun investigations, which reporting was a substantial factor in causing the guilty pleas of two of the responsible individuals;
- Upon conclusion of the internal investigation, continuing to cooperate with the DOJ and SEC in their parallel investigations, which cooperation included making numerous current and former employees available for interviews and testimony in the United States and abroad, and responding promptly to requests for documentary evidence, much of which was located in remote international locations;
- Expanding, enhancing, and, where appropriate, centralizing its worldwide legal, accounting, and international audit functions;

- Issuing an enhanced, stand-alone FCPA policy and conducting worldwide training upon implementation of that policy;
- Retaining new senior management with substantial international experience and understanding of FCPA requirements;
- Acknowledging responsibility for the misconduct; and
- Delaying pursuit of civil remedies against certain former employees so as not to prejudice the DOJ's criminal investigation of the individuals.

The above cooperative and remedial steps were specifically outlined in the DPA and represent model remedial steps by a company discovering and promptly investigating bribery conduct. The Willbros resolution offers important guidance on how mid-size companies uncovering serious misconduct by senior management in multiple countries can still manage to avoid a felony conviction for both the parent and its subsidiaries.

AC.   *United States v. AGA Medical Corp.*[213]

▶ **Misconduct Category:**	Kickback payments to physicians at state-owned hospitals to purchase medical products
▶ **Country:**	China
▶ **Foreign Government Officials:**	High-ranking officials at state-owned hospital
▶ **Improper Payment Dollar Value:**	$480,000
▶ **Penalty:**	$2 million
▶ **Other:**	Voluntary disclosure by a small U.S. private company; DPA; use of Chinese distributor to make improper payments.

In June 2008, AGA Medical Corporation of Plymouth, Minnesota, agreed to pay the DOJ a $2 million criminal penalty in connection with corrupt payments made to Chinese government officials. AGA is a privately held medical device manufacturer with approximately $150 million in annual sales. The DOJ entered into a DPA with AGA and filed a criminal information against the company in the U.S. District Court for the District of Minnesota alleging two series of corrupt payments.[214] First, between 1997 and 2005, AGA, one of its high-ranking officers, and other employees agreed to make improper payments to doctors in China through AGA's local distributor. The doctors involved were employed by government-owned hospitals. Second, from 2000 to 2002, as it sought patents for its products, AGA and one of its high-ranking officers agreed to make corrupt payments to Chinese government officials through their local Chinese distributor.

AGA, which voluntarily disclosed and thoroughly reviewed the improper payments, cooperated fully with the U.S. government, enhanced its corporate compliance policies and procedures, and engaged an independent corporate monitor. In recognition of these efforts, the DOJ agreed to a three-year DPA. The case makes clear that the DOJ will fully pursue small companies for antibribery conduct even if such companies have small overseas sales and limited compliance resources, and voluntarily disclose.

AD. **U.S. Department of Justice Faro Technologies, Inc. Agreement;[215]** ***In re* Faro Technologies, Inc. Agreement;[216] *SEC v. Meza*[217]**

▶ **Misconduct Category:**	Corrupt payments termed "referral fees"; use of shell company to pay Chinese officials to "avoid exposure" and to secure business
▶ **Country:**	China
▶ **Foreign Government Officials:**	Employees of state-owned or state-controlled companies
▶ **Improper Payment Dollar Value:**	$444,992
▶ **Combined Penalties:**	Faro: $2.95 million; Meza: $30,000 civil penalty and $26,707 in disgorgement of profits and prejudgment interest
▶ **Other:**	10 to 15 percent kickbacks to employees of state-owned customers; two-year NPA; small company; voluntary disclosure and cooperation; independent monitor; Faro secured $4.5 million in sales and approximately $1.4 million in net profit. One employee e-mailed Faro officers and managers about whether he could "do business the Chinese way" and was advised by the company's outside lawyer in China that making payments violated Chinese law. One e-mail stated, "I wish we didn't have to pay this bribery."

In June 2008, Faro Technologies, Inc., entered into an NPA and agreed to pay the DOJ a $1.1 million penalty in connection with corrupt payments to Chinese government officials. Faro, a Florida-based public company, specializes in computerized measurement devices and software and had a net income of $18 million in 2007. It began selling its products in China in 2003 through a subsidiary, Faro China. In 2004 and 2005, in order to secure business there, a Faro employee authorized other Faro employees to make corrupt payments to employees of Chinese state-owned or state-controlled entities. These payments were internally termed "referral fees" and disguised as such, and helped to secure contracts worth approximately $4.5 million. In addition, in 2005, Faro employees began routing the corrupt payments to Chinese officials through a shell company, and wrote internal e-mails explaining that they did so to "avoid exposure." One employee wrote in an e-mail, "Actually, I wish we didn't have to pay this bribery. While in Beijing, I saw in the news in CCTV that the Chinese government will start enforcing the laws against bribery too. Be careful!!!" Faro falsely recorded at least $238,000 in improper payments in its books and records, terming the bribe payments "referral fees." Moreover, between May 2003 and February 2006, Faro did not maintain a system of internal controls regarding foreign sales sufficient to comply with the FCPA.

Faro voluntarily disclosed the improper payments and made a thorough review of them, cooperated with the DOJ investigation, implemented and committed to implement enhanced compliance policies and procedures, and agreed to engage an independent corporate monitor. In recognition of its voluntary disclosure and other efforts, the DOJ agreed to a two-year NPA. The SEC simultaneously instituted a settled enforcement action against Faro whereby Faro agreed to pay approximately $1.85 million in disgorgement of profits and prejudgment interest, and consented to the entry of a cease-and-desist order.

In August 2009, the SEC filed a settled enforcement action against Oscar H. Meza, formerly the director of Asia Pacific Sales for Faro. The SEC alleged that beginning in 2004, Meza authorized a former Faro subsidiary employee to make improper payments totaling $444,492 over the next two years, generating $4.5 million in sales and approximately $1.4 million in net profit. Meza agreed to pay a $30,000 civil penalty as well as $26,707 in disgorgement of profits and prejudgment interest. Meza was charged with antibribery books-and-records and internal controls violations, and aiding and abetting Faro's violations of the same.

AE.   *United States v. Naaman;*[218] *SEC v. Naaman & Turner;*[219] *SEC v. Jennings*[220]

▶ **Misconduct Category:**	Naaman, as agent for Innospec, Inc., and its subsidiaries, paid over $7.5 million over seven years to secure contracts to sell tetraethyl lead as an Oil-for-Food program component
▶ **Countries:**	Iraq and Indonesia
▶ **Foreign Government Officials:**	Senior Iraqi Ministry of Oil (MoO) officials and officials of Pertamina, an Indonesian-owned oil company
▶ **Improper Payment Dollar Value:**	$7.5 million ($4 million in kickbacks to the Iraqi government and $3.5 million in bribes to senior Iraqi government officials), including cash payments, travel, and the purchase of a Mercedes-Benz
▶ **Combined Penalties:**	Naaman sentenced to 30 months in jail and ordered to pay a $250,000 criminal fine. Turner: $40,000 disgorgement; Naaman: $877,000 disgorgement and prejudgment interest and $438,038 penalty, which will be satisfied by payment of a criminal fine of equal amounts.

▶ **Other:**

Naaman extradited from Germany; despite belated cooperation with U.S. and U.K. governments, DOJ sought for Naaman 90-month sentence or 25 percent discount off of agreed reasonable guideline number of 120 months; Jennings made false SOX certifications; e-mail references to "the Indonesian way" and "commissions."

▶ **Related Matters:**

United States v. Innospec Ltd.; *Regina v. Innospec Ltd. (U.K.)*

In August 2008, Ousama Naaman, 60, of Abu Dhabi, United Arab Emirates, was charged in the U.S. District Court for the District of Columbia with one count of conspiracy to commit wire fraud and to violate the FCPA and two counts of violating the FCPA. Naaman, a Lebanese-Canadian citizen, was arrested on July 30, 2009, in Frankfurt, Germany. The DOJ obtained extradition of Naaman from Germany to the United States.[221] In March 2010, Naaman pled guilty to conspiracy to commit wire fraud, substantive FCPA violations, and other charges in Washington, D.C.

According to the indictment, from 2001 to 2003, acting on behalf of a publicly traded U.S. chemical company and its subsidiary, Naaman allegedly offered and paid 10 percent kickbacks to the Iraqi government in exchange for five contracts under the UN Oil-for-Food program (OFFP). Naaman allegedly negotiated the contracts, including a 10 percent increase in the price to cover the kickback. In exchange for handling the kickbacks, Naaman allegedly received 2 percent of the contract value, in addition to the 2 percent commission he was paid for securing the contracts. The U.S. company inflated its prices in contracts approved by the OFFP to cover the cost of the kickbacks.

In addition, according to the indictment, in 2006 Naaman, a Canadian, allegedly paid $150,000 in bribes on behalf of the U.S. company to Iraqi Ministry of Oil (MoO) officials to ensure that a competing product manufactured by a different company failed a field test, keeping the competing product out of the Iraqi market. Naaman is alleged then to have provided the U.S. company with false invoices, on the basis of which the U.S. company reimbursed him for bribes paid to the Iraq officials. In December 2011, Naaman was sentenced to 30 months in prison and ordered to pay a $250,000 fine.

In August 2010, the SEC charged David P. Turner,[222] a former business director at Innospec, Inc., and Naaman, the company's third-party agent in Iraq, with violating the FCPA by engaging in widespread bribery of Iraqi government officials to land contracts under the OFFP and continue selling a fuel additive to Iraq after the program ended. Bribes also were paid to Indonesian officials to enable Innospec to sell the fuel additive to Indonesian state-owned oil companies. Both Turner and Naaman agreed to settle the SEC's charges against them.

According to the SEC complaint, Turner and Naaman played key roles in Innospec's bribery activities in Iraq, which began with the company's participation in

the OFFP in 2001 and extended until at least 2008. Turner also actively participated in the bribery scheme in Indonesia, which began as early as 2000 and continued until 2005. Innospec, a manufacturer and distributor of fuel additives and
specialty chemicals, made illicit payments of more than $6.3 million and promised
an additional $2.8 million in bribes to government officials in Iraq and Indonesia
to sell tetraethyl lead (TEL). The contracts that Innospec obtained in exchange for
the bribes were worth approximately $176 million.

The SEC alleged that Naaman paid kickbacks to Iraq on Innospec's behalf so
that the company could obtain five OFFP contracts for the sale of TEL to the Iraqi
MoO and its component oil refineries. Naaman aided Innospec in obtaining the
OFFP contracts by paying kickbacks equaling 10 percent of the contract value on
three of the contracts. When the program ended shortly before Innospec was to
pay promised kickbacks on the two remaining contracts, Innospec kept the promised payments as part of its profit. When Innospec's internal auditors questioned
Turner about the nature of the commission payments that were made to Naaman
under the OFFP, Turner made false statements to the auditors and concealed the
fact that the commission payments to Naaman included kickbacks to the Iraqi
government in return for contracts.

The SEC alleged that after the OFFP ended in late 2003, Turner and Naaman
continued to pay bribes to Iraqi officials in order to secure TEL business contracts
from Iraq. In one e-mail, Naaman informed Turner and other management that
Iraqi officials were demanding a 2 percent kickback related to one TEL order. Naaman stated, "We are sharing most of our profits with Iraqi officials. Otherwise, our
business will stop and we will lose the market. We have to change our strategy and
do more compensation to get the rewards." In his response to the e-mail, Turner
confirmed that the requested kickback would be paid through an additional 2 percent "commission" to Naaman.

According to the SEC complaint, Turner and senior Innospec officials also
directed Naaman to pay a bribe of $155,000 to Iraqi officials to ensure the fail-
ure of a 2006 field trial test of MMT, a fuel product manufactured by a competitor of Innospec. Turner and other Innospec officials also authorized payments,
through Naaman, to fund lavish trips for Iraqi officials, including the seven-day
honeymoon of one official. Innospec officials and Turner also arranged for Naaman to pay thousands of dollars in cash to Iraqi officials for "pocket money" on
trips funded by Innospec.

The SEC complaint also alleged that Turner and senior Innospec officials autho-
rized and directed the payment of bribes to Indonesian government officials to win
contracts for Innospec. More than $2.8 million in bribes was funneled through an
Indonesian agent. These involved bribes paid annually to a senior official at BP
Migas, "special commissions" paid to a Swiss account, and a "one off" payment of
$300,000. On one occasion, a managing director of Innospec informed Turner that
Innospec had provided payments to its Indonesian agent to fund the purchase of a
Mercedes-Benz for a Pertamina official.

Turner agreed to disgorge $40,000 in profits in order to settle the SEC's charges
against him. Despite facing significant financial penalties, none were sought

against him based on, among other things, his extensive and ongoing cooperation in the investigation. Naaman agreed to disgorge $810,076 plus prejudgment
interest of $67,030, and pay a penalty of $438,038 that will be deemed satisfied by
a criminal order requiring him to pay a criminal fine that is at least equal to the
civil penalty amount. Naaman cooperated in the investigation after his extradition
to the United States.

In January 2011, the SEC charged Paul W. Jennings, a former chief executive
officer at Innospec, Inc., with violating the FCPA by approving bribes to government officials to obtain and retain business. According to the SEC's complaint
filed in the U.S. District Court for the District of Columbia, Jennings played a
key role in Innospec's bribery activities in Iraq and Indonesia. The SEC alleged
that Innospec made payments totaling more than $1.6 million and promised an
additional $884,480 to MoO officials. For example, in an October 2005 e-mail
copying Jennings, an Iraqi agent said that Iraqi officials were demanding a 2
percent kickback and that "[w]e are sharing most of our profits with Iraqi officials. Otherwise, our business will stop and we will lose the market. We have to
change our strategy and do more compensation to get the rewards." The kickback and later payments were paid by increasing the agent's commission, which
Jennings approved. The SEC's complaint also alleged that Jennings was aware of
the scheme to pay an official at the Trade Bank of Iraq in exchange for a favorable exchange rate on letters of credit. Another scheme involved a bribe to ensure
the failure of a field test of a competitor product. A confidential MoO report for
the field trial test was shared with Jennings. Bribes were offered to secure a 2008
long-term purchase agreement that would have caused approximately $850,000
to be shared with Iraqi officials. The agreement, however, did not go forward
due to the investigation and ultimate discovery by U.S. regulators of widespread
bribery by Innospec.

According to the SEC complaint, Innospec also paid bribes to Indonesian government officials from at least 2000 to 2005 in order to win contracts worth more
than $48 million from state-owned oil and gas companies in Indonesia. Jennings
became aware of and approved payments beginning in mid- to late 2004. Various
euphemisms to refer to the bribery were commonly used in e-mails and in discussions with Jennings and others at Innospec, including "the Indonesian Way," "the
Lead Defense Fund," and "TEL optimization." Bribery discussions were held on a
flight in the United States and even discussed at Jennings's performance review in
2005. In one bribery scheme with Pertamina, an Indonesian state-owned oil and
gas company, Innospec agreed, with approval by Jennings, to the "one off payment" of $300,000 to their Indonesian agent with the understanding that it would
be passed on to an Indonesian official.

The SEC's complaint also alleged that from 2004 to February 2009, Jennings
signed annual certifications that were provided to auditors where he falsely stated
that he had complied with Innospec's Code of Ethics incorporating the company's
FCPA policy. Jennings also signed annual and quarterly personal certifications pursuant to the Sarbanes-Oxley Act of 2002 (SOX) in which he made false certifications concerning the company's books and records and internal controls.

AF.   *United States v. Nexus Technologies Inc., Nguyen, Lukas, Nguyen & Nguyen*[223]

▶ **Misconduct Category:**	Payments to secure supply contracts described as "commissions" in company records
▶ **Country:**	Vietnam
▶ **Foreign Government Officials:**	Ministries of Transport, Industry, and Public Safety officials
▶ **Improper Payment Dollar Value:**	$150,000
▶ **Combined Penalties:**	Nam Nguyen: 16 months in jail; An Nguyen: nine months in jail; Lukas and Kim Nguyen: two years of probation and fine of $1,000 and $20,000, respectively. Company agreed to cease operations and dissolve ("death penalty" after court declared it a "criminal enterprise").
▶ **Other:**	Lukas's cooperation led to Nguyen and corporate pleas.

In September 2008, U.S. citizens Nam Nguyen, 52, of Houston; Joseph Lukas, 59, of Smithville, N.J.; Kim Nguyen, 39, of Philadelphia; and An Nguyen, 32, of Philadelphia were charged, along with Nexus Technologies Inc., a privately owned export company with offices in Philadelphia, New Jersey, and Vietnam that purchased a wide variety of equipment and technology, on one count of conspiracy to bribe Vietnamese public officials in violation of the FCPA and four substantive counts of violating the FCPA.

According to the indictment, Nexus Technologies Inc. sold equipment, including underwater mapping equipment, bomb containment equipment, helicopter parts, chemical detectors, satellite communication parts, and air tracking systems, for export to agencies of the government of Vietnam. The indictment alleged that from approximately 1999 through 2008, the defendants engaged in a conspiracy to pay Vietnamese government officials bribes in order to secure lucrative contracts for Nexus Technologies Inc. Over the course of the scheme, the defendants are alleged to have paid at least $150,000 in bribes to foreign officials in Vietnam. The defendants' customers in Vietnam are alleged to have included multiple Vietnamese government agencies, including the commercial branches of Vietnam's Ministries of Transport, Industry, and Public Safety. Nam Nguyen allegedly negotiated contracts and bribes with officials of Vietnamese government agencies, while Lukas negotiated with vendors in the United States. Kim Nguyen and An Nguyen allegedly arranged for the transfer of funds at Nam Nguyen's direction. In June 2009, Lukas, a partner in Nexus Technologies until 2005, cooperated and pled guilty to one conspiracy count and one substantive FCPA count.[224]

In March 2010, the Nguyens and Nexus pled guilty. Nam Nguyen, the president and owner of the company, was sentenced to 16 months in prison; his sibling, An Nguyen, was sentenced to nine months in prison, and his other sibling, Kim Nguyen, was sentenced to two years of probation and ordered to pay a $20,000 fine. Lukas was also sentenced to two years of probation and ordered to pay a $1,000 fine. Nexus pled guilty to all charges filed in an October 30, 2009 superseding indictment and agreed to cease operation and dissolve.[225]

AG.   *United States v. Stanley;*[226] *SEC v. Stanley*[227]

▶ **Misconduct Category:**	Use of U.K. and Japanese "consultants" to pay massive bribes to senior Nigerian government officials to obtain $6 billion worth of contracts
▶ **Country:**	Nigeria
▶ **Foreign Government Officials:**	Executive branch
▶ **Improper Payment Dollar Value:**	$182 million
▶ **Combined Penalties:**	Restitution of $10.8 million. Although subject to a seven-year plea agreement, Stanley was sentenced to only 30 months in prison.
▶ **Other:**	Engineering, procurement, and construction (EPC) contracts in Nigeria worth $6 billion; seven-year incarceration plea agreement; $10.8 million forfeiture
▶ **Related Matters:**	*United States v. Kellogg, Brown & Root LLC; SEC v. Halliburton Co. & KBR Inc.; United States v. Snamprogetti B.V.; SEC v. ENI, SpA & Snamprogetti; United States v. Technip SA; SEC v. Technip SA; United States v. JGC Corp.; United States v. Tesler & Chodan*

In September 2008, Albert Jackson "Jack" Stanley, a former officer and director of Kellogg, Brown & Root, Inc. (KBR), a Texas-based global engineering and construction company, pled guilty to conspire to violate the FCPA and to violate the federal fraud statutes. The decade-long conspiracy included two separate schemes: bribery of Nigerian officials to obtain engineering, procurement, and construction contracts worth more than $6 billion, and conspiring to commit mail and wire fraud as part of a separate kickback scheme.

Between 1995 and 2004, KBR was part of a joint venture with three other companies awarded contracts by the government-owned company Nigeria LNG Ltd. (NLNG), to build liquefied natural gas (LNG) facilities on Bonny Island, Nigeria. Stanley was the senior representative of KBR on the joint venture's steering committee. He admitted that he authorized the joint venture to hire "agents" (Consulting Companies A and B) to bribe Nigerian officials, and that he met with senior officials in the executive branch of the Nigerian government to ask them to designate a representative with whom the joint venture could negotiate bribes. The joint venture paid $132 million to Consulting Company A and over $50 million to Consulting Company B during the bribery scheme; Stanley admitted that he intended for the agents' fees to be used, in part, to bribe Nigerian government officials. In a separate action, Stanley pled guilty to conspiracy to commit mail and wire fraud to defraud KBR and others. He admitted to receiving about $10.8 million in kick-backs from a consultant he caused KBR and its predecessor company to hire in connection with worldwide LNG projects.

Stanley faced a maximum penalty of ten years in prison and a $500,000 fine. Under his plea agreement, he had agreed to a seven-year sentence and the payment of $10.8 million in restitution. However, in February 2012, the 69-year old Stanley was sentenced to 30 months in prison and ordered to pay a $1,000 fine. He claimed that alcoholism had played a role in compromising his values.[228] In a separate civil action, the SEC charged Stanley in September 2008 with violating the antibribery provisions of the FCPA and related provisions of the federal securities laws. Stanley consented to injunctive relief and to cooperate with the SEC's ongoing investigation.

AH. *United States v. Green & Green*[229]

▶ **Misconduct Category:**	Sham contracts and sales commissions to pay bribes for film festival management contracts to the president of the Bangkok International Film Festival, which the Thailand Tourism Authority administered and funded
▶ **Country:**	Thailand
▶ **Foreign Government Official:**	Former governor of Thailand Tourism Authority
▶ **Improper Payment Dollar Value:**	$1.8 million
▶ **Combined Penalties:**	Greens each sentenced to six months in prison, six months of home confinement, and two and one-half years of probation despite DOJ request for ten years' incarceration; Greens ordered to pay jointly and severally $250,000 in restitution
▶ **Other:**	Contract's value $14 million; tax and money laundering counts. Very light sentence due to poor health of 77-year-old Gerald Green.

In October 2008, the United States charged Gerald and Patricia Green, a film producer and his wife of West Hollywood, California, in the Central District of California, with paying bribes totaling $1.8 million to obtain management contracts worth $14 million. The same couple had been indicted in January 2008 on federal charges of bribing a Thai government official, the former governor of the Tourism Authority of Thailand, his daughter, and a friend. The Greens paid these bribes during 2002 to 2007. As charged in the superseding indictment, the Greens conspired with others to make the bribes and used different business entities, some with phony business addresses and telephone numbers, in order to conceal the large sums they were being paid under the contracts. They disguised these bribes as "sales commissions." The indictment, which sought forfeiture, charged the Greens with one count of conspiracy to violate the FCPA by paying bribes to a foreign public official and by engaging in money laundering; ten substantive counts of violating the FCPA; seven counts of money laundering; one count of a transaction in criminally derived property; and two counts of false subscription of tax returns. The Greens were convicted by a jury in September 2009. After repeated delays, in August 2010 the Greens were sentenced to six months in prison, followed by six months of home confinement and two and a half years of probation. They were also ordered jointly and severally to pay restitution of $250,000. The United States, which had sought the maximum sentence of ten years' incarceration, initially appealed the Greens' sentences, but dropped the appeal in August 2011.

AI.   *United States v. Aibel Group Ltd.*[230]

▶ **Misconduct Category:**	Use of major international freight forwarder to obtain preferential treatment during the customs process
▶ **Country:**	Nigeria
▶ **Foreign Government Officials:**	Nigerian Customs Service officials
▶ **Improper Payment Dollar Value:**	$2.1 million
▶ **Combined Penalties:**	$4.2 million (with Aibel Group's guilty plea and sentence, the combined penalties paid by Vetco entities for the 2004, 2007, and 2008 guilty pleas now exceed $46 million)
▶ **Other:**	Voluntary disclosure of problems post-DPA; guilty plea to FCPA conspiracy and money laundering; violation of 2007 DPA resulting in an additional organizational probation term requiring a two-year reporting obligation to the U.S. government; combined financial penalties for Vetco-related entities exceed $46 million.
▶ **Related Matters:**	*United States v. Vetco Gray U.K. Ltd., Vetco Gray Controls Inc. & Vetco Controls Ltd.*

In November 2008, Aibel Group Ltd., a United Kingdom corporation, pled guilty to a two-count superseding information charging a conspiracy to violate the FCPA and a substantive anti-money laundering in the Southern District of Texas. At the same time, Aibel Group admitted that it was not in compliance with a DPA it had entered into with the DOJ in February 2007 regarding the same underlying conduct. As part of the plea agreement, Aibel Group agreed to pay a $4.2 million criminal fine.

Beginning in February 2001, Aibel Group's predecessor company and several affiliated companies began providing engineering and procurement services, as well as subsea construction equipment, for Nigeria's first deepwater oil drilling operation, known as the Bonga Project. From at least September 2002 to at least

April 2005, Aibel Group admitted to conspiring with others to make at least 378 corrupt payments totaling approximately $2.1 million to Nigerian Customs Service officials in an effort to induce those officials to give the defendants preferential treatment during the customs process. These corrupt payments were paid through a major international freight-forwarding and customs clearance company to the Nigerian officials, and were coordinated largely through an affiliated company's offices in Houston.

This is the third time since July 2004 that entities affiliated with Aibel Group have pled guilty to violating the FCPA. On July 6, 2004, Vetco Gray U.K. Ltd., previously named ABB Vetco Gray U.K. Ltd., and an affiliated company pled guilty to violating the antibribery provisions of the FCPA in connection with the payment of more than $1 million in bribes to officials of the National Petroleum Investment Management Services, a Nigerian government agency that evaluates and approves potential bidders for contract work on oil exploration projects. ABB Vetco Gray U.K. Ltd. was renamed Vetco Gray U.K. Ltd. after its upstream oil and gas businesses and assets of its parent corporation, ABB Handels-und Verwaltungs AG (ABB), were acquired by a group of private equity entities.

In February 2007, Vetco Gray Controls Inc., Vetco Gray Controls Ltd., and Vetco Gray U.K. Ltd. (collectively referred to as the Vetco Gray entities), wholly owned subsidiaries of Vetco International Ltd., pled guilty to violating the antibribery provisions, *infra*. At the same time, Aibel Group, another wholly owned subsidiary of Vetco International Ltd., entered into the 2004 DPA with which Aibel Group admitted it was not in compliance. As part of the February 2007 plea, Vetco Gray Controls Inc., Vetco Gray Controls Ltd., and Vetco Gray U.K. Ltd. agreed to pay a combined $26 million criminal fine. Subsequent to the 2007 guilty pleas, the Vetco Gray entities were sold. The Vetco Gray entities have been in compliance with the terms of their respective plea agreements.

The resolution of the criminal investigation against Aibel Group in November 2008 and its affiliates in 2007 resulted, in large part, from the actions of the companies in voluntarily disclosing the matter to the Justice Department and the companies' agreement to take significant remedial steps. In addition to the $4.2 million criminal fine, Aibel Group was ordered in 2008 to serve a two-year term of organizational probation that requires, among other things, that it submit periodic reports regarding its progress in implementing antibribery compliance measures. The combined penalties paid by Vetco entities in 2004, 2007, and 2008 exceeded $46 million.

AJ. *United States v. Siemens AG;*[231] *SEC v. Siemens*[232]

▶ **Misconduct Category:**	"Systematic and widespread effort to make and to hide hundreds of millions of dollars in bribe payments across the globe": Consulting firm; cash payments; off-the-books slush funds; and use of shell companies in at least 11 countries
▶ **Countries:**	Argentina, Bangladesh, China, France, Iraq, Israel, Mexico, Russia, Turkey, Venezuela, and Vietnam

▶ **Foreign Government Officials:**   Various governmental officials in 11 countries, including two presidents, cabinet ministers in Argentina, and officials of state-owned telegraph and telephone board

▶ **Improper Payment Dollar Value:** $1.3 billion

▶ **Combined Penalties:** $1.7 billion ($850 million to German authorities; $450 million criminal penalty to DOJ; $350 million in disgorgement of profits; and $100 million to World Bank)

▶ **Other:**   Largest FCPA fine ever; first criminal plea to books-and-records and internal controls violations (avoidance of bribery conviction and near certain government debarment and suspension); joint announcement of resolution by German and U.S. law enforcement officials; four-year monitorship—foreign national to serve as monitor; massive global internal investigation (34 countries, 1,750 interviews, and 800 informational meetings); state-of-the-art ten-element compliance model; $100 million World Bank settlement and up to four-year Russian ban of Siemens unit in Russia

▶ **Related Matters:**   *United States v. Sharef, Steffen, Truppel, Bock, Signer, Reichert, Sergi & Czysch; SEC v. Sharif, Bock, Sergi, Signer, Steffen, Truppel, & Regendantz*

In December 2008, Siemens AG of Munich, Germany, and three subsidiaries (Siemens Argentina, Siemens Bangladesh, and Siemens Venezuela) pled guilty in the U.S. District Court for the District of Columbia, to various FCPA violations and agreed to pay DOJ, SEC, and German authorities over $1.6 billion in penalties in the largest FCPA antibribery enforcement case ever. Siemens AG pled guilty to a two-count indictment charging criminal violations of the FCPA's internal controls and books-and-records provisions. Siemens is a global company with industry (transport, building, and utilities), energy, and healthcare sectors that have over 405,000 employees. By pleading guilty to the Act's accounting provisions, the parent company avoided a corruption conviction and government debarment in numerous jurisdictions. Further, pleas by three non–European subsidiaries likely avoided government debarment of Siemens in the European Community. The U.S. and German authorities concluded that Siemens and various subsidiaries had made improper payments exceeding $1.3 billion in various countries including Argentina, Bangladesh, France, Iraq, Turkey, and Venezuela. Siemens agreed to pay U.S. authorities penalties totaling $450 million to the DOJ and $350 million in disgorgement of wrongful profits to the SEC. The company agreed to pay German authorities $850 million in similar penalties and disgorgement of profits.

In the wake of multiple searches of officers' and employees' homes in Germany, Siemens AG and its subsidiaries discovered FCPA violations after initiating an internal investigation of unprecedented scope. According to the DOJ, from the 1990s through 2007 Siemens engaged in a "systematic and widespread effort to make and to hide hundreds of millions of dollars in bribe payments across the globe."[233] From 2001 to 2007 Siemens and various subsidiaries paid more than $800 million in bribes. Efforts by Siemens executives involved off-the-books slush fund accounts and shell companies to facilitate bribes, and false entries on the company's books and records, for example, falsely recording bribes as consulting fees and accumulating profit reserves as a liability on company books and then using these funds to facilitate bribe payments.[234]

The company shared the results of its investigation with DOJ and SEC officials and continuously cooperated extensively and authentically with the DOJ in its ongoing investigation; took appropriate disciplinary actions against individual wrongdoers, including senior management; and took remedial action, including the complete restructuring of Siemens AG and the implementation of a sophisticated compliance program and organization. The ten minimum elements of the compliance program required under the plea agreement are as follows:

1. A compliance code with a clearly articulated corporate policy against violations of the FCPA, including its antibribery, books-and-records, and internal controls provisions, and other applicable counterparts (collectively, the "anticorruption laws").

2. A system of financial and accounting procedures, including a system of internal accounting controls, designed to ensure the maintenance of fair and accurate books, records, and accounts.

3. Promulgation of compliance standards and procedures designed to reduce the prospect of violations of the anticorruption laws and Siemens's compliance code. These standards and procedures shall apply to all directors, officers, and employees and, where necessary and appropriate, outside parties acting on behalf of Siemens in foreign jurisdictions, including agents, consultants, representatives, distributors, teaming partners, and joint venture partners (collectively referred to as "agents and business partners").

4. The assignment of responsibilities to one or more senior corporate officials of Siemens AG for the implementation and oversight of compliance with policies, standards, and procedures regarding the anticorruption laws. Such corporate official(s) shall have the authority to report matters directly to the audit or compliance committee of Siemens AG's Supervisory Board.

5. Mechanisms designed to ensure that the policies, standards, and procedures of Siemens regarding the anticorruption laws are effectively communicated to all directors, officers, employees, and, where necessary and appropriate, agents and business partners. These mechanisms shall include (a) periodic training for all such directors, officers, employees, and, where necessary and appropriate, agents and business partners; and (b) annual certifications by all such directors, officers, employees, and, where necessary and appropriate, agents and business partners, certifying compliance with the training requirements.

6. An effective system for reporting suspected criminal conduct and/or violations of the compliance policies, standards, and procedures regarding the anticorruption laws for directors, officers, and, as necessary and appropriate, agents and business partners.

7. Appropriate disciplinary procedures to address, among other things, violations of the anticorruption laws of Siemens's compliance code by directors, officers, and employees.
8. Appropriate due diligence requirements pertaining to the retention and oversight of agents and business partners.
9. Standard provisions in agreements, contracts, and renewals thereof with all agents and business partners that are designed to prevent violations of the FCPA and other applicable anticorruption laws, which provisions may, depending upon the circumstances, include (a) anticorruption representations and undertakings related to compliance with the anticorruption laws; (b) rights to conduct audits of the books and records of the agent or business partner to ensure compliance with the foregoing; and (c) rights to terminate an agent or business partner as a result of any breach of anticorruption laws, and regulations or representations and undertakings related to such matters.
10. Periodic testing of the compliance code, standards, and procedures designed to evaluate their effectiveness in detecting and reducing violations of the anticorruption laws and Siemens's internal controls system and compliance code.

There are several significant features about the Siemens settlement in addition to the massive $1.7 billion in penalties. First, the parent company was not charged with bribery, enabling it to likely avoid government debarment in a large number of jurisdictions. Second, Siemens AG pled guilty to the FCPA's internal controls provision—the first time this section has been charged criminally. Third, while monitorships have become standard FCPA resolutions, the Siemens monitorship extends four years—a year longer than the common three-year term—and the monitor was for the first time to be a non-U.S. citizen, Dr. Theo Waizul, the former German minister of finance. Fourth, the announcement of the Siemens resolution was a joint one by the DOJ, SEC, and Munich prosecutors, signaling even greater coordination with foreign authorities in the antibribery arena. Fifth, the penalty, while massive by any measure, could have been more severe. Under the applicable corporate guidelines,[235] Siemens's criminal fine range was $1.35 billion to $2.7 billion.

The company received credit at sentencing for (1) substantial assistance in the investigation; (2) extraordinary efforts to uncover evidence of prior corrupt activities (34 countries, 1,750 interviews, and 800 informational meetings, and 1.5 million hours of billable time by outside counsel and accounting professionals); and (3) extensive commitment to restructure and remediate its operations to make it a worldwide leader in transparent and responsible corporate practices going forward. The company collected and preserved over 100 million documents and produced to the DOJ over 24,000 documents, amounting to over 100,000 pages. The Siemens case makes clear that there is almost no limit to corporate penalties, that companies will be expected to conduct thorough internal investigations, that multijurisdictional cooperation is here to stay, and that remedial measures must be thorough, global, and real.

In July 2009, Siemens AG reached a settlement with the World Bank, agreeing to pay $100 million over the next 15 years to aid anticorruption efforts and agreeing to forgo bidding on any of the development bank's projects for two years. The World Bank's investigation focused on an urban-transport project the bank financed in Moscow. Under the agreement, Siemens's Russian unit faces a ban of up to four years on projects there, but the comprehensive settlement meant the global industrial conglomerate would not face additional World Bank sanctions involving subsidiaries in other countries.[236]

AK.   *United States v. Hioki*[237]

► **Misconduct Category:**	Local sales agent payments to state-owned customers to secure business
► **Countries:**	Argentina, Brazil, Ecuador, Mexico, and Venezuela
► **Foreign Government Officials:**	Officials of state-owned companies
► **Improper Payment Dollar Value:**	$1 million plus
► **Penalty:**	$80,000 and two-year jail sentence for antitrust and FCPA misconduct
► **Other:**	Parallel Antitrust Division and Fraud Section investigation of marine hose industry bid rigging; plea to conspiracy to violate both the FCPA and antitrust law
► **Related Matter:**	*United States v. Bridgestone Corp.*

In December 2008, Misao Hioki, a Japanese marine hose executive with Bridgestone Corporation, pled guilty to both antitrust and FCPA violations and was sentenced to two years in jail and fined $80,000 for his participation in the conspiracies. With respect to his FCPA misconduct, the United States charged that from January 2004 through around May 2007, Hioki and his coconspirators:

- Supervised Bridgestone's International Engineered Products (IEP) department employees both in Japan and in regional subsidiaries, including a U.S. subsidiary of the company in the United States, who were responsible for selling the company's products in Latin America;
- Contracted with local sales agents in many of the Latin American countries where Bridgestone sought IEP sales;
- Developed relationships with employees of the government-owned enterprises with which Bridgestone sought to do business;
- Negotiated with employees of government-owned businesses in Argentina, Brazil, Ecuador, Mexico, Venezuela, and possibly other countries to make corrupt payments to those foreign officials to secure business for Bridgestone and its U.S. subsidiary;
- Approved the making of corrupt payments to the foreign government officials through the local sales agents, to secure business for Bridgestone and its U.S. subsidiary;
- Paid the local sales agents a commission for each sale and, if a corrupt payment to the customer through the local sales agent was involved with the sale, concealed that payment within the commission payment made to the local sales agent; and
- Coordinated these corrupt payments in Latin America through the U.S. subsidiary's offices in the United States including its Houston office.

The Hioki case demonstrates how different divisions of the DOJ can work closely together. Here, the Antitrust Division was investigating marine hose cartel activity in Europe and Japan and later discovered information of possible FCPA violations in Latin America. The Antitrust Division shared the information with the Fraud Section of the Criminal Division of the DOJ, which supervises FCPA matters nationwide. Hioki was induced to cooperate in both investigations and agreed to a two-year sentence.

AL.   *United States v. Fiat S.p.A.;*[238] *United States v. Iveco S.p.A.;*[239]
       United States v. CNH Italia S.p.A.;[240] *United States v. CNH France S.A.;*[241]
       SEC v. Fiat S.p.A & CNH Global N.V.[242]

▶ **Misconduct Category:**	Use of agents and a distributor in Jordan and Lebanon to make payments to Iraqi government to obtain truck and truck parts contracts under the UN Oil-for-Food program
▶ **Country:**	Iraq
▶ **Foreign Government Officials:**	None
▶ **Improper Payment Dollar Value:**	$4.4 million
▶ **Combined Penalties:**	$17.8 million ($7 million criminal penalty, $3.6 million SEC civil penalty, and $7.2 million in disgorgement of profits)
▶ **Other:**	DPA; UN Oil-for-Food program; none of the charged entities was incorporated or headquartered in the United States; three-year DPA; use of conspiracy to commit wire fraud charges; exceptional international law enforcement cooperation

In December 2008, the DOJ and SEC announced that the automobile manufacturer Fiat, based in Turin, Italy, agreed to enter into a three-year DPA and to pay a total of $17.8 million to both agencies to resolve an FCPA investigation of Oil-for-Food program improper payments. Criminal informations were filed against three Fiat subsidiaries in the U.S. District Court for the District of Columbia; Iveco S.p.A. (Iveco) and CNH Italia S.p.A. (CNH Italia) were each charged with one count of conspiracy to commit wire fraud and to violate the books-and-records provisions of the FCPA. CNH France S.A. (CNH France) was charged with conspiracy to commit wire fraud. Employees and agents of the three subsidiaries made improper payments to the Iraqi government in order to obtain contracts with Iraqi ministries to provide industrial pumps, gears, and other equipment. Between 2000 and 2002, Iveco, CNH Italia, and CNH France paid a total of approximately $4.4 million to the Iraqi government by inflating the price of contracts by 10 percent before submitting the contracts to the United Nations for approval, and concealed from the UN the fact that the price contained a kickback to the Iraqi government. Iveco and CNH Italia also inaccurately recorded the kickback payments as "commissions" and "service fees" for its agents in its books and records.

Fiat agreed to pay $7 million in criminal penalties to the DOJ for improper payments to Iraqi ministers in connection with the UN Oil-for-Food program. Fiat and CNH Global, its Netherlands subsidiary, reached an SEC settlement in the U.S. District Court for the District of Columbia whereby they agreed to pay $3.6 million in civil penalties and $7.2 million in disgorgement of profits in connection with contracts for which subsidiaries paid kickbacks to the Iraqi government. The Fiat resolution is noteworthy for the fact that none of the entities charged was incorporated or headquartered in the United States, and very little of the misconduct occurred in the United States.

AM. *United States v. Kellogg, Brown & Root LLC;*[243]
     SEC v. Halliburton Co. & KBR, Inc.[244]

▶ **Misconduct Category:**	Joint venture partners' payments to agents in U.K. and Japan of $182 million to funnel bribes to Nigerian officials and secure lucrative Bonny Island liquefied natural gas (LNG) project contracts worth $6 billion.
▶ **Country:**	Nigeria
▶ **Foreign Government Officials:**	High-level officials of Nigerian federal government, Nigerian National Petroleum Corporation (NNPC), and Nigeria LNG Limited (NLNG)
▶ **Improper Payment Dollar Value:**	$182 million
▶ **Combined Penalties:**	$579 million ($402 million DOJ penalty and $177 million SEC disgorgement of profits)
▶ **Other:**	Second-largest FCPA fine—$402 million for a decade-long conspiracy; appointment of an independent consultant. SEC complaint charged subsidiary KBR, Inc. with aiding and abetting for "knowingly or recklessly substantially assist[ing]" its parent Halliburton Inc. with violations of books-and-records and internal controls provisions.
▶ **Related Matters:**	*United States v. Stanley; United States v. Technip SA; SEC v. Technip SA; United States v. Snamprogetti; SEC v. ENI, SpA & Snamprogetti; United States v. Tesler & Chodan; United States v. JGC Corp.; United States v. Marubeni Corp.*

In February 2009, Kellogg Brown & Root (KBR) pled guilty in the Southern District of Texas to conspiring to violate the FCPA and to four substantive violations of the antibribery provisions. Houston-based KBR is engaged in the business of providing engineering, procurement, and construction (EPC) services around the world, including designing and building liquefied natural gas (LNG) production plants. The criminal information alleged that beginning in 1994 and to 2004, KBR, along with three other joint venture partners, paid bribes to high-level Nigerian government officials to win EPC contracts to build the Bonny Island LNG project in the delta region of Nigeria. Members of the four-company joint venture paid two agents (Jeffrey Tesler in London and Wojciech Chodan in Tokyo) $182 million to funnel bribes to high-level Nigerian government officials and win construction contracts worth more than $6 billion.[245]

KBR CEO Albert Jack Stanley, utilizing a joint venture steering committee, engaged the two agents who in turn paid bribes from the $182 million in consulting fees they received from the joint venture to senior officials of the Nigerian federal government; to officers of the Nigerian National Petroleum Corporation (NNPC), a Nigerian government-owned company charged with development of Nigeria's oil and gas wealth and regulation of the country's oil and gas industry; and to officers of Nigeria LNG Limited (NLNG), an entity created by the Nigerian government to develop the Bonny Island project and the entity that awarded the EPC contracts. NNPC owned 49 percent of NLNG while its other owners were multinational companies. The indictment and plea agreement alleged that NNPC and NLNG were instrumentalities of the Nigerian federal government and that their officers and employees were "foreign officials" for purposes of the FCPA. Under the plea agreement, KBR was required to pay a criminal fine of $402 million and to retain a monitor for three years. This fine is the second-largest FCPA criminal fine—behind only the Siemens $450 million criminal fine of December 2008.

In a related proceeding, the SEC charged KBR, Inc., an agent of U.S. issuer Halliburton Company (Halliburton), with violations of the antibribery provisions, and KBR and Halliburton, KBR's former parent company, with engaging in books-and-records and internal controls violations relating to the bribery. Signally, the SEC charged in its third claim for relief subsidiary KBR Inc. with aiding and abetting for "knowingly or recklessly substantially assisting" its parent Halliburton with violations of the accounting provisions.[246] KBR and Halliburton agreed to pay $177 million in disgorgement of profits to settle the SEC's charges. The SEC $177 million sanction and the DOJ $402 million criminal penalty, totaling $579 million, represented the largest combined FCPA settlement ever paid by U.S. companies. In addition to a three-year monitor, the settlement imposed an independent consultant upon Halliburton to review its policies and procedures as they relate to compliance with the FCPA.

AN.   *United States v. Tesler & Chodan*[247]

▶ **Misconduct Category:**   Recipients of $182 million in "consulting contracts" to funnel bribes to senior Nigerian government officials to obtain $6 billion worth of liquefied natural gas project contracts in the Niger Delta

▶ Country:	Nigeria
▶ Foreign Government Officials:	Top-level executive-branch officials and high-level petroleum industry officials of state-owned oil company—the Nigerian National Petroleum Corporation (NNPG) and the Nigerian LNG Limited (NLNG)
▶ Improper Payment Dollar Value:	Approximately $182 million
▶ Combined Penalties:	Tesler and Chodan pled guilty and agreed to cooperate. Tesler was sentenced to 21 months in prison and Chodan to one year of probation. Tesler agreed to record a forfeiture of nearly $149 million and Chodan to a forfeiture of $726,885.
▶ Other:	Use of Gibraltar-based consulting company and Japanese trading company to pay $182 million in bribes to Nigerian officials in order to obtain EPC contracts valued at $6 billion; largest individual forfeiture in FCPA history
▶ Related Matters:	*United States v. KBR*; *United States v. Snamprogetti SA*; *United States v. Technip SA*; *United States v. Stanley*; *United States v. JGC Corp.*; *United States v. Marubeni Corp.*

In February 2009, Jeffrey Tesler of London and Wojciech Chodan of Maidenhead, England, were charged with one count of conspiracy to violate the FCPA and ten substantive violations under a sealed indictment filed in the U.S. District Court for the Southern District of Texas.[248] Specifically, the two U.K. citizens were charged with a decade-long scheme to bribe Nigerian government officials to obtain engineering, procurement, and construction (EPC) contracts. The EPC contracts to build liquefied natural gas (LNG) facilities on Bonny Island, Nigeria, were valued at more than $6 billion. The indictment sought forfeiture of more than $130 million from the defendants. In March 2009, Tesler was arrested by the London Metropolitan Police and fought extradition for two years. Both Tesler and Chodan returned to the United States, agreed to cooperate with the U.S. government, and pled guilty. Tesler was sentenced to 21 months' incarceration and Chodan received probation.

Tesler was hired in 1995 as an agent of a four-company joint venture—TSKJ (Technip, Snamprogetti, KBR, and JGC Corporation (JGC))—that was awarded four EPC contracts by Nigeria LNG Ltd. (NLNG) between 1995 and 2004 to build LNG facilities on Bonny Island. The government-owned Nigerian National Petroleum Corporation (NNPC) was the largest shareholder of NLNG, owning 49 percent of the company. Chodan was a former salesperson and consultant of a United Kingdom subsidiary of Kellogg, Brown & Root Inc. (KBR), one of the four joint venture companies. At so-called "cultural meetings," Chodan and other coconspirators discussed the use of Tesler and other agents to pay bribes to Nigerian officials to secure the officials' support for awarding the EPC contracts to the joint venture.

The indictment alleged that the joint venture hired Tesler to bribe high-level Nigerian government officials, including top-level executive-branch officials, and another agent to bribe lower-level Nigerian government officials, including employees of NLNG. At crucial junctures before the award of the EPC contracts, KBR's former CEO, Albert Jackson "Jack" Stanley, and others allegedly met with three successive holders of a top-level office in the executive branch of the Nigerian government to ask the office holder to designate a representative with whom the joint venture should negotiate the bribes. Stanley and others allegedly negotiated bribe amounts with the office holders' representatives and agreed to hire Tesler and the other agent to pay the bribes. Stanley's sentencing has been repeatedly postponed. The TSKJ joint venture entered into a series of consulting contracts with a Gibraltar corporation allegedly controlled by Tesler to which the joint venture paid approximately $132 million to a Gibraltar-based consulting company, Tri-Star Investments Ltd., for Tesler to use to bribe high-level Nigerian government officials; the joint venture also paid the Japanese trading company $50 million to pay lower-level government officials. On behalf of the joint venturers, Tesler wire-transferred bribe payments to or for the benefit of various Nigerian government officials, including officials of the executive branch, NNPC, and NLNG, and for the benefit of a political party in Nigeria.

The U.K. High Court rejected Tesler's extradition challenge in January 2011. He thereafter waived extradition and, in March 2011, pleaded guilty in the Southern District of Texas to one substantive FCPA violation and to conspiring to violate the FCPA. He also agreed to a record FCPA individual forfeiture of $148,964,568.67.[249] In February 2012, Tesler was sentenced to 21 months in prison and ordered to pay a $25,000 fine. At the same time, Chodan, 74, was sentenced to one year of probation and ordered to pay a $20,000 fine.[250]

In a related criminal case, KBR's successor company, Kellogg, Brown & Root LLC, of Texas, pled guilty in February 2009 to FCPA charges related to its participation in the scheme to bribe Nigerian government officials. The company agreed to pay a combined DOJ and SEC fine of $579 million. Both Tesler and Chodan reported to KBR president Stanley, who also pled guilty and agreed to a seven-year sentence and a $10.8 million forfeiture. In 2012, Stanley, then 69, received a sentence of only 30 months and a $1,000 fine.

AO.   *United States v. Latin Node, Inc.*[251]

▶ **Misconduct Category:**   Payments to third parties to pass on to
                                telecommunication officials to obtain
                                interconnection agreement and reduced
                                rates

▶ **Countries:**   Honduras and Yemen

▶ **Foreign Government Officials:**	Officials of state-owned telecommunication company; officials at the Ministry of Telecommunications; son of the president of Yemen
▶ **Improper Payment Dollar Value:**	$2,250,000
▶ **Penalty:**	$2 million
▶ **Other:**	Inadequate preclosing due diligence; misconduct discovered during eLandia International Inc.'s postclosing discovery; postacquisition voluntary disclosure to DOJ, and full cooperation and implementation and remedial actions, including termination of senior Latin Node management who had knowledge of or involvement in violations; plea by nonoperating subsidiary may have avoided government debarment; no independent monitor, Latin Node dissolved

In April 2009, Latin Node Inc. (Latinode), a privately held Florida corporation, pled guilty in the Southern District of Florida to violation of the FCPA in connection with improper payments in Honduras and Yemen. The company agreed to pay a $2 million fine during a three-year period.[252]

LatiNode, a wholesale telecommunications provider of protocol technology, admitted that from March 2004 to June 2007, it paid or caused to be paid $1,099,899 in payments to third parties, knowing that some or all of those funds would be passed on as bribes to officials of Hondutel, the state-owned telecom of Honduras. LatiNode admitted it paid bribes to obtain an interconnection agreement and to reduce the rate per minute under the interconnection agreement. The payments were made through a Miami bank account with the knowledge and approval of senior LatiNode executives. Recipients of the payments included a member of the interconnection agreement award evaluation committee, the deputy general manager of Hondutel, and a senior Hondutel in-house attorney.

LatiNode also admitted that from July 2005 to April 2006, it made 17 payments totaling approximately $1,150,654 to Yemeni officials and to a third-party consultant with the knowledge that some or all of the funds would be passed on to Yemeni officials in exchange for favorable interconnection rates in Yemen. Intended payment recipients included the son of the Yemeni president, the vice president of operations at Tele Yemen, the Yemeni government-owned telecommunications company, other officials of Tele Yemen, and officials of the Yemeni Ministry of Telecommunications.

Elandia International Inc. first learned of the improper payments during postclosing discovery after it acquired LatiNode and disclosed the misconduct to the DOJ. Further, it conducted an internal investigation, shared the factual results with the DOJ, and terminated senior LatiNode management who had involvement in or knowledge of the improper payments. While no monitor requirement was imposed, LatiNode was dissolved, negating any need for a monitor.

AP.   *United States v. Carson, Carson, Cosgrove, Edmonds, Ricotti &*
       Kim; United States v. Covino & Morlock;[253] *United States v. Control*
       Components, Inc.[254]

▶ **Misconduct Category:**	263 corrupt payments to obtain contracts in over 30 countries
▶ **Countries:**	China, Greece, Malaysia, South Korea, and United Arab Emirates
▶ **Foreign Government Officials:**	State-owned energy company officials
▶ **Improper Payment Dollar Value:**	$49 million in bribes to officials and $1.95 million in bribes to officers and employees of private companies
▶ **Combined Penalties:**	CCI corporate fine of $18.2 million; Stuart Carson received four months in prison and $20,000 fine; Rose Carson received six months of home confinement, $20,000 fine, and 200 hours of community service; Cosgrove received 13 months of home confinement; Edmunds received four months in prison and four months home confinement
▶ **Other:**	Voluntary disclosure by company; charging of eight executives was then an FCPA individual charging record, demonstrating the DOJ's commitment to pursue individual wrongdoers; destruction of records count against former director of sales for China and Taiwan; private bribes charged under the Travel Act; independent corporate compliance monitor for three years

In April 2009, the DOJ charged six former executives of Control Components Inc. (CCI), an Orange County, California–based valve company, in the Central District of California with a conspiracy to secure contracts by paying bribes to officials of foreign state-owned energy companies, as well as officers and employees of foreign and domestic private companies. According to the DOJ press release, bribes totaling $6.85 million resulted in net profits to the company of approximately $46.5 million. The indictment alleged that from approximately 2003 to 2007, the defendants and others caused 263 corrupt payments in more than 30 countries. Alleged corrupt payments were made to foreign officials of state-owned entities, including Jiangsu Nuclear Power Corporation (China), Guohua Electric Power (China), China Petroleum Materials and Equipment Corporation, Petro China, Dongfang Electric Corporation (China), China National Offshore Oil Corporation, Korea Hydro and Nuclear Power, Petronas (Malaysia), and National Petroleum Construction Company (UAE).

The charges against the seven executives include conspiracy to violate the FCPA and the Travel Act, substantive FCPA and Travel Act violations, and the destruction of records in connection with a matter within the jurisdiction of a department or agency of the United States. In 2009, former CCI executives Mario Covino and Richard Morlock pleaded guilty to the conspiracy charge and substantive FCPA charges and are expected to testify in the 2012 trial of two executives. In April 2011, Ricotti pled guilty, and in April 2012 Stuart and Rose Carson pled guilty. In November 2012, former CEO Stuart Carson, age 72, was sentenced to four months in prison and to eight months of home confinement, and was ordered to pay a $20,000 fine. His wife Rose, age 48, was sentenced to six months of home confinement, fined $20,000, and ordered to perform 200 hours of community service. In May 2012, former director of international sales Cosgrove pled guilty, and in September 2012 was sentenced to nine months home confinement over the government's request for 15 months in prison. In June 2012 Edmunds pled guilty and in November 2012 was sentenced to five months in prison and four months of home confinement. The charges against Kim, the former president of CCI's Korean office, are pending.[255] Kim, of Korea, is currently a fugitive.

In July 2009, CCI pled guilty to violations of the FCPA and the Travel Act in a bribery scheme to secure contracts in approximately 30 countries. CCI admitted it paid approximately $4.9 million to officials of state-owned companies and approximately $1.95 million in bribes to officers and employees of foreign privately owned companies. As part of a plea agreement, CCI agreed to pay a criminal fine of $18.2 million; to create, implement, and maintain a comprehensive antibribery compliance program; to retain an independent compliance monitor for a three-year term; to review the design and implementation of CCI's antibribery compliance program; to make periodic reports to the DOJ; to serve a three-year term of organized probation; and to continue to cooperate with the DOJ in its investigation.

AQ.   U.S. DOJ–Helmerich & Payne Inc. Agreement;[256] *In re* Helmerich & Payne, Inc.[257]

▶ **Misconduct Category:**	Bribes to customs officials to import and export goods that were not within regulation, to import goods that could not be lawfully exported, and to evade higher duties
▶ **Countries:**	Argentina and Venezuela
▶ **Foreign Government Officials:**	Customs officials
▶ **Improper Payment Dollar Value:**	Unknown
▶ **Combined Penalties:**	$1.375 million ($1 million penalty and $375,000 disgorgement of profits including prejudgment interest)
▶ **Other:**	Voluntary disclosure; two-year DOJ NPA; SEC consent decree

In July 2009, Helmerich & Payne (H&P), a Tulsa, Oklahoma–based contract supplier of oil drilling rigs, equipment, and personnel to the United States and South America, entered into an NPA with the Department of Justice relating to improper payments by H&P to Argentine and Venezuelan government officials. H&P was required to pay a $1 million penalty to resolve the allegations, to continue to cooperate, and to take future remedial steps. In a related matter, H&P settled with the SEC and agreed to pay $375,000 disgorgement of profits, including prejudgment interest.

H&P acknowledged that its subsidiaries, employees, and agents paid Argentine and Venezuelan customs officials in order to import and export goods that were not within regulation, to import goods that could not lawfully be imported, and to evade higher duties. As a result of H&P's voluntary disclosure and thorough self-investigation of the underlying conduct, the cooperation provided to the DOJ, and its extensive remedial efforts, the DOJ agreed not to prosecute H&P or its subsidiaries for making improper payments, provided the company pays the penalty, continues to cooperate, and implements further remedial measures under the two-year agreement.

AR. *United States v. AGCO Corp.;*[258] *SEC v. AGCO Corp.*[259]

▶ **Misconduct Category:**	Kickbacks in connection with sales of foreign equipment
▶ **Country:**	Iraq
▶ **Foreign Government Officials:**	Ministry of Agriculture
▶ **Improper Payment Dollar Value:**	$5.9 million
▶ **Combined Penalties:**	$19.9 million ($1.6 million criminal penalty; $2.4 million civil penalty; and disgorgement of profits of $13.9 million plus $2 million in prejudgment interest)
▶ **Other:**	UN Oil-for-Food program; DPA; lax internal Audit and Legal Department oversight; use of fictitious "after-sales service funds" to generate 40 percent kickbacks to Iraq government ministry

In September 2009, AGCO Corporation, a Duluth, Georgia, manufacturer and supplier of agricultural equipment and its subsidiaries, entered into a DPA relating to $5.9 million in kickback payments in connection with foreign sales of equipment under 16 contracts to Iraq under the UN Oil-for-Food program. The kickbacks were characterized as "after-sales service funds," but no bona fide services were performed.

In 2000, AGCO's Iraq business manager learned from its Jordanian agent that the Iraqi Ministry of Agriculture was demanding a 10 percent kickback as a condition of awarding contracts to AGCO, which was seeking to increase its market share in Iraq. To conceal the scheme, AGCO's employees created a fictional account denoted as "Ministry Accrual." The kickbacks were recorded in this account, which AGCO employees made appear was being used to pay an agent for his after-sales commissions. The accrual account was created by AGCO Ltd.'s marketing staff and had virtually no oversight from its finance department. Marketing and finance employees in the United Kingdom, France, and Denmark were instrumental in concealing the scheme whereby some contract prices were inflated by 10 percent to cover the kickbacks to the Iraqi Ministry. One AGCO employee described the finance department employees as "blind leaders" who input information into AGCO's books without any adequate oversight role. Not only did AGCO's Internal Audit Department ignore newer problems with the sales process, but AGCO's legal department was aware that the company was conducting sales under the program into Iraq, a sanctioned country, but failed to ensure that the sanctions of the UN rules and regulations were followed.

Pursuant to the DPA filed in the District Court for the District of Columbia, AGCO agreed to a $1.6 million penalty with the SEC. The parent company consented to a government injunction from future violations of section 13(b)(2)(A) and section 13(b)(2)(B) of the Securities Exchange Act of 1934, and ordered AGCO to disgorge $13,907,393 in profits, plus $2 million in prejudgment interest and a civil penalty of $2.4 million.

AS.   United States v. Jumet[260]

▶ **Misconduct Category:**	Use of a foreign shell corporation owned by government official to funnel payments to the official to obtain contracts to maintain lighthouse and buoys
▶ **Country:**	Panama
▶ **Foreign Government Officials:**	Administrator of Panama's National Maritime Ports Authority (APN) and high-ranking executive official of the Republic of Panama
▶ **Improper Payment Dollar Value:**	$200,000+
▶ **Combined Penalties:**	87-month jail sentence, $15,000 fine, and three years of supervised release
▶ **Other:**	Second-longest FCPA prison sentence ever
▶ **Related Matters:**	United States v. Warwick

In a November 2009 plea filed in the Eastern District of Virginia, Charles Paul Edward Jumet admitted that from at least 1997 through approximately July 2003, he and others conspired to make corrupt payments totaling more than $200,000 to the former administrator and deputy administrator of Panama's National Maritime Port Authority and to a former, high-ranking elected executive official of the Republic of Panama in order to assist his company, Port Engineering Consultants Corporation (PECC), in receiving lighthouse and buoy maintenance contracts.

In his guilty plea, Jumet also admitted that he knowingly made a false statement to federal agents about a December 1997 "dividend" check payable to the bearer in the amount of $18,000, which was endorsed and deposited into an account belonging to the former, high-ranking elected executive official. Jumet admitted that he had falsely claimed that this "dividend" check was a donation for the high-ranking official's reelection campaign. Jumet also admitted that the "dividend" check was in fact given to the former official as a corrupt payment for allowing PECC to receive the contract from the Panamanian government.

In December 1997, the Panamanian government awarded PECC a no-bid, 20-year concession to perform the maintenance duty. In exchange for the concession, Jumet and others authorized corrupt payments to Panamanian government officials. In 2000, Panama's Comptroller General's Office suspended the contract while it investigated the government's decision to award PECC a contract without soliciting any bids from other firms. In 2003, the Panama government resumed making payments to PECC. As part of his plea agreement, Jumet agreed to cooperate with the DOJ in its ongoing investigation.

In April 2010, Jumet was sentenced to 87 months in prison. In addition to the prison term, he was ordered to pay a $15,000 fine and to serve three years of supervised release following the prison term. The 87-month sentence is the second-longest prison term imposed against an individual for violating the FCPA and the longest period of incarceration for a defendant who has pled guilty to an FCPA offense.

AT.   *United States v. O'Shea;*[261] *United States v. Basurto*[262]

▶ **Misconduct Category:**	General manager authorization of payments to multiple officials at Mexican utility in return for lucrative network management contracts
▶ **Country:**	Mexico
▶ **Foreign Government Officials:**	Officials of Comisión Federal de Electricidad
▶ **Alleged Improper Payment Dollar Value:**	$900,000
▶ **Combined Penalties:**	O'Shea: None. Basurto: time served (22 months)
▶ **Other:**	Acquittal of O'Shea; guilty plea by Basurto
▶ **Related Matters:**	*United States v. Aguilar; United States v. ABB Inc.; United States v. ABB Ltd.; United States v. Aibel Group Ltd.; United States v. Vetco Gray Co. Ltd.; United States v. ABB Vetco Gray Inc.*

In November 2009, John Joseph O'Shea, the former general manager of a Sugar Land, Texas–based business, was arrested for his alleged role in a conspiracy to bribe Mexican government officials to secure contracts with the Comisión Federal de Electridad (CFE), a Mexican state-owned utility company. O'Shea, 57, was charged in an 18-count indictment returned in the Southern District of Texas with conspiracy, violations of the FCPA, international money laundering, and falsification of records in a federal investigation. The indictment alleged that while acting as the general manager of a Texas business unit of a U.S. subsidiary of a Swiss corporation, O'Shea arranged and authorized payments to multiple officials at CFE in exchange for lucrative contracts. According to the indictment, the Texas unit's primary business was to provide products and services to electrical utilities, many of them foreign state-owned utilities, for network management in power generation, transmission, and distribution.[263]

The indictment alleged that the Texas business unit managed by O'Shea contracted with a Mexican company, Esimex, to serve as its sales representative in Mexico, whereby the Mexican company received a percentage of the revenue generated from business with Mexican governmental utilities, including CFE. The Texas business unit received multiple contracts with CFE for goods and services related to CFE's network while using the Mexican company as its sales representative. Fernando Maya Basurto, 47, of Mexico City, was a principal of the Mexican company, performing work for the Texas business unit on its contracts with CFE.

In December 1997, CFE awarded the Texas business unit a contract, known as the SITRACEN contract, to significantly upgrade the backbone of Mexico's electrical network system. The SITRACEN contract generated more than $44 million in revenue for the Texas business unit. Then, in approximately October 2003, CFE awarded the Texas business unit a multiyear contract for maintenance and upgrades of the SITRACEN contract, referred to as the Evergreen contract.

For the Evergreen contract, the indictment alleged that O'Shea, Basurto, officials at CFE, and others agreed that approximately 10 percent of the revenue the Texas business unit received from CFE would be returned to CFE officials as corrupt payments. The indictment alleged that the Evergreen contract, a sole source award, generated more than $37 million in revenue for the Texas business unit. The indictment alleged that it was also agreed that O'Shea would receive approximately 1 percent of the contract revenue as kickback payments. O'Shea, Basurto, and others allegedly used false invoices from Mexican companies as a basis to make international wire transfers that purported to be legitimate payments for "technical services" and "maintenance support services." The indictment alleged these were actually corrupt payments and the companies did not do any work for the Texas business unit. O'Shea, Basurto, and others allegedly also made additional "commission" payments to Basurto and his family that were further transferred to CFE officials. According to the indictment, in connection with the Evergreen contract, O'Shea authorized more than $900,000 in corrupt payments to CFE officials before an internal investigation by the Swiss corporation stopped the transfers. ABB, the Swiss corporation, then voluntarily disclosed the payments to the DOJ and SEC and said it was fully cooperating with their investigations.

In addition, the indictment alleged that O'Shea, Basurto, and others engaged in a cover-up after O'Shea was terminated from the Texas business unit, which included fabricating documents that purported to be evidence of a legitimate business relationship between the Texas business unit and the Mexican companies that provided the false invoices. According to the indictment, Basurto and O'Shea exchanged e-mails in which they discussed draft language for fake correspondence and a fake contract.

Basurto pleaded guilty on November 16, 2009, before U.S. District Judge Lynn Hughes in Houston to a one-count information charging him for his role in the conspiracy. In his plea, Basurto admitted that while he acted as a sales representative for the Texas business unit, he conspired with others to make corrupt payments to CFE officials, helped launder the bribe monies, and engaged in a cover-up to obstruct the investigations of the Department of Justice and the SEC. Basurto also admitted that he submitted false invoices and helped fabricate correspondence in contemplation of federal investigations into the bribery. As part of his plea agreement, Basurto agreed to cooperate with the DOJ in its ongoing investigation and the trial of O'Shea.

After the DOJ presented its case against O'Shea, Judge Hughes of the Southern District of Texas granted a defense motion for acquittal. In announcing his ruling, Judge Hughes said he found that the government's chief witness, an Esimex principal awaiting sentencing on conspiracy charges, could not tie O'Shea to the alleged crimes. The judge found that O'Shea's conduct, including efforts to renew an ABB-Esimex contract, was reasonably explained by lawful motives. The court also expressed concern that the government had granted immunity to Esimex's founder, Fernando Basurto, Sr., allowing him to disclose selective information to the government, while refusing to grant immunity to an important defense witness even six to seven years after the facts at issue. Basurto Sr. did not testify; the government relied instead on his cooperating son's testimony.

Judge Hughes severed the substantive counts from the money laundering, conspiracy, and obstruction counts. He tried the substantive counts but allowed evidence of the conspiracy and obstruction. Judge Hughes granted a Rule 29 motion on the substantive tried counts at the end of the government's case-in-chief. Faced with both the fact that the money laundering count was effectively nullified by the Rule 29 and the prospect of retrying a conspiracy and obstruction case with the same witnesses that the court had found lacked personal knowledge, the DOJ dismissed the remaining counts.[264]

AU. *United States v. Esquenazi, Rodriguez, Antoine, Duperval & Grandison*[265]

▶ **Misconduct Category:**	Use of shell companies to receive and forward improper payments to Haiti government telecommunication officials to obtain preferred telecommunications rates
▶ **Country:**	Haiti
▶ **Foreign Government Officials:**	Haiti Teleco officials
▶ **Improper Payment Dollar Value:**	$800,000
▶ **Combined Penalties:**	Antoine: four years in jail, $1,852,209 in restitution, and $1,580,771 in forfeiture; Esquenazi: 15 years in jail; Rodriguez: seven years in jail; Duperval: nine years in jail and $497,321 in forfeiture; Grandison: awaiting trial
▶ **Other:**	First use of conspiracy and money laundering statutes to charge foreign officials. Esquenazi's 15-year jail sentence is the longest period of incarceration ever handed down in a U.S. foreign bribery case.

In December 2009, the DOJ unsealed a Southern District of Florida indictment charging two Florida executives of a Miami-based telecommunications company, the president of a Florida-based Telecom Consulting Services Corporation, and two former Haitian government officials for their alleged role in a foreign bribery, wire fraud, and money laundering scheme. The indictment alleged that the defendants participated in a scheme from November 2001 through March 2005, during which time the Florida telecommunications company paid more than $800,000 to shell companies to be used to bribe foreign officials of the Republic of Haiti's state-owned telecommunications company, Telecommunications D'Haiti (Haiti Teleco).

Terra Telecommunications Corporation executed a series of contracts with Haiti Teleco that allowed the company's customers to place telephone calls to Haiti. The alleged corrupt payments were authorized by the telecommunication company's president and vice president and were allegedly paid to successive Haitian government officials at Haiti Teleco. The purpose of the bribes was to obtain various business advantages from the Haitian officials for the telecommunications company, including issuing preferred telecommunications rates, reducing the number of minutes for which payment was owed, and giving a variety of credits toward sums owed, as well as to defraud the Republic of Haiti of revenue. To conceal the bribe payments, the defendants allegedly used shell companies to receive and forward on payments. In addition, they allegedly created false records claiming that the payments were for "consulting services," which were never intended or performed.

Signally, the former Haitian officials were charged with conspiracy to commit money laundering. The two, Robert Antoine and Jean Rene Duperval, had been directors of international relations for telecommunications at Haiti Teleco. While foreign officials may not be charged with substantive FCPA violations, there is no prohibition against charging a federal conspiracy to commit money laundering. This was the first time the DOJ charged foreign officials in an FCPA matter. In March 2010, Antoine pled guilty and was sentenced in June 2010 to four years in prison and ordered to pay $1,852,209 in restitution and to forfeit $1,580,771. In August 2011 Esquenazi and Rodriguez were convicted by a jury. In October 2011 Esquenazi received the stiffest FCPA sentence ever—15 years—while Rodriguez was sentenced to seven years in jail. In March 2012, Duperval was convicted by a jury on all counts for his role in a scheme to launder bribes. In May 2012, he was sentenced to nine years in jail and ordered to forfeit $497,321.[266] Grandson is awaiting trial.

The DOJ commended Haiti's financial intelligence unit, the Unité Centrale de Renseignements Financiers (UCREF), the Bureau des Affaires Financières et Economiques (BAFE), and the Haiti Ministry of Justice and Public Security. The prosecution is further indication of increased international law enforcement cooperation in antibribery investigations.

AV.   *U.S. DOJ–UTStarcom, Inc. Agreement;*[267] *SEC v. UTStarcom*[268]

▶ **Misconduct Category:**   Improper travel and entertainment expenses; improper executive training programs at U.S. universities; sham consultants, work visas issued under false pretenses to obtain contracts

▶ **Countries:**   China, Mongolia, and Thailand

▶ **Foreign Government Officials:**   Employees of state-owned telecommunications companies and their family members

▶ **Improper Payment Dollar Value:** $11 million plus

▶ **Combined Penalties:** $3 million ($1.5 million DOJ penalty; $1.5 million SEC fine)

▶ **Other:**   NPA; hundreds of overseas trips purportedly for training; conduct included sightseeing trips under the guise of training; $600 bottles of wine; bribe to obtain a Mongolian licensee fee; DOJ NPA and SEC consent decree; credit for voluntary disclosure and full cooperation; worldwide investigation, FCPA training, and other proactive remedial efforts; annual compliance reports and certifications to the SEC for four years

In December 2009, UTStarcom Inc. (UTSI) entered into an NPA with the DOJ, agreeing to pay a $1.5 million fine for violations of the FCPA by providing travel and other things of value to foreign officials, specifically employees at state-owned telecommunications companies in the People's Republic of China (PRC). At the same time, the SEC obtained an identical penalty and obtained permanent injunctive relief in the Northern District of California. UTSI, a publicly traded Delaware-based corporation headquartered in California, is a global telecommunications company that designs, manufactures, and sells network equipment and handsets and has historically done most of its business in China with government-controlled municipal and provincial telecommunications companies through its wholly owned subsidiary UTStarcom China, Co. Ltd. (UTS-China).

The SEC alleged that UTStarcom's wholly owned subsidiary in China paid nearly $7 million between 2002 and 2007 for hundreds of overseas trips by employees of Chinese government-controlled telecommunications companies that were customers of UTStarcom, purportedly to provide customer training. It is part of UTS-China's standard practice to include as part of its internal sales contracts for wireless networks a provision for UTS-China to pay for some of the customer's employees to attend the purported training overseas after installation of the network. In reality, the trips were entirely or primarily for sightseeing popular tourist attractions in the United States, including Hawaii, Las Vegas, and New York City. Most trips lasted two weeks and cost $5,000 per customer employee. Also the trips were supposed to be for training at UTSI training facilities when UTSI had no training facilities at the purported training locations and conducted no training.

On at least seven occasions between 2002 and 2004, UTSI allegedly paid for executive training programs at U.S. universities that were attended by managers and other employees of government customers in China. The programs covered general management topics and were not specifically related to UTSI's products or business. UTSI paid for all expenses associated with the program, which totaled more than $4 million and included travel, tuition, room and board, field trips to tourist destinations, and a cash allowance of between $800 and $3,000 per person. UTSI accounted for the cost of the programs as "marketing expenses." The company's senior management believed that the executive training programs helped it obtain or retain business.

On at least ten occasions between 2001 and 2005, UTSI provided or offered full-time employment with UTSI in the United States, including salaries and other benefits, to employees of government customers or their family members in China and Thailand. In reality, these individuals never worked for UTSI in any capacity. However, phony annual performance reviews were placed in personnel files for the individuals to document their employment and UTSI improperly accounted for the payments to the individuals as "employee compensation." UTStarcom provided the individuals with work visas, when in reality the individuals did not work for UTStarcom.

In 2004, UTSI submitted a bid for a sales contract to a government-controlled telecommunications company in Thailand. While its bid was under consideration, UTSI's general manager in Thailand spent nearly $10,000 on French wine as a gift to agents of the government, including rare bottles that cost more than $600 each. The manager also spent $13,000 for entertainment expenses to secure the same contract. UTSI's former chief executive officer and executive vice president of UTS-China approved the payments. UTSI reimbursed the expenditures and accounted for them as marketing expenses. In 2005, UTSI attempted to expand its business into Mongolia, and UTSI's EVP and the CEO of UTS-China authorized a $1.5 million payment to a Mongolian company pursuant to a purported consulting agreement and told UTSI's board of directors the $1.5 million was a license fee paid to the Mongolian government. In reality, the license fee was only $50,000 and the Mongolian company used a portion of that $1.5 million to make payments to at least one Mongolian government official to help UTSI obtain a favorable ruling in a dispute over its license. In 2007, the former parent EVP and CEO of its Chinese subsidiary authorized a $200,000 payment to a Chinese company pursuant to a purported consulting agreement. Although the payment was accounted for as a consulting expense, in reality there was a sham consulting company and the payment was made as part of an effort to obtain contracts from a Chinese government customer.

In 2006, after learning of alleged bribe payments, the parent company's audit committee initiated an internal investigation into potential FCPA violations, which UTSI expanded in 2007 and 2008 to cover all of its operations worldwide. UTSI adopted new FCPA-related policies and procedures, hired additional finance and internal compliance personnel, implemented stronger internal accounting controls, and conducted FCPA training at all of its major offices around the world. In reaching its NPA resolution, the DOJ recognized UTSI's voluntary disclosure, thorough self-investigation of the underlying conduct, the cooperation provided by the company to the department, and the company's remedial efforts. In the related administrative proceeding, UTStarcom agreed to settle SEC charges and pay a $1.5 million penalty and to provide the SEC with annual FCPA compliance reports and certifications for four years.[269]

AW.   *United States v. Warwick*[270]

▶ Misconduct Category:	Use of a foreign shell corporation owned by government official to funnel payments to the official to obtain contracts to maintain lighthouse and buoys
▶ Country:	Panama
▶ Foreign Government Officials:	Administrator of Panama's National Maritime Ports Authority (APN) and high-ranking executive official of the Republic of Panama
▶ Improper Payment Dollar Value:	$200,000+
▶ Combined Penalties:	37-month jail sentence and forfeiture of $331,000
▶ Other:	Fifth-longest FCPA sentence
▶ Related Matters:	*United States v. Jumet*

In December 2009, John W. Warwick was charged in the Eastern District of Virginia in a one-count indictment charging him with conspiring to make corrupt payments to foreign government officials for the purpose of securing business for Ports Engineering Consultants Corporation (PECC) in violation of the FCPA.[271] PECC, a company incorporated under the laws of Panama, was affiliated with an engineering firm based in Virginia Beach. According to the indictment, PECC was created so that Warwick, coconspirator Charles Jumet, the engineering firm, and others could corruptly obtain certain maritime contracts from the Panamanian government. The conspiracy count alleged Warwick and Jumet participated in a conspiracy to pay money secretly to Panamanian government officials for awarding contracts to PECC to maintain lighthouses and buoys along Panama's waterway. In December 1997, the Panamanian government awarded PECC a no-bid 20-year concession to perform these duties. Upon receipt of the concession, Warwick, Jumet, and others authorized corrupt payments to be made to the Panamanian government officials.

Warwick pled guilty in February 2010. In connection with his guilty plea, Warwick admitted that at least from 1997 through approximately July 2003, he, Jumet, and others conspired to make corrupt payments totaling more than $200,000 to the former administrator and deputy administrator of the Panama Maritime Authority and to a former, high-ranking elected executive official of the Republic of Panama. As part of his plea agreement, Warwick agreed to forfeit $331,000. In June 2010, Warwick was sentenced to 37 months in jail; the DOJ recommended a sentence of 40 months within the guideline range of 37 to 46 months.[272]

Jumet pleaded guilty in November 2009 to a two-count criminal information charging him with conspiring to make corrupt payments to foreign government officials for the purpose of securing business for PECC, in violation of the FCPA, and making a false statement. Jumet was sentenced to 87 months in jail, the second-longest FCPA sentence ever.

AX.   *United States v. Alvirez* (One of 16 Indictments in FBI Sting Operation)[273]

▶ **Misconduct Category:**   Scheme to pay bribes to minister of
                                    defense in African country to win a
                                    purported $15 million security contract to
                                    outfit the country's presidential guard

▶ **Country:**   Gabon

▶ **Foreign Government Official:** Fictitious minister of defense of Gabon

▶ **Improper Payment Dollar Value:** $3 million commission (20 percent to win
                                    $15 million deal)

▶ **Combined Penalties:**   Many defendants are awaiting fair trials;
                                    sentencing of cooperating defendants has
                                    been postponed

▶ **Other:**   Largest single investigation and
                                    prosecution against individuals in FCPA
                                    history; 21 search warrants executed
                                    in United States and United Kingdom
                                    by 150 FBI agents and others; criminal
                                    forfeiture claim; mass arrests while
                                    attending Las Vegas industry trade show
                                    (Shot Show Case). The first "Shot Show"
                                    trial in June 2011 resulted in a mistrial
                                    when jurors could not reach unanimous
                                    verdicts; a second "Shot Show" trial
                                    resulted in a hung jury. In February 2012,
                                    the government moved to dismiss with
                                    prejudice the superseding indictment and
                                    all underlying indictments against the
                                    remaining defendants.

▶ **Related Matter:**   *United States v. Bistrong*

In January 2010, 22 executives and employees of companies in the military and law enforcement products industry were arrested for engaging in schemes to bribe foreign government officials to obtain and retain business. All but one of the defendants were arrested in Las Vegas while attending an industry trade show.[274] The 16 indictments returned in the District of Columbia stemmed from an FBI undercover operation that focused on allegations of foreign bribery in the military and law enforcement products industry. Two years later, the United States, after two hung juries, moved to dismiss with prejudice the superseding indictment and all underlying indictments against the remaining defendants. The case was a clear and major setback for the Fraud Section and its FCPA enforcement effort. In this highly publicized investigation, three defendants pled guilty, three were acquitted, and the charges against 16 were dismissed.

The 16 indictments represented the largest single investigation and prosecution against individuals in the history of DOJ's enforcement of the FCPA. The indictments were returned on December 11, 2009, by a grand jury in Washington, D.C., but filed under seal until the arrests in January 2010. In connection with these indictments, approximately 150 FBI agents executed 14 search warrants in locations across the country, including Bull Shoals, Ark.; San Francisco; Miami; Ponte Vedra Beach, Fla.; Sarasota, Fla.; St. Petersburg, Fla.; Sunrise, Fla.; University Park, Fla.; Decatur, Ga.; Stearns, Ky.; Upper Darby, Pa.; and Woodbridge, Va. Additionally, the United Kingdom's City of London Police executed seven search warrants in connection with their own investigations into companies involved in the foreign bribery conduct that formed the basis for the indictments.

The indictments alleged that the defendants engaged in a scheme to pay bribes to the minister of defense for an unidentified country in Africa. In fact, the scheme was part of the undercover operation, with no actual involvement from any minister of defense. As part of the undercover operation, the defendants allegedly agreed to pay a 20 percent "commission" to a sales agent whom the defendants believed represented the minister of defense for a country in Africa in order to win a portion of a $15 million deal to outfit the country's presidential guard. In reality, the "sales agent" was an undercover FBI agent. The defendants were told that half of that "commission" would be paid directly to the minister of defense. The defendants allegedly agreed to create two price quotations in connection with the deals, with one quote representing the true cost of the goods and the second quote representing the true cost, plus the 20 percent "commission." The defendants also allegedly agreed to engage in a small "test" deal to show the minister of defense that he would personally receive the 10 percent bribe. The defendants purportedly sent e-mail messages that confirmed their decisions.[275]

The indictments charged the executives and employees of the various companies in the military and law enforcement product industries listed below. The resolutions as to each are noted.

- Daniel Alvirez, 32 (pled guilty but later dismissed), and Lee Allen Tolleson, 25 (mistrial and acquittal), the president and the director of acquisitions and logistics at a company in Bull Shoals, Ark., that manufactures and sells law enforcement and military equipment;
- Helmie Ashiblie, 44 (dismissal), the vice president and founder of a company in Woodbridge, Va., that supplies tactical bags and other security-related articles for law enforcement agencies and governments worldwide;
- Andrew Bigelow, 40 (mistrial and dismissal), the managing partner and director of government programs for a Sarasota, Fla., company that sells machine guns, grenade launchers, and other small arms and accessories;
- R. Patrick Caldwell, 61 (acquitted by jury), and Stephen Gerard Giordanella, 50 (judgment of acquittal by court), the current and former chief executive officers of a Sunrise, Fla., company that designs and manufactures concealable and tactical body armor;
- Yochanan R. Cohen, a/k/a Yochi Cohen, 47 (dismissal), the chief executive officer of a San Francisco company that manufactures security equipment, including body armor and ballistic plates;
- Haim Geri, 50 (pleaded guilty, but later dismissed), the president of a North Miami Beach, Fla., company that serves as a sales agent for companies in the law enforcement and military products industries;

- Amaro Goncalves, 49 (dismissal), the vice president of sales for Smith & Wesson, a Springfield, Mass., company that designs and manufactures firearms, firearm safety/security products, rifles, firearms systems, and accessories;
- John Gregory Godsey, a/k/a Greg Godsey, 37 (acquitted by jury), and Mark Frederick Morales, 37, the owner and the agent of a Decatur, Ga., company that sells ammunition and other law enforcement and military equipment;
- Saul Mishkin, 38 (dismissal), the owner and chief executive officer of an Aventura, Fla., company that sells law enforcement and military equipment;
- John M. Mushriqui, 28 (acquitted), and Jeana Mushriqui, 30 (acquitted), the director of international development and the general counsel/U.S. manager of an Upper Darby, Pa., company that manufactures and exports bulletproof vests and other law enforcement and military equipment;
- David R. Painter, 56 (dismissal), and Lee M. Wares, 43 (dismissed), the chairman and a director of a United Kingdom company that markets armored vehicles;
- Pankesh Patel, 43 (mistrial and dismissal), the managing director of a United Kingdom company that acts as sales agent for companies in the law enforcement and military products industries;
- Ofer Paz, 50 (dismissed), the president and chief executive officer of an Israeli company that acts as a sales agent for companies in the law enforcement and military products industries;
- Jonathan M. Spiller, 58 (pleaded guilty, but later dismissed), the owner and president of a Ponte Vedra Beach, Fla., company that markets and sells law enforcement and military equipment;
- Israel Weisler, a/k/a Wayne Weisler, 63 (dismissal), and Michael Sachs, 66, owners and co-chief executive officers of a Stearns, Ky., company that designs, manufactures, and sells armor products, including body armor; and
- John Benson Wier III, 46 (mistrial and dismissal), the president of a St. Petersburg, Fla., company that sells tactical and ballistic equipment.

Each of the original indictments alleged that the defendants conspired to violate the FCPA, conspired to engage in money laundering and engaged in substantive violations of the FCPA. The indictments also seek criminal forfeiture of the defendants' ill-gotten gains. In March 2010, a two-count superseding information was filed against Daniel Alvirez alleging two conspiracies. The first alleged that Alvirez conspired with Lee Allen Tolleson and others to bribe the minister of defense of Gabon, as alleged in the original indictment. A second new conspiracy alleged that Alvirez and his coconspirators conspired to bribe Ministry of Defense officials in the Republic of Georgia in order to win contracts for the sale of ammunition and food. In April 2010, the grand jury issued a superseding indictment against all 22 defendants, thereby consolidating the 16 separate cases. The same day, prosecutors proposed a plan for grouping the defendants into four manageable units for trial. In March 2011, Alvirez pleaded guilty to both counts of conspiracy to violate the FCPA.[276] In 2011, Jonathan Spiller and Haim Geri each pleaded guilty to one count of conspiracy to violate the FCPA and agreed to cooperate with the government.

In 2011 D.C. District Judge Leon divided the Shot Show cases into four trials. The first trial involving defendants Pankesh Patel, Andrew Bigalow, John Benson Weir, and Lee Allen Tolleson proceeded in June 2011 and resulted in a mistrial on July 7, 2011, when jurors were unable to reach unanimous verdicts after seven days of deliberations. The second trial resulted in a hung jury against two defendants after three others were acquitted. The jury was reportedly troubled by the sting operation and that the agents and informant Bistrong never used the word "bribe" or "kickback" on tape; instead, they called the payment a "commission." The informant admitted to accepting $1.3 million in kickbacks from suppliers during his business trips, using prostitutes, and having an expensive cocaine habit. In granting the government's motion to dismiss, Judge Leon applauded federal prosecutors for seeking dismissal of the charges but also criticized them for engaging in what the judge called a "long and sad chapter in the annals of white collar criminal enforcement."[277]

AY.   *United States v. Bistrong*[278]

▶ **Misconduct Category:**	"Success Fee" to agent for the United Nations to obtain body armor; rigging of pepper spray bid specifications in the Netherlands and advising a colleague to use a Nigerian national's shell company for kickbacks to secure fingerprint ink contract
▶ **Countries:**	United Nations (a Public International Organization); Netherlands; Nigeria; Iraq (Export Violations) through the United Arab Emirates
▶ **Foreign Government Officials:**	UN procurement official; National Police Services Agency of the Netherlands (KLPD) procurement officer; and Nigerian National Independent Election Commission (NIEC) official
▶ **Improper Payment Dollar Value:**	$4.4 million
▶ **Combined Penalties:**	18 months in prison
▶ **Other:**	Defendant is "Individual 1" in the 22-defendant FBI sting of the military and law enforcement equipment industry and was not called by the government in the first Shot Show trial that resulted in a mistrial when the jury could not reach unanimous verdicts. Bistrong was sentenced to 18 months in prison despite government recommendation of five years' probation due to his five-year "extraordinary cooperation."
▶ **Related Matter:**	*United States v. Alvirez et al.* (Shot Show Case); Armor Holdings Inc. DPA; *SEC v. Armor Holdings Inc.*

In January 2010, the DOJ charged Richard T. Bistrong in the U.S. District Court for the District of Columbia with conspiracy to make corrupt payments to foreign officials, to falsify books and records, and to export controlled goods without authorization. Bistrong, a former vice president for international sales at Armor Holdings of Jacksonville, Florida, was accused of paying bribes to get contracts to supply helmets, armored vests, pepper spray, and other protective gear to United Nations peace-keeping authorities and a Dutch law enforcement agency.

Specifically, beginning in July 2001, Bistrong's employer, Armor Holdings, allegedly paid a UN agent more than $200,000 in commissions under a "success fee" arrangement for UN contracts, knowing a portion of the payments would go to a UN procurement official to induce that official to provide nonpublic inside information to the UN agent and to cause the UN to award body armor contracts to Bistrong's employer. Further, the information charged that beginning in 2001, Bistrong allegedly schemed with a Dutch agent to rig a bid on a tender issued by the National Police Services Agency of the Netherlands (KPLD) for a supply of pepper spray. At the request of a Norwegian sales agent and a Dutch agent, a KPLD procurement officer used his influence within KPLD to cause the KPLD to issue a tender specifying a specific type of pepper spray manufactured by Bistrong's employer and no other bidder, as opposed to an alternative pepper spray manufactured by a competitor that the KPLD was considering. After the award of the pepper spray contract to his employer, Bistrong and the Norwegian sales agent caused the company to pay the Dutch agent $15,000 for "marketing services," knowing that some or all of that money would be passed on to the Dutch procurement officer.

Finally, the information charged that as part of the conspiracy, in 2006 Bistrong urged a fellow employee who was a Colombian citizen to not pay directly a Nigerian official of the Independent National Election Commission (INEC) to secure the sales of fingerprint inkpads to INEC, but instead to arrange for the official to designate a company to which a kickback should be paid. INEC never in fact purchased the inkpads.

Bistrong was also charged with conspiring to violate export control laws and specifically to export without a proper license ballistic armor, vests, and helmets to the Kurdistan Regional Government, which was located in Iraq. Armor reportedly disclosed the matter to the DOJ and SEC, and Bistrong was terminated before BAE Systems acquired the company in 2007.[279] On September 15, 2010, Bistrong pled guilty to one count of conspiracy to violate the FCPA and other statutes. He cooperated with the DOJ, did not testify in the June 2011 first Shot Show trial, but did testify in the second Shot Show trial in the fall of 2011 where his testimony was greatly discredited.[280]

On July 31, 2012, Judge Richard Leon sentenced Bistrong to 18 months in prison. The government argued that Bistrong should receive probation due to his five-year "extraordinary cooperation" in the unsuccessful sting operation. Twenty-two defendants were charged, but after three acquittals and two mistrials, Judge Leon granted the DOJ's request to drop the case in February 2012. Judge Leon said he understood Bistrong's cooperation but questioned the government's probation recommendation. He commented that Bistrong had already received benefits from the government by pleading to lesser charges and added, "We certainly don't want the moral of the story to be: Steal big. Violate the law big. Cooperate big. Probation."[281]

AZ.   *United States v. BAE Systems plc;*[282] *In re* BAE Systems plc[283]

▶ **Misconduct Category:**	Use of "Marketing Advisors" through offshore shell companies to ensure favoritism in foreign government military sales
▶ **Countries:**	Kingdom of Saudi Arabia (KSA), Hungary, and Czech Republic
▶ **Foreign Government Officials:**	KSA public officials who would influence KSA fighter jet sales; gain to BAES of $200 million from false statements to U.S. government
▶ **Improper Payment Dollar Value:**	$200 million plus
▶ **Combined Penalties:**	$450 million ($400 million to U.S. and £30 million to U.K. authorities and Tanzania); $79 million penalty with the U.S. Department of State in May 2011
▶ **Other:**	False statements made to the U.S. Secretary of Defense and the DOJ regarding BAES's anticorruption compliance measures and failure to honor certain compliance undertakings; despite the third-largest criminal penalty ever imposed in an FCPA matter, no FCPA bribery count charged thereby likely avoiding government debarment; U.K. citizen to serve as corporate monitor for three-year period; largest fine in Department of State history ($79 million) imposed in 2010

In February 2010, the United States charged BAE Systems plc (BAES), formerly known as British Aerospace, in the U.S. District Court for the District of Columbia with a conspiracy to (1) knowingly impair the lawful functions of the Department of Defense and the Department of State and (2) commit offenses against the United States, to wit: knowingly and willfully make false or fraudulent statements[284] and knowingly and willfully cause to be filed export license applications with the State Department's Directorate of Defense Trade Controls, that is, "applications that failed to properly disclose fees on commissions made, offered, and agreed to be made, directly or indirectly, in connection with sales of defense articles."[285] The improper payments furthered deals to lease SAAB/Grippen fighter jets to Hungary and the Czech Republic. In March 2010, BAES, one of the largest defense contractors in both Europe and the United States, pled guilty and agreed to pay a $400 million fine,[286] the third-largest criminal penalty in an FCPA investigation. BAES also agreed to the appointment of a monitor, a U.K. citizen acceptable to the DOJ for a period not to exceed three years.

Simultaneously with the filing of criminal information in the United States, Britain's Serious Fraud Office (SFO) announced that it had reached an agreement with the BAES whereby the company will plead guilty to failing to keep reasonably accurate accounting records in relation to its activities in Tanzania. BAES agreed to pay £30 million comprising a financial order to be determined by a Crown Court judge, with the balance to be paid "as an ex gratia payment for the benefit of the people of Tanzania."[287]

The U.S. and U.K. resolutions with Europe's largest military contractor ended two long-running investigations. While the criminal information filed in the United States did not name any individuals, prior published reports had indicated that BAES made payments exceeding $2 billion to Prince Bandar bin Sultan, the Kingdom's former ambassador to the United States, and to Prince Turki bin Nasser, who controlled the Saudi air force.[288] The criminal information stated that BAES's U.S. subsidiary was not involved in any of the illegal activities.[289] The absence of a substantive FCPA count likely aided BAES in avoiding a government debarment or suspension. The use of a conspiracy count predicated on false statements to U.S. government agencies also may have avoided problematic FCPA jurisdictional bases as most payments in the case appear to have been made wholly outside the United States. Still, the DOJ case serves as a warning that companies who pledge a compliance program and significant reforms to the DOJ or other government agencies should ensure that such promises are monitored, maintained, and kept.

In May 2011, BAES and the U.S. Department of State (DOS) reached a civil settlement in connection with violations of the U.S. defense export control regulations, to wit: the Arms Export Control Act (ACEA) and the International Traffic in Arms Regulations (ITAR) (22 C.F.R. Parts 120 to 130), that were the subject of the company's March 2010 criminal disposition with the DOJ. Under the four-year term of the consent agreement, BAES agreed to pay in fines and in remedial compliance measures an aggregate civil penalty of $79 million, the largest civil penalty in DOS history. The DOS agreed to consider suspension of $10 million of this amount for qualified pre- and postconsent agreement remedial compliance measures. BAES also agreed to oversight and auditing of its export compliance program for the duration of the consent agreement.[290] The violations were identified by the DOS during a review of BAES's conduct following its March 2010 criminal conviction for conspiracy to violate the AECA and the ITAR. Per the Proposed Charging Letter, BAES allegedly committed an estimated 2,591 violations of the ITAR in connection with unauthorized brokering of U.S. defense articles and services, failure to register as a broker, failure to file annual broker reports, causing unauthorized brokering, failure to report the payment of fees or commissions associated with defense transactions, and failure to maintain records involving ITAR-controlled transactions.[291]

In response to the 2010 criminal conviction, the DOS elected to impose a statutory debarment on BAES, but in accordance with the AECA, after a thorough review of the circumstances surrounding the conviction, and a finding that appropriate steps had been taken to mitigate law enforcement concerns, the DOS determined to concurrently rescind the statutory debarment. The DOS also released the administrative hold it imposed immediately following the conviction on BAES-related license authorization requests. The DOS imposed, however, a policy of denial on three BAES subsidiaries, because of their substantial involvement in activities related to the conviction. These subsidiaries are BAE Systems CS&S International, Red Diamond Trading Ltd., and Poseidon Trading Investments Ltd., including their divisions and business units, and successor entities. There will remain an initial presumption of denial for all applications involving these entities, unless upon case-by-case review the DOS determines that it is in the foreign policy or national security interests of the United States to provide an approval.[292]

BA.   *United States v. Innospec Inc.;*[293] *SEC v. Innospec;*[294]
       Regina v. Innospec Ltd. (U.K.)[295]

► **Misconduct Category:**	United Nations Oil-for-Food program; Cuban embargo violation; bribery of officials of state-owned oil company to obtain chemical contracts
► **Countries:**	Iraq and Indonesia
► **Foreign Government Officials:**	Iraqi Ministry of Oil (MoO) officials and officials of Pertamina, an Indonesian state-owned oil company
► **Improper Payment Dollar Value:**	$7.05 million, including cash, travel, and purchase of a Mercedes-Benz
► **Combined Penalties:**	$40.2 million ($14.1 million criminal penalty; $11.2 million SEC disgorgement of profits; $2.2 million Office of Foreign Assets Control (OFAC) payment; and $12.7 million U.K. criminal penalty)
► **Other:**	Independent monitor for three years; export violations; DOJ referral of matter to U.K. Serious Fraud Office (SFO); first corruption-related settlement between the DOJ, SEC, and the U.K. Serious Fraud Office
► **Related Matters:**	See *United States v. Naaman; SEC v. Naaman & Turner; SEC v. Jennings*

In March 2010, Innospec Inc., a Delaware corporation with executive offices in the United Kingdom, pleaded guilty in the District of Columbia to defrauding the United Nations (UN), to violating the FCPA, and to violating the U.S. embargo against Cuba. Innospec, previously known as Octel Corporation, pleaded guilty to a 12-count information charging wire fraud in connection with Innospec's payment of kickbacks to the former Iraqi government under the UN Oil-for-Food program (OFFP), as well as FCPA violations in connection with bribe payments it made to officials in the Iraqi Ministry of Oil. Innospec also admitted to selling chemicals to Cuban power plants, in violation of the U.S. embargo against Cuba. Innospec manufactures and sells specialty chemicals and is the world's only manufacturer of the antiknock compound tetraethyl lead, used in leaded gasoline.

As part of the plea agreement with the DOJ, Innospec agreed to pay a $14.1 million U.S. criminal fine and to retain an independent compliance monitor for a minimum of three years to oversee the implementation of a robust anticorruption and export control compliance program and report periodically to the DOJ. Innospec also agreed to fully cooperate with the DOJ and other U.S. and foreign authorities in ongoing investigations of corrupt payments by Innospec employees and agents.

According to court documents, from 2000 to 2003, Innospec's Swiss subsidiary, Alcor, was awarded five contracts valued at more than $40 million to sell tetraethyl lead to refineries run by the Iraqi Ministry of Oil under the OFFP. To obtain these contracts, Innospec admitted that Alcor paid or promised to pay at least $4 million in kickbacks to the former Iraqi government. Court documents detail how Alcor inflated the price of the contracts by approximately 10 percent to cover the cost of the kickbacks before submitting them to the UN for approval, and then falsely characterized the payments on the company's books and records as "commissions" paid to Ousama Naaman, its agent in Iraq. Naaman, Innospec's agent in Iraq, was indicted in the District of Columbia on August 8, 2008, and later arrested in Frankfurt, Germany, on July 30, 2009, based on a U.S. arrest warrant. The United States obtained Naaman's extradition from Germany.

Innospec also admitted to paying and promising to pay more than $1.5 million in bribes, in the form of cash and travel, to officials of the Iraqi Ministry of Oil to secure sales of tetraethyl lead in Iraq from 2004 to 2008, as well as to paying $150,000 in 2006 to officials in the Iraqi Ministry of Oil to ensure that a competing product to tetraethyl lead was not approved for use in Iraqi refineries. Innospec admitted that the illicit payments were recorded as "commissions" on the basis of false invoices, which were incorporated into the company's books and records.

According to the plea agreement, Innospec admitted that a subsidiary sold nearly $20 million in oil soluble fuel additives from 2001 to 2004 to state-owned Cuban power plants without a license from the Office of Foreign Asset Controls (OFAC), in violation of the Trading with the Enemy Act (TWEA). In addition, Innospec acknowledged in court documents that it paid approximately $2.9 million in bribes to Indonesian government officials to secure sales.

In a related matter, Innospec settled a civil complaint filed by the SEC, charging Innospec with violating the FCPA's antibribery, internal controls, and books-and-records provisions in connection with the misconduct described in court documents. Innospec agreed to disgorge $11.2 million in profits to the SEC. Innospec also agreed to pay $2.2 million to resolve outstanding matters with the OFAC related to the U.S. embargo (Cuban Assets Control Regulations) against Cuba.

In another related matter brought by the United Kingdom's Serious Fraud Office (SFO), Innospec's British subsidiary, Innospec Ltd., pleaded guilty in the Southwark Crown Court in London in connection with the corrupt payments to Indonesian officials. (See chapter 11.) In connection with these charges, Innospec Ltd agreed to pay a criminal penalty of $12.7 million. The SFO's case was developed as a result of a DOJ referral in October 2007. The Crown Court was troubled by the Innospec three-party (U.S. DOJ, U.K. SFO, and Innospec Ltd.) plea agreement and warned the SFO not to bring such a fait accompli agreement before it again. U.K. courts do not routinely accept plea agreements between the DOJ and criminal defendants as most U.S. district courts do. (See chapter 11 at VIII.C.)

BB.   *United States v. Daimler AG;*[296] *United States v. DaimlerChrysler*
      Automotive Russia SAO (DCAR);[297] *United States v. Export & Trade*
      Finance GmbH;[298] *United States v. DaimlerChrysler China Ltd. (DCCL)*[299]

▶ **Misconduct Category:**

"Repeated and Systematic" bribes over a ten-year period in 22 countries largely to secure commercial vehicle sales; use of corporate ledger accounts, cash desks, offshore bank accounts, deceptive pricing arrangements, and third-party intermediaries; improper payments in the form of commissions through phony sales intermediaries, rogue business partners; delegation; travel and gifts abuses; use of U.S.–based agents to facilitate bribe payments; UN Oil-for-Food program in Iraq

▶ **Countries:**

Bulgaria, China, Croatia, Egypt, Ghana, Greece, Hungary, Indonesia, Iraq, Ivory Coast, Latvia, Liberia, Montenegro, Nigeria, North Korea, Poland, Russia, Serbia, Thailand, Turkey, Turkmenistan, Uzbekistan, and Vietnam

▶ **Foreign Government Officials:**

Senior government officials in 22 countries

▶ **Improper Payment Dollar Value:**

In excess of $50 million

▶ **Combined Penalties:**

$185 million

▶ **Other:**

Fourth-largest FCPA fine to date; DPA for parent and Chinese subsidiary; guilty pleas by Russian sales and German finance subsidiaries; criminal penalties of subsidiaries set off and credited as to parent's $93.6 million criminal penalty; $91.4 million SEC disgorgement; three-year independent compliance monitor; payments continued after the investigation began; gift of a $600,000 armored Mercedes G500 to a senior Liberian official paid through a Liberian dealership; disregard of internal audit warnings in 1986 and 2000; "excellent" cooperation, including a worldwide internal investigation involving dozens of countries and every major market in which the company does business; termination or separation of 45 employees and inception of antibribery program reformation prior to finalization of DOJ resolution; "virtually a non-existent FCPA compliance program";[300] extension of DPA in April 2012 for eight months until 12/31/2012.

In April 2010, Daimler AG, a German corporation, and three of its subsidiaries resolved charges related to an FCPA investigation into the company's worldwide sales practices in the U.S. District Court for the District of Columbia.[301] The United States stated that Daimler had made at least $56 million in improper payments over a period of ten years.[302] The SEC investigation began in 2004 when a DaimlerChrysler Corporation auditor claimed he was terminated for complaining about bribery payments. The auditor filed a whistleblower complaint with the U.S. Department of Labor, alleging that he learned of secret bank accounts used to bribe foreign officials in 2001. Daimler became subject to the FCPA in 1993 when its predecessor Daimler-Benz AG registered a class of securities under section 12 of the Exchange Act. Daimler AG entered into a DPA and agreed to the filing of a criminal information charging that company with one count of conspiracy to violate the books-and-records provisions of the FCPA and one count of violating those provisions. In total, Daimler AG and its subsidiaries will pay $93.6 million in criminal fines and penalties. On the same date, Daimler AG resolved a related civil complaint filed by the SEC. Daimler AG agreed to pay $91.4 million in disgorgement of profits relating to those violations.

Daimler AG's Russian subsidiary, DaimlerChrysler Automotive Russia SAO (DCAR), now known as Mercedes-Benz Russia SAO, and its German subsidiary, Export and Trade Finance GmbH (ETF), each pleaded guilty to criminal informations charging the companies with one count of conspiracy to violate the antibribery provisions of the FCPA and one count of violating those provisions. As part of the plea agreements, DCAR and ETF agreed to pay criminal fines of $27.26 million and $29.12 million, respectively. Both these fines were credited by the parent's payment of $93.4 million. Daimler AG's Chinese subsidiary DaimlerChrysler China Ltd. (DCCL), now known as Daimler North East Asia Ltd., also entered into a DPA and agreed to the filing of a criminal information charging it with one count of conspiracy to violate the antibribery provisions of the FCPA and one count of violating those provisions.

According to court documents, Daimler AG, whose shares trade on multiple exchanges in the United States, engaged in a long-standing practice of paying bribes to foreign government officials through a variety of mechanisms, including the use of corporate ledger accounts known internally as "third-party accounts" or "TPAs," corporate "cash desks," offshore bank accounts, deceptive pricing arrangements, and third-party intermediaries. Daimler AG and its subsidiaries made hundreds of improper payments worth tens of millions of dollars to foreign officials in at least 22 countries—including China, Croatia, Egypt, Greece, Hungary, Indonesia, Iraq, Ivory Coast, Latvia, Montenegro, Nigeria, Russia, Serbia, Thailand, Turkey, Turkmenistan, Uzbekistan, Vietnam, and others—to assist in securing contracts with government customers for the purchase of Daimler vehicles. For example, Daimler obtained a sales contract to supply 100 trucks to the government of Liberia by providing a free armored Mercedes G500 vehicle worth nearly $600,000 to a senior government official. Daimler then arranged to pay its outside dealer in Liberia $600,000, which was mischaracterized as commission, and which the dealer then used to pay for the vehicle. The deceptive structuring of the deal made it appear as if the dealer had purchased the vehicle when, in fact, Daimler employees gifted the vehicle to the Liberian government official as a bribe.[303] The contracts in the above countries were valued at hundreds of millions of dollars.

In some cases, Daimler AG or its subsidiaries wire-transferred these improper payments to U.S. bank accounts, or to the foreign bank accounts of U.S. shell companies, in order for those entities to pass on the bribes. Within Daimler AG and its subsidiaries, bribe payments were often identified and recorded as "commissions," "special discounts," and/or "nützliche Aufwendungen" or "N.A." payments, which translates to "useful payment" or "necessary payment," and was understood by certain Daimler employees to mean "official bribe." Certain corrupt payments continued as late as January 2008, after the DOJ had begun its investigation. In all cases, Daimler AG improperly recorded these corrupt payments in its corporate books and records. Daimler AG admitted that it earned more than $50 million in profits from corrupt transactions with a nexus to the territory of the United States. Daimler AG also admitted that it agreed to pay kickbacks to the former Iraqi government in connection with contracts to sell vehicles to Iraq under the UN's Oil-for-Food program.

In connection with its guilty plea, DCAR admitted that it made improper payments to Russian federal and municipal government officials to secure contracts to sell vehicles by overinvoicing the customer and paying the excess amount back to the government officials, or to other designated third parties that provided no legitimate services to DCAR or Daimler AG. When requested, DCAR or Daimler AG employees caused the wire transfer of payments from Daimler AG's bank accounts in Germany to, among other destinations, U.S. and Latvian bank accounts held by shell companies with the understanding that the money, in whole or in part, was for the benefit of Russian government officials.

In connection with its guilty plea, ETF admitted that it made corrupt payments directly to Croatian government officials and to third parties, including two U.S.-based corporate entities, with the understanding that the payments would be passed on, in whole or in part, to Croatian government officials, to assist in securing the sale of 210 fire trucks.

In connection with its DPA, DCCL admitted that it made improper payments in the form of commissions, delegation travel, and gifts for the benefit of Chinese government officials or their designees in connection with sales of commercial vehicles and Unimogs to various Chinese government customers. DCCL admitted that, in certain cases, it used U.S.-based agents to facilitate the bribe payments.

The SEC complaint criticized Daimler's internal audit, legal, and finance and accounting departments, alleging that they played important roles in the subversion of internal controls and obfuscation of corporate records.[304] Describing a "lax system of internal controls," the complaint alleged that the company's FCPA compliance program, its U.S.-based Chrysler division outside, was "virtually non-existent" even though the company had thousands of employees and dozens of affiliates and business units selling vehicles to foreign governments and government-related entities in many foreign countries.[305] Further, despite adopting a corporate Integrity Code in July 1999, which included antibribery provisions, the company, according to the SEC, failed to adequately enforce those provisions or train employees outside the United States on corporate compliance.[306] The DPA required the company to ensure that it had a regular ten-element compliance program and system of internal controls.[307]

The DOJ described Daimler's cooperation in the investigation as "excellent," pointing out that the vehicle manufacturer conducted a worldwide internal investigation, involving dozens of countries and every major market in which the company does business.[308] The government noted disciplinary actions resulted in sanctions against over 60 company employees with approximately 45 employees terminated or separated under termination agreements.[309] It commended Daimler for beginning to reform its antibribery program while the investigation was still going on, without waiting[310] until the disposition with the DOJ. Under the terms of the DOJ DPA, Daimler AG agreed to retain an independent compliance monitor for a three-year period to oversee the company's continued implementation and maintenance of an FCPA compliance program, and to make reports to the company and the Department of Justice. DCAR, ETF, and DCCL are covered by the monitoring provisions of the DPA with their parent company. Daimler AG also agreed to fully cooperate with ongoing investigations by U.S. and foreign authorities into the company's corrupt payments.

In April 2012 Daimler and the DOJ filed an amendment to the March 22, 2010 DPA which extended the term to December 31, 2012.[311] The amendment did not explain the reason for the extension, but stated that on or before October 31, 2012, the monitor would certify whether the compliance program of Daimler, including its policies and procedures, was reasonably designed to prevent and detect violations within Daimler of the FCPA and the applicable anticorruption laws.

BC.   *United States v. Technip, S.A.;*[312] *SEC v. Technip, S.A.*[313]

▶ **Misconduct Category:**	Decade-long scheme by four joint venture partners (KBR, Technip, Snamprogetti Netherlands B.V., and a Japanese engineering firm) to enter into sham consultancy agreements to bribe Nigerian officials to obtain engineering, procurement, and construction (EPC) contracts.
▶ **Country:**	Nigeria
▶ **Foreign Government Officials:**	"Top-level officials in executive branch of Nigeria"
▶ **Improper Payment Dollar Value:**	$182 million
▶ **Combined Penalties:**	$338 million ($240 million in DOJ criminal penalty and $98 million disgorgement of profits and prejudgment interest to SEC)
▶ **Other:**	Payments to U.K. and Japanese agents who were occasionally described as "cultural advisors" totaled $182 million. Failure to conduct any due diligence on these agents. Two-year DPA; joint venture scheme has led to more than $1.28 billion in criminal and civil penalties to date; Snamprogetti and Technip share largest DPA fine in FCPA history—possibly to avoid EU debarment and suspension; DOJ recognized cooperation by authorities in United States, France, Italy, Switzerland, and the United Kingdom.

▶ **Related Matters:**   *United States v. Stanley; United States v. KBR; United States v. Snamprogetti B.V.; SEC v. ENI SpA & Snamprogetti; United States v. Snamprogetti; SEC v. KBR; United States v. JGC Corp.; United States v. Tesler & Chodan; United States v. Marubeni Corp.*

In June 2010, Technip, S.A., a global engineering, construction, and services company based in Paris, agreed to pay a $240 million criminal penalty to resolve charges related to the FCPA for its participation in a decade-long scheme to bribe Nigerian government officials to obtain engineering, procurement, and construction (EPC) contracts. The EPC contracts to build liquefied natural gas (LNG) facilities on Bonny Island, Nigeria, were valued at more than $6 billion. The DOJ filed a DPA and a two-count criminal information in the U.S. District Court for the Southern District of Texas charging Technip with one count of conspiracy and one count of violating the FCPA. Technip's American depositary shares traded on the New York Stock Exchange from 2001 until 2007.

Technip, Snamprogetti B.V., Kellogg Brown & Root Inc. (KBR), and JGC Corporation (JGC) were part of a four-company joint venture (TSKJ) that was awarded four EPC contracts by Nigeria LNG Ltd. (NLNG) between 1995 and 2004 to build LNG facilities on Bonny Island. The government-owned Nigerian National Petroleum Corporation (NNPC) was the largest shareholder of NLNG, owning 49 percent of the company. The TSKJ joint venture operated through entities incorporated in Madeira, Portugal.

According to court documents, the joint venture authorized the hiring of two agents, Jeffrey Tesler, the U.K. agent, and a Japanese trading company, to pay bribes to a range of Nigerian government officials, including top-level executive-branch officials, to assist the joint venture in obtaining the EPC contracts. The U.K. agent paid the high-ranking officials while the Japanese agent paid lower-level Nigerian officials. A senior executive of Technip, KBR's former CEO, Albert "Jack" Stanley, and others met with successive holders of a top-level office in the executive branch of the Nigerian government to ask the office holders to designate a representative with whom the joint venture should negotiate bribes to Nigerian government officials. The joint venture paid approximately $132 million to a Gibraltar corporation controlled by Tesler and more than $50 million to Wojciech Chodan of the Japanese trading company during the course of the bribery scheme. The joint venture partners intended for these payments to be used, in part, for bribes to Nigerian government. The U.K. and Japanese agents were sometimes referred to as "Cultural Advisors." Two clear lessons emerge from the Technip resolution: (1) joint venture partners must ensure that the legal entity has adequate antibribery controls; and (2) such controls should include quality due diligence and ongoing supervision of agents, consultants, or similar third parties.[314]

Under the terms of the two-year DPA, Technip agreed, among other things, to retain an independent compliance monitor for a two-year period to review the design and implementation of Technip's compliance program and to cooperate with the department in ongoing investigations. If Technip abided by the DPA's terms, the DOJ agreed to dismiss the criminal information when the term of the agreement expires.

Technip also reached a settlement of a related civil complaint filed by the SEC charging it with violating the FCPA's antibribery, books-and-records, and internal controls provisions. The books-and-records and circumvention of internal controls claims alleged that Technip failed to conduct any due diligence on the agents. The SEC criticized the fact that while Technip required potential agents to complete a basic questionnaire, "[N]o additional due diligence was required such as interview of the agent or a background check or beyond that provided by the answers to the questionnaire." As part of that settlement, Technip agreed to pay $98 million in disgorgement of profits. Technip was a U.S. issuer between August 30, 2001, and November 14, 2007, as American depositary shares, representing ordinary shares of Technip, were registered with and traded on the New York Stock Exchange.

BD.   *United States v. Snamprogetti Netherlands B.V.;*[315]
      SEC v. Eni, S.p.A. & Snamprogetti Netherlands, B.V.[316]

▶ **Misconduct Category:**	Decade-long scheme by joint venture partners (KBR, Technip, Snamprogetti, and JGC) to enter into sham consultancy agreements to bribe Nigerian officials to obtain engineering, procurement, and construction (EPC) contracts.
▶ **Country:**	Nigeria
▶ **Foreign Government Officials:**	"Top-level officials in executive branch of Nigeria"
▶ **Improper Payment Dollar Value:**	$182 million
▶ **Combined Penalties:**	$365 million ($240 million in DOJ criminal penalty and $125 million in disgorgement of profits to SEC)
▶ **Other:**	Payments to U.K. and Japanese agents who were occasionally described as "cultural advisors" totaled $182 million. Failure to conduct any due diligence of these agents hired through the joint venture in which the ongoing participated (25 percent interest). Two-year DPA; joint venture scheme has led to more than $1.28 billion in criminal and civil penalties to date; Snamprogetti and Technip share largest DPA fine in FCPA history—possibly to avoid EU debarment and suspension, cooperation with authorities in the United States, France, Italy, and Switzerland.
▶ **Related Matters:**	*United States v. KBR; SEC v. KBR & Halliburton; United States v. Technip SA; SEC v. Technip SA; United States v. Stanley; United States v. JGC Corp.; United States v. Tesler & Chodan; United States v. Marubeni Corp.*

In July 2010, Snamprogetti Netherlands B.V. (Snamprogetti), a global engineering, construction, and services company based in Paris, agreed to pay a $240 million criminal penalty to resolve charges related to the FCPA for its participation in a decade-long scheme to bribe Nigerian government officials to obtain engineering, procurement, and construction (EPC) contracts. During the relevant time period, Snamprogetti was a Dutch wholly owned subsidiary of Snamprogetti S.p.A., an Italian EPC company headquartered in Milan. Snamprogetti S.p.A. was, in turn, a wholly owned subsidiary of ENI during the relevant period. ENI common stock and American depositary shares are listed on the New York Stock Exchange. The EPC contracts to build liquefied natural gas (LNG) facilities on Bonny Island, Nigeria, were valued at more than $6 billion. The DOJ filed a DPA and a two-count criminal information in the U.S. District Court for the Southern District of Texas charging Snamprogetti with one count of conspiracy and one count of violating the FCPA. Technip's American depositary shares traded on the New York Stock Exchange from 2001 until 2007.

Snamprogetti, Kellogg Brown & Root Inc. (KBR), Technip, S.A., and JGC Corporation (JGC) were part of a four-company joint venture (TSKJ) that was awarded four EPC contracts by Nigeria LNG Ltd. (NLNG) between 1995 and 2004 to build LNG facilities on Bonny Island. The government-owned Nigerian National Petroleum Corporation (NNPC) was the largest shareholder of NLNG, owning 49 percent of the company. The joint venture operated through entities incorporated in Madeira, Portugal.

According to court documents, the joint venture authorized the hiring of two agents, Jeffrey Tesler, the U.K. agent, and Wojciech Chodan of a Japanese trading company in order to pay bribes to a range of Nigerian government officials, including top-level executive-branch officials, to assist the joint venture in obtaining the EPC contracts. A senior executive of Technip, KBR's former CEO, Albert Jackson "Jack" Stanley, and others met with successive holders of a top-level office in the executive branch of the Nigerian government to ask the office holders to designate a representative with whom the joint venture should negotiate bribes to Nigerian government officials. The joint venture paid approximately $132 million to a Gibraltar corporation controlled by Tesler and more than $50 million to the Japanese trading company controlled by Chodan during the course of the bribery scheme. The joint venture partners intended for these payments to be used, in part, for bribes to Nigerian government. The U.K. and Japanese agents were sometimes referred to as "Cultural Advisors."

Under the terms of a two-year DPA, Snamprogetti, its current parent company, Saipem S.p.A., and its former parent company, ENI S.p.A. (ENI), agreed, among other things, to ensure that their compliance programs satisfied certain standards and to cooperate with the DOJ in ongoing investigations. If Snamprogetti and its owner and former parent companies abide by the DPA's terms, the DOJ agrees to dismiss the criminal information when the term of the agreement expires.

In July 2010, Snamprogetti and its former parent company, ENI S.p.A. (ENI), also reached a settlement of a related civil complaint filed by the SEC, charging Snamprogetti with violating the FCPA's antibribery provisions, falsifying books and records, and circumventing internal controls and charging ENI with violating the FCPA's books-and-records and internal controls provisions.[317] As part of the internal controls claim, the SEC alleged that Snamprogetti failed to conduct due diligence of the agents. ENI, Snamprogetti's indirect parent, approved Snamprogetti's entry into the JV but there is no allegations it participated in JV activities or knew of the wrongdoing. ENI is alleged to have to failed to assure that Snamprogetti conducted due diligence on agents hired through joint ventures in which Snamprogetti participated.[318] As part of that settlement, Snamprogetti and ENI agreed jointly to pay $125 million in disgorgement of profits relating to those violations.

BE.   U.S. Alliance One International Inc. Agreement; *United States v. Alliance One International AG; United States v. Alliance One Tobacco Osh LLC;*[319] *SEC v. Alliance One International Inc.*[320]

▶ **Misconduct Category:**	Bribes paid to Thai government officials to secure contracts with the Thailand Tobacco Monopoly and bribes paid to Kyrgyzstan government officials in connection with its purchase of Kyrgyz tobacco
▶ **Countries:**	Thailand and Kyrgyzstan (DOJ and SEC); China, Greece, and Indonesia (SEC)
▶ **Foreign Government Officials:**	Thailand Tobacco Monopoly employees; Kyrgyzstan Tamekesi, a tobacco regulatory agency; akims, provincial government officials in Kyrgyzstan
▶ **Improper Payment Dollar Value:**	$4.575 million
▶ **Combined Penalties:**	$19.45 million (DOJ criminal penalties of $9.45 million and SEC disgorgement of profits of $10 million)
▶ **Other:**	NPA for parent Alliance One International Inc.; guilty pleas by Swiss and Kyrgyzstan subsidiaries; independent compliance monitor; key illustration of successor liability.
▶ **Related Matters:**	Universal Corporation; Universal Leaf Tabacos Ltda.; *United States v. Elkin*

In August 2010, Alliance One International AG (AOIAG), a Swiss subsidiary of Alliance One International Inc. (Alliance One), a global tobacco leaf merchant headquartered in Morrisville, North Carolina, pleaded guilty to a three-count criminal information in the U.S. District Court for the Western District of Virginia, charging it with conspiring to violate the FCPA, violations of the antibribery provisions of the FCPA, and violations of the books-and-records provisions of the FCPA. The charges relate to bribes paid to Thai government officials to secure contracts with the Thailand Tobacco Monopoly, a Thai government agency, for the sale of tobacco leaf. Alliance One Tobacco Osh LLC (AOI-Kyrgyzstan), a Kyrgyzstan corporation, also pleaded guilty to a separate three-count criminal information charging it with conspiracy to violate the FCPA, violations of the antibribery provisions of the FCPA, and violations of the books-and-records provisions of the FCPA relating to bribes paid to Kyrgyzstan government officials in connection with its purchase of Kyrgyz tobacco.

The DOJ and Alliance One entered into an NPA in which the U.S. parent company agreed to cooperate with the ongoing investigation and to retain an independent compliance monitor for a minimum of three years to oversee the implementation of an antibribery and anticorruption compliance program and to report periodically to the DOJ.

According to court documents, Alliance One is an independent leaf tobacco merchant that purchases, processes, and sells tobacco to manufacturers of consumer tobacco products worldwide. Alliance One was formed in 2005 as the result of a merger of Dimon Incorporated and Standard Commercial Corporation, both of which were wholesale leaf tobacco merchants. The guilty pleas relate to conduct that was committed by employees and agents of foreign subsidiaries of both Dimon and Standard prior to the merger. As part of the plea agreements, AOIAG agreed to pay a fine of $5.25 million and AOI-Kyrgyzstan agreed to pay a fine of $4.2 million for a total of $9.45 million in criminal fines.

According to court documents, from 2000 to 2004, Dimon and Standard sold Brazilian-grown tobacco to the Thailand Tobacco Monopoly. Each of the companies retained sales agents in Thailand, and collaborated through those agents to apportion tobacco sales to the Thailand Tobacco Monopoly among themselves, coordinate their sales prices, and pay kickbacks to officials of the Thailand Tobacco Monopoly in order to ensure that each company would share in the Thai tobacco market. Each of the companies made annual sales to the Thailand Tobacco Monopoly. To secure the sales contracts, each company admitted it paid kickbacks to certain Thailand Tobacco Monopoly representatives based on the number of kilograms of tobacco sold to the Thailand Tobacco Monopoly. To obtain these contracts, Dimon paid bribes totaling $542,590 and Standard paid bribes totaling $696,160, for a total of $1,238,750 in bribes paid to the Thailand Tobacco Monopoly officials over four years.

In addition, according to court documents, AOI-Kyrgyzstan admitted that employees of Dimon's Kyrgyz subsidiary paid a total of approximately $3 million in bribes from 1996 to 2004 to various officials in the Republic of Kyrgyzstan, including officials of the Kyrgyzstan Tamekesi, a government entity that controlled and regulated the sale and export of tobacco in Kyrgyzstan. Also, according to court documents, the employees paid bribes totaling $254,262 to five local provincial government officials, known as *akims*, to obtain permission to purchase tobacco from local growers during the same period. In addition, the employees paid approximately $82,000 in bribes to officers of the Kyrgyz Tax Police in order to avoid penalties and lengthy tax investigations.

In a related SEC matter, the parent company Alliance One International Inc. settled a civil complaint filed, charging it with violating the FCPA's antibribery, internal controls, and books-and-records provisions in connection with the above misconduct. Alliance One agreed to disgorge approximately $10 million in ill-gotten gains to the SEC. The SEC complaint alleged that Dimon made improper payments to the officials in Greece and Indonesia and that Standard also made an improper payment to a political candidate and provided gifts, travel, and entertainment expenses to foreign officials in the Asia region, including China and Thailand. The SEC alleged that "despite . . . extensive international operations" the company "had failed to establish a program to monitor compliance with the FCPA by its employees, agents, and subsidiaries."

BF.   *United States v. Elkin;*[321] *SEC v. Elkin, Myers, Reynolds & Williams*

▶ **Misconduct Category:**   Bribery of officials who regulate and tax tobacco to obtain export licenses and to gain access to government processing facilities

▶ **Country:**   Kyrgyzstan

▶ **Foreign Government Officials:**   Kyrgyz tax inspection police, Kyrgyz Tameski, a tobacco regulatory agency, and akims—local Provincial government officials in Kyrgyzstan[322]

▶ **Improper Payment Dollar Value:** $3 million

▶ **Combined Penalties:**   Elkin: Three years probation and $5,000 criminal fine; SEC penalties against Myers and Reynolds of $40,000 each

▶ **Related Matters:**   Alliance One International Inc.; *United States v. Alliance One International AG; United States v. Alliance One Tobacco Osh LLC;* Universal Corporation; Universal Leaf Tabacos Ltda.

In August 2010, Bobby Jay Elkin, Jr., a former Kyrgyzstan country manager for Alliance One International, pleaded guilty to a one-count criminal investigation for his role in a conspiracy to pay bribes to officials of the Republic of Kyrgyzstan. At sentencing, the cooperating Elkin faced a government-recommended penalty of five years in prison and a $250,000 fine. Under the U.S. Sentencing Guidelines, he had faced 90 to 121 months in jail. In October 2010, the district court sentenced Elkin to three years of probation and a $5,000 fine.

Elkin admitted to conspiring to make corrupt payments totaling more than $3 million to government officials in Kyrgyzstan from 1996 through 2004 for the purpose of securing business advantages for his employer. Elkin admitted he made cash payments to officials of Kyrgyz Tameski, a tobacco authority and instrumentality of the government, in order to obtain export licenses and to gain access to government-owned tobacco processing facilities. According to court documents, the payments were based on the number of kilograms of Kyrgyz tobacco Elkin's employer purchased and processed for export. In addition, Elkin admitted he made cash payments to local government officials, known as *akims*, to obtain permission to purchase tobacco from local growers, and to the Kyrgyz Tax Inspection Police to influence their decisions and avoid lengthy tax inspections and penalties. In the SEC proceeding, Elkin, Myers, Reynolds, and Williams consented to a permanent injunction, and Myers and Reynolds were ordered to pay penalties of $40,000 each.

BG.   *United States v. Mercator Corp.*[323]

▶ **Misconduct Category:**	Unlawful gift of luxury items to influence government decisions
▶ **Country:**	Kazakhstan
▶ **Foreign Government Officials:**	Senior officials
▶ **Improper Payment Dollar Value:**	Two snowmobiles
▶ **Penalty:**	$32,000 fine
▶ **Other:**	Purchase of two snowmobiles, shipment to Kazakhstan for delivery to government official
▶ **Related Matters:**	*United States v. Giffen; United States v. Williams*

In August 2010, the Mercator Corporation, a merchant bank with offices in New York, pleaded guilty in the Southern District of New York to one count of making an unlawful payment to a senior government official of the Republic of Kazakhstan. According to court documents, Mercator advised Kazakhstan in connection with various transactions related to the sale of portions of Kazakhstan's oil and gas wealth. Three senior officials in the government of Kazakhstan had the power to substantially influence whether Mercator obtained and retained lucrative business, as well as the authority to pay Mercator substantial success fees if certain oil transactions closed, as well as to decide whether or not those transactions would close. According to court documents, Mercator was therefore dependent upon the goodwill of those senior officials, and in an effort to maintain its lucrative position, Mercator caused the purchase of two snowmobiles in November 1999. The snowmobiles were shipped to Kazakhstan for delivery to one of the officials. Mercator faced a maximum fine of the greater of $2 million or twice the gross gain or loss resulting from the offense.

On the same date, James H. Giffen, Mercator's chairman, pleaded guilty to one count of failing to disclose control of a Swiss bank account on his income tax return. Giffen filed a U.S. Individual Income Tax Return, Form 1040, on March 27, 1997, for himself for the calendar year 1996, which failed to report that he maintained an interest in, and a signature and other authority over, a bank account in Switzerland in the name of Condor Capital Management, a British Virgin Islands corporation he controlled. In December 2010 a Southern District of New York judge declined to sentence Giffen to jail.

In 2007, the United States brought a separate, related civil forfeiture action in the U.S. District Court in Manhattan against approximately $84 million on deposit in Switzerland. The civil complaint alleged that the funds were traceable to unlawful payments to senior Kazakh officials in connection with oil and gas transactions arranged by Mercator for Kazakhstan. According to a 2007 agreement between the United States, Switzerland, and Kazakhstan, the funds are being used by a nongovernmental organization in Kazakhstan, independent of the Kazakh government, to benefit underprivileged Kazakh children.

BH.   U.S. DOJ–Universal Corp. Agreement; *United States v. Universal Leaf Tabacos Ltda.;*[324] *SEC v. Universal Corp.*[325]

▶ **Misconduct Category:**	Bribes paid to the employees of Thailand Tobacco Monopoly for the sale of Brazilian tobacco
▶ **Countries:**	Thailand (DOJ and SEC); Mozambique and Malawi (SEC)
▶ **Foreign Government Officials:**	Thailand Tobacco Monopoly officials; improper payments to high-ranking Malawian government officials and a political opposition leader; Mozambican Ministry of Agriculture and Fisheries; high-ranking officials and their wives; tax officials in Greece and Indonesia; gifts, travel, and entertainment expenses in China and Thailand
▶ **Improper Payment Dollar Value:**	$697,000
▶ **Combined Penalties:**	$9.9 million (DOJ criminal penalties of $4.4 million and SEC disgorgement of $4.5 million)
▶ **Other:**	NPA for parent company due, in part, to "preexisting compliance" program, and Universal Corporation's guilty plea for Brazilian subsidiary; independent compliance monitor for three years
▶ **Related Matters:**	Alliance One International Inc; *United States v. Alliance One International AG; United States v. Alliance One Tobacco Osh LLC; United States v. Elkin*

In August 2010, the DOJ filed a two-count information in the Eastern District of Virginia charging Universal Leaf Tabacos Ltda. (Universal Brazil), a subsidiary of Universal Corporation, with conspiring to violate the antibribery provisions and books-and-records provisions of the FCPA and with violating the antibribery provisions of the FCPA relating to bribes paid to employees of Thailand Tobacco Monopoly, a Thai government agency, for the sale of Brazilian tobacco. The DOJ also filed a plea agreement signed by Universal Brazil whereby the company admitted to the conduct contained in the charging document. In addition, Universal Corporation and the DOJ entered into a separate NPA. According to the plea agreement and the NPA, Universal Brazil agreed to pay a $4.4 million criminal fine, and Universal Corporation and Universal Brazil agreed to retain an independent compliance monitor for a minimum of three years to oversee the implementation of an antibribery and anticorruption compliance program and to report periodically to the DOJ.

Universal Brazil admitted that the company paid approximately $697,000 in kickbacks to the Thailand Tobacco Monopoly officials. Court documents detail how the companies conspired to set the price of the tobacco sales, pay the kickbacks to the officials, and then falsely characterized the "special expenses" on each of the companies' respective books and records as "commissions" paid to their sales agents.

In a related matter Universal Corporation, a Virginia corporation, settled a civil complaint filed by the SEC, charging it with violating from 2002 through 2007 the FCPA's antibribery, internal controls, and books-and-records provisions in connection with misconduct in Thailand, Mozambique, and Malawi. Universal Leaf agreed to disgorge approximately $4.5 million in profits to resolve the civil matter. Improper payments to government officials and/or their family members totaling $165,000 in Mozambique were falsely described in books and records as "commissions," "consulting fees," and "travel advances." Improper payments to two Malawian government officials and to a political opposition leader totaled $850,000 and were made through a Belgian subsidiary. They were variously and improperly recorded as "fees for service," "commission for brokers [sic] fees," "expenses . . . relating to Malawi tobacco purchasing requirements" and "donations made to the Malawi government."

BI. *United States v. Aguilar & Aguilar*[326]

▶ **Misconduct Category:**	Bribes by Mexican sales representatives to U.S. company of officials of Mexican state-owned utility to obtain contract awards
▶ **Country:**	Mexico
▶ **Foreign Government Officials:**	Officials of Comisión Federal de Electricidad (CFE), a Mexican state-owned electric utility
▶ **Improper Payment Dollar Value:**	In excess of $1 million
▶ **Combined Penalties:**	Angela Aguilar sentenced to time served in custody (approximately nine months); Enrique Aguilar is a fugitive
▶ **Other:**	Sales representatives purchase $1.8 million yacht and $297,500 Ferrari for a CFE official; payment of more than $170,000 worth of American Express bills and sending of $600,000 to relatives of state-owned utility official
▶ **Related Matter:**	*United States v. Lindsey Manufacturing Co., Lindsey & Lee*

In September 2010 Enrique Aguilar and Angela Aguilar, two intermediaries and directors of Grupo Internacional de Asesores S.A. (Grupo), were indicted in the Central District of California for their alleged roles in a conspiracy to pay and launder bribes to Mexican government officials at the Comisión Federal de Electricidad (CFE), a state-owned utility company. CFE is responsible for supplying electricity in Mexico and contracts with Mexican and foreign companies for goods and services to help supply electricity services to its customers. Enrique Faustino Aguilar Noriega, 56, of Cuernavaca, Mexico, was charged in a seven-count indictment, with conspiracy to violate the FCPA, substantive FCPA violations, money laundering conspiracy, and money laundering. Angela Maria Gomez Aguilar, 55, of Cuernavaca, was charged with money laundering conspiracy and money laundering.

The indictment alleged that Enrique and Angela Aguilar were directors of Grupo, which purported to provide sales representation services for companies doing business with CFE. According to the indictment, Grupo was hired by Lindsey Manufacturing Company (Lindsey), an Azusa, California–based company to serve as its sales representative in Mexico and to obtain contracts for it from CFE. Grupo received a percentage of the revenue that Lindsey company realized from its contracts with CFE. The Azusa-based company manufactured emergency restoration systems and other equipment used by electrical utility companies. Many Lindsey clients were foreign, state-owned utilities, including CFE, which was one of the company's most significant customers.

From approximately February 2002 until March 2009, Enrique Aguilar and his coconspirators allegedly orchestrated a scheme in which Enrique Aguilar was paid a 30 percent commission on all the goods and services Lindsey sold to CFE, even though this was a significantly higher commission than previous sales representatives for the company had received. The indictment alleges that Enrique Aguilar's coconspirators understood that all or part of the 30 percent commission would be used to pay bribes to Mexican officials in exchange for CFE awarding contracts to the Azusa-based company. The costs of goods and services sold to CFE allegedly were increased by 30 percent to ensure that the added cost of paying Enrique Aguilar was absorbed by CFE and not the Azusa-based company.

Enrique Aguilar allegedly caused fraudulent invoices to be submitted from Grupo to the Azusa-based company for 30 percent of the contract price. According to the indictment, a coconspirator would then wire the money requested in the fraudulent invoices into Grupo's brokerage account, allegedly knowing that the invoices were fraudulent and the funds were being used as bribes. Enrique and Angela Aguilar allegedly then laundered the money in the Grupo brokerage account to make concealed payments for the benefit of CFE officials. According to the indictment, the two purchased a yacht for approximately $1.8 million and a Ferrari for $297,500 for a CFE official on August 10, 2010. According to the indictment, Enrique and Angela Aguilar also paid more than $170,000 worth of American Express bills for a CFE official and sent approximately $600,000 to relatives of a CFE official. Angela Aguilar was arrested on a criminal complaint when she traveled to Houston from Mexico. In May 2011, she was convicted by a jury of money laundering and in June sentenced to time served (approximately nine months in custody without bail). Enrique Aguilar remains a fugitive.

BJ.   *United States v. ABB Inc.;*[327] *United States v. ABB Ltd.-Jordan;*[328]
       SEC v. ABB Ltd.;[329] *United States v. ABB Ltd.*[330]

▶ **Misconduct Category:**	Bribes of Mexican utility officials through third-party sales representative; UN Oil-for-Food program kickbacks made in the form of bank guarantees and cash payments
▶ **Countries:**	Iraq and Mexico
▶ **Foreign Government Officials:**	Comisión Federal de Electricidad (CFE—state-owned utility) officials
▶ **Improper Payment Dollar Value:**	$2.4 million
▶ **Combined Penalties:**	$58 million: $19 million DOJ criminal penalties and $39 million SEC penalties ($22.5 million SEC disgorgement of profits and interest and $16.5 million civil penalty)
▶ **Other:**	DPA for parent; guilty pleas by two subsidiaries (one U.S. and one Jordanian); enhanced and corporate compliance reporting and responsibilities; independent compliance consultant

In September 2010, ABB Ltd., a Swiss corporation, and two of its subsidiaries, U.S.–based ABB Ltd. and Jordan-based ABB Ltd.-Jordan, resolved its charges related to the FCPA. ABB Inc. pleaded guilty to two criminal informations charging it with an antibribery violation and conspiracy to violate the same. ABB Inc. admitted that one of its business units based in Sugarland, Texas, ABB Network Management (ABB NM), paid bribes from 1997 to 2004 that totaled $1.9 million to officials at Comisión Federal de Electricidad (CFE), a Mexican state-owned utility company, in order to obtain business with government-owned power companies. In exchange for these bribes, ABB NM received contracts worth more than $81 million in revenue. ABB NM's sales representative in Mexico was used to make the bribery payments to CFE officials.

ABB Ltd.-Jordan admitted that it paid kickbacks to the Iraqi government in connection with contracts to sell vehicles under the UN Oil-for-Food program. It admitted that from 2000 to 2004, the Jordanian subsidiary paid more than $500,000 in kickbacks to the former Iraqi government to secure contracts with the General Company for Electricity Energy Production, the Baghdad Mayoralty, and the State Company Baghdad Electricity Distribution, all of which were regional companies of the Iraqi Electricity Commission, an Iraqi government agency. As a result, ABB Ltd.-Jordan and its subsidiary received 11 purchase orders for electrical equipment and seven worth more than $5.9 million.

The parent company ABB Ltd. entered into a DPA and agreed to pay a $19 million criminal penalty. ABB Ltd. further agreed to fully cooperate with investigators of U.S. and foreign authorities of the company's corrupt payments and to adhere to a set of enhanced corporate compliance and reporting obligations, which include the recommendations of an independent compliance consultant.

In a related matter, in September 2010, ABB Ltd. settled with the SEC on similar allegations. According to the SEC complaint, the Oil-for-Food contracts obtained as a result of the kickback schemes generated $13.5 million in revenues and $3.8 million in profits. It agreed to pay $39 million in the SEC matter: $22.5 million in disgorgement of profits and prejudgment interest and a $16.5 million civil penalty.

BK.   *United States v. Lindsey Manufacturing Co., Lindsey & Lee*[331]

▶ **Misconduct Category:**	Bribes by Mexican sales representatives of Azusa, California, manufacturer to officers of Comisíon Federal de Electricidad (CFE), a major state-owned electric utility in Mexico to award contracts
▶ **Country:**	Mexico
▶ **Foreign Government Officials:**	Officers of CFE, Mexican state-owned electric utility
▶ **Improper Payment Dollar Value:**	In excess of $1 million
▶ **Combined Penalties:**	Indictment dismissed due to prosecutorial misconduct in August 2011
▶ **Other:**	Sales representative gave a $297,500 Ferrari to a government official; Keith Lindsey, Steven Lee, Angela Aguilar, and the company proceeded to trial, were convicted in May 2011. On December 11, 2011, Judge Matz of the Central District of California issued an order dismissing the indictment against the company, Lindsey, and Lee due to prosecutorial misconduct; district court ruling that CFE is an instrumentality and its officers are government officials for purposes of the FCPA
▶ **Related Matter:**	*United States v. Aguilar & Aguilar*

In October 2010 Lindsey Manufacturing Company, an Azusa, California, company, and two of its executives, Keith E. Lindsey and Steven K. Lee, were indicted in the Central District of California for their alleged roles in a conspiracy to pay bribes to Mexican government officials at the Comisión Federal de Electricidad (CFE), a state-owned utility company. Lindsey Manufacturing makes emergency restoration systems and other equipment used by electrical utility companies.

Lindsey, 65, of La Canada, California; Lee, 60, of Diamond Bar, California; and Lindsey Manufacturing Company each were charged in an eight-count superseding indictment with conspiracy to violate the FCPA and substantive FCPA violations. The superseding indictment also charged Enrique Faustino Aguilar Noriega, 56, and Angela Maria Gomez Aguilar, 55, both of Cuernavaca, Mexico, who were previously indicted on September 15, 2010. Enrique Aguilar was charged with the conspiracy to violate the FCPA and FCPA violations. Enrique and Angela Aguilar each were charged with conspiracy to commit money laundering and money laundering.

According to the superseding indictment, CFE was responsible for supplying electricity in Mexico, and contracts with Mexican and foreign companies for goods and services to help supply electricity services to its customers. Enrique and Angela Aguilar were directors of Grupo Internacional de Asesores S.A. (Grupo), which purported to provide sales representation services for companies doing business with CFE.

The superseding indictment alleged that Lindsey Manufacturing hired Grupo to serve as its sales representative in Mexico and to obtain contracts for it from CFE and that many of Lindsey Manufacturing's clients were foreign, state-owned utilities, including CFE, which was one of the company's most significant customers. Grupo received a percentage of the revenue Lindsey Manufacturing realized from its contracts with CFE.

From approximately February 2002 until March 2009, Lindsey Manufacturing, Lindsey, Lee, and Enrique Aguilar allegedly orchestrated a scheme in which Enrique Aguilar was paid a 30 percent commission on all the goods and services Lindsey Manufacturing sold to CFE, even though this was a significantly higher commission than previous sales representatives for the company had received. The superseding indictment alleged that Lindsey and Lee understood that all or part of the 30 percent commission would be used to pay bribes to Mexican officials in exchange for CFE awarding contracts to Lindsey Manufacturing Company. The costs of goods and services sold to CFE allegedly were increased by 30 percent to ensure that the added cost of paying Enrique Aguilar was absorbed by CFE and not Lindsey Manufacturing.

Enrique Aguilar allegedly caused fraudulent invoices to be submitted from Grupo to Lindsey Manufacturing for 30 percent of the contract price. According to the superseding indictment, Lindsey and Lee then caused the money requested in the fraudulent invoices to be wired into Grupo's brokerage account, allegedly knowing that the invoices were fraudulent and the funds were being used as bribes.

Enrique and Angela Aguilar allegedly then laundered the money in the Grupo brokerage account to make concealed payments for the benefit of CFE officials. According to the indictment, Enrique and Angela Aguilar purchased a yacht for approximately $1.8 million named the Dream Seeker and a Ferrari for $297,500 for a CFE official. According to the indictment, Enrique and Angela Aguilar also paid more than $170,000 worth of American Express bills for a CFE official and sent approximately $600,000 to relatives of a CFE official.

In April 2011, Lindsey, Lee, and Angela Aguilar proceeded to trial and were convicted of all counts by a jury in May. In December 2011, Judge Matz issued an order dismissing the indictment with prejudice due to a host of prosecutorial misconduct, finding that

> The government's misconduct went way beyond the delayed and incomplete production of the Guernsey grand jury transcripts. It included procuring search and seizure warrants through materially

false and misleading affidavits; improperly obtaining attorney-client privileged communications; violating court orders; questioning witnesses improperly; failing timely to produce information required under *Jencks*; and engaging in questionable behavior during closing arguments. Even if the suppression of the Guernsey transcripts did not constitute a *Brady* violation, overall the Government's conduct was improper, and it warrants exercise of the Court's supervisory powers.[332]

Angela Aguilar was sentenced to time served while awaiting trial in custody for approximately nine months. Enrique Aguilar remains a fugitive.

BL.   U.S. DOJ–Noble Corp. Agreement;[333] *SEC v. Noble Corp.*[334]

▶ **Misconduct Category:**	Bribes paid through freight forwarder to customs officials to obtain preferential treatment in customs matters
▶ **Country:**	Nigeria
▶ **Foreign Government Officials:**	Nigerian Customs Service officials
▶ **Improper Payment Dollar Value:**	$74,000
▶ **Combined Penalties:**	$8.09 million ($2.59 million in DOJ criminal penalties and $5.5 million in SEC disgorgement of profits and prejudgment interest)
▶ **Other:**	NPA due to Noble's early voluntary disclosure, thorough self-investigation of the underlying conduct, full real-time cooperation with the DOJ, implementation of extensive remedial measures; and annual reporting to DOJ; Noble recorded some of its bribes as "facilitating payments"; the Noble NPA and below USSG sentence may signal the DOJ and SEC's recognition of the need for greater credit to cooperating companies
▶ **Related Matters:**	*United States v. Panalpina, United States v. Pride International, United States v. Shell Nigeria Exploration & Production Co., United States v. Tidewater, and United States v. Transocean; SEC v. GlobalSantaFe Corp.; SEC v. Jackson & Ruehlen; SEC v. O'Rourke*

In November 2010, the DOJ and Noble Corporation (Noble), a Cayman Islands corporation with worldwide oil and gas drilling operations and headquarters in Sugar Land, Texas, reached an NPA in which Noble admitted that it had paid approximately $74,000 to a Nigerian freight-forwarding agent, acknowledged that certain employees knew that some of the payments would be passed on as bribes to Nigerian customs officials, and admitted that Noble falsely recorded the bribe payments as legitimate business expenses in its corporate books, records, and accounts.

As part of the NPA, Noble agreed to pay a $2.59 million criminal penalty. The NPA recognized Noble's discovery of the violations through its own investigation and early voluntary disclosure, thorough self-investigation of the underlying conduct, full real-time cooperation with the DOJ and SEC, the existence of a pre-existing compliance program, and extensive remedial measures undertaken by the company.[335] As a result of these factors, among others, the DOJ agreed not to prosecute Noble or its subsidiaries for the bribe payments, provided that Noble satisfies its ongoing NPA obligations, including providing annual, written reports to the DOJ on its progress and experience.

In a related civil enforcement action brought by the SEC, Noble agreed to pay approximately $5.5 million in disgorgement of profits and prejudgment interest. Noble recorded some of the payments to Nigerian customs officials in its "facilitating payment" account. Because the payments did not qualify as facilitating payments under the FCPA, the SEC alleged that Noble created false books and records by recording the payments as such. On the eve of trial in July 2014, Jackson consented to an injunction for being a control person for Noble's books-and-records violations and Ruehlen consented to an injunction for aiding and abetting books-and-records violations. No civil penalty was imposed on either individual.[336]

In February 2013, the Supreme Court in *Gabelli v. SEC* held that the five-year statute of limitations under 28 U.S.C. § 2462 runs as applied to the government from when the fraud occurred, not when it is discovered. This opinion, which came down after the SEC had charged defendants in 2012 with conduct occurring between 2003 and 2007, likely was limited in its option in pursuing civil penalties against Jackson and Ruehlen.[337]

BM.   *United States v. Panalpina World Transport (Holding) Ltd.;*[338]
      United States v. Panalpina Inc.; SEC v. Panalpina, Inc.[339]

▶ **Misconduct Category:**	Freight-forwarder payment of bribes to numerous public officials on behalf of customers to circumvent local rules and regulations relating to the import of goods and materials into foreign jurisdictions
▶ **Countries:**	Angola, Azerbaijan, Brazil, Kazakhstan, Nigeria, Russia, and Turkmenistan
▶ **Foreign Government Officials:**	Nigerian Customs Service officials
▶ **Improper Payment Dollar Value:**	$27 million
▶ **Combined Penalties:**	More than $81 million ($70.56 million DOJ criminal penalty and SEC $11.3 million in disgorgement of profits); Panalpina paid over $30 million in bribes to Nigerian government officials; criminal penalty slightly less than USSG minimum

▶ **Other:**

DPA for Swiss parent company and guilty plea by U.S. subsidiary; Panalpina spawned industry-wide investigation focusing primarily on Nigeria Customs Service abuses; government theory in essence charged that Panalpina aided and abetted select issuer-customers by paying bribes to customs officials to avoid duties and expedite imported goods; no monitor requirement despite six-year multicountry misconduct due to Panalpina's significant commitment to build a compliance department during the government investigation

▶ **Related Matters:**

Noble, *United States v. Pride International, United States v. Shell Nigeria Exploration & Production Co., United States v. Tidewater; United States v. Transocean; SEC v. GlobalSantaFe Corp.*; Panalpina and these companies agreed to pay combined DOJ criminal penalties and SEC disgorgement of profit amounts of over $236 million.

In November 2010 Panalpina World Transport (Holding) Ltd., a global freight-forwarding and logistics services firm based in Basel, Switzerland, and its U.S.–based subsidiary, Panalpina Inc., admitted that the companies, through subsidiaries and affiliates (collectively Panalpina), engaged in a scheme to pay bribes to numerous foreign officials on behalf of many of its customers in the oil and gas industry. They did so in order to circumvent local rules and regulations relating to the import of goods and materials into numerous foreign jurisdictions. Panalpina admitted that between 2002 and 2007, it paid thousands of bribes totaling at least $27 million to foreign officials in at least seven countries, including Angola, Azerbaijan, Brazil, Kazakhstan, Nigeria, Russia, and Turkmenistan; the company provides global freight-forwarding and logistics services in approximately 160 jurisdictions. In November, Panalpina's customers, including Shell Nigeria Exploration and Production Company Ltd. (SNEPCO), Transocean Inc., and Tidewater Marine International Inc., admitted that they approved of or condoned the payment of bribes on their behalf in Nigeria and falsely recorded the bribe payments made on their behalf as legitimate business expenses in their corporate books, records, and accounts.

The government theory was that Panalpina, through its subsidiaries, made improper payments to Nigerian Customs Service (NCS) officials in the course of providing a variety of shipping, freight-forwarding, and logistics services, including customs service and transportation services, on behalf of issuer-customers, including express courier service and temporary importations. The charges for the improper payments were later invoiced to the issuer-customers with descriptions intended to aid the issuer-customers in concealing the nature of the improper payments in their books, records, and accounts. False descriptions included "local processing fees," "interventions," "special handing," and "administration/transport charges."[340] Between 2002 and 2007, Panalpina Nigeria paid over $30 million in improper payments to Nigerian government officials. The company admitted that it engaged in similar misconduct during roughly the same period in Angola, Azerbaijan, Brazil, Kazakhstan, Russia, and Turkmenistan.[341]

As part of the resolution, the DOJ filed a criminal information charging Panalpina World Transport with conspiring to violate and violating the antibribery provisions of the FCPA. The DOJ and parent company Panalpina World Transport agreed to resolve the charges by entering into a DPA. The DOJ also filed a criminal information charging Panalpina Inc. with conspiring to violate the books-and-records provisions of the FCPA and with aiding and abetting certain customers in violating the books-and-records provisions of the FCPA and Panalpina Inc. agreed to plead guilty. The agreements require the payment by Panalpina of a $70.56 million criminal penalty.

Under the terms of the three-year DPA, Panalpina World Transport is required to fully cooperate with U.S. and foreign authorities in any ongoing investigations of the company's corrupt payments. In addition, it is required to implement and adhere to a set of enhanced corporate compliance and reporting obligations. In a related civil enforcement action brought by the SEC, Panalpina Inc. agreed to pay approximately $11.3 million in disgorgement of profits.

The DOJ criminal penalty of $70.56 million was slightly less than the minimum prescribed by the USSG. In reaching an agreement with Panalpina World Transport (PWT), the DOJ considered that (1) PWT conducted comprehensive antibribery compliance investigations of operations of PWT's subsidiaries in seven countries, as well as separate investigations related to U.S. and Swiss operations; (2) PWT conducted a review of certain transactions and operations conducted by its subsidiaries or agents in another 36 countries; (3) PWT promptly and voluntarily reported its findings from all investigations to the DOJ, including arranging to provide information from foreign jurisdictions that significantly facilitated the DOJ's access to such information; (4) PWT mandated employee cooperation from the top down and ensured the availability of more than 300 employees and former employees for interviews during the following the investigations; (5) PWT instituted a limited employee amnesty program to encourage employee cooperation with the investigations; (6) PWT expanded the scope of the investigations where necessary to ensure thorough and effective review of potentially improper practices, and promptly and voluntarily reported any improper payments identified after internal and DOJ investigations had begun; (7) after initially not cooperating with the investigation for several months, PWT fully cooperated with the DOJ's investigation of this matter, as well as the SEC's investigation, and on the whole exhibited exemplary cooperation with the DOJ investigation; (8) PWT provided substantial assistance to the DOJ and the SEC in its investigation of its directors, officers, employees, agents, lawyers, consultants, contractors, subcontractors, subsidiaries, and customers relating to violations of the FCPA; (9) PWT agreed to continue to cooperate with the DOJ in any ongoing investigation of the conduct of PWT and its directors, officers, employees, agents, lawyers, consultants, subcontractors, subsidiaries, and customers relating to violations of the FCPA; and (10) PWT undertook substantial remedial measures, including

a. creating a compliance department, with a reporting line to the board of directors, and providing it with the authority and resources required to assess global operations and recommend and implement necessary changes in business practices;

b. implementing a compliance program, including an upgraded code of conduct and on-site compliance audits, and enhancing the program throughout the investigation;

c. drafting upgraded compliance policies and implementing them globally through enhanced training;

d. conducting systematic risk assessments in high-risk countries and working with compliance counsel to conduct numerous on-site compliance audits;

e. developing mechanisms to review and evaluate the legality of hundreds of processes on a global basis to ensure compliance;

f. retaining and promoting senior management with the most significant commitment to compliance within the company to ensure the appropriate "tone at the top";

g. overseeing significant turnover of personnel globally, including individuals who departed because they were unwilling to work within the new compliance standards implemented worldwide;

h. coordinating its compliance and internal audit functions to ensure implementation of policies and procedures and monitoring of the company's global remediation progress;

i. voluntarily and independently hiring its own outside compliance counsel to advise and assist the company in undertaking further remedial measures and compliance enhancements as contemplated by this agreement; and

j. of its own initiative and at a substantial cost, closing down its operations and withdrawing from Nigeria to avoid potential ongoing improper conduct.

The Panalpina freight-forwarder investigation led to the subpoenaing of numerous international oil and gas drilling contractors. On the date the Panalpina charges were returned, Noble, SNEPCO, Pride International, Tidewater, and Transocean agreed to pay a total of $86 million to the DOJ in criminal penalties, and the SEC announced settlements with companies, which involve civil disgorgement, interest, and penalties totaling approximately $68.7 million. Combined, freight-forwarder Panalpina and the oil and drilling issuer-customer companies agreed to pay the U.S. government more than $236 million.

BN. *United States v. Pride International Inc.; United States v. Pride Forasol S.A.S.;*[342] *SEC v. Pride International Inc.*[343]

▶ **Misconduct Category:**   Bribes paid to government officials to extend drilling contracts in Venezuela, to secure a favorable administrative judicial decision for a rig in India, and to avoid customs duties and penalties on equipment operating in Mexico

▶ **Countries:**   India, Mexico, and Venezuela (DOJ); Congo, Kazakhstan, Libya, Mexico, Nigeria, and Saudi Arabia (SEC)

▶ **Foreign Government Officials:**   Petróleos de Venezuela (PDVSA) director; judge of the Customs, Excise, and Gold Appellate Tribunal (CEGAT) in India, an administrative judicial tribunal; and customs administrator operations assistant for the Mexican Customs Service

▶ **Improper Payment Dollar Value:** $800,000

▶ **Combined Penalties:** $56.1 million ($32.625 million in DOJ criminal penalties and $23.5 million in SEC disgorgement of profits and prejudgment interest). DOJ criminal penalty less than half of USSG minimum fine.

▶ **Other:**   DPA for U.S. parent company Pride International and guilty plea by wholly owned French subsidiary Pride Forasol S.A.S.; periodic compliance reporting to DOJ during three-year DPA; bribes for Indian judge recorded as "regular fees" in newly created "miscellaneous fees" account; PDVSA director bribes paid through a Miami bank account; Indian judge bribes paid through a Dubai bank account; Mexican bribe recorded as an "electricity maintenance" expense; Pride provided substantial assistance to the DOJ in its investigation of Panalpina; no monitor requirement. In November 2012 Pride became the first company to have its FCPA DPA period terminated early.

▶ **Related Matters:**   Noble, *United States v. Panalpina, United States v. Shell Nigeria Exploration & Production Co., United States v. Tidewater; United States v. Transocean; SEC v. GlobalSantaFe Corp.; SEC v. Benton*

In November 2010, Pride International Inc., a Houston-based offshore drilling company, and Pride Forasol S.A.S., a wholly owned French subsidiary of Pride International (collectively Pride), admitted that Pride paid a total of approximately $800,000 in bribes directly and indirectly to government officials in Venezuela, India, and Mexico. According to court documents, the bribes were paid to extend drilling contracts for three rigs operating offshore in Venezuela; to secure a favorable administrative judicial decision relating to a customs dispute for a rig imported into India; and to avoid the payment of customs duties and penalties relating to a rig and equipment operating in Mexico. During the course of the investigation, Pride provided information and substantially assisted in the investigation of Panalpina.

Pride International was charged in a criminal information filed with conspiring to violate the antibribery and books-and-records provisions of the FCPA; violating the antibribery provisions of the FCPA; and violating the books-and-records provisions of the FCPA. The DOJ and Pride International agreed to resolve the charges by entering into a DPA. The DOJ also filed a criminal information charging Pride Forasol with conspiring to violate the antibribery provisions of the FCPA; violating the antibribery provisions of the FCPA; and aiding and abetting the violation of the books-and-records provisions of the FCPA. Pride Forasol has agreed to plead guilty to the charges. The agreements require the payment of a $32.625 million criminal penalty, which was less than half the minimum fine of $72.5 million under the USSG. Among the individual facts and circumstances that the DOJ considered were (1) during a routine audit, bribery misconduct was discovered; (2) Pride International voluntarily and timely disclosed to the DOJ and the SEC the misconduct described in the Information and Statement of Facts, which was unknown to the DOJ and the SEC at the time; (3) Pride International conducted a thorough internal investigation of that misconduct; (4) Pride International voluntarily initiated a comprehensive antibribery compliance review of Pride International's business operations in certain other high-risk countries; (5) Pride International regularly reported its findings to the DOJ; (6) Pride International cooperated in the DOJ's investigation of this matter, as well as the SEC's investigation; (7) Pride International undertook, of its own accord, remedial measures, including the enhancement of its FCPA compliance program, and agreed to maintain and enhance, as appropriate, its FCPA compliance program; and (8) Pride International agreed to continue to cooperate with the DOJ in any ongoing investigation of the conduct of Pride International and its employees, agents, consultants, contractors, subcontractors, and subsidiaries relating to violations of the FCPA.[344]

In a related civil enforcement action brought by the SEC, Pride International agreed to pay approximately $23.5 million in disgorgement of profits and prejudgment interest.[345] The SEC complaint alleged books-and-records and internal controls violations in the Congo, Kazakhstan, Libya, Mexico, Nigeria, and Saudi Arabia. In November 2012 the DOJ agreed to terminate Pride's DPA early. In 2011 Pride was acquired by Ensco plc, which agreed to adopt and enforce the compliance conditions of the DPA. Pride is the first subject of an FCPA DPA to have its DPA term terminated early.

BO. *United States v. Shell Nigeria Exploration & Production Co.;*[346] *In re* **Royal Dutch Shell plc and Shell International Exploration & Production Inc.**[347]

► **Misconduct Category:** Freight forwarder provided payments to subcontractors with the knowledge the funds would be used to pay Nigerian customs officials to import materials and equipment

► **Country:** Nigeria

► **Foreign Government Officials:** Nigerian Customs Service officials

► **Improper Payment Dollar Value:** $2 million

► Combined Penalties:	$48.15 million ($30 million criminal penalty; $18.15 million in SEC disgorgement of profits and prejudgment interest)
► Other:	DPA; DOJ criminal penalty 13 percent below USSG minimum guideline.
► Related Matters:	*United States v. Panalpina,* Noble, *United States v. Pride International, United States v. Tidewater; United States v. Transocean;* SEC v. *GlobalSantaFe Corp.*

In November 2010, a criminal information was filed in the Southern District of Texas charging Shell Nigeria Exploration and Production Company (SNEPCO), a Nigerian subsidiary of Royal Dutch Shell plc (RDS), with conspiring to violate the antibribery and books-and-records provisions of the FCPA, and with aiding and abetting a violation of the books-and-records provisions. Royal Dutch Shell is the owner of a global group of energy and petrochemicals companies. The charges relate to approximately $2 million SNEPCO paid to its subcontractors with the knowledge that some or all of the money would be paid as bribes to Nigerian customs officials by Panalpina to import materials and equipment into Nigeria. To resolve the matter, the DOJ and Shell entered into a DPA that requires, among other things, SNEPCO to pay a $30 million criminal penalty. The $30 million criminal penalty was approximately 13 percent below the USSG minimum fine. Among the facts the DOJ considered in reaching this resolution were (1) SNEPCO and RDS cooperated with the DOJ's investigation of SNEPCO and RDS entities; (2) SNEPCO and RDS undertook remedial measures, including the implementation of an enhanced compliance program; (3) SNEPCO and RDS agreed to continue to cooperate with the DOJ in any ongoing investigation of the conduct of SNEPCO and its directors, employees, agents, consultants, contractors, subcontractors, subsidiaries, affiliates, and others relating to violations of the FCPA; and (4) the impact on SNEPCO and other RDS entities, including collateral consequences, of a guilty plea or criminal conviction.

Under the terms of the three-year DPA, Shell is required to fully cooperate with U.S. and foreign authorities in any ongoing investigations of the companies' corrupt payments. In addition, it is required to implement and adhere to a set of enhanced corporate compliance and reporting obligations. In a related civil enforcement action brought by the SEC, Royal Dutch Shell and a U.S. subsidiary, Shell International Exploration and Production Inc., agreed to pay approximately $18.15 million in disgorgement of profits and prejudgment interest.

BP.   *United States v. Tidewater Marine International Inc.;*[348]
       SEC v. Tidewater Inc.[349]

► Misconduct Category:	Bribes paid through its freight forwarder to customs officials and tax inspectors to disregard customs regulations and to secure favorable tax assessments
► Countries:	Azerbaijan and Nigeria

▶ **Foreign Government Officials:**   Azerbaijan tax inspectors and Nigerian Customs Service officials

▶ **Improper Payment Dollar Value:** $1.76 million

▶ **Combined Penalties:** $15.65 million ($7.35 million criminal penalty and $8.3 million in SEC disgorgement of profits, prejudgment of interest, and civil penalties)

▶ **Other:**   DPAs for parent Tidewater Inc. and Cayman Islands subsidiary criminal penalty 30 percent below USSG minimum fine

▶ **Related Matters:**   *United States v. Panalpina, United States v. Pride International, Shell Nigeria Exploration & Production Co., United States v. Transocean; SEC v. GlobalSantaFe Corp.,* Noble

In November 2010, the DOJ filed a criminal information in the Southern District of Texas charging Tidewater Marine International Inc. (TMII), a Cayman Island subsidiary of Tidewater Inc. (TDW), with conspiring to violate the antibribery and books-and-records provisions of the FCPA, and with violating the books-and-records provisions of the FCPA. Tidewater Inc. is a global operator of offshore service and supply vessels for energy exploration headquartered in New Orleans. The charges filed against TMII relate to approximately $160,000 in bribes paid through its employees and agents to tax inspectors in Azerbaijan to improperly secure favorable tax assessments and approximately $1.6 million in bribes paid through Panalpina to Nigerian customs officials to induce the officials to disregard Nigerian customs regulations relating to the importation of vessels into Nigerian waters. To resolve the matter, the DOJ and Tidewater have entered into a DPA that requires, among other things, Tidewater Marine to pay a $7.35 million criminal penalty. Under the terms of the three-year DPA, Tidewater Inc. is required to fully cooperate with U.S. and foreign authorities in any ongoing investigations of the companies' corrupt payments. In addition, it is required to implement and adhere to a set of enhanced corporate compliance and reporting obligations.

The DOJ agreed to a criminal penalty of $7.35 million, which was 30 percent below the minimum fine described by the USSG. Among the facts that the DOJ considered in reaching this resolution were (1) TMII and TDW promptly commenced an internal investigation into its dealings with Panalpina after becoming aware of information indicating potential issues with its freight-forwarding agent; (2) promptly after commencing its internal investigation, TMII and TDW voluntarily disclosed the conduct described in the Information and its Statement of Facts to the DOJ; (3) TMII and TDW voluntarily expanded their internal investigation to numerous operations and areas of the world outside Nigeria where no misconduct had been reported or suspected, and reported all relevant findings to the DOJ; (4) TMII and TDW hired a general counsel with substantial international compliance experience, appointed him the chief compliance officer, and established a corporate compliance committee; (5) TMII and TDW issued an enhanced, stand-alone FCPA compliance policy, substantially revised its code of conduct, as well as additional relevant policies and procedures, including a vetting and approval process for third-party service providers and business partners upon implementation of that policy, and instituted a worldwide training program for employees; (6) TMII and TDW expanded their internal investigation to cover additional countries and business activities; (7) TMII and TDW cooperated with the DOJ's investigation, including sharing all relevant investigation findings and making available numerous current and former employees; (8) TMII and TDW exhibited leadership in the oil and gas industry by leading an oil and gas industry initiative, both in the United States and abroad, to address the misconduct at issue; (9) TMII and TDW implemented an enhanced compliance program; (10) TDW, on behalf of TMII, agreed to provide a written report to the DOJ on its progress and experience in maintaining and, as appropriate, enhancing its compliance policies and procedures; and (11) TMII and TDW agreed to continue to cooperate with the DOJ in any ongoing investigation of the conduct of TMII and its directors, employees, agents, consultants, contractors, subcontractors, subsidiaries, affiliates, and others relating to violations of the FCPA.

In a related civil enforcement action brought by the SEC, Tidewater Inc. agreed to pay approximately $8.3 million in disgorgement of profits and prejudgment interest and civil penalties. Bribes to the Azerbaijan officials were described as "payment of taxes" and were recorded in an account tracking "professional services" expenses. Bribery payments to Nigerian agents were recorded in an expense account titled Other Vessel Costs.

BQ.   *United States v. Transocean Inc.;*[350] *SEC v. Transocean Inc.*[351]

▶ **Misconduct Category:**	Bribes paid through freight-forwarding agents to Nigerian customs officials to circumnavigate customs regulations
▶ **Country:**	Nigeria
▶ **Foreign Government Officials:**	Nigerian Customs Service officials
▶ **Improper Payment Dollar Value:**	$90,000
▶ **Combined Penalties:**	$20.64 million ($13.44 million DOJ criminal penalty and $7.2 million in SEC disgorgement of profits and prejudgment interest)
▶ **Other:**	DPA; no monitor requirement; criminal penalty approximately 20 percent below USSG minimum guideline
▶ **Related Matters:**	*United States v. Panalpina, United States v. Pride International, Shell Nigeria Exploration & Production Co., United States v. Tidewater; SEC v. GlobalSantaFe Corp.*

In November 2010, Transocean Inc., a Cayman Islands subsidiary of Transocean Ltd. (collectively Transocean), was charged in a Southern District of Texas criminal information with conspiring to violate the antibribery and books-and-records provisions of the FCPA; violating the antibribery provision of the FCPA; and aiding and abetting the violation of the books-and-records provisions of the FCPA. Transocean Ltd. is the world's largest provider of offshore oil drilling services and equipment based in Vernier, Switzerland. The charges relate to approximately $90,000 in bribes paid by Transocean Inc.'s freight-forwarding agents to Nigerian customs officials to circumvent Nigerian customs regulations regarding the import of goods and materials and the import of Transocean's deepwater oil rigs into Nigerian waters. The DOJ and Transocean agreed to enter into a DPA that requires, among other things, Transocean Inc. to pay a $13.44 million criminal penalty. Under the terms of the three-year DPA, Transocean was required to fully cooperate with U.S. and foreign authorities in any ongoing investigations of the companies' corrupt payments. In addition, it was required to implement and adhere to a set of enhanced corporate compliance and reporting obligations.

The $13.44 million DOJ penalty was approximately 20 percent less than the minimum fine prescribed under the USSG. In reaching an agreement, the DOJ considered the following facts (1) Transocean and Transocean personnel in Nigeria promptly commenced an internal investigation into dealings between Transocean's Nigeria operations and Panalpina after becoming aware of information indicating potential issues with its freight-forwarding agent; (2) Transocean expanded its internal investigation to numerous operations and areas of the world outside Nigeria where no misconduct had been reported or suspected, and reported all relevant findings to the DOJ; (3) a subsidiary of Transocean Ltd., Transocean Offshore Deepwater Drilling Inc., hired a new chief compliance officer with substantial experience in corporate ethics and anticorruption compliance policies; the compliance officer, who is an officer of Transocean Ltd., is responsible for the oversight of compliance for Transocean Ltd. and all of its subsidiaries and affiliates, including Transocean; (4) Transocean Ltd. established a specific internal audit team of well-trained auditors to focus on fraud, FCPA compliance, and antibribery issues at Transocean Ltd.'s worldwide operations; (5) Transocean Ltd. issued a revised FCPA compliance policy and revised its code of conduct, instituted a worldwide FCPA training program for its companies' employees, and implemented a well-defined due diligence process for retaining third-party service providers and business partners that interact with government officials; (6) Transocean and Transocean Ltd. cooperated with the DOJ's investigation, including sharing all relevant investigation findings and making available numerous current and former employees; (7) Transocean and Transocean Ltd. agreed to provide a written report to the DOJ on their progress and experience in maintaining and, as necessary and appropriate, enhancing their compliance policies and procedures; and (8) Transocean and Transocean Ltd. agreed to continue to cooperate with the DOJ in any ongoing investigation of the conduct of Transocean and its directors, employees, agents, consultants, contractors, subcontractors, subsidiaries, and any affiliate it controls relating to violations of the FCPA.

In a related civil enforcement action brought by the SEC, Transocean agreed to disgorge approximately $7.2 million in profits and prejudgment interest. The SEC complaint noted that after customer issues related to the use of Panalpina began to surface publicly, Transocean conducted an internal investigation and proceeded with a policy allowing only limited use of Panalpina; nonetheless, Transocean, on 11 subsequent occasions, while using Panalpina, did not pay applicable customs duties or value-added taxes. The total customs duties that Transocean avoided using Panalpina's Pancourier service for 404 shipments was $1,480,419.[352]

BR.   U.S. DOJ–RAE Systems Inc. Agreement[353]

▶ **Misconduct Category:**	Cash payments to Chinese government officials through third-party agent on behalf of joint ventures
▶ **Country:**	China
▶ **Foreign Government Officials:**	Fire department, emergency response department, and provincial environmental agency officials
▶ **Improper Payment Dollar Value:**	$400,000
▶ **Combined Penalties:**	$3 million (DOJ: $1.7 million criminal fine; SEC: $1,147,800 in disgorgement of profits and $109,212 in prejudgment interest)
▶ **Other:**	NPA; lax or nonexistent due diligence in joint venture due diligence; highlights need to implement internal controls to stop postacquisition payments

In December 2010, RAE Systems Inc., a California-based, publicly traded chemical and radiation detection system manufacturer, settled FCPA charges with the DOJ and the SEC arising from the payment of approximately $400,000 to Chinese government officials on behalf of two of RAE's majority-owned joint ventures in China. Between 2004 and 2008, the joint ventures provided their third-party agents with cash advances generated through false or misleading invoices, portions of which were passed on to Chinese officials. RAE allegedly uncovered this practice during preacquisition due diligence for one of the joint ventures, but failed to implement a system of internal controls sufficient to stop the payments postacquisition. With respect to the other joint venture, RAE allegedly failed to conduct any FCPA due diligence in connection with the transaction, despite a number of red flags, and, as a result, the company continued to make improper payments following the acquisition.

To resolve the criminal allegations, RAE entered into an NPA with the DOJ, agreeing to pay a $1.7 million fine. It also agreed to submit periodic reports to the DOJ regarding its compliance with the agreements. The DOJ cited RAE's substantial cooperation in the investigation and voluntary disclosure of the conduct as factors relevant to the decision to resolve the matter with an NPA. In a related matter, RAE consented to the entry of a civil injunction with the SEC against future violations of the FCPA's accounting provisions and agreed to disgorge $1,147,800 in allegedly ill-gotten profits, plus $109,212 in prejudgment interest.

BS.   *United States v. Granados & Caceres;*[354] *United States v. Salvoch*[355] *& Vasquez*[356]

▶ **Misconduct Category:**   Payments to officers and senior attorney of a wholly state-owned telecommunications company to reduce long-distance rates and obtain other economic benefits; fraudulent consulting contracts

▶ **Country:**   Honduras

▶ **Foreign Government Officials:**   General manager of Hondutel, wholly owned telecommunications company; senior attorney for Hondutel; and minister of Honduran government

▶ **Improper Payment Dollar Value:** $500,000

▶ **Combined Penalties:**   Granados: 46 months in jail; Caceres: 23 months in jail; Salvoch: ten months in prison and three years of supervised release; Vasquez: three year's probation and $7,500 fine

▶ **Other:**   International money laundering charges filed; sensitive e-mails included "One would meet with these criminals," adding, "but I will solve this problem for you, I promise. Not only will we get [a preferential rate], but the capacity we need. I have something to reveal to them in exchange for what I'm going to ask from them," and "No governmental official (from Hondutel or from the government) can appear" on the consulting contract.

▶ **Related Matters:**   *United States v. Latin Node Inc.*

In December 2010, Jorge Granados and Manuel Caceres, the former chief executive officer and the vice president of business development, respectively, for Miami-based telecommunications company Latin Node Inc. (LatiNode), were charged in the Southern District of Florida for allegedly paying more than $500,000 in bribes to government officials in Honduras under the antibribery provisions of the Foreign Corrupt Practices Act (FCPA), and for alleged international money laundering. The 19-count indictment, returned by a federal grand jury in Miami on December 14, 2010, was unsealed on December 20, 2010, and the defendants were arrested in Miami at that time.

According to court documents, LatiNode provided wholesale telecommunications services using Internet protocol technology to countries throughout the world, including Honduras. In December 2005, LatiNode learned that it was the sole winner of an "interconnection agreement" with Empresa Hondureña de Telecomunicaciones (Hondutel), the wholly state-owned telecommunications authority in Honduras. The agreement permitted LatiNode to use Hondutel's telecommunications lines in order to establish a network between Honduras and the United

States and provide long-distance services between the two countries. LatiNode was required to pay Hondutel a set rate per minute for calls to Honduras.

According to the indictment, soon after winning the contract with Hondutel, defendants Granados and Caceres sought a reduction in the rates payable to Hondutel. The defendants also learned that a newly elected high-ranking government official's friend had been made a manager of Hondutel, who considered rescinding the agreement with LatiNode. Caceres allegedly informed Granados and another LatiNode executive by e-mail that "it would be necessary to 'give' something to the [Hondutel] general manager. . . . I will try this with [the manager]." Caceres said that he would "meet with these criminals," adding "But I will solve this problem for you, I promise. Not only will we get a preferential rate but the capacity we need. I have some things to reveal to them in exchange for what I'm going to ask of them."

According to the indictment, the defendants and other LatiNode executives agreed to a secret deal to pay bribes to the manager, as well as to a senior attorney for Hondutel who acted as the manager's "straw man," and to a minister of the Honduran government who became a representative on the Hondutel board of directors. The alleged bribes were paid in exchange for keeping the interconnection agreement in place and receiving reduced rates and other economic benefits from Hondutel. Between September 2006 and June 2007, the defendants allegedly paid more than $500,000 in bribes to the officials, concealing many of the payments by laundering the money through LatiNode subsidiaries in Guatemala and to accounts in Honduras controlled by the Honduran government officials.

As the payments grew, according to the indictment, the defendants allegedly became concerned about the rising costs of the scheme and the possibility of detection. On one occasion, according to the indictment, Caceres forwarded to Granados an e-mail from the senior attorney, identifying four bank accounts to receive the bribe payments. Caceres told Granados, "I recommend sending [the manager] $100,000 tomorrow to the bank accounts and in the amounts according to the instructions in [the senior attorney's] e-mail. We have stretched the rope to the maximum, but we are reaching the limit and we don't want to break it. This payment will create tolerance for any late payments to Hondutel, avoiding the removal of capacity; on the contrary, it will help to get them to increase it for us." According to the indictment Granados approved the payments, and another LatiNode executive facilitated the wire transfers.

In early 2007, according to public filings, eLandia International Inc. announced an agreement to acquire LatiNode. The indictment alleged that the defendants took additional measures to conceal the illicit payments during the acquisition due diligence process. Specifically, according to the indictment, Granados allegedly urged Caceres to formalize the secret rate reduction deal with the Honduran officials, as the issue could cause a "HUGE" problem during the process. The defendants also allegedly urged the Honduran officials to sign fraudulent "consulting contracts" that would disguise the true nature of the relationship. Caceres explained to the officials in an e-mail that, "[n]o government official (from Hondutel or from the government) can appear" on the consulting contract, and that future payments "will come from eLandia through Servicios IP, a firm of ours in Guatemala."

On April 7, 2009, LatiNode pleaded guilty to a one-count information charging the company with a criminal violation of the FCPA. As part of the plea agreement, LatiNode agreed to pay a $2 million fine. The resolution of the criminal investigation of LatiNode reflected, in large part, the actions of eLandia in disclosing potential FCPA violations to the DOJ after eLandia's acquisition of LatiNode and discovery of the improper payments.

On May 19, 2011, Granados pleaded guilty in Miami to conspiracy to violate the antibribery provisions of the Foreign Corrupt Practices Act (FCPA). In September 2011, Granada was sentenced to 46 months in prison to be followed by two years of supervised release. In December 2010, criminal informations were filed against Manuel Salvoch, the chief financial officer of LatiNode, and Juan Pablo Vasquez, the chief commercial officer of Latin Node, charging them with conspiracy to violate the FCPA. Salvoch, Vasquez, and Caceres pleaded guilty to conspiracy to violate the FCPA on January 12, 2011, January 21, 2011, and May 18, 2011, respectively. In April 2012, Vasquez received three years' probation and a $7,500 fine, and Caceres was sentenced to 23 months in jail. In June 2012, Salvoch was sentenced to ten months in prison and three years of supervised release.

BT.   *United States v. Alcatel-Lucent France SA, Alcatel-Lucent Trade International A.G. & Alcatel Centroamerica S.A.; United States v. Alcatel-Lucent SA*[357]

▶ **Misconduct Category:**	Public and private bribes through agents and consultants to obtain or retain business
▶ **Countries:**	Angola, Bangladesh, Costa Rica, Ecuador, Honduras, Ivory Coast, Malaysia, Mali, Nicaragua, Nigeria, Taiwan, and Uganda
▶ **Foreign Government Officials:**	Senior government officials in executive branches, plus Taiwanese legislators
▶ **Improper Payment Dollar Value:**	Tens of millions of dollars
▶ **Combined Penalties:**	$137 million (DOJ penalty of $92 million and SEC disgorgement of profits of $45.3 million)
▶ **Other:**	Cessation of use of third-party sales and marketing agents; retention of independent compliance monitor for three years; payment of $10 million fine for corruption to Costa Rican government; former president of Costa Rica Miguel Angel Rodriguez sentenced in Costa Rica to five years in jail.
▶ **Related Matters:**	*United States v. Sapsizian & Valverde*

In December 2010, Alcatel-Lucent S.A. and three of its subsidiaries agreed to pay the DOJ a combined $92 million penalty to resolve an FCPA investigation into the worldwide sales practices of Alcatel S.A. prior to its 2006 merger with Lucent

Technologies Inc. As part of the agreed resolution, the DOJ filed a criminal infor-
mation in the U.S. District Court for the Southern District of Florida charging
Alcatel-Lucent with one count of violating the internal controls provisions of the
FCPA, and one count of violating the books-and-records provisions of the FCPA.
The DOJ and Alcatel-Lucent agreed to resolve the charges by entering into a DPA
for a term of three years.

The DOJ also filed a criminal information charging three subsidiaries: Alcatel-
Lucent France S.A., formerly known as Alcatel CIT S.A.; Alcatel-Lucent Trade International A.G., formerly known as Alcatel Standard A.G.; and Alcatel Centroamerica
S.A., formerly known as Alcatel de Costa Rica S.A. The three subsidiaries were each
charged with conspiring to violate the antibribery, books-and-records, and internal
controls provisions of the FCPA. Each of the three subsidiaries agreed to plead
guilty to the charges.

In addition to the $92 million penalty, Alcatel-Lucent and its three subsidiar-
ies agreed to implement rigorous compliance enhancements. Alcatel-Lucent also
agreed to retain an independent compliance monitor for a three-year period to
oversee the company's implementation and maintenance of an enhanced FCPA
compliance program and to submit yearly reports to the DOJ. The charging documents and penalty reflect, among other things, that there was limited and inadequate cooperation by the company for a substantial period of time, but that after
the merger, Alcatel-Lucent substantially improved its cooperation with the DOJ's
investigation. In addition, the DOJ also credited Alcatel-Lucent for, on its own initiative and at a substantial financial cost, making an unprecedented pledge to stop
using third-party sales and marketing agents in conducting its worldwide business.

Alcatel-Lucent was formed in late 2006 after Lucent Technologies merged with
Alcatel, a French telecommunications equipment and services company. Starting in
the 1990s and continuing through late 2006, Alcatel pursued many of its business
opportunities around the world through subsidiaries like Alcatel CIT and Alcatel de
Costa Rica using third-party agents and consultants who were retained by Alcatel
Standard. This business model was shown to be prone to corruption, as consultants
were repeatedly used as conduits for bribe payments to foreign officials and business
executives of private customers to obtain or retain business in many countries.

Alcatel-Lucent's three subsidiaries paid millions of dollars in improper payments
to foreign officials for the purpose of obtaining and retaining business in Costa Rica,
Honduras, Malaysia, and Taiwan. In addition to the improper payments, Alcatel-
Lucent also admitted that it violated the internal controls and books-and-records
provisions of the FCPA related to the hiring of third-party agents in Kenya, Nigeria,
Bangladesh, Ecuador, Nicaragua, Angola, Ivory Coast, Uganda, and Mali. Overall,
Alcatel-Lucent admitted that the company earned approximately $48.1 million in
profits as a result of these improper payments.

Specifically, Alcatel CIT won three contracts in Costa Rica worth a combined
total of more than $300 million as a result of corrupt payments to government offi-
cials and from which Alcatel reaped a profit of more than $23 million, according
to court documents. Alcatel CIT wired more than $18 million to two consultants
in Costa Rica, which had been retained by Alcatel Standard, in connection with
obtaining business in that country. According to court documents, more than half

of this money was then passed on by the consultants to various Costa Rican government officials, including then president Miguel Angel Rodriguez, for assisting Alcatel CIT and Alcatel de Costa Rica in obtaining and retaining business. As part of the scheme, the consultants created phony invoices that they then submitted to Alcatel CIT. Senior Alcatel executives approved the retention of and payments to the consultants despite obvious indications that the consultants were performing little or no legitimate work.

In addition, Alcatel Standard hired a consultant in Honduras who was a perfume distributor with no experience in telecommunications. The consultant was retained after being personally selected by the brother of a senior Honduran government official. Alcatel CIT executives knew that a significant portion of the money paid to the consultant would be paid to the family of the senior Honduran government official in exchange for favorable treatment of Alcatel CIT. As a result of these payments, Alcatel CIT was able to retain contracts worth approximately $47 million and from which Alcatel earned $870,000.

In addition, according to court documents, Alcatel Standard retained two consultants on behalf of another Alcatel subsidiary in Taiwan to assist in obtaining an axle counting contract worth approximately $19.2 million. Alcatel and its joint venture paid these two consultants more than $950,000 despite the fact that neither consultant had telecommunications experience. Alcatel Standard's purpose for hiring the consultants was so that Alcatel SEL could funnel payments through the consultants to Taiwanese legislators who had influence in the award of the contract. Alcatel earned approximately $4.34 million from this contract.

In a related matter, the SEC reached a settlement filed in December 2010 in which Alcatel-Lucent consented to the entry of a permanent injunction against FCPA violations and agreed to pay $45,372,000 in disgorgement and prejudgment interest. Alcatel-Lucent also agreed with the SEC to comply with certain undertakings regarding its FCPA compliance program.

In January 2011, Alcatel-Lucent also agreed to pay $10 million to settle a corruption case brought by the government of Costa Rica arising out of the bribery of Costa Rican officials by the company. The settlement marked the first time in Costa Rica's history that a foreign corporation agreed to pay the government damages for corruption. In April 2011, a Costa Rican court sentenced former president Miguel Angel Rodriguez to five years in prison after finding him guilty of bribes from Alcatel. Rodriguez, who resigned in 2004 when the scandal first broke, also was barred from public office for 12 years. Rodriguez allegedly received over $800,000 in payments from Alcatel during his presidency (1998–2002) for helping Alcatel get a $149 million government contract to provide 400,000 cell phone lines.[358]

BU. *United States v. Maxwell Technologies Inc.*; *SEC v. Maxwell Technologies Inc.*;[359] *United States v. Riedo*[360]

▶ **Misconduct Category:**	Sales agent bribes to secure contract with state-owned manufacturers over a seven-year period and false characterization of same as "sales commission expenses"
▶ **Country:**	China

► **Foreign Government Officials:**   Chinese officials of state-owned enterprises

► **Improper Payment Dollar Value:** $2.5 million

► **Combined Penalties:** $13.65 million ($8 million DOJ fine; $5.654 million in disgorgement of profits including $700,000 in prejudgment interest to SEC)

► **Other:**   DPA; voluntary disclosure and cooperation; incriminating e-mail: "this is a well-known issue . . . no more emails please"; SEC Complaint: "Internal controls wholly inadequate" and Maxwell code of conduct had only a brief section on the FCPA agreement to an enhanced compliance program

In January 2011, Maxwell Technologies Inc. (Maxwell), a publicly traded manufacturer of energy-storage and power-delivery products based in San Diego, agreed to pay an $8 million criminal penalty to resolve FCPA charges for bribing Chinese government officials from 2002 to 2009 to secure sales of Maxwell's products to state-owned manufacturers of electric utility infrastructure in several Chinese provinces. A two-count civil information filed in the U.S. District Court for the Southern District of California charged Maxwell with one count of violating the FCPA's antibribery provisions and one count of violating the FCPA's books-and-records provisions. Specifically, Maxwell's wholly owned Swiss subsidiary, Maxwell Technologies S.A., engaged a Chinese sales agent to sell Maxwell's high-voltage capacitors in China. From at least July 2002 through May 2009, Maxwell S.A. paid more than $2.5 million to its Chinese agent to secure contracts with Chinese customers, including contracts for the sale of Maxwell's high-voltage capacitor products to state-owned manufacturers of electrical utility infrastructure. The agent in turn used Maxwell S.A.'s money to bribe officials at the state-owned entities in connection with the sales contracts. The contracts generated more than $15.4 million in revenues and $5.6 million in profits for Maxwell. Maxwell S.A. paid its Chinese agent approximately $165,000 in 2002 and increased the payments to the agent to $1.1 million in 2008. In its books and records, Maxwell mischaracterized the bribes inter alia as "sales commission expenses." According to court documents, Maxwell's U.S. management discovered the bribery scheme in late 2002. Maxwell voluntarily disclosed the FCPA violations to the DOJ and the SEC.

Under the terms of the three-year DPA. Maxwell agreed, among other things, to implement an enhanced compliance program and internal controls capable of preventing and detecting FCPA violations, to report periodically to the DOJ concerning Maxwell's compliance efforts, and to cooperate with the DOJ in ongoing investigations. The DOJ will dismiss the criminal information when the term of the agreement expires.

Maxwell also reached a settlement of a related civil complaint filed by the SEC charging Maxwell with violating the FCPA's antibribery, books-and-records, internal controls, and disclosure provisions. The SEC alleged that the bribes were classified in invoices as either "Extra Amount" or "Special Arrangement" fees. Former management at Maxwell knew of the bribery scheme in late 2002 when an employee indicated in an e-mail that a payment made in connection with a sale in China appeared to be "a kick-back, pay-off, bribe, whatever you want to call it, . . . in violation of U.S. trade laws." A U.S.–based Maxwell executive replied, "This is a well-known issue" and warned, "No more emails, please."[361] The SEC described the controls designed to prevent payments to foreign officials as "wholly inadequate" and that the company's code of conduct only had a brief section on the FCPA[362] and the employees did not receive FCPA training. As part of its SEC settlement, Maxwell agreed to pay $5.654 million in disgorgement of profits and nearly $700,000 in prejudgment interest.

In October 2013, Alain Riedo, former vice president and general manager of Maxwell S.A. from 2002 to 2006, was indicted in the Southern District of California and charged with conspiracy to violate the FCPA, bribery, falsification of books and records, and circumventing internal accounting controls. A bench warrant has been issued for the fugitive Swiss citizen.

BV.   *United States v. Tyson Foods Inc.;*[363] *SEC v. Tyson Foods Inc.*[364]

▶ **Misconduct Category:**	Bribes paid to government meat inspectors to keep them from disrupting the operations of meat-production facilities
▶ **Country:**	Mexico
▶ **Foreign Government Officials:**	Veterinarians with Mexico Department of Agriculture
▶ **Improper Payment Dollar Value:**	$90,000
▶ **Combined Penalties:**	$5.2 million ($4 million DOJ fine and $1.2 million SEC disgorgement, plus prejudgment interest); DOJ penalty approximately 20 percent under low end of the USSG
▶ **Other:**	Use of spouses on phantom subsidiary payroll; in-house counsel instructed Mexican subsidiary to cease making payments two years after Tyson Foods' officials first learned of subsidiary's illicit payments; Tyson de Mexico subsidiary produces only 1 percent of company's revenues; two-year DPA; voluntary disclosure and cooperation; semiannual reporting on compliance program to the DOJ

In February 2011, Tyson Foods Inc., a food products producer based in Springdale, Arkansas, agreed to pay a $4 million DOJ criminal penalty to resolve an investigation into improper payments by company representatives to government-employed inspection veterinarians in Mexico. Any company that exports meat products from Mexico must participate in an inspection program, supervised by the Mexican Department of Agriculture. The inspection program at each facility is supervised by an on-site veterinarian employed by the Mexican government to ensure that all exports conform to Mexican health and safety laws.

A criminal information filed in the U.S. District Court in the District of Columbia in connection with the DPA charged Tyson with conspiracy to violate the FCPA and with violating the FCPA during the years 2004 to 2006. Tyson acknowledged responsibility for the actions of its subsidiaries, employees, and agents who made improper payments to government-employed veterinarians who inspected two of its chicken processing plants in Gomez Palacio, Mexico. Tyson's Mexican subsidiary, Tyson de Mexico, paid approximately $90,000 between 2004 and 2006, to two publicly employed veterinarians who inspected its Mexican plants, resulting in profits of approximately $880,000. The payments were made both directly to the veterinarians and indirectly through their wives, who Tyson de Mexico listed on its payroll, although neither performed any services for Tyson. The bribe payments were made to keep the veterinarians from disrupting the operations of the meat-production facilities. When payments to the spouses were terminated in 2004, Tyson representatives agreed to increase the amount paid to the veterinarians to match the amount previously paid to their spouses. In 2006, Tyson's counsel learned of the improper payments in Mexico and ordered them to stop.

In addition to agreeing to pay a $4 million penalty, approximately 20 percent below the low end of the U.S. Sentencing Guidelines ($5.40 million), Tyson agreed to implement rigorous internal controls and cooperate fully with the DOJ and report to the DOJ on its compliance program semiannually. The government recognized Tyson's voluntary disclosure, thorough self-investigation of the underlying conduct and implementation of remedial measures. Provided Tyson abided by the terms of the two-year agreement, the DOJ agreed to dismiss the criminal information. In a related matter, Tyson reached a settlement with the SEC under which it agreed to pay more than $1.2 million in disgorgement of profits, including prejudgment interest. Tyson de Mexico produces food products that comprise approximately 1 percent of Tyson Foods' total net sales. Approximately 93 percent of the parent company's employees are based in the United States. This case confirms that the DOJ and SEC will hold a U.S.-based parent company responsible for the bribery misconduct of a very small foreign subsidiary.

BW.   *United States v. JGC Corp.*[365]

▶ **Misconduct Category:**	Joint venture partners' payments to agents in the United Kingdom and Japan totaling $182 million in order to obtain engineering, production, and construction contracts
▶ **Country:**	Nigeria
▶ **Foreign Government Officials:**	High-level officials
▶ **Improper Payment Dollar Value:**	$182 million
▶ **Penalty:**	$218.8 million

▶ **Other:**

First Japanese company charged with FCPA violations; DPA for two years; sixth-largest FCPA fine—$218.8 million; appointment of an independent compliance consultant for two years; assistance by authorities in France, Italy, Switzerland, and the United Kingdom. Criminal penalties for the four JV partners (the others are KBR, Technip, and Snamprogetti) exceeded $1.1 billion.

▶ **Related Matter:**

United States v. Stanley; United States v. Technip, S.A.; United States v. Snamprogetti B.V.; SEC v. ENI SpA & Snamprogetti B.V.; United States v. Tesler & Chodan; United States v. KBR; SEC v. Halliburton Co. & KBR Inc.; United States v. Marubeni Corp.

In April 2011, JGC Corporation agreed to pay a $218.8 million criminal penalty to resolve FCPA charges for its participation in a decade-long scheme to bribe Nigerian government officials to obtain engineering, procurement, and construction (EPC) contracts. JGC is a Japanese engineering and construction company headquartered in Yokohama, Japan. The DOJ filed a DPA and a two-count criminal information in the U.S. District Court for the Southern District of Texas charging JGC with one count of conspiracy and one count of aiding and abetting violations of the FCPA. The four joint venture partners have paid over $1.5 billion in criminal and civil penalties.

JGC, Kellogg Brown & Root Inc. (KBR), Technip S.A., and Snamprogetti Netherlands B.V. composed the four-company TSKJ joint venture that was awarded four EPC contracts by Nigeria LNG Ltd. (NLNG) between 1995 and 2004 to build LNG facilities on Bonny Island. The government-owned Nigerian National Petroleum Corporation (NNPC) was the largest shareholder of NLNG, owning 49 percent of the company. The EPC contracts to build liquefied natural gas (LNG) facilities on Bonny Island, Nigeria, were valued at more than $6 billion.

JGC authorized the joint venture to hire two agents—Jeffrey Tesler and a Japanese trading company—to pay bribes to a range of Nigerian government officials, to assist JGC and the joint venture in obtaining the EPC contracts. The joint venture hired Tesler as a consultant to pay bribes to high-level Nigerian government officials, including top-level executive-branch officials, and hired the Japanese trading company to pay bribes to lower-level Nigerian government officials. At crucial junctures preceding the award of EPC contracts, JGC's coconspirators met with successive holders of a top-level office in the executive branch of the Nigerian government to ask the office holders to designate a representative with whom TSKJ should negotiate bribes to Nigerian government officials. TSKJ paid approximately $132 million to a Gibraltar corporation controlled by Tesler and more than $50 million to the Japanese trading company during the course of the bribery scheme. According to court documents, JGC intended for these payments to be used, in part, for bribes to Nigerian government officials.

Under the terms of the two-year DPA, JGC agreed to retain an independent compliance consultant for a term of two years to review the design and implementation of its compliance program, to enhance its compliance program to ensure that it satisfies certain standards, and to cooperate with the DOJ in ongoing investigations.

In a related criminal case, KBR's successor company, Kellogg Brown & Root LLC, pleaded guilty in February 2009 to FCPA charges for its participation in the scheme to bribe Nigerian government officials. Kellogg Brown & Root LLC was ordered to pay a $402 million fine and to retain an independent compliance monitor for a three-year period to review the design and implementation of its compliance program. In another related criminal case, the DOJ filed a DPA and criminal information against Technip in June 2010. Technip agreed to pay a $240 million criminal penalty and to retain an independent compliance monitor for two years. In July 2010, the DOJ filed a DPA and criminal information against Snamprogetti, which also agreed to pay a $240 million criminal penalty. The corporate criminal penalties against the four JV partners exceeded $1.1 billion.

In other related criminal cases, KBR's former CEO, Albert "Jack" Jackson Stanley, pleaded guilty in September 2008 to conspiring to violate the FCPA for his participation in the bribery scheme. Tesler and Wojciech J. Chodan, a former salesperson and consultant of a United Kingdom subsidiary of KBR, were indicted in February 2009 on FCPA-related charges for their participation in the bribery scheme. In March 2011, Tesler was extradited from the United Kingdom and subsequently pleaded guilty to conspiring to violate and violating the FCPA and agreed to forfeit $148,964,568. In December 2010, Chodan was extradited from the United Kingdom and subsequently pleaded guilty to conspiring to violate the FCPA and agreed to forfeit $726,885. In February 2012, Tesler was sentenced to 21 months in prison and Chodan to one year of probation. Significant assistance was provided by the SEC's Division of Enforcement and by authorities in France, Italy, Switzerland, and the United Kingdom.

BX.   U.S. DOJ–Comverse Technology, Inc. Agreement; *SEC v. Comverse Technology Inc.*[366]

▶ **Misconduct Category:**	Improper payments through agent to officials of a partially state-owned telecommunications company to obtain purchase orders
▶ **Country:**	Greece
▶ **Foreign Government Officials:**	Employees of Hellenic Telecommunications Organisation SA (OTE), telecommunications provider partially owned by the Hellenic Republic (government of Greece)
▶ **Improper Payment Dollar Value:**	$56,000
▶ **Combined Penalties:**	$2.8 million ($1.2 million criminal penalty to the DOJ and $1.6 million in disgorgement of profits and prejudgment interest to the SEC)
▶ **Other:**	NPA; books-and-records violations only

In April 2011, Comverse Technology Inc. (CTI), a New York City–headquartered corporation, agreed to pay a $1.2 million penalty for FCPA violations as part of an NPA. CTI, through its main operating subsidiary Comverse Inc. and Comverse Inc.'s subsidiaries, is a global provider of software and software systems for communication and billing services.

According to the NPA, CTI has accepted responsibility for violating the books-and-records provisions of the FCPA arising from and related to CTI's failure to record accurately certain improper payments that were made between 2003 and 2006 by employees and a third-party agent of Comverse Inc. subsidiaries to individuals connected to OTE, a Greek telecommunications provider partially owned by the Hellenic Republic, in order to obtain purchase orders. The payments, totaling approximately $536,000, were inaccurately characterized as legitimate agent commissions in the books and records of Comverse Ltd., a wholly owned subsidiary of Comverse Inc. that is based in Tel Aviv, Israel.

The NPA recognized the company's thorough self-investigation and the results of its investigation, voluntary disclosure of the underlying conduct, and full cooperation with the DOJ. CTI had undertaken extensive remedial efforts and overhauled its overall compliance culture, including through the implementation of mandatory training programs focused on anticorruption and the use of third-party agents and intermediaries, as well as more rigorous accounting controls for the approval of third-party payments.

As a result of these mitigating factors, the DOJ agreed not to prosecute CTI or its subsidiaries for failing to maintain accurate books and records, provided that CTI satisfied its obligations under the agreement for a period of two years. Those obligations included ongoing cooperation, payment of the $1.2 million criminal penalty, and the continued implementation of rigorous internal controls. In a related matter filed in the Eastern District of New York, CTI reached a settlement in April 2011 with the SEC in which it agreed to pay approximately $1.6 million in disgorgement and prejudgment interest.[367]

BY.   *United States v. Depuy, Inc.;*[368] *SEC v. Johnson & Johnson;*[369]
       Crown v. Dougall[370]

▶ **Misconduct Category:**	Bribes to public doctors and administrators who selected Johnson & Johnson surgical implants, who awarded tenders, and who prescribed Johnson & Johnson pharmaceutical products. Payment of secret kickbacks to Iraq under the UN Oil-for-Food program to obtain 19 contracts involving humanitarian relief. 17th UN Oil-for-Food program case.
▶ **Countries:**	Greece, Iraq, Poland, and Romania
▶ **Foreign Government Officials:**	Public doctors and administrators
▶ **Improper Payment Dollar Value:**	In excess of $7.5 million

▶ **Combined Penalties:**	$70 million (DOJ criminal penalties of $21.4 million and SEC disgorgement of profits and prejudgment interest of $48.6 million) in the United States; $7.8 million to U.K. Serious Fraud Office regarding Greek improper payments.
▶ **Other:**	DPA; misuse of foreign agents; slush funds; sham civil contracts with doctors and offshore companies in the Isle of Man; and travel and entertainment abuses. Postacquisition internal controls failures DPA. Industry-wide assistance in the DOJ FCPA investigation resulted in no corporate monitorship but a requirement to report to the DOJ every six months on the company's enhanced compliance effort for the duration of the DPA. Greece seized assets of Johnson & Johnson subsidiary DePuy Hellas. DOJ criminal penalty 25 percent discount below low end of USSG. Robert John Dougall, the first cooperating defendant in a U.K. SFO foreign bribery investigation, was spared jail.

In April 2011, Johnson & Johnson (J&J), a global manufacturer of medical devices, pharmaceuticals, and consumer healthcare products headquartered in New Brunswick, New Jersey, agreed to pay a $21.4 million criminal penalty as part of a DPA with the DOJ to resolve improper payments by J&J subsidiaries to government officials in Greece, Poland, and Romania. The DPA also resolved kickbacks paid to the government of Iraq under the United Nations Oil-for-Food program (OFFP) in order to obtain 19 contracts involving humanitarian relief. J&J accepted and acknowledged that the United States would file a criminal information charging DePuy Inc. with FCPA violations and that J&J would be bound by the letter DPA.[371]

J&J acknowledged responsibility for the actions of its subsidiaries, employees, and agents who made various improper payments to publicly employed healthcare providers in Greece, Poland, and Romania in order to induce the purchase of medical devices and pharmaceuticals manufactured by J&J subsidiaries. J&J also acknowledged that kickbacks were paid on behalf of J&J subsidiary companies to the government of Iraq under the OFFP in order to secure contracts to provide humanitarian supplies. The criminal information, filed in the U.S. District Court in the District of Columbia in connection with the DPA, charged J&J wholly owned subsidiary DePuy Inc. with conspiracy and violations of the FCPA in connection with the payments to public physicians in Greece. J&J acquired DePuy Inc. in 1998 and failed to promptly detect and curb that company's improper payment practices.

The DOJ recognized J&J's timely voluntary disclosure, and thorough and wide-reaching self-investigation of the underlying conduct; the extraordinary cooperation provided by the company to the department, the SEC, and multiple foreign enforcement authorities, including significant assistance in the industry-wide investigation; and the extensive remedial efforts and compliance improvements undertaken by the company. J&J received an internal complaint, began an investigation in March 2006, and made a report to the SEC and DOJ, which, in turn, made a referral to the U.K. Serious Fraud Office in October 2007. The DOJ stated J&J received a reduction in its criminal fine as a result of its cooperation in the ongoing investigation of other companies and individuals, as outlined in the U.S. Sentencing Guidelines, including the company's "role in identifying improper practices in the life sciences industry." J&J's fine was also reduced in light of its anticipated resolution in the United Kingdom. Due to J&J's preexisting compliance and ethics programs, extensive remediation, and improvement of its compliance systems and internal controls, as well as the enhanced compliance undertakings included in the agreement, J&J was not required to retain a corporate monitor, but it must report to the DOJ on implementation of its remediation and enhanced compliance efforts every six months for the duration of the DPA.

In addition to and building upon the commitments enumerated in the recent DOJ compliance program requirements,[372] Johnson & Johnson and its subsidiaries and operating companies (collectively J&J) agreed that they had or would undertake the following enhanced compliance obligations, at a minimum, for the duration of their agreement:

General

1. J&J will:
   a. Appoint a senior corporate executive with significant experience with compliance with the FCPA, including its antibribery, books-and-records, and internal controls provisions, as well as other applicable anticorruption laws and regulations (hereinafter "anticorruption laws and regulations") to serve as Chief Compliance Officer. The Chief Compliance Officer will have reporting obligations directly to the Audit Committee of the Board of Directors.
   b. Appoint heads of compliance within each business sector and corporate function. These compliance heads will have reporting obligations to the Chief Compliance Officer and the Audit Committee.
   c. Maintain a global compliance leadership team, including regional compliance leaders and business segment compliance leaders, with responsibility for overseeing its company-wide compliance program. That leadership team will have reporting obligations directly to the Chief Compliance Officer.
2. J&J shall institute gifts, hospitality, and travel policies and procedures in each jurisdiction that are appropriately designed to prevent violations of the anticorruption laws and regulations. At a minimum, these policies shall contain the following restrictions regarding government officials, including but not limited to public healthcare providers, administrators, and regulators:
   a. Gifts must be modest in value, appropriate under the circumstances, and given in accordance with anticorruption laws and regulations, including those of the government official's home country;

b. Hospitality shall be limited to reasonably priced meals, accommodations, and incidental expenses that are part of product education and training programs, professional training, and conferences or business meetings;

c. Travel shall be limited to product education and training programs, professional training, and conferences or business meetings; and

d. Gifts, hospitality, and travel shall not include expenses for anyone other than the official.

Complaints, Reports, and Compliance Issues

3. J&J shall maintain its mechanisms for making and handling reports and complaints related to potential violations of anticorruption laws and regulations, including referral for review and response to a standing committee that includes internal audit, legal, and compliance personnel, and will ensure that reasonable access is provided to an anonymous, toll-free hotline as well as to an anonymous electronic complaint form, where anonymous reporting is legally permissible.

4. J&J will ensure that its Sensitive Issue Triage Committee reviews and responds to FCPA and corruption issues promptly and consistently; this Triage Committee will include members from J&J's internal audit, legal, and compliance functions.

Risk Assessments and Audits

5. J&J will conduct risk assessments of markets where J&J has government customers and/or other anticorruption compliance risks on a staggered, periodic basis. Such risk assessments shall occur at reasonable intervals and include a review of trends in interactions with government officials, including healthcare providers, to identify new risk areas. On the basis of those assessments, as needed, J&J will modify compliance implementation to minimize risks observed through the risk assessment process.

6. J&J will conduct periodic audits specific to the detection of violations of anticorruption laws and regulations (FCPA Audits). Specifically, J&J will identify no less than five operating companies[373] that are high risk for corruption because of their sector and location and will conduct FCPA Audits of those operating companies at least once every three years. High risk operating companies shall be identified based on J&J's risk assessment process in consultation with the Chief Compliance Officer, sector compliance leaders, corporate internal audit, and the Law Department, taking into account multiple risk factors including, but not limited to: a high degree of interaction with government officials; the existence of internal reports of potential corruption risk; a high corruption risk based on certain corruption indexes; and financial audit results. The list of high risk operating companies shall be reviewed annually and updated as necessary. FCPA Audits of other operating companies that pose corruption risk shall occur no less than once every five years.[374] Each FCPA Audit shall include:

a. On-site visits by an audit team comprised of qualified auditors who have received FCPA and anticorruption training;

b. Where appropriate, participation in the on-site visits by personnel from the compliance and legal functions;

c. Review of a statistically representative sample appropriately adjusted for the risks of the market, of contracts with and payments to individual healthcare providers;

d. Creation of action plans resulting from issues identified during audits; these action plans will be shared with appropriate senior management, including the Chief Compliance Officer, and will contain mandatory undertakings designed to enhance anticorruption compliance, repair process weaknesses, and deter violations; and

e. Where appropriate, feasible, and permissible under local law, review of the books and records of distributors that, in the view of the audit team, may present corruption risk.

Acquisitions

7. J&J will ensure that new business entities are only acquired after thorough FCPA and anticorruption due diligence by legal, accounting, and compliance personnel. Where such anticorruption due diligence is not practicable prior to acquisition of a new business for reasons beyond J&J's control, or due to any applicable law, rule, or regulation, J&J will conduct FCPA and anticorruption due diligence subsequent to the acquisition and report to the Department any corrupt payments, falsified books and records, or inadequate internal controls as required by Paragraph 11 of the deferred prosecution agreement.

8. J&J will ensure that J&J's policies and procedures regarding the anticorruption laws and regulations apply as quickly as is practicable, but in any event no less than one year postclosing, to newly-acquired businesses, and will promptly:

a. Train directors, officers, employees, agents, consultants, representatives, distributors, joint venture partners, and relevant employees thereof, who present corruption risk to J&J, on the anticorruption laws and regulations and J&J's related policies and procedures; and

b. Conduct an FCPA-specific audit of all newly-acquired businesses within 18 months of acquisition.

Relationships with Third Parties

9. J&J will conduct due diligence reviews of sales intermediaries, including agents, consultants, representatives, distributors, and joint venture partners. At a minimum, such due diligence shall include:

a. A review of the qualifications and business reputation of the sales intermediaries;

b. A rationale for the use of the sales intermediary; and

c. A review of FCPA risk areas.

10. Such due diligence will be conducted by local businesses and reviewed by local healthcare compliance officers. New intermediaries that have not worked for the company prior to the date of this agreement, or where due diligence raises any red flags, shall be reviewed by a regional compliance officer with specific knowledge of and responsibility for anticorruption due diligence of sales intermediaries. Due diligence will be conducted prior to retention of any new agent, consultant, representative, distributor, or joint venture partner and for all such intermediaries will be updated no less than once every three years.

11. Where necessary and appropriate and where permitted by applicable law, J&J shall include standard provisions designed to prevent violations of the FCPA and other applicable anticorruption laws and regulations in agreements, contracts, grants, and renewals thereof with agents, distributors, and business partners, including:
    a. Anticorruption representations and undertakings relating to compliance with the anticorruption laws and regulations;
    b. Rights to conduct audits of the books and records of the agent, distributor, or business partner that are related to their business with J&J; and
    c. Rights to terminate the agent, distributor, or business partner as a result of any breach of anticorruption laws and regulations or representations and undertakings related to such anticorruption laws and regulations.

Training

12. J&J shall provide:
    a. Annual training on anticorruption laws and regulations to directors, officers, executives, and employees who could present corruption risk to J&J.
    b. Enhanced and in-depth FCPA training for all internal audit, financial, and legal personnel involved in FCPA audits, due diligence reviews, and acquisition of new businesses.
    c. Training as necessary based on risk profiles to relevant third parties acting on the company's behalf that may interact with government officials at least once every three years.

13. J&J shall implement a system of annual certifications from senior managers in each of J&J's corporate-level functions, divisions, and business units in each foreign country confirming that their local standard operating procedures adequately implement J&J's anticorruption policies and procedures, including training requirements, and that they are not aware of any FCPA or other corruption issues that have not already been reported to corporate compliance.[375]

In April 2011, J&J also reached a settlement of a related SEC civil complaint, charging it with violating the FCPA's antibribery provisions, falsifying books and records, and failing to implement internal controls. Under this settlement J&J

agreed to pay the SEC more than $48.6 million in disgorgement of profits, including prejudgment interest. As part of the internal controls claim, the SEC alleged that J&J failed to conduct due diligence on its Greek distributor, which allowed bribery at an acquired subsidiary to continue postacquisition and paid a consultant outside of Greece to avoid bribery detection.

Finally, J&J also settled an investigation by the U.K. Serious Fraud Office (SFO) into the company's improper payments in Greece and agreed to pay a $7.8 million fine to the SFO. The DOJ acknowledged the significant assistance provided by the Athens Economic Crime Squad in Greece; the Regional Prosecutor's Office in Radom, Poland; and the United Kingdom's SFO. Greek authorities have frozen assets of DePuy Hellas worth $5.875 million.

In April 2010, former DePuy International managing director Robert John Dougall pleaded guilty at Southwark Crown Court in London to making £4.5 million ($6.8 million) in corrupt payments to Greek medical professionals within the state-controlled healthcare system. That month he was sentenced to 12 months in prison. The U.K. Serious Fraud Office stated that from 2002 to 2005, Dougall arranged the payment of commissions to surgeons as an inducement to use DePuy's products, and asked a court of appeal to suspend the sentence due to his cooperation. In May 2010, the court of appeal decided to suspend Dougall's sentence, but warned that agreements the SFO makes with whistleblowers will have no bearing on sentences.[376] DePuy International, which was acquired by J&J in 1999, makes and sells orthopedic devices. The DePuy payments were made through agents and offshore accounts. The SFO said its investigation began "following a referral by the U.S. Department of Justice in October 2007." Dougall, it said, is the first "co-operating defendant" in a major SFO corruption investigation.[377] He had signed a formal agreement with the SFO that enabled the U.K. court to take his assistance into account.

BZ.   U.S. DOJ–Armor Holdings Inc. Agreement; *SEC v. Armor Holdings Inc.*[378]

▶ **Misconduct Category:**	Inflated commissions to third-party agents used to bribe UN procurement officers utilizing sham consulting agreements to award body armor contracts
▶ **Country:**	United Nations
▶ **Foreign Government Officials:**	United Nations officials
▶ **Improper Payment Dollar Value:**	$4.6 million
▶ **Combined Penalties:**	$15.98 million: $10.29 million DOJ penalty and $5.69 million SEC ($3.68 million SEC penalty and $2 million disgorgement and prejudgment interest)
▶ **Other:**	NPA; BAE Systems acquired Armor in 2007; former Armor vice president Richard Bistrong became an undercover cooperating individual in the Shot Show indictments; company required to file compliance reports every six months; voluntary disclosure and cooperation
▶ **Related Matter:**	*United States v. Bistrong*

In July 2011 Armor Holdings Inc. entered into an NPA with the DOJ to pay a $10.29 million penalty to resolve violations of the FCPA. In addition to the $10.29 million penalty, the agreement required that Armor continue to implement rigorous internal controls and that it cooperate fully with the DOJ. According to the agreement, at the time of the conduct at issue, Armor was headquartered in Jacksonville, Florida, and was listed on the New York Stock Exchange. At that time, the company manufactured security products, vehicle armor systems, protective equipment, and other products primarily for use by military, law enforcement, security, and corrections personnel. On July 31, 2007, Armor was acquired by BAE Systems Inc. and is currently a subsidiary of BAE.

According to the NPA, Armor accepted responsibility for its subsidiary's payment of more than $200,000 in commissions to a third-party sales agent, a portion of which it knew was to be passed on to a UN procurement official to induce the official to award two separate UN contracts to Armor's subsidiary. The contracts were for the sale of approximately $6 million of body armor. The agents caused the Armor subsidiary to enter into a sham consulting agreement with a third-party intermediary for purportedly legitimate services in connection with the sale of goods to the UN. The subsidiary agreed to pay the intermediary a success fee in the form of a percentage of value of any contract obtained from the UN. Armor also acknowledged that it falsely recorded the commission payments on its books and records. In addition, Armor admitted that it kept off its books and records approximately $4.4 million in additional payments to agents and other third-party intermediaries used by its Products Group to assist it in obtaining business from foreign government customers. Armor acknowledged that it failed to devise and maintain an appropriate system of internal accounting controls.

The DOJ recognized Armor's complete voluntary disclosure of the conduct; its internal investigation and cooperation with the DOJ and the SEC; the fact that the conduct took place prior to the acquisition of Armor by BAE; and Armor's extensive remedial efforts undertaken before and after its acquisition by BAE. Due to Armor's implementation of BAE's due diligence protocols and review processes, its application of BAE's compliance policies and internal controls to all Armor businesses, its extensive remediation and improvement of its compliance systems and internal controls, as well as the enhanced compliance undertakings included in the agreement, Armor is not required to retain a corporate monitor. Armor was required to report to the DOJ on implementation of its remediation and enhanced compliance efforts every six months for the duration of the agreement. In a related matter, Armor reached a settlement with the SEC and agreed to pay $1,552,306 in disgorgement of profits, $458,438 prejudgment interest, and a civil money penalty of $3,680,000.

CA. *United States v. Bridgestone Corp.*[379]

▶ **Misconduct Category:**	Conspiracy to use local sales agents to bribe state-owned officials to secure sales of marine hose in Latin America
▶ **Country:**	Mexico
▶ **Foreign Government Officials:**	State-owned oil company (Pemex)

▶ **Improper Payment Dollar Value:**	Unspecified
▶ **Combined Penalties:**	$28 million (includes criminal antitrust penalty)
▶ **Other:**	Conspiracy to bribe foreign government officials and to rig bids; first FCPA–antitrust corporate prosecution; "Read and Destroy" instructions on facsimiles that contained information related to corrupt payments; DOJ agrees to "substantially reduced fine due to cooperation"
▶ **Related Matter:**	*United States v. Hioki*

In September 2011 Bridgestone Corporation agreed to plead guilty and to pay a $28 million criminal fine for its role in conspiracies to rig bids and to make corrupt payments to foreign government officials in Latin America related to the sale of marine hose and other industrial products manufactured by the company and sold throughout the world.[380] A two-count criminal information was filed in the U.S. District Court in Houston against Bridgestone, a Tokyo-headquartered manufacturer of marine hose and other industrial products, charging the company with conspiring to violate the Sherman Act and the FCPA. According to court documents, Bridgestone conspired to rig bids, fix prices, and allocate market shares of marine hose in the United States and elsewhere and, separately, conspired to make corrupt payments to government officials in various Latin American countries to obtain and retain business. Bridgestone participated in the conspiracies from as early as January 1999, and continuing until as late as May 2007. Under the terms of the plea agreement, Bridgestone agreed to cooperate fully in the DOJ's ongoing antitrust and FCPA investigations.

The DOJ charged that, in order to secure sales of marine hose in Latin America, Bridgestone authorized and approved corrupt payments to foreign government officials employed at state-owned entities. Bridgestone's local sales agents agreed to pay employees of state-owned customers a percentage of the total value of proposed sales. According to the criminal information, the state-owned entity was Petroleos Mexicanos (Pemex), the national oil company of Mexico. When Bridgestone secured a sale, it would pay the local sales agent a "commission" consisting of not only the local sales agent's actual commission but also the corrupt payments to be made to employees of the state-owned customer. The local sales agent then was responsible for passing the agreed-upon corrupt payment to the employees of the customer. Bridgestone took steps in some instances to conceal improper payments by writing "Read and Destroy" on facsimiles that contained information related to corrupt payments.

In 2008 Misao Hioki, the former general manager of Bridgestone's international engineered products department, pleaded guilty and was sentenced for his role in the FCPA conspiracy. He was sentenced to two years in prison in December 2008. Under the corporate plea agreement, the DOJ recognized Bridgestone's cooperation with the investigations, including conducting a worldwide internal investigation, voluntarily making employees available for interviews, and collecting, analyzing, and providing to the department voluminous evidence and information. In addition, the plea agreement acknowledged Bridgestone's extensive remediation, including restructuring the relevant part of its business, terminating many of its third-party agents, and taking remedial actions with respect to employees responsible for many of the corrupt payments. Under the terms of the plea agreement, Bridgestone committed to continuing to enhance its compliance program and internal controls. As a result of these mitigating factors, the DOJ agreed to recommend a substantially reduced fine.

CB.   *U.S. DOJ–Aon Corp. Agreement;*[381] *SEC v. Aon Corp.*[382]

▶ **Misconduct Category:**	Misuse of training and education funds in connection with reinsurance business for overseas travel with spouses and for uses that could not be determined from books and records and payments made to third-party facilitators to obtain insurance business
▶ **Countries:**	Bangladesh, Costa Rica, Egypt, Indonesia, Myanmar, UAE, and Vietnam
▶ **Foreign Government Officials:**	Officials of Instituto Nacional De Seguros State Insurance Company (INS) (state-owned insurance company of Costa Rica)
▶ **Improper Payment Dollar Value:**	Over $3.6 million
▶ **Combined Penalties:**	$16.26 million ($1.76 million DOJ penalty and $14.5 million SEC disgorgement and prejudgment interest)
▶ **Other:**	NPA for parent Aon Corporation due to extraordinary cooperation; Aon conducted a global investigation of its operations; timely and complete disclosure of improper payments; and early and extensive remedial efforts.
▶ **Related Matters:**	Aon Limited; prior financial penalty of £5.25 million to the U.K. Financial Services Authority (FSA) and the FSA's close and continuous supervisory oversight of Aon Ltd. was also a factor in a substantially reduced monetary penalty.

In December 2011, Aon Corporation, a publicly traded corporation headquartered in Chicago and one of the largest insurance brokerage firms in the world, entered into an NPA with the DOJ to pay a $1.76 million penalty to resolve FCPA violations. Aon's United Kingdom subsidiary, Aon Limited, administered certain training and education funds in connection with its reinsurance business with Instituto Nacional de Seguros (INS), Costa Rica's state-owned insurance company. The supposed purpose of the funds was to provide education and training for INS officials. However, between 1997 and 2005, Aon Limited used a significant portion of the funds to reimburse INS officials for non-training-related activity, including travel with spouses to overseas tourist destinations, or for uses that could not be determined from Aon's books and records. Many of the invoices and other records for trips taken by INS officials did not provide any business purpose for the expenditures, or showed that the expenses were clearly not related to a legitimate business purpose.

As part of the NPA, Aon admitted that Aon Limited's accounting books and records related to the funds, which were consolidated into Aon's books and records, did not accurately and fairly reflect the purpose for which the expenses were incurred. Aon also admitted that it failed to devise and maintain an adequate system of internal accounting controls with respect to foreign sales activities sufficient to ensure compliance with the FCPA. In addition to the monetary penalty, the agreement required that Aon Corporation adhere to rigorous compliance, bookkeeping and internal controls standards and cooperate fully with the DOJ.

The DOJ entered into the NPA with Aon as a result of Aon's extraordinary cooperation with the DOJ and the SEC; timely and complete disclosure of improper payments in Costa Rica and other countries that it discovered during its thorough investigation of its global operations; early and extensive remedial efforts; the prior financial penalty of £5.25 million that Aon Limited paid to the United Kingdom's Financial Services Authority (FSA);[383] and the FSA's close and continuous supervisory oversight over Aon Limited. The DOJ stated that these factors also led to a substantially reduced monetary penalty.

In a related matter, Aon Corporation reached an SEC settlement and agreed to pay approximately $14.5 million in disgorgement and prejudgment interest. The SEC complaint alleged that Aon's subsidiaries made over $3.6 million in improper payments to various parties between 1983 and 2007 as a means of obtaining or retaining insurance business in those countries.[384] The complaint alleged that some of the improper payments were made directly or indirectly to foreign government officials who could award business directly to Aon subsidiaries, who were in position to influence others who could award business to Aon subsidiaries, or who could otherwise provide favorable business treatment for the company's interests. The complaint alleged that these payments were not accurately reflected in Aon's books and records, and that Aon failed to maintain an adequate internal controls system reasonably designed to detect and prevent the improper payments.

According to the SEC's complaint, the improper payments made by Aon's subsidiaries fell into two general categories: (1) training, travel, and entertainment provided to employees of foreign government-owned clients and third parties; and (2) payments made to third-party facilitators. Aon subsidiaries made these payments in various countries around the world, including Costa Rica, Egypt, Vietnam, Indonesia, United Arab Emirates, Myanmar, and Bangladesh. The complaint alleged that Aon realized over $11.4 million in profits from these improper payments. Aon agreed to pay disgorgement of $11,416,814 in profits, together with prejudgment interest of $3,128,206, for a total of $14,545,020.[385]

CC.   *United States v. Magyar Telekom Plc; United States–Deutsche Telekom Nonprosecution Agreement;[386] SEC v. Magyar Telekom Plc & Deutsche Telekom, AG[387]*

▶ **Misconduct Category:**   Fictitious consulting consultant and improper lobbying payments to obtain regulatory benefits

▶ **Countries:**   Macedonia and Montenegro

▶ **Foreign Government Officials:**	Officials of the different ruling parties in Macedonia
▶ **Improper Payment Dollar Value:**	$15 million
▶ **Combined Penalties:**	Magyar Telekom: $59.6 criminal penalty and $31.2 million SEC disgorgement and prejudgment interest; Deutsch Telekom: $4.36 million penalty
▶ **Other:**	ADR jurisdiction for parent Deutsche Telekom; DPA for Magyar Telekom; NPA for Deutsche Telekom; voluntary disclosure and "thorough global investigation concerning bribery and related misconduct."
▶ **Related Matters:**	*SEC v. Straub, Balogh & Morvai*[388]

In December 2011, Magyar Telekom Plc., a Hungarian telecommunications company, and Deutsche Telekom AG, a German telecommunications company and majority owner of Magyar Telekom, agreed to pay a combined $63.9 million criminal penalty to resolve an FCPA investigation into activities by Magyar Telekom and its subsidiaries in Macedonia and Montenegro.[389]

The DOJ filed a criminal information against Magyar Telekom and a two-year DPA in the U.S. District Court for the Eastern District of Virginia. The three-count information charges Magyar Telekom with one count of violating the antibribery provisions of the FCPA and two counts of violating the books-and-records provisions of the FCPA. At the time of the charged conduct, Magyar Telekom's American depositary receipts traded on the New York Stock Exchange (NYSE). As part of the DPA, Magyar Telekom agreed to pay a $59.6 million penalty for its illegal activity, implement an enhanced compliance program, and submit annual reports regarding its efforts in implementing the enhanced compliance measures and remediating past problems.

According to court documents, Magyar Telekom's scheme in Macedonia stemmed from potential legal changes being made to the telecommunications market in that country. In early 2005, the Macedonian government tried to liberalize the Macedonian telecommunications market in a way that Magyar Telekom deemed detrimental to its Macedonian subsidiary, Makedonski Telekommunikacii AD Skopje (MakTel). Throughout the late winter and spring of 2005, Magyar Telekom executives, with the help of Greek intermediaries, lobbied Macedonian government officials to prevent the implementation of the new telecommunications laws and regulations.

Magyar Telekom eventually entered into an agreement with certain high-ranking Macedonian government officials to resolve its concerns about the legal changes. In the secret agreement, a so-called "protocol of cooperation," Macedonian government officials agreed to delay the entrance of a third mobile license into the Macedonian telecommunications market, as well as other regulatory benefits. Magyar Telekom executives signed two copies of the protocol of cooperation, each with high-ranking officials of the different ruling parties of Macedonia. The Magyar Telekom executives then kept the only executed copies outside of Magyar Telekom's company records.

According to court documents, in order to secure the benefits in the protocol of cooperation, the Magyar Telekom executives engaged in a course of conduct with consultants, intermediaries and other third parties, including through sham consultancy contracts with entities owned and controlled by a Greek intermediary, to pay €4.875 million (approximately $6 million) under circumstances in which they knew, or were aware of a high probability that circumstances existed in which, all or part of such payment would be passed on to Macedonian officials. The sham contracts were recorded as legitimate on MakTel's books and records, which were consolidated into Magyar Telekom's financials. Deutsche Telekom, which owned approximately 60 percent of Magyar Telekom, reported the results of Magyar Telekom's operations in its consolidated financial statements.

Additionally, the criminal information charged Magyar Telekom with falsifying its books and records in regard to its activity in Montenegro. According to the court filing, Magyar Telekom made improper payments in connection with its acquisition of a state-owned telecommunications company in Montenegro. These payments were documented on Magyar Telekom's books and records through the execution of four bogus contracts. For example, two of the contracts were backdated and concealed the true counterparties, and no legitimate services were provided under the contracts even though the contracts were for €4.47 million.

The DOJ also entered into a two-year NPA with Magyar Telekom's parent company, Deutsche Telekom, for its failure to keep books and records that accurately detailed the activities of Magyar Telekom. Deutsche Telekom, which is headquartered in Germany, agreed to pay a $4.36 million penalty in connection with the inaccurate books and records and to enhance its compliance program. At the time of the conduct, Deutsche Telekom's American depositary receipts traded on the NYSE.

Both agreements acknowledged Magyar Telekom and Deutsche Telekom's voluntary disclosure of the FCPA violations to the department and the leadership of Magyar Telekom's audit committee in pursuing a "thorough global internal investigation concerning bribery and related misconduct." In addition, the agreements highlighted that the companies had already undertaken remedial measures and had committed to further remedial steps through the implementation of an enhanced compliance program.

In a related matter, the SEC announced civil charges against Magyar Telekom and Deutsche Telekom, as well as three former Magyar Telecom executives: Elek Straub, former chairman and CEO; Andras Balogh, former director of central strategic organization; and Tamas Morvai, former director of business development and acquisitions. Magyar Telekom and Deutsche Telekom consented to the entry of a permanent injunction against FCPA violations. Magyar Telecom agreed to pay $31.2 million in disgorgement and prejudgment interest. Significant assistance was provided by international legal partners in Switzerland, Germany, Greece, Hungary, and the Republic of Macedonia.

CD.   *United States v. Sharef, Steffen, Truppel, Bock, Signer, Reichert, Sergi & Czysch;*[390] *SEC v. Sharif, Bock, Sergi, Signer, Steffen, Truppel & Regendantz*[391]

▶ **Misconduct Category:**   Decade-long scheme to bribe senior Argentine officials to obtain $1 billion national identity card contract

▶ **Country:**	Argentina
▶ **Foreign Government Officials:**	Two presidents and cabinet ministers in two presidential administrations
▶ **Improper Payment Dollar Value:**	$100 million
▶ **Combined Penalties:**	$40,000 SEC civil penalty as to Regendantz and $275,000 SEC civil penalty as to Sharef
▶ **Other:**	The December 2011 criminal charges against eight Siemens officers are a follow-on to the December 2008 indictment of Siemens and its subsidiaries, which resulted in record combined U.S., German, and World Bank fines of $1.7 billion; in addition to FCPA violations, conspiracy to commit money laundering, conspiracy to commit wire fraud, and substantive wire fraud violations were charged
▶ **Related Matters:**	*United States v. Siemens Aktiengesellschaft* (2008); *SEC v. Siemens Aktiengesellschaft* (2008);

In December 2011, eight former executives and agents of Siemens AG and its subsidiaries were charged for allegedly engaging in a decade-long scheme to bribe senior Argentine government officials to secure, implement, and enforce a $1 billion contract with the Argentine government to produce national identity cards. The defendants charged in the indictment are Uriel Sharef, a former member of the central executive committee of Siemens AG; Herbert Steffen, a former chief executive officer of Siemens Argentina; Andres Truppel, a former chief financial officer of Siemens Argentina; Ulrich Bock, Stephan Signer, and Eberhard Reichert, former senior executives of Siemens Business Services; and Carlos Sergi and Miguel Czysch, who served as intermediaries and agents of Siemens in the bribe scheme. The indictment charged the defendants and their coconspirators with conspiracy to violate the FCPA and the wire fraud statute, money laundering conspiracy, and wire fraud. At the same time, the SEC filed related civil charges against seven individuals, *infra*, six of whom were charged in the criminal case.

According to the indictment, the government of Argentina issued a tender for bids in 1994 to replace an existing system of manually created national identity booklets with state-of-the-art national identity cards or *documentos nacionales de identi* (the DNI project). The value of the DNI project was $1 billion. In 1998, the Argentine government awarded the DNI project to a special-purpose subsidiary of Siemens AG.

The indictment alleged that during the bidding and implementation phases of the project, the defendants and their coconspirators caused Siemens to commit to paying nearly $100 million in bribes to sitting officials of the Argentine government, members of the opposition party, and candidates for office who were likely to come to power during the performance of the project. According to the indictment, members of the conspiracy worked to conceal the illicit payments through various means. For instance, Bock made cash withdrawals from Siemens AG general-purpose accounts in Germany totaling approximately $10 million, transported the cash across the border into Switzerland, and deposited the funds into

Swiss bank accounts for transfer to officials. Bock, Truppel, Reichert, and other conspirators also allegedly caused Siemens to wire transfer more than $7 million in bribes to a bank account in New York disguised as a foreign exchange hedging contract relating to the DNI project. Over the duration of the conspiracy, the conspirators allegedly relied on at least 17 offshore shell companies associated with Sergi, Czysch, and other intermediaries to disguise and launder the funds, often documenting the payments through fake consulting contracts.

In May 1999, according to the indictment, the Argentine government suspended the DNI project, due in part to instability in the local economy and an impending presidential election. When a new government took power in Argentina, and in the hopes of getting the DNI project resumed, members of the conspiracy allegedly committed Siemens to paying additional bribes to the incoming officials and to satisfying existing obligations to officials of the outgoing administration, many of whom remained in influential positions within the government.

When the project was terminated in May 2001, members of the conspiracy allegedly responded with a multifaceted strategy to overcome the termination. According to the indictment, the conspirators sought to recover the anticipated proceeds of the DNI project, notwithstanding the termination, by causing Siemens AG to file a fraudulent arbitration claim against the Republic of Argentina in Washington, D.C. The claim alleged wrongful termination of the contract for the DNI project and demanded nearly $500 million in lost profits and expenses. Members of the conspiracy allegedly caused Siemens to actively hide from the tribunal the fact that the contract for the DNI project had been secured by means of bribery and corruption, including tampered witness statements and pleadings that falsely denied the existence of corruption.

The indictment also alleged that members of the conspiracy continued the bribe scheme, in part to prevent disclosure of the bribery in the arbitration and to ensure Siemens' ability to secure future government contracts in Argentina and elsewhere in the region. In four installments between 2002 and 2007, members of the conspiracy allegedly caused Siemens to pay approximately $28 million in further satisfaction of the obligations. Conspirators continued to conceal these additional payments through various means. For example, according to the DOJ, Sharef, Truppel, and other members of the conspiracy allegedly caused Siemens to transfer approximately $9.5 million through fictitious transactions involving a Siemens business division that had no role in the DNI project. They also caused Siemens to pay an additional $8.8 million in 2007 under the legal cover of a separate arbitration initiated in Switzerland by the intermediaries to enforce a sham $27 million contract from 2001 between Siemens Business Services and Mfast Consulting, a company controlled by their coconspirator intermediaries, which consolidated existing bribe commitments into one contract. The conspirators caused Siemens to quietly settle the arbitration, keeping all evidence of corruption out of the proceeding. The settlement agreement included a provision preventing Sergi, Czysch, and another intermediary from testifying in, or providing information to, the Washington arbitration.

Siemens's corrupt procurement of the DNI project was not exposed during the lifespan of the conspiracy, and, in February 2007, the arbitral tribunal in

Washington sided with Siemens AG, awarding the company nearly $220 million on its DNI claims, plus interest. On August 12, 2009, following Siemens' corporate resolutions with the U.S. and German authorities, new management of Siemens caused Siemens AG to forgo its right to receive the award and, as a result, the company never claimed the award money.

The indictment charged the defendants with conspiracy to violate the antibribery, books-and-records, and internal controls provisions of the FCPA; conspiracy to commit wire fraud; conspiracy to commit money laundering; and substantive wire fraud. The criminal defendants all live in either Germany, Switzerland, or Argentina. The United States has not been able to extradite the eight executives from those countries. The individual charges followed by three years the December 15, 2008, guilty pleas by Siemens AG and its subsidiary, Siemens S.A. (Siemens Argentina), to criminal violations of the FCPA. As part of the company's plea agreement, Siemens AG and Siemens Argentina agreed to pay fines of $448.5 million and $500,000, respectively.

In a parallel civil action, the SEC announced charges against senior former executives and agents of Siemens: Sharef, Steffen, Truppel, Bock, Sergi, Stephan, Signer, and Bernd Regendantz. The SEC charged that during the relevant 2001 to 2007 time period, defendants Sharef, Bock, Sergi, Signer, Steffen, Truppel, and Regendantz each had a role in authorizing, negotiating, facilitating, or concealing bribe payments in connection with the DNI contract. Siemens employed a group of consultants, designated the Project Group and led by defendant Sergi, to serve as payment intermediaries between the company and the Argentine government officials.

According to the SEC, each of the defendants violated section 30A of the Exchange Act by engaging in the bribery of government officials in Argentina. Each defendant also aided and abetted Siemens' violations of section 30A. The defendants also violated Exchange Act section 13(b)(5) and Rule 13b2-1 thereunder by authorizing or directing others to falsify documents, including invoices and sham consulting contracts, in furtherance of the bribery scheme. Defendant Regendantz violated Rule 13b2-2 by signing false internal certifications pursuant to the Sarbanes-Oxley Act (SOX). All defendants aided and abetted Siemens' violations of Exchange Act sections 13(b)(2)(A) and 13(b)(2)(B) by substantially assisting in Siemens' failure to maintain internal controls to detect and prevent bribery of government officials in Argentina, and by substantially assisting in the improper recording of the bribe payments in Siemens' accounting books and records. The SEC's complaint sought permanent injunctive relief, disgorgement, and civil penalties from the defendants. During the course of the bribery scheme, over $100 million in bribes were paid, approximately $31.3 million of which were made after March 12, 2001, when Siemens became a U.S. issuer subject to U.S. securities laws.

Defendant Regendantz consented to the SEC's allegations in December 2011 and to the entry of a final judgment that permanently enjoined him from future violations of sections 30A and 13(b)(5) of the Exchange Act, and Rules 13b2-1 and 13b2-2 thereunder, and from aiding and abetting violations of Exchange Act sections 30A, 13(b)(2)(A), and 13(b)(2)(B). The SEC ordered him to pay a civil penalty of $40,000, deemed satisfied by Regendantz' payment of a €30,000 administrative fine ordered by the Public Prosecutor General in Munich, Germany. Sharef, a former officer and board member of Siemens AG, settled with the SEC in April 2013 and agreed to pay $275,000. In February 2013, Judge Scheindlin of the Southern District of New York dismissed the SEC case as to former Siemens Argentina CEO Steffen (see chapter 2, section III.A.2). In February 2014, the same judge entered default judgments against Signer and Bock in the SEC trial and ordered Signer to pay a $524,000 civil penalty and Bock to pay an additional $413,957 in disgorgement. On May 15, 2014, Siemens delisted its American depository receipts (ADRs) on the New York Stock Exchange and no longer has periodic reporting obligations with the SEC.[392]

The individual charges follow, in large part, the actions of Siemens AG and its audit committee in disclosing potential FCPA violations to the DOJ after the Munich Public Prosecutor's Office initiated an investigation. Siemens AG and its subsidiaries disclosed these violations after initiating an internal FCPA investigation of unprecedented scope; shared the results of that investigation; cooperated extensively and authentically with the department in its ongoing investigation; and took remedial action, including the complete restructuring of Siemens AG and the implementation of a sophisticated compliance program and organization. The DOJ and the SEC collaborated with the Munich Public Prosecutor's Office to bring this case.

CE.   *United States v. Marubeni Corp.*

▶ **Misconduct Category:**	Payment as agent of consortium of bribes to Nigerian government officials to obtain $6 billion in engineering procurement and construction (EPC) contracts
▶ **Country:**	Nigeria
▶ **Foreign Government Officials:**	Lower-level government official and holder of top-level office in the executive branch of the Nigerian government
▶ **Improper Payment Dollar Value:**	Unspecified as to Marubeni
▶ **Combined Penalties:**	$54.6 million
▶ **Other:**	Two-year deferred prosecution agreement (DPA); retention of independent corporate compliance consultant; participation with consortium partner in improper payments
▶ **Related Matters:**	*United States v. Kellogg Brown & Root; United States v. Technip; United States v. JGC; United States v. Snamprogetti; United States v. Stanley; United States v. Tesler & Chodan; United States v. Marubeni Corp.* (2014)

In January 2012, Marubeni Corporation, a Japanese trading company headquartered in Tokyo, agreed to pay a $54.6 million criminal penalty to resolve FCPA charges related to participation in a decade-long scheme to bribe Nigerian government officials to obtain engineering, procurement, and construction (EPC) contracts.[393] The DOJ filed a DPA and a criminal information against Marubeni in the

U.S. District Court for the Southern District of Texas. The two-count information charged Marubeni with one count of conspiracy and one count of aiding and abetting violations of the FCPA.

According to court documents, Marubeni was hired as an agent by the four-company TSKJ joint venture to help TSKJ obtain and retain EPC contracts to build liquefied natural gas (LNG) facilities on Bonny Island, Nigeria, by offering to pay and paying bribes to Nigerian government officials, among other means. TSKJ was composed of Technip S.A., Snamprogetti Netherlands B.V., Kellogg Brown & Root Inc. (KBR), and JGC Corporation. Between 1995 and 2004, TSKJ was awarded four EPC contracts, valued at more than $6 billion, by Nigeria LNG Ltd. to build the LNG facilities on Bonny Island. The government-owned Nigerian National Petroleum Corporation was the largest shareholder of NLNG, owning 49 percent of the company.

According to court documents, to assist in obtaining and retaining the EPC contracts, the joint venture hired two agents—Marubeni and Jeffrey Tesler, a U.K. solicitor—to pay bribes to a wide range of Nigerian government officials. The joint venture hired Tesler as a consultant to pay bribes to high-level Nigerian government officials, including top-level executive-branch officials, and hired Marubeni to pay bribes to lower-level Nigerian government officials. At crucial junctures preceding the award of EPC contracts, a number of coconspirators, including on two occasions an employee of Marubeni, met with successive holders of a top-level office in the executive branch of the Nigerian government to ask the office holders to designate a representative with whom TSKJ should negotiate bribes to Nigerian government officials. TSKJ paid approximately $132 million to a Gibraltar corporation controlled by Tesler and $51 million to Marubeni during the course of the bribery scheme and intended for these payments to be used, in part, for bribes to Nigerian government officials.

Under the two-year DPA, Marubeni agreed to retain a corporate compliance consultant for a term of two years to review the design and implementation of its compliance program, to enhance its compliance program to ensure that it satisfies certain standards and to cooperate with the department in ongoing investigations.

In a related criminal case, KBR's successor company, Kellogg Brown & Root LLC, pleaded guilty in February 2009 to FCPA-related charges for its participation in the scheme to bribe Nigerian government officials. Kellogg Brown & Root LLC was ordered to pay a $402 million fine and to retain an independent compliance monitor for a three-year period to review the design and implementation of its compliance program. In another related criminal case, the DOJ filed a DPA and criminal information against Technip in June 2010. According to that agreement, Technip agreed to pay a $240 million criminal penalty and to retain an independent compliance monitor for two years. In July 2010, the DOJ filed a DPA and criminal information against Snamprogetti, which also agreed to pay a $240 million criminal penalty. In April 2011, the DOJ filed a DPA and criminal information against JGC, in which JGC agreed to pay a $218.8 million criminal penalty and to retain an independent compliance consultant for two years.

In other related criminal cases, KBR's former CEO, Albert "Jack" Stanley, pleaded guilty in September 2008 to conspiring to violate the FCPA for his participation in the bribery scheme. Tesler and Wojciech J. Chodan, a former salesperson and consultant of a United Kingdom subsidiary of KBR, were indicted in February 2009 on FCPA-related charges for their participation in the bribery scheme. In March 2011, Tesler was extradited from the United Kingdom and subsequently pleaded guilty to conspiring to violate and violating the FCPA and agreed to forfeit $148,964,568. In December 2010, Chodan was extradited from the United Kingdom and subsequently pleaded guilty to conspiring to violate the FCPA and agreed to forfeit $726,885. In 2012 Stanley was sentenced to 30 months in jail, Tesler was sentenced to 21 months in jail, and Chodan was sentenced to one year of probation. The DOJ press release for Marubeni indicated that significant assistance was provided by authorities in France, Italy, Switzerland, and the United Kingdom.[394]

CF.   *United States v. Smith & Nephew, Inc.*[395]

▶ **Misconduct Category:**	Use of distributor discounts to pay, through distributor shell companies, cash and other things of value to Greek publicly owned health providers to induce purchases of medical device products
▶ **Country:**	Greece
▶ **Foreign Government Officials:**	Publicly employed healthcare providers
▶ **Improper Payment Dollar Value:**	Less than $9.4 million
▶ **Combined Penalties:**	$22.2 million (DOJ: $16.8 million; SEC: $5.4 million disgorgement of profits, including prejudgment interest)
▶ **Other:**	DPA; Hybrid monitor: 18-month independent compliance monitor

In February 2012, Smith & Nephew Inc., a Delaware corporation, entered into a DPA[396] with the DOJ to resolve improper payments by the company and certain affiliates in violation of the FCPA. Smith & Nephew Inc., headquartered in Memphis, Tennessee, is a wholly owned subsidiary of Smith & Nephew plc, an English company traded on the New York Stock Exchange. The company manufactures and sells medical devices worldwide. Smith & Nephew acknowledged responsibility for the actions of its affiliates, subsidiaries, employees, and agents who made various improper payments to publicly employed healthcare providers in Greece from 1998 until 2008 to secure lucrative business. According to the criminal information filed in the U.S. District Court in the District of Columbia in connection with the agreement, Smith & Nephew, through certain executives, employees and affiliates, agreed to sell products at full list price to a Greek distributor based in Athens, and then pay the amount of the distributor discount to an offshore shell company controlled by the distributor. These off-the-books funds were then used by the distributor to pay cash incentives and other things of value to publicly employed Greek healthcare providers to induce the purchase of Smith & Nephew products. In total, from 1998 to 2008, Smith & Nephew, its affiliates and employees authorized the payment of approximately $9.4 million to the distributor's shell companies, some or all of which was passed on to physicians to corruptly induce them to purchase medical devices manufactured by Smith & Nephew.

The agreement recognized Smith & Nephew's cooperation with the DOJ's investigation, thorough self-investigation of the underlying conduct, and the remedial efforts and compliance improvements undertaken by the company. As part of the agreement, Smith & Nephew agreed to pay a $16.8 million penalty and implement rigorous internal controls, cooperate fully with the DOJ, and retain a compliance monitor for 18 months—half the length of what most monitorships have been. In a related matter, Smith & Nephew reached a settlement with the SEC under which Smith & Nephew agreed to pay $5.4 million in disgorgement of profits, including prejudgment interest.

CG.   *United States v. Biomet, Inc.;*[397] *SEC v. Biomet, Inc.*[398]

▶ **Misconduct Category:**	Kickbacks as high as 20 percent of pack sale to publicly employed doctors in Argentina: use of a distributor in Brazil to bribe publicly employed doctors; use of a distributor in China who provided publicly employed doctors with money and travel in exchange for their purchases of Biomet medical device products
▶ **Countries:**	Argentina, Brazil, and China
▶ **Foreign Government Officials:**	Publicly employed doctors
▶ **Improper Payment Dollar Value:**	$1.5 million
▶ **Combined Penalties:**	Over $22 million (DOJ: $17.2 million; SEC: $5.4 million)
▶ **Other:**	DPA; independent compliance monitor for 18 months; payment disguised as "commissions," "royalties," "consulting fees," and "scientific incentives"; third medical device company to resolve FCPA investigation of industry; highly incriminating e-mails with distributors; awareness of payments by internal audit and executives as early as 2000; use of a distributor to bribe publicly employed doctors with 10–20 percent of value of medical devices; improper company-sponsored overseas travel that included sightseeing and other entertainment;[399] discount for cooperation against other companies and individuals

In March 2012 Biomet Inc., headquartered in Warsaw, Indiana, which manufactures and sells medical devices worldwide and is listed on the NASDAQ, entered into a DPA with the DOJ to resolve improper payments by the company and its subsidiaries in violation of the FCPA. According to the criminal information filed in the U.S. District Court in the District of Columbia in connection with the DPA, Biomet, its subsidiaries, employees, and agents made various improper payments from approximately 2000 to 2008 to publicly employed healthcare providers in Argentina, Brazil, and China to secure lucrative business with hospitals. During this time, more than

$1.5 million in direct and indirect corrupt payments were made. In addition, at the end of each fiscal year, Biomet, its executives, employees, and agents falsely recorded the payments on its books and records as "commissions," "royalties," "consulting fees," and "scientific incentives" to conceal the true nature of the payments.

As part of the agreement, Biomet agreed to pay a $17.28 million criminal penalty and was required to implement rigorous internal controls, cooperate fully with the DOJ, and retain a compliance monitor for 18 months. The DPA recognized Biomet's cooperation with the DOJ's investigation; thorough and wide-reaching self-investigation of the underlying conduct; and the remedial efforts and compliance improvements undertaken by the company. In addition, Biomet received a reduction in its penalty as a result of its cooperation in the ongoing investigation of other companies and individuals.

In a related matter, Biomet settled with the SEC and agreed to pay $5.4 million in disgorgement of profits, including prejudgment interest. According to the SEC's complaint filed in federal court in Washington D.C., employees of Biomet Argentina SA paid kickbacks as high as 15 to 20 percent of each sale to publicly employed doctors in Argentina. Phony invoices were used to justify the payments, and the bribes were falsely recorded as "consulting fees" or "commissions" in Biomet's books and records.[400] Executives and internal auditors at Biomet's Indiana headquarters were aware of the payments as early as 2000, but failed to stop it.

The SEC alleged that Biomet's U.S. subsidiary Biomet International used a distributor to bribe publicly employed doctors in Brazil by paying them as much as 20 percent of the value of their medical device purchases. Payments were openly discussed in communications between the distributor, Biomet International employees, and Biomet's executives and internal auditors in the United States. For example, a February 2002 internal Biomet memorandum about a limited audit of the distributor's books stated:

> Brazilian Distributor makes payments to surgeons that may be considered as a kickback. These payments are made in cash that allows the surgeon to receive income tax free. . . . The accounting entry is to increase a prepaid expense account. In the consolidated financials sent to Biomet, these payments were reclassified to expense in the income statement.[401]

According to the SEC's complaint, two additional subsidiaries—Biomet China and Scandimed AB—sold medical devices through a distributor in China who provided publicly employed doctors with money and travel in exchange for their purchases of Biomet products. Beginning as early as 2001, the distributor exchanged e-mails with Biomet employees that explicitly described the bribes he was arranging on the company's behalf. For example, one e-mail stated:

> [Doctor] is the department head of [public hospital]. [Doctor] uses about 10 hips and knees a month and it's on an uptrend, as he told us over dinner a week ago. . . . Many key surgeons in Shanghai are buddies of his. A kind word on Biomet from him goes a long way for us. Dinner

has been set for the evening of the 24th. It will be nice. But dinner aside, I've got to send him to Switzerland to visit his daughter.[402]

The SEC alleged that some e-mails described the way that vendors would deliver cash to surgeons upon completion of surgery, and others discussed the amount of payments. The distributor explained in one e-mail that 25 percent in cash would be delivered to a surgeon upon completion of surgery. Biomet sponsored travel for 20 Chinese surgeons in 2007 to Spain, where a substantial part of the trip was devoted to sightseeing and other entertainment. Biomet consented to the entry of a court order requiring payment of $4,432,998 in disgorgement and $1,142,733 in prejudgment interest to the SEC. Biomet is permanently enjoined from future FCPA violations.

The Biomet matter is part of a DOJ industry-wide investigation into bribery by medical device companies of healthcare providers and administrators employed by government institutions. Previously, Johnson & Johnson and Smith & Nephew Inc. agreed to pay criminal penalties and entered into DPAs related to the ongoing investigation.

CH.   *United States v. BizJet International Sales & Support, Inc.*[403]
       Lufthansa Technik AG Nonprosecution Agreement[404]

▶ **Misconduct Category:**	Bribes to various government aircraft officials and use of a shell company owned and operated by a BizJet sales manager to pay officials to secure aircraft maintenance, repair and service contracts
▶ **Countries:**	Mexico and Panama
▶ **Foreign Government Officials:**	Captains and colonels in Mexico Federal Police and Mexican president's air fleet; a director of air services for the governor of the Mexican State of Sinaloa; and a chief mechanic at the Panama Aviation Authority
▶ **Improper Payment Dollar Value:**	$560,000 plus
▶ **Combined Penalties:**	$11.8 million
▶ **Other:**	BizJet: DPA; and Lufthansa Technik: NPA; combined fine is 30 percent off low end of the Guidelines. Use of the terms "commissions," "incentives" or "referral fees" to conceal payments. Presentation at 2005 board of directors meeting at which executives discussed with the board that the decision as to where an aircraft was sent for maintenance was made by the potential customer's director of maintenance or chief pilot who were demanding $30,000 to $40,000 in commissions and BizJet would pay referral fees in order to gain market share; compliance self-assessment permitted.
▶ **Related Matters:**	*United States v. Kovalewski, DuBois, Jensen & Uhl*

In March 2012 BizJet International Sales and Support Inc., a provider of aircraft maintenance, repair, and overhaul (MRO) services based in Tulsa, Oklahoma, agreed to pay an $11.8 million criminal penalty to resolve FCPA charges involving the bribery of government officials in Latin America to secure contracts to perform aircraft MRO services for government agencies. The DOJ filed a one-count criminal information charging BizJet with conspiring to violate the FCPA's anti-bribery provisions and a DPA in the U.S. District Court for the Northern District of Oklahoma. According to court documents, BizJet paid bribes to officials employed by the Mexican Policia Federal Preventiva, the Mexican Coordinacion General de Transportes Aereos Presidenciales, the air fleet for the Gobierno del Estado de Sinaloa, the air fleet for the Gobierno del Estado de Sonora, and the Republica de Panama Autoridad Aeronautica Civil. In many instances, BizJet paid the bribes directly to the foreign officials. In other instances, BizJet funneled the bribes through a California shell company owned and operated by a BizJet sales manager. BizJet executives orchestrated, authorized, and approved the unlawful payments. The bribes exceeded $560,000[405] and resulted in contracts worth in excess of $7 million. In 2005 two senior executives explained to the BizJet board of directors that the decision of where an aircraft is sent for maintenance work is generally made by the potential customer's director of maintenance or chief pilot and that these individuals were demanding $30,000 to $40,000 in commissions and that BizJet would pay referral fees in order to gain market share.[406] Payments were recorded as "commissions," "incentives," or "referral fees."[407]

Under the terms of the agreement the DOJ agreed to defer prosecution of BizJet for three years. In addition to the monetary penalty, BizJet agreed to cooperate with the DOJ in ongoing investigations, to report periodically to the DOJ concerning BizJet's compliance efforts, and to continue to implement an enhanced compliance program and internal controls designed to prevent and detect FCPA violations. In addition, BizJet's indirect parent company, Lufthansa Technik AG, itself a German provider of aircraft-related services, entered into an NPA with the DOJ in connection with the unlawful payments by BizJet and its directors, officers, employees, and agents. The DOJ agreed not to prosecute Lufthansa Technik provided that Lufthansa Technik satisfies its obligations under the agreement for a period of three years. Those obligations include ongoing cooperation and the continued implementation of rigorous internal controls.

The agreements acknowledged BizJet's and Lufthansa Technik's voluntary disclosure of the FCPA violations to the DOJ and their extraordinary cooperation, including conducting an extensive internal investigation, voluntarily making U.S. and foreign employees available for interviews, and collecting, analyzing, and organizing voluminous evidence and information for the DOJ. In addition, BizJet and Lufthansa Technik engaged in extensive remediation, including terminating the officers and employees responsible for the corrupt payments, enhancing their due diligence protocol for third-party agents and consultants, and heightening review of proposals and other transactional documents for all BizJet contracts. The DOJ stated that it worked closely with law enforcement counterparts in Mexico and Panama in this matter.

CI.   *United States v. Peterson;*[408] *SEC v. Peterson;*[409] *Declination of Morgan Stanley*

▶ **Misconduct Category:**   Real estate scam by former Morgan Stanley managing director with official of a Chinese state-owned entity (SOE) in order to obtain an interest in the SOE's property

▶ **Country:**   People's Republic of China

▶ **Foreign Government Officials:** Official of Yongye Enterprise (Group) Co. Ltd., a large state-owned and state-controlled real estate investment entity

▶ **Improper Payment Dollar Value:** $1.8 million

▶ **Combined Penalties:**   Nine months in jail for Peterson

▶ **Other:**   Morgan Stanley was not charged by either the DOJ or the SEC due to its internal compliance program. As a regulated investment bank, its internal controls program is required by law to be much more comprehensive than a typical public company. Arguably the first successful public FCPA "rogue employee/company victim" defense.

In April 2012, Garth Peterson, a former managing director for Morgan Stanley's Real Estate Group in the People's Republic of China, pleaded guilty in the Eastern District of New York to a one-count criminal information charging him with conspiring to evade internal accounting controls that Morgan Stanley was required to maintain under the Foreign Corrupt Practices Act (FCPA). Signally, his employer Morgan Stanley was not charged by either the DOJ or the SEC.

According to court documents, Morgan Stanley maintained a system of internal controls meant to ensure accountability for its assets and to prevent employees from offering, promising, or paying anything of value to foreign government officials. Morgan Stanley's internal policies, which were updated regularly to reflect regulatory developments and specific risks, prohibited bribery and addressed corruption risks associated with the giving of gifts, business entertainment, travel, lodging, meals, charitable contributions, and employment. Morgan Stanley frequently trained its employees on its internal policies, the FCPA, and other anticorruption laws. Between 2002 and 2008, Morgan Stanley trained various groups of Asia-based personnel on anticorruption policies 54 times. During the same period, Morgan Stanley trained Peterson on the FCPA seven times and reminded him to comply with the FCPA at least 35 times. Morgan Stanley's compliance personnel regularly monitored transactions, randomly audited particular employees, transactions, and business units, and tested to identify illicit payments. Moreover, Morgan Stanley conducted extensive due diligence on all new business partners and imposed stringent controls on payments made to business partners.

According to court documents, Peterson conspired with others to circumvent Morgan Stanley's internal controls in order to transfer a multimillion-dollar ownership interest in a Shanghai building to himself and a Chinese public official with whom he had a personal friendship. The corruption scheme began when Peterson encouraged Morgan Stanley to sell an interest in a Shanghai real estate deal to Shanghai Yongye Enterprise (Group) Co. Ltd., a state-owned and state-controlled entity through which Shanghai's Luwan District managed its own property and facilitated outside investment in the district. Peterson falsely represented to others within Morgan Stanley that Yongye was purchasing the real estate interest, when in fact Peterson knew the interest would be conveyed to a shell company controlled by him, a Chinese public official associated with Yongye and a Canadian attorney. After Peterson and his coconspirators falsely represented to Morgan Stanley that Yongye owned the shell company, Morgan Stanley sold the real estate interest in 2006 to the shell company at a discount to the interest's actual 2006 market value. As a result, the conspirators realized an immediate paper profit of more than $2.5 million. After the sale, Peterson and his coconspirators continued to claim falsely that Yongye owned the shell company, which in reality they owned. In the years since Peterson and his coconspirators gained control of the real estate interest, they periodically accepted equity distributions and the real estate interest has appreciated in value.

In 2012, Peterson was sentenced to nine months in jail despite the government's request for a five- to six-year sentence. After considering all the available facts and circumstances, including that Morgan Stanley constructed and maintained a system of internal controls, which provided reasonable assurances that its employees were not bribing government officials, the DOJ declined to bring any enforcement action against Morgan Stanley related to Peterson's conduct. The company voluntarily disclosed this matter and cooperated throughout the DOJ's investigation. On the same day, the SEC announced civil charges and a settlement with Peterson.

The DOJ is likely to cite the *Peterson* case as an example of awarding a declination to a company that has a strong compliance program in place. However, this case involved the highly regulated financial service industry where institutions must have far more internal controls than most public companies. It also involved an officer who secretly victimized his employer in a $1.8 million fraud. Whether companies in unregulated industries that have compliance programs that are far less sophisticated and training that is much less frequent will obtain declinations remains to be seen. Still, Peterson holds up clear hope for companies that are in large part a victim of a rogue officer or employee, and it serves as a continuing lesson that all companies are wise to regularly review and enhance their compliance efforts.

CJ.   *United States v. Data Systems & Solutions LLC*[410]

▶ **Misconduct Category:**	Funneling of bribes through subcontractors in the United States and Lithuania to secure contracts to perform nuclear power plant services
▶ **Country:**	Lithuania
▶ **Foreign Government Officials:**	Lithuanian nuclear power plant official

▶ **Improper Payment Dollar Value:**   Unspecified

▶ **Penalty:** $8.82 million

▶ **Other:**   DPA; compliance self-assessment requirement

In June 2012, Data Systems & Solutions LLC (DS&S), a company based in Reston, Virginia, that provides design, installation, maintenance, and other services at nuclear and fossil fuel power plants, agreed to pay an $8.82 million criminal penalty to resolve FCPA violations. The DOJ filed a two-count criminal information in the Eastern District of Virginia charging DS&S with conspiring to violate, and violating, the FCPA's antibribery provisions.

According to court documents, DS&S paid bribes to officials employed by the Ignalina Nuclear Power Plant, a state-owned nuclear power plant in Lithuania, to secure contracts to perform services for the plant. To disguise the scheme, the bribes were funneled through several subcontractors located in the United States and abroad. The subcontractors, in turn, made repeated payments to high-level officials at Ignalina via check or wire transfer.

The DOJ also filed a DPA with DS&S. Under the terms of the agreement, the DOJ will defer prosecution of DS&S for two years. In addition to the monetary penalty, DS&S agreed to cooperate, to report periodically to the DOJ concerning DS&S's compliance efforts, and to continue to implement an enhanced compliance program and internal controls designed to prevent and detect FCPA violations. If DS&S abides by the terms of the DPA, the DOJ will dismiss the criminal information when the three-year term expires.

The DPA acknowledged DS&S's extraordinary cooperation, including conducting an extensive, thorough, and swift internal investigation; providing to the department extensive information and evidence; and responding promptly and fully with the government. In addition, DS&S engaged in extensive remediation, including terminating the officers and employees responsible for the corrupt payments; instituting a more rigorous compliance program; enhancing its due diligence protocol for third-party agents and subcontractors; strengthening its ethics policies; providing FCPA training for all agents and subcontractors; and establishing heightened review of most foreign transactions.

CK.   U.S. DOJ–NORDAM Group Inc. Agreement[411]

▶ **Misconduct Category:**   Sales representation agreements with fictitious entities to secure aircraft maintenance, repair, and overhaul service contracts

▶ **Country:**   China

▶ **Foreign Government Officials:**   Employees of state-owned airlines

▶ **Improper Payment Dollar Value:** $1.5 million

▶ **Penalty:** $2 million

▶ **Other:**	Voluntary disclosure; NPA; inability to pay and continued viability of the company a factor in lesser monetary penalty.[412] E-mail: "On this deal, we also need to cover our friends inside"; compliance self-assessment requirement

In July 2012, the NORDAM Group Inc. (NORDAM), a provider of aircraft maintenance, repair, and overhaul (MRO) services based in Tulsa, Oklahoma, entered into an NPA with the DOJ to pay a $2 million penalty to resolve violations of the FCPA. According to the agreement, NORDAM, its subsidiaries, and affiliates paid bribes to employees of airlines created, controlled, and exclusively owned by the People's Republic of China in order to secure contracts to perform MRO services for those airlines. The bribes, which were referred to internally as "commissions" and "facilitator fines," were paid both directly and indirectly to the airline employees who were referred to internally as "internal guys," "internal ghosts," or "our friends inside." In an effort to disguise the bribes, three employees of NORDAM's affiliate entered into sales representation agreements with fictitious entities and then used the money paid by NORDAM to those entities to pay bribes to the airline employees. In all, NORDAM, its wholly owned subsidiary Nordam Singapore Pte Ltd., and an affiliate, World Aviation Associates Pte Ltd., paid as high as $1.5 million in bribes to secure roughly $2.48 million in profits from state-owned and state-controlled customers in China. In addition to the monetary penalty, NORDAM agreed to cooperate with the DOJ for the three-year term of the agreement, to report periodically to the DOJ concerning NORDAM's compliance efforts, and to continue to implement an enhanced compliance program and internal controls designed to prevent and detect FCPA violations.

The DOJ entered into an NPA with NORDAM as a result of NORDAM's timely, voluntary, and complete disclosure of the conduct; its cooperation with the DOJ; and its remedial efforts. In addition, the NPA recognized that a fine below the standard range under the U.S. Sentencing Guidelines was appropriate because NORDAM fully demonstrated to the DOJ, and an independent accounting expert retained by the DOJ verified, that a fine exceeding $2 million would substantially jeopardize the company's continued viability.

CL.   *United States v. Orthofix International, N.V.;*[413]
       SEC v. Orthofix International N.V.[414]

▶ **Misconduct Category:**	Bribes in form of cash, laptop computers, televisions, and appliances to obtain medical device sales contracts
▶ **Country:**	Mexico
▶ **Foreign Government Officials:**	Officials at Instituto Mexicano del Seguno Social (the Mexican social security administration), and administrative and purchasing directors of state-owned or controlled hospitals

▶ **Improper Payment Dollar Value:** $300,000

▶ **Penalty:** $7.4 million ($5.2 million in SEC disgorgement: $4.98 million disgorgement and $242,000 in prejudgment interest; and DOJ: $2.2 million criminal penalty)

▶ **Other:**   DPA; lax oversight; bribes referred to as "chocolates"; annual reporting by Orthofix chief compliance officer to DOJ; Orthofix criticized for failing to translate compliance materials; compliance monitoring and self-assessment

In July 2012, Orthofix International, a Texas-based medical device company, entered into a three-year DPA with the DOJ, filed in the Eastern District of Texas, and agreed to pay a $2.22 million criminal penalty. Promeca S.A. de C.V. (Promeca) headquartered in Mexico City, was an indirectly wholly owned subsidiary of Orthofix N.V. that distributed Orthofix N.V.'s medical nails and fixators in Mexico. From 2003 to March 2010, with the knowledge of one senior Orthofix executive, Promeca and its employees paid $300,000 to Mexican officials in return for agreements with the Instituto Mexicano del Seguro Social (IMSS), the social security administration of Mexico, and its hospitals to purchase millions of dollars in Orthofix products. Orthofix N.V. and Orthofix Inc. personnel based in the United States oversaw Promeca's activities, reviewed and approved Promeca's annual budgets, and had the authority to hire and fire Promeca's officers. Promeca personnel colloquially referred to the illicit payments as "chocolates," a term commonly understood within Promeca and by the Orthofix executive to describe a supplier's improper payments to purchasers of medical supplies and devices in exchange for an agreement to buy the supplier's goods.

In 2003, a Promeca executive won the right to sell Orthofix N.V. products to state-owned or controlled hospitals by agreeing to pay to Mexican hospital deputy administrator and purchasing director a percentage of collected sales revenue generated through sales to the hospitals. To implement this agreement, the Promeca executive periodically reviewed a report of sales revenue collected from the hospitals. He then submitted requests for expense advancements payable to himself, cashed the resulting checks with the assistance of Promeca's office messenger, and delivered the cash to another Promeca executive. From 2003 until 2006, the other Promeca executive and additional Promeca employees delivered to the deputy administrator cash payments equal to as much as 10 percent of Promeca's collected sales to one hospital and for an additional year cash payments to a purchasing director equal to as much as 6 percent of Promeca's collected sales to the hospital. From 2003 until 2007, another Promeca executive and additional Promeca employees delivered to another purchasing director cash payments equal to as much as 5 percent of Promeca's collected sales to a second hospital. Beginning in July 2007 Promeca stopped making cash payments to the second purchasing director and instead leased a vehicle for him to drive. This government official drove the leased car for nearly three years.

In 2008, IMSS began holding national tenders for medical device contracts with hospitals that IMSS owned and controlled. To obtain contracts under the national tenders in or around 2008 and 2009, a Promeca executive agreed to pay certain IMSS officials a percentage of Promeca's sales revenue collected under the contracts that IMSS awarded to Promeca. To accomplish this agreement, a Promeca executive regularly reported to IMSS officials the amount of collected sales revenue from the national tender contracts. IMSS officials then used fictitious companies to issue to Promeca invoices for medical equipment or training in an amount equal to the payments due to the IMSS officials plus a value-added tax (VAT) to make the invoices appear to be legitimate. Promeca then paid the invoiced amounts to the front companies incorporated by the IMSS officials. Promeca recorded the bribe-related expenses on its books and records as "promotional expenses," payments for medical equipment, and training-related expenses, none of which reflected the true purpose for which the expenditures were made. Promeca consistently overspent in these categories the budget that it had communicated to Orthofix N.V. and Orthofix Inc.

In July 2012, the SEC charged the company with violating the FCPA for the same conduct. The SEC alleged that the "chocolates" came in the form of cash, laptop computers, televisions, and appliances that were provided directly to Mexican government officials or indirectly through front companies that the officials owned. It further alleged the bribery scheme lasted for several years and yielded nearly $5 million in illegal profits for the Orthofix subsidiary. Orthofix agreed to pay a total of $5.2 million to settle the SEC's charges: $4,983,644 in disgorgement and more than $242,000 in prejudgment interest. It also agreed to certain undertakings, including monitoring its FCPA compliance program and reporting back to the SEC for a two-year period.

According to the SEC's complaint also filed in the U.S. District Court for the Eastern District of Texas, Promeca falsely recorded the bribes as cash advances and falsified its invoices to support the expenditures, describing them as, for example, meals and new automobile tires. Later, when the bribes become much larger, Promeca falsely recorded them as promotional and training costs. Because of the bribery scheme, Promeca's training and promotional expenses were significantly over budget. Orthofix did launch an inquiry into these expenses, but did very little to investigate or diminish the excessive spending. Later, upon discovery of the bribe payments through a Promeca executive, Orthofix immediately self-reported the matter to the SEC and implemented significant remedial measures. The company terminated the Promeca executives who orchestrated the bribery scheme. Orthofix was criticized for distributing compliance materials but neglecting to have them translated into Spanish. Under the DPA, Orthofix's chief compliance officer must report to the DOJ annually.

CM.   *United States v. Pfizer H.C.P. Corp.;*[415] *SEC v. Pfizer Inc.*[416]

| ▶ **Misconduct Category:** | Sham consulting contracts, exclusive distributorship and improper travel and cash payments to influence approval of registrations of Pfizer products and the award of pharmaceutical tenders and the level of sales of Pfizer products to state-owned hospitals |

▶ **Countries:**   Bulgaria, Croatia, Kazakhstan, and Russia

▶ **Foreign Government Officials:**   Hospital administrators, publicly employed
                                          regulators, purchase committee members, and
                                          public healthcare professionals

▶ **Improper Payment Dollar Value:**   In excess of $2 million

▶ **Penalty:** $60 million ($15 million penalty; $45 million
                                          disgorgement of profit and prejudgment
                                          interest

▶ **Other:**   Voluntary disclosure; DPA; DOJ elected not
                                          to pursue preacquisition improper payment
                                          conduct of Wyeth; compliance self-assessment

In August 2012, Pfizer H.C.P. Corporation, an indirect wholly owned subsidiary of
Pfizer Inc., agreed to pay a $15 million penalty to resolve an investigation of FCPA
violations under a DPA.[417] In a related matter, Pfizer Inc., a global pharmaceutical,
animal health, and consumer product company headquartered in New York City,
and Wyeth LLC reached settlements with the SEC under which Pfizer Inc. agreed
to pay more than $26.3 million in disgorgement of profits, including prejudgment
interest, to resolve concerns involving the conduct of its subsidiaries. Wyeth, which
had been acquired by Pfizer Inc. in 2009, agreed to pay $18.8 million in disgorge-
ment of profits, including prejudgment interest, to resolve concerns involving the
conduct of Wyeth subsidiaries.

As part of the resolution, the DOJ filed a two-count criminal information
charging Pfizer H.C.P. with conspiracy and violations of the FCPA in connection with improper payments made to government officials, including publicly employed regulators and healthcare professionals in Bulgaria, Croatia,
Kazakhstan, and Russia. Both the information and the DPA were filed in the
U.S. District Court in the District of Columbia. According to court documents,
Pfizer H.C.P. made a broad range of improper payments to numerous government officials in Bulgaria, Croatia, Kazakhstan, and Russia—including hospital
administrators, members of regulatory and purchasing committees, and other
healthcare professionals—and sought to improperly influence government decisions in these countries regarding the approval and registration of Pfizer Inc.
products, the award of pharmaceutical tenders, and the level of sales of Pfizer Inc.
products. According to court documents, Pfizer H.C.P. used numerous mechanisms to improperly influence government officials, including sham consulting
contracts, an exclusive distributorship, and improper travel and cash payments.
Pfizer H.C.P. admitted that between 1997 and 2006, it paid more than $2 million
of bribes to government officials in Bulgaria, Croatia, Kazakhstan, and Russia.
Pfizer H.C.P. also admitted that it made more than $7 million in profits as a
result of the bribes.

The DPA recognized the timely voluntary disclosure by Pfizer H.C.P.'s parent company, Pfizer Inc.; the thorough and wide-reaching self-investigation of
the underlying and related conduct; the significant cooperation provided by the
company to the DOJ and the SEC; and the early and extensive remedial efforts
and the substantial and continuing improvements Pfizer Inc. has made to its

global anticorruption compliance procedures. Pfizer H.C.P. received a reduction in its penalty as a result of Pfizer Inc.'s cooperation in the ongoing investigation of other companies and individuals. In addition to the $15 million penalty, the agreement required Pfizer Inc. to continue to implement rigorous internal controls and to cooperate fully with the DOJ. Due to Pfizer Inc.'s extensive remediation and improvement of its compliance systems and internal controls, as well as the enhanced compliance undertakings included in the agreement, Pfizer H.C.P. was not required to retain a corporate monitor, but Pfizer Inc. must periodically report to the DOJ on implementation of its remediation and enhanced compliance efforts for the duration of the agreement.

In the 18 months following its acquisition of Wyeth, Pfizer Inc., in consultation with the DOJ, conducted a due diligence and investigative review of the Wyeth business operations and integrated Pfizer Inc.'s internal controls system into the former Wyeth business entities. The DOJ considered these extensive efforts and the SEC resolution in its determination not to pursue a criminal resolution for the preacquisition conduct of Wyeth subsidiaries.

CN.   U.S. DOJ–Tyco International Ltd. Agreement;[418] *United States v. Tyco Valves & Controls Middle East*;[419] *SEC v. Tyco International Ltd.*[420]

▶ **Misconduct Category:**   Improper "sham" commissions to sales agents for the purpose of making payments to employees of government customers in order to obtain oil and gas company contracts of SOE; technical consultant; cash or gifts to officials of design institutes in China; misuse of distributors; improper entertainment; trips; forged seals in China; falsification of travel expenses

▶ **Countries:**   China, Congo, Croatia, Egypt, France, Germany, India, Libya, Madagascar, Malaysia, Mauritania, Niger, Poland, Saudi Arabia, Serbia, Syria, Thailand, Turkey, and the United Arab Emirates

▶ **Foreign Government Officials:**   Officials of Saudi Aramco state-owned and controlled oil and gas company; Ministry of Public Security (China); officials of design institutes in China; employees of government customers; a Thai consultant who was an intermediary to government officials; family members of public healthcare professionals; public healthcare officials; and public doctors

▶ **Improper Payment Dollar Value:**   Substantially in excess of $472,222

▶ **Penalty:**   More than $26 million ($13.68 million to DOJ as part of NPA; and SEC $10.5 million in disgorgement plus $2.5 million in prejudgment interest)

▶ **Other:**   NPA for parent Tyco, criminal plea to
                                conspiracy to violate the FCPA for Tyco Valves
                                & Controls Middle East Inc. subsidiary;
                                Tyco International Ltd.'s violations of 2006
                                Southern District of New York consent decree
                                and injunction; review of 454 entities in 50
                                countries and quarterly ethics training of 4,000
                                Tyco middle managers; creation of a corporate
                                ombudsman's office; termination of over 90
                                employees, including supervisors, because of
                                FCPA compliance concerns; exit from business
                                operations in high-risk areas; e-mail: "Hell,
                                everyone knows you have to bribe somebody
                                to do business in Turkey. Nevertheless, I'll play
                                it dumb if [a subsidiary's agent] should call";
                                compliance self-assessment

▶ **Related Matters:**   *SEC v. Tyco International Ltd.* (2006)[421]

In September 2012, Tyco International Ltd. (Tyco)—together with subsidiary Tyco Valves & Controls Middle East Inc., which pleaded guilty to a criminal charge for conspiring to violate the FCPA—agreed to pay more than $26 million to resolve the conspiracy charge with the DOJ and charges with the SEC. As part of the more than $26 million, Tyco—a company based in Switzerland that manufactures and sells products related to security, fire protection, and energy—agreed to pay to the DOJ a $13.68 million penalty for falsifying books and records in connection with payments by its subsidiaries to government officials in various countries in order to obtain and retain business.

Tyco Valves & Controls Middle East Inc. (TVC ME)—an indirect, wholly owned subsidiary of Tyco that sold and marketed valves and other industrial equipment throughout the Middle East for the oil, gas, petrochemical, commercial construction, water treatment, and desalination industries—pleaded guilty to conspiring to violate the antibribery provisions of the FCPA. According to the criminal information to which TVC ME pleaded guilty, the subsidiary paid bribes to officials employed by Saudi Aramco, an oil and gas company controlled and managed by the government of the Kingdom of Saudi Arabia, in order to obtain contracts with Saudi Aramco. The district court sentenced TVC ME to pay a $2.1 million fine, which was included as part of the $13.68 million penalty.

As part of the settlement, the DOJ entered into an NPA with the parent Tyco International Ltd. According to the NPA, a number of Tyco's subsidiaries made payments, both directly and indirectly, to government officials in order to obtain and retain business with private and state-owned entities, and falsely described the payments in Tyco's corporate books, records, and accounts as legitimate charges. From 1999 to 2009, Tyco knowingly conspired to falsify its books and records in connection with these payments. In addition to the monetary penalty, Tyco and TVC ME also agreed to cooperate with the DOJ, to report periodically to the DOJ concerning the companies' compliance efforts, and to continue to implement an enhanced compliance program and internal controls designed to prevent and detect FCPA violations.

In the NPA, the DOJ acknowledged Tyco's timely, voluntary, and complete disclosure; its cooperation, including a global internal investigation concerning bribery and related misconduct; and its extensive remediation. That remediation included the implementation of an enhanced compliance program, the termination of employees responsible for the improper payments and falsification of books and records, the severing of contracts with the responsible third-party agents, and the closing of subsidiaries due to compliance failures.

In the parallel civil proceedings, Tyco consented with the SEC to a proposed final judgment that ordered it to pay $10,564,992 in disgorgement and $2,566,517 in prejudgment interest—which, together with the DOJ penalty, totals more than $26 million. Most of the SEC charges relate to Tyco's violations of a 2006 injunction. Specifically, in April 2006, the SEC filed a settled accounting fraud, disclosure, and FCPA injunctive action against Tyco, pursuant to which the parent company consented to entry of a final judgment enjoining it from violations of the antifraud, periodic reporting, books-and-records, internal controls, proxy disclosure, and antibribery provisions of the federal securities laws and ordering it to pay $1 in disgorgement and a $50 million civil penalty.[422] The U.S. District Court for the Southern District of New York entered the settled final judgment against Tyco on May 1, 2006. At the time of this settlement, Tyco had already committed to and commenced a review of its FCPA compliance and a global, comprehensive internal investigation of possible additional FCPA violations. As a result of that review and investigation, certain FCPA violations came to light for which the misconduct occurred, or the benefit to Tyco continued, after the 2006 injunction. Those FCPA violations are alleged in the September 2012 SEC complaint.

As its global review and investigation progressed, Tyco voluntarily disclosed this conduct to the SEC and took significant, broad-spectrum remedial measures. Those remedial measures include the initial FCPA review of every Tyco legal operating entity, ultimately including 454 entities in 50 separate countries; active monitoring and evaluation of all of Tyco's agents and other relevant third-party relationships; quarterly ethics and compliance training by over 4,000 middle managers; FCPA-focused on-site reviews of higher risk entities; creation of a corporate ombudsman's office and numerous segment-specific compliance counsel positions; exit from several business operations in high-risk areas; and the termination of over 90 employees, including supervisors, because of FCPA-compliance concerns.

The FCPA misconduct reported by Tyco that led to the 2012 enforcement action showed that Tyco's books and records were misstated as a result of at least 12 different, postinjunction illicit payment schemes occurring at Tyco subsidiaries across the globe. The schemes frequently entailed illicit payments to foreign officials that were inaccurately recorded so as to conceal the nature of the payments. Those inaccurate entries were incorporated into Tyco's books and records.[423] Tyco also failed to devise and maintain internal controls sufficient to provide reasonable assurances that all transactions were properly recorded in the company's books, records, and accounts. As reflected in the 2012 SEC complaint, numerous Tyco subsidiaries engaged in violative conduct, the conduct was carried out by several different methods, and the conduct occurred over a lengthy period of time and continued even after the 2006 injunction.

1. Turkey

TE M/A-COM, Inc. (M/A-COM) was an indirect, wholly owned subsidiary of Tyco incorporated in Florida with its principal place of business in Lowell, Massachusetts. M/A-COM operated within the Electronics segment of Tyco until the split of Tyco and Tyco Electronics Ltd. (TE) in or about June 2007, when it became a unit of TE. TE divested all of the assets of M/A-COM in or about 2008. MIA-COM, through its SIGINT Products business unit, retained a New York City–based sales agent who made illicit payments in connection with a September 2006 sale of microwave equipment to an instrumentality of the Turkish government. The agent, who was contractually designated as M/A-COM's sales agent for Turkey, sold the equipment to the entity controlled by Turkey at a markup over the M/A-COM invoice price. The microwave receivers were shipped from Hunt Valley, Maryland to the agent in New York, who then shipped them to Turkey via New York, New York. Employees of M/A-COM were aware that the agent was paying foreign government customers to obtain orders. One internal e-mail stated, "Hell, everyone knows you have to bribe somebody to do business in Turkey. Nevertheless, I'll play it dumb if [M/A-COM's agent] should call."

Tyco exerted control over M/A-COM in part by utilizing dual roles for its officers. At the time of the September 2006 transaction, four high-level Tyco officers were also officers of M/A-COM, including one who was M/A-COM's president. Additionally, one of those Tyco officers served as one of five members of M/A-COM's board of directors. While there is no indication that any of these individuals knew of the illegal conduct described herein, through the corporate structure used to hold M/A-COM and through the dual roles of these officers, Tyco controlled M/A-COM. As a result, M/A-COM was Tyco's agent for purposes of the September 2006 transaction, and the transaction was squarely within the scope of M/A-COM's agency. The benefit obtained by Tyco as a result of the September 2006 deal was $44,513.

2. China

Tyco Thermal Controls (Huzhou) Co., Ltd. (TTC Huzhou) and Tyco Thermal Controls (Shanghai) Co., Ltd. TIC Shanghai) were indirect, wholly owned subsidiaries of Tyco incorporated in China. TIC Huzhou was formed in or about October 2003, when Tyco acquired a company that manufactured electrical cables. Because TIC Huzhou did not have its own sales or marketing staff, TIC Shanghai was largely responsible for sales of TTC Huzhou's products. (Collectively, these entities are referred to as TIC China.) In or about June 2005, TTC China signed a contract with the Chinese Ministry of Public Security for $770,000, but reportedly paid approximately $3,700 to the "site project team" of a state-owned corporation to obtain the contract. This amount was improperly recorded in TTC China's books and records as a commission, when in fact part of that amount was passed along to the end user. TTC China's financial results were incorporated in Tyco's publicly filed financial statements. Tyco' s benefit as a result of these illicit payments was $192,500.

3. Germany

Tyco Waterworks Deutschland GmbH (TWW Germany) was an indirect, wholly owned subsidiary of Tyco incorporated in Germany. TWW Germany manufactured, marketed, and sold industrial valves for the water, gas, sewage, chemical, and processing industries. These products were sold worldwide through a network of sales representatives. Customers included government entities, such as municipal waterworks, and private contractors. Tyco divested itself of TWW Germany in or about 2010. TWW Germany and/or its agents failed to enact and/or follow policies governing the retention and payment of third-party agents/distributors.

TWW Germany and/or its agents paid or promised to pay third parties to secure contracts or avoid penalties or fines in several countries: the People's Republic of China, Croatia, India, Libya, Saudi Arabia, Serbia, Syria, and the United Arab Emirates. The payments were ostensibly booked as commissions and in a manner that did not reflect the ultimate recipients of the funds. The payments related to projects ongoing from October 2004 to 2009. In fact the payments were not commissions, but were used to pay employees of government customers and for other purposes. These entries were consolidated within Tyco and, as a result, caused Tyco's books and records to be misstated. Tyco's benefit as a result of these illicit payments was $4,684,966.

4. *France, Madagascar, Mauritania, Niger, and The Congo*

Tyco Fire & Integrated Solutions France (TFIS France) was an indirect, wholly owned subsidiary of Tyco that was incorporated in France. TFIS France sold fire extinguishing and detection products to residential customers and commercial businesses. TFIS France and/or its agents made payments to individuals from 2005 to 2009 for "business introduction services." One of the individuals receiving payments was a security officer at a government-owned mining company in Mauritania, and a substantial amount of the payments made before 2007 ultimately were deposited in that government official's personal bank account in France. These payments were not supported by written contracts or invoices and were not accurately recorded in TFIS France's books and records. In addition, TFIS France and/or its agents paid sham "commissions" to approximately 12 other intermediaries in four countries (Mauritania, the Congo, Niger, and Madagascar). The inaccurate entries were incorporated into Tyco' s books and records. Tyco's benefit as a result of these illicit payments was $1,256,389.

5. *HK and China*

Tyco Flow Control Hong Kong Limited (TFC HK) and Beijing Valve Co. Ltd. (Keystone) were indirect, wholly owned subsidiaries of Tyco that were incorporated under the laws of Hong Kong and China, respectively. TFC HK and Keystone sold valves and controls products to commercial and government customers through direct sales and local distributors. TFC HK and Keystone failed to follow Tyco's internal controls policies and procedures governing the retention and payment of third-party agents/distributors. TFC HK and Keystone also failed to maintain an appropriate system to ensure accuracy in its books and records regarding payments to sales agents and distributors. Between 2005 and August 2006, THC HK and Keystone paid approximately $246,000 to an agent in connection with sales to a large, government-owned Chinese petrochemical company, although Tyco is unable to ascertain what, if any, legitimate services were performed by the agent. As a result,

Tyco's books and records were misstated. Tyco's benefit as a result of these illicit payments was $181,504.

TFC HK and Keystone also had other improper arrangements with agents. Approximately $137,000 was paid to agencies owned by approximately eight Keystone sales employees in 2005 and 2006, and those employees in turn transferred some portion of that amount in cash or gifts to government officials, including design institutes, in the People's Republic of China. The amounts in question were incorrectly recorded as proper commissions to hide the fact that the payments were made to companies owned by Keystone employees. As a result, Tyco's books and records were misstated. Tyco's benefit as a result of these illicit payments was $196,584.

6. *Thailand*

ADT Sensormatic Thailand Ltd. (ADT Thailand) was an indirect, wholly owned subsidiary of Tyco that was incorporated in Thailand. ADT Thailand designed, installed, and serviced mechanical, electrical, fire protection, security, and traffic systems in Southeast Asia. From in or about 2000 to in or about 2006, ADT Thailand maintained inaccurate books and records in connection with multiple transactions and failed to implement policies to ensure accurate record-keeping.

In connection with a contract to install a CCTV system in the Thai Parliament House in 2006, ADT Thailand paid over $50,000 to a Thai entity that acted as a consultant. The invoice related to this payment refers to "renovation work," but Tyco is unable to ascertain what, if any, work was done. As a result, Tyco's books and records were misstated. Tyco's benefit as a result of these illicit payments was $104,117.

7. *Malaysia*

Tyco Fire, Security & Services Malaysia SDN BHD (TFS Malaysia) was an indirect, wholly owned subsidiary of Tyco that was incorporated in Malaysia. TFS Malaysia designed, installed, serviced, and commissioned mechanical, electrical, fire protection, security, and traffic systems in Malaysia. From 2000 to 2007, TFS Malaysia used intermediaries to pay the employees of its customers when bidding on contracts. Payments were made to approximately 26 employees of customers, and one of those payees was an employee of a government-controlled entity. TFS Malaysia inaccurately described these expenses as "commissions" and failed to maintain policies sufficient to prohibit such payments. As a result, Tyco's books and records were misstated. Tyco's benefit as a result of these illicit payments was $45,972.

8. *Egypt*

From in or about 2004 to in or about 2008, an Egyptian agent of TFIS UK wired approximately $282,022 to a former employee's personal bank account with the understanding that the money would be used in connection with entertainment expenses for representatives of a company majority-owned by the Egyptian government. A portion of the funds was used to pay for lodging, meals, transportation, spending money, and entertainment expenses for that company's officials on two trips to the United Kingdom in 2005 and 2006 and two trips to the United States in 2007 and 2008. TFIS UK made payments pursuant to inflated invoices submitted by the company's Egyptian agent, who wired funds to the former employees to be used to entertain foreign officials.

TFIS UK's books and records did not accurately reflect TFIS UK's understanding that the funds would be used for entertainment of government officials, and TFIS UK did not maintain sufficient internal controls over its payments to agents. As a result, Tyco's books and records were misstated. Tyco's benefit as a result of these illicit payments was $1,589,374.

9. Saudi Arabia

Tyco Healthcare Saudi Arabia (THC Saudi Arabia) was an operational entity within Tyco Healthcare AG, an indirect, wholly owned subsidiary of Tyco that was incorporated in Switzerland. THC Saudi Arabia operated within the Healthcare segment of Tyco until the split of Tyco and Covidien in or about June 2007, when it became a unit of Covidien. Beginning in or about December 2000 and continuing into at least June 2006, THC Saudi Arabia's distributor in Saudi Arabia used a "control account" to make payments at THC Saudi Arabia's direction to doctors and hospital officials in Saudi Arabia, including those employed by agencies or instrumentalities of the Saudi government. The control account was not a bank account, but rather a general ledger account.

While some disbursements from the control account were used for legitimate expenses, several items were booked improperly as "promotional expenses" and "sales development" expenses. As a result, Tyco's books and records were misstated. In connection with the transactions related to these inaccurate books and records, Tyco's benefit was approximately $1,900,600.

10. China (Shanghai)

Tyco Healthcare International Trading (Shanghai) Co., Ltd. (THC China) was an indirect, wholly owned subsidiary of Tyco that was incorporated in China. THC China operated within the Healthcare segment of Tyco until the split of Tyco and Covidien Public Limited Company (Covidien) in or about June 2007, when it became a unit of Covidien. From in or about September 2004 to in or about January 2007, employees of THC China submitted approximately 33 expense claims related to entertainment of public healthcare officials of the People's Republic of China (PRC). THC China then reimbursed those expenses. Some of the expenses were supported by fictitious receipts, including references to a nonexistent company. In connection with the expenses, at least one THC China employee forged receipts and applied a "seal" for a bogus company. Employees forged receipts because the actual expenditures were prohibited under Tyco' s internal guidelines.

From 2001 to 2008, THC China employees submitted false itineraries and other documentation that did not properly identify travel expenses incurred in connection with medical conferences. The inaccurate record-keeping related to payment by THC China for trips or portions of trips for publicly employed doctors in the PRC. As a result, Tyco's books and records were misstated. In connection with the transactions related to these inaccurate books and records, Tyco's benefit was approximately $353,800.

11. Poland

Tyco Healthcare Polska Sp.z.o.o. (THC Polska) was an indirect, wholly owned subsidiary of Tyco that was incorporated in Poland. THC Polska operated within the Healthcare segment of Tyco until the split of Tyco and Covidien in or about June 2007, when it became a unit of Covidien. From in or about January 2005 to in or about December 2007, THC Polska used "service contracts" to hire public healthcare professionals in Poland for various purposes, including conducting training sessions, performing clinical studies, and distributing marketing materials. Approximately five such service contracts involved falsified records and approximately 26 other service contracts involved incomplete and inaccurate records, including some related expenses paid by THC Polska to family members of healthcare professionals. As a result, Tyco's books and records were misstated. In connection with the transactions related to these inaccurate books and records, Tyco's benefit was approximately $14,673.

CO.   *United States v. Kowalewski, Jensen, DuBois & Uhl*

▶ **Misconduct Category:**	Bribes to various government aircraft officials and use of a shell company owned and operated by a BizJet sales manager to pay officials to secure aircraft maintenance, repair, and service contracts
▶ **Countries:**	Brazil, Mexico, and Panama
▶ **Foreign Government Officials:**	Captains and colonels in Mexico Federal Police and Mexican president's air fleet; air services for the governor of the Mexican State of Sinaloa
▶ **Improper Payment Dollar Value:**	$560,000 plus
▶ **Combined Penalties:**	DuBois and Uhl, eight months of house confinement each; Kowalewski, time served and $15,000 fine
▶ **Other:**	USSG § 5K1.1 departure for Uhl and DuBois illustrate substantial benefits of individual cooperation, avoiding sentences of up to five and ten years, respectively, in jail; use of a shell company by Jensen; Jensen is believed to remain abroad.
▶ **Related Matters:**	*United States v. BizJet International Sales & Support Inc.;* Lufthansa Technik AG nonprosecution agreement (NPA)

In April 2013, charges were unsealed against Bernd Kowalewski, the former president and chief executive officer of BizJet; Jald Jensen, the former sales manager at BizJet; Peter DuBois, the former vice president of sales and marketing at BizJet; and Neal Uhl, the former vice president of finance at BizJet. The four former executives of BizJet alleged that the U.S.-based subsidiary of Lufthansa Technik AG, which provides aircraft maintenance, repair, and overhaul (MRO) services, paid bribes to officials employed by the Mexican Policia Federal Preventiva, the Mexican Coordinacion General de Transportes Aereos Presidenciales, the air fleet for the Gobierno del Estado de Sinaloa in Mexico, the air fleet for the Estado De Roraima in Brazil, and the Republica de Panama Autoridad Aeronautica Civil in exchange for those officials' assistance in securing contracts for BizJet to perform MRO services.[424]

The charges alleged that the defendants, in many instances, paid bribes directly to foreign officials in Mexico, Panama, and Brazil for assistance in securing contracts. In other instances, the defendants allegedly funneled bribes through a shell company owned and operated by Jensen. The shell company, Avionica International & Associates Inc., allegedly operated under the pretense of providing aircraft maintenance brokerage services but in reality laundered money related to BizJet's bribery scheme. Avionica was located at Jensen's personal residence in Van Nuys, California, and Jensen was the only officer, director, and employee.

In March 2012, BizJet entered into a three-year DPA with the DOJ and agreed to an $11.8 million monetary penalty to resolve charges related to the corrupt conduct. That agreement acknowledged BizJet's voluntary disclosure, extraordinary cooperation, and extensive remediation in this case. In 2012, Lufthansa Technik received an NPA due to its voluntary disclosure and extraordinary cooperation.

DuBois and Uhl pled guilty on January 5, 2012, to criminal informations, and their pleas were unsealed in April 2013. DuBois pled guilty to one count of conspiracy to violate the FCPA and one count of violating the FCPA. Uhl pled guilty to one count of conspiracy to violate the FCPA. Both received exceptional cooperation credit and downward departures under section 5K1.1 of the United States Sentencing Guidelines. DuBois's sentence was reduced from a sentencing guidelines range of 108 to 120 months in prison to probation and eight months home detention based on his cooperation in the government's investigation. Uhl's sentence was similarly reduced for cooperation from a guidelines range of 60 months in prison to probation and eight months' home detention.

Kowalewski and Jensen were charged by an indictment filed in U.S. District Court for the Northern District of Oklahoma on January 5, 2012, with conspiring to violate the FCPA and to launder money, as well as substantive charges of violating the FCPA and money laundering. In March 2014, Kowalewski waived extradition from Amsterdam in March 2014, returned to the United States, and pled guilty in the Northern District of Oklahoma to the FCPA conspiracy charge in July 2014. On November 18, 2014, Kowalewski was sentenced to time served and fined $15,000. Jensen is believed to remain abroad.

CP.   *United States v. Parker Drilling Co.;*[425] *SEC v. Parker Drilling Co.*[426]

▶ **Misconduct Category:**	Use of intermediary to make payments to Nigerian officials to influence decisions involving adherence to local customs and tax laws, including "entertainment"
▶ **Countries:**	Nigeria
▶ **Foreign Government Officials:**	Customs officials

▶ **Improper Payment Dollar Value:**	Less than $1.25 million paid to agent
▶ **Combined Penalties:**	$15.85 million ($11.76 million DOJ penalty and SEC $4.09 million disgorgement and prejudgment interest)
▶ **Other:**	Three-year deferred prosecution agreement; entertainment of Nigerian government officials; inadequate due diligence and poor agency contract
▶ **Related Matters:**	Noble, *United States v. Pride International, United States v. Shell Nigeria Exploration & Production Co., United States v. Tidewater; United States v. Transocean; SEC v. GlobalSantaFe Corp.;* Panalpina and these companies agreed to pay combined DOJ criminal penalties and SEC disgorgement of profit amounts of over $236 million.

In April 2013, Parker Drilling Company, a publicly listed drilling services company, headquartered in Houston, agreed to pay an $11.76 million penalty to resolve charges related to the FCPA for authorizing payment to an intermediary, knowing that the payment would be used to corruptly influence the decisions of a Nigerian government panel reviewing Parker Drilling's adherence to Nigerian customs and tax laws. The investigation of Parker Drilling stemmed from the DOJ's Panalpina-related investigations, which previously yielded criminal resolutions with Panalpina and five oil and gas service companies and subsidiaries and resulted in more than $156 million in criminal penalties.

The DOJ filed a deferred prosecution agreement and a criminal information against Parker Drilling in U.S. District Court for the Eastern District of Virginia. The one-count information charges Parker Drilling with violating the FCPA's anti-bribery provisions. According to court documents, in 2001 and 2002, Panalpina World Transport (Nigeria) Limited, working on Parker Drilling's behalf, avoided certain costs associated with complying with Nigeria's customs laws by fraudulently claiming that Parker Drilling's rigs had been exported and then reimported into Nigeria. In late 2002, Nigeria formed a government commission, commonly called the Temporary Import (TI) Panel, to examine whether Nigeria's Customs Service had collected certain duties and tariffs that Nigeria was due. In December 2002, the TI Panel commenced proceedings against Parker Drilling. The TI Panel later determined that Parker Drilling had violated Nigeria's customs laws and assessed a $3.8 million fine against Parker Drilling.

According to court documents, rather than pay the assessed fine, Parker Drilling contracted indirectly with an intermediary agent to resolve its customs issues. The agent's résumé represented he had spent around 15 years as "Executive Managing Director" of his own companies and had spent two years before as a mechanical engineer. It did not reflect any past experience working in Nigeria or handling customs issues. Parking Drilling conducted no additional due diligence into the Nigerian agent's qualifications. In January 2004, Parker Drilling entered into an agreement with the Nigerian agent whereby the latter would "act as a consultant to [a law firm] to provide professional assistance resolving these issues in Nigeria." The agent agreement did not specify the amount or basis of calculating the fees and expenses that the agent could charge other than to require an initial retainer of $50,000 and to provide for an unexplained "success fee." The company wired the agent $500,000 as soon as the agent signed the contract. On one occasion, the agent e-mailed outside U.S. counsel, "there is nothing more serious than landing in Nigeria without money to resolve the problems. . . . Therefore, please make sure that you transfer the funds today."[427]

From January to May 2004, Parker Drilling transferred $1.25 million to the agent, who reported spending a portion of the money on various things including entertaining government officials. E-mails in which the agent requested additional money from Parker Drilling referenced the agent's interactions with Nigeria's Ministry of Finance, State Security Service, and a delegation from the Nigerian president's office. Two senior executives within Parker Drilling at the time reviewed and approved the agent's invoices, knowing that the invoices arbitrarily attributed portions of the money that Parker Drilling transferred to the agent to various fees and expenses. The agent succeeded in reducing Parker Drilling's Temporary Import Panel fines from $3.8 million to just $750,000.

Under the terms of the DPA, the DOJ agreed to defer prosecution of Parker Drilling for three years. Parker Drilling agreed, among other things, to implement an enhanced compliance program and internal controls capable of preventing and detecting FCPA violations, to report periodically to the DOJ concerning Parker Drilling's compliance efforts, and to cooperate with the department in ongoing investigations. If Parker Drilling abides by the terms of the DPA, the DOJ will dismiss the criminal information when the three-year term expires.

In agreeing to a DPA, the DOJ took into account a number of factors: Parker Drilling conducted an extensive, multiyear investigation into the charged conduct; engaged in widespread remediation, including ending its business relationships with officers, employees, or agents primarily responsible for the corrupt payments; enhancing scrutiny of high-risk third-party agents and transactions; increasing training and testing requirements; and instituting heightened review of proposals and other transactional documents for all the company's contracts; otherwise significantly enhanced its compliance program and internal controls; and agreed to continue to cooperate with the DOJ in any ongoing investigation of the conduct.

Parker Drilling also reached a settlement of a related civil complaint filed by the SEC charging it with violating the FCPA's antibribery, books-and-records, and internal controls provisions. The SEC alleged that Parker Drilling authorized payments to a Nigerian agent totaling $1.25 million, knowing that the agent intended to use the funds to "entertain" Nigerian officials involved in resolving the company's ongoing customs problems.[428] As part of the SEC settlement, Parker Drilling agreed to pay $3.05 million in disgorgement and $1.04 million in prejudgment interest relating to those violations.

CQ.   DOJ Ralph Lauren Corp. Agreement;[429] SEC Ralph Lauren Corp. Agreement[430]

▶ **Misconduct Category:**	Bribes paid to obtain paperwork and/or the clearance of merchandise and to on occasion avoid inspection entirely
▶ **Countries:**	Argentina
▶ **Foreign Government Officials:**	Customs Officers
▶ **Improper Payment Dollar Value:**	$593,000
▶ **Combined Penalties:**	$1,616,845: $882,000 DOJ penalty; SEC disgorgement $734,846, including $141,845.79 in prejudgment interest
▶ **Other:**	First SEC FCPA nonprosecution agreement (NPA); bribe payments over a four-year period totaled $593,000; 18-element DOJ compliance program; Ralph Lauren ceased operations in Argentina; likely alternative jurisdiction theory, although not expressly stated in NPA

In April 2013, Ralph Lauren Corporation (RLC), a New York-based apparel company, agreed to pay an $882,000 penalty to resolve DOJ allegations that it violated the FCPA by bribing government officials in Argentina to obtain improper customs clearance of merchandise. According to the NPA, the manager of RLC's subsidiary in Argentina bribed customs officials in Argentina over the span of five years to improperly obtain paperwork necessary for goods to clear customs; to permit clearance of items without the necessary paperwork and/or the clearance of prohibited items; and, on occasion, to avoid inspection entirely. RLC's employee disguised the payments by funneling them through a customs clearance agency, which created fake invoices to justify the improper payments. During these five years, RLC did not have an anticorruption program and did not provide any anticorruption training or oversight with respect to its subsidiary in Argentina.[431] The bribe payments and gifts to Argentine officials totaled $593,000 during a four-year period.[432]

In addition to the monetary penalty, RLC agreed to cooperate with the DOJ, to report periodically to the DOJ concerning RLC's compliance efforts, and to continue to implement an enhanced compliance program and internal controls designed to prevent and detect FCPA violations. The DOJ NPA acknowledged RLC's extensive, thorough, and timely cooperation, including self-disclosure of the misconduct, voluntarily making employees available for interviews, making voluntary document disclosures, conducting a worldwide risk assessment, and making multiple presentations to the DOJ on the status and findings of the internal investigation and the risk assessment. In addition, RLC engaged in early and extensive remediation, including conducting extensive FCPA training for employees worldwide; enhancing the company's existing FCPA policy;

implementing an enhanced gift policy and other enhanced compliance, control, and anticorruption policies and procedures; enhancing its due diligence protocol for third-party agents; terminating culpable employees and a third-party agent; instituting a whistleblower hotline; and hiring a designated corporate compliance attorney.

Under the DOJ NPA, RLC agreed to an 18-element corporate compliance program. The elements of that program are in substantially identical form found in the discussion of Avon Products Inc., *infra*.

In a related matter, the SEC announced a nonprosecution agreement with RLC in which RLC agreed to pay $734,846 in disgorgement and prejudgment interest. The SEC NPA is the first that the SEC has entered into involving FCPA misconduct. NPAs are part of the SEC Enforcement Division's Cooperation Initiative, which rewards cooperation in SEC investigations. The SEC credited RLC's cooperation efforts including

- reporting preliminary findings of its internal investigation to the staff within two weeks of discovering the illegal payments and gifts;
- voluntarily and expeditiously producing documents;
- providing English-language translations of documents to the staff;
- summarizing witness interviews that the company's investigators conducted overseas; and
- making overseas witnesses available for staff interviews and bringing witnesses to the United States.

The SEC determined not to charge Ralph Lauren Corporation with violations of the FCPA due to the company's prompt reporting of the violations on its own initiative, the completeness of the information it provided, and its extensive, thorough, and real-time cooperation with the SEC's investigation. Ralph Lauren Corporation's cooperation saved the agency substantial time and resources ordinarily consumed in investigations of comparable conduct.[433]

According to the SEC NPA, the bribes occurred during a period when Ralph Lauren Corporation lacked meaningful anticorruption compliance and control mechanisms over its Argentine subsidiary. The misconduct came to light as a result of the company adopting measures to improve its worldwide internal controls and compliance efforts, including implementation of an FCPA compliance training program in Argentina. Under the SEC NPA, Ralph Lauren Corporation agreed to pay $593,000 in disgorgement and $141,846 in prejudgment interest. The SEC took into account the significant remedial measures undertaken by Ralph Lauren Corporation, including a comprehensive new compliance program throughout its operations. Among Ralph Lauren Corporation's remedial measures were new compliance training, termination of employment and business arrangements with all individuals involved in the wrongdoing, and strengthening its internal controls and its procedures for third-party due diligence. Ralph Lauren Corporation also conducted a risk assessment of its major operations worldwide to identify any other compliance problems. Ralph Lauren Corporation ceased operations in Argentina.

CR. *United States v. Lujan, Hurtado & Clarke;*[434] *United States v. Gonzalez de Hernandez; SEC v. Clarke, Hurtado, Pabon, Rodolfo, Lujan, Chinea & DeMeneses*[435]

▶ **Misconduct Category:**   Bribery scheme with officials of state-owned economic development banks in Venezuela in order to obtain lucrative bond work involving "pay-to-play" arrangements

▶ **Country:**   Venezuela

▶ **Foreign Government Officials:** Officials of state economic development banks

▶ **Improper Payment Dollar Value:** In excess of $1.5 million

▶ **Combined Penalties:**   Awaiting sentencing

▶ **Other:**   Prosecution of large broker-dealer network

In May 2013, Ernesto Lujan, Jose Alejandro Hurtado, and Tomas Alberto Clarke Bethancourt, three employees of Direct Access Partners (DAP), a New York-based U.S. broker-dealer, were charged in New York federal court with conspiring to violate the FCPA, to violate the Travel Act, and to commit money laundering, as well as substantive counts of these offenses. In August 2013, Lujan, Hurtado, and Clarke pled guilty. These charges related to a scheme to bribe foreign official Maria de los Angeles Gonzalez de Hernandez at Banco de Desarrollo Económico y Social de Venezuela (BANDES), a state economic development bank in Venezuela, in exchange for receiving trading business from BANDES. Lujan, Hurtado, and Clarke each also pleaded guilty to an additional charge of conspiring to violate the FCPA in connection with a similar scheme to bribe a foreign official employed by Banfoandes, another state economic development bank in Venezuela, and to conspiring to obstruct an examination by the SEC of the New York-based broker-dealer where all three defendants had worked, to conceal the true facts of the broker-dealer's relationship with BANDES.

Lujan, Hurtado, and Clarke each pleaded guilty to the same six offenses and face a maximum penalty of five years in prison on each count except money laundering, which carries a maximum penalty of 20 years in prison. Lujan, Clarke, and Hurtado await sentencing.

According to the informations filed against Lujan, Hurtado, and Clarke, the criminal complaints previously filed, and statements made during the plea proceedings, Lujan, Clarke, and Hurtado worked or were associated with the broker-dealer, principally through its Miami offices. In 2008, the broker-dealer established a group called the Global Markets Group, which included Lujan, Clarke, and Hurtado, and which offered fixed-income trading services to institutional clients.

One of the broker-dealer's clients was BANDES, which operated under the direction of the Venezuelan Ministry of Finance. The Venezuelan government had a majority ownership interest in BANDES and provided it with substantial funding. Gonzalez was an official at BANDES and oversaw the development bank's overseas trading activity. At her direction, BANDES conducted substantial trading through the broker-dealer. Most of the trades executed by the broker-dealer on behalf of BANDES involved fixed-income investments for which the broker-dealer charged the bank a markup on purchases and a markdown on sales.

The broker-dealer also conducted business with Banfoandes, another state development bank in Venezuela that, along with its 2009 successor Banco Bicentenario, operated under the direction of the Venezuelan Ministry of Finance. Banfoandes acted as a financial agent of the Venezuelan government in order to promote economic and social development by, among other things, offering credit to low-income Venezuelans. The Banfoandes foreign official was responsible for some of Banfoandes's foreign investments.

Court records state that from early 2009 through 2012, Lujan, Clarke, and Hurtado participated in a bribery scheme in which Gonzalez allegedly directed trading business she controlled at BANDES to the broker-dealer, and in return, agents and employees of the broker-dealer split the revenue the broker-dealer generated from this trading business with Gonzalez. During this time period, the broker-dealer generated over $60 million in markups and markdowns from trades with BANDES. Agents and employees of the broker-dealer, including Lujan, Clarke, and Hurtado, devised a split with Gonzalez of the commissions paid by BANDES to the broker-dealer. E-mails, account records and other documents collected from the broker-dealer and other sources reveal that Gonzalez allegedly received a substantial share of the revenue generated by the broker-dealer for BANDES-related trades. Specifically, Gonzalez allegedly received kickbacks and payments from broker-dealer agents and employees that were frequently in six-figure amounts.

To further conceal the scheme, the kickbacks to Gonzalez were often paid using intermediary corporations and offshore accounts that she held in Switzerland, among other places. For instance, Lujan, Clarke, and Hurtado used accounts they controlled in Switzerland to transfer funds to an account Gonzalez allegedly controlled in Switzerland. Additionally, Hurtado and his spouse received substantial compensation from the broker-dealer, portions of which Hurtado transferred to an account allegedly held by Gonzalez in Miami and to an account held by an associate of Gonzalez in Switzerland. Hurtado also sought and allegedly received reimbursement from Gonzalez for the U.S. income taxes he had paid on money that he used to make kickback payments to Gonzalez. Lujan and Clarke also derived substantial profit from their roles in the bribery scheme.

According to court records, beginning in or about November 2010, the SEC commenced a periodic examination of the broker-dealer, and from November 2010 through March 2011 the SEC's examination staff made several visits to the broker-dealer's offices in Manhattan. In early 2011, Lujan, Clarke, and Hurtado discussed their concern that the SEC was examining the broker-dealer's relationship with BANDES and asking questions regarding certain e-mails and other information that the SEC examination staff had discovered. Lujan, Clarke, and Hurtado agreed that they would take steps to conceal the true facts of the broker-dealer's relationship with BANDES, including deleting e-mails. Lujan, Clarke, and Hurtado then, in fact, deleted e-mails. Additionally as part of this effort to obstruct the

SEC examination, Clarke lied to SEC examination staff in response to an interview question about his relationship to an individual who had received purported foreign associate payments relating to BANDES.

In a related scheme, from 2008 through mid-2009, Lujan, Clarke, and Hurtado paid bribes to the Banfoandes foreign official, who, in exchange, directed Banfoandes trading business to the broker-dealer. Gonzalez was charged in a criminal complaint and arrested on May 3, 2013 in connection with the BANDES bribery scheme. In November 2013, Gonzalez pled guilty in the Southern District of New York to conspiracy to violate the Travel Act and to commit money laundering. In December 2014, Chinea and DeMeneses each pled guilty to conspiracy to violate the FCPA and one Travel Act count.

CS.   *United States v. Total S.A.;*[436] *In re* Total S.A.[437]

▶ **Misconduct Category:**	Payments to an intermediary through purported consulting agreements to obtain oil rights in major Iranian oil and gas fields. Unlawful payments falsely described as "business development expenses."
▶ **Country:**	Iran
▶ **Foreign Government Officials:**	Chairman of state-owned and state-controlled engineering company
▶ **Improper Payment Dollar Value:**	$60 million
▶ **Combined Penalties:**	$398.2 million (SEC $153 million in disgorgement and prejudgment interest; and DOJ monetary penalty of $245.2 million.
▶ **Other:**	Three-year deferred prosecution agreement (DPA) and independent corporate compliance consultant requirement. Referral of Total chief executive officer and other individuals to French criminal court for violations of French criminal law. First coordinated effort by U.S. and French law enforcement authorities in corruption area.

In May 2013, Total, S.A., a French oil and gas company that trades on the New York Stock Exchange, agreed to pay a $245.2 million monetary penalty to resolve charges related to violations of the FCPA in connection with illegal payments made through third parties to a government official in Iran to obtain valuable oil and gas concessions. As part of the agreed resolution, the DOJ filed a criminal information in U.S. District Court for the Eastern District of Virginia charging Total with one count of conspiracy to violate the antibribery provisions of the FCPA, one count of violating the internal controls provision of the FCPA, and one count of violating the books-and-records provision of the FCPA. The DOJ and Total agreed to resolve the charges by entering into a deferred prosecution agreement (DPA) for a term of three years. In addition to the monetary penalty, Total also agreed to cooperate with the DOJ and foreign law enforcement to retain an independent corporate compliance monitor for a period of three years and to continue to implement an enhanced compliance program and internal controls designed to prevent and detect FCPA violations.

Simultaneously, the SEC entered into a cease-and-desist order against Total in which the company agreed to pay an additional $153 million in disgorgement and prejudgment interest. Total also agreed with the SEC to comply with certain undertakings regarding its FCPA compliance program, including the retention of a compliance consultant. In addition, French enforcement authorities announced on the same date that they had requested that Total, Total's chairman and chief executive officer, and two additional individuals be referred to the criminal court for violations of French law, including France's foreign bribery law.

According to the DPA, in 1995 Total sought to reenter the Iranian oil and gas market by attempting to obtain a contract with the National Iranian Oil Company (NIOC) to develop the Sirri A and E oil and gas fields. In May 1995, Total entered into negotiations with an Iranian official who served as the chairman of an Iranian state-owned and state-controlled engineering company. Total subsequently entered into a purported consulting agreement pursuant to which Total would corruptly make payments to an intermediary designated by the Iranian official to secure NIOC signing a development agreement with Total for the Sirri A and E project, which NIOC did in July 1995. The consulting agreement contained no specific payment terms, but instead stated that the intermediary would provide "economic and marketing research support" upon "Consulting Service Requests." Total mischaracterized the bribes in its books and records as legitimate "business development expenses."[438] Over the next two and a half years, Total paid approximately $16 million in bribes under the purported consulting agreement.

In 1997, Total sought to negotiate a contract with NIOC to develop a portion of the South Pars gas field, the world's largest gas field. At the direction of the Iranian official, Total and a second intermediary entered into another purported consulting agreement that called for Total to make large payments to the intermediary. In September 1997, Total executed a contract with NIOC that granted it a 40 percent interest in developing phases two and three of the South Pars gas field. Over the next seven years, Total made unlawful payments of approximately $44 million pursuant to the second purported consulting agreement.

In sum, between 1995 and 2004, at the direction of the Iranian official, Total corruptly made approximately $60 million in bribe payments under the agreements for the purpose of inducing the Iranian official to use his influence in connection with Total's efforts to obtain and retain lucrative oil rights in the Sirri A and E and South Pars oil and gas fields. Total mischaracterized the unlawful payments as "business development expenses" when they were, in fact, bribes designed to corruptly influence a foreign official. Further, Total failed to implement effective internal accounting controls, permitting the consulting agreements' true nature and true participants to be concealed and thereby failing to maintain accountability for assets.

CT.   *United States v. Diebold Incorporated;*[439] *SEC v. Diebold, Inc.*[440]

▶ **Misconduct Category:**	Payment of bribes in connection with the sale of automated teller machines (ATMs) to state-owned and private banks; things of value included European vacations and trips to popular tourist destinations in the U.S., including Las Vegas, Napa Valley, and Disneyland; funneling of bribes through a distributor
▶ **Countries:**	China, Indonesia, and Russia
▶ **Foreign Government Officials:**	Employees and officials of state-owned or state-controlled banks
▶ **Improper Payment Dollar Value:**	$1.747 million
▶ **Combined Penalties:**	$48.7 (DOJ: $25.2 million penalty; SEC: $22.9 million in disgorgement and prejudgment interest)
▶ **Other:**	Three-year deferred prosecution agreement; voluntary disclosure; extensive internal investigation and cooperation; 18-month independent compliance monitor; payments of $1.6 million to government-owned bank officials in China, and more than $147,000 to bribe officials at government banks in Indonesia. Bribes paid to privately owned banks in Russia resulted in books-and-records violations for the publicly traded company.

In October 2013, Diebold Inc. (Diebold), an Ohio-based provider of integrated self-service delivery and security systems, including automated teller machines (ATMs), agreed to pay a $25.2 million penalty to resolve allegations that it violated the FCPA by bribing government officials in China and Indonesia and falsifying records in Russia in order to obtain and retain contracts to provide ATMs to state-owned and private banks in those countries. A two-count information filed in U.S. District Court for the Northern District of Ohio charged Diebold with conspiring to violate the FCPA's antibribery and books-and-records provisions and violating the FCPA's books-and-records provisions. The DOJ agreed to defer prosecution for three years and, if Diebold abides by the terms of the deferred prosecution agreement, the DOJ will dismiss the criminal information when the agreement's term expires. The agreement acknowledged Diebold's voluntary disclosure and extensive internal investigation and cooperation.

According to court documents, Diebold paid bribes and falsified documents in connection with the sale of ATMs to bank customers in China, Indonesia, and Russia. With respect to China and Indonesia, the court documents alleged that from 2005 to 2010, in order to secure and retain business with bank customers, including state-owned and -controlled banks, Diebold repeatedly provided things of value, including payments, gifts, and nonbusiness travel for employees of the banks, totaling approximately $1.75 million. Diebold's subsidiary in China provided government officials with annual company gifts ranging from less than $100 to more than $600. Officials also were treated to European vacations. For example, eight officials at a government-owned bank in China enjoyed a two-week trip at Diebold's expense that included stays in Paris, Brussels, Amsterdam, Cologne, Frankfurt, Munich, Salzburg, Vienna, Klagenfurt, Venice, Florence, and Rome. Destinations of leisure trips for other officials included Australia, New Zealand, and Bali. In total, Diebold spent approximately $1.6 million to bribe government-owned bank officials in China, and more than $147,000 to bribe officials at government banks in Indonesia. Among the tourist destinations of U.S. trips were the Grand Canyon, Napa Valley, Disneyland, and Universal Studios, as well as Las Vegas, New York City, Chicago, and Washington, D.C. Diebold attempted to disguise the payments and benefits through various means, including by making payments through third parties designated by the banks and by inaccurately recording leisure trips for bank employees as "training."

From 2005 to 2008, Diebold's Russian subsidiary paid approximately $1.2 million in connection with the sale of ATMs to private banks in Russia. The court documents allege that during this period, Diebold created and entered into false contracts with a distributor in Russia for services that the distributor was not performing. The distributor, in turn, used the money that Diebold paid to it, in part, to pay bribes to employees of Diebold's privately owned bank customers. The distributor payments were falsely recorded as legitimate business expenses.[441] In addition to the monetary penalty, Diebold agreed to implement rigorous internal controls, cooperate fully with the DOJ, and retain a compliance monitor for at least 18 months.

In a related matter, Diebold reached a settlement with the SEC and agreed to pay approximately $22.97 million in disgorgement and prejudgment interest.[442] In addition to the bribery conduct, the SEC alleged Diebold falsified its books and records to hide approximately $1.2 million in bribes paid to employees at privately owned banks.

CU.   *United States v. Weatherford International Limited;*[443]
      United States v. Weatherford Services, Ltd.;[444] *SEC v.*
      Weatherford International[445]

▶ **Misconduct Category:**	UN Oil-for-Food Program
▶ **Countries:**	Albania, Algeria, and Iraq; export countries Cuba, Iran, Syria, and Sudan
▶ **Foreign Government Officials:**	State-owned oil company drilling manager; tax authorities
▶ **Improper Payment Dollar Value:**	Unspecified
▶ **Combined Penalties:**	$252,690,606

▶ **Other:**

Two-year deferred prosecution agreement; investigation expanded to cover violations of the International Emergency Economic Powers Act (IEEPA) and the Trading with the Enemy Act (TWEA) involving Cuba, Iran, Sudan, and Syria, and leading to penalties of $141 million; improper conduct through joint venture; week-long trip for government official to Italy with a Portugal honeymoon trip for daughter of state-owned oil company manager; trip to FIFA World Cup soccer tournament in Germany.

In November 2013, three subsidiaries of Weatherford International Limited (Weatherford International), a Swiss oil services company that trades on the New York Stock Exchange, agreed to plead guilty to antibribery provisions of the FCPA and export controls violations under the International Emergency Economic Powers Act (IEEPA) and the Trading with the Enemy Act (TWEA). Weatherford International and its subsidiaries also agreed to pay more than $252 million in penalties and fines.

Weatherford Services Limited (Weatherford Services), a subsidiary of Weatherford International, agreed to plead guilty to violating the antibribery provisions of the FCPA. As part of a coordinated FCPA resolution, the DOJ also filed a criminal information in U.S. District Court for the Southern District of Texas charging Weatherford International with one count of violating the internal controls provisions of the FCPA. To resolve the charge, Weatherford International agreed to pay an $87.2 million criminal penalty as part of a deferred prosecution agreement with the DOJ.

In a separate matter, Weatherford International and four of its subsidiaries agreed to pay a combined $100 million to resolve a criminal and administrative export controls investigation conducted by the U.S. Attorney's Office for the Southern District of Texas, the Department of Commerce's Bureau of Industry and Security (BIS), and the Department of the Treasury's Office of Foreign Assets Control (OFAC). As part of the resolution of that investigation, Weatherford International agreed to enter into a deferred prosecution agreement for a term of two years, and two of its subsidiaries have agreed to plead guilty to export controls charges. In a related FCPA matter, the SEC filed a settlement in which Weatherford International consented to the entry of a permanent injunction against FCPA violations and agreed to pay $65,612,360 in disgorgement, prejudgment interest, and civil penalties. Weatherford International also agreed with the SEC to comply with certain undertakings regarding its FCPA compliance program, including the retention of an independent corporate compliance monitor.

The combined investigations resulted in the conviction of three Weatherford subsidiaries, the entry by Weatherford International into two deferred prosecution agreements and a civil settlement, and the payment of a total of $252,690,606 in penalties and fines.

1. FCPA Violations

According to court documents filed by the DOJ, prior to 2008, Weatherford International knowingly failed to establish an effective system of internal accounting controls designed to detect and prevent corruption, including FCPA violations. The company failed to implement these internal controls despite operating in an industry with a substantial corruption risk profile, and despite growing its global footprint in large part by purchasing existing companies, often themselves in countries with high corruption risks. As a result, a permissive and uncontrolled environment existed within which employees of certain of Weatherford International's wholly owned subsidiaries in Africa and the Middle East were able to engage in corrupt conduct over the course of many years, including both bribery of foreign officials and fraudulent misuse of the United Nations' Oil-for-Food Program.

Court documents state that Weatherford Services employees established and operated a joint venture in Africa with two local entities controlled by foreign officials and their relatives from 2004 through at least 2008. The foreign officials selected the entities with which Weatherford Services would partner, and Weatherford Services and Weatherford International employees knew that the members of the local entities included foreign officials' relatives and associates. Notwithstanding the fact that the local entities did not contribute capital, expertise, or labor to the joint venture, neither Weatherford Services nor Weatherford International investigated why the local entities were involved in the joint venture. The sole purpose of those local entities, in fact, was to serve as conduits through which Weatherford Services funneled hundreds of thousands of dollars in payments to the foreign officials controlling them. In exchange for the payments they received from Weatherford Services through the joint venture, the foreign officials awarded the joint venture lucrative contracts, gave Weatherford Services inside information about competitors' pricing, and took contracts away from Weatherford Services' competitors and awarded them to the joint venture.

Additionally, Weatherford Services employees in Africa bribed a foreign official so that he would approve the renewal of an oil services contract, according to court documents. Weatherford Services funneled bribery payments to the foreign official through a freight-forwarding agent it retained via a consultancy agreement in July 2006. Weatherford Services generated sham purchase orders for consulting services the freight-forwarding agent never performed, and the freight-forwarding agent, in turn, generated sham invoices for those same nonexistent services. When paid for those invoices, the freight-forwarding agent passed at least some of those monies on to the foreign official with the authority to approve Weatherford Services' contract renewal. In exchange for these payments, the foreign official awarded the renewal contract to Weatherford Services in 2006.

Further, according to court documents, in a third scheme in the Middle East, from 2005 through 2011, employees of Weatherford Oil Tools Middle East Limited (WOTME), another Weatherford International subsidiary, awarded improper "volume discounts" to a distributor who supplied Weatherford International products to a government-owned national oil company, believing that those discounts were being used to create a slush fund with which to make bribe payments to decision makers at the national oil company. Between 2005 and 2011, WOTME paid approximately $15 million in volume discounts to the distributor.

Weatherford International's failure to implement effective internal accounting controls also permitted corrupt conduct relating to the United Nations' Oil-for-Food Program to occur, according to court documents. Between about February 2002 and about July 2002, WOTME paid approximately $1,470,128 in kickbacks to the government of Iraq on nine contracts with Iraq's Ministry of Oil, as well as other ministries, to provide oil drilling and refining equipment. WOTME falsely recorded these kickbacks as other, seemingly legitimate, types of costs and fees. Further, WOTME concealed the kickbacks from the UN by inflating contract prices by 10 percent. According to court documents, these corrupt transactions in Africa and the Middle East earned Weatherford International profits of $54,486,410, which were included in the consolidated financial statements that Weatherford International filed with the SEC.

In addition to the guilty plea by Weatherford Services, the DPA entered into by Weatherford International and the DOJ requires the company to cooperate with law enforcement, retain an independent corporate compliance monitor for at least 18 months, and continue to implement an enhanced compliance program and internal controls designed to prevent and detect future FCPA violations. The agreement acknowledges Weatherford International's cooperation in this matter, including conducting a thorough internal investigation into bribery and related misconduct, and its extensive remediation and compliance improvement efforts.

2. *Export Control Violations*

According to court documents filed in a separate matter, between 1998 and 2007, Weatherford International and some its subsidiaries engaged in conduct that violated various U.S. export control and sanctions laws by exporting or reexporting oil and gas drilling equipment to, and conducting Weatherford business operations in, sanctioned countries without the required U.S. government authorization. In addition to the involvement of employees of several Weatherford International subsidiaries, some Weatherford International executives, managers, or employees on multiple occasions participated in, directed, approved, and facilitated the transactions and the conduct of its various subsidiaries.

This conduct involved persons within the U.S.-based management structure of Weatherford International participating in conduct by Weatherford International foreign subsidiaries, and the unlicensed export or reexport of U.S.-origin goods to Cuba, Iran, Sudan, and Syria. Weatherford subsidiaries Precision Energy Services Colombia Ltd. (PESC) and Precision Energy Services Ltd. (PESL), both headquartered in Canada, conducted business in Cuba. Weatherford's subsidiary WOTME, headquartered in the United Arab Emirates (UAE), conducted business in the countries of Iran, Sudan, and Syria. Weatherford's subsidiary Weatherford Production Optimisation f/k/a eProduction Solutions U.K. Ltd. (eProd-U.K.), headquartered in the United Kingdom, conducted business in the country of Iran. Weatherford generated approximately $110 million in revenue from its illegal transactions in Cuba, Iran, Syria, and Sudan.

To resolve these charges, Weatherford and its subsidiaries agreed to pay a total penalty of $100 million, with a $48 million monetary penalty paid pursuant to the DPA, $2 million paid in criminal fines pursuant to the two guilty pleas, and a $50 million civil penalty paid pursuant to a Department of Commerce settlement agreement to resolve 174 violations charged by Commerce's BIS. Weatherford International and certain of its affiliates are also signing a $91 million settlement agreement with the Department of the Treasury to resolve their civil liability arising out of the same underlying course of conduct, which is to be deemed satisfied by the payments above.

CV.   *United States v. Bilfinger SE*[446]

▶ **Misconduct Category:**	Inflation of joint venture bid price by 3 percent to cover cost of paying bribes to Nigerian government officials
▶ **Country:**	Nigeria
▶ **Foreign Government Officials:**	Officials of Nigerian National Petroleum Corporation (NNPC), National Petroleum Investment Management Services, a subsidiary of NNPC
▶ **Improper Payment Dollar Value:**	$6 million
▶ **Combined Penalties:**	$32 million
▶ **Other:**	Three-year DPA; independent corporate monitor for 18 months
▶ **Related Matters:**	*United States v. Willbros Group Inc. & Willbros International Inc.; United States v. Brown; United States v. Steph; United States v. Tillery; United States v. Novak; SEC v. Willbros Group Inc.*

In December 2013 Bilfinger SE, an international engineering and services company based in Mannheim, Germany, agreed to pay a $32 million penalty to resolve charges that it violated the FCPA by bribing government officials of the Federal Republic of Nigeria to obtain and retain contracts related to the Eastern Gas Gathering System (EGGS) project, which was valued at approximately $387 million.

As part of the resolution, the DOJ filed a three-count criminal information in U.S. District Court for the Southern District of Texas charging Bilfinger with violating and conspiring to violate the FCPA's antibribery provisions. The DOJ and Bilfinger agreed to resolve the charges by entering into a deferred prosecution agreement for a term of three years. In addition to the monetary penalty, Bilfinger agreed to implement rigorous internal controls, continue cooperating fully with the department, and retain an independent corporate compliance monitor for at least 18 months. The agreement acknowledged Bilfinger's cooperation with the DOJ and its remediation efforts.

According to court documents, from late 2003 through June 2005, Bilfinger conspired with Willbros Group Inc. and others to make corrupt payments total-ing more than $6 million to Nigerian government officials to assist in obtain-ing and retaining contracts related to the EGGS project. Bilfinger and Willbros formed a joint venture to bid on the EGGS project and inflated the price of the joint venture's bid by 3 percent to cover the cost of paying bribes to Nige-rian officials. As part of the conspiracy, Bilfinger employees bribed Nigerian officials with cash that Bilfinger employees sent from Germany to Nigeria. At another point in the conspiracy, when Willbros employees encountered diffi-culty obtaining enough money to make their share of the bribe payments, Bil-finger loaned them $1 million, with the express purpose of paying bribes to the Nigerian officials.

Related to this case against Bilfinger, the DOJ previously filed criminal charges in the Southern District of Texas against two companies and four executives and consultants in connection with the EGGS bribery. (See section VI.AB.)

CW. U.S. DOJ- Archer Daniels Midland Co. Agreement;
United States v. Alfred C. Toepfer International Ukraine Ltd.;[447]
SEC v. Archer Daniels Midland[448]

▶ **Misconduct Category:**	Payment of bribes to two vendors and, in turn, to value-added tax (VAT) officials to obtain $100 million in tax refunds
▶ **Countries:**	Ukraine, Venezuela
▶ **Foreign Government Officials:**	Tax officials
▶ **Improper Payment Dollar Value:**	$20 million
▶ **Combined Penalties:**	$54 million ($17.8 million in criminal penalties and $36.5 million in disgorgement and prejudgment interest)
▶ **Other:**	ADM, the parent company, received an NPA, the DOJ recognizing ADM's early and extensive remedial efforts.

In December 2013, Alfred C. Toepfer International Ukraine Ltd. (ACTI Ukraine), a subsidiary of Archer Daniels Midland Company (ADM) of Decatur, Illinois, pleaded guilty and agreed to pay more than $17 million in criminal fines to resolve charges that it paid bribes through vendors to Ukrainian government officials to obtain value-added tax (VAT) refunds, in violation of the FCPA.

ACTI Ukraine pleaded guilty in the Central District of Illinois to one count of conspiracy to violate the antibribery provisions of the FCPA and agreed to pay $17.8 million in criminal fines. The DOJ also entered into a nonprosecution agree-ment (NPA) with ADM in connection with the company's failure to implement an adequate system of internal financial controls to address the making of improper payments both in Ukraine and by an ADM joint venture in Venezuela.

According to the charges, from 2002 to 2008, ACTI Ukraine, a trader and seller of commodities based in the Ukraine, together with Alfred C. Toepfer International G.m.b.H. (ACTI Hamburg), another subsidiary of ADM, paid third-party vendors to pass on bribes to Ukrainian government officials to obtain VAT refunds. The charges allege that, in total, ACTI Ukraine and ACTI Hamburg paid roughly $22 million to two vendors, nearly all of which was to be passed on to Ukrainian government officials to obtain over $100 million in VAT refunds, resulting in a benefit to ACTI Ukraine and ACTI Hamburg of roughly $41 million.

According to the NPA with ADM, a number of concerns were expressed to ADM executives, including an e-mail calling into question potentially illegal "donations" by ACTI Ukraine and ACTI Hamburg to recover the VAT refunds, yet nonetheless failed to implement sufficient antibribery compliance policies and procedures to prevent corrupt payments.

In addition to the monetary penalty, ADM and ACTI Ukraine also agreed to cooperate with the DOJ, to periodically report the companies' compliance efforts, and to continue implementing enhanced compliance programs and internal controls designed to prevent and detect FCPA violations.

In a parallel action, ADM consented with the SEC to a proposed final judgment that ordered the company to pay roughly $36.5 million in disgorgement and prejudgment interest, bringing the total amount of U.S. criminal and regulatory penalties to be paid by ADM and its subsidiary to more than $54 million.

The agreements acknowledged ADM's timely, voluntary, and thorough disclosure of the conduct; ADM's extensive cooperation with the department, including conducting a worldwide risk assessment and corresponding global internal investigation, making numerous presentations to the DOJ on the status and findings of the internal investigation, voluntarily making current and former employees available for interviews, and compiling relevant documents by category for the DOJ; and ADM's early and extensive remedial efforts.

CX.   *United States v. Alcoa World Alumina LLC;*[449] *SEC v. Alcoa Inc.*[450]

▶ **Misconduct Category:**	Corrupt payment in excess of $110 million to Bahraini officials to obtain influence in contract negotiations between Alcoa and Aluminum Bahrain B.S.C. (Alba), a major state-owned aluminum company
▶ **Country:**	Bahrain
▶ **Foreign Government Officials:**	Members of the Bahrain royal family who controlled the tender process and members of the board of directors and senior management of the state-owned aluminum company
▶ **Improper Payment Dollar Value:**	$110 million

▶ **Combined Penalties:** $384 million (DOJ: $209 million; SEC: $175 million in disgorgement)

▶ **Other:**   Alcoa did not conduct due diligence or otherwise seek to determine whether there was a legitimate purpose for a middleman; SEC Administrative Proceeding

In January 2014, Alcoa World Alumina LLC, a majority-owned and controlled global alumina sales company of Alcoa, Inc., agreed to plead guilty and pay $223 million in criminal fines and forfeiture to resolve charges that it used an international middleman in London with security offshore to pay officials of the Kingdom of Bahrain. At the same time, issuer Alcoa Inc. agreed to settle with the SEC and pay $175 million in disgorgement, resulting in a combined fine of $384 million.

Alcoa World Alumina pled guilty in the Western District of Pennsylvania to one count of violating the antibribery provisions of the FCPA in connection with a 2004 corrupt transaction, to pay a criminal fine of $209 million, and to administratively forfeit $14 million. As part of the plea agreement, Alcoa Inc. has agreed to maintain and implement an enhanced global anticorruption compliance program.

The court filings alleged that Alcoa of Australia, another Alcoa-controlled entity, originally secured a long-term alumina supply agreement with Aluminium Bahrain B.S.C. (Alba), an aluminum smelter controlled by the government of Bahrain. At the request of certain members of Bahrain's royal family who controlled the tender process, Alcoa of Australia inserted a London-based middleman with close ties to certain royal family members as a sham sales agent and agreed to pay him a corrupt commission intended to conceal bribe payments, according to court papers. Over time, Alcoa of Australia expanded the relationship with the middleman, identified as a consultant in the court filings, to begin invoicing increasingly larger volumes of alumina sales through his shell companies, which permitted the consultant to make larger bribe payments to certain government officials, according to court filings.

As admitted in the DOJ charging documents, in 2004, Alcoa World Alumina corruptly secured a long-term alumina supply agreement with Alba by agreeing to purportedly sell over 1.5 million metric tons of alumina to Alba through offshore shell companies owned by the consultant. The sham distributorship permitted the consultant to mark up the price of alumina by approximately $188 million from 2005 to 2009, the duration of the corrupt supply agreement. Court filings allege that the consultant used the markup to pay tens of millions in corrupt kickbacks to Bahraini government officials, including senior members of Bahrain's royal family. To conceal the illicit payments, the consultant and the government officials used various offshore bank accounts, including accounts held under aliases, at several major financial institutions around the world, including in Guernsey, Luxembourg, Liechtenstein, and Switzerland.

The SEC also settled with global aluminum producer and issuer Alcoa Inc. for violating the FCPA when its subsidiaries repeatedly paid bribes to government officials in Bahrain to maintain a key source of business. The SEC investigation found that more than $110 million in corrupt payments were made to Bahraini officials with influence over contract negotiations between Alcoa and a major government-operated aluminum plant. Alcoa's subsidiaries used a London-based consultant with connections to Bahrain's royal family as an intermediary to negotiate with government officials and funnel the illicit payments to retain Alcoa's business as a supplier to the plant. Alcoa lacked sufficient internal controls to prevent and detect the bribes, which were improperly recorded in Alcoa's books and records as legitimate commissions or sales to a distributor.

According to the SEC's order instituting settled administrative proceedings, Alcoa is a global provider of not only primary or fabricated aluminum, but also smelter grade alumina—the raw material that is supplied to plants called smelters that produce aluminum. Alcoa refines alumina from bauxite that it extracts in its global mining operations. From 1989 to 2009, one of the largest customers of Alcoa's global bauxite and alumina refining business was Aluminium Bahrain B.S.C. (Alba), which is considered one of the largest aluminum smelters in the world. Alba is controlled by Bahrain's government, and Alcoa's mining operations in Australia were the source of the alumina that Alcoa supplied to Alba. Alcoa's Australian subsidiary retained a consultant to assist in negotiations for long-term alumina supply agreements with Alba and Bahraini government officials. A manager at the subsidiary described the consultant as "well versed in the normal ways of Middle East business" and one who "will keep the various stakeholders in the Alba smelter happy. . . ." Despite the red flags inherent in this arrangement, Alcoa's subsidiary inserted the intermediary into the Alba sales supply chain, and the consultant generated the funds needed to pay bribes to Bahraini officials. Money used for the bribes came from the commissions that Alcoa's subsidiary paid to the consultant as well as price markups the consultant made between the purchase price of the product from Alcoa and the sale price to Alba.

The SEC's order found that Alcoa did not conduct due diligence or otherwise seek to determine whether there was a legitimate business purpose for the use of a middleman. Recipients of the corrupt payments included senior Bahraini government officials, members of Alba's board of directors, and Alba senior management. For example, after Alcoa's subsidiary retained the consultant to lobby a Bahraini government official, the consultant's shell companies made two payments totaling $7 million in August 2003 for the benefit of the official. Two weeks later, Alcoa and Alba signed an agreement in principle to have Alcoa participate in Alba's plant expansion. In October 2004, the consultant's shell company paid $1 million to an account for the benefit of that same government official, and Alba went on to reach another supply agreement in principle with Alcoa. Around the time that agreement was executed, the consultant's companies made three payments totaling $41 million to benefit another Bahraini government official as well.

The SEC's cease-and-desist order found that Alcoa violated sections 30A, 13(b)(2)(A), and 13(b)(2)(B) of the Securities Exchange Act of 1934. Alcoa agreed to pay

$175 million in disgorgement of ill-gotten gains, of which $14 million was satisfied by the company's payment of forfeiture in the parallel criminal matter. Alcoa agreed to pay a criminal fine of $209 million.

CY.   *United States v. PetroTiger Ltd;*[451] *United States v. Sigelman,*
      Hammerskjold & Weisman[452]

▶ **Misconduct Category:**	Bribery to state-owned oil company official for a lucrative oil services contract
▶ **Country:**	Colombia
▶ **Foreign Government Officials:**	Official of Ecopetrol SA, the Colombian state-owned and -controlled oil company
▶ **Improper Payment Dollar Value:**	Unspecified
▶ **Combined Penalties:**	Hammerskjold and Weisman await sentencing, while Sigelman awaits trial
▶ **Other:**	Payments to bank account of wife of foreign official for purported consulting services she did not perform were deposited into a Philippine bank account of Engelman and were referred to as "the Manila split"; general counsel of PetroTiger pled guilty and was disbarred by New York state

In January 2014, Joseph Sigelman, 42, formerly of Miami and the Philippines, and Knut Hammarskjold, 42, of Greenville, S.C., two former chief executive officers of PetroTiger Ltd.—a British Virgin Islands oil and gas company with operations in Colombia and offices in New Jersey—were charged for their alleged participation in a scheme to pay bribes to foreign government officials in violation of the FCPA, to defraud PetroTiger, and to launder proceeds of those crimes. In addition, PetroTiger's former general counsel Gregory Weisman pleaded guilty to bribery and fraud charges in connection with the same scheme. The three paid bribes to an official in Colombia in exchange for the official's assistance in securing approval for an oil services contract worth roughly $39 million.

Sigelman and Hammarskjold were charged by sealed complaints filed in the District of New Jersey on November 8, 2013, with conspiracy to commit wire fraud, conspiracy to violate the FCPA, conspiracy to launder money and substantive violations of the FCPA. Sigelman was arrested on January 3, 2014, in the Philippines. He awaits trial.

Weisman pleaded guilty on November 8, 2013, to a criminal information charging one count of conspiracy to violate the FCPA and to commit wire fraud. The charges and guilty plea were also unsealed. In November 2014, a New York appellate court upheld his disbarment from the practice of law. Hammarskjold was arrested November 20, 2013, at Newark Liberty International Airport. In February 2014, he pled guilty to one count of conspiracy to violate the FCPA and to commit wire fraud.

The charges alleged the defendants made three separate payments from PetroTiger's bank account in the United States to the official's bank account in Colombia to secure approval from Colombia's state-owned and -controlled oil company for a lucrative oil services contract in the country. To conceal the bribes, the defendants first attempted to make the payments to a bank account in the name of the foreign official's wife, for purported consulting services she did not perform. The charges alleged that Sigelman and Hammarskjold provided Weisman invoices including her bank account information. The defendants made the payments directly to the official's bank account when attempts to transfer the money to his wife's account failed.

In addition, court documents alleged that the defendants attempted to secure kickback payments at the expense of PetroTiger's board members and were negotiating an acquisition of another company on behalf of PetroTiger, including on behalf of several members of PetroTiger's board of directors who were helping to fund the acquisition. In exchange for negotiating a higher purchase price for the acquisition, two of the owners of the target company agreed to kick back to the defendants a portion of the increased purchase price. According to the charges, to conceal the kickback payments, the defendants had the payments deposited into Sigelman's bank account in the Philippines, created a "side letter" to falsely justify the payments, and used the code name "Manila Split" to refer to the payments among themselves.

CZ.   *United States v. Cilins*[453]

▶ **Misconduct Category:**	Obstruction of justice of ongoing grand jury investigation of bribes to obtain mining concessions in the Republic of Guinea
▶ **Country:**	Republic of Guinea
▶ **Foreign Government Officials:**	Guinean government ministers and senior officials and former wife of a deceased Guinean government official
▶ **Improper Payment Dollar Value:**	Offer of millions of dollars to secure mining concessions contract
▶ **Combined Penalties:**	Two years of imprisonment, $75,000 fine, and forfeiture of $20,000
▶ **Other:**	Attempt to induce a witness, the former wife of a deceased Guinean government official, to sign an affidavit containing numerous false statements

In March 2014, Frederic Cilins, 51, a French citizen, pled guilty in the Southern District of New York to obstructing a federal criminal investigation into whether a mining company paid bribes to win lucrative mining rights in the Republic of Guinea. Cilins pleaded guilty to a one-count superseding information, which alleged that he agreed to pay money to induce a witness to destroy, or provide to him for destruction, documents sought by the FBI. According to the superseding information, those documents related to allegations concerning the payment of bribes to obtain mining concessions in the Simandou region of the Republic of Guinea.

According to publicly filed documents, Cilins allegedly attempted to obstruct an ongoing Manhattan federal grand jury investigation concerning potential violations of the FCPA and laws proscribing money laundering. Court documents stated the federal grand jury was investigating whether a particular mining company and its affiliates—on whose behalf Cilins had been working—transferred into the United States funds in furtherance of a scheme to obtain and retain valuable mining concessions in the Republic of Guinea's Simandou region. During monitored and recorded phone calls and face-to-face meetings, Cilins agreed to pay substantial sums of money to induce a witness to the bribery scheme to turn over documents to Cilins for destruction, which Cilins knew had been requested by the FBI and needed to be produced before a federal grand jury.

Court documents alleged that Cilins sought to induce the witness to sign an affidavit containing numerous false statements regarding matters under investigation by the grand jury. Court documents also alleged that the documents Cilins sought to destroy included original copies of contracts between the mining company and its affiliates and the former wife of a now-deceased Guinean government official, who at the relevant time held an office in Guinea that allowed him to influence the award of mining concessions. The contracts allegedly related to a scheme by which the mining company and its affiliates offered the wife of the Guinean official millions of dollars, which were to be distributed to the official's wife as well as ministers or senior officials of Guinea's government whose authority might be needed to secure the mining rights.

According to court documents, the official's wife incorporated a company in 2008 that agreed to take all necessary steps to secure the valuable mining rights for the mining company's subsidiary. That same contract stipulated that $2 million was to be transferred to the official's wife's company and an additional sum was to be "distributed among persons of good will who may have contributed to facilitating the granting of" the valuable mining rights. According to the complaint, in 2008, the mining company and its affiliates also agreed to give 5 percent of its ownership of particular mining areas in Guinea to the official's wife. In July 2014, Cilins was sentenced to serve two years of imprisonment, to pay a fine of $75,000, and to forfeit approximately $20,000 that was seized from him at the time of his arrest.

DA.   *United States v. Marubeni Corp.;*[454] *United States v. Pierucci, Rothschild, Hoskins & Pomponi*[455]

▶ **Misconduct Category:**   Bribery of Indonesian member of Parliament and public electricity company official to win an electricity contract for itself and its partner, Alstom SA

▶ **Country:**	Indonesia
▶ **Foreign Government Officials:**	Member of Indonesian Parliament and officials of state-owned and state-controlled electricity company
▶ **Improper Payment Dollar Value:**	Unspecified
▶ **Combined Penalties:**	$88 million
▶ **Other:**	Marubeni paid $54.6 million criminal penalty in early 2012 to resolve FCPA charges for its role as an agent of the KBR-led TSKJ joint venture; e-mails addressing whether the agent would give officials "rewards" that they would consider "satisfactory" or "only give them pocket money and disappear"; Marubeni's refusal to cooperate resulted in a fire in the middle of the applicable USSG guidelines
▶ **Related Matters:**	*United States v. Marubeni Corp.* (2012); *United States v. Alstom S.A.*; *United States v. Alstom Network Schweiz AG*; *United States v. Alstom Power Inc.* (DPA); *United States v. Alstom Grid Inc.* (DPA)

In March 2014, Marubeni Corporation, a major Japanese trading company involved in the handling of products and provision of services in a broad range of sectors around the world, including power generation, entered a plea of guilty for its participation in a scheme to pay bribes to high-ranking government officials in Indonesia to secure a lucrative power project.

Marubeni entered a plea of guilty to an eight-count criminal information filed in the U.S. District Court for the District of Connecticut, charging Marubeni with one count of conspiracy to violate the antibribery provisions of the FCPA and seven counts of violating the FCPA. Marubeni admitted its criminal conduct and agreed to pay a criminal fine of $88 million.

As part of the plea agreement, Marubeni agreed to maintain and implement an enhanced global anticorruption compliance program and to cooperate with the DOJ's ongoing investigation. The plea agreement cited Marubeni's decision not to cooperate with the DOJ's investigation when given the opportunity to do so, its lack of an effective compliance and ethics program at the time of the offense, its failure to properly remediate, and the lack of its voluntary disclosure of the conduct as some of the factors considered by the DOJ in reaching an appropriate resolution.

Frederic Pierucci, who was the vice president of global boiler sales at Marubeni's consortium partner, Alstom Inc. (Alstom), pleaded guilty on July 29, 2013, to one count of conspiring to violate the FCPA and one count of violating the FCPA. David Rothschild, a former vice president of regional sales at Alstom, pleaded guilty on November 2, 2012, to one count of conspiracy to violate the FCPA. Lawrence

Hoskins, a former senior vice president for the Asia region for Alstom Inc., and William Pomponi, a former vice president of regional sales at Alstom, were charged in a second superseding indictment on July 30, 2013. Pomponi and Hoskins pled guilty in July 2014. Only Hoskins awaits trial. In December 2014, Alstom S.A., a French power conglomerate, pled guilty to violating the books-and-records and internal controls provision in connection with bribes in Indonesia, Saudi Arabia, Egypt, and the Bahamas, and agreed to pay a record $772 million fine. In addition, Alstom Network Schweiz AG, a Swiss subsidiary, pleaded guilty to conspiring to violate the antibribery provision of the FCPA. The U.S. subsidiary Alstom Power Inc. and Alstom Grid Inc. entered into DPAs.

According to court filings, Marubeni and its employees, together with others, paid bribes to officials in Indonesia—including a high-ranking member of the Indonesian Parliament and high-ranking members of Perusahaan Listrik Negara (PLN), the state-owned and state-controlled electricity company in Indonesia—in exchange for assistance in securing a $118 million contract, known as the Tarahan project, for Marubeni and its consortium partner to provide power-related services for the citizens of Indonesia. To conceal the bribes, Marubeni and Alstom retained two consultants purportedly to provide legitimate consulting services on behalf of the power company and its subsidiaries in connection with the Tarahan project. The primary purpose for hiring the consultants, however, was to use the consultants to pay bribes to Indonesian officials.

As admitted in court documents, Marubeni and its coconspirators retained the first consultant in the fall of 2002. However, in the fall of 2003, before the Tarahan contract had been awarded, Marubeni and its coconspirators determined that the first consultant was not bribing key officials at PLN effectively. One e-mail between employees of the power company's subsidiary in Indonesia described a meeting between Marubeni employees, employees of its consortium partner, and PLN officials during which the PLN officials expressed "concern" that if Marubeni and its consortium partner win the project, whether the agent would give the officials "rewards" that they would consider "satisfactory," or "only give them pocket money and disappear. Nothing has been shown by the agent that the agent is willing to spend money." Shortly thereafter, a Marubeni employee sent an e-mail to other employees at Marubeni and its consortium partner stating that "unfortunately our agent almost did not execute his function at all, so far. In case we don't take immediate action now now [sic], we don't have any chance to get this project forever."

As a result, Marubeni and its consortium partner decided to reduce the first consultant's commission from 3 percent of the total contract value to 1 percent, and pay the remaining 2 percent to a second consultant who could more effectively bribe officials at PLN. In an e-mail between two employees of Marubeni's consortium partner, they discussed a meeting between Marubeni, an executive from the consortium partner, and the first consultant, stating that the first consultant "committed to convince [the member of Parliament] that 'one' [percent] is enough."

Marubeni and its coconspirators were successful in securing the Tarahan project and subsequently made payments to the consultants for the purpose of bribing the Indonesian officials. Marubeni and its coconspirators paid hundreds of thousands of dollars into the first consultant's bank account in Maryland to be used to bribe the member of Parliament. The consultant then allegedly transferred the bribe money to a bank account in Indonesia for the benefit of the official.

DB.   *United States v. Chinea & DeMeneses;*[456] *SEC v. Chinea & DeMeneses*[457]

▶ **Misconduct Category:**	Bribery by broker-dealer officers to a senior official of a state economic development bank in return for the official's steering of brokerage business
▶ **Country:**	Venezuela
▶ **Foreign Government Officials:**	Officials of state-owned economic development bank
▶ **Improper Payment Dollar Value:**	In excess of $1.5 million
▶ **Combined Penalties:**	Four years in jail for each defendant
▶ **Other:**	Checks payable to foreign finders
▶ **Related Matters:**	*United States v. Lujan, Hurtad & Clarke; United States v. Gonzalez de Hernandez; SEC v. Clarke, Hurtado, Pabon, Rodolfo, Lujan, Chinea & DeMeneses*

In April 2014, Benito Chinea, the chief executive officer, and Joseph DeMeneses, the managing partner of a New York–based U.S. broker-dealer, were arrested on felony charges arising from a conspiracy to pay bribes to a senior official in Venezuela's state economic development bank, Banco de Desarollo Económico y Social de Venezuela (BANDES). Chinea, 47, was arrested in Manalapan, N.J., where he resides, and DeMeneses, 44, was arrested in Fairfield, Conn., where he resides. In a separate action, the SEC announced civil charges against Chinea, DeMeneses, and others involved in the bribery scheme.

Chinea and DeMeneses conspired with others to pay and launder bribes to Maria de los Angeles Gonzalez de Hernandez, a senior official in Venezuela's state-owned economic development bank, in exchange for her directing BANDES's financial trading business to the broker-dealer. DeMeneses was also charged with conspiring to obstruct an examination of the broker-dealer by the U.S. Securities and Exchange Commission (SEC) to conceal the true facts of the broker-dealer's relationship with BANDES.

According to the allegations in the unsealed indictment, as well as other documents previously filed in Manhattan federal court, Chinea and DeMeneses worked at the headquarters of the broker-dealer in New York City. In 2008, the broker-dealer established a group called the Global Markets Group (GMG), which offered fixed-income trading services for institutional clients in the purchase and sale of foreign sovereign debt. One of the broker-dealer's GMG clients was BANDES, which operated under the direction of the Venezuelan Ministry of Finance. Gonzalez was an official at BANDES and oversaw the development bank's overseas trading activity. At her direction, BANDES conducted substantial trading through the broker-dealer. Most of the trades executed by the broker-dealer on behalf of BANDES involved fixed-income investments for which the broker-dealer charged the bank a commission.

From late 2008 through 2012, Chinea and DeMeneses, together with three Miami-based broker-dealer employees, Ernesto Lujan, Tomas Alberto Clarke Bethancourt, and Jose Alejandro Hurtado, participated in a bribery scheme in which Gonzalez directed trading business she controlled at BANDES to the broker-dealer, and in return, agents and employees of the broker-dealer split the revenue the broker-dealer generated from this trading business with Gonzalez. During this time period, the broker-dealer generated over $60 million in commissions from trades with BANDES. In order to conceal their conduct, Chinea, DeMeneses, and their coconspirators routed the payments to Gonzalez, frequently in six-figure amounts, through third parties posing as "foreign finders" and into offshore bank accounts. In several instances, Chinea personally signed checks worth millions of dollars that were made payable to one of these purported "foreign finders" and later deposited in a Swiss bank account.

As a result of the bribery scheme, BANDES quickly became the broker-dealer's most profitable customer. As the relationship continued, however, Gonzalez became increasingly unhappy about the untimeliness of the payments due her from the broker-dealer, and she threatened to suspend BANDES's business. In response, DeMeneses and Clarke agreed to pay Gonzalez approximately $1.5 million from their personal funds. Chinea and DeMeneses agreed to use broker-dealer funds to reimburse DeMeneses and Clarke for these bribe payments. To conceal their true nature, Chinea and DeMeneses agreed to hide these reimbursements in the broker-dealer's books as sham loans from the broker-dealer to corporate entities associated with DeMeneses and Clarke.

Court documents also alleged that beginning in or around November 2010, the SEC commenced a periodic examination of the broker-dealer, and from November 2010 through March 2011, the SEC's exam staff made several visits to the broker-dealer's offices in Manhattan. In or about early 2011, DeMeneses and others involved in the scheme discussed that the SEC was examining the broker-dealer's relationship with BANDES. DeMeneses and others agreed they would take steps to conceal the true facts of the broker-dealer's relationship with BANDES, including by deleting e-mails, in order to hide the actual relationship from the SEC.

Chinea and DeMeneses were each charged with one count of conspiracy to violate the FCPA and the Travel Act, five counts of violating the FCPA, and five counts of violating of the Travel Act. Chinea and DeMeneses were also charged with one count of conspiracy to commit money laundering and three counts of money laundering. DeMeneses was further charged with one count of conspiracy to obstruct justice. In December 2014, Chinea and DeMeneses each pled guilty to conspiracy to violate the FCPA and one Travel Act count. On March 27, 2015, each was sentenced to four years in jail.

Previously, on August 29 and August 30, 2013, Lujan, Hurtado, and Clarke each pleaded guilty in Manhattan federal court to conspiring to violate the FCPA, to violate the Travel Act, and to commit money laundering, as well as substantive counts of these offenses, relating, among other things, to the scheme involving bribe payments to Gonzalez. On November 18, 2013, Gonzalez pleaded guilty in Manhattan to conspiring to violate the Travel Act and to commit money laundering, as well as substantive counts of these offenses, for her role in the corrupt scheme.

DC.   *United States v. Firtash, Knopp, Gevorgyan, Lal, Sunderalingam & Rao*[458]

▶ **Misconduct Category:**	Bribes to secure licenses to mine titanium and other minerals in project expected to generate $500 million annually
▶ **Country:**	India
▶ **Foreign Government Officials:**	State and central government mining officials
▶ **Improper Payment Dollar Value:**	$18.5 million
▶ **Combined Penalties:**	Unknown
▶ **Other:**	In addition to an FCPA conspiracy, defendants were charged with racketeering conspiracy, money laundering conspiracy, and interstate travel in aid of racketeering; Rao is a Member of Parliament in India and a former official of the state government of Andhra Pradesh; Firtash signals the steps the U.S. will take to arrest foreign nationals overseas. The purported Ukrainian billionaire waived extradition.

In April 2014, a federal indictment returned in Chicago under seal in June 2013 was unsealed and charged six foreign nationals, including a Ukrainian businessman and a government official in India, with participating in an alleged international racketeering conspiracy involving bribes of state and central government officials in India to allow the mining of titanium minerals. Five of the six defendants were also charged with conspiracy to violate the FCPA, among other offenses.

Beginning in 2006, the defendants allegedly conspired to pay at least $18.5 million in bribes to secure licenses to mine minerals in the eastern coastal Indian state of Andhra Pradesh. The mining project was expected to generate more than $500 million annually from the sale of titanium products, including sales to unnamed "Company A," headquartered in Chicago.

Dmitry Firtash, aka "Dmytro Firtash" and "DF," 48, a Ukrainian national and purported billionaire, was arrested March 12, 2014, in Vienna, Austria. Firtash was released from custody on March 21, 2014, after posting €125 million (approximately $174 million) bail, and he pledged to remain in Austria until the end of extradition proceedings.

Five other defendants remain at large: Andras Knopp, 75, a Hungarian business-man; Suren Gevorgyan, 40, of Ukraine; Gajendra Lal, 50, an Indian national and permanent resident of the United States who formerly resided in Winston-Salem, N.C.; Periyasamy Sunderalingam, aka "Sunder," 60, of Sri Lanka; and K.V.P. Ramachandra Rao, aka "KVP" and "Dr. KVP," 65, a Member of Parliament in India who was an official of the state government of Andhra Pradesh and a close advisor to the now-deceased chief minister of the State of Andhra Pradesh, Y.S. Rajasekhara Reddy.

The five-count indictment was returned under seal by a federal grand jury in Chicago on June 20, 2013. All six defendants were charged with one count each of racketeering conspiracy and money laundering conspiracy, and two counts of inter-state travel in aid of racketeering. Five defendants, excluding Rao, were charged with one count of conspiracy to violate the FCPA.

As alleged in court documents, Firtash controls Group DF, an international conglomerate of companies that was directly and indirectly owned by Group DF Limited, a British Virgin Islands company. Group DF companies include Ostchem Holding AG, an Austrian company in the business of mining and processing minerals, including titanium; Global Energy Mining and Minerals Limited, a Hungarian company, and Bothli Trade AG, a Swiss company, for which Global Energy Mining and Minerals was the majority shareholder. In April 2006, Bothli Trade and the state government of Andhra Pradesh agreed to set up a joint venture to mine various minerals, including ilmenite, a mineral which may be processed into various titanium-based products such as titanium sponge, a porous form of the mineral that occurs in the processing of titanium ore.

In February 2007, Company A entered into an agreement with Ostchem Holding, through Bothli Trade, to work toward a further agreement that would allow Bothli Trade the ability to supply 5 million to 12 million pounds of titanium sponge from the Indian project to Company A on an annual basis. The mining project required licenses and approval of both the Andhra Pradesh state government and the central government of India before the licenses could be issued.

As alleged in the indictment, the defendants used U.S. financial institutions to engage in the international transmission of millions of dollars for the purpose of bribing Indian public officials to obtain approval of the necessary licenses for the project. They allegedly financed the project and transferred and concealed bribe payments through Group DF, and used threats and intimidation to advance the interests of the enterprise's illegal activities.

According to the indictment, Firtash was the leader of the enterprise and caused the participation of certain Group DF companies in the project. Firtash allegedly met with Indian government officials, including Chief Minister Reddy, to discuss the project and its progress, and authorized payment of at least $18.5 million in bribes to both state and central government officials in India to secure the approval of licenses for the project. Firtash also allegedly directed his subordinates to create documents to make it falsely appear that money transferred for the purpose of paying these bribes was transferred for legitimate commercial purposes, and he appointed various subordinates to oversee efforts to obtain the licenses through bribery.

As alleged in the indictment, Knopp supervised the enterprise and, together with Firtash, met with Indian government officials. Knopp also met with Company A representatives to discuss supplying titanium products from the project. Gevorgyan allegedly traveled to Seattle and met with Company A representatives. Gevorgyan also engaged in other activities, including allegedly signing false documents, monitoring bribe payments and coordinating transfers of money to be used for bribes. Lal, also known as "Gaj," allegedly engaged in similar activities, reported to Firtash and Knopp on the status of obtaining licenses, and recommended whether, and in what manner, to pay certain bribes to government officials. Lal has not submitted to U.S. jurisdiction.

The indictment further alleged that Sunderalingam met with Rao to determine the total amount of bribes and advised others on the results of the meeting, and he identified various foreign bank accounts held in the names of nominees outside India that could be used to funnel bribes to Rao. Rao allegedly solicited bribes for himself and others in return for approving licenses for the project, and he warned other defendants concerning the threat of a possible law enforcement investigation of the project.

The indictment listed 57 transfers of funds between various entities, some controlled by Group DF, in various amounts totaling more than $10.59 million beginning April 28, 2006, through July 13, 2010. The indictment seeks forfeiture from Firtash of his interests in Group DF Limited and its assets, including 14 companies registered in Austria and 18 companies registered in the British Virgin Islands, as well as 127 other companies registered in Cyprus, Germany, Hungary, the Netherlands, Seychelles, Switzerland, the United Kingdom and one unknown jurisdiction and all funds in 41 bank accounts in several of those same countries. Furthermore, the indictment seeks forfeiture from all six defendants of more than $10.59 million.

DD. *United States v. ZAO Hewlett-Packard A.O. (HP Russia);*[459]
SEC v. Hewlett-Packard Co.[460]

▶ **Misconduct Category:**	Bribery of Russian officials to secure a large technology contract with the Office of the Prosecutor General of the Russian Federation; corrupt payments totaling more than $600,000 to Director of Polish National Police Agency Commission; and improper payments under a commission arrangement through a channel partner for Pemex officials in Mexico
▶ **Country:**	Mexico, Poland, and Russia
▶ **Foreign Government Officials:**	Information technology directors
▶ **Improper Payment Dollar Value:**	Over $7 million
▶ **Combined Penalties:**	$108 million (DOJ: $76.7 million in criminal penalties and forfeiture; SEC: $31.4 million in disgorgement, prejudgment interest, and civil penalties)

▶ **Other:**   Government trifecta: Guilty plea for HP
                                Russia; deferred prosecution agreement
                                (DPA) for HP Poland; and nonprosecution
                                agreement (NPA) for HP Mexico. Pressure
                                to win $150 million in Russian business
                                viewed as "golden key" to additional
                                business with Russian government agencies;
                                evidence of bags filled with hundreds of
                                thousands of dollars of cash; provisions
                                of HP desktops and laptops; misuse of
                                channel partner; use of anonymous e-mail
                                accounts and prepaid mobile telephones to
                                avoid detection; use of offshore accounts
                                in Switzerland; Las Vegas trip with private
                                flight over Grand Canyon.

In April 2014, ZAO Hewlett-Packard A.O. (HP Russia), an international subsidiary of the California technology company Hewlett-Packard Company (HP Co.), agreed to plead guilty in the U.S. District Court for the Northern District of California to felony violations of the FCPA and admit its role in bribing Russian government officials to secure a large technology contract with the Office of the Prosecutor General of the Russian Federation. The criminal information charged HP Russia with conspiracy and substantive violations of the antibribery and accounting provisions of the FCPA. In addition, the government is entering into criminal resolutions with HP subsidiaries in Poland and Mexico relating to contracts with Poland's national police agency and Mexico's state-owned petroleum company, respectively. Pursuant to a DPA, the DOJ filed a criminal information charging Hewlett-Packard Polska, Sp. Z.o.o. (HP Poland) with violating the accounting provisions of the FCPA. Hewlett-Packard Mexico, S. de R.L. de C.V. (HP Mexico) entered into a nonprosecution agreement with the DOJ pursuant to which it will forfeit proceeds and admit and accept responsibility for its misconduct as set forth in a statement of facts.

In total, the three HP entities agreed to pay $76,760,224 in criminal penalties and forfeiture. In a related FCPA matter, the SEC filed a proposed final judgment to which issuer Hewlett-Packard Company consented. Under the terms of the proposed final judgment, the parent company agreed to pay the SEC $31,472,250 in disgorgement, prejudgment interest, and civil penalties, bringing the total amount of U.S. criminal and regulatory penalties paid by the parent and its subsidiaries (collectively, HP) to more than $108 million.

1. Russia

According to court documents, in 1999, the Russian government announced a project to automate the computer and telecommunications infrastructure of its Office of the Prosecutor General of the Russian Federation (GPO). Not only was that project itself worth more than $100 million, but HP Russia viewed it as the "golden key" that could unlock the door to another $100 to $150 million dollars in business with Russian government agencies. To secure a contract for the first phase of project, ultimately valued at more than €35 million, HP Russia executives and other employees structured the deal to create a secret slush fund totaling several million dollars, at least part of which was intended for bribes to Russian government officials.

As admitted in a statement of facts, HP Russia created excess profit margins for the slush fund through an elaborate buy-back deal structure, whereby (1) HP sold the computer hardware and other technology products called for under the contract to a Russian channel partner, (2) HP bought the same products back from an intermediary company at a nearly €8 million markup and paid the intermediary an additional €4.2 million for purported services, and (3) HP sold the same products to the GPO at the increased price. The payments to the intermediary were then largely transferred through a cascading series of shell companies—some of which were directly associated with government officials—registered in the United States, United Kingdom, British Virgin Islands, and Belize. Many of these payments from the intermediary were laundered through offshore bank accounts in Switzerland, Lithuania, Latvia, and Austria. Portions of the funds were spent on travel, cars, jewelry, clothing, expensive watches, swimming pool technology, furniture, household appliances, and other luxury goods. To keep track of these corrupt payments, the conspirators inside HP Russia kept two sets of books: secret spreadsheets that detailed the categories of recipients of the corrupt funds and sanitized versions that hid the corrupt payments from others outside of HP Russia. They also entered into off-the-books side agreements. As one example, an HP Russia executive executed a letter agreement to pay €2.8 million in purported "commission" fees to a U.K.-registered shell company, which was linked to a director of the Russian government agency responsible for managing the GPO project. HP Russia never disclosed the existence of the agreement to internal or external auditors or management outside of HP Russia and conducted no due diligence of the shell company. In September 2014, Judge D. Lowell Jensen of the Northern District of California accepted HP Russia's plea of guilty and imposed a $58,772,250 fine.

2. Poland

According to an agreed DPA statement of facts, in Poland, from 2006 through at least 2010, HP Poland falsified HP books and records and circumvented HP internal controls to execute and conceal a scheme to corruptly secure and maintain millions of dollars in technology contracts with the Komenda Główna Policji (KGP), the Polish National Police agency. HP Poland made corrupt payments totaling more than $600,000 in the form of cash bribes and gifts, travel, and entertainment to the KGP's Director of Information and Communications Technology. Among other things, HP Poland gave the government official bags filled with hundreds of thousands of dollars of cash; provided the official with HP desktop and laptop computers, mobile devices, and other products; and took the official on a leisure trip to Las Vegas, which included drinks, dining, entertainment, and a private tour flight over the Grand Canyon. To covertly communicate with the official about the corrupt scheme, an HP Poland executive used anonymous e-mail accounts, prepaid mobile telephones, and other methods meant to evade detection.

3. Mexico

In Mexico, according to the NPA, HP Mexico falsified corporate books and records and circumvented HP internal controls in connection with contracts to sell hardware, software, and licenses to Mexico's state-owned petroleum company, Petroleos Mexicanos (Pemex). To secure the contracts, HP Mexico understood that it had to retain a certain third-party consultant with close ties to senior executives of Pemex. HP agreed to pay a $1.41 million "commission" to the consultant and hid the payments by inserting into the deal structure another third party, which had been approved by HP as a channel partner. HP Mexico made the commission payment to the channel partner, which in turn forwarded the payments to the consultant. Shortly thereafter, the consultant paid one of the Pemex officials approximately to $125,000.

Court filings acknowledged HP Co.'s extensive cooperation with the DOJ, including conducting a robust internal investigation, voluntarily making U.S. and foreign employees available for interviews, and collecting, analyzing, and organizing voluminous evidence for the DOJ. Court filings also acknowledged the extensive anticorruption remedial efforts undertaken by the parent company, including taking appropriate disciplinary action against culpable employees and enhancing its internal accounting, reporting, and compliance functions.

DE. *United States v. Bio-Rad Laboratories, Inc.;*[461] *In re* Bio-Rad Laboratories Inc.[462]

▶ **Misconduct Category:**	Unlawful payments in Vietnam and Thailand to obtain or retain business
▶ **Countries:**	Russia, Thailand, and Vietnam
▶ **Foreign Government Officials:**	Purportedly officials of the Russian Ministry of Health
▶ **Improper Payment Dollar Value:**	$7.5 million
▶ **Combined Penalties:**	$55 million ($14.35 million DOJ criminal penalty; $40.7 million in SEC disgorgement and prejudgment interest)
▶ **Other:**	Nonprosecution agreement (NPA); company is charged by the SEC with paying agent commissions of 15–30 percent while demonstrating a conscious disregard for the high probability that the Russian agents were not performing services and were passing along at least a portion of their commissions to Russian government officials; instruction in e-mail to lower-level employee to "talk with codes"; Vietnamese bribes recorded as "commissions"; "advertising fees" and "training fees"; very little due diligence on Thai acquisition. Two-year compliance and remediation reporting requirement to the DOJ; first agreement to require that prior to the conclusion of the reporting period, Bio-Rad's CEO and CFO must "certify to [DOJ] that the Company has met its disclosure (to disclose new misconduct) obligations."

In November 2014, Bio-Rad Laboratories Inc. (Bio-Rad), a Hercules, California–based medical diagnostics and life sciences manufacturing and sales company, agreed to pay a $14.35 million criminal penalty to the DOJ to resolve allegations that it violated the FCPA by falsifying its books and records and failing to implement adequate internal controls in connection with sales it made in Russia.

According to the company's admissions in the nonprosecution agreement (NPA), Bio-Rad SNC, a Bio-Rad subsidiary located in France, retained and paid intermediary companies commissions of 15–30 percent purportedly in exchange for various services in connection with certain governmental sales in Russia even though distribution costs were estimated to range between 2 percent and 2.5 percent. The intermediary companies, however, did not perform these services. Several high-level managers at Bio-Rad, responsible for overseeing Bio-Rad's business in Russia, reviewed and approved the commission payments to the intermediary companies despite knowing that the intermediary companies were not performing such services. These managers knowingly caused the payments to be falsely recorded on Bio-Rad SNC's and, ultimately, Bio-Rad's books. Bio-Rad, through several of its managers, also failed to implement adequate controls, as well as adequate compliance systems, with regard to its Russian operations while knowing that the failure to implement such controls allowed the intermediary companies to be paid significantly above-market commissions for little or no services.[463]

The DOJ entered into a nonprosecution agreement with the company due, in large part, to Bio-Rad's self-disclosure of the misconduct and full cooperation with the DOJ's investigation. That cooperation included voluntarily making U.S. and foreign employees available for interviews, voluntarily producing documents from overseas, and summarizing the findings of its internal investigation. In addition, Bio-Rad engaged in significant remedial actions, including enhancing its anticorruption policies globally, improving its internal controls and compliance functions, developing and implementing additional due diligence and contracting procedures for intermediaries, and conducting extensive anticorruption training throughout the organization.

In addition to the monetary penalty, Bio-Rad agreed to continue to cooperate with the DOJ, to report periodically to the DOJ for a two-year period concerning Bio-Rad's compliance efforts, and to continue to implement an enhanced compliance program and internal controls designed to prevent and detect FCPA violations. It is required to disclose to the Fraud Section any credible evidence of possible corrupt payments. The Bio-Rad NPA is the first agreement to require that before conclusion of the two-year reporting period, Bio-Rad's CEO and CFO must "certify to [DOJ] that the Company has met its disclosure obligations" subject to the false statement statute (18 U.S.C. § 1001).

In a related matter, the SEC announced that it had entered into a cease-and-desist order against Bio-Rad in which the parent company agreed to pay $40.7 million in disgorgement and prejudgment interest in connection with the company's sales in Russia, as well as in Thailand and Vietnam. The SEC investigation found that Bio-Rad lacked sufficient internal controls to prevent approximately $7.5 million in bribes over a five-year period and improperly recorded the payments as legitimate expenses, including commissions, advertising, and training fees. Red flags include agents who "did not have resources to perform the contracted-for services" and "commissions were excessive and were paid to banks in Latvia and Lithuania." Red flags surfaced repeatedly over five years. According to the SEC, the improper payments allowed Bio-Rad to earn $35 million in illicit profits.[464] The SEC recognized Bio-Rad's thorough Audit Committee investigation, which included over 100 in-person interviews, the collection of millions of documents, the production of tens of thousands of documents, and forensic auditing.

DF. United States v. Dallas Airmotive, Inc.[465]

▶ **Misconduct Category:**	Bribery to officials of Latin American air forces and gubernatorial offices in order to secure government contracts
▶ **Countries:**	Argentina, Brazil, and Peru
▶ **Foreign Government Officials:**	Officials of Brazilian and Peruvian Air Forces and offices of governors in Argentina and Brazil
▶ **Improper Payment Dollar Value:**	Not specified
▶ **Combined Penalties:**	$14 million
▶ **Other:**	Bribe payments described as "commissions" and "consulting fees"; paid vacations for government offices; use of personal e-mails to arrange improper payments and expensive hotel accommodations

In December 2014, Dallas Airmotive Inc., a provider of aircraft engine maintenance, repair, and overhaul (MRO-provider) services based in Grapevine, Texas, admitted to violations of the FCPA and agreed to pay a $14 million criminal penalty to resolve charges that it bribed Latin American government officials in order to secure lucrative government contracts. A criminal information, filed in federal court in the Northern District of Texas as part of a deferred prosecution agreement (DPA), charged Dallas Airmotive with one count of conspiring to violate the FCPA and one count of violating the FCPA's antibribery provisions.

According to Dallas Airmotive's detailed admissions in the statement of facts accompanying the DPA, between 2008 and 2012, the company bribed officials of the Brazilian Air Force, the Peruvian Air Force, the Office of the Governor of the Brazilian State of Roraima, and the Office of the Governor of the San Juan Province in Argentina. Dallas Airmotive used various methods to convey the bribe payments, including by entering into agreements with front companies affiliated with foreign officials, making payments to third-party representatives with the understanding that funds would be directed to foreign officials, and directly providing things of value, such as paid vacations, to foreign officials. Dallas Airmotive is the third MRO-provider to resolve FCPA charges.

DG. *United States v. Avon Products (China) Co., Ltd.*,[466]
     United States v. Avon Products, Inc.,[467] *SEC v. Avon*
     Products, Inc.[468]

▶ **Misconduct Category:**	Improper payments of more than $8 million in gifts, cash, and nonbusiness meals, travel, and entertainment to Chinese governmental officials in order to obtain and retain business benefits for Avon China, including one of the first direct selling licenses in China
▶ **Country:**	China
▶ **Foreign Government Officials:**	Various Chinese government licensing officials, including individuals associated with the Ministry of Commerce (MOFCOM) and the state and regional Administrations for Industry and Commerce (AICs)
▶ **Improper Payment Dollar Value:**	$8 million
▶ **Combined Penalties:**	$135 million ($61,648,000 DOJ criminal penalty, $52,850,000 disgorgement of benefits, and $14,515,013.13 in prejudgment interest)
▶ **Other:**	Guilty plea by a wholly owned Chinese subsidiary and a three-year DPA by parent corporation. The massive fine is likely the result in substantial part of Avon's failure in 2005 in the wake of an audit report to halt improper practices and to further conceal the same. In 2007, parent company executives falsely reported to the Compliance Committee that the FCPA matters in China, including widespread improper gifts and payments to government officials, were "unsubstantiated." In 2008 Avon finally began a full-blown internal investigation after its CEO received a putative whistleblower letter. Avon is required to retain an independent compliance monitor to review its FCPA compliance program for a period of 18 months, followed by an 18-month period of self-reporting on its compliance efforts.

In December 2014 Avon Products (China) Co. Ltd. (Avon China), a wholly owned subsidiary of the New York-based cosmetics company Avon Products Inc. (Avon), pleaded guilty in the Southern District of New York to conspiring to violate the accounting provisions of the FCPA to conceal more than $8 million in gifts, cash, and nonbusiness meals, travel, and entertainment it gave to Chinese government officials in order to obtain and retain business benefits for Avon China. Avon China and Avon admitted the improper accounting and payments, and Avon entered into a three-year deferred prosecution agreement (DPA) to resolve the investigation. Criminal informations were filed against Avon and Avon China, and Avon China entered its guilty plea and was sentenced.

Avon China pleaded guilty to a criminal information charging the company with conspiring to violate the books-and-records provisions of the FCPA. Avon, the parent company, entered into a deferred prosecution agreement and admitted its criminal conduct, including its role in the conspiracy and its failure to implement internal controls. Pursuant to the DPA, the DOJ filed a criminal information charging Avon with conspiring to violate the books-and-records provisions of the FCPA and violating the internal controls provisions of the FCPA. In total, the Avon entities will pay $67,648,000 in criminal penalties. Avon also agreed to implement rigorous internal controls, cooperate fully with the department and retain a compliance monitor for at least 18 months. Avon settled a related FCPA matter with the SEC, and agreed to pay an additional $67,365,013 in disgorgement and prejudgment interest, bringing the total amount of U.S. criminal and regulatory penalties paid by Avon and Avon China to $135,013,013.

According to the companies' admissions, from at least 2004 through 2008, Avon and Avon China conspired to falsify Avon's books and records by falsely describing the nature and purpose of certain Avon China transactions. Specifically, the companies sought to disguise over $8 million in gifts, cash, and nonbusiness travel, meals, and entertainment that Avon China executives and employees gave to government officials in China in order to obtain and retain business benefits for Avon China. Avon needed their approval for direct selling in China. Avon received approval to test direct selling in China in 2005. In March 2006, Avon became one of the first companies to receive a direct selling license. Some examples of payments alleged in the SEC complaint included payments for travel within China or to the United States or Europe, corporate box seats to the China Open tennis tournament; gifts of Louis Vuitton merchandise, Gucci bags, and Tiffany pens; and $1.65 million for meals and entertainment. (See chapter 6, section IV.I for further details.) Avon China attempted to disguise the payments and benefits through various means, including falsely describing the nature or purpose of, or participants associated with such expenses, and falsely recording payments to a third-party intermediary as payments for legitimate consulting services.

The companies also admitted that in late 2005 Avon learned through an internal audit report that Avon China was routinely providing things of value to Chinese government officials and failing to properly document them. Instead of ensuring the practice was halted, fixing the false books and records, disciplining the culpable individuals, and implementing appropriate controls to address this problem, the companies took steps to conceal the conduct, despite knowing that Avon China's books and records, and ultimately Avon's books and records and consolidated financial statements, would continue to be inaccurate. Avon management had consulted an outside law firm, directed that reforms be instituted at the subsidiary, and sent an internal audit team to follow up. Ultimately, however, no such reforms were instituted at the Chinese subsidiary. In January 2007, an Avon executive reported to the Compliance Committee that the matter regarding potential FCPA violations at the China subsidiary had been closed as "unsubstantiated," even though that executive and other parent company executives and attorneys knew of the subsidiary's previous and continuing practice of giving things of value to government officials, ongoing false books and records, and the failure to implement adequate internal controls. Avon finally began a full-blown internal investigation in 2008 after its CEO received a letter from a whistleblower.

Court filings acknowledge Avon's cooperation with the DOJ, including conducting an extensive internal investigation in China and other relevant countries; voluntarily making U.S. and foreign employees available for interviews; its voluntary disclosure of its employees' and its subsidiary's employees' misconduct, which came relatively soon after the company received a whistleblower letter alleging misconduct but years after certain senior executives of the company had learned of and sought to hide the misconduct in China; collecting, analyzing, translating, and organizing voluminous evidence; and the company's extensive remediation, including terminating the employees responsible for the misconduct, enhancing its compliance program and internal controls, and significantly increasing the resources available for compliance and internal audit. The *Avon* resolution demonstrates the high costs of failing to stop misconduct when discovered and to remediate promptly.

DH. *United States v. Alstom S.A. (Alstom)*;[469]
     United States v. Alstom Network Schweiz AG;[470]
     U.S. DOJ–Alstom Power Inc. Agreement;[471]
     U.S. DOJ of Justice–Alstom Grid Inc. Agreement[472]

▶ **Misconduct Category:**   Bribes totaling $75 million paid to government officials, including officials of state-owned entities, to secure $4 billion worth of power, grid, and transportation projects around the world.

▶ **Countries:**   Bahamas, Egypt, Indonesia, Saudi Arabia, and Taiwan

▶ **Foreign Government Officials:**   Officials of state-owned electric companies and member of Indonesian Parliament

▶ **Improper Payment Dollar Value:** $75 million

▶ **DOJ Penalty:** $772 million

▶ **Other:**

Largest FCPA criminal penalty in DOJ history. Decade-long widespread schemes to bribe government officials to secure energy projects. Parent company Alstrom S.A. pled guilty to falsifying books and records and failing to implement adequate internal controls. A Swiss subsidiary pled guilty to conspiracy to violate the antibribery provisions, while two U.S. subsidiaries entered into DPAs for related conduct. Alstom's refusal to fully cooperate for years, its prior misconduct resolutions with the World Bank and various other companies, misconduct that continued for years after it was discovered by internal audit, the involvement of high-level officers, and the length and breadth of the misconduct contributed to the massive DOJ fine. Internal documents reflected the use of code names for consultants such as "Mr. Geneva," "Mr. Paris," "London," "Quiet Man," and "Old Friend." No meaningful due diligence conducted on consultants despite blowing red flags. Alstom likely avoided a full-blown independent FCPA monitorship due to its already existing World Bank monitorship.

▶ **Related Matters:**

United States v. Pierucci; United States v. Rothschild; United States v. Pomponi; United States v. Hoskins; United States v. Marubeni

In December 2014, Alstom S.A. (Alstom), a French power generation and transportation company, pleaded guilty and agreed to pay a record $772,290,000 DOJ criminal fine to resolve charges related to a widespread scheme involving tens of millions of dollars in bribes in countries around the world, including Indonesia, Saudi Arabia, Egypt, and the Bahamas.

Alstom pleaded guilty to a two-count criminal information filed in the U.S. District Court for the District of Connecticut, charging the parent company with violating the FCPA by falsifying its books and records and failing to implement adequate internal controls. By not pleading guilty to a felony, the parent company likely avoided suspension and debarment consequences. Alstom admitted its criminal conduct and agreed to pay a criminal penalty of $772,290,000. A sentencing hearing is set for June 2015. In addition, Alstom Network Schweiz AG, formerly Alstom Prom, Alstom's Swiss subsidiary, pleaded guilty to a criminal information charging the company with conspiracy to violate the antibribery provisions of the FCPA. Alstom Power Inc. and Alstom Grid Inc., two U.S. subsidiaries, both entered into three-year deferred prosecution agreements, admitting that they conspired to violate the antibribery provisions of the FCPA. Alstom Power is headquartered in Windsor, Connecticut, and Alstom Grid, formerly Alstom T&D, was headquartered in New Jersey. Because Alstom shares are not publicly traded on a U.S. stock exchange, there was no SEC enforcement action.

According to the companies' admissions, Alstom, Alstom Prom, Alstom Power, and Alstom Grid, through various executives and employees, paid bribes to government officials and falsified books and records in connection with power, grid, and transportation projects for state-owned entities around the world, including in Indonesia, Egypt, Saudi Arabia, the Bahamas, and Taiwan. In Indonesia, for example, Alstom, Alstom Prom, and Alstom Power paid bribes to government officials—including a high-ranking member of the Indonesian Parliament and high-ranking members of Perusahaan Listrik Negara, the state-owned electricity company in Indonesia—in exchange for assistance in securing several contracts to provide power-related services valued at approximately $375 million. In total, Alstom paid more than $75 million to secure $4 billion in projects around the world, with a profit to the company of approximately $296 million.

Alstom and its subsidiaries also attempted to conceal the bribery scheme by retaining consultants purportedly to provide consulting services on behalf of the companies, but who actually served as conduits for corrupt payments to the government officials. Certain consultants proposed for retention had no expertise or experience in the industry sector in which Alstom was working to secure a project. Other consultants were located in countries different from the project countries. At other times, the consultants asked to be paid in a currency or in a bank account located in a country other than where the consultant or the project was located. Alstom maintained an unwritten policy to discourage, where possible, consultancy arrangements that would subject Alstom to the jurisdiction of the United States. To effectuate this policy, the company typically used consultants who were not based in the United States and whose currencies were other than U.S. dollars. On multiple occasions, more than one consultant was retained on the same project, ostensibly to perform the same services. Despite "red flags," the consultants were retained without meaningful due diligence. Internal Alstom documents referred to some of the consultants in code, including "Mr. Geneva," "Mr. Paris," "London," "Quiet Man," and "Old Friend."

The plea agreement cited many factors considered by the DOJ in reaching an appropriate resolution, including Alstom's failure to voluntarily disclose the misconduct even though it was aware of related misconduct at a U.S. subsidiary that previously resolved corruption charges with the DOJ in connection with a power project in Italy; Alstom's refusal to fully cooperate with the DOJ's investigation for several years; the breadth of the companies' misconduct, which spanned many years, occurred in countries around the globe and in several business lines, and involved sophisticated schemes to bribe high-level government officials; Alstom's lack of an effective compliance and ethics program at the time of the conduct; and Alstom's prior criminal misconduct, including conduct that led to resolutions with various other governments and the World Bank. In June 2014, Alstom agreed to sell most of its energy business to General Electric and stated that pursuant to its discussions with the DOJ, it would not be able to transfer its $772 million fine to GE.[473]

After the DOJ charged several Alstom executives in late 2012 and unsealed three informations in April 2013, Alstom began providing thorough cooperation, including assisting the DOJ's prosecution of other companies and individuals. To date, the DOJ has announced charges against five individuals, including four corporate executives of Alstom and its subsidiaries, for alleged corrupt conduct involving Alstom. Frederic Pierucci, Alstom's former vice president of global boiler sales, pleaded guilty on July 29, 2013, to conspiring to violate the FCPA and a charge of violating the FCPA for his role in the Indonesia bribery scheme. David Rothschild, Alstom Power's former vice president of regional sales, pleaded guilty on November 2, 2012, to conspiracy to violate the FCPA. William Pomponi, Alstom Power's former vice president of regional sales, pleaded guilty on July 17, 2014, to conspiracy to violate the FCPA. Lawrence Hoskins, Alstom's former senior vice president for the Asia region, was charged in a second superseding indictment on July 30, 2013, and is pending trial in the District of Connecticut in June 2015. The high-ranking member of Indonesian Parliament was also convicted in Indonesia of accepting bribes from Alstom, and is currently serving a three-year term of imprisonment.

In connection with a corrupt scheme in Egypt, Asem Elgawhary, the general manager of an entity working on behalf of the Egyptian Electricity Holding Company, a state-owned electricity company, pleaded guilty on December 4, 2014, in the District of Maryland to mail fraud, conspiring to launder money, and tax fraud for accepting kickbacks from Alstom and other companies. In his plea agreement, Elgawhary agreed to serve 42 months in prison and forfeit approximately $5.2 million in proceeds.

The corporate compliance program required of Alstom SA includes the following 18 elements:

High-Level Commitment

1. The Company will ensure that its directors and senior management provide strong, explicit, and visible support and commitment to its corporate policy against violations of the anticorruption laws and its compliance code.

Policies and Procedures

2. The Company will maintain, or where necessary establish, a clearly articulated and visible corporate policy against violations of the FCPA and other applicable foreign law counterparts (collectively, the "anticorruption laws,"), which policy shall be memorialized in a written compliance code.

3. The Company will maintain, or where necessary establish, compliance policies and procedures designed to reduce the prospect of violations of the anticorruption laws and the Company's compliance code, and the Company will take appropriate measures to encourage and support the observance of ethics and compliance policies and procedures against violation of the anticorruption laws by personnel at all levels of the Company. These anticorruption policies and procedures shall apply to all directors, officers, and employees and, where necessary and appropriate, outside parties acting on behalf of the Company in a foreign jurisdiction, including but not limited to, agents and intermediaries,

consultants, representatives, distributors, teaming partners, contractors and suppliers, consortia, and joint venture partners (collectively, "agents and business partners"). The Company shall notify all employees that compliance with the policies and procedures is the duty of individuals at all levels of the company. Such policies and procedures shall address:

    a. gifts;

    b. hospitality, entertainment, and expenses;

    c. customer travel;

    d. political contributions;

    e. charitable donations and sponsorships;

    f. facilitation payments; and

    g. solicitation and extortion.

4. The Company will ensure that it has a system of financial and accounting procedures, including a system of internal controls, reasonably designed to ensure the maintenance of fair and accurate books, records, and accounts. This system should be designed to provide reasonable assurances that:

    a. transactions are executed in accordance with management's general or specific authorization;

    b. transactions are recorded as necessary to permit preparation of financial statements in conformity with generally accepted accounting principles or any other criteria applicable to such statements, and to maintain accountability for assets;

    c. access to assets is permitted only in accordance with management's general or specific authorization; and

    d. the recorded accountability for assets is compared with the existing assets at reasonable intervals and appropriate action is taken with respect to any differences.

Periodic Risk-Based Review

5. The Company will develop these compliance policies and procedures on the basis of a risk assessment addressing the individual circumstances of the Company, in particular the foreign bribery risks facing the Company, including, but not limited to, its geographical organization, interactions with various types and levels of government officials, industrial sectors of operation, involvement in joint venture arrangements, importance of licenses and permits in the Company's operations, degree of governmental oversight and inspection, and volume and importance of goods and personnel clearing through customs and immigration.

6. The Company shall review its anticorruption compliance policies and procedures no less than annually and update them as appropriate to ensure their continued effectiveness, taking into account relevant developments in the field and evolving international and industry standards.

Proper Oversight and Independence

7. The Company will assign responsibility to one or more senior corporate executives of the Company for the implementation and oversight of the

Company's anticorruption compliance code, policies, and procedures. Such corporate official(s) shall have direct reporting obligations to independent monitoring bodies, including internal audit, the Company's Board of Directors, or any appropriate committee of the Board of Directors, and shall have an adequate level of autonomy from management as well as sufficient resources and authority to maintain such autonomy.

Training and Guidance

8. The Company will maintain, or where necessary establish, mechanisms designed to ensure that its anticorruption compliance code, policies, and procedures are effectively communicated to all directors, officers, employees, and, where necessary and appropriate, agents and business partners. These mechanisms shall include: (a) periodic training for all directors and officers, all employees in positions of leadership or trust, positions that require such training (e.g., internal audit, sales, legal, compliance, finance), or positions that otherwise pose a corruption risk to the Company, and, where necessary and appropriate, agents and business partners; and (b) annual certifications by all such directors, officers, employees, agents, and business partners, certifying compliance with the training requirements.

9. The Company will maintain, or where necessary establish, an effective system for providing guidance and advice to directors, officers, employees, and, where necessary and appropriate, agents and business partners, on complying with the Company's anticorruption compliance code, policies, and procedures, including when they need advice on an urgent basis or in any foreign jurisdiction in which the Company operates.

Internal Reporting and Investigation

10. The Company will maintain, or where necessary establish, an effective system for internal and, where possible, confidential reporting by, and protection of, directors, officers, employees, and, where appropriate, agents and business partners concerning violations of the anticorruption laws or the Company's anticorruption compliance code, policies, and procedures.

11. The Company will maintain, or where necessary establish, an effective and reliable process with sufficient resources for responding to, investigating, and documenting allegations of violations of the anticorruption laws or the Company's anticorruption compliance code, policies, and procedures.

Enforcement and Discipline

12. The Company will maintain, or where necessary establish, mechanisms designed to effectively enforce its compliance code, policies, and procedures, including appropriately incentivizing compliance and disciplining violations.

13. The Company will maintain, or where necessary establish, appropriate disciplinary procedures to address, among other things, violations of the anticorruption laws and the Company's anticorruption compliance

code, policies, and procedures by the Company's directors, officers, and employees. Such procedures should be applied consistently and fairly, regardless of the position held by, or perceived importance of, the director, officer, or employee. The Company shall implement procedures to ensure that where misconduct is discovered, reasonable steps are taken to remedy the harm resulting from such misconduct, and to ensure that appropriate steps are taken to prevent further similar misconduct, including assessing the internal controls, compliance code, policies, and procedures and making modifications necessary to ensure the overall anticorruption compliance program is effective.

Third-Party Relationships

14. The Company will maintain, or where necessary establish, appropriate risk-based due diligence and compliance requirements pertaining to the retention and oversight of all agents and business partners, including:
    a. properly documented due diligence pertaining to the hiring and appropriate and regular oversight of agents and business partners;
    b. informing agents and business partners of the Company's commitment to abiding by anticorruption laws, and of the Company's anticorruption compliance code, policies, and procedures; and
    c. seeking a reciprocal commitment from agents and business partners.

15. Where necessary and appropriate, the Company will include standard provisions in agreements, contracts, and renewals thereof with all agents and business partners that are reasonably calculated to prevent violations of the anticorruption laws, which may, depending upon the circumstances, include: (a) anticorruption representations and undertakings relating to compliance with the anticorruption laws; (b) rights to conduct audits of the books and records of the agent or business partner to ensure compliance with the foregoing; and (c) rights to terminate an agent or business partner as a result of any breach of the anticorruption laws, the Company's compliance code, policies, or procedures, or the representations and undertakings related to such matters.

Mergers and Acquisitions

16. The Company will maintain, or where necessary establish, policies and procedures for mergers and acquisitions requiring that the Company conduct appropriate risk-based due diligence on potential new business entities, including appropriate FCPA and anticorruption due diligence by legal, accounting, and compliance personnel. *If the Company discovers any corrupt payments or inadequate internal controls as part of its due diligence of newly acquired entities or entities merged with the Company, it shall report such conduct to the Department.*

17. The Company will ensure that the Company's compliance code, policies, and procedures regarding the anticorruption laws apply as quickly as is practicable to newly acquired businesses or entities merged with the Company and will promptly:

a. train the directors, officers, employees, agents, and business partners consistent with Paragraph 8 above on the anticorruption laws and the Company's compliance code, policies, and procedures regarding anti-corruption laws; and

b. where warranted, conduct an FCPA-specific audit of all newly acquired or merged businesses as quickly as practicable.

Monitoring and Testing

18. The Company will conduct periodic reviews and testing of its anticorruption compliance code, policies, and procedures designed to evaluate and improve their effectiveness in preventing and detecting violations of anticorruption laws and the Company's anticorruption code, policies, and procedures, taking into account relevant developments in the field and evolving international and industry standards.[474]

VII. PRACTICAL ADVICE IN INTERPRETING FCPA PROSECUTIONS, ENFORCEMENT ACTIONS, DOJ FCPA OPINION RELEASES, AND DOJ AND SEC CHARGING CRITERIA

Because there is a dearth of FCPA case law, counsel must carefully review DOJ prosecutions, DPAs, and NPAs, and SEC enforcement actions in the FCPA area. While not controlling as a matter of law, these resolutions can help guide clients through a challenging and evolving enforcement area. Some rules of thumb in reviewing the growing number of government charges, resolutions, and opinion releases include:

- Read each DOJ press release or SEC litigation release and DOJ indictment, information or SEC complaint carefully for what it says and does not say. For example, does the resolution require a monitorship or simply impose an independent consultant or self-reporting requirement? Is the DOJ criminal penalty within or below the United States Sentencing Guidelines' recommended range? Does the SEC settlement through disgorgement of profits and pre-judgment interest in effect negate any financial benefit or credit off the DOJ's USSG calculation? Does the press release suggest an ongoing investigation crossover into a related industry? For example, the Vetco Gray 2007 settlement spawned an investigation of Panalpina, a major international freight forwarder, and its customers leading to fines exceeding $235 million.
- Review favorable DOJ or SEC resolutions for their recognition of important compliance program and remedial measure efforts, for example, Siemens, Willbros, Noble, Pride International, Maxwell Technologies, and Johnson & Johnson and, in the case of Morgan Stanley, avoidance of any adverse action in the *Garth Peterson* resolution.
- Review the resolutions for language that portends follow-on individual DOJ prosecutions and/or SEC enforcement actions. For example, the Schnitzer Steel criminal resolution led to a later SEC enforcement action against Schnitzer Steel CEO Robert Philip.

- Do not overlook and ignore the lessons of seemingly minor resolutions. For example, the SEC's Delta & Pine Land settlement signals a low dollar enforcement threshold for improper payments ($8,300/year), notwithstanding the company's voluntary disclosure and complete cooperation with the SEC.
- Assume that some of the DOJ and/or SEC settlement total dollar figures are approximations or estimates and may reflect what the U.S. government thought it could prove in court as opposed to what it believes the actual figures may have been.
- Review what role a company's settlement with a foreign government authority may have played in the U.S. law enforcement settlement. For example, the Statoil settlement with the government of Norway likely reduced its U.S. fines.
- Consider how the DOJ penalties in a published settlement correspond to U.S. Sentencing Guideline calculations under the Alternative Fines Act.
- Contrast the improper payment totals and resulting criminal penalties in first-offender cases versus recidivist cases (e.g., Baker Hughes, Vetco Gray, IBM, and Marubeni), to understand the fine multiplier the government may have used against recidivists.
- Consider whether proactive third-party due diligence and timely anticorruption training may lessen the need for an independent monitor or reduce a fine.
- Consider what types of misconduct are increasingly the focus of DOJ and SEC authorities, for example, Chinese travel and entertainment in the Lucent, Diebold, Bruker, and Avon resolutions; merger and acquisition activity in the Titan, InVision, Latin Node, and Johnson & Johnson cases; improper use of consultants as in the Alcoa, KBR, and Alstom resolutions; or misuse of Chinese design institutes in the ITT, Avery Dennison, Rockwell Automation, or Watts Water Technologies resolutions.
- Review the jurisdictional basis and theory underlying any DOJ or SEC action against foreign nationals or subsidiaries; for example, an act in furtherance may be as insignificant as an e-mail in the United States.
- Consider why FCPA accounting violations were brought instead of more egregious bribery violations; was there insufficient proof of bribes, questionable things of value, or credit for exceptional cooperation or an issue with government debarment and suspension if there were a bribery conviction? (See Siemens AG resolution.)
- Review the SEC filings of any public company whose conduct is similar to the client's.
- Determine what specific remedial actions led the DOJ to not insist on a felony conviction; for example, Willbros's substantial FCPA cooperation against former employees resulted in DPAs for both the parent and subsidiary. Study and implement where possible the most recent 18 articulated compliance program elements to demonstrate an awareness and recognition of the DOJ's pronouncements and resolutions.
- Consider why a resolution required or waived the imposition of a monitor. For example, the majority of UN Oil-for-Food program prosecution settlements have not required an independent monitor. In Ingersoll-Rand and Paradigm, federal authorities permitted a "monitor-lite." Panalpina, due to

its thorough internal investigation and remedial actions during the U.S. government investigation, avoided a monitorship.

- Consider whether potential government debarment played a role in which charges were ultimately filed; for example, Siemens and Alstom were not charged with bribery conduct for worldwide improper payments, but rather with criminal books-and-records and internal controls violations, thereby avoiding likely mandatory EU debarment. Were the DPA penalties for Royal Dutch Shell and its Nigerian subsidiary SNEPCO substantial in order to avoid a conviction that might bar Shell from government contracts?

- Note how often the DOJ penalties and SEC civil fines and forfeitures nearly match; for example, in the *Avon Products* matter each obtained fines of $67 million; in *Daimler*, the DOJ fine was $93.6 million, the SEC component $91.4 million.

- Ascertain any industry, government program, or regional enforcement patterns. For example, the UN Oil-for-Food program cases did not result in FCPA bribery charges, because improper payments were made to a foreign government (Iraq) and not foreign government officials.

- Scan the index of DOJ FCPA Opinion Releases (appendix 5) and consider any factually similar opinions.

- Consider the revenues and size of the subsidiary involved. Tyson Foods makes clear that misconduct at a very small foreign subsidiary (1 percent of sales) can expose a parent to DOJ and SEC enforcement actions.

- Consider whether the settlement or underlying document gives guidance on a particular foreign operation issue or policy; for example, the Wabtech NPA indicated that a $31.50 monthly payment to avoid recurrent audits may not be a legal "facilitating payment."

- Examine whether there are any local law references or resolutions such as in the Alcatel-Lucent or Statoil matters.

- Review the SEC/DOJ publication *FCPA: Resource Guide to the United States Foreign Corrupt Practices Act* (2012) for particular guidance (appendix 4).

- Review the nine corporate charging criteria and commentary in *Principles of Federal Prosecution of Business Organizations* (appendix 9).

- Review the 13 SEC *Seaboard* charging criteria in any SEC investigation (appendix 11).

- Consider any section 20(a) Reports of the SEC, for example, Titan and Halliburton cases offering guidance to securities counsel handling mergers and acquisitions.

- For compliance program best practices, study the various elements of the corporate compliance programs approved and articulated in the most recent FCPA resolutions, for example, Alstom and Avon Products.

VIII. ADDITIONAL RESOURCES

- Margaret Ayres & Bethany Hipp, *Selected Trends in Enforcement of Anti-Corruption Laws throughout the World, in* THE FOREIGN CORRUPT PRACTICES ACT 2009: COPING WITH HEIGHTENED ENFORCEMENT RISKS (PLI Course Handbook B-1737, 2009).

- Peter B. Clark & Jennifer A. Suprenant, Siemens—Potential Interplay of FCPA Charges and Mandatory Debarment under the Public Procurement Directive of the European Union, ABA National Institute on White Collar Crime (San Francisco, Mar. 5–6, 2009).
- Gibson, Dunn & Crutcher LLP, 2014 Year-End FCPA Update (Jan. 5, 2015), http://www.gibsondunn.com/publications/pages/2014-Year-End-FCPA -Update.aspx.
- Jay G. Martin, Compliance with the Foreign Corrupt Practices Act and the Developing International Anti-Corruption Environment (unpublished manuscript, on file at Baker Hughes Inc.).
- Press releases and litigation releases involving FCPA cases at DOJ and SEC websites (http://www.justice.gov and http://www.sec.gov).
- Shearman & Sterling, FCPA Digest (Jan. 2015) (comprehensive listing of every FCPA case since 1977), http://www.shearman.com.
- Crim. Div., U.S. Dep't of Justice & Enforcement Div., U.S. Sec. & Exch. Comm., FCPA: A Resource Guide to the U.S. Foreign Corrupt Practices Act (2012), http://www.justice.gov/criminal/fraud/fcpa/guidance/ or http://www.sec.gov /spotlight/fcpa.shtml (appendix 4).
- Philip Urofsky et al., *Recent Trends and Patterns in Enforcement of the U.S. Foreign Corrupt Practices Act*, (Jan. 5, 2015) Shearman & Sterling LLP, http://www .shearman.com/en/newsinsights/publications/2015/01/fcpa-digest.

NOTES

1. Pub. L. No. 107-204, 116 Stat. 745 (codified at 15 U.S.C. §§ 7201 *et seq.*).

2. Pub. L. No. 111-203, H.R. 4173 (codified at 15 U.S.C. ch. 2B, § 21F Securities Whistleblower Incentives and Protection Act); SEC Release for Rules Implementing the Whistleblower Provisions of Section 21F of Securities Exchange Act of 1934 (May 25, 2011), http://www.sec.gov/rule/final/2011/34-64545.pdf.

3. Press Release, U.S. Dep't of Justice, BAE Systems PLC Pleads Guilty and Ordered to Pay $400 Million Criminal Fine (Mar. 1, 2010), http://www.justice.gov/opa /pr/2010/March/10-CRM-209.html.

4. Press Release, U.S. Dep't of Justice, Assistant Attorney General Leslie R. Caldwell Speaks at the Launch of the Organisation for Economic Co-operation and Development Foreign Bribery Report (Dec. 2, 2014), http://www.justice.gov/opa/speech /assistant-attorney-general-leslie-r-caldwell-speaks-launch-oraganization-economic-co.

5. United States v. Alstom, S.A., 3:14-cr-00246-JBA (D. Conn. Dec. 22, 2014).

6. Robert W. Tarun & Peter P. Tomczak, *Introductory Essay for the 25th Anniversary White Collar Crime Survey: A Proposal for a United States Department of Justice Foreign Corrupt Practices Act Leniency Policy*, 47 Am. Crim. L. Rev. 153 (Spring 2010).

7. Crim. Div., U.S. Dep't of Justice & Enforcement Div., U.S. Sec. & Exch. Comm., FCPA: A Resource Guide to the U.S. Foreign Corrupt Practices Act (2012) [hereinafter Resource Guide], http://www.justice.gov/criminal/fraud/fcpa/guidance/ or http://www.sec.gov/spotlight/fcpa.shtml (appendix 4).

8. *See* 15 U.S.C. § 78dd-1(a).

9. *See* 15 U.S.C. § 78dd-3(a).

10. GIBSON DUNN, 2014 YEAR-END FCPA UPDATE 6 (Jan. 5, 2015), http://www .gibsondunn.com/publications/pages/2014-Year-End-FCPA-Update.aspx.

11. *Id. See* Jean Eaglesham, *SEC Is Steering More Trials to Judges It Appoints*, WALL ST. J., Oct. 21, 2014, http://www.wsj.com/articles/sec-is-steering-more-trials-to-judges-it -appoints-1413849590.

12. Yin Wilczek, *SEC to Unveil FCPA Actions against Individuals by Year's End*, BNA CORP. COUNSEL WKLY. (Oct. 10, 2014), http://www.bna.com/sec-unveil-fcpa-n17179896476/.

13. *See, e.g.*, United States v. ABB Vetco Gray Inc.; United States v. Statoil Inc.; United States v. SSI Int'l Far E. Ltd.; United States v. Siemens AG; United States v. Willbros Group Inc.; United States v. York Int'l Group.

14. Criminal Information, United States v. Monsanto Co., No. 05-CR-00008 (D.D.C. filed Jan. 6, 2005).

15. *See, e.g.*, Admin. Proceeding Order, *In re* Delta & Pine Land Co. & Turk Deltap- ine, Inc., SEC Release No. 56,138, Admin. Proceeding File No. 3-12712, Litig. Release No. 20,214 (July 26, 2007).

16. Remarks of Assistant Attorney General of the Criminal Division of the DOJ Leslie R. Caldwell at ABA Nat'l Inst. on White Collar Crime (New Orleans, Mar. 6, 2015).

17. Press Release, U.S. Dep't of Justice, Aibel Group Ltd. Pleads Guilty to Foreign Bribery and Agrees to Pay $4.2 Million in Criminal Fines (Nov. 21, 2008), http://www .usdoj.gov/opa/pr/2008/November/08-crm-1041.html.

18. Complaint, SEC v. Peterson, No. CV-12-2033-JBW (E.D.N.Y. filed Apr. 25, 2012), Litig. Release No. 22,346 (Apr. 25, 2012).

19. Press Release, U.S. Dep't of Justice, RAE Systems Agrees to Pay $1.7 Million Criminal Penalty to Resolve Violations of the Foreign Corrupt Practices Act (Dec. 10, 2010), http://www.justice.gov/opa/pr/2010/December/10-crm-1428.html.

20. Richard Grime & Alison Fischer, *Obvious and Not-So-Obvious Consequences for the Risk of FCPA Enforcement*, ABA Nat'l Inst. on White Collar Crime (San Francisco, Mar. 5–6, 2009) (citing Judith Burns, *U.S. Justice Department Probing Oil Operation in Nigeria*, DOW JONES NEWS WIRE, July 25, 2007; *Oil Field Services Firm under Fire in Africa*, PETROL. INTELLIGENCE WKLY., Oct. 22. 2007).

21. *See* Robert W. Tarun & Peter P. Tomczak, *Introductory Essay: A Proposal for a United States Department of Justice Foreign Corrupt Practices Act Leniency Policy*, 47 AM. CRIM. L. REV. (Spring 2010).

22. RESOURCE GUIDE, *supra* note 7, at 82–83.

23. STEVEN L. SKALAK ET AL., A GUIDE TO FORENSIC ACCOUNTING INVESTIGATION (2d ed. 2011).

24. U.S. Dep't of Justice, Foreign Corrupt Practices Act, http://www.justice.gov /criminal/fraud/fcpa; U.S. Sec. & Exch. Comm'n, Spotlight on Foreign Corrupt Prac- tices Act, http://www.sec.gov/spotlight/fcpa.shtml.

25. http://www.shearman.com.

26. Admin. Proceeding Order, SEC v. Int'l Bus. Machs. Corp., Litig. Release No. 16,839, 73 SEC Docket 3049 (Dec. 21, 2000).

27. Securities Exchange Act of 1934 § 13(b)(2)(A).

28. Admin. Proceeding Order, *In re* Baker Hughes Inc., Exchange Act Release No. 44,784, 75 SEC Docket 1808 (Sept. 12, 2001).

29. No. 01-CV-3105 (S.D. Tex. 2001).

30. No. 01-CV-3106 (S.D. Tex. 2001).

31. *In re* Chiquita Brands Int'l, Inc., Exchange Act Release No. 44,902, 75 SEC Docket 2308 (Oct. 3, 2001).

32. Complaint, SEC v. Bell S. Corp., No. 1:02-CV-0113 (N.D. Ga. filed Jan. 15, 2002), Litig. Release No. 17,310 (Jan. 15, 2002).

33. Complaint, *In re* Bellsouth Corp., Exchange Act Release No. 45,279, Litig. Release No. 17,310 (Jan. 15, 2002).

34. *Id.*

35. Admin. Proceeding Order, *In re* BJ Servs. Co., Exchange Act Release No. 49,390, Admin. Proceeding File No. 3-11427 (Mar. 10, 2004).

36. Complaint, *In re* Schering-Plough Corp., Exchange Act Release No. 49,838, 82 S.E.C. Docket 3644, Litig. Release No. 18,740 (June 9, 2004).

37. No. 1:04-CV-00945 (D.D.C. filed June 9, 2004).

38. SEC Release No. 53,732 (Apr. 27, 2006).

39. 06-CV-249 (S.D.N.Y. filed Apr. 17, 2006).

40. Litig. Release No. 19,657, Accounting and Auditing Enforcement Release No. 2414 (Apr. 17, 2006), http://www.sec.gov/litigation/litreleases/2006/lr19657.htm.

41. *Tyco*, Complaint at ¶¶ 47–55.

42. Complaint, SEC v. Pillor, No. C-06-4906-WHA (N.D. Cal. filed Aug. 15, 2006).

43. Litig. Release No. 19,803 (Aug. 15, 2006), http://www.sec.gov/litigation/litreleases/2006/lr19803.htm.

44. *Pillor*, Complaint at ¶ 29.

45. *Id.* at ¶¶ 15 (Thailand), 19 (Philippines), & 22 (Thailand).

46. Burns & Sullivan, *Navigating the FCPA's Complex Scienter Requirements*, BLOOMBERG FINANCE L.P. (Apr. 1, 2009), http://www.gibsondunn.com/publications/Pages/NavigatingtheFCPAsComplex?ScienterRequirements.aspx.

47. Complaint, SEC v. Dow Chem. Co., No. 07-CV-00336 (D.D.C. filed Feb. 13, 2007), Litig. Release No. 20,000 (Feb. 13, 2007).

48. SEC Admin. Proceeding File No. 3-12567 (Feb. 13, 2007).

49. SEC Release No. 56,138, Admin. Proceeding File No. 3-12712 (July 26, 2007).

50. Complaint, SEC v. Delta & Pine Land Co., No. 1:07-CV-01352 (RWR) (D.D.C. filed July 25, 2007).

51. Litig. Release No. 20,251 (Aug. 23, 2007), http://www.sec.gov/litigation/litreleases/2007/lr20251.htm.

52. SEC Release No. 56,533, Admin. Proceeding File No. 3-12833 (Sept. 26, 2007).

53. Complaint, SEC v. Srinivasan, No. 07-CV-01699 (D.D.C. filed Sept. 25, 2007).

54. *Id.*

55. Admin. Proceeding Order, *In re* Elec. Data Sys. Corp., SEC Release No. 20,296, Exchange Act Release No. 56,519, Admin. Proceeding File No. 3-12825 (Sept. 25, 2007).

56. Complaint, SEC v. Chevron Corp., No. 07-CV-10299 (S.D.N.Y. filed Nov. 14, 2007), Litig. Release No. 20,363 (Nov. 14, 2007).

57. Litig. Release No. 20,410 (Dec. 20, 2007), http://www.sec.gov/litigation/litreleases/2007/lr20410.htm.

58. Letter from Loni A. Leonovicz, Dep't of Justice, to John L. Hardiman, Sullivan & Cromwell LLP (Dec. 20, 2007), *http://www.justice.gov.*

59. No. 1:08-CV-01478-EGS (D.D.C.), http://www.sec.gov/litigation/litreleases/2008/lr20690.htm (Aug. 27, 2008). See also Press Release, U.S. Sec. & Exch. Comm'n, SEC Files

Settled Enforcement Action Charging Con-way Inc. with Violations of the Foreign Corrupt Practices Act (Aug. 27, 2008), http://www.sec.gov/litigation/litreleases/2008/lr20690.htm.

60. Complaint, SEC v. ITT Corp., No. 09-CV-00272-RJL (D.D.C. filed Feb. 11, 2009), http://www.sec.gov/litigation/complaints/2009/comp20896.pdf.

61. Complaint, SEC v. Wurzel, No. 09-Civ-01005-RWR (D.D.C. filed May 29, 2009).

62. SEC Exchange Act Release No. 34-60005, Accounting and Auditing Enforcement Release No. 2981 (May 29, 2009).

63. *Id.* at 2, Corrected Order Instituting Cease and Desist Proceedings.

64. Complaint, SEC v. Nature's Sunshine Prods., Inc., No. 09-CV-672 (D. Utah filed July 31, 2009), Litig. Release No. 21,162 (July 31, 2009), http://www.sec.gov /litigation/litreleases/2009/lr21162.htm; Press Release, U.S. Sec. & Exch. Comm'n, SEC Charges Natures' Sunshine Products, Inc. with Making Illegal Foreign Payments (July 31, 2009), http://www.sec.gov/litigation/litreleases/2009/lr21162.htm.

65. Complaint, SEC v. Avery Dennison Corp., No. 09-CV-5493 (C.D. Cal. filed July 28, 2009), Litig. Release No. 21,156 (July 28, 2009).

66. Complaint, SEC v. Benton, No. 09-CV-03963 (S.D. Tex. filed Dec. 11, 2009), Litig. Release No. 21,335 (Dec. 14, 2009), http://www.sec.gov/litigation/litreleases/2009 /lr21335.htm.

67. Complaint, SEC v. NATCO Group Inc., No. 10-CV-98 (S.D. Tex. filed Jan. 11, 2010), Litig. Release No. 21,374 (Jan. 11, 2010), http://www.sec.gov/litigation /litreleases/2010/lr21374.htm.

68. S. Rep. No. 95-1114, at 11 (1977), *reprinted in* 1977 U.S.C.C.A.N. 4098, 4108.

69. SEC v. Veraz Networks, Inc., No. CV-10-2849-PVT (N.D. Cal. filed June 29, 2010), Litig. Release No. 21,581 (June 29, 2010), http://www.sec.gov/litigation /litreleases/2010/lr21581.htm.

70. Press Release, Sec. & Exch. Comm'n, SEC Charges General Electric and Two Subsidiaries with FCPA Violations (July 27, 2010), http://www.sec.gov/news /press/2010/2010-133.htm.

71. *Id.*

72. No. 10-CV-01890 (J. Collyer) (D.D.C. filed Nov. 4, 2010).

73. SEC v. Jennings, No. 11-CV-00144-RMC (D.D.C. filed Jan. 24, 2011), Litig. Release No. 21,822 (Jan. 24, 2011), http://www.sec.gov/litigation/litreleases/2011 /lr21822.htm.

74. Complaint, SEC v. Int'l Bus. Machs. Corp., No. 11-CV-00563-RJL (D.D.C. filed Mar. 18, 2011).

75. *Judge Leon, the SEC, IBM, and the FCPA*, Corp. Crime Rep., Jan. 3, 2013, http:// www.corporatecrimereporter.com/news/200/judgeleonibmsecfcpa01032013.

76. SEC Litig. Release No. 64,123 (Mar. 24, 2011).

77. SEC Exchange Act Release No. 64,380, Accounting and Auditing Enforcement Release No. 3274 (May 3, 2011).

78. Press Release, U.S. Sec. & Exch. Comm'n, Tenaris to Pay $5.4 Million in SEC's First-Ever Deferred Prosecution Agreement (May 17, 2011), http://www.sec.gov/news /press/2011/2011-112.htm.

79. *See* Letter from Jerrob Duffy, U.S. Dep't of Justice Criminal Div., to Robert J. Giuffra, Sullivan & Cromwell LLP (Mar. 14, 2011) (outlining NPA).

80. *See id.* at app. A.

81. *See id.* at A2 (Statement of Facts).

82. SEC Release No. 64,978 (July 27, 2011).

83. SEC Exchange Act Release No. 65,555, Accounting and Auditing Release No. 3328 (Oct. 13, 2011).

84. In February 2009, the SEC entered into a consent decree involving design institute abuses with ITT Corp. SEC v. ITT Corp., No. 09-CV-00272 (Rptr.) (D.D.C. filed Feb. 11, 2009).

85. 15 U.S.C. § 78m(b)(2)(B).

86. No. 4:12-CV-00563 (S.D. Tex. filed Feb. 24, 2012).

87. No. 4:12-CV-00564 (S.D. Tex. filed Feb. 24, 2012).

88. Press Release, U.S. Sec. & Exch. Comm'n, SEC Charges Three Oil Services Executives with Bribing Customs Officials in Nigeria (Feb. 12, 2012). http://www.sec gov/news/press/2012/2012-32.htm.

89. Litig. Release No. 23,038, SEC Settles Pending Civil Action against Noble Executives Mark A. Jackson and James J. Ruehlen (July 7, 2014), http://www.sec.gov /litigation/litreleases/2014/lr23038.htm.

90. Gabelli v. SEC, 568 U.S. ____, 133 S. Ct. 1216 (2013).

91. CV-12-4310-CRB (N.D. Cal.).

92. Press Release, U.S. Sec. & Exch. Comm'n, SEC Charges Oracle Corporation with FCPA Violations Related to Secret Side Funds in India (Aug. 16, 2012), http:// www.sec.gov/news/press/2012/2012-158.htm.

93. Complaint at ¶ 9.

94. *Oracle*, Complaint at ¶ 20.

95. SEC Admin. Proceeding File No. 3-15132.

96. Press Release, U.S. Sec. & Exch. Comm'n, SEC Charges Germany-Based Allianz SE with FCPA Violations (Dec. 17, 2012), http://www.sec.gov/news/press/2012/2012 -266.htm.

97. Most of the account introducers were deemed by the SEC to be foreign officials because they were employees of Indonesian state-owned entities and acted in an official government capacity to procure or retain insurance contracts from Allianz on government projects.

98. In late 2010, Allianz reported to the staff that Manroland AG, an entity in which Allianz had invested in through its private equity arm, was under investigation by German tax authorities. The German tax investigation focused on the tax-deductibility of certain sales-related expenses, many of which occurred after Allianz ceased being an issuer. None of the irregularities in payments involve government projects or payments to foreign officials.

99. 1:12-CV-02045 (D.D.C. filed Dec. 20, 2012).

100. *Id.* at ¶ 6.

101. Press Release, U.S. Sec. & Exch. Comm'n, SEC Charges Eli Lilly and Company with FCPA Violations (Dec. 20, 2012), http://www.sec.gov/news/press/2012/2012-273 .htm.

102. *Id.*

103. *Id.*

104. This section on misconduct in Russia is largely taken from Press Release, U.S. Sec. & Exch. Comm'n, SEC Charges Eli Lilly and Company with FCPA Violations, (Dec. 20, 2012), http://www.sec.gov/news/press/2012/2012-273.htm.

105. *Eli Lilly & Co.*, Complaint at ¶¶ 25–43.

106. This section on misconduct in China is largely taken from *id.*, Complaint at ¶¶ 16–21.

107. This section on distributor misconduct in Brazil is largely taken from *id.*, Complaint at ¶¶ 22–24.

108. This section on misconduct in Poland is largely taken from *id.*, Complaint at ¶¶ 7–15.

109. Complaint at ¶ 46.

110. Press Release, SEC Charges Eli Lilly and Company with FCPA Violations, *supra* note 104.

111. Litig. Release No. 69,327, Admin. Proceeding File No. 3-15265 (Apr. 5, 2013).

112. Press Release, U.S. Sec. & Exch. Comm'n, SEC Charges Stryker Corporation with FCPA Violations (Oct. 24, 2013), http://www.sec.gov/News/PressRelease/Detail/PressRelease/1370540044262.

113. Admin. Proceeding File No. 3-15986 (July 28, 2014), http://www.sec.gov/litigation/admin/2014/34-7267.8.pdf.

114. Press Release, U.S. Sec. & Exch. Comm'n, SEC Charges Smith & Wesson with FCPA Violations (July 28, 2014), http://www.sec.gov/News/PressRelease/Detail/PressRelease/1370542384677; *see also* R. Daniel O'Connor, Geoff Atkins & Lauren M. Modelski, *Smith & Wesson Agrees to Pay $2 Million to Settle SEC Probe into FCPA Violations*, 12 Corp. L. & Accountability Rep. 879 (Aug. 1, 2014).

115. Release No. 73,437, Administrative Proceeding No. 3-16216 (Oct. 27, 2014), http://www.sec.gov/litigation/admin/2014/34-73437.pdf.

116. Press Release, U.S. Sec. & Exch. Comm'n, SEC Sanctions Two Former Defense Contractor Employees for FCPA Violations (Nov. 17, 2014), http://www.sec.gov/News/PressRelease/Detail/PressRelease/1370543472839.

117. *In re* Bruker Corp., Exchange Act Release No. 73,835, Admin. Proceeding File No. 3-16314 (Dec. 15, 2014).

118. Press Release, U.S. Sec. Exch. Comm'n, SEC Charges Massachusetts-Based Scientific Instruments Manufacturer with FCPA Violations (Dec. 15, 2014), http://www.sec.gov/News/PressRelease/Detail/PressRelease/1370543708934.

119. *Id.*

120. *Id.*

121. *Id.* at 4.

122. Complaint, United States v. Metcalf & Eddy, Inc., No. 99-CIV-12566 (D. Mass. filed Dec. 14, 1999).

123. Consent and Undertaking of Metcalf & Eddy, Inc., No. 99-CIV-12566-NG (D. Mass. filed Dec. 14, 1999).

124. *Id.* ¶¶ 4, 7.

125. No. 02-CR-40 (D.D.C. 2002).

126. Press Release, U.S. Dep't of Justice, Former World Bank Employee Sentenced for Taking Kickbacks and Assisting in the Bribery of a Foreign Official (Apr. 25, 2008), http://www.justice.gov/opa/pr/2008/April/08-crm-341.html.

127. Criminal Information, United States v. Basu, No. 02-CR-475-RWR (D.D.C. filed Nov. 18, 2002).

128. *Id.*

129. Criminal Information, United States v. Sengupta, No. 02-CR-40 (D.D.C. filed Jan. 30, 2002).

130. United States v. Syncor Taiwan, Inc., No. 02-CR-01244 (C.D. Cal. filed Dec. 5, 2002).

131. Complaint, SEC v. Syncor Int'l Corp., No. 02-CV-0241-EGS (D.D.C. filed Dec. 10, 2002).

132. Complaint, SEC v. Fu, No. 07-CV-01735-EGS (D.D.C. filed Sept. 28, 2007).

133. Complaint, SEC v. Syncor Int'l Corp., No. 02-CV-0241-EGS (D.D.C. filed Dec. 10, 2002).

134. Complaint, SEC v. Fu, No. 07-CV-01735-EGS (D.D.C. filed Sept. 28, 2007).

135. *Id.*; SEC Litig. Release No. 20,310 (filed Sept. 28, 2007).

136. United States v. Giffen, 326 F. Supp. 2d 497 (S.D.N.Y. 2004).

137. No. 03-CR-406 (S.D.N.Y. 2003).

138. United States v. Bodmer, 342 F. Supp. 2d 176 (S.D.N.Y. 2004).

139. Press Release, U.S. Att'y's Off., S.D.N.Y., U.S. Announces Charges in Massive Bribe Scheme to Bribe Senior Government Officials in the Republic of Azerbaijan (Oct. 6, 2005).

140. Criminal Information, United States v. ABB Vetco Gray, Inc. & ABB Vetco Gray U.K. Ltd., No. 04-CR-0279 (S.D. Tex. filed June 22, 2004).

141. No. 1-04-CV-1141-RBW (D.D.C. filed July 6, 2009).

142. Criminal Information, United States v. Monsanto Co., No. 05-CR-00008 (D.D.C. filed Jan. 6, 2005).

143. Complaint, SEC v. Monsanto, No. 05-CV-14 (D.D.C. filed Jan. 6, 2005), Litig. Release No. 2159 (Jan. 6, 2005).

144. Monsanto Co. Exchange Act Release No. 50,798, 2005 WL 38787, para. G, § 4 (Jan. 6, 2005).

145. Press Release, U.S. Dep't of Justice, InVision Technologies, Inc. Enters into Agreement with United States (Dec. 6, 2004), http://www.justice.gov/opa/pr/2004/December/04_crm_780.htm.

146. Complaint, SEC v. GE InVision, Inc., No. 05-CV-00660 (N.D. Cal. filed Feb. 14, 2005).

147. Complaint, SEC v. Pillor, No. C-06-4906-WHA (N.D. Cal. filed Aug. 15, 2006).

148. *Id.* ¶ 29.

149. Criminal Information, United States v. Titan Corp., No. 05-CR-0314-BEN (S.D. Cal. filed Mar. 1, 2005).

150. Complaint, SEC v. Titan Corp., No. 05-CV-0411 (D.D.C. filed Mar. 1, 2005).

151. Criminal Information, United States v. Head, No. 06-CR-01380 (S.D. Cal. filed June 23, 2006).

152. Complaint, SEC v. Titan Corp., No. 05-CV-0411 (JR) (D.D.C. filed Mar. 1, 2005).

153. Report of Investigation Pursuant to Section 21(a) of the Securities Exchange Act of 1934 and Commission Statement on Potential Exchange Act 10(b) and Section 14(a) Liability, Exchange Act Release No. 51,283 (Mar. 1, 2005), http://www.sec.gov/litigation/investreport/34-51238.htm.

154. Section 21(a) of the Exchange Act allows the SEC, in its discretion, to "make such investigations as it deems necessary to determine whether any person has violated,

is violating or is about to violate any provision of this title" and "to publish information concerning any such violation." Such reports enable the SEC to broadly discuss its position regarding the conduct in question.

155. Bruce V. Bigelow, *Titan Ex-Exec Admits Role in Benin Bribery*, SAN DIEGO UNION-TRIB., June 24, 2006, http://www.signonsandiego.com/uniontrib/20060624 /news_1b24plea.html.

156. Press Release, U.S. Dep't of Justice, Micrus Corp. Enters into Agreement to Resolve Potential Foreign Corrupt Practices Act Liability (Mar. 2, 2005), http://www .justice.gov/opa/pr/2005/March/05_crm_090.htm.

157. Criminal Information, United States v. Diagnostic Prods. Corp., No. 05-CR-482 (C.D. Cal. filed May 20, 2005).

158. SEC Admin. Proceeding File No. 3-11933 (May 20, 2005).

159. Press Release, U.S. Dep't of Justice, DPC (Tianjin) Ltd. Charged with Violating the Foreign Corrupt Practices Act (May 20, 2005), http://www.justice.gov/opa /pr/2005/May/05_crm_282.htm.

160. Press Release, U.S. Att'y's Off., S.D.N.Y., U.S. Announces Charges in Massive Scheme to Bribe Senior Government Officials in the Republic of Azerbaijan (Oct. 6, 2005).

161. United States v. Kozeny, 541 F.3d 166 (2d Cir. 2008).

162. Memorandum Opinion and Order, United States v. Kozeny , 05-CR-518-SAS (2d Cir. Oct. 21, 2008) (citing S. REP. No. 95-114, at 10–11 (1977), *reprinted in* 1977 U.S.C.C.A.N. 4098, 4108).

163. Press Release, U.S. Dep't of Justice, Former Alcatel CIT Executive Sentenced for Paying $2.5 Million in Bribes to Senior Costa Rican Officials (Sept. 23, 2008), http:// www.justice.gov/opa/pr/2008/September/08-crm-848.html.

164. Criminal Information, United States v. Statoil ASA, No. 06-CR-00960 (S.D.N.Y. filed Oct. 13, 2006).

165. SEC Admin. Proceeding File No. 3-12453 (Oct. 13, 2006).

166. No. CV-06-398 (filed Oct. 10, 2006).

167. SEC Admin. Proceeding File No. 2-17456 (Oct. 16, 2006). *See In re* Schnitzer Steel Indus., Inc., Order Imposing and Instituting Cease-and-Desist Proceedings, Exchange Act Release No. 54,606, 89 SEC Docket 302 (Oct. 16, 2006), http://www.sec .gov/litigation/admin/2006/34-54606.pdf.

168. Complaint, SEC v. Philip, No. 07-CV-1836 (D. Or. filed Dec. 13, 2007), Litig. Release No. 20,397 (Dec. 13, 2007).

169. *Id.*

170. Criminal Information, United States v. Vetco Gray Controls Inc., No. 07-CR-00004 (S.D. Tex. filed Jan. 5, 2007).

171. Criminal Information, United States v. Baker Hughes Svcs. Int'l, Inc., No. H-07-CR-129 (S.D. Tex. filed Apr. 11, 2007).

172. No. 07-CV-01408 (S.D. Tex. 2007).

173. No. H-07-130 (S.D. Tex. filed Apr. 11, 2007).

174. Press Release, SEC Charges Baker Hughes with Foreign Bribery and with Violating 2001 Commission Cease-and-Desist Order (Apr. 26, 2007), http://www.sec.gov /news/press/2007/2007-77.htm; SEC v. Fearnley, No H-07-130 (S.D. Tex order entered Jan. 26, 2010).

175. Press Release, U.S. Dep't of Justice, Baker Hughes Subsidiary Pleads Guilty to Bribing Kazakh Official and Agrees to Pay $11 Million Criminal Fine as Part of the

Largest Combined Sanction Ever Imposed in FCPA Case (Apr. 26, 2007), http://www
.justice.gov/opa/pr/2007/April/07_crm_296.html.

176. *Id.*

177. Press Release, U.S. Dep't of Justice, Congressman William Jefferson Indicted
on Bribery, Racketeering, Money Laundering, Obstruction of Justice, and Related
Charges (June 4, 2007), http://www.justice.gov/opa/pr/2007/June/07_crm_402.html.

178. Press Release, U.S. Dep't of Justice, Former Congressman William J. Jefferson
Sentenced to 13 Years in Prison for Bribery and Other Charges (Nov. 13, 2009), http://
www.justice.gov/opa/pr/2009/November/09-crm-1231.html.

179. Press Release, U.S. Dep't of Justice, Paradigm B.V. Agrees to Pay $1 Million
Penalty to Resolve Foreign Bribery Issues in Multiple Countries (Sept. 24, 2007), http://
www.justice.gov/opa/pr/2007/September/07_crm_751.html.

180. Press Release, U.S. Dep't of Justice, Ingersoll-Rand Agrees to Pay $2.5 Million
Fine in Connections with Payment of Kickbacks under the UN Oil for Food Program,
http://www.justice.gov/opa/pr/2007/October/07_crm_872.html.

181. Complaint, SEC v. Ingersoll-Rand Co., No. 07-CV-1955 (D.D.C. filed Oct. 31,
2007), Litig. Release No. 20,353 (Oct. 31, 2007).

182. Criminal Information, United States v. Thermo King Ireland Ltd., No. 07-CR-
00296 (D.D.C. filed Oct. 31, 2007); Criminal Information, United States v. Ingersoll-Rand
Italiana SpA, No. 07-CR-00294 (D.D.C. filed Oct. 31, 2007).

183. Complaint, SEC v. Ingersoll-Rand Co., No. 107-CV-01955 (D.D.C. filed Oct.
31, 2007).

184. Press Release, U.S. Dep't of Justice, Justice Department Agrees to Defer Prosecution of York International Corporation in Connection with Payment of Kickbacks
under the UN Oil for Food Program (Oct. 1, 2007), http://www.justice.gov/opa/pr
/2007/October/07_crm_783.html; Deferred Prosecution Agreement, United States v.
York Int'l Corp., No. 07-cr-00253 (D.D.C. filed Oct. 15, 2007).

185. *Id.*

186. Complaint, SEC v. York Int'l Corp., No. 07-CV-01750 (D.D.C. filed Oct. 1,
2007).

187. Plea Agreement, United States v. Steph, No. 07-CR-307 (S.D. Tex. filed Nov. 5,
2007).

188. Indictment, United States v. Tillery & Novak, No. 08-CR-022 (S.D. Tex. filed
Jan. 17, 2008).

189. Press Release, U.S. Dep't of Justice, Former Willbros International Consultant Pleads Guilty to $6 Million Foreign Bribery Scheme (Nov. 12, 2009), http://www
.justice.gov/opa/pr/2009/November/09-crm-1220.html.

190. Press Release, U.S. Dep't of Justice, Former Willbros International Executive
and Consultant Charged in $6 Million Foreign Bribery Conspiracy (Dec. 19, 2008),
http://www.justice.gov/opa/pr/2008/December/08-crm-1137.html.

191. Press Release, U.S. Dep't of Justice, Lucent Technologies Inc. Agrees to Pay $1
Million Fine to Resolve FCPA Allegations (Dec. 21, 2007), http://www.justice.gov/opa
/pr/2007/December/07_crm_1028.html.

192. No. 07-CV-02301 (D.D.C. 2007).

193. In December 2006, Lucent merged with Alcatel SA of France to form Alcatel-
Lucent, headquartered in Paris.

194. Press Release, U.S. Dep't of Justice, Lucent Technologies Inc. Agrees to Pay $1 Million Fine to Resolve FCPA Allegations (Dec. 21, 2007), http://www.justice.gov/opa/pr/2007/December/07_crm_1028.html.

195. Complaint, SEC v. Lucent Techs. Inc., No. 07-CV-02301-RBW (D.D.C. filed Dec. 21, 2007), Litig. Release No. 20,414.

196. Press Release, U.S. Dep't of Justice, Westinghouse Air Brake Technologies Corporation Agrees to Pay $300,000 Penalty to Resolve Foreign Bribery Violations in India (Feb. 14, 2008), http://www.justice.gov/opa/pr/2008/February/08_crm_116.html.

197. No. 08-CV-706 (E.D. Pa. 2008).

198. Complaint, SEC v. Westinghouse Air Brake Techs. Corp., No. 08-CV-706, SEC Litig. Release No. 20,457 (E.D. Pa. filed Feb. 14, 2008).

199. Press Release, U.S. Dep't of Justice, Flowserve Corp. to Pay $4 Million Penalty for Kickback Payments to the Iraqi Government under the UN Oil for Food Program (Feb. 21, 2008), http://www.justice.gov/opa/pr/2008/February/08_crm_132.html.

200. No. 08 CV-00294 (D.D.C. filed Feb. 21, 2008).

201. No. 08-CR-00035 (D.D.C. 2008).

202. Complaint, SEC v. Flowserve Corp., No. 08-CV-00294-EGS (D.D.C. filed Feb. 21, 2008), Litig. Release No. 20,461.

203. Press Release, U.S. Dep't of Justice, AB Volvo to Pay $7 Million Penalty for Kickback Payments to the Iraqi Government under the UN Oil for Food Program (Mar. 20, 2008), http://www.justice.gov/opa/pr/2008/March/08_crm_220.html.

204. *Id.*

205. *Id.*; SEC v. AB Volvo, No. 08-CV-00473 (JB) (D.D.C. filed Mar. 18, 2008), Litig. Release No. 20,504 (Mar. 20, 2008).

206. Press Release, U.S. Dep't of Justice, Former Pacific Consolidated Industries LP Executive Pleads Guilty in Connection with Bribes Paid to U.K. Ministry of Defence Official (May 8, 2008), http://www.justice.gov/opa/pr/2008/May/08-crm-394.html.

207. Leo Winston Smith was indicted in April 2007 for his role in the scheme and pled guilty on September 3, 2009. The DOJ asked for a 37-month sentence. In December 2010 Smith, age 75, was sentenced to six months in jail followed by six months of home confinement.

208. The U.K.-MOD official was investigated by U.K. authorities, pled guilty in the United Kingdom to accepting bribes from PCI, and was sentenced to two years in prison.

209. Press Release, U.S. Dep't of Justice, Willbros Group Inc. Enters Deferred Prosecution Agreement and Agrees to Pay $22 Million Penalty for FCPA Violations (May 14, 2008), http://www.justice.gov/opa/pr/2008/May/08-crm-417.html.

210. Complaint, SEC v. Willbros Group Inc., No. 08-CV-01494 (S.D. Tex.–Hous. filed May 14, 2008), Litig. Release No. 20,571 (May 14, 2008).

211. Press Release, U.S. Dep't of Justice, Willbros Group Inc. Enters Deferred Prosecution Agreement and Agrees to Pay $22 Million Penalty for FCPA Violations (May 14, 2008), http://www.justice.gov/opa/pr/2008/May/08-crm-417.html.

212. Complaint, SEC v. Willbros Group Inc., No. 08-CV-01494 (S.D. Tex.–Hous. filed May 14, 2008), SEC Litig. Release No. 20,571 (May 14, 2008).

213. Press Release, U.S. Dep't of Justice, AGA Medical Corporation Agrees to Pay $2 Million Penalty and Enter Deferred Prosecution Agreement for FCPA Violations (June 3, 2008), http://www.justice.gov/opa/pr/2008/June/08-crm-491.html.

214. No. 0:08-CR-00172 (D. Minn. 2008).

215. Press Release, U.S. Dep't of Justice, Faro Technologies Inc. Agrees to Pay $1.1 Million Penalty and Enter Non-Prosecution Agreement for FCPA Violations (June 5, 2008), http://www.justice.gov/opa/pr/2008/June/08-crm-505.html.

216. SEC Admin. Proceeding File No. 3-13059 (June 5, 2008).

217. Complaint, SEC v. Oscar H. Meza, No. 09-CV-01648 (D.D.C. filed Aug. 28, 2009), Litig. Release No. 21,190 (Aug. 28, 2009).

218. Superseding Information, Criminal No. 08-246 ESH (D.D.C. filed June 24, 2010).

219. 10-CV-013019 (D.D.C. Aug. 25, 2010).

220. 11-CV-00144 (D.D.C. Jan. 24, 2011).

221. Press Release, U.S. Dep't of Justice, Canadian National Charged with Foreign Bribery and Paying Kickbacks under the Oil for Food Program (July 31, 2009), http://www.justice.gov/opa/pr/2009/July/09-crm-757.html.

222. Press Release, U.S. Sec. & Exch. Comm'n, SEC Charges Two Individuals for Roles in Innospec FCPA Scheme (Aug. 5, 2010), http://www.sec.gov/news/press/2010/2010-141.htm.

223. Indictment, United States v. Nguyen, 08-CR-00522 (E.D. Pa. filed Sept. 4, 2008); Press Release, U.S. Dep't of Justice, Philadelphia Export Company and Employees Indicted for Paying Bribes to Foreign Officials (Sept. 5, 2008), http://www.justice.gov/opa/pr/2008/September/08-crm-782.html.

224. Press Release, U.S. Dep't of Justice, Former Executive of Philadelphia Company Pleads Guilty to Paying Bribes to Vietnamese Officials (June 29, 2009), http://www.justice.gov/opa/pr/2009/June/09-crm-635.html.

225. Press Release, U.S. Dep't of Justice, Former Nexus Technologies Inc. Employees and Partner Sentenced for Roles in Foreign Bribery Scheme Involving Vietnamese Officials (Sept. 16, 2010), http://www.justice.gov/opa/pr/2010/September/10-crm-1032.html.

226. Criminal Information, United States v. Stanley, No. 08-CR-597 (S.D. Tex. filed Aug. 29, 2008), http://s3.amazonaws.com/propublica/assets/docs/stanley_information_080829.pdf.

227. Complaint, SEC v. Stanley, No. 08-CV-02680 (S.D. Tex. filed Sept. 3, 2008).

228. A.P. Wire, *Ex-KBR Chief Gets 30 Months for Nigeria Bribery*, CBS News, Feb. 24, 2012, http://www.cbsnews.com/8301-201_162-57384333/ex-kbr-chief-gets-30-months-for-nigeria-bribery/.

229. Press Release, U.S. Att'y's Off., C.D. Cal., Film Executive and Spouse Indicted for Paying Bribes to a Thai Tourism Official to Obtain Lucrative Contracts (Oct. 2, 2008), http://www.justice.gov/usao/cac/Pressroom/pr2008/134.html.

230. Press Release, U.S. Dep't of Justice, Aibel Group Ltd. Pleads Guilty to Foreign Bribery and Agrees to Pay $4.2 Million in Criminal Fines (Nov. 21, 2008), http://www.justice.gov/opa/pr/2008/November/08-crm-1041.html.

231. Criminal Information, United States v. Siemens AG, No. 08-CR-367 (D.D.C. Dec. 12, 2008).

232. Complaint, SEC v. Siemens AG, No. 08-CV-02167 (D.D.C. filed Dec. 12, 2008).

233. Press Release, U.S. Dep't of Justice, Siemens AG and Three Subsidiaries Plead Guilty to Foreign Corrupt Practices Act Violations and Agree to Pay $450 Million

in Combined Criminal Fines (Dec. 15, 2008), http://www.justice.gov/opa/pr/2008
/December/08-crm-1105.html.

234. *Id.*

235. U.S. Sentencing Guidelines Manual § 8C2.7.

236. Vanessa Fuhrmans, *Siemens Settles with World Bank on Bribes*, Wall St. J., July 3, 2009, at B1.

237. Press Release, U.S. Dep't of Justice, Japanese Executive Pleads Guilty, Sentenced to Two Years in Jail for Participating in Conspiracies to Rig Bids and Bribe Foreign Officials to Purchase Marine Hose and Related Products (Dec. 10, 2008), http://www.justice.gov/opa/pr/2008/December/08-at-1084.html.

238. Press Release, U.S. Dep't of Justice, Fiat Agrees to $7 Million Fine in Connection with Payment of $4.4 Million in Kickbacks by Three Subsidiaries under the U.N. Oil for Food Program (Dec. 22, 2008), http://www.justice.gov/opa/pr/2008/December/08-crm-1140.html.

239. No. 08-CR-00377-RJL (D.D.C. Dec. 22, 2008).

240. No. 08-CR-00378-RJL (D.D.C. Dec. 22, 2008).

241. No. 08-CR-00379-RJL (D.D.C. Dec. 22, 2008).

242. No. 08-CV-02211 (D.D.C. Dec. 22, 2008).

243. Criminal Information, United States v. Kellogg Brown & Root LLC, No. 09-CR-00071 (S.D. Tex.–Hous. Div. filed Feb. 6, 2009).

244. Complaint, SEC v. Halliburton Co. & KBR Inc., No. 09-CV-0399 (S.D. Tex. filed Feb. 11, 2009).

245. The former chief executive officer of KBR is Albert Jack Stanley, discussed *supra*.

246. *See, e.g.*, Complaint, ¶¶ 47–52, SEC v. Halliburton Co. & KBR Inc., No. 09-CV-0399 (S.D. Tex. filed Feb. 11, 2009).

247. Press Release, U.S. Dep't of Justice, Two U.K. Citizens Charged by United States with Bribing Nigerian Government Officials to Obtain Lucrative Contracts as Part of KBR Joint Venture Scheme (Mar. 5, 2009), http://www.justice.gov/opa/pr/2009/March/09-crm-192.html.

248. Indictment, United States v. Tesler & Chodan, No. 09-CR-00098 (S.D. Tex. filed Feb. 17, 2009).

249. Plea Agreement, United States v. Tesler, No. 09-CR-00098 ((S.D. Tex. filed Mar. 11, 2011).

250. Press Release, U.S. Dep't of Justice, Former Chairman and CEO of Kellogg, Brown & Root Sentenced to 30 Months in Prison for Foreign Bribery and Kickback Schemes (Feb. 23, 2012), http://www.justice.gov/opa/pr/2012/February/12-crm-249.html.

251. Criminal Information, United States v. Latin Node, Inc., No. 09-CR-20239-PCH (S.D. Fla. filed Mar. 23, 2009).

252. Press Release, U.S. Dep't of Justice, Latin Node Inc. Pleads Guilty to Foreign Corrupt Practices Act Violation and Agrees to Pay a $2 Million Criminal Fine (Apr. 7, 2009), http://www.justice.gov/opa/pr/2009/April/09-crm-318.html.

253. Press Release, U.S. Dep't of Justice, Six Former Executives of California Valve Company Charged in $46 Million Foreign Bribery Conspiracy (Apr. 8, 2009), http://www.justice.gov/opa/pr/2009/April/09-crm-322.html.

254. *Id.*

255. Press Release, U.S. Dep't of Justice, Two Former Executives of California Valve Company Plead Guilty to Foreign Bribery Offenses (Apr. 7, 2012), http://www.justice gov/opa/pr/2012/April/12-crm-485.html.

256. Press Release, U.S. Dep't of Justice, Helmerich & Payne Agrees to Pay $1 Million Penalty to Resolve Allegations of Foreign Bribery in South America (July 30, 2009). http://www.justice.gov/opa/pr/2009/July/09-crm-741.html.

257. Exchange Act Release No. 60,400 (July 30, 2009), http://www.sec.gov /litigation/admin/2009/34-60400.pdf.

258. Press Release, U.S. Dep't of Justice, AGCO Corp. to Pay $1.6 Million in Connection with Payments to the Former Iraqi Government under the UN Oil-for-Food Program (Sept. 30, 2009), http://www.justice.gov/opa/pr/2009/September/09-crm-1056 .html.

259. Complaint, SEC v. AGCO Corp., No. 09-CV-01865 (RMU) (D.D.C. filed Sept. 30, 2009), Litig. Release No. 21,229 (Sept. 30, 2009).

260. Criminal No. 3:09-CR-397 (E.D. Va. filed Nov. 10, 2009).

261. Indictment, United States v. O'Shea, No. H-90-629 (S.D. Tex. filed Nov. 16, 2009).

262. Superseding Criminal Information No. 09-CR-325 (S.D. Tex. filed No. 16, 2009).

263. Press Release, U.S. Dep't of Justice, Former General Manager of Texas Business Arrested for Role in Alleged Scheme to Bribe Officials at Mexican State-Owned Electrical Utility (Nov. 23, 2009), http://www.justice.gov/opa/pr/2009/November/09 -crm-1265.html.

264. E-mail from Joel Androphy, counsel for John Joseph O'Shea, to author (Mar. 21, 2012) (on file with author).

265. Indictment, United States v. Esquenazi, No. 09-CR-21010-JEM (S.D. Fla.— Miami filed Dec. 4, 2009); Press Release, U.S. Dep't of Justice, Two Florida Executives, One Florida Intermediary and Two Former Haitian Government Officials Indicted for Their Alleged Participation in Foreign Bribery Scheme, http://www.justice.gov/opa /pr/2009/December/09-crm-1307.html.

266. Press Release, U.S. Dep't of Justice, Former Haitian Government Official Convicted in Miami for Role in Scheme to Launder Bribes Paid by Telecommunications Company (Mar. 13, 2012), http://www.justice.gov/opa/pr/2012/March/12-crm-310 .html.

267. Press Release, U.S. Dep't of Justice, UTStarcom Agrees to Pay $1.5 Million Penalty for Acts of Foreign Bribery in China (Dec. 31, 2009) http://www.justice.gov /opa/pr/2009/December/09-crm-1390.html.

268. Complaint, SEC v. UTStarcom Inc., No. 09-CV-6094 (JSW) (N.D. Cal. filed Dec. 31, 2009), Litig. Release No. 21,357 (Dec. 31, 2009), http://www.sec.gov/litigation /litreleases/2009/lr21357.htm.

269. *Id.*

270. Crim. No. 09 CR-449 (E.D. Va. filed Dec. 15, 2009).

271. *Id.*

272. Government's Sentencing Memorandum at 1, United States v. Warwick, No. 3:09-CR 447, (E.D. Va. filed June 14, 2010).

273. Press Release, U.S. Dep't of Justice, Twenty-Two Executives and Employees of Military and Law Enforcement Products Companies Charged in Foreign Bribery Scheme (Jan. 19, 2010), http://www.justice.gov/opa/pr/2010/January/10-crm-048.html.

274. Diana B. Henriques, *FBI Snares Weapons Executives in Bribery Sting*, N.Y. TIMES, Jan. 21, 2010, at A3.

275. *Id.*

276. Superseding Criminal Information, United States v. Alvirez, No. 09-CR-348 (RJL) (D.D.C. filed Mar. 5, 2010).

277. Del Quentin Wilber, *Charges Dismissed against 16 Accused of Bribing Foreign Official in Sting*, WASH. POST, Feb. 21, 2012, http://articles.washingtonpost.com/2012-02-21/local/35443860_1_informant-fbi-agents-defense-attorneys.

278. Information, 1:10-CR-00021-RJL (D.D.C. filed Jan. 21, 2010).

279. Diana B. Henriques, *Supplier Accused of Bribes for U.N. Contracts*, N.Y. TIMES, Jan. 23, 2010, http://www.nytimes.com/2010/01/23/business/23sting.html.

280. *Id.*

281. C.M. Matthews, *Cooperator Gets 18 Months in Complicated Bribery Case*, WALL ST. J. CORRUPTION CURRENTS BLOG (July 31, 2012), http://blogs.wsj.com/corruption-currents/2012/07/31/cooperator-gets-18-months-in-complicated-bribery-case/.

282. Criminal Information, United States v. BAE Sys. plc., No. 1:10-cr-00035-JDB (D.D.C. filed Feb. 4, 2010).

283. U.S. Dep't of State, Bureau of Political Military Affairs, Washington, D.C., Order dated May 16, 2011.

284. 18 U.S.C. § 1001.

285. 22 U.S.C. § 1778.

286. Press Release, U.S. Dep't of Justice, BAE Systems PLC Pleads Guilty and Ordered to Pay $400 Million Criminal Fine (Mar. 1, 2010), http://www.justice.gov/opa/pr/2010/March/10-crm-209.html.

287. Press Release, U.K. Serious Fraud Office, BAE Systems plc (Feb. 5, 2010), http://www.sfo.gov.uk/press-room/press-release-archive/press-releases-2010/bae-systems-plc.aspx.

288. Christopher Drew & Nicola Clark, *BAE Settles Corruption Charges*, N.Y. TIMES, Feb. 6, 2010, http://www.nytimes.com/2010/02/06/business/global/06bribe.html.

289. Criminal Information at ¶ 2.

290. Press Release, U.S. Dep't of State, BAE Systems plc Enters Civil Settlement of Alleged Violations of the AECA and ITAR and Agrees to Civil Penalty of $79 Million (May 17, 2011), http://www.state.gov/r/pa/prs/ps/2011/05/163530.htm.

291. *Id.*

292. *Id.*

293. 10-CR-00061 (D.D.C. filed Mar. 17, 2010).

294. 1:10-CV-00448 (D.D.C. filed Mar. 17, 2010).

295. Press Release, U.S. Dep't of Justice, Innospec Inc. Pleads Guilty to FCPA Charges and Defrauding the United Nations; Admits to Violating the U.S. Embargo against Cuba (Mar. 18, 2010), http://www.justice.gov/opa/pr/2010/March/10-crm-278.html.

296. Criminal Information, United States v. Daimler AG, No. 10-CR-00063-RJL (D.D.C. filed Mar. 22, 2010).

297. Criminal Information, United States v. DaimlerChrysler Russia SAO, No. 10-CR-00064-RJL (D.D.C. filed Mar. 22, 2010).

298. Criminal Information, United States v. Daimler Exp. & Trade Fin. GmbH, No. 10-CR-00065-RJL (D.D.C. filed Mar. 22, 2010).

299. Criminal Information, United States v. DaimlerChrysler China Ltd., No. 10-CR-00066-RJL (D.D.C. filed Mar. 22, 2010).

300. Complaint, SEC v. Daimler AG, No. 10-CR-00473-RJL (D.D.C. filed Mar. 22, 2010).

301. Press Release, U.S. Dep't of Justice, Daimler AG and Three Subsidiaries Resolve Foreign Corrupt Practices Act Investigation and Agree to Pay $93.6 Million in Criminal Penalties (Apr. 1, 2010), http://www.justice.gov/opa/pr/2010/April/10-crm-360.html.

302. Press Release, U.S. Sec. & Exch. Comm'n, SEC Charges Daimler AG with Global Bribery (Apr. 1, 2010), http://www.sec.gov/news/press/2010/2010-51.htm.

303. Complaint, ¶ 58, SEC v. Daimler AG, No. 10-CR-00473-RJL (D.D.C. filed Mar. 22, 2010).

304. *Id.* ¶ 5.

305. *Id.* ¶ 15.

306. *Id.* ¶ 17.

307. Criminal Information, United States v. Daimler AG, No. 10-CR-00063-RJL (D.D.C. filed Mar. 22, 2010), and Attachment C: Corporate Compliance Program to Plan Agreement.

308. United States' Sentencing Memorandum at 15 sec. d (Daimler's Cooperation and Remediation Efforts), Criminal Information, United States v. Daimler AG, No. 10-CR-00063-RJL (D.D.C. filed Mar. 22, 2010).

309. *Id.*

310. *Id.*

311. Amendment to the Deferred Prosecution Agreement, Criminal Information, United States v. Daimler AG, No. 18-063 (RJL) (D.D.C. filed Apr. 4, 2012).

312. *See* U.S. Dep't of Justice, Press Release, Technip S.A. Resolves Foreign Corrupt Practices Act Investigation and Agrees to Pay $240 Million Criminal Fine (June 28, 2010) http://www.justice.gov/opa/pr/2010/June/10-crm-751.html.

313. Complaint, SEC v. Technip, No. 10-CV-02289 (S.D. Tex. filed June 28, 2010).

314. Philip Urofsky et al., *Recent Trends and Patterns in Enforcement of the U.S. Foreign Corrupt Practices Act, in* THE FOREIGN CORRUPT PRACTICES ACT 2011 (PLI Course Handbook 13-1883).

315. *See* Press Release, U.S. Dep't of Justice, Snamprogetti Netherlands B.V. Resolves Foreign Corrupt Practices Act Investigation and Agrees to Pay $240 Million Criminal Penalty (July 7, 2010) http://www.justice.gov/opa/pr/2010/July/10-crm-780.html.

316. Complaint, SEC v. ENI, S.p.A., & Snamprogetti Netherlands B.V., No. 10-CV-2414 (S.D. Tex. filed July 7, 2010).

317. *Id.*

318. *Id.*

319. Press Release, U.S. Dep't of Justice, Alliance One International Inc. and Universal Corporation Resolve Related FCPA Matters Involving Bribes Paid to Foreign Government Officials (Aug. 6, 2010), http://www.justice.gov/opa/pr/2010/August/10-crm-903.html.

320. No. 10-CV-01319 (D.D.C. filed Aug. 6, 2010).

321. No. 10-CR-00015 (E.D. Va. filed Aug. 3, 2010).

322. In Kyrgyzstan, each local government unit is headed by an *akim*, who exercises authority over the sale of tobacco by the growers within the municipality or local geographic area. Plea Agreement, exh. A, Statement of Facts, at ¶ 10 (Aug. 3, 2010).

323. Criminal Information, United States v. Mercator Corp., No. 03-CR-404 (S.D.N.Y. filed Aug. 6, 2010), *superseding* Information filed Aug. 6, 2010.

324. Press Release, U.S. Dep't of Justice, Alliance One International Inc. and Universal Corporation Resolve Related FCPA Matters Involving Bribes Paid to Foreign Government Officials (Aug. 6, 2010), http://www.justice.gov/opa/pr/2010/August/10 -crm-903.html.

325. No. 10-CV-01318 (D.D.C. filed Aug. 6, 2010).

326. Press Release, U.S. Dep't of Justice, Two Intermediaries Indicated for Their Alleged Participation in Scheme to Bribe Officials at State-Owned Electrical Utility in Mexico (Sept. 15, 2010), http://www.justice.gov/opa/pr/2010/September/10-crm-1034 .html.

327. Criminal Information, United States v. ABB, Inc., No. 10-CR-664 (S.D. Tex. filed Sept. 29, 2010).

328. Criminal Information, United States v. ABB Ltd.-Jordan, No. 10-CR-665 (S.D. Tex. filed Sept. 29, 2010).

329. Complaint, SEC v. ABB Ltd., 10-CV-01648 (D.D.C. filed Sept. 29, 2010), Litig. Release No. 21,673 (Sept. 29, 2010).

330. Press Release, U.S. Dep't of Justice, ABB Ltd. and Two Subsidiaries Resolve Foreign Corrupt Practices Act Investigation and Will Pay $19 Million in Criminal Penalties (Sept. 29, 2010). http://www.justice.gov/opa/pr/2010/September/10-crm-1096.html.

331. Press Release, U.S. Dep't of Justice, California Company and Two Executives Indicted for Their Alleged Participation in Scheme to Bribe Officials at State-Owned Electrical Utility in Mexico (Oct. 21, 2010), http://www.justice.gov/opa/pr/2010 /October/10-crm-1185.html.

332. United States v. Lindsey Mfg. Co., No. 2:10-CR-01031-AHM (Dec. 1, 2010), Opinion at 34–35.

333. Press Release, U.S. Dep't of Justice, Oil Services Companies and a Freight Forwarding Company Agree to Resolve Foreign Bribery Investigations and to Pay More Than $156 Million in Criminal Penalties (Nov. 4, 2010), http://www.justice.gov/opa /pr/2010/November/10-crm-1251.html.

334. No. 10-CV-4336 (S.D. Tex. filed Nov. 4, 2010).

335. *See* Letter from Stacy Luck, U.S. Dep't of Justice, to Mary Spearing, Baker & Botts (Nov. 4, 2010) (regarding Noble Corp. nonprosecution agreement).

336. Litig. Release No. 23,038, SEC Settles Pending Civil Action against Noble Executives Mark A. Jackson and James J. Ruehlen (July 7, 2014), http://www.sec.gov /litigation/litreleases/2014/lr23038.htm.

337. Gabelli v. SEC, 568 U.S. ____, 133 S. Ct. 1216 (2013).

338. Press Release, U.S. Dep't of Justice, Oil Services Companies and a Freight Forwarding Company Agree to Resolve Foreign Bribery Investigations and to Pay More Than $156 Million in Criminal Penalties (Nov. 4, 2010), http://www.justice.gov/opa /pr/2010/November/10-crm-1251.html.

339. No. 10-CV-4334 (S.D. Tex. filed Nov. 4, 2010).

340. Information, ¶¶ 17, 19, United States v. Panalpina, Inc., No. 10-CR-00765 (S.D. Tex. filed Nov. 4, 2010).

341. Deferred Prosecution Agreement, Attached Statement of Facts.

342. Press Release, U.S. Dep't of Justice, Oil Services Companies and a Freight Forwarding Company Agree to Resolve Foreign Bribery Investigations and to Pay More Than $156 Million in Criminal Penalties (Nov. 4, 2010), http://www.justice.gov/opa/pr/2010/November/10-crm-1251.html.

343. No. 10-CV-4335 (S.D. Tex. filed Nov. 4, 2010).

344. Deferred Prosecution Agreement, Relevant Considerations, ¶¶ 6, 8.

345. Id.

346. Press Release, U.S. Dep't of Justice, Oil Services Companies and a Freight Forwarding Company Agree to Resolve Foreign Bribery Investigations and to Pay More Than $156 Million in Criminal Penalties (Nov. 4, 2010), http://www.justice.gov/opa/pr/2010/November/10-crm-1251.html.

347. Securities Exchange Act of 1934, Release No. 63,243 (Nov. 4, 2010).

348. Press Release, U.S. Dep't of Justice, Oil Services Companies and a Freight Forwarding Company Agree to Resolve Foreign Bribery Investigations and to Pay More Than $156 Million in Criminal Penalties (Nov. 4, 2010), http://www.justice.gov/opa/pr/2010/November/10-crm-1251.html.

349. No. 10-CV-04180 (E.D. La. filed Nov. 4, 2010).

350. Press Release, U.S. Dep't of Justice, Oil Services Companies and a Freight Forwarding Company Agree to Resolve Foreign Bribery Investigations and to Pay More Than $156 Million in Criminal Penalties (Nov. 4, 2010), http://www.justice.gov/opa/pr/2010/November/10-crm-1251.html.

351. No. 10-CV-01891 (D.D.C. filed Nov. 4, 2010).

352. Id. ¶¶ 30, 33–34.

353. Press Release, U.S. Dep't of Justice, RAE Systems Agrees to Pay $1.7 Million Criminal Penalty to Resolve Violation of the Foreign Corrupt Practices Act (Dec. 20, 2010), http://www.justice.gov/opa/pr/2010/December/10-crm-1428.html.

354. Press Release, U.S. Dep't of Justice, Foreign Senior Executives of Latin Node Inc. Charged with Bribing Honduran Officials and Money Laundering (Dec. 20, 2010), http://www.justice.gov/opa/pr/2010/December/10-crm-1463.html.

355. No. 10-20893 (S.D. Fl. filed Dec. 17, 2010).

356. No. 10-20894 (S.D. Fl. filed Dec. 17, 2010).

357. SEC v. Innospec, Inc., No. 10-CV-00448 (RMC) (D.D.C. filed Mar. 18, 2010), Litig. Release No. 21,454 (Mar. 18, 2010), http://www.sec.gov/litigation/litreleases/2010/lr21454.htm.

358. Oscar Nunez Olivas, *Costa Rican Ex-President Found Guilty of Corruption*, AGENCE FRANCE-PRESSE, Apr. 28, 2011, http://www.afp.com/afpcom/en.

359. Press Release, U.S. Dep't of Justice, Maxwell Technologies Inc. Resolves Foreign Corrupt Practices Act Investigation and Agrees to Pay $8 Million Criminal Penalty (Jan. 31, 2011), http://www.justice.gov/opa/pr/2011/January/11-crm-129.html.

360. 13-CR-03789-JM (S.D. Cal. filed Oct. 15, 2013).

361. Complaint, ¶ 16, SEC v. Maxwell Techs., Inc., No. 11-CV-00258 (D.D.C. filed Jan. 31, 2011), Litig. Release No. 21,832 (Jan. 31, 2011), http://www.sec.gov/litigation/litreleases/2011/lr21832.htm.

362. *Id.*, Complaint at ¶ 24.

363. Press Release, U.S. Dep't of Justice, Tyson Foods Inc. Agrees to Pay $4 Million Criminal Penalty to Resolve Foreign Bribery Allegations (Feb. 10, 2011), http://www.justice.gov/opa/pr/2011/February/11-crm-171.html.

364. SEC v. Tyson Foods, Inc., No. 11-CV-00350 (D.D.C. filed Feb. 10, 2011), Litig. Release No. 21,851 (Feb. 10, 2011), http://www.sec.gov/litigation/litreleases/2011/lr21851.htm.

365. Press Release, U.S. Dep't of Justice, JGC Corporation Resolves Foreign Corrupt Practices Act Investigation and Agrees to Pay a $218.8 million Criminal Penalty (Apr. 6, 2011), http://www.justice.gov/opa/pr/2011/April/11-crm-431.html.

366. Litig. Release No. 21,920 (Apr. 7, 2011), http://www.sec.gov/litigation/litreleases/2011/lr21920: SEC v. Comverse Technology, No. 11-cv-1704-LDW (E.D.N.Y. filed Apr. 7, 2011).

367. *Id.*

368. Criminal Information, United States v. DePuy, Inc. No. 11-CR-00099 (D.D.C. filed Apr. 8, 2011); SEC v. Johnson & Johnson, No. 11-CV-00686 (D.D.C. filed Apr. 8, 2011), Litig. Release No. 21,922 (Apr. 8, 2011).

369. Complaint, SEC v. Johnson & Johnson, No. 11-CV-00686 (D.D.C. filed Apr. 8, 2011).

370. Press Release, U.K. Serious Fraud Office, British Executive Jailed for Part in Greek Health Corruption (Apr. 14, 2010), http://www.sfo.gov.uk/press-room/press-release-archive/press-releases-2010/british-executive-jailed-for-part-in-greek-healthcare-corruption.aspx.

371. Letter from Paul Pelletier, U.S. Dep't of Justice, to Erica A. Dubelier, Reed & Smith (Jan. 1, 2011) at 1.

372. *See, e.g.*, Maxwell Technologies Corporate Compliance Program, Attachment C to DPA.

373. The footnote at this place in the agreement states: "For purposes of this agreement, 'operating company' shall mean a pharmaceutical, medical device, or consumer company located in a single country that may include multiple J&J franchises."

374. The footnote at this place in the agreement states: "For those operating companies that are determined not to pose corruption risk, J&J will conduct periodic FCPA audits, or will incorporate FCPA components into financial audits."

375. *See* Attachment D, Enhanced Compliance Obligations.

376. Sean Farrell, *SFO Whistleblower Robert Dougall Is Spared Prison*, Telegraph (U.K.), May 14, 2010, http://www.telegraph.co.uk/finance/newsbysector/pharmaceuticalsandchemicals/7720824/SFO-whistleblower-Robert-Dougall-is-spared-prison.html.

377. Press Release, U.K. Serious Fraud Office, British Executive Jailed for Part in Greek Health Corruption (14 Apr. 2010), http://www.sfo.gov.uk/press-room/press-release-archive/press-releases-2010/british-executive-jailed-for-part-in-greek-healthcare-corruption.aspx.

378. Press Release, U.S. Dep't of Justice, Armor Holdings Agrees to Pay $10.2 Million Penalty to Resolve Violations of the Foreign Corrupt Practices Act (July 13, 2011), http://www.justice.gov/opa/pr/2011/July/11-crm-911.html; Press Release, U.S. Sec. & Exch. Comm'n., Sec Charges Armor Holdings, Inc. with FCPA Violations in Connection with Sales to the United Nations (July 13, 2011), http://www.sec.gov/news/press/2011/2011-146.htm.

379. Criminal Information, United States v. Bridgestone Corp., No. 11-CR-651 (S.D. Tex. filed Sept. 15, 2011).

380. *Id.*

381. Press Release, U.S. Dep't of Justice, Aon Corporation Agrees to Pay a $1.76 Million Criminal Penalty to Resolve Violations of the Foreign Corrupt Practices Act (Dec. 20, 2011), http://www.justice.gov/opa/pr/2011/December/11-crm-1678.html.

382. SEC v. Aon Corp., No. 1-11-CV-02256 (D.D.C. filed Dec. 20, 2011), Litig. Release No. 22,203 (Dec. 20, 2011), http://www.sec.gov/litigation/litreleases/2011/lr22203.htm.

383. Press Release, U.K. Fin. Servs. Auth., FSA Fines Aon Limited £5.25 Million for Failings in Its Anti-Bribery and Corruption Systems and Controls (Jan. 8, 2009), http://www.fsa.gov.uk/library/communication/pr/2009/004.shtml.

384. No. 1:11-CV-02256 (D.D.C. filed Dec. 20, 2011).

385. *Id.*

386. Criminal Information No. 1:1CR00597 (E.D. Va. filed Dec. 29, 2011).

387. No. 11 CIV 9646 (S.D.N.Y. filed Dec. 29, 2011).

388. No. 11 CIV 9645 (S.D.N.Y. filed Dec. 29, 2011).

389. Press Release, U.S. Dep't of Justice, Magyar Telekom and Deutsche Telekom Resolve Foreign Corrupt Practices Act Investigation and Agree to Pay Nearly $64 Million in Combined Criminal Penalties (Dec. 29, 2011), http://www.justice.gov/opa/pr/2011/December/11-crm-1714.html.

390. Press Release, U.S. Dep't of Justice, Eight Former Senior Executives and Agents of Siemens Charged in Alleged $100 Million Foreign Bribe Scheme (Dec. 13, 2011), http://www.justice.gov/opa/pr/2011/December/11-crm-1626.html.

391. Litig. Release No. 22,190 (Dec. 13, 2011), http://www.sec.gov/litigation/litreleases/2011/lr22190: SEC v. Uriel Sharef, Ulrich Bock, Carlos Sergi, Stephan Signer, Herbert Steffen, Andres Truppel and Bernd Regendantz, No. 11-cv-9070 (SDNY filed Dec. 13, 2011).

392. www.siemens.com/investor/pool/en/investor_relations/delisting_faq_en.pdf.

393. Press Release, U.S. Dep't of Justice, Marubeni Corporation Resolves Foreign Corrupt Practices Act Investigation and Agrees to Pay A $54.6 Million Criminal Penalty (Jan. 17, 2012), http://www.justice.gov/opa/pr/2012/January/12-crm-060.html.

394. *Id.*

395. 1:12-CR-30 (RBW) (D.D.C. Feb. 6, 2012).

396. Press Release, U.S. Dep't of Justice, Medical Device Company Smith & Nephew Resolves Foreign Corrupt Practices Act Investigation (Feb. 6, 2012), http://www.justice.gov/opa/pr/2012/February/12-crm-166.html.

397. No. 12-CR-080-RBW (D.D.C.).

398. No. 1:12-CV-00450 (D.D.C. filed Mar. 26, 2012).

399. Press Release, U.S. Dep't of Justice, Third Medical Device Company Resolves Foreign Corrupt Practices Act Investigation (Mar. 26, 2012), http://www.justice.gov/opa/pr/2012/March/12-crm-373.html.

400. Press Release, U.S. Sec. & Exch. Comm'n, SEC Charges Medical Device Company Biomet with Foreign Bribery (Mar. 26, 2012) http://www.sec.gov/news/press/2012/2012-50.htm.

401. *Id.*

402. *Id.*

403. Criminal Information, United States v. BizJet Int'l Sales & Support, Inc., No. 12-CR-061-CVE (N.D. Okla. filed Mar. 14, 2012).

404. Press Release, U.S. Dep't of Justice, BizJet International Sales and Support Inc., Resolves Foreign Corrupt Practices Act Investigation and Agrees to Pay $11.8 Million Criminal Penalty (Mar. 14, 2012), http://www.justice.gov/opa/pr/2012/March/12-crm-321.html.

405. Deferred Prosecution Agreement Attachment A: Statement of Facts ¶¶ 25–44.

406. *Id.* ¶ 24.

407. Information at ¶ 21a.

408. Press Release, U.S. Dep't of Justice, Former Morgan Stanley Managing Director Pleads Guilty for Role in Evading Internal Controls Required by FCPA (Apr. 25, 2012), http://www.justice.gov/opa/pr/2012/April/12-crm-534.html.

409. Criminal Information, SEC v. Peterson, No. CV12-2033-JBW (E.D.N.Y. filed Apr. 25, 2012), Litig. Release No. 22,346 (Apr. 25, 2012).

410. Press Release, U.S. Dep't of Justice, Data Systems & Solutions LLC Resolves Foreign Corrupt Practices Act Violations and Agrees to Pay $8.82 Million Criminal Penalty (June 18, 2012), http://www.justice.gov/opa/pr/2012/June/12-crm-768.html.

411. Press Release, U.S. Dep't of Justice, The Nordam Group Inc. Resolves Foreign Corrupt Practices Act Violations and Agrees to Pay $2 Million Penalty (July 17, 2012), http://www.justice.gov/opa/pr/2012/July/12-crm-881.html.

412. Letter from U.S. Dep't of Justice to Carlos F. Ortiz, LeClairRyan (July 6, 2012), http://www.justice.gov/criminal/fraud/fcpa/cases/nordam-group/2012-07-17-nordam-npa.pdf.

413. Criminal Information, United States v. Orthofix, No. 4:12-CR-00150-RAS-DDB (E.D. Tex. filed July 12, 2012); Deferred Prosecution Agreement.

414. Press Release, U.S. Sec. & Exch. Comm'n, SEC Charges Orthofix International with FCPA Violations (July 10, 2012), http://www.sec.gov/news/press/2012/2012-133.htm.

415. Criminal Information, United States v. Pfizer H.C.P. Corp., No. 12-CR-169 (D.D.C. filed Aug. 7, 2012), Deferred Prosecution Agreement.

416. Complaint, SEC v. Pfizer Inc., No. 1:12-CV-01303 (D.D.C. filed Aug. 7, 2012).

417. Press Release, U.S. Dep't of Justice, Pfizer H.C.P. Corp. Agrees to Pay $15 Million Penalty to Resolve Foreign Bribery Investigation (Aug. 7, 2012), http://www.justice.gov/opa/pr/2012/August/12-crm-980.html.

418. Press Release, U.S. Dep't of Justice, Subsidiary of Tyco International Ltd. Pleads Guilty, Is Sentenced for Conspiracy to Violate Foreign Corrupt Practices Act (Sept. 24, 2012), http://www.justice.gov/opa/pr/2012/September/12-crm-1149.html.

419. No. 1:12-CR-00148 (E.D. Va. filed Sept. 24, 2012).

420. Complaint, SEC v. Tyco Int'l Ltd, No. 1:12-CV-01583 (D.D.C. filed Sept. 24, 2012), Litig. Release No. 22,491 (Sept. 24, 2012).

421. No. 06-CV-2942 (S.D.N.Y. filed Apr. 17, 2006).

422. *Id.*

423. 15 U.S.C. § 78m(b)(2)(A).

424. Press Release, U.S. Dep't of Justice, Four Former Executives of Lufthansa Subsidiary Bizjet Charged with Foreign Bribery (Apr. 5, 2013), http://www.justice.gov/opa/pr/four-former-executives-lufthansa-subsidiary-bizjet-charged-foreign-bribery.

425. 1:13-cr-00176-6BL (E.D. Va. Apr. 16, 2012). Press Release, Parker Drilling Company Resolves FCPA Investigation and Agrees to Pay $11.76 Million Penalty (Apr. 16, 2013), http://www.justice.gov/opa/pr/2013/April/13-crm-431.html.

426. Press Release, U.S. Sec. & Exch. Comm'n, SEC Charges Parker Drilling Company with Violating the Foreign Corrupt Practices Act (Apr. 16, 2013), http://www.sec .gov/litigation/litreleases/2013/lr22672.htm.

427. Deferred Prosecution Agreement Statement of Facts at A-7, ¶ 33 (filed Apr. 16, 2013).

428. *Id.*

429. Press Release, U.S. Dep't of Justice, Ralph Lauren Corporation Resolves Foreign Corrupt Practices Act Investigation and Agrees to Pay $882,000 Monetary Penalty (Apr. 22, 2013), http://www.justice.gov/opa/pr/2013/april/13-CRM-456.html.

430. Press Release, U.S. Sec. & Exch. Comm'n, SEC Announces Non-Prosecution Agreement with Ralph Lauren Corporation Involving FCPA Misconduct (Apr. 22, 2013), http://www.sec.gov/news/press/2013/2013-65.htm.

431. *Id.*

432. *Id.*

433. Press Release, SEC Announces Non-Prosecution Agreement with Ralph Lauren Corporation Involving FCPA Misconduct, *supra* note 430.

434. Press Release, U.S. Dep't of Justice, Three Former Broker-Dealer Employees Plead Guilty in Manhattan Federal Court to Bribery of Foreign Officials, Money Laundering and Conspiracy to Obstruct Justice (Aug. 30, 2013), http://www.justice.gov /opa/pr/three-former-broker-dealer-employees-plead-guilty-manhattan-federal-court -bribery-foreign.

435. 13 cv 3074 (JMF) (S.D.N.Y. Apr. 14, 2014).

436. Criminal Information, United States v. Total, S.A., No. 13-CR-00239-LO (E.D. Va. filed May 29, 2013); Press Release, U.S. Dep't of Justice, French Oil and Gas Company, Total, S.A. Charged in the United States and France in Connection with International Bribery Scheme (May 29, 2013), http://www.justice.gov/opa/pr/2013 /May/13-crm-613.html.

437. *In re* Total, S.A., Exchange Act Release No. 69,654, Admin. Proceeding File No. 3-15338 (May 29, 2013), http://www.sec.gov/litigation/admin/2013/34-69654.pdf.

438. Press Release, U.S. Sec. & Exch. Comm'n, SEC Charges Total S.A. for Illegal Payments to Iranian Official (May 29, 2013), http://www.sec.gov/news/press/2013/2013 -94.htm.

439. Press Release, U.S. Dep't of Justice, Diebold Incorporated Resolves Foreign Corrupt Practices Act Investigation and Agrees to Pay $25.2 Million Criminal Penalty (Oct. 22, 2013), http://www.justice.gov/opa/pr/2013/October/13-crm-1118 .html.

440. Press Release, U.S. Sec. & Exch. Comm'n, SEC Charges Diebold with FCPA Violations (Oct. 22, 2013), http://www.sec.gov/News/PressRelease/Detail/Press Release/1370539977273.

441. *Id.*

442. Press Release, U.S. Sec. & Exch. Comm'n, SEC Charges Diebold with FCPA Violations (Oct. 22, 2013), http://www.sec.gov/News/PressRelease/1370539977273.

443. Press Release, U.S. Dep't of Justice, Three Subsidiaries of Weatherford International Limited Agree to Plead Guilty to FCPA and Export Control Violations (Nov. 26, 2013), http://www.justice.gov/opa/pr/2013/November/13-crm-1260.html.

444. 13-CR-734 (S.D. Tex. Nov. 16, 2013).

445. Press Release, U.S. Sec. & Exch. Comm'n, SEC Charges Weatherford International with FCPA Violations (Nov. 26, 2013), http://www.sec.gov/News/PressRelease/Detail/PressRelease/1370540415694.

446. Press Release, U.S. Dep't of Justice, German Engineering Firm Bilfinger Resolves Foreign Corrupt Practices Act Charges and Agrees to Pay $32 Million Criminal Penalty (Dec. 11, 2013), http://www.justice.gov/opa/pr/2013/December/13-crm-1297.html.

447. Press Release, U.S. Dep't of Justice, ADM Subsidiary Pleads Guilty to Conspiracy to Violate the Foreign Corrupt Practices Act (Dec. 20, 2013), http://www.justice.gov/opa/pr/adm-subsidiary-pleads-guilty-conspiracy-violate-foreign-corrupt-practices-act.

448. 2:13-cv-02279 (C.D. Ill. Dec. 20, 2013).

449. 14-cr-00007 (W.D. Pa. Jan. 9, 2014).

450. Press Release, U.S. Sec. & Exch. Comm'n, SEC Charges Alcoa with FCPA Violations (Jan. 9, 2014), http://www.sec.gov/News/PressRelease/Detail/PressRelease/1370540596936.

451. Press Release, U.S. Dep't of Justice, Foreign Bribery Charges Unsealed against Former Chief Executive Officers of Oil Services Company (Jan. 6, 2014), http://www.justice.gov/opa/pr/2014/January/14-crm-007.html.

452. 14-CR-00263-JEI (D.N.J. Nov. 8, 2013).

453. 13 Crim. 315 (S.D.N.Y. Apr. 25, 2013); Press Release, U.S. Dep't of Justice, French Citizen Pleads Guilty to Obstructing Criminal Investigation to Alleged Bribes Paid to Win Mining Rights in the Republic of Guinea (Mar. 10, 2014), http://www.justice.gov/opa/pr/french-citizen-pleads-guilty-obstructing-criminal-investigation-alleged-bribes-paid-win.

454. Press Release, U.S. Dep't of Justice, Marubeni Corporation Agrees to Plead Guilty to Foreign Bribery Charges and to Pay an $88 Million Fine (Mar. 19, 2014), http://www.justice.gov/opa/pr/2014/March/14-crm-290.html.

455. http://www.justice.gov/opa/pr/marubeni-corporation-agrees-plead-guilty-foreign-bribery-charges-and-pay-88-million-fine.

456. Indictment, 14 CRIM 240-DLC (Apr. 10, 2014); Press Release, U.S. Dep't of Justice, CEO and Managing Partner of Wall Street Broker-Dealer Charged with Massive International Bribery Scheme (Apr. 14, 2014), http://www.justice.gov/opa/pr/2014/April/14-crm-381.html.

457. Press Release, U.S. Sec. & Exch. Comm'n, SEC Charges Brokerage Firm Executives in Kickback Scheme to Secure Business of Venezuelan Bank (Apr. 14, 2013), http://www.sec.gov/News/PressRelease/Detail/PressRelease/1370541487258.

458. Press Release, U.S. Dep't of Justice, Six Defendants Indicated in Alleged Conspiracy to Bribe Government Officials in India to Mine Titanium Minerals (Apr. 2, 2014), http://www.justice.gov/opa/pr/2014/April/14-crm-333.html.

459. CR-14-00201-DLJ (N.D. Cal.); April 9, 2014 Press Release, Hewlett-Packard Russia Agrees to Plead Guilty to Foreign Bribery (Apr. 9, 2014), http://www.justice.gov/opa/pr/2014/April/14-crm-358.html.

460. Press Release, U.S. Sec. & Exch. Comm'n, SEC Charges Hewlett-Packard with FCPA Violations (Apr. 9, 2014), http://www.sec.gov/News/PressRelease/Detail /PressRelease/1370541453075.

461. *See* Letter from Andrew Genton, U.S. Dep't of Justice, to Douglas N. Greenburg, Latham & Watkins (Nov. 3, 2014) (regarding Bio-Rad Laboratories nonprosecution agreement).

462. Litig. Release No. 73,496 (Nov. 3, 2014), http://www.sec.gov/litigation/admin /2014/34-73496.pdf.

463. Press Release, U.S. Dep't of Justice, Bio-Rad Laboratories Resolves Foreign Corrupt Practices Act Investigation and Agrees to Pay $14.35 Million Penalty (Nov. 3, 2014), http://www.justice.gov/opa/pr/bio-rad-laboratories-resolves-foreign-corrupt -practices-act-investigation-and-agrees-pay-1435.

464. Press Release, U.S. Sec. & Exch. Comm'n, SEC Charges California-Based Bio-Rad Laboratories with FCPA Violations (Nov. 3, 2014), http://www.sec.gov /News/PressRelease/Detail/PressRelease/1370543347364.

465. Press Release, U.S. Dep't of Justice, Dallas Airmotive Inc. Admits Foreign Corrupt Practices Act Violations and Agrees to Pay $14 Million Criminal Penalty (Dec. 10, 2014), http://www.justice.gov/opa/pr/dallas-airmotive-inc-admits-foreign-corrupt -practices-act-violations-and-agrees-pay-14.

466. S1 14 Cr. 828-GBD (Superseding Information, S.D.N.Y. 2014).

467. Letter from William J. Stellmach to Evan R. Chesler and Benjamin Gruenstein, Cravath, Swaine & Moore LLP (Dec. 15, 2014).

468. 14 CV 9956 (S.D.N.Y. Dec. 15, 2014).

469. United States v. Alstom, S.A., 3:14-cr-00246-JBA (D. Conn. Dec. 22, 2014).

470. United States v. Alstom Network Schweiz AG, 3:14-cr-00245-JBA (D. Conn. Dec. 22, 2014).

471. United States v. Alstom Grid, Inc., 3:14-cr-00247-JBA (D. Conn. Dec. 22, 2014).

472. United States v. Alstom Power, Inc., 3:14-cr-00248-JBA (D. Conn. Dec. 23, 2014).

473. Danielle Ivory, *Alstom to Plead Guilty and Pay U.S. a $772 Million Fine in a Bribery Scheme*, N.Y. TIMES, Dec. 23, 2014, at B3.

474. Nonprosecution Agreement, Ralph Lauren Corp. (DOJ Apr. 22, 2013) Attachment B, Corporate Compliance Program, http://www.justice.gov/criminal/fraud/fcpa /cases/ralph-lauren/Ralph-Lauren-NPA-Executed.pdf.

CHAPTER 11

United Kingdom Bribery Act 2010, Corporate Criminal Liability, and Corporate Prosecution Guidance

I. INTRODUCTION

This chapter focuses on (1) the U.K. Bribery Act 2010 (Bribery Act or the Act) offense of bribery of a foreign public official (section 6 of the Bribery Act), which is most analogous to the bribery provisions of the U.S. Foreign Corrupt Practices Act (FCPA); (2) the U.K. strict liability offense for failure of a company to prevent bribery by others on its behalf (section 7 of the Bribery Act); (3) the adequate procedures defense under the Bribery Act as amplified in the U.K. Ministry of Justice's Bribery Guidance of March 2011 (MOJ Guidance); (4) a summary of the MOJ Guidance's 11 case studies; (5) a summary of the principal similarities and differences between the Bribery Act and the FCPA; (6) a discussion of the 2013 Deferred Prosecution Agreements legislation and the Deferred Prosecution Agreement Code jointly issued by the Crown Prosecution Service (CPS) and the Serious Fraud Office[1] (SFO); (7) a review of the Joint Prosecution Guidance that relates to the Bribery Act and the Corporate Prosecution Guidance that addresses the broader issue of corporate prosecutions; (8) the corporate criminal liability principles that guide U.K. prosecutorial authorities in corporate investigations and prosecutions; (9) the U.K. Sentencing Council Definitive Guideline for Bribery Offences; and (10) practical guidance for multinational companies seeking to comply with the Bribery Act.

With respect to corporate criminal liability, U.S. counsel must be aware of the very different U.K. identification principle under which a company will only be prosecuted if the acts were done by the controlling mind and will of the company, that is, by senior managers or directors. (See section IX.A.2.b.) The purpose of this chapter is to provide practical advice to companies and their counsel facing corruption issues and investigations in the United Kingdom that may subject their businesses and executives to the broad jurisdictional reach of the Bribery Act.

II. BRIBERY ACT 2010

A. Overview of Four Bribery Offenses

The Bribery Act is an Act of the Parliament of the United Kingdom that covers its criminal law relating to bribery.[2] Following both Labour and Conservative Party support, the 19-section Bribery Bill received Royal Assent on April 8, 2010, becoming the Bribery Act 2010 and eventually become effective on July 1, 2011. The Act repeals all previous statutory and common law provisions in relation to bribery, replacing them instead with four bribery offenses (two general offenses, a discrete offense of bribery of a foreign official, and a new corporate offense of failing to prevent bribery). The Bribery Act does not apply to conduct that took place before it came into force on July 1, 2011. Conduct before that date remains subject to the preexisting law, which in many respects was very similar to the Act, other than the Act contains the broad section 7 corporate offense of failing to prevent bribery.

The Act addresses only bribery, which is generally defined as giving someone a financial or other advantage to perform his or her functions or activities improperly, or to reward that person for already having done so. "Financial or other advantage" is not defined in the Bribery Act and is left to the fact finder. The four bribery offenses under the Act can be committed by individuals and corporations:

1. Offering a bribe (section 1);
2. Receiving a bribe (section 2);[3]
3. Bribery of a foreign public official (section 6); and
4. The failure of a commercial organization (corporation or partnership) to prevent bribery on its behalf (section 7).

Only the third and fourth Bribery Act offenses (sections 6 and 7 of the Bribery Act) are discussed in this chapter. Sections 1 and 2 apply to commercial bribery, that is, private bribery involving nongovernment officials or employees.

The penalties for committing a crime under the Act are a maximum of 10 years' imprisonment for an individual along with an *unlimited fine* for corporations,[4] and the potential for the confiscation or civil recovery of property (e.g., the disgorgement of profits) under the Proceeds of Crime Act 2002 (POCA), as well as the disqualification of directors under the Company Directors Disqualification Act of 1986.

B.   Recent U.K. Foreign Bribery Prosecutions

Foreign bribery prosecutions and civil recovery proceedings against companies are a relatively recent development in the United Kingdom and have been brought thus far under the common law and statutes that preceded the Bribery Act. The first case in which the SFO used its civil recovery powers was against Balfour Beatty plc in 2008 and resulted in a £2.25 million penalty. Balfour Beatty was part of a joint venture to build the Bibliotheca Alexandrina, a library in Alexandria, Egypt. The company investigated irregularities and reported the matter to the SFO in April 2005. The SFO investigated and ultimately agreed to a civil recovery order, the first such order made under POCA. The civil recovery order allowed Balfour Beatty, a major engineering and construction services company, to avoid being debarred from public works contracts. Since this action, the SFO has obtained ten other corporate resolutions relating to improper foreign payments with the amounts recovered by the SFO from the companies involved ranging from £5 million to £30 million:

- Mabey & Johnson Ltd. (2009)—£6.5m
- AMEC plc (2009)—£5m (civil recovery)

- Innospec Inc. (U.S.) & Innospec Ltd. (U.K.) (2010)—U.S. $17m and £9m (U.S./U.K.)
- BAE Systems plc (2010)—U.S. $400m and £30m (U.S./U.K.)
- M.W. Kellogg Ltd. (2011)—U.S. $400m and £7m (U.S./U.K.) (civil recovery)
- Johnson & Johnson and DePuy Ltd. (2011)—U.S. $70m and £5m (U.S./U.K.) (civil recovery)
- Weir Group (2011)—£17m[5]
- Macmillan Publishers Ltd. (2011)—£11.2m (civil recovery)
- Oxford Publishing (2012)—£1.9m (civil recovery)
- Smith and Ouzman Ltd. (2014)—corporation and two employees awaiting sentence

The 2014 trial of Smith and Ouzman Ltd. resulted in the SFO's first conviction of a corporation after a trial for bribery of a foreign official.[6] The printing firm and two former employees were convicted of corruptly agreeing to make payments to public officials in order to obtain business contracts in Kenya and Mauritania, in violation of the Prevention of Corruption Act of 1906.

Five of the ten bribery resolutions since 2008 have resulted in civil rather than criminal sanctions, largely as a result of disclosure and cooperation by the companies. (See Self-Reporting discussion in section VIII.B.3). However, since taking control of the SFO in 2012, Director David Green Q.C. has made it clear on several occasions that he looks less favorably on civil recovery as an option for the SFO than his predecessor did and that the SFO is a prosecutorial agency first and foremost.

In the United Kingdom, as in the United States, foreign bribery prosecutions of individuals have been significantly fewer. With the Bribery Act having only become effective on July 1, 2011, the SFO has had to use older statutes for misconduct before July 2011. It is presently investigating Alstom, GlaxoSmithKline, and Rolls Royce, among other companies, for potential bribery violations.

In developing comprehensive foreign public official bribery legislation and policies, the United Kingdom has borrowed from the 1997 OECD Anti-Bribery Convention on Combating Bribery of Foreign Public Officials in International Business Transactions (OECD Convention) as well as the U.S. Department of Justice and Securities and Exchange Commission's FCPA enforcement policies. The SFO staff have developed close working relationships with their U.S. counterparts and can be expected to consider U.S. policies; see, for example, the 2014 Deferred Prosecution Agreement legislation and code.

U.S. efforts to enforce the law in this area were gradual and at times halting in the first 20 years following the 1977 enactment of the FCPA. Foreign bribery enforcement certainly remains at essentially an infancy stage in the United Kingdom, but there is no doubt that the Bribery Act gives the SFO the legislative tools to tackle overseas corruption where it sees fit. In addition, the SFO and its new legislation and policies will likely serve as an anticorruption catalyst for other nations in Europe and elsewhere, marking the end of an era where one superpower attempted to enforce global anticorruption largely alone. Finally, U.S. counsel need to consider the broad corporate money laundering reporting obligations in the United Kingdom.

III. BRIBERY OF FOREIGN PUBLIC OFFICIALS

Section 6 of the Bribery Act makes bribery of a foreign public official a stand-alone distinct offense, consistent with the requirements of the 1997 OECD Anti-Bribery Convention on Combating Bribery of Foreign Public Officials.[7] The offense can be committed by both individuals and corporations. There are at least five key elements to understand in connection with a section 6 offense: (1) the combined mental state required to commit the offense; (2) the conduct required to commit the offense; (3) the meaning of the phrase foreign public official; (4) the jurisdiction of the offense; and (5) the meaning of "consent and connivance."

A. Mental State

Sections 1 and 2 of the Bribery Act address the requisite combined mental state.

> (1) A person ("P") who bribes a foreign public official ("F") is guilty of an offence if P's intention is to influence F in F's capacity as a foreign public official.
> (2) P must also intend to obtain or retain—
>   (a) business, or
>   (b) an advantage in the conduct of business.

There are two separate and distinct elements to the mental state: (1) P must intend to influence the foreign public official in his capacity as a public official, and (2) P must intend to bribe in order to obtain or retain business or an advantage in the conduct of the business. The MOJ Guidance states that the policy underlying this offense is "the need to prohibit the influencing of decision-making in the context of public business opportunities by the inducement of personal enrichment of foreign public officials, or to others at the official's request, assent or acquiescence."[8] Like the U.S. FCPA, the Bribery Act not only covers improper conduct that directly results in "obtaining and retaining business," for example, bribes to secure large government contracts, but also improper conduct that obtains or retains "an advantage in the conduct of the business," such as bribes to "fix" local tax or customs issues or to obtain permits or licenses. The Bribery Act business purpose language is broader than the related OECD or FCPA language as it encompasses one who intends to obtain or retain business or an advantage in the conduct of business[9] and not an improper advantage in the conduct of international business.[10]

B. Conduct

Section 6(3) addresses the requisite conduct of the offense—that is, what a person must do in order to commit the offense. It provides:

> P bribes F if, and only if—
> (a) directly or through a third party, P offers, promises, or gives any financial or other advantage—
>   (i)   to F, or
>   (ii) to another person at F's request or with F's assent or acquiescence, and

(b) F is neither permitted nor required by the written law applicable to F to be influenced in F's capacity as a foreign public official by the offer, promise, or gift.

A person will be guilty of this new offense if he or she promises, offers, or gives a financial or other advantage to a foreign public official, either directly or through a third party, where such an advantage is not legitimately due.

The inclusion of "through a third party" in subsection (3) is intended to address and prohibit the use of intermediaries to bribe a government official. There is a narrow exception where the written law of the country of the foreign public official allows or requires the official to accept the advantage offered. In such circumstances, no crime will be committed.

Under the foreign public official bribery offense, U.K. prosecutors are required to show not only that an "advantage" was offered, promised, or given to the official or to another person at the official's request, assent, or acquiescence, but that the official was not permitted or required to be influenced by the written law applicable to the foreign official.[11] There is no requirement to prove that the public official acted improperly as a result of the offer or giving; this is a significant distinction between the Bribery Act and the OECD Anti-Bribery Convention. As under the U.S. FCPA, a section 6 offense applies only to the briber, and not to the recipient or foreign public official who receives or agrees to receive such a bribe.

C. Foreign Public Official

Section 6(5) of the Bribery Act broadly provides both an institutional and functional definition of "foreign public official." Specifically, it defines a foreign public official as an individual who

(a) holds a legislative, administrative, or judicial position of any kind, whether appointed or elected, of a country or territory outside the United Kingdom (or any subdivision of such a country or territory),

(b) exercises a public function—
   (i) for or on behalf of a country or territory outside the United Kingdom (or any subdivision of such a country or territory), or
   (ii) for any public agency or public enterprise of that country or territory (or subdivision), or

(c) is an official or agent of a public international organisation.

Section 6(5)(b) includes individuals who exercise a public function for any public agency or public enterprise, such as professionals working for public health agencies and officers exercising public functions in state-owned enterprises.[12] This subsection is analogous to the FCPA's "instrumentality" language and concept.

With respect to SFO fraud investigation priorities, Director Green has stated:

> The SFO must focus on top drawer fraud. By that I mean:
> - cases which undermine confidence in UK plc and the City of London in particular;
> - cases which compromise the level playing field to which investors are entitled;

- *serious bribery and corruption, national or international;*
- those other cases which may have a particularly strong public interest dimension, or which represent a striking new species of fraud.

    The SFO is here to use its unique set up and capability to do the most difficult and serious investigations and (where appropriate) prosecutions; those that others cannot do.[13]

D. Jurisdiction

Section 12 sets forth the scope or territorial application of the Act's provisions. To come within the purview under section 6's bribery of a foreign public official offense (as well as section 1 and 2 offenses), a person must have either committed a crime inside the United Kingdom, or acted or omitted to act outside of the United Kingdom in a way that would have constituted a crime had it happened in the United Kingdom, and the person must have a "close connection" to the United Kingdom by virtue of being a British national or ordinarily resident in the United Kingdom, or a company incorporated in the United Kingdom, or a Scottish partnership.[14] Thus, a resident in the United Kingdom or of British citizenry or a corporation in the United Kingdom can commit an offense, regardless of whether the acts or commissions take place there.

E. Consent and Connivance

Section 14 of the Bribery Act addresses the offense of "consent and connivance." Under a section 6 offense (as well as a section 1 or 2 offense) that is committed by a corporation, if the offense is proved to have been committed with the "consent and connivance" of a senior officer of the corporation or a person purporting to act in such a capacity, the senior officer or person (as well as the corporation) is guilty of the offense and subject to prosecution and punishment,[15] so long as the senior officer or person purporting to act in such capacity has a close connection to the United Kingdom.[16] For purposes of this section, "senior officer," in relation to a corporation, means "a director, manager, secretary, or other similar officer" of the corporation.[17]

    Leading U.K. white-collar criminal lawyer Monty Raphael has explained the history of "consent and connivance" in *Blackstone's Guide to the Bribery Act 2010*:

> Consent and connivance provisions are commonplace in regulatory statutes, such as those dealing with health and safety. The meaning of "consent and connive" has been shown to be flexible. The Law Commission has previously likened the terms to those of encouragement or tolerance. In its broadest consideration of these terms, carried out ahead of a lengthy consultation period on reform of the law of bribery, the Law Commission said this of the concept of connivance:
>
>   "[I]t is wider than that provided for by the doctrine of complicity. First, in theory it is possible for someone to 'connive' at the commission of an offence (to know it may occur but to do nothing to prevent its commission) without providing actual assistance or encouragement. Secondly, connivance may occur through reckless conduct (knowing

that there is a risk of offending but doing nothing) whereas, speaking in very broad terms, complicity requires intention or knowledge as to the offending behaviour."

The Law Commission goes on to assert that "connivance at the culpable actions of the corporate perpetrator may be reckless on the part of a high-ranking member of an organisation, as well as the intentional or knowing."[18]

"Consent" would certainly suggest the involvement of active knowledge and agreement on the part of the senior officer.

Commenting on a similar provision in the Health and Safety at Work Act 1974, Lord Hope, in *R v. Chargot*, commented that: "[N]o fixed rule can be laid down as to what the prosecution must identify and prove in order to establish that the officer's state of mind was such as to amount to consent, connivance or neglect."[19]

The MOJ Guidance does not shed any new light on section 14's "consent and connivance" offense. It remains to be seen how "flexible" the SFO will be in bringing charges of an offense whose very words connote some flexibility.

F.   Facilitation Payments

Facilitation payments, sometimes referred to as "speed" or "grease" payments, are unofficial payments made to public officials in order to secure or expedite the performance of a routine or necessary action. There is no U.K. exemption under the Bribery Act or otherwise for facilitating payments.[20]

IV.   FAILURE OF COMPANIES TO PREVENT BRIBERY

A.   Offense

Section 7 of the Bribery Act creates the unprecedented and controversial offense of failure of commercial organizations (companies or partnerships) to prevent bribery by others on their behalf. This strict liability section, which applies only to corporate bodies and not individuals, provides in principal part:

(1) A relevant commercial organisation ("C") is guilty of an offence under this section if a person ("A") associated with C bribes another person intending—
   (a) to obtain or retain business for C, or
   (b) to obtain or retain an advantage in the conduct of business for C.
(2) But it is a defence for C to prove that C had in place adequate procedures designed to prevent persons associated with C from undertaking such conduct.
(3) For the purposes of this section, A bribes another person if, and only if, A
   (a) is, or would be, guilty of an offence under section 1 or 6 (whether or not A has been prosecuted for such an offence), or
   (b) would be guilty of such an offence if section 12(2)(c) and (4) were omitted.

This strict corporate liability offense arises where a person associated with a company, for example, an employee, agent, or subsidiary, bribes another to obtain or retain business or a business advantage. The defense to section 7 liability is adequate procedures (see section IV), which a company must prove by "the balance of probabilities"[21]—the equivalent of "preponderance of the evidence" in U.S. courts.

B. Relevant Commercial Organization

Under section 7(5) "relevant commercial organization" means:

(a) a body which is incorporated under the law of any part of the United Kingdom and which carries on a business (whether there or elsewhere),
(b) any other body corporate (wherever incorporated) which carries on a business, or part of a business, in any part of the United Kingdom,
(c) a partnership which is formed under the law of any part of the United Kingdom and which carries on a business (whether there or elsewhere), or
(d) any other partnership (wherever formed) which carries on a business, or part of a business, in any part of the United Kingdom.

A relevant commercial organization (RCO) thus includes various business organizations formed under the laws of the United Kingdom as well as foreign corporations that carry on a business, or part of a business, in any part of the United Kingdom. As noted in the MOJ Guidance, the key concept is that a corporation "carries on or does business in the U.K.," of which courts will be the final arbiter depending on the particular facts of each case.[22] The term "carries on a business" is neither defined in the Act nor the explanatory notes. Factors that may perhaps affect a jury interpreting the "carrying on business" language and upholding a foreign corporation's activities as "carrying on business" in the United Kingdom include the repetition or continuity of a company's activities in the United Kingdom, a foreign company's management or control over such activities and its pursuit of profits in the United Kingdom.[23] Further, the determination of whether an organization or entity constitutes an RCO under either of these tests is to be determined by applying "a common sense approach."[24]

The concept of "carrying on business" was considered by the U.K. Court of Appeal in the 2014 Akzo Nobel N.V. judgment regarding the application of antitrust law. Although not considering the concept from the Act's perspective, the judgment is nevertheless informative. The Court of Appeal adopted a wide interpretation of the meaning of "carrying on a business in the U.K.," stating that this will be a fact-intensive question, and will depend on the answer to two questions:

1. Is there a business being carried on in (or partly in) the U.K.?, and
2. Is the target person sufficiently involved in that business that it can be said to be carrying it on, whether alone or with others?[25]

Interestingly, the MOJ Guidance provides that the "carrying on business" test will not be satisfied by "the mere fact that a company's securities have been admitted to the U.K. Listing Authority's Official List and therefore admitted to trading on the London Stock Exchange" or by the organization "having a U.K. subsidiary . . . , in itself . . . , since a subsidiary may act independently of its parent or other group companies."[26]

C. Associated Persons

A company or partnership can be guilty of the failure to prevent a bribery offense if the bribery is carried out by an associated person. Section 8(1) defines the term "associated person" for purposes of imposing section 7 liability as any person or entity "who performs services for or on behalf of a relevant commercial organization." Section 8(3) makes clear an associated person can be a company's employee, agent, or subsidiary. Pursuant to section 8(4), whether a person or entity "performs services for or on behalf of" an organization "is to be determined by reference to all the relevant circumstances and not merely by reference to the nature of the relationship" between the person or entity and the company.

In March 2011 the director of the SFO and the director of Public Prosecutions issued Joint Prosecution Guidance on the Bribery Act (Joint Prosecution Guidance). The Joint Prosecution Guidance on "associated persons" reinforces this contextual standard, and further notes that through the phrase "performs services for or on behalf of," the offense of failing to prevent bribery has "a broad scope so as to embrace the whole range of persons connected to an organization who might be capable of committing bribery on the organization's behalf."[27] Contractors and suppliers may therefore be "associated" persons to the extent they perform services for, as opposed to merely sell the goods of, an organization.[28]

Under sections 7 and 8 of the Bribery Act, the offense of a company failing to prevent bribery can be committed without a company or one of its officers or a putative "directing mind" having any knowledge, belief or intentions, or mental state at all about the events in question.[29]

Multinational companies with a nexus to the United Kingdom should be particularly mindful of whether participants in their joint ventures and multitiered supply chains qualify as "associated persons." The MOJ Guidance introduces the concept of control in analyzing these issues. Joint venture participants may be liable for the acts of the joint venture, though the Guidance distinguishes between joint ventures operated through a separate legal entity and those conducted through a contract arrangement.[30] In a contractual joint venture, "[t]he degree of control that a participant has over that arrangement is likely to be one of the 'relevant circumstances' that would be taken into account in deciding whether a person who paid a bribe in the conduct of the joint venture business was 'performing services for or on behalf of' a participant in that arrangement."[31] Notably, the MOJ Guidance disclaims the imposition of liability based on indirect benefits that are lacking in intention to benefit a specific business entity (such as the parent company).[32]

With regard to multitiered supply chains, the MOJ Guidance acknowledges that a company's contractual relationship, dealings, and control may extend to only the first layer or prime contractor.[33] Accordingly, it envisions that the primary method to safeguard against bribery conduct by members of the supply chain will be procedures established contractually and in succession down the supply chain by members in privity with one another and per the request of member(s) up the supply chain.[34] Examples of prophylactic practices and provisions for supply-chain members are "risk-based due diligence and the use of anti-bribery terms and conditions."[35]

V. "ADEQUATE PROCEDURES" DEFENSE TO FAILURE OF COMPANIES TO PREVENT BRIBERY OFFENSE

Under section 7(2) of the Bribery Act, a corporation has a full defense to a section 7 offense if it can show that the commercial organization had in place "adequate procedures designed to prevent persons associated with [the company] from undertaking such conduct." Signally, the Act does not require "perfect procedures" but rather "adequate procedures."

On March 30, 2011, the Ministry of Justice (MOJ) issued the Bribery Act 2010 Guidance (MOJ Guidance) (appendix 17), outlining inter alia procedures that companies can put into place to prevent persons associated with them from bribing others in contravention of section 7 of the Bribery Act.[36] In addressing the four offenses and the adequate procedures defense, the MOJ Guidance discusses jurisdiction over foreign companies, "associated persons" including joint ventures, corporate hospitality, facilitation payments, and mandatory debarment, and further offers 11 case studies based on hypothetical scenarios. These are designed to illustrate the application of the principles for small, medium, and large organizations, *infra*.

In October 2012 the new director of the SFO (David Green) modified the office's existing anticorruption guidance and issued three new policies with respect to facilitating payments, business expenditures (corporate hospitality), and self-reporting.[37] While the revised policies are thought to be "a change in tone or emphasis rather than a substantive shift in the SFO's approval,"[38] the SFO has made clear that the "SFO's primary role is to investigate and prosecute" and the revised policies will carry "no presumption in favor of civil settlements in any circumstance."[39] These new SFO policies are discussed in section VI of this chapter.

The Joint Prosecution Guidance, which relates specifically to the Bribery Act, noted that a single act of bribery does not necessarily mean that a company's procedures are inadequate. Under the Act's explanatory notes, the burden of proof with respect to establishing an adequate procedures defense is on the corporation, with the burden of proof being "on the balance of probabilities."

The "adequate procedures" discussion in the MOJ Guidance has been especially welcome given the concerns of many companies about the broad liability imposed under section 7(1) of the Bribery Act. Signally, the adequate procedures defense does not apply to offenses outside section 7. Thus, a U.K. company or a foreign corporation with a close connection to the United Kingdom can still be convicted of section 6 foreign public official bribery once the identification principle outlined in *Tesco Supermarkets Ltd. v. Nattrass* is satisfied.[40]

The MOJ Guidance language could be interpreted to limit the circumstances where the adequate procedures defense is available. For example, its Introduction reads:

> The Act creates a new offence under Section 7 which can be committed
> by commercial organizations which fail to prevent persons associated

with them from committing bribery on their behalf. It is a full defence for an organisation to prove that despite a particular case of bribery, it nonetheless had adequate procedures in place to prevent persons associated with it from bribery.[41]

In later discussing government policy and section 7 of the Bribery Act, the MOJ Guidance states:

> The objective of the Act is not to bring the full force of the criminal law to bear upon well run commercial organizations that experience *an isolated incidence of bribery on their behalf.* So in order to achieve an appropriate balance, Section 7 provides a full defence. This is in recognition of the fact that no bribery prevention regime will be capable of preventing bribery at all times. However, the defence is also included in order to encourage commercial organisations to push procedures to prevent bribery by persons associated with them.[42]

A. Overview of the Six Principles Necessary to Establish an Adequate Procedures Defense

The March 2011 MOJ Guidance provides welcome insight into what constitute "adequate procedures," to form a full defense to strict liability for corporations and partnerships under section 7 of the Bribery Act. The onus of this defense remains on companies. In designing policies and procedures to mitigate the risk of bribery conduct, companies should heed six, nonprescriptive principles and adopt a risk-based approach to managing bribery risks:

1. *Proportionate procedures.* Under the fundamental and first principle of proportionality, the MOJ Guidance acknowledges that the adequacy of procedures must be evaluated under a bribery risk-based approach and in appreciation to the size and nature of the organization and its operations, and the people associated with it. Indeed, the Foreword to the MOJ Guidance by the then Secretary of State for Justice Kenneth Clarke and the Introduction specifically disclaim a "one size fits all" application of the Bribery Act in determining the adequacy of an organization's procedures.[43] Common topics to be addressed by organizations' procedures include, among others, (a) involvement of top-level management; (b) due diligence of current and potential associated persons; (c) hospitality and gifts; (d) financial and commercial controls, including the accurate and transparent recording of transactions and financial information; and (e) whistleblowing procedures.

2. *Top-level commitment.* The Guidance emphasizes the important role of senior directors, officers, and employees in creating an organizational culture that does not tolerate bribery conduct. Moreover, the antibribery message from top-level management should be communicated throughout the business organization and reinforced through formal statements. However, as noted U.K. compliance authority Eoin O'Shea has pointed out, "More important

than warm words from a CEO is actual support for the (compliance) program, in particular the provision of resources to those tasked with operating it."[44] Appropriate leaders in the organization (board members and/or senior executives) should also be actively engaged in establishing and implementing antibribery procedures and provide sufficient staff to carry out a program.

3. *Risk assessment.* Pursuant to the MOJ Guidance, business organizations should periodically conduct and document a bribery risk-based assessment that evaluates both external and internal risks. External risks may be divided into five categories: (a) country risk; (b) sector risk; (c) transaction risk; (d) business opportunity risk; and (e) business partnership risk. These external risks may be compounded by internal risks such as poor training, organizational cultures that promote excessive risk taking, poor financial controls, and unclear antibribery policies and senior management messages.

4. *Due diligence.* Elevating due diligence to a distinct principle, the MOJ Guidance "encourage[s] commercial organizations to put in place due diligence procedures that adequately inform the application of proportionate measures designed to prevent persons associated with them from bribing on their behalf." Due diligence procedures function both to assess and mitigate bribery risk. The precise methods, scope, and updating of due diligence are determined under a proportionate and risk-based approach, though thorough due diligence should be undertaken prior to retaining local agents or entering into a joint venture, merger or acquisition.

5. *Communication (including training).* The MOJ Guidance observes that business organizations should promote compliance with and understanding of their antibribery procedures through communication and training. Communications (external and internal) by an organization reduce the incidence of bribery conduct by increasing awareness and knowledge of antibribery procedures. External communications can discourage associated persons from engaging in bribery conduct. As previously noted, internal communications transmit the antibribery message from the organization's senior managers (i.e., the "tone from the top"). External and internal communications will differ in tone, substance, and method and scope of dissemination. An important antibribery communication procedure is "a secure, confidential and accessible means" for employees and third parties to report bribery conduct or comment on the effectiveness of antibribery procedures.

Training should be provided to employees as well as "associated persons" selected under a risk-based analysis. The MOJ Guidance notes the possibility of mandatory general training for new employees and certain agents (again determined under a risk-based analysis), but further recommends that training be customized "to the specific risks associated with specific posts," and for organizations to consider providing special training to employees in more sensitive positions or in higher-risk environments. The commitment to training is ongoing, and should be regularly reviewed. Under the MOJ Guidance, the effectiveness of the training is more important than its form (live or online).

6. *Monitoring and review.* Companies must monitor and review their procedures, and make improvements and adjustments in light of changing circumstances, including reports or changes in countries in which the organization conducts business. Companies may use various internal and external means, such as staff surveys and feedback from training, to periodically evaluate its procedures. The MOJ Guidance further urges companies to consider formal periodic reporting to senior management, testing, and verification of antibribery procedures by outside parties, and obtaining certified compliance with independent antibribery standards, such as ones established by industry groups or multilateral bodies.

The practical application of the Six Principles is made clearer through 11 hypothetical case studies that are part of the MOJ Guidance. Commentators, however, already have begun debating the case studies' actual value in providing certainty and guidance to companies subject to the Bribery Act.

B. The Six Principles in Detail

1. *Principle 1: A Commercial Organization's Procedures*

A commercial organization's procedures to prevent bribery by persons associated with it must be proportionate to the bribery risks it faces and to the nature, scale, and complexity of the commercial organization's activities. They must also be clear, practical, accessible, and effectively implemented and enforced.

The thrust of the first principle and throughout the MOJ Guidance is that companies should take a risk-based approach to bribery and to preventing persons associated with them from bribing. The principle of "proportionality" makes clear that the level of risk will not only be linked to the size of the company and the nature and complexity of its business, but will vary with the type and nature of persons associated with the company (e.g., third-party agents representing a company in negotiations with foreign public officials would require much more in the way of protective procedures).

The MOJ Guidance for Principle 1 suggests that a company may wish to cover in its prevention policies:

- Its commitment to bribery prevention (see Principle 2);
- Its general approach to mitigation of specific bribery risks, such as those arising from the conduct of intermediaries and agents, or those associated with hospitality and promotional expenditures, facilitation payments, or political and charitable donations or contributions (see Principle 3 on Risk Assessment); and
- An overview of its strategy to implement its bribery prevention policies.

Further, the MOJ Guidance offers a nonexhaustive list of 14 topics that a solid bribery procedure might embrace depending on the particular risks faced:

- The involvement of the organization's top-level management (see Principle 2);
- Risk assessment procedures (see Principle 3);

- Due diligence of existing or prospective associated person (see Principle 4);
- The provision of gifts, hospitality, and promotional expenditure; charitable and political donations; or demands for facilitation payments;
- Direct and indirect employment, including recruitment, terms and conditions, disciplinary action, and remuneration;
- Governance of business relationships with all other associated persons including precontractual and postcontractual agreements;
- Financial and commercial controls such as adequate bookkeeping, auditing, and approval of expenditures;
- Transparency of transactions and disclosure of information;
- Decision making, such as delegation of authority procedures, separation of functions, and the avoidance of conflicts of interest;
- Enforcement, detailing discipline processes and sanctions for breaches of the organization's antibribery rules;
- The reporting of bribery including "speak up" or whistleblowing procedures;
- The detail of the process by which the organization plans to implement its bribery prevention procedures, for example, how its policy will be applied to individual projects and to different parts of the organization;
- The communication of the organization's policies and procedures, and training in their application (see Principle 5); and
- The monitoring, review, and evaluation of bribery prevention procedures (see Principle 6).

2.   Principle 2: Top-Level Commitment

The top-level management of a commercial organization (be it a board of directors, the owners, or any other equivalent body or person) must be committed to preventing bribery by persons associated with it. They foster a culture within the organization in which bribery is never acceptable.

This principle mirrors the U.S. compliance mantra of "tone at the top" and focuses on procedures that (1) communicate a company's antibribery stance; and (2) involve to an appropriate degree top-level persons in developing bribery prevention procedures. The MOJ Guidance indicates that effective formal statements that demonstrate top-level commitment are likely to include

- a commitment to carry out business fairly, honestly, and openly;
- a commitment to zero tolerance toward bribery;
- the consequences of breaching the policy for employees and managers; for other associated persons, the consequences of breaching contractual provisions relating to bribery prevention (this could include a reference to avoiding doing business with others who do not commit to doing business without bribery as a "best practice" objective);
- articulation of the business benefits of rejecting bribery (reputational, and customer and business partner confidence);
- reference to the range of bribery prevention procedures the commercial organization has or is putting in place, including any protection and procedures for confidential reporting of bribery (whistleblowing);

- key individuals and departments involved in the development and implementation of the organization's bribery prevention procedures; and
- reference to the organization's involvement in any collective action against bribery in, for example, the same business sector.

With respect to top-level involvement, the MOJ Guidance indicates that top-level engagement is likely to include the following elements:

- selection and training of senior managers to lead antibribery work where appropriate;
- leadership on key measures such as a code of conduct;
- endorsement of all bribery prevention related publications;
- leadership in awareness raising and encouraging transparent dialogue throughout the organization so as to seek to ensure effective dissemination of antibribery policies and procedures to employees, subsidiaries, and associated persons;
- engagement with relevant associated persons and external bodies, such as sectoral organizations and the media, to help articulate the organization's policies;
- specific involvement in high-profile and critical decision making where appropriate;
- assurance of risk assessment; and
- general oversight of breaches of procedures and the provision of feedback to the board or equivalent, where appropriate, on levels of compliance.

The not infrequent senior management practice of delegating compliance responsibilities down will not meet the spirit or letter of the MOJ Guidance. Senior management should be fully engaged in compliance and make its footprints visible.

3.   *Principle 3: Risk Assessment*

The commercial organization assesses the nature and extent of its exposure to potential external and internal risks of bribery on its behalf by persons associated with it. The assessment is periodic, informed, and documented.

a.   Basic Characteristics

The MOJ Guidance for Principle 3 indicates that risk assessment procedures will usually reflect the following five basic characteristics:

1. Oversight of the risk assessment by top-level management;
2. Appropriate resourcing—this should reflect the scale of the organization's business and the need to identify and prioritize all relevant risks;
3. Identification of the internal and external information sources that will enable risk to be assessed and reviewed;
4. Due diligence inquiries (see Principle 4); and
5. Accurate and appropriate documentation of the risk assessment and its conclusions.

The MOJ Guidance goes on to distinguish among five broad groups of external risks and five internal factors that may add to the level of corruption risk.

b.   The Five External Risks

1.   *Country risk.* This is evidenced by perceived high levels of corruption; an absence of effectively implemented antibribery legislation; and a failure of the foreign government, media, local business community, and civil society effectively to promote transparent procurement and investment policies.
2.   *Sectoral risk.* Some sectors are higher risk than others. Higher-risk sectors include the extractive industries and the large scale infrastructure industries.
3.   *Transaction risk.* Certain types of transactions give rise to higher risks, for example, charitable or political contributions, licenses and permits, and transactions relating to public procurement.
4.   *Business opportunity risk.* Such risks might arise in high value projects or with projects involving many contractors or intermediaries; or with projects that are not apparently undertaken at market prices or that do not have a clear legitimate objective.
5.   *Business partnership risk.* Certain relationships may involve higher risk, for example, the use of intermediaries in transactions with foreign public officials; consortia or joint venture partners; and relationships with politically exposed persons where the proposed business relationship involves, or is linked to, a prominent public official.

Too often multinational companies conflate these five external risks, but each is worthy of separate regular analysis and reassessment.

c.   Five Internal Factors

The five internal factors that affect corruption risk are

1.   deficiencies in employee training, skills, and knowledge;
2.   bonus culture that rewards excessive risk taking;
3.   lack of clarity in the organization's policies on, and procedures for, hospitality and promotional expenditure, and political or charitable contributions;
4.   lack of clear financial controls; and
5.   lack of a clear antibribery message from the top-level management.

Companies have more control over their internal factors than their external risks and can be expected to manage the former more effectively.

d.   "Periodic, Informed, and Documented"

Risk assessment is the principle that offers the greatest challenge and the best opportunity to demonstrate a company's commitment to "adequate procedures." While the above five external risks and five internal factors identify very helpful specific risks for counsel to consider, one should keep in mind the final sentence of the third principle: "The assessment is periodic, informed, and documented." For most multinational companies "periodic" will be at least annually. To be "informed," any risk assessment should involve oversight by top-level management and likely include the input of legal, compliance, financial, accounting, audit, sales, human resources, and country managers. One or two persons cursorily reviewing and concluding that the above ten factors or risks are "unchanged" is not likely to be viewed as "informed" by law enforcement authorities. Finally, "documentation" is critical for not only analyzing risks but, if necessary, proving to the SFO or a fact finder that the risk assessment was real, periodic, and informed at the company—and much more than "adequate." Without a solid, contemporaneous record of its risk assessment, a company may fail to prove the third and, arguably, swing principle in the SFO's "adequate procedures" calculus.

4. Principle 4: Due Diligence

The commercial organization must apply due diligence procedures, taking a proportionate and risk-based approach, in respect of persons who perform or will perform services for or on behalf of the organization, in order to mitigate identified bribery risks.

a.   Third-Party Intermediaries

The primary focus of this principle is on the due diligence of local third-party intermediaries, but the MOJ Guidance also points out the important implications of due diligence in the merger and acquisitions context. It comments that due diligence procedures are both a form of bribery assessment (Principle 3) and a means of mitigating risks. It further recognizes that a person "associated" with a company as set forth in section 8 of the Act can embrace a wide variety of business relationships and that related risks will vary enormously as well. By example, it offers that the appropriate level of due diligence for an information technology services contractor may be low, while an intermediary assisting in the establishment of business in foreign markets will typically require a much higher level of due diligence.[45] The MOJ Guidance reminds companies that employees are presumed to be associated persons of a company, and thus, an employer may wish to incorporate in its recruitment and human resources procedures an appropriate level of due diligence, depending on the level or responsibility of the applicant. The MOJ Guidance allows that due diligence is unlikely to be needed in relation to lower risk posts.[46]

The MOJ Guidance warns of the situation where local law or convention dictates the use of local agents and the difficulty of a company extricating itself from a business relationship once entered. In high-risk situations the MOJ Guidance makes clear the need for ongoing due diligence and suggests there is a greater need for prospective and existing associated companies than associated individuals. Potential due diligence efforts include "direct requests for details on the background, expertise and business experience, of relevant individuals."[47]

b.   Transaction Due Diligence

The MOJ Guidance is surprisingly brief on providing advice with respect to merger and acquisition due diligence. However, in 2012, Transparency International U.K., in coordination with Skadden Arps and Kroll Advisory Solutions, finalized a comprehensive analysis of transactions titled *Anti-Bribery Guidance for Transactions: Guidance for Anti-Bribery Due Diligence in Mergers, Acquisitions and Investments*[48] (Antibribery Transaction Guide). Due diligence is an area where businesspersons in the midst of closing a deal often eschew the need for any detailed antibribery due diligence, the costs associated with the same and defer it—too often indefinitely. For these important constituents, counsel will need to emphasize that due diligence can fully shield a company from criminal liability.

The Antibribery Due Diligence for Transactions Guide is republished in its entirety in appendix 18. The first section—the Bribery Due Diligence process—carries an especially important lesson: begin the bribery portion of the due diligence process at the very beginning, as it may require more time and investigation than other parts of a due diligence review. If the bribery portion is placed near the end of the due diligence exercise or is delayed, there is a real risk that it will not be completed or given adequate attention, and a company may acquire a target with serious bribery issues and not receive, if later discovered, a sympathetic reception from anticorruption prosecutors and regulators in the United Kingdom, the United States, or elsewhere.

Transparency International U.K. has identified six reasons why investments in companies that have committed bribery represent an ongoing risk:

1. The target or purchaser may face criminal, civil, and financial sanctions;
2. Corrupt partners are unreliable and may be involved with or obligated to dubious entities and people;
3. Deals are at great risk of collapse;
4. Market value may be distorted;
5. Associates of the target may make a purchaser liable to investigation and prosecution; and
6. A corrupt target may introduce dishonesty and corruption to the purchaser's own activities.[49]

The Antibribery Transaction Guide has also identified five consequences of prior bribery by a target company and the associated costs:

1. Diminished asset value and returns
   • Reduced investment and portfolio valuations
   • Acquisition of an overvalued asset
2. Investigations and convictions
   • Criminal, civil, and financial proceedings against the company
   • Stringent settlement agreements
   • Appointment of court monitors
   • Diversion of management and board time
   • Extensive professional fees
3. Business instability
   • Aborted deals
   • Reputational damage and media attention
   • Acquired business proves dysfunctional
   • Diminished exit opportunities
   • Debarment from government contracts
   • Director disqualification
   • Regulatory authority restrictions
   • Employee demotivation
   • Loss of key people in investee companies if they are convicted of an offense

4. Liability of directors, partners, and officials
   • Criminal and civil penalties
   • Debarment from office
   • Professional damage
5. Media attention[50]

Many businesspersons who have not been involved in a government anticorruption investigation dismiss the above consequences as exaggerated while those who have undergone the experience can quickly attest to their toll.

c.   Due Diligence Process

The Antibribery Transaction Guide offers a six-step due diligence process from the initiation of the purchase idea to postcompletion monitoring. The six steps are

1. initiating the process;
2. initial screening;
3. detailed analysis;
4. decision;
5. postacquisition due diligence; and
6. postacquisition integration and monitoring.[51]

   Among this guidance's many excellent signposts is one that addresses initial screening: "Don't rely upon someone else's due diligence work. Risk approaches and risk circumstances are never the same. Each transaction is a fresh start."[52]

d.   Transparency International U.K. Due Diligence Checklist

In 2012 Transparency International U.K. issued a final report titled *Anti-Bribery Due Diligence for Transactions* that provides a useful Mergers and Acquisitions Due Diligence Checklist.[53] Specifically, the anticorruption organization cautions that this checklist should not be used as a "tick-box approach" for due diligence, but, rather, to prompt thinking about the areas to be considered during mergers and acquisitions due diligence. The checklist poses 59 questions to consider in due diligence for mergers, acquisitions, and investments broken into 11 categories. Many questions will be familiar to transactional and anticorruption counsel, but the ones italicized below by category are those that can offer particular value to standard due diligence questions and are perhaps not necessarily intuitive.
   Bribery due diligence process:

1. *Is the bribery due diligence integrated into the due diligence process from the start?*
2. *Have milestones been set for the bribery due diligence?*
3. Is the timetable adequate for effective antibribery due diligence?
4. Have the deal and due diligence teams been trained in their company's antibribery program including the significance of relevant legislation?
5. *Have the deal and due diligence teams been trained in antibribery due diligence?*
6. Is there a process implemented for coordination across functions?
7. Has legal privilege been established with use of general counsel and external legal advisors?

8. *Is there a process for dealing with any bribery discovered during the due diligence?*
9. *Is the person responsible for antibribery due diligence at a sufficiently senior level to influence the transaction's decision makers?*

Geographical and sector data:

10. Is the target dependent on operations in countries where corruption is prevalent?
11. *Does the target operate in sectors known to be prone to high risk of bribery?*
12. *Are competitors suspected to be actively using bribery in the target's markets?*

Business model risks:

13. Does the organizational structure of the target foster an effective antibribery program or present risks?
14. *Is the target dependent on large contracts or critical licenses?*
15. *Does the target implement an adequate antibribery program in its subsidiaries?*
16. *Is the target reliant on agents or other intermediaries?*
17. *Has the target been assessed for its exposure to use of intermediaries that operate in countries and sectors prone to corruption risks?*
18. Does it have policies and effective systems to counter risks related to intermediaries?
19. Does the target require contractual antibribery standards of its suppliers?
20. *Does the target's organizational structure present bribery risks, for example, diversified structure?*
21. Is the target reliant on outsourcing and if so do the contracted outsourcers show evidence of commitment and effective implementation of the target's antibribery program?

Legislative footprint:

22. Is the target subject to the U.K. Bribery Act and/or the U.S. FCPA?
23. Are there equivalent laws from other jurisdictions that are relevant?

Organizational:

24. *Does the target's board and leadership show commitment to embedding antibribery in their company?*
25. Does the target exhibit a culture of commitment to ethical business conduct? (Use evidence such as results of employee surveys)
26. *Has the senior management of the target carried out an assessment of bribery risk in the business?*
27. Have there been any corruption allegations or convictions related to members of the target's board or management?
28. Have the main shareholders or investors in the target had a history of activism related to the integrity of the target?
29. *Have there been any corruption allegations or convictions related to the main shareholders or investors in the target?*
30. Does the target have an active audit committee that oversees anticorruption effectively?

Antibribery program:

31. Does the target have an antibribery program that matches that recommended by Transparency International U.K.?[54]
32. *Is the antibribery program based on an adequate risk-based approach?*
33. *Is the antibribery program implemented and effective?*

Key bribery risks:

34. *Has the target been assessed for its exposure to risk of paying large bribes in public contracts or to kickbacks?*
35. Has the target been assessed for risks attached to hospitality and gifts?
36. Has the target been assessed for risks attached to travel expenses?
37. Has the target been assessed for risks attached to political contributions?
38. Has the target been assessed for risks attached to charitable donations and sponsorships?
39. Has the target been assessed for risks attached to facilitation payments?

Foreign public officials (FPOs):

40. *Is there an implemented policy and process for identifying and managing situations where FPOs are associated with intermediaries, customers, and prospects?*
41. Have any FPOs been identified that are associated with intermediaries, customers, and prospects?
42. Is there an implemented policy and process for identifying and managing situations where politically exposed people are associated with intermediaries, customers, and prospects?
43. Have any FPOs been identified that present particular risk?
44. Is there evidence or suspicion that subsidiaries or intermediaries are being used to disguise or channel corrupt payments to FPOs or others?

Financial and ledger analysis:

45. Have the financial tests listed on page 11 of the MOJ Guidance (appendix 17) been carried out?
46. *Are the beneficiaries of banking payments clearly identifiable?*
47. *Is there evidence of payments being made to intermediaries in countries different to where the intermediary is located and if so are the payments valid?*
48. *Is there evidence of regular orders being placed in batches just below the approval level?*
49. *Are payments rounded, especially in currencies with large denominations?*
50. *Are suppliers appointed for valid reasons?*
51. *Is there evidence of suppliers created for bribery, for example, just appointed for the transaction, no VAT registration?*
52. Is there evidence of special purpose vehicles created to act as channels for bribery?

Incidents:

53. *Has a schedule and description been provided of pending or threatened government, regulatory, or administrative proceedings, inquiries, or investigations or litigation related to bribery and other corruption?*

54. *Has the target provided a schedule of any internal investigations over the past five years into bribery allegations?*

55. Has the target been involved in any bribery incidents or investigations not reported by the target?

56. *Has the target sanctioned any employees or directors in the past five years for violations related to bribery?*

57. *Has the target sanctioned any business partners in the past five years for violations related to bribery?*

58. Is there an implemented policy and procedure for reporting bribery when discovered during due diligence?

Audit reports:

59. *Has the target provided any reviews, reports, or audits, internal and external, carried out on the implementation of its antibribery program?*[55]

5.   Principle 5: Communication (Including Training)

The commercial organization must seek to ensure that its bribery prevention policies and procedures are embedded and understood throughout the organization through internal and external communication, including training, that is proportionate to the risks it faces.

a.   Communication

The MOJ Guidance for this principle indicates that information can assist in more effective monitoring, evaluation, and review of bribery provisions while training provides the knowledge and skills needed to employ a company's procedures and address bribery-related situations that may arise. In dividing communications into internal and external categories, the MOJ Guidance indicates that internal communications must convey "tone at the top" and include "policies on particular areas such as decision making, financial control, hospitality and promotional expenditure, facilitation payments, training, charitable and political donations and penalties for breach of rules and the articulation of management roles at different levels." Internal communications should also embrace "speak up" procedures that allow internal or external parties to express bribery concerns or to offer suggested improvements.[56] External communications of bribery prevention policies can include "information on bribery prevention procedures and controls, sanctions, results of internal surveys, rules governing recruitment, procurement and tendering."[57]

b.   Training

With regard to training, the MOJ Guidance reiterates the theme of proportionality but states that some training is likely to be effective in firmly establishing an anti-bribery culture. It suggests that tailored training may be appropriate for higher-risk functions such as purchasing, contracting, distribution and marketing, and working in high-risk countries.[58] The training guidance does not prefer traditional, classroom, or seminar formats, such as e-learning and other web-based tools, over others. The objective of training is to make sure that employees or other associated persons develop a firm understanding of what the relevant policies and procedures mean in practice for them.[59] This principle is one of the easier ones for a company to satisfy. What may prove important in deciding whether to recognize procedures as adequate is whether the rogue employees, agents, or other third parties in fact received training. For this reason companies should take extra steps to make sure all employees, agents, and third parties receive some form of annual anticorruption training and that there are certifications to prove the same.

6. *Principle 6: Monitoring and Review*

The commercial organization must monitor and review procedures designed to prevent bribery by persons associated with it and make improvements where necessary.

   The commentary to the sixth and final principle emphasizes that the bribery risks anyone faces change over time so the policies and procedures necessary to reduce the risks are also likely to change. In addition to regular monitoring, the MOJ Guidance urges companies to review their processes in the context of external factors such as government changes in countries where they operate, incidents of bribery, and negative press reports. Systems and procedures that a company can utilize to deter, detect, and investigate bribery and monitor the ethical quality of transactions include internal financial control mechanisms; staff surveys; questionnaires and feedback from training; formal periodic reviews and reports for top-level management; information publication from relevant trade bodies or regulators; and external verification or assurance of the effectiveness of antibribery procedures. A critical piece to satisfying the sixth principle is likely the input and visibility of a company's internal audit department. If the internal audit staff are active and regularly conducting anticorruption assessments and making recommendations that are seriously taken by management, the company has a much better chance of satisfying this important principle.

VI. OTHER RELEVANT U.K. ANTIBRIBERY GUIDANCE

A. MOJ Appendix A's 11 Case Studies

Appendix A of the MOJ Guidance offers 11 case studies with hypothetical scenario guidance involving nine subjects:

Case Study	Principle	Subject	Hypothetical Scenario
No. 1	Principle 1: Proportionate Procedures	Facilitation payments	Company acquires new customer in foreign country where it operates through its agent company; "inspection fees" are rumored.
No. 2	Principle 1: Proportionate Procedures	Proportionate procedures	Use of consultants to facilitate business opportunities and assist in tenders.
No. 3	Principles 1: Proportionate Procedures; and 6: Monitoring and Review	Joint venture	Joint venture has equal interests with local partner who is to interact with local government officials.

Case Study	Principle	Subject	Hypothetical Scenario
No. 4	Principles 1: Proportionate Procedures; and 5: Communications (including training)	Hospitality and promotional expenditure	Engineering firm hosts annual hospitality events at various sporting venues and pays for travel and accommodation of foreign government officials.
No. 5	Principle 3: Risk Assessment	Assessing risks	Small manufacturer seeks to open in a foreign market and is uncertain how to assess risks.
No. 6	Principle 4: Due Diligence	Due diligence of agents	Manufacturer seeks to enter market in emerging foreign country where local competition requires foreign company to operate through a local agent.
No. 7	Principle 5: Communication and Training	Communication training	Small manufacturer has a local foreign individual agent to assist in winning a contract in a high-risk country.
No. 8	Principles 1: Proportionate Procedures; 4: Due Diligence; and 6: Monitoring and Review	Community benefits and charitable donations	Local government official suggests donation to local charity at time exporter is seeking import license.
No. 9	Principle 4: Due Diligence	Due diligence of agents	Small company historically relies on agents in high-risk country and is offered a new business opportunity through a new agent. An agreement needs to be concluded quickly.
No. 10	Principle 2: Top-Level Commitment	Top-level commitment	Senior manager is dedicating time to participation in the development of an industry-wide antibribery initiative, and top-level management is considering how it can further this initiative.
No. 11	Principle 1: Proportionate Procedures	Proportionate procedures	A small export trading company operates through agents in a number of foreign countries and wishes to develop proportionate and risk-based bribery presentation procedures.

A company and its counsel contemplating a course of action involving one of the above nine subjects or scenarios should carefully review the applicable case study(ies) and hypothetical scenarios.

B. Hospitality and Business Expenditure

The MOJ Guidance also clarified several concerns relating to section 6 of the Bribery Act (Bribery of foreign public officials). One particular topic of substantial interest in the United Kingdom has been hospitality. The Guidance reflected the MOJ's intention not to criminalize "[b]ona fide hospitality and promotional, or other business expenditure which seeks to improve the image of a commercial organization, better to present products and services, or establish cordial relations," though it recognizes that hospitality can be employed as bribes.[60] It emphasized the need for the government to demonstrate a corrupt intent, that is, "sufficient connection between the advantage and the intention to influence and secure business or a business advantage."[61]

The MOJ Guidance makes it clear that "it is unlikely . . . that incidental provision of a routine business courtesy will raise the inference that it was intended to have a direct impact on decision-making, particularly where such hospitality is commensurate with the reasonable and proportionate norms for the particular industry" without evidence of a corrupt intent.[62] The MOJ Guidance further notes that "reasonable travel and accommodation" offered to demonstrate products, assets, and services, or "as a matter of genuine mutual convenience," including "some reasonable hospitality for the individual and his or her partner" in the form of a sporting or other entertainment event, are not prohibited.[63] By way of example, the MOJ Guidance expressly states that an invitation to foreign clients to attend a Six Nations rugby match as part of a public relations exercise designed to cement good relations or enhance knowledge in the company's field is very unlikely to violate section 1 of the Bribery Act as there is unlikely to be evidence or intention to induce proper performances of a relevant function. The MOJ Guidance stresses, however, that these expenditures would be scrutinized in light of the facts and circumstances of each particular situation. In March 2011 companies were urged to review under the MOJ Guidance their hospitality procedures and policies in light of both the Guidance's hospitality discussion and its Case Study No. 4.

However, in October 2012 the SFO in a revised policy on business expenditure (hospitality) stated that the new policy reaffirmed that corporate hospitality is a legitimate and an important part of doing business but cautioned that it "will prosecute offenders who disguise bribes as business expenditures" (hospitality and the like) but only if (1) the case is a serious or complex one that falls within the SFO's remit;[64] and (2) whether the SFO concludes an offender that should be prosecuted "under the Code for Crown Prosecutors."[65]

C. Facilitating Payments

In the wake of this legislation and pending official MOJ Guidance, many U.K. entities were concerned about facilitation payment liability. While the Bribery Act of 2010 does not permit or provide any exception for "grease" payments, the MOJ Guidance recognizes the problems that companies face in some parts of the world and in certain industries. It states that eradication of facilitation payments is a long-term objective and will require the efforts of governments, international bodies, and industry groups.[66] Immediately following its discussion of facilitation payments, the MOJ Guidance states that the common law defense of duress is available in circumstances to avoid loss of life, limb, or liberty. Thus, employees who feel threatened physically by a demand for facilitating payments would have a duress defense. Finally, in addressing facilitation payments, hospitality, and promotional expenditures, the MOJ Guidance directs prosecutors to consider very carefully what is in the public interest before deciding whether to prosecute.[67] In October 2012 the SFO issued revised guidance on facilitating payments, stating that the SFO's primary role is one of investigation and prosecution, that "facilitating payments are illegal" and that it will prosecute if it is in the public interest to do so.[68] In issuing this policy, the SFO no doubt intended to make clear that it retains the discretion to charge any company that encourages or permits facilitating payments.

D. Joint Ventures

The March 2011 MOJ Guidance recognizes that joint ventures "come in many forms, sometimes operating through a separate legal entity, but at other times through contractual arrangements."[69] It provides that "In the case of a joint venture operating through a separate legal entity, a bribe paid by the joint venture entity may lead to liability for a member of the joint venture if the joint venture is performing services for the member and the bribe is paid with the intention of benefiting that member." However, it explains that the existence of a joint venture entity will not of itself mean that it is "associated" with any of its members. A bribe paid on behalf of the joint venture entity by one of its employees or agents will therefore not trigger liability for members of the joint venture simply by virtue of them benefiting indirectly from the bribe through their investment in or ownership of the joint venture.[70]

Where the joint venture is conducted through a contractual arrangement, the MOJ Guidance states that the degree of control that a participant has over that arrangement is likely to be one of the "relevant circumstances" that will be taken into account in deciding whether a person who paid a bribe in the conduct of the joint venture business was "performing services for or on behalf of" a participant in that arrangement. The MOJ Guidance offers the example when an employee of a participant who has paid a bribe in order to benefit his employer is not to be regarded as a person "associated" with all the other participants in the joint venture. Ordinarily, a participant's employee will, according to the MOJ Guidance, be presumed to be a person performing services for and on behalf of his employer. Likewise, an agent engaged by a participant in a contractual joint venture is likely to be regarded as a person associated with that participant in the absence of evidence that the agent is acting on behalf of the contractual joint venture as a whole.[71]

Even where an agent, a subsidiary, or another person acting for a member of a joint venture is performing services for the organization, an offense will be committed only if that agent, subsidiary, or other person intended to obtain or retain business or an advantage in the conduct of business for the organization. The fact that an organization benefits indirectly from a bribe is very unlikely, in itself, to amount to proof of the specific intention required by the offense. The MOJ Guidance explains that without proof of the required intention, liability will not accrue through simple corporate ownership or investment, or through the payment of dividends or provision of loans by a subsidiary to its parent.[72]

The MOJ Guidance offers the example of a bribe on a subsidiary's behalf by one of its employees or agents and concludes that this will not automatically result in liability on the part of its parent company, or any other subsidiaries of the parent company, so long as it cannot be shown the employee or agent intended to obtain or retain business or a business advantage for the parent company or other subsidiaries.[73] This is the case even though the parent company or subsidiaries may benefit indirectly from the bribe. By the same token, liability for a parent company may arise where a subsidiary is the "person" that pays a bribe that it intends will result in its parent obtaining or retaining business or vice versa.[74] The MOJ Guidance offers much more than general commentary and advice on joint ventures. Defenses based on the thoughtful U.K. guidance are likely to carry some weight in arguments before the DOJ and SEC in joint venture scenarios since the MOJ has addressed this common legal entity in international business transactions in more detail than its U.S. counterparts.

E.   Corruption Indicators

The SFO has published on its website a nonexhaustive list of 19 corruption indicators that companies, compliance officers, and counsel should be alert to:

1. Abnormal cash payments;
2. Pressure exerted for payments to be made urgently or ahead of schedule;
3. Payments being made through a third-party country—for example, goods or services supplied to country "A" but payment is being made, usually to a shell company in country "B";
4. An abnormally high commission percentage being paid to a particular agency that may be split into two accounts for the same agent, often in different jurisdictions;
5. Private meetings with public contractors or companies hoping to tender for contracts;
6. Lavish gifts being received;
7. An individual who never takes time off even if ill, or holidays, or insists on dealing with specific contractors himself or herself;
8. Making unexpected or illogical decisions accepting projects or contracts;
9. The unusually smooth process of cases where an individual does not have the expected level of knowledge or expertise;
10. Abuse of the decision process or delegated powers in specific cases;
11. Agreeing to contracts not favorable to the organization either because of the terms or the time period;
12. Unexplained preference for certain contractors during tendering period;
13. Avoidance of independent checks on the tendering or contracting processes;
14. Raising barriers around specific roles or departments that are key in the tendering or contracting processes;
15. Bypassing normal tendering or contracting procedures;
16. Invoices being agreed in excess of the contract without reasonable cause;
17. Missing documents or records regarding meetings or decisions;
18. Company procedures or guidelines not being followed; and
19. The payment of, or making funds available for, high value expenses or school fees (or similar) on behalf of others.[75]

The list is, not surprisingly, similar to red flags and examples found in U.S. FCPA enforcement cases and the DOJ–SEC *Resource Guide to the U.S. Foreign Corrupt Practices Act* (2012).[76]

VII. SUMMARY OF PRINCIPAL SIMILARITIES AND DIFFERENCES BETWEEN THE FCPA AND THE U.K. BRIBERY ACT 2010

The U.K. Bribery Act and the MOJ Guidance share many similar features with their American counterpart, FCPA. There are also meaningful distinctions between the two statutory regimes.

A. Similarities

- Each has an offense for bribery of a foreign public official, obligated by the 1997 OECD Convention on Combating Bribery of Foreign Public Officials in International Business Transactions.
- Neither statute authorizes prosecution of a foreign public official.
- Neither statute offers a de minimis exception.
- Each statute contains "business advantage language," confirming that the scope of each foreign bribery offense is much broader than simply conduct designed to obtain or retain business, that is, significant government contracts.
- Each country has a foreign bribery offense law enforcement unit staffed by a relatively small group of dedicated prosecutors or regulators in each nation's capital.
- Each offense carries a potential for massive corporate fines—unlimited in the United Kingdom while the United States provides up to $256 million per count or more under the Alternative Fines Act.
- Each regime views disgorgement of profits as a sanction—the United Kingdom explicitly addresses confiscation while the SEC has adopted the practice of disgorging profits and obtaining prejudgment interest.
- Each regime addresses whistleblowers—the United Kingdom in its Principle 1 "speak up" discussion and the United States separately in the Dodd-Frank Amendment Final Whistleblower Rules promulgated in May 2011.
- The United Kingdom's "adequate procedures" discussion in the MOJ Guidance contains many principles and elements well familiar to FCPA practitioners and corporate compliance officers who have designed and reviewed effective compliance programs, for example, top-level commitment ("tone at the top"); enforcement detailing discipline process; and training and monitoring under the U.S. Sentencing Guidelines.
- Comparatively few individuals have been prosecuted for foreign official bribery offenses by either the U.S. or U.K. authorities.

B. Differences

The table shows some of the significant differences between the Bribery Act 2010 and the FCPA.

U.K. Bribery Act	FCPA
Covers bribery in both the public and private sectors	Covers only bribery of foreign governmental officials (broadly defined)

U.K. Bribery Act	FCPA
Covers both active and passive bribery domestically, i.e., both persons giving bribes and recipients	Does not cover the recipients
Does not cover foreign political parties, foreign political party officials, or foreign political party candidates	Covers foreign political party officials, foreign political parties, and foreign political party candidates
Covers "domestic" bribery in the United Kingdom	Does not cover "domestic" bribery in the United States
Covers all companies "carrying on business" in whole or in part in the United Kingdom	Covers issuers and "domestic concerns" and others in territorial terms
Employees of state-owned or state-controlled entities are not necessarily FPOs	Employees of state-owned or controlled entities are generally considered FPOs
No exception for travel, lodging, and hospitality	Affirmative defense for reasonable and bona fide expenditures directly related to the promotion, demonstration, or explanation of products or services; or the execution or performance of a contract with a foreign government or agency thereof
No exception for "facilitating payments"	Permits modest "facilitating payments"
Criminal penalties only	Civil and criminal penalties
Section 7 (failure of commercial organization to prevent bribery) strict liability for corporations and partnerships	Traditional corporate criminal liability, e.g., proof beyond a reasonable doubt
"Adequate procedures" is a defense for companies that fail to prevent bribery from taking place (section 7(2))	Strong compliance is a mitigating factor, but not a defense
No requirement of dishonesty or corruption	Explicit "corrupt" intent requirement
No formal advance guidance procedure is in place for the SFO	The DOJ offers a formal FCPA Opinion Release Procedure
Has no books-and-records or internal controls provisions*	Has accounting provisions (books-and-records and internal controls provisions)
Section 14 "Consent and Connivance" liability	Similar to "aiding and abetting" principles in the United States
Has in essence a misdemeanor (summary) offense available to the SFO	Only felony charges are available to the DOJ
No statute of limitations	In general, a five-year statute of limitations

* The United Kingdom has the Companies Act.

C. Corporate Plea Agreements

In the United States, federal district courts routinely, if not almost always, recognize and approve plea agreements entered into by the Department of Justice and corporate defendants. As a result, boards of directors of companies entering into such agreements with the United States proceed with a high degree of confidence that any agreement negotiated between DOJ prosecutors and corporate counsel will be honored and represent the final court-approved resolution. In contrast, U.K. courts, as the *R v. Innospec Ltd.* case makes clear, are nowhere near as prone to accept plea agreements and representations by the parties.

While a prosecutor in the United Kingdom may discuss a basis for a plea and agree to it,[77] a court is not bound by any agreement and must itself establish the basis on which it is to sentence.[78] In cases involving serious or complex fraud, the U.K. court must be provided with full details so as to understand the facts of the case and the history of the plea discussions, make an assessment through a hearing on whether the plea agreement is in the interests of justice, and decide the appropriate sentence.[79] Although sentencing submissions may draw a court's attention to any applicable range in a guideline, they should not include a specific sentence or agreed range.[80]

At the March 26, 2010, sentencing of Innospec Ltd. at the Crown Court at Southwark, the Honorable Lord Justice Thomas eloquently made clear that

> [T]he SFO cannot enter into an agreement under the laws of England and Wales with an offender as to the penalty in respect of the offence charged.... The Practice Direction reflects the constitutional principle that, save in minor matters such as monitoring offences, the imposition of a sentence is a matter for the judiciary. Principles of transparent and open justice require a court sitting in public itself first to determine by a hearing in open court the extent of the criminal conduct on which the offender has entered the plea and then, on the basis of its determination as to the conduct, the appropriate sentence. It is in the public interest, particularly in relation to the crime of corruption.... A court must rigorously scrutinize in open court in the interests of transparency and good governance the basis of that plea and to see whether it reflects the public interest. This has always been the position under the law of England and Wales. Agreements and submissions of the type put forward in this case have no effect.... I have concluded that the Director of the SFO has no power to enter into the arrangements made and no such arrangements should be made again.[81]

Had Innospec not had been faced with a serious inability to pay and had this not been the first case where a "global settlement" had been sought and presented in concurrent criminal proceedings brought by the United States and United Kingdom, the Crown Court might well not have approved the plea agreement and fine on the basis that it felt the fine failed to recognize the seriousness of the offense. The uncertainty of court approval of corporate plea agreements negotiated with the SFO as part of global agreements is an issue of substantial concern to U.S.-based companies and their boards of directors who seek clear certainty in anticorruption resolutions where their counsel have often negotiated in good faith for months and agreed to have the multinational corporations pay huge sums to resolve matters.

VIII. DEFERRED PROSECUTION AGREEMENTS

Deferred prosecution agreements (DPAs) became effective in the United Kingdom in February 2014. DPAs in the United Kingdom are agreements reached under judicial supervision between the prosecutor and an organization, for example, a company. A major difference between this mechanism in the United States and the United Kingdom is the degree of judicial oversight over the entire process in the United Kingdom and transparency from beginning to end. In the United States, the DOJ has long negotiated DPAs with corporations, and courts have, in all but rare cases, approved them. Four High Court judges in the United Kingdom have been specifically appointed to handle DPAs. U.K. counsel representing companies need to carefully review Schedule 17 of the Crime and Courts Act 2013[82] (the Act) and the Code of Practice[83] (DPA Code) issued by the director of Crown Prosecution Service and director of the Serious Fraud Office pursuant to paragraph 6(1) of Schedule 17 of the Act.

A. Deferred Prosecution Agreements: Schedule 17 of the Crime and Courts Act 2013

Only a corporation, a partnership, or an unincorporated association may enter into a U.K. DPA. Individuals are ineligible. A DPA must contain a statement of facts relating to each alleged offense, which may include an admission by the company.[84] The statement of facts must include details where possible of any financial gain or loss, with reference to key documents to be attached.[85] There is no requirement for formal admissions with respect to the offenses charged, but it will be necessary for the party to admit the contents and meaning of key documents referred to in the statement of facts.[86] The basis of the DPA and its terms will be explained in an agreed written application to the court.[87] A DPA must specify an expiration date, which is the date on which the DPA shall cease to have effect if it has not already been terminated due to a breach.[88]

Among other things, under a DPA, a company may be required

1. to pay to the prosecutor a financial penalty;
2. to compensate victims of the alleged offense;
3. to donate money to a charity or other third party;
4. to disgorge any corporate profits from the alleged offense; and
5. to implement a compliance program or make changes to an existing compliance program relating to the company's policies or to the training of its employees or both.[89]

The amount of any financial penalty agreed to by the prosecutor and the company must be "broadly comparable to the fine that a court would have imposed on the company on conviction for the alleged offense following a guilty plea.[90]

Unlike courts in the United States, courts in the United Kingdom are very involved in DPAs from the negotiation onward. Often, negotiations between the prosecutor and company begin but *before* the terms of the DPA are agreed. The prosecutor must apply to the Crown Court for a declaration that

1. entering into a DPA with the company is likely to be in the interests of justice; and
2. the proposed terms of the DPA are fair, reasonable, and proportionate.[91]

The court must give reasons on whether or not to make a declaration satisfying (1) and (2).[92]

The prosecutor may make a further application to the court if following the original or an earlier application, the court has declined to make a declaration.[93] A hearing at which an application is determined must be held in private, any declaration must be made in private, and any revisions for or against a declaration must be in private.[94]

Once a prosecutor and a company have agreed on the terms of a DPA, the prosecutor must again apply to the Crown Court to set the above-referenced (1) and (2) terms for a final hearing. If the court decides to approve the DPA and make the above-referenced declaration, it must do so and give its reasons in open court and, upon approval, the prosecutor must publish

1. the DPA;
2. the declaration of the court and the reasons for the decision;
3. in the case where the court initially declined to make a declaration, the Court's reason for that decision; and
4. the court's declaration and the reasons for its decision to make that declaration.[95]

A prosecutor may postpone publication to avoid prejudicing other proceedings.[96]

A prosecutor who believes that a company has failed to comply with the terms of a DPA may make an application to the Crown Court. On such application, the court must decide whether, on balance of probabilities (a preponderance standard), the company has failed to comply with the DPA.[97] If the company has failed to comply with the DPA's terms, the court may

1. invite the prosecutor and company to agree to proposals to remedy the failure; or
2. terminate the DPA.[98]

The prosecutor and the company may agree to vary the DPA's terms if

1. the court has invited the parties to vary the terms as a result of the company's failure to abide by the terms; and
2. variation of the DPA is necessary to avoid failure by the company with its terms in circumstances that were not, and could not have been, foreseen by the prosecutor or the company at the time that the DPA was agreed to.[99]

The court must again declare that such variation is in the interests of justice, and the terms of the DPA, as varied, are fair, reasonable, and proportionate.[100] The prosecutor must also publish the DPA as varied and the court's declaration and the reasons for its decision to make the declaration that approves the variation. The Act applies to numerous criminal offenses, including the Proceeds of Crime Act 2002 (money laundering)[101] and the Bribery Act 2010, and specifically:

1. Section 1 (bribery of another person);
2. Section 2 (being bribed);
3. Section 6 (bribery of public officials); and
4. Section 7 (failure of commercial organization to prevent bribery).[102]

B.   Deferred Prosecution Agreement Code

In February 2014, the directors of the Crown Prosecution Service (CPS) and the Serious Fraud Office (SFO) jointly issued their Deferred Prosecution Agreement Code of Practice (DPA Code). As the SFO press release at that time made clear, "A DPA may be appropriate where the public interest is not best served by mounting a prosecution. Entering into the agreement will be a fully transparent public event and the process will be approved and supervised by a judge."[103] The DPA Code thus fulfills the transparency mandate of the Crime and Courts Act 2013.

1.   *Prosecutorial Discretion*

The DPA Code makes clear that a DPA is "a discretionary tool created by the Act to provide a way of responding to alleged criminal conduct."[104] The prosecutor may invite a company to enter into negotiations to agree to a DPA as an alternative to prosecution.[105] More specifically, the DPA states:

> An invitation to negotiate a DPA is a matter for the prosecutor's discretion. A (company) has no right to be invited to negotiate a DPA. The SFO and the CPS are first and foremost prosecutors and it will only be in specific circumstances deemed by their directors to be appropriate that they will decide to offer a DPA instead of pursuing the full prosecution of the alleged conduct. In many cases, criminal prosecution will continue to be the appropriate course of action. *An invitation to enter DPA discussions is not a guarantee that a DPA will be offered at the conclusion of the discussion.*[106]

2.   *Public Interest Factors*

In addition to the public factors in the Code for Crown Prosecutors, additional public interest factors in favor of prosecution include the following:

1. A history of similar conduct (including prior criminal, civil, and regulatory enforcement actions against P (person) and/or its directors/partners and/or majority shareholders). Failing to prosecute in circumstances where there have been repeated or serious breaches of the law may not be a proportionate response and may not provide adequate deterrent effects.
2. The conduct alleged is part of the established business practices of P.
3. The offense was committed at a time when P had no or an ineffective corporate compliance program and it has not been able to demonstrate a significant improvement in its compliance program since then.

4. P has been previously subject to warning, sanctions, or criminal charges and had nonetheless failed to take adequate action to prevent future unlawful conduct, or had continued to engage in the conduct.

5. Failure to notify the wrongdoing within reasonable time of the offending conduct[107] coming to light.

6. Reporting the wrongdoing but failing to verify it, or reporting it knowing or believing it to be inaccurate, misleading, or incomplete.

7. Significant level of harm caused directly or indirectly to the victims of the wrongdoing or a substantial adverse impact to the integrity or confidence of markets, local or national governments.[108]

Public interest factors against prosecution include the following:

1. Cooperation: Considerable weight may be given to a genuinely proactive approach adopted by P's management team when the offending is brought to their notice, involving within a reasonable time of the offending coming to light reporting P's offending otherwise unknown to the prosecutor and taking remedial actions including, where appropriate, compensating victims. In applying this factor the prosecutor needs to establish whether sufficient information about the operation and conduct of P has been supplied in order to assess whether P has been cooperative. Cooperation will include identifying relevant witnesses, disclosing their accounts and the documents shown to them. Where practicable it will involve making the witnesses available for interview when requested. It will further include providing a report in respect of any internal investigation including source documents.

2. A lack of a history of similar conduct involving prior criminal, civil and regulatory enforcement actions against P and/or its directors/partners and/or majority shareholders; The prosecutor should contact relevant regulatory departments (including where applicable those overseas) to ascertain whether there are existing investigations in relation to P and/or its directors/partners and/or majority shareholders.

3. The existence of a proactive corporate compliance program[109] both at the time of offending and at the time of reporting but that failed to be effective in this instance.

4. The offending represents isolated actions by individuals, for example by a rogue director.

5. The offending is not recent and P in its current form is effectively a different entity from that which committed the offenses—for example it has been taken over by another organization, it no longer operates in the relevant industry or market, P's management team has completely changed, disciplinary action has been taken against all of the culpable individuals, including dismissal where appropriate, or corporate structures or processes have been changed to minimize the risk of a repetition of offending.

6. A conviction is likely to have disproportionate consequences for P, under domestic law, the law of another jurisdiction including but not limited to that of the European Union, always bearing in mind the seriousness of the offense and any other relevant public interest factors.

7. A conviction is likely to have collateral effects on the public, P's employees and shareholders or P's and/or institutional pension holders.[110]

3. Self-Reporting

1. The prosecutor, in giving weight to P's self-report, will consider the totality of information that P provides to the prosecutor. It must be remembered that when P self-reports, it will have been incriminated by the actions of individuals. It will ordinarily be appropriate that those individuals be investigated and where appropriate prosecuted. P must ensure in its provision of material as part of the self-report that it does not withhold material that would jeopardize an effective investigation and where appropriate prosecution of those individuals. To do so would be a strong factor in favor of prosecution.[111]
2. The prosecutor will also consider how early P self-reports and the extent that P involves the prosecutor in the early stages of an investigation (for example, in order to discuss work plans, timetabling, or to provide the opportunity to the prosecutor to give direction and where appropriate commence an early criminal investigation where it can use statutory powers in particular against individuals).[112]
3. The prosecutor will consider whether any actions taken by P by not self-reporting earlier may have prejudiced the investigation into P or the individuals that incriminate P. In particular the prosecutor will critically assess the manner of any internal investigation to determine whether its conduct could have led to material being destroyed or the gathering of first accounts from suspects being delayed to the extent that the opportunity for fabrication has been afforded. Internal investigations that lead to such adverse consequences may militate against the use of DPAs.[113]

4. Invitation Process

If the prosecutor decides to offer a corporate entity the opportunity to enter into DPA negotiations, it will do so by way of a formal letter of invitation outlining the basis on which any negotiations will proceed.[114] That letter will constitute the beginning of the DPA negotiation period, which period will end on either the withdrawal of one or both parties from the process, or the approval/refusal by the court of a DPA at a final hearing. Neither party will be obliged to give reasons for withdrawal from negotiations. However in the event of withdrawal from negotiations by the prosecutor it will ordinarily be appropriate to provide the corporation with the gist of the reasons for doing so. In some instances this may not be possible without prejudicing the investigation.[115]

All parties should keep in mind that DPAs are entirely voluntary agreements. The prosecutor is under no obligation to invite the corporate entity to negotiate a DPA, and the corporate entity is under no obligation to accept that invitation should it be made. The terms of a DPA are similarly voluntary, and neither party is obliged to agree any particular term therein. The Act does not, and this DPA Code cannot, alter the law on legal professional privilege.[116]

DPA negotiations must be transparent. The prosecutor must:

1. Ensure that a full and accurate record of negotiations is prepared and retained. It is essential that a full written record is kept of every key action and event in the discussion process, including details of every offer or concession made by each party, and the reasons for every decision taken by the prosecutor. Meetings between the parties should be minuted and the minutes agreed and signed;
2. Ensure that the prosecution and the corporate entity have obtained sufficient information from each other so each can play an informed part in the negotiations;
3. Ensure that documentation and any other material relevant to the matters the prosecutor is considering prosecuting is retained by the corporate entity for any future prosecution;
4. Ensure that the proposed DPA placed before the court fully and fairly reflects the corporate entity's alleged offending; and
5. Not agree to additional matters with the corporate entity that are not recorded in the DPA and not made known to the court.[117]

5.   *Financial Penalties and Discounts*

The Deferred Prosecution Agreement statute provides that any financial penalty is to be broadly comparable to a fine that the court would have imposed following a guilty plea.[118] This is intended to enable the parties and courts to have regard for relevant preexisting sentencing principles and guidelines in order to determine the appropriate level for a financial penalty in a particular case. This should include consideration of the corporation's means, and its ability to pay should be given priority over a penalty.[119]

The extent of the discretion available when considering a financial penalty is broad. The discount for a guilty plea will be applied by the sentencing court after it has taken into account all relevant considerations, including any assistance given by the corporation. The level of the discount to reflect the corporation's assistance would depend on the circumstances and the level of assistance given, and the parties must be guided by sentencing practice, statute, and preexisting case law on the matter. A financial penalty must provide for a discount equivalent to that which would be afforded by an early guilty plea. Current guidelines provide for a one-third discount for a plea at the earliest opportunity.[120]

6.   *Monitors*

The DPA Code expressly addresses monitors. A U.K. prosecutor must carefully consider before commencing with a DPA, whether the corporation already has a genuinely proactive and effective corporate compliance program. The use of monitors will be approached with care. The appointment of a monitor will depend upon the factual circumstances of each case and must always be "fair, reasonable and proportionate."[121]

a.   Primary Responsibility

A monitor's primary responsibility is to assess and monitor the corporation's internal controls, advise of necessary compliance improvements that will reduce the risk of future recurrence of the conduct subject to the DPA, and report specified misconduct to the prosecutor.

b.   Payment of Costs

A corporation is responsible for payment of all the costs of the selection, appointment, remuneration of the monitor, and reasonable costs of the prosecutor associated with the monitorship during the monitoring period. In assessing whether a term of monitoring may satisfy the statutory test, the prosecutor should give consideration to the costs of such a term as these may be relevant.

c.   Access to the Business

A corporation must afford to the monitor complete access to all relevant aspects of its business during the course of the monitoring period as requested by the monitor. The DPA Code expressly provides that any legal professional privilege that may exist in respect of investigating compliance issues that arise during the monitorship is unaffected by the Act, the DPA Code, or a DPA.[122]

d.   Confidentiality

Monitors' reports and associated correspondence are to be designated confidential with disclosure restricted to the prosecutor, the corporation, and the court, save as otherwise permitted by law.

e.   Terms

Terms included in the monitor's agreement may include, but are not limited to, ensuring that the corporation has in place:[123]

1.   A code of conduct;
2.   An appropriate training and education program;
3.   Internal procedures for reporting conduct issues that enable officers and employees to report issues in a safe and confidential manner;
4.   Processes for identifying key strategic risk areas;
5.   Reasonable safeguards to approve the appointment of representatives and payment of commissions;
6.   A gifts and hospitality policy;
7.   Reasonable procedures for undertaking due diligence on potential projects, acquisitions, business partners, agents, representatives, distributors, subcontractors, and suppliers;
8.   Procurement procedures that minimize the opportunity of misconduct;
9.   Contract terms between the corporation and its business partners, subcontractors, distributors, and suppliers that include express contractual obligations and remedies in relation to misconduct;
10.   Internal management and audit processes that include reasonable controls against misconduct where appropriate;
11.   Policies and processes in all of its subsidiaries and operating businesses, and joint ventures in which it has management control, and that the corporation uses reasonable endeavors to ensure that the joint ventures in which it does not have management control, together with key subcontractors and

representatives, are familiar with and are required to abide by its code of conduct to the extent possible;

12. Procedures compatible with money laundering regulations;
13. Policies regarding charitable and political donations;
14. Terms related to external controls, for example, procedures for selection of appropriate charities;
15. Policies relating to internal investigative resources, employee disciplinary procedures; and compliance screening of prospective employees;
16. Policies relating to the extent to which senior management takes responsibility for implementing relevant practices and procedures;
17. Mechanisms for review of the effectiveness of relevant policies and procedures across business and jurisdictions in which the corporation operates;
18. Compensation structures that remove incentives for unethical behavior.[124]

C. Other Issues Around Corporate Self-Reporting

1. SFO Policy

The SFO has enunciated a clear policy on corporate self-reporting: "[I]f on the evidence there is a realistic prospect of conviction, the SFO will prosecute if it is in the public interest to do so. The fact that a corporate body has reported itself will be a relevant consideration to the extent set out in the Guidance on Corporate Prosecutions.[125] That Guidance explains that, for a self-report to be taken into consideration as a public interest factor tending against prosecution, it must form part of a "genuinely proactive approach adopted by the corporate management team when the offending is brought to their notice."[126] Self-reporting is no guarantee that a prosecution will not follow. Each case will turn on its own facts.[127] The SFO's primary law enforcement role remains "to investigate and prosecute"; there is to be no presumption in favor of civil settlements in any circumstances.[128] Finally, in cases where the SFO does not prosecute a self-reporting corporate body, it reserves the right (1) to prosecute it for any unreported violations of the law; and (2) lawfully to provide information on the reported violation to other bodies (such as foreign police forces).[129]

2. Waiver of Attorney-Client Privilege and First Accounts of Witnesses

As regards the question of privilege, the SFO largely respects the sanctity of the attorney-client privilege. However, in recent speeches it has been made clear that questionable assertions of privilege by companies that self-report to the SFO will be viewed in a dim light when the office decides whether the company has provided sufficient cooperation to warrant being offered a DPA. This is especially the case for assertions of privilege over first-hand accounts of witnesses. The current position of the SFO in relation to assertions of privilege is probably best summed up in a recent speech by Alun Milford (the SFO's general counsel):

> If the company's stance in asserting privilege over part of its fact-finding exercise makes it harder for us to build a sustainable case against other suspects, I cannot see how that stance can possibly contribute to the public interest case against prosecuting the company, not least when, rather than engage constructively with us, the company chose

instead to instruct lawyers to speak to witnesses before us and thereby set out to throw an impenetrable web of confidentiality all over the evidence they generated. The position is even starker if the company's stance is that it has no criminal liability and that it is simply trying to assist our investigation into others. We do not necessarily accept that assertions of privilege are well-founded. Like everything else in the law, all depends on the facts of the case. Where we do not accept that the claim is well-founded, we are prepared to litigate. Of course, any such litigation would be a last resort: we want our focus to be on the investigation, not satellite litigation. Even if we do accept that the facts of the case point to privilege attaching, we see nothing objectionable in principle in inviting a company to waive this privilege and this privilege alone. For the avoidance of any doubt, we are not interested in seeing the advice clients received from their lawyers. We just want accurate and complete first accounts of witnesses, and we do not understand why a truly cooperative company would deny us them. It is unhelpful of your clients to put their interest in civil proceedings ahead of assisting our criminal investigation.[130]

U.S. prosecutors and regulators have not insisted upon production of first-hand accounts of witnesses.

IX. GUIDANCE ON CORPORATE PROSECUTIONS AND CORPORATE CRIMINAL LIABILITY; AND BRIBERY ACT 2010: JOINT PROSECUTION GUIDANCE OF THE SFO AND CPS

A. Guidance on Corporate Prosecutions

The director of Public Prosecutions, the director of the Serious Fraud Office, and the director of the Revenue and Customs Prosecutions Office have issued Guidance on Corporate Prosecutions (Corporate Prosecution Guidance).[131] This broad guidance is to be distinguished from the more narrow Joint Prosecution Guidance that relates specifically to the Bribery Act.

The Corporate Prosecution Guidance should be carefully considered by counsel representing companies subject to investigation for bribery that conduct business in the United Kingdom (England, Scotland, Wales, and Northern Ireland). It defines a company as "a legal person capable of being prosecuted, and should not be treated differently from an individual because of its artificial personality."[132] While a company normally means a company registered under the Companies Act 2006, a company can also be one registered under equivalent legislation in another jurisdiction.[133]

1. General Principles

The Corporate Prosecution Guidance sets forth three general principles:

1. A thorough enforcement of the criminal law against corporate offenders, where appropriate, will have a deterrent effect, protect the public and support ethical business practices. Prosecuting corporations, where

appropriate, will capture the full range of criminality involved and thus lead to increased public confidence in the criminal justice system.

2. Prosecutions of a company should not be seen as a substitute for the prosecution of criminally culpable individuals such as directors, officers, employees, or shareholders. Prosecuting such individuals provides a strong deterrent against future corporate wrongdoing. Equally, when considering prosecuting individuals, it is important to consider the possible liability of the company where the criminal conduct is for corporate gain.

3. It is usually best to have all connected offenders prosecuted together at the same time. However there are circumstances where the prosecution of a company will take place before the prosecution of connected individuals or vice versa. This may occur where there is going to be delay in initiating proceedings which could result in unfairness to one or more parties.[134]

2. *Establishing Corporate Liability*

The Corporate Prosecution Guidance distinguishes between vicarious liability and nonvicarious liability:

- *Vicarious liability for the acts of a company's employees/agents.* This has some limited application at common law, for example, in relation to public nuisance. Many statutory or regulatory offenses impose strict liability upon employers (corporate and human) to ensure compliance with the relevant regulatory legislation.
- *Non-vicarious liability arising from the so-called identification principle.* The identification principle determines whether an offender was "a directing mind and will" of the company. It applies to all types of offenses, including those that require *mens rea*[135] such as Section 6 of the Bribery Act (bribery of foreign public officials).

a. Vicarious Liability

In explaining vicarious liability, the Corporate Prosecution Guidance states in pertinent part:

1. A corporate employer is vicariously liable for the acts of its employees and agents where a natural person would be similarly liable (*Mousell Bros. Ltd. v. London and North Western Railway Co.* [1917] 2 KB 836).

2. When determining if a company is vicariously liable, you must first consider the terms of the statute creating the offense. It may require mens rea, yet impose vicarious liability. Conversely, it may create strict liability without specifically imposing vicarious liability.

3. Normally vicarious liability will arise from offenses of strict liability. These are offenses which do not require intention, recklessness, or even negligence as to one or more elements in the *actus reus*. If a strict liability offense is committed by an employee of a company in the course of his employment, the company may also be criminally liable. It is likely that any corporate prosecution will be linked to the prosecution of a controlling officer and/or other employees.[136]

b. Nonvicarious Liability, the Identification Principle,
and the "Directing Mind and Will" Imputation

In addressing nonvicarious liability and offenses requiring mens rea, the Corporate Prosecution Guidance explains the identification principle and highlights the leading case of *Tesco Supermarkets Ltd. v. Nattrass*. The identification principle requires action by at least one senior officer, for example, a managing director, who carries out the functions of management and speaks and acts as the company.[137] The Corporate Prosecution Guidance makes four key points with respect to nonvicarious liability:

1. Companies are legal persons. They may also be criminally responsible for offenses requiring mens rea by application of the identification principle. This is where "the acts and state of mind' of those who represent the 'directing mind and will" will be imputed to the company—*Lennards Carrying Co and Asiatic Petroleum* [1915] AC 705, *Bolton Engineering Co. v. Graham* [1957] 1 QB 159 (per Denning LJ) and *R v. Andrews Weatherfoil* 56 C App R 31 CA.

2. The leading case of *Tesco Supermarkets Ltd. v. Nattrass* [1972] AC 153 restricts the application of this principle to the actions of the Board of Directors, the Managing Director and perhaps other superior officers who carry out functions of management and speak and act as the company.

3. This identification principle acknowledges the existence of corporate officers who are the embodiment of the company when acting in its business. Their acts and states of mind are deemed to be those of the company and they are deemed to be "controlling officers" of the company. Criminal acts by such officers will not only be offenses for which the company can be prosecuted because of their status within the company. A company may be liable for the act of its servant even though that act was done in fraud of the company itself—*Moore v. I. Bressler, Ltd.* [1944] 2 All ER 515.

4. In seeking to identify the "directing mind" of a company, prosecutors will need to consider the constitution of the company concerned (with the aid of memoranda/articles of association/actions of directors of the company in general meeting) and consider any reference in statutes to the offenses committed by officers of a company. Certain regulatory offenses may require a more purposive interpretation in addition to the primary rules of attribution. In these types of offenses, corporate liability may be determined by the construction of a particular statute, irrespective of the "directing mind" principle. (See the approach of the Privy Council in *Meridian Global Funds Management Asia Ltd. v. Securities Commission* [1995] 2 AC 500 PC) and in relation to offenses under The Health and Safety at Work etc. Act 1974 see *R v. British Steel plc* [1995] 1 W.L.R. 1356.[138]

Thus, unlike broad U.S. corporate criminal liability principles, the identification principle in the United Kingdom narrows corporate criminal liability to circumstances where only the "directing mind" of a senior officer or person can be imputed to a company.

3.   Prosecutorial or Evidential Considerations

The Corporate Prosecution Guidance also addresses "evidential" considerations that govern crown prosecutors in developing viable corporate criminal cases whether involving bribery or not. Notably, the U.K. prosecutorial authorities expressly reject what in the United States is known as the "collective knowledge doctrine"[139] and thereby predictably requires a mens rea of at least one controlling officer or employee. The Joint Guidance states that at a smaller corporation guilty knowledge can more easily be attributed to the controlling officer and therefore to the company itself while a company with a diffuse structure may present evidential obstacles.

1.   The legal basis of any corporate prosecution must be fully considered at review and noted in detail on the file. Evidential difficulties may arise where the company concerned has a diffuse structure, because of the need to link the offense to a controlling officer. The smaller the corporation, the more likely it will be that guilty knowledge can be attributed to the controlling officer. The smaller the corporation, the more likely it will be that guilty knowledge can be attributed to the controlling officer and therefore to the company itself.

2.   In a corporate prosecution, prosecutors must identify the correct corporate entity from the outset. It is crucial that prosecutors ensure that the corporation is fully and accurately named in the summons/indictment. If necessary, a company search should be conducted. Later amendment of the name may not be possible (Marco (Croydon) Ltd trading as A&J Bull Containers v. Metropolitan Police [1984] RTR 24).

3.   The evidence must set out relevant employer/employee relationships, in order that both corporate liability and the admissibility of any admissions by an employee against a defendant corporation may be established (Edwards v. Brooks (Milk Ltd.) [1963] 3 All ER 62).

4.   In offenses requiring mens rea, the controlling officer(s) must be clearly identified and their status and functions established. The required mens rea of at least one controlling officer of the company must also be established.

5.   Where a number of officers in a company have been concerned in the act of omission giving rise to a potential offense but none individually has the required mens rea, it is not permissible to aggregate all states of mind of the officers to prove a dishonest state of mind: Armstrong v. Strain [1952] 1 All ER 139. See also R V P&O European Ferries (Dover) Ltd. & others [1991] 93 Cr App R 72.

6.   It is important to prosecute not only the corporation but those who are in control. Certain types of offenses (for example false accounting and regulatory offenses) committed by a body corporate with the consent of connivance of a director/manager/secretary of a company make those officers criminally liable. When proceeding against company officers in these circumstances the offense by the body corporate must be proved, but it is not always possible to secure the conviction of the company, and this is not required (R v. Dickson and Wright 94 Cr App 7).

Prosecutors may consider proceedings against the company officers where the company has been dissolved, for example.

7. Dissolution of a company has the same effect as the death of a human defendant inasmuch as the company ceases to exist. It is possible, however, to apply for an order to declare the dissolution void or to restore the corporation to the register. Criminal proceedings can only be instituted by leave of the Court responsible for the winding up or liquidation.[140]

4. *Public Interest Considerations*

The Corporate Prosecution Guidance outlines three general public interest factors to be considered in evaluating the appropriateness of a corporate prosecution:

1. Where the evidence provides a realistic prospect of conviction, the prosecutor must consider whether or not a prosecution is in the public interest, in accordance with the Code for Crown Prosecutors. The more serious the offense, the more likely it is that prosecution will be needed in the public interest. Indicators of seriousness include not just the value of any gain or loss, but also the risk of harm to the public, to unidentified victims, shareholders, employees, creditors and to the stability and integrity of financial markets and international trade. The impact of the offending in other countries, and not just the consequences in the UK, should be taken into account.

2. Prosecutors must balance factors for and against prosecution carefully and fairly. Public interest factors that can affect the decision to prosecute usually depend on the seriousness of the offense and of the circumstances of the suspect. Some factors may increase the need to prosecute, but others may suggest that another course of action would be better. A prosecution will usually take place unless there are public interest factors against prosecution which clearly outweigh those tending in favor of prosecution.

3. In addition to the public interest factors set out in section 5 of the Code for Crown Prosecutors, the following factors may be of relevance in deciding whether the prosecution of a company is required in the public interest as the proper response to alleged corporate offending. This list of additional public interest factors is not intended to be exhaustive. The factors that will apply will depend on the facts of each case.[141]

The Corporate Prosecution Guidance also provides a nonexhaustive list of six public interest factors in favor of corporate prosecution:

1. A history of similar conduct (including prior criminal, civil and regulatory enforcement actions against it); failing to prosecute in circumstances where there have been repeated and flagrant breaches of the law may not be a proportionate response and may not provide adequate deterrent effects;

2. The conduct alleged is part of the established business practices of the company;

3. The offense was committed at a time when the company had an ineffective corporate compliance program;

4. The company had been previously subject to warning, sanctions or criminal charges and had nonetheless failed to take adequate action to prevent future unlawful conduct, or had continued to engage in the conduct;

5. Failure to report wrongdoing within reasonable time of the offending coming to light; (the prosecutor will also need to consider whether it is appropriate to charge the company officers responsible for the failures/breaches); and

6. Failure to report properly and fully the true extent of the wrongdoing.[142]

Conversely, the Corporate Prosecution Guidance lists eight public interest factors against a corporate prosecution:

1. A genuinely proactive approach adopted by the corporate management team when the offending is brought to their notice, involving self-reporting and remedial actions, including the compensation of victims:

    In applying this factor the prosecutor needs to establish whether sufficient information about the operation of the company in its entirety has been supplied in order to assess whether the company has been proactively compliant. This will include making witnesses available and disclosure of the details of any internal investigation.

2. A lack of a history of similar conduct involving prior criminal, civil and regulatory enforcement actions against the company; contact should be made with the relevant regulatory departments to ascertain whether investigations are being conducted in relation to the due diligence of the company;

3. The existence of a genuinely proactive and effective corporate compliance program.

4. The availability of civil or regulatory remedies that are likely to be effective and more proportionate:

    Appropriate alternatives to prosecution may include civil recovery orders combined with a range of agreed regulatory measures. However, the totality of the offending needs to have been identified. A fine after conviction may not be the most effective and just outcome if the company cannot pay. The prosecutor should refer to the Attorney's Guidance on Civil Recovery (see Proceeds of Crime Act 2002: Section 2A [Contribution to the reduction of crime] Joint Guidance given by the Secretary of State and Her Majesty's Attorney General) and on the appropriate use of Serious Crime Prevention Orders.

5. The offending represents isolated actions by individuals, for example by a rogue director.

6. The offending is not recent in nature, and the company in its current form is effectively a different body to that which committed the offenses—for example it has been taken over by another company, it no longer operates in the relevant industry or market, all of the culpable individuals have left or been dismissed, or corporate structures or

processes have been changed in such a way as to make a repetition of the offending impossible.

7. A conviction is likely to have adverse consequences for the company under European Law, always bearing in mind the seriousness of the offense and any other relevant public interest factors.

    Any candidate or tenderer (including company directors and any person having powers of representation, decision or control) who has been convicted of fraud relating to the protection of the financial interests of the European Communities, corruption, or a money laundering offense is excluded from participation in public contracts within the EU. (Article 45 of Directive 2004/18/EC of the European Parliament and of the Council on the coordination of procedures for the award of public works contracts, public supply contracts and public service contracts). The Directive is intended to be draconian in its effect, and companies can be assumed to have been aware of the potential consequences at the time when they embarked on the offending. Prosecutors should bear in mind that a decision not to prosecute because the Directive is engaged will tend to undermine its deterrent effect.

8. The company is in the process of being wound up.[143]

The third factor rewards a *genuinely* proactive and effective compliance program in place. The fifth factor offers support to nonprosecution or declination of a company that is the victim of a rogue officer.[144] The seventh factor is plainly mindful of the public contract debarment consequences for companies convicted of fraud in the European Community.

B. Joint Prosecution Guidance on U.K. Bribery Act 2010

The more narrow Joint Prosecution Guidance relates specifically to the Bribery Act and offers inter alia additional guidance factors tending in favor of and against prosecution under section 6 foreign public official bribery, as well as other offenses under the Act.

Factors tending in favor of prosecution:

- Large or repeated payments are more likely to attract a significant sentence;
- Facilitation payments that are planned for or accepted as part of a standard way of conducting business may indicate the offense was premeditated (Code 4.16e);
- Payments may indicate an element of active corruption of the official in the way the offense was committed; and
- Where a commercial organization has a clear and appropriate policy setting out procedures an individual should follow if facilitation payments are requested and these have not been correctly followed.

Factors tending against prosecution:

- A single small payment is likely to result in only a nominal penalty;
- The payment(s) came to light as a result of a genuinely proactive approach involving self-reporting and remedial action (additional factor (a) in the Guidance on Corporate Prosecutions);

- Where a commercial organization has a clear and appropriate policy setting out procedures an individual should follow if facilitation payments are requested and these have been correctly followed; and
- The payer was in a vulnerable position arising from the circumstances in which the payment was demanded.

Counsel should review this Joint Prosecution Guidance when representing a bribery target or subject.

X. U.K. SENTENCING COUNCIL DEFINITIVE GUIDELINE FOR BRIBERY OFFENSES

In 2014, the U.K. Sentencing Council issued definitive guidelines for, inter alia, bribery offenses for both individual offenders aged 18 and older and organizations that are sentenced on or after October 1, 2014, regardless of the date of the offenses.[145] Courts are required to follow the sentencing guidelines, unless the court is satisfied that it would be contrary to the interests of justice to do so.

The guidelines specify offense ranges or the range of sentences appropriate for bribery and a number of categories that reflect varying degrees of seriousness. The Council has identified a starting point within each category.

Starting points define the position within a category from which to start calculating a provisional sentence. A court is to then consider aggravating and mitigating factors. Starting points and ranges apply to all offenders whether they have pleaded guilty or been convicted after trial. Credit for a guilty plea is taken into consideration only after the appropriate sentence has been identified.

A. Individuals

For individuals, the Sentencing Guideline prescribes that the court follow eight steps:

1. Determine the offense category;
2. Determine point and category range;
3. Consider any factors that indicate a reduction, such as assistance to the prosecution;
4. Make reduction for guilty pleas;
5. Totality principle (where an offender is sentenced for more than one offense) or where the offender is already serving a sentence, consider whether the total sentence is just and proportionate;
6. Consider confiscation, compensation, and ancillary orders;
7. Give reasons for, and explain the effect of, the sentence; and
8. Allow for time spent on bail.

Steps 1 and 2 are the most demanding.

In determining the offense category (Step 1), the court should assess both culpability and harm. The level of culpability for which there are three rankings (high, medium, and lesser) is determined by weighing of all the factors of the case to determine the offender's role, the extent to which the conduct was planned, and the sophistication with which it was carried out.

Culpability is demonstrated by one or more of the following:

1. *High Culpability*
   - A leading role where offending is part of a group activity;
   - Involvement of others through pressure, influence;
   - Abuse of position of significant power or trust or responsibility;
   - Intended corruption (directly or indirectly) of a senior official performing a public function;
   - Intended corruption (directly or indirectly) of a law enforcement officer;
   - Sophisticated nature of offense/significant planning;
   - Offending conducted over sustained period of time; or
   - Motivated by expectation of substantial financial, commercial, or political gain.

2. *Medium Culpability*
   - All other cases where characteristics for categories A or C are not present;
   - A significant role where offending is part of a group activity.

3. *Lesser Culpability*
   - Involved through coercion, intimidation, or exploitation;
   - Not motivated by personal gain;
   - Peripheral role in organized activity;
   - Opportunistic "one-off" offense; very little or no planning; or
   - Limited awareness or understanding of extent of corrupt activity.

Harm is demonstrated by one or more of the following factors.

a. Category 1
   - Serious detrimental effect on individuals (for example, by provision of substandard goods or services resulting from the corrupt behavior);
   - Serious environmental impact;
   - Serious undermining of the proper function of local or national government, business, or public services; or
   - Substantial actual or intended financial gain to offender or another loss caused to others.

b. Category 2
   - Significant detrimental effect on individuals;
   - Significant environmental impact;
   - Significant undermining of the proper function of local or national government, business, or public services; or
   - Significant actual or intended financial gain to offender or another loss caused to others; or
   - Risk of category 1 harm.

c. Category 3
   - Limited detrimental impact on individuals, the environment, government, business, or public services; or
   - Risk of category 2 harm.

d. Category 4
- Risk of category 3 harm.

"Risk of harm" involves consideration of both the likelihood of harm occurring and the extent of it if it does. Risk of harm is less serious than the same actual harm. Where the offense has caused risk of harm but no (or much less) actual harm, the normal approach is to move to the next category of harm down. This may not be appropriate if either the likelihood or extent of potential harm is particularly high.

Having determined the category in Step 1, Step 2 proceeds to use the corresponding starting point to reach a sentence within the category range below. The starting point applies to all offenders irrespective of previous convictions.

Harm	A	B	C
Category 1	**Starting point** 7 years' custody **Category range** 5–8 years' custody	**Starting point** 5 years' custody **Category range** 3–6 years' custody	**Starting point** 3 years' custody **Category range** 18 months'–4 years' custody
Category 2	**Starting point** 5 years' custody **Category range** 3–6 years' custody	**Starting point** 3 years' custody **Category range** 18 months'–4 years' custody	**Starting point** 18 months' custody **Category range** 26 weeks'–3 years' custody
Category 3	**Starting point** 3 years' custody **Category range** 18 months'–4 years' custody	**Starting point** 18 months' custody **Category range** 26 weeks'–3 years' custody	**Starting point** 26 weeks' custody **Category range** Medium level community order–1 year's custody
Category 4	**Starting point** 18 months' custody **Category range** 26 weeks'–3 years' custody	**Starting point** 26 weeks' custody **Category range** Medium level community order–1 year's custody	**Starting point** Medium level community order **Category range** B and B fine–High level community order

The table below contains a nonexhaustive list of factors that increase or reduce seriousness.

Factors Increasing Seriousness	Factors Reducing Seriousness or Reflecting Personal Mitigation
Statutory Aggravating Factors	No previous convictions *or* no relevant/recent convictions
Previous convictions, having regard to (1) the nature of the offense to which the conviction relates and its relevance to the current offense, and (2) the time that has elapsed since the conviction	Remorse

Factors Increasing Seriousness	Factors Reducing Seriousness or Reflecting Personal Mitigation
Offense committed while on bail	Good character and/or exemplary conduct
Other Aggravating Factors	Little or no prospect of success
Steps taken to prevent victims reporting or obtaining assistance and/or from assisting or supporting the prosecution	Serious medical conditions requiring urgent, intensive, or long-term treatment
Attempts to conceal/dispose of evidence	Age and/or lack of maturity where it affects the responsibility of the offender
Established evidence of community/wider impact	Lapse of time since apprehension where this does not arise from the conduct of the offender
Failure to comply with current court orders	Mental disorder or learning disability
Offense committed on license	Sole or primary career for dependent relatives
Offenses taken into consideration	Offender cooperated with investigation, made early admissions, and/or voluntarily reported offending
Failure to respond to warnings about behavior	
Offenses committed across borders	
Blame wrongly placed on others	
Pressure exerted on another party	
Offense committed to facilitate other criminal activity	

Pursuant to Step 3, a court may reduce a sentence of an offender who has, pursuant to a written agreement, assisted or offered to assist the investigation or prosecution in relation to that offense or another offense. The court will take into account the extent and nature of the assistance given or offered.

Step 4 allows for a potential reduction for a guilty plea in accordance with the Sentencing Council's Guilty Plea Guideline.[146] The recommended approach for guilty plea credit is that (1) the court decides the sentence for the offense, taking into account aggravating and mitigating factors and any other offenses that have been formally admitted; (2) the court selects the amount of the reduction by reference to the sliding scale, *infra*; (3) the court applies the reduction; and (4) the court usually pronounces what the sentence would have been but for the reduction as a result of the guilty plea.[147]

The level of reduction is intended to reflect the stage at which the offender indicated a willingness to admit guilt to the offense—the sliding scale, in general, provides a recommendation:

1. One-third reduction where the guilty plea was entered at the first reasonable opportunity in relation to the offense for which sentence is being imposed;
2. One-quarter reduction where a trial date has been set; and
3. One-tenth reduction for a guilty plea entered at the "door of the court" or after trial has begun.

B. Corporations

For corporations, sentencing is a ten-step process:

1. Compensation—considering a compensation order to pay compensation for any personal injury, loss, or damage resulting from the offense, having regard for the evidence and the means of the offender;
2. Confiscation, where the Crown asks for it or the court thinks it may be appropriate;
3. Determining the offense category—with reference to culpability and harm;
4. Starting point and range;
5. Adjustment of fine with the objective of orders made, compensation, confiscation, and fine being the removal of all gain, appropriate additional punishment, and deterrence;
6. Consideration of any factors that would indicate a reduction, such as assistance to the prosecution;
7. Reduction for guilty pleas;
8. Ancillary orders;
9. Totality principle; and
10. Reasons—court has only to give reasons and explain the effect of the sentence.

Steps 3 and 4 for corporations are the most detailed. To determine the offense category (Step 3), a court will review to assess culpability the following nonexhaustive characteristics.

1. High Culpability

- Corporation plays a leading role in organized, planned unlawful activity (whether acting alone or with others);
- Willful obstruction of detection (for example destruction of evidence, misleading investigators, suborning employees);
- Involving others through pressure or coercion (for example, employees or suppliers);
- Targeting of vulnerable victims or a large number of victims;
- Corruption of local or national government officials or ministers;
- Corruption of officials performing a law enforcement role;
- Abuse of dominant market position or position of trust or responsibility;
- Offending committed over a sustained period of time; and
- Culture of willful disregard of commission of offenses by employees or agents with no effort to put effective systems in place (section 7 Bribery Act only).

2. Medium Culpability

- Corporation plays a significant role in unlawful activity organized by others;
- Activity not unlawful from the outset;
- Corporation reckless in making false statement (section 7 VAT Act 1994);
- All other cases where characteristics for categories A or C are not present.

3. *Lesser Culpability*

- Corporation plays a minor, peripheral role in unlawful activity organized by others;
- Some effort made to put bribery prevention measures in place but insufficient to amount to a defense (section 7 Bribery Act only); and
- Involvement through coercion, intimidation, or exploitation.

For offenses under the Bribery Act, the appropriate figure will normally be the gross profit from the contract obtained, retained, or sought as a result of the offending. An alternative measure for offenses under section 7 may be the likely cost avoided by failing to put in place appropriate measures to prevent bribery.

Having determined the culpability level at Step 3, the court should, for Step 4, use the table below to determine the starting point within the category range below. The starting point applies to all offenders irrespective of plea or previous convictions.

The harm figure at Step 3 is multiplied by the relevant percentage figure representing culpability.

Culpability Level

	A	B	C
Harm figure multiplier	**Starting point** 300% **Category range** 250% to 400%	**Starting point** 200% **Category range** 100% to 300%	**Starting point** 100% **Category range** 20% to 150%

Having determined the appropriate starting point, the court should then consider adjustment within the category range for aggravating or mitigating features. In some cases, having considered these factors, it may be appropriate to move outside the identified category range. (See below for a nonexhaustive list of aggravating and mitigating factors.)

Factors Increasing Seriousness	**Factors Reducing Seriousness or Reflecting Personal Mitigation**
Previous relevant convictions or subject to previous relevant civil or regulatory enforcement action	No previous relevant convictions or previous relevant civil or regulatory enforcement action
Corporation or subsidiary set up to commit fraudulent activity	Victims voluntary reimbursed/compensated
Fraudulent activity endemic within corporation	No actual loss to victims
Attempts made to conceal misconduct	Corporation cooperated with investigation, made early admissions and/or voluntarily reported offending
Substantial harm (whether financial or otherwise) suffered by victims of offending or by third parties affected by offending	Offending committed under previous director(s)/manager(s)

Factors Increasing Seriousness	Factors Reducing Seriousness or Reflecting Personal Mitigation
Risk of harm greater than actual or intended harm (for example in banking/ credit fraud)	Little or no actual gain to corporation from offending
Substantial harm caused to integrity or confidence of markets	
Substantial harm caused to integrity of local or national governments	
Serious nature of underlying criminal activity (money laundering offenses)	
Offense committed across borders of jurisdictions	

In the United Kingdom, a corporate defendant must produce to the court comprehensive financial accounts for the past three years. The failure to produce relevant financial information on request can lead to the conclusion that the company can pay any appropriate fine.

In adjusting the fine imposed on a company, the Definitive Guideline directs the court to consider the following nonexhaustive six factors in adjusting the level of the fine:

1. Fine fulfills the objectives of punishment, deterrence, and removal of gain;
2. The value, worth or available means of the offender;
3. Fine impairs offender's ability to make restitution to victims;
4. Impact of fine on offender's ability to implement effective compliance programs;
5. Impact of fine on employment of staff, service users, customers, and local economy (but not shareholders); and
6. Impact of fine on performance of public or charitable function.

C. Comparison of the U.S. Sentencing Guidelines and the U.K. Definitive Guidelines for Convicted Bribery Defendants

The factors that U.S. and U.K. courts are considering for sentences of both individuals and corporate defendants convicted of bribery are, not surprisingly, very similar. Although the few U.K. bribery prosecutions to date have not led to much use of the 2007 Definitive Guidance, certain general observations are possible. First, jail term for individuals in the United States can be much greater. Second, fines for corporations are, for now, much greater in U.S. courts.

Third, reductions for guilty pleas in the United Kingdom focus far more on the timeliness of a guilty plea with the recommended maximum deduction only one-third for a pea at the first reasonable opportunity. The U.K. guilty plea reductions do not seem drafted for corporations, but rather for individuals. Finally, the court's role in and explanation of the reasons for imposing a particular reduced sentence are much greater and more transparent in the United Kingdom.

XI. PRACTICAL MULTINATIONAL ADVICE REGARDING THE U.K. BRIBERY ACT 2010

- Multinational companies (MNCs) should consider revising their codes of conduct and policies and procedures to make them more global, less U.S.-centric, and mindful of the conflicting, in parts, U.K. Bribery Act and FCPA laws. It is usually easier to step up to a higher, global compliance standard than to try to navigate between the FCPA and Bribery Act statutes.

- Senior officers and "directing minds" (*Tesco Supermarkets Ltd. v. Nattrass*) especially need anticorruption training and familiarity with bribery red flags since they may still be prosecuted if the identification principle is satisfied and their state of mind may determine whether the company is held liable, notwithstanding that adequate procedures for the corporation may be in place and protect it.

- MNCs should thoroughly examine the MOJ Guidance (appendix 17) for the Six Principles and develop checklists of recommended practices. While an MNC need not adopt each recommended practice, it should analyze each and have a basis or reason for declining to adopt particular guidance or recommended practices. Like the DOJ–SEC *Resource Guide to the U.S. Foreign Corrupt Practices Act* (2012) (appendix 4), the MOJ Guidance is an advocacy piece representing U.K. law enforcement's view of its foreign official bribery statute.

- MNCs should be sure to address both public and private sector bribery in their codes of conduct, policies, and procedures.

- MNCs should thoroughly review and address the adequate procedures defense and draft a timetable for full implementation in order to avail themselves of the defense to the strict corporate liability offense (failure of a company to prevent bribery) under section 7 of the Bribery Act. Given the breadth of the concept of "associated persons," companies should ensure that agents, contractors, and joint venture partners are adequately trained on corruption laws.

- MNCs should recognize the risk-based nature of the U.K. antibribery enforcement scheme and undertake a thorough and regular risk assessment of their global operations—considering the input of legal, financial, sales, internal audit, human resources and accounting personnel, regional and country managers, and antibribery counsel.

- An MNC should consider what contemporaneous record it could establish before a court demonstrating its fulfillment of the MOJ Guidance's Six Principles underlining the adequate procedures defense and who among its senior officers could testify in support of the record—since that is precisely what it might have to do before the SFO staff or a U.K. court.

- The Risk Assessment principle (Principle 3) affords companies the most opportunity to demonstrate *or* fail to demonstrate their commitment to the Six Principles and implementation of adequate procedures. A detailed written analysis of the five external risks and the five internal factors can make a powerful record of the company's commitment to avoiding bribes by employers, agents, subsidiaries, joint venture parties, and others. Conversely, a one-time perfunctory memo "analyzing" these risk categories and issues is unlikely to be persuasive in establishing an adequate procedures defense. An annual risk assessment should ideally include the input of country managers, the general counsel and regional lawyers, senior sales officers, the chief compliance officer, the chief executive and financial officers, the head of internal audit, and FCPA expert counsel. Companies may wish to consider sharing an annual risk analysis with the board of directors or a compliance committee.

- Any risk assessment must be periodic, informed, and documented (Principle 3). Periodic should be at least annually. Informed means a management team should consider the company's internal risks and external risks, *supra*. Documented means there should be an ample annual record of the materials and legal developments management considered and a detailed memorandum assessing both internal and external risks.

- Joint ventures are addressed specifically in the U.K. Bribery Act's MOJ Guidance (appendix 17). MNCs contemplating joint ventures should carefully review paragraphs 40–42 of the MOJ Guidance and Case Study Number 3 in its appendix A.

- Counsel defending companies before the SFO should fully understand the identification principle of *Tesco Supermarkets Ltd. v. Nattrass* and be conversant with the Corporate Prosecution Guidance and the Joint Prosecution Guidance. The Corporate Prosecution Guidance relates to the broader issue of corporate prosecutions in the U.K. while the Joint Prosecution Guidance relates specifically to the Bribery Act.

- The SFO is unlikely to charge MNCs for hospitality events that are reasonable and proportionate. The Joint Prosecution Guidance contains specific examples of permissible one-day hospitality designed no doubt to assuage those who have expressed concerns about arbitrary prosecutions of routine hospitality of government officials.

- In October 2012 the SFO issued a new self-reporting policy that would appear to make civil resolutions of even self-reporting companies much less certain. Moreover, there are distinct differences from the United States, such as waiver of privileged interview notes and memoranda, that counsel representing a company subject to the Bribery Act's jurisdiction must understand and analyze.

- While the MOJ Guidance stresses a core principle of proportionality that suggests fewer policies and procedures may be necessary for smaller organizations, MNCs should be mindful that a company considered small in the United States may well be viewed as a mid-sized or large organization in the United Kingdom.

- MNCs and their boards of directors should not assume that U.K. courts will as a matter of course recognize and accept plea agreements between them and the SFO and/or between them, the SFO, and the DOJ. Indeed, they should assume U.K. courts will conduct an independent, transparent hearing to determine whether any proposed plea agreement is in the public interest.

- Government debarment and suspension are more likely to be imposed in the United Kingdom than in the United States for bribery-related convictions, raising the stakes for government contractors in the United Kingdom and making timely implementation of adequate procedures all the more critical.

- MNCs should design and implement genuinely proactive and effective compliance programs. Paper compliance programs will be obvious and not persuade authorities not to bring a corporate prosecution.

XII. RESOURCES

- Marcus Asner, Drew Harker, Keith Korenchuk, & Jennifer Hogan, *The U.K.'s SFO Provides Additional Guidance on Its Approach to Investigating Allegations of Overseas Companies*, BLOOMBERG L. REP. RISK & COMPLIANCE 2010.
- Bribery Act 2010, ch. 23, http://www.legislation.gov.uk/ukpga/2010/23 (appendix 3).
- Bribery Act, 2010 Explanatory Notes, http://www.legislation.gov.uk/ukpga /2010/23/ notes/contents (appendix 3).
- Crime and Courts Act 2013, Schedule 17 Deferred Prosecution Agreements, http://www.legislation.gov.uk/ukpga/2013/22/schedule/17/enacted.
- Gibson, Dunn, U.K. Government and Serious Fraud Office Publish Guidance on the Bribery Act (March 31, 2011), http://www.gibsondunn.com /publications/Documents/UKGovernmentAndSeriousFraudOffice-Publish GuidanceOnBriberyAct.pdf.
- EOIN O'SHEA, THE BRIBERY ACT 2010: A PRACTICAL GUIDE (Jordan 2011).
- PHILIP MONTAGUE RAPHAEL, BLACKSTONE'S GUIDE TO THE BRIBERY ACT 2010 (Oxford Univ. Press 2010).
- Regina v. Innospec Ltd., March 26, 2010, Sentencing Remarks of Lord Justice Thomas in the Crown Court of Southwark, http://www.judiciary.gov.uk /media/judgments/2010/innospec.
- Sentencing Guidelines Council, Fraud, Bribery and Money Laundering Offences, Definitive Guideline (October 1, 2014), https://www.sentencingcouncil.org .uk/wp-content/uploads/Fraud_bribery_and_money_laundering_offences_-_ Definitive_guideline.pdf.
- Sentencing Guidelines Council, Reduction in Sentence for a Guilty Plea Definitive Guideline (Rev. 2007), https://www.sentencingcouncil.org.uk/wp -content/uploads/Reduction_in_Sentence_for_a_Guilty_Plea_-Revised_2007 .pdf.
- Serious Fraud Office and Crown Prosecution Service Deferred Prosecution Agreements Code of Practice, Crime and Courts Act 2013 (Nov. 2, 2014), http://www.sfo.gov.uk/media/264623/deferred%20prosecution%20 agreements%20cop.pdf.
- Transparency International, U.K. Anti-Bribery Guidance for Transactions: Guidance for Anti-Bribery Due Diligence in Mergers, Acquisitions and Investments (2012) (appendix 18).
- U.K. Ministry of Justice, Bribery Act 2010 Guidance and Quick Start Guide (March 30, 2011), http://www.justice.gov.uk/guidance/bribery.htm (appendix 17).
- F. Joseph Warin, Charles Falconer & Michael Diamant, *The British Are Coming!: Britain Changes Its Law on Foreign Bribery and Joins the International Fight against Corruption*, 46 TEX. INT'L L.J. 1 (2010).

NOTES

1. The CPS is the principal prosecuting authority for England and Wales, acting independently in criminal cases investigated by the police and others. The SFO is the lead agency for investigating and prosecuting cases of serious domestic and overseas offenses under the Bribery Act.

2. Appendix 3. Two excellent resources for understanding the Bribery Act 2010 are EOIN O'SHEA, THE BRIBERY ACT 2010: A PRACTICAL GUIDE (Jordan 2011), and PHILIP MONTAGUE RAPHAEL, BLACKSTONE'S GUIDE TO THE BRIBERY ACT 2010 (Oxford Univ. Press 2010).

3. Sections 1 and 2 of the Act cover the two "general bribery offenses." The crime of active bribery is described in section 1 as occurring when a person offers, gives, or promises to give a "financial or other advantage" to another individual in exchange for "improperly" performing a "relevant function or activity." Section 2 covers the passive offense of being bribed, which is defined as requesting, accepting, or agreeing to accept such an advantage, in exchange for improperly performing such a function or activity. (appendix 3.)

4. Section 12.

5. Matthew Cowie, former SFO prosecutor, Distinguishing the Bribery Act from the FCPA, PowerPoint presentation at ACI FCPA Boot Camp (Chicago, Ill., June 27, 2011).

6. Press Release, Serious Fraud Office, U.K. Printing Company and Two Men Found Guilty in Corruption Trial (Dec. 22, 2014), www.sfo.gov.uk/press-room/latest -press-releases-2014/uk-printing-company-and-two-men-found-guilty-in-corruption -trial.

7. *See* OECD Anti-Bribery Convention on Combating Bribery of Foreign Public Officials, pt. 1, http://www.oecd.org/dataoecd/4/18/38028044.pdf (appendix 2).

8. U.K. Ministry of Justice, Bribery Act 2010 Guidance, at 11, para. 23, http:// www.justice.gov.uk/guidance/docs/bribery-act-2010-guidance.pdf [hereinafter MOJ Guidance] (reprinted as appendix 17).

9. Bribery Act 2010, ch. 23, section 6(2)(b).

10. OECD art. 1; FCPA.

11. MOJ Guidance, *supra* note 8, at 11–12, para. 24.

12. *Id.* at 11, para. 22.

13. David Green, CB QC, Director, Serious Fraud Office, Tenth Annual Corporate Accountability Conference at PricewaterhouseCoopers (June 14, 2012) (emphasis added), http://www.sfo.gov.uk/about-us/our-views/director%27s-speeches/speeches-2012 /10th-annual-corporate-accountability-conference-held-at-pricewaterhousecoopers-on-14 -june-2012.aspx.

14. Bribery Act 2010, ch. 23, sections 12(1)–(4); MOJ Guidance, *supra* note 8, at 1, para. 5.

15. Bribery Act 2010, ch. 23, section 14(2).

16. *Id.* section 14(3).

17. *Id.* section 14(4).

18. Law Commission paras. 9.21–9.37.

19. MONTY RAPHAEL, BLACKSTONE'S GUIDE TO THE BRIBERY ACT 2010, at 106 (Oxford Univ. Press 2010) (quoting Lord Hope, R v. Chargot, [2008] UKHL 73, [2009] 1 WLR 1).

20. Bribery Act 2010: Joint Prosecution Guidance of the Director of the Serious Fraud Office and the Director of Public Prosecutions 8.

21. MOJ Guidance, *supra* note 8, at 15, para. 33.

22. *Id.* at 15, para. 34.

23. Eoin O'Shea, The Bribery Act 2010: A Practical Guide 137–38 (Jordan 2011).

24. MOJ Guidance, *supra* note 8, at 15–16, paras. 35–36.

25. Akzo Nobel N.V. v. Competition Comm'n [2014] EWCA Civ 482.

26. MOJ Guidance, *supra* note 8, at 16, para. 39.

27. *Id.* para. 37.

28. *Id.* para. 38.

29. O'Shea, *supra* note 23, at 132, section 8.10.

30. MOJ Guidance, *supra* note 8, at 17, paras. 40–41.

31. *Id.* at 16, para. 41.

32. *Id.* at 17–18, para. 42.

33. *Id.* at 16, para. 39.

34. *See id.*

35. *Id.*

36. Section 9 of the Act required the Secretary of State of Justice to publish guidance on the interpretation of the section 7 offense. On March 30, 2011, the Secretary of State published a 43-page guidance on the interpretation and use of the Act. MOJ Guidance, *supra* note 8.

37. Serious Fraud Office, Revised Policies (Oct. 9, 2012), http://www.sfo.gov.uk/press-room/latest-press-releases/press-releases-2012/revised-policies.aspx.

38. Jones Day, Serious Fraud Office's Revised Guidance on the U.K. Bribery Act (Oct. 2012), http://www.jonesday.com/serious_fraud.

39. http://www.sfo.gov.uk/bribery—corruption/the-bribery-act/questions-and-answers.aspx.

40. [1972] AC 153; O'Shea, *supra* note 23, at 134.

41. MOJ Guidance, *supra* note 8, at 6, para. 1.

42. *Id.* at 8, para. 11 (emphasis added).

43. *Id.* at 6–7, paras. 5–6.

44. O'Shea, *supra* note 23, at 179, section 9.7.3.

45. *Id.* at 27, section 4.3.

46. *Id.* at 28, section 4.6.

47. *Id.* at 27, section 4.5.

48. Transparency Int'l U.K., Anti-Bribery Due Diligence for Transactions: Guidance for Anti-Bribery Due Diligence in Mergers, Acquisitions, and Investments (2012), http://www.transparency.org.uk/our-work/publications/227-anti-bribery-due-diligence-for-transactions (appendix 18).

49. *Id.*

50. *Id.*

51. *Id.*

52. *Id.*

53. *Id.*

54. *Id.*

55. *Id.*

56. *Id.* at 29, para. 5.3.

57. *Id.* para. 5.4.

58. *Id.* at 30, para. 5.6.

59. *Id.* para. 5.8.

60. *Id.* at 12, para. 26.

61. *Id.*

62. *Id.* at 13, para. 30.

63. *Id.* at 14, para. 31.

64. The SFO may still refer a matter it does not consider an offence under the Act to the City of London Police.

65. http://www.sfo.gov.uk/bribery-corruption/the-bribery-act/question-and -answers.aspx.

66. MOJ Guidance, *supra* note 8, at 18, paras. 45–46.

67. *Id.* at 19, para. 50.

68. http://www.sfo.gov.uk/bribery-corruption/the-bribery-act/question-and -answers.aspx.

69. MOJ Guidance, *supra* note 8, at 17, para. 40.

70. *Id.*

71. *Id.*

72. *Id.* at 17–18.

73. *Id.*

74. *Id.*

75. Serious Fraud Office, Corruption Indicators, http://www.sfo.gov.uk/bribery —corruption/corruption-indicators.aspx.

76. Appendix 4.

77. Consolidated Criminal Practice Direction, IV.45.10–45.15.

78. *Id. See also* R v. Underwood (2005).

79. Consolidated Criminal Practice Direction, IV.45.16–45.28.

80. R v. Innospec Ltd., Mar. 26, 2010 (sentencing remarks of Lord Justice Thomas), http://www.judiciary.gov.uk/media/judgments/2010/innospec.

81. *Id.*

82. http://www.legislation.gov.uk/ukpga/2013/22/schedule/17/enacted.

83. http://sfo.gov.uk/media/264623/deferred%20prosecution%20agreements%20 cop.pdf.

84. Act 5(1).

85. DPA Code of Practice, Crime and Courts Act 2013 (Nov. 2, 2014) at 6.1ii, http://www.sfo.gov.uk/media/264623/deferred%20prosecution%20agreements%20cop .pdf.

86. *Id.* at 6.3.

87. *Id.* at 7.3.

88. Act 5(2).

89. Act 5(3).

90. Act 5(4).

91. Act 7(1).

92. Act 7(2).

93. Act 7(3).

94. Act 7(4).

95. Act 8(7).

96. *Id.*

97. Act 9(2).

98. Act 9(3).

99. Act 10(1).

100. Act 10(8).

101. Act 23.

102. Act 26.

103. Press Release, Serious Fraud Office, Deferred Prosecution Agreements: New Guidance for Prosecutors (14 Feb. 2014), http://www.sfo.gov.uk/press-room/latest -press-releases/press-releases-2014/deferred-prosecution-agreements-new-guidance-for -prosecutors.aspx.

104. DPA Code of Practice, Crime and Courts Act 2013 (Nov. 2, 2014) at 1.1, http:// www.sfo.gov.uk/media/264623/deferred%20prosecution%20agreements%20cop.pdf.

105. *Id.*

106. *Id.* at 2.1 (emphasis added).

107. For what is reasonable, *see* paragraph 2.9 of the DPA Code of Practice, Crime and Courts Act 2013 (Nov. 2, 2014).

108. *Id.* at 2.8.1.

109. The prosecutor may choose to bring in external resource to assist in the assessment of P's compliance culture and program for example as described in any self-report.

110. *Id.* at 2.8.2.

111. *Id.* at 2.9.1.

112. *Id.* at 2.9.2.

113. *Id.* at 2.9.3.

114. *Id.* at 3.1.

115. *Id.* at 3.2.

116. *Id.* at 3.3.

117. *Id.* at 3.4.

118. Schedule 17, para. 5(4).

119. DPA Code at 8.3.

120. *Id.* at 8.4.

121. DPA Code at 7.11.

122. *Id.* at 7.14.

123. These policies and procedures are not intended to provide an indication of what can amount to adequate procedures under Bribery Act 2010 section 7.

124. DPA Code of Practice, Crime and Courts Act 2013 (Nov. 2, 2014) at 7.21, http:// www.sfo.gov.uk/media/264623/deferred%20prosecution%20agreements%20cop.pdf.

125. *Id.*

126. *Id.*

127. SFO, Corporate Self-Reporting (Oct. 9, 2012), http://www.sfo.gov.uk/bribery -corruption/corporate-self-reporting.aspx.

128. SFO Questions and Answers, http://www.sfo.gov.uk/bribery-corruption/the bribery-act-questions-and-answers.aspx.

129. *Id.*

130. Alun Milford, SFO General Counsel, Annual Employer Bar Conference, Corporate Criminal Liability and Deferred Prosecution Agreements (Mar. 26, 2014), http://www.sfo.gov.uk/about-us/our-views/other-speeches/speeches-2014/corporate-criminal-liability-and-deferred-prosecution-agreements.aspx.

131. SFO, Guidance on Corporate Prosecutions, http://www.sfo.gov.uk/media/65217/joint_guidance_on_corporate_prosecutions.pdf.

132. *Id.* at 1, ¶ 4.

133. *Id.* at 2, ¶ 5.

134. *Id.* at 2, ¶¶ 7–9.

135. *Id.* at 2–3, ¶ 10.

136. *Id.* at 3–4, ¶¶ 14–16.

137. [1972] AC 153.

138. *Id.* at 4–5, ¶¶ 17–20. This principle is consistent with U.S. law; however, government agencies may in their discretion decline a case against a company that is also a victim. See discussion of United States v. Peterson and SEC v. Peterson, *supra* chapter 10, in which the DOJ and SEC declined to prosecute Peterson's employer Morgan Stanley.

139. *See, e.g.,* United States v. Bank of New England, 821 F.2d 844 (1st Cir.), *cert. denied,* 484 U.S. 943 (1987). The U.S. DOJ has not brought a contested "collective knowledge" doctrine-based FCPA prosecution, but this doctrine may have influenced settlement discussions in eventually settled FCPA cases.

140. SFO, Guidance on Corporate Prosecutions, *supra* note 131, at 5–6, ¶¶ 21–27.

141. *Id.* at 6–7, ¶¶ 30–32.

142. *Id.* at 7–8.

143. *Id.* at 8–9.

144. See discussion of United States v. Peterson and SEC v. Peterson, *supra* chapter 10, in which the DOJ and SEC declined to prosecute Peterson's employer Morgan Stanley.

145. http://www.sentencingcouncil.org.uk.

146. Reduction in Sentence for a Guilty Plea (Rev. 2007), http://sentencingcouncil.judiciary.gov.uk/docs/Reduction_in_Sentence_for_a_Guilty_Plea_-Revised_2007.pdf.

147. *Id.* at section C.3.1.

APPENDIX 1

United States Foreign
Corrupt Practices Act

TEXT OF THE FOREIGN CORRUPT PRACTICES ACT
Current through Pub. L. 105-366 (November 10, 1998)
UNITED STATES CODE
TITLE 15. COMMERCE AND TRADE
CHAPTER 2B—SECURITIES EXCHANGES

§ 78M. PERIODICAL AND OTHER REPORTS

(a) Reports by issuer of security; contents

Every issuer of a security registered pursuant to section 78l of this title shall file with the Commission, in accordance with such rules and regulations as the Commission may prescribe as necessary or appropriate for the proper protection of investors and to insure fair dealing in the security—

(1)   such information and documents (and such copies thereof) as the Commission shall require to keep reasonably current the information and documents required to be included in or filed with an application or registration statement filed pursuant to section 78l of this title, except that the Commission may not require the filing of any material contract wholly executed before July 1, 1962.

(2)   such annual reports (and such copies thereof), certified if required by the rules and regulations of the Commission by independent public accountants, and such quarterly reports (and such copies thereof), as the Commission may prescribe. Every issuer of a security registered on a national securities exchange shall also file a duplicate original of such information, documents, and reports with the exchange.

(b) Form of report; books, records, and internal accounting; directives

(1)   The Commission may prescribe, in regard to reports made pursuant to this chapter, the form or forms in which the required information shall be set forth, the items or details to be shown in the balance sheet and the earnings statement, and the methods to be followed in the preparation of reports, in the appraisal or valuation of assets and liabilities, in the determination of depreciation and depletion, in the differentiation of recurring

and nonrecurring income, in the differentiation of investment and operating income, and in the preparation, where the Commission deems it necessary or desirable, of separate and/or consolidated balance sheets or income accounts of any person directly or indirectly controlling or controlled by the issuer, or any person under direct or indirect common control with the issuer; but in the case of the reports of any person whose methods of accounting are prescribed under the provisions of any law of the United States, or any rule or regulation thereunder, the rules and regulations of the Commission with respect to reports shall not be inconsistent with the requirements imposed by such law or rule or regulation in respect of the same subject matter (except that such rules and regulations of the Commission may be inconsistent with such requirements to the extent that the Commission determines that the public interest or the protection of investors so requires.)

(2) Every issuer which has a class of securities registered pursuant to section 78l of this title and every issuer which is required to file reports pursuant to section 78o(d) of this title shall—

(A) make and keep books, records, and accounts, which, in reasonable detail, accurately and fairly reflect the transactions and dispositions of the assets of the issuer; and

(B) devise and maintain a system of internal accounting controls sufficient to provide reasonable assurances that—

(i)   transactions are executed in accordance with management's general or specific authorization;

(ii) transactions are recorded as necessary (I) to permit preparation of financial statements in conformity with generally accepted accounting principles or any other criteria applicable to such statements, and (II) to maintain accountability for assets;

(iii) access to assets is permitted only in accordance with management's general or specific authorization; and

(iv) the recorded accountability for assets is compared with the existing assets at reasonable intervals and appropriate action is taken with respect to any differences.

(3) (A) With respect to matters concerning the national security of the United States, no duty or liability under paragraph (2) of this subsection shall be imposed upon any person acting in cooperation with the head of any Federal department or agency responsible for such matters if such act in cooperation with such head of a department or agency was done upon the specific, written directive of the head of such department or agency pursuant to Presidential authority to issue such directives. Each directive issued under this paragraph shall set forth the specific facts and circumstances with respect to which the provisions of this paragraph are to be invoked. Each such directive shall, unless renewed in writing, expire one year after the date of issuance.

(B) Each head of a Federal department or agency of the United States who issues such a directive pursuant to this paragraph shall maintain a complete file of all such directives and shall, on October 1 of each year, transmit a summary of matters covered by such directives in force at any time during the previous year to the Permanent Select Committee on Intelligence of the House of Representatives and the Select Committee on Intelligence of the Senate.

(4) No criminal liability shall be imposed for failing to comply with the requirements of paragraph (2) of this subsection except as provided in paragraph (5) of this subsection.

(5) No person shall knowingly circumvent or knowingly fail to implement a system of internal accounting controls or knowingly falsify any book, record, or account described in paragraph (2).

(6) Where an issuer which has a class of securities registered pursuant to section 78l of this title or an issuer which is required to file reports pursuant to section 78o(d) of this title holds 50 per centum or less of the voting power with respect to a domestic or foreign firm, the provisions of paragraph (2) require only that the issuer proceed in good faith to use its influence, to the extent reasonable under the issuer's circumstances, to cause such domestic or foreign firm to devise and maintain a system of internal accounting controls consistent with paragraph (2). Such circumstances include the relative degree of the issuer's ownership of the domestic or foreign firm and the laws and practices governing the business operations of the country in which such firm is located. An issuer which demonstrates good faith efforts to use such influence shall be conclusively presumed to have complied with the requirements of paragraph (2).

(7) For the purpose of paragraph (2) of this subsection, the terms "reasonable assurances" and "reasonable detail" mean such level of detail and degree of assurance as would satisfy prudent officials in the conduct of their own affairs.

§ 78DD-1. PROHIBITED FOREIGN TRADE PRACTICES BY ISSUERS

(a) Prohibition

It shall be unlawful for any issuer which has a class of securities registered pursuant to section 78l of this title or which is required to file reports under section 78o(d) of this title, or for any officer, director, employee, or agent of such issuer or any stockholder thereof acting on behalf of such issuer, to make use of the mails or any means or instrumentality of interstate commerce corruptly in furtherance of an offer, payment, promise to pay, or authorization of the payment of any money, or offer, gift, promise to give, or authorization of the giving of anything of value to—

(1) any foreign official for purposes of—

(A) (i) influencing any act or decision of such foreign official in his official capacity, (ii) inducing such foreign official to do or omit to do any act in violation of the lawful duty of such official, or (iii) securing any improper advantage; or

(B) inducing such foreign official to use his influence with a foreign government or instrumentality thereof to affect or influence any act or decision of such government or instrumentality, in order to assist such issuer in obtaining or retaining business for or with, or directing business to, any person;

(2) any foreign political party or official thereof or any candidate for foreign political office for purposes of—
   (A) (i) influencing any act or decision of such party, official, or candidate in its or his official capacity, (ii) inducing such party, official, or candidate to do or omit to do an act in violation of the lawful duty of such party, official, or candidate, or (iii) securing any improper advantage; or
   (B) inducing such party, official, or candidate to use its or his influence with a foreign government or instrumentality thereof to affect or influence any act or decision of such government or instrumentality,

in order to assist such issuer in obtaining or retaining business for or with, or directing business to, any person; or

(3) any person, while knowing that all or a portion of such money or thing of value will be offered, given, or promised, directly or indirectly, to any foreign official, to any foreign political party or official thereof, or to any candidate for foreign political office, for purposes of—
   (A) (i) influencing any act or decision of such foreign official, political party, party official, or candidate in his or its official capacity, (ii) inducing such foreign official, political party, party official, or candidate to do or omit to do any act in violation of the lawful duty of such foreign official, political party, party official, or candidate, or (iii) securing any improper advantage; or
   (B) inducing such foreign official, political party, party official, or candidate to use his or its influence with a foreign government or instrumentality thereof to affect or influence any act or decision of such government or instrumentality,

in order to assist such issuer in obtaining or retaining business for or with, or directing business to, any person.

(b) Exception for routine governmental action

Subsections (a) and (g) of this section shall not apply to any facilitating or expediting payment to a foreign official, political party, or party official the purpose of which is to expedite or to secure the performance of a routine governmental action by a foreign official, political party, or party official.

(c) Affirmative defenses

It shall be an affirmative defense to actions under subsection (a) or (g) of this section that—

(1) the payment, gift, offer, or promise of anything of value that was made, was lawful under the written laws and regulations of the foreign official's, political party's, party official's, or candidate's country; or

(2)   the payment, gift, offer, or promise of anything of value that was made, was a reasonable and bona fide expenditure, such as travel and lodging expenses, incurred by or on behalf of a foreign official, party, party official, or candidate and was directly related to—

    (A)   the promotion, demonstration, or explanation of products or services; or

    (B)   the execution or performance of a contract with a foreign government or agency thereof.

(d) Guidelines by Attorney General

Not later than one year after August 23, 1988, the Attorney General, after consultation with the Commission, the Secretary of Commerce, the United States Trade Representative, the Secretary of State, and the Secretary of the Treasury, and after obtaining the views of all interested persons through public notice and comment procedures, shall determine to what extent compliance with this section would be enhanced and the business community would be assisted by further clarification of the preceding provisions of this section and may, based on such determination and to the extent necessary and appropriate, issue—

(1)   guidelines describing specific types of conduct, associated with common types of export sales arrangements and business contracts, which for purposes of the Department of Justice's present enforcement policy, the Attorney General determines would be in conformance with the preceding provisions of this section; and

(2)   general precautionary procedures which issuers may use on a voluntary basis to conform their conduct to the Department of Justice's present enforcement policy regarding the preceding provisions of this section.

The Attorney General shall issue the guidelines and procedures referred to in the preceding sentence in accordance with the provisions of subchapter II of chapter 5 of Title 5 and those guidelines and procedures shall be subject to the provisions of chapter 7 of that title.

(e) Opinions of Attorney General

(1)   The Attorney General, after consultation with appropriate departments and agencies of the United States and after obtaining the views of all interested persons through public notice and comment procedures, shall establish a procedure to provide responses to specific inquiries by issuers concerning conformance of their conduct with the Department of Justice's present enforcement policy regarding the preceding provisions of this section. The Attorney General shall, within 30 days after receiving such a request, issue an opinion in response to that request. The opinion shall state whether or not certain specified prospective conduct would, for purposes of the Department of Justice's present enforcement policy, violate the preceding provisions of this section. Additional requests for opinions may be filed with the Attorney General regarding other specified prospective conduct

that is beyond the scope of conduct specified in previous requests. In any action brought under the applicable provisions of this section, there shall be a rebuttable presumption that conduct, which is specified in a request by an issuer and for which the Attorney General has issued an opinion that such conduct is in conformity with the Department of Justice's present enforcement policy, is in compliance with the preceding provisions of this section. Such a presumption may be rebutted by a preponderance of the evidence. In considering the presumption for purposes of this paragraph, a court shall weigh all relevant factors, including but not limited to whether the information submitted to the Attorney General was accurate and complete and whether it was within the scope of the conduct specified in any request received by the Attorney General. The Attorney General shall establish the procedure required by this paragraph in accordance with the provisions of subchapter II of chapter 5 of Title 5 and that procedure shall be subject to the provisions of chapter 7 of that title.

(2) Any document or other material which is provided to, received by, or prepared in the Department of Justice or any other department or agency of the United States in connection with a request by an issuer under the procedure established under paragraph (1), shall be exempt from disclosure under section 552 of Title 5 and shall not, except with the consent of the issuer, be made publicly available, regardless of whether the Attorney General responds to such a request or the issuer withdraws such request before receiving a response.

(3) Any issuer who has made a request to the Attorney General under paragraph (1) may withdraw such request prior to the time the Attorney General issues an opinion in response to such request. Any request so withdrawn shall have no force or effect.

(4) The Attorney General shall, to the maximum extent practicable, provide timely guidance concerning the Department of Justice's present enforcement policy with respect to the preceding provisions of this section to potential exporters and small businesses that are unable to obtain specialized counsel on issues pertaining to such provisions. Such guidance shall be limited to responses to requests under paragraph (1) concerning conformity of specified prospective conduct with the Department of Justice's present enforcement policy regarding the preceding provisions of this section and general explanations of compliance responsibilities and of potential liabilities under the preceding provisions of this section.

(f) Definitions

For purposes of this section

(1) (A) The term "foreign official" means any officer or employee of a foreign government or any department, agency, or instrumentality thereof, or of a public international organization, or any person acting in an official capacity for or on behalf of any such government or department,

agency, or instrumentality, or for or on behalf of any such public international organization.

(B) For purposes of subparagraph (A), the term "public international organization" means—

(i) an organization that is designated by Executive Order pursuant to section 1 of the International Organizations Immunities Act (22 U.S.C. § 288); or

(ii) any other international organization that is designated by the President by Executive Order for the purposes of this section, effective as of the date of publication of such order in the Federal Register.

(2) (A) A person's state of mind is "knowing" with respect to conduct, a circumstance, or a result if—

(i) such person is aware that such person is engaging in such conduct, that such circumstance exists, or that such result is substantially certain to occur; or

(ii) such person has a firm belief that such circumstance exists or that such result is substantially certain to occur.

(B) When knowledge of the existence of a particular circumstance is required for an offense, such knowledge is established if a person is aware of a high probability of the existence of such circumstance, unless the person actually believes that such circumstance does not exist.

(3) (A) The term "routine governmental action" means only an action which is ordinarily and commonly performed by a foreign official in—

(i) obtaining permits, licenses, or other official documents to qualify a person to do business in a foreign country;

(ii) processing governmental papers, such as visas and work orders;

(iii) providing police protection, mail pick-up and delivery, or scheduling inspections associated with contract performance or inspections related to transit of goods across country;

(iv) providing phone service, power and water supply, loading and unloading cargo, or protecting perishable products or commodities from deterioration; or

(v) actions of a similar nature.

(B) The term "routine governmental action" does not include any decision by a foreign official whether, or on what terms, to award new business to or to continue business with a particular party, or any action taken by a foreign official involved in the decision-making process to encourage a decision to award new business to or continue business with a particular party.

(g) Alternative Jurisdiction

(1) It shall also be unlawful for any issuer organized under the laws of the United States, or a State, territory, possession, or commonwealth of the United States or a political subdivision thereof and which has a class

of securities registered pursuant to section 12 of this title or which is required to file reports under section 15(d) of this title, or for any United States person that is an officer, director, employee, or agent of such issuer or a stockholder thereof acting on behalf of such issuer, to corruptly do any act outside the United States in furtherance of an offer, payment, promise to pay, or authorization of the payment of any money, or offer, gift, promise to give, or authorization of the giving of anything of value to any of the persons or entities set forth in paragraphs (1), (2), and (3) of this subsection (a) of this section for the purposes set forth therein, irrespective of whether such issuer or such officer, director, employee, agent or stockholder makes use of the mails or any means or instrumentals of interstate commerce in furtherance of such offer, gift payment promise, or authorization.

(2)   As used in this subsection, the term "United States person" means a national of the United States (as defined in section 101 of the Immigration and Nationality Act (8 U.S.C. § 1101)) or any corporation, partnership, association, joint-stock company, business trust, unincorporated organization, or sole proprietorship organized under the laws of the United States or any State, territory, possession, or commonwealth of the United States, or any political subdivision thereof.

§ 78DD-2.   PROHIBITED FOREIGN TRADE PRACTICES BY DOMESTIC CONCERNS

(a) Prohibition

It shall be unlawful for any domestic concern, other than an issuer which is subject to section 78dd-1 of this title, or for any officer, director, employee, or agent of such domestic concern or any stockholder thereof acting on behalf of such domestic concern, to make use of the mails or any means or instrumentality of interstate commerce corruptly in furtherance of an offer, payment, promise to pay, or authorization of the payment of any money, or offer, gift, promise to give, or authorization of the giving of anything of value to—

(1)   any foreign official for purposes of—
   (A) (i) influencing any act or decision of such foreign official in his official capacity, (ii) inducing such foreign official to do or omit to do any act in violation of the lawful duty of such official, or (iii) securing any improper advantage; or
   (B) inducing such foreign official to use his influence with a foreign government or instrumentality thereof to affect or influence any act or decision of such government or instrumentality,

in order to assist such domestic concern in obtaining or retaining business for or with, or directing business to, any person;

(2)   any foreign political party or official thereof or any candidate for foreign political office for purposes of—

(A) (i) influencing any act or decision of such party, official, or candidate in its or his official capacity, (ii) inducing such party, official, or candidate to do or omit to do an act in violation of the lawful duty of such party, official, or candidate, or (iii) securing any improper advantage; or

(B) inducing such party, official, or candidate to use its or his influence with a foreign government or instrumentality thereof to affect or influence any act or decision of such government or instrumentality,

in order to assist such domestic concern in obtaining or retaining business for or with, or directing business to, any person;

(3) any person, while knowing that all or a portion of such money or thing of value will be offered, given, or promised, directly or indirectly, to any foreign official, to any foreign political party or official thereof, or to any candidate for foreign political office, for purposes of—

(A) (i) influencing any act or decision of such foreign official, political party, party official, or candidate in his or its official capacity, (ii) inducing such foreign official, political party, party official, or candidate to do or omit to do any act in violation of the lawful duty of such foreign official, political party, party official, or candidate, or (iii) securing any improper advantage; or

(B) inducing such foreign official, political party, party official, or candidate to use his or its influence with a foreign government or instrumentality thereof to affect or influence any act or decision of such government or instrumentality,

in order to assist such domestic concern in obtaining or retaining business for or with, or directing business to, any person.

(b) Exception for routine governmental action

Subsections (a) and (i) of this section shall not apply to any facilitating or expediting payment to a foreign official, political party, or party official the purpose of which is to expedite or to secure the performance of a routine governmental action by a foreign official, political party, or party official.

(c) Affirmative defenses

It shall be an affirmative defense to actions under subsection (a) or (i) of this section that—

(1) the payment, gift, offer, or promise of anything of value that was made, was lawful under the written laws and regulations of the foreign official's, political party's, party official's, or candidate's country; or

(2) the payment, gift, offer, or promise of anything of value that was made, was a reasonable and *bona fide* expenditure, such as travel and lodging expenses, incurred by or on behalf of a foreign official, party, party official, or candidate and was directly related to

(A) the promotion, demonstration, or explanation of products or services; or

(B) the execution or performance of a contract with a foreign government or agency thereof.

(d) Injunctive relief

(1) When it appears to the Attorney General that any domestic concern to which this section applies, or officer, director, employee, agent, or stockholder thereof, is engaged, or about to engage, in any act or practice constituting a violation of subsection (a) or (i) of this section, the Attorney General may, in his discretion, bring a civil action in an appropriate district court of the United States to enjoin such act or practice, and upon a proper showing, a permanent injunction or a temporary restraining order shall be granted without bond.

(2) For the purpose of any civil investigation which, in the opinion of the Attorney General, is necessary and proper to enforce this section, the Attorney General or his designee are empowered to administer oaths and affirmations, subpoena witnesses, take evidence, and require the production of any books, papers, or other documents which the Attorney General deems relevant or material to such investigation. The attendance of witnesses and the production of documentary evidence may be required from any place in the United States, or any territory, possession, or commonwealth of the United States, at any designated place of hearing.

(3) In case of contumacy by, or refusal to obey a subpoena issued to, any person, the Attorney General may invoke the aid of any court of the United States within the jurisdiction of which such investigation or proceeding is carried on, or where such person resides or carries on business, in requiring the attendance and testimony of witnesses and the production of books, papers, or other documents. Any such court may issue an order requiring such person to appear before the Attorney General or his designee, there to produce records, if so ordered, or to give testimony touching the matter under investigation. Any failure to obey such order of the court may be punished by such court as a contempt thereof.

All process in any such case may be served in the judicial district in which such person resides or may be found. The Attorney General may make such rules relating to civil investigations as may be necessary or appropriate to implement the provisions of this subsection.

(e) Guidelines by Attorney General

Not later than 6 months after August 23, 1988, the Attorney General, after consultation with the Securities and Exchange Commission, the Secretary of Commerce, the United States Trade Representative, the Secretary of State, and the Secretary of the Treasury, and after obtaining the views of all interested persons through public notice and comment procedures, shall determine to what extent compliance with this section would be enhanced and the business community would be assisted by further clarification of the preceding provisions of this section and may, based on such determination and to the extent necessary and appropriate, issue—

(1) guidelines describing specific types of conduct, associated with common types of export sales arrangements and business contracts, which for purposes of the Department of Justice's present enforcement policy, the Attorney General determines would be in conformance with the preceding provisions of this section; and

(2) general precautionary procedures which domestic concerns may use on a voluntary basis to conform their conduct to the Department of Justice's present enforcement policy regarding the preceding provisions of this section.

The Attorney General shall issue the guidelines and procedures referred to in the preceding sentence in accordance with the provisions of subchapter II of chapter 5 of Title 5 and those guidelines and procedures shall be subject to the provisions of chapter 7 of that title.

(f) **Opinions of Attorney General**

(1) The Attorney General, after consultation with appropriate departments and agencies of the United States and after obtaining the views of all interested persons through public notice and comment procedures, shall establish a procedure to provide responses to specific inquiries by domestic concerns concerning conformance of their conduct with the Department of Justice's present enforcement policy regarding the preceding provisions of this section. The Attorney General shall, within 30 days after receiving such a request, issue an opinion in response to that request. The opinion shall state whether or not certain specified prospective conduct would, for purposes of the Department of Justice's present enforcement policy, violate the preceding provisions of this section. Additional requests for opinions may be filed with the Attorney General regarding other specified prospective conduct that is beyond the scope of conduct specified in previous requests. In any action brought under the applicable provisions of this section, there shall be a rebuttable presumption that conduct, which is specified in a request by a domestic concern and for which the Attorney General has issued an opinion that such conduct is in conformity with the Department of Justice's present enforcement policy, is in compliance with the preceding provisions of this section.

Such a presumption may be rebutted by a preponderance of the evidence. In considering the presumption for purposes of this paragraph, a court shall weigh all relevant factors, including but not limited to whether the information submitted to the Attorney General was accurate and complete and whether it was within the scope of the conduct specified in any request received by the Attorney General. The Attorney General shall establish the procedure required by this paragraph in accordance with the provisions of subchapter II of chapter 5 of Title 5 and that procedure shall be subject to the provisions of chapter 7 of that title.

(2) Any document or other material which is provided to, received by, or prepared in the Department of Justice or any other department or agency of the United States in connection with a request by a domestic concern under the procedure established under paragraph (1), shall be exempt from disclosure under section 552 of Title 5 and shall not, except with the consent of the domestic concern, be made publicly available, regardless of whether the Attorney General response to such a request or the domestic concern withdraws such request before receiving a response.

(3) Any domestic concern who has made a request to the Attorney General under paragraph (1) may withdraw such request prior to the time the Attorney General issues an opinion in response to such request. Any request so withdrawn shall have no force or effect.

(4) The Attorney General shall, to the maximum extent practicable, provide timely guidance concerning the Department of Justice's present enforcement policy with respect to the preceding provisions of this section to potential exporters and small businesses that are unable to obtain specialized counsel on issues pertaining to such provisions. Such guidance shall be limited to responses to requests under paragraph (1) concerning conformity of specified prospective conduct with the Department of Justice's present enforcement policy regarding the preceding provisions of this section and general explanations of compliance responsibilities and of potential liabilities under the preceding provisions of this section.

(g) Penalties

(1) (A) Any domestic concern that is not a natural person and that violates subsection (a) or (i) of this section shall be fined not more than $2,000,000.

(B) Any domestic concern that is not a natural person and that violates subsection (a) or (i) of this section shall be subject to a civil penalty of not more than $10,000 imposed in an action brought by the Attorney General.

(2) (A) Any natural person that is an officer, director, employee, or agent of a domestic concern, or stockholder acting on behalf of such domestic concern, who willfully violates subsection (a) or (i) of this section shall be fined not more than $100,000 or imprisoned not more than 5 years, or both.

(B) Any natural person that is an officer, director, employee, or agent of a domestic concern, or stockholder acting on behalf of such domestic concern, who violates subsection (a) or (i) of this section shall be subject to a civil penalty of not more than $10,000 imposed in an action brought by the Attorney General.

(3) Whenever a fine is imposed under paragraph (2) upon any officer, director, employee, agent, or stockholder of a domestic concern, such fine may not be paid, directly or indirectly, by such domestic concern.

(h) Definitions

For purposes of this section:

(1)   The term "domestic concern" means—

   (A) any individual who is a citizen, national, or resident of the United States; and

   (B) any corporation, partnership, association, joint-stock company, business trust, unincorporated organization, or sole proprietorship which has its principal place of business in the United States, or which is organized under the laws of a State of the United States or a territory, possession, or commonwealth of the United States.

(2)   (A) The term "foreign official" means any officer or employee of a foreign government or any department, agency, or instrumentality thereof, or of a public international organization, or any person acting in an official capacity for or on behalf of any such government or department, agency, or instrumentality, or for or on behalf of any such public international organization.

   (B) For purposes of subparagraph (A), the term "public international organization" means—

     (i)   an organization that has been designated by Executive order pursuant to Section 1 of the International Organizations Immunities Act (22 U.S.C. § 288); or

     (ii) any other international organization that is designated by the President by Executive order for the purposes of this section, effective as of the date of publication of such order in the Federal Register.

(3)   (A) A person's state of mind is "knowing" with respect to conduct, a circumstance, or a result if—

     (i)   such person is aware that such person is engaging in such conduct, that such circumstance exists, or that such result is substantially certain to occur; or

     (ii) such person has a firm belief that such circumstance exists or that such result is substantially certain to occur.

   (B) When knowledge of the existence of a particular circumstance is required for an offense, such knowledge is established if a person is aware of a high probability of the existence of such circumstance, unless the person actually believes that such circumstance does not exist.

(4)   (A) The term "routine governmental action" means only an action which is ordinarily and commonly performed by a foreign official in—

     (i)   obtaining permits, licenses, or other official documents to qualify a person to do business in a foreign country;

     (ii)   processing governmental papers, such as visas and work orders;

     (iii) providing police protection, mail pick-up and delivery, or scheduling inspections associated with contract performance or inspections related to transit of goods across country;

(iv) providing phone service, power and water supply, loading and unloading cargo, or protecting perishable products or commodities from deterioration; or

(v) actions of a similar nature.

(B) The term "routine governmental action" does not include any decision by a foreign official whether, or on what terms, to award new business to or to continue business with a particular party, or any action taken by a foreign official involved in the decision-making process to encourage a decision to award new business to or continue business with a particular party.

(5) The term "interstate commerce" means trade, commerce, transportation, or communication among the several States, or between any foreign country and any State or between any State and any place or ship outside thereof, and such term includes the intrastate use of—

(A) a telephone or other interstate means of communication, or

(B) any other interstate instrumentality.

(i) Alternative Jurisdiction

(1) It shall also be unlawful for any United States person to corruptly do any act outside the United States in furtherance of an offer, payment, promise to pay, or authorization of the payment of any money, or offer, gift, promise to give, or authorization of the giving of anything of value to any of the persons or entities set forth in paragraphs (1), (2), and (3) of subsection (a), for the purposes set forth therein, irrespective of whether such United States person makes use of the mails or any means or instrumentality of interstate commerce in furtherance of such offer, gift, payment, promise, or authorization.

(2) As used in this subsection, a "United States person" means a national of the United States (as defined in section 101 of the Immigration and Nationality Act (8 U.S.C. § 1101)) or any corporation, partnership, association, joint-stock company, business trust, unincorporated organization, or sole proprietorship organized under the laws of the United States or any State, territory, possession, or commonwealth of the United States, or any political subdivision thereof.

§ 78DD-3. PROHIBITED FOREIGN TRADE PRACTICES BY PERSONS OTHER THAN ISSUERS OR DOMESTIC CONCERNS

(a) Prohibition

It shall be unlawful for any person other than an issuer that is subject to section 30A of the Securities Exchange Act of 1934 or a domestic concern, as defined in section 104 of this Act, or for any officer, director, employee, or agent of such person or any stockholder thereof acting on behalf of such person, while in the territory of the United States, corruptly to make use of the mails or any means or instrumentality of interstate commerce or to do any other act in furtherance of an offer, payment, promise to pay, or authorization of the payment of any money, or offer, gift, promise to give, or authorization of the giving of anything of value to

(1) any foreign official for purposes of—

    (A) (i) influencing any act or decision of such foreign official in his official capacity, (ii) inducing such foreign official to do or omit to do any act in violation of the lawful duty of such official, or (iii) securing any improper advantage; or

    (B) inducing such foreign official to use his influence with a foreign government or instrumentality thereof to affect or influence any act or decision of such government or instrumentality,

in order to assist such person in obtaining or retaining business for or with, or directing business to, any person;

(2) any foreign political party or official thereof or any candidate for foreign political office for purposes of—

    (A) (i) influencing any act or decision of such party, official, or candidate in its or his official capacity, (ii) inducing such party, official, or candidate to do or omit to do an act in violation of the lawful duty of such party, official, or candidate, or (iii) securing any improper advantage; or

    (B) inducing such party, official, or candidate to use its or his influence with a foreign government or instrumentality thereof to affect or influence any act or decision of such government or instrumentality,

in order to assist such person in obtaining or retaining business for or with, or directing business to, any person; or

(3) any person, while knowing that all or a portion of such money or thing of value will be offered, given, or promised, directly or indirectly, to any foreign official, to any foreign political party or official thereof, or to any candidate for foreign political office, for purposes of—

    (A) (i) influencing any act or decision of such foreign official, political party, party official, or candidate in his or its official capacity, (ii) inducing such foreign official, political party, party official, or candidate to do or omit to do any act in violation of the lawful duty of such foreign official, political party, party official, or candidate, or (iii) securing any improper advantage; or

    (B) inducing such foreign official, political party, party official, or candidate to use his or its influence with a foreign government or instrumentality thereof to affect or influence any act or decision of such government or instrumentality,

in order to assist such person in obtaining or retaining business for or with, or directing business to, any person.

(b) Exception for routine governmental action

Subsection (a) of this section shall not apply to any facilitating or expediting payment to a foreign official, political party, or party official the purpose of which is to expedite or to secure the performance of a routine governmental action by a foreign official, political party, or party official.

(c) Affirmative defenses

It shall be an affirmative defense to actions under subsection (a) of this section that—

(1)   the payment, gift, offer, or promise of anything of value that was made, was lawful under the written laws and regulations of the foreign official's, political party's, party official's, or candidate's country; or

(2)   the payment, gift, offer, or promise of anything of value that was made, was a reasonable and bona fide expenditure, such as travel and lodging expenses, incurred by or on behalf of a foreign official, party, party official, or candidate and was directly related to—

(A)   the promotion, demonstration, or explanation of products or services; or

(B)   the execution or performance of a contract with a foreign government or agency thereof.

(d) Injunctive relief

(1)   When it appears to the Attorney General that any person to which this section applies, or officer, director, employee, agent, or stockholder thereof, is engaged, or about to engage, in any act or practice constituting a violation of subsection (a) of this section, the Attorney General may, in his discretion, bring a civil action in an appropriate district court of the United States to enjoin such act or practice, and upon a proper showing, a permanent injunction or a temporary restraining order shall be granted without bond.

(2)   For the purpose of any civil investigation which, in the opinion of the Attorney General, is necessary and proper to enforce this section, the Attorney General or his designee are empowered to administer oaths and affirmations, subpoena witnesses, take evidence, and require the production of any books, papers, or other documents which the Attorney General deems relevant or material to such investigation. The attendance of witnesses and the production of documentary evidence may be required from any place in the United States, or any territory, possession, or commonwealth of the United States, at any designated place of hearing.

(3)   In case of contumacy by, or refusal to obey a subpoena issued to, any person, the Attorney General may invoke the aid of any court of the United States within the jurisdiction of which such investigation or proceeding is carried on, or where such person resides or carries on business, in requiring the attendance and testimony of witnesses and the production of books, papers, or other documents. Any such Court may issue an order requiring such person to appear before the Attorney General or his designee, there to produce records, if so ordered, or to give testimony touching the matter

under investigation. Any failure to obey such order of the court may be punished by such court as a contempt thereof.

(4) All process in any such case may be served in the judicial district in which such person resides or may be found. The Attorney General may make such rules relating to civil investigations as may be necessary or appropriate to implement the provisions of this subsection.

(e) Penalties

(1) (A) Any juridical person that violates subsection (a) of this section shall be fined not more than $2,000,000.

(B) Any juridical person that violates subsection (a) of this section shall be subject to a civil penalty of not more than $10,000 imposed in an action brought by the Attorney General,

(2) (A) Any natural person who willfully violates subsection (a) of this section shall be fined not more than $100,000 or imprisoned not more than 5 years, or both.

(B) Any natural person who violates subsection (a) of this section shall be subject to a civil penalty of not more than $10,000 imposed in an action brought by the Attorney General.

(3) Whenever a fine is imposed under paragraph (2) upon any officer, director, employee, agent, or stockholder of a person, such fine may not be paid, directly or indirectly, by such person.

(f) Definitions

For purposes of this section:

(1) The term "person," when referring to an offender, means any natural person other than a national of the United States (as defined in 8 U.S.C. § 1101) or any corporation, partnership, association, joint-stock company, business trust, unincorporated organization, or sole proprietorship organized under the law of a foreign nation or a political subdivision thereof.

(2) (A) The term "foreign official" means any officer or employee of a foreign government or any department, agency, or instrumentality thereof, or of a public international organization, or any person acting in an official capacity for or on behalf of any such government or department, agency, or instrumentality, or for or on behalf of any such public international organization.

(B) For purposes of subparagraph (A), the term "public international organization" means—

(i) an organization that has been designated by Executive Order pursuant to Section 1 of the International Organizations Immunities Act (22 U.S.C. § 288); or

(ii) any other international organization that is designated by the President by Executive order for the purposes of this section, effective as of the date of publication of such order in the Federal Register.

(3) (A) A person's state of mind is "knowing" with respect to conduct, a circumstance, or a result if—

   (i) such person is aware that such person is engaging in such conduct, that such circumstance exists, or that such result is substantially certain to occur; or

   (ii) such person has a firm belief that such circumstance exists or that such result is substantially certain to occur.

   (B) When knowledge of the existence of a particular circumstance is required for an offense, such knowledge is established if a person is aware of a high probability of the existence of such circumstance, unless the person actually believes that such circumstance does not exist.

(4) (A) The term "routine governmental action" means only an action which is ordinarily and commonly performed by a foreign official in—

   (i) obtaining permits, licenses, or other official documents to qualify a person to do business in a foreign country;

   (ii) processing governmental papers, such as visas and work orders;

   (iii) providing police protection, mail pickup and delivery, or scheduling inspections associated with contract performance or inspections related to transit of goods across country;

   (iv) providing phone service, power and water supply, loading and unloading cargo, or protecting perishable products or commodities from deterioration; or

   (v) actions of a similar nature.

   (B) The term "routine governmental action" does not include any decision by a foreign official whether, or on what terms, to award new business to or to continue business with a particular party, or any action taken by a foreign official involved in the decision-making process to encourage a decision to award new business to or continue business with a particular party.

(5) The term "interstate commerce" means trade, commerce, transportation, or communication among the several States, or between any foreign country and any State or between any State and any place or ship outside thereof, and such term includes the intrastate use of—

   (A) a telephone or other interstate means of communication, or

   (B) any other interstate instrumentality.

§ 78FF. PENALTIES

(a) Willful violations; false and misleading statements

Any person who willfully violates any provision of this chapter (other than section 78dd-1 of this title), or any rule or regulation thereunder the violation of which is made unlawful or the observance of which is required under the terms of this chapter, or any person who willfully and knowingly makes, or causes to be made, any statement in any application, report, or document required to be filed under this chapter or any rule or regulation thereunder or any undertaking contained in a registration statement as provided in subsection (d) of section 78o of this title, or by any self-regulatory organization in connection with an application for membership or participation therein or to become associated with a member thereof, which statement was false or misleading with respect to any material fact, shall upon conviction be fined not more than $5,000,000, or imprisoned not more than 20 years, or both, except that when such person is a person other than a natural person, a fine not exceeding $25,000,000 may be imposed; but no person shall be subject to imprisonment under this section for the violation of any rule or regulation if he proves that he had no knowledge of such rule or regulation.

(b) Failure to file information, documents, or reports

Any issuer which fails to file information, documents, or reports required to be filed under subsection (d) of section 78o of this title or any rule or regulation thereunder shall forfeit to the United States the sum of $100 for each and every day such failure to file shall continue. Such forfeiture, which shall be in lieu of any criminal penalty for such failure to file which might be deemed to arise under subsection (a) of this section, shall be payable into the Treasury of the United States and shall be recoverable in a civil suit in the name of the United States.

(c) Violations by issuers, officers, directors, stockholders, employees, or agents of issuers

(1) (A) Any issuer that violates subsection (a) or (g) of section 78dd-1 of this title shall be fined not more than $2,000,000.

(B) Any issuer that violates subsection (a) or (g) of section 78dd-1 of this title shall be subject to a civil penalty of not more than $10,000 imposed in an action brought by the Commission.

(2) (A) Any officer, director, employee, or agent of an issuer, or stockholder acting on behalf of such issuer, who willfully violates subsection (a) or (g) of section 78dd-1 of this title shall be fined not more than $100,000, or imprisoned not more than 5 years, or both.

(B) Any officer, director, employee, or agent of an issuer, or stockholder acting on behalf of such issuer, who violates subsection (a) or (g) of section 78dd-1 of this title shall be subject to a civil penalty of not more than $10,000 imposed in an action brought by the Commission.

(3) Whenever a fine is imposed under paragraph (2) upon any officer, director, employee, agent, or stockholder of an issuer, such fine may not be paid, directly or indirectly, by such issuer.

APPENDIX 2

OECD Convention

Convention on Combating Bribery of Foreign Officials in International Business Transactions[1]

Adopted by the Negotiating Conference on 21 November 1977

PREAMBLE

The Parties,

Considering that bribery is a widespread phenomenon in international business transactions, including trade and investment, which raises serious moral and political concerns, undermines good governance and economic development, and distorts international competitive conditions;

Considering that all countries share a responsibility to combat bribery in international business transactions;

Having regard to the Revised Recommendation on Combating Bribery in International Business Transactions, adopted by the Council of the Organisation for Economic Co-operation and Development (OECD) on 23 May 1977, C(97)123/FINAL, which, *inter alia*, called for effective measures to deter, prevent and combat the bribery of foreign public officials in connection with international business transactions, in particular the prompt criminalization of such bribery in an effective and coordinated manner and in conformity with the agreed common elements set out in that Recommendation and with the jurisdictional and other basic legal principles of each country;

Welcoming other recent developments which further advance international understanding and co-operation in combating bribery of public officials, including actions of the United Nations, the World Bank, the International Monetary Fund, the World Trade Organisation, the Organisation of American States, the Council of Europe and the European Union;

Welcoming the efforts of companies, business organisations and trade unions as well as other non-governmental organisations to combat bribery;

Recognising the role of governments in the prevention of solicitation of bribes from individuals and enterprises in international business transactions;

Recognising that achieving progress in this field requires not only efforts on a national level but also multilateral co-operation, monitoring and follow-up;

Recognising that achieving equivalence among the measures to be taken by the Parties in an essential object and purpose of the Convention, which requires that the Convention be ratified without derogations affecting this equivalence;

---

1. OECD Doc. DAFFE/IME/BR(97)20, *reprinted in* 37 LL.M. 1 (1998).

Have agreed as follows:

ARTICLE 1 – THE OFFICIAL BRIBERY OF FOREIGN PUBLIC OFFICIALS

 1. Each Party shall take such measures as may be necessary to establish that it is a criminal offence under its law for any person intentionally to offer, promise or give any undue pecuniary or other advantage, whether directly or through intermediaries, to a foreign public official, for that official or for a third party, in order that the official act or refrain from acting in relation to the performance of official duties, in order to obtain or retain business or other improper advantage in the conduct of international business.
 2. Each Party shall take any measures necessary to establish that complicity in, including incitement, aiding and abetting, or authorization of an act of bribery of a foreign public official, shall be a criminal offence. Attempt and conspiracy to bribe a foreign public official shall be criminal offences to the same extent as attempt and conspiracy to bribe a public official of that Party.
 3. The offences set out in paragraphs 1 and 2 above are hereinafter referred to as "bribery of a foreign public official."
 4. For the purpose of this Convention:
    a. "foreign public official" means any person holding a legislative, administrative or judicial office of a foreign country, whether appointed or elected; any person exercising a public function for a foreign country, including for a public agency or public enterprise; and any official or agent of a public international organisation;s
    b. "foreign country" includes all levels and subdivisions of government, from national to local;
    c. "act or refrain from acting in relation to the performance of official duties" includes any use of the public official's position, whether or not within the official's authorized competence.

ARTICLE 2 – RESPONSIBILITY OF LEGAL PERSONS

Each Party shall take such measures as may be necessary, in accordance with its legal principles, to establish the liability of legal persons for the bribery of a foreign public official.

ARTICLE 3 – SANCTIONS

 1. The bribery of a foreign public official shall be punishable by effective, proportionate and dissuasive criminal penalties. The range of penalties shall be comparable to that applicable to the bribery of the Party's own public officials and shall, in the case of natural persons, include deprivation of liberty sufficient to enable effective mutual legal assistance and extradition.
 2. In the event that, under the legal system of a Party, criminal responsibility is not applicable to legal persons, that Party shall ensure that legal persons shall be subject to effective, proportionate and dissuasive non-criminal sanctions, including monetary sanctions, for bribery of foreign public officials.
 3. Each Party shall take such measures as may be necessary to provide that the bribe and the proceeds of the bribery of a foreign public official, or property the value of which corresponds to that of such proceeds, are subject to

seizure and confiscation or that monetary sanctions of comparable effect are applicable.

4. Each Party shall consider the imposition of additional civil or administrative sanctions upon a person subject to sanctions for the bribery of a foreign public official.

ARTICLE 4 – JURISDICTION

1. Each Party shall take such measures as may be necessary to establish its jurisdiction over the bribery of a foreign public official when the offence is committed in whole or in part in its territory.
2. Each Party which has jurisdiction to prosecute its nationals for offences committed abroad shall take such measures as may be necessary to establish its jurisdiction to do so in respect of the bribery of a foreign public official, according to the same principles.
3. When more than one Party has jurisdiction over an alleged offence described in this Convention, the Parties involved shall, at the request of one of them, consult with a view to determining the most appropriate jurisdiction for prosecution.
4. Each Party shall review whether its current basis for jurisdiction is effective in the fight against the bribery of foreign public officials and, if it is not, shall take remedial steps.

ARTICLE 5 – ENFORCEMENT

Investigation and prosecution of the bribery of a foreign public official shall be subject to the applicable rules and principles of each Party. They shall not be influenced by considerations of national economic interest, the potential effect upon relations with another State or the identity of the natural or legal persons involved.

ARTICLE 6 – STATUTE OF LIMITATIONS

Any statute of limitations applicable to the offence of bribery of a foreign public official shall allow an adequate period of time for the investigation and prosecution of this offence.

ARTICLE 7 – MONEY LAUNDERING

Each Party which has made bribery of its own public official a predicate offence for the purpose of the application of its money laundering legislation shall do so on the same terms for the bribery of a foreign public official, without regard to the place where the bribery occurred.

ARTICLE 8 – ACCOUNTING

1. In order to combat bribery of foreign public officials effectively, each Party shall take such measures as may be necessary, within the framework of its laws and regulations regarding the maintenance of books and records, financial statement disclosures, and accounting and auditing standards, to prohibit the establishment of off-the-books accounts, the making of off-the-books or inadequately identified transactions, the recording of non-existent expenditures, the entry of liabilities with incorrect identification of their object, as well as the use of false documents, by companies

subject to those laws and regulations, for the purpose of bribing foreign public officials or of hiding such bribery.

2. Each Party shall provide effective, proportionate and dissuasive civil, administrative or criminal penalties for such omission and falsifications in respect of the books, records, accounts and financial statements of such companies.

ARTICLE 9 – MUTUAL LEGAL ASSISTANCE

1. Each Party shall, to the fullest extent possible under its laws and relevant treaties and arrangements, provide prompt and effective legal assistance to another Party for the purpose of criminal investigations and proceedings brought by a Party concerning offenses within the scope of this Convention and for non-criminal proceedings within the scope of this Convention brought by a Party against a legal person. The requested Party shall inform the requesting Party, without delay, of any additional information or documents needed to support the request for assistance and, where requested, of the status and outcome of the request for assistance.

2. Where a Party makes mutual legal assistance conditional upon the existence of dual criminality, dual criminality shall be deemed to exist if the offense for which the assistance is sought is within the scope of this Convention.

3. A Party shall not decline to render mutual legal assistance for criminal matters within the scope of this Convention on the ground of bank secrecy.

ARTICLE 10 – EXTRADITION

1. Bribery of a foreign public official shall be deemed to be included as an extraditable offence under the laws of the Parties and the extradition treaties between them.

2. If a Party which makes extradition conditional on the existence of an extradition treaty receives a request for extradition from another Party with which it has no extradition treaty, it may consider this Convention to be the legal basis for extradition in respect of the offence of bribery of a foreign public official.

3. Each Party shall take any measures necessary to assure either that it can extradite its nationals or that it can prosecute its nationals for the offence of bribery of a foreign public official. A Party which declines to request to extradite a person for bribery of a foreign public official solely on the ground that the person is its national shall submit the case to its competent authorities for the purpose of prosecution.

4. Extradition for bribery of a foreign public official is subject to the conditions set out in the domestic law and applicable treaties and arrangements of each Party. Where a Party makes extradition conditional upon the existence of dual criminality, that condition shall be deemed to be fulfilled if the offence for which extradition is sought is within the scope of Article 1 of this Convention.

ARTICLE 11 – RESPONSIBLE AUTHORITIES

For purposes of Article 4, paragraph 3, on consultation, Article 9, on mutual legal assistance and Article 10, on extradition, each Party shall notify to the Secretary-General of the OECD an authority or authorities responsible for making and receiving requests, which shall serve as channel of communication for these matters for that Party, without prejudice to other arrangements between Parties.

ARTICLE 12 – MONITORING AND FOLLOW-UP

The Parties shall co-operate in carrying out a programme of systematic follow-up to monitor and promote the full implementation of this Convention. Unless otherwise decided by consensus of the Parties, this shall be done in the framework of the OECD Working Group on Bribery in International Business Transactions and according to its terms of reference, or within the framework and terms of reference of any successor to its functions, and Parties shall bear the costs of the programme in accordance with the rules applicable to that body.

ARTICLE 13 – SIGNATURE AND ACCESSION

1. Until its entry into force, this Convention shall be open for signature by OECD members and by non-members which have been invited to become full participants in its Working Group on Bribery in International Business Transactions.

2. Subsequent to its entry into force, this Convention shall be open to accession by any nonsignatory which is a member of the OECD or has become a full participant in the Working Group on Bribery in International Business Transactions or any successor to its functions. For each such nonsignatory, the Convention shall enter into force on the sixtieth day following the date of deposit of its instrument of accession.

ARTICLE 14 – RATIFICATION AND DEPOSITARY

1. This Convention is subject to acceptance, approval or ratification by the Signatories, in accordance with their respective laws.

2. Instruments of acceptance, approval, ratification or accession shall be deposited with the Secretary-General of the OECD, who shall serve as depositary of this Convention.

ARTICLE 15 – ENTRY INTO FORCE

1. This convention shall enter into force on the sixtieth day following the date upon which five of the ten countries which have the ten largest export shares set out in (annexed), and which represent by themselves at least sixty per cent of the combined total exports of those ten countries, have deposited their instruments of acceptance, approval, or ratification. For each signatory depositing its instrument after such entry into force, the Convention shall enter into force on the sixtieth day after deposit of its instrument.

2. If, after 31 December 1998, the Convention has not entered into force under paragraph 1 above, any signatory which has deposited its instrument of acceptance, approval or ratification may declare in writing to the Depositary its readiness to accept entry into force of this Convention under this paragraph 2. The Convention shall enter into force for such a signatory on the sixtieth day following the date upon which such declarations have been deposited by at least two signatories. For each signatory depositing its declaration after such entry into force, the Convention shall enter into force on the sixtieth day following the date of deposit.

ARTICLE 16 – AMENDMENT

Any Party may propose the amendment of this Convention. A proposed amendment shall be submitted to the Depositary which shall communicate it to the other Parties at least sixty days before convening a meeting of the Parties to consider the proposed amendment. An amendment adopted by consensus of the parties, or by such other means as the Parties may determine by consensus, shall enter into force sixty days after the deposit of an instrument of ratification, acceptance or approval by all of the Parties, or in such other circumstances as may be specified by the Parties at the time of adoption of the amendment.

ARTICLE 17 – WITHDRAWAL

A Party may withdraw from this Convention by submitting written notification to the Depositary. Such withdrawal shall be effective one year after the date of the receipt of the notification. After withdrawal, co-operation shall continue between the Parties and the Party which has withdrawn on all requests for assistance or extradition made before the effective date of withdrawal which remain pending.

Concerning Belgium-Luxembourg: Trade statistics for Belgium and Luxembourg are available only on a combined basis for the two countries. For purposes of Article 15, paragraph 1 of the Convention, if either Belgium or Luxembourg deposits its instrument of acceptance, approval or ratification, or if both Belgium and Luxembourg deposit their instruments of acceptance, approval or ratification, it shall be considered that one of the countries which have the ten largest exports shares has deposited its instrument and the joint exports of both countries will be counted towards the 60 percent of combined total exports of those ten countries, which is required for entry into force under this provision.

APPENDIX 3

Bribery Act 2010

CHAPTER 23

CONTENTS

ELIZABETH II   c. 23

Bribery Act 2010

2010 CHAPTER 23

An Act to make provision about offences relating to bribery; and for connected
purposes.   [8th April 2010]

B E IT ENACTED by the Queen's most Excellent Majesty, by and with the advice and
consent of the Lords Spiritual and Temporal, and Commons, in this present
Parliament assembled, and by the authority of the same, as follows: —

General bribery offences

1   Offences of bribing another person

(1)   A person ("P") is guilty of an offence if either of the following cases applies.

(2)   Case 1 is where —
    (a)   P offers, promises or gives a financial or other advantage to another
        person, and
    (b)   P intends the advantage —
        (i)   to induce a person to perform improperly a relevant function or
            activity, or
        (ii)   to reward a person for the improper performance of such a
            function or activity.

(3)   Case 2 is where —
    (a)   P offers, promises or gives a financial or other advantage to another
        person, and
    (b)   P knows or believes that the acceptance of the advantage would itself
        constitute the improper performance of a relevant function or activity.

(4)   In case 1 it does not matter whether the person to whom the advantage is
offered, promised or given is the same person as the person who is to perform,
or has performed, the function or activity concerned.

(5)   In cases 1 and 2 it does not matter whether the advantage is offered, promised or given by P directly or through a third party.

2   Offences relating to being bribed

(1)   A person ("R") is guilty of an offence if any of the following cases applies.

(2)   Case 3 is where R requests, agrees to receive or accepts a financial or other advantage intending that, in consequence, a relevant function or activity should be performed improperly (whether by R or another person).

(3)   Case 4 is where—
   (a)   R requests, agrees to receive or accepts a financial or other advantage, and·
   (b)   the request, agreement or acceptance itself constitutes the improper performance by R of a relevant function or activity.

(4)   Case 5 is where R requests, agrees to receive or accepts a financial or other advantage as a reward for the improper performance (whether by R or another person) of a relevant function or activity.

(5)   Case 6 is where, in anticipation of or in consequence of R requesting, agreeing to receive or accepting a financial or other advantage, a relevant function or activity is performed improperly—
   (a)   by R, or
   (b)   by another person at R's request or with R's assent or acquiescence.

(6)   In cases 3 to 6 it does not matter—
   (a)   whether R requests, agrees to receive or accepts (or is to request, agree to receive or accept) the advantage directly or through a third party,
   (b)   whether the advantage is (or is to be) for the benefit of R or another person.

(7)   In cases 4 to 6 it does not matter whether R knows or believes that the performance of the function or activity is improper.

(8)   In case 6, where a person other than R is performing the function or activity, it also does not matter whether that person knows or believes that the performance of the function or activity is improper.

3   Function or activity to which bribe relates

(1)   For the purposes of this Act a function or activity is a relevant function or activity if—
   (a)   it falls within subsection (2), and
   (b)   meets one or more of conditions A to C.

(2)   The following functions and activities fall within this subsection—
   (a)   any function of a public nature,
   (b)   any activity connected with a business,
   (c)   any activity performed in the course of a person's employment,
   (d)   any activity performed by or on behalf of a body of persons (whether corporate or unincorporate).

(3)   Condition A is that a person performing the function or activity is expected to perform it in good faith.

(4) Condition B is that a person performing the function or activity is expected to perform it impartially.

(5) Condition C is that a person performing the function or activity is in a position of trust by virtue of performing it.

(6) A function or activity is a relevant function or activity even if it —
   (a) has no connection with the United Kingdom, and
   (b) is performed in a country or territory outside the United Kingdom.

(7) In this section "business" includes trade or profession.

4   **Improper performance to which bribe relates**

(1) For the purposes of this Act a relevant function or activity —
   (a) is performed improperly if it is performed in breach of a relevant expectation, and
   (b) is to be treated as being performed improperly if there is a failure to perform the function or activity and that failure is itself a breach of a relevant expectation.

(2) In subsection (1) "relevant expectation" —
   (a) in relation to a function or activity which meets condition A or B, means the expectation mentioned in the condition concerned, and
   (b) in relation to a function or activity which meets condition C, means any expectation as to the manner in which, or the reasons for which, the function or activity will be performed that arises from the position of trust mentioned in that condition.

(3) Anything that a person does (or omits to do) arising from or in connection with that person's past performance of a relevant function or activity is to be treated for the purposes of this Act as being done (or omitted) by that person in the performance of that function or activity.

5   **Expectation test**

(1) For the purposes of sections 3 and 4, the test of what is expected is a test of what a reasonable person in the United Kingdom would expect in relation to the performance of the type of function or activity concerned.

(2) In deciding what such a person would expect in relation to the performance of a function or activity where the performance is not subject to the law of any part of the United Kingdom, any local custom or practice is to be disregarded unless it is permitted or required by the written law applicable to the country or territory concerned.

(3) In subsection (2) "written law" means law contained in —
   (a) any written constitution, or provision made by or under legislation, applicable to the country or territory concerned, or
   (b) any judicial decision which is so applicable and is evidenced in published written sources.

Bribery of foreign public officials

6   Bribery of foreign public officials

(1)   A person ("P") who bribes a foreign public official ("F") is guilty of an offence if P's intention is to influence F in F's capacity as a foreign public official.

(2)   P must also intend to obtain or retain —
    (a)   business, or
    (b)   an advantage in the conduct of business.

(3)   P bribes F if, and only if —
    (a)   directly or through a third party, P offers, promises or gives any financial or other advantage —
        (i)   to F, or
        (ii)   to another person at F's request or with F's assent or acquiescence, and
    (b)   F is neither permitted nor required by the written law applicable to F to be influenced in F's capacity as a foreign public official by the offer, promise or gift.

(4)   References in this section to influencing F in F's capacity as a foreign public official mean influencing F in the performance of F's functions as such an official, which includes —
    (a)   any omission to exercise those functions, and
    (b)   any use of F's position as such an official, even if not within F's authority.

(5)   "Foreign public official" means an individual who —
    (a)   holds a legislative, administrative or judicial position of any kind, whether appointed or elected, of a country or territory outside the United Kingdom (or any subdivision of such a country or territory),
    (b)   exercises a public function —
        (i)   for or on behalf of a country or territory outside the United Kingdom (or any subdivision of such a country or territory), or
        (ii)   for any public agency or public enterprise of that country or territory (or subdivision), or
    (c)   is an official or agent of a public international organisation.

(6)   "Public international organisation" means an organisation whose members are any of the following —
    (a)   countries or territories,
    (b)   governments of countries or territories,
    (c)   other public international organisations,
    (d)   a mixture of any of the above.

(7)   For the purposes of subsection (3)(b), the written law applicable to F is —
    (a)   where the performance of the functions of F which P intends to influence would be subject to the law of any part of the United Kingdom, the law of that part of the United Kingdom,
    (b)   where paragraph (a) does not apply and F is an official or agent of a public international organisation, the applicable written rules of that organisation,

(c)   where paragraphs (a) and (b) do not apply, the law of the country or territory in relation to which F is a foreign public official so far as that law is contained in—

    (i)   any written constitution, or provision made by or under legislation, applicable to the country or territory concerned, or

    (ii)   any judicial decision which is so applicable and is evidenced in published written sources.

(8)   For the purposes of this section, a trade or profession is a business.

Failure of commercial organisations to prevent bribery

7   Failure of commercial organisations to prevent bribery

(1)   A relevant commercial organisation ("C") is guilty of an offence under this section if a person ("A") associated with C bribes another person intending—

    (a)   to obtain or retain business for C, or

    (b)   to obtain or retain an advantage in the conduct of business for C.

(2)   But it is a defence for C to prove that C had in place adequate procedures designed to prevent persons associated with C from undertaking such conduct.

(3)   For the purposes of this section, A bribes another person if, and only if, A—

    (a)   is, or would be, guilty of an offence under section 1 or 6 (whether or not A has been prosecuted for such an offence), or

    (b)   would be guilty of such an offence if section 12(2)(c) and (4) were omitted.

(4)   See section 8 for the meaning of a person associated with C and see section 9 for a duty on the Secretary of State to publish guidance.

(5)   In this section—

"partnership" means—

    (a)   a partnership within the Partnership Act 1890, or

    (b)   a limited partnership registered under the Limited Partnerships Act 1907,

or a firm or entity of a similar character formed under the law of a country or territory outside the United Kingdom,

"relevant commercial organisation" means—

    (a)   a body which is incorporated under the law of any part of the United Kingdom and which carries on a business (whether there or elsewhere),

    (b)   any other body corporate (wherever incorporated) which carries on a business, or part of a business, in any part of the United Kingdom,

    (c)   a partnership which is formed under the law of any part of the United Kingdom and which carries on a business (whether there or elsewhere), or

    (d)   any other partnership (wherever formed) which carries on a business, or part of a business, in any part of the United Kingdom,

and, for the purposes of this section, a trade or profession is a business.

8   Meaning of associated person

(1)   For the purposes of section 7, a person ("A") is associated with C if (disregarding any bribe under consideration) A is a person who performs services for or on behalf of C.

(2)   The capacity in which A performs services for or on behalf of C does not matter.

(3)   Accordingly A may (for example) be C's employee, agent or subsidiary.

(4)   Whether or not A is a person who performs services for or on behalf of C is to be determined by reference to all the relevant circumstances and not merely by reference to the nature of the relationship between A and C.

(5)   But if A is an employee of C, it is to be presumed unless the contrary is shown that A is a person who performs services for or on behalf of C.

9   Guidance about commercial organisations preventing bribery

(1)   The Secretary of State must publish guidance about procedures that relevant commercial organisations can put in place to prevent persons associated with them from bribing as mentioned in section 7(1).

(2)   The Secretary of State may, from time to time, publish revisions to guidance under this section or revised guidance.

(3)   The Secretary of State must consult the Scottish Ministers before publishing anything under this section.

(4)   Publication under this section is to be in such manner as the Secretary of State considers appropriate.

(5)   Expressions used in this section have the same meaning as in section 7.

Prosecution and penalties

10   Consent to prosecution

(1)   No proceedings for an offence under this Act may be instituted in England and Wales except by or with the consent of —
    (a)   the Director of Public Prosecutions,
    (b)   the Director of the Serious Fraud Office, or
    (c)   the Director of Revenue and Customs Prosecutions.

(2)   No proceedings for an offence under this Act may be instituted in Northern Ireland except by or with the consent of —
    (a)   the Director of Public Prosecutions for Northern Ireland, or
    (b)   the Director of the Serious Fraud Office.

(3)   No proceedings for an offence under this Act may be instituted in England and Wales or Northern Ireland by a person —
    (a)   who is acting —
        (i)   under the direction or instruction of the Director of Public Prosecutions, the Director of the Serious Fraud Office or the Director of Revenue and Customs Prosecutions, or
        (ii)   on behalf of such a Director, or

(b)   to whom such a function has been assigned by such a Director,

except with the consent of the Director concerned to the institution of the proceedings.

(4)   The Director of Public Prosecutions, the Director of the Serious Fraud Office and the Director of Revenue and Customs Prosecutions must exercise personally any function under subsection (1), (2) or (3) of giving consent.

(5)   The only exception is if —

(a)   the Director concerned is unavailable, and

(b)   there is another person who is designated in writing by the Director acting personally as the person who is authorised to exercise any such function when the Director is unavailable.

(6)   In that case, the other person may exercise the function but must do so personally.

(7)   Subsections (4) to (6) apply instead of any other provisions which would otherwise have enabled any function of the Director of Public Prosecutions, the Director of the Serious Fraud Office or the Director of Revenue and Customs Prosecutions under subsection (1), (2) or (3) of giving consent to be exercised by a person other than the Director concerned.

(8)   No proceedings for an offence under this Act may be instituted in Northern Ireland by virtue of section 36 of the Justice (Northern Ireland) Act 2002 (delegation of the functions of the Director of Public Prosecutions for Northern Ireland to persons other than the Deputy Director) except with the consent of the Director of Public Prosecutions for Northern Ireland to the institution of the proceedings.

(9)   The Director of Public Prosecutions for Northern Ireland must exercise personally any function under subsection (2) or (8) of giving consent unless the function is exercised personally by the Deputy Director of Public Prosecutions for Northern Ireland by virtue of section 30(4) or (7) of the Act of 2002 (powers of Deputy Director to exercise functions of Director).

(10)   Subsection (9) applies instead of section 36 of the Act of 2002 in relation to the functions of the Director of Public Prosecutions for Northern Ireland and the Deputy Director of Public Prosecutions for Northern Ireland under, or (as the case may be) by virtue of, subsections (2) and (8) above of giving consent.

11   Penalties

(1)   An individual guilty of an offence under section 1, 2 or 6 is liable —

(a)   on summary conviction, to imprisonment for a term not exceeding 12 months, or to a fine not exceeding the statutory maximum, or to both,

(b)   on conviction on indictment, to imprisonment for a term not exceeding 10 years, or to a fine, or to both.

(2)   Any other person guilty of an offence under section 1, 2 or 6 is liable —

(a)   on summary conviction, to a fine not exceeding the statutory maximum,

(b)   on conviction on indictment, to a fine.

(3)   A person guilty of an offence under section 7 is liable on conviction on indictment to a fine.

(4) The reference in subsection (1)(a) to 12 months is to be read —

    (a) in its application to England and Wales in relation to an offence committed before the commencement of section 154(1) of the Criminal Justice Act 2003, and

    (b) in its application to Northern Ireland,

as a reference to 6 months.

Other provisions about offences

12   Offences under this Act: territorial application

(1) An offence is committed under section 1, 2 or 6 in England and Wales, Scotland or Northern Ireland if any act or omission which forms part of the offence takes place in that part of the United Kingdom.

(2) Subsection (3) applies if —

    (a) no act or omission which forms part of an offence under section 1, 2 or 6 takes place in the United Kingdom,

    (b) a person's acts or omissions done or made outside the United Kingdom would form part of such an offence if done or made in the United Kingdom, and

    (c) that person has a close connection with the United Kingdom.

(3) In such a case —

    (a) the acts or omissions form part of the offence referred to in subsection (2)(a), and

    (b) proceedings for the offence may be taken at any place in the United Kingdom.

(4) For the purposes of subsection (2)(c) a person has a close connection with the United Kingdom if, and only if, the person was one of the following at the time the acts or omissions concerned were done or made —

    (a) a British citizen,

    (b) a British overseas territories citizen,

    (c) a British National (Overseas),

    (d) a British Overseas citizen,

    (e) a person who under the British Nationality Act 1981 was a British subject,

    (f) a British protected person within the meaning of that Act,

    (g) an individual ordinarily resident in the United Kingdom,

    (h) a body incorporated under the law of any part of the United Kingdom,

    (i) a Scottish partnership.

(5) An offence is committed under section 7 irrespective of whether the acts or omissions which form part of the offence take place in the United Kingdom or elsewhere.

(6) Where no act or omission which forms part of an offence under section 7 takes place in the United Kingdom, proceedings for the offence may be taken at any place in the United Kingdom.

(7) Subsection (8) applies if, by virtue of this section, proceedings for an offence are to be taken in Scotland against a person.

(8) Such proceedings may be taken —

    (a) in any sheriff court district in which the person is apprehended or in custody, or

    (b) in such sheriff court district as the Lord Advocate may determine.

(9) In subsection (8) "sheriff court district" is to be read in accordance with section 307(1) of the Criminal Procedure (Scotland) Act 1995.

13   Defence for certain bribery offences etc.

(1) It is a defence for a person charged with a relevant bribery offence to prove that the person's conduct was necessary for —

    (a) the proper exercise of any function of an intelligence service, or

    (b) the proper exercise of any function of the armed forces when engaged on active service.

(2) The head of each intelligence service must ensure that the service has in place arrangements designed to ensure that any conduct of a member of the service which would otherwise be a relevant bribery offence is necessary for a purpose falling within subsection (1)(a).

(3) The Defence Council must ensure that the armed forces have in place arrangements designed to ensure that any conduct of —

    (a) a member of the armed forces who is engaged on active service, or

    (b) a civilian subject to service discipline when working in support of any person falling within paragraph (a),

which would otherwise be a relevant bribery offence is necessary for a purpose falling within subsection (1)(b).

(4) The arrangements which are in place by virtue of subsection (2) or (3) must be arrangements which the Secretary of State considers to be satisfactory.

(5) For the purposes of this section, the circumstances in which a person's conduct is necessary for a purpose falling within subsection (1)(a) or (b) are to be treated as including any circumstances in which the person's conduct —

    (a) would otherwise be an offence under section 2, and

    (b) involves conduct by another person which, but for subsection (1)(a) or (b), would be an offence under section 1.

(6) In this section —

"active service" means service in —

    (a) an action or operation against an enemy,

    (b) an operation outside the British Islands for the protection of life or property, or

    (c) the military occupation of a foreign country or territory,

"armed forces" means Her Majesty's forces (within the meaning of the Armed Forces Act 2006),

"civilian subject to service discipline" and "enemy" have the same meaning as in the Act of 2006,

"GCHQ" has the meaning given by section 3(3) of the Intelligence Services Act 1994,

"head" means —

    (a) in relation to the Security Service, the Director General of the Security Service,

(b)   in relation to the Secret Intelligence Service, the Chief of the Secret Intelligence Service, and

(c)   in relation to GCHQ, the Director of GCHQ,

"intelligence service" means the Security Service, the Secret Intelligence Service or GCHQ,

"relevant bribery offence" means—

(a)   an offence under section 1 which would not also be an offence under section 6,

(b)   an offence under section 2,

(c)   an offence committed by aiding, abetting, counselling or procuring the commission of an offence falling within paragraph (a) or (b),

(d)   an offence of attempting or conspiring to commit, or of inciting the commission of, an offence falling within paragraph (a) or (b), or

(e)   an offence under Part 2 of the Serious Crime Act 2007 (encouraging or assisting crime) in relation to an offence falling within paragraph (a) or (b).

14   Offences under sections 1, 2 and 6 by bodies corporate etc.

(1)   This section applies if an offence under section 1, 2 or 6 is committed by a body corporate or a Scottish partnership.

(2)   If the offence is proved to have been committed with the consent or connivance of—

(a)   a senior officer of the body corporate or Scottish partnership, or

(b)   a person purporting to act in such a capacity,

the senior officer or person (as well as the body corporate or partnership) is guilty of the offence and liable to be proceeded against and punished accordingly.

(3)   But subsection (2) does not apply, in the case of an offence which is committed under section 1, 2 or 6 by virtue of section 12(2) to (4), to a senior officer or person purporting to act in such a capacity unless the senior officer or person has a close connection with the United Kingdom (within the meaning given by section 12(4)).

(4)   In this section—

"director", in relation to a body corporate whose affairs are managed by its members, means a member of the body corporate,

"senior officer" means—

(a)   in relation to a body corporate, a director, manager, secretary or other similar officer of the body corporate, and

(b)   in relation to a Scottish partnership, a partner in the partnership.

15   Offences under section 7 by partnerships

(1)   Proceedings for an offence under section 7 alleged to have been committed by a partnership must be brought in the name of the partnership (and not in that of any of the partners).

(2)   For the purposes of such proceedings—

    (a)   rules of court relating to the service of documents have effect as if the partnership were a body corporate, and

    (b)   the following provisions apply as they apply in relation to a body corporate—

        (i)   section 33 of the Criminal Justice Act 1925 and Schedule 3 to the Magistrates' Courts Act 1980,

       (ii)   section 18 of the Criminal Justice Act (Northern Ireland) 1945 (c. 15 (N.I.)) and Schedule 4 to the Magistrates' Courts (Northern Ireland) Order 1981 (S.I. 1981/1675 (N.I.26)),

     (iii)   section 70 of the Criminal Procedure (Scotland) Act 1995.

(3)   A fine imposed on the partnership on its conviction for an offence under section 7 is to be paid out of the partnership assets.

(4)   In this section "partnership" has the same meaning as in section 7.

Supplementary and final provisions

16   Application to Crown

This Act applies to individuals in the public service of the Crown as it applies to other individuals.

17   Consequential provision

(1)   The following common law offences are abolished—

    (a)   the offences under the law of England and Wales and Northern Ireland of bribery and embracery,

    (b)   the offences under the law of Scotland of bribery and accepting a bribe.

(2)   Schedule 1 (which contains consequential amendments) has effect.

(3)   Schedule 2 (which contains repeals and revocations) has effect.

(4)   The relevant national authority may by order make such supplementary, incidental or consequential provision as the relevant national authority considers appropriate for the purposes of this Act or in consequence of this Act.

(5)   The power to make an order under this section—

    (a)   is exercisable by statutory instrument,

    (b)   includes power to make transitional, transitory or saving provision,

    (c)   may, in particular, be exercised by amending, repealing, revoking or otherwise modifying any provision made by or under an enactment (including any Act passed in the same Session as this Act).

(6)   Subject to subsection (7), a statutory instrument containing an order of the Secretary of State under this section may not be made unless a draft of the instrument has been laid before, and approved by a resolution of, each House of Parliament.

(7)   A statutory instrument containing an order of the Secretary of State under this section which does not amend or repeal a provision of a public general Act or of devolved legislation is subject to annulment in pursuance of a resolution of either House of Parliament.

(8) Subject to subsection (9), a statutory instrument containing an order of the Scottish Ministers under this section may not be made unless a draft of the instrument has been laid before, and approved by a resolution of, the Scottish Parliament.

(9) A statutory instrument containing an order of the Scottish Ministers under this section which does not amend or repeal a provision of an Act of the Scottish Parliament or of a public general Act is subject to annulment in pursuance of a resolution of the Scottish Parliament.

(10) In this section—

"devolved legislation" means an Act of the Scottish Parliament, a Measure of the National Assembly for Wales or an Act of the Northern Ireland Assembly,

"enactment" includes an Act of the Scottish Parliament and Northern Ireland legislation,

"relevant national authority" means—

(a) in the case of provision which would be within the legislative competence of the Scottish Parliament if it were contained in an Act of that Parliament, the Scottish Ministers, and

(b) in any other case, the Secretary of State.

18   Extent

(1) Subject as follows, this Act extends to England and Wales, Scotland and Northern Ireland.

(2) Subject to subsections (3) to (5), any amendment, repeal or revocation made by Schedule 1 or 2 has the same extent as the provision amended, repealed or revoked.

(3) The amendment of, and repeals in, the Armed Forces Act 2006 do not extend to the Channel Islands.

(4) The amendments of the International Criminal Court Act 2001 extend to England and Wales and Northern Ireland only.

(5) Subsection (2) does not apply to the repeal in the Civil Aviation Act 1982.

19   Commencement and transitional provision etc.

(1) Subject to subsection (2), this Act comes into force on such day as the Secretary of State may by order made by statutory instrument appoint.

(2) Sections 16, 17(4) to (10) and 18, this section (other than subsections (5) to (7)) and section 20 come into force on the day on which this Act is passed.

(3) An order under subsection (1) may—

(a) appoint different days for different purposes,

(b) make such transitional, transitory or saving provision as the Secretary of State considers appropriate in connection with the coming into force of any provision of this Act.

(4) The Secretary of State must consult the Scottish Ministers before making an order under this section in connection with any provision of this Act which would be within the legislative competence of the Scottish Parliament if it were contained in an Act of that Parliament.

(5)   This Act does not affect any liability, investigation, legal proceeding or penalty for or in respect of —

    (a)   a common law offence mentioned in subsection (1) of section 17 which is committed wholly or partly before the coming into force of that subsection in relation to such an offence, or

    (b)   an offence under the Public Bodies Corrupt Practices Act 1889 or the Prevention of Corruption Act 1906 committed wholly or partly before the coming into force of the repeal of the Act by Schedule 2 to this Act.

(6)   For the purposes of subsection (5) an offence is partly committed before a particular time if any act or omission which forms part of the offence takes place before that time.

(7)   Subsections (5) and (6) are without prejudice to section 16 of the Interpretation Act 1978 (general savings on repeal).

20   Short title

This Act may be cited as the Bribery Act 2010.

SCHEDULES

SCHEDULE 1

Section 17(2)

CONSEQUENTIAL AMENDMENTS

Ministry of Defence Police Act 1987 (c. 4)

1   In section 2(3)(ba) of the Ministry of Defence Police Act 1987 (jurisdiction of members of Ministry of Defence Police Force) for "Prevention of Corruption Acts 1889 to 1916" substitute "Bribery Act 2010".

Criminal Justice Act 1987 (c. 38)

2   In section 2A of the Criminal Justice Act 1987 (Director of SFO's pre-investigation powers in relation to bribery and corruption: foreign officers etc.) for subsections (5) and (6) substitute −

"(5)   This section applies to any conduct −
   (a)   which, as a result of section 3(6) of the Bribery Act 2010, constitutes an offence under section 1 or 2 of that Act under the law of England and Wales or Northern Ireland, or
   (b)   which constitutes an offence under section 6 of that Act under the law of England and Wales or Northern Ireland."

International Criminal Court Act 2001 (c. 17)

3   The International Criminal Court Act 2001 is amended as follows.

4   In section 54(3) (offences in relation to the ICC: England and Wales) −
   (a)   in paragraph (b) for "or" substitute ", an offence under the Bribery Act 2010 or (as the case may be) an offence", and
   (b)   in paragraph (c) after "common law" insert "or (as the case may be) under the Bribery Act 2010".

5   In section 61(3)(b) (offences in relation to the ICC: Northern Ireland) after "common law" insert "or (as the case may be) under the Bribery Act 2010".

International Criminal Court (Scotland) Act 2001 (asp 13)

6   In section 4(2) of the International Criminal Court (Scotland) Act 2001 (offences in relation to the ICC) −
   (a)   in paragraph (b) after "common law" insert "or (as the case may be) under the Bribery Act 2010", and
   (b)   in paragraph (c) for "section 1 of the Prevention of Corruption Act 1906 (c.34) or at common law" substitute "the Bribery Act 2010".

Serious Organised Crime and Police Act 2005 (c. 15)

7   The Serious Organised Crime and Police Act 2005 is amended as follows.

8   In section 61(1) (offences in respect of which investigatory powers apply) for
        paragraph (h) substitute—
              "(h)   any offence under the Bribery Act 2010."

9   In section 76(3) (financial reporting orders: making) for paragraphs (d) to (f)
        substitute—
              "(da)   an offence under any of the following provisions of the
                       Bribery Act 2010—
                            section 1 (offences of bribing another person),
                            section 2 (offences relating to being bribed),
                            section 6 (bribery of foreign public officials),".

10   In section 77(3) (financial reporting orders: making in Scotland) after
        paragraph (b) insert—
              "(c)   an offence under section 1, 2 or 6 of the Bribery Act 2010."

Armed Forces Act 2006 (c. 52)

11   In Schedule 2 to the Armed Forces Act 2006 (which lists serious offences the
        possible commission of which, if suspected, must be referred to a service
        police force), in paragraph 12, at the end insert—
              "(aw)   an offence under section 1, 2 or 6 of the Bribery Act
                       2010."

Serious Crime Act 2007 (c. 27)

12   The Serious Crime Act 2007 is amended as follows.

13   (1) Section 53 of that Act (certain extra-territorial offences to be prosecuted only
        by, or with the consent of, the Attorney General or the Advocate General for
        Northern Ireland) is amended as follows.

     (2) The existing words in that section become the first subsection of the section.

     (3) After that subsection insert—

              "(2)   Subsection (1) does not apply to an offence under this Part to which
                      section 10 of the Bribery Act 2010 applies by virtue of section 54(1)
                      and (2) below (encouraging or assisting bribery)."

14   (1) Schedule 1 to that Act (list of serious offences) is amended as follows.

     (2) For paragraph 9 and the heading before it (corruption and bribery: England
        and Wales) substitute—

        "Bribery

              9   An offence under any of the following provisions of the Bribery
                       Act 2010—
                            (a)   section 1 (offences of bribing another person);
                            (b)   section 2 (offences relating to being bribed);
                            (c)   section 6 (bribery of foreign public officials)."

(3) For paragraph 25 and the heading before it (corruption and bribery: Northern Ireland) substitute —

"*Bribery*

25   An offence under any of the following provisions of the Bribery Act 2010 —
   (a)   section 1 (offences of bribing another person);
   (b)   section 2 (offences relating to being bribed);
   (c)   section 6 (bribery of foreign public officials)."

SCHEDULE 2   Section 17(3)

REPEALS AND REVOCATIONS

Short title and chapter	*Extent of repeal or revocation*
Public Bodies Corrupt Practices Act 1889 (c. 69)	The whole Act.
Prevention of Corruption Act 1906 (c. 34)	The whole Act.
Prevention of Corruption Act 1916 (c. 64)	The whole Act.
Criminal Justice Act (Northern Ireland) 1945 (c. 15 (N.I.))	Section 22.
Electoral Law Act (Northern Ireland) 1962 (c. 14 (N.I.))	Section 112(3).
Increase of Fines Act (Northern Ireland) 1967 (c. 29 (N.I.))	Section 1(8)(a) and (b).
Criminal Justice (Miscellaneous Provisions) Act (Northern Ireland) 1968 (c. 28 (N.I.))	In Schedule 2, the entry in the table relating to the Prevention of Corruption Act 1906.
Local Government Act (Northern Ireland) 1972 (c. 9 (N.I.))	In Schedule 8, paragraphs 1 and 3.
Civil Aviation Act 1982 (c. 16)	Section 19(1).
Representation of the People Act 1983 (c. 2)	In section 165(1), paragraph (b) and the word "or" immediately before it.
Housing Associations Act 1985 (c. 69)	In Schedule 6, paragraph 1(2).
Criminal Justice Act 1988 (c. 33)	Section 47.
Criminal Justice (Evidence etc.) (Northern Ireland) Order 1988 (S.I. 1988/1847 (N.I.17))	Article 14.
Enterprise and New Towns (Scotland) Act 1990 (c. 35)	In Schedule 1, paragraph 2.
Scotland Act 1998 (c. 46)	Section 43.

Short title and chapter	Extent of repeal or revocation
Anti-terrorism, Crime and Security Act 2001 (c. 24)	Sections 108 to 110.
Criminal Justice (Scotland) Act 2003 (asp 7)	Sections 68 and 69.
Government of Wales Act 2006 (c. 32)	Section 44.
Armed Forces Act 2006 (c. 52)	In Schedule 2, paragraph 12(l) and (m).
Local Government and Public Involvement in Health Act 2007 (c. 28)	Section 217(1)(a). Section 244(4). In Schedule 14, paragraph 1.
Housing and Regeneration Act 2008 (c. 17)	In Schedule 1, paragraph 16.

Printed in the UK by The Stationery Office Limited under the authority and superintendence of Carol Tullo, Controller of Her Majesty's Stationery Office and Queen's Printer of Acts of Parliament

4/2010   445945   19585

These notes refer to the Bribery Act 2010 (c.23)

BRIBERY ACT 2010

EXPLANATORY NOTES

INTRODUCTION

1.   These explanatory notes relate to the Bribery Act 2010 (c. 23) which received Royal Assent on 8 April 2010. They have been prepared by the Ministry of Justice in order to assist the reader in understanding the Act. They do not form part of the Act and have not been endorsed by Parliament.

2.   The notes need to be read in conjunction with the Act. They are not, and are not meant to be, a comprehensive description of the Act. So where a section or part of a section does not seem to require explanation or comment, none is given.

SUMMARY

3.   The purpose of the Act is to reform the criminal law of bribery to provide for a new consolidated scheme of bribery offences to cover bribery both in the United Kingdom (UK) and abroad.

4.   The Act replaces the offences at common law and under the Public Bodies Corrupt Practices Act 1889, the Prevention of Corruption Act 1906 and the Prevention of Corruption Act 1916 (known collectively as the Prevention of Corruption Acts 1889 to 1916 and which will be repealed: see Schedule 2) with two general offences. The first covers the offering, promising or giving of an advantage (broadly, offences of bribing another person). The second deals with the requesting, agreeing to receive or accepting of an advantage (broadly, offences of being bribed). The formulation of these two offences abandons the agent/principal relationship on which the previous law was based in favour of a model based on an intention to induce improper conduct. The Act also creates a discrete offence of bribery of a foreign public official and a new offence where a commercial organisation fails to prevent bribery.

5.   The other main provisions of the Act include:

    •   replacing the requirement for the Attorney General's consent to prosecute a bribery offence with a requirement that the offences in the Act may only be instituted by, or with the consent of, the Director of the relevant prosecuting authority.

    •   a maximum penalty of 10 years imprisonment for all the offences, except the offence relating to commercial organisations, which will carry an unlimited fine;

    •   extra-territorial jurisdiction to prosecute bribery committed abroad by persons ordinarily resident in the UK as well as UK nationals and UK corporate bodies;

    •   a defence for conduct that would constitute a bribery offence where the conduct was necessary for the proper exercise of any function of the intelligence services or the armed forces engaged on active service.

BACKGROUND

6.   The reform of the law on bribery dates back to the Nolan Committee's *Report on Standards in Public Life* in 1995 (Cm 2850I), which was set up in response to concerns

These notes refer to the Bribery Act 2010 (c.23)

about unethical conduct by those in public office, and its suggestion that the Law Commission might usefully take forward the consolidation of the statute law on bribery. The Law Commission first made proposals for reform of bribery in a 1998 report (*Legislating the Criminal Code: Corruption*, Report No. 248).

7. The Government then set up a working group of stakeholders which met over the period 1998-2000, and this was followed in June 2000 by a Government White Paper on corruption (*Raising Standards and Upholding Integrity: the prevention of Corruption* Cm 4759). This was positively received and led to the publication of a draft Corruption Bill in 2003 (*Corruption Draft Legislation* Cm 5777). That draft Bill was then subjected to pre-legislative scrutiny by a Joint Committee of Parliament which reported in July 2003 (*Joint Committee on the Draft Corruption Bill Session 2002-03 Report and Evidence* HL 157, HC 705). The draft Bill failed to win broad support, in particular the Joint Committee was critical of the retention of the agent/principal relationship as the basis for the offence.

8. The Government responded to the Joint Committee's report in December 2003 (*The Government Reply to the Report from the Joint Committee on the Draft Corruption Bill* Session 2002-03 HL 157, HC 705, Cm 6068). In its response, the Government accepted the Report's recommendations in part but expressed reservations about the suggestions made by the Committee in relation to how the offences should be structured given its rejection of the principal/agent model. A Government consultation exercise, *Bribery: Reform of the Prevention of Corruption Acts and SFO powers in cases of bribery of foreign officials*, followed in 2005. The Government concluded that, although there remained support for reform, there was no clear consensus on the form it should take. It was therefore decided to refer the matter back to the Law Commission for a further review.

9. The Law Commission's terms of reference were to consider the full range of options for consolidating and reforming the law on bribery. The Law Commission issued a consultation paper, *Reforming Bribery* (Consultation Paper No. 185), in October 2007. The Law Commission published its report *Reforming Bribery* (Report No. 313) on 20 November 2008.

10. The Government presented a draft Bribery Bill (Cm 7570) to Parliament on 25 March 2009 which built on the proposals in the Law Commission's report. A Joint Committee of Parliament was established to undertake pre-legislative scrutiny of the draft Bill. It reported on 28 July 2009 (*Joint Committee on the Draft Bribery Bill, First Report, Session 2008-09*, HL115, HC430 – I & II). The Government responded to the Joint Committee's report on 20 November 2009 (*Government Response to the conclusions and recommendations of the Joint Committee Report on the Draft Bribery Bill*, Cm7748).

TERRITORIAL EXTENT

11. Section 18 sets out the territorial extent of the Act. Its main substantive provisions extend throughout the UK.

Territorial application: Scotland

12. A legislative consent motion was agreed by the Scottish Parliament on 11 February 2010 under the Sewel Convention. The Convention was triggered as the Act makes provision concerning the criminal law of Scotland in relation to bribery. The Sewel Convention provides that Westminster will not normally legislate with regard to devolved matters in Scotland without the consent of the Scottish Parliament.

These notes refer to the Bribery Act 2010 (c.23)

Territorial application: Wales

13.   The Act applies to Wales as it does to the rest of the UK. It does not change the position as regards the National Assembly for Wales nor does it affect the powers of the Welsh Ministers.

Territorial application: Northern Ireland

14.   The Act applies to Northern Ireland as it does to the rest of the UK. It does not change the position as regards the Northern Ireland Assembly.

COMMENTARY ON SECTIONS

Section 1: Offences of bribing another person

15.   This section defines the offence of bribery as it applies to the person who offers, promises or gives a financial or other advantage to another. That person is referred to in the section as P. The meaning of "financial or other advantage" is left to be determined as a matter of common sense by the tribunal of fact. Section 1 distinguishes two cases: Case 1 (*subsection (2)*) and Case 2 (*subsection (3)*).

16.   Case 1 concerns cases in which the advantage is intended to bring about an improper performance by another person of a relevant function or activity, or to reward such improper performance. The nature of a "relevant function or activity" is addressed in section 3. The nature of "improper performance" is defined in section 4.

17.   It is sufficient for the purposes of the offence that P intended to induce or reward impropriety in relation to a function or activity falling within section 3(2) to (5). It is not necessary that the person to whom the advantage is offered, promised or given be the same person as the person who is to engage in the improper performance of an activity or function, or who has already done so (*subsection (4)*).

18.   Case 2 concerns cases in which P knows or believes that the acceptance of the advantage offered, promised or given in itself constitutes the improper performance of a function or activity as defined in section 3.

19.   *Subsection (5)* makes it clear that, in Cases 1 and 2, the advantage can be offered, promised or given by P directly or through someone else.

Section 2: Offences relating to being bribed

20.   This section defines the offence of bribery as it applies to the recipient or potential recipient of the bribe, who is called R. It distinguishes four cases, namely Case 3 to Case 6.

21.   In Cases 3, 4 and 5 there is a requirement that R "requests, agrees to receive or accepts" an advantage, whether or not R actually receives it. This requirement must then be linked with the "improper performance" of a relevant function or activity. As with section 1, the nature of this function or activity is addressed in section 3, and "improper performance" is defined in section 4.

22.   The link between the request, agreement to receive or acceptance of an advantage and improper performance may take three forms:

   •   R may intend improper performance to follow as a consequence of the request, agreement to receive or acceptance of the advantage (Case 3, in *subsection (2)*);

   •   requesting, agreeing to receive or accepting the advantage may itself amount to improper performance of the relevant function or activity (Case 4, in *subsection (3)*);

- alternatively, the advantage may be a reward for performing the function or activity improperly (Case 5, in *subsection (4)*).

23. In Cases 3 and 5, it does not matter whether the improper performance is by R or by another person. In Case 4, it must be R's requesting, agreeing to receive or acceptance of the advantage which amounts to improper performance, subject to *subsection (6)*.

24. In Case 6 (*subsection (5)*) what is required is improper performance by R (or another person, where R requests it, assents to or acquiesces in it). This performance must be in anticipation or in consequence of a request, agreement to receive or acceptance of an advantage.

25. *Subsection (6)* is concerned with the role of R in requesting, agreeing to receive or accepting advantages, or in benefiting from them, in Cases 3 to 6. First, this subsection makes it clear that in Cases 3 to 6 it does not matter whether it is R, or someone else through whom R acts, who requests, agrees to receive or accepts the advantage (*subsection (6)(a)*). Secondly, *subsection (6)* indicates that the advantage can be for the benefit of R, or of another person (*subsection (6)(b)*).

26. *Subsection (7)* makes it clear that in Cases 4 to 6, it is immaterial whether R knows or believes that the performance of the function is improper. Additionally, by *subsection (8)*, in Case 6 where the function or activity is performed by another person, it is immaterial whether that person knew or believed that the performance of the function is improper.

Section 3: Function or activity to which bribe relates

27. This section defines the fields within which bribery can take place, in other words the types of function or activity that can be improperly performed for the purposes of sections 1 and 2. The term "relevant function or activity" is used for this purpose.

28. The purpose of the section is to ensure that the law of bribery applies equally to public and to selected private functions without discriminating between the two. Accordingly the functions or activities in question include all functions of a public nature and all activities connected with a business, trade or profession. The phrase "functions of a public nature" is the same phrase as is used in the definition of "public authority" in section 6(3)(b) of the Human Rights Act 1998 but it is not limited in the way it is in that Act. In addition, the functions or activities include all activities performed either in the course of employment or on behalf of any body of persons: these two categories straddle the public/private divide.

29. Not every defective performance of one of these functions for reward or in the hope of advantage engages the law of bribery. *Subsections (3) to (5)* make clear that there must be an expectation that the functions be carried out in good faith (condition A), or impartially (condition B), or the person performing it must be in a position of trust (condition C).

30. *Subsection (6)* provides that the functions or activities in question may be carried out either in the UK or abroad, and need have no connection with the UK. This preserves the effect of section 108(1) and (2) of the Anti-terrorism, Crime and Security Act 2001 (which is repealed by the Act).

Section 4: Improper performance to which bribe relates

31. Section 4 defines "improper performance" as performance which breaches a relevant expectation, as mentioned in condition A or B (*subsections (3) and (4)* of section 3 respectively) or any expectation as to the manner in which, or reasons for which, a function or activity satisfying condition C (*subsection (5)* of section 3) will be performed. *Subsection (1)(b)* states that an omission can in some circumstances amount to improper "performance".

These notes refer to the Bribery Act 2010 (c.23)

32.   *Subsection (3)* addresses the case where R is no longer engaged in a given function or activity but still carries out acts related to his or her former function or activity. These acts are treated as done in performance of the function or activity in question.

Section 5: Expectation test

33.   Section 5 provides that when deciding what is expected of a person performing a function or activity for the purposes of sections 3 and 4, the test is what a reasonable person in the UK would expect of a person performing the relevant function or activity. *Subsection (2)* makes it clear that in deciding what a reasonable person in the UK would expect in relation to functions or activities the performance of which is not subject to UK laws, local practice and custom must not be taken into account unless such practice or custom is permitted or required by written law. *Subsection (3)* defines what is meant by "written law" for the purposes of this section.

Section 6: Bribery of foreign public officials

34.   This section creates a separate offence of bribery of a foreign public official. This offence closely follows the requirements of the Organisation for Economic Cooperation and Development (OECD) *Convention on Combating Bribery of Foreign Public Officials in International Business Transactions* (http://www.oecd.org/document/21/0,3343,en_2649_34859_2017813_1_1_1_1,00.html).

35.   Unlike the general bribery offences in sections 1 and 2, the offence of bribery of a foreign public official only covers the offering, promising or giving of bribes, and not the acceptance of them. The person giving the bribe must intend to influence the recipient in the performance of his or her functions as a public official, and must intend to obtain or retain business or a business advantage.

36.   Foreign public officials are defined in *subsection (5)* to include both government officials and those working for international organisations. The definition draws on Article 1.4(a) of the OECD Convention. Similarly, the definition of "public international organisation" in *subsection (6)* draws on Commentary 17 to the OECD Convention.

The conduct element

37.   The conduct element of the offence – what a person must do in order to commit the offence – is set out in *subsection (3)*. The offence may be committed in a number of ways.

38.   If a person (P) offers, promises or gives any advantage to a foreign public official (F) with the requisite intention (see below), and the written law applicable to F neither permits nor requires F to be influenced in his or her capacity as a foreign public official by the offer, promise or gift, then P commits an offence.

39.   The "written law" applicable to F is defined in *subsection (7)* as the law of the relevant part of the UK where the performance of F's functions would be subject to that law. Where the performance of F's functions would not be subject to the law of a part of the UK, the written law is either the applicable rules of a public international organisation, or the law of the country or territory in relation to which F is a foreign public official as contained in its written constitution, provision made by or under legislation or judicial decisions that are evidenced in writing.

40.   The offence will also be committed if the advantage is offered to someone other than the official, if that happens at the official's request, or with the official's assent or acquiescence.

41.   It does not matter whether the offer, promise or gift is made directly to the official or through a third party (*subsection (3)(a)*).

These notes refer to the Bribery Act 2010 (c.23)

42. The language of the OECD Convention is mirrored in the phrases "obtain or retain business" in *subsection (2)* and "offers, promises or gives" and "advantage" in *subsection (3)*, and in the words "public function" in *subsection (5)(b)*.

The fault element

43. The fault element of the offence – what a person must intend in order to commit the offence – is specified in *subsections (1), (2) and (4)*.

44. *Subsections (1) and (4)* have the effect that, in order to commit the offence, a person must intend to influence a foreign public official in the performance of his or her functions as a public official, including any failure to exercise those functions and any use of his or her position, even if he or she does not have authority to use the position in that way.

45. In order to commit the offence a person must also intend to obtain or retain business or an advantage in the conduct of business (*subsection (2)*).

46. The effect of *subsection (8)* is that "business" includes what is done in the course of a trade or profession.

Section 7: Failure of commercial organisations to prevent bribery

47. Section 7 creates an offence of failing to prevent bribery which can only be committed by a relevant commercial organisation.

48. "Relevant commercial organisation" is defined (at *subsection (5)*) as:

   • a body incorporated under the law of any part of the UK and which carries on business whether there or elsewhere,

   • a partnership that is formed under the law of any part of the UK and which carries on business there or elsewhere, or

   • any other body corporate or partnership wherever incorporated or formed which carries on business in any part of the UK.

49. *Subsection (5)* also provides that "business" includes a trade or profession and includes what is done in the course of a trade or profession.

50. The offence is committed where a person (A) who is associated with the commercial organisation (C) bribes another person with the intention of obtaining or retaining business or an advantage in the conduct of business for C. *Subsection (2)* provides that it is a defence for the commercial organisation to show it had adequate procedures in place to prevent persons associated with C from committing bribery offences. Although not explicit on the face of the Act, in accordance with established case law, the standard of proof the defendant would need to discharge in order to prove the defence is the balance of probabilities.

51. *Subsection (3)* provides that "bribery" in the context of this offence relates only to the offering, promising or giving of a bribe contrary to sections 1 and 6 (there is no corresponding offence of failure to prevent the taking of bribes). Applying ordinary principles of criminal law, the reference to offences under section 1 and 6 include being liable for such offences by way of aiding, abetting, counselling or procuring (secondary liability). *Subsection (3)* also makes clear that there is no need for the prosecution to show that the person who committed the bribery offence has already been successfully prosecuted. The prosecution must, however, show that the person would be guilty of the offence were that person prosecuted under this Act. Finally, *subsection (3)(b)* makes clear that there is no need for A to have a close connection to the UK as defined in section 12; rather, so long as C falls within the definition of "relevant commercial organisation" that should be enough to provide courts in the UK with jurisdiction.

These notes refer to the Bribery Act 2010 (c.23)

Section 8: Meaning of associated person

52.   Section 8 provides that A is associated with C for the purposes of section 7, if A performs services for, or on behalf of C. It also ensures that section 7 relates to the actual activities being undertaken by A at the time rather than A's general position. The section expressly states that A may be the commercial organisation's employee, agent or subsidiary. But where A is an employee it is to be presumed that A is performing services for or on behalf of C unless the contrary is shown.

Section 9: Guidance about commercial organisations preventing bribery

53.   This section requires the Secretary of State to publish guidance on procedures that relevant commercial organisations can put in place to prevent bribery by persons associated with them *(subsection (1))*. The Secretary of State may revise such guidance or publish revised guidance from time to time *(subsection (2))*. The Scottish Ministers must be consulted before publication *(subsection (3))*. The guidance may be published in such a manner as the Secretary of State considers appropriate *(subsection (4))*. The Government has indicated its intention to publish guidance ahead of the commencement of section 7 of the Act (Hansard, House of Lords, 2 February 2010, Vol. 717, col.143).

Section 10: Consent to prosecution

54.   A prosecution under the Act in England and Wales can only be brought with the consent of the Director of one of the three senior prosecuting authorities, that is to say the Director of Public Prosecutions, the Director of the Serious Fraud Office and the Director of Revenue and Customs Prosecutions *(subsections (1) and (3))*. Under *subsection (4)*, the relevant Director must exercise the consent function personally. However, where the Director is unavailable (for example where he or she is out of the country or is incapacitated) another person who has been designated in writing by the Director to exercise any such function may do so, but must do so personally *(subsections (5) and (6))*. Provisions of other legislation which would allow another person to exercise the functions of one of the Directors do not apply to the Directors' consent functions under section 10 *(subsection (7))*

55.   A prosecution in Northern Ireland can only be brought with the consent of the Director of Public Prosecutions for Northern Ireland or the Director of the Serious Fraud Office *(subsections (2), (3) and (8))*. Under *subsection (9)* the Director of Public Prosecutions for Northern Ireland must exercise the consent function personally unless the consent function is exercised by the Deputy Director (again personally) by virtue of section 30(4) and (7) of the Justice (Northern Ireland) Act 2002. Under *subsection (10)*, section 36 of the 2002 Act, which provides for the delegation of the Director's functions, does not apply in relation to the Director's functions of giving consent to prosecutions under the Act.

Section 11: Penalties

56.   Any offence under the Act committed by an individual under sections 1, 2 or 6 is punishable either by a fine or imprisonment for up to 10 years (12 months on summary conviction in England and Wales or Scotland or 6 months in Northern Ireland), or both. An offence committed by a person other than an individual is punishable by a fine. In either case, the fine may be up to the statutory maximum (currently £5000 in England and Wales or Northern Ireland, £10000 in Scotland) if the conviction is summary, and unlimited if it is on indictment. The section 7 offence can only be tried upon indictment.

57.   Section 154 of the Criminal Justice Act 2003, which is not yet in force, sets the maximum sentence that can be imposed by a Magistrates' Court in England and Wales at 12 months. Where an offence under this Act is committed before section 154 comes into force, the Magistrates' Court's power is limited to 6 months *(subsection (4)(a))*.

These notes refer to the Bribery Act 2010 (c.23)

Section 12: **Offences under this Act: territorial application**

58.   *Subsection (1)* provides that the offences in sections 1, 2 or 6 are committed in any part of the UK if any part of the conduct element takes place in that part of the UK.

59.   The effect of *subsections (2) to (4)* is that, even though all the actions in question take place abroad, they still constitute the offence if the person performing them is a British national or ordinarily resident in the UK, a body incorporated in the UK or a Scottish partnership.

60.   *Subsection (5)* makes it clear that for the purposes of the offence in section 7 (failure of commercial organisation to prevent bribery) it is immaterial where the conduct element of the offence occurs.

61.   *Subsections (7) to (9)* provide that where proceedings are to be taken in Scotland against a person, such proceedings may be taken in any sheriff court district in which the person is apprehended or in custody, or in such sheriff district as the Lord Advocate may determine.

Section 13: **Defence for certain bribery offences etc.**

62.   Section 13 deals with the legitimate functions of the intelligence services or the armed forces which may require the use of a financial or other advantage to accomplish the relevant function. The section provides a defence where a person charged with a relevant bribery offence can prove that it was necessary for:

- the proper exercise of any function of one of the intelligence services; or

- the proper exercise of any function of the armed forces when engaged on active service.

Although not explicit on the face of the Act, in accordance with established case law, the standard of proof the defendant would need to discharge in order to prove the defence is the balance of probabilities.

63.   The head of each intelligence service is required under *subsection (2)* to ensure that each service has in place arrangements designed to ensure that the conduct of a member of the service that would otherwise amount to a relevant bribery offence is necessary for a purpose set out in *subsection (1)(a)*. A similar requirement is placed on the Defence Council under *subsection (3)* to ensure that the armed forces have arrangements in place designed to ensure that the conduct of any member of the armed forces engaged on active service or a civilian subject to service discipline working in support of military personnel so engaged is necessary for a purpose set out in *subsection (1)(b)*. Under *subsection (4)*, the arrangements must be ones that the relevant Secretary of State considers to be satisfactory.

64.   *Subsection (5)* provides that a person's conduct is to be treated as necessary for the purposes of *subsection (1)(a) or (b)* in circumstances where the person's conduct would otherwise be an offence under section 2 and involves conduct on the part of another person which would amount to an offence under section 1 but for the defence in *subsection (1)*. In other words, *subsection (5)* has the effect that a recipient of a bribe paid by a member of the intelligence services or armed forces is covered by the defence in any case where the person offering or paying the bribe is able to rely on the section 13 defence.

65.   As well as providing definitions for other terms used in the section, *subsection (6)* makes it clear that a "relevant bribery offence" means an offence under section 1 or 2, including one committed by aiding, abetting, counselling or procuring such an offence, and related inchoate offences. "Relevant bribery offence" does not include a section 1 offence which would also amount to an offence of bribing a foreign public official under section 6. This addresses concerns raised by the Joint Committee on the 2003

draft Corruption Bill in relation to, in particular, compliance with the UK's obligations under the OECD Convention (see paragraph 152, HL 157 and HC 705, 31 July 2003).

Section 14: *Offences under sections 1, 2 and 6 by bodies corporate etc.*

66.   Section 14 is aimed at individuals who consent or connive at bribery, contrary to section 1, 2 or 6, committed by a body corporate (of any kind) or Scottish partnership. It does not apply to the offence in section 7.

67.   The first step is to ascertain that the body corporate or Scottish partnership has indeed been guilty of an offence under section 1, 2 or 6. That established, the section provides that a director, partner or similar senior manager of the body is guilty of the same offence if he or she has consented to or connived in the commission of the offence. In a body corporate managed by its members, the same applies to members. In relation to a Scottish partnership, the provision applies to partners.

68.   It should be noted that in this situation, the body corporate or Scottish partnership and the senior manager are both guilty of the main bribery offence. This section does not create a separate offence of "consent or connivance".

69.   *Subsection (3)* makes clear that for a "senior officer" or similar person to be guilty he or she must have a close connection to the UK as defined in section 12(4).

Section 15: *Offences under section 7 by partnerships*

70.   Section 15 deals with proceedings for an offence under section 7 against partnerships. Such proceedings must be brought in the name of the partnership (and not the partners) (*subsection (1)*); certain rules of court and statutory provisions which apply to bodies corporate are deemed to apply to partnerships (*subsection (2)*); and any fine imposed on the partnership on conviction must be paid out of the partnership assets (*subsection (3)*).

Section 16: *Application to Crown*

71.   Section 16 applies the Act to individuals in the public service of the Crown. Such individuals will therefore be liable to prosecution if their conduct in the discharge of their duties constitutes an offence under the Act.

Section 17: *Consequential provision*

72.   This section abolishes the common law offences of bribery and embracery (bribery etc of jurors), as well as the common law offence in Scotland of accepting a bribe, and gives effect to Schedules 1 and 2, which contain consequential amendments and repeals.

73.   *Subsections (4) to (10)* of this section create a power for the Secretary of State (or, as the case may be, Scottish Ministers) to make supplementary, incidental or consequential provision by order. The order making power is subject to the affirmative resolution procedure where it amends a public general Act or devolved legislation, otherwise the negative resolution procedure applies.

Section 18: *Extent*

74.   This section provides that the Act extends to the whole of the UK and that any amendments or repeals of a provision of an enactment have the same extent as that provision. However the amendment of and repeals in the Armed Forces Act 2006 do not extend to the Channel Islands and the amendments of the International Criminal Court Act 2001 and the repeal in the Civil Aviation Act 1982 do not extend to the Channel Islands, Isle of Man or the British overseas territories

Section 19: Commencement and transitional provision etc.

75.   This section provides for commencement. Details are in paragraph 107 below. A commencement order made under this section may appoint different days for different purposes and may contain transitory, transitional or saving provisions. The section also contains express saving provisions so that any offence committed or partly committed before the operative provisions of the Act come into force must be dealt with under the old law.

Section 20: Short title

76.   This section deals with citation.

Schedule 1

77.   This Schedule contains consequential amendments to other legislation. These are as follows.

Ministry of Defence Police Act 1987

78.   Section 2 of that Act gives the Ministry of Defence Police the same powers as normal police, in relation to services property or personnel, including with regard to offences involving the bribery of such persons. That Act is amended to refer to offences under this Act rather than those under the Prevention of Corruption Acts 1889 to 1916.

Criminal Justice Act 1987

79.   Section 2A of that Act gives the Director of the Serious Fraud Office power to investigate corruption offences. The amendment replaces the references to the Prevention of Corruption Acts with references to offences under this Act. The offences in question are the bribery of foreign officials (section 6), and the general bribery offence (sections 1 and 2) where the functions in question are performed outside or unconnected with the UK.

International Criminal Court Act 2001

80.   Sections 54 and 61 of that Act set out the relevant domestic offences in relation to the International Criminal Court in the law of England and Wales, and Northern Ireland respectively. The amendments make clear that offences under this Act are also relevant domestic offences.

International Criminal Court (Scotland) Act 2001

81.   Section 4 of that Act sets out the relevant domestic offences under Scots law in relation to the International Criminal Court. The amendment updates the references to the Prevention of Corruption Act 1906 and to the common law by substituting a reference to the offences under the Act.

Serious Organised Crime and Police Act 2005

82.   Chapter 1 of Part 2 of that Act gives investigatory powers to the Director of Public Prosecutions and other prosecuting authorities in relation to offences listed in section 61. This list was amended by SI 2006/1629 to include common law bribery and offences under the Prevention of Corruption Acts. These offences are now replaced by the offences under this Act.

83.   A similar amendment applies to section 76 (and section 77 in respect of Scotland), which gives the court power to make a financial reporting order in dealing with a person convicted of (among other offences) corruption offences.

These notes refer to the Bribery Act 2010 (c.23)

Armed Forces Act 2006

84.   Schedule 2 of that Act lists serious civilian offences the possible commission of which, if suspected, must be referred to a service police force. The list of civilian offences is amended to include the offences under this Act.

Serious Crime Act 2007

85.   Section 53 of that Act requires the Attorney General's consent prior to commencing proceedings where there is an international element to an offence of encouraging or assisting crime under the 2007 Act. This amendment ensures that the requirement for the Attorney General's consent will not apply in the case of encouraging or assisting bribery by excluding from section 53 any offence to which section 10 (consent to prosecution) of this Act applies.

86.   The Serious Crime Act also creates a power to make a "serious crime prevention order" in relation to offences listed in Schedule 1 of the Act. Part 1 of that Schedule, relating to offences in England and Wales, includes offences under the Prevention of Corruption Acts. Those offences are replaced with offences under sections 1, 2 and 6 of this Act. A corresponding amendment is made in Part 2 of the same Schedule in relation to Northern Ireland.

Schedule 2

87.   This Schedule contains repeals and revocations.

88.   The three Prevention of Corruption Acts are repealed in their entirety. These offences are wholly replaced by the offences under this Act.

89.   Criminal Justice Act (Northern Ireland) 1945 (c. 15 (N.I)) – section 22 amended section 4 of the Public Bodies Corrupt Practices Act 1889 and section 2(1) of the Prevention of Corruption Act 1906 to provide for proceedings to be taken in Northern Ireland only with the consent of the Attorney General for Northern Ireland. Given the 1889 and 1906 Acts will be repealed the section will become redundant.

90.   Electoral Law Act (Northern Ireland) 1962 (c.14 (N.I.)) - section 112(3) amended paragraphs (c) and (d) of section 2 of the 1889 Act and will be redundant following the repeal of the 1889 Act.

91.   Increase of Fines Act (Northern Ireland) 1967 (c. 29 (N.I.)) – section 1(8)(a) and (b) provide that a court may impose a fine whether greater or less than the amount limited by section 2 of the Public Bodies Corrupt Practices Act 1889 or section 1(1) of the Prevention of Corruption Act 1906 respectively. These references will become redundant once those two Acts are repealed.

92.   Criminal Justice (Miscellaneous Provisions) Act (Northern Ireland) 1968 (c. 28 (N.I)) – the entry in the table in Schedule 2 relating to the Prevention of Corruption Act 1906 increased the penalty in Northern Ireland for the offence under section 1(1) of the 1906 Act from 4 months imprisonment to 6 months imprisonment. That entry will become redundant upon repeal of the 1906 Act.

93.   Local Government Act (Northern Ireland) 1972 (c.9 (N.I.)) – paragraph 1 of Schedule 8 amended the 1889 Act and will be redundant following the repeal of the 1889 Act.

94.   Civil Aviation Act 1982 (c. 16) – section 19(1) designates the Civil Aviation Authority as a public authority for the purposes of the Prevention of Corruption Acts 1889-1916 and will be redundant once they are repealed.

95.   Representation of the People Act 1983 (c. 2) – section 165(1) makes certain provision where a candidate at a Parliamentary or local election engages as agent or canvasser an individual who has been convicted and disenfranchised, including under the Public

Bodies Corrupt Practices Act 1889. That entry becomes redundant upon repeal of the 1889 Act.

96.   Housing Associations Act 1985 (c. 69) – paragraph 1(2) of Schedule 6 provides that the Housing Corporation is a public body for the purposes of the Prevention of Corruption Acts 1889 to 1916. That paragraph becomes redundant upon repeal of those Acts.

97.   Criminal Justice Act 1988 (c. 33) – section 47 inserts provisions about penalties into the three Prevention of Corruption Acts, and becomes redundant upon repeal of those Acts.

98.   Criminal Justice (Evidence etc.) (Northern Ireland) Order 1988 (S.I. 1988/1847 (N.I.17)) – article 14(1) amended paragraph (a) of section 2 of the 1889 Act and will be redundant following the repeal of the 1889 Act.

99.   Enterprise and New Towns (Scotland) Act 1990 (c. 35) – paragraph 2 of Schedule 1 provides that Scottish Enterprise and Highlands and Islands Enterprise are public bodies for the purposes of the Prevention of Corruption Acts 1889 to 1916. That paragraph becomes redundant upon repeal of those Acts.

100.   Scotland Act 1998 (c. 46) – section 43 provides that the Scottish Parliament shall be a public body for the purposes of the Prevention of Corruption Acts 1889 to 1916. This section will be redundant once those Acts are repealed.

101.   Anti-terrorism, Crime and Security Act 2001 (c. 24) – sections 108 to 110, which extend the geographical scope of the offences under the Prevention of Corruption Acts 1889 to 1916, will be redundant once those Acts are repealed.

102.   Criminal Justice (Scotland) Act 2003 (asp7) – sections 68 and 69, which extend the geographical scope of the offences under the Prevention of Corruption Acts 1889 to 1916, will be redundant once those Acts are repealed.

103.   Government of Wales Act 2006 (c.32) – section 44 provides that the Welsh Assembly and the Assembly Commission shall be public bodies for the purposes of the Prevention of Corruption Acts 1889 to 1916. This section will be redundant once those Acts are repealed.

104.   Armed Forces Act 2006 (c. 52) – those paragraphs in the list in Schedule 2 which refer to offences under the Prevention of Corruption Acts are repealed. This repeal is a corollary of the amendment to that list in Schedule 1 to this Act.

105.   Local Government and Public Involvement in Health Act 2007 (c. 28) – section 217(1) (a) gives the Secretary of State power to define an "entity under the control of a local authority" and an "entity jointly controlled by bodies that include a local authority" for the purposes of section 4(2) of the Prevention of Corruption Act 1916. Section 217(1)(a) becomes redundant upon the repeal of the 1916 Act. Paragraph 1 of Schedule 14 to the 2007 Act, which contains amendments to the 1916 Act and section 244(4) which makes provision as to the extent of a repeal contained in that paragraph, are also repealed.

106.   Housing and Regeneration Act 2008 (c.17) – paragraph 16 of Schedule 1 provides that the Home and Communities Agency is a public body for the purposes of the Prevention of Corruption Acts 1889 to 1916. This section will be redundant once those Acts are repealed.

COMMENCEMENT

107.   Sections 16, 17(4) to (10), 18, 19(1) to (4) and 20 of the Act came into force on Royal Assent. The remainder of the Act will be brought into force by one or more commencement orders.

These notes refer to the Bribery Act 2010 (c.23)

HANSARD REFERENCES

108.   The following table sets out the dates and Hansard references for each stage of the Bribery Bill's passage through Parliament.

Stage	Date	Hansard Reference
House of Lords		
Introduction	19 November 2009	Vol 715 Col 27
Second Reading	9 December 2009	Vol 715 Col 1085-1126
Committee	7 January 2010 13 January 2010	Vol 716 GC21-GC72 Vol 716 GC83 – GC118
Report	2 February 2010	Vol 717 Col 117-187
Third Reading	8 February 2010	Vol 717 Col 481-502
House of Commons		
First Reading	9 February 2010	No debate
Second Reading	3 March 2010	Vol 506 Col 945-983
Committee	16 March 2010 18 March 2010 23 March 2010	Hansard Public Bill Committee
Report	7 April 2010	Vol 508 Col 1005-1009
Third Reading	7 April 2010	Vol 508 Col 1009-1015
Consideration of Amendments		
Lords consideration of Commons amendments	8 April 2010	Vol 718 Col 1704-1713
Royal Assent	8 April 2010	Lords: Vol 718 Col 1738 Commons: Vol 508 Col 1256

APPENDIX 4

U.S. DOJ and SEC *A Resource Guide to the U.S. Foreign Corrupt Practices Act*

A Resource Guide to the U.S. Foreign Corrupt Practices Act

By the Criminal Division of the U.S. Department of Justice and
the Enforcement Division of the U.S. Securities and Exchange Commission

This guide is intended to provide information for businesses and individuals regarding the U.S. Foreign Corrupt Practices Act (FCPA). The guide has been prepared by the staff of the Criminal Division of the U.S. Department of Justice and the Enforcement Division of the U.S. Securities and Exchange Commission. It is non-binding, informal, and summary in nature, and the information contained herein does not constitute rules or regulations. As such, it is not intended to, does not, and may not be relied upon to create any rights, substantive or procedural, that are enforceable at law by any party, in any criminal, civil, or administrative matter. It is not intended to substitute for the advice of legal counsel on specific issues related to the FCPA. It does not in any way limit the enforcement intentions or litigating positions of the U.S. Department of Justice, the U.S. Securities and Exchange Commission, or any other U.S. government agency.

Companies or individuals seeking an opinion concerning specific prospective conduct are encouraged to use the U.S. Department of Justice's opinion procedure discussed in Chapter 9 of this guide.

This guide is United States Government property. It is available to the public free of charge online at www.justice.gov/criminal/fraud/fcpa and www.sec.gov/spotlight/fcpa.shtml.

A RESOURCE GUIDE TO THE
U.S. FOREIGN CORRUPT PRACTICES ACT

By the Criminal Division of the U.S. Department of Justice and
the Enforcement Division of the U.S. Securities and Exchange Commission

FOREWORD

We are pleased to announce the publication of *A Resource Guide to the U.S. Foreign Corrupt Practices Act*. The Foreign Corrupt Practices Act (FCPA) is a critically important statute for combating corruption around the globe. Corruption has corrosive effects on democratic institutions, undermining public accountability and diverting public resources from important priorities such as health, education, and infrastructure. When business is won or lost based on how much a company is willing to pay in bribes rather than on the quality of its products and services, law-abiding companies are placed at a competitive disadvantage—and consumers lose. For these and other reasons, enforcing the FCPA is a continuing priority at the Department of Justice (DOJ) and the Securities and Exchange Commission (SEC).

The *Guide* is the product of extensive efforts by experts at DOJ and SEC, and has benefited from valuable input from the Departments of Commerce and State. It endeavors to provide helpful information to enterprises of all shapes and sizes— from small businesses doing their first transactions abroad to multi-national corporations with subsidiaries around the world. The *Guide* addresses a wide variety of topics, including who and what is covered by the FCPA's anti-bribery and accounting provisions; the definition of a "foreign official"; what constitute proper and improper gifts, travel and entertainment expenses; the nature of facilitating payments; how successor liability applies in the mergers and acquisitions context; the hallmarks of an effective corporate compliance program; and the different types of civil and criminal resolutions available in the FCPA context. On these and other topics, the *Guide* takes a multi-faceted approach, setting forth in detail the statutory requirements while also providing insight into DOJ and SEC enforcement practices through hypotheticals, examples of enforcement actions and anonymized declinations, and summaries of applicable case law and DOJ opinion releases.

The *Guide* is an unprecedented undertaking by DOJ and SEC to provide the public with detailed information about our FCPA enforcement approach and priorities. We are proud of the many lawyers and staff who worked on this project, and hope that it will be a useful reference for companies, individuals, and others interested in our enforcement of the Act.

Lanny A. Breuer
Assistant Attorney General
Criminal Division
Department of Justice

Robert S. Khuzami
Director of Enforcement
Securities and Exchange Commission

November 14, 2012

CONTENTS

Corporate bribery is bad business. In our free market system it is basic that the sale of products should take place on the basis of price, quality, and service. Corporate bribery is fundamentally destructive of this basic tenet. Corporate bribery of foreign officials takes place primarily to assist corporations in gaining business. Thus foreign corporate bribery affects the very stability of overseas business. Foreign corporate bribes also affect our domestic competitive climate when domestic firms engage in such practices as a substitute for healthy competition for foreign business.[1]

—United States Senate, 1977

INTRODUCTION

Congress enacted the U.S. Foreign Corrupt Practices Act (FCPA or the Act) in 1977 in response to revelations of widespread bribery of foreign officials by U.S. companies. The Act was intended to halt those corrupt practices, create a level playing field for honest businesses, and restore public confidence in the integrity of the marketplace.[2]

The FCPA contains both anti-bribery and accounting provisions. The anti-bribery provisions prohibit U.S. persons and businesses (domestic concerns), U.S. and foreign public companies listed on stock exchanges in the United States or which are required to file periodic reports with the Securities and Exchange Commission (issuers), and certain foreign persons and businesses acting while in the territory of the United States (territorial jurisdiction) from making corrupt payments to foreign officials to obtain or retain business. The accounting provisions require issuers to make and keep accurate books and records and to devise and maintain an adequate system of internal accounting controls. The accounting provisions also prohibit individuals and businesses from knowingly falsifying books and records or knowingly circumventing or failing to implement a system of internal controls.

The Department of Justice (DOJ) and the Securities and Exchange Commission (SEC) share FCPA enforcement authority and are committed to fighting foreign bribery through robust enforcement. An important component of this effort is education, and this resource guide, prepared by DOJ and SEC staff, aims to provide businesses and individuals with information to help them abide by the law, detect and prevent FCPA violations, and implement effective compliance programs.

The Costs of Corruption

Corruption is a global problem. In the three decades since Congress enacted the FCPA, the extent of corporate bribery has become clearer and its ramifications in a transnational economy starker. Corruption impedes economic growth by diverting public resources from important priorities such as health, education, and infrastructure. It undermines democratic values and public accountability and weakens the rule of law.[3] And it threatens stability and security by facilitating criminal activity within and across borders, such as the illegal trafficking of people, weapons, and drugs.[4] International corruption also undercuts good governance and impedes U.S. efforts to promote freedom and democracy, end poverty, and combat crime and terrorism across the globe.[5]

Corruption is also bad for business. Corruption is anti-competitive, leading to distorted prices and disadvantaging honest businesses that do not pay bribes. It increases the cost of doing business globally and inflates the cost of government contracts in developing countries.[6] Corruption also introduces significant uncertainty into business transactions: Contracts secured through bribery may be legally unenforceable, and paying bribes on one contract often results in corrupt officials making ever-increasing demands.[7] Bribery has destructive effects within a business as well, undermining employee confidence in a company's management and fostering a permissive atmosphere for other kinds of corporate misconduct, such as employee self-dealing, embezzlement,[8] financial fraud,[9] and anti-competitive behavior.[10] Bribery thus raises the risks of doing business, putting a company's bottom line and reputation in jeopardy. Companies that pay bribes to win business ultimately undermine their own long-term interests and the best interests of their investors.

Historical Background

Congress enacted the FCPA in 1977 after revelations of widespread global corruption in the wake of the Watergate political scandal. SEC discovered that more than 400 U.S. companies had paid hundreds of millions of dollars in bribes to foreign government officials to secure business overseas.[11] SEC reported that companies were using secret "slush funds" to make illegal campaign contributions in the United States and corrupt payments to foreign officials abroad and were falsifying their corporate financial records to conceal the payments.[12]

Congress viewed passage of the FCPA as critical to stopping corporate bribery, which had tarnished the image of U.S. businesses, impaired public confidence in the financial integrity of U.S. companies, and hampered the efficient functioning of the markets.[13] As Congress

> No problem does more to alienate citizens from their political leaders and institutions, and to undermine political stability and economic development, than endemic corruption among the government, political party leaders, judges, and bureaucrats.
>
> — *USAID Anti-Corruption Strategy*

recognized when it passed the FCPA, corruption imposes enormous costs both at home and abroad, leading to market inefficiencies and instability, sub-standard products, and an unfair playing field for honest businesses.[14] By enacting a strong foreign bribery statute, Congress sought to minimize these destructive effects and help companies resist corrupt demands, while addressing the destructive foreign policy ramifications of transnational bribery.[15] The Act also prohibited off-the-books accounting through provisions designed to "strengthen the accuracy of the corporate books and records and the reliability of the audit process which constitute the foundations of our system of corporate disclosure."[16]

In 1988, Congress amended the FCPA to add two affirmative defenses: (1) the local law defense; and (2) the reasonable and bona fide promotional expense defense.[17] Congress also requested that the President negotiate an international treaty with members of the Organisation for Economic Co-operation and Development (OECD) to prohibit bribery in international business transactions by many of the United States' major trading partners.[18] Subsequent negotiations at the OECD culminated in the Convention on Combating Bribery of Foreign Officials in International Business Transactions (Anti-Bribery Convention), which, among other things, required parties to make it a crime to bribe foreign officials.[19]

DOJ Contact Information

Deputy Chief (FCPA Unit)
Fraud Section, Criminal Division
Bond Building
1400 New York Ave, N.W.
Washington, DC 20005

Telephone: (202) 514-7023
Facsimile: (202) 514-7021
Email: FCPA.Fraud@usdoj.gov

chapter 1
Introduction

In 1998, the FCPA was amended to conform to the requirements of the Anti-Bribery Convention. These amendments expanded the FCPA's scope to: (1) include payments made to secure "any improper advantage"; (2) reach certain foreign persons who commit an act in furtherance of a foreign bribe while in the United States; (3) cover public international organizations in the definition of "foreign official"; (4) add an alternative basis for jurisdiction based on nationality; and (5) apply criminal penalties to foreign nationals employed by or acting as agents of U.S. companies.[20] The Anti-Bribery Convention came into force on February 15, 1999, with the United States as a founding party.

National Landscape: Interagency Efforts

DOJ and SEC share enforcement authority for the FCPA's anti-bribery and accounting provisions.[21] They also work with many other federal agencies and law enforcement partners to investigate and prosecute FCPA violations, reduce bribery demands through good governance programs and other measures, and promote a fair playing field for U.S. companies doing business abroad.

Department of Justice

DOJ has criminal FCPA enforcement authority over "issuers" (i.e., public companies) and their officers,

directors, employees, agents, or stockholders acting on the issuer's behalf. DOJ also has both criminal and civil enforcement responsibility for the FCPA's anti-bribery provisions over "domestic concerns"—which include (a) U.S. citizens, nationals, and residents and (b) U.S. businesses and their officers, directors, employees, agents, or stockholders acting on the domestic concern's behalf—and certain foreign persons and businesses that act in furtherance of an FCPA violation while in the territory of the United States. Within DOJ, the Fraud Section of the Criminal Division has primary responsibility for all FCPA matters.[22] FCPA matters are handled primarily by the FCPA Unit within the Fraud Section, regularly working jointly with U.S. Attorneys' Offices around the country.

DOJ maintains a website dedicated to the FCPA and its enforcement at http://www.justice.gov/criminal/fraud/fcpa/. The website provides translations of the FCPA in numerous languages, relevant legislative history, and selected documents from FCPA-related prosecutions and resolutions since 1977, including charging documents, plea agreements, deferred prosecution agreements, non-prosecution agreements, press releases, and other relevant pleadings and court decisions. The website also provides copies of opinions issued in response to requests by companies and individuals under DOJ's FCPA opinion procedure. The procedures for submitting a request for an opinion can be found at http://www.justice.gov/criminal/fraud/fcpa/docs/frgncrpt.pdf and are discussed further in Chapter 9. Individuals and companies wishing to disclose information about potential FCPA violations are encouraged to contact the FCPA Unit at the telephone number or email address above.

Securities and Exchange Commission

SEC is responsible for civil enforcement of the FCPA over issuers and their officers, directors, employees, agents,

Individuals and companies with information about possible FCPA violations by issuers may report them to the Enforcement Division via SEC's online Tips, Complaints and Referral system, http://www.sec.gov/complaint/tipscomplaint.shtml. They may also submit information to SEC's Office of the Whistleblower through the same online system or by contacting the Office of the Whistleblower at (202) 551-4790. Additionally, investors with questions about the FCPA can call the Office of Investor Education and Advocacy at (800) SEC-0330.

For more information about SEC's Whistleblower Program, under which certain eligible whistleblowers may be entitled to a monetary award if their information leads to certain SEC actions, see Chapter 8.

Law Enforcement Partners

DOJ's FCPA Unit regularly works with the Federal Bureau of Investigation (FBI) to investigate potential FCPA violations. The FBI's International Corruption Unit has primary responsibility for international corruption and fraud investigations and coordinates the FBI's national FCPA enforcement program. The FBI also has a dedicated FCPA squad of FBI special agents (located in the Washington Field Office) that is responsible for investigating many, and providing support for all, of the FBI's FCPA investigations. In addition, the Department of Homeland Security and the Internal Revenue Service-Criminal Investigation regularly investigate potential FCPA violations. A number of other agencies are also involved in the fight against international corruption, including the Department of Treasury's Office of Foreign Assets Control, which has helped lead a number of FCPA investigations.

or stockholders acting on the issuer's behalf. SEC's Division of Enforcement has responsibility for investigating and prosecuting FCPA violations. In 2010, SEC's Enforcement Division created a specialized FCPA Unit, with attorneys in Washington, D.C. and in regional offices around the country, to focus specifically on FCPA enforcement. The Unit investigates potential FCPA violations; facilitates coordination with DOJ's FCPA program and with other federal and international law enforcement partners; uses its expert knowledge of the law to promote consistent enforcement of the FCPA; analyzes tips, complaints, and referrals regarding allegations of foreign bribery; and conducts public outreach to raise awareness of anti-corruption efforts and good corporate governance programs.

The FCPA Unit maintains a "Spotlight on FCPA" section on SEC's website at http://www.sec.gov/spotlight/fcpa.shtml. The website, which is updated regularly, provides general information about the Act, links to all SEC enforcement actions involving the FCPA, including both federal court actions and administrative proceedings, and contains other useful information.

Departments of Commerce and State

Besides enforcement efforts by DOJ and SEC, the U.S. government is also working to address corruption abroad and level the playing field for U.S. businesses through the efforts of the Departments of Commerce and State. Both Commerce and State advance anti-corruption and good governance initiatives globally and regularly assist U.S. companies doing business overseas in several important ways. Both agencies encourage U.S. businesses to seek the assistance of U.S embassies when they are confronted with bribe solicitations or other corruption-related issues overseas.[23]

The Department of Commerce offers a number of important resources for businesses, including the International Trade Administration's United States and Foreign Commercial Service (Commercial Service). The Commercial Service has export and industry specialists located in over 100 U.S. cities and 70 countries who are available to provide counseling and other assistance to U.S. businesses, particularly small and medium-sized companies, regarding exporting their products and services. Among other things, these specialists can help a U.S. company conduct due diligence when choosing business partners or agents overseas. The International Company Profile Program, for instance, can be part of a U.S. business' evaluation of potential overseas business partners.[24] Businesses may contact the Commercial Service through its website, http://export.gov/eac/, or directly at its domestic and foreign offices.[25]

Additionally, the Department of Commerce's Office of the General Counsel maintains a website, http://www.commerce.gov/os/ogc/transparency-and-anti-bribery-initiatives, that contains recent articles and speeches, links to translations of the FCPA, a catalogue of anti-corruption resources, and a list of international conventions and initiatives. The Trade Compliance Center in the Department of Commerce's International Trade Administration hosts a website with anti-bribery resources, http://tcc.export.gov/Bribery. This website contains an online form through which U.S. companies can report allegations of foreign bribery by foreign competitors in international business transactions.[26] The Department of Commerce also provides information to companies through a number of U.S. and international publications designed to assist firms in complying with anti-corruption laws. For example, the Department of Commerce has included a new anti-corruption section in its Country Commercial Guides, prepared by market experts at U.S. embassies worldwide, that contains information on market conditions for more than 100 countries, including information on the FCPA for exporters.[27]

chapter 1
Introduction

The Department of Commerce has also published a guide, *Business Ethics: A Manual for Managing a Responsible Business Enterprise in Emerging Market Economies*, which contains information about corporate compliance programs for businesses involved in international trade.[28]

The Departments of Commerce and State also provide advocacy support, when determined to be in the national interest, for U.S. companies bidding for foreign government contracts. The Department of Commerce's Advocacy Center, for example, supports U.S. businesses competing against foreign companies for international contracts, such as by arranging for the delivery of an advocacy message by U.S. government officials or assisting with unanticipated problems such as suspected bribery by a competitor.[29] The Department of State's Bureau of Economic and Business Affairs (specifically, its Office of Commercial and Business Affairs) similarly assists U.S. firms doing business overseas by providing advocacy on behalf of U.S. businesses and identifying risk areas for U.S. businesses; more information is available on its website, http://www.state.gov/e/eb/cba/. Also, the Department of State's economic officers serving overseas provide commercial advocacy and support for U.S. companies at the many overseas diplomatic posts where the Commercial Service is not represented.

The Department of State promotes U.S. government interests in addressing corruption internationally through country-to-country diplomatic engagement; development of and follow-through on international commitments relating to corruption; promotion of high-level political engagement (e.g., the G20 Anticorruption Action Plan); public outreach in foreign countries; and support for building the capacity of foreign partners to combat corruption. In fiscal year 2009, the U.S. government provided more than $1 billion for anti-corruption and related good governance assistance abroad.

The Department of State's Bureau of International Narcotics and Law Enforcement Affairs (INL) manages U.S. participation in many multilateral anti-corruption political and legal initiatives at the global and regional level. INL also funds and coordinates significant efforts to assist countries with combating corruption through legal reform, training, and other capacity-building efforts. Inquiries about the U.S. government's general anti-corruption efforts and implementation of global and regional anti-corruption initiatives may be directed to INL on its website, http://www.state.gov/j/inl/c/crime/corr/index.htm, or by email to: anticorruption@state.gov. In addition, the U.S. Agency for International Development (USAID) has developed several anti-corruption programs and publications, information about which can be found at http://www.usaid.gov/what-we-do/democracy-human-rights-and-governance/promoting-accountability-transparency. Finally, the Department of State's brochure "Fighting Global Corruption: Business Risk Management," available at http://www.ogc.doc.gov/pdfs/Fighting_Global_Corruption.pdf, provides guidance about corporate compliance programs as well as international anti-corruption initiatives.

International Landscape: Global Anti-Corruption Efforts

In recent years, there has been a growing international consensus that corruption must be combated, and the United States and other countries are parties to a number of international anti-corruption conventions. Under these conventions, countries that are parties undertake commitments to adopt a range of preventive and criminal law measures to combat corruption. The conventions incorporate review processes that allow the United States to monitor other countries to ensure that they are meeting their international obligations. Likewise, these processes in turn permit other parties to monitor the United States' anti-corruption laws and enforcement to ensure that such enforcement and legal frameworks are consistent with the United States' treaty obligations.[30] U.S. officials regularly address the subject of corruption with our foreign counterparts to raise awareness of the importance of fighting corruption and urge stronger enforcement of anti-corruption laws and policies.

OECD Working Group on Bribery and the Anti-Bribery Convention

The OECD was founded in 1961 to stimulate economic progress and world trade. As noted, the Anti-Bribery Convention requires its parties to criminalize the bribery of foreign public officials in international business transactions.[31] As of November 1, 2012, there were 39 parties to the Anti-Bribery Convention: 34 OECD member countries (including the United States) and five non-OECD member countries (Argentina, Brazil, Bulgaria, the Russian Federation, and South Africa). All of these parties are also members of the OECD Working Group on Bribery (Working Group).[32]

The Working Group is responsible for monitoring the implementation of the Anti-Bribery Convention, the 2009 Recommendation of the Council for Further Combating Bribery of Foreign Public Officials in International Business Transactions, and related instruments. Its members meet quarterly to review and monitor implementation of the Anti-Bribery Convention by member states around the world. Each party undergoes periodic peer review.[33] This peer-review monitoring system is conducted in three phases. The Phase 1 review includes an in-depth assessment of each country's domestic laws implementing the Convention. The Phase 2 review examines the effectiveness of each country's laws and anti-bribery efforts. The final phase is a permanent cycle of peer review (the first cycle of which is referred to as the Phase 3 review) that evaluates a country's enforcement actions and results, as well as the country's efforts to address weaknesses identified during the Phase 2 review.[34] All of the monitoring reports for the parties to the Convention can be found on the OECD website and can be a useful resource about the foreign bribery laws of the OECD Working Group member countries.[35]

The United States was one of the first countries to undergo all three phases of review. The reports and appendices can be found on DOJ's and SEC's websites.[36] In its

Phase 3 review of the United States, which was completed in October 2010, the Working Group commended U.S. efforts to fight transnational bribery and highlighted a number of best practices developed by the United States. The report also noted areas where the United States' anti-bribery efforts could be improved, including consolidating publicly available information on the application of the FCPA and enhancing awareness among small- and medium-sized companies about the prevention and detection of foreign bribery. This guide is, in part, a response to these Phase 3 recommendations and is intended to help businesses and individuals better understand the FCPA.[37]

U.N. Convention Against Corruption

The United States is a state party to the United Nations Convention Against Corruption (UNCAC), which was adopted by the U.N. General Assembly on October 31, 2003, and entered into force on December 14, 2005.[38] The United States ratified the UNCAC on October 30, 2006. The UNCAC requires parties to criminalize a wide range of corrupt acts, including domestic and foreign bribery and related offenses such as money laundering and obstruction of justice. The UNCAC also establishes guidelines for the creation of anti-corruption bodies, codes of conduct for public officials, transparent and objective systems of procurement, and enhanced accounting and auditing standards for the private sector. A peer review mechanism assesses the implementation of the UNCAC by parties to the Convention, with a focus in the first round on criminalization and law enforcement as well as international legal cooperation.[39] The United States has been reviewed under the Pilot Review Programme, the report of which is available on DOJ's website. As of November 1, 2012, 163 countries were parties to the UNCAC.[40]

Other Anti-Corruption Conventions

The Inter-American Convention Against Corruption (IACAC) was the first international anti-corruption convention, adopted in March 1996 in Caracas, Venezuela, by members of the Organization of American States.[41]

The IACAC requires parties (of which the United States is one) to criminalize both foreign and domestic bribery. A body known as the Mechanism for Follow-Up on the Implementation of the Inter-American Convention Against Corruption (MESICIC) monitors parties' compliance with the IACAC. As of November 1, 2012, 31 countries were parties to MESICIC.

The Council of Europe established the Group of States Against Corruption (GRECO) in 1999 to monitor countries' compliance with the Council of Europe's anti-corruption standards, including the Council of Europe's Criminal Law Convention on Corruption.[42] These standards include prohibitions on the solicitation and receipt of bribes, as well as foreign bribery. As of November 1, 2012, GRECO member states, which need not be members of the Council of Europe, include more than 45 European countries and the United States.[43]

The United States has been reviewed under both MESICIC and GRECO, and the reports generated by those reviews are available on DOJ's website.

THE FCPA: ANTI-BRIBERY PROVISIONS

The FCPA addresses the problem of international corruption in two ways: (1) the anti-bribery provisions, which are discussed below, prohibit individuals and businesses from bribing foreign government officials in order to obtain or retain business and (2) the accounting provisions, which are discussed in Chapter 3, impose certain record keeping and internal control requirements on issuers, and prohibit individuals and companies from knowingly falsifying an issuer's books and records or circumventing or failing to implement an issuer's system of internal controls. Violations of the FCPA can lead to civil and criminal penalties, sanctions, and remedies, including fines, disgorgement, and/or imprisonment.

In general, the FCPA prohibits offering to pay, paying, promising to pay, or authorizing the payment of money or anything of value to a foreign official in order to influence any act or decision of the foreign official in his or her official capacity or to secure any other improper advantage in order to obtain or retain business.[44]

Who Is Covered by the Anti-Bribery Provisions?

The FCPA's anti-bribery provisions apply broadly to three categories of persons and entities: (1) "issuers" and their officers, directors, employees, agents, and shareholders; (2) "domestic concerns" and their officers, directors, employees, agents, and shareholders; and (3) certain persons and entities, other than issuers and domestic concerns, acting while in the territory of the United States.

Issuers—15 U.S.C. § 78dd-1

Section 30A of the Securities Exchange Act of 1934 (the Exchange Act), which can be found at 15 U.S.C. § 78dd-1, contains the anti-bribery provision governing issuers.[45] A company is an "issuer" under the FCPA if it has a class of securities registered under Section 12 of the Exchange Act[46] or is required to file periodic and other reports with SEC under Section 15(d) of the Exchange Act.[47] In practice, this means that any company with a class of securities listed on a national securities exchange in the United States, or any company with a class of securities quoted in the over-the-counter market in the United States and required to file periodic reports with SEC, is an issuer. A company thus need not be a U.S. company to be an issuer. Foreign companies with American Depository Receipts that are listed on a U.S. exchange are also issuers.[48] As of December 31, 2011, 965 foreign companies were registered with SEC.[49] Officers, directors, employees, agents, or stockholders acting on behalf of an issuer (whether U.S. or foreign nationals), and any co-conspirators, also can be prosecuted under the FCPA.[50]

Domestic Concerns—15 U.S.C. § 78dd-2

The FCPA also applies to "domestic concerns."[51] A domestic concern is any individual who is a citizen, national, or resident of the United States, or any corporation, partnership, association, joint-stock company, business trust, unincorporated organization, or sole proprietorship that is organized under the laws of the United States or its states, territories, possessions, or commonwealths or that has its principal place of business in the United States.[52] Officers,

directors, employees, agents, or stockholders acting on behalf of a domestic concern, including foreign nationals or companies, are also covered.[53]

Territorial Jurisdiction—15 U.S.C. § 78dd-3

The FCPA also applies to certain foreign nationals or entities that are not issuers or domestic concerns.[54] Since 1998, the FCPA's anti-bribery provisions have applied to foreign persons and foreign non-issuer entities that, either directly or through an agent, engage in *any* act in furtherance of a corrupt payment (or an offer, promise, or authorization to pay) while in the territory of the United States.[55] Also, officers, directors, employees, agents, or stockholders acting on behalf of such persons or entities may be subject to the FCPA's anti-bribery prohibitions.[56]

What Jurisdictional Conduct Triggers the Anti-Bribery Provisions?

The FCPA's anti-bribery provisions can apply to conduct both inside and outside the United States. Issuers and domestic concerns—as well as their officers, directors, employees, agents, or stockholders—may be prosecuted for using the U.S. mails or any means or instrumentality of interstate commerce in furtherance of a corrupt payment to a foreign official. The Act defines "interstate commerce" as "trade, commerce, transportation, or communication among the several States, or between any foreign country and any State or between any State and any place or ship outside thereof ...."[57] The term also includes the *intrastate* use of any interstate means of communication, or any other interstate instrumentality.[58] Thus, placing a telephone call or sending an e-mail, text message, or fax from, to, or through the United States involves interstate commerce—as does sending a wire transfer from or to a U.S. bank or otherwise using the U.S. banking system, or traveling across state borders or internationally to or from the United States.

Those who are not issuers or domestic concerns may be prosecuted under the FCPA if they directly, or through an agent, engage in *any* act in furtherance of a corrupt payment while in the territory of the United States, regardless of whether they utilize the U.S. mails or a means or instrumentality of interstate commerce.[59] Thus, for example, a foreign national who attends a meeting in the United States that furthers a foreign bribery scheme may be subject to prosecution, as may any co-conspirators, even if they did not themselves attend the meeting. A foreign national or company may also be liable under the FCPA if it aids and abets, conspires with, or acts as an agent of an issuer or domestic concern, regardless of whether the foreign national or company itself takes any action in the United States.[60]

In addition, under the "alternative jurisdiction" provision of the FCPA enacted in 1998, U.S. companies or persons may be subject to the anti-bribery provisions even if they act outside the United States.[61] The 1998 amendments to the FCPA expanded the jurisdictional coverage of the Act by establishing an alternative basis for jurisdiction, that is, jurisdiction based on the nationality principle.[62] In particular, the 1998 amendments removed the requirement that there be a use of interstate commerce (e.g., wire, email, telephone call) for acts in furtherance of a corrupt payment

to a foreign official by U.S. companies and persons occurring wholly outside of the United States.[63]

What Is Covered?—The Business Purpose Test

The FCPA applies only to payments intended to induce or influence a foreign official to use his or her position "in order to assist ... in obtaining or retaining business for or with, or directing business to, any person."[64] This requirement is known as the "business purpose test" and is broadly interpreted.[65]

Not surprisingly, many enforcement actions involve bribes to obtain or retain government contracts.[66] The FCPA also prohibits bribes in the conduct of business or

Hypothetical: FCPA Jurisdiction

Company A, a Delaware company with its principal place of business in New York, is a large energy company that operates globally, including in a number of countries that have a high risk of corruption, such as Foreign Country. Company A's shares are listed on a national U.S. stock exchange. Company A enters into an agreement with a European company (EuroCo) to submit a joint bid to the Oil Ministry to build a refinery in Foreign Country. EuroCo is not an issuer.

Executives of Company A and EuroCo meet in New York to discuss how to win the bid and decide to hire a purported third-party consultant (Intermediary) and have him use part of his "commission" to bribe high-ranking officials within the Oil Ministry. Intermediary meets with executives at Company A and EuroCo in New York to finalize the scheme. Eventually, millions of dollars in bribes are funneled from the United States and Europe through Intermediary to high-ranking officials at the Oil Ministry, and Company A and EuroCo win the contract. A few years later, a front page article alleging that the contract was procured through bribery appears in Foreign Country, and DOJ and SEC begin investigating whether the FCPA was violated.

Based on these facts, which entities fall within the FCPA's jurisdiction?

All of the entities easily fall within the FCPA's jurisdiction. Company A is both an "issuer" and a "domestic concern" under the FCPA, and Intermediary is an "agent" of Company A. EuroCo and Intermediary are also subject to the FCPA's territorial jurisdiction provision based on their conduct while in the United States. Moreover, even if EuroCo and Intermediary had never taken any actions in the territory of the United States, they can still be subject to jurisdiction under a traditional application of conspiracy law and may be subject to substantive FCPA charges under *Pinkerton* liability, namely, being liable for the reasonably foreseeable substantive FCPA crimes committed by a co-conspirator in furtherance of the conspiracy.

Examples of Actions Taken to Obtain or Retain Business

- Winning a contract

- Influencing the procurement process

- Circumventing the rules for importation of products

- Gaining access to non-public bid tender information

- Evading taxes or penalties

- Influencing the adjudication of lawsuits or enforcement actions

- Obtaining exceptions to regulations

- Avoiding contract termination

---

to gain a business advantage.[67] For example, bribe payments made to secure favorable tax treatment, to reduce or eliminate customs duties, to obtain government action to prevent competitors from entering a market, or to circumvent a licensing or permit requirement, all satisfy the business purpose test.[68]

In 2004, the U.S. Court of Appeals for the Fifth Circuit addressed the business purpose test in *United States v. Kay* and held that bribes paid to obtain favorable tax treatment—which reduced a company's customs duties and sales taxes on imports—could constitute payments made to "obtain or retain" business within the meaning of the FCPA.[69] The court explained that in enacting the FCPA, "Congress meant to prohibit a range of payments wider than only those that directly influence the acquisition or retention of government contracts or similar commercial or industrial arrangements."[70] The *Kay* court found that "[t]he congressional target was bribery paid to engender assistance in improving the business opportunities of the payor or his beneficiary, irrespective of whether that assistance be direct or indirect, and irrespective of whether it be related to administering the law, awarding, extending, or renewing a contract, or executing or preserving an agreement."[71] Accordingly, *Kay*

held that payments to obtain favorable tax treatment can, under appropriate circumstances, violate the FCPA:

> Avoiding or lowering taxes reduces operating costs and thus increases profit margins, thereby freeing up funds that the business is otherwise legally obligated to expend. And this, in turn, enables it to take any number of actions to the disadvantage of competitors. Bribing foreign officials to lower taxes and customs duties certainly *can* provide an unfair advantage over competitors and thereby be of assistance to the payor in obtaining or retaining business.

> * * *

> [W]e hold that Congress intended for the FCPA to apply broadly to payments intended to assist the payor, either directly or indirectly, in obtaining or retaining business for some person, and that bribes paid to foreign tax officials to secure illegally reduced customs and tax liability constitute a type of payment that can fall within this broad coverage.[72]

Paying Bribes to Customs Officials

In 2010, a global freight forwarding company and six of its corporate customers in the oil and gas industry resolved charges that they paid bribes to customs officials. The companies bribed customs officials in more than ten countries in exchange for such benefits as:

- evading customs duties on imported goods

- improperly expediting the importation of goods and equipment

- extending drilling contracts and lowering tax assessments

- obtaining false documentation related to temporary import permits for drilling rigs

- enabling the release of drilling rigs and other equipment from customs officials

In many instances, the improper payments at issue allowed the company to carry out its existing business, which fell within the FCPA's prohibition on corrupt payments made for the purpose of "retaining" business. The seven companies paid a total of more than $235 million in civil and criminal sanctions and disgorgement.

13

In short, while the FCPA does not cover every type of bribe paid around the world for every purpose, it does apply broadly to bribes paid to help obtain or retain business, which can include payments made to secure a wide variety of unfair business advantages.[73]

What Does "Corruptly" Mean?

To violate the FCPA, an offer, promise, or authorization of a payment, or a payment, to a government official must be made "corruptly."[74] As Congress noted when adopting the FCPA, the word "corruptly" means an intent or desire to wrongfully influence the recipient:

> The word "corruptly" is used in order to make clear that the offer, payment, promise, or gift, must be intended to induce the recipient to misuse his official position; for example, wrongfully to direct business to the payor or his client, to obtain preferential legislation or regulations, or to induce a foreign official to fail to perform an official function.[75]

Where corrupt intent is present, the FCPA prohibits paying, offering, or promising to pay money or anything of value (or authorizing the payment or offer).[76] By focusing on intent, the FCPA does not require that a corrupt act succeed in its purpose.[77] Nor must the foreign official actually solicit, accept, or receive the corrupt payment for the bribe payor to be liable.[78] For example, in one case, a specialty chemical company promised Iraqi government officials approximately $850,000 in bribes for an upcoming contract. Although the company did not, in the end, make the payment (the scheme was thwarted by the U.S. government's investigation), the company still violated the FCPA and was held accountable.[79]

Also, as long as the offer, promise, authorization, or payment is made corruptly, the actor need not know the identity of the recipient; the attempt is sufficient.[80] Thus, an executive who authorizes others to pay "whoever you need to" in a foreign government to obtain a contract has violated the FCPA—even if no bribe is ultimately offered or paid.

What Does "Willfully" Mean and When Does It Apply?

In order for an individual defendant to be criminally liable under the FCPA, he or she must act "willfully."[81] Proof of willfulness is not required to establish corporate criminal or civil liability,[82] though proof of corrupt intent is.

The term "willfully" is not defined in the FCPA, but it has generally been construed by courts to connote an act committed voluntarily and purposefully, and with a bad purpose, i.e., with "knowledge that [a defendant] was doing a 'bad' act under the general rules of law."[83] As the Supreme Court explained in *Bryan v. United States*, "[a]s a general matter, when used in the criminal context, a 'willful' act is one undertaken with a 'bad purpose.' In other words, in order to establish a 'willful' violation of a statute, 'the Government must prove that the defendant acted with knowledge that his conduct was unlawful.'"[84]

Notably, as both the Second Circuit and Fifth Circuit Courts of Appeals have found, the FCPA does not require the government to prove that a defendant was specifically aware of the FCPA or knew that his conduct violated the FCPA.[85] To be guilty, a defendant must act with a bad purpose, i.e., know generally that his conduct is unlawful.

What Does "Anything of Value" Mean?

In enacting the FCPA, Congress recognized that bribes can come in many shapes and sizes—a broad range of unfair benefits[86]—and so the statute prohibits the corrupt "offer, payment, promise to pay, or authorization of the payment of any money, or offer, gift, promise to give, or authorization of the giving of *anything of value* to" a foreign official.[87]

An improper benefit can take many forms. While cases often involve payments of cash (sometimes in the guise of "consulting fees" or "commissions" given through intermediaries), others have involved travel expenses and expensive gifts. Like the domestic bribery statute, the FCPA does not contain a minimum threshold amount for corrupt gifts or payments.[88] Indeed, what might be considered a modest payment in the United States could be a larger and much more significant amount in a foreign country.

Regardless of size, for a gift or other payment to violate the statute, the payor must have corrupt intent—that is, the intent to improperly influence the government official. The corrupt intent requirement protects companies that engage in the ordinary and legitimate promotion of their businesses while targeting conduct that seeks to improperly induce officials into misusing their positions. Thus, it is difficult to envision any scenario in which the provision of cups of coffee, taxi fare, or company promotional items of nominal value would ever evidence corrupt intent, and neither DOJ nor SEC has ever pursued an investigation on the basis of such conduct. Moreover, as in all areas of federal law enforcement, DOJ and SEC exercise discretion in deciding which cases promote law enforcement priorities and justify investigation. Certain patterns, however, have emerged: DOJ's and SEC's anti-bribery enforcement actions have focused on small payments and gifts only when they comprise part of a systemic or long-standing course of conduct that evidences a scheme to corruptly pay foreign officials to obtain or retain business. These assessments are necessarily fact specific.

Cash

The most obvious form of corrupt payment is large amounts of cash. In some instances, companies have maintained cash funds specifically earmarked for use as bribes. One U.S. issuer headquartered in Germany disbursed corrupt payments from a corporate "cash desk" and used offshore bank accounts to bribe government officials to win contracts.[89] In another instance, a four-company joint venture used its agent to pay $5 million in bribes to a Nigerian political party.[90] The payments were made to the agent in suitcases of cash (typically in $1 million installments), and, in one instance, the trunk of a car when the cash did not fit into a suitcase.[91]

Gifts, Travel, Entertainment, and Other Things of Value

A small gift or token of esteem or gratitude is often an appropriate way for business people to display respect for each other. Some hallmarks of appropriate gift-giving are when the gift is given openly and transparently, properly recorded in the giver's books and records, provided only to reflect esteem or gratitude, and permitted under local law.

Items of nominal value, such as cab fare, reasonable meals and entertainment expenses, or company promotional items, are unlikely to improperly influence an official, and, as a result, are not, without more, items that have resulted in enforcement action by DOJ or SEC. The larger or more extravagant the gift, however, the more likely it was given with an improper purpose. DOJ and SEC enforcement cases thus have involved single instances of large, extravagant gift-giving (such as sports cars, fur coats, and other luxury items) as well as widespread gifts of smaller items as part of a pattern of bribes.[92] For example, in one case brought by DOJ and SEC, a defendant gave a government official a country club membership fee and a generator, as well as household maintenance expenses, payment of cell phone bills, an automobile worth $20,000, and limousine services. The same official also received $250,000 through a third-party agent.[93]

In addition, a number of FCPA enforcement actions have involved the corrupt payment of travel and entertainment expenses. Both DOJ and SEC have brought cases where these types of expenditures occurred in conjunction with other conduct reflecting systemic bribery or other clear indicia of corrupt intent.

A case involving a California-based telecommunications company illustrates the types of improper travel and entertainment expenses that may violate the FCPA.[94] Between 2002 and 2007, the company spent nearly $7 million on approximately 225 trips for its customers in order to obtain systems contracts in China, including for employees of Chinese state-owned companies to travel to popular tourist destinations in the United States.[95] Although the trips were purportedly for the individuals to conduct training at

Examples of Improper
Travel and Entertainment

- a $12,000 birthday trip for a government decision-maker from Mexico that included visits to wineries and dinners

- $10,000 spent on dinners, drinks, and entertainment for a government official

- a trip to Italy for eight Iraqi government officials that consisted primarily of sightseeing and included $1,000 in "pocket money" for each official

- a trip to Paris for a government official and his wife that consisted primarily of touring activities via a chauffeur-driven vehicle

the company's facilities, in reality, no training occurred on many of these trips and the company had no facilities at those locations. Approximately $670,000 of the $7 million was falsely recorded as "training" expenses.[96]

Likewise, a New Jersey-based telecommunications company spent millions of dollars on approximately 315 trips for Chinese government officials, ostensibly to inspect factories and train the officials in using the company's equipment.[97] In reality, during many of these trips, the officials spent little or no time visiting the company's facilities, but instead visited tourist destinations such as Hawaii, Las Vegas, the Grand Canyon, Niagara Falls, Disney World, Universal Studios, and New York City.[98] Some of the trips were characterized as "factory inspections" or "training" with government customers but consisted primarily or entirely of sightseeing to locations chosen by the officials, typically lasting two weeks and costing between $25,000 and $55,000 per trip. In some instances, the company gave the government officials $500 to $1,000 per day in spending money and paid all lodging, transportation, food, and entertainment expenses. The company either failed to record these expenses or improperly recorded them as "consulting fees" in its corporate books and records. The

company also failed to implement appropriate internal controls to monitor the provision of travel and other things of value to Chinese government officials.[99]

Companies also may violate the FCPA if they give payments or gifts to third parties, like an official's family members, as an indirect way of corruptly influencing a foreign official. For example, one defendant paid personal bills and provided airline tickets to a cousin and close friend of the foreign official whose influence the defendant sought in obtaining contracts.[100] The defendant was convicted at trial and received a prison sentence.[101]

As part of an effective compliance program, a company should have clear and easily accessible guidelines and processes in place for gift-giving by the company's directors, officers, employees, and agents. Though not necessarily appropriate for every business, many larger companies have automated gift-giving clearance processes and have set clear monetary thresholds for gifts along with annual limitations, with limited exceptions for gifts approved by appropriate management. Clear guidelines and processes can be an effective and efficient means for controlling gift-giving, deterring improper gifts, and protecting corporate assets.

The FCPA does not prohibit gift-giving. Rather, just like its domestic bribery counterparts, the FCPA prohibits the payments of bribes, including those disguised as gifts.

Charitable Contributions

Companies often engage in charitable giving as part of legitimate local outreach. The FCPA does not prohibit charitable contributions or prevent corporations from acting as good corporate citizens. Companies, however, cannot use the pretense of charitable contributions as a way to funnel bribes to government officials.

For example, a pharmaceutical company used charitable donations to a small local castle restoration charity headed by a foreign government official to induce the official to direct business to the company. Although the charity was a bona fide charitable organization, internal documents at the pharmaceutical company's subsidiary established that the payments were not viewed as charitable contributions but rather as "dues" the subsidiary was required to pay for assistance from the government official. The payments constituted a significant portion of the subsidiary's total promotional donations budget and were structured to allow the subsidiary to exceed its authorized limits. The payments

Hypothetical: Gifts, Travel, and Entertainment

Company A is a large U.S. engineering company with global operations in more than 50 countries, including a number that have a high risk of corruption, such as Foreign Country. Company A's stock is listed on a national U.S. stock exchange. In conducting its business internationally, Company A's officers and employees come into regular contact with foreign officials, including officials in various ministries and state-owned entities. At a trade show, Company A has a booth at which it offers free pens, hats, t-shirts, and other similar promotional items with Company A's logo. Company A also serves free coffee, other beverages, and snacks at the booth. Some of the visitors to the booth are foreign officials.

Is Company A in violation of the FCPA?

No. These are legitimate, bona fide expenditures made in connection with the promotion, demonstration, or explanation of Company A's products or services. There is nothing to suggest corrupt intent here. The FCPA does not prevent companies from promoting their businesses in this way or providing legitimate hospitality, including to foreign officials. Providing promotional items with company logos or free snacks as set forth above is an appropriate means of providing hospitality and promoting business. Such conduct has never formed the basis for an FCPA enforcement action.

At the trade show, Company A invites a dozen current and prospective customers out for drinks, and pays the moderate bar tab. Some of the current and prospective customers are foreign officials under the FCPA. Is Company A in violation of the FCPA?

No. Again, the FCPA was not designed to prohibit all forms of hospitality to foreign officials. While the cost here may be more substantial than the beverages, snacks, and promotional items provided at the booth, and the invitees specifically selected, there is still nothing to suggest corrupt intent.

Two years ago, Company A won a long-term contract to supply goods and services to the state-owned Electricity Commission in Foreign Country. The Electricity Commission is 100% owned, controlled, and operated by the government of Foreign Country, and employees of the Electricity Commission are subject to Foreign Country's domestic bribery laws. Some Company A executives are in Foreign Country for meetings with officials of the Electricity Commission. The General Manager of the Electricity Commission was recently married, and during the trip Company A executives present a moderately priced crystal vase to the General Manager as a wedding gift and token of esteem. Is Company A in violation of the FCPA?

No. It is appropriate to provide reasonable gifts to foreign officials as tokens of esteem or gratitude. It is important that such gifts be made openly and transparently, properly recorded in a company's books and records, and given only where appropriate under local law, customary where given, and reasonable for the occasion.

During the course of the contract described above, Company A periodically provides training to Electricity Commission employees at its facilities in Michigan. The training is paid for by the Electricity Commission as part of the contract. Senior officials of the Electricity Commission inform Company A that they want to inspect the facilities and ensure that the training is working well. Company A pays for the airfare, hotel, and transportation for the

(cont'd)

17

Electricity Commission senior officials to travel to Michigan to inspect Company A's facilities. Because it is a lengthy international flight, Company A agrees to pay for business class airfare, to which its own employees are entitled for lengthy flights. The foreign officials visit Michigan for several days, during which the senior officials perform an appropriate inspection. Company A executives take the officials to a moderately priced dinner, a baseball game, and a play. Do any of these actions violate the FCPA?

No. Neither the costs associated with training the employees nor the trip for the senior officials to the Company's facilities in order to inspect them violates the FCPA. Reasonable and bona fide promotional expenditures do not violate the FCPA. Here, Company A is providing training to the Electricity Commission's employees and is hosting the Electricity Commission senior officials. Their review of the execution and performance of the contract is a legitimate business purpose. Even the provision of business class airfare is reasonable under the circumstances, as are the meals and entertainment, which are only a small component of the business trip.

Would this analysis be different if Company A instead paid for the senior officials to travel first-class with their spouses for an all-expenses-paid, week-long trip to Las Vegas, where Company A has no facilities?

Yes. This conduct almost certainly violates the FCPA because it evinces a corrupt intent. Here, the trip does not appear to be designed for any legitimate business purpose, is extravagant, includes expenses for the officials' spouses, and therefore appears to be designed to corruptly curry favor with the foreign government officials. Moreover, if the trip were booked as a legitimate business expense—such as the provision of training at its facilities—Company A would also be in violation of the FCPA's accounting provisions. Furthermore, this conduct suggests deficiencies in Company A's internal controls.

Company A's contract with the Electricity Commission is going to expire, and the Electricity Commission is offering the next contract through its tender process. An employee of the Electricity Commission contacts Company A and offers to provide Company A with confidential, non-public bid information from Company A's competitors if Company A will pay for a vacation to Paris for him and his girlfriend. Employees of Company A accede to the official's request, pay for the vacation, receive the confidential bid information, and yet still do not win the contract. Has Company A violated the FCPA?

Yes. Company A has provided things of value to a foreign official for the purpose of inducing the official to misuse his office and to gain an improper advantage. It does not matter that it was the foreign official who first suggested the illegal conduct or that Company A ultimately was not successful in winning the contract. This conduct would also violate the FCPA's accounting provisions if the trip were booked as a legitimate business expense and suggests deficiencies in Company A's internal controls.

also were not in compliance with the company's internal policies, which provided that charitable donations generally should be made to healthcare institutions and relate to the practice of medicine.[102]

Proper due diligence and controls are critical for charitable giving. In general, the adequacy of measures taken to prevent misuse of charitable donations will depend on a risk-based analysis and the specific facts at hand. In Opinion Procedure Release No. 10-02, DOJ described the due diligence and controls that can minimize the likelihood of an FCPA violation. In that matter, a Eurasian-based subsidiary of a U.S. non-governmental organization was asked by an agency of a foreign government to make a grant to a local microfinance institution (MFI) as a prerequisite to the subsidiary's transformation to bank status. The subsidiary proposed contributing $1.42 million to a local MFI to satisfy the request. The subsidiary undertook an extensive, three-stage due diligence process to select the proposed grantee and imposed significant controls on the proposed grant, including ongoing monitoring and auditing, earmarking funds for capacity building, prohibiting compensation of board members, and implementing anti-corruption compliance provisions. DOJ explained that it would not take any enforcement action because the company's due diligence and the controls it planned to put in place sufficed to prevent an FCPA violation.

Other opinion releases also address charitable-type grants or donations. Under the facts presented in those releases, DOJ approved the proposed grant or donation,[103] based on due diligence measures and controls such as:

- certifications by the recipient regarding compliance with the FCPA;[104]
- due diligence to confirm that none of the recipient's officers were affiliated with the foreign government at issue;[105]
- a requirement that the recipient provide audited financial statements;[106]
- a written agreement with the recipient restricting the use of funds;[107]
- steps to ensure that the funds were transferred to a valid bank account;[108]

- confirmation that the charity's commitments were met before funds were disbursed;[109] and
- on-going monitoring of the efficacy of the program.[110]

Legitimate charitable giving does not violate the FCPA. Compliance with the FCPA merely requires that charitable giving not be used as a vehicle to conceal payments made to corruptly influence foreign officials.

Five Questions to Consider When Making Charitable Payments in a Foreign Country:

1. What is the purpose of the payment?

2. Is the payment consistent with the company's internal guidelines on charitable giving?

3. Is the payment at the request of a foreign official?

4. Is a foreign official associated with the charity and, if so, can the foreign official make decisions regarding your business in that country?

5. Is the payment conditioned upon receiving business or other benefits?

Who Is a Foreign Official?

The FCPA's anti-bribery provisions apply to corrupt payments made to (1) "any foreign official"; (2) "any foreign political party or official thereof"; (3) "any candidate for foreign political office"; or (4) any person, while knowing that all or a portion of the payment will be offered, given, or promised to an individual falling within one of these three categories.[111] Although the statute distinguishes between a "foreign official," "foreign political party or official thereof," and "candidate for foreign political office," the term "foreign official" in this guide generally refers to an individual falling within any of these three categories.

The FCPA defines "foreign official" to include:

> any officer or employee of a foreign government or any department, agency, or instrumentality thereof,

or of a public international organization, or any person acting in an official capacity for or on behalf of any such government or department, agency, or instrumentality, or for or on behalf of any such public international organization.[112]

As this language makes clear, the FCPA broadly applies to corrupt payments to "any" officer or employee of a foreign government and to those acting on the foreign government's behalf.[113] The FCPA thus covers corrupt payments to low-ranking employees and high-level officials alike.[114]

The FCPA prohibits payments to foreign *officials*, not to foreign *governments*.[115] That said, companies contemplating contributions or donations to foreign governments should take steps to ensure that no monies are used for corrupt purposes, such as the personal benefit of individual foreign officials.

Department, Agency, or Instrumentality of a Foreign Government

Foreign officials under the FCPA include officers or employees of a department, agency, or instrumentality of a foreign government. When a foreign government is organized in a fashion similar to the U.S. system, what constitutes a government department or agency is typically clear (e.g., a ministry of energy, national security agency, or transportation authority).[116] However, governments can be organized in very different ways.[117] Many operate through state-owned and state-controlled entities, particularly in such areas as aerospace and defense manufacturing, banking and finance, healthcare and life sciences, energy and extractive industries, telecommunications, and transportation.[118] By including officers or employees of agencies and instrumentalities within the definition of "foreign official," the FCPA accounts for this variability.

The term "instrumentality" is broad and can include state-owned or state-controlled entities. Whether a particular entity constitutes an "instrumentality" under the FCPA requires a fact-specific analysis of an entity's ownership, control, status, and function.[119] A number of courts have approved final jury instructions providing a non-exclusive

list of factors to be considered:

- the foreign state's extent of ownership of the entity;
- the foreign state's degree of control over the entity (including whether key officers and directors of the entity are, or are appointed by, government officials);
- the foreign state's characterization of the entity and its employees;
- the circumstances surrounding the entity's creation;
- the purpose of the entity's activities;
- the entity's obligations and privileges under the foreign state's law;
- the exclusive or controlling power vested in the entity to administer its designated functions;
- the level of financial support by the foreign state (including subsidies, special tax treatment, government-mandated fees, and loans);
- the entity's provision of services to the jurisdiction's residents;
- whether the governmental end or purpose sought to be achieved is expressed in the policies of the foreign government; and
- the general perception that the entity is performing official or governmental functions.[120]

Companies should consider these factors when evaluating the risk of FCPA violations and designing compliance programs.

DOJ and SEC have pursued cases involving instrumentalities since the time of the FCPA's enactment and have long used an analysis of ownership, control, status, and function to determine whether a particular entity is an agency or instrumentality of a foreign government. For example, the second-ever FCPA case charged by DOJ involved a California company that paid bribes through a Mexican corporation to two executives of a state-owned

Mexican national oil company.[121] And in the early 1980s, DOJ and SEC brought cases involving a $1 million bribe to the chairman of Trinidad and Tobago's racing authority.[122]

DOJ and SEC continue to regularly bring FCPA cases involving bribes paid to employees of agencies and instrumentalities of foreign governments. In one such case, the subsidiary of a Swiss engineering company paid bribes to officials of a state-owned and controlled electricity commission. The commission was created by, owned by, and controlled by the Mexican government, and it had a monopoly on the transmission and distribution of electricity in Mexico. Many of the commission's board members were cabinet-level government officials, and the director was appointed by Mexico's president.[123] Similarly, in another recent case, Miami telecommunications executives were charged with paying bribes to employees of Haiti's state-owned and controlled telecommunications company. The telecommunications company was 97% owned and 100% controlled by the Haitian government, and its director was appointed by Haiti's president.[124]

While no one factor is dispositive or necessarily more important than another, as a practical matter, an entity is unlikely to qualify as an instrumentality if a government does not own or control a majority of its shares. However, there are circumstances in which an entity would qualify as an instrumentality absent 50% or greater foreign government ownership, which is reflected in the limited number of DOJ or SEC enforcement actions brought in such situations. For example, in addition to being convicted of funneling millions of dollars in bribes to two sitting presidents in two different countries, a French issuer's three subsidiaries were convicted of paying bribes to employees of a Malaysian telecommunications company that was 43% owned by Malaysia's Ministry of Finance. There, notwithstanding its minority ownership stake in the company, the Ministry held the status of a "special shareholder," had veto power over all major expenditures, and controlled important operational decisions.[125] In addition, most senior company officers were political appointees, including the Chairman and Director, the Chairman of the Board of the Tender Committee, and the Executive Director.[126] Thus,

despite the Malaysian government having a minority shareholder position, the company was an instrumentality of the Malaysian government as the government nevertheless had substantial control over the company.

Companies and individuals should also remember that, whether an entity is an instrumentality of a foreign government or a private entity, commercial (i.e., private-to-private) bribery may still violate the FCPA's accounting provisions, the Travel Act, anti-money laundering laws, and other federal or foreign laws. Any type of corrupt payment thus carries a risk of prosecution.

Public International Organizations

In 1998, the FCPA was amended to expand the definition of "foreign official" to include employees and representatives of public international organizations.[127] A "public international organization" is any organization designated as such by Executive Order under the International Organizations Immunities Act, 22 U.S.C. § 288, or any other organization that the President so designates.[128] Currently, public international organizations include entities such as the World Bank, the International Monetary Fund, the World Intellectual Property Organization, the World Trade Organization, the OECD, the Organization of American States, and numerous others. A comprehensive list of organizations designated as "public international organizations" is contained in 22 U.S.C. § 288 and can also be found on the U.S. Government Printing Office website at http://www.gpo.gov/fdsys/.

How Are Payments to Third Parties Treated?

The FCPA expressly prohibits corrupt payments made through third parties or intermediaries.[129] Specifically, it covers payments made to "any person, while knowing that all or a portion of such money or thing of value will be offered, given, or promised, directly or indirectly,"[130] to a foreign official. Many companies doing business in a foreign country retain a local individual or company to help them conduct business. Although these foreign agents may provide entirely legitimate advice regarding local customs and procedures and may help facilitate business transactions, companies should be aware of the risks involved in engaging third-party agents or intermediaries. The fact that a bribe is paid by a third party does not eliminate the potential for criminal or civil FCPA liability.[131]

For instance, a four-company joint venture used two agents—a British lawyer and a Japanese trading company—to bribe Nigerian government officials in order to win a series of liquefied natural gas construction projects.[132] Together, the four multi-national corporations and the Japanese trading company paid a combined $1.7 billion in civil and criminal sanctions for their decade-long bribery scheme. In addition, the subsidiary of one of the companies pleaded guilty and a number of individuals, including the British lawyer and the former CEO of one of the companies' subsidiaries, received significant prison terms.

Similarly, a medical device manufacturer entered into a deferred prosecution agreement as the result of corrupt payments it authorized its local Chinese distributor to pay to Chinese officials.[133] Another company, a manufacturer of specialty chemicals, committed multiple FCPA violations through its agents in Iraq: a Canadian national and the Canadian's companies. Among other acts, the Canadian national paid and promised to pay more than $1.5 million in bribes to officials of the Iraqi Ministry of Oil to secure sales of a fuel additive. Both the company and the Canadian national pleaded guilty to criminal charges and resolved civil enforcement actions by SEC.[134]

In another case, the U.S. subsidiary of a Swiss freight forwarding company was charged with paying bribes on behalf of its customers in several countries.[135] Although the U.S. subsidiary was not an issuer under the FCPA, it was an "agent" of several U.S. issuers and was thus charged directly with violating the FCPA. Charges against the freight forwarding company and seven of its customers resulted in over $236.5 million in sanctions.[136]

Because Congress anticipated the use of third-party agents in bribery schemes—for example, to avoid actual knowledge of a bribe—it defined the term "knowing" in a way that prevents individuals and businesses from avoiding liability by putting "any person" between themselves and

chapter 2
The FCPA:
Anti-Bribery Provisions

the foreign officials.[137] Under the FCPA, a person's state of mind is "knowing" with respect to conduct, a circumstance, or a result if the person:

- is aware that [he] is engaging in such conduct, that such circumstance exists, or that such result is substantially certain to occur; or
- has a firm belief that such circumstance exists or that such result is substantially certain to occur.[138]

Thus, a person has the requisite knowledge when he is aware of a high probability of the existence of such circumstance, unless the person actually believes that such circumstance does not exist.[139] As Congress made clear, it meant to impose liability not only on those with actual knowledge of wrongdoing, but also on those who purposefully avoid actual knowledge:

[T]he so-called "head-in-the-sand" problem—variously described in the pertinent authorities as "conscious disregard," "willful blindness" or "deliberate ignorance"—should be covered so that management officials could not take refuge from the Act's prohibitions by their unwarranted obliviousness to any action (or inaction), language or other "signaling device" that should reasonably alert them of the "high probability" of an FCPA violation.[140]

Common red flags associated with third parties include:

- excessive commissions to third-party agents or consultants;
- unreasonably large discounts to third-party distributors;
- third-party "consulting agreements" that include only vaguely described services;
- the third-party consultant is in a different line of business than that for which it has been engaged;
- the third party is related to or closely associated with the foreign official;

- the third party became part of the transaction at the express request or insistence of the foreign official;
- the third party is merely a shell company incorporated in an offshore jurisdiction; and
- the third party requests payment to offshore bank accounts.

Businesses may reduce the FCPA risks associated with third-party agents by implementing an effective compliance program, which includes due diligence of any prospective foreign agents.

United States v. Kozeny, et al.

In December 2011, the U.S. Court of Appeals for the Second Circuit upheld a conscious avoidance instruction given during the 2009 trial of a businessman who was convicted of conspiring to violate the FCPA's anti-bribery provisions by agreeing to make payments to Azeri officials in a scheme to encourage the privatization of the Azerbaijan Republic's state oil company. The court of appeals found that the instruction did not lack a factual predicate, citing evidence and testimony at trial demonstrating that the defendant knew corruption was pervasive in Azerbaijan; that he was aware of his business partner's reputation for misconduct; that he had created two U.S. companies in order to shield himself and other investors from potential liability for payments made in violation of the FCPA; and that the defendant expressed concerns during a conference call about whether his business partner and company were bribing officials.

The court of appeals also rejected the defendant's contention that the conscious avoidance charge had improperly permitted the jury to convict him based on negligence, explaining that ample evidence in the record showed that the defendant had "serious concerns" about the legality of his partner's business practices "and worked to avoid learning exactly what [he] was doing," and noting that the district court had specifically instructed the jury not to convict based on negligence.

What Affirmative Defenses Are Available?

The FCPA's anti-bribery provisions contain two affirmative defenses: (1) that the payment was lawful under the written laws of the foreign country (the "local law" defense), and (2) that the money was spent as part of demonstrating a product or performing a contractual obligation (the "reasonable and bona fide business expenditure" defense). Because these are affirmative defenses, the defendant bears the burden of proving them.

The Local Law Defense

For the local law defense to apply, a defendant must establish that "the payment, gift, offer, or promise of anything of value that was made, was lawful under the written laws and regulations of the foreign official's, political party's, party official's, or candidate's country."[141] The defendant must establish that the payment was lawful under the foreign country's written laws and regulations at the time of the offense. In creating the local law defense in 1988, Congress sought "to make clear that the absence of written laws in a foreign official's country would not by itself be sufficient to satisfy this defense."[142] Thus, the fact that bribes may not be prosecuted under local law is insufficient to establish the defense. In practice, the local law defense arises infrequently, as the written laws and regulations of countries rarely, if ever, permit corrupt payments. Nevertheless, if a defendant can establish that conduct that otherwise falls within the scope of the FCPA's anti-bribery provisions was lawful under written, local law, he or she would have a defense to prosecution.

In *United States v. Kozeny*, the defendant unsuccessfully sought to assert the local law defense regarding the law of Azerbaijan. The parties disputed the contents and applicability of Azeri law, and each presented expert reports and testimony on behalf of their conflicting interpretations. The court ruled that the defendant could not invoke the FCPA's affirmative defense because Azeri law did not actually legalize the bribe payment. The court concluded that an exception under Azeri law relieving bribe payors who voluntarily disclose bribe payments to the authorities of criminal liability did not make the bribes legal.[143]

Reasonable and Bona Fide Expenditures

The FCPA allows companies to provide reasonable and bona fide travel and lodging expenses to a foreign official, and it is an affirmative defense where expenses are directly related to the promotion, demonstration, or explanation of a company's products or services, or are related to a company's execution or performance of a contract with a foreign government or agency.[144] Trips that are primarily for personal entertainment purposes, however, are not bona fide business expenses and may violate the FCPA's anti-bribery provisions.[145] Moreover, when expenditures, bona fide or not, are mischaracterized in a company's books and records, or where unauthorized or improper expenditures occur due to a failure to implement adequate internal controls, they may also violate the FCPA's accounting provisions. Purposeful mischaracterization of expenditures may also, of course, indicate a corrupt intent.

DOJ and SEC have consistently recognized that businesses, both foreign and domestic, are permitted to pay for reasonable expenses associated with the promotion of their products and services or the execution of existing contracts. In addition, DOJ has frequently provided guidance about legitimate promotional and contract-related expenses—addressing travel and lodging expenses in particular—through several opinion procedure releases. Under the circumstances presented in those releases,[146] DOJ opined that the following types of expenditures on behalf of foreign officials did not warrant FCPA enforcement action:

- travel and expenses to visit company facilities or operations;
- travel and expenses for training; and
- product demonstration or promotional activities, including travel and expenses for meetings.

Whether any particular payment is a bona fide expenditure necessarily requires a fact-specific analysis. But the following non-exhaustive list of safeguards, compiled from several releases, may be helpful to businesses in evaluating whether a particular expenditure is appropriate or may risk violating the FCPA:

- Do not select the particular officials who will participate in the party's proposed trip or program[147] or else select them based on pre-determined, merit-based criteria.[148]
- Pay all costs directly to travel and lodging vendors and/or reimburse costs only upon presentation of a receipt.[149]
- Do not advance funds or pay for reimbursements in cash.[150]
- Ensure that any stipends are reasonable approximations of costs likely to be incurred[151] and/or that expenses are limited to those that are necessary and reasonable.[152]
- Ensure the expenditures are transparent, both within the company and to the foreign government.[153]
- Do not condition payment of expenses on any action by the foreign official.[154]
- Obtain written confirmation that payment of the expenses is not contrary to local law.[155]
- Provide no additional compensation, stipends, or spending money beyond what is necessary to pay for actual expenses incurred.[156]
- Ensure that costs and expenses on behalf of the foreign officials will be accurately recorded in the company's books and records.[157]

In sum, while certain expenditures are more likely to raise red flags, they will not give rise to prosecution if they are (1) reasonable, (2) bona fide, and (3) directly related to (4) the promotion, demonstration, or explanation of products or services or the execution or performance of a contract.[158]

chapter 2
The FCPA:
Anti-Bribery Provisions

What Are Facilitating or Expediting Payments?

The FCPA's bribery prohibition contains a narrow exception for "facilitating or expediting payments" made in furtherance of routine governmental action.[159] The facilitating payments exception applies only when a payment is made to further "routine governmental action" that involves non-discretionary acts.[160] Examples of "routine governmental action" include processing visas, providing police protection or mail service, and supplying utilities like phone service, power, and water. Routine government action does *not* include a decision to award new business or to continue business with a particular party.[161] Nor does it include acts that are within an official's discretion or that would constitute misuse of an official's office.[162] Thus, paying an official a small amount to have the power turned on at a factory might be a facilitating payment; paying an inspector to ignore the fact that the company does not have a valid permit to operate the factory would not be a facilitating payment.

Examples of "Routine Governmental Action"

An action which is ordinarily and commonly performed by a foreign official in—

- obtaining permits, licenses, or other official documents to qualify a person to do business in a foreign country;

- processing governmental papers, such as visas and work orders;

- providing police protection, mail pickup and delivery, or scheduling inspections associated with contract performance or inspections related to transit of goods across country;

- providing phone service, power and water supply, loading and unloading cargo, or protecting perishable products or commodities from deterioration; or

- actions of a similar nature.

Whether a payment falls within the exception is not dependent on the size of the payment, though size can be telling, as a large payment is more suggestive of corrupt intent to influence a non-routine governmental action. But, like the FCPA's anti-bribery provisions more generally, the facilitating payments exception focuses on the *purpose* of the payment rather than its value. For instance, an Oklahoma-based corporation violated the FCPA when its subsidiary paid Argentine customs officials approximately $166,000 to secure customs clearance for equipment and materials that lacked required certifications or could not be imported under local law and to pay a lower-than-applicable duty rate. The company's Venezuelan subsidiary had also paid Venezuelan customs officials approximately $7,000 to permit the importation and exportation of equipment and materials not in compliance with local regulations and to avoid a full inspection of the imported goods.[163] In another case, three subsidiaries of a global supplier of oil drilling products and services were criminally charged with authorizing an agent to make at least 378 corrupt payments (totaling approximately $2.1 million) to Nigerian Customs Service officials for preferential treatment during the customs process, including the reduction or elimination of customs duties.[164]

Labeling a bribe as a "facilitating payment" in a company's books and records does not make it one. A Swiss offshore drilling company, for example, recorded payments to its customs agent in the subsidiary's "facilitating payment" account, even though company personnel believed the payments were, in fact, bribes. The company was charged with violating both the FCPA's anti-bribery and accounting provisions.[165]

Although true facilitating payments are not illegal under the FCPA, they may still violate local law in the countries where the company is operating, and the OECD's Working Group on Bribery recommends that all countries encourage companies to prohibit or discourage facilitating payments, which the United States has done regularly.[166] In addition, other countries' foreign bribery laws, such as the United Kingdom's, may not contain an exception for facilitating payments.[167] Individuals and companies should therefore be aware that although true facilitating payments are permissible under the FCPA, they may still subject a company or individual to sanctions. As with any expenditure, facilitating payments may still violate the FCPA if they are not properly recorded in an issuer's books and records.[168]

Hypothetical: Facilitating Payments

Company A is a large multi-national mining company with operations in Foreign Country, where it recently identified a significant new ore deposit. It has ready buyers for the new ore but has limited capacity to get it to market. In order to increase the size and speed of its ore export, Company A will need to build a new road from its facility to the port that can accommodate larger trucks. Company A retains an agent in Foreign Country to assist it in obtaining the required permits, including an environmental permit, to build the road. The agent informs Company A's vice president for international operations that he plans to make a one-time small cash payment to a clerk in the relevant government office to ensure that the clerk files and stamps the permit applications expeditiously, as the agent has experienced delays of three months when he has not made this "grease" payment. The clerk has no discretion about whether to file and stamp the permit applications once the requisite filing fee has been paid. The vice president authorizes the payment.

A few months later, the agent tells the vice president that he has run into a problem obtaining a necessary environmental permit. It turns out that the planned road construction would adversely impact an environmentally sensitive and protected local wetland. While the problem could be overcome by rerouting the road, such rerouting would cost Company A $1 million more and would slow down construction by six months. It would also increase the transit time for the ore and reduce the number of monthly shipments. The agent tells the vice president that he is good friends with the director of Foreign Country's Department of Natural Resources and that it would only take a modest cash payment to the director and the "problem would go away." The vice president authorizes the payment, and the agent makes it. After receiving the payment, the director issues the permit, and Company A constructs its new road through the wetlands.

Was the payment to the clerk a violation of the FCPA?

No. Under these circumstances, the payment to the clerk would qualify as a facilitating payment, since it is a one-time, small payment to obtain a routine, non-discretionary governmental service that Company A is entitled to receive (i.e., the stamping and filing of the permit application). However, while the payment may qualify as an exception to the FCPA's anti-bribery provisions, it may violate other laws, both in Foreign Country and elsewhere. In addition, if the payment is not accurately recorded, it could violate the FCPA's books and records provision.

Was the payment to the director a violation of the FCPA?

Yes. The payment to the director of the Department of Natural Resources was in clear violation of the FCPA, since it was designed to corruptly influence a foreign official into improperly approving a permit. The issuance of the environmental permit was a discretionary act, and indeed, Company A should not have received it. Company A, its vice president, and the local agent may all be prosecuted for authorizing and paying the bribe.

Does the FCPA Apply to Cases of Extortion or Duress?

Situations involving extortion or duress will not give rise to FCPA liability because a payment made in response to true extortionate demands under imminent threat of physical harm cannot be said to have been made with corrupt intent or for the purpose of obtaining or retaining business.[169] In enacting the FCPA, Congress recognized that real-world situations might arise in which a business is compelled to pay an official in order to avoid threats to health and safety. As Congress explained, "a payment to an official to keep an oil rig from being dynamited should not be held to be made with the requisite corrupt purpose."[170]

Mere *economic* coercion, however, does not amount to extortion. As Congress noted when it enacted the FCPA: "The defense that the payment was demanded on the part of a government official as a price for gaining entry into a market or to obtain a contract would not suffice since at some point the U.S. company would make a conscious decision whether or not to pay a bribe."[171] The fact that the payment was "first proposed by the recipient ... does not alter the corrupt purpose on the part of the person paying the bribe."[172]

This distinction between extortion and economic coercion was recognized by the court in *United States v. Kozeny*. There, the court concluded that although an individual who makes a payment under duress (i.e., upon threat of physical harm) will not be criminally liable under the FCPA,[173] a bribe payor who claims payment was demanded as a price for gaining market entry or obtaining a contract "cannot argue that he lacked the intent to bribe the official because he made the 'conscious decision' to pay the official."[174] While the bribe payor in this situation "could have turned his back and walked away," in the oil rig example, "he could not."[175]

Businesses operating in high-risk countries may face real threats of violence or harm to their employees, and payments made in response to imminent threats to health or safety do not violate the FCPA.[176] If such a situation arises, and to ensure the safety of its employees, companies should immediately contact the appropriate U.S. embassy for assistance.

Principles of Corporate Liability for Anti-Bribery Violations

General principles of corporate liability apply to the FCPA. Thus, a company is liable when its directors, officers, employees, or agents, acting within the scope of their employment, commit FCPA violations intended, at least in part, to benefit the company.[177] Similarly, just as with any other statute, DOJ and SEC look to principles of parent-subsidiary and successor liability in evaluating corporate liability.

Parent-Subsidiary Liability

There are two ways in which a parent company may be liable for bribes paid by its subsidiary. First, a parent may have participated sufficiently in the activity to be directly liable for the conduct—as, for example, when it directed its subsidiary's misconduct or otherwise directly participated in the bribe scheme.

Second, a parent may be liable for its subsidiary's conduct under traditional agency principles. The fundamental characteristic of agency is control.[178] Accordingly, DOJ and SEC evaluate the parent's control—including the parent's knowledge and direction of the subsidiary's actions, both generally and in the context of the specific transaction—when evaluating whether a subsidiary is an agent of the parent. Although the formal relationship between the parent and subsidiary is important in this analysis, so are the practical realities of how the parent and subsidiary actually interact.

If an agency relationship exists, a subsidiary's actions and knowledge are imputed to its parent.[179] Moreover, under traditional principles of *respondeat superior*, a company is liable for the acts of its agents, including its employees, undertaken within the scope of their employment and intended, at least in part, to benefit the company.[180] Thus, if an agency relationship exists between a parent and a subsidiary, the parent is liable for bribery committed by the subsidiary's employees. For example, SEC brought an administrative action against a parent for bribes paid by the president of its indirect, wholly owned subsidiary. In that matter, the subsidiary's president reported directly to the CEO of the parent issuer, and the issuer routinely identified the president as a member of its senior management in its annual filing with SEC and in annual reports. Additionally, the parent's legal department approved the retention of the third-party agent through whom the bribes were arranged despite a lack of documented due diligence and an agency agreement that violated corporate policy; also, an official of the parent approved one of the payments to the third-party agent.[181] Under these circumstances, the parent company had sufficient knowledge and control of its subsidiary's actions to be liable under the FCPA.

Successor Liability

Companies acquire a host of liabilities when they merge with or acquire another company, including those arising out of contracts, torts, regulations, and statutes. As a general legal matter, when a company merges with or acquires another company, the successor company assumes the predecessor company's liabilities.[182] Successor liability is an integral component of corporate law and, among other things, prevents companies from avoiding liability by reorganizing.[183] Successor liability applies to all kinds of civil and criminal liabilities,[184] and FCPA violations are no exception. Whether successor liability applies to a particular corporate transaction depends on the facts and the applicable state, federal, and foreign law. Successor liability does not, however, create liability where none existed before. For example, if an issuer were to acquire a foreign company that was not previously subject to the FCPA's jurisdiction, the mere acquisition of that foreign company would not retroactively create FCPA liability for the acquiring issuer.

DOJ and SEC encourage companies to conduct pre-acquisition due diligence and improve compliance programs and internal controls after acquisition for a variety of reasons. First, due diligence helps an acquiring company to accurately value the target company. Contracts obtained through bribes may be legally unenforceable, business obtained illegally may be lost when bribe payments are stopped, there may be liability for prior illegal conduct, and the prior corrupt acts may harm the acquiring company's reputation and future business prospects. Identifying these issues before an acquisition allows companies to better

evaluate any potential post-acquisition liability and thus properly assess the target's value.[185] Second, due diligence reduces the risk that the acquired company will continue to pay bribes. Proper pre-acquisition due diligence can identify business and regional risks and can also lay the foundation for a swift and successful post-acquisition integration into the acquiring company's corporate control and compliance environment. Third, the consequences of potential violations uncovered through due diligence can be handled by the parties in an orderly and efficient manner through negotiation of the costs and responsibilities for the investigation and remediation. Finally, comprehensive due diligence demonstrates a genuine commitment to uncovering and preventing FCPA violations.

In a significant number of instances, DOJ and SEC have declined to take action against companies that voluntarily disclosed and remediated conduct and cooperated with DOJ and SEC in the merger and acquisition context.[186] And DOJ and SEC have only taken action against successor companies in limited circumstances, generally in cases involving egregious and sustained violations or where the successor company directly participated in the violations or failed to stop the misconduct from continuing after the acquisition. In one case, a U.S.-based issuer was charged with books and records and internal controls violations for continuing a kickback scheme originated by its predecessor.[187] Another recent case involved a merger between two tobacco leaf merchants, where prior to the merger each company committed FCPA violations through its foreign subsidiaries, involving multiple countries over the course of many years. At each company, the bribes were directed by the parent company's senior management. The two issuers then merged to form a new public company. Under these circumstances—the merger of two public companies that had each engaged in

---

Practical Tips to Reduce FCPA Risk in Mergers and Acquisitions

Companies pursuing mergers or acquisitions can take certain steps to identify and potentially reduce FCPA risks:

- **M&A Opinion Procedure Release Requests:** One option is to seek an opinion from DOJ in anticipation of a potential acquisition, such as occurred with Opinion Release 08-02. That case involved special circumstances, namely, severely limited pre-acquisition due diligence available to the potential acquiring company, and, because it was an opinion release (i.e., providing certain assurances by DOJ concerning prospective conduct), it necessarily imposed demanding standards and prescriptive timeframes in return for specific assurances from DOJ, which SEC, as a matter of discretion, also honors. Thus, obtaining an opinion from DOJ can be a good way to address specific due diligence challenges, but, because of the nature of such an opinion, it will likely contain more stringent requirements than may be necessary in all circumstances.

- **M&A Risk-Based FCPA Due Diligence and Disclosure:** As a practical matter, most acquisitions will typically not require the type of prospective assurances contained in an opinion from DOJ. DOJ and SEC encourage companies engaging in mergers and acquisitions to: (1) conduct thorough risk-based FCPA and anti-corruption due diligence on potential new business acquisitions; (2) ensure that the acquiring company's code of conduct and compliance policies and procedures regarding the FCPA and other anti-corruption laws apply as quickly as is practicable to newly acquired businesses or merged entities; (3) train the directors, officers, and employees of newly acquired businesses or merged entities, and when appropriate, train agents and business partners, on the FCPA and other relevant anti-corruption laws and the company's code of conduct and compliance policies and procedures; (4) conduct an FCPA-specific audit of all newly acquired or merged businesses as quickly as practicable; and (5) disclose any corrupt payments discovered as part of its due diligence of newly acquired entities or merged entities. DOJ and SEC will give meaningful credit to companies who undertake these actions, and, in appropriate circumstances, DOJ and SEC may consequently decline to bring enforcement actions.

---

bribery—both the new entity and the foreign subsidiaries were liable under the FCPA. The new parent entered into a non-prosecution agreement with DOJ and settled a civil action with SEC, while the company's subsidiaries, which also merged, pleaded guilty.[188]

More often, DOJ and SEC have pursued enforcement actions against the predecessor company (rather than the acquiring company), particularly when the acquiring company uncovered and timely remedied the violations or when the government's investigation of the predecessor company preceded the acquisition. In one such case, an Ohio-based health care company's due diligence of an acquisition target uncovered FCPA violations by the target's subsidiary, and, before the merger was completed, the subsidiary's violations were disclosed to DOJ and SEC. The subsidiary pleaded guilty and paid a $2 million criminal fine,[189] the acquisition target settled with SEC and paid a $500,000 civil penalty,[190]

and no successor liability was sought against the acquiring entity. In another case, a Pennsylvania-based issuer that supplied heating and air conditioning products and services was subject to an ongoing investigation by DOJ and SEC at the time that it was acquired; DOJ and SEC resolved enforcement actions only against the predecessor company, which had by that time become a wholly owned subsidiary of the successor company.[191]

DOJ and SEC have also brought actions only against a predecessor company where its FCPA violations are discovered after acquisition. For example, when a Florida-based U.S. company discovered in post-acquisition due diligence that the telecommunications company (a domestic concern) it had acquired had engaged in foreign bribery, the successor company disclosed the FCPA violations to DOJ. It then conducted an internal investigation, cooperated fully with DOJ, and took appropriate remedial action—including terminating senior management at the acquired company. No enforcement action was taken against the successor, but the predecessor company pleaded guilty to one count of violating the FCPA and agreed to pay a $2 million fine.[192] Later, four executives from the predecessor company were convicted of FCPA violations, three of whom received terms of imprisonment.[193]

On occasion, when an enforcement action has been taken against a predecessor company, the successor seeks assurances that it will not be subject to a future enforcement action. In one such case, a Dutch predecessor resolved FCPA charges with DOJ through a deferred prosecution agreement.[194] While both the predecessor and successor signed the agreement, which included a commitment to ongoing cooperation and an improved compliance program, only the predecessor company was charged; in signing the agreement, the successor company gained the certainty of conditional release from criminal liability, even though it was not being pursued for FCPA violations.[195] In another case, after a Connecticut-based company uncovered FCPA violations by a California company it sought to acquire, both companies voluntarily disclosed the conduct to DOJ and SEC.[196] The predecessor company resolved its criminal liability through a non-prosecution agreement with DOJ that included an $800,000 monetary penalty and also settled with SEC, paying a total of $1.1 million in disgorgement, pre-judgment interest, and civil penalties. The successor company proceeded with the acquisition and separately entered into a non-prosecution agreement with DOJ in which it agreed, among other things, to ensure full performance of the predecessor company's non-prosecution agreement. This agreement provided certainty to the successor concerning its FCPA liability.[197]

Importantly, a successor company's voluntary disclosure, appropriate due diligence, and implementation of an effective compliance program may also decrease the likelihood of an enforcement action regarding an acquired company's post-acquisition conduct when pre-acquisition due diligence is not possible.[198]

chapter 2

The FCPA:
Anti-Bribery Provisions

Hypothetical: Successor Liability Where Acquired Company Was Not Previously Subject to the FCPA

Company A is a Delaware corporation with its principal offices in the United States and whose shares are listed on a national U.S. exchange. Company A is considering acquiring Foreign Company, which is not an issuer or a domestic concern. Foreign Company takes no actions within the United States that would make it subject to territorial jurisdiction. Company A's proposed acquisition would make Foreign Company a subsidiary of Company A.

Scenario 1:

Prior to acquiring Foreign Company, Company A engages in extensive due diligence of Foreign Company, including: (1) having its legal, accounting, and compliance departments review Foreign Company's sales and financial data, its customer contracts, and its third-party and distributor agreements; (2) performing a risk-based analysis of Foreign Company's customer base; (3) performing an audit of selected transactions engaged in by Foreign Company; and (4) engaging in discussions with Foreign Company's general counsel, vice president of sales, and head of internal audit regarding all corruption risks, compliance efforts, and any other corruption-related issues that have surfaced at Foreign Company over the past ten years. This due diligence aims to determine whether Foreign Company has appropriate anti-corruption and compliance policies in place, whether Foreign Company's employees have been adequately trained regarding those policies, how Foreign Company ensures that those policies are followed, and what remedial actions are taken if the policies are violated.

During the course of its due diligence, Company A learns that Foreign Company has made several potentially improper payments in the form of an inflated commission to a third-party agent in connection with a government contract with Foreign Country. Immediately after the acquisition, Company A discloses the conduct to DOJ and SEC, suspends and terminates those employees and the third-party agent responsible for the payments, and makes certain that the illegal payments have stopped. It also quickly integrates Foreign Company into Company A's own robust internal controls, including its anti-corruption and compliance policies, which it communicates to its new employees through required online and in-person training in the local language. Company A also requires Foreign Company's third-party distributors and other agents to sign anti-corruption certifications, complete training, and sign new contracts that incorporate FCPA and anti-corruption representations and warranties and audit rights.

Based on these facts, could DOJ or SEC prosecute Company A?

No. Although DOJ and SEC have jurisdiction over Company A because it is an issuer, neither could pursue Company A for conduct that occurred prior to its acquisition of Foreign Company. As Foreign Company was neither an issuer nor a domestic concern and was not subject to U.S. territorial jurisdiction, DOJ and SEC have no jurisdiction over its pre-acquisition misconduct. The acquisition of a company does not create jurisdiction where none existed before.

Importantly, Company A's extensive pre-acquisition due diligence allowed it to identify and halt the corruption. As there was no continuing misconduct post-acquisition, the FCPA was not violated.

Scenario 2:

Company A performs only minimal and pro forma pre-acquisition due diligence. It does not conduct a risk-based analysis, and its review of Foreign Company's data, contracts, and third-party and distributor agreements is cursory. Company A acquires Foreign Company and makes it a wholly owned subsidiary. Although Company A circulates its compliance policies to all new personnel after the acquisition, it does not translate the compliance policies into the local language or train its new personnel or third-party agents on anti-corruption issues.

A few months after the acquisition, an employee in Company A's international sales office (Sales Employee) learns from a legacy Foreign Company employee that for years the government contract that generated most of Foreign Company's revenues depended on inflated commissions to a third-party agent "to make the right person happy at Foreign Government Agency." Sales Employee is told that unless the payments continue the business will likely be lost, which would mean that Company A's new acquisition would quickly become a financial failure. The payments continue for two

(cont'd)

years after the acquisition. After another employee of Company A reports the long-running bribe scheme to a director at Foreign Government Agency, Company A stops the payments and DOJ and SEC investigate.

Based on these facts, would DOJ or SEC charge Company A?

Yes. DOJ and SEC have prosecuted companies like Company A in similar circumstances. Any charges would not, however, be premised upon successor liability, but rather on Company A's post-acquisition bribe payments, which themselves created criminal and civil liability for Company A.

Scenario 3:

Under local law, Company A's ability to conduct pre-acquisition due diligence on Foreign Company is limited. In the due diligence it does conduct, Company A determines that Foreign Company is doing business in high-risk countries and in high-risk industries but finds no red flags specific to Foreign Company's operations. Post-acquisition, Company A conducts extensive due diligence and determines that Foreign Company had paid bribes to officials with Foreign Government Agency. Company A takes prompt action to remediate the problem, including following the measures set forth in Opinion Procedure Release No. 08-02. Among other actions, it voluntarily discloses the misconduct to DOJ and SEC, ensures all bribes are immediately stopped, takes remedial action against all parties involved in the corruption, and quickly incorporates Foreign Company into a robust compliance program and Company A's other internal controls.

Based on these facts, would DOJ or SEC prosecute Company A?

DOJ and SEC have declined to prosecute companies like Company A in similar circumstances. Companies can follow the measures set forth in Opinion Procedure Release No. 08-02, or seek their own opinions, where adequate pre-acquisition due diligence is not possible.

Hypothetical: Successor Liability Where Acquired Company Was Already Subject to the FCPA

Both Company A and Company B are Delaware corporations with their principal offices in the United States. Both companies' shares are listed on a national U.S. exchange.

Scenario 1:

Company A is considering acquiring several of Company B's business lines. Prior to the acquisition, Company A engages in extensive due diligence, including: (1) having its legal, accounting, and compliance departments review Company B's sales and financial data, its customer contracts, and its third-party and distributor agreements; (2) performing a risk-based analysis of Company B's customer base; (3) performing an audit of selected transactions engaged in by Company B; and (4) engaging in discussions with Company B's general counsel, vice president of sales, and head of internal audit regarding all corruption risks, compliance efforts, and any other major corruption-related issues that have surfaced at Company B over the past ten years. This due diligence aims to determine whether Company B has appropriate anti-corruption and compliance policies in place, whether Company B's employees have been adequately trained regarding those policies, how Company B ensures that those policies are followed, and what remedial actions are taken if the policies are violated.

During the course of its due diligence, Company A learns that Company B has made several potentially improper payments in connection with a government contract with Foreign Country. As a condition of the acquisition, Company A requires Company B to disclose the misconduct to the government. Company A makes certain that the illegal payments

(cont'd)

have stopped and quickly integrates Company B's business lines into Company A's own robust internal controls, including its anti-corruption and compliance policies, which it communicates to its new employees through required online and in-person training in the local language. Company A also requires Company B's third-party distributors and other agents to sign anti-corruption certifications, complete training, and sign new contracts that incorporate FCPA and anti-corruption representations and warranties and audit rights.

Based on these facts, would DOJ or SEC prosecute?

DOJ and SEC have declined to prosecute companies like Company A in similar circumstances. DOJ and SEC encourage companies like Company A to conduct extensive FCPA due diligence. By uncovering the corruption, Company A put itself in a favorable position, and, because the corrupt payments have stopped, Company A has no continuing liability. Whether DOJ and SEC might charge Company B depends on facts and circumstances beyond the scope of this hypothetical. DOJ would consider its *Principles of Federal Prosecution of Business Organizations* and SEC would consider the factors contained in the *Seaboard Report*, both of which are discussed in Chapter 5. In general, the more egregious and long-standing the corruption, the more likely it is that DOJ and SEC would prosecute Company B. In certain limited circumstances, DOJ and SEC have in the past declined to bring charges against acquired companies, recognizing that acquiring companies may bear much of the reputational damage and costs associated with such charges.

Scenario 2:

Company A plans to acquire Company B. Although, as in Scenario 1, Company A conducts extensive due diligence, it does not uncover the bribery until after the acquisition. Company A then makes certain that the illegal payments stop and voluntarily discloses the misconduct to DOJ and SEC. It quickly integrates Company B into Company A's own robust internal controls, including its anti-corruption and compliance policies, which it communicates to its new employees through required online and in-person training in the local language. Company A also requires Company B's third-party distributors and other agents to sign anti-corruption certifications, complete training, and sign new contracts that incorporate FCPA and anti-corruption representations and warranties and audit rights.

Based on these facts, would DOJ or SEC prosecute?

Absent unusual circumstances not contemplated by this hypothetical, DOJ and SEC are unlikely to prosecute Company A for the pre-acquisition misconduct of Company B, provided that Company B still exists in a form that would allow it to be prosecuted separately (e.g., Company B is a subsidiary of Company A). DOJ and SEC understand that no due diligence is perfect and that society benefits when companies with strong compliance programs acquire and improve companies with weak ones. At the same time, however, neither the liability for corruption—nor the harms caused by it—are eliminated when one company acquires another. Whether DOJ and SEC will pursue a case against Company B (or, in unusual circumstances, Company A) will depend on consideration of all the factors in the *Principles of Federal Prosecution of Business Organizations* and the *Seaboard Report*, respectively.

Scenario 3:

Company A merges with Company B, which is in the same line of business and interacts with the same Foreign Government customers, and forms Company C. Due diligence before the merger reveals that both Company A and Company B have been engaging in similar bribery. In both cases, the bribery was extensive and known by high-level management within the companies.

Based on these facts, would DOJ or SEC prosecute?

Yes. DOJ and SEC have prosecuted companies like Company C on the basis of successor liability. Company C is a combination of two companies that both violated the FCPA, and their merger does not eliminate their liability. In addition, since Company C is an ongoing concern, DOJ and SEC may impose a monitorship to ensure that the bribery has ceased and a compliance program is developed to prevent future misconduct.

Additional Principles of Criminal Liability for Anti-Bribery Violations: Aiding and Abetting and Conspiracy

chapter 2
The FCPA:
Anti-Bribery Provisions

Under federal law, individuals or companies that aid or abet a crime, including an FCPA violation, are as guilty as if they had directly committed the offense themselves. The aiding and abetting statute provides that whoever "commits an offense against the United States or aids, abets, counsels, commands, induces or procures its commission," or "willfully causes an act to be done which if directly performed by him or another would be an offense against the United States," is punishable as a principal.[199] Aiding and abetting is not an independent crime, and the government must prove that an underlying FCPA violation was committed.[200]

Individuals and companies, including foreign nationals and companies, may also be liable for conspiring to violate the FCPA—i.e., for *agreeing* to commit an FCPA violation—even if they are not, or could not be, independently charged with a substantive FCPA violation. For instance, a foreign, non-issuer company could be convicted of conspiring with a domestic concern to violate the FCPA. Under certain circumstances, it could also be held liable for the domestic concern's substantive FCPA violations under *Pinkerton v. United States*, which imposes liability on a defendant for reasonably foreseeable crimes committed by a co-conspirator in furtherance of a conspiracy that the defendant joined.[201]

A foreign company or individual may be held liable for aiding and abetting an FCPA violation or for conspiring to violate the FCPA, even if the foreign company or individual did not take any act in furtherance of the corrupt payment while in the territory of the United States. In conspiracy cases, the United States generally has jurisdiction over all the conspirators where at least one conspirator is an issuer, domestic concern, or commits a reasonably foreseeable overt act within the United States.[202] For example, if a foreign company or individual conspires to violate the FCPA with someone who commits an overt act within the United States, the United States can prosecute the foreign company or individual for the conspiracy. The same principle applies to aiding and abetting violations. For instance,

even though they took no action in the United States, Japanese and European companies were charged with conspiring with and aiding and abetting a domestic concern's FCPA violations.[203]

Additional Principles of Civil Liability for Anti-Bribery Violations: Aiding and Abetting and Causing

Both companies and individuals can be held civilly liable for aiding and abetting FCPA anti-bribery violations if they knowingly or recklessly provide substantial assistance to a violator.[204] Similarly, in the administrative proceeding context, companies and individuals may be held liable for causing FCPA violations.[205] This liability extends to the subsidiaries and agents of U.S. issuers.

In one case, the U.S. subsidiary of a Swiss freight forwarding company was held civilly liable for paying bribes on behalf of its customers in several countries.[206] Although the U.S. subsidiary was not an issuer for purposes of the FCPA, it was an "agent" of several U.S. issuers. By paying bribes on behalf of its issuers' customers, the subsidiary both directly violated and aided and abetted the issuers' FCPA violations.

What Is the Applicable Statute of Limitations?

Statute of Limitations in Criminal Cases

The FCPA's anti-bribery and accounting provisions do not specify a statute of limitations for criminal actions. Accordingly, the general five-year limitations period set forth in 18 U.S.C. § 3282 applies to substantive criminal violations of the Act.[207]

In cases involving FCPA conspiracies, the government may be able to reach conduct occurring before the five-year limitations period applicable to conspiracies under 18 U.S.C. § 371. For conspiracy offenses, the government generally need prove only that one act in furtherance of the conspiracy occurred during the limitations period, thus enabling the government to prosecute bribes paid or accounting violations occurring more than five years prior to the filing of formal charges.[208]

There are at least two ways in which the applicable limitations period is commonly extended. First, companies or individuals cooperating with DOJ may enter into a tolling agreement that voluntarily extends the limitations period. Second, under 18 U.S.C. § 3292, the government may seek a court order suspending the statute of limitations posed in a criminal case for up to three years in order to obtain evidence from foreign countries. Generally, the suspension period begins when the official request is made by the U.S. government to the foreign authority and ends on the date on which the foreign authority takes final action on the request.[209]

Statute of Limitations in Civil Actions

In civil cases brought by SEC, the statute of limitations is set by 28 U.S.C. § 2462, which provides for a five-year limitation on any "suit or proceeding for the enforcement of any civil fine, penalty, or forfeiture." The five-year period begins to run "when the claim first accrued." The five-year limitations period applies to SEC actions seeking civil penalties, but it does not prevent SEC from seeking equitable remedies, such as an injunction or the disgorgement of ill-gotten gains, for conduct pre-dating the five-year period. In cases against individuals who are not residents of the United States, the statute is tolled for any period when the defendants are not "found within the United States in order that proper service may be made thereon."[210] Furthermore, companies or individuals cooperating with SEC may enter into tolling agreements that voluntarily extend the limitations period.

chapter 2
The FCPA:
Anti-Bribery Provisions

THE FCPA: ACCOUNTING PROVISIONS

In addition to the anti-bribery provisions, the FCPA contains accounting provisions applicable to public companies. The FCPA's accounting provisions operate in tandem with the anti-bribery provisions[211] and prohibit off-the-books accounting. Company management and investors rely on a company's financial statements and internal accounting controls to ensure transparency in the financial health of the business, the risks undertaken, and the transactions between the company and its customers and business partners. The accounting provisions are designed to "strengthen the accuracy of the corporate books and records and the reliability of the audit process which constitute the foundations of our system of corporate disclosure."[212]

The accounting provisions consist of two primary components. First, under the "books and records" provision, issuers must make and keep books, records, and accounts that, in reasonable detail, accurately and fairly reflect an issuer's transactions and dispositions of an issuer's assets.[213] Second, under the "internal controls" provision, issuers must devise and maintain a system of internal accounting controls sufficient to assure management's control, authority, and responsibility over the firm's assets.[214]

These components, and other aspects of the accounting provisions, are discussed in greater detail below.

Although the accounting provisions were originally enacted as part of the FCPA, they do not apply only to bribery-related violations. Rather, the accounting provisions ensure that all public companies account for all of their assets and liabilities accurately and in reasonable detail, and they form the backbone for most accounting fraud and issuer disclosure cases brought by DOJ and SEC.[215]

What Is Covered by the Accounting Provisions?

Books and Records Provision

Bribes, both foreign and domestic, are often mischaracterized in companies' books and records. Section 13(b)(2)(A) of the Exchange Act (15 U.S.C. § 78m(b)(2)(A)), commonly called the "books and records" provision, requires issuers to "make and keep books, records, and accounts, which, in reasonable detail, accurately and fairly reflect the transactions and dispositions of the assets of the issuer."[216] The "in reasonable detail" qualification was adopted by Congress "in light of the concern that such a standard, if unqualified, might connote a degree of exactitude and precision which is unrealistic."[217] The addition of this phrase was intended to make clear "that the issuer's records should reflect transactions in conformity with accepted methods of recording economic events and effectively prevent off-the-books slush funds and payments of bribes."[218]

The term "reasonable detail" is defined in the statute as the level of detail that would "satisfy prudent officials in the conduct of their own affairs."[219] Thus, as Congress noted when it adopted this definition, "[t]he concept of reasonableness of necessity contemplates the weighing of a number of relevant factors, including the costs of compliance."[220]

Although the standard is one of reasonable detail, it is never appropriate to mischaracterize transactions in a company's books and records.[221] Bribes are often concealed under the guise of legitimate payments, such as commissions or consulting fees.

In instances where all the elements of a violation of the anti-bribery provisions are not met—where, for example, there was no use of interstate commerce—companies nonetheless may be liable if the improper payments are inaccurately recorded. Consistent with the FCPA's approach to prohibiting payments of any value that are made with a corrupt purpose, there is no materiality threshold under the books and records provision. In combination with the internal controls provision, the requirement that issuers maintain books and records that accurately and fairly reflect the corporation's transactions "assure[s], among other things, that the assets of the issuer are used for proper corporate purpose[s]."[222] As with the anti-bribery provisions, DOJ's and SEC's enforcement of the books and records provision has typically involved misreporting of either large bribe payments or widespread inaccurate recording of smaller payments made as part of a systemic pattern of bribery.

Bribes Have Been Mischaracterized As:

- Commissions or Royalties
- Consulting Fees
- Sales and Marketing Expenses
- Scientific Incentives or Studies
- Travel and Entertainment Expenses
- Rebates or Discounts
- After Sales Service Fees
- Miscellaneous Expenses
- Petty Cash Withdrawals
- Free Goods
- Intercompany Accounts
- Supplier / Vendor Payments
- Write-offs
- "Customs Intervention" Payments

Internal Controls Provision

The payment of bribes often occurs in companies that have weak internal control environments. Internal controls over financial reporting are the processes used by companies to provide reasonable assurances regarding the reliability of financial reporting and the preparation of financial statements. They include various components, such as: a control environment that covers the tone set by the organization regarding integrity and ethics; risk assessments; control activities that cover policies and procedures designed to ensure that management directives are carried out (e.g., approvals, authorizations, reconciliations, and segregation of duties); information and communication; and monitoring. Section 13(b)(2)(B) of the Exchange Act (15 U.S.C. § 78m(b)(2)(B)), commonly called the "internal controls" provision, requires issuers to:

> devise and maintain a system of internal accounting controls sufficient to provide reasonable assurances that—
> (i) transactions are executed in accordance with management's general or specific authorization;
> (ii) transactions are recorded as necessary (I) to permit preparation of financial statements in conformity with generally accepted accounting principles or any other criteria applicable to such statements, and (II) to maintain accountability for assets;
> (iii) access to assets is permitted only in accordance with management's general or specific authorization; and
> (iv) the recorded accountability for assets is compared with the existing assets at reasonable intervals and appropriate action is taken with respect to any differences ....[223]

Like the "reasonable detail" requirement in the books and records provision, the Act defines "reasonable assurances" as "such level of detail and degree of assurance as would satisfy prudent officials in the conduct of their own affairs."[224]

The Act does not specify a particular set of controls that companies are required to implement. Rather, the internal controls provision gives companies the flexibility to develop and maintain a system of controls that is appropriate to their particular needs and circumstances.

An effective compliance program is a critical component of an issuer's internal controls. Fundamentally, the design of a company's internal controls must take into account the operational realities and risks attendant to the company's business, such as: the nature of its products or services; how the products or services get to market; the nature of its work force; the degree of regulation; the extent of its government interaction; and the degree to which it has operations in countries with a high risk of corruption. A company's compliance program should be tailored to these differences. Businesses whose operations expose them to a high risk of corruption will necessarily devise and employ different internal controls than businesses that have a lesser exposure to corruption, just as a financial services company would be expected to devise and employ different internal controls than a manufacturer.

A 2008 case against a German manufacturer of industrial and consumer products illustrates a systemic internal controls problem involving bribery that was unprecedented in scale and geographic reach. From 2001 to 2007, the company created elaborate payment schemes—including slush

Companies with ineffective internal controls often face risks of embezzlement and self-dealing by employees, commercial bribery, export control problems, and violations of other U.S. and local laws.

funds, off-the-books accounts, and systematic payments to business consultants and other intermediaries—to facilitate bribery. Payments were made in ways that obscured their purpose and the ultimate recipients of the money. In some cases, employees obtained large amounts of cash from cash desks and then transported the cash in suitcases across international borders. Authorizations for some payments were placed on sticky notes and later removed to avoid any permanent record. The company made payments totaling approximately $1.36 billion through various mechanisms, including $805.5 million as bribes and $554.5 million for unknown purposes.[225] The company was charged with internal controls and books and records violations, along with anti-bribery violations, and paid over $1.6 billion to resolve the case with authorities in the United States and Germany.[226]

The types of internal control failures identified in the above example exist in many other cases where companies were charged with internal controls violations.[227] A 2010 case against a multi-national automobile manufacturer involved bribery that occurred over a long period of time in multiple countries.[228] In that case, the company used dozens of ledger accounts, known internally as "internal third party accounts," to maintain credit balances for the benefit of government officials.[229] The accounts were funded through several bogus pricing mechanisms, such as "price surcharges," "price inclusions," or excessive commissions.[230] The company also used artificial discounts or rebates on sales contracts to generate the money to pay the bribes.[231] The bribes also were made through phony sales intermediaries and corrupt business partners, as well as through the use of cash desks.[232] Sales executives would obtain cash from the company in amounts as high as hundreds of thousands of dollars, enabling the company to obscure the purpose and recipients of the money paid to government officials.[233] In addition to bribery charges, the company was charged with internal controls and books and records violations.

Good internal controls can prevent not only FCPA violations, but also other illegal or unethical conduct by the company, its subsidiaries, and its employees. DOJ and SEC have repeatedly brought FCPA cases that also involved other types of misconduct, such as financial fraud,[234] commercial bribery,[235] export controls violations,[236] and embezzlement or self-dealing by company employees.[237]

Potential Reporting and Anti-Fraud Violations

Issuers have reporting obligations under Section 13(a) of the Exchange Act, which requires issuers to file an annual report that contains comprehensive information about the issuer. Failure to properly disclose material information about the issuer's business, including material revenue, expenses, profits, assets, or liabilities related to bribery of foreign government officials, may give rise to anti-fraud and reporting violations under Sections 10(b) and 13(a) of the Exchange Act.

For example, a California-based technology company was charged with reporting violations, in addition to violations of the FCPA's anti-bribery and accounting provisions, when its bribery scheme led to material misstatements in its SEC filings.[238] The company was awarded contracts procured through bribery of Chinese officials that generated material revenue and profits. The revenue and profits helped the company offset losses incurred to develop new products expected to become the company's future source of revenue growth. The company improperly recorded the bribe payments as sales commission expenses in its books and records.

Companies engaged in bribery may also be engaged in activity that violates the anti-fraud and reporting provisions. For example, an oil and gas pipeline company and its employees engaged in a long-running scheme to use the company's petty cash accounts in Nigeria to make a variety of corrupt payments to Nigerian tax and court officials using false invoices.[239] The company and its employees also engaged in a fraudulent scheme to minimize the company's tax obligations in Bolivia by using false invoices to claim false offsets to its value-added tax obligations. The scheme resulted in material overstatements of the company's net income in the company's financial statements, which violated the Exchange Act's anti-fraud and reporting provisions. Both schemes also violated the books and records and internal controls provisions.

What Are Management's Other Obligations?

Sarbanes-Oxley Act of 2002

In 2002, in response to a series of accounting scandals involving U.S. companies, Congress enacted the Sarbanes-Oxley Act (Sarbanes-Oxley or SOX),[240] which strengthened the accounting requirements for issuers. All issuers must comply with Sarbanes-Oxley's requirements, several of which have FCPA implications.

SOX Section 302 (15 U.S.C. § 7241)—Responsibility of Corporate Officers for the Accuracy and Validity of Corporate Financial Reports

Section 302 of Sarbanes-Oxley requires that a company's "principal officers" (typically the Chief Executive Officer (CEO) and Chief Financial Officer (CFO)) take responsibility for and certify the integrity of their company's financial reports on a quarterly basis. Under Exchange Act Rule 13a-14, which is commonly called the "SOX certification" rule, each periodic report filed by an issuer must include a certification signed by the issuer's principal executive officer and principal financial officer that, among other things, states that: (i) based on the officer's knowledge, the report contains no material misstatements or omissions; (ii) based on the officer's knowledge, the relevant financial statements are accurate in all material respects; (iii) internal controls are properly designed; and (iv) the certifying officers have disclosed to the issuer's audit committee and auditors all significant internal control deficiencies.

SOX Section 404 (15 U.S.C. § 7262)—Reporting on the State of a Company's Internal Controls over Financial Reporting

Sarbanes-Oxley also strengthened a company's required disclosures concerning the state of its internal control over financial reporting. Under Section 404, issuers are required to present in their annual reports management's conclusion regarding the effectiveness of the company's internal controls over financial reporting. This statement must also assess the effectiveness of such internal controls and procedures. In addition, the company's independent auditor must attest to and report on its assessment of the effectiveness of the company's internal controls over financial reporting.

As directed by Section 404, SEC has adopted rules requiring issuers and their independent auditors to report to the public on the effectiveness of the company's internal controls over financial reporting.[241] These internal controls include those related to illegal acts and fraud—including acts of bribery—that could result in a material misstatement of the company's financial statements.[242] In 2007, SEC issued guidance on controls over financial reporting.[243]

SOX Section 802 (18 U.S.C. §§ 1519 and 1520)— Criminal Penalties for Altering Documents

Section 802 of Sarbanes-Oxley prohibits altering, destroying, mutilating, concealing, or falsifying records, documents, or tangible objects with the intent to obstruct, impede, or influence a potential or actual federal investigation. This section also prohibits any accountant from knowingly and willfully violating the requirement that all audit or review papers be maintained for a period of five years.

Who Is Covered by the Accounting Provisions?

Civil Liability for Issuers, Subsidiaries, and Affiliates

The FCPA's accounting provisions apply to every issuer that has a class of securities registered pursuant to Section 12 of the Exchange Act or that is required to file annual or other periodic reports pursuant to Section 15(d) of the Exchange Act.[244] These provisions apply to any issuer whose securities trade on a national securities exchange in the United States, including foreign issuers with exchange-traded American Depository Receipts.[245] They also apply

chapter 3
The FCPA:
Accounting Provisions

to companies whose stock trades in the over-the-counter market in the United States and which file periodic reports with the Commission, such as annual and quarterly reports. Unlike the FCPA's anti-bribery provisions, the accounting provisions do not apply to private companies.[246]

Although the FCPA's accounting requirements are directed at "issuers," an issuer's books and records include those of its consolidated subsidiaries and affiliates. An issuer's responsibility thus extends to ensuring that subsidiaries or affiliates under its control, including foreign subsidiaries and joint ventures, comply with the accounting provisions. For instance, DOJ and SEC brought enforcement actions against a California company for violating the FCPA's accounting provisions when two Chinese joint ventures in which it was a partner paid more than $400,000 in bribes over a four-year period to obtain business in China.[247] Sales personnel in China made the illicit payments by obtaining cash advances from accounting personnel, who recorded the payments on the books as "business fees" or "travel and entertainment" expenses. Although the payments were made exclusively in China by Chinese employees of the joint venture, the California company failed to have adequate internal controls and failed to act on red flags indicating that its affiliates were engaged in bribery. The California company paid $1.15 million in civil disgorgement and a criminal monetary penalty of $1.7 million.

Companies may not be able to exercise the same level of control over a minority-owned subsidiary or affiliate as they do over a majority or wholly owned entity. Therefore, if a parent company owns 50% or less of a subsidiary or affiliate, the parent is only required to use good faith efforts to cause the minority-owned subsidiary or affiliate to devise and maintain a system of internal accounting controls consistent with the issuer's own obligations under the FCPA.[248] In evaluating an issuer's good faith efforts, all the circumstances—including "the relative degree of the issuer's ownership of the domestic or foreign firm and the laws and practices governing the business operations of the country in which such firm is located"—are taken into account.[249]

Civil Liability for Individuals and Other Entities

Companies (including subsidiaries of issuers) and individuals may also face civil liability for aiding and abetting or causing an issuer's violation of the accounting provisions.[250] For example, in April 2010, SEC charged four individuals—a Country Manager, a Senior Vice President of Sales, a Regional Financial Director, and an International Controller of a U.S. issuer—for their roles in schemes to bribe Kyrgyz and Thai government officials to purchase tobacco from their employer. The complaint alleged that, among other things, the individuals aided and abetted the issuer company's violations of the books and records and internal controls provisions by "knowingly provid[ing] substantial assistance to" the parent company.[251] All four executives settled the charges against them, consenting to the entry of final judgments permanently enjoining them from violating the accounting and anti-bribery provisions, with two executives paying civil penalties.[252] As in other areas of federal securities law, corporate officers also can be held liable as control persons.[253]

Similarly, in October 2011, SEC brought an administrative action against a U.S. water valve manufacturer and a former employee of the company's Chinese subsidiary for violations of the FCPA's accounting provisions.[254] The Chinese subsidiary had made improper payments to employees of certain design institutes to create design specifications that favored the company's valve products. The payments were disguised as sales commissions in the subsidiary's books and records, thereby causing the U.S. issuer's books and records to be inaccurate. The general manager of the subsidiary, who approved the payments and knew or should have known that they were improperly recorded, was ordered to cease-and-desist from committing or causing violations of the accounting provisions, among other charges.[255]

Additionally, individuals and entities can be held directly civilly liable for falsifying an issuer's books and records or for circumventing internal controls. Exchange Act Rule 13b2-1 provides: "No person shall, directly or indirectly, falsify or cause to be falsified, any book, record or account subject to [the books and records provision] of the Securities Exchange Act."[256] And Section 13(b)(5) of the Exchange Act (15 U.S.C. § 78m(b)(5)) provides that "[n]o person shall knowingly circumvent or knowingly fail to implement a system of internal accounting controls or knowingly falsify any book, record, or account ...."[257] The Exchange Act defines "person" to include a "natural person, company, government, or political subdivision, agency, or instrumentality of a government."[258]

An issuer's officers and directors may also be held civilly liable for making false statements to a company's auditor. Exchange Act Rule 13b2-2 prohibits officers and directors from making (or causing to be made) materially false or misleading statements, including an omission of material facts, to an accountant. This liability arises in connection with any audit, review, or examination of a company's financial statements or in connection with the filing of any document with SEC.[259]

Finally, the principal executive and principal financial officer, or persons performing similar functions, can be held liable for violating Exchange Act Rule 13a-14 by signing false personal certifications required by SOX. Thus, for example, in January 2011, SEC charged the former CEO of a U.S. issuer for his role in schemes to bribe Iraqi government officials in connection with the United Nations Oil-For-Food Programme and to bribe Iraqi and Indonesian officials to purchase the company's fuel additives. There, the company used false invoices and sham consulting contracts to support large bribes that were passed on to foreign officials through an agent, and the bribes were mischaracterized as legitimate commissions and travel fees in the company's books and records. The officer directed and authorized the bribe payments and their false recording in the books and records. He also signed annual and quarterly SOX certifications in which he falsely represented that the company's financial statements were fairly presented and the company's internal controls sufficiently designed, as well as annual representations to the company's external auditors where he falsely stated that he complied with the company's code of ethics and was unaware of any violations of the code of ethics by anyone else. The officer was charged with aiding and abetting violations of the books and records and internal controls provisions, circumventing internal

controls, falsifying books and records, making false statements to accountants, and signing false certifications.[260] He consented to the entry of an injunction and paid disgorgement and a civil penalty.[261] He also later pleaded guilty in the United Kingdom to conspiring to corrupt Iraqi and Indonesian officials.[262]

Criminal Liability for Accounting Violations

Criminal liability can be imposed on companies and individuals for knowingly failing to comply with the FCPA's books and records or internal controls provisions.[263] As with the FCPA's anti-bribery provisions, individuals are only subject to the FCPA's criminal penalties for violations of the accounting provisions if they acted "willfully."[264]

For example, a French company was criminally charged with failure to implement internal controls and failure to keep accurate books and records, among other violations.[265] As part of its deferred prosecution agreement, the company admitted to numerous internal control failures, including failure to implement sufficient anti-bribery compliance policies, maintain a sufficient system for the selection and approval of consultants, and conduct appropriate audits of payments to purported "business consultants."[266] Likewise, a German company pleaded guilty to internal controls and books and records violations where, from 2001 through 2007, it made payments totaling approximately $1.36 billion through various mechanisms, including $805.5 million as bribes and $554.5 million for unknown purposes.[267]

Individuals can be held criminally liable for accounting violations. For example, a former managing director of a U.S. bank's real estate business in China pleaded guilty to conspiring to evade internal accounting controls in order to transfer a multi-million dollar ownership interest in a Shanghai building to himself and a Chinese public official with whom he had a personal friendship. The former managing director repeatedly made false representations to his employer about the transaction and the ownership interests involved.[268]

Conspiracy and Aiding and Abetting Liability

As with the FCPA's anti-bribery provisions, companies (including subsidiaries of issuers) and individuals may face criminal liability for conspiring to commit or for aiding and abetting violations of the accounting provisions.

For example, the subsidiary of a Houston-based company pleaded guilty both to conspiring to commit and to aiding and abetting the company's books and records and anti-bribery violations.[269] The subsidiary paid bribes of over $4 million and falsely characterized the payments as "commissions," "fees," or "legal services," consequently causing the company's books and records to be inaccurate. Although the subsidiary was not an issuer and therefore could not be charged directly with an accounting violation, it was criminally liable for its involvement in the parent company's accounting violation.

Similarly, a U.S. subsidiary of a Swiss freight forwarding company that was not an issuer was charged with conspiring to commit and with aiding and abetting the books and records violations of its customers, who were issuers and therefore subject to the FCPA's accounting provisions.[270] The U.S. subsidiary substantially assisted the issuer-customers in violating the FCPA's books and records provision by masking the true nature of the bribe payments in the invoices it submitted to the issuer-customers.[271] The subsidiary thus faced criminal liability for its involvement in the issuer-customers' FCPA violations even though it was not itself subject to the FCPA's accounting provisions.

Auditor Obligations

All public companies in the United States must file annual financial statements that have been prepared in conformity with U.S. Generally Accepted Accounting Principles (U.S. GAAP). These accounting principles are among the most comprehensive in the world. U.S. GAAP requires an accounting of all assets, liabilities, revenue, and expenses as well as extensive disclosures concerning the company's operations and financial condition. A company's financial statements should be complete and fairly represent the company's financial condition.[272] Thus, under U.S. GAAP, any payments to foreign government officials must be properly accounted for in a company's books, records, and financial statements.

U.S. laws, including SEC Rules, require issuers to undergo an annual external audit of their financial statements and to make those audited financial statements available to the public by filing them with SEC. SEC Rules and the rules and standards issued by the Public Company Accounting Oversight Board (PCAOB) under SEC oversight, require external auditors to be independent of the companies that they audit. Independent auditors must comply with the rules and standards set forth by the PCAOB when they perform an audit of a public company. These audit standards govern, for example, the auditor's responsibility concerning material errors, irregularities, or illegal acts by a client and its officers, directors, and employees. Additionally, the auditor has a responsibility to obtain an understanding of an entity's internal controls over financial reporting as part of its audit and must communicate all significant deficiencies and material weaknesses identified during the audit to management and the audit committee.[273]

Under Section 10A of the Exchange Act, independent auditors who discover an illegal act, such as the payment of bribes to domestic or foreign government officials, have certain obligations in connection with their audits of public companies.[274] Generally, Section 10A requires auditors who become aware of illegal acts to report such acts to appropriate levels within the company and, if the company fails to take appropriate action, to notify SEC.

chapter 3
The FCPA:
Accounting Provisions

OTHER RELATED U.S. LAWS

Businesses and individuals should be aware that conduct that violates the FCPA's anti-bribery or accounting provisions may also violate other statutes or regulations. Moreover, payments to foreign government officials and intermediaries may violate these laws even if all of the elements of an FCPA violation are not present.

Travel Act

The Travel Act, 18 U.S.C. § 1952, prohibits travel in interstate or foreign commerce or using the mail or any facility in interstate or foreign commerce, with the intent to distribute the proceeds of any unlawful activity or to promote, manage, establish, or carry on any unlawful activity.[275] "Unlawful activity" includes violations of not only the FCPA, but also state commercial bribery laws. Thus, bribery between private commercial enterprises may, in some circumstances, be covered by the Travel Act. Said differently, if a company pays kickbacks to an employee of a private company who is not a foreign official, such private-to-private bribery could possibly be charged under the Travel Act.

DOJ has previously charged both individual and corporate defendants in FCPA cases with violations of the Travel Act.[276] For instance, an individual investor was convicted of conspiracy to violate the FCPA and the Travel Act in 2009 where the relevant "unlawful activity" under the Travel Act was an FCPA violation involving a bribery scheme in Azerbaijan.[277] Also in 2009, a California company that engaged in both bribery of foreign officials in violation of the FCPA and commercial bribery in violation of California state law pleaded guilty to conspiracy to violate the FCPA and the Travel Act, among other charges.[278]

Money Laundering

Many FCPA cases also involve violations of anti-money laundering statutes.[279] For example, two Florida executives of a Miami-based telecommunications company were convicted of FCPA and money laundering conduct where they conducted financial transactions involving the proceeds of specified unlawful activities—violations of the FCPA, the criminal bribery laws of Haiti, and wire fraud—in order to conceal and disguise these proceeds. Notably, although foreign officials cannot be prosecuted for FCPA violations,[280] three former Haitian officials involved in the same scheme were convicted of money laundering.[281]

Mail and Wire Fraud

The mail and wire fraud statutes may also apply. In 2006, for example, a wholly owned foreign subsidiary of a U.S. issuer pleaded guilty to both FCPA and wire fraud counts where the scheme included overbilling the subsidiary's customers—both government and private—and using part of the overcharged money to pay kickbacks to the customers' employees. The wire fraud charges alleged that the subsidiary had funds wired from its parent's Oregon bank account to off-the-books bank accounts in South Korea that were controlled by the subsidiary. The funds, amounting to almost $2 million, were then paid to managers of state-owned and private steel production companies in China and South Korea as illegal commission payments and kickbacks that were disguised as refunds, commissions, and other seemingly legitimate expenses.[282]

Certification and Reporting Violations

Certain other licensing, certification, and reporting requirements imposed by the U.S. government can also be implicated in the foreign bribery context. For example, as a condition of its facilitation of direct loans and loan guarantees to a foreign purchaser of U.S. goods and services, the Export-Import Bank of the United States requires the U.S. supplier to make certifications concerning commissions, fees, or other payments paid in connection with the financial assistance and that it has not and will not violate the FCPA.[283] A false certification may give rise to criminal liability for false statements.[284]

Similarly, manufacturers, exporters, and brokers of certain defense articles and services are subject to registration, licensing, and reporting requirements under the Arms Export Control Act (AECA), 22 U.S.C. § 2751, *et seq.*, and its implementing regulations, the International Traffic in Arms Regulations (ITAR), 22 C.F.R. § 120, *et seq.* For example, under AECA and ITAR, all manufacturers and exporters of defense articles and services must register with the Directorate of Defense Trade Controls. The sale of defense articles and services valued at $500,000 or more triggers disclosure requirements concerning fees and commissions, including bribes, in an aggregate amount of $100,000 or more.[285] Violations of AECA and ITAR can result in civil and criminal penalties.[286]

Tax Violations

Individuals and companies who violate the FCPA may also violate U.S. tax law, which explicitly prohibits tax deductions for bribes, such as false sales "commissions" deductions intended to conceal corrupt payments.[287] Internal Revenue Service-Criminal Investigation has been involved in a number of FCPA investigations involving tax violations, as well as other financial crimes like money laundering.

chapter 4
**Other Related
U.S. Laws**

GUIDING PRINCIPLES OF ENFORCEMENT

What Does DOJ Consider When Deciding Whether to Open an Investigation or Bring Charges?

Whether and how DOJ will commence, decline, or otherwise resolve an FCPA matter is guided by the *Principles of Federal Prosecution* in the case of individuals, and the *Principles of Federal Prosecution of Business Organizations* in the case of companies.

DOJ *Principles of Federal Prosecution*

The *Principles of Federal Prosecution*, set forth in Chapter 9-27.000 of the U.S. Attorney's Manual,[288] provide guidance for DOJ prosecutors regarding initiating or declining prosecution, selecting charges, and plea-bargaining. The *Principles of Federal Prosecution* provide that prosecutors should recommend or commence federal prosecution if the putative defendant's conduct constitutes a federal offense and the admissible evidence will probably be sufficient to obtain and sustain a conviction unless (1) no substantial federal interest would be served by prosecution; (2) the person is subject to effective prosecution in another jurisdiction; or (3) an adequate non-criminal alternative to prosecution exists. In assessing the existence of a substantial federal interest, the prosecutor is advised to "weigh all relevant considerations," including the nature and seriousness of the offense; the deterrent effect of prosecution; the person's culpability in connection with the offense; the person's history with respect to criminal activity; the person's willingness to cooperate in the investigation or prosecution of others; and the probable sentence or other consequences if the person is convicted. The *Principles of Federal Prosecution* also set out the considerations to be weighed when deciding whether to enter into a plea agreement with an individual defendant, including the nature and seriousness of the offense and the person's willingness to cooperate, as well as the desirability of prompt and certain disposition of the case and the expense of trial and appeal.[289]

DOJ *Principles of Federal Prosecution of Business Organizations*

The *Principles of Federal Prosecution of Business Organizations*, set forth in Chapter 9-28.000 of the U.S. Attorney's Manual,[290] provide guidance regarding the resolution of cases involving corporate wrongdoing. The *Principles of Federal Prosecution of Business Organizations* recognize that resolution of corporate criminal cases by means other than indictment, including non-prosecution and deferred prosecution agreements, may be appropriate in certain circumstances. Nine factors are considered in conducting an investigation, determining whether to charge a corporation, and negotiating plea or other agreements:

- the nature and seriousness of the offense, including the risk of harm to the public;
- the pervasiveness of wrongdoing within the corporation, including the complicity in, or the condoning of, the wrongdoing by corporate management;
- the corporation's history of similar misconduct, including prior criminal, civil, and regulatory enforcement actions against it;
- the corporation's timely and voluntary disclosure of wrongdoing and its willingness to cooperate in the investigation of its agents;
- the existence and effectiveness of the corporation's pre-existing compliance program;
- the corporation's remedial actions, including any efforts to implement an effective corporate compliance program or improve an existing one, replace responsible management, discipline or terminate wrongdoers, pay restitution, and cooperate with the relevant government agencies;
- collateral consequences, including whether there is disproportionate harm to shareholders, pension holders, employees, and others not proven personally culpable, as well as impact on the public arising from the prosecution;
- the adequacy of the prosecution of individuals responsible for the corporation's malfeasance; and
- the adequacy of remedies such as civil or regulatory enforcement actions.

As these factors illustrate, in many investigations it will be appropriate for a prosecutor to consider a corporation's pre-indictment conduct, including voluntary disclosure, cooperation, and remediation, in determining whether to seek an indictment. In assessing a corporation's cooperation, prosecutors are prohibited from requesting attorney-client privileged materials with two exceptions—when a

corporation or its employee asserts an advice-of-counsel defense and when the attorney-client communications were in furtherance of a crime or fraud. Otherwise, an organization's cooperation may only be assessed on the basis of whether it disclosed the *relevant facts* underlying an investigation—and not on the basis of whether it has waived its attorney-client privilege or work product protection.[291]

What Does SEC Consider When Deciding Whether to Open an Investigation or Bring Charges?

SEC's *Enforcement Manual*, published by SEC's Enforcement Division and available on SEC's website,[292] sets forth information about how SEC conducts investigations, as well as the guiding principles that SEC staff considers when determining whether to open or close an investigation and whether civil charges are merited. There are various ways that potential FCPA violations come to the attention of SEC staff, including: tips from informants or whistleblowers; information developed in other investigations; self-reports or public disclosures by companies; referrals from other offices or agencies; public sources, such as media reports and trade publications; and proactive investigative techniques, including risk-based initiatives. Investigations can be formal, such as where SEC has issued a formal order of investigation that authorizes its staff to issue investigative subpoenas for testimony and documents, or informal, such as where the staff proceeds with the investigation without the use of investigative subpoenas.

In determining whether to open an investigation and, if so, whether an enforcement action is warranted, SEC staff considers a number of factors, including: the statutes or rules potentially violated; the egregiousness of the potential violation; the potential magnitude of the violation; whether the potentially harmed group is particularly vulnerable or at risk; whether the conduct is ongoing; whether the conduct can be investigated efficiently and within the statute of limitations period; and whether other authorities, including federal or state agencies or regulators, might be better suited to investigate the conduct. SEC staff also may consider whether the case involves a possibly widespread industry practice that should be addressed, whether the case involves a recidivist, and whether the matter gives SEC an opportunity to be visible in a community that might not otherwise be familiar with SEC or the protections afforded by the securities laws.

For more information about the Enforcement Division's procedures concerning investigations, enforcement actions, and cooperation with other regulators, see the *Enforcement Manual* at http://www.sec.gov/divisions/enforce.shtml.

Self-Reporting, Cooperation, and Remedial Efforts

While the conduct underlying any FCPA investigation is obviously a fundamental and threshold consideration in deciding what, if any, action to take, both DOJ and SEC place a high premium on self-reporting, along with cooperation and remedial efforts, in determining the appropriate resolution of FCPA matters.

Criminal Cases

Under DOJ's *Principles of Federal Prosecution of Business Organizations*, federal prosecutors consider a company's cooperation in determining how to resolve a corporate criminal case. Specifically, prosecutors consider whether the company made a voluntary and timely disclosure as well as the company's willingness to provide relevant information and evidence and identify relevant actors inside and outside the company, including senior executives. In addition, prosecutors may consider a company's remedial actions, including efforts to improve an existing compliance program or appropriate disciplining of wrongdoers.[293] A company's remedial measures should be meaningful and illustrate its recognition of the seriousness of the misconduct, for example, by taking steps to implement the personnel, operational, and organizational changes necessary to establish an awareness among employees that criminal conduct will not be tolerated.[294]

The *Principles of Federal Prosecution* similarly provide that prosecutors may consider an individual's willingness

to cooperate in deciding whether a prosecution should be undertaken and how it should be resolved. Although a willingness to cooperate will not, by itself, generally relieve a person of criminal liability, it may be given "serious consideration" in evaluating whether to enter into a plea agreement with a defendant, depending on the nature and value of the cooperation offered.[295]

The U.S. Sentencing Guidelines similarly take into account an individual defendant's cooperation and voluntary disclosure. Under § 5K1.1, a defendant's cooperation, if sufficiently substantial, may justify the government filing a motion for a reduced sentence. And under § 5K2.16, a defendant's voluntary disclosure of an offense prior to its discovery—if the offense was unlikely to have been discovered otherwise—may warrant a downward departure in certain circumstances.

Chapter 8 of the Sentencing Guidelines, which governs the sentencing of organizations, takes into account an organization's remediation as part of an "effective compliance and ethics program." One of the seven elements of such a program provides that after the detection of criminal conduct, "the organization shall take reasonable steps to respond appropriately to the criminal conduct and to prevent further similar criminal conduct, including making any necessary modifications to the organization's compliance and ethics program."[296] Having an effective compliance and ethics program may lead to a three-point reduction in an organization's culpability score under § 8C2.5, which affects the fine calculation under the Guidelines. Similarly, an organization's self-reporting, cooperation, and acceptance of responsibility may lead to fine reductions under § 8C2.5(g) by decreasing the culpability score. Conversely, an organization will not qualify for the compliance program reduction when it unreasonably delayed reporting the offense.[297] Similar to § 5K1.1

for individuals, organizations can qualify for departures pursuant to § 8C4.1 of the Guidelines for cooperating in the prosecution of others.

Civil Cases

SEC's Framework for Evaluating Cooperation by Companies

SEC's framework for evaluating cooperation by companies is set forth in its 2001 *Report of Investigation Pursuant to Section 21(a) of the Securities Exchange Act of 1934 and Commission Statement on the Relationship of Cooperation to Agency Enforcement Decisions,* which is commonly known as the *Seaboard Report*.[298] The report, which explained the Commission's decision not to take enforcement action against a public company for certain accounting violations caused by its subsidiary, details the many factors SEC considers in determining whether, and to what extent, it grants leniency to companies for cooperating in its investigations and for related good corporate citizenship. Specifically, the report identifies four broad measures of a company's cooperation:

- self-policing prior to the discovery of the misconduct, including establishing effective compliance procedures and an appropriate tone at the top;
- self-reporting of misconduct when it is discovered, including conducting a thorough review of the nature, extent, origins, and consequences of the misconduct, and promptly, completely, and effectively disclosing the misconduct to the public, to regulatory agencies, and to self-regulatory organizations;
- remediation, including dismissing or appropriately disciplining wrongdoers, modifying and improving internal controls and procedures to prevent recurrence of the misconduct, and appropriately compensating those adversely affected; and
- cooperation with law enforcement authorities, including providing SEC staff with all information relevant to the underlying violations and the company's remedial efforts.

Since every enforcement matter is different, this analytical framework sets forth general principles but does not limit SEC's broad discretion to evaluate every case individually on its own unique facts and circumstances. Similar to SEC's treatment of cooperating individuals, credit for cooperation by companies may range from taking no enforcement action to pursuing reduced sanctions in connection with enforcement actions.

SEC's Framework for Evaluating Cooperation by Individuals

In 2010, SEC announced a new cooperation program for individuals.[299] SEC staff has a wide range of tools to facilitate and reward cooperation by individuals, from taking no enforcement action to pursuing reduced sanctions in connection with enforcement actions. Although the evaluation of cooperation depends on the specific circumstances, SEC generally evaluates four factors to determine whether, to what extent, and in what manner to credit cooperation by individuals:

- the assistance provided by the cooperating individual in SEC's investigation or related enforcement actions, including, among other things: the value and timeliness of the cooperation, including whether the individual was the first to report the misconduct to SEC or to offer his or her cooperation; whether the investigation was initiated based upon the information or other cooperation by the individual; the quality of the cooperation, including whether the individual was truthful and the cooperation was complete; the time and resources conserved as a result of the individual's cooperation; and the nature of the cooperation, such as the type of assistance provided;
- the importance of the matter in which the individual provided cooperation;
- the societal interest in ensuring that the cooperating individual is held accountable for his or her misconduct, including the severity of the individual's misconduct, the culpability of the individual, and the efforts undertaken by the individual to remediate the harm; and

- the appropriateness of a cooperation credit in light of the profile of the cooperating individual.

Corporate Compliance Program

In a global marketplace, an effective compliance program is a critical component of a company's internal controls and is essential to detecting and preventing FCPA violations.[300] Effective compliance programs are tailored to the company's specific business and to the risks associated with that business. They are dynamic and evolve as the business and the markets change.

An effective compliance program promotes "an organizational culture that encourages ethical conduct and a commitment to compliance with the law."[301] Such a program protects a company's reputation, ensures investor value and confidence, reduces uncertainty in business transactions, and secures a company's assets.[302] A well-constructed, thoughtfully implemented, and consistently enforced compliance and ethics program helps prevent, detect, remediate, and report misconduct, including FCPA violations.

In addition to considering whether a company has self-reported, cooperated, and taken appropriate remedial actions, DOJ and SEC also consider the adequacy of a company's compliance program when deciding what, if any, action to take. The program may influence whether or not charges should be resolved through a deferred prosecution agreement (DPA) or non-prosecution agreement (NPA), as well as the appropriate length of any DPA or NPA, or the term of corporate probation. It will often affect the penalty amount and the need for a monitor or self-reporting.[303] As discussed above, SEC's *Seaboard Report* focuses, among other things, on a company's self-policing prior to the discovery of the misconduct, including whether it had established effective compliance procedures.[304] Likewise, three of the nine factors set forth in DOJ's *Principles of Federal Prosecution of Business Organizations* relate, either directly or indirectly, to a compliance program's design and implementation, including the pervasiveness of wrongdoing within the company, the existence and effectiveness of the company's pre-existing compliance program, and the company's remedial actions.[305] DOJ also considers the U.S.

Sentencing Guidelines' elements of an effective compliance program, as set forth in § 8B2.1 of the Guidelines.

These considerations reflect the recognition that a company's failure to prevent every single violation does not necessarily mean that a particular company's compliance program was not generally effective. DOJ and SEC understand that "no compliance program can ever prevent all criminal activity by a corporation's employees,"[306] and they do not hold companies to a standard of perfection. An assessment of a company's compliance program, including its design and good faith implementation and enforcement, is an important part of the government's assessment of whether a violation occurred, and if so, what action should be taken. In appropriate circumstances, DOJ and SEC may decline to pursue charges against a company based on the company's effective compliance program, or may otherwise seek to reward a company for its program, even when that program did not prevent the particular underlying FCPA violation that gave rise to the investigation.[307]

DOJ and SEC have no formulaic requirements regarding compliance programs. Rather, they employ a common-sense and pragmatic approach to evaluating compliance programs, making inquiries related to three basic questions:

- Is the company's compliance program well designed?
- Is it being applied in good faith?
- Does it work?[308]

This guide contains information regarding some of the basic elements DOJ and SEC consider when evaluating compliance programs. Although the focus is on compliance with the FCPA, given the existence of anti-corruption laws in many other countries, businesses should consider designing programs focused on anti-corruption compliance more broadly.[309]

56

Hallmarks of Effective Compliance Programs

Individual companies may have different compliance needs depending on their size and the particular risks associated with their businesses, among other factors. When it comes to compliance, there is no one-size-fits-all program. Thus, the discussion below is meant to provide insight into the aspects of compliance programs that DOJ and SEC assess, recognizing that companies may consider a variety of factors when making their own determination of what is appropriate for their specific business needs.[310] Indeed, small- and medium-size enterprises likely will have different compliance programs from large multi-national corporations, a fact DOJ and SEC take into account when evaluating companies' compliance programs.

Compliance programs that employ a "check-the-box" approach may be inefficient and, more importantly, ineffective. Because each compliance program should be tailored to an organization's specific needs, risks, and challenges, the information provided below should not be considered a substitute for a company's own assessment of the corporate compliance program most appropriate for that particular business organization. In the end, if designed carefully, implemented earnestly, and enforced fairly, a company's compliance program—no matter how large or small the organization—will allow the company generally to prevent violations, detect those that do occur, and remediate them promptly and appropriately.

Commitment from Senior Management and a Clearly Articulated Policy Against Corruption

Within a business organization, compliance begins with the board of directors and senior executives setting the proper tone for the rest of the company. Managers and employees take their cues from these corporate leaders. Thus, DOJ and SEC consider the commitment of corporate leaders to a "culture of compliance"[311] and look to see if this high-level commitment is also reinforced and implemented by middle managers and employees at all levels of a business. A well-designed compliance program that is

not enforced in good faith, such as when corporate management explicitly or implicitly encourages employees to engage in misconduct to achieve business objectives, will be ineffective. DOJ and SEC have often encountered companies with compliance programs that are strong on paper but that nevertheless have significant FCPA violations because management has failed to effectively implement the program even in the face of obvious signs of corruption. This may be the result of aggressive sales staff preventing compliance personnel from doing their jobs effectively and of senior management, more concerned with securing a valuable business opportunity than enforcing a culture of compliance, siding with the sales team. The higher the financial stakes of the transaction, the greater the temptation for management to choose profit over compliance.

A strong ethical culture directly supports a strong compliance program. By adhering to ethical standards, senior managers will inspire middle managers to reinforce those standards. Compliant middle managers, in turn, will encourage employees to strive to attain those standards throughout the organizational structure.[312]

In short, compliance with the FCPA and ethical rules must start at the top. DOJ and SEC thus evaluate whether senior management has clearly articulated company standards, communicated them in unambiguous terms, adhered to them scrupulously, and disseminated them throughout the organization.

Code of Conduct and Compliance Policies and Procedures

A company's code of conduct is often the foundation upon which an effective compliance program is built. As DOJ has repeatedly noted in its charging documents, the most effective codes are clear, concise, and accessible to all employees and to those conducting business on the company's behalf. Indeed, it would be difficult to effectively implement a compliance program if it was not available in the local language so that employees in foreign subsidiaries can access and understand it. When assessing a compliance program, DOJ and SEC will review whether the company has taken steps to make certain that the code of conduct remains current and effective and whether a company has periodically reviewed and updated its code.

Whether a company has policies and procedures that outline responsibilities for compliance within the company, detail proper internal controls, auditing practices, and documentation policies, and set forth disciplinary procedures will also be considered by DOJ and SEC. These types of policies and procedures will depend on the size and nature of the business and the risks associated with the business. Effective policies and procedures require an in-depth understanding of the company's business model, including its products and services, third-party agents, customers, government interactions, and industry and geographic risks. Among the risks that a company may need to address include the nature and extent of transactions with foreign governments, including payments to foreign officials; use of third parties; gifts, travel, and entertainment expenses; charitable and political donations; and facilitating and expediting payments. For example, some companies with global operations have created web-based approval processes to review and approve routine gifts, travel, and entertainment involving foreign officials and private customers with clear monetary limits and annual limitations. Many of these systems have built-in flexibility so that senior management, or in-house legal counsel, can be apprised of and, in appropriate circumstances, approve unique requests. These types of systems can be a good way to conserve corporate resources while, if properly implemented, preventing and detecting potential FCPA violations.

Regardless of the specific policies and procedures implemented, these standards should apply to personnel at all levels of the company.

Oversight, Autonomy, and Resources

In appraising a compliance program, DOJ and SEC also consider whether a company has assigned responsibility for the oversight and implementation of a company's compliance program to one or more specific senior executives within an organization.[313] Those individuals must have appropriate authority within the organization,

adequate autonomy from management, and sufficient resources to ensure that the company's compliance program is implemented effectively.[314] Adequate autonomy generally includes direct access to an organization's governing authority, such as the board of directors and committees of the board of directors (e.g., the audit committee).[315] Depending on the size and structure of an organization, it may be appropriate for day-to-day operational responsibility to be delegated to other specific individuals within a company.[316] DOJ and SEC recognize that the reporting structure will depend on the size and complexity of an organization. Moreover, the amount of resources devoted to compliance will depend on the company's size, complexity, industry, geographical reach, and risks associated with the business. In assessing whether a company has reasonable internal controls, DOJ and SEC typically consider whether the company devoted adequate staffing and resources to the compliance program given the size, structure, and risk profile of the business.

Risk Assessment

Assessment of risk is fundamental to developing a strong compliance program, and is another factor DOJ and SEC evaluate when assessing a company's compliance program.[317] One-size-fits-all compliance programs are generally ill-conceived and ineffective because resources inevitably are spread too thin, with too much focus on low-risk markets and transactions to the detriment of high-risk areas. Devoting a disproportionate amount of time policing modest entertainment and gift-giving instead of focusing on large government bids, questionable payments to third-party consultants, or excessive discounts to resellers and distributors may indicate that a company's compliance program is ineffective. A $50 million contract with a government agency in a high-risk country warrants greater scrutiny than modest and routine gifts and entertainment. Similarly, performing identical due diligence on all third-party agents, irrespective of risk factors, is often counterproductive, diverting attention and resources away from those third parties that pose the most significant risks. DOJ and SEC will give meaningful credit to a company that implements in good faith a comprehensive, risk-based compliance program, even if that program does not prevent an infraction in a low risk area because greater attention and resources had been devoted to a higher risk area. Conversely, a company that fails to prevent an FCPA violation on an economically significant, high-risk transaction because it failed to perform a level of due diligence commensurate with the size and risk of the transaction is likely to receive reduced credit based on the quality and effectiveness of its compliance program.

As a company's risk for FCPA violations increases, that business should consider increasing its compliance procedures, including due diligence and periodic internal audits. The degree of appropriate due diligence is fact-specific and should vary based on industry, country, size, and nature of the transaction, and the method and amount of third-party compensation. Factors to consider, for instance, include risks presented by: the country and industry sector, the business opportunity, potential business partners, level of involvement with governments, amount of government regulation and oversight, and exposure to customs and immigration in conducting business affairs. When assessing a company's compliance program, DOJ and SEC take into account whether and to what degree a company analyzes and addresses the particular risks it faces.

Training and Continuing Advice

Compliance policies cannot work unless effectively communicated throughout a company. Accordingly, DOJ and SEC will evaluate whether a company has taken steps to ensure that relevant policies and procedures have been communicated throughout the organization, including through periodic training and certification for all directors, officers, relevant employees, and, where appropriate, agents and

business partners.[318] For example, many larger companies have implemented a mix of web-based and in-person training conducted at varying intervals. Such training typically covers company policies and procedures, instruction on applicable laws, practical advice to address real-life scenarios, and case studies. Regardless of how a company chooses to conduct its training, however, the information should be presented in a manner appropriate for the targeted audience, including providing training and training materials in the local language. For example, companies may want to consider providing different types of training to their sales personnel and accounting personnel with hypotheticals or sample situations that are similar to the situations they might encounter. In addition to the existence and scope of a company's training program, a company should develop appropriate measures, depending on the size and sophistication of the particular company, to provide guidance and advice on complying with the company's ethics and compliance program, including when such advice is needed urgently. Such measures will help ensure that the compliance program is understood and followed appropriately at all levels of the company.

Incentives and Disciplinary Measures

In addition to evaluating the design and implementation of a compliance program throughout an organization, enforcement of that program is fundamental to its effectiveness.[319] A compliance program should apply from the board room to the supply room—no one should be beyond its reach. DOJ and SEC will thus consider whether, when enforcing a compliance program, a company has appropriate and clear disciplinary procedures, whether those procedures are applied reliably and promptly, and whether they are commensurate with the violation. Many companies have found that publicizing disciplinary actions internally, where appropriate under local law, can have an important deterrent effect, demonstrating that unethical and unlawful actions have swift and sure consequences.

DOJ and SEC recognize that positive incentives can also drive compliant behavior. These incentives can take many forms such as personnel evaluations and promotions, rewards for improving and developing a company's compliance program, and rewards for ethics and compliance leadership.[320] Some organizations, for example, have made adherence to compliance a significant metric for management's bonuses so that compliance becomes an integral part of management's everyday concern. Beyond financial incentives, some companies have highlighted compliance within their organizations by recognizing compliance professionals and internal audit staff. Others have made working in the company's compliance organization a way to advance an employee's career. SEC, for instance, has encouraged companies to embrace methods to incentivize ethical and lawful behavior:

> [M]ake integrity, ethics and compliance part of the promotion, compensation and evaluation processes as well. For at the end of the day, the most effective way to communicate that "doing the right thing" is a priority, is to reward it. Conversely, if employees are led to believe that, when it comes to compensation and career advancement, all that counts is short-term profitability, and that cutting ethical corners is an acceptable way of getting there, they'll perform to that measure. To cite an example from a different walk of life: a college football coach can be told that the graduation rates of his players are what matters, but he'll know differently if the sole focus of his contract extension talks or the decision to fire him is his win-loss record.[321]

No matter what the disciplinary scheme or potential incentives a company decides to adopt, DOJ and SEC will consider whether they are fairly and consistently applied across the organization. No executive should be above compliance, no employee below compliance, and no person within an organization deemed too valuable to be disciplined, if warranted. Rewarding good behavior and sanctioning bad behavior reinforces a culture of compliance and ethics throughout an organization.

Third-Party Due Diligence and Payments

DOJ's and SEC's FCPA enforcement actions demonstrate that third parties, including agents, consultants, and distributors, are commonly used to conceal the payment of bribes to foreign officials in international business transactions. Risk-based due diligence is particularly important with third parties and will also be considered by DOJ and SEC in assessing the effectiveness of a company's compliance program.

Although the degree of appropriate due diligence may vary based on industry, country, size and nature of the transaction, and historical relationship with the third-party, some guiding principles always apply.

First, as part of risk-based due diligence, companies should understand the qualifications and associations of its third-party partners, including its business reputation, and relationship, if any, with foreign officials. The degree of scrutiny should increase as red flags surface.

Second, companies should have an understanding of the business rationale for including the third party in the transaction. Among other things, the company should understand the role of and need for the third party and ensure that the contract terms specifically describe the services to be performed. Additional considerations include payment terms and how those payment terms compare to typical terms in that industry and country, as well as the timing of the third party's introduction to the business. Moreover, companies may want to confirm and document that the third party is actually performing the work for which it is being paid and that its compensation is commensurate with the work being provided.

Third, companies should undertake some form of ongoing monitoring of third-party relationships.[322] Where appropriate, this may include updating due diligence periodically, exercising audit rights, providing periodic training, and requesting annual compliance certifications by the third party.

In addition to considering a company's due diligence on third parties, DOJ and SEC also assess whether the company has informed third parties of the company's

Compliance Program Case Study

Recent DOJ and SEC actions relating to a financial institution's real estate transactions with a government agency in China illustrate the benefits of implementing and enforcing a comprehensive risk-based compliance program. The case involved a joint venture real estate investment in the Luwan District of Shanghai, China, between a U.S.-based financial institution and a state-owned entity that functioned as the District's real estate arm. The government entity conducted the transactions through two special purpose vehicles ("SPVs"), with the second SPV purchasing a 12% stake in a real estate project.

The financial institution, through a robust compliance program, frequently trained its employees, imposed a comprehensive payment-approval process designed to prevent bribery, and staffed a compliance department with a direct reporting line to the board of directors. As appropriate given the industry, market, and size and structure of the transactions, the financial institution (1) provided extensive FCPA training to the senior executive responsible for the transactions and (2) conducted extensive due diligence on the transactions, the local government entity, and the SPVs. Due diligence on the entity included reviewing Chinese government records; speaking with sources familiar with the Shanghai real estate market; checking the government entity's payment records and credit references; conducting an on-site visit and placing a pretextual telephone call to the entity's offices; searching media sources; and conducting background checks on the entity's principals. The financial institution vetted the SPVs by obtaining a letter with designated bank account information from a Chinese official associated with the government entity (the "Chinese Official"); using an international law firm to request and review 50 documents from the SPVs' Canadian attorney; interviewing the attorney; and interviewing the SPVs' management.

Notwithstanding the financial institution's robust compliance program and good faith enforcement of it, the company failed to learn that the Chinese Official personally owned nearly 50% of the second SPV (and therefore a nearly 6% stake in the joint venture) and that the SPV was used as a vehicle for corrupt payments. This failure was due, in large part, to misrepresentations by the Chinese Official, the financial institution's executive in charge of the project, and the SPV's attorney that the SPV was 100% owned and controlled by the government entity. DOJ and SEC declined to take enforcement action against the financial institution, and its executive pleaded guilty to conspiracy to violate the FCPA's internal control provisions and also settled with SEC.

---

compliance program and commitment to ethical and lawful business practices and, where appropriate, whether it has sought assurances from third parties, through certifications and otherwise, of reciprocal commitments. These can be meaningful ways to mitigate third-party risk.

Confidential Reporting and Internal Investigation

An effective compliance program should include a mechanism for an organization's employees and others to report suspected or actual misconduct or violations of the company's policies on a confidential basis and without fear of retaliation.[323] Companies may employ, for example, anonymous hotlines or ombudsmen. Moreover, once an allegation is made, companies should have in place an efficient, reliable,

and properly funded process for investigating the allegation and documenting the company's response, including any disciplinary or remediation measures taken. Companies will want to consider taking "lessons learned" from any reported violations and the outcome of any resulting investigation to update their internal controls and compliance program and focus future training on such issues, as appropriate.

Continuous Improvement: Periodic Testing and Review

Finally, a good compliance program should constantly evolve. A company's business changes over time, as do the environments in which it operates, the nature of its customers, the laws that govern its actions, and the standards of its industry. In addition, compliance programs that do not just exist on paper but are followed in practice will inevitably uncover compliance weaknesses and require enhancements. Consequently, DOJ and SEC evaluate whether companies regularly review and improve their compliance programs and not allow them to become stale.

According to one survey, 64% of general counsel whose companies are subject to the FCPA say there is room for improvement in their FCPA training and compliance programs.[324] An organization should take the time to review and test its controls, and it should think critically about its potential weaknesses and risk areas. For example, some companies have undertaken employee surveys to measure their compliance culture and strength of internal controls, identify best practices, and detect new risk areas. Other companies periodically test their internal controls with targeted audits to make certain that controls on paper are working in practice. DOJ and SEC will give meaningful credit to thoughtful efforts to create a sustainable compliance program if a problem is later discovered. Similarly, undertaking proactive evaluations before a problem strikes can lower the applicable penalty range under the U.S. Sentencing Guidelines.[325] Although the nature and the frequency of proactive evaluations may vary depending on the size and complexity of an organization, the idea behind such efforts is the same: continuous improvement and sustainability.[326]

Mergers and Acquisitions: Pre-Acquisition Due Diligence and Post-Acquisition Integration

In the context of the FCPA, mergers and acquisitions present both risks and opportunities. A company that does not perform adequate FCPA due diligence prior to a merger or acquisition may face both legal and business risks.[327] Perhaps most commonly, inadequate due diligence can allow a course of bribery to continue—with all the attendant harms to a business's profitability and reputation, as well as potential civil and criminal liability.

In contrast, companies that conduct effective FCPA due diligence on their acquisition targets are able to evaluate more accurately each target's value and negotiate for the costs of the bribery to be borne by the target. In addition,

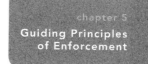

chapter 5
Guiding Principles
of Enforcement

such actions demonstrate to DOJ and SEC a company's commitment to compliance and are taken into account when evaluating any potential enforcement action. For example, DOJ and SEC declined to take enforcement action against an acquiring issuer when the issuer, among other things, uncovered the corruption at the company being acquired as part of due diligence, ensured that the corruption was voluntarily disclosed to the government, cooperated with the investigation, and incorporated the acquired company into its compliance program and internal controls. On the other hand, SEC took action against the acquired company, and DOJ took action against a subsidiary of the acquired company.[328] When pre-acquisition due diligence is not possible, DOJ has described procedures, contained in Opinion Procedure Release No. 08-02, pursuant to which companies can nevertheless be rewarded if they choose to conduct thorough post-acquisition FCPA due diligence.[329]

FCPA due diligence, however, is normally only a portion of the compliance process for mergers and acquisitions. DOJ and SEC evaluate whether the acquiring company promptly incorporated the acquired company into all of its internal controls, including its compliance program. Companies should consider training new employees, reevaluating third parties under company standards, and, where appropriate, conducting audits on new business units.

For example, as a result of due diligence conducted by a California-based issuer before acquiring the majority interest in a joint venture, the issuer learned of corrupt payments to obtain business. However, the issuer only implemented its internal controls "halfway" so as not to "choke the sales engine and cause a distraction for the sales guys." As a result, the improper payments continued, and the issuer was held liable for violating the FCPA's internal controls and books and records provisions.[330]

Other Guidance on Compliance and International Best Practices

In addition to this guide, the U.S. Departments of Commerce and State have both issued publications that contain guidance regarding compliance programs. The Department of Commerce's International Trade Administration has published *Business Ethics: A Manual for Managing a Responsible Business Enterprise in Emerging Market Economies*,[331] and the Department of State has published *Fighting Global Corruption: Business Risk Management*.[332]

There is also an emerging international consensus on compliance best practices, and a number of inter-governmental and non-governmental organizations have issued guidance regarding best practices for compliance.[333] Most notably, the OECD's 2009 Anti-Bribery Recommendation and its Annex II, *Good Practice Guidance on Internal Controls, Ethics, and Compliance*,[334] published in February 2010, were drafted based on consultations with the private sector and civil society and set forth specific good practices for ensuring effective compliance programs and measures for preventing and detecting foreign bribery. In addition, businesses may wish to refer to the following resources:

- Asia-Pacific Economic Cooperation—*Anti-Corruption Code of Conduct for Business*;[335]
- International Chamber of Commerce—*ICC Rules on Combating Corruption*;[336]
- Transparency International—*Business Principles for Countering Bribery*;[337]
- United Nations Global Compact—*The Ten Principles*;[338]
- World Bank—*Integrity Compliance Guidelines*;[339] and
- World Economic Forum—*Partnering Against Corruption–Principles for Countering Bribery*.[340]

Hypothetical: Third-Party Vetting

Part 1: Consultants

Company A, a U.S. issuer headquartered in Delaware, wants to start doing business in a country that poses high risks of corruption. Company A learns about a potential $50 million contract with the country's Ministry of Immigration. This is a very attractive opportunity to Company A, both for its profitability and to open the door to future projects with the government. At the suggestion of the company's senior vice president of international sales (Sales Executive), Company A hires a local businessman who assures them that he has strong ties to political and government leaders in the country and can help them win the contract. Company A enters into a consulting contract with the local businessman (Consultant). The agreement requires Consultant to use his best efforts to help the company win the business and provides for Consultant to receive a significant monthly retainer as well as a success fee of 3% of the value of any contract the company wins.

What steps should Company A consider taking before hiring Consultant?

There are several factors here that might lead Company A to perform heightened FCPA-related due diligence prior to retaining Consultant: (1) the market (high-risk country); (2) the size and significance of the deal to the company; (3) the company's first time use of this particular consultant; (4) the consultant's strong ties to political and government leaders; (5) the success fee structure of the contract; and (6) the vaguely-defined services to be provided. In order to minimize the likelihood of incurring FCPA liability, Company A should carefully vet Consultant and his role in the transaction, including close scrutiny of the relationship between Consultant and any Ministry of Immigration officials or other government officials. Although there is nothing inherently illegal about contracting with a third party that has close connections to politicians and government officials to perform legitimate services on a transaction, this type of relationship can be susceptible to corruption. Among other things, Company A may consider conducting due diligence on Consultant, including background

(cont'd)

and reference checks; ensuring that the contract spells out exactly what services and deliverables (such as written status reports or other documentation) Consultant is providing; training Consultant on the FCPA and other anti-corruption laws; requiring Consultant to represent that he will abide by the FCPA and other anti-corruption laws; including audit rights in the contract (and exercising those rights); and ensuring that payments requested by Consultant have the proper supporting documentation before they are approved for payment.

Part 2: Distributors and Local Partners

Assume the following alternative facts:

Instead of hiring Consultant, Company A retains an often-used local distributor (Distributor) to sell Company A's products to the Ministry of Immigration. In negotiating the pricing structure, Distributor, which had introduced the project to Company A, claims that the standard discount price to Distributor creates insufficient margin for Distributor to cover warehousing, distribution, installation, marketing, and training costs and requests an additional discount or rebate, or, in the alternative, a contribution to its marketing efforts, either in the form of a lump sum or as a percentage of the total contract. The requested discount/allowance is significantly larger than usual, although there is precedent at Company A for granting this level of discount in unique circumstances. Distributor further advises Company A that the Ministry's procurement officials responsible for awarding the contract have expressed a strong preference for including a particular local company (Local Partner) in the transaction as a subcontractor of Company A to perform installation, training, and other services that would normally have been performed by Distributor or Company A. According to Distributor, the Ministry has a solid working relationship with Local Partner, and it would cause less disruption for Local Partner to perform most of the on-site work at the Ministry. One of the principals (Principal 1) of the Local Partner is an official in another government ministry.

What additional compliance considerations do these alternative facts raise?

As with Consultant in the first scenario above, Company A should carefully vet Distributor and Local Partner and their roles in the transaction in order to minimize the likelihood of incurring FCPA liability. While Company A has an established relationship with Distributor, the fact that Distributor has requested an additional discount warrants further inquiry into the economic justification for the change, particularly where, as here, the proposed transaction structure contemplates paying Local Partner to provide many of the same services that Distributor would otherwise provide. In many cases, it may be appropriate for distributors to receive larger discounts to account for unique circumstances in particular transactions. That said, a common mechanism to create additional margin for bribe payments is through excessive discounts or rebates to distributors. Accordingly, when a company has pre-existing relationships with distributors and other third parties, transaction-specific due diligence—including an analysis of payment terms to confirm that the payment is commensurate with the work being performed—can be critical even in circumstances where due diligence of the distributor or other third party raises no initial red flags.

Company A should carefully scrutinize the relationship among Local Partner, Distributor, and Ministry of Immigration officials. While there is nothing inherently illegal about contracting with a third party that is recommended by the end-user, or even hiring a government official to perform legitimate services on a transaction unrelated to his or her government job, these facts raise additional red flags that warrant significant scrutiny. Among other things, Company A would be well-advised to require Principal 1 to verify that he will have no role in the Ministry of Immigration's decision to award the contract to Company A, notify the Ministry of Immigration and his own ministry of his proposed involvement in the transaction, and certify that he will abide by the FCPA and other anti-corruption laws and that his involvement in the transaction is permitted under local law.

(cont'd)

Assume the following additional facts:

Under its company policy for a government transaction of this size, Company A requires both finance and compliance approval. The finance officer is concerned that the discounts to Distributor are significantly larger than what they have approved for similar work and will cut too deeply into Company A's profit margin. The finance officer is also skeptical about including Local Partner to perform some of the same services that Company A is paying Distributor to perform. Unsatisfied with Sales Executive's explanation, she requests a meeting with Distributor and Principal 1. At the meeting, Distributor and Principal 1 offer vague and inconsistent justifications for the payments and fail to provide any supporting analysis, and Principal 1 seems to have no real expertise in the industry. During a coffee break, Distributor comments to Sales Executive that the finance officer is naïve about "how business is done in my country." Following the meeting, Sales Executive dismisses the finance officer's concerns, assuring her that the proposed transaction structure is reasonable and legitimate. Sales Executive also reminds the finance officer that "the deal is key to their growth in the industry."

The compliance officer focuses his due diligence on vetting Distributor and Local Partner and hires a business investigative firm to conduct a background check. Distributor appears reputable, capable, and financially stable and is willing to take on real risk in the project, financial and otherwise. However, the compliance officer learns that Distributor has established an off-shore bank account for the transaction. The compliance officer further learns that Local Partner's business was organized two years ago and appears financially stable but has no expertise in the industry and has established an off-shore shell company and bank account to conduct this transaction. The background check also reveals that Principal 1 is a former college roommate of a senior official of the Ministry of Immigration. The Sales Executive dismisses the compliance officer's concerns, commenting that what Local Partner does with its payments "isn't our problem." Sales Executive also strongly objects to the compliance officer's request to meet with Principal 1 to discuss the off-shore company and account, assuring him that it was done for legitimate tax purposes and complaining that if Company A continues to "harass" Local Partner and Distributor, they would partner with Company A's chief competitor. The compliance officer and the finance officer discuss their concerns with each other but ultimately sign off on the deal even though their questions had not been answered. Their decision is motivated in large part by their conversation with Sales Executive, who told them that this was the region's most important contract and that the detailed FCPA questionnaires and robust anti-corruption representations in the contracts placed the burden on Distributor and Local Partner to act ethically.

Company A goes forward with the Distributor and Local Partner agreements and wins the contract after six months. The finance officer approves Company A's payments to Local Partner via the offshore account, even though Local Partner's invoices did not contain supporting detail or documentation of any services provided. Company A recorded the payments as legitimate operational expenses on its books and records. Sales Executive received a large year-end bonus due to the award of the contract.

In fact, Local Partner and Distributor used part of the payments and discount margin, respectively, to funnel bribe payments to several Ministry of Immigration officials, including Principal 1's former college roommate, in exchange for awarding the contract to Company A. Thousands of dollars are also wired to the personal offshore bank account of Sales Executive.

How would DOJ and SEC evaluate the potential FCPA liability of Company A and its employees?

This is not the case of a single "rogue employee" circumventing an otherwise robust compliance program. Although Company A's finance and compliance officers had the correct instincts to scrutinize the structure and economics of the transaction and the role of the third parties, their due diligence was incomplete. When the initial inquiry identified significant red flags, they approved the transaction despite knowing that their concerns were unanswered or the answers they received raised additional concerns and red flags. Relying on due diligence questionnaires and anti-corruption representations is insufficient, particularly when the risks are readily apparent. Nor can Company A or its employees shield themselves from liability because it was Distributor and Local Partner—rather than Company A directly—that made the payments.

The facts suggest that Sales Executive had actual knowledge of or was willfully blind to the consultant's payment of the bribes. He also personally profited from the scheme (both from the kickback and from the bonus he received from the company) and intentionally discouraged the finance and compliance officers from learning the full story. Sales Executive is therefore subject to liability under the anti-bribery, books and records, and internal controls provisions of the FCPA, and others may be as well. Company A may also be liable for violations of the anti-bribery, books and records, and internal controls provisions of the FCPA given the number and significance of red flags that established a high probability of bribery and the role of employees and agents acting on the company's behalf.

chapter 5
**Guiding Principles
of Enforcement**

FCPA PENALTIES, SANCTIONS, AND REMEDIES

What Are the Potential Consequences for Violations of the FCPA?

The FCPA provides for different criminal and civil penalties for companies and individuals.

Criminal Penalties

For each violation of the anti-bribery provisions, the FCPA provides that corporations and other business entities are subject to a fine of up to $2 million.[341] Individuals, including officers, directors, stockholders, and agents of companies, are subject to a fine of up to $100,000 and imprisonment for up to five years.[342]

For each violation of the accounting provisions, the FCPA provides that corporations and other business entities are subject to a fine of up to $25 million.[343] Individuals are subject to a fine of up to $5 million and imprisonment for up to 20 years.[344]

Under the Alternative Fines Act, 18 U.S.C. § 3571(d), courts may impose significantly higher fines than those provided by the FCPA—up to twice the benefit that the defendant sought to obtain by making the corrupt payment, as long as the facts supporting the increased fines are included in the indictment and either proved to the jury beyond a reasonable doubt or admitted in a guilty plea proceeding.[345]

Fines imposed on individuals may not be paid by their employer or principal.[346]

U.S. Sentencing Guidelines

When calculating penalties for violations of the FCPA, DOJ focuses its analysis on the U.S. Sentencing Guidelines (Guidelines)[347] in all of its resolutions, including guilty pleas, DPAs, and NPAs. The Guidelines provide a very detailed and predictable structure for calculating penalties for all federal crimes, including violations of the FCPA. To determine the appropriate penalty, the "offense level" is first calculated by examining both the severity of the crime and facts specific to the crime, with appropriate reductions for cooperation and acceptance of responsibility, and, for business entities, additional factors such as voluntary disclosure, cooperation, preexisting compliance programs, and remediation.

The Guidelines provide for different penalties for the different provisions of the FCPA. The initial offense level for violations of the anti-bribery provisions is determined under § 2C1.1, while violations of the accounting provisions are assessed under § 2B1.1. For individuals, the initial offense level is modified by factors set forth in Chapters 3, 4, and 5 of the Guidelines[348] to identify a final offense level. This final offense level, combined with other factors, is used to determine whether the Guidelines would recommend that incarceration is appropriate, the length of any term of incarceration, and the appropriate amount of any fine. For corporations, the offense level is modified by factors particular to organizations as described in Chapter 8 to determine the applicable organizational penalty.

For example, violations of the anti-bribery provisions are calculated pursuant to § 2C1.1. The offense level is determined by first identifying the base offense level;[349] adding additional levels based on specific offense characteristics, including whether the offense involved more than one bribe, the value of the bribe or the benefit that was conferred, and the level of the public official;[350] adjusting the offense level based on the defendant's role in the offense;[351] and using the total offense level as well as the defendant's criminal history category to determine the advisory guideline range.[352] For violations of the accounting provisions assessed under § 2B1.1, the procedure is generally the same, except that the specific offense characteristics differ. For instance, for violations of the FCPA's accounting provisions, the offense level may be increased if a substantial part of the scheme occurred outside the United States or if the defendant was an officer or director of a publicly traded company at the time of the offense.[353]

For companies, the offense level is calculated pursuant to §§ 2C1.1 or 2B1.1 in the same way as for an individual—by starting with the base offense level and increasing it as warranted by any applicable specific offense characteristics. The organizational guidelines found in Chapter 8, however, provide the structure for determining the final advisory guideline fine range for organizations. The base fine consists of the greater of the amount corresponding to the total offense level, calculated pursuant to the Guidelines, or the pecuniary gain or loss from the offense.[354] This base fine is then multiplied by a culpability score that can either reduce the fine to as little as five percent of the base fine or increase the recommended fine to up to four times the amount of the base fine.[355] As described in § 8C2.5, this culpability score is calculated by taking into account numerous factors such as the size of the organization committing the criminal

acts; the involvement in or tolerance of criminal activity by high-level personnel within the organization; and prior misconduct or obstructive behavior. The culpability score is reduced if the organization had an effective pre-existing compliance program to prevent violations and if the organization voluntarily disclosed the offense, cooperated in the investigation, and accepted responsibility for the criminal conduct.[356]

Civil Penalties

Although only DOJ has the authority to pursue criminal actions, both DOJ and SEC have civil enforcement authority under the FCPA. DOJ may pursue civil actions for anti-bribery violations by domestic concerns (and their officers, directors, employees, agents, or stockholders) and foreign nationals and companies for violations while in the United States, while SEC may pursue civil actions against issuers and their officers, directors, employees, agents, or stockholders for violations of the anti-bribery and the accounting provisions.[357]

For violations of the anti-bribery provisions, corporations and other business entities are subject to a civil penalty of up to $16,000 per violation.[358] Individuals, including officers, directors, stockholders, and agents of companies, are similarly subject to a civil penalty of up to $16,000 per violation,[359] which may not be paid by their employer or principal.[360]

For violations of the accounting provisions, SEC may obtain a civil penalty not to exceed the greater of (a) the gross amount of the pecuniary gain to the defendant as a result of the violations or (b) a specified dollar limitation. The specified dollar limitations are based on the egregiousness of the violation, ranging from $7,500 to $150,000 for an individual and $75,000 to $725,000 for a company.[361] SEC may obtain civil penalties both in actions filed in federal court and in administrative proceedings.[362]

Collateral Consequences

In addition to the criminal and civil penalties described above, individuals and companies who violate the FCPA may face significant collateral consequences, including suspension or debarment from contracting with the federal government, cross-debarment by multilateral development banks, and the suspension or revocation of certain export privileges.

Debarment

Under federal guidelines governing procurement, an individual or company that violates the FCPA or other criminal statutes may be barred from doing business with the federal government. The Federal Acquisition Regulations (FAR) provide for the potential suspension or debarment of companies that contract with the government upon conviction of or civil judgment for bribery, falsification or destruction of records, the making of false statements, or "[c]ommission of any other offense indicating a lack of business integrity or business honesty that seriously and directly affects the present responsibility of a Government contractor or subcontractor."[363] These measures are not intended to be punitive and may be imposed only if "in the public's interest for the Government's protection."[364]

Under the FAR, a decision to debar or suspend is discretionary. The decision is not made by DOJ prosecutors or SEC staff, but instead by independent debarment authorities within each agency, such as the Department of Defense or the General Services Administration, which analyze a number of factors to determine whether a company should be suspended, debarred, or otherwise determined to be ineligible for government contracting. Such factors include whether the contractor has effective internal control systems in place, self-reported the misconduct in a timely manner, and has taken remedial measures.[365] If a cause for debarment exists, the contractor has the burden of demonstrating to the satisfaction of the debarring official that it is presently responsible and that debarment is not necessary.[366] Each federal department and agency determines the eligibility of contractors with whom it deals. However, if one department or agency debars or suspends a contractor, the debarment or suspension applies to the entire executive branch of the federal government, unless a department or agency shows compelling reasons not to debar or suspend the contractor.[367]

Although guilty pleas, DPAs, and NPAs do not result in automatic debarment from U.S. government contracting,

committing a federal crime and the factual admissions underlying a resolution are factors that the independent debarment authorities may consider. Moreover, indictment alone can lead to suspension of the right to do business with the government.[368] The U.S. Attorney's Manual also provides that when a company engages in fraud against the government, a prosecutor may not negotiate away an agency's right to debar or delist the company as part of the plea bargaining process.[369] In making debarment determinations, contracting agencies, including at the state and local level, may consult with DOJ in advance of awarding a contract. Depending on the circumstances, DOJ may provide information to contracting authorities in the context of the corporate settlement about the facts and circumstances underlying the criminal conduct and remediation measures undertaken by the company, if any. This information sharing is not advocacy, and the ultimate debarment decisions are squarely within the purview of the independent debarment authorities. In some situations, the contracting agency may impose its own oversight requirements in order for a company that has admitted to violations of federal law to be awarded federal contracts, such as the Corporate Integrity Agreements often required by the Department of Health and Human Services.

Cross-Debarment by Multilateral Development Banks

Multilateral Development Banks (MDBs), like the World Bank, also have the ability to debar companies and individuals for corrupt practices.[370] Each MDB has its own process for evaluating alleged corruption in connection with MDB-funded projects. When appropriate, DOJ and SEC work with MDBs to share evidence and refer cases. On April 9, 2010, the African Development Bank Group, the Asian Development Bank, the European Bank for

Reconstruction and Development, the Inter-American Development Bank Group, and the World Bank Group entered into an agreement under which entities debarred by one MDB will be sanctioned for the same misconduct by other signatory MDBs.[371] This cross-debarment agreement means that if a company is debarred by one MDB, it is debarred by all.[372]

Loss of Export Privileges

Companies and individuals who violate the FCPA may face consequences under other regulatory regimes, such as the Arms Export Control Act (AECA), 22 U.S.C. § 2751, *et seq.*, and its implementing regulations, the International Traffic in Arms Regulations (ITAR), 22 C.F.R. § 120, *et seq.* AECA and ITAR together provide for the suspension, revocation, amendment, or denial of an arms export license if an applicant has been indicted or convicted for violating the FCPA.[373] They also set forth certain factors for the Department of State's Directorate of Defense Trade Controls (DDTC)[374] to consider when determining whether to grant, deny, or return without action license applications for certain types of defense materials. One of those factors is whether there is reasonable cause to believe that an applicant for a license has violated (or conspired to violate) the FCPA; if so, the Department of State "may disapprove the application."[375] In addition, it is the policy of the Department of State not to consider applications for licenses involving any persons who have been convicted of violating the AECA or convicted of conspiracy to violate the AECA.[376] In an action related to the criminal resolution of a U.K. military products manufacturer, the DDTC imposed a "policy of denial" for export licenses on three of the company's subsidiaries that were involved in violations of AECA and ITAR.[377]

When Is a Compliance Monitor or Independent Consultant Appropriate?

One of the primary goals of both criminal prosecutions and civil enforcement actions against companies that violate the FCPA is ensuring that such conduct does not occur again. As a consequence, enhanced compliance and reporting requirements may be part of criminal and civil resolutions of FCPA matters. The amount of enhanced compliance and kind of reporting required varies according to the facts and circumstances of individual cases.

In criminal cases, a company's sentence, or a DPA or NPA with a company, may require the appointment of an independent corporate monitor. Whether a monitor is appropriate depends on the specific facts and circumstances of the case. In 2008, DOJ issued internal guidance regarding the selection and use of corporate monitors in DPAs and NPAs with companies. Additional guidance has since been issued.[378] A monitor is an independent third party who assesses and monitors a company's adherence to the compliance requirements of an agreement that was designed to reduce the risk of recurrence of the company's misconduct. Appointment of a monitor is not appropriate in all circumstances, but it may be appropriate, for example, where a company does not already have an effective internal compliance program or needs to establish necessary internal controls. In addition, companies are sometimes allowed to engage in self-monitoring, typically in cases when the company has made a voluntary disclosure, has been fully cooperative, and has demonstrated a genuine commitment to reform.

Factors DOJ and SEC Consider When Determining Whether a Compliance Monitor Is Appropriate Include:

- Seriousness of the offense

- Duration of the misconduct

- Pervasiveness of the misconduct, including whether the conduct cuts across geographic and/ or product lines

- Nature and size of the company

- Quality of the company's compliance program at the time of the misconduct

- Subsequent remediation efforts

In civil cases, a company may similarly be required to retain an independent compliance consultant or monitor to provide an independent, third-party review of the company's internal controls. The consultant recommends improvements, to the extent necessary, which the company must adopt. When both DOJ and SEC require a company to retain a monitor, the two agencies have been able to coordinate their requirements so that the company can retain one monitor to fulfill both sets of requirements.

The most successful monitoring relationships are those in which the company embraces the monitor or consultant. If the company takes the recommendations and suggestions seriously and uses the monitoring period as a time to find and fix any outstanding compliance issues, the company can emerge from the monitorship with a stronger, long-lasting compliance program.

chapter 6

FCPA Penalties, Sanctions, and Remedies

RESOLUTIONS

What Are the Different Types of Resolutions with DOJ?

Criminal Complaints, Informations, and Indictments

Charges against individuals and companies are brought in three different ways under the Federal Rules of Criminal Procedure: criminal complaints, criminal informations, and indictments.

DOJ may agree to resolve criminal FCPA matters against companies either through a declination or, in appropriate cases, a negotiated resolution resulting in a plea agreement, deferred prosecution agreement, or non-prosecution agreement. For individuals, a negotiated resolution will generally take the form of a plea agreement, which may include language regarding cooperation, or a non-prosecution cooperation agreement. When negotiated resolutions cannot be reached with companies or individuals, the matter may proceed to trial.

Plea Agreements

Plea agreements—whether with companies or individuals—are governed by Rule 11 of the Federal Rules of Criminal Procedure. The defendant generally admits to the facts supporting the charges, admits guilt, and is convicted of the charged crimes when the plea agreement is presented to and accepted by a court.

The plea agreement may jointly recommend a sentence or fine, jointly recommend an analysis under the U.S. Sentencing Guidelines, or leave such items open for argument at the time of sentencing.

Deferred Prosecution Agreements

Under a deferred prosecution agreement, or a DPA as it is commonly known, DOJ files a charging document with the court,[379] but it simultaneously requests that the prosecution be deferred, that is, postponed for the purpose of allowing the company to demonstrate its good conduct. DPAs generally require a defendant to agree to pay a monetary penalty, waive the statute of limitations, cooperate with the government, admit the relevant facts, and enter into certain compliance and remediation commitments, potentially including a corporate compliance monitor. DPAs describe the company's conduct, cooperation, and remediation, if any, and provide a calculation of the penalty pursuant to the U.S. Sentencing Guidelines. In addition to being publicly filed, DOJ places all of its DPAs on its website. If the company successfully completes the term of the agreement (typically two or three years), DOJ will then move to dismiss the filed charges. A company's successful completion of a DPA is not treated as a criminal conviction.

Non-Prosecution Agreements

Under a non-prosecution agreement, or an NPA as it is commonly known, DOJ maintains the right to file charges but refrains from doing so to allow the company to demonstrate its good conduct during the term of the NPA. Unlike a DPA, an NPA is not filed with a court but is instead maintained by the parties. In circumstances where an NPA is with a company for FCPA-related offenses, it is made available to the public through DOJ's website. The requirements of an NPA are similar to those of a DPA, and generally require a waiver of the statute of limitations, ongoing cooperation, admission of the material facts, and compliance and remediation commitments, in addition to payment of a monetary penalty. If the company complies with the agreement throughout its term, DOJ does not file criminal charges. If an individual complies with the terms of his or her NPA, namely, truthful and complete cooperation and continued law-abiding conduct, DOJ will not pursue criminal charges.

Declinations

As discussed above, DOJ's decision to bring or decline to bring an enforcement action under the FCPA is made pursuant to the *Principles of Federal Prosecution*, in the case of individuals, and the *Principles of Federal Prosecution of Business Organizations*, in the case of companies. As described, in the case of individuals, the *Principles of Federal Prosecution* advise prosecutors to weigh all relevant considerations, including:

- federal law enforcement priorities;
- the nature and seriousness of the offense;
- the deterrent effect of prosecution;
- the person's culpability in connection with the offense;
- the person's history of criminal activity;
- the person's willingness to cooperate in the investigation or prosecution of others; and
- the probable sentence or other consequences if the person is convicted.[380]

The *Principles of Federal Prosecution* provide additional commentary about each of these factors. For instance, they explain that prosecutors should take into account federal law enforcement priorities because federal law enforcement and judicial resources are not sufficient to permit prosecution of every alleged offense over which federal jurisdiction exists. The deterrent effect of prosecution should also be kept in mind because some offenses, "although seemingly not of great importance by themselves, if commonly committed would have a substantial cumulative impact on the community."[381]

As discussed above, the *Principles of Federal Prosecution of Business Organizations* require prosecutors to consider nine factors when determining whether to prosecute a corporate entity for an FCPA violation, including the nature and seriousness of the offense; the pervasiveness of wrongdoing within the company; the company's history of similar conduct; the existence and effectiveness of the company's pre-existing compliance program; and the adequacy of remedies, such as civil or regulatory enforcement actions.

Pursuant to these guidelines, DOJ has declined to prosecute both individuals and corporate entities in numerous cases based on the particular facts and circumstances presented in those matters, taking into account the available evidence.[382] To protect the privacy rights and other interests of the uncharged and other potentially interested parties, DOJ has a long-standing policy not to provide, without the party's consent, non-public information on matters it has declined to prosecute. To put DOJ's declinations in context, however, in the past two years alone, DOJ has declined several dozen cases against companies where potential FCPA violations were alleged.

As mentioned above, there are rare occasions in which, in conjunction with the public filing of charges against an individual, it is appropriate to disclose that a company is not also being prosecuted. That was done in a recent case where a former employee was charged but the former corporate employer was not.[383]

What Are the Different Types of Resolutions with SEC?

Civil Injunctive Actions and Remedies

In a civil injunctive action, SEC seeks a court order compelling the defendant to obey the law in the future. Violating such an order can result in civil or criminal contempt proceedings. Civil contempt sanctions, brought by SEC, are remedial rather than punitive in nature and serve one of two purposes: to compensate the party injured as a result of the violation of the injunction or force compliance with the terms of the injunction.

Where a defendant has profited from a violation of law, SEC can obtain the equitable relief of disgorgement of ill-gotten gains and pre-judgment interest and can also obtain civil money penalties pursuant to Sections 21(d)(3) and 32(c) of the Exchange Act. SEC may also seek ancillary relief (such as an accounting from a defendant). Pursuant to Section 21(d)(5), SEC also may seek, and any federal court may grant, any other equitable relief that may be appropriate or necessary for the benefit of investors, such as enhanced remedial measures or the retention of an independent compliance consultant or monitor.

Civil Administrative Actions and Remedies

SEC has the ability to institute various types of administrative proceedings against a person or an entity that it believes has violated the law. This type of enforcement action is brought by SEC's Enforcement Division and is litigated before an SEC administrative law judge (ALJ). The ALJ's decision is subject to appeal directly to the Securities and Exchange Commission itself, and the Commission's decision is in turn subject to review by a U.S. Court of Appeals.

Administrative proceedings provide for a variety of relief. For regulated persons and entities, such as broker-dealers and investment advisers and persons associated with them, sanctions include censure, limitation on activities, suspension of up to twelve months, and bar from association or revocation of registration. For professionals such as attorneys and accountants, SEC can order in Rule 102(e) proceedings that the professional be censured, suspended, or barred from practicing before SEC.[384] SEC staff can seek an order from an administrative law judge requiring the respondent to cease and desist from any current or future violations of the securities laws. In addition, SEC can obtain disgorgement, pre-judgment interest, and civil money penalties in administrative proceedings under Section 21B of the Exchange Act, and also can obtain other equitable relief, such as enhanced remedial measures or the retention of an independent compliance consultant or monitor.

Deferred Prosecution Agreements

A deferred prosecution agreement is a written agreement between SEC and a potential cooperating individual or company in which SEC agrees to forego an enforcement action against the individual or company if the individual or company agrees to, among other things: (1) cooperate truthfully and fully in SEC's investigation and related enforcement actions; (2) enter into a long-term tolling agreement; (3) comply with express prohibitions and/or undertakings during a period of deferred prosecution; and (4) under certain circumstances, agree either to admit or not to contest underlying facts that SEC could assert to establish a violation of the federal securities laws. If the agreement is violated during the period of deferred prosecution, SEC staff may recommend an enforcement action to the Commission against the individual or company for the original misconduct as well as any additional misconduct. Furthermore, if the Commission authorizes the enforcement action, SEC staff may use any factual admissions made by the cooperating individual or company in support of a motion for summary judgment, while maintaining the ability to bring an enforcement action for any additional misconduct at a later date.

In May of 2011, SEC entered into its first deferred prosecution agreement against a company for violating the FCPA.[385] In that case, a global manufacturer of steel pipe products violated the FCPA by bribing Uzbekistan government officials during a bidding process to supply pipelines for transporting oil and natural gas. The company made almost $5 million in profits when it was subsequently awarded several contracts by the Uzbekistan government. The company discovered the misconduct during a worldwide review of its operations and brought it to the government's attention. In addition to self-reporting, the company conducted a thorough internal investigation; provided complete, real-time cooperation with SEC and DOJ staff; and undertook extensive remediation, including enhanced anti-corruption procedures and training. Under the terms of the DPA, the company paid $5.4 million in disgorgement and prejudgment interest. The company also paid a $3.5 million monetary penalty to resolve a criminal investigation by DOJ through an NPA.[386]

For further information about deferred prosecution agreements, see SEC's *Enforcement Manual*.[387]

Non-Prosecution Agreements

A non-prosecution agreement is a written agreement between SEC and a potential cooperating individual or company, entered into in limited and appropriate circumstances, that provides that SEC will not pursue an enforcement action against the individual or company if the individual or company agrees to, among other things: (1) cooperate truthfully and fully in SEC's investigation and related enforcement actions; and (2) comply, under certain circumstances, with express undertakings. If the agreement is violated, SEC staff retains its ability to recommend an enforcement action to the Commission against the individual or company.

For further information about non-prosecution agreements, see SEC's *Enforcement Manual*.[388]

Termination Letters and Declinations

As discussed above, SEC's decision to bring or decline to bring an enforcement action under the FCPA is made pursuant to the guiding principles set forth in SEC's *Enforcement Manual*. The same factors that apply to SEC staff's determination of whether to recommend an enforcement action against an individual or entity apply to the decision to close an investigation without recommending enforcement action.[389]

Generally, SEC staff considers, among other things:

- the seriousness of the conduct and potential violations;
- the resources available to SEC staff to pursue the investigation;
- the sufficiency and strength of the evidence;
- the extent of potential investor harm if an action is not commenced; and
- the age of the conduct underlying the potential violations.

SEC has declined to take enforcement action against both individuals and companies based on the facts and circumstances present in those matters, where, for example, the conduct was not egregious, the company fully cooperated, and the company identified and remediated the misconduct quickly. SEC Enforcement Division policy is to notify individuals and entities at the earliest opportunity when the staff has determined not to recommend an enforcement action against them to the Commission. This notification takes the form of a termination letter.

In order to protect the privacy rights and other interests of the uncharged and other potentially interested parties, SEC does not provide non-public information on matters it has declined to prosecute.

What Are Some Examples of Past Declinations by DOJ and SEC?

Neither DOJ nor SEC typically publicizes declinations but, to provide some insight into the process, the following are recent, anonymized examples of matters DOJ and SEC have declined to pursue:

Example 1: Public Company Declination

DOJ and SEC declined to take enforcement action against a public U.S. company. Factors taken into consideration included:

chapter 7
Resolutions

- The company discovered that its employees had received competitor bid information from a third party with connections to the foreign government.
- The company began an internal investigation, withdrew its contract bid, terminated the employees involved, severed ties to the third-party agent, and voluntarily disclosed the conduct to DOJ's Antitrust Division, which also declined prosecution.
- During the internal investigation, the company uncovered various FCPA red flags, including prior concerns about the third-party agent, all of which the company voluntarily disclosed to DOJ and SEC.
- The company immediately took substantial steps to improve its compliance program.

Example 2: Public Company Declination

DOJ and SEC declined to take enforcement action against a public U.S. company. Factors taken into consideration included:

- With knowledge of employees of the company's subsidiary, a retained construction company paid relatively small bribes, which were wrongly approved by the company's local law firm, to foreign building code inspectors.
- When the company's compliance department learned of the bribes, it immediately ended the conduct, terminated its relationship with the construction company and law firm, and terminated or disciplined the employees involved.
- The company completed a thorough internal investigation and voluntarily disclosed to DOJ and SEC.
- The company reorganized its compliance department, appointed a new compliance officer dedicated to anti-corruption, improved the training and compliance program, and undertook a review of all of the company's international third-party relationships.

Example 3: Public Company Declination

DOJ and SEC declined to take enforcement action against a U.S. publicly held industrial services company for

bribes paid by a small foreign subsidiary. Factors taken into consideration included:

- The company self-reported the conduct to DOJ and SEC.
- The total amount of the improper payments was relatively small, and the activity appeared to be an isolated incident by a single employee at the subsidiary.
- The profits potentially obtained from the improper payments were very small.
- The payments were detected by the company's existing internal controls. The company's audit committee conducted a thorough independent internal investigation. The results of the investigation were provided to the government.
- The company cooperated fully with investigations by DOJ and SEC.
- The company implemented significant remedial actions and enhanced its internal control structure.

Example 4: Public Company Declination

DOJ and SEC declined to take enforcement action against a U.S. publicly held oil-and-gas services company for small bribes paid by a foreign subsidiary's customs agent. Factors taken into consideration included:

- The company's internal controls timely detected a potential bribe before a payment was made.
- When company management learned of the potential bribe, management immediately reported the issue to the company's General Counsel and Audit Committee and prevented the payment from occurring.
- Within weeks of learning of the attempted bribe, the company provided in-person FCPA training to employees of the subsidiary and undertook

an extensive internal investigation to determine whether any of the company's subsidiaries in the same region had engaged in misconduct.

- The company self-reported the misconduct and the results of its internal investigation to DOJ and SEC.
- The company cooperated fully with investigations by DOJ and SEC.
- In addition to the immediate training at the relevant subsidiary, the company provided comprehensive FCPA training to all of its employees and conducted an extensive review of its anti-corruption compliance program.
- The company enhanced its internal controls and record-keeping policies and procedures, including requiring periodic internal audits of customs payments.
- As part of its remediation, the company directed that local lawyers rather than customs agents be used to handle its permits, with instructions that "no matter what, we don't pay bribes"—a policy that resulted in a longer and costlier permit procedure.

Example 5: Public Company Declination

DOJ and SEC declined to take enforcement action against a U.S. publicly held consumer products company in connection with its acquisition of a foreign company. Factors taken into consideration included:

- The company identified the potential improper payments to local government officials as part of its pre-acquisition due diligence.
- The company promptly developed a comprehensive plan to investigate, correct, and remediate any FCPA issues after acquisition.
- The company promptly self-reported the issues prior to acquisition and provided the results of its investigation to the government on a real-time basis.
- The acquiring company's existing internal controls and compliance program were robust.
- After the acquisition closed, the company implemented a comprehensive remedial plan, ensured that all improper payments stopped, provided

extensive FCPA training to employees of the new subsidiary, and promptly incorporated the new subsidiary into the company's existing internal controls and compliance environment.

Example 6: Private Company Declination

In 2011, DOJ declined to take prosecutorial action against a privately held U.S. company and its foreign subsidiary. Factors taken into consideration included:

- The company voluntarily disclosed bribes paid to social security officials in a foreign country.
- The total amount of the bribes was small.
- When discovered, the corrupt practices were immediately terminated.
- The conduct was thoroughly investigated, and the results of the investigation were promptly provided to DOJ.
- All individuals involved were either terminated or disciplined. The company also terminated its relationship with its foreign law firm.
- The company instituted improved training and compliance programs commensurate with its size and risk exposure.

chapter 7
Resolutions

WHISTLEBLOWER PROVISIONS AND PROTECTIONS

Assistance and information from a whistleblower who knows of possible securities law violations can be among the most powerful weapons in the law enforcement arsenal. Through their knowledge of the circumstances and individuals involved, whistleblowers can help SEC and DOJ identify potential violations much earlier than might otherwise have been possible, thus allowing SEC and DOJ to minimize the harm to investors, better preserve the integrity of the U.S. capital markets, and more swiftly hold accountable those responsible for unlawful conduct.

The Sarbanes-Oxley Act of 2002 and the Dodd-Frank Act of 2010 both contain provisions affecting whistleblowers who report FCPA violations. Sarbanes-Oxley prohibits issuers from retaliating against whistleblowers and provides that employees who are retaliated against for reporting possible securities law violations may file a complaint with the Department of Labor, for which they would be eligible to receive reinstatement, back pay, and other compensation.[390] Sarbanes-Oxley also prohibits retaliation against employee whistleblowers under the obstruction of justice statute.[391]

In 2010, the Dodd-Frank Act added Section 21F to the Exchange Act, addressing whistleblower incentives and protections. Section 21F authorizes SEC to provide monetary awards to eligible individuals who voluntarily come forward with high quality, original information that leads to an SEC enforcement action in which over $1,000,000 in sanctions is ordered.[392] The awards range is between 10% and 30% of the monetary sanctions recovered by the government. The Dodd-Frank Act also prohibits employers from retaliating against whistleblowers and creates a private right of action for employees who are retaliated against.[393]

Furthermore, businesses should be aware that retaliation against a whistleblower may also violate state, local, and foreign laws that provide protection of whistleblowers.

On August 12, 2011, the final rules for SEC's Whistleblower Program became effective. These rules set forth the requirements for whistleblowers to be eligible for awards consideration, the factors that SEC will use to determine the amount of the award, the categories of individuals who are excluded from award consideration, and the categories of individuals who are subject to limitations in award considerations.[394] The final rules strengthen incentives for employees to report the suspected violations internally through internal compliance programs when appropriate, although it does not require an employee to do so in order to qualify for an award.[395]

Individuals with information about a possible violation of the federal securities laws, including FCPA violations, should submit that information to SEC either online through SEC's Tips, Complaints, and Referrals (TCR) Intake and Resolution System (available at https://denebleo.sec.gov/TCRExternal/disclaimer.xhtml) or by mailing or faxing a completed Form TCR to the Commission's Office of the Whistleblower.

Whistleblowers can submit information anonymously. To be considered under SEC's whistleblower program as eligible for a reward, however, the information must be submitted on an anonymous whistleblower's behalf by an attorney.[396] Whether or not a whistleblower reports anonymously, SEC is committed to protecting the identity of a whistleblower to the fullest extent possible under the statute.[397] SEC's Office of the Whistleblower administers SEC's Whistleblower Program and answers questions from the public regarding the program. Additional information regarding SEC's Whistleblower Program, including answers to frequently asked questions, is available online at http://www.sec.gov/whistleblower.

> **SEC Office of the Whistleblower**
>
> 100 F Street NE, Mail Stop 5971
> Washington, DC 20549
> Facsimile: (703) 813-9322
> Online Report Form: http://www.sec.gov/whistleblower

chapter 8
**Whistleblower
Provisions and
Protections**

DOJ OPINION PROCEDURE

DOJ's opinion procedure is a valuable mechanism for companies and individuals to determine whether proposed conduct would be prosecuted by DOJ under the FCPA.[398] Generally speaking, under the opinion procedure process, parties submit information to DOJ, after which DOJ issues an opinion about whether the proposed conduct falls within its enforcement policy. All of DOJ's prior opinions are available online.[399] Parties interested in obtaining such an opinion should follow these steps:[400]

First, those seeking an opinion should evaluate whether their question relates to actual, prospective conduct.[401] The opinion procedure cannot be used to obtain opinions on purely historical conduct or on hypothetical questions. DOJ will not consider a request unless that portion of the transaction for which an opinion is sought involves only prospective conduct, although the transaction as a whole may have components that already have occurred. An executed contract is not a prerequisite and, in most—if not all—instances, an opinion request should be made before the requestor commits to proceed with a transaction.[402] Those seeking requests should be aware that FCPA opinions relate only to the FCPA's anti-bribery provisions.[403]

Second, before making the request, the company or individual should check that they are either an issuer or a domestic concern, as only those categories of parties can

receive an opinion.[404] If the transaction involves more than one issuer or domestic concern, consider making a request for an opinion jointly, as opinions only apply to the parties that request them.[405]

Third, those seeking an opinion must put their request in writing. The request must be specific and accompanied by all relevant and material information bearing on the conduct and circumstances for which an opinion is requested. Material information includes background information, complete copies of all operative documents, and detailed statements of all collateral or oral understandings, if any. Those seeking opinions are under an affirmative obligation to make full and true disclosures.[406] Materials disclosed to DOJ will not be made public without the consent of the party submitting them.[407]

Fourth, the request must be signed. For corporate requestors, the signatory should be an appropriate senior officer with operational responsibility for the conduct that is the subject of the request and who has been designated by the corporation's chief executive officer. In appropriate cases, DOJ also may require the chief executive officer to sign the request. Those signing the request must certify that it contains a true, correct, and complete disclosure with respect to the proposed conduct and the circumstances of the conduct.[408]

Fifth, an original and five copies of the request should be addressed to the Assistant Attorney General in charge of the Criminal Division, Attention: FCPA Opinion Group.[409] The mailing address is P.O. Box 28188 Central Station, Washington, D.C. 20038. DOJ also asks that you send an electronic courtesy copy to FCPA.Fraud@usdoj.gov.

DOJ will evaluate the request for an FCPA opinion.[410] A party may withdraw a request for an opinion at any time prior to the release of an opinion.[411] If the request is complete and all the relevant information has been submitted, DOJ will respond to the request by issuing an opinion within 30 days.[412] If the request is incomplete, DOJ will identify for the requestor what additional information or documents are required for DOJ to review the request. Such information must be provided to DOJ promptly. Once the additional information has been received, DOJ will issue an opinion within 30 days of receipt of that additional information.[413] DOJ's FCPA opinions state whether, for purposes of DOJ's present enforcement policy, the prospective conduct would violate either the issuer or domestic concern anti-bribery provisions of the FCPA.[414] DOJ also may take other positions in the opinion as it considers appropriate.[415] To the extent that the opinion concludes that the proposed conduct would not violate the FCPA, a rebuttable presumption is created that the requestor's conduct that was the basis of the opinion is in compliance with the FCPA.[416] In order to provide non-binding guidance to the business community, DOJ makes versions of its opinions publicly available on its website.[417]

If, after receiving an opinion, a party is concerned about prospective conduct that is beyond the scope of conduct specified in a previous request, the party may submit an additional request for an opinion using the procedures outlined above.[418]

chapter 9
**DOJ Opinion
Procedure**

CONCLUSION

The FCPA was designed to prevent corrupt practices, protect investors, and provide a fair playing field for those honest companies trying to win business based on quality and price rather than bribes. Following Congress' leadership in enacting the FCPA 35 years ago, and through determined international diplomatic and law enforcement efforts in the time since, laws like the FCPA prohibiting foreign bribery have been enacted by most of the United States' major trading partners.

This guide is designed to provide practical advice about, and useful insights into, our enforcement considerations. For businesses desiring to compete fairly in foreign markets, it is our goal to maximize those businesses' ability to comply with the FCPA in the most effective and efficient way suitable to their business and the markets in which they operate. Through our ongoing efforts with the U.S. and international business and legal communities and non-governmental organizations, DOJ and SEC can continue effectively to protect the integrity of our markets and reduce corruption around the world.

(The Appendix of *A Resource Guide to the U.S. Foreign Corrupt Practices Act* is the act itself. 15 U.S.C. 78 dd-1, 78 dd-2, 78 dd-3, 78m and 78ff. See Appendix 1 of THE FCPA HANDBOOK for the entire Foreign Corrupt Practices Act)

ENDNOTES

[1] S. Rep. No. 95-114, at 4 (1977) [hereinafter S. Rep. No. 95-114], *available at* http://www.justice.gov/criminal/fraud/fcpa/history/1977/senaterpt-95-114.pdf.

[2] *Id.*; H.R. Rep. No. 95-640, at 4-5 (1977) [hereinafter H. R. Rep. No. 95-640], *available at* http://www.justice.gov/criminal/fraud/fcpa/history/1977/houseprt-95-640.pdf. The House Report made clear Congress's concerns:

> The payment of bribes to influence the acts or decisions of foreign officials, foreign political parties or candidates for foreign political office is unethical. It is counter to the moral expectations and values of the American public. But not only is it unethical, it is bad business as well. It erodes public confidence in the integrity of the free market system. It short-circuits the marketplace by directing business to those companies too inefficient to compete in terms of price, quality or service, or too lazy to engage in honest salesmanship, or too intent upon unloading marginal products. In short, it rewards corruption instead of efficiency and puts pressure on ethical enterprises to lower their standards or risk losing business.

Id.

[3] *See, e.g.*, U.S. Agency for Int'l Dev., USAID Anticorruption Strategy 5-6 (2005), *available at* http://transition.usaid.gov/policy/ads/200/200mbo.pdf. The growing recognition that corruption poses a severe threat to domestic and international security has galvanized efforts to combat it in the United States and abroad. *See, e.g.*, Int'l Anti-Corruption and Good Governance Act of 2000, Pub. L. No. 106-309, § 202, 114 Stat. 1090 (codified as amended at 22 U.S.C. §§ 2151-2152 (2000)) (noting that "[w]idespread corruption endangers the stability and security of societies, undermines democracy, and jeopardizes the social, political, and economic development of a society. . . . [and that] [c]orruption facilitates criminal activities, such as money laundering, hinders economic development, inflates the costs of doing business, and undermines the legitimacy of the government and public trust").

[4] *See* Maryse Tremblay & Camille Karbassi, *Corruption and Human Trafficking* 4 (Transparency Int'l, Working Paper No. 3, 2011), *available at* http://issuu.com/transparencyinternational/docs/ti-working_paper_human_trafficking_28_jun_2011; U.S. Agency for Int'l Dev., Foreign Aid in the National Interest 40 (2002), *available at* http://pdf.usaid.gov/pdf_docs/PDABW900.pdf ("No problem does more to alienate citizens from their political leaders and institutions, and to undermine political stability and economic development, than endemic corruption among the government, political party leaders, judges, and bureaucrats. The more endemic the corruption is, the more

likely it is to be accompanied by other serious deficiencies in the rule of law: smuggling, drug trafficking, criminal violence, human rights abuses, and personalization of power.").

[5] President George W. Bush observed in 2006 that "the culture of corruption has undercut development and good governance and . . . . impedes our efforts to promote freedom and democracy, end poverty, and combat international crime and terrorism." President's Statement on Kleptocracy, 2 Pub. Papers 1504 (Aug. 10, 2006), *available at* http://georgewbush-whitehouse.archives.gov/news/releases/2006/08/20060810.html. The administrations of former President George W. Bush and President Barack Obama both recognized the threats posed to security and stability by corruption. For instance, in issuing a proclamation restricting the entry of certain corrupt foreign public officials, former President George W. Bush recognized "the serious negative effects that corruption of public institutions has on the United States' efforts to promote security and to strengthen democratic institutions and free market systems. . . ." Proclamation No. 7750, 69 Fed. Reg. 2287 (Jan. 14, 2004). Similarly, President Barack Obama's National Security Strategy paper, released in May 2010, expressed the administration's efforts and commitment to promote the recognition that "pervasive corruption is a violation of basic human rights and a severe impediment to development and global security." The White House, National Security Strategy 38 (2010), *available at* http://www.whitehouse.gov/sites/default/files/rss_viewer/national_security_strategy.pdf.

[6] *See, e.g.*, Int'l Chamber of Commerce, et al., Clean Business Is Good Business: The Business Case Against Corruption (2008), *available at* http://www.unglobalcompact.org/docs/news_events/8.1/clean_business_is_good_business.pdf; World Health Org., *Fact Sheet No. 335, Medicines: Corruption and Pharmaceuticals* (Dec. 2009), *available at* http://www.who.int/mediacentre/factsheets/fs335/en/; Daniel Kaufmann, *Corruption: The Facts*, Foreign Pol'y, Summer 1997, at 119-20; Paolo Mauro, *Corruption and Growth*, 110 Q. J. Econ. 681, 683, 705 (1995) (finding that "corruption lowers private investment . . . [and] reduc[es] economic growth . . ."); The World Bank, The Data Revolution: Measuring Governance and Corruption, (Apr. 8, 2004), *available at* http://go.worldbank.org/87JUY8GJH0.

[7] *See, e.g.*, *The Corruption Eruption*, Economist (Apr. 29, 2010), *available at* http://www.economist.com/node/16005114 ("The hidden costs of corruption are almost always much higher than companies imagine. Corruption inevitably begets ever more corruption: bribe-takers keep returning to the trough and bribe-givers open themselves up to blackmail."); Daniel Kaufmann and Shang-Jin Wei, *Does "Grease Money" Speed Up the Wheels of Commerce?* 2 (Nat'l Bureau of Econ. Research, Working Paper No. 7093, 1999), *available at* http://www.nber.org/papers/w7093.pdf ("Contrary to the 'efficient grease' theory, we find

that firms that pay more bribes are also likely to spend more, not less, management time with bureaucrats negotiating regulations, and face higher, not lower, cost of capital.").

[8] For example, in a number of recent enforcement actions, the same employees who were directing or controlling the bribe payments were also enriching themselves at the expense of the company. *See, e.g.,* Complaint, SEC v. Peterson, No. 12-cv-2033 (E.D.N.Y. 2012), ECF No. 1, *available at* http://www.sec.gov/litigation/complaints/2012/comp-pr2012-78.pdf; Criminal Information, United States v. Peterson, No. 12-cr-224 (E.D.N.Y. 2012), ECF No. 7 [hereinafter *United States v. Peterson*], *available at* http://www.justice.gov/criminal/fraud/fcpa/cases/petersong/petersong-information.pdf; Plea Agreement, United States v. Stanley, No. 08-cr-597 (S.D. Tex. 2008), ECF No. 9 [hereinafter *United States v. Stanley*], *available at* http://www.justice.gov/criminal/fraud/fcpa/cases/stanleya/09-03-08stanley-plea-agree.pdf; Plea Agreement, United States v. Sapsizian, No. 06-cr-20797 (S.D. Fla. 2007), ECF No. 42 [hereinafter *United States v. Sapsizian*], *available at* http://www.justice.gov/criminal/fraud/fcpa/cases/sapsizianc/06-06-07sapsizian-plea.pdf.

[9] *See, e.g.,* Complaint, SEC v. Tyco Int'l Ltd., 06-cv-2942 (S.D.N.Y. 2006), ECF No. 1 [hereinafter *SEC v. Tyco Int'l*], *available at* http://www.sec.gov/litigation/complaints/2006/comp19657.pdf; Complaint, SEC v. Willbros Group, Inc., No. 08-cv-1494 (S.D. Tex. 2008), ECF No. 1 [hereinafter *SEC v. Willbros*], *available at* http://www.sec.gov/litigation/complaints/2008/comp20571.pdf.

[10] *See* Plea Agreement, United States v. Bridgestone Corp., No. 11-cr-651 (S.D. Tex. 2011), ECF No. 21, *available at* http://www.justice.gov/criminal/fraud/fcpa/cases/bridgestone/10-05-11bridgestone-plea.pdf.

[11] *See* S. Rep. No. 95-114, at 6; H.R. Rep. No. 95-640, at 4; *see also* A. Carl Kotchian, *The Payoff: Lockheed's 70-Day Mission to Tokyo,* Saturday Rev., Jul. 9, 1977, at 7.

[12] U.S. Sec. and Exchange Comm., Report of the Securities and Exchange Commission on Questionable and Illegal Corporate Payments and Practices 2-3 (1976).

[13] *See* H.R. Rep. No. 95-640, at 4-5; S. Rep. No. 95-114, at 3-4.

[14] H.R. Rep. No. 95-640, at 4-5; S. Rep. No. 95-114, at 4. The Senate Report observed, for instance, that "[m]anagements which resort to corporate bribery and the falsification of records to enhance their business reveal a lack of confidence about themselves," while citing the Secretary of the Treasury's testimony that "'[p]aying bribes—apart from being morally repugnant and illegal in most countries—is simply not necessary for the successful conduct of business here or overseas.'" *Id.*

[15] *See* S. Rep. No. 100-85, at 46 (1987) (recounting FCPA's historical background and explaining that "a strong antibribery statute could help U.S. corporations resist corrupt demands . . . .") [hereinafter S. Rep. No. 100-85].

[16] S. Rep. No. 95-114, at 7.

[17] Omnibus Trade and Competitiveness Act of 1988, Pub. L. No. 100-418, § 5003, 102 Stat. 1107, 1415-25 (1988); *see also* H.R. Rep. No. 100-576, at 916-24 (1988) (discussing FCPA amendments, including changes to standard of liability for acts of third parties) [hereinafter H.R. Rep. No. 100-576].

[18] *See* Omnibus Trade and Competitiveness Act of 1988, § 5003(d). The amended statute included the following directive:

> It is the sense of the Congress that the President should pursue the negotiation of an international agreement, among the members of the Organization of Economic Cooperation and Development, to govern persons from those countries concerning acts prohibited with respect to issuers and domestic concerns by the amendments made by this section. Such international agreement should include a process by which problems and conflicts associated with such acts could be resolved.

Id.; *see also* S. Rep. No. 105-277, at 2 (1998) (describing efforts by Executive Branch to encourage U.S. trading partners to enact legislation similar to FCPA following 1988 amendments) [hereinafter S. Rep. No. 105-277].

[19] Convention on Combating Bribery of Foreign Public Officials in International Business Transactions art. 1.1, Dec. 18, 1997, 37 I.L.M. 1 [hereinafter Anti-Bribery Convention]. The Anti-Bribery Convention requires member countries to make it a criminal offense "for any person intentionally to offer, promise or give any undue pecuniary or other

advantage, whether directly or through intermediaries, to a foreign public official, for that official or for a third party, in order that the official act or refrain from acting in relation to the performance of official duties, in order to obtain or retain business or other improper advantage in the conduct of international business." The Convention and its commentaries also call on all parties (a) to ensure that aiding and abetting and authorization of an act of bribery are criminal offenses, (b) to assert territorial jurisdiction "broadly so that an extensive physical connection to the bribery act is not required," and (c) to assert nationality jurisdiction consistent with the general principles and conditions of each party's legal system. *Id.* at art. 1.2, cmts. 25, 26.

[20] *See* International Anti-Bribery and Fair Competition Act of 1998, Pub. L. 105-366, 112 Stat. 3302 (1998); *see also* S. Rep. No. 105-277, at 2-3 (describing amendments to "the FCPA to conform it to the requirements of and to implement the OECD Convention").

[21] There is no private right of action under the FCPA. *See, e.g.,* Lamb v. Phillip Morris, Inc., 915 F.2d 1024, 1028-29 (6th Cir. 1990); McLean v. Int'l Harvester Co., 817 F.2d 1214, 1219 (5th Cir. 1987).

[22] U.S. Dept. of Justice, U.S. Attorneys' Manual § 9-47.110 (2008) [hereinafter USAM], *available at* http://www.justice.gov/usao/eousa/foia_reading_room/usam/.

[23] Go to http://export.gov/worldwide_us/index.asp for more information.

[24] Additional information about publicly available market research and due diligence assistance is available online. *See* In'l Trade Admin., *Market Research and Due Diligence, available at* http://export.gov/salesandmarketing/eg_main_018204.asp. The International Company Profile reports include a listing of the potential partner's key officers and senior management; banking relationships and other financial information about the company; and market information, including sales and profit figures and potential liabilities. They are not, however, intended to substitute for a company's own due diligence, and the Commercial Service does not offer ICP in countries where Dun & Bradstreet or other private sector vendors are already performing this service. *See* In'l Trade Admin., *International Company Profile, available at* http://export.gov/salesandmarketing/eg_main_018198.asp.

[25] The Commercial Services' domestic and foreign offices can also be found at http://export.gov/usoffices/index.asp and http://export.gov/worldwide_us/index.asp.

[26] This form can be located at http://tcc.export.gov/Report_a_Barrier/index.asp.

[27] *See* In'l Trade Admin., "Doing Business In" Guides, *available at* http://export.gov/about/eg_main_016806.asp.

[28] The Business Ethics Manual is available at http://www.ita.doc.gov/goodgovernance/business_ethics/manual.asp.

[29] Information about the Advocacy Center can be found at http://export.gov/advocacy.

[30] Reports on U.S. compliance with these treaties can be found at http://www.justice.gov/criminal/fraud/fcpa/intlagree/.

[31] *See* Statement on Signing the International Anti-Bribery and Fair Competition Act of 1998, 34 Weekly Comp. Pres. Doc. 2290, 2291 (Nov. 10, 1998) ("U.S. companies have had to compete on an uneven playing field . . . . The OECD Convention . . . is designed to change all that. Under the Convention, our major competitors will be obligated to criminalize the bribery of foreign public officials in international business transactions.").

[32] Colombia is also a member of the Working Group and is expected to accede to the Anti-Bribery Convention.

[33] OECD, *Country Monitoring of the OECD Anti-Bribery Convention, available at* http://www.oecd.org/document/12/0,3746,en_2649_34859_35692940_1_1_1_1,00.html.

[34] OECD, *Phase 3 Country Monitoring of the OECD Anti-Bribery Convention, available at* http://www.oecd.org/document/31/0,3746,en_2649_34859_44684959_1_1_1_1,00.html.

[35] OECD, *Country Reports on the Implementation of the OECD Anti-Bribery Convention, available at* http://www.oecd.org/document/24/0,3746,en_2649_34859_1933144_1_1_1_1,00.html.

[36] The OECD Phase 1, 2, and 3 reports on the United States, as well as the U.S. responses to questionnaires, are available at http://www.justice.gov/criminal/fraud/fcpa/intlagree.

[37] *See* OECD Working Group on Bribery, *United States: Phase 3, Report on the Application of the Convention on Combating Bribery of Foreign*

Public Officials in International Business Transactions and the 2009 Revised Recommendation on Combating Bribery in International Business Transactions, Oct. 2010, at 61-62 (recommending that the United States "[c]onsolidate and summarise publicly available information on the application of the FCPA in relevant sources"), *available at* http://www.oecd.org/dataoecd/10/49/46213841.pdf.

[38] United Nations Convention Against Corruption, Oct. 31, 2003, S. Treaty Doc. No. 109-6, 2349 U.N.T.S. 41, *available at* http://www.unodc.org/documents/treaties/UNCAC/Publications/Convention/08-50026_E.pdf [hereinafter UNCAC].

[39] For more information about the UNCAC review mechanism, see *Mechanism for the Review of Implementation of the United Nations Convention Against Corruption*, United Nations Office on Drugs and Crime, *available at* http://www.unodc.org/documents/treaties/UNCAC/Publications/ReviewMechanism-BasicDocuments/Mechanism_for_the_Review_of_Implementation_-_Basic_Documents_-_E.pdf.

[40] For information about the status of UNCAC, see United Nations Office on Drugs and Crime, *UNCAC Signature and Ratification Status as of 12 July 2012, available at* http://www.unodc.org/unodc/en/treaties/CAC/signatories.html.

[41] Organization of American States, Inter-American Convention Against Corruption, Mar. 29, 1996, 35 I.L.M. 724, *available at* http://www.oas.org/juridico/english/treaties/b-58.html. For additional information about the status of the IACAC, see Organization of American States, Signatories and Ratifications, *available at* http://www.oas.org/juridico/english/Sigs/b-58.html.

[42] Council of Europe, Criminal Law Convention on Corruption, Jan. 27, 1999, 38 I.L.M. 505, *available at* http://conventions.coe.int/Treaty/en/Treaties/html/173.htm.

[43] For additional information about GRECO, see Council of Europe, *Group of States Against Corruption, available at* http://www.coe.int/t/dghl/monitoring/greco/default_EN.asp. The United States has not yet ratified the GRECO convention.

[44] The text of the FCPA statute is set forth in the appendix. *See also* Jury Instructions at 21-27, United States v. Esquenazi, No. 09-cr-21010 (S.D. Fla. Aug. 5, 2011), ECF No. 520 [hereinafter *United States v. Esquenazi*] (FCPA jury instructions); Jury Instructions at 14-25, United States v. Kay, No. 01-cr-914 (S.D. Tex. Oct. 6, 2004), ECF No. 142 (same), *aff'd*, 513 F.3d 432, 446-52 (5th Cir. 2007), *reh'g denied*, 513 F.3d 461 (5th Cir. 2008) [hereinafter *United States v. Kay*]; Jury Instructions at 76-87, United States v. Jefferson, No. 07-cr-209 (E.D. Va. July 30, 2009), ECF No. 684 [hereinafter *United States v. Jefferson*] (same); Jury Instructions at 8-10, United States v. Green, No. 08-cr-59 (C.D. Cal. Sept. 11, 2009), ECF No. 288 [hereinafter *United States v. Green*] (same); Jury Instructions at 23-29, United States v. Bourke, No. 05-cr-518 (S.D.N.Y. July 2009) [hereinafter *United States v. Bourke*] (same, not docketed); Jury Instructions at 2-8, United States v. Mead, No. 98-cr-240 (D.N.J. Oct. 1998) [hereinafter *United States v. Mead*] (same).

[45] The provisions of the FCPA applying to issuers are part of the Securities Exchange Act of 1934 [hereinafter Exchange Act]. The anti-bribery provisions can be found at Section 30A of the Exchange Act, 15 U.S.C. § 78dd-1.

[46] 15 U.S.C. § 78*l*.

[47] 15 U.S.C. § 78*o*(d).

[48] SEC enforcement actions have involved a number of foreign issuers. *See, e.g.*, Complaint, SEC v. Magyar Telekom Plc., *et al.*, No. 11-cv-9646 (S.D.N.Y. Dec. 29, 2011), ECF No. 1 (German and Hungarian companies), *available at* http://www.sec.gov/litigation/complaints/2011/comp22213-co.pdf; Complaint, SEC v. Alcatel-Lucent, S.A., No. 10-cv-24620 (S.D. Fla. Dec. 27, 2010), ECF No. 1 [hereinafter *SEC v. Alcatel-Lucent*] (French company), *available at* http://www.sec.gov/litigation/complaints/2010/comp21795.pdf; Complaint, SEC v. ABB, Ltd., No. 10-cv-1648 (D.D.C. Sept. 29, 2010), ECF No. 1 [hereinafter *SEC v. ABB*] (Swiss company), *available at* http://www.sec.gov/litigation/complaints/2010/comp-pr2010-175.pdf; Complaint, SEC v. Daimler AG, No. 10-cv-473 (D.D.C. Apr. 1, 2010), ECF No. 1 [hereinafter *SEC v. Daimler AG*] (German company), *available at* http://sec.gov/litigation/complaints/2010/comp-pr2010-51.pdf; Complaint, SEC v. Siemens Aktiengesellschaft, No. 08-cv-2167 (D.D.C. Dec. 12, 2008), ECF No. 1 [hereinafter *SEC v. Siemens AG*] (Germany company), *available at* http://www.sec.gov/litigation/

complaints/2008/comp20829.pdf. Certain DOJ enforcement actions have likewise involved foreign issuers. *See, e.g.*, Criminal Information, United States v. Magyar Telekom, Plc., No. 11-cr-597 (E.D. Va. Dec. 29, 2011), ECF No. 1, *available at* http://www.justice.gov/criminal/fraud/fcpa/cases/magyar-telekom/2011-12-29-information-magyar-telekom.pdf; Non-Pros. Agreement, In re Deutsche Telekom AG (Dec. 29, 2011), *available at* http://www.justice.gov/criminal/fraud/fcpa/cases/deutsche-telekom/2011-12-29-deustche-telekom-npa.pdf; Criminal Information, United States v. Alcatel-Lucent, S.A., No. 10-cr-20907 (S.D. Fla. Dec. 27, 2010), ECF No. 1 [hereinafter *United States v. Alcatel-Lucent, S.A.*], *available at* http://www.justice.gov/criminal/fraud/fcpa/cases/alcatel-etal/12-27-10alcatel-et-al-info.pdf; Criminal Information, United States v. Daimler AG, No. 10-cr-63 (D.D.C. Mar. 22, 2010), ECF No. 1 [hereinafter *United States v. Daimler AG*], *available at* http://www.justice.gov/criminal/fraud/fcpa/cases/daimler/03-22-10daimlerag-info.pdf; Criminal Information, United States v. Siemens Aktiengesellschaft, No. 08-cr-367 (D.D.C. Dec. 12, 2008), ECF No. 1 [hereinafter *United States v. Siemens AG*], *available at* http://www.justice.gov/criminal/fraud/fcpa/cases/siemens/12-12-08siemensakt-info.pdf.

[49] See http://www.sec.gov/divisions/corpfin/internatl/companies.shtml.

[50] *See, e.g.*, Complaint, SEC v. Turner, *et al.*, No. 10-cv-1309 (D.D.C. Aug. 4, 2010), ECF No. 1 [hereinafter, *SEC v. Turner*] (charging a Lebansese/Canadian agent of a UK company listed on U.S. exchange with violating the FCPA for bribes of Iraqi officials), *available at* http://www.sec.gov/litigation/complaints/2010/comp21615.pdf; Indictment, United States v. Naaman, No. 08-cr-246 (D.D.C. Aug. 7, 2008), ECF No. 3 [hereinafter *United States v. Naaman*] (same), *available at* http://www.justice.gov/criminal/fraud/fcpa/cases/naamano/08-07-08naaman-indict.pdf; Complaint, SEC v. Elkin, *et al.*, No. 10-cv-661 (D.D.C. Apr. 28, 2010), ECF No. 1 [hereinafter *SEC v. Elkin*] (charging an employee of U.S. publicly traded company with violating FCPA for bribery of officials in Kyrgyzstan), *available at* http://www.sec.gov/litigation/complaints/2010/comp21509.pdf; Criminal Information, United States v. Elkin, No. 10-cr-15 (W.D. Va. Aug. 3, 2010), ECF No. 8 [hereinafter *United States v. Elkin*] (same), *available at* http://www.justice.gov/criminal/fraud/fcpa/cases/elkin/08-03-10elkin-information.pdf; Indictment, United States v. Tesler, *et al.*, No. 09-cr-98 (S.D. Tex. Feb. 17, 2009), ECF No. 1 [hereinafter *United States v. Tesler*] (charging a British agent of U.S. publicly traded company with violating FCPA for bribery of Nigerian officials), *available at* http://www.justice.gov/criminal/fraud/fcpa/cases/tesler/tesler-indict.pdf; Superseding Indictment, *United States v. Sapsizian*, et al., *supra* note 8, ECF 32 (charging a French employee of French company traded on a U.S. exchange with violating the FCPA).

[51] 15 U.S.C. § 78dd-2.

[52] 15 U.S.C. § 78dd-2(h)(1).

[53] 15 U.S.C. § 78dd-2(a). *See, e.g.*, Superseding Indictment, United States v. Nexus Technologies, *et al.*, No. 08-cr-522 (E.D. Pa. Oct. 28, 2009), ECF No. 106 [hereinafter *United States v. Nexus Technologies*] (private U.S. company and corporate executives charged with violating FCPA for bribes paid in Vietnam), *available at* http://www.justice.gov/criminal/fraud/fcpa/cases/nguyenn/09-04-08nguyen-indict.pdf; Indictment, *United States v. Esquenazi*, *supra* note 44, (private U.S. company and corporate executives charged with FCPA violations for bribes paid in Haiti), *available at* http://www.justice.gov/criminal/fraud/fcpa/cases/esquenazij/12-08-09esquenazi-indict.pdf.

[54] 15 U.S.C. § 78dd-3(a). As discussed above, foreign companies that have securities registered in the United States or that are required to file periodic reports with the SEC, including certain foreign companies with American Depository Receipts, are covered by the FCPA's anti-bribery provisions governing "issuers" under 15 U.S.C. § 78dd-1.

⁵⁵ *See* International Anti-Bribery and Fair Competition Act of 1998, Pub. L. 105-366, 112 Stat. 3302 (1998); 15 U.S.C. § 78dd-3(a); *see also* U.S. DEPT. OF JUSTICE, CRIMINAL RESOURCE MANUAL § 9-1018 (Nov. 2000) (the Department "interprets [Section 78dd-3(a)] as conferring jurisdiction whenever a foreign company or national *causes* an act to be done within the territory of the United States by any person acting as that company's or national's agent."). This interpretation is consistent with U.S. treaty obligations. *See* S. REP. NO. 105-2177 (1998) (expressing Congress' intention that the 1998 amendments to the FCPA "conform it to the requirements of and to implement the OECD Convention."); Anti-Bribery Convention at art. 4.1, *supra* note 19 ("Each Party shall take such measures as may be necessary to establish its jurisdiction over the bribery of a foreign public official when the offence is committed in whole or in part in its territory.").

⁵⁶ 15 U.S.C. § 78dd-3(a); *see, e.g.,* Criminal Information, United States v. Alcatel-Lucent France, S.A., *et al.,* No. 10-cr-20906 (S.D. Fla. Dec. 27, 2010), ECF No. 1 [hereinafter *United States v. Alcatel-Lucent France*] (subsidiary of French publicly traded company convicted of conspiracy to violate FCPA), *available at* http://www.justice.gov/criminal/fraud/fcpa/cases/alcatel-lucent-sa-etal/12-27-10alcatel-et-al-info.pdf; Criminal Information, United States v. DaimlerChrysler Automotive Russia SAO, No. 10-cr-64 (D.D.C. Mar. 22, 2010), ECF No. 1 (subsidiary of German publicly traded company convicted of violating FCPA), *available at* http://www.justice.gov/criminal/fraud/fcpa/cases/daimler/03-22-10daimlerrussia-info.pdf; Criminal Information, United States v. Siemens S.A. (Argentina), No. 08-cr-368 (D.D.C. Dec. 12, 2008), ECF No. 1 (subsidiary of German publicly traded company convicted of violating FCPA), *available at* http://www.justice.gov/criminal/fraud/fcpa/cases/siemens/12-12-08siemensargen-info.pdf.

⁵⁷ *See* 15 U.S.C. §§ 78dd-2(h)(5) (defining "interstate commerce"), 78dd-3(f)(5) (same); *see also* 15 U.S.C. §78c(a)(17).

⁵⁸ 15 U.S.C. §§ 78dd-2(h)(5), 78dd-3(f)(5).

⁵⁹ *See* 15 U.S.C. § 78dd-3.

⁶⁰ Criminal Information, United States v. JGC Corp., No. 11-cr-260 (S.D. Tex. Apr. 6, 2011), ECF No. 1 [hereinafter *United States v. JGC Corp.*], *available at* http://www.justice.gov/criminal/fraud/fcpa/cases/jgc-corp/04-6-11jgc-corp-info.pdf; Criminal Information, United States v. Snamprogetti Netherlands B.V., No. 10-cr-460 (S.D. Tex. Jul. 7, 2010), ECF No. 1 [hereinafter *United States v. Snamprogetti*], *available at* http://www.justice.gov/criminal/fraud/fcpa/cases/snamprogetti/07-07-10snamprogetti-info.pdf.

⁶¹ *See* 15 U.S.C. §§ 78dd-1(g) ("irrespective of whether such issuer or such officer, director, employee, agent, or stockholder makes use of the mails or any means or instrumentality of interstate commerce in furtherance of such offer, gift, payment, promise, or authorization"), 78dd-2(i) (1) ("irrespective of whether such United States person makes use of the mails or any means or instrumentality of interstate commerce in furtherance of such offer, gift, payment, promise, or authorization").

⁶² S. REP. NO. 105-277 at 2 ("[T]he OECD Convention calls on parties to assert nationality jurisdiction when consistent with national legal and constitutional principles. Accordingly, the Act amends the FCPA to provide for jurisdiction over the acts of U.S. businesses and nationals in furtherance of unlawful payments that take place wholly outside the United States. This exercise of jurisdiction over U.S. businesses and nationals for unlawful conduct abroad is consistent with U.S. legal and constitutional principles and is essential to protect U.S. interests abroad.").

⁶³ *Id.* at 2-3.

⁶⁴ 15 U.S.C. §§ 78dd-1(a), 78dd-2(a), 78dd-3(a).

⁶⁵ *See* H.R. REP. NO. 95-831, at 12 (referring to "business purpose" test).

⁶⁶ *See, e.g.,* Complaint, *SEC v. Siemens AG, supra* note 48; Criminal Information, *United States v. Siemens AG, supra* note 48.

⁶⁷ In amending the FCPA in 1988, Congress made clear that the business purpose element, and specifically the "retaining business" prong, was meant to be interpreted broadly:

> The Conferees wish to make clear that the reference to corrupt payments for "retaining business" in present law is not limited to the renewal of contracts or other business, but also includes a prohibition against corrupt payments related to the execution or performance of contracts or the carrying out of existing business, such as a payment to a foreign

official for the purpose of obtaining more favorable tax treatment. The term should not, however, be construed so broadly as to include lobbying or other normal representations to government officials.

H.R. REP. NO. 100-576, at 1951-52 (internal citations omitted).

⁶⁸ *See, e.g.,* Complaint, SEC v. Panalpina, Inc., No. 10-cv-4334 (S.D. Tex. Nov. 4, 2010), ECF No. 1 [hereinafter *SEC v. Panalpina, Inc.*], *available at* http://www.sec.gov/litigation/complaints/2010/comp21727.pdf; Criminal Information, United States v. Panalpina, Inc., No. 10-cr-765 (S.D. Tex. Nov. 4, 2010), ECF No. 1 [hereinafter *United States v. Panalpina, Inc.*], *available at* http://www.justice.gov/criminal/fraud/fcpa/cases/panalpina-inc/11-04-10panalpina-info.pdf; Criminal Information, United States v. Panalpina World Transport (Holding) Ltd., No. 10-cr-769 (S.D. Tex. Nov. 4, 2010), ECF No. 1, *available at* http://www.justice.gov/criminal/fraud/fcpa/cases/panalpina-world/11-04-10panalpina-world-info.pdf; *see also* Press Release, U.S. Sec. and Exchange Comm., SEC Charges Seven Oil Services and Freight Forwarding Companies for Widespread Bribery of Customs Officials (Nov. 4, 2010) ("The SEC alleges that the companies bribed customs officials in more than 10 countries in exchange for such perks as avoiding applicable customs duties on imported goods, expediting the importation of goods and equipment, extending drilling contracts, and lowering tax assessments."), *available at* http://www.sec.gov/news/press/2010/2010-214.htm; Press Release, U.S. Dept. of Justice, Oil Services Companies and a Freight Forwarding Company Agree to Resolve Foreign Bribery Investigations and to Pay More Than $156 Million in Criminal Penalties (Nov. 4, 2010) (logistics provider and its subsidiary engaged in scheme to pay thousands of bribes totaling at least $27 million to numerous foreign officials on behalf of customers in oil and gas industry "to circumvent local rules and regulations relating to the import of goods and materials into numerous foreign jurisdictions"), *available at* http://www.justice.gov/opa/pr/2010/November/10-crm-1251.html.

⁶⁹ United States v. Kay, 359 F.3d 738, 755-56 (5th Cir. 2004).

⁷⁰ *Id.* at 749. Indeed, the *Kay* court found that Congress' explicit exclusion of facilitation payments from the scope of the FCPA was evidence that "Congress intended for the FCPA to prohibit *all other* illicit payments that are intended to influence non-trivial official foreign action in an effort to aid in obtaining or retaining business for some person." *Id.* at 749-50 (emphasis added).

⁷¹ *Id.* at 750.

⁷² *Id.* at 749-55.

⁷³ *Id.* at 756 ("It still must be shown that the bribery was intended to produce an effect—here, through tax savings—that would 'assist in obtaining or retaining business.'").

⁷⁴ The FCPA does not explicitly define "corruptly," but in drafting the statute Congress adopted the meaning ascribed to the same term in the domestic bribery statute, 18 U.S.C. § 201(b). *See* H.R. REP. NO. 95-640, at 7.

⁷⁵ The House Report states in full:

> The word "corruptly" is used in order to make clear that the offer, payment, promise, or gift, must be intended to induce the recipient to misuse his official position; for example, wrongfully to direct business to the payor or his client, to obtain preferential legislation or regulations, or to induce a foreign official to fail to perform an official function. The word "corruptly" connotes an evil motive or purpose such as that required under 18 U.S.C. 201(b) which prohibits domestic bribery. As in 18 U.S.C. 201(b), the word "corruptly" indicates an intent or desire wrongfully to influence the recipient. It does not require that the act [be] fully consummated or succeed in producing the desired outcome.

Id. The Senate Report provides a nearly identical explanation of the meaning of the term:

> The word "corruptly" is used in order to make clear that the offer, payment, promise, or gift, must be intended to induce the recipient to misuse his official position in order to wrongfully direct business to the payor or his client, or to obtain

APPENDIX
Endnotes

preferential legislation or a favorable regulation. The word "corruptly" connotes an evil motive or purpose, an intent to wrongfully influence the recipient.
S. REP. No. 95-114, at 10.
[76] *See* 15 U.S.C. §§ 78dd-1(a), 78dd-2(a), 78dd-3(a).
[77] *See, e.g.,* Complaint, SEC v. Monsanto Co., No. 05-cv-14 (D.D.C. Jan. 6, 2005) (among other things, the company paid a $50,000 bribe to influence an Indonesian official to repeal an unfavorable law, which was not repealed despite the bribe), *available at* http://www.sec.gov/litigation/complaints/comp19023.pdf; Criminal Information, United States v. Monsanto Co., No. 05-cr-8 (D.D.C. Jan. 6, 2005), *available at* http://www.justice.gov/criminal/fraud/fcpa/cases/monsanto-co/01-06-05monsanto-info.pdf.
[78] Jury instructions in FCPA cases have defined "corruptly" consistent with the definition found in the legislative history. *See, e.g.,* Jury Instructions at 22-23, *United States v. Esquenazi, supra* note 44; Jury Instructions at 10, *United States v. Green, supra* note 44; Jury Instructions at 35, *United States v. Jefferson, supra* note 44; Jury Instructions at 25, *United States v. Bourke, supra* note 44; Jury Instructions at 17, *United States v. Kay, supra* note 44; Jury Instructions at 5, *United States v. Mead, supra* note 44.
[79] *See* Complaint, SEC v. Innospec, Inc., No. 10-cv-448 (D.D.C. Mar. 18, 2010), ECF No. 1 [hereinafter *SEC v. Innospec*], *available at* http://www.sec.gov/litigation/complaints/2010/comp21454.pdf; Criminal Information at 8, United States v. Innospec Inc., No. 10-cr-61 (D.D.C. Mar. 17, 2010), ECF No. 1 [hereinafter *United States v. Innospec*], *available at* http://www.justice.gov/criminal/fraud/fcpa/cases/innospec-inc/03-17-10innospec-info.pdf.
[80] *See* Complaint, *SEC v. Innospec, supra* note 79; Criminal Information, *United States v. Innospec, supra* note 79.
[81] *See* 15 U.S.C. §§ 78dd-1(c)(2)(A), 78dd-2(g)(2)(A), and 78dd-3(3)(2)(A).
[82] *Compare* 15 U.S.C. § 78ff(c)(1)(A) (corporate criminal liability under issuer provision) *with* § 78ff(c)(2)(A) (individual criminal liability under issuer provision); *compare* 15 U.S.C. § 78dd-2(g)(1)(A) (corporate criminal liability under domestic concern provision) *with* § 78dd-2(g)(2)(A) (individual criminal liability under issuer provision); *compare* 15 U.S.C. § 78dd-3(e)(1)(A) (corporate criminal liability for territorial provision) *with* § 78dd-3(e)(2)(A) (individual criminal liability for territorial provision). However, companies still must act corruptly. *See* Section 30A(a), 15 U.S.C. § 78dd-1(a); 15 U.S.C. §§ 78dd-2(a), 78dd-3(a).
[83] United States v. Kay, 513 F.3d 432, 448 (5th Cir. 2007); *see also* Jury Instructions at 38, *United States v. Esquenazi, supra* note 44; Jury Instructions at 10, *United States v. Green, supra* note 44; Jury Instructions at 35, *United States v. Jefferson, supra* note 44; Jury Instructions at 25, *United States v. Bourke, supra* note 44; Jury Instructions at 5, *United States v. Mead, supra* note 44.
[84] Bryan v. United States, 524 U.S. 184, 191-92 (1998) (construing "willfully" in the context of 18 U.S.C. § 924(a)(1)(A)) (quoting Ratzlaf v. United States, 510 U.S. 135, 137 (1994)); *see also* Kay, 513 F.3d at 446-51 (discussing *Bryan* and term "willfully" under the FCPA).
[85] *Kay,* 513 F.3d at 447-48; Stichting Ter Behartiging Van de Belangen Van Oudaandeelhouders In Het Kapitaal Van Saybolt Int'l B.V. v. Schreiber, 327 F.3d 173, 181 (2d Cir. 2003).
[86] The phrase "anything of value" is not defined in the FCPA, but the identical phrase under the domestic bribery statute has been broadly construed to include both *tangible* and *intangible* benefits. *See, e.g.,* United States v. Moore, 525 F.3d 1033, 1048 (11th Cir. 2008) (rejecting defendant's objection to instruction defining sex as a "thing of value," which "unambiguously covers intangible considerations"); United States v. Gorman, 807 F.2d 1299, 1304-05 (6th Cir. 1986) (holding that loans and promises of future employment are "things of value"); United States v. Williams, 705 F.2d 603, 622-23 (2d Cir. 1983) (approving jury instruction that stock could be a "thing of value" if defendant believed it had value, even though the shares had no commercial value, and noting that "[t]he phrase 'anything of value' in bribery and related statutes has consistently been given a broad meaning").
[87] Section 30A(a), 15 U.S.C. § 78dd-1(a); 15 U.S.C. §§ 78dd-2(a), 78dd-3(a) (emphasis added).
[88] Like the FCPA, the domestic bribery statute, 18 U.S.C. § 201, prohibits

giving, offering, or promising "anything of value." Numerous domestic bribery cases under Section 201 have involved "small" dollar bribes. *See, e.g.,* United States v. Franco, 632 F.3d 880, 882-84 (5th Cir. 2011) (affirming bribery convictions of inmate for paying correctional officer $325 to obtain cell phone, food, and marijuana, and noting that 18 U.S.C. § 201 does not contain minimum monetary threshold); United States v. Williams, 216 F.3d 1099, 1103 (D.C. Cir. 2000) (affirming bribery conviction for $70 bribe to vehicle inspector); United States v. Traitz, 871 F.2d 368, 396 (3rd Cir. 1989) (affirming bribery conviction for $100 bribe paid to official of Occupational Health and Safety Administration); United States v. Hsieh Hui Mei Chen, 754 F.2d 817, 822 (9th Cir. 1985) (affirming bribery convictions including $100 bribe to immigration official); United States v. Bishton, 463 F.2d 887, 889 (D.C. Cir. 1972) (affirming bribery conviction for $100 bribe to division chief of District of Columbia Sewer Operations Division).
[89] Complaint, *SEC v. Daimler AG, supra* note 48; Criminal Information, *United States v. Daimler AG, supra* note 48.
[90] Complaint, SEC v. Halliburton Company and KBR, Inc., No. 09-cv-399 (S.D. Tex. Feb. 11, 2009), ECF No 1 [hereinafter *SEC v. Halliburton and KBR*], *available at* http://www.sec.gov/litigation/complaints/2009/comp20897.pdf; Criminal Information, United States v. Kellogg Brown & Root LLC, No. 09-cr-71, ECF No. 1 (S.D. Tex. Feb. 6, 2009) [hereinafter *United States v. KBR*], *available at* http://www.justice.gov/criminal/fraud/fcpa/cases/kelloggb/02-06-09kbr-info.pdf.
[91] Complaint, *SEC v. Halliburton and KBR, supra* note 90; Criminal Information, *United States v. KBR, supra* note 90.
[92] *See, e.g.,* Complaint, SEC v. RAE Sys. Inc., No. 10-cv-2093 (D.D.C. Dec. 10, 2010), ECF No. 1 [hereinafter *SEC v. RAE Sys., Inc.*] (fur coat, among other extravagant gifts), *available at* http://www.sec.gov/litigation/complaints/2010/comp21770.pdf; Non-Pros. Agreement, In re RAE Sys. Inc. (Dec. 10, 2010) [hereinafter *In re RAE Sys. Inc.*] (same), *available at* http://www.justice.gov/criminal/fraud/fcpa/cases/rae-systems/12-10-10rae-systems.pdf; Complaint, *SEC v. Daimler AG, supra* note 48 (armored Mercedes Benz worth €300,000); Criminal Information, *United States v. Daimler AG, supra* note 48 (same).
[93] *See* Complaint, SEC v. ABB Ltd, No. 04-cv-1141 (D.D.C. July 6, 2004), ECF No. 1, *available at* http://www.sec.gov/litigation/complaints/comp18775.pdf; Criminal Information, United States v. ABB Vetco Gray Inc., *et al.,* No. 04-cr-279 (S.D. Tex. June 22, 2004), ECF No 1 [hereinafter *United States v. ABB Vetco Gray*], *available at* http://www.justice.gov/criminal/fraud/fcpa/cases/abb/06-22-04abbvetco-info.pdf.
[94] Complaint, SEC v. UTStarcom, Inc., No. 09-cv-6094 (N.D. Cal. Dec. 31, 2009), ECF No. 1 [hereinafter *SEC v. UTStarcom*], *available at* http://www.sec.gov/litigation/complaints/2009/comp21357.pdf; Non-Pros. Agreement, In re UTStarcom Inc. (Dec. 31, 2009) [hereinafter *In re UTStarcom*], *available at* http://www.justice.gov/criminal/fraud/fcpa/cases/utstarcom-inc/12-31-09utstarcom-agree.pdf.
[95] Complaint, *SEC v. UTStarcom, supra* note 94; Non-Pros. Agreement, *In re UTStarcom, supra* note 94.
[96] Complaint, *SEC v. UTStarcom, supra* note 94; Non-Pros. Agreement, *In re UTStarcom, supra* note 94.
[97] Complaint, SEC v. Lucent Technologies Inc., No. 07-cv-2301 (D.D.C. Dec. 21, 2007), ECF No.1 [hereinafter *SEC v. Lucent*], *available at* http://www.sec.gov/litigation/complaints/2007/comp20414.pdf; Non-Pros. Agreement, In re Lucent Technologies (Nov. 14, 2007) [hereinafter *In re Lucent*], *available at* http://www.justice.gov/criminal/fraud/fcpa/cases/lucent-tech/11-14-07lucent-agree.pdf.
[98] Complaint, *SEC v. Lucent, supra* note 97; Non-Pros. Agreement, *In re Lucent, supra* note 97.
[99] The company consented to the entry of a final judgment permanently

enjoining it from future violations of the books and records and internal controls provisions and paid a civil penalty of $1,500,000. Complaint, *SEC v. Lucent*, *supra* note 97. Additionally, the company entered into a non-prosecution agreement with DOJ and paid a $1,000,000 monetary penalty. Non-Pros. Agreement, *In re Lucent*, *supra* note 97.
[100] United States v. Liebo, 923 F.2d 1308, 1311 (8th Cir. 1991).
[101] Judgment, United States v. Liebo, No. 89-cr-76 (D. Minn. Jan. 31, 1992), *available at* http://www.justice.gov/criminal/fraud/fcpa/cases/liebor/1992-01-31-liebor-judgment.pdf.
[102] Complaint, SEC v. Schering-Plough Corp., No. 04-cv-945 (D.D.C. June 9, 2004), ECF No. 1, *available at* http://www.sec.gov/litigation/complaints/comp18740.pdf; Admin. Proceeding Order, In the Matter of Schering-Plough Corp., Exchange Act Release No. 49838 (June 9, 2004) (finding that company violated FCPA accounting provisions and imposing $500,000 civil monetary penalty), *available at* http://www.sec.gov/litigation/admin/34-49838.htm.
[103] FCPA opinion procedure releases can be found at http://www.justice.gov/criminal/fraud/fcpa/. In the case of the company seeking to contribute the $1.42 million grant to a local MFI, DOJ noted that it had undertaken each of these due diligence steps and controls, in addition to others, that would minimize the likelihood that anything of value would be given to any officials of the Eurasian country. U.S. DEPT. OF JUSTICE, FCPA OP. RELEASE 10-02 (July 16, 2010), *available at* http://www.justice.gov/criminal/fraud/fcpa/opinion/2010/1002.pdf.
[104] U.S. DEPT. OF JUSTICE, FCPA OP. RELEASE 95-01 (Jan. 11, 1995), *available at* http://www.justice.gov/criminal/fraud/fcpa/opinion/1995/9501.pdf.
[105] *Id.*
[106] *Id.*
[107] U.S. DEPT. OF JUSTICE, FCPA OP. RELEASE 97-02 (Nov. 5, 1997), *available at* http://www.justice.gov/criminal/fraud/fcpa/opinion/1997/9702.pdf; U.S. DEPT. OF JUSTICE, FCPA OP. RELEASE 06-01 (Oct. 16, 2006), *available at* http://www.justice.gov/criminal/fraud/fcpa/opinion/2006/0601.pdf.
[108] U.S. DEPT. OF JUSTICE, FCPA OP. RELEASE 06-01 (Oct. 16, 2006).
[109] *Id.*
[110] *Id.*
[111] *See* Section 30A(a)(1)-(3) of the Exchange Act, 15 U.S.C. § 78dd-1(a)(1)-(3); 15 U.S.C. §§ 78dd-2(a)(1)-(3), 78dd-3(a)(1)-(3).
[112] Section 30A(f)(1)(A) of the Exchange Act, 15 U.S.C. § 78dd-1(f)(1)(A); 15 U.S.C. §§ 78dd-2(h)(2)(A), 78dd-3(f)(2)(A).
[113] Under the FCPA, any person "acting in an official capacity for or on behalf of" a foreign government, a department, agency, or instrumentality thereof, or a public international organization, is a foreign official. Section 30A(f)(1)(A), 15 U.S.C. § 78dd-1(f)(1)(A); 15 U.S.C. §§ 78dd-2(h)(2)(A), 78dd-2(f)(2)(A). *See also* U.S. DEPT. OF JUSTICE, FCPA OP. RELEASE No. 10-03, at 2 (Sept. 1, 2010), *available at* http://www.justice.gov/criminal/fraud/fcpa/opinion/2010/1003.pdf (listing safeguards to ensure that consultant was not acting on behalf of foreign government).
[114] *But see* Sections 30A(b) and f(3)(A) of the Exchange Act, 15 U.S.C. § 78dd-1(b) & (f)(3); 15 U.S.C. §§ 78dd-2(b) & (h)(4), 78dd-3(b) & (f)(4) (facilitating payments exception).
[115] Even though payments to a foreign government may not violate the anti-bribery provisions of the FCPA, such payments may violate other U.S. laws, including wire fraud, money laundering, and the FCPA's accounting provisions. This was the case in a series of matters brought by DOJ and SEC involving kickbacks to the Iraqi government through the United Nations Oil-for-Food Programme. *See, e.g.*, Complaint, *SEC v. Innospec*, *supra* note 79; Criminal Information, *United States v. Innospec*, *supra* note 79; Complaint, SEC v. Novo Nordisk A/S, No. 09-cv-862 (D.D.C. May 11, 2009), ECF No. 1, *available at* http://www.sec.gov/litigation/complaints/2009/comp21033.pdf; Criminal Information, United States v. Novo Nordisk A/S, No. 09-cr-126 (D.D.C. May 11, 2009), ECF No. 1, *available at* http://www.justice.gov/criminal/fraud/fcpa/cases/nordiskn/05-11-09novo-info.pdf; Complaint, SEC v. Ingersoll-Rand Company Ltd., No. 07-cv-1955 (D.D.C. Oct. 31, 2007), ECF No. 1, *available at* http://www.sec.gov/litigation/complaints/2007/comp20353.pdf; Criminal Information, United States v. Ingersoll-Rand Italiana SpA, No. 07-cr-294 (D.D.C. Oct. 31, 2007), ECF No. 1, *available at* http://www.justice.gov/criminal/fraud/fcpa/cases/ingerand-italiana/10-31-07ingersollrand-info.pdf; Complaint,

SEC v. York Int'l Corp., No. 07-cv-1750 (D.D.C. Oct. 1, 2007), ECF No. 1 [hereinafter *SEC v. York Int'l Corp.*], *available at* http://www.sec.gov/litigation/complaints/2007/comp20319.pdf; Criminal Information, United States v. York Int'l Corp., No. 07-cr-253 (D.D.C. Oct. 1, 2007), ECF No. 1 [hereinafter *United States v. York Int'l Corp.*], *available at* http://www.justice.gov/criminal/fraud/fcpa/cases/york/10-01-07york-info.pdf; Complaint, SEC v. Textron Inc., No. 07-cv-1505 (D.D.C. Aug. 23, 2007), ECF No. 1 [hereinafter *SEC v. Textron*], *available at* http://www.sec.gov/litigation/complaints/2007/comp20251.pdf; Non-Pros. Agreement, In re Textron Inc. (Aug. 23, 2007), *available at* http://www.justice.gov/criminal/fraud/fcpa/cases/textron-inc/08-21-07textron-agree.pdf. DOJ has issued opinion procedure releases concerning payments (that were, in essence, donations) to government agencies or departments. *See* U.S. DEPT. OF JUSTICE, FCPA OP. RELEASE 09-01 (Aug. 3, 2009) (involving donation of 100 medical devices to foreign government), *available at* http://www.justice.gov/criminal/fraud/fcpa/opinion/2009/0901.pdf; U.S. DEPT. OF JUSTICE, FCPA OP. RELEASE 06-01 (Oct. 16, 2006) (involving contribution of $25,000 to regional customs department to pay incentive rewards to improve local enforcement of anti-counterfeiting laws), *available at* http://www.justice.gov/criminal/fraud/fcpa/opinion/2006/0601.pdf.
[116] The United States has some state-owned entities, like the Tennessee Valley Authority, that are instrumentalities of the government. McCarthy v. Middle Tenn. Elec. Membership Corp., 466 F.3d 399, 411 n.18 (6th Cir. 2006) ("[T]here is no question that TVA is an agency and instrumentality of the United States.") (internal quotes omitted).
[117] During the period surrounding the FCPA's adoption, state-owned entities held virtual monopolies and operated under state-controlled price-setting in many national industries around the world. *See generally* WORLD BANK, BUREAUCRATS IN BUSINESS: THE ECONOMICS AND POLITICS OF GOVERNMENT OWNERSHIP, WORLD BANK POLICY RESEARCH Report at 78 (1995); SUNITA KIKERI AND AISHETU KOLO, STATE ENTERPRISES, THE WORLD BANK GROUP (Feb. 2006), *available at* http://rru.worldbank.org/documents/publicpolicyjournal/304Kikeri_Kolo.pdf.
[118] *Id.* at 1 ("[A]fter more than two decades of privatization, government ownership and control remains widespread in many regions—and in many parts of the world still dominates certain sectors.").
[119] To date, consistent with the approach taken by DOJ and SEC, all district courts who have considered this issue have concluded that this is an issue of fact for a jury to decide. *See* Order, United States v. Carson, 2011 WL 5101701, No. 09-cr-77 (C.D. Cal. May 18, 2011), ECF No. 373 [hereinafter *United States v. Carson*]; United States v. Aguilar, 783 F. Supp. 2d 1108 (C.D. Cal. 2011); Order, *United States v. Esquenazi*, *supra* note 44, ECF No. 309; *see also* Order, United States v. O'Shea, No. 09-cr-629 (S.D. Tex. Jan. 3, 2012), ECF No. 142; Order, United States v. Nguyen, No. 08-cr-522 (E.D. Pa. Dec. 30, 2009), ECF No. 144. These district court decisions are consistent with the acceptance by district courts around the country of over 35 guilty pleas by individuals who admitted to violating the FCPA by bribing officials of state-owned or state-controlled entities. *See* Government's Opposition to Defendants' Amended Motion to Dismiss Counts One Through Ten of the Indictment at 18, *United States v. Carson*, *supra* note 119, ECF No. 332; Exhibit I, *United States v. Carson*, *supra* note 119, ECF No. 335 (list of examples of enforcement actions based on foreign officials of state-owned entities).
[120] Jury Instructions, *United States v. Esquenazi*, *supra* note 44, ECF No. 520; Order at 5 and Jury Instructions, *United States v. Carson*, *supra* note 119, ECF No. 373 and ECF No. 549; *Aguilar*, 783 F. Supp. 2d at 1115.
[121] Criminal Information, United States v. C.E. Millier Corp., *et al.*, No. 82-cr-788 (C.D. Cal. Sept. 17, 1982), *available at* http://www.justice.gov/criminal/fraud/fcpa/cases/ce-miller/1982-09-17-ce-miller-information.pdf.
[122] *See* Complaint, SEC v. Sam P. Wallace Co., Inc., *et al.*, No. 81-cv-1915 (D.D.C. Aug. 31, 1982); Criminal Information, United States v. Sam P. Wallace Co., Inc., No. 83-cr-34 (D.P.R. Feb. 23, 1983), *available at* http://www.justice.gov/criminal/fraud/fcpa/cases/sam-wallace-company/1983-02-23-sam-wallace-company-information.pdf; *see also* Criminal Information, United States v. Goodyear Int'l Corp., No. 89-cr-156 (D.D.C. May 11, 1989) (Iraqi Trading Company identified as "instrumentality of the Government of the Republic of Iraq"), *available at* http://www.justice.gov/criminal/fraud/fcpa/cases/goodyear/1989-

05-11-goodyear-information.pdf.

123 *See* Complaint, *SEC v. ABB*, *supra* note 48; Criminal Information at 3, United States v. ABB Inc., No. 10-cr-664 (S.D. Tex. Sept. 29, 2010), ECF No. 1 [hereinafter *United States v. ABB*], *available at* http://www.justice.gov/criminal/fraud/fpca/cases/abb/09-20-10abbinc-info.pdf; Constitución Política de los Estados Unidos Mexicanos [C.P.], as amended, art. 27, Diario Oficial de la Federación [DO], 5 de Febrero de 1917 (Mex.); Ley Del Servicio Publico de Energia Electrica, as amended, art. 1-3, 10, Diario Oficial de la Federación [DO], 22 de Diciembre de 1975 (Mex.).

124 *See* Indictment at 2, *United States v. Esquenazi*, *supra* note 44, ECF No. 3; Affidavit of Mr. Louis Gary Lissade at 1-9, *id.*, ECF No. 417-2.

125 Criminal Information at 30-31, *United States v. Alcatel-Lucent France*, *supra* note 56, ECF No. 10.

126 *Id.*

127 *See* International Anti-Bribery and Fair Competition Act of 1998, Pub. L. 105-366 § 2, 112 Stat. 3302, 3303, 3305, 3308 (1998).

128 Section 30A(F)(1)(B) of the Exchange Act, 15 U.S.C. § 78dd-1(f)(1)(B); 15 U.S.C. §§ 78dd-2(h)(2)(B), 78dd-3(f)(2)(B).

129 Third parties and intermediaries themselves are also liable for FCPA violations. Section 30A(a) of the Exchange Act, 15 U.S.C. § 78dd-1(a); 15 U.S.C. §§ 78dd-2(a), and 78dd-3(a).

130 Section 30A(a)(3) of the Exchange Act, 15 U.S.C. § 78dd-1(a)(3); 15 U.S.C. §§ 78dd-2(a)(3), 78dd-3(a)(3).

131 *See, e.g.*, Complaint, SEC v. Johnson & Johnson, No. 11-cv-686 (D.D.C. Apr. 8, 2011) [hereinafter *SEC v. Johnson & Johnson*] (bribes paid through Greek and Romanian agents)), *available at* http://www.sec.gov/litigation/complaints/2011/comp21922.pdf; Criminal Information, United States v. DePuy, Inc., No. 11-cr-99 (D.D.C. Apr. 8, 2011), ECF No. 1 [hereinafter *United States v. DePuy*] (bribes paid through Greek agents), *available at* http://www.justice.gov/criminal/fraud/fpca/cases/depuy-inc/04-08-11depuy-info.pdf; Complaint, *SEC v. ABB*, *supra* note 48 (bribes paid through Mexican agents); Criminal Information, *United States v. ABB*, *supra* note 123 (same); Criminal Information, United States v. Int'l Harvester Co., No. 82-cr-244 (S.D. Tex. Nov. 17, 1982) (bribes paid through Mexican agent), *available at* http://www.justice.gov/criminal/fraud/fpca/cases/international-harvester/1982-11-17-international-harvester-information.pdf.

132 *See* Criminal Information, United States v. Marubeni Corp., No. 12-cr-22 (S.D. Tex. Jan. 17, 2012), ECF No. 1 [hereinafter *United States v. Marubeni*], *available at* http://www.justice.gov/criminal/fraud/fpca/cases/marubeni/2012-01-17-marubeni-information.pdf; Criminal Information, *United States v. JGC Corp.*, *supra* note 60, ECF No. 1; Criminal Information, *United States v. Snamprogetti*, *supra* note 60, ECF No. 1; Complaint, SEC v. ENI, S.p.A. and Snamprogetti Netherlands B.V., No. 10-cv-2414 (S.D. Tex. July 7, 2010), ECF No. 1, *available at* http://www.sec.gov/litigation/complaints/2010/comp-pr2010-119.pdf; Criminal Information, United States v. Technip S.A., No. 10-cr-439 (S.D. Tex. June 28, 2010), ECF No. 1 [hereinafter *United States v. Technip*], *available at* http://www.justice.gov/criminal/fraud/fpca/cases/technip-sa/06-28-10-technip-%20information.pdf; Complaint, SEC v. Technip, No. 10-cv-2289 (S.D. Tex. June 28, 2010), ECF No. 1 [hereinafter *SEC v. Technip*], *available at* http://www.sec.gov/litigation/complaints/2010/comp-pr2010-110.pdf; Indictment, *United States v. Tesler*, *supra* note 50; Complaint, *SEC v. Halliburton and KBR*, *supra* note 90; Criminal Information, *United States v. KBR*, *supra* note 90; Criminal Information, *United States v. Stanley*, No. 08-cr-597 (S.D. Tex. Sept. 3, 2008), ECF No. 1, *available at* http://justice.gov/criminal/fraud/fpca/cases/stanleya/08-29-08stanley-info.pdf.

133 *See* Criminal Information, United States v. AGA Medical Corp., No. 08-cr-172, ECF No. 1 (D. Minn. June 3, 2008), *available at* http://www.justice.gov/criminal/fraud/fpca/cases/agamedcorp/06-03-08aga-info.pdf.

134 Complaint, *SEC v. Innospec*, *supra* note 79; Criminal Information, *United States v. Innospec*, *supra* note 79; Superseding Criminal Information, *United States v. Naaman*, *supra* note 50, ECF No. 15, *available at* http://www.justice.gov/criminal/fraud/fpca/cases/naamano/06-24-10naaman-supsersed-info.pdf; Complaint, *SEC v. Turner*, *supra* note 50.

135 *See* sources cited *supra* note 68.

136 *See* sources cited *supra* note 68.

137 Section 30A(a)(3) of the Exchange Act, 15 U.S.C. § 78dd-1(a)(3); 15

U.S.C. §§ 78dd-2(a)(3), 78dd-3(a)(3).

138 *See* Section 30A(f)(2)(A) of the Exchange Act, 15 U.S.C. § 78dd-1(f)(2)(A); 15 U.S.C. §§ 78dd-2(h)(3)(A), 78dd-3(f)(3)(A).

139 *See* Section 30A(f)(2)(B) of the Exchange Act, 15 U.S.C. § 78dd-1(f)(2)(B); 15 U.S.C. §§ 78dd-2(h)(3)(B), 78dd-3(f)(3)(B). The "knowing" standard was intended to cover "both prohibited actions that are taken with 'actual knowledge' of intended results as well as other actions that, while falling short of what the law terms 'positive knowledge,' nevertheless evidence a conscious disregard or deliberate ignorance of known circumstances that should reasonably alert one to the high probability of violations of the Act." H.R. REP. NO. 100-576, at 920; *see also* Omnibus Trade and Competitiveness Act of 1988, Pub. L. No. 100-418, § 5003, 102 Stat. 1107, 1423-24 (1988).

140 H.R. REP. NO. 100-576, at 920 (1988).

141 Section 30A(c)(1) of the Exchange Act, 15 U.S.C. § 78dd-1(c)(1); 15 U.S.C. §§ 78dd-2(c)(1), 78dd-3(c)(1).

142 H.R. REP. NO. 100-576, at 922. The conferees also noted that "[i]n interpreting what is 'lawful under the written laws and regulations' . . . the normal rules of legal construction would apply." *Id.*

143 *See* United States v. Kozeny, 582 F. Supp. 2d 535, 537-40 (S.D.N.Y. 2008). Likewise, the court found that a provision under Azeri law that relieved bribe payors of criminal liability if they were extorted did not make the bribe payments legal. Azeri extortion law precludes the prosecution of the payor of the bribes for the illegal payments, but it does not make the payments legal. *Id.* at 540-41.

144 Section 30A(c)(2)(A), (B) of the Exchange Act, 15 U.S.C. § 78dd-1(c)(2); 15 U.S.C. §§ 78dd-2(c)(2), 78dd-3(c)(2).

145 For example, the Eighth Circuit Court of Appeals found that providing airline tickets to a government official in order to corruptly influence that official may form the basis for a violation of the FCPA's anti-bribery provisions. *See Liebo*, 923 F. 2d at 1311-12.

146 *See generally* U.S. DEPT. OF JUSTICE, FCPA OP. RELEASE 11-01 (June 30, 2011) (travel, lodging, and meal expenses of two foreign officials for two-day trip to United States to learn about services of U.S. adoption service provider), *available at* http://www.justice.gov/criminal/fraud/fpca/opinion/2011/11-01.pdf; U.S. DEPT. OF JUSTICE, FCPA OP. RELEASE 08-03 (July 11, 2008) (stipends to reimburse minimal travel expenses of local, government-affiliated journalists attending press conference in foreign country), *available at* http://www.justice.gov/criminal/fraud/fpca/opinion/2008/0803.pdf; U.S. DEPT. OF JUSTICE, FCPA OP. RELEASE 07-02 (Sept. 11, 2007) (domestic travel, lodging, and meal expenses of six foreign officials for six-week educational program), *available at* http://www.justice.gov/criminal/fraud/fpca/opinion/2007/0702.pdf; U.S. DEPT. OF JUSTICE, FCPA OP. RELEASE 07-01 (July 24, 2007) (domestic travel, lodging, and meal expenses of six foreign officials for four-day educational and promotional tour of U.S. company's operations sites), *available at* http://www.justice.gov/criminal/fraud/fpca/opinion/2007/0701.pdf; U.S. DEPT. OF JUSTICE, FCPA OP. RELEASE 04-04 (Sept. 3, 2004) (travel, lodging, and modest per diem expenses of five foreign officials to participate in nine-day study tour of mutual insurance companies), *available at* http://www.justice.gov/criminal/fraud/fpca/opinion/2004/0404.pdf; U.S. DEPT. OF JUSTICE, FCPA OP. RELEASE 04-03 (June 14, 2004) (travel, lodging, meal, and insurance expenses for twelve foreign officials and one translator on ten-day trip to three U.S. cities to meet with U.S. public sector officials), *available at* http://www.justice.gov/criminal/fraud/fpca/opinion/2004/0403.pdf; U.S. DEPT. OF JUSTICE, FCPA OP. RELEASE 04-01 (Jan. 6, 2004) (seminar expenses, including receptions, meals, transportation and lodging costs, for one-and-a-half day comparative law seminar on labor and employment law in foreign country), *available at* http://www.justice.gov/criminal/fraud/fpca/

opinion/2004/0401.pdf; U.S. Dept. of Justice, FCPA Op. Release 96-01 (Nov. 25, 1996) (travel, lodging, and meal expenses of regional government representatives to attend training courses in United States), *available at* http://www.justice.gov/criminal/fraud/fcpa/opinion/1996/9601.pdf; U.S. Dept. of Justice, FCPA Op. Release 92-01 (Feb. 1992) (training expenses so that foreign officials could effectively perform duties related to execution and performance of joint-venture agreement, including seminar fees, airfare, lodging, meals, and ground transportation), *available at* http://www.justice.gov/criminal/fraud/fcpa/review/1992/r9201.pdf.

[147] U.S. Dept. of Justice, FCPA Op. Release 11-01 (June 30, 2011); U.S. Dept. of Justice, FCPA Op. Release 07-02 (Sept. 11, 2007); U.S. Dept. of Justice, FCPA Op. Release 07-01 (July 24, 2007); U.S. Dept. of Justice, FCPA Op. Release 04-04 (Sept. 3, 2004); U.S. Dept. of Justice, FCPA Op. Release 04-03 (June 14, 2004); U.S. Dept. of Justice, FCPA Op. Release 04-01 (Jan. 6, 2004).

[148] U.S. Dept. of Justice, FCPA Op. Release 96-01 (Nov. 25, 1996).

[149] U.S. Dept. of Justice, FCPA Op. Release 11-01 (June 30, 2011); U.S. Dept. of Justice, FCPA Op. Release 07-02 (Sept. 11, 2007); U.S. Dept. of Justice, FCPA Op. Release 07-01 (July 24, 2007); U.S. Dept. of Justice, FCPA Op. Release 04-04 (Sept. 3, 2004); U.S. Dept. of Justice, FCPA Op. Release 04-01 (Jan. 6, 2004).

[150] U.S. Dept. of Justice, FCPA Op. Release 04-01 (Jan. 6, 2004).

[151] U.S. Dept. of Justice, FCPA Op. Release 08-03 (July 11, 2008).

[152] U.S. Dept. of Justice, FCPA Op. Release 11-01 (June 30, 2011); U.S. Dept. of Justice, FCPA Op. Release 92-01 (Feb. 1992).

[153] U.S. Dept. of Justice, FCPA Op. Release 08-03 (July 11, 2008).

[154] *Id.*

[155] *Id.*; U.S. Dept. of Justice, FCPA Op. Release 04-03 (June 14, 2004); U.S. Dept. of Justice, FCPA Op. Release 04-01 (Jan. 6, 2004); U.S. Dept. of Justice, FCPA Op. Release 07-01 (July 24, 2007).

[156] U.S. Dept. of Justice, FCPA Op. Release 11-01 (June 30, 2011); U.S. Dept. of Justice, FCPA Op. Release 07-02 (Sept. 11, 2007); U.S. Dept. of Justice, FCPA Op. Release 07-01 (July 24, 2007); U.S. Dept. of Justice, FCPA Op. Release 04-04 (Sept. 3, 2004); U.S. Dept. of Justice, FCPA Op. Release 04-03 (June 14, 2004); U.S. Dept. of Justice, FCPA Op. Release 04-01 (Jan. 6, 2004).

[157] U.S. Dept. of Justice, FCPA Op. Release 07-01 (July 24, 2007); U.S. Dept. of Justice, FCPA Op. Release 08-03 (July 11, 2008).

[158] For example, DOJ has previously approved expenditures on behalf of family members or for entertainment purposes under certain, limited circumstances. *See, e.g.*, U.S. Dept. of Justice, FCPA Rev. P. Release 83-02 (July 26, 1983) (declining to take enforcement action against company seeking to provide promotional tour for foreign official and wife, where both had already planned a trip to the United States at their own expense and company proposed to pay only for all reasonable and necessary actual domestic expenses for the extension of their travel to allow the promotional tour, which would not exceed $5,000), *available at* http://www.justice.gov/criminal/fraud/fcpa/review/1983/r8302.pdf.

[159] Unlike the local law and bona fide expenditures defenses, the facilitating payments exception is not an affirmative defense to the FCPA. Rather, payments of this kind fall outside the scope of the FCPA's bribery prohibition. Prior to 1988, the "facilitating payments" exception was incorporated into the definition of "foreign official," which excluded from the statute's purview officials whose duties were primarily ministerial or clerical. *See* Foreign Corrupt Practices Act of 1977, Pub. L. No. 95-213, § 104(d)(2), 91 Stat. 1494, 1498 (1977) (providing that the term foreign official "does not include any employee of a foreign government or any department, agency, or instrumentality thereof whose duties are essentially ministerial or clerical"). The original exception thus focused on the duties of the recipient, rather than the purpose of the payment. In practice, however, it proved difficult to determine whether a foreign official's duties were "ministerial or clerical." S. Rep. No. 100-85, at 53. Responding to criticism that the statutory language "does not clearly reflect Congressional intent and the boundaries of the prohibited conduct," Congress revised the FCPA to define the exception in terms of the purpose of the payment. H. Rep. No. 100-40, pt. 2, at 77. In doing so, Congress reiterated that while its policy to exclude facilitating payments reflected practical considerations of enforcement, "such payments should not be condoned." *Id.* The enacted language reflects this narrow purpose.

[160] In exempting facilitating payments, Congress sought to distinguish them as "payments which merely move a particular matter toward an eventual act or decision or which do not involve any discretionary action," giving the examples of "a gratuity paid to a customs official to speed the processing of a customs document" or "payments made to secure permits, licenses, or the expeditious performance of similar duties of an essentially ministerial or clerical nature which must of necessity be performed in any event." H.R. Rep. No. 95-640, at 8.

[161] Section 30A(f)(3)(B) of the Exchange Act, 15 U.S.C. § 78dd-1(f)(3)(B); 15 U.S.C. §§ 78dd-2(h)(4)(B), 78dd-3(f)(4)(B).

[162] In a 2004 decision, the Fifth Circuit emphasized this precise point, commenting on the limited nature of the facilitating payments exception:

> A brief review of the types of routine governmental actions enumerated by Congress shows how limited Congress wanted to make the grease exceptions. Routine governmental action, for instance, includes "obtaining permits, licenses, or other official documents to qualify a person to do business in a foreign country," and "scheduling inspections associated with contract performance or inspections related to transit of goods across country." Therefore, routine governmental action does not include the issuance of *every* official document or *every* inspection, but only (1) documentation that qualifies a party to do business and (2) scheduling an inspection—very narrow categories of largely non-discretionary, ministerial activities performed by mid- or low-level foreign functionaries.

United States v. Kay, 359 F.3d 738, 750-51 (5th Cir. 2004) (internal footnote omitted) (emphasis in original).

[163] Non-Pros. Agreement, In re Helmerich & Payne, Inc. (July 29, 2009) [hereinafter *In re Helmerich & Payne*], *available at* http://www.justice.gov/criminal/fraud/fcpa/cases/helmerich-payne/06-29-09helmerich-agree.pdf; Admin. Proceeding Order, In the Matter of Helmerich & Payne, Inc., Exchange Act Release No. 60400 (July 30, 2009) [hereinafter *In the Matter of Helmerich & Payne*], *available at* http://www.sec.gov/litigation/admin/2009/34-60400.pdf.

[164] Criminal Information, Vetco Gray Controls Inc., *et al.*, No. 07-cr-4 No. (S.D. Tex. Jan. 5, 2007), ECF Nos. 1-2, *available at* http://www.justice.gov/criminal/fraud/fcpa/cases/vetco-controls/02-06-07vetcogray.pdf.

[165] Complaint, SEC v. Noble Corp., No. 10-cv-4336 (S.D. Tex. Nov. 4, 2010), ECF No. 1, *available at* http://www.sec.gov/litigation/complaints/2010/comp21728.pdf; Non-Pros. Agreement, In re Noble Corp. (Nov. 4, 2010), *available at* http://www.justice.gov/criminal/fraud/fcpa/cases/noble-corp/11-04-10noble-corp-npa.pdf; *see also* sources cited *supra* note 68.

[166] Working Group on Bribery, *2009 Recommendation of the Council for Further Combating Bribery of Foreign Public Officials in International Business Transactions*, at § VI (recommending countries should periodically review their policies and approach to facilitation payments and should encourage companies to prohibit or discourage facilitation payments "in view of the corrosive effect of small facilitation payments, particularly on sustainable economic development and the rule of law"); Working Group on Bribery, *United States: Phase 3*, at 24 (Oct. 15, 2010), *available at* http://www.oecd.org/dataoecd/10/49/46213841.pdf (commending United States for steps taken in line with 2009 recommendation to encourage companies to prohibit or discourage facilitation payments).

[167] Facilitating payments are illegal under the U.K. Bribery Act 2010, which came into force on July 1, 2011, and were also illegal under prior U.K. legislation. *See* Bribery Act 2010, c.23 (Eng.), *available at* http://www.legislation.gov.uk/ukpga/2010/23/contents; *see also* U.K. Ministry of Justice, *The Bribery Act 2010: Guidance About Procedures Which Relevant Commercial Organisations Can Put into Place to Prevent Persons Associated with Them from Bribing (Section 9 of the Bribery Act 2010)*, at 18 (2011), *available at* http://www.justice.gov.uk/guidance/docs/bribery-act-2010-guidance.pdf.

[168] *See, e.g.*, Non-Pros. Agreement, *In re Helmerich & Payne*, *supra* note 163; Admin. Proceeding Order, *In the Matter of Helmerich & Payne*, *supra* note 163.

[169] In order to establish duress or coercion, a defendant must demonstrate that the defendant was under unlawful, present, immediate, and

APPENDIX
Endnotes

impending threat of death or serious bodily injury; that the defendant did not negligently or recklessly create a situation where he would be forced to engage in criminal conduct (e.g., had been making payments as part of an ongoing bribery scheme); that the defendant had no reasonable legal alternative to violating the law; and that there was a direct causal relationship between the criminal action and the avoidance of the threatened harm. *See* Eleventh Circuit Pattern Jury Instr., Special Instr. No. 16 (2003); *see also* Fifth Circuit Pattern Jury Instr. No. 1.36 (2001); Sixth Circuit Pattern Jury Instr. No. 6.05 (2010); Seventh Circuit Pattern Jury Instr. No. 6.08 (1998); Ninth Circuit Pattern Jury Instr. No. 6.5 (2010); 1A Kevin F. O'Malley, Jay E. Grenig, Hon. William C. Lee, *Federal Jury Practice and Instructions* § 19.02 (6th ed. 2008 & Supp. 2012).

[170] S. Rep. No. 95-114, at 11.

[171] *Id*. at 10.

[172] *Id*. at 11.

[173] United States v. Kozeny, 582 F. Supp. 2d 535, 540 n.31 (S.D.N.Y. 2008).

[174] *Kozeny*, 582 F. Supp. 2d at 540 (citing S. Rep. No. 95-114, at 10-11).

[175] *Id*.

[176] These payments, however, must be accurately reflected in the company's books and records so that the company and its management are aware of the payments and can assure that the payments were properly made under the circumstances. For example, in one instance, a Kazakh immigration prosecutor threatened to fine, jail, or deport employees of a U.S. company's subsidiary. Believing the threats to be genuine, the employees in Kazakhstan sought guidance from senior management of the U.S. subsidiary and were authorized to make the payments. The employees then paid the government official a total of $45,000 using personal funds. The subsidiary reimbursed the employees, but it falsely recorded the reimbursements as "salary advances" or "visa fines." The parent company, which eventually discovered these payments, as well as other improperly booked cash payments made to a Kazakhstani consultant to obtain visas, was charged with civil violations of the accounting provisions. Admin. Proceeding Order, In the Matter of NATCO Group Inc., Exchange Act Release No. 61325 (Jan. 11, 2010), *available at* http://www.sec.gov/litigation/admin/2010/34-61325.pdf (imposing cease-and-desist order and $65,000 civil monetary penalty).

[177] *See* Jury Instructions at 21, United States v. Aguilar, No. 10-cr-1031 (C.D. Cal. May 16, 2011), ECF No. 511.

[178] *See, e.g.*, Pacific Can Co. v. Hewes, 95 F.2d 42, 46 (9th Cir. 1938) ("Where one company is controlled by another, the former acts not for itself but as directed by the latter, the same as an agent, and the principal is liable for the acts of its agent within the scope of the agent's authority."); United States v. NYNEX Corp., 788 F. Supp. 16, 18 n.3 (D.D.C. 1992) (holding that "[a] corporation can of course be held criminally liable for the acts of its agents," including "the conduct of its subsidiaries.").

[179] *Pacific Can Co.*, 95 F.2d at 46; *NYNEX Corp.*, 788 F. Supp. at 18 n.3.

[180] *See, e.g.*, Standard Oil Co. v. United States, 307 F.2d 120, 127 (5th Cir. 1962).

[181] Admin. Proceeding Order, In the Matter of United Industrial Corp., Exchange Act Release No. 60005 (May 29, 2009), *available at* http://www.sec.gov/litigation/admin/2009/34-60005.pdf; *see also* Lit. Release No. 21063, *SEC v. Worzel* (May 29, 2009), *available at* http://www.sec.gov/litigation/litreleases/2009/lr21063.htm.

[182] *See, e.g.*, Philip Urofsky, *What You Don't Know Can Hurt You: Successor Liability Resulting From Inadequate FCPA Due Diligence in M&A Transactions*, 1763 PLI/Corp. 631, 637 (2009) ("As a legal matter, when one corporation acquires another, it assumes any existing liabilities of that corporation, including liability for unlawful payments, regardless of whether it knows of them."). Whether or not successor liability applies to a particular corporate transaction depends on the facts involved and state, federal, and, potentially, foreign law.

[183] *See, e.g.*, Carolyn Lindsey, *More Than You Bargained for: Successor Liability Under the U.S. Foreign Corrupt Practices Act*, 35 Ohio N.U. L. Rev. 959, 966 (2009) ("Allowing a company to escape its debts and liabilities by merging with another entity is considered to lead to an unjust result.").

[184] *See, e.g.*, Melrose Distillers, Inc. v. United States, 359 U.S. 271, 274 (1959) (affirming criminal successor liability for antitrust violations); United States v. Alamo Bank of Texas, 880 F.2d 828, 830 (5th Cir. 1989) (affirming criminal successor liability for Bank Secrecy Act violations); United States v. Polizzi, 500 F.2d 856, 907 (9th Cir. 1974) (affirming criminal successor liability for conspiracy and Travel Act violations); United States v. Shields Rubber Corp., 732 F. Supp. 569, 571-72 (W.D. Pa. 1989) (permitting criminal successor liability for customs violations); *see also* United States v. Mobile Materials, Inc., 776 F.2d 1476, 1477 (10th Cir. 1985) (allowing criminal post-dissolution liability for antitrust, mail fraud, and false statement violations);.

[185] Complaint, SEC v. The Titan Corp., No. 05-cv-411 (D.D.C. Mar. 1, 2005) (discovery of FCPA violations during pre-acquisition due diligence protected potential acquiring company and led to termination of merger agreement), *available at* http://www.sec.gov/litigation/complaints/comp19107.pdf; Criminal Information, United States v. Titan Corp., No. 05-cr-314 (S.D. Cal. Mar. 1, 2005) (same) [hereinafter *United States v. Titan Corp.*], *available at* http://www.justice.gov/criminal/fraud/fcpa/cases/titan-corp/03-01-05titan-info.pdf.

[186] For a discussion of declinations, see Chapter 7.

[187] *See* Complaint, SEC v. El Paso Corp., No. 07-cv-899 (S.D.N.Y. Feb. 7, 2007), ECF No. 1 [hereinafter *SEC v. El Paso Corp.*] (charging company with books and records and internal controls charges for improper payments to Iraq under U.N. Oil-for-Food Programme), *available at* http://www.sec.gov/litigation/complaints/2007/comp19991.pdf.

[188] Complaint, SEC v. Alliance One Int'l, Inc., No. 10-cv-1319 (D.D.C. Aug. 6, 2010), ECF No. 1, *available at* http://www.sec.gov/litigation/complaints/2010/comp21618-alliance-one.pdf; Non-Pros. Agreement, In re Alliance One Int'l, Inc. (Aug. 6, 2010), *available at* http://www.justice.gov/criminal/fraud/fcpa/cases/alliance-one/08-06-10alliance-one-npa.pdf; Criminal Information, United States v. Alliance One Int'l AG, No. 10-cr-17 (W.D. Va. Aug. 6, 2010), ECF No. 3, *available at* http://www.justice.gov/criminal/fraud/fcpa/cases/alliance-one/08-06-10alliance-one-info.pdf; Criminal Information, United States v. Alliance One Tobacco Osh, LLC, No. 10-cr-16 (W.D. Va. Aug. 6, 2010), ECF No. 3, *available at* http://www.justice.gov/criminal/fraud/fcpa/cases/alliance-one/08-06-10alliance-one-tobaccoinfo.pdf.

[189] *See* Criminal Information, United States v. Syncor Taiwan, Inc., No. 02-cr-1244 (C.D. Cal. Dec. 5, 2002), ECF No. 1, *available at* http://www.justice.gov/criminal/fraud/fcpa/cases/syncor-taiwan/12-05-02syncor-taiwan-info.pdf; Plea Agreement, United States v. Syncor Taiwan, Inc., No. 02-cr-1244 (C.D. Cal. Dec. 9, 2002), ECF No. 14, *available at* http://www.justice.gov/criminal/fraud/fcpa/cases/syncor-taiwan/12-03-02syncor-taiwan-plea-agree.pdf.

[190] *See* Complaint, SEC v. Syncor Int'l Corp., No. 02-cv-2421 (D.D.C. Dec. 10, 2002), ECF No. 1, *available at* http://www.sec.gov/litigation/complaints/comp17887.htm; SEC v. Syncor International Corp., SEC Lit. Rel. 17997, (Dec. 10, 2002), *available at* http://www.sec.gov/litigation/litreleases/lr17887.htm.

[191] *See* Complaint, *SEC v. York Int'l Corp.*, *supra* note 115; Criminal Information, *United States v. York Int'l Corp.*, *supra* note 115.

[192] *See* Criminal Information, United States v. Latin Node, Inc., No. 09-cr-20239 (S.D. Fla. Mar. 23, 2009), ECF No. 1, *available at* http://www.justice.gov/criminal/fraud/fcpa/cases/litton-applied/03-23-09latinnode-info.pdf; eLandia Int'l Inc., Annual Report (Form 10-K), at 20 (Apr. 2, 2009), *available at* http://www.sec.gov/Archives/edgar/data/1352819/000119312509070961/d10k.htm.

[193] *See* Criminal Information, United States v. Salvoch, No. 10-cr-20893 (S.D. Fla. Dec. 17, 2010), ECF No. 3, *available at* http://www.justice.gov/criminal/fraud/fcpa/cases/salvoch/12-17-10salvoch-info.pdf; Criminal Information, United States v. Vasquez, No. 10-cr-20894 (S.D. Fla. Dec. 17, 2010), ECF No. 3, *available at* http://www.justice.gov/criminal/fraud/fcpa/cases/vasquezjp/12-17-10vasquez-juan-info.pdf; Indictment, United States v. Granados, *et al.*, No. 10-cr-20881, (S.D.

Fla. Dec. 14, 2010), ECF No. 3, *available at* http://www.justice.gov/criminal/fraud/fcpa/cases/granados-jorge/12-21-10granados-indict.pdf.

[194] *See* Deferred Pros. Agreement, *United States v. Snamprogetti*, *supra* note 60, ECF No. 3, *available at* http://www.justice.gov/criminal/fraud/fcpa/cases/snamprogetti/07-07-10snamprogetti-dpa.pdf.

[195] *Compare* Criminal Information, *United States v. Snamprogetti*, *supra* note 60, *with* Deferred Pros. Agreement, *United States v. Snamprogetti*, *supra* note 60, ECF No. 3.

[196] *See* Press Release, General Electric Co., General Electric Agrees to Acquire InVision (Mar. 15, 2004), *available at* http://www.ge.com/files/usa/company/investor/downloads/sharpeye_press_release.pdf; Press Release, U.S. Dept. of Justice, InVision Tech. Inc. Enters into Agreement with the United States (Dec. 6, 2004), *available at* http://www.justice.gov/opa/pr/2004/December/04_crm_780.htm; Company News; *G.E. Gets InVision, a Maker of Bomb Detectors*, N.Y. TIMES, Dec. 7, 2004, at C4.

[197] Non-Pros. Agreement, In re InVision (Dec. 3, 2004), *available at* http://www.justice.gov/criminal/fraud/fcpa/cases/invision-tech/12-03-04invisiontech-agree.pdf; Non-Pros. Agreement, In re General Elec. Co., (Dec. 3, 2004), *available at* http://www.justice.gov/criminal/fraud/fcpa/cases/invision-tech/12-03-04invisiontech-agree-ge.pdf; Complaint, SEC v. GE InVision, Inc., f/k/a InVision Technologies, Inc., No. 05-cv-660, (N.D. Cal. Feb. 14, 2005), ECF No. 1, *available at* http://www.sec.gov/litigation/complaints/comp19078.pdf.

[198] *See* U.S. DEPT. OF JUSTICE, FCPA OP. RELEASE 08-02 (June 13, 2008), *available at* http://www.justice.gov/criminal/fraud/fcpa/opinion/2008/0802.pdf; *see also* Press Release, U.S. Dept. of Justice, Pfizer H.C.P. Corp. Agrees to Pay $15 Million Penalty to Resolve Foreign Bribery Investigation (Aug. 7, 2012) ("In the 18 months following its acquisition of Wyeth, Pfizer Inc., in consultation with the department, conducted a due diligence and investigative review of the Wyeth business operations and integrated Pfizer Inc.'s internal controls system into the former Wyeth business entities. The department considered these extensive efforts and the SEC resolution in its determination not to pursue a criminal resolution for the pre-acquisition improper conduct of Wyeth subsidiaries."), *available at* http://www.justice.gov/opa/pr/2012/August/12-crm-980.html.

[199] 18 U.S.C. § 2.

[200] In enacting the FCPA in 1977, Congress explicitly noted that "[t]he concepts of aiding and abetting and joint participation would apply to a violation under this bill in the same manner in which those concepts have always applied in both SEC civil actions and in implied private actions brought under the securities laws generally." H.R. REP. No. 95-640, at 8.

[201] *Pinkerton* held that a conspirator may be found guilty of a substantive offense committed by a co-conspirator in furtherance of the conspiracy if the co-conspirator's acts were reasonably foreseeable. *See* Pinkerton v. United States, 328 U.S. 640, 647-48 (1946).

[202] *See* United States v. MacAllister, 160 F.3d 1304, 1307 (11th Cir. 1998); United States v. Winter, 509 F.2d 975, 982 (5th Cir. 1975).

[203] *See* Criminal Information, *United States v. Marubeni*, *supra* note 132; Criminal Information, *United States v. JGC Corp.*, *supra* note 60; Criminal Information, *United States v. Snamprogetti*, *supra* note 60; *see also* Criminal Information, *United States v. Technip*, *supra* note 132.

[204] Section 20(e) of the Exchange Act, "Prosecution of Persons Who Aid and Abet Violations," explicitly provides that, for purposes of a civil action seeking injunctive relief or a civil penalty, "any person that knowingly or recklessly provides substantial assistance to another person in violation of a provision of this chapter, or of any rule or regulation issued under this chapter, shall be deemed to be in violation of such provision to the same extent as the person to whom such assistance is provided." Section 20(e) of the Exchange Act, 15 U.S.C. § 78t(e).

[205] Under Section 21C(a) of the Exchange Act, the SEC may impose a cease-and-desist order through the SEC's administrative proceedings upon any person who is violating, has violated, or is about to violate any provision of the Exchange Act or any rule or regulation thereunder, and upon any other person that is, was, or would be a cause of the violation, due to an act or omission the person knew or should have known would contribute to such violation. Section 21C(a) of the Exchange Act,15 U.S.C. § 78u-3(a).

[206] *See* Complaint, *SEC v. Panalpina, Inc.*, *supra* note 68.

[207] 18 U.S.C. § 3282(a) provides: "Except as otherwise expressly provided by law, no person shall be prosecuted, tried, or punished for any offense,

not capital, unless the indictment is found or the information is instituted within five years next after such offense shall have been committed."

[208] *See* Grunewald v. United States, 353 U.S. 391, 396-97 (1957) (holding government must prove conspiracy still existed and at least one overt act was committed within the statute of limitations); Fiswick v. United States, 329 U.S. 211, 216 (1946) ("The statute of limitations, unless suspended, runs from the last overt act during the existence of the conspiracy. The overt acts averred and proved may thus mark the duration, as well as the scope, of the conspiracy.") (citation omitted); *see generally* Julie N. Sarnoff, *Federal Criminal Conspiracy*, 48 AM. CRIM. L. REV. 663, 676 (Spring 2011).

[209] 18 U.S.C. § 3292.

[210] 28 U.S.C. § 2462.

[211] S. REP. No. 95-114, at 3 (noting that, in the past, "corporate bribery has been concealed by the falsification of corporate books and records," that the accounting provisions "remove [] this avenue of coverup," and that "[t]aken together, the accounting requirements and criminal [anti-bribery] prohibitions . . . should effectively deter corporate bribery of foreign government officials").

[212] S. REP. No. 95-114, at 7.

[213] Section 13(b)(2)(A) of the Exchange Act, 15 U.S.C. § 78m(b)(2)(A).

[214] Section 13(b)(2)(B) of the Exchange Act, 15 U.S.C. § 78m(b)(2)(B).

[215] The accounting provisions contain a narrow exemption related to national security and the protection of classified information. Under this "national security" provision, "no duty or liability [under Section 13(b)(2) of the Exchange Act] shall be imposed upon any person acting in cooperation with the head of any federal department or agency responsible for such matters if such act in cooperation with such head of a department or agency was done upon the specific, written directive of the head of such department or agency pursuant to Presidential authority to issue such directives." Section 13(b)(3) of the Exchange Act, 15 U.S.C. § 78m(b)(3). As Congress made clear, however, the exception is narrowly tailored and intended to prevent the disclosure of classified information. H.R. REP. 94-831, at 11, *available at* http://www.justice.gov/criminal/fraud/fcpa/history/1977/corruptrpt-94-831.pdf.

[216] Section 13(b)(2)(A) of the Exchange Act, 15 U.S.C. § 78m(b)(2)(A).

[217] H.R. REP. No. 94-831, at 10.

[218] *Id.*

[219] Section 13(b)(7) of the Exchange Act, 15 U.S.C. § 78m(b)(7).

[220] H.R. REP. No. 100-576, at 917 (1988), *available at* http://www.justice.gov/criminal/fraud/fcpa/history/1988/tradeact-100-418.pdf. Congress rejected the addition of proposed cost-benefit language to the definition "in response to concerns that such a statutory provision might be abused and weaken the accounting provisions at a time of increasing concern about audit failures and financial fraud and resultant recommendations by experts for stronger accounting practices and audit standards." *Id.*

[221] *See, e.g.*, Complaint, SEC v. Biomet, Inc., No. 12-cv-454 (D.D.C. Mar. 26, 2012), ECF No. 1 [hereinafter *SEC v. Biomet*], *available at* http://www.sec.gov/litigation/complaints/2012/comp22306.pdf; Criminal Information, United States v. Biomet, Inc., No. 12-cr-80 (D.D.C. Mar. 26, 2012) [hereinafter *United States v. Biomet*], *available at* http://www.justice.gov/criminal/fraud/fcpa/cases/biomet/2012-03-26-biomet-information.pdf; Complaint, SEC v. Smith & Nephew Inc., No. 12-cv-187 (D.D.C. Feb. 6, 2012), ECF No. 1, *available at* http://www.sec.gov/litigation/complaints/2012/comp22252.pdf; Criminal Information, United States v. Smith & Nephew plc., No. 12-cr-30 (D.D.C. Feb. 6, 2012), ECF No. 1, *available at* http://www.justice.gov/criminal/fraud/fcpa/cases/smith-nephew/2012-02-06-s-n-information.pdf; Complaint, *SEC v. Johnson & Johnson*, *supra* note 131; Criminal Information, *United States v. DePuy*, *supra* note 131; Complaint, SEC v. Maxwell Technologies Inc., No. 11-cv-258 (D.D.C. Jan. 31, 2011), ECF No. 1 [hereinafter *SEC v. Maxwell Technologies*], *available at* http://www.sec.gov/litigation/complaints/2011/comp21832.pdf; Criminal Information, United States v. Maxwell Technologies Inc., No. 11-cr-329 (S.D. Cal. Jan. 31, 2011), ECF No. 1, *available at* http://www.justice.gov/criminal/fraud/fcpa/cases/maxwell/01-31-11maxwell-tech-info.pdf; Complaint, SEC v. Transocean, Inc., No. 10-cv-1891 (D.D.C. Nov. 4, 2010), ECF No. 1, *available at* http://www.sec.gov/litigation/complaints/2010/comp21725.pdf; Criminal Information, United States v. Transocean, Inc., No. 10-cr-768 (S.D. Tex. Nov. 4, 2010), ECF No. 1, *available at* http://www.justice.gov/criminal/fraud/fcpa/cases/transocean-inc/11-04-10transocean-info.pdf.

222 S. Rep. No. 95-114, at 7.

223 Section 13(b)(2)(B) of the Exchange Act, 15 U.S.C. § 78m(b)(2)(B).

224 Section 13(b)(7) of the Exchange Act, 15 U.S.C. § 78m(b)(7).

225 *See* Complaint, *SEC v. Siemens AG, supra* note 48; Criminal Information, *United States v. Siemens AG, supra* note 48.

226 Complaint, *SEC v. Siemens AG, supra* note 48; Criminal Information, *United States v. Siemens AG, supra* note 48; Press Release, U.S. Dept. of Justice, Siemens AG and Three Subsidiaries Plead Guilty to Foreign Corrupt Practices Act Violations and Agree to Pay $450 Million in Combined Criminal Fines (Dec. 15, 2008), *available at* http://www.justice.gov/opa/pr/2008/December/08-crm-1105.html.

227 *See, e.g.,* Complaint, *SEC v. Biomet, supra* note 221 (bribes paid to government healthcare providers in which phony invoices were used to justify payments and bribes were falsely recorded as "consulting fees" or "commissions" in company's books and records); Criminal Information, *United States v. Biomet, supra* note 221 (same); *SEC v. Alcatel-Lucent, supra* note 48 (bribes paid to foreign officials to secure telecommunications contracts where company lacked proper internal controls and permitted books and records to falsified); *United States v. Alcatel-Lucent, S.A., supra* note 48 (same).

228 Complaint, *SEC v. Daimler AG, supra* note 48; Criminal Information, *United States v. Daimler AG, supra* note 48.

229 *Id.*

230 *Id.*

231 *Id.*

232 *Id.*

233 *Id.*

234 *See, e.g.,* Complaint, *SEC v. Tyco Int'l, supra* note 9; Complaint, SEC v. Willbros, No. 08-cv-1494 (S.D. Tex. May 14, 2008), ECF No. 1, *available at* http://www.sec.gov/litigation/complaints/2008/comp20571.pdf.

235 *See, e.g.,* Complaint, *SEC v. Siemens AG, supra* note 48; Complaint, *SEC v. York Int'l Corp., supra* note 115; Complaint, *SEC v. Textron, supra* note 115; Criminal Information, United States v. Control Components, Inc., No. 09-cr-162 (C.D. Cal. July 22, 2009), ECF No. 1 [hereinafter *United States v. Control Components*], *available at* http://www.justice.gov/criminal/fraud/fcpa/cases/control-inc/07-22-09cci-info.pdf; Criminal Information, United States v. SSI Int'l Far East, Ltd., No. 06-cr-398, ECF No. 1 (D. Or. Oct. 10, 2006) [hereinafter *United States v. SSI Int'l*], *available at* http://www.justice.gov/criminal/fraud/fcpa/cases/ssi-intl/10-10-06ssi-information.pdf.

236 *See, e.g.,* Complaint, *SEC v. El Paso Corp., supra* note 187; Complaint, *SEC v. Innospec, supra* note 79; Complaint, SEC v. Chevron Corp., 07-cv-10299 (S.D.N.Y. Nov. 14, 2007), ECF No. 1, *available at* http://www.sec.gov/litigation/complaints/2007/comp20363.pdf.

237 Plea Agreement, *United States v. Stanley, supra* note 8; Plea Agreement, *United States v. Sapsizian, supra* note 8.

238 *See* Complaint, *SEC v. Maxwell Technologies, supra* note 221.

239 *See* Complaint, *SEC v. Willbros Group, supra* note 9.

240 15 U.S.C. § 7201, *et seq.*

241 Exchange Act Rule 13a-15, 17 C.F.R. § 240.13a-15; Exchange Act Rule 15d-15, 17 C.F.R. § 240.15d-15; Item 308 of Regulation S-K, 17 C.F.R. § 229.308; Item 15, Form 20-F, *available at* http://www.sec.gov/about/forms/form20-f.pdf; General Instruction (B), Form 40-F (for foreign private issuers), *available at* http://www.sec.gov/about/forms/form40-f.pdf.

242 *See* U.S. Sec. and Exchange Comm., Commission Guidance Regarding Management's Report on Internal Control over Financial Reporting Under Section 13(a) or 15(d) of the Securities Exchange Act of 1934, Release No. 33-8810 (June 27, 2007), *available at* http://www.sec.gov/rules/interp/2007/33-8810.pdf.

243 *Id.*

244 Foreign Corrupt Practices Act of 1977, Pub. L. No. 95-213, § 102, 91 Stat. 1494 (1977).

245 *See supra* note 48; *SEC v. Technip, supra* note 132, (French company); *United States v. Technip, supra* note 132, (same); *see also* Admin. Proceeding Order, In re Diageo plc, Exchange Act Release No. 64978 (SEC July 27, 2011) (UK company), *available at* http://www.sec.gov/litigation/admin/2011/34-64978.pdf; Admin. Proceeding Order, In re Statoil, ASA, Exchange Act Release No. 54599 (SEC May 29, 2009) (Norwegian company), *available at* http://www.sec.gov/litigation/admin/2006/34-54599.pdf; Criminal Information, United States v.

Statoil, ASA, No. 06-cr-960 (S.D.N.Y. Oct. 13, 2006) (same), *available at* http://www.justice.gov/criminal/fraud/fcpa/cases/statoil-asa-inc/10-13-09statoil-information.pdf.

246 Although private companies are not covered by the books and records and internal controls provisions of the FCPA and do not fall within SEC's jurisdiction, such companies generally are required by federal and state tax laws and state corporation laws to maintain accurate books and records sufficient to properly calculate taxes owed. Further, most large private companies maintain their books and records to facilitate the preparation of financial statements in conformity with GAAP to comply with financial institutions' lending requirements.

247 *See SEC v. RAE Sys. Inc., supra* note 92; *In re RAE Sys., supra* note 92.

248 *See* Section 13(b)(6) of the Exchange Act, 15 U.S.C. § 78m(b) (6), which provides that where an issuer "holds 50 per centum or less of the voting power with respect to a domestic or foreign firm," the issuer must "proceed in good faith to use its influence, to the extent reasonable under the issuer's circumstances, to cause such domestic or foreign firm to devise and maintain a system of internal accounting controls consistent with [Section 13(b)(2)]."

249 *See* 15 U.S.C. § 78m(b)(6). Congress added the language in subsection 78m(b)(6) to the FCPA in 1988, recognizing that "it is unrealistic to expect a minority owner to exert a disproportionate degree of influence over the accounting practices of a subsidiary." H.R. Rep. No. 100-576, at 917. The Conference Report noted that, with respect to minority owners, "the amount of influence which an issuer may exercise necessarily varies from case to case. While the relative degree of ownership is obviously one factor, other factors may also be important in determining whether an issuer has demonstrated good-faith efforts to use its influence." *Id.; see also* S. Rep. No. 100-85, at 50.

250 Section 20(e) of the Exchange Act, titled "Prosecution of Persons Who Aid and Abet Violations," explicitly provides that for purposes of a civil action seeking injunctive relief or a civil penalty, "any person that knowingly or recklessly provides substantial assistance to another person in violation of a provision of this title, or of any rule or regulation issued under this title, shall be deemed to be in violation of such provision to the same extent as the person to whom such assistance is provided." *See* Section 20(e) of the Exchange Act, 15 U.S.C. § 78t(e).

251 *See* Complaint at 11-12, *SEC v. Elkin, supra* note 50, ECF 1.

252 *SEC v. Elkin, supra* note 50, ECF 6-9 (final judgments).

253 *See, e.g.,* Complaint, SEC v. Nature's Sunshine Products, Inc., et al., No. 09-cv-672 (D. Utah, July 31, 2009), ECF No. 2, *available at* http://www.sec.gov/litigation/litreleases/2009/lr21162.htm.

254 *See* Admin. Proceeding Order, In re Watts Water Technologies, Inc. and Leesen Chang, Exchange Act Release No. 65555 (SEC Oct. 13, 2011), *available at* http://www.sec.gov/litigation/admin/2011/34-65555.pdf.

255 *Id.* at 2, 4, 6-7.

256 Exchange Act Rule 13b2-1, 17 C.F.R. § 240.13b2-1.

257 15 U.S.C. § 78m(b)(5).

258 Section 3(a)(9) of the Exchange Act, 15 U.S.C. § 78c(a)(9).

259 Exchange Act Rule 13b2-2, 17 C.F.R. § 240.13b2-2

260 Complaint, SEC v. Jennings, No. 11-cv-1444 (D.D.C. Jan. 24, 2011), ECF No. 1, *available at* http://www.sec.gov/litigation/complaints/2011/comp21822.pdf.

261 Complaint, *id.,* ECF No. 1; Final Judgment, *id.,* ECF No. 3.

262 Serious Fraud Office, Innospec Ltd: Former CEO admits bribery to falsify product tests (July 30, 2012), *available at* http://www.sfo.gov.uk/press-room/latest-press-releases/press-releases-2012/innospec-ltd--former-ceo-admits-bribery-to-falsify-product-tests.aspx.

263 15 U.S.C. § 78m(b)(4)-(5). Congress adopted this language in 1988 in

order to make clear that, consistent with enforcement policy at the time, criminal penalties would not be imposed "for inadvertent or insignificant errors in books and records, or inadvertent violations of accounting controls." *See* S. Rep. No. 100-85, at 49; H.R. Rep. No. 100-576, at 916 ("The Conferees intend to codify current Securities and Exchange Commission (SEC) enforcement policy that penalties not be imposed for insignificant or technical infractions or inadvertent conduct.").

[264] 15 U.S.C. § 78ff(a).

[265] *See United States v. Alcatel-Lucent, S.A., supra* note 48; *see also United States v. Alcatel-Lucent France, supra* note 56.

[266] *See* Deferred Prosecution Agreement, *United States v. Alcatel-Lucent, S.A., supra* note 48, ECF No. 10, *available at* http://www.justice.gov/criminal/fraud/fcpa/cases/alcatel-etal/02-22-11alcatel-dpa.pdf.

[267] *See* Plea Agreement, *United States v. Siemens AG, supra* note 48, ECF No. 14, *available at* http://www.justice.gov/criminal/fraud/fcpa/cases/siemens/12-15-08siemensakt-plea.pdf.

[268] *See* Minute Entry of Guilty Plea, *United States v. Peterson, supra* note 8, ECF 13; *see also* Press Release, U.S. Dept. of Justice, Former Morgan Stanley Managing Director Pleads Guilty for Role in Evading Internal Controls Required by FCPA (Apr. 23, 2012), *available at* http://www.justice.gov/opa/pr/2012/April/12-crm-534.html.

[269] *See* Criminal Information, United States v. Baker Hughes Svcs. Int'l, No. 07-cr-129 (S.D. Tex. Apr. 11, 2007), ECF No. 1, *available at* http://www.justice.gov/criminal/fraud/fcpa/cases/baker-hughs/04-11-07bakerhughesintl-info.pdf.

[270] *See United States v. Panalpina, Inc., supra* note 68.

[271] *Id.*

[272] *See* FASB Statement of Financial Accounting Concepts No. 2, ¶¶ 63-80.

[273] PCAOB Auditing Standard No. 12 and PCAOB AU Section 325.

[274] *See* Section 10A of the Exchange Act, 15U.S.C. § 78j-1.

[275] 18 U.S.C. § 1952.

[276] *See, e.g., United States v. Nexus Technologies, supra* note 53; Criminal Information, United States v. Robert Richard King, *et al.,* No. 01-cr-190 (W.D. Mo. June 27, 2001), *available at* http://www.justice.gov/criminal/fraud/fcpa/cases/kingr-etal/05-03-02king-robert-indict.pdf; Superseding Indictment, *United States v. Mead, supra* note 44; Criminal Information, United States v. Saybolt North America Inc., *et al.,* No. 98-cr-10266 (D. Mass. Aug. 18, 1998), *available at* http://www.justice.gov/criminal/fraud/fcpa/cases/saybolt/08-10-98saybolt-info.pdf.

[277] *See* Second Superseding Indictment, United States v. Kozeny, No. 05-cr-518 (S.D.N.Y. May 26, 2009), ECF No. 203, *available at* http://www.justice.gov/criminal/fraud/fcpa/cases/kozenyv/05-26-09bourke2nd-supersed-indict.pdf; Judgment, United States v. Bourke, No. 05-cr-518 (S.D.N.Y. Nov. 12, 2009), ECF No. 253, *available at* http://www.justice.gov/criminal/fraud/fcpa/cases/kozenyv/11-12-09bourke-judgment.pdf.

[278] Plea Agreement, *United States v. Control Components, supra* note 235, ECF No. 7; *see also* Order, *United States v. Carson, supra* note 119, ECF No. 440 (denying motion to dismiss counts alleging Travel Act violations), *available at* http://www.justice.gov/criminal/fraud/fcpa/cases/carsons/2011-09-20-carson-minutes-denying-motion-to-dismiss.pdf.

[279] *See, e.g.,* Criminal Information, *United States v. Esquenazi, supra* note 44; Criminal Information, *United States v. Green, supra* note 44; Criminal Information, United States v. General Elec. Co., No. 92-cr-87 (S.D. Ohio July 22, 1992), *available at* http://www.justice.gov/criminal/fraud/fcpa/cases/general-electric/1992-07-22-general-electric-information.pdf.

[280] Foreign officials may "not be charged with violating the FCPA itself, since the [FCPA] does not criminalize the receipt of a bribe by a foreign official." United States v. Blondek, 741 F.Supp. 116, 117 (N.D. Tex. 1990), *aff'd* United States v. Castle, 925 F.2d 831 (5th Cir. 1991) ("We hold that foreign officials may not be prosecuted under 18 U.S.C. § 371 for conspiring to violate the FCPA."). Foreign officials, however, can be charged with violating the FCPA when the foreign official acts as an intermediary of a bribe payment. *See, e.g.,* Information, United States v. Basu, No. 02-cr-475 (D.D.C. Nov. 26, 2002) (World Bank employee charged with wire fraud and FCPA violations for facilitating bribe payments to another World Bank official and Kenyan government official), *available at* http://www.justice.gov/criminal/fraud/fcpa/cases/basu/11-26-02basu-info.pdf; Information, United States v. Sengupta, No. 02-cr-40 (D.D.C. Jan. 30, 2002), *available at* http://www.justice.gov/criminal/fraud/fcpa/cases/sengupta/01-30-02sengupta-info.pdf.

[281] *See, e.g.,* Judgments, *United States v. Esquenazi, supra* note 44, ECF Nos. 182, 816, 824 (judgments against foreign official defendants).

[282] Criminal Information, *United States v. SSI Int'l, supra* note 235 (alleging violations of 18 U.S.C. §§ 1343, 1346); Plea Agreement, *United States v. SSI Int'l, supra* note 235, (Oct. 10, 2006), *available at* http://www.justice.gov/criminal/fraud/fcpa/cases/control-inc/07-24-09cci-plea-agree.pdf.

[283] *See* Ex-Im Bank, Form of Exporter's Certificate, EBD-M-56 (Jan. 2007), *available at* http://www.exim.gov/pub/ins/pdf/ebd-m-56.pdf.

[284] *See* 18 U.S.C. § 1001.

[285] 22 C.F.R. §§ 130.2, 130.9.

[286] For example, in *United States v. BAE Systems plc*, BAE pleaded guilty to conspiring to defraud the United States by impairing and impeding its lawful functions, to making false statements about its FCPA compliance program, and to violating the AECA and ITAR. BAE paid a $400 million fine and agreed to an independent corporate monitor to ensure compliance with applicable anti-corruption and export control laws. Criminal Information and Plea Agreement, United States v. BAE Sys. plc, No. 10-cr-35 (D.D.C. Mar. 1, 2010), ECF Nos.1, 8, *available at* http://www.justice.gov/criminal/fraud/fcpa/cases/bae-system/02-01-10baesystems-info.pdf and http://www.justice.gov/criminal/fraud/fcpa/cases/bae-system/03-01-10baesystems-plea-agree.pdf. In an action based on the same underlying facts as the criminal guilty plea, BAE entered a civil settlement with the Directorate of Defense Trade Controls for violations of AECA and ITAR, including over 2500 ITAR violations that included a failure to report the payment of fees or commissions associated with defense transactions and failure to maintain records involving ITAR-controlled transactions. BAE paid $79 million in penalties, and the State Department imposed a "policy of denial" for export licenses on three BAE subsidiaries involved in the wrongful conduct. Consent Agreement between BAE Sys. plc and Defense Trade Controls at 17-20, Bureau of Political-Military Affairs, U.S. Dept. of State (May 16, 2011), *available at* http://www.pmddtc.state.gov/compliance/consent_agreements/pdf/BAES_CA.pdf; Proposed Charging Letter, In re Investigation of BAE Systems plc Regarding Violations of the Arms Export Control Act and the International Traffic in Arms Regulations, U.S. Dept. of State (May 2011), *available at* http://www.pmddtc.state.gov/compliance/consent_agreements/pdf/BAES_PCL.pdf.

[287] 26 U.S.C. § 162(c)(1); *see also* Plea Agreement, United States v. Smith, No. 07-cr-69 (C.D. Cal. Sept. 3, 2009), ECF No. 89, *available at* http://www.justice.gov/criminal/fraud/fcpa/cases/smithl/09-03-09smithl-plea-agree.pdf; Criminal Information, *United States v. Titan Corp., supra* note 185.

[288] *See* USAM § 9-27.000.

[289] *See* USAM § 9-27.420 (setting forth considerations to be weighed when determining whether it would be appropriate to enter into plea agreement).

[290] *See* USAM § 9-28.000 *et seq.*

[291] *See* USAM § 9-28.710 (discussing attorney-client and work product protections).

[292] *See* http://www.sec.gov/divisions/enforce/enforcementmanual.pdf.

[293] *See* USAM§ 9-28.300.A; *see also* USAM § 9-28.700.B (explaining benefits of cooperation for both government and corporation).

[294] *See* USAM § 9-28.900 (discussing restitution and remediation). The commentary further provides that prosecutors should consider and weigh whether the corporation appropriately disciplined wrongdoers and a corporation's efforts to reform, including its quick recognition of the flaws in the program and its efforts to improve the program. *Id.*

[295] *See* USAM §§ 9-27.230, 9-27.420.

[296] U.S. Sentencing Guidelines § 8B2.1(b)(7) (2011).

[297] *Id.* § 8C2.5(f)(2) (2011).

[298] U.S. Sec. and Exchange Comm., Report of Investigation Pursuant to Section 21(a) of the Securities Exchange Act of 1934 and Commission Statement on the Relationship of Cooperation to Agency Enforcement Decisions, SEC Rel. Nos. 34-44969 and AAER-1470 (Oct. 23, 2001) [hereinafter *Seaboard* Report] *available at* http://www.sec.gov/litigation/investreport/34-44969.htm.

[299] U.S. Sec. and Exchange Comm., Policy Statement Concerning Cooperation by Individuals in its Investigations and Related Enforcements Actions, 17 C.F.R. § 202.12 (Jan. 10, 2010), *available at* http://www.sec.gov/rules/

policy/2010/34-61340.pdf.

300 *See* U.S. Sentencing Guidelines at § 8B2.1(a)(2).

301 U.S. Sentencing Guidelines § 8B2.1(b).

302 *See generally* Debbie Troklus, *et al.*, Compliance 101: How to build and maintain an effective compliance and ethics program, Society of Corp. Compliance and Ethics (2008) 3-9 [hereinafter Compliance 101] (listing reasons to implement compliance program, including protecting company's reputation, creating trust between management and employees, preventing false statements to customers, creating efficiencies and streamlining processes, detecting employee and contractor fraud and abuse, ensuring high-quality products and services, and providing "early warning" system of inappropriate actions); Transparency Int'l, Business Principles for Countering Bribery: Small and Medium Enterprise (SME) Edition 5 (2008) (citing benefits of anti-bribery program like protecting reputation, creating record of integrity enhances opportunities to acquire government business, protecting company assets otherwise squandered on bribes); Mark Pieth, Harmonising Anti-Corruption Compliance: The OECD Good Practice Guidance 45-46 (2011) [hereinafter Harmonising Anti-Corruption Compliance] (citing need for compliance program to prevent and detect in-house risks, such as workplace security or conflicts of interest, and external risks, like anti-trust violations, embargo circumvention, environmental hazards, and money laundering).

303 Debarment authorities, such as the Department of Defense or the General Services Administration, may also consider a company's compliance program when deciding whether to debar or suspend a contractor. Specifically, the relevant regulations provide that the debarment authority should consider "[w]hether the contractor had effective standards of conduct and internal control systems in place at the time of the activity which constitutes cause for debarment or had adopted such procedures prior to any Government investigation of the activity cited as a cause for debarment," and "[w]hether the contractor has instituted or agreed to institute new or revised review and control procedures and ethics training programs." 48 C.F.R. § 9.406-1(a).

304 *Seaboard* Report, *supra* note 298; U.S. Sec. and Exchange Comm., Report of Investigation Pursuant to Section 21(a) of the Securities Exchange Act of 1934 and Commission Statement on the Relationship of Cooperation to Agency Enforcement Decisions, SEC Rel. No. 44969 (Oct. 23, 2001), *available at* http://www.sec.gov/litigation/investreport/34-44969.htm.

305 USAM § 9-28.300. When evaluating the pervasiveness of wrongdoing within the corporation, prosecutors are advised that while it may be appropriate to charge a corporation for minor misconduct where the wrongdoing was pervasive, "it may not be appropriate to impose liability upon a corporation, *particularly one with a robust compliance program in place*, under a strict *respondeat superior* theory for the single isolated act of a rogue employee." *Id.* § 9-28.500.A (emphasis added). Prosecutors should also consider a company's compliance program when examining any remedial actions taken, including efforts to implement an effective compliance program or to improve an existing one. As the commentary explains, "although the inadequacy of a corporate compliance program is a factor to consider when deciding whether to charge a corporation, that corporation's quick recognition of the flaws in the program and its efforts to improve the program are also factors to consider as to appropriate disposition of a case." *Id.* § 9-28.900.B. Finally, the Principles of Federal Prosecution of Business Organizations provides that prosecutors should consider the existence and effectiveness of the corporation's pre-existing compliance program in determining how to treat a corporate target. *Id.* § 9-28.800.

306 *See* USAM § 9-28.800.B; *see also* U.S. Sentencing Guidelines § 8B2.1(a) (2011) ("The failure to prevent or detect the instant offense does not necessarily mean that the program is not generally effective in preventing and detecting criminal conduct.").

307 *See* Press Release, U.S. Dept. of Justice, Former Morgan Stanley Managing Director Pleads Guilty for Role in Evading Internal Controls Required by FCPA (Apr. 25, 2012) (declining to bring criminal case against corporate employer that "had constructed and maintained a system of internal controls, which provided reasonable assurances that its employees were not bribing government officials"), *available at* http://www.justice.gov/opa/pr/2012/April/12-crm-534.html; Press Release, U.S. Sec. and Exchange Comm., SEC Charges Former Morgan Stanley

Executive with FCPA Violations and Investment Adviser Fraud, No. 2012-78 (Apr. 25, 2012) (indicating corporate employer was not charged in the matter and had "cooperated with the SEC's inquiry and conducted a thorough internal investigation to determine the scope of the improper payments and other misconduct involved"), *available at* http://www.sec.gov/news/press/2012/2012-78.htm.

308 *See* USAM § 9-28.800.B.

309 *See, e.g.*, Int'l Chamber of Commerce, ICC Rules on Combating Corruption (2011) [hereinafter ICC Rules on Combating Corruption], *available at* http://www.iccwbo.org/uploadedFiles/ICC/policy/business_in_society/Statements/ICC_Rules_on_Combating_Corruption_2011edition.pdf; Transparency Int'l, Business Principles for Countering Bribery (2d ed. 2009) [hereinafter Business Principles for Countering Bribery], *available at* http://www.transparency.org/global_priorities/private_sector/business_principles/; United Kingdom Ministry of Justice, The Bribery Act of 2010, Guidance about procedures which relevant commercial organisations can put into place to prevent persons associated with them from bribing (2010), *available at* http://www.justice.gov.uk/downloads/legislation/bribery-act-2010-guidance.pdf; World Bank Group, Integrity Compliance Guidelines (2011) [hereinafter Integrity Compliance Guidelines], *available at* http://siteresources.worldbank.org/INTDOII/Resources/Integrity_Compliance_Guidelines.pdf; Asia-Pacific Economic Cooperation, APEC Anti-corruption Code of Conduct for Business (2007) [hereinafter APEC Anti-corruption Code], *available at* http://www.apec.org/Groups/SOM-Steering-Committee-on-Economic-and-Technical-Cooperation/Task-Groups/~/media/Files/Groups/ACT/07_act_codebrochure.ashx; Int'l Chamber of Commerce, Transparency Int'l, United Nations Global Compact, and World Economic Forum, Resisting Extortion and Solicitation in International Transactions: A Company Tool for Employee Training (2011), *available at* http://www3.weforum.org/docs/WEF_PACI_RESIST_Report_2011.pdf; Int'l Chamber of Commerce, et al., Clean Business Is Good Business, *available at* http://www3.weforum.org/docs/WEF_PACI_BusinessCaseFightingCorruption_2011.pdf; World Economic Forum, Partnering Against Corruption – Principles for Countering Bribery (2009) [hereinafter Partnering Against Corruption], *available at* http://www3.weforum.org/docs/WEF_PACI_Principles_2009.pdf; Working Group on Bribery, OECD, Good Practice Guidance on Internal Controls, Ethics, and Compliance 2010, [hereinafter OECD Good Practice Guidance] *available at* http://www.oecd.org/dataoecd/5/51/44884389.pdf; U.N. Global Compact, The Ten Principles [hereinafter The Ten Principles] *available at* http://www.unglobalcompact.org/aboutTheGC/TheTenPrinciples/index.html.

310 This is also reflected in the *Sentencing Guidelines*, which recognizes that no single, formulaic set of requirements should be imposed, but instead focuses on a number of factors like applicable industry practice or the standards called for by any applicable governmental regulation, the size of the organization, and whether the organization has engaged in similar misconduct in the past. *See* U.S. Sentencing Guidelines § 8B2.1 & app. note 2 (2011).

311 This was underscored by then-SEC Commissioner Cynthia Glassman in 2003 in a speech on the SEC's implementation of the Sarbanes-Oxley Act: "[T]he ultimate effectiveness of the new corporate governance rules will be determined by the 'tone at the top.' Adopting a code of ethics means little if the company's chief executive officer or its directors make clear, by conduct or otherwise, that the code's provisions do not apply

116

to them. . . . Corporate officers and directors hold the ultimate power and responsibility for restoring public trust by conducting themselves in a manner that is worthy of the trust that is placed in them." Cynthia Glassman, SEC Implementation of Sarbanes-Oxley: The New Corporate Governance, Remarks at National Economists Club (April 7, 2003), *available at* http://www.sec.gov/news/speech/spch040703cag.htm .

[312] Indeed, research has found that "[e]thical culture is the single biggest factor determining the amount of misconduct that will take place in a business." ETHICS RESOURCE CENTER, 2009 NATIONAL BUSINESS ETHICS SURVEY: ETHICS IN THE RECESSION (2009), at 41. Metrics of ethical culture include ethical leadership (tone at the top), supervisor reinforcement of ethical behavior (middle management reinforcement), and peer commitment (supporting one another in doing the right thing). ETHICS RESOURCE CENTER, 2011 NATIONAL BUSINESS ETHICS SURVEY: WORKPLACE ETHICS IN TRANSITION (2012) at 19. Strong ethical cultures and strong ethics and compliance programs are related, as data show that a well-implemented program helps lead to a strong ethical culture. *Id.* at 34. "Understanding the nature of any gap between the desired culture and the actual culture is a critical first step in determining the nature of any ethics-based risks inside the organization." David Gebler, *The Role of Culture* at 1.7, *in* SOCIETY OF CORPORATE COMPLIANCE AND ETHICS, THE COMPLETE COMPLIANCE AND ETHICS MANUAL (2011). To create an ethical culture, attention must be paid to norms at all levels of an organization, including the "tone at the top," "mood in the middle," and "buzz at the bottom." *Id.* 1.9-1.10.

[313] *See, e.g.,* U.S. SENTENCING GUIDELINES § 8B2.1(2)(B)-(C) (2011).

[314] *Id.*

[315] *Id.*

[316] *Id.*

[317] *See, e.g.,* ETHICS AND COMPLIANCE OFFICER ASSOCIATION FOUNDATION, THE ETHICS AND COMPLIANCE HANDBOOK: A PRACTICAL GUIDE FROM LEADING ORGANIZATIONS (2008) at 13-26 [hereinafter THE ETHICS AND COMPLIANCE HANDBOOK].

[318] *See* U.S. SENTENCING GUIDELINES § 8B2.1(b)(4) (2011).

[319] *See* U.S. SENTENCING GUIDELINES § 8B2.1(b)(6) (2011) ("The organization's compliance and ethics program shall be promoted and enforced consistently throughout the organization through (A) appropriate incentives to perform in accordance with the compliance and ethics program; and (B) appropriate disciplinary measures for engaging in criminal conduct and for failing to take reasonable steps to prevent or detect criminal conduct.").

[320] *See, e.g.,* JOSEPH E. MURPHY, SOCIETY OF CORP. COMPLIANCE AND ETHICS, USING INCENTIVES IN YOUR COMPLIANCE AND ETHICS PROGRAM (2011) at 1; THE ETHICS AND COMPLIANCE HANDBOOK, *supra* note 317, at 111-23.

[321] Stephen M. Cutler, Director, Division of Enforcement, SEC, *Tone at the Top: Getting It Right*, Second Annual General Counsel Roundtable (Dec. 3, 2004), *available at* http://www.sec.gov/news/speech/spch120304smc.htm.

[322] *See, e.g.,* ICC RULES ON COMBATING CORRUPTION, *supra* note 309, at 8.

[323] *See, e.g.* U.S. SENTENCING GUIDELINES § 8B2.1(b)(5)(C); COMPLIANCE 101, *supra* note 302, at 30-33.

[324] Corporate Board Member/FTI Consulting 2009 Legal Study, *Buckle Up. Boards and General Counsel May Face a Bumpy Ride in 2009*, at 5 ("Interestingly, while 67% of general counsel say their company is subject to compliance under the FCPA, 64% of those say there is room for improvement in their FCPA training and compliance programs.").

[325] *See* U.S. SENTENCING GUIDELINES § 8B2.1(b)(5)(B) ("The organization shall take reasonable steps . . . to evaluate periodically the effectiveness of the organization's compliance and ethics program.").

[326] *See, e.g.,* COMPLIANCE 101, *supra* note 302, at 60-61; THE ETHICS AND COMPLIANCE HANDBOOK, *supra* note 317, at 155-60; BUSINESS PRINCIPLES FOR COUNTERING BRIBERY, *supra* note 309, at 14.

[327] *See, e.g.,* Michael M. Mannix and David S. Black., *Compliance Issues in M&A: Performing Diligence on the Target's Ethics and Compliance Program* at 5.71-5.81, *in* SOCIETY OF CORPORATE COMPLIANCE AND ETHICS, THE COMPLETE COMPLIANCE AND ETHICS MANUAL (2011).

[328] Complaint, SEC v. Syncor International Corp., *supra* note 190; Criminal Information, United States v. Syncor Taiwan, Inc., *supra* note 189.

[329] U.S. DEPT. OF JUSTICE, FCPA OP. RELEASE 08-02 (June 13, 2008), *available at* http://justice.gov/criminal/fraud/fcpa/opinion/2008/0802.pdf.

[330] Complaint, SEC v. Rae Sys., Inc., *supra* note 92; Non-Pros. Agreement, *In re Rae Sys. Inc.*, *supra* note 92.

[331] U.S. DEPT. OF COMMERCE, BUSINESS ETHICS: A MANUAL FOR MANAGING A RESPONSIBLE BUSINESS ENTERPRISE IN EMERGING MARKET ECONOMIES (2004), *available at* http://www.ita.doc.gov/goodgovernance/adobe/bem_manual.pdf.

[332] U.S. DEPT. OF STATE, FIGHTING GLOBAL CORRUPTION: BUSINESS RISK MANAGEMENT (2d ed. 2001), *available at* http://www.ogc.doc.gov/pdfs/Fighting_Global_Corruption.pdf.

[333] *See* HARMONISING ANTI-CORRUPTION COMPLIANCE, *supra* note 302, at 46 ("Anti-corruption compliance is becoming more and more harmonised worldwide.").

[334] OECD GOOD PRACTICE GUIDANCE, *supra* note 309.

[335] APEC ANTI-CORRUPTION CODE, *supra* note 309.

[336] ICC RULES ON COMBATING CORRUPTION, *supra* note 309.

[337] BUSINESS PRINCIPLES FOR COUNTERING BRIBERY, *supra* note 309.

[338] THE TEN PRINCIPLES, *supra* note 309.

[339] INTEGRITY COMPLIANCE GUIDELINES, *supra* note 309.

[340] PARTNERING AGAINST CORRUPTION, *supra* note 309.

[341] 15 U.S.C. §§ 78dd-2(g)(1)(A), 78dd-3(e)(1)(A), 78ff(c)(1)(A).

[342] 15 U.S.C. §§ 78dd-2(g)(2)(A), 78dd-3(e)(2)(A), 78ff(c)(2)(A).

[343] 15 U.S.C. § 78ff(a).

[344] 15 U.S.C. § 78ff(a).

[345] 18 U.S.C. § 3571(d); *see Southern Union v. United States*, 132 S. Ct. 2344, 2350-51 & n.4 (2012).

[346] 15 U.S.C. §§ 78dd-2(g)(3), 78dd-3(e)(3), 78ff(c)(3).

[347] The U.S. Sentencing Guidelines are promulgated by the U.S. Sentencing Commission:

> The United States Sentencing Commission ("Commission") is an independent agency in the judicial branch composed of seven voting and two non-voting *ex-officio* members. Its principal purpose is to establish sentencing policies and practices for the federal criminal justice system that will assure the ends of justice by promulgating detailed guidelines prescribing the appropriate sentences for offenders convicted of federal crimes. The Guidelines and policy statements promulgated by the Commission are issued pursuant to Section 994(a) of Title 28, United States Code.

U.S. SENTENCING GUIDELINES § 1A1.1 (2011).

[348] *Id.* at ch. 3-5.

[349] *Id.* § 2C1.1.

[350] *Id.* § 2C1.1(b).

[351] *Id.* § 3B1.1.

[352] *Id.* at ch. 4, § 5A.

[353] *Id.* § 2B1.1(b)(10)(B), 2B1.1(b)(18)(A).

[354] *Id.* § 8C2.4 (a).

[355] *Id.* § 8C2.5.

[356] *Id.* § 8C2.5(f), 8C2.5(g).

[357] DOJ has exercised this civil authority in limited circumstances in the last thirty years. *See, e.g.,* United States & SEC v. KPMG Siddharta Siddharta & Harsono, *et al.*, No. 01-cv-3105 (S.D. Tex. 2001) (entry of injunction barring company from future FCPA violations based on allegations that company paid bribes to Indonesian tax official in order to reduce the company's tax assessment); United States v. Metcalf & Eddy, Inc., No. 99-cv-12566 (D. Mass. 1999) (entry of injunction barring company from future FCPA violations and requiring maintenance of compliance program based on allegations that it paid excessive marketing and promotional expenses such as airfare, travel expenses, and per diem to an Egyptian official and his family); United States v. American Totalisator Co. Inc., No. 93-cv-161 (D. Md. 1993) (entry of injunction barring company from future FCPA violations based on allegations that it paid money to its Greek agent with knowledge that all or some of the money paid would be offered, given, or promised to Greek foreign officials in connection with sale of company's system and spare parts); United States v. Eagle Bus Manufacturing, Inc., No. 91-cv-171 (S.D. Tex. 1991) (entry of injunction barring company from future FCPA violations based on allegations that employees of the company participated in

bribery scheme to pay foreign officials of Saskatchewan's state-owned transportation company $50,000 CAD in connection with sale of buses); United States v. Carver, *et al.*, No. 79-cv-1768 (S.D. Fla. 1979) (entry of injunction barring company from future FCPA violations based on allegations that Carver and Holley, officers and shareholders of Holcar Oil Corp., paid $1.5 million to Qatar foreign official to secure an oil drilling concession agreement); United States v. Kenny, *et al.*, No. 79-cv-2038 (D.D.C. 1979) (in conjunction with criminal proceeding, entry of injunction barring company from future FCPA violations for providing illegal financial assistance to political party to secure renewal of stamp distribution agreement).

358 15 U.S.C. §§ 78dd-2(g)(1)(B), 78dd-3(e)(1)(B), 78ff(c)(1)(B); *see also* 17 C.F.R. § 201.1004 (providing adjustments for inflation).

359 15 U.S.C. §§ 78dd-2(g)(2)(B), 78dd-3(e)(2)(B), 78ff(c)(2)(B); *see also* 17 C.F.R. § 201.1004 (providing adjustments for inflation).

360 15 U.S.C. §§ 78dd-2(g)(3), 78dd-3(e)(3), 78ff(c)(3); *see also* 17 C.F.R. § 201.1004 (providing adjustments for inflation).

361 Section 21(B)(b) of the Exchange Act, 15 U.S.C. § 78u(d)(3); *see also* 17 C.F.R. § 201.1004 (providing adjustments for inflation).

362 *See* Securities Enforcement Remedies and Penny Stock Reform Act of 1990, Pub. L. No. 101-429, 104 Stat. 931 §§ 202, 301, 401, and 402 (codified in scattered sections of Title 15 of the United States Code).

363 48 C.F.R. §§ 9.406-2, 9.407-2.

364 48 C.F.R. § 9.402(b).

365 *See* 48 C.F.R. §§ 9.406-1, 9.407-1(b)(2). Section 9.406-1 sets forth the following non-exhaustive list of factors:

> (1) Whether the contractor had effective standards of conduct and internal control systems in place at the time of the activity which constitutes cause for debarment or had adopted such procedures prior to any Government investigation of the activity cited as a cause for debarment.
> (2) Whether the contractor brought the activity cited as a cause for debarment to the attention of the appropriate Government agency in a timely manner.
> (3) Whether the contractor fully investigated the circumstances surrounding the cause for debarment and, if so, made the result of the investigation available to the debarring official.
> (4) Whether the contractor cooperated fully with Government agencies during the investigation and any court or administrative action.
> (5) Whether the contractor has paid or has agreed to pay all criminal, civil, and administrative liability for the improper activity, including any investigative or administrative costs incurred by the Government, and has made or agreed to make full restitution.
> (6) Whether the contractor has taken appropriate disciplinary action against the individuals responsible for the activity which constitutes cause for debarment.
> (7) Whether the contractor has implemented or agreed to implement remedial measures, including any identified by the Government.
> (8) Whether the contractor has instituted or agreed to institute new or revised review and control procedures and ethics training programs.
> (9) Whether the contractor has had adequate time to eliminate the circumstances within the contractor's organization that led to the cause for debarment.
> (10) Whether the contractor's management recognizes and understands the seriousness of the misconduct giving rise to the cause for debarment and has implemented programs to prevent recurrence.

366 48 C.F.R. § 9.406-1(a).

367 Exec. Order No. 12,549, 51 Fed. Reg. 6,370 (Feb. 18, 1986); Exec. Order No. 12,689, 54 Fed. Reg. 34131 (Aug. 18, 1989).

368 48 C.F.R. § 9.407-2(b).

369 USAM § 9-28.1300 (2008).

370 *See, e.g.*, AFRICAN DEVELOPMENT BANK GROUP, INTEGRITY

AND ANTI-CORRUPTION PROGRESS REPORT 2009-2010 7, 14 ("As the premier financial development institution in Africa, the AfDB is determined to root out misconduct, fraud and corruption within its own ranks as well as in the implementation of the projects it finances. In order to do so, the Bank created an anti-corruption and fraud investigation division in November 2005 as its sole investigative body. The unit became operational in June 2006 and commenced investigations in January 2007. . . . Investigations conducted by the IACD [Integrity and Anti-Corruption Department] are not criminal proceedings; they are administrative in nature. Sanctions range from personnel disciplinary actions, such as separation, to loan cancellation and debarment for contractors, which can be temporary or permanent."), *available at* http://www.afdb.org/fileadmin/uploads/afdb/Documents/Publications/Integrity%20and%20Anti-Corruption.pdf; The World Bank Group, *Procurement: Sanctions Committee* ("The World Bank's debarment process was first formulated in July, 1996, and the Sanctions Committee was established in November 1998 to review allegations and recommend sanctions to the President. Written procedures were issued in August 2001 and are posted on the Bank's website, along with the sanction actions."), *available at* http://web.worldbank.org/WBSITE/EXTERNAL/PROJECTS/PROCUREMENT/0,,contentMDK:5000 2288~pagePK:84271~piPK:84287~theSitePK:84266,00.html.

371 *See* African Development Bank Group, Asian Development Bank, European Bank for Reconstruction and Development, Inter-American Development Bank Group and World Bank Group, *Agreement for Mutual Enforcement of Debarment Decisions* (Apr. 9, 2010), *available at* http://siteresources.worldbank.org/NEWS/Resources/AgreementForMutualEnforcementofDebarmentDecisions.pdf.

372 *Id.*; *see also* The World Bank Group, *Cross-Debarment Accord Steps Up Fight Against Corruption* (Apr. 9, 2010) ("'With today's cross-debarment agreement among development banks, a clear message on anticorruption is being delivered: Steal and cheat from one, get punished by all,' said World Bank Group President Robert B. Zoellick."), *available at* http://web.worldbank.org/WBSITE/EXTERNAL/NEWS/0,,contentMDK:2 2535805~pagePK:64257043~piPK:437376~theSitePK:4607,00.html.

373 22 C.F.R. §§ 126.7(a)(3)-(4), 120.27(a)(6).

374 Authority under the AECA is delegated to the DDTC. *See* 22 C.F.R. § 120.1(a).

375 22 U.S.C. § 2778(g)(1)(A)(vi), (g)(3)(B).

376 22 C.F.R. § 127.7(c).

377 *See supra* note 286.

378 *See* Gary G. Grindler, Acting Dep. Att'y Gen., U.S. Dept. of Justice, Mem. to the Heads of Department Components and United States Attorneys on Additional Guidance on the Use of Monitors in Deferred Prosecution Agreements and Non-Prosecution (May 25, 2010), *available at* http://www.justice.gov/dag/dag-memo-guidance-monitors.pdf; Lanny A. Breuer, Assist. Att'y Gen., Dep't of Justice, Mem. to All Criminal Division Personnel on Selection of Monitors in Criminal Division Matters (June 24, 2009), *available at* http://www.justice.gov/criminal/fraud/fcpa/docs/response3-supp-appx-3.pdf; *see also* Craig S. Morford, Acting Dep. Att'y Gen., U.S. Dept. of Justice, Mem. to the Heads of Department Components and United States Attorneys on Selection and Use of Monitors in Deferred Prosecution Agreements and Non-Prosecution Agreements with Corporations (Mar. 7, 2008), *available at* http://www.justice.gov/dag/morford-useofmonitorsmemo-03072008.pdf.

379 Historically, DOJ had, on occasion, agreed to DPAs with companies that were not filed with the court. That is no longer the practice of DOJ.

380 USAM § 9-27.230.

381 USAM § 9-27.230.B.

382 DOJ has recently declined matters where some or all of the following

circumstances were present: (1) a corporation voluntarily and fully disclosed the potential misconduct; (2) corporate principles voluntarily engaged in interviews with DOJ and provided truthful and complete information about their conduct; (3) a parent company conducted extensive pre-acquisition due diligence of potentially liable subsidiaries and engaged in significant remediation efforts post-acquisition; (4) a company provided information about its extensive compliance policies, procedures, and internal controls; (5) a company agreed to a civil resolution with the Securities and Exchange Commission while also demonstrating that criminal declination was appropriate; (6) only a single employee was involved in the improper payments; and (7) the improper payments involved minimal funds compared to overall business revenues.

[383] *See* Criminal Information, *United States v. Peterson, supra* note 8, Press Release, U.S. Dept. of Justice, Former Morgan Stanley Managing Director Pleads Guilty for Role in Evading Internal Controls Required by FCPA (Apr. 25, 2012), *available at* http://www.justice.gov/opa/pr/2012/April/12-crm-534.html ("After considering all the available facts and circumstances, including that Morgan Stanley constructed and maintained a system of internal controls, which provided reasonable assurances that its employees were not bribing government officials, the Department of Justice declined to bring any enforcement action against Morgan Stanley related to Peterson's conduct. The company voluntarily disclosed this matter and has cooperated throughout the department's investigation."); *see also* Press Release, U.S. Sec. and Exchange Comm., SEC Charges Former Morgan Stanley Executive with FCPA Violations and Investment Adviser Fraud (Apr. 25, 2012), *available at* http://www.sec.gov/news/press/2012/2012-78.htm ("Morgan Stanley, which is not charged in the matter, cooperated with the SEC's inquiry and conducted a thorough internal investigation to determine the scope of the improper payments and other misconduct involved.").

[384] SEC Rules of Practice, 17 C.F.R. § 201.102(e).

[385] Deferred Pros. Agreement, In the Matter of Tenaris, S.A. (May 17, 2011), *available at* http://www.sec.gov/news/press/2011/2011-112-dpa.pdf; *see also* Press Release, U.S. Sec. and Exchange Comm., Tenaris to Pay $5.4 Million in SEC's First-Ever Deferred Prosecution Agreement (May 17, 2011), *available at* http://www.sec.gov/news/press/2011/2011-112.htm.

[386] *See* Non-Pros. Agreement, In re Tenaris, S.A. (May 17, 2011), *available at* http://www.justice.gov/criminal/fraud/fcpa/cases/tenaris-sa/2011-03-14-tenaris.pdf.

[387] *See* U.S. Sec. and Exchange Comm., Enforcement Manual § 6.2.3. (March 9, 2012), *available at* http://www.sec-gov/divisions/enforce/enforcementmanual.pdf.

[388] *See id.* § 6.2.4.

[389] *See id.* § 2.6.

[390] 18 U.S.C. § 1514A(c).

[391] 18 U.S.C. § 1513(e).

[392] 15 U.S.C. § 78u-6(a)(3). The new provision defines "original information" to mean information that:
> (A) is derived from the independent knowledge or analysis of a whistleblower; (B) is not known to the Commission from any other source, unless the whistleblower is the original source of the information; and (C) is not exclusively derived from an allegation made in a judicial or administrative hearing, in a governmental report, hearing, audit, or investigation, or from the news media, unless the whistleblower is a source of the information.

[393] 15 U.S.C. § 78u-6; *see also* Dodd-Frank Wall Street Reform and Consumer Protection Act, Pub. L. No. 111-203, § 922, 124 Stat. 1376, 1841-49 (2010).

[394] For detailed information about the program, including eligibility requirements and certain limitations that apply, see Section 922 of the Dodd-Frank Wall Street Reform and Consumer Protection Act, *available at* http://www.sec.gov/about/offices/owb/dodd-frank-sec-922.pdf, and the final rules on eligibility, Exchange Act Rule 21F-8, 17 C.F.R. § 240.21F-8.

[395] For example, the rules: (1) make a whistleblower eligible for an award if the whistleblower reports original information internally, and the company informs the SEC about the violations; (2) give whistleblowers 120 days to report information to the SEC after first reporting internally and still be treated as if he or she had reported to the SEC

at the earlier reporting date , thus preserving their "place in line" for a possible whistleblower award from the SEC; and (3) provide that a whistleblower's voluntary participation in an entity's internal compliance and reporting systems is a factor that can increase the amount of an award, and that a whistleblower's interference with internal compliance and reporting system is a factor that can decrease the amount of an award. *See* Exchange Act Rule 21F, 17 C.F.R. § 240.21F.

[396] *See* Exchange Act Rule 21F-7(b), 17 C.F.R. § 240.21F-7(b).

[397] For example, SEC staff will not disclose a whistleblower's identity in response to requests under the Freedom of Information Act. However, there are limits on SEC's ability to shield a whistleblower's identity, and in certain circumstances SEC must disclose it to outside entities. For example, in an administrative or court proceeding, SEC may be required to produce documents or other information that would reveal the whistleblower's identity. In addition, as part of ongoing SEC investigatory responsibilities, SEC staff may use information provided by a whistleblower during the course of the investigation. In appropriate circumstances, SEC may also provide information, subject to confidentiality requirements, to other governmental or regulatory entities. Exchange Act Rule 21F-7(a), 17 C.F.R. 240.21F-7(a).

[398] Although SEC does not have an opinion procedure release process, it has declared its decision to follow the guidance announced through DOJ's FCPA Opinion Release Procedure. U.S. Sec. and Exchange Comm., SEC Release No. 34-17099 (Aug. 29, 1980), *available at* http://www.sec.gov/news/digest/1980/dig082980.pdf. SEC Release No. 34-17099 stated that, to encourage issuers to take advantage of the DOJ's FCPA Review Procedure, as a matter of prosecutorial discretion, SEC would "not take enforcement action alleging violations of Section 30A in any case where an issuer has sought and obtained an FCPA Review letter from the Department, prior to May 31, 1981, stating that the Department will not take enforcement action under Section 30A with respect to the transaction involved." *Id.* The release further noted that it would revisit this policy once the DOJ had evaluated the results of the FCPA Review Procedure after its first year of operation. A second release stated that the SEC would continue to adhere to the policy announced in Release No. 34-17099. U.S. Sec. and Exchange Comm., SEC Release No. 34-18255 (Nov. 13, 1981), *available at* http://www.sec.gov/news/digest/1981/dig111381.pdf.

[399] Both DOJ's opinion procedure releases (from 1993 to present) and review procedure releases (from 1980-1992) are available at http://www.justice.gov/criminal/fraud/fcpa/opinion.

[400] The full regulations relating to DOJ's opinion procedure are available at http://www.justice.gov/criminal/fraud/fcpa/docs/frgncrpt.pdf.

[401] 28 C.F.R. § 80.1.

[402] 28 C.F.R. § 80.3.

[403] 28 C.F.R. § 80.12 ("Neither the submission of a request for an FCPA Opinion, its pendency, nor the issuance of an FCPA Opinion, shall in any way alter the responsibility of an issuer to comply with the accounting requirements of 15 U.S.C. 78m(b)(2) and (3).").

[404] 28 C.F.R. § 80.4.

[405] 28 C.F.R. § 80.5.

[406] 28 C.F.R. § 80.6.

[407] 28 C.F.R. § 80.14(a). This non-disclosure policy applies regardless of whether DOJ responds to the request or the party withdraws the request before receiving a response. *Id.*

[408] 28 C.F.R. § 80.6.

[409] 28 C.F.R. § 80.2.

[410] In connection with any request for an FCPA opinion, DOJ may conduct whatever independent investigation it believes appropriate. 28 C.F.R. § 80.7.

[411] 28 C.F.R. § 80.15. Once a request is withdrawn, it has no effect. However, DOJ reserves the right to retain a copy of any FCPA opinion request, documents, and information submitted during the opinion release procedure for any governmental purpose, subject to the restrictions on disclosures in 28 C.F.R. § 80.14.

[412] 28 C.F.R. § 80.8.

[413] 28 C.F.R. § 80.7. "Such additional information, if furnished orally, must be confirmed in writing promptly. The same person who signed the initial request must sign the written, supplemental information and must again certify it to be a true, correct and complete disclosure of the requested information." *Id.*

[414] 28 C.F.R. § 80.9 ("No oral clearance, release or other statement

purporting to limit the enforcement discretion of the Department of Justice may be given. The requesting issuer or domestic concern may rely only upon a written FCPA opinion letter signed by the Attorney General or his designee.").

[415] 28 C.F.R. § 80.8. FCPA opinions do not bind or obligate any agency other than DOJ. They also do not affect the requesting party's obligations to any other agency or under any statutory or regulatory provision other than those specifically cited in the particular FCPA opinion. 28 C.F.R. § 80.11. If the conduct for which an FCPA opinion is requested is subject to approval by any other agency, such FCPA opinion may not be taken to indicate DOJ's views on any legal or factual issues before that other agency. 28 C.F.R. § 80.13.

[416] 28 C.F.R. § 80.10. DOJ can rebut this presumption by a preponderance of the evidence. A court determining whether the presumption has been rebutted weighs all relevant factors, including whether the submitted information was accurate and complete and the activity was within the scope of conduct specified in the request. *Id.* As of September 2012, DOJ has never pursued an enforcement action against a party for conduct that formed the basis of an FCPA opinion stating that the prospective conduct would violate DOJ's present enforcement policy.

[417] As a general matter, DOJ normally anonymizes much of the information in its publicly released opinions and includes the general nature and circumstances of the proposed conduct. DOJ does not release the identity of any foreign sales agents or other types of identifying information. 28 C.F.R. § 80.14(b). However, DOJ may release the identity of the requesting party, the foreign country in which the proposed conduct is to take place, and any actions DOJ took in response to the FCPA opinion request. *Id.* If a party believes that an opinion contains proprietary information, it may request that DOJ remove or anonymize those portions of the opinion before it is publicly released. 28 C.F.R. § 80.14(c).

[418] 28 C.F.R. § 80.16.

APPENDIX
Endnotes

FCPA Unit
Fraud Section, Criminal Division
U.S. Department of Justice
1400 New York Avenue, N.W.
Washington, DC 20005
http://www.justice.gov/criminal/fraud/fcpa/

FCPA Unit
Enforcement Division
U.S. Securities & Exchange Commission
100 F Street, NE
Washington, DC 20549
http://www.sec.gov/spotlight/fcpa.shtml

APPENDIX 5

DOJ FCPA Opinion Releases Index

Foreign Corrupt Practices Act
U.S. Department of Justice
Opinion Procedure Releases
1993 through December 2012

FCPA Opinion Procedure Release No.	Date	Subject	Country
93-01	04/20/1993	COMMERCIAL Major commercial organization proposing to supply management services to entity owned by government of a former Eastern Bloc country.	Former Eastern Bloc Country
93-02	05/11/1993	DEFENSE American company seeking to enter into a sales agreement to sell defense equipment to foreign country's armed forces.	Foreign Country
94-01	05/13/1994	CONSULTING American company and wholly-owned subsidiary seeking to enter into a consulting relationship with foreign individual who is general director of a state-owned enterprise.	Foreign Country
95-01	01/11/1995	DONATION US-based energy company planning to acquire and operate a plant in a South Asian country and make a prospective donation to charitable organization and foreign public limited liability company near the plant.	South Asian Nation

FCPA Opinion Procedure Release No.	Date	Subject	Country
95-02	09/14/1995	OFFSET OBLIGATIONS Two American companies seeking to enter into two transactions in a foreign country have to fulfill off-set obligations in foreign country as a result of contracts entered.	Foreign Country
96-01	11/25/1996	NON-PROFIT FUNDING Non-profit corporation seeking to sponsor and provide funds to representatives from ten foreign countries to attend environmental protection training courses in the United States.	Ten Regional Nations
96-02	11/25/1996	MARKETING US company seeking to manufacture and sell off equipment used in commercial and military aircraft to state-owned enterprise of foreign country.	Foreign Country
97-01	02/27/1997	COMMERCIAL Wholly-owned subsidiary of US company submitting a bid to sell and service high technology equipment with private company in foreign country.	Foreign Country
97-02	11/05/1997	DONATION US-based utility company seeking to donate funds to government entity in Asian country to build a school near plant to be built by US-based utility company.	Asian Nation
98-01	02/23/1998	ENVIRONMENTAL CLEAN-UP US-based industrial and service company seeking to arrange to pay environmental contamination liability imposed on it by the Nigerian government and to clean up contaminated site.	Nigeria

FCPA Opinion Procedure Release No.	Date	Subject	Country
98-02	08/05/1998	MILITARY Wholly-owned subsidiary of US company submitting a bid to foreign-owned entity to sell and service military training program and enter into several agreements with private company in same foreign country.	Foreign Country
00-01	03/29/2000	COMPENSATION US law firm seeking to provide payments and benefits to foreign partner of a US law firm, who took a leave of absence from the law firm to become a high-ranking Foreign Government Official.	Foreign Country
01-01	05/24/2001	COMMERCIAL US company seeking to enter into a joint venture with a French company which is contributing pre-existing contracts and transactions to joint venture at risk *if* any of these contracts procured by French company was obtained or maintained through bribery.	France
01-02	07/18/2001	COMMERCIAL US company seeking to avoid any impropriety in situation where chairman of foreign company (who is also an advisor to his country's senior government official) which will form a consortium with a partially owned US company will be bidding on prospective government business.	Foreign Country
01-03	12/11/2001	COMMERCIAL Wholly-owned US subsidiary seeking to submit a bid to a foreign government for sale of equipment to government with the assistance of a foreign dealer who informed it that payments have been made or would be made by dealer to government officials so that bid is accepted.	Foreign Country

FCPA Opinion Procedure Release No.	Date	Subject	Country
03-01	01/15/2003	ACQUISITION OF COMPANY US issuer while acquiring another US company with both US and foreign subsidiaries learned that officers of foreign subsidiary authorized and made payments to foreign state owned entities to obtain or retain business.	Foreign Country
04-01	01/06/2004	EVENT SPONSORING US law firm seeking to sponsor, present and pay costs for a Comparative Law Seminar on Labor & Employment Law in conjunction with a ministry of the People's Republic of China.	People's Republic of China
04-02	07/12/2004	ACQUISITION OF COMPANIES Investment group acquiring certain companies and assets from ABB Ltd. relating to upstream oil, gas and petrochemical businesses, which had been charged with FCPA violations relating to transactions involving business in several foreign countries, including Nigeria.	Foreign Countries, including Nigeria
04-03	06/14/2004	EVENT SPONSORING American law firm sponsoring and paying for travel expenses related to a trip to US *for* 12 ministry officials from the People's Republic of China to discuss employment issues.	People's Republic of China
04-04	09/03/2004	EVENT SPONSORING US company providing funds for a Study Tour of foreign officials who are members of committee drafting insurance regulations in foreign country.	Foreign Country

FCPA Opinion Procedure Release No.	Date	Subject	Country
06-01	10/16/2006	BENEVOLENT CONTRIBUTION Delaware corporation with headquarters in Switzerland seeking to contribute $25,000 to a regional Customs department or Ministry of Finance in an African country as part of a pilot project to improve local enforcement of anti-counterfeiting laws.	African Nation
06-02	12/31/2006	RETENTION OF LAW FIRM Wholly-owned US subsidiary in foreign country seeking to retain law firm to aid in obtaining foreign exchange from government agency by preparing application and representing company for a substantial flat fee.	Foreign Country
07-01	07/24/2007	EDUCATIONAL FUNDING Issuer seeking to cover domestic expenses for a trip to US of a six-person delegation of the government of an Asian country for educational and promotional tour of the Issuer's US operations sites.	Asian Nation
07-02	09/11/2007	EDUCATIONAL FUNDING US insurance company proposing to pay domestic expenses of six junior mid-level officials of a foreign government for education programs at its US headquarters in order to familiarize the officials with operation of the US insurance company.	Foreign Country
07-03	12/21/2007	PAYMENT OF LEGAL EXPENSES Permanent resident of the US proposing to make a payment required by a family court judge in an Asian country to cover litigation-related costs.	Asian Nation

FCPA Opinion Procedure Release No.	Date	Subject	Country
08-01	01/15/2008	INVESTMENT Wholly-owned foreign subsidiary of US issuer seeking to undertake a prospective majority investment in a foreign company which is responsible for managing certain public services for a major foreign municipality.	Foreign Country
08-02	06/13/2008	ACQUISITION OF COMPANY Halliburton Company and its subsidiaries considering making an additional bid to acquire the entire share capital of a company based in the United Kingdom, a company which is traded on the London Stock Exchange and operates in over 50 countries.	United Kingdom
08-03	07/11/2008	FUNDING FOR JOURNALISTS TRACE International, Inc. proposing to pay certain expenses for approximately 20 journalists employed by media outlets based in the People's Republic of China to enable them to attend a press conference being held by TRACE in Shanghai.	People's Republic of China
09-01	08/08/2009	MEDICAL SAMPLES A medical device designer and manufacturer proposing to provide a foreign government, not a foreign official, free sample devices, each worth $19,000.	Foreign Country
10-01	04-19-2010	DUAL EMPLOYMENT Contract with US government agency to help construct a certain facility in a foreign country, which along with US government agency approved facility director who is to earn $60,000 over a year while also a paid officer of an agency of the foreign country.	Foreign Country

FCPA Opinion Procedure Release No.	Date	Subject	Country
10-02	04-16-2010	GRANTS Non-profit, US-based microfinance institution (MFI) whose mission is to provide loans and other beneficial services to world's lowest-income entrepreneurs and contemplated grants to a short list of institutions with potential FCPA issues.	Foreign Country
10-03	09-01-2010	CONSULTANT Engagement of consultant represents by "domestic concern"/ limited partnership where consultant has separate and unrelated representation of foreign government.	Foreign Country
11-01	06-30-2011	TRAVEL & LODGING Travel to US and lodging for foreign officials to learn more about adoption services business.	Foreign Countries
12-01	9-18-2012	CONSULTANT Royal Family Member Partner in a consultancy providing lobbying services in the United States.	Foreign Countries
12-02	10-18-2012	TRAVEL & LODGING Travel to and hosting in the US 18 government officials to learn more about processing adoptions in foreign countries.	Foreign Countries
13-01	12-19-2013	CHARITABLE Requestor, a partner in a law firm, sought to pay medical expenses of $13,500–$20,500 for a foreign official's daughter.	Foreign Country
14-01	03-17-2014	SHAREHOLDINGS Purchase of foreign shareholder/ now foreign government official's minority interest in an investment bank where he had worked prior to accepting a senior government post.	Foreign Country

FCPA Opinion Procedure Release No.	Date	Subject	Country
14-02	11-07-2014	PRE-ACQUISITION DUE DILIGENCE Pre-acquisition due diligence identified improper payments which lacked US jurisdiction. Discussion of successor criminal liability.	Foreign Country

APPENDIX 6

U.K. Serious Fraud Office and Crown Prosecution Service Deferred Prosecution Agreements code of practice

Deferred Prosecution Agreements Code of Practice

Crime and Courts Act 2013

Deferred Prosecution Agreements
Code of Practice

Crime and Courts Act 2013

CONTENTS

Introduction

This Deferred Prosecution Agreement Code of Practice ("DPA Code") is issued by the Director of Public Prosecutions and Director of the Serious Fraud Office pursuant to paragraph 6(1) of Schedule 17 to the Crime and Courts Act 2013 ("the Act").

Prosecutors should have regard to this DPA Code when:

i. Negotiating Deferred Prosecution Agreements ("DPAs") with an organisation ("P") whom the prosecutor is considering prosecuting for an offence specified in the Act;

ii. Applying to the court for the approval of a DPA;

and

iii. Overseeing DPAs after their approval by the court, in particular in relation to variation, breach, termination and completion.

1.1. A DPA is a discretionary tool created by the Act to provide a way of responding to alleged criminal conduct. The prosecutor may invite P to enter into negotiations to agree a DPA as an alternative to prosecution.

1.2. In order to enter a DPA the prosecutor is to apply the following two stage test. Prosecutors must be satisfied and record that:

EVIDENTIAL STAGE

i. Either:
a) the evidential stage of the Full Code Test in the Code for Crown Prosecutors is satisfied or, if this is not met, that
b) there is at least a reasonable suspicion based upon some admissible evidence that P has committed the offence, and there are reasonable grounds for believing that a continued investigation would provide further admissible evidence within a reasonable period of time, so that all the evidence together would be capable of establishing a realistic prospect of conviction in accordance with the Full Code Test.

And

PUBLIC INTEREST STAGE

ii. The public interest would be properly served by the prosecutor not prosecuting but instead entering into a DPA with P in accordance with the criteria set out below.

1.3 The Prosecutor should first consider whether the test in paragraph 1.2 i a) is met. If it is not met consideration may be given to the test under paragraph 1.2 i b).

1.4 For the purposes of 1.2 i b) a reasonable time period will depend on all the facts and circumstances of the case, including its size, type and complexity.

1.5 If a DPA is considered appropriate by the relevant Director, having determined that either limb of the evidential stage is met, and that the public interest is best served by entering into a DPA, the prosecutor will (where the court approves the DPA) prefer an indictment. The indictment will however then immediately be suspended pending the satisfactory performance, or otherwise, of the DPA.

1.6 In cases where neither limb of the evidential stage can be met by the conclusion of any DPA negotiations and it is not considered appropriate to continue the criminal investigation, the prosecutor should consider whether a Civil Recovery Order is appropriate. Attention is drawn to the Attorney General's guidance to prosecuting bodies on their asset recovery powers under the Proceeds of Crime Act 2002, issued 5 November 2009.

NEGOTIATIONS

2.1   An invitation to negotiate a DPA is a matter for the prosecutor's discretion. P has no right to be invited to negotiate a DPA. The SFO and the CPS are first and foremost prosecutors and it will only be in specific circumstances deemed by their Directors to be appropriate that they will decide to offer a DPA instead of pursuing the full prosecution of the alleged conduct. In many cases, criminal prosecution will continue to be the appropriate course of action. An invitation to enter DPA discussions is not a guarantee that a DPA will be offered at the conclusion of the discussions.

2.2   Where the prosecutor is satisfied that:

i.   either the evidential stage of the Full Code Test in the Code for Crown Prosecutors is met, or there is a reasonable suspicion based upon some admissible evidence that P has committed an offence;

ii.   the full extent of the alleged offending has been identified;

and

iii.   the public interest would likely be met by a DPA,

then the prosecutor may initiate DPA negotiations with any P who is being investigated with a view to prosecution in connection with an offence specified in the Act.

2.3   When considering whether a DPA may be appropriate the prosecutor will have regard to existing Codes of Practice and Guidance, in particular:

i.   The Code for Crown Prosecutors;

ii.   The Joint Prosecution Guidance on Corporate Prosecutions ("the Corporate Prosecution Guidance");

iii.   Bribery Act 2010: Joint Prosecution Guidance ("the Bribery Act Guidance");

iv.   The DPA Code.

2.4   Where either limb of the evidential stage is passed, the prosecutor must consider whether or not a prosecution is in the public interest. The more serious the offence, the more likely it is that prosecution will be required in the public interest. Indicators of seriousness include not just the value of any gain or loss, but also the risk of harm to the public, to unidentified victims, shareholders, employees and creditors and to the stability and integrity of financial markets and international trade. The impact of the offending in other countries, and not just the consequences in the UK, should be taken into account.

2.5   Prosecutors must balance factors for and against prosecution carefully and fairly. Public interest factors that can affect the decision to prosecute usually depend on the seriousness of the offence, which includes the culpability of P and the harm to the victim.
A prosecution will usually take place unless there are public interest factors against prosecution which clearly outweigh those tending in favour of prosecution.

2.6   In applying the public interest factors when considering whether to charge, seek to enter a DPA or take no further criminal action the prosecutor undertakes a balancing exercise of the factors that tend to support prosecution and those that do not. This is an exercise of discretion. Which factors are considered relevant and what weight is given to each are matters for the individual prosecutor. It is quite possible that one public interest factor alone may outweigh a number of other factors which tend in the opposite direction. Decisions will be made on an individual case by case basis.

4

2. Factors that the prosecutor may take into account when deciding whether to enter into a DPA

2.7   Prosecutors should have regard when considering the public interest stage to the UK's commitment to abide by the OECD Convention on "Combating Bribery of Foreign Public Officials in International Business Transactions" in particular Article 5. Investigation and prosecution of the bribery of a foreign public official should not be influenced by considerations of national economic interest, the potential effect upon relations with another State or the identity of the natural or legal persons involved.

2.8   The prosecutor should have regard to the public interest factors set out in the Code for Crown Prosecutors. In addition the following non-exhaustive factors will be of relevance in deciding whether a prosecution is appropriate or not in order to satisfy the public interest:

2.8.1 Additional public interest factors in favour of prosecution

   i.   A history of similar conduct (including prior criminal, civil and regulatory enforcement actions against P and/or its directors/partners and/or majority shareholders). Failing to prosecute in circumstances where there have been repeated or serious breaches of the law may not be a proportionate response and may not provide adequate deterrent effects.

   ii. The conduct alleged is part of the established business practices of P.

   iii. The offence was committed at a time when P had no or an ineffective corporate compliance programme and it has not been able to demonstrate a significant improvement in its compliance programme since then.

   iv. P has been previously subject to warning, sanctions or criminal charges and had nonetheless failed to take adequate action to prevent future unlawful conduct, or had continued to engage in the conduct.

   v.   Failure to notify the wrongdoing within reasonable time of the offending conduct[1] coming to light.

   vi. Reporting the wrongdoing but failing to verify it, or reporting it knowing or believing it to be inaccurate, misleading or incomplete.

   vii. Significant level of harm caused directly or indirectly to the victims of the wrongdoing or a substantial adverse impact to the integrity or confidence of markets, local or national governments.

2.8.2 Additional public interest factors against prosecution

   i.   Co-operation: Considerable weight may be given to a genuinely proactive approach adopted by P's management team when the offending is brought to their notice, involving within a reasonable time of the offending coming to light reporting P's offending otherwise unknown to the prosecutor and taking remedial actions including, where appropriate, compensating victims. In applying this factor the prosecutor needs to establish whether sufficient information about the operation and conduct of P has been supplied in order to assess whether P has been co-operative. Co-operation will include identifying relevant witnesses, disclosing their accounts and the documents shown to them. Where practicable it will involve making the witnesses available for interview when requested. It will further include providing a report in respect of any internal investigation including source documents.

   ii. A lack of a history of similar conduct involving prior criminal, civil and regulatory enforcement actions against P and/or its directors/partners and/or majority shareholders; The prosecutor should contact relevant regulatory departments (including where applicable those overseas) to ascertain whether there are existing investigations in relation to P and/or its directors/partners and/or majority shareholders;

[1] For what is reasonable see paragraph 2.9 below

iii. The existence of a proactive corporate compliance programme[2] both at the time of offending and at the time of reporting but which failed to be effective in this instance;

iv. The offending represents isolated actions by individuals, for example by a rogue director;

v. The offending is not recent and P in its current form is effectively a different entity from that which committed the offences – for example it has been taken over by another organisation, it no longer operates in the relevant industry or market, P's management team has completely changed, disciplinary action has been taken against all of the culpable individuals, including dismissal where appropriate, or corporate structures or processes have been changed to minimise the risk of a repetition of offending;

vi. A conviction is likely to have disproportionate consequences for P, under domestic law, the law of another jurisdiction including but not limited to that of the European Union, always bearing in mind the seriousness of the offence and any other relevant public interest factors;[3]

vii. A conviction is likely to have collateral effects on the public, P's employees and shareholders or P's and/or institutional pension holders.

2.9   With respect to the "Additional public interest factors against prosecution", at paragraph 2.8.2 i. above:

2.9.1 The prosecutor in giving weight to P's self-report will consider the totality of information that P provides to the prosecutor. It must be remembered that when P self-reports it will have been incriminated by the actions of individuals. It will ordinarily be appropriate that those individuals be investigated and where appropriate prosecuted. P must ensure in its provision of material as part of the self-report that it does not withhold material that would jeopardise an effective investigation and where appropriate prosecution of those individuals. To do so would be a strong factor in favour of prosecution.

2.9.2 The prosecutor will also consider how early P self-reports, the extent that P involves the prosecutor in the early stages of an investigation (for example, in order to discuss work plans, timetabling, or to provide the opportunity to the prosecutor to give direction and where appropriate commence an early criminal investigation where it can use statutory powers in particular against individuals).

2.9.3 The prosecutor will consider whether any actions taken by P by not self-reporting earlier may have prejudiced the investigation into P or the individuals that incriminate P. In particular the prosecutor will critically assess the manner of any internal investigation to determine whether its conduct could have led to material being destroyed or the gathering of first accounts from suspects being delayed to the extent that the opportunity for fabrication has been afforded. Internal investigations which lead to such adverse consequences may militate against the use of DPAs.

2.10   The Bribery Act Guidance provides factors tending in favour of or against prosecution in respect of each offence under the Bribery Act 2010. In doing so it refers to the Code for Crown Prosecutors, the Corporate Prosecution Guidance and unique considerations appropriate to the particular bribery offence being considered. A prosecutor in considering the public interest under the Code for Crown Prosecutors in respect of a bribery offence must therefore also consider the current Bribery Act Guidance offered in respect of the particular offence under consideration.

---

[2] The prosecutor may choose to bring in external resource to assist in the assessment of P's compliance culture and programme for example as described in any self-report.

[3] Any candidate or tenderer (including company directors and any person having powers of representation, decision or control) who has been convicted of fraud relating to the protection of the financial interests of the European Communities, corruption, or a money laundering offence is mandatorily excluded from participation in public contracts within the EU. Discretionary exclusion may follow in respect of a conviction for a criminal offence.

3. Process for invitation to enter into negotiations

3.1 If the prosecutor decides to offer P the opportunity to enter into DPA negotiations, it will do so by way of a formal letter of invitation outlining the basis on which any negotiations will proceed.

3.2 That letter will constitute the beginning of the DPA negotiation period, which period will end on either the withdrawal of one or both parties from the process, or the approval/refusal by the court of a DPA at a final hearing. Neither party will be obliged to give reasons for withdrawal from negotiations. However in the event of withdrawal from negotiations by the prosecutor it will ordinarily be appropriate to provide P with the gist of the reasons for doing so. In some instances this may not be possible without prejudicing the investigation.

3.3 All parties should keep in mind that DPAs are entirely voluntary agreements. The prosecutor is under no obligation to invite P to negotiate a DPA and P is under no obligation to accept that invitation should it be made. The terms of a DPA are similarly voluntary, and neither party is obliged to agree any particular term therein. The Act does not, and this DPA Code cannot, alter the law on legal professional privilege.

3.4 DPA negotiations must be transparent. The prosecutor must:

  i. Ensure that a full and accurate record of negotiations is prepared and retained. It is essential that a full written record is kept of every key action and event in the discussion process, including details of every offer or concession made by each party, and the reasons for every decision taken by the prosecutor. Meetings between the parties should be minuted and the minutes agreed and signed;

  ii. Ensure that the prosecution and P have obtained sufficient information from each other so each can play an informed part in the negotiations;

  iii. Ensure that documentation and any other material relevant to the matters the prosecutor is considering prosecuting is retained by P for any future prosecution;

  iv. Ensure that the proposed DPA placed before the court fully and fairly reflects P's alleged offending; and

  v. The prosecutor must not agree additional matters with P which are not recorded in the DPA and not made known to the court.

THE LETTER OF INVITATION

3.5 In order to initiate the DPA negotiations, the prosecutor will first send P a letter containing:

  i. Confirmation of the prosecutor's decision to offer P the opportunity to enter into DPA negotiations;

  ii. A request for confirmation of whether P wishes to enter into negotiations in accordance with the Act and this DPA Code; and

  iii. A timeframe within which P must notify the prosecutor whether it accepts the invitation to enter into DPA negotiations.

UNDERTAKINGS

3.6 Where P agrees to engage in DPA negotiations, the prosecutor should send P a letter setting out the way in which the discussions will be conducted. This letter should make undertakings in respect of:

  i. the confidentiality of the fact that DPA negotiations are taking place;

  ii. the confidentiality of information provided by the prosecutor and P in the course of the DPA negotiations.

3.7   In doing so the undertaking will make clear:

i.   the use which may be made by the prosecutor of information provided by P pursuant to paragraph 13 of Schedule 17 to the Act;

ii.   that the law in relation to the disclosure of unused material may require the prosecutor to provide information received during the course of DPA negotiations to a defendant in criminal proceedings; and

iii.   that the information may be disclosed as permitted by law.

3.8   The letter should also include:

i.   a statement of the prosecutor's responsibility for disclosure of material pursuant to this DPA Code;

ii.   a warning that the provision by P of inaccurate, misleading or incomplete information where P knew or ought to have known that the information was inaccurate, misleading or incomplete may lead to a prosecution of P:

a.   for an offence consisting of the provision of such inaccurate, misleading or incomplete information, and/or

b.   for an offence or offences which are the subject of an agreed DPA; and

iii.   the practical means by which the discussions will be conducted including appropriate time limits.

3.9   The prosecutor will require P to provide an undertaking:

i.   that information provided by the prosecutor in the course of DPA negotiations will be treated as confidential and will not be disclosed to any other party, other than for the purposes of the DPA negotiations or as required by law; and

ii.   all documentation or other material relevant to the matters the prosecutor is considering prosecuting is retained until P is released from the obligation to do so by the prosecutor.

3.10   In exceptional circumstances and where permitted by law the prosecutor may agree in writing to different terms regarding the confidentiality of information. Ordinarily the decision to vary confidentiality terms will be dealt with on a case by case basis at the point that the disclosure is considered. In deciding whether to make such an exceptional variation, for example in relation to a disclosure of information to third parties, the prosecutor will take into account that statutory and common law safeguards already exist in respect of disclosure of information to third parties.

3.11   Until the issues of confidentiality, use of and retention of information have been agreed to the satisfaction of both parties, and the agreement reflected in signed undertakings, the prosecutor must not continue with the substantive DPA negotiations.

4. Subsequent use of information obtained
by a prosecutor during the DPA negotiation period

4.1 The use to which information obtained by a prosecutor during the DPA negotiation period may subsequently be put is dealt with at paragraph 13 of Schedule 17 to the Act. The use of any particular item is therefore governed by that legislation.

4.2 It is recognised that there is a balance to be struck between encouraging all parties to be able to negotiate freely, and the risk that P may seek knowingly (or when it should have known) to induce the prosecutor to enter into a DPA on an inaccurate, misleading or incomplete basis.

4.3 If P provides inaccurate, misleading or incomplete information where P knew or ought to have known that the information was inaccurate, misleading or incomplete, the prosecutor may instigate fresh proceedings against P for the same alleged offence in accordance with paragraph 11 of Schedule 17 to the Act notwithstanding any DPA that may have been approved.

4.4 There are two contexts within which information obtained by the prosecutor during the DPA negotiation period may subsequently be used.

   i. Where a DPA is approved by the court under paragraph 8 of Schedule 17 to the Act the legislation provides (at paragraph 13 (1) and (2) of Schedule 17) that the statement of facts contained in the DPA may be used in subsequent criminal proceedings as an admission in accordance with section 10 of the Criminal Justice Act 1967.

   ii. Where a DPA has not been concluded and the prosecutor chooses to pursue criminal proceedings against P, the material described in paragraph 13(6) of Schedule 17 to the Act may only be used in the limited circumstances described in paragraphs 13 (4) and (5) of Schedule 17 to the Act.

4.5 Apart from the material described at paragraph 13(6) of Schedule 17 to the Act, there is no limitation on the use to which other information obtained by a prosecutor during the DPA negotiation period may subsequently be put during criminal proceedings brought against P, or against anyone else (so far as the rules of evidence permit).

4.6 By way of non-exhaustive example, if the DPA negotiations fail the following types of document provided to a prosecutor in those negotiations would be available to be used by the prosecutor subject to the rules of evidence in a subsequent prosecution of P:

   i. pre-existing contemporary key documentation such as contracts, accountancy records including payments of any kind, any records evidencing the transfer of money, emails or other communications etc. provided to the prosecutor by P;

   ii. any internal or independent investigation report carried out by P and disclosed to the prosecutor prior to the DPA negotiation period commencing;

   iii. any interview note or witness statement obtained from an employee of P and disclosed to the prosecutor prior to the DPA negotiation period commencing;

   iv. any document obtained by the prosecutor at any time obtained from any source other than P; and

   v. any information obtained by the prosecutor as a result of enquiries made as a result of information provided by P at any time.

5. Unused Material and Disclosure

5.1. Negotiations to enter into a DPA will necessarily take place prior to the institution of proceedings and the statutory disclosure rules will therefore not be engaged at this early stage.

5.2. P should have sufficient information to play an informed part in the negotiations. The purpose of disclosure here is to ensure that negotiations are fair and that P is not misled as to the strength of the prosecution case. The prosecutor must always be alive to the potential need to disclose material in the interests of justice and fairness in the particular circumstances of any case. For instance, disclosure ought to be made of information that might undermine the factual basis of conclusions drawn by P from material disclosed by P. A statement of the prosecutor's duty of disclosure will be included in the terms and conditions letter provided to P at the outset of the negotiations.

5.3. Consideration should be given to reasonable and specific requests for disclosure by P. Where the need for such disclosure is not apparent to the prosecutor, any disclosure may depend on what P chooses to reveal to the prosecutor about its case in order to justify the request.

5.4. The investigator's duty to pursue reasonable lines of inquiry in accordance with the CPIA 1996 Code of Practice is not affected by the introduction of DPAs or the application of this Code. What is reasonable in each case will depend upon the particular circumstances.

5.5. Before the final DPA hearing the prosecutor must obtain from the investigator enquiring into the alleged offence or offences information that will enable the prosecutor to make a written declaration to the court, as required by Criminal Procedure Rule 12.2 (3) (b), namely that:

i. the investigator enquiring into the offence or alleged offences has certified that no information has been supplied which the investigator knows to be inaccurate, misleading or incomplete; and

ii. the prosecutor has complied with the prosecution obligation to disclose material to the defendant.

5.6. To satisfy (ii) above, the prosecutor should request that the investigator provide written certification to the prosecutor that any material retained by the investigator which may satisfy the test for prosecution disclosure as outlined in this DPA Code has been drawn to the attention of the prosecutor.

5.7 Where a DPA is approved by the court and a bill of indictment is preferred upon entering into a DPA, the CPIA will apply. However, the immediate suspension of the indictment will have the effect of immediately suspending with it the disclosure obligations imposed. The statutory disclosure obligations and standard directions providing time limits for compliance will only apply if the suspension is lifted in the event of termination of the DPA and the prosecution of P.

5.8 The disclosure duty of the prosecutor as outlined in this DPA Code is a continuing one and the prosecutor must disclose to P any material that comes to light after the DPA has been agreed which satisfies the test for disclosure above.

6. Statement of facts

6.1. The application must include a statement of facts which must:

i. give particulars relating to each alleged offence;

ii. include details where possible of any financial gain or loss, with reference to key documents that must be attached.

6.2. The parties should resolve any factual issues necessary to allow the court to agree terms of the DPA on a clear, fair and accurate basis. The court does not have the power to adjudicate upon factual differences in DPA proceedings.

6.3. There is no requirement for formal admissions of guilt in respect of the offences charged by the indictment though it will be necessary for P to admit the contents and meaning of key documents referred to in the statement of facts.

6.4. In the event that P is prosecuted for the alleged offence addressed by a court approved DPA, the statement of facts would be admissible against P in accordance with section 10 of the Criminal Justice Act 1967 in any subsequent criminal proceedings.

7. Terms

7.1. A DPA may include a broad range of terms, some of which are detailed in a non-exhaustive list in paragraph 5(3) of Schedule 17 to the Act.

7.2. The prosecutor and P are required to agree the terms of a DPA[4] which are fair, reasonable and proportionate. What terms are fair, reasonable and proportionate, including the length of the DPA, will be determined on a case by case basis. The terms may consist of a combination of requirements and it will normally be fair, reasonable and proportionate for there to be a financial penalty. It is particularly desirable that measures should be included that achieve redress for victims, such as payment of compensation. Paragraph 5 of Schedule 17 to the Act suggests that a possible term of a DPA is the recovery of the reasonable costs of the prosecutor in relation to the alleged offence or the DPA. The prosecutor should ordinarily seek to recover these costs, including the costs of the investigation where they have been incurred by the prosecutor.

7.3. The basis of the DPA and its terms will be explained in an agreed written application to the court.

7.4. The terms must set out clearly the measures with which P must comply. Clarity is important so P understands what is required. Further, in the event of breach of a term drafting ambiguity will complicate breach proceedings.

7.5. The terms must be proportionate to the offence and tailored to the specific facts of the case.

7.6. The DPA must specify the end date.

7.7. The following will normally be requirements of the DPA:

i. that the DPA relates only to the offences particularised in the counts of the draft indictment;[5]

ii. a warranty provided by both P and with P's consent, its legal advisers[6] that the information provided to the prosecutor throughout the DPA negotiations and upon which the DPA is based does not knowingly, contain inaccurate, misleading or incomplete information relevant to the conduct P has disclosed to the prosecutor.

iii. a requirement on P to notify the prosecutor and to provide where requested any documentation or other material that it becomes aware of whilst the DPA is in force which P knows or suspects would have been relevant to the offences particularised in the draft indictment.

7.8. The following will normally be terms of a DPA:

i. A financial order;

ii. The payment of the reasonable costs of the prosecutor;

iii. Co-operation with an investigation related to the alleged offence(s)[7].

[4] The length of a DPA will need to be sufficient to be capable of permitting compliance with other terms such as financial penalties paid in instalments, monitoring and co-operation with the investigations and trials into individuals.
[5] Prosecutors should not agree to a term that would prevent P from being prosecuted for conduct not included in the indictment even where the conduct has been disclosed during the course of DPA negotiations but not charged.
[6] The SRA Code of Conduct sets out in Chapter 5 the duties of a solicitor when conducting litigation or acting as an advocate. There are obligations on a solicitor:
a. Not to attempt to deceive or knowingly or recklessly mislead the court [O5.1],
b. Not to be complicit in any other person deceiving or misleading the court [O5.2], and
c. Where relevant to inform their client of circumstances in which their duties to the court outweigh their obligations to their client [O5.4].
[7] For example in respect of individuals. The obligation would include the provision of material to be used in evidence and for the purposes of disclosure.

12

7. Terms

7.9. The suggested financial terms may include but are not confined to: compensating victims; payment of a financial penalty; payment of the prosecutor's costs; donations to charities which support the victims of the offending; disgorgement of profits. There is no requirement to include all or any of these terms all of which are a matter of negotiation with P and subject to judicial oversight. The following should be noted:

i. A late payment may constitute a breach of the DPA leading to breach and termination. It may however be appropriate to make provision for short delays pursuant to paragraph 5 (5) of Schedule 17 to the Act requiring the payment of interest on any payment(s) not paid by the date agreed and specify the rate that applies[8].

ii. Where payment of a donation, compensation, financial penalty and/or costs is an agreed term of the DPA, the starting point should be that monies are ordered to be paid within seven days of the final hearing and this should be a standard term unless not fair, reasonable or proportionate.

iii. Where a financial penalty is to be imposed, the figure agreed must approximate to what would have been imposed had P pleaded guilty (see section 8).

iv. There should be a transparent and consistent approach to the setting of a financial penalty that is analogous to the sentencing framework for setting fines so the parties and the court will know before they enter into the process what the appropriate starting point is.

v. Financial penalties and disgorgements of profits will be paid to the prosecutor and then passed to the Consolidated Fund. Charitable donations and compensation will be paid by P directly or through an intermediary agreed by the parties and approved by the court as part of the DPA. P will provide confirmation and supporting evidence to the prosecutor of this as required.

7.10 Other terms that may be agreed might include:

i. prohibiting P from engaging in certain activities.

ii. financial reporting obligations.

iii. putting in place a robust compliance and/or monitoring programme.

iv. co-operation with sector wide investigations.

MONITORS

7.11 An important consideration for entering into a DPA is whether P already has a genuinely proactive and effective corporate compliance programme. The use of monitors should therefore be approached with care. The appointment of a monitor will depend upon the factual circumstances of each case and must always be fair, reasonable and proportionate.

7.12 A monitor's primary responsibility is to assess and monitor P's internal controls, advise of necessary compliance improvements that will reduce the risk of future recurrence of the conduct subject to the DPA and report specified misconduct to the prosecutor.

7.13 Where the terms require a monitor to be appointed it is the responsibility of P to pay all the costs of the selection, appointment, remuneration of the monitor, and reasonable costs of the prosecutor associated with the monitorship during the monitoring period. In assessing whether a term of monitoring may satisfy the statutory

---

[8] The rate should ordinarily be not less than the rate of interest payable on post judgment debts at the date when the DPA is approved

13

test the prosecutor should give consideration to the costs of such a term as these may be relevant.

7.14 P shall afford to the monitor complete access to all relevant aspects of its business during the course of the monitoring period as requested by the monitor. Any legal professional privilege that may exist in respect of investigating compliance issues that arise during the monitorship is unaffected by the Act, this DPA Code or a DPA.

7.15 As part of the DPA negotiations P should provide the prosecutor and the court with details of three potential monitors, including relevant qualifications, specialist knowledge and experience; any associations the monitor has or has had with P and/or associated companies and/or person(s) or any named companies or person(s) that feature in the DPA to avoid any conflict of interest; and an estimate of costs of the monitorship.

7.16 P should indicate their preferred monitor with reasons for the preference.

7.17 The prosecutor should ordinarily accept P's preferred monitor. However where the prosecutor considers there to be a conflict of interest or that the monitor is inappropriate, or does not have the requisite experience and authority, they may reject the proposed appointment. Similarly the court may register its dissatisfaction with the selection by not approving the proposed term.

7.18 Where monitorship is proposed to be a term of a DPA, before the DPA is approved the monitor will be selected, provisionally appointed, the terms of the monitorship agreed by the parties to the DPA, a detailed work plan for the first year (to include the method of review and frequency of reporting to the prosecutor) and an outline work plan for the remainder of the monitoring period agreed with the monitor including provisions

or limits as to costs. The monitor's report should include a breakdown of his proposed costs, and on what matters costs are incurred.

7.19 Terms of the DPA should include the length of time the monitors should be appointed. Provision should however be made in the DPA that if the monitor is satisfied that P's policies are functioning properly such that there is no need for further monitoring, the monitor may inform the prosecutor who will, subject to being satisfied through discussion with the monitor that the monitor's views are reasonable, agree to the termination or suspension of the monitor's appointment. Conversely the DPA should provide that, if the monitor and the prosecutor agree that P has not, or it appears will not by the end of the monitoring period have successfully satisfied its obligations with respect to the monitor's mandate, the term of the monitorship will be extended provided that no extension exceeds the length of the DPA.

7.20 Monitors' reports and associated correspondence shall be designated confidential with disclosure restricted to the prosecutor, P and the court, save as otherwise permitted by law.

7.21 No two monitoring programmes will be the same, given the varying facts and circumstances of each case including the nature and size of P. Terms included in the monitor's agreement may include, but are not limited to, ensuring that P has in place[9]:

i. a code of conduct;

ii. an appropriate training and education programme;

iii. internal procedures for reporting conduct issues which enable officers and employees to report issues in a safe and confidential manner;

[9] These policies and procedures are not intended to provide an indication of what can amount to adequate procedures under s. 7 Bribery Act 2010.

iv. processes for identifying key strategic risk areas;

v. reasonable safeguards to approve the appointment of representatives and payment of commissions;

vi. a gifts and hospitality policy;

vii. reasonable procedures for undertaking due diligence on potential projects, acquisitions, business partners, agents, representatives, distributors, sub-contractors and suppliers;

viii. procurement procedures which minimise the opportunity of misconduct;

ix. contract terms between P and its business partners, subcontractors, distributors, and suppliers include express contractual obligations and remedies in relation to misconduct;

x. internal management and audit processes which include reasonable controls against misconduct where appropriate;

xi. policies and processes in all of its subsidiaries and operating businesses, and joint ventures in which it has management control, and that P uses reasonable endeavours to ensure that the joint ventures in which it does not have management control, together with key subcontractors and representatives, are familiar with and are required to abide by its code of conduct to the extent possible;.

xii. procedures compatible with money laundering regulations;

xiii. policies regarding charitable and political donations;

xiv. terms related to external controls, e.g. procedures for selection of appropriate charities;

xv. policies relating to internal investigative resources, employee disciplinary procedures; and compliance screening of prospective employees;

xvi. policies relating to the extent to which senior management takes responsibility for implementing relevant practices and procedures;

xvii. mechanisms for review of the effectiveness of relevant policies and procedures across business and jurisdictions in which P operates;

xviii. compensation structures that remove incentives for unethical behaviour.

7.22 In designing a monitoring programme regard should be had to contemporary external guidance on compliance programmes[10].

---

[10] At the time of publishing guidance can be found in the Ministry of Justice Bribery Act 2010: Guidance to help commercial organisations prevent bribery, the OECD Good Practice Guide on Internal Controls, Ethics and Compliance, the BS 10500 Anti-Bribery System Standard, the US Sentencing Commission's Federal Sentencing Guidelines Manual, in particular its guidance on effective compliance and ethics programmes, and the guidance on corporate compliance programmes in the US Department of Justice's Principles of Federal Prosecution of Business.

8. Financial Penalty

8.1. The prosecutor represents the public interest, and should assist with the identification of appropriate terms by drawing the judge's attention where possible and relevant to the following information:

i. any victim statement or other information available to the prosecutor as to the impact of the alleged offence on the victim;

ii. any statutory provisions relevant to the offender and the offences under consideration;

iii. any relevant Sentencing Council Guidelines and guideline cases; and

iv. the aggravating and mitigating factors of the alleged offence under consideration.

8.2. Such information where available and relevant should form part of the agreed written application to be provided to the court at the final hearing.

8.3. Any financial penalty is to be broadly comparable to a fine that the court would have imposed upon P following a guilty plea.[11] This is intended to enable the parties and courts to have regard to relevant pre-existing sentencing principles and guidelines in order to determine the appropriate level for a financial penalty in an individual case. This should include consideration of P's means and where compensation is appropriate, this should be given priority over a penalty.

8.4. The extent of the discretion available when considering a financial penalty is broad. The discount for a guilty plea is applied by the sentencing court after it has taken into account all relevant considerations, including any assistance given by P. The level of the discount to reflect P's assistance would depend on the circumstances and the level of assistance given, and the parties should be guided by sentencing practice, statute and pre-existing case law on this matter. A financial penalty must provide for a discount equivalent to that which would be afforded by an early guilty plea. Current guidelines provide for a one third discount for a plea at the earliest opportunity.

8.5. To be considered as voluntary and therefore mitigating, co-operation should be over and above mere compliance with any coercive[12] measures.

---

[11] Schedule 17, Paragraph 5 (4).
[12] Such as notices under s 2 (1) Criminal Justice Act 1987 issued by the Serious Fraud Office

9. Preliminary hearing(s)

9.1. The Criminal Procedure Rules make provision for the contents of the application[13].

9.2. The prosecutor should contact a court designated to approve DPAs in order to request a listing and in doing so provide a realistic time estimate for a preliminary hearing.

9.3. The draft proposed application and any supporting documents must be submitted on a confidential basis to the court before the preliminary hearing.

9.4. The application must explain why the agreement is in the interests of justice and fair, reasonable and proportionate. In so explaining the prosecutor must address issues such as concurrent jurisdiction, on-going and/or subsequent ancillary proceedings, any conduct outwith the scope of the DPA which P has disclosed to the prosecutor but which does not form part of the draft indictment on account of the test at paragraph 1.2 above not having been satisfied.

9.5. Consideration should be given at the preliminary hearing to additional relevant issues such as timing of subsequent hearings.

9.6. The appropriate manner and timing of a preliminary hearing will vary on a case by case basis, and the court may adjourn a preliminary hearing if it requires more information about the facts or terms of a proposed DPA before it can make the full declaration under paragraph 7(1) of Schedule 17 to the Act.

10. Application for Approval

10.1. The Criminal Procedure Rules make provision for the contents of the application for final approval[14]. They further provide that an application for final approval should be sought as soon as practicable once the court has made a declaration under paragraph 7(1) of Schedule 17 to the Act and the parties have settled the terms of the DPA.

10.2. The basis of the DPA and its terms will be explained in an agreed written application accompanied by the proposed final terms of the DPA, agreed case statement with any supporting documents and the prosecutor's confirmation of which evidential test has been met. These documents must be submitted to the court on a confidential basis before the application for approval.

10.3. Issues germane to whether the DPA is in the interests of justice and its terms being fair, reasonable and proportionate such as concurrent jurisdiction, on-going and/or subsequent ancillary proceedings, must also be addressed by the prosecutor in the application for approval.

10.4. The application for approval of the DPA may be in private. This is likely to be almost always necessary as the prosecutor and P will be uncertain as to whether the court will grant a declaration under paragraph 8 (1). For the parties to make an application in open court which was refused might lead to the uncertainties and destabilisation that private preliminary hearings are designed to avoid.

10.5. The court may adjourn an application for approval if it requires more information about the facts or terms of a proposed DPA before it can make the declaration under paragraph 8(1) of Schedule 17 to the Act.

13,14 Crim PR 12

11. Declaration in Open Court

11.1. If a DPA is approved, the court must make a declaration to that effect along with reasons in an open hearing[15].

11.2. Once the declaration has been made in open court the prosecutor will, unless prevented from doing so by an enactment or by an order from the Court, publish on its website:

 i. the DPA;

 ii. the declaration of the court pursuant to paragraph 8 (1) of Schedule 17 to the Act with the reasons for making such a declaration;

 iii. the declaration of the court pursuant to paragraph 7 (1) of Schedule 17 to the Act with the reasons for making such a declaration; and

 iv. if appropriate, any initial refusal to make such a declaration with reasons for declining.

11.3. Immediate publication may be prevented by any enactment or order that postponement is necessary to avoid a substantial risk of prejudice to the administration of justice in any legal proceedings. P's offence and the sanctions provided for in the DPA will be made public as soon as it is safe to do so.

[15] See paragraph 15.4 in respect of listing

18

12. Breach of a DPA

12.1. Paragraph 9 of Schedule 17 to the Act deals with the situation where P is, or is believed by the prosecutor to be, in breach of a term of a DPA that has been approved at a final hearing.

ALLEGING AND PROVING BREACH OF A DPA

12.2. If, prior to the expiry of the DPA, it is believed that P is in breach of it, where possible the prosecutor should ask P to rectify the alleged breach immediately. In cases of minor breaches, it may be possible for a solution to be reached efficiently in this way, without the need for either an application under paragraph 9 of Schedule 17 to the Act or a variation of the DPA under paragraph 10 of Schedule 17 to the Act. The prosecutor will nevertheless still be required to publish details of the breach pursuant to paragraph 9 (8) of Schedule 17 to the Act. The prosecutor should also notify the court of any such developments.

12.3. If the prosecutor is unable to secure a satisfactory outcome in this way, it may apply to the court seeking a finding that P is in breach of the term as alleged, and explaining the remedy it seeks as a result. The question of whether or not there has been a breach of a term is to be judged on the balance of probabilities. The successful party may seek its costs of an application under paragraph 9 of Schedule 17[16].

12.4. If the court finds that P is in breach of a term of the DPA it may invite the parties to agree a suitable proposed remedy. If agreement can be reached, that proposed remedy must then be presented to the court by way of an application in accordance with paragraph 10 of Schedule 17 to the Act. The court will approve the variation only if that variation is in the interests of justice and the terms of the DPA as varied are fair, reasonable and proportionate. It is anticipated that this mechanism should generally be used to rectify relatively minor breaches of a DPA where the parties have been unable to agree a remedy without the involvement of the court.

TERMINATION FOLLOWING BREACH OF A DPA

12.5. Where the alleged breach is more material or the parties are unable to agree a suitable remedy or the court does not approve a proposed remedy, the court may order that the DPA be terminated. If the court makes such an order the DPA shall cease to take effect from that point onwards, and the prosecutor may apply to have the suspension of the indictment covered by the DPA lifted in accordance with paragraph 2 of Schedule 17 to the Act.

12.6. Where a DPA has been terminated in this way, P is not entitled to the return of any monies paid under the DPA prior to its termination, or to any other relief for detriment arising from its compliance with the DPA up to that point (for example the costs of a monitoring programme). The prosecutor may seek from P the costs of an application under paragraph 9 of schedule 17 to the Act[17].

---

[16][17] Crim PR 76.1 (c)

POST TERMINATION PROCESS

12.7. Should the DPA be terminated it will be usual for the prosecutor to apply for the suspension of the indictment to be lifted and P to be prosecuted. The application to lift the suspension need not be made at the time that the DPA is terminated.

12.8. The lifting of the suspension would reinstitute criminal proceedings. Given the manner in which the earlier investigation was concluded and/or the passage of time since the DPA was concluded the prosecutor may not be in a position to commence criminal proceedings immediately. Further investigation and preparation may be needed in order for the prosecutor to be trial ready.

12.9. Before re-opening proceedings, the prosecutor must be satisfied that the Full Code Test under the Code for Crown Prosecutors is met in relation to each charge. The court will have been informed at the final hearing if the original charge was pursuant to the second limb of the evidential stage at paragraph 1.2 i b) above, in which case the prosecutor will now need to be satisfied that the more stringent evidential stage of the Full Code Test is met. Furthermore the public interest position will need reassessing in light of the breach.

12.10. If the prosecutor requires time before being in a position to re-open proceedings the court should be informed of the prosecutor's proposed course of action and then kept informed of progress.

13.1. Paragraph 10 of Schedule 17 to the Act deals with the situation where it becomes necessary to vary the terms of a DPA that has been approved.

13.2. There are two possible situations in which variation may be necessary.

i. The first is where a breach has occurred in respect of which the prosecutor has applied under paragraph 9 of Schedule 17, and the court has invited the parties to agree a solution to that breach, which the court then has to consider whether to approve.

ii. The second situation is where a breach has not yet occurred, but, absent the variation, is likely to. A variation in this category will only be approved by the court if it arises from circumstances that were not, and could not have been, foreseen by the prosecutor or P at the time that the DPA was agreed[18]. What circumstances a court considers to be adequate in these types of cases will have to be decided on a case by case basis. Variation of a DPA is not a mechanism that exists for mere convenience or efficiency. A DPA is a serious sanction for criminal conduct and will have been approved by the court on that basis. In the vast majority of cases the terms of a DPA that are approved at a final hearing should be strictly complied with in their entirety, failing which P risks prosecution.

13.3. In both situations, it is the prosecutor that must apply to the court to seek a declaration that a variation is acceptable. P does not have a right to apply to the court for a variation; it may only ask the prosecutor for a variation.

13.4. If a variation is approved, the court must give its declaration to that effect in an open hearing. Costs of an application under paragraph 10 of Schedule 17 to the Act may be sought[19].

---

[18] Paragraph 10(1)(b) of Schedule 17 to the Act
[19] Crim PR 76.1 (c)

14. Discontinuance

14.1. On expiry of the DPA, the prosecutor should give notice to the court that it does not want proceedings to continue, in accordance with paragraph 11(1) of Schedule 17 to the Act.

14.2. Where considered necessary, consultation with the investigator and any monitor should take place prior to discontinuance.

14.3. Discontinuance notices should be sent to the court as soon as practicable after the decision to discontinue, and copies should be sent to P and the investigator.

14.4. The notice should state:

   i.   The effective date of discontinuance;

   ii. The offences to be discontinued;

   iii. Confirmation that the DPA has expired.

14.5. A DPA will ordinarily expire on the date specified in the agreement. However, this will not always be the case, and prosecutors should be aware of the various circumstances under paragraph 11 of Schedule 17 to the Act in which a DPA is to be treated as having or not having expired.

14.6. No notice of discontinuance is needed where the court terminates the DPA: see paragraph 11(5)(b) of Schedule 17 to the Act.

14.7. In contrast to discontinuance under the section 23A of the Prosecutions of Offences Act 1985, once proceedings are discontinued under paragraph 11(1), fresh proceedings against P for the same offence may not be instituted unless the conditions specified in paragraph 11(3) of Schedule 17 to the Act (provision of inaccurate, misleading or incomplete information by P) are satisfied.

15. Applications in Private

15.1. Where an application in private is contemplated all parties should consider whether the hearing can be heard in public as a starting point and if not, whether as much as possible of the hearing can be heard in public.

15.2. An application for a private hearing might be made for example where it is necessary to avoid a substantial risk of prejudice to the administration of justice in any legal proceedings.

15.3. The court will not identify the parties to a private application.

15.4. Where the application to approve the DPA is in private it would be normally appropriate for reasons of transparency and open justice for the parties to request the court to delay the making of a declaration approving a DPA in open court so that a listing might be publicised in the normal manner.

15.5. All communications with the court in respect of a DPA will be confidential and the use of secure email should be the preferred means to maintain confidentiality.

16. Publishing decisions and postponement

16.1. Transparency remains a key aspect of the success and proper operation of DPAs, and accordingly Schedule 17 of the Act requires in prescribed circumstances the prosecutor to publish on its website orders made by the court or decisions made by the prosecutor.

16.2. All requirements to publish under this section are subject to any enactment or order of the court under paragraph 12 of Schedule 17 to the Act preventing such publication from being made.

16.3. There is no requirement to publish a conclusion reached by a prosecutor alone that no breach has in fact occurred so that no application to the court has been made.

Crown Prosecution Service
Rose Court
2 Southwark Bridge
London SE1 9HS

Telephone: +44 (0)20 3357 0000

www.CPS.gov.uk

Serious Fraud Office
2-4 Cockspur Street
London SW1Y 5BS

Telephone: +44 (0)20 7239 7272

www.SFO.gov.uk
Designed by the SFO Graphics Unit

APPENDIX 7

FCPA Acquisition Due Diligence Checklist

- Corporate Information
  - Names and Addresses of Target's Officers, Directors, Management Level Employees, Owners and Principal Shareholders (private company)
  - Names and Addresses of Target's Officers, Directors, Management Level Employees, Owners and Shareholders with Interests of 10% or More (public company)
  - Identification of any Officers, Directors, Management Level Employees, Owners or Principal Shareholders Who are:
    - Current or Former Government Officials or Employees
    - Close Family Members of Government Officials or Employees
- FCPA or Anti-Bribery Compliance Policies and Procedures
  - Statement of Corporate Compliance Policy
  - Internal FCPA or Anti-Bribery Compliance Procedures
  - FCPA or Anti-Bribery Compliance Training Materials
    - PowerPoint Presentations
    - Handouts
    - Attendance Lists
    - Acknowledgment Forms
  - Internal Accounting Control Procedures
  - Appropriate Translation of Compliance Policies and Procedures
- International Business Activities
  - Countries in which Target has Business Operations
  - Countries in which Target makes sales to Government Entities (including State-Owned Commercial Enterprises)
    - Evaluation of Countries against *Transparency International* Corruption Perception Index (CPI)
  - List of all Registrations, Licenses, Permits and other Government Approvals held by Target to do business in each Country
  - Identification of each Government Agency responsible for administering Registration, Licensing, Permits and Approvals
    - Copies of all Correspondence with Government Agencies relating to Registration, Licensing, Permits and Approvals

- List of all Consultants and other Intermediaries engaged to Perform Services in connection with Registration, Licensing, Permits or Approvals from Government Agencies
  - Copies of Contracts with those Consultants and other Intermediaries
  - Records of all Compensation paid to Consultants and other Intermediaries
- Sales to Government Entities (including State-Owned Commercial Enterprises)
  - List of all Government Entities to which Target Sells or Supplies Goods or Services
  - Percentage of Target's Total Business with Government Entities
  - Copies of all Contracts to Sell or Supply Goods or Services to Government Entities
    - Include Copies of Subcontracts to Supply Goods or Services to Government Contractors
    - Copies of Sales Records under Government Contracts
  - List of all Payments, along with Payment Records, to Third Parties, including Consultants, Sales Representatives, Agents and Other Intermediaries, made in connection with any Government Contract or Subcontract
- Relationships with Intermediaries
  - List of all Distributors, Sales Representatives, Agents, Resellers, Freight Forwarders, Consultants, Customs Brokers and Other Intermediaries Retained by Target for any Purpose
    - List of Intermediaries Engaged by Target for the Purpose of Promoting Sales of the Target's Goods or Services to Government Entities (including State-Owned Commercial Enterprises)
    - Copies of Contracts with all Intermediaries
    - Description of Services Performed by each such Intermediary
    - Compensation Arrangements and Payment Records of all Payments to Intermediaries
  - Description of Approval Process for the Retention of Intermediaries
    - Background Check and Due Diligence Materials on each Intermediary
    - Records of Approval of each Intermediary
  - Records and Reports of any Investigation or Termination of any Intermediary based on Anti-Corruption Concerns
- Dealings with Government Officials
  - Records of all Payments and Gifts to any Government Officials
  - Records of all Hospitality (travel, meals, lodging) provided to any Government Officials
  - Approval Process for Payments, Gifts and Hospitality for Government Officials
    - Purpose for each Payment, Gift or Hospitality
    - Actual Approvals for each Payment, Gift or Hospitality
    - Legal Opinions on Legality of each Payment, Gift or Hospitality
  - Accounting Records Reflecting each Payment, Gift or Hospitality
- Contributions and Donations
  - Contributions to Political Parties
  - Contributions to Candidates for Political Office

- Donations to Government Agencies
- Donations to Charitable Organizations
- Approval Process for Contributions and Donations
    - Purpose or Rationale for each Contribution and Donation
    - Actual Approvals for each Contribution and Donation
    - Legal Opinions on Legality of each Contribution and Donation (especially political contributions)
- Accounting Records Reflecting each Contribution and Donation
- Compliance Reviews, Violations and Enforcement Actions
    - Internal Procedures on Compliance Reviews
        - Reports of Compliance Audits
        - Follow-Up Actions in Response to Compliance Audits
    - Records and Reports of Internal Compliance Investigations
    - Records and Reports of External (Government) Compliance Investigations
    - Documents relating to Threatened, Pending and Completed Administrative and Judicial Enforcement Actions and Proceedings
    - Voluntary Disclosures of Suspected Violations to Government Agencies
    - Local Legal Opinions Relating to Anti-Corruption Issues
- List of all Funds, Assets, Accounts and Transactions not recorded or reflected on the Target's Books and Records
- Internet Searches
    - Target
    - Officers and Directors
    - Management Level Employees
    - Owners or Principal Shareholders (all private companies and 10% or more shareholders of public companies)

APPENDIX 8

American College of Trial Lawyers' *Recommended Practices for Companies and Their Counsel in Conducting Internal Investigations* (February 2008)

RECOMMENDED PRACTICES FOR COMPANIES AND THEIR COUNSEL IN CONDUCTING INTERNAL INVESTIGATIONS

Approved by the Board of Regents
February 2008

AMERICAN COLLEGE OF TRIAL LAWYERS

The American College of Trial Lawyers, founded in 1950, is composed of the best of the trial bar from the United States and Canada. Fellowship in the College is extended by invitation only, after careful investigation, to those experienced trial lawyers who have mastered the art of advocacy and those whose professional careers have been marked by the highest standards of ethical conduct, professionalism, civility and collegiality. Lawyers must have a minimum of 15 years' experience before they can be considered for Fellowship. Membership in the College cannot exceed 1% of the total lawyer population of any state or province. Fellows are carefully selected from among those who represent plaintiffs and those who represent defendants in civil cases; those who prosecute and those who defend persons accused of crime. The College is thus able to speak with a balanced voice on important issues affecting the administration of justice. The College strives to improve and elevate the standards of trial practice, the administration of justice and the ethics of the trial profession.

◆ ◆ ◆

"In this select circle, we find pleasure and charm in the illustrious company of our contemporaries and take the keenest delight in exalting our friendships."

—Hon. Emil Gumpert,
Chancellor-Founder, ACTL

American College of Trial Lawyers
19900 MacArthur Boulevard, Suite 610
Irvine, California 92612
Telephone: (949) 752-1801
Facsimile: (949) 752-1674
E-mail: nationaloffice@actl.com
Website: www.actl.com

AMERICAN COLLEGE OF TRIAL LAWYERS

CHANCELLOR-FOUNDER
Hon. Emil Gumpert
(1895—1982)

OFFICERS
MIKEL L. STOUT, *President*
JOHN J. (JACK) DALTON, *President-Elect*
GREGORY P. JOSEPH, *Secretary*
JOAN A. LUKEY, *Treasurer*
DAVID J. BECK, *Immediate Past President*

BOARD OF REGENTS

DAVID J. BECK
Houston, Texas

PAUL D. BEKMAN
Baltimore, Maryland

J. DONALD COWAN, JR.
Greensboro, North Carolina

JOHN J. (JACK) DALTON
Atlanta, Georgia

MICHEL DÉCARY, Q.C.
Montréal, Québec

FRANCIS X. DEE
Newark, New Jersey

BRUCE W. FELMLY
Manchester, New Hampshire

PAUL T. FORTINO
Portland, Oregon

PHILLIP R. GARRISON
Springfield, Missouri

ROBERT A. GOODIN
San Francisco, California

CHRISTY D. JONES
Jackson, Mississippi

GREGORY P. JOSEPH
New York, New York

PHILIP J. KESSLER
Detroit, Michigan

JOAN A. LUKEY
Boston, Massachusetts

PAUL S. MEYER
Costa Mesa, California

JOHN S. SIFFERT
New York, New York

MIKEL L. STOUT
Wichita, Kansas

ROBERT W. TARUN
Chicago, Illinois

JOHN H. TUCKER
Tulsa, Oklahoma

CHILTON DAVIS VARNER
Atlanta, Georgia

• ii •

AMERICAN COLLEGE OF TRIAL LAWYERS

PAST PRESIDENTS

1950-51 EMIL GUMPERT*
Los Angeles, California
1951-52 C. RAY ROBINSON*
Merced, California
1952-53 CODY FOWLER*
Tampa, Florida
1953-54 E. D. BRONSON*
San Francisco, California
1954-55 CODY FOWLER*
Tampa, Florida
1955-56 WAYNE E. STICHTER*
Toledo, Ohio
1956-57 JESSE E. NICHOLS*
Oakland, California
1957-58 LEWIS C. RYAN*
Syracuse, New York
1958-59 ALBERT E. JENNER, JR.*
Chicago, Illinois
1959-60 SAMUEL P. SEARS*
Boston, Massachusetts
1960-61 LON HOCKER*
Woods Hole, Massachusetts
1961-62 LEON JAWORSKI*
Houston, Texas
1962-63 GRANT B. COOPER*
Los Angeles, California
1963-64 WHITNEY NORTH SEYMOUR*
New York, New York
1964-65 BERNARD G. SEGAL*
Philadelphia, Pennsylvania
1965-66 EDWARD L. WRIGHT*
Little Rock, Arkansas
1966-67 FRANK G. RAICHLE*
Buffalo, New York
1967-68 JOSEPH A. BALL*
Long Beach, California
1968-69 ROBERT W. MESERVE*
Boston, Massachusetts
1969-70 HON. LEWIS F. POWELL, JR.*
Washington, District of Columbia
1970-71 BARNABAS F. SEARS*
Chicago, Illinois
1971-72 HICKS EPTON*
Wewoka, Oklahoma
1972-73 WILLIAM H. MORRISON*
Portland, Oregon
1973-74 ROBERT L. CLARE, JR.*
New York, New York
1974- AUSTIN W. LEWIS*
New Orleans, Louisiana
1975-76 THOMAS E. DEACY, JR.
Kansas City, Missouri
1976-77 SIMON H. RIFKIND*
New York, New York
1977-78 KRAFT W. EIDMAN*
Houston, Texas
1978-79 MARCUS MATTSON*
Los Angeles, California

1979-80 JAMES E. S. BAKER*
Chicago, Illinois
1980-81 JOHN C. ELAM*
Columbus, Ohio
1981-82 ALSTON JENNINGS*
Little Rock, Arkansas
1982-83 LEON SILVERMAN
New York, New York
1983-84 GAEL MAHONY
Boston, Massachusetts
1984-85 GENE W. LAFITTE
New Orleans, Louisiana
1985-86 GRIFFIN B. BELL
Atlanta, Georgia
1986-87 R. HARVEY CHAPPELL, JR.
Richmond, Virginia
1987-88 MORRIS HARRELL*
Dallas, Texas
1988-89 PHILIP W. TONE*
Chicago, Illinois
1989-90 RALPH I. LANCASTER, JR.
Portland, Maine
1990-91 CHARLES E. HANGER*
San Francisco, California
1991-92 ROBERT B. FISKE, JR.
New York, New York
1992-93 FULTON HAIGHT*
Santa Monica, California
1993-94 FRANK C. JONES
Atlanta, Georgia
1994-95 LIVELY M. WILSON
Louisville, Kentucky
1995-96 CHARLES B. RENFREW
San Francisco, California
1996-97 ANDREW M. COATS
Oklahoma City, Oklahoma
1997-98 EDWARD BRODSKY*
New York, New York
1998-99 E. OSBORNE AYSCUE, JR.
Charlotte, North Carolina
1999-2000 MICHAEL E. MONE
Boston, Massachusetts
2000-2001 EARL J. SILBERT
Washington, District of Columbia
2001-2002 STUART D. SHANOR
Roswell, New Mexico
2002-2003 WARREN B. LIGHTFOOT
Birmingham, Alabama
2003-2004 DAVID W. SCOTT, Q.C.
Ottawa, Ontario
2004-2005 JAMES W. MORRIS, III
Richmond, Virginia
2005-2006 MICHAEL A. COOPER,
New York, New York
2006-2007 DAVID J. BECK
Houston, Texas

* Deceased

FEDERAL CRIMINAL PROCEDURE COMMITTEE

CHAIR
DOUGLAS R. YOUNG, SAN FRANCISCO, CA

VICE-CHAIR
CHUCK MEADOWS, DALLAS, TX

MEMBERS

LESLIE I. BALLIN, MEMPHIS, TN
MARK E. BECK, LOS ANGELES, CA
RICHARD W. BECKLER, WASHINGTON, DC
MARTHA A. BOERSCH, SAN FRANCISCO, CA
BILL W. BRISTOW, JONESBORO, AR
DAVID M. BRODSKY, NEW YORK, NY
JAMES J. BROSNAHAN, SAN FRANCISCO, CA
NANCI L. CLARENCE, SAN FRANCISCO, CA
JOHN D. CLINE, SAN FRANCISCO, CA
ARTHUR T. DONATO, JR., MEDIA, PA
ROBERT J. DONATONI, WEST CHESTER, PA
DAVID F. DUMOUCHEL, DETROIT, MI
HON. NANCY GERTNER, BOSTON, MA
EDWARD L. GREENSPAN, Q.C., TORONTO, ON
HON. SAM E. HADDON, GREAT FALLS, MT
LINDA DALE HOFFA, PHILADELPHIA, PA
MURRAY J. JANUS, RICHMOND, VA
HON. D. LOWELL JENSEN, OAKLAND, CA
HON. JOSEPH D. JOHNSON, TOPEKA, KS
PAULA M. JUNGHANS, WASHINGTON, DC
NEIL A. KAPLAN, SALT LAKE CITY, UT
DALE P. KELBERMAN, BALTIMORE, MD
HON. MATTHEW F. KENNELLY, CHICAGO, IL
JOHN J. KENNEY, NEW YORK, NY
LARRY H. KRANTZ, NEW YORK, NY
GARY LOZOW, DENVER, CO
MARK J. MACDOUGALL, WASHINGTON, DC

GERARD P. MARTIN, BALTIMORE, MD
JOHN P. MCDONALD, SOMERVILLE, NJ
DANIEL E. MONNAT, WICHITA, KS
ANN C. MOORMAN, BERKELEY, CA
ROBERT G. MORVILLO, NEW YORK, NY
BRIAN O'NEILL, LOS ANGELES, CA
THOMAS J. ORLOFF, OAKLAND, CA
TAI H. PARK, NEW YORK, NY
LESTER A. PINES, MADISON, WI
JOHN P. PUCCI, NORTHAMPTON, MA
HON. JED S. RAKOFF, NEW YORK, NY
JAMES D. RIDDET, SANTA ANA, CA
MICHELE A. ROBERTS, WASHINGTON, DC
N. SCOTT ROSENBLUM, ST. LOUIS, MO
ANDREW J. SAVAGE, III, CHARLESTON, SC
HARRY L. SHORSTEIN, JACKSONVILLE, FL
J. MICHAEL SMALL, ALEXANDRIA, LA
LEON F. SPIES, IOWA CITY, IA
MARK J. STEIN, NEW YORK, NY
CHARLES A. STILLMAN, NEW YORK, NY
JAMES C. THOMAS, DETROIT, MI
KAREN S. TOWNSEND, MISSOULA, MT
DOUGLAS A. TRANT, KNOXVILLE, TN
ROBERT L. ULLMANN, BOSTON, MA
JOHN W. VAUDREUIL, MADISON, WI
ROBERT C. WEAVER, JR., PORTLAND, OR
MATT J. WHITWORTH, KANSAS CITY, MO

REGENT LIAISON
ROBERT W. TARUN, CHICAGO, IL

EX OFFICIO
ELIZABETH K. AINSLIE, PHILADELPHIA, PA

TABLE OF CONTENTS

RECOMMENDED PRACTICES FOR
COMPANIES AND THEIR COUNSEL IN
CONDUCTING INTERNAL INVESTIGATIONS*

I.   Purpose of the Paper

Since 2001, over 2,500 public companies have retained outside counsel to conduct internal investigations into suspected wrong-doing by corporate executives and employees. These investigations have included inquiries into suspected violations of the Foreign Corrupt Practices Act; alleged options backdating activities; alleged violations of the antitrust, environmental, import/export, and other laws; and financial statement improprieties.[1] The Federal Criminal Procedure Committee of the American College of Trial Lawyers has observed counsel implementing a wide variety of procedures and protocols in conducting corporate internal investigations for issuers and public companies in particular. The result has been variances both in treatment of officers and employees and in outcomes of the investigations for such officers and employees and the corporations themselves. The Committee has sought to determine, and now recommends, what it believes to be the fairest and most effective practices for conducting internal investigations of possible corporate wrongdoing. Although the principles articulated in this paper are tailored to internal investigations by issuers and public companies where significant allegations of malfeasance are alleged or suspected, many of these principles may be applied in the context of other entities and smaller investigations.

---

*   The principal draftsman of this report was David M. Brodsky (New York, N.Y.). He was assisted by a subcommittee of the Federal Criminal Procedure Committee of the American College of Trial Lawyers consisting of its Chair Douglas R. Young (San Francisco, CA.), Fellows Nanci Clarence (San Francisco, CA.), James Brosnahan (San Francisco, CA.), John S. Siffert (New York, N.Y.), Robert G. Morvillo (New York, N.Y.), the Honorable Nancy Gertner (US District Court, District of Massachusetts), and Regent Liaison Robert W. Tarun (Chicago, IL.). Fellow Cristina Arguedas (Berkeley, CA.) also reviewed this report.

1   *See, e.g.,* the Wall Street Journal Options Scoreboard, where 143 public companies are listed as having conducted internal investigations into suspected options backdating, http://online.wsj.com/public/resources/documents/info-optionsscore06-full.html.

A sample of the internal investigations conducted by different law firms reveals the diversity of the matters under internal investigation since 2001:

- representation of Fortune 100 Company in a Special Litigation Committee investigation involving derivative shareholder claims against directors and officers regarding false financial statements and conflicts of interest arising out of acquisitions;
- representation of the Audit Committee of leading lessor of shipping containers and chassis in an internal investigation arising from an accounting restatement;
- representation of the Corporate Governance Committee of a major transportation company in a review of its corporate governance structure;
- representation of the Audit Committee of a large semiconductor company in an internal investigation involving alleged accounting improprieties and self-dealing;
- representation of the Audit Committee of a major computer data storage company regarding an investigation involving revenue recognition issues at one of the companies subsidiaries;
- representation of a leading fiber optics company in an internal investigation;
- representation of an Audit Committee into allegations of insider trading by certain directors and those affiliated with them
- representation of a U.S. public company and its U.S. subsidiary corresponding to the Japanese subsidiary in an investigation involving improper labeling of the grade and quality of plastics being used in computer monitors and other electronics equipment being shipped around the world, including the U.S.; and
- representation of an Audit Committee of one of the world's largest industrial corporations into the activities of foreign subsidiaries relating to energy plant inspections.

◆ 1 ◆

II.   Initial Organizational Issues

A.   Factors to Consider When Evaluating Whether to Commence an Internal Investigation When Allegations Have Been Lodged of Significant Corporate Malfeasance Or Where an Outside Auditor Suspects Illegality

Internal investigations typically result from discovery -- by the Company, the media, an external auditor, or a whistleblower -- of circumstances that raise a serious concern of potential liability or financial misconduct. The investigations are thus meant to determine the validity and seriousness of the circumstances alleged or disclosed and what action, if any, the Company should take consistent with the best interests of the shareholders. Among the possible responsive actions are remediation, market disclosure, and preparation for, and defense of, potential prosecutorial and regulatory actions or civil lawsuits. Depending on whose conduct is the focus of the investigation, senior management, the Board of Directors, an audit committee or a special committee of disinterested directors may decide to commence an investigation. There are some respected corporate lawyers who counsel that Boards should resist the trend of having audit committees or special committees of independent directors routinely investigating whistleblower complaints and the like.[2]

Whether to commence an internal investigation may be a discretionary decision, supra, or in limited circumstances may be prescribed by statute. In the latter case, Section 10A of the Exchange Act requires external auditors, who detect or otherwise become aware that an illegal act has or may have occurred, to determine whether it is likely such an illegal act has occurred and the effect of any illegal act on the Company's financial statements. Auditors look to the Company to investigate and evaluate such possible illegalities and then assess whether the Company and the Board of Directors have taken "timely and appropriate remedial actions" regarding such possible illegalities. In this regard, the methodology used in "10A investigations" is not materially different from an internal investigation commenced on the company's own initiative, and therefore, for the purposes of this paper they will be treated collectively.

Outside of the 10A context, there are several circumstance that have traditionally triggered the initiation of internal investigations by senior management, a Board, audit committee or special committee:

a.   Receipt of a whistleblower letter or communication that raises allegations of misconduct by senior or significant members of management;

b.   Shareholder demand in the nature of an actual or threatened derivative action against directors and officers, possibly leading to formation of a Special Litigation Committee;

c.   Allegations of misconduct raised by external auditor, internal auditor, or compliance;

d.   Board member suspicion of misconduct by officers or employees;

e.   Receipt of subpoena or informal request for information by a government or self-regulatory organization (SRO), or an announcement by a government agency or SRO of suspicions of misconduct by the Company or industry; or

f.   Allegations of misconduct by the media, watchdog groups, or academics.

---

2   Andrew Ross Sorkin, *Questioning an Adviser's Advice*, N.Y. TIMES, Jan. 8, 2008 (interview of Martin Lipton).

In addition, although there have been no reported enforcement actions under the section yet, the "reporting up" provisions of the Sarbanes-Oxley Act of 2002 require in-house counsel to ensure that the corporation takes appropriate steps in response to allegations of wrongdoing.

B.   External Factors, Such as The Existence or Anticipated Existence of a Parallel Government Investigation or Shareholder Lawsuit, Should Be Considered When Making Decisions About How To Conduct and Document An Internal Investigation

There is a reasonable likelihood that any major internal investigation will be followed by, or conducted parallel to, an actual (or anticipated) external investigation by (one or more of): the Department of Justice, Securities and Exchange Commission, NYSE (or other self regulatory organization ("SRO")), a state attorney general or local district attorney, or other enforcement or regulatory authority. The Company and the Board may also be facing civil lawsuits, including shareholder class actions and derivative suits, pertaining to the alleged misconduct; and in certain instances, may be dealing with criminal investigations initiated by federal and, more recently, state prosecutors.[3]

The existence or threatened existence of any of these external events necessarily affects how the Company, Board, audit or independent committee, and outside counsel conduct and document an internal investigation. As discussed more fully below, counsel and the Company should anticipate that all documents created, facts uncovered, and witness statements made to them, may be disclosed to the government or regulator, and also may be discoverable by a private plaintiff. This assumption should be a factor in all major decisions about the procedure and protocol for any major internal investigation. In particular, the company, the Board or its independent committees, and counsel may want, or may be forced, to make an early determination about whether and how they will "cooperate" with government or regulatory investigations.

During approximately the last decade, driven by regulatory policies promulgated by the Department of Justice,[4] the Securities and Exchange Commission and other regulators,[5] and

---

3   *See, e.g.*, Mark Gimein, *Eliot Spitzer: The Enforcer*, Fortune, Sept. 16, 2002, at 77; Charles Gasparino & Paul Beckett, *Quick Fix May Elude Citigroup and Weill*, Wall St. J., Sept. 10, 2002, at C1; Gregory Zuckerman & Mitchell Pacelle, *Now, Telecom Deals Face Scrutiny*, Wall St. J., June 28, 2002, at C1.

4   *See* text, *infra* at n. 7-10, 13-14.

5   *See* "Report of Investigation Pursuant to Section 21(a) of the Securities Exchange Act of 1934 and Commission Statement on the Relationship of Cooperation to Agency Enforcement Decisions," issued on October 23, 2001 as Releases 44969 and 1470, available at http://www.sec.gov/litigation/investreport/34-44969.htm, and referred to as the "Seaboard Report." The Seaboard Report is the SEC's current policy regarding waiver of privilege and work product, and sets forth the criteria that it will consider in determining the extent to which organizations will be granted credit for cooperating with the agency's staff by discovering, self-reporting, and remedying illegal conduct, which cooperation, or lack thereof, in the eyes of the staff will be taken into consideration when the SEC decides what, if any, enforcement action to take. The Seaboard Report has been read by practitioners as encouraging companies not to assert, or to waive, their attorney-client privilege, work product, and other legal protections as a sign of full cooperation. *See* Seaboard Report at paragraph 8, criteria no. 11, and footnote 3.

Another example of a regulatory agency promulgating similar policies is the Commodity Futures Trading Commission ("CFTC"), the Enforcement Division of which issued an Enforcement Advisory on August 11, 2004, entitled "Cooperation Factors in Enforcement Division Sanction Recommendations," promoting the waiver of appropriate privileges. The CFTC issued a revised Enforcement Advisory eliminating the waiver language on March 1, 2007. *See* http://www.abanet.org/poladv/priorities/privilegewaiver/acprivilege.html.

the U.S. Sentencing Commission, the passage of federal legislation mandating certain activities by independent auditors and Audit Committees, and civil litigation, there has been a renewed emphasis on companies' expanding the scope of their cooperation with governmental investigations, and even initiating them, by conducting extensive internal investigations into perceived corporate misconduct in order to achieve longer-term benefits at the hands of such regulators and avoid what could be punitive reactions by regulators and auditors.

Since the mid-1990s, the principal focus of law enforcement and regulatory authorities in the United States has been to develop policies and guidelines designed to induce corporations and other business entities to waive, or not assert, applicable attorney-client and work-product privileges and protections.[6] In 1999, after several years of informal policies at various United States Attorney's Offices (principally the Southern District of New York), the Department of Justice formally adopted what came to be known as the "Holder Memorandum," after Eric Holder, then Deputy Attorney General of the United States. The Holder Memorandum, although advisory, set forth standards by which a corporation would be judged cooperative in a federal criminal investigation.[7] One factor was whether the corporation waived or did not assert privileges protecting the confidentiality of communications.

In 2002, then Deputy Attorney General Larry Thompson promulgated a revision of the Holder Memorandum, this time making mandatory the use of the factors in judging whether a corporation was sufficiently cooperative, including whether applicable privileges were waived or not asserted.[8] Among the most controversial of the nine additional factors in the Thompson Memorandum were those addressed to indicia of corporate "cooperation," including a willingness to waive or not assert the attorney-client privilege and the attorney work-product doctrine[9] and a willingness to deny advancement of fees and expenses and indemnification coverage.[10]

---

[6] *See* United States Attorneys' Criminal Resource Manual, Art. 162, §VI.B; United States Sentencing Guidelines Manual §8C2.5(g)(2001); the SEC's Seaboard Report, http://www.sec.gov/litigation/investreport/34-44969.htm; *see also* the EPA Voluntary Disclosure Program, the HHS Provider Self-Disclosure Protocol, and the Department of Justice Antitrust Corporate Leniency Policy.

[7] *See generally* Memorandum from Eric Holder, Jr., Deputy Attorney General, to All Heads of Department Components and U.S.Attorneys (June 16, 1999) (including attachment entitled "Federal Prosecution of Corporations"), *reprinted in* Criminal Resource Manual, arts. 161, 162, *available at* http://www.usdoj.gov/usao/eousa/foia_reading_room/usam/title9/crm00100.htm.

[8] *See* US DOJ, Principles of Federal Prosecution of Business Organizations (Jan. 20, 2003) (the "Thompson Memorandum"), *available at* http://www.usdoj.gov/dag/cftf/business_organizations.pdf.

[9] Regarding the attorney-client privilege and work-product doctrine, the Thompson Memorandum stated, in relevant part, that "[o]ne factor the prosecutor may weigh in assessing the adequacy of a corporation's cooperation is the completeness of its disclosure including, if necessary, a waiver of the attorney-client and work product protections, both with respect to its internal investigation and with respect to communications among specific officers, directors, and employees and counsel. Such waivers permit the government to obtain statements of possible witnesses, subjects and targets, without having to negotiate individual cooperation or immunity agreements."

[10] Regarding denial of advancement of fees and expenses, the Thompson Memorandum stated, in relevant part, that "a corporation's promise of support to culpable employees and agents...through the advancing of attorneys' fees...may be considered by the prosecutor in weighing the extent and value of a corporation's cooperation."

In 2004, following the general trend of policy reflected in the Thompson Memorandum, the United States Sentencing Commission adopted an amendment that a corporation's waiver of the attorney-client privilege and work product protections would be a prerequisite for obtaining a reduction by a corporation in its culpability score.

The adoption of these policies by the Department of Justice and other regulatory entities have made inroads into historic policies protecting privilege and work-product in favor of policies promoting cooperation with governmental agencies and maximizing the effectiveness and efficiency of governmental investigations.[11] Companies formerly expected that the work product of their counsel prepared as a result of an internal investigation (and advice given as a result of such investigation) would be protected. Instead, however, many have come to learn that, upon the initiation of a governmental inquiry (formal or informal, and whether the company is a target or not) such expectations of confidentiality have in many cases been illusory. Internal investigations, conducted by and at the direction of legal counsel, are a critical tool by which companies and their boards learn about violations of law, breaches of duty and other misconduct that may expose the company to liability and damages. They are also an essential predicate to enabling companies to take remedial action and to formulate defenses, where appropriate. But internal investigations no longer have clear and predictable protections of confidentiality in the current environment, viewed as a "culture of waiver."[12]

Following significant criticism by business organizations and bar associations, these principles were superseded in 2006 by the so-called McNulty Memorandum.[13] The McNulty Memorandum reaffirms many of the factors to be considered by federal prosecutors when conducting corporate investigations and deciding whether to indict corporations or considering corporate plea agreements, but places some procedural restrictions and additional procedural reviews on prosecutors regarding their ability to request waivers of corporate attorney-client privileges or work-product

---

11   Joint Drafting Committee of the American College of Trial Lawyers, *The Erosion of the Attorney-Client Privilege and Work Product Doctrine in Federal Criminal Investigations* (March 2002), *available at* http://www.actl.com/AM/Template. cfm?Section=All_Publications&Template=/CM/ContentDisplay.cfm&ContentFileID=68.

12   "The Decline of the Attorney-Client Privilege in the Corporate Context," Survey Results, Presented to the United States Congress and the United States Sentencing Commission, March 2006, http://www.nacdl.org/public.nsf/whitecollar/wcnews024/$FILE/A-C_PrivSurvey.pdf, and http://www.acca.com/public/attyclntprvlg/coalitionussctestimony031506.pdf ("Survey Results").

13   *See* Principles of Federal Prosecution of Business Organizations (December 12, 2006) (the "McNulty Memorandum"), *available at* http://www.usdoj.gov/dag/speech/2006/mcnulty_memo.pdf

protections.[14][15] Despite these additional restrictions and reviews, there is little practical difference between the McNulty Memorandum and its predecessors: all maintain the position that waivers of the privilege and work product protections will be bases for favorable treatment of corporations and thus will still provide significant motivation for defense attorneys zealously representing their corporate clients to offer waivers without prosecutors having to ask. Since the main focus of both DOJ Memoranda is an evaluation of how the DOJ evaluates the "authenticity of a corporation's cooperation with a government investigation," including waivers, the McNulty Memorandum will still provide significant motivation for defense attorneys zealously representing their corporate clients to offer waivers without prosecutors having to ask.

In 2001, the SEC announced its own cooperation policy when it decided to take no action against Seaboard Corporation despite evidence that its former controller had caused the company's books and records to be inaccurate and its financial reports misstated. The Commission outlined thirteen factors it would consider in determining cooperation.[16]

In 2006, the SEC updated its standards for imposing civil penalties on corporations.[17] As explained in the Commission's Statement,

---

14   The McNulty Memorandum lists nine factors that "prosecutors must consider…in reaching a decision as to the proper treatment of a corporate target":

    (1)   the nature and seriousness of the offense including the risk of harm to the public and any policies and priorities relating to the particular categories of crime;

    (2)   the pervasiveness of wrongdoing within the business organization including complicity in or condonation of the wrongdoing by management;

    (3)   the history of similar conduct within the company including prior criminal, civil and regulatory enforcement actions against the company;

    (4)   the timely and voluntary disclosure of wrongdoing and the company's willingness to cooperate in the investigation of its own agents;

    (5)   the existence and adequacy of the company's pre-existing compliance program;

    (6)   the company's remedial actions, including efforts to implement an effective compliance program or improve an existing one, efforts to replace responsible management, efforts to discipline or terminate wrongdoers, efforts to pay restitution, and efforts to cooperate with government agencies;

    (7)   collateral consequences, including disproportionate harm to shareholders, pension holders and employees not proven personally culpable, and impact on the public arising from the prosecution;

    (8)   the adequacy of the prosecution of individuals who are responsible for the corporation's malfeasance; and

    (9)   adequacy of civil, regulatory enforcement actions or other remedies. *Id.*

15   We note also that as this paper is being published, Congress is considering the "Attorney-Client Privilege Protection Act," which would impose a bar on federal investigations requesting companies to waive privilege or to refuse to advance fees (H. 3013, passed by the U.S. House of Representatives on November 13, 2007; S.186, now before the U.S. Senate Judiciary Committee).

16   *Report of Investigation Pursuant to Section 21(a) of the Securities Exchange Act of 1934 and Commission Statement on the Relationship of Cooperation to Agency Enforcement Decisions*, Release No. 44969, Oct. 23, 2001, *available at* http://www.sec.gov/litigation/investreport/34-44969.htm.

17   Statement of the Securities and Exchange Commission Concerning Financial Penalties, January 4, 2006, *available at* http://www.sec.gov/news/press/2006-4.htm; *see also* Litigation Release No. 19520, January 4, 2006, *SEC v. McAfee, Inc.*, Civil Action No. 06-009 (PJH) (N.D. Cal. 2006); *see also* Baker and Holbrook, "SEC Statement Clarifies Corporate Penalties – A Bit," National Law Journal, March 13, 2006.

"whether, and if so to what extent, to impose civil penalties against a corporation… turns principally on two considerations: The presence or absence of a direct benefit to the corporation as a result of the violation…[and] [t]he degree to which the penalty will recompense or further harm the injured shareholders."

Several additional factors the Commission will take into account include:

(1)   The need to deter the particular type of offense;
(2)   The extent of injury to innocent parties;
(3)   Whether complicity in the violation is widespread throughout the corporation;
(4)   The level of intent on the part of the perpetrators;
(5)   The degree of difficulty in detecting the particular type of offense;
(6   Presence or lack of remedial steps by the corporation;
(7)   Extent of cooperation with the Commission and other law enforcement agencies.

Despite the DOJ memoranda and SEC guidance discussed above, in most cases, the precise benefits of the Company's cooperation, if any, cannot be known at the outset of an investigation. Indeed, many companies that have cooperated with the government have received stiff financial penalties, albeit perhaps lower than if no cooperation had been proffered.[18] In the area of enforcement of the Foreign Corrupt Practices Act, Assistant Attorney General Alice Fischer has stated that, although not in the "best interests of law enforcement to make promises about lenient treatment in cases where the magnitude, duration, or high-level management involvement in the disclosed conduct may warrant a guilty plea and a significant penalty,…there is *always a benefit* to corporate cooperation, including voluntary disclosure, as contemplated by the Thompson memo. …*[I]f you are doing the things you should be doing* – whether it is self-policing, self-reporting, conducting proactive risk assessments, improving your controls and procedures, training on the FCPA, or *cooperating with an investigation* after it starts – *you will get a benefit*. It may not mean that you or your client will get a complete pass, but *you will get a real, tangible benefit*" (emphasis added).[19] While the number of DOJ-deferred prosecution or non-prosecution agreements has increased recently, many corporations and their counsel continue to believe that the benefits of cooperation have not been tangible and have, with certain DOJ divisions and sections or U.S. Attorney offices, been far too unclear. Some companies, after due consideration, have decided, in the face of a grand jury subpoena or allegation of wrongdoing, neither to conduct an internal investigation nor to cooperate with government authorities.

Signally, the Antitrust Division has a very clear standard – that parties who cooperate fully receive amnesty and reduced civil penalties. The Antitrust Criminal Penalty Enhancement

18   For a discussion of the Securities and Exchange Commission's response to cooperation through the end of 2004, *see* Tim Reason, *The Limits of Mercy: The Cost of Cooperation with the SEC is High. The Cost of Not Cooperating is Even Higher*, CFO Magazine, April 2005, *available at* http://www.cfo.com/article.cfm/3804652/c_3805512?f=magazine_featured.

19   Prepared Remarks of Alice S. Fisher at the ABA National Institute on the Foreign Corrupt Practices Act, October 16, 2006, *available at* http://www.usdoj.gov/criminal/fraud/docs/reports/speech/2006/10-16-06AAGFCPASpeech.pdf.

and Reform Act, adopted in 2004, increases the criminal penalties for violations, but also increases the incentives for self-reporting and cooperation in criminal antitrust matters. Corporations and individuals reporting their involvement in antitrust violations may receive immunity from the DOJ's Antitrust Division under its leniency program, insulating successful applicants from criminal fines and imprisonment. The legislation thus creates strong incentives for antitrust violators to be the first to self-report their violations and thus insulate themselves from criminal prosecution, though not from the likely civil litigation to follow.[20] In a statement issued after the bill was signed into law, Assistant Attorney General for Antitrust R. Hewitt Pate stated that the Act would make the DOJ's Corporate Leniency Program "even more effective."[21]

As emphasized in the College's 2002 report *The Erosion of the Attorney-Client Privilege and Work Product Doctrine in Federal Criminal Investigations,*[22] the attorney-client privilege and work product doctrine play a central role in corporate governance and remain essential to the due administration of the American criminal justice system. A waiver of these protections should not be taken lightly. This paper assumes that while a company, board, or audit or independent committee will consider, first and foremost, whether and how to conduct an internal investigation so as to protect the interests of the company and its stakeholders, it will also be cognizant of the importance of the attorney-client privilege and work-product protections in our society. (See also footnote 15, preceding.)

C.   The Role of the Board and Management in Conducting and Overseeing the Investigation

The relative participation of management and the Board in an internal investigation is a function principally of the nature of the allegations. Where the alleged or suspected conduct involves senior officers or serious employee misconduct, or where the corporate entity is the focal point of a government inquiry, it is important that management, including usually the General Counsel's office, not be, and not be perceived to be, in charge of the internal investigation. An investigation carried out by management, or a corporate department (such as an internal audit department), likely will not be afforded credibility. Furthermore, the continuing involvement in the conduct of the investigation by board members and officers whose conduct is at issue may taint the ability to preserve the privilege as well as the appearance of impartiality.[23]

Rather, the Board of Directors should delegate the task of overseeing the conduct of the internal investigation and retaining counsel to conduct the investigation to the Audit Committee of the Board, the independent members of the Audit Committee, or alternatively, some group of independent Board members forming a Special Committee (hereinafter, jointly referred to as the "Independent Committee").

---

20   H.R. 1086, 108th Cong., Title II, §201-221(2004). The benefits to the second, third or fourth cooperating company in Antitrust Division investigations are significantly less.

21   Press Release, Department of Justice, Assistant Attorney General for Antitrust, R. Hewitt Pate, Issues Statement on Enactment of Antitrust Criminal Penalty Enhancement And Reform Act of 2004 (June 23, 2004), *available at* http://www.usdoj.gov/atr/public/press_releases/2004/204319.htm.

22   http://www.actl.com/AM/Template.cfm?Section=All_Publications&Template=/CM/ContentDisplay.cfm&ContentFileID=68

23   *See Ryan v. Gifford,* 2007 WL 4259557 (Del. Ch. Nov. 30, 2007) (*Ryan I*); *Ryan v. Gifford,* 2008 Del. Ch. LEXIS 2 (Del. Ch. Jan. 2, 2008) (*Ryan II*).

D.   Independent Outside Counsel Should Be Retained To Conduct Significant Internal Investigations

At least since the era of Enron, WorldCom, Adelphia, and other corporate scandals, government prosecutors, regulators,[24] and, increasingly, the Company's independent auditors, have looked askance at the choice of regular outside corporate counsel to conduct a sensitive inquiry. This skepticism is based on the fear that regular corporate counsel may have a motive to avoid criticizing, and thus alienating, senior management, the source of perhaps sizeable past and future law firm revenues. Regular counsel may also have given advice on matters related to the subject of the investigation and members of the firm may become witnesses in the internal, or subsequent external, investigation. Similarly, the government and outside auditors will likely be concerned that the Company's regular outside counsel's business and social familiarity with the Company's management or implicated directors will cause counsel to pull punches to avoid alienating friends. However, there may be select circumstances where regular outside counsel's knowledge of a corporation's business, special expertise, and distance from the core investigation issues and subjects permit it to conduct an objective investigation. In some cases, in fact, the government agency most interested in the investigation may agree in advance that regular counsel is the most viable choice to conduct the investigation so long as the objectivity of the effort is assured.

The Company is best served to portray itself to the government, its independent auditors, the investment community, and the media as having complete integrity and a commitment to uncovering the facts. Thus, choosing independent counsel with few if any prior ties to the Company ("Special Counsel")[25] has become commonplace and is generally regarded as the first step in convincing governmental authorities of the "authenticity" of its cooperation.[26] Such Special Counsel are perceived as not beholden to the Company and able to view facts in an objective manner, neither biased in favor of the Company or its management, nor, indeed, the governmental authorities.[27]

There are several consequences to the bias in favor of Special Counsel:

First, placing a higher value on the perception of independence than on the experience of existing counsel comes at a price: existing counsel's familiarity with the people and practices of the corporate client is lost, and the absence of such, while it might satisfy the perceptions

---

24   *See* speech by SEC Commissioner Campos, "How to be an Effective Board Member," August 15, 2006, at http://www.sec. gov/news/speech/2006/spch081506rcc.htm ("…when circumstances indicate possible wrongdoing, the audit committee and the board should have their own independent advisors, investigators, and lawyers. As guided by Sarbanes-Oxley, the board and its committees should 'engage independent counsel and other advisors, as it determines necessary to carry out its duties' and should not rely exclusively on the corporation's advisors and lawyers").

25   The term "Special Counsel" is used in the same sense as the term "independent counsel" is generally used by other authors and papers. In our view, counsel that have been used occasionally by companies for individual matters should not be precluded from being selected as Special Counsel; rather, we recommend that whatever counsel is chosen, such firm not have had a substantial prior relationship with the Company.

26   Bennett, Kriegel, Rauh, and Walker, "Internal Investigations and the Defense of Corporations in the Sarbanes-Oxley Era," 62 Bus.Law.55, 57 (Nov. 2006)(hereinafter, "Bennett").

27   Indeed, some firms have specialized in the conduct of internal investigations, at the possible risk that such consistent conducting of internal investigations may tend to align the Special Counsel regularly with the interests of the regulators, rather than the Company and its shareholders.

of the regulators and independent auditors, could well cause a consequential cost increase to the public company and its shareholders.[28]

Second, the bias sometimes results in the self-perception that Special Counsel are hired in order to find wrongdoing and thus to justify the Special Committee's judgment that wrongdoing may have occurred. In this regard, it is incumbent on the Independent Committee, as well as the Special Counsel, to ensure that the Special Counsel mandate is to investigate the validity of the allegations and not to ferret out some perceived concerns for the sake of justifying what inevitably is the significant cost of the investigation.

It should be the goal of the Independent Committee, in seeking to determine the truth of the underlying allegations, to safeguard and act in the best interests of the shareholders, as well as to prevent the internal investigation from impairing the reputations of employees, officers, and directors of the Company not found to have engaged in wrongdoing. To those ends, Special Counsel should be instructed to engage in investigative tactics designed to get at the truth, including using their investigative, technological, and professional capabilities.

The Independent Committee should be aware that Special Counsel, left unchecked, could succumb to the abuses that are an occupational hazard of special prosecutors as described by then-Attorney General Robert Jackson, and cited by Justice Scalia:

> If the prosecutor is obliged to choose his case, it follows that he can choose his defendants. Therein is the most dangerous power of the prosecutor: that he will pick people that he thinks he should get, rather than cases that need to be prosecuted. With the law books filled with a great assortment of crimes, a prosecutor stands a fair chance of finding at least a technical violation of some act on the part of almost anyone. In [such cases], it is not a question of discovering the commission of a crime and then looking for the man who has committed it, it is a question of picking the man and then searching the law books, or putting investigators to work, to pin some offense on him.[29]

Third, in the current and foreseeable regulatory environment, the findings of Special Counsel are more likely to be credited by prosecutors, regulators, or private counsel (*e.g.*, when justifying settlement of a class or derivative lawsuit) if the Special Counsel is independent – *i.e.*, without a substantial prior relationship with the company or its senior management.

---

28 *See* announcement by Dell Corporation of the cost of $135 million to it in retaining Special Counsel and forensic accountants to investigate issues resulting in a restatement of net income for 2003 through 2005 of between $50 and $150 million on total net income of $12 billion for that period. According to the Form 8-K, the investigation was done by 125 lawyers from Special Counsel and 250 accountants who conducted 233 interviews of 146 Dell employees and reviewed 5 million documents. *See* http://www.sec.gov/Archives/edgar/data/826083/000095013407018421/d49260e8vk.htm.

29 R. Jackson, The Federal Prosecutor, Address Delivered at the Second Annual Conference of United States Attorneys, April 1, 1940, quoted in *Morrison, Independent Counsel v. Olson, et al.*, 487 U.S. 654 (1988) (Scalia, J., dissenting).

E.   The Independent Committee and Special Counsel Should Determine The Appropriate Scope of the Inquiry and the Rules of the Road

The Board should pass a resolution broadly authorizing the Independent Committee to retain counsel and their agents (e.g., auditors or other experts), conduct an investigation, and report its ultimate findings to the Board. The Independent Committee should retain the Special Counsel in writing. Special Counsel's retention letter should state the allegations under review and the scope of the inquiry, and make clear that Counsel is to advise the Independent Committee of its legal rights and obligations, as well as potential liabilities. Absent a conflict, the general counsel or regular outside counsel will advise the Company of its related rights and obligations and liabilities. The scope of the Special Counsel's engagement can be expanded in appropriate circumstances, and that expansion should also be confirmed in writing by the Independent Committee.

The scope of Special Counsel's mandate as set forth in the retention letter should be determined by the Independent Committee, in consultation with the Board, and state whether the Committee shall act for the Board or investigate and report to the Board for action. In defining the scope of the investigation, the Independent Committee must decide whether to provide Special Counsel at the outset with a broad mandate to find any and all suspected corporate wrongdoing, or a narrower mandate, at least at the outset, to examine only specific allegations or suspicions. In the latter case, Special Counsel should reassess with the Independent Committee whether additional suspicions should form the basis for a separate investigation by this or other Special Counsel or by regular counsel.

The Independent Committee and Special Counsel should also agree upon specific reporting procedures and protocols for documenting the investigation (such as the designation of all communications with legends such as "ATTORNEY-CLIENT PRIVILEGED" and, where applicable, "ATTORNEY WORK PRODUCT"). The goal at the outset should be frequent updating by oral reporting. Careful consideration should be given to the extent to which written reports should be rendered, if at all, during or at the conclusion of the inquiry. There is typically limited utility and great risk in creating interim written reports of investigation. Such interim reports run the risk of creating confusion and credibility issues, as well as potential unfairness to officers or employees who are the subjects of the investigations, if facts discovered in the latter part of the investigation are inconsistent with preliminary factual determinations or interim substantive findings.

The Board of Directors, in consultation with the Independent Committee, should also determine whether and to what extent Special Counsel may waive the Company's attorney-client privilege or its own work product protections in its dealings with regulators or other third parties.[30] We question whether there are any circumstances where Special Counsel, either on its own or with the authority of the Independent Committee, but without specific authority from the Board of Directors, should waive the Company's attorney-client privilege. We recommend that the Special Counsel not be given the authority to make such waiver decisions without prior full deliberation by the Independent Committee and the full Board, with the latter being encouraged to take advice from regular or other counsel on this decision.[31]

Nor should Special Counsel be allowed to condition its retention by the Independent Committee upon a pre-retention decision by the Independent Committee to waive all privileges. Furthermore, the engagement letter for Special Counsel should make clear that Special Counsel's work product, data, and document collection and analysis belong to the Independent Committee and the Company, not to Special Counsel, and should be returned to the Independent Committee and Company upon completion of the investigation, for possible use by the Company in its defense of possible third party or government claims.

There are times when it is far more efficient in terms of both cost and time for an outside expert to assist Special Counsel in the course of its investigations. Under Sarbanes-Oxley, the Audit Committee (which may well be functioning as the Independent Committee) has the authority to retain expert assistance in the course of an investigation.[32] The Independent Committee should exercise that authority by permitting Special Counsel to retain additional professionals, including forensic auditors, investigators, and public relations advisers, where necessary and with appropriate consultation with the Committee.

The choice of a particular expert and the manner in which it is retained are critical junctures in an investigation. In order to protect the attorney-client privilege and general confidentiality of communications between Special Counsel and its additional professionals, it is not advisable to choose professionals who also regularly or generally are employed by the Company to perform similar services, unless a very convincing case can be made that the Special Counsel's professionals are different and separated from the Company's regular professionals. In some situations, Special Counsel have conferred with prosecutors and regulators and obtained the prior approval of experts well-known to the company.

---

30   *See In re Qwest Communications International Inc. Securities Litigation*, 450 F.3d 1179 (10 Cir. 2006), in which the Court held that a company's turning over to the SEC and DOJ of internal investigative documents, pursuant to a confidentiality agreement, constituted a waiver of the attorney-client and work product privileges, and rejected the doctrine of "selective waiver" or "limited waiver." See also *U.S. v. Reyes,* 2006 U.S. Dist. Lexis 94456 (N.D. Cal. Dec. 22, 2006), holding that investigating counsel's oral report to DOJ and SEC summarizing otherwise privileged internal investigation interviews created a waiver, and rejecting the concept of "selective waiver." In connection therewith, the Judicial Conference of the United .States proposed and the U.S. Senate Judiciary has reported favorably to the Senate for a floor vote S. 2450, which would enact new Rule 502 of the Federal Rules of Evidence, placing, *inter alia*, new restrictions on waivers of the attorney-client privilege, such as limitations on the scope of a waiver and inadvertent disclosure and new procedures on the effectiveness of confidentiality orders. See http://www.uscourts.gov/rules/index2.html#sen502. Notably, however, the Judicial Conference did not recommend and the Senate Judiciary Committee did not adopt any version of the "selective waiver" doctrine.

31   We note the possibility that Special Counsel may unintentionally induce an inadvertent waiver of the corporate attorney-client privilege if there are communications by Company's officers or Board members directly with Special Counsel, rather than through the Independent Committee. See *Ryan v. Gifford*, 2007 WL 4259557 (Del. Ch. Nov. 30, 2007) (*Ryan I*); see generally, Gregory P. Joseph, "Privilege Developments I," The National Law Journal, February 11, 2008. However, the confines of this paper do not allow for analysis and recommendations with respect to this circumstance.

32   15 U.S.C. 78f(m)(5) ("AUTHORITY TO ENGAGE ADVISERS- Each audit committee shall have the authority to engage independent counsel and other advisers, as it determines necessary to carry out its duties.")

Experts should sign retention agreements that make clear their engagement is in contemplation of providing assistance for legal advice. Conclusions of independent experts also improve the appearance to outsiders (*i.e.*, government agencies and auditors) that the investigation is in fact independent.

F.   Communications to, and Indemnification of, Company Employees

Numerous management and employee morale issues will likely arise during the course of an internal investigation, especially where long-standing practices or the conduct of senior employees are under investigation. These issues should be addressed promptly by the Independent Committee, usually by a memorandum to all affected employees to keep employees abreast of general information about the purpose and expected length of the inquiry, the expectation of the Audit Committee that all employees will cooperate with the inquiry and with Special Counsel, and the need to preserve all data related to the investigation.

Importantly, the Independent Committee should explicitly communicate what constitutes "cooperation" of an employee during an internal investigation, and that an employee's refusal to cooperate in this regard may result in dismissal. In most circumstances, the cooperation of employees should include: (1) the provision, upon request, of all documents related to company business whether kept in the employee's office, home, or personal computer; (2) strict compliance with all document hold and retention notices; and (3) submission to interviews by Special Counsel.[33]

The Independent Committee should make an early determination of the extent to which employees of the Company will be authorized to retain separate representation by counsel whose fees will be advanced or indemnified, either through existing indemnification policies or new policies designed for the scope of the internal investigation (a decision that is largely governed by state law and the entity's bylaws). The Company should give consideration to distributing a memorandum to employees notifying them of the nature of any prospective investigation, the possible need for witness interviews, the Company's ability to recommend counsel for individual employees, the possibility that the Company will be responsible for advancing fees and expenses for the employee's representation, and the absolute requirement that any employee being interviewed tell the truth to Special Counsel.[34]

Whether to indemnify or advance legal fees (and the scope of any such indemnification or advancement) to employees has become a significant area of controversy under the

---

33   We distinguish the situation where an employee must cooperate fully with an internal investigation, including making himself available for an interview , or be subject to employment sanctions including possible discharge, from the situation where an employee invokes constitutional protections under the Fifth Amendment not to testify before a governmental body. In the latter situation, we do not think it appropriate for a Company to sanction the employee's invocation of constitutional rights by penalty or discharge. Nor, importantly, do we think it appropriate for governmental bodies to consider a corporation non-cooperative if it does not discharge or sanction an employee who invokes such protections, see *infra* at 22. We note the observation of the U.S. Supreme Court in *Slochower v. Board of Higher Education*, 350 US 551, 557-58 (1956) that ". . . a witness may have a reasonable fear of prosecution and yet be innocent of any wrongdoing. The privilege serves to protect the innocent who might otherwise be ensnared by ambiguous circumstances..." and do not think a Company should be in any way penalized for respecting an employee's invocation of such constitutional right.

34   *See Bennett*, at 65.

Thompson Memorandum and will likely continue to be under the McNulty Memorandum.[35] Under the Thompson Memorandum, in making charging decisions with respect to entities, prosecutors were required to consider whether the entity was supporting "culpable employees and agents . . . through the advancing of attorney's fees."[36] In June 2006, just months before the Department of Justice issued revised guidelines through the McNulty Memorandum, a district court in the Southern District of New York held this provision of the Thompson Memorandum unconstitutional in connection with the government's prosecution of several former KPMG employees for participation in the creation of allegedly fraudulent tax shelters.[37] In that case, the court held that the government's exertion of pressure on KPMG to refuse to advance legal fees for certain of its former employees violated those employees' Fifth and Sixth Amendment rights.[38]

In response, the McNulty Memorandum softened the DOJ's guidance. Under the McNulty Memorandum, federal prosecutors "*generally* should not take into account whether a corporation is advancing attorneys' fees to employees or agents under investigation and indictment;" but may take indemnification of employees into account in "extremely rare cases" in which "the totality of the circumstances show[s] that [the advancement of fees] was intended to impede a government investigation."[39] It is yet unclear whether a federal prosecutor's invocation of this aspect of the McNulty Memorandum in "extremely rare" circumstances would survive constitutional challenge. (Judge Kaplan's initial holdings with respect to the broader provisions of the Thompson Memorandum are currently before the Second Circuit.) It is also not clear the extent to which provisions of the McNulty Memorandum dealing with corporations' waiving the applicable privileges or not denying indemnity to employees under investigation are actually being followed by the line Assistant U.S. Attorneys, by whom most investigations are being conducted.[40]

As a general matter, the SEC for its part has generally not considered, and in our view should not consider, whether an entity has chosen to indemnify or advance legal fees

---

35   See generally, *United States v. Stein*, 435 F.Supp.2d 330 (SDNY 2006); *see also United States v. Stein* 452 F. Supp. 2d 230 (S.D.N.Y. 2006), *vacated by Stein v. KPMG LLP*) 486 F.3d 753 (2d Cir. 2007); *United States v. Stein*, 488 F.Supp.2d 350 (S.D.N.Y. 2007); *see also SEC v. Lucent Technologies*, Litigation Release No. 18715 / May 17, 2004, *available at* http://www. sec.gov/litigation/litreleases/lr18715.htm (Lucent fined $25 million for non-cooperation in that, *inter alia*, after reaching an agreement in principle with the staff to settle the case, and without being required to do so by state law or its corporate charter, Lucent expanded the scope of employees who could be indemnified against the consequences of the SEC enforcement action and failed over a period of time to provide timely and full disclosure to the staff on a key issue concerning indemnification of employees.)

36   *Thompson Memorandum, supra* n. 8, at 7-8.

37   435 F. Supp. 2d at 365-69.

38   *Id.* at 356-360.

39   *Id.* at 360-365.

40   In a survey conducted in 2007 by the Association of Corporate Counsel and the National Association of Criminal Defense Lawyers, corporate members were contacted via email and invited to participate confidentially in a survey to determine whether there had been or continued to be instances of prosecutorial abuse in the coercion of the waiver of their clients' attorney-client privilege or work product protection or denial of the rights to counsel or job security protections for their employees in the corporate investigation process. In a report to the U.S. Senate Judiciary Committee by the former Chief Justice of the Delaware Supreme Court, E. Norman Veasey, numerous instances of such coerced waivers and other abuses were cited, including several where Assistant U.S. Attorneys either did not know of the McNulty Memorandum, or were unfamiliar with its modifications of prior Department of Justice Practices. *See* Letter to Senate Judiciary Committee, dated September 13, 2007, *available at* http://www. abanet.org/poladv/abaday07/acpresources.html

for its employees or former employees, in determining whether the entity has been sufficiently "cooperative." (However, in 2004, the SEC took action against Lucent in part because the company "expanded the scope of employees that could be indemnified against the consequences of this SEC enforcement action," after it had reached "an agreement in principle with the staff to settle the case, and without being required to do so by state law or its corporate charter."[41]) The SEC has explicitly barred settling parties from recovering penalty payments through indemnification agreements. This policy, adopted in 2004 to purportedly "enhance deterrence and accountability," "require[s] settling parties to forgo any rights they may have to indemnification, reimbursement by insurers, or favorable tax treatment of penalties."[42] We question whether such a policy is fair to employees who may have engaged in what the SEC perceives as wrongdoing but did not do so as so-called "rogue" employees, but rather in furtherance of what they may have mistakenly believed was corporate policy. We also question what legitimate interest the SEC or, for that matter, any agency of the government has in interfering in any way with a corporation's legal right to pay the legal fees and expenses of past and present employees in defense of an investigation, trial, or appeal; with the exception of making payments for the purpose of the employee's committing acts of obstruction of justice by, for example, destroying documents, threatening witnesses, or suborning perjury.

Based upon the treatment by the SEC and the courts of indemnification and advancement of fees issues, we recommend that Independent Committees adopt a written policy at the outset of an internal investigation regarding the scope of indemnity and advancement that will be followed, presumably in adherence to its by-laws, applicable state laws, and other corporate and regulatory governance policies. The policy should include the possibility that, at the outset, the Independent Committee could desire to expand the scope of indemnity to include employees who might not be covered by the by-laws but are likely witnesses, subjects or targets of the inquiry, as well as independent contractors or acting officers of companies or their subsidiaries who perform important executive functions but are not literally within the company's standard indemnity policies. It is not recommended that, to curry favor with the regulators or governmental authorities, those individuals performing such functions be excluded from indemnification or advancement.

III.   Creating an Accurate Factual Record: Document Review & Witness Interviews

Given the attention being given by prosecutors and regulators to document preservation and production, the expedient collection and review of relevant documents, and interviewing of relevant witnesses, are principal steps in ensuring an accurate factual record.

A.   Mechanics of a Litigation Hold

At the outset of an investigation, counsel (likely Special Counsel in collaboration with regular or internal counsel) should identify the universe of documents that must be *preserved*,

---

41   *"Lucent Settles SEC Enforcement Action Charging the Company with $1.1 Billion Accounting Fraud,"* http://www.sec.gov/news/press/2004-67.htm. ("Companies whose actions delay, hinder or undermine SEC investigations will not succeed," said Paul Berger, Associate Director of Enforcement. "Stiff sanctions and exposure of their conduct will serve as a reminder to companies that only genuine cooperation serves the best interests of investors.")

42   Speech by Stephen Cutler, Director of Division of Enforcement, 24th Annual Ray Garrett Jr. Corporate & Securities Law Institute, April 29, 2004, http://www.sec.gov/news/speech/spch042904smc.htm.

as opposed to the universe of documents that must be *collected*. Counsel should not send a blanket email request that all relevant documents be forwarded to a central source.

The first step should be the identification of all relevant employees who are the likely sources of documents; preliminary interviews should be conducted by regular outside counsel and internal counsel to determine such relevant employees. Then, internal counsel should send an email direction to relevant employees stating, in essence, that no documents, including electronic documents and attachments, may be destroyed without explicit approval of counsel, see *infra*.

Third, regular counsel should engage in an analysis of relevant documents to determine if others should be included in the "litigation hold." This is especially important when the organization affected by the internal inquiry is in many disparate locations. For electronic documents, this may include communicating with the "key players" to learn how they stored information. Because of the amendments to the Federal Rules of Civil Procedure pertaining to e-discovery that went into effect on December 1, 2006, internal counsel should already have prepared and have available guides to all sources of "electronically stored information" in the Company, *see* Rule 16(f), and should be prepared to institute a litigation hold on all such materials.[43]

External counsel should oversee compliance with a litigation hold, using reasonable efforts to continually monitor the party's retention and production of relevant documents.[44] Once the relevant documents are obtained, all documents should be logged in the same way that one would during traditional litigation. A revised document storage and retention policy should be established as early as possible following the collection of relevant documents. This should involve the segregation of relevant backup electronic media, which in some cases may necessitate counsel's taking physical possession of backup tapes.[45]

As with traditional litigation, care should be taken to avoid over- or under-production during discovery. Over-producing data, especially in light of the volume of electronic media, can greatly drive up fees without yielding additional relevant data. An even greater risk of over-production or uncontrolled production is the waiver of privilege, which can result when documents are produced in their native application formats without care being taken to reveal metadata or

---

43   Among the varieties of electronically stored information, or "ESI," is one particular type called "metadata," defined by one Federal Magistrate Judge, as "(i) information embedded in a ESI in Native File [the electronic format of the application in which such ESI is normally created, viewed and/or modified] that is not ordinarily viewable or printable from the application that generated, edited, or modified such Native File; and (ii) information generated automatically by the operation of a computer or other information technology system when a Native File is created, modified, transmitted, deleted or otherwise manipulated by a user of such system." Suggested Protocol for Discovery of Electronically Stored Information, *In re Electronically Stored Information*, U.S.D.C., D.Md (Magistrate Judge Paul Grimm)(2007), *available at* http://www.mdd.uscourts.gov/news/news/ESIProtocol.pdf at pgs. 2-3. Metadata has provided Special Counsel with the ability to view drafts of documents and emails, including electronic information concerning the creation, formation, editing of such document, as well as the author or viewer of such edits and the dates of creation and viewing.

44   *See Zubulake v. UBS Warburg*, 2004 WL 1620866 (S.D.N.Y. July 20, 2004) ("Zubulake V"). *See also Telecom International Am. Ltd. V. AT&T Corp.*, 189 F.R.D. 76, 81 (S.D.N.Y. 1999) ("Once on notice [that evidence is relevant], the obligation to preserve evidence runs first to counsel, who then has a duty to advise and explain to the client its obligations to retain pertinent documents that may be relevant to the litigation") (citing *Kansas-Nebraska Natural Gas Co. v. Marathon Oil Co.*, 109 F.R.D. 12, 18 (D.Neb. 1983)).

45   *In re Electronically Stored Information, supra* n. 41, at 10.

maintain relationships between attachments and emails. Under-production and spoliation during the discovery process may result in sanctions ranging from adverse inference instructions[46] to default judgments because of counsel's insufficient actions[47] to monetary fines.[48]

B.   Document Collection & Review

Document collection is usually accomplished by the Company's regular outside and internal counsel, and then review of the documents and interviewing of witnesses by Special Counsel. The relevant universe of hard-copy and electronic documents must be identified and collected as early as possible in the investigative process, even before Special Counsel is retained, so that all available information will be preserved and there will be a sufficient factual background to identify relevant witnesses and conduct efficient interviews by asking the appropriate questions and being able to refresh witnesses' recollections.

Inside counsel and internal technology experts can be particularly helpful in identifying processes and sources of documents, and in coordinating the document collection process; each should play a major role in supervising the gathering, production, and preservation of documents, including electronic documents. However, once the Independent Committee has been appointed and Special Counsel retained, we recommend that the function of document analysis should be that of the Special Counsel and retained technology professionals to retrieve, host, and analyze electronic and hard documents. Internal technology professionals should be used only in those circumstances in which the Company has a sufficiently sophisticated staff that is trained in issues that may become critical in a subsequent litigation (*i.e.*, chain of custody) or in a government investigation (*i.e.*, the preservation of metadata).

C.   Witness Interviews

After relevant documents are reviewed (assuming time permits), Special Counsel should identify the relevant witnesses and begin conducting the interviews. Investigating lawyers should be aware that they could become witnesses in a criminal or civil procedure where an issue arises as to what statements a witness made to them during the investigation. In certain cases, such as when the scope of the issues are unclear, it may make sense for Special Counsel to begin the interview process before all relevant documents can be digested. Careful consideration should be given as to who should attend each interview both for reasons of obtaining objective responses and for ensuring the appearance of obtaining objective responses. Whether inside counsel should be present during the employee interviews is an issue that should receive special attention. The risks of having internal counsel present at the interview include inadvertently chilling the employee's ability to be forthcoming and having the employee incorrectly perceive that she is represented personally

---

46   *See In Re Seroquel Products Liability Litigation,* 244 F.R.D. 650 (M.D.Fla., Aug. 21, 2007) (granting in part a motion for sanctions against the defendant for failure to produce the discovery in usable format).

47   *See Metropolitan Opera Assoc., Inc. v. Local 100, Hotel Employees & Restaurant Employees International Union,* 212 F.R.D. 178, 222 (S.D.N.Y. 2003).

48   *See In the Matter of Banc of America Securities LLC,* Admin. Proc. File No. 3-11425, Mar. 10, 2004, *available at* http:// www. sec.gov/litigation/admin/34-49386.htm (fining Banc of America $10,000,000 for violating sections 17(a) and 17(b) of the Exchange Act for failure to produce documents during a Commission investigation).

by the internal counsel. It may also inadvertently trigger concerns by external auditors or regulators that inside counsel may herself be a potential wrongdoer, and thus inappropriately present when interviews are being conducted. At the very least, the issue should be thoroughly vetted with the Independent Committee before inside counsel takes a seat at the investigating table.

In some instances, it may be necessary for the Company to hire separate legal counsel for employees who are being interviewed that may have — or may appear to have — interests adverse to the Company. However, depending upon the Company's by-laws, it should not be necessary to retain such counsel until such adversity becomes sufficiently clear, or until an employee makes a reasonable request for separate counsel. An employee may on her own choose to seek the advice of counsel and ask that counsel be present for the interview. Absent exigent circumstances, *e.g.*, the need to immediately conduct interviews in order to qualify for corporate amnesty under Antitrust Division Corporate Leniency Program, a company should not refuse to grant such a request for counsel. However, as indicated earlier, an employee should be advised that his failure timely to cooperate – which includes fully submitting to interviews by Special Counsel – may result in adverse employment consequences including dismissal.

Special Counsel should be especially wary of the situation that arises frequently in the course of an internal investigation, when an employee who is otherwise without counsel is about to be interviewed and, before or as an interview is being conducted, asks whether she needs to consult counsel, or if she retains counsel, would the Company pay for such counsel. Special Counsel is best advised under these circumstances to remind the witness that he does not represent her and that if she wishes to speak to counsel, the Special Counsel would be willing to adjourn the interview for a reasonable time to allow such consultation, and, assuming that the Company's by-laws so allow, to consider the Company's indemnification of the employee's costs of counsel and advancement of fees and expenses.

As discussed above, advance preparation for such contingencies should include consultation with the Independent Committee at the outset of the engagement regarding the scope of the Company's obligations to indemnify and advance fees to categories of directors, officers, and employees.

The Independent Committee should also decide whether Special Counsel will agree with counsel for employees to make documents available to them for review before conducting interviews. Absent special circumstances such as valid concerns of possible witness tampering, obstruction of justice, other evidence of attempts to disrupt the integrity of the internal investigation, or an inability to retrieve and review voluminous documentation, Special Counsel generally should not interview witnesses before the witnesses have had a chance to review relevant documents. We specifically disapprove of Special Counsel's attempting to interview a witness who has not been given an adequate opportunity to refresh his recollection as to prior events by reviewing key hard or electronic documents, or Special Counsel's succumbing to pressure from prosecutors or regulators to attempt to do so, in an effort to trap a witness into a misstatement, which would otherwise not occur if the witness were properly refreshed with all relevant documents and electronic communications. This is particularly true since the government has indicted several executives in obstruction of justice cases in recent years based on alleged misstatements to outside counsel during the course of an investigation.[49] Accordingly, before interviews of officers and employees, and whenever practical, Special Counsel should make available to counsel for employees the topics and documents that will be covered in the interview, and allow employees to obtain copies of their documentary files, including calendars and electronic data.

At the outset of the interview, in addition to providing an overview of the investigation and the purpose of the interview, Special Counsel should make very clear that (1) Special Counsel represents the Company (or the Independent Committee, as the case may be); (2) Special Counsel is not the employee's lawyer and does not represent the employee's interests separate from those of its own client; (3) the conversation is protected by the attorney-client privilege, but the privilege belongs to the Company; and therefore (4) the Company can choose to waive its privilege and disclose all or part of what the employee has told Special Counsel during the interview to external auditors, the government, regulators, or others. Employees also should be apprised of their rights and responsibilities if they are contacted by regulators or prosecutors and asked to subject themselves to an interview, including the ability, without employment sanction, to invoke constitutional rights.

In light of the position taken by the DOJ, as indicated above, that an employee can be indicted for obstruction of justice under 18 U.S.C. 1512, if she lies to private counsel conducting an internal investigation, where she knows that her statements may be shared with a government agency such as the SEC or DOJ conducting its own investigation, we recommend that Special Counsel advise employees at the outset of the interview whether the Company has made a decision to waive the attorney-client privilege and work product protections, or is likely to do so, and to disclose the memorandum of interview to governmental authorities. In recent years, the government has brought several such cases.[50] It should be anticipated that an employee, being so advised, would seek individual counsel and Special Counsel should be prepared to accommodate the request for an adjournment to seek such counsel.

The interviews should be memorialized in a manner consistent with the attorney work-product doctrine and the ultimate purpose of the investigation. A memorandum should be prepared by Special Counsel of the substance of each witness's interview as close in time to the interview as possible. Ultimate decisions on the contents of the memorandum of a witness's interview should be Special Counsel's. However, fairness, and the possible use of such memoranda in follow-up inquiries by Special Counsel, regulators, or prosecutors, causes us to recommend that counsel for witnesses be given reasonable opportunity to review the memoranda for substance and to recommend possible modifications (which Special Counsel may, but is not compelled to, adopt, especially where the recommended modifications are, in Special Counsel's opinion, contrary to what was stated at the interview) so as to avoid misstating or mischaracterizing a witness's statements and

---

49   See text, *infra*, at n. 50.

50   *Id.*

to address adverse inferences that may be submitted in company proffers.[51] Special Counsel should consider reading, explaining the substance of, or showing a draft of the memorandum of interview of the witness to counsel for interviewed witnesses to review for accuracy but not to keep a copy thereof.[52]

      In addition, if a final written report is to be prepared, we recommend that tentative conclusions as to witnesses' conduct should, as a matter of fairness and completeness, be shared with counsel for present or former employees whose conduct is under examination for possible correction, modification or explanation. Again, we do not suggest that Special Counsel is obligated to adopt any modification suggested, but rather only to give any suggestion whatever weight is in Special Counsel's opinion warranted under the circumstances.

      The question of the extent to which, if at all, privileged and work-product protected material should be made available to the company's independent auditors, if, as would be expected, they so request, is highly complex.[53] There is little, if any, authority to support the view that dissemination of privileged information to an independent auditor does not create a waiver of the privilege. With respect to the production to external auditors of Special Counsel's work product prepared in anticipation of litigation, the decisions are inconsistent regarding whether doing so constitutes a waiver.[54] In the latter circumstance, we believe that entry into a written agreement with the independent auditor, acknowledging the confidentiality of the information shared and assuring that it will be held in confidence *might* be effective in some jurisdictions despite *Medinol*. However, under current case law, it is doubtful that any written confidentiality agreement with the independent auditor with respect to privileged material could prevent a waiver from being found. Notwithstanding

---

51   *See U.S. v. Kumar, E.D.N.Y., DOJ News Release, September 22, 2004* ("Former Computer Associates executives indicted on securities fraud, obstruction charges"), *available at* http://www.usdoj.gov/opa/pr/2004/September/04_crm_642.htm ("Shortly after being retained, the company's law firm met with [executives] in order to inquire into their knowledge of the practices that were the subject of the government investigations. During these meetings, the defendants … allegedly presented to the law firm an assortment of false justifications to explain away evidence of the 35-day month practice. The indictment alleges that [the defendants] … intended … that the company's law firm would present these false justifications to the U.S. Attorney's Office, the SEC and the FBI in an attempt to persuade the government that the 35-day month practice never existed").

52   We note the possible argument that disclosure to a witness or her counsel of the substance of a draft memorandum of interview or of tentative conclusions as to a witness's conduct may be deemed a waiver of the corporate privilege and perhaps Special Counsel's work product. We believe that risk of the success of such argument may be able to be mitigated by conditioning such limited disclosure upon the execution of a narrow "common interest" agreement between Special Counsel and counsel for the witness, premised upon the common interest that exists to prevent inadvertent factual errors and conclusions based thereon from being made by Special Counsel and the Independent Committee. See *Ryan v. Gifford I, supra* ("Under [the common interest] exception [to the attorney-client privilege],… for the communication to remain privileged even after its disclosure to others, the "others [must] have interests that are 'so parallel and non-adverse that, at least with respect to the transaction involved, they may be regarded as acting as joint venturers.'" *Saito v. McKesson HBOC, Inc.,* No. 18553, 2002 WL 31657622, at *4 (Del. Ch. Nov. 13, 2002) (citing *Jedwab v. MGM Grand Hotels, Inc.,* No. 8077, 1986 WL 3426, at *2 (Del. Ch. Mar. 20, 1986))."

53   See Brodsky, Palmer, and Malionek, "The Auditor's Need For Its Client's Detailed Information vs. The Client's Need to Preserve the Attorney-Client Privilege and Work Product Protection: The Debate, The Problems, and Proposed Solutions," http://www.abanet.org/buslaw/attorneyclient/publichearing20050211/schedule.shtml

54   *See Medinol, Ltd. v. Boston Scientific Corp.*, 214 F.R.D. 113 (S.D.N.Y. 2002) (holding that the disclosure of an internal investigation report to outside auditors waives both the attorney-client and work-product privileges, because the auditor's interests are not necessarily aligned with the corporation's interests). *But see Merrill Lynch & Co., Inc. v. Allegheny Energy, Inc.*, 2004 WL 2389822 (S.D.N.Y. 2004) (holding that the disclosure of internal investigation reports to outside auditors, while waiving the attorney-client privilege, does not waive the work product privilege because under the facts of the case the auditor and the corporation is not the equivalent of the type of tangible adversarial relationship contemplated by the work product doctrine).

the resulting dilemma to the Independent Committee and the Board of Directors, we believe there may well be circumstances where the independent auditor will insist that presentation of privileged material is a *sine qua non* for the certification of financial statements. Under those circumstances, a Board may have no choice but to authorize the delivery of such materials. However, we recommend that all other alternative courses of action be first explored with the independent auditors before such an outcome. We further recommend that Special Counsel be advised by the Board and Independent Committee at the outset of the engagement <u>not to share</u> information with the Company's external auditors without the written, fully informed consent of both the Independent Committee and the Company's Board. We recommend that the Board formally consider and decide the production and waiver issue before any steps leading to waiver are taken.

IV.   <u>Developing a Record of the Investigation</u>

During the course of the investigation, we recommend that Special Counsel keep and continuously update a record of witnesses and documents examined, documents shown to witnesses, and issues being raised. We also recommend that the Independent Committee be regularly updated on the course of the investigation. Under certain circumstances, these updates, especially those being done in the early stages of an inquiry, should be made orally, because the possibility exists that preliminary information gathered or early conclusions formed may well prove to be inaccurate or incomplete; premature recording of such information or conclusions could well be prejudicial to the company as well as implicated employees. In particular, once the Special Counsel has conveyed early impressions to the Independent Committee (based on preliminary reviews of documents and early interviews), those impressions may, as a practical matter, prove embarrassing to modify or be impossible to eradicate from the minds of the Independent Committee.

Once the investigation has been completed, Special Counsel must report its findings, conclusions, and bases to the Board, the Audit Committee, or the Independent Committee, as the case may be. Careful and early consideration must be given to whether the ultimate form of the report will be written or oral, and the effect of preparing a report on issues concerning the corporate attorney-client privilege and work product protections. The form of the report and the nature of its preliminary dissemination should be analyzed because of the likelihood that some version of the report will likely make it into the hands of government authorities or plaintiffs' attorneys, resulting in the substantial risk of enhanced civil litigation against the Company, and the officers and directors. If the report is to be written, careful consideration must be given to whether it will be posted on a website[55], and whether it will be turned over to prosecutors, regulators, and the independent auditor. [56]

Special Counsel should be careful to remind the governing body that the report's conclusions are ultimately that of the Independent Committee, not just Special Counsel, and that the Board members have fiduciary responsibilities to draw their own conclusions as to the evidence presented, and should not simply accept the conclusions as drawn by Special Counsel without a full understanding of the bases for such conclusions.

V.   The External Investigation

A.   Role of Special Counsel in Follow-on Investigations and Civil Litigation.

The Company may be tempted to use the services or work product of its Special Counsel in connection with its defense of external investigations and civil litigation. However, many experienced General Counsel and practitioners believe that Special Counsel should not be used as Company defense counsel, lest the independence of the Special Counsel be brought into question, and the legitimacy of the inquiry be compromised. We recommend that such follow-up inquiries be handled by counsel other than Special Counsel; otherwise, the view of Special Counsel as being independent of management will likely be dissipated, and external auditors, as well as regulators or prosecutors, are likely to disregard the work of such Special Counsel as being the product of bias.

B.   Use of Work Product of Special Counsel

As to whether the documents and database accumulated by the Special Counsel may be utilized by Company or employee counsel to minimize expenses to the Company and maximize the speed of preparation, we recommend that, absent genuine regulatory concerns regarding possible obstruction of justice, such documents and databases should be available for that use, once stripped of the evidence of the internal thought processes of Special Counsel.

Among the more difficult issues facing Company counsel that has inherited such document depositary and work product is the extent to which such should be made available to counsel for present or former employees, who are likely also facing civil litigation and regulatory

---

55   Posting a copy of an internal investigative report to the Independent Committee on a website or otherwise making it available to the public runs the risk of waiving both the protections of the work product doctrine and the corporate attorney-client privilege. *In re Kidder Peabody Securities Litigation*, 168 F.R.D. 459, 467, 469-70 (SDNY 1996) ("The decision to release the report appears, in retrospect, to have been virtually a foregone conclusion from the outset since this was a crucial aspect of Kidder's public relations strategy… In practical terms this means that Kidder's waiver by publication requires disclosure of those portions of the interview documents that are specifically alluded to in the [Special Counsel] report.")

56   *See Ryan v. Gifford,* 2007 WL 4259557 (Del. Ch. Nov. 30, 2007) (*Ryan I*), where it was held that delivery of a report by a special investigative committee, set up following the filing of a derivative action, to a Board of Directors consisting of several directors who were also named as defendants in the derivative action, constituted a full waiver of the privilege as to all communications between the committee and its counsel, including all correspondence between the special committee and its counsel, the investigation report, and all correspondence between the company and counsel to the special committee. Several unusual factors contributed to the finding of waiver. For example, because the directors were present at the committee's report in their personal, not fiduciary, capacities, the Court found the privilege had been waived, particularly as their personal attorneys were present and they used the committee's findings in their individual defenses. Furthermore, the special committee lacked sufficient authority to take action independent of the other board members.

investigations. Although outside the strict boundaries of this paper, we again believe that, absent genuine concerns about obstruction of justice, fairness dictates that such materials be made available on an individualized basis to such present or former employees, especially since it is likely that they have also been made available already to the Department of Justice, SEC, or other regulators.[57] Accordingly, we also recommend that the presumption be that the work product of Special Counsel such as witness interviews conducted by Special Counsel should be made available, on an individualized basis, to counsel for present or former employees, again, absent genuine concerns of obstruction of justice.

VI.   Recommendations

1.   An organization should take steps to consider an internal investigation when allegations have been lodged of significant corporate malfeasance or where an outside auditor gives notice that it suspects the possibility of illegal corporate activity. A Board of Directors, an audit, or a special committee may in select circumstances conclude that it is not in the best interests of the Company to investigate, disclose to, or cooperate with the government. In reaching the decision as to what is in the best interests of the shareholders, the Board, audit committee, or special committee may weigh and consider published prosecutorial and regulatory policies, related cases and dispositions, DOJ and/or SEC statements and the impact and costs of actual or anticipated litigation on the Company.

2.   Where the alleged or suspected conduct involves senior officers or serious employee misconduct, or where the corporate entity is the focal point of a government inquiry, management, including usually the general counsel's office, should not be, and should not be perceived to be, in charge of the internal investigation.

3.   A committee of the Board of Directors consisting of the independent members of the Board (the "Independent Committee") should be delegated the task by the Board of Directors of overseeing the conduct of the internal investigation when allegations have been lodged of significant corporate malfeasance or where an outside auditor gives notice that it suspects the possibility of illegal corporate activity and retaining counsel to conduct the investigation.

4.   The goal of the Independent Committee should be to seek to determine the truth of the underlying allegations, to safeguard and act in the best interests of the shareholders, and to prevent the internal investigation from impairing the reputations of employees, officers, and directors of the Company not found to have engaged in wrongdoing.

5.   The Board should pass a resolution broadly authorizing the Independent Committee to retain counsel and their agents, conduct an investigation, and report its ultimate findings to the Board. In order to preserve communications between the Committee and the Board as privileged, the Committee should have authority to take action independent of the Board.

---

57   It should be noted that the Department of Justice is on record in at least one option backdating case that disclosure of witness interview memoranda of Special Counsel to counsel for derivative plaintiffs, and other parties, would constitute premature disclosure of the substance of testimony from potential Government witnesses and would facilitate efforts by subjects and potential criminal defendants to manufacture evidence and tailor their testimony and defenses to conform to the Government's proof. *In re UnitedHealth Group Shareholder Derivative Litigation*, USDC, D.Minn., Civil No. 06-1216JMR/FLN.

6.   Outside counsel which has not had a substantial prior relationship with the Company and its senior management ("Special Counsel") should be retained to conduct significant internal investigations.

7.   The Independent Committee should retain the Special Counsel in writing. Special Counsel's engagement letter should state the allegations under review, the scope of the inquiry, and make clear that Special Counsel is to advise the Company of its legal rights and obligations, as well as its potential liabilities.

8.   The scope of the Special Counsel's engagement can be expanded in appropriate circumstances, and that expansion should also be confirmed in writing by the Independent Committee.

9.   The Special Counsel should be instructed to engage in investigative tactics designed to get at the truth of the underlying allegations of wrongdoing, including using such investigative, technological, and professional techniques of which they are capable.

10.   It should not be the goal of the Special Counsel, absent specific mandate from the Independent Committee, to investigate any perceived wrongdoing by corporate officers or employees wherever it may occur.

11.   The Independent Committee and Special Counsel should also agree upon specific reporting procedures and protocols for documenting the investigation.

12.   The Independent Committee should also determine whether and to what extent Special Counsel may waive the Company's attorney-client privilege or its own work product protections in its dealings with regulators or other third parties. The waiver of these protections is a major corporate decision that requires full and frank discussion of the benefits of these privileges and the impact of a waiver on prosecutorial, regulatory or parallel proceedings. In few, if any, cases, should Special Counsel be given the authority to make such waiver decisions on its own without prior full deliberation by the Independent Committee and the full Board, with the latter being encouraged to take advice from regular or other counsel on this decision.

13.   Special Counsel should not be allowed to condition its retention by the Independent Committee upon a pre-retention decision by the Independent Committee to waive all privileges.

14.   The engagement letter for Special Counsel should make clear that Special Counsel's work product, data, and document collection and analysis belongs to the Independent Committee and their Special Counsel, and upon completion of the investigation, may, in appropriate circumstances, be shared under the common interest privilege with the Company for possible use in its defense of third party or government claims. Any sharing of the materials with any director-defendants should be done only if it is clear those directors are acting in their fiduciary, not individual, capacities; to this end, their individual counsel should not be present and the directors should not use those materials in their individual defenses, or else the common interest privilege could be waived.

15.   The Independent Committee should authorize the Special Counsel in writing to retain additional professionals, including forensic auditors, investigators, and public relations advisers, where necessary.

16.   Experts should sign retention agreements that make clear their engagement is in contemplation of providing assistance for legal advice.

17.   The Independent Committee should consider promptly addressing management and employee morale issues by a memorandum to all affected employees to keep employees abreast of general information about the purpose and expected length of the inquiry, and the expectation that all employees will cooperate with the inquiry and with Special Counsel.

18.   The Independent Committee should explicitly communicate what constitutes "cooperation" of an employee during an internal investigation, and that an employee's refusal timely to cooperate in this regard may result in dismissal. In most circumstances, the cooperation of employees should include: (1) the provision upon request of all documents related to company business whether kept in the employee's office, home, or personal computer; (2) strict compliance with all document hold and retention notices; and (3) submission to interviews by Special Counsel.

19.   At the outset of an investigation, the Independent Committee should adopt a written policy regarding the scope of indemnity and advancement to directors, officers and employees, or others affiliated with the Company, in adherence to its by-laws, other corporate governance policies or new policies designed for the scope of the internal investigation.

20.   The Independent Committee should also consider, at the outset of an internal investigation, adopting a written policy expanding the scope of indemnity to include employees otherwise not covered by normal indemnification policies, and independent contractors or acting officers of companies or their subsidiaries who perform important executive functions but are not literally within the company's standard indemnity policies. The adoption of any expanded indemnification or advancement policy should be adhered to, once adopted, and not thereafter expanded to include those originally excluded, unless the scope of the investigation is altered.

21.   The Independent Committee should give careful consideration to distributing a memorandum to affected employees notifying them of the nature of any prospective investigation, the possible need for witness interviews, the ability of the Company to recommend counsel for individual employees, the possibility that the Company will be responsible for advancing fees and expenses for the employee's representation, and the requirement that any employee asked to give an interview cooperate and tell the truth to Special Counsel.

22.   External counsel should oversee compliance with a litigation hold, using reasonable efforts to continually monitor the party's retention and production of relevant hard-copy and electronic documents.

23.   The relevant universe of hard-copy and electronic documents must be identified and collected as early as possible in the investigative process, even before Special Counsel is retained.

24.   Special Counsel and retained forensic professionals should conduct document review and analysis of electronic and hard documents.

25.   Assuming time permits, after review and analysis of documents, Special Counsel should identify the relevant witnesses and begin conducting the interviews.

26.   At the outset of the interview, Special Counsel should advise each witness that (1) the Special Counsel represents the Independent Committee, (2) Special Counsel is not the employee's lawyer and does not represent the employee's interests; (3) statements made to the Special Counsel should be truthful; (4) the interview is protected by the attorney-client privilege, but the privilege belongs to the Company; and (5) the Independent Committee can unilaterally choose to waive its privilege and disclose all or part of what the employee has told Special Counsel during the interview to external auditors, the government, regulators, or others.

27.   The Independent Committee and Special Counsel should give careful consideration as to whether inside counsel should attend witness interviews, with an eye to maximizing the possibility of obtaining objective responses and to ensuring the appearance of obtaining objective responses.

28.   Special Counsel should advise employees at the outset of the interview whether the Company has made a decision to waive the attorney-client privilege and work product protections, or is likely to do so, and to disclose the memorandum of interview to governmental agencies such as the SEC or DOJ that is conducting its own investigation.

29.   Special Counsel should tell witnesses at the outset of the interview that the Department of Justice has taken the position that an employee can be indicted for obstruction of justice under 18 U.S.C. § 1512, if he or she lies to private counsel conducting an internal investigation, where he or she knows that his or her statements may be shared with a government agency such as the SEC or DOJ that is conducting its own investigation.

30.   Absent special circumstances such as valid concerns of possible witness tampering, obstruction of justice, other evidence of attempts to disrupt the integrity of the internal investigation or the unavailability of hard-copy or electronic documents, Special Counsel should make available to witnesses or their counsel the topics and documents that will be covered in the interview, and allow employees to obtain copies of their documentary files, including calendars and electronic data.

31.   Absent special circumstances such as valid concerns of possible witness tampering, obstruction of justice, or other evidence of attempts to disrupt the integrity of the internal investigation, Special Counsel should not generally interview witnesses before they have had a reasonable opportunity to review relevant documents.

32.   Absent special circumstances such as valid concerns of possible witness tampering, obstruction of justice, or other evidence of attempts to disrupt the integrity of an investigation, Special Counsel should resist attempts by prosecutors or regulators to seek the Special Counsel's interview of a witness who has not been given an opportunity to refresh his recollection as to prior events.

33.   Special Counsel should not advise an employee whether he or she should seek the advice of individual counsel, lest the employee misunderstand the role of Special Counsel as being the exclusive representative of the Independent Committee. Under these circumstances Special Counsel should remind the witness that the Special Counsel does not represent the witness and that if he or she wishes to speak to counsel, the Special Counsel will adjourn the interview for a short time to allow such consultation, and, if previously authorized by the Independent Committee, to provide recommendations of counsel.

34.   Special Counsel should memorialize the substance of each witness interview as close in time to the interview as possible and in a manner consistent with the attorney work-product doctrine and the ultimate purpose of the investigation.

35.   Absent special circumstances such as valid concerns of possible witness tampering, obstruction of justice, or other evidence of attempts to disrupt the integrity of an investigation, Special Counsel should give counsel for witnesses an opportunity to suggest modifications to the memoranda so as to avoid misstating or mischaracterizing a witness's statements. Special Counsel should consider reading, explaining the substance of, or showing a draft of the memorandum of the interview of the witness to counsel for interviewed witnesses to review for accuracy, but not to keep a copy thereof.

36.   Absent special circumstances such as valid concerns of possible witness tampering, obstruction of justice, or other evidence of attempts to disrupt the integrity of an investigation, if a final written report is to be prepared, Special Counsel should share tentative conclusions as to witnesses' conduct with counsel for present or former employees whose conduct is under examination for possible correction or modification.

37.   If the company's independent auditors request access to privileged information or the Special Counsel's work product, the Independent Committee should first explore all other alternative courses of action, but should not have the power or authority to decide the issue on its own. The Independent Committee should give careful consideration to such request and make a recommendation to the Board. The Special Counsel should be advised by the Board and Independent Committee at the outset of the engagement not to share information with the Company's external auditors without the written, fully informed consent of both the Independent Committee and the Company's Board.

38.   We recommend that the Board formally consider and decide the issue of production to the independent auditors before any steps leading to waiver are taken. In light of inconsistent decisions regarding whether production of Special Counsel's work product to external auditors constitutes a waiver of the work product protections, it is important to enter into a written confidentiality and common interest agreement with external auditors that allows for work product information to be provided without a waiver issue arising.

39.   During the course of the investigation, Special Counsel should keep and continuously update a record of witnesses and documents examined, documents shown to witnesses, and issues raised.

40.   Special Counsel should regularly update the Independent Committee on the course of the investigation. In the early stages of an inquiry, updates should generally be made orally, because of the possibility that preliminary information gathered or early conclusions formed might prove to be inaccurate or incomplete, and prejudicial to the company as well as employees implicated by them.

41.   Upon the completion of the investigation, Special Counsel should report its findings and the conclusions, and the bases therefor, to the Board, the Audit Committee, or the Independent Committee, as the case may be. Special Counsel should be careful to remind the governing body that the report's conclusions are ultimately that of the Independent Committee, not just Special Counsel, and that the Board members have fiduciary responsibilities to draw their own conclusions as to the evidence presented.

42.   Before presentation of the final report, the Independent Committee and Special Counsel should again give careful consideration to whether the ultimate form of the report will be written, oral or PowerPoint, to whom it will be provided, and how it will be published.

43.   Special Counsel should not be used as Company defense counsel in civil or criminal litigation or investigations that follow the internal investigation.

44.   Absent genuine regulatory concerns regarding possible obstruction of justice, the database of documents and selected work product, once stripped of the evidence the internal thought processes of Special Counsel, should be made available for use by any Special Litigation Committee, counsel to the Company, and on an individualized basis, to counsel for present or former employees.

APPENDIX 9

Title 9, Chapter 9-28.000 Principles of Federal Prosecution of Business Organizations (U.S. Department of Justice)[1]

---

1. While these guidelines refer to corporations, they apply to the consideration of the prosecution of all types of business organizations, including partnerships, sole proprietorships, government entities, and unincorporated associations.

9-28.001   DUTIES OF FEDERAL PROSECUTORS AND DUTIES OF CORPORATE LEADERS

The prosecution of corporate crime is a high priority for the Department of Justice. By investigating allegations of wrongdoing and by bringing charges where appropriate for criminal misconduct, the Department promotes critical public interests. These interests include, to take just a few examples: (1) protecting the integrity of our free economic and capital markets; (2) protecting consumers, investors, and business entities that compete only through lawful means; and (3) protecting the American people from misconduct that would violate criminal laws safeguarding the environment.

In this regard, federal prosecutors and corporate leaders typically share common goals. For example, directors and officers owe a fiduciary duty to a corporation's shareholders, the corporation's true owners, and they owe duties of honest dealing to the investing public in connection with the corporation's regulatory filings and public statements. The faithful execution of these duties by corporate leadership serves the same values in promoting public trust and confidence that our criminal cases are designed to serve.

A prosecutor's duty to enforce the law requires the investigation and prosecution of criminal wrongdoing if it is discovered. In carrying out this mission with the diligence and resolve necessary to vindicate the important public interests discussed above, prosecutors should be mindful of the common cause we share with responsible corporate leaders. Prosecutors should also be mindful that confidence in the Department is affected both by the results we achieve and by the real and perceived ways in which we achieve them. Thus, the manner in which we do our job as prosecutors—including the professionalism we demonstrate, our willingness to secure the facts in a manner that encourages corporate compliance and self-regulation, and also our appreciation that corporate prosecutions can potentially harm blameless investors, employees, and others—affects public perception of our mission. Federal prosecutors recognize that they must maintain public confidence in the way in which they exercise their charging discretion. This endeavor requires the thoughtful analysis of all facts and circumstances presented in a given case. As always, professionalism and civility play an important part in the Department's discharge of its responsibilities in all areas, including the area of corporate investigations and prosecutions.

[new August 2008]

9-28.200   GENERAL CONSIDERATIONS OF CORPORATE LIABILITY

A.   General Principle: Corporations should not be treated leniently because of their artificial nature nor should they be subject to harsher treatment. Vigorous enforcement of the criminal laws against corporate wrongdoers, where appropriate, results in great benefits for law enforcement and the public, particularly in the area of white collar crime. Indicting corporations for wrongdoing enables the government to be a force for positive change of corporate culture, and a force to prevent, discover, and punish serious crimes.

B.   Comment: In all cases involving corporate wrongdoing, prosecutors should consider the factors discussed further below. In doing so, prosecutors should be aware of the public benefits that can flow from indicting a corporation in appropriate cases. For instance, corporations are likely to take immediate remedial steps when one is indicted for criminal misconduct that is pervasive throughout a particular industry, and thus an indictment can provide a unique opportunity for deterrence on a broad scale. In addition, a corporate indictment may result in specific deterrence by changing the culture of the indicted corporation and the behavior of its employees. Finally, certain crimes that carry with them a substantial risk of great public harm—e.g., environmental crimes or sweeping financial frauds—may be committed by a business entity, and there may therefore be a substantial federal interest in indicting a corporation under such circumstances.

In certain instances, it may be appropriate, upon consideration of the factors set forth herein, to resolve a corporate criminal case by means other than indictment. Non-prosecution and deferred prosecution agreements, for example, occupy an important middle ground between declining prosecution and obtaining the conviction of a corporation. These agreements are discussed further in USAM 9-28.1000. Likewise, civil and regulatory alternatives may be appropriate in certain cases, as discussed in USAM 9-28.1100.

Where a decision is made to charge a corporation, it does not necessarily follow that individual directors, officers, employees, or shareholders should not also be charged. Prosecution of a corporation is not a substitute for the prosecution of criminally culpable individuals within or without the corporation. Because a corporation can act only through individuals, imposition of individual criminal liability may provide the strongest deterrent against future corporate wrongdoing. Only rarely should provable individual culpability not be pursued, particularly if it relates to high-level corporate officers, even in the face of an offer of a corporate guilty plea or some other disposition of the charges against the corporation.

Corporations are "legal persons," capable of suing and being sued, and capable of committing crimes. Under the doctrine of *respondeat superior*, a corporation may be held criminally liable for the illegal acts of its directors, officers, employees, and agents. To hold a corporation liable for these actions, the government must establish that the corporate agent's actions (i) were within the scope of his duties and (ii) were intended, at least in part, to benefit the corporation. In all cases involving wrongdoing by corporate agents, prosecutors should not limit their focus solely to individuals or the corporation, but should consider both as potential targets.

Agents may act for mixed reasons—both for self-aggrandizement (both direct and indirect) and for the benefit of the corporation, and a corporation may be held liable as long as one motivation of its agent is to benefit the corporation. *See United States v. Potter*, 463 F.3d 9, 25 (1st Cir. 2006) (stating that the test to determine whether an agent is acting within the scope of employment is "whether the agent is performing acts of the kind which he is authorized to perform, and those acts are motivated, at least in part, by an intent to benefit the corporation."). In *United States v. Automated Medical Laboratories, Inc.*, 770 F.2d 399 (4th Cir. 1985), for example, the Fourth Circuit affirmed a corporation's conviction for the actions of a subsidiary's employee despite the corporation's claim that the employee was acting for his own benefit, namely his "ambitious nature and his desire to ascend the corporate ladder." *Id.* at 407. The court stated, "Partucci was clearly acting in part to benefit AML since his advancement within the corporation depended on AML's well-being and its lack of difficulties with the FDA." *Id.*; see also *United States v. Cincotta*, 689 F.2d 238, 241-42 (1st Cir. 1982) (upholding a corporation's conviction, notwithstanding the substantial personal benefit reaped by its miscreant agents, because the fraudulent scheme required money to pass through the corporation's treasury and the fraudulently obtained goods were resold to the corporation's customers in the corporation's name).

Moreover, the corporation need not even necessarily profit from its agent's actions for it to be held liable. In *Automated Medical Laboratories*, the Fourth Circuit stated:

> [B]enefit is not a "touchstone of criminal corporate liability; benefit at best is an evidential, not an operative, fact." Thus, whether the agent's actions ultimately redounded to the benefit of the corporation is less significant than whether the agent acted with the intent to benefit the corporation. The basic purpose of requiring that an agent have acted with the intent to benefit the corporation, however, is to insulate the corporation from criminal liability for actions of its agents which may be *inimical* to the interests of the corporation or which may have been undertaken solely to advance the interests of that agent or of a party other than the corporation.

770 F.2d at 407 (internal citation omitted) (quoting *Old Monastery Co. v. United States*, 147 F.2d 905, 908 (4th Cir. 1945)).

[new August 2008]

9-28.300   FACTORS TO BE CONSIDERED

A.   General Principle: Generally, prosecutors apply the same factors in determining whether to charge a corporation as they do with respect to individuals.

See USAM 9-27.220 *et seq.* Thus, the prosecutor must weigh all of the factors normally considered in the sound exercise of prosecutorial judgment: the sufficiency of the evidence; the likelihood of success at trial; the probable deterrent, rehabilitative, and other consequences of conviction; and the adequacy of non-criminal approaches. *See id.* However, due to the nature of the corporate "person," some additional factors are present. In conducting an investigation, determining whether to bring charges, and negotiating plea or other agreements, prosecutors should consider the following factors in reaching a decision as to the proper treatment of a corporate target:

- the nature and seriousness of the offense, including the risk of harm to the public, and applicable policies and priorities, if any, governing the prosecution of corporations for particular categories of crime (see USAM 9-28.400);
- the pervasiveness of wrongdoing within the corporation, including the complicity in, or the condoning of, the wrongdoing by corporate management (see USAM 9-28.500);
- the corporation's history of similar misconduct, including prior criminal, civil, and regulatory enforcement actions against it (see USAM 9-28.600);
- the corporation's timely and voluntary disclosure of wrongdoing and its willingness to cooperate in the investigation of its agents (see USAM 9-28.700);
- the existence and effectiveness of the corporation's pre-existing compliance program (see USAM 9-28.800);
- the corporation's remedial actions, including any efforts to implement an effective corporate compliance program or to improve an existing one, to replace responsible management, to discipline or terminate wrongdoers, to pay restitution, and to cooperate with the relevant government agencies (see USAM 9-28.900);
- collateral consequences, including whether there is disproportionate harm to shareholders, pension holders, employees, and others not proven personally culpable, as well as impact on the public arising from the prosecution (see USAM 9-28.1000);
- the adequacy of the prosecution of individuals responsible for the corporation's malfeasance; and
- the adequacy of remedies such as civil or regulatory enforcement actions (see USAM 9-28.1100).

B.   Comment: The factors listed in this section are intended to be illustrative of those that should be evaluated and are not an exhaustive list of potentially relevant considerations. Some of these factors may not apply to specific cases, and in some cases one factor may override all others. For example, the nature and seriousness of the offense may be such as to warrant prosecution regardless of the other factors. In most cases, however, no single factor will be dispositive. In addition, national law enforcement policies in various enforcement areas may require that more or less weight be given to certain of these factors than to others. Of course, prosecutors must exercise their thoughtful and pragmatic judgment in applying and balancing these factors, so as to achieve a fair and just outcome and promote respect for the law.

In making a decision to charge a corporation, the prosecutor generally has substantial latitude in determining when, whom, how, and even whether to prosecute for violations of federal criminal law. In exercising that discretion, prosecutors should consider the following statements of principles that summarize the considerations they should weigh and the practices they should follow in discharging their prosecutorial responsibilities. In doing so, prosecutors should ensure that the general purposes of the criminal law—assurance of warranted punishment, deterrence of further criminal conduct, protection of the public from dangerous and fraudulent conduct, rehabilitation of offenders, and restitution for victims and affected communities— are adequately met, taking into account the special nature of the corporate "person."

[new August 2008]

9-28.400   SPECIAL POLICY CONCERNS

A.   General Principle: The nature and seriousness of the crime, including the risk of harm to the public from the criminal misconduct, are obviously primary factors in determining whether to charge a corporation. In addition, corporate conduct, particularly that of national and multi-national corporations, necessarily intersects with federal economic, tax, and criminal law enforcement policies. In applying these Principles, prosecutors must consider the practices and policies of the appropriate Division of the Department, and must comply with those policies to the extent required by the facts presented.

B.   Comment: In determining whether to charge a corporation, prosecutors should take into account federal law enforcement priorities as discussed above. *See* USAM 9-27.230. In addition, however, prosecutors must be aware of the specific policy goals and incentive programs established by the respective Divisions and regulatory agencies. Thus, whereas natural persons may be given incremental degrees of credit (ranging from immunity to lesser charges to sentencing considerations) for turning themselves in, making statements against their penal interest, and cooperating in the government's investigation of their own and others' wrongdoing, the same approach may not be appropriate in all circumstances with respect to corporations. As an example, it is entirely proper in many investigations for a prosecutor to consider the corporation's pre-indictment conduct, e.g., voluntary disclosure, cooperation, remediation or restitution, in determining whether to seek an indictment. However, this would not necessarily be appropriate in an antitrust investigation, in which antitrust violations, by definition, go to the heart of the corporation's business. With this in mind, the Antitrust Division has established a firm policy, understood in the business community, that credit should not be given at the charging stage for a compliance program and that amnesty is available only to the first corporation to make full disclosure to the government. As another example, the Tax Division has a strong preference for prosecuting responsible individuals, rather than entities, for corporate tax offenses. Thus, in determining whether or not to charge a corporation, prosecutors must consult with the Criminal, Antitrust, Tax, Environmental and Natural Resources, and National Security Divisions, as appropriate.

[new August 2008]

9-28.500   PERVASIVENESS OF WRONGDOING WITHIN THE CORPORATION

A.   General Principle: A corporation can only act through natural persons, and it is therefore held responsible for the acts of such persons fairly attributable to it. Charging a corporation for even minor misconduct may be appropriate where the wrongdoing was pervasive and was undertaken by a large number of employees, or by all the employees in a particular role within the corporation, or was condoned by upper management. On the other hand, it may not be appropriate to impose liability upon a corporation, particularly one with a robust compliance program in place, under a strict *respondeat superior* theory for the single isolated act of a rogue employee. There is, of course, a wide spectrum between these two extremes, and a prosecutor should exercise sound discretion in evaluating the pervasiveness of wrongdoing within a corporation.

B.   Comment: Of these factors, the most important is the role and conduct of management. Although acts of even low-level employees may result in criminal liability, a corporation is directed by its management and management is responsible for a corporate culture in which criminal conduct is either discouraged or tacitly encouraged. As stated in commentary to the Sentencing Guidelines:

> Pervasiveness [is] case specific and [will] depend on the number, and degree of responsibility, of individuals [with] substantial authority . . . who participated in, condoned, or were willfully ignorant of the offense. Fewer individuals need to be involved for a finding of pervasiveness if those individuals exercised a relatively high degree of authority. Pervasiveness can occur either within an organization as a whole or within a unit of an organization.

USSG § 8C2.5, cmt. (n. 4).

[new August 2008]

9-28.600   THE CORPORATION'S PAST HISTORY

A.   General Principle: Prosecutors may consider a corporation's history of similar conduct, including prior criminal, civil, and regulatory enforcement actions against it, in determining whether to bring criminal charges and how best to resolve cases.

B.   Comment: A corporation, like a natural person, is expected to learn from its mistakes. A history of similar misconduct may be probative of a corporate culture that encouraged, or at least condoned, such misdeeds, regardless of any compliance programs. Criminal prosecution of a corporation may be particularly appropriate where the corporation previously had been subject to non-criminal guidance, warnings, or sanctions, or previous criminal charges, and it either had not taken adequate action to prevent future unlawful conduct or had continued to engage in the misconduct in spite of the warnings or enforcement actions taken against it. The corporate structure itself (e.g., the creation or existence of subsidiaries or operating divisions) is not dispositive in this analysis, and enforcement actions taken against the corporation or any of its divisions, subsidiaries, and affiliates may be considered, if germane. *See* USSG § 8C2.5(c), cmt. (n. 6).

[new August 2008]

9-28.700   THE VALUE OF COOPERATION

A.   General Principle: In determining whether to charge a corporation and how to resolve corporate criminal cases, the corporation's timely and voluntary disclosure of wrongdoing and its cooperation with the government's investigation may be relevant factors. In gauging the extent of the corporation's cooperation, the prosecutor may consider, among other things, whether the corporation made a voluntary and timely disclosure, and the corporation's willingness to provide relevant information and evidence and identify relevant actors within and outside the corporation, including senior executives.

Cooperation is a potential mitigating factor, by which a corporation—just like any other subject of a criminal investigation—can gain credit in a case that otherwise is appropriate for indictment and prosecution. Of course, the decision not to cooperate by a corporation (or individual) is not itself evidence of misconduct, at least where the lack of cooperation does not involve criminal misconduct or demonstrate consciousness of guilt (e.g., suborning perjury or false statements, or refusing to comply with lawful discovery requests). Thus, failure to cooperate, in and of itself, does not support or require the filing of charges with respect to a corporation any more than with respect to an individual.

B.   Comment: In investigating wrongdoing by or within a corporation, a prosecutor is likely to encounter several obstacles resulting from the nature of the corporation itself. It will often be difficult to determine which individual took which action on behalf of the corporation. Lines of authority and responsibility may be shared among operating divisions or departments, and records and personnel may be spread throughout the United States or even among several countries. Where the criminal conduct continued over an extended period of time, the culpable or knowledgeable personnel may have been promoted, transferred, or fired, or they may have quit or retired. Accordingly, a corporation's cooperation may be critical in identifying potentially relevant actors and locating relevant evidence, among other things, and in doing so expeditiously.

This dynamic—i.e., the difficulty of determining what happened, where the evidence is, and which individuals took or promoted putatively illegal corporate actions—can have negative consequences for both the government and the corporation that is the subject or target of a government investigation. More specifically, because of corporate attribution principles concerning actions of corporate officers and employees (*see, e.g., supra* section II), uncertainty about exactly who authorized or directed apparent corporate misconduct can inure to the detriment of a corporation. For example, it may not matter under the law which of several possible executives or leaders in a chain of command approved of or authorized criminal conduct; however, that information if known might bear on the propriety of a particular disposition short of indictment of the corporation. It may not be in the interest of a corporation or the government for a charging decision to be made in the absence of such information, which might occur if, for example, a statute of limitations were relevant and authorization by any one of the officials were enough to justify a charge under the law. Moreover, and at a minimum, a protracted government investigation of such an issue could, as a collateral consequence, disrupt the corporation's business operations or even depress its stock price.

For these reasons and more, cooperation can be a favorable course for both the government and the corporation. Cooperation benefits the government—and ultimately shareholders, employees, and other often blameless victims—by allowing prosecutors and federal agents, for example, to avoid protracted delays, which compromise their ability to quickly uncover and address the full extent of widespread corporate crimes. With cooperation by the corporation, the government may be able to reduce tangible losses, limit damage to reputation, and preserve assets for restitution. At the same time, cooperation may benefit the corporation by enabling the government to focus its investigative resources in a manner that will not unduly disrupt the corporation's legitimate business operations. In addition, and critically, cooperation may benefit the corporation by presenting it with the opportunity to earn credit for its efforts.

[new August 2008]

9-28.710   ATTORNEY-CLIENT AND WORK PRODUCT PROTECTIONS

The attorney-client privilege and the attorney work product protection serve an extremely important function in the American legal system. The attorney-client privilege is one of the oldest and most sacrosanct privileges under the law. *See Upjohn v. United States*, 449 U.S. 383, 389 (1981). As the Supreme Court has stated, "[i]ts purpose is to encourage full and frank communication between attorneys and their clients and thereby promote broader public interests in the observance of law and administration of justice." *Id.* The value of promoting a corporation's ability to seek frank and comprehensive legal advice is particularly important in the contemporary global business environment, where corporations often face complex and dynamic legal and regulatory obligations imposed by the federal government and also by states and foreign governments. The work product doctrine serves similarly important goals.

For these reasons, waiving the attorney-client and work product protections has never been a prerequisite under the Department's prosecution guidelines for a corporation to be viewed as cooperative. Nonetheless, a wide range of commentators and members of the American legal community and criminal justice system have asserted that the Department's policies have been used, either wittingly or unwittingly, to coerce business entities into waiving attorney-client privilege and work-product protection. Everyone agrees that a corporation may freely waive its own privileges if it chooses to do so; indeed, such waivers occur routinely when corporations are victimized by their employees or others, conduct an internal investigation, and then disclose the details of the investigation to law enforcement officials in an effort to seek prosecution of the offenders. However, the contention, from a broad array of voices, is that the Department's position on attorney-client privilege and work product protection waivers has promoted an environment in which those protections are being unfairly eroded to the detriment of all.

The Department understands that the attorney-client privilege and attorney work product protection are essential and long-recognized components of the American legal system. What the government seeks and needs to advance its legitimate (indeed, essential) law enforcement mission is not waiver of those protections, but rather the facts known to the corporation about the putative criminal misconduct under review. In addition, while a corporation remains free to convey non-factual or "core" attorney-client communications or work product—if and only if the corporation voluntarily chooses to do so—prosecutors should not ask for such waivers and are directed not to do so. The critical factor is whether the corporation has provided the facts about the events, as explained further herein.

[new August 2008]

9-28.720   COOPERATION: DISCLOSING THE RELEVANT FACTS

Eligibility for cooperation credit is not predicated upon the waiver of attorney-client privilege or work product protection. Instead, the sort of cooperation that is most valuable to resolving allegations of misconduct by a corporation and its officers, directors, employees, or agents is disclosure of the relevant *facts* concerning such misconduct. In this regard, the analysis parallels that for a non-corporate defendant, where cooperation typically requires disclosure of relevant factual knowledge and not of discussions between an individual and his attorneys.

Thus, when the government investigates potential corporate wrongdoing, it seeks the relevant facts. For example, how and when did the alleged misconduct occur? Who promoted or approved it? Who was responsible for committing it? In this respect, the investigation of a corporation differs little from the investigation of an individual. In both cases, the government needs to know the facts to achieve a just and fair outcome. The party under investigation may choose to cooperate by disclosing the facts, and the government may give credit for the party's disclosures. If a corporation wishes to receive credit for such cooperation, which then can be considered with all other cooperative efforts and circumstances in evaluating how fairly to proceed, then the corporation, like any person, must disclose the relevant facts of which it has knowledge.[2]

---

2. There are other dimensions of cooperation beyond the mere disclosure of facts, of course. These can include, for example, providing non-privileged documents and other evidence, making witnesses available for interviews, and assisting in the interpretation of complex business records. This section of the Principles focuses solely on the disclosure of facts and the privilege issues that may be implicated thereby.

(a) Disclosing the Relevant Facts – Facts Gathered Through Internal Investigation

Individuals and corporations often obtain knowledge of facts in different ways. An individual knows the facts of his or others' misconduct through his own experience and perceptions. A corporation is an artificial construct that cannot, by definition, have personal knowledge of the facts. Some of those facts may be reflected in documentary or electronic media like emails, transaction or accounting documents, and other records. Often, the corporation gathers facts through an internal investigation. Exactly how and by whom the facts are gathered is for the corporation to decide. Many corporations choose to collect information about potential misconduct through lawyers, a process that may confer attorney-client privilege or attorney work product protection on at least some of the information collected. Other corporations may choose a method of fact-gathering that does not have that effect—for example, having employee or other witness statements collected after interviews by non-attorney personnel. Whichever process the corporation selects, the government's key measure of cooperation must remain the same as it does for an individual: has the party timely disclosed the relevant facts about the putative misconduct? That is the operative question in assigning cooperation credit for the disclosure of information—*not* whether the corporation discloses attorney-client or work product materials. Accordingly, a corporation should receive the same credit for disclosing facts contained in materials that are not protected by the attorney-client privilege or attorney work product as it would for disclosing identical facts contained in materials that are so protected.[3] On this point the Report of the House Judiciary Committee, submitted in connection with the attorney-client privilege bill passed by the House of Representatives (H.R. 3013), comports with the approach required here:

> [A]n . . . attorney of the United States may base cooperation credit on the facts that are disclosed, but is prohibited from basing cooperation credit upon whether or not the materials are protected by attorney-client privilege or attorney work product. As a result, an entity that voluntarily discloses should receive the same amount of cooperation credit for disclosing facts that happen to be contained in materials not protected by attorney-client privilege or attorney work product as it would receive for disclosing identical facts that are contained in materials protected by attorney-client privilege or attorney work product. There should be no differentials in an assessment of cooperation (i.e., neither a credit nor a penalty) based upon whether or not the materials disclosed are protected by attorney-client privilege or attorney work product.

H.R. Rep. No. 110-445 at 4 (2007).

---

3. By way of example, corporate personnel are typically interviewed during an internal investigation. If the interviews are conducted by counsel for the corporation, certain notes and memoranda generated from the interviews may be subject, at least in part, to the protections of attorney-client privilege and/or attorney work product. To receive cooperation credit for providing factual information, the corporation need not produce, and prosecutors may not request, protected notes or memoranda generated by the lawyers' interviews. To earn such credit, however, the corporation does need to produce, and prosecutors may request, relevant factual information—including relevant factual information acquired through those interviews, unless the identical information has otherwise been provided—as well as relevant non-privileged evidence such as accounting and business records and emails between non-attorney employees or agents.

In short, so long as the corporation timely discloses relevant facts about the putative misconduct, the corporation may receive due credit for such cooperation, regardless of whether it chooses to waive privilege or work product protection in the process.[4] Likewise, a corporation that does not disclose the relevant facts about the alleged misconduct—for whatever reason—typically should not be entitled to receive credit for cooperation.

Two final and related points bear noting about the disclosure of facts, although they should be obvious. First, the government cannot compel, and the corporation has no obligation to make, such disclosures (although the government can obviously compel the disclosure of certain records and witness testimony through subpoenas). Second, a corporation's failure to provide relevant information does not mean the corporation will be indicted. It simply means that the corporation will not be entitled to mitigating credit for that cooperation. Whether the corporation faces charges will turn, as it does in any case, on the sufficiency of the evidence, the likelihood of success at trial, and all of the other factors identified in Section III above. If there is insufficient evidence to warrant indictment, after appropriate investigation has been completed, or if the other factors weigh against indictment, then the corporation should not be indicted, irrespective of whether it has earned cooperation credit. The converse is also true: The government may charge even the most cooperative corporation pursuant to these Principles if, in weighing and balancing the factors described herein, the prosecutor determines that a charge is required in the interests of justice. Put differently, even the most sincere and thorough effort to cooperate cannot necessarily absolve a corporation that has, for example, engaged in an egregious, orchestrated, and widespread fraud. Cooperation is a relevant potential mitigating factor, but it alone is not dispositive.

(b) Legal Advice and Attorney Work Product

Separate from (and usually preceding) the fact-gathering process in an internal investigation, a corporation, through its officers, employees, directors, or others, may have consulted with corporate counsel regarding or in a manner that concerns the legal implications of the putative misconduct at issue. Communications of this sort, which are both independent of the fact-gathering component of an internal investigation and made for the purpose of seeking or dispensing legal advice, lie at the core of the attorney-client privilege. Such communications can naturally have a salutary effect on corporate behavior—facilitating, for example, a corporation's effort to comply with complex and evolving legal and regulatory regimes.[5] Except as noted in subparagraphs (b)(i) and (b)(ii) below, a corporation need not disclose

---

4. In assessing the timeliness of a corporation's disclosures, prosecutors should apply a standard of reasonableness in light of the totality of circumstances.

5. These privileged communications are not necessarily limited to those that occur contemporaneously with the underlying misconduct. The would include, for instance, legal advice provided by corporate counsel in an internal investigation report. Again, the key measure of cooperation is the disclosure of factual information known to the corporation, not the disclosure of legal advice or theories rendered in connection with the conduct at issue (subject to the two exceptions noted in U.S.A.M. 9-28.720(b)(i-ii)).

and prosecutors may not request the disclosure of such communications as a condition for the corporation's eligibility to receive cooperation credit.

Likewise, non-factual or core attorney work product—for example, an attorney's mental impressions or legal theories—lies at the core of the attorney work product doctrine. A corporation need not disclose, and prosecutors may not request, the disclosure of such attorney work product as a condition for the corporation's eligibility to receive cooperation credit.

(i) Advice of Counsel Defense in the Instant Context

Occasionally a corporation or one of its employees may assert an advice-of-counsel defense, based upon communications with in-house or outside counsel that took place prior to or contemporaneously with the underlying conduct at issue. In such situations, the defendant must tender a legitimate factual basis to support the assertion of the advice-of-counsel defense. *See, e.g., Pitt v. Dist. of Columbia*, 491 F.3d 494, 504-05 (D.C. Cir. 2007); *United States v. Wenger*, 427 F.3d 840, 853-54 (10th Cir. 2005); *United States v. Cheek*, 3 F.3d 1057, 1061-62 (7th Cir. 1993). The Department cannot fairly be asked to discharge its responsibility to the public to investigate alleged corporate crime, or to temper what would otherwise be the appropriate course of prosecutive action, by simply accepting on faith an otherwise unproven assertion that an attorney—perhaps even an unnamed attorney—approved potentially unlawful practices. Accordingly, where an advice-of-counsel defense has been asserted, prosecutors may ask for the disclosure of the communications allegedly supporting it.

(ii) Communications in Furtherance of a Crime or Fraud

Communications between a corporation (through its officers, employees, directors, or agents) and corporate counsel that are made in furtherance of a crime or fraud are, under settled precedent, outside the scope and protection of the attorney-client privilege. *See United States v. Zolin*, 491 U.S. 554, 563 (1989); *United States v. BDO Seidman, LLP*, 492 F.3d 806, 818 (7th Cir. 2007). As a result, the Department may properly request such communications if they in fact exist.

[new August 2008]

9-28.730 OBSTRUCTING THE INVESTIGATION

Another factor to be weighed by the prosecutor is whether the corporation has engaged in conduct intended to impede the investigation. Examples of such conduct could include: inappropriate directions to employees or their counsel, such as directions not to be truthful or to conceal relevant facts; making representations or submissions that contain misleading assertions or material omissions; and incomplete or delayed production of records.

In evaluating cooperation, however, prosecutors should not take into account whether a corporation is advancing or reimbursing attorneys' fees or providing counsel to employees, officers, or directors under investigation or indictment. Likewise, prosecutors may not request that a corporation refrain from taking such action. This prohibition is not meant to prevent a prosecutor from asking questions about an attorney's representation of a corporation or its employees, officers, or directors, where otherwise appropriate under the law.[6] Neither is it intended to limit the otherwise applicable reach of criminal obstruction of justice statutes such as 18 U.S.C. § 1503. If the payment of attorney fees were used in a manner that would otherwise constitute criminal obstruction of justice—for example, if fees were advanced on the condition that an employee adhere to a version of the facts that the corporation and the employee knew to be false—these Principles would not (and could not) render inapplicable such criminal prohibitions.

Similarly, the mere participation by a corporation in a joint defense agreement does not render the corporation ineligible to receive cooperation credit, and prosecutors may not request that a corporation refrain from entering into such agreements. Of course, the corporation may wish to avoid putting itself in the position of being disabled, by virtue of a particular joint defense or similar agreement, from providing some relevant facts to the government and thereby limiting its ability to seek such cooperation credit. Such might be the case if the corporation gathers facts from employees who have entered into a joint defense agreement with the corporation, and who may later seek to prevent the corporation from disclosing the facts it has acquired. Corporations may wish to address this situation by crafting or participating in joint defense agreements, to the extent they choose to enter them, that provide such flexibility as they deem appropriate.

Finally, it may on occasion be appropriate for the government to consider whether the corporation has shared with others sensitive information about the investigation that the government provided to the corporation. In appropriate situations, as it does with individuals, the government may properly request that, if a corporation wishes to receive credit for cooperation, the information provided by the government to the corporation not be transmitted to others—for example, where the disclosure of such information could lead to flight by individual subjects, destruction of evidence, or dissipation or concealment of assets.

[new August 2008]

9-28.740   OFFERING COOPERATION: NO ENTITLEMENT TO IMMUNITY

A corporation's offer of cooperation or cooperation itself does not automatically entitle it to immunity from prosecution or a favorable resolution of its case. A corporation should not be able to escape liability merely by offering up its directors, officers, employees, or agents. Thus, a corporation's willingness to cooperate is not determinative; that factor, while relevant, needs to be considered in conjunction with all other factors.

[new August 2008]

---

6. Routine questions regarding the representation status of a corporation and its employees, including how and by whom attorneys' fees are paid, sometimes arise in the course of an investigation under certain circumstances—to take one example, to assess conflict-of-interest issues. Such questions can be appropriate and this guidance is not intended to prohibit such limited inquiries.

9-28.750   QUALIFYING FOR IMMUNITY, AMNESTY, OR REDUCED SANCTIONS THROUGH VOLUNTARY DISCLOSURES

In conjunction with regulatory agencies and other executive branch departments, the Department encourages corporations, as part of their compliance programs, to conduct internal investigations and to disclose the relevant facts to the appropriate authorities. Some agencies, such as the Securities and Exchange Commission and the Environmental Protection Agency, as well as the Department's Environmental and Natural Resources Division, have formal voluntary disclosure programs in which self-reporting, coupled with remediation and additional criteria, may qualify the corporation for amnesty or reduced sanctions. Even in the absence of a formal program, prosecutors may consider a corporation's timely and voluntary disclosure in evaluating the adequacy of the corporation's compliance program and its management's commitment to the compliance program. However, prosecution and economic policies specific to the industry or statute may require prosecution notwithstanding a corporation's willingness to cooperate. For example, the Antitrust Division has a policy of offering amnesty only to the first corporation to agree to cooperate. Moreover, amnesty, immunity, or reduced sanctions may not be appropriate where the corporation's business is permeated with fraud or other crimes.

[new August 2008]

9-28.760   OVERSIGHT CONCERNING DEMANDS FOR WAIVERS OF ATTORNEY-CLIENT PRIVILEGE OR WORK PRODUCT PROTECTION BY CORPORATIONS CONTRARY TO THIS POLICY

The Department underscores its commitment to attorney practices that are consistent with Department policies like those set forth herein concerning cooperation credit and due respect for the attorney-client privilege and work product protection. Counsel for corporations who believe that prosecutors are violating such guidance are encouraged to raise their concerns with supervisors, including the appropriate United States Attorney or Assistant Attorney General. Like any other allegation of attorney misconduct, such allegations are subject to potential investigation through established mechanisms.

[new August 2008]

9-28.800   CORPORATE COMPLIANCE PROGRAMS

A. General Principle: Compliance programs are established by corporate management to prevent and detect misconduct and to ensure that corporate activities are conducted in accordance with applicable criminal and civil laws, regulations, and rules. The Department encourages such corporate self-policing, including voluntary disclosures to the government of any problems that a corporation discovers on its own. However, the existence of a compliance program is not sufficient, in and of itself, to justify not charging a corporation for criminal misconduct undertaken by its officers, directors, employees, or agents. In addition, the nature of some crimes, e.g., antitrust violations, may be such that national law enforcement policies mandate prosecutions of corporations notwithstanding the existence of a compliance program.

B.   Comment: The existence of a corporate compliance program, even one that specifically prohibited the very conduct in question, does not absolve the corporation from criminal liability under the doctrine of *respondeat superior. See United States v. Basic Constr. Co.,* 711 F.2d 570, 573 (4th Cir. 1983) ("[A] corporation may be held criminally responsible for antitrust violations committed by its employees if they were acting within the scope of their authority, or apparent authority, and for the benefit of the corporation, even if . . . such acts were against corporate policy or express instructions."). As explained in *United States v. Potter,* 463 F.3d 9 (1st Cir. 2006), a corporation cannot "avoid liability by adopting abstract rules" that forbid its agents from engaging in illegal acts, because "[e]ven a specific directive to an agent or employee or honest efforts to police such rules do not automatically free the company for the wrongful acts of agents." *Id.* at 25-26. *See also United States v. Hilton Hotels Corp.,* 467 F.2d 1000, 1007 (9th Cir. 1972) (noting that a corporation "could not gain exculpation by issuing general instructions without undertaking to enforce those instructions by means commensurate with the obvious risks"); *United States v. Beusch,* 596 F.2d 871, 878 (9th Cir. 1979) ("[A] corporation may be liable for acts of its employees done contrary to express instructions and policies, but . . . the existence of such instructions and policies may be considered in determining whether the employee in fact acted to benefit the corporation.").

While the Department recognizes that no compliance program can ever prevent all criminal activity by a corporation's employees, the critical factors in evaluating any program are whether the program is adequately designed for maximum effectiveness in preventing and detecting wrongdoing by employees and whether corporate management is enforcing the program or is tacitly encouraging or pressuring employees to engage in misconduct to achieve business objectives. The Department has no formulaic requirements regarding corporate compliance programs. The fundamental questions any prosecutor should ask are: Is the corporation's compliance program well designed? Is the program being applied earnestly and in good faith? Does the corporation's compliance program work? In answering these questions, the prosecutor should consider the comprehensiveness of the compliance program; the extent and pervasiveness of the criminal misconduct; the number and level of the corporate employees involved; the seriousness, duration, and frequency of the misconduct; and any remedial actions taken by the corporation, including, for example, disciplinary action against past violators uncovered by the prior compliance program, and revisions to corporate compliance programs in light of lessons learned.[7] Prosecutors should also consider the promptness of any disclosure of wrongdoing to the government. In evaluating compliance programs, prosecutors may consider whether the

---

7. For a detailed review of these and other factors concerning corporate compliance programs, see USSG § 8B2.1.

corporation has established corporate governance mechanisms that can effectively detect and prevent misconduct. For example, do the corporation's directors exercise independent review over proposed corporate actions rather than unquestioningly ratifying officers' recommendations; are internal audit functions conducted at a level sufficient to ensure their independence and accuracy; and have the directors established an information and reporting system in the organization reasonably designed to provide management and directors with timely and accurate information sufficient to allow them to reach an informed decision regarding the organization's compliance with the law. *See, e.g., In re Caremark Int'l Inc. Derivative Litig.*, 698 A.2d 959, 968-70 (Del. Ch. 1996).

Prosecutors should therefore attempt to determine whether a corporation's compliance program is merely a "paper program" or whether it was designed, implemented, reviewed, and revised, as appropriate, in an effective manner. In addition, prosecutors should determine whether the corporation has provided for a staff sufficient to audit, document, analyze, and utilize the results of the corporation's compliance efforts. Prosecutors also should determine whether the corporation's employees are adequately informed about the compliance program and are convinced of the corporation's commitment to it. This will enable the prosecutor to make an informed decision as to whether the corporation has adopted and implemented a truly effective compliance program that, when consistent with other federal law enforcement policies, may result in a decision to charge only the corporation's employees and agents or to mitigate charges or sanctions against the corporation.

Compliance programs should be designed to detect the particular types of misconduct most likely to occur in a particular corporation's line of business. Many corporations operate in complex regulatory environments outside the normal experience of criminal prosecutors. Accordingly, prosecutors should consult with relevant federal and state agencies with the expertise to evaluate the adequacy of a program's design and implementation. For instance, state and federal banking, insurance, and medical boards, the Department of Defense, the Department of Health and Human Services, the Environmental Protection Agency, and the Securities and Exchange Commission have considerable experience with compliance programs and can be helpful to a prosecutor in evaluating such programs. In addition, the Fraud Section of the Criminal Division, the Commercial Litigation Branch of the Civil Division, and the Environmental Crimes Section of the Environment and Natural Resources Division can assist United States Attorneys' Offices in finding the appropriate agency office(s) for such consultation.

[new August 2008]

9-28.900 RESTITUTION AND REMEDIATION

A. General Principle: Although neither a corporation nor an individual target may avoid prosecution merely by paying a sum of money, a prosecutor may consider the corporation's willingness to make restitution and steps already taken to do so. A prosecutor may also consider other remedial actions, such as improving an existing compliance program or disciplining wrongdoers, in determining whether to charge the corporation and how to resolve corporate criminal cases.

B.   Comment: In determining whether or not to prosecute a corporation, the government may consider whether the corporation has taken meaningful remedial measures. A corporation's response to misconduct says much about its willingness to ensure that such misconduct does not recur. Thus, corporations that fully recognize the seriousness of their misconduct and accept responsibility for it should be taking steps to implement the personnel, operational, and organizational changes necessary to establish an awareness among employees that criminal conduct will not be tolerated.

Among the factors prosecutors should consider and weigh are whether the corporation appropriately disciplined wrongdoers, once those employees are identified by the corporation as culpable for the misconduct. Employee discipline is a difficult task for many corporations because of the human element involved and sometimes because of the seniority of the employees concerned.

Although corporations need to be fair to their employees, they must also be committed, at all levels of the corporation, to the highest standards of legal and ethical behavior. Effective internal discipline can be a powerful deterrent against improper behavior by a corporation's employees. Prosecutors should be satisfied that the corporation's focus is on the integrity and credibility of its remedial and disciplinary measures rather than on the protection of the wrongdoers.

In addition to employee discipline, two other factors used in evaluating a corporation's remedial efforts are restitution and reform. As with natural persons, the decision whether or not to prosecute should not depend upon the target's ability to pay restitution. A corporation's efforts to pay restitution even in advance of any court order is, however, evidence of its acceptance of responsibility and, consistent with the practices and policies of the appropriate Division of the Department entrusted with enforcing specific criminal laws, may be considered in determining whether to bring criminal charges. Similarly, although the inadequacy of a corporate compliance program is a factor to consider when deciding whether to charge a corporation, that corporation's quick recognition of the flaws in the program and its efforts to improve the program are also factors to consider as to appropriate disposition of a case.

[new August 2008]

9-28.1000   COLLATERAL CONSEQUENCES

A.   General Principle: Prosecutors may consider the collateral consequences of a corporate criminal conviction or indictment in determining whether to charge the corporation with a criminal offense and how to resolve corporate criminal cases.

B.   Comment: One of the factors in determining whether to charge a natural person or a corporation is whether the likely punishment is appropriate given the nature and seriousness of the crime. In the corporate context, prosecutors may take into account the possibly substantial consequences to a corporation's employees, investors, pensioners, and customers, many of whom may, depending on the size and nature of the corporation and their role in its operations, have played no role in the criminal conduct, have been unaware of it, or have been unable to prevent it. Prosecutors should also be aware of non-penal sanctions that may accompany a criminal charge, such as potential suspension or debarment from eligibility for government contracts or federally funded programs such as health care programs. Determining whether or not such non-penal sanctions are appropriate or required in a particular case is the responsibility of the relevant agency, and is a decision that will be made based on the applicable statutes, regulations, and policies.

Virtually every conviction of a corporation, like virtually every conviction of an individual, will have an impact on innocent third parties, and the mere existence of such an effect is not sufficient to preclude prosecution of the corporation. Therefore, in evaluating the relevance of collateral consequences, various factors already discussed, such as the pervasiveness of the criminal conduct and the adequacy of the corporation's compliance programs, should be considered in determining the weight to be given to this factor. For instance, the balance may tip in favor of prosecuting corporations in situations where the scope of the misconduct in a case is widespread and sustained within a corporate division (or spread throughout pockets of the corporate organization). In such cases, the possible unfairness of visiting punishment for the corporation's crimes upon shareholders may be of much less concern where those shareholders have substantially profited, even unknowingly, from widespread or pervasive criminal activity. Similarly, where the top layers of the corporation's management or the shareholders of a closely-held corporation were engaged in or aware of the wrongdoing, and the conduct at issue was accepted as a way of doing business for an extended period, debarment may be deemed not collateral, but a direct and entirely appropriate consequence of the corporation's wrongdoing.

On the other hand, where the collateral consequences of a corporate conviction for innocent third parties would be significant, it may be appropriate to consider a non-prosecution or deferred prosecution agreement with conditions designed, among other things, to promote compliance with applicable law and to prevent recidivism. Such agreements are a third option, besides a criminal indictment, on the one hand, and a declination, on the other. Declining prosecution may allow a corporate criminal to escape without consequences. Obtaining a conviction may produce a result that seriously harms innocent third parties who played no role in the criminal conduct. Under appropriate circumstances, a deferred prosecution or non-prosecution agreement can help restore the integrity of a company's operations and preserve the financial viability of a corporation that has engaged in criminal conduct, while preserving the government's ability to prosecute a recalcitrant corporation that materially breaches the agreement. Such agreements achieve other important objectives as well, like prompt restitution for victims.[8] Ultimately, the appropriateness of a criminal charge against a corporation, or some lesser alter-

---

8. Prosecutors should note that in the case of national or multi-national corporations, multi-district or global agreements may be necessary. Such agreements may only be entered into with the approval of each affected district or the appropriate Department official. See U.S.A.M. 9-27.641.

native, must be evaluated in a pragmatic and reasoned way that produces a fair outcome, taking into consideration, among other things, the Department's need to promote and ensure respect for the law.

[new August 2008]

9-28.1100   OTHER CIVIL OR REGULATORY ALTERNATIVES

A. General Principle: Non-criminal alternatives to prosecution often exist and prosecutors may consider whether such sanctions would adequately deter, punish, and rehabilitate a corporation that has engaged in wrongful conduct. In evaluating the adequacy of non-criminal alternatives to prosecution—e.g., civil or regulatory enforcement actions—the prosecutor may consider all relevant factors, including:

1. the sanctions available under the alternative means of disposition;
2. the likelihood that an effective sanction will be imposed; and
3. the effect of non-criminal disposition on federal law enforcement interests.

B. Comment: The primary goals of criminal law are deterrence, punishment, and rehabilitation. Non-criminal sanctions may not be an appropriate response to a serious violation, a pattern of wrongdoing, or prior non-criminal sanctions without proper remediation. In other cases, however, these goals may be satisfied through civil or regulatory actions. In determining whether a federal criminal resolution is appropriate, the prosecutor should consider the same factors (modified appropriately for the regulatory context) considered when determining whether to leave prosecution of a natural person to another jurisdiction or to seek non-criminal alternatives to prosecution. These factors include: the strength of the regulatory authority's interest; the regulatory authority's ability and willingness to take effective enforcement action; the probable sanction if the regulatory authority's enforcement action is upheld; and the effect of a non-criminal disposition on federal law enforcement interests. *See* USAM 9-27.240, 9-27.250.

[new August 2008]

9-28.1200   SELECTING CHARGES

A. General Principle: Once a prosecutor has decided to charge a corporation, the prosecutor at least presumptively should charge, or should recommend that the grand jury charge, the most serious offense that is consistent with the nature of the defendant's misconduct and that is likely to result in a sustainable conviction.

B. Comment: Once the decision to charge is made, the same rules as govern charging natural persons apply. These rules require "a faithful and honest application of the Sentencing Guidelines" and an "individualized assessment of the extent to which particular charges fit the specific circumstances of the case, are consistent with the purposes of the Federal criminal code, and maximize the impact of Federal resources on crime." *See* USAM 9-27.300. In making this determination, "it is appropriate that the attorney for the government consider, *inter alia*, such factors as the [advisory] sentencing guideline range yielded by the charge, whether the penalty yielded by such sentencing range . . . is proportional to the seriousness of the defendant's conduct, and whether the charge achieves such purposes of the criminal law as punishment, protection of the public, specific and general deterrence, and rehabilitation."

[new August 2008]

9-28.1300 PLEA AGREEMENTS WITH CORPORATIONS

A. General Principle: In negotiating plea agreements with corporations, as with individuals, prosecutors should generally seek a plea to the most serious, readily provable offense charged. In addition, the terms of the plea agreement should contain appropriate provisions to ensure punishment, deterrence, rehabilitation, and compliance with the plea agreement in the corporate context. Although special circumstances may mandate a different conclusion, prosecutors generally should not agree to accept a corporate guilty plea in exchange for non-prosecution or dismissal of charges against individual officers and employees.

B   Comment: Prosecutors may enter into plea agreements with corporations for the same reasons and under the same constraints as apply to plea agreements with natural persons. *See* USAM 9-27.400-530. This means, *inter alia*, that the corporation should generally be required to plead guilty to the most serious, readily provable offense charged. In addition, any negotiated departures or recommended variances from the advisory Sentencing Guidelines must be justifiable under the Guidelines or 18 U.S.C. § 3553 and must be disclosed to the sentencing court. A corporation should be made to realize that pleading guilty to criminal charges constitutes an admission of guilt and not merely a resolution of an inconvenient distraction from its business. As with natural persons, pleas should be structured so that the corporation may not later "proclaim lack of culpability or even complete innocence." *See* USAM 9-27.420(b)(4), 9-27.440, 9-27.500. Thus, for instance, there should be placed upon the record a sufficient factual basis for the plea to prevent later corporate assertions of innocence.

A corporate plea agreement should also contain provisions that recognize the nature of the corporate "person" and that ensure that the principles of punishment, deterrence, and rehabilitation are met. In the corporate context, punishment and deterrence are generally accomplished by substantial fines, mandatory restitution, and institution of appropriate compliance measures, including, if necessary, continued judicial oversight or the use of special masters or corporate monitors. *See* USSG §§ 8B1.1, 8C2.1, *et seq*. In addition, where the corporation is a government contractor, permanent or temporary debarment may be appropriate. Where the corporation was engaged in fraud against the government (e.g., contracting fraud), a prosecutor may not negotiate away an agency's right to debar or delist the corporate defendant.

In negotiating a plea agreement, prosecutors should also consider the deterrent value of prosecutions of individuals within the corporation. Therefore, one factor that a prosecutor may consider in determining whether to enter into a plea agreement is whether the corporation is seeking immunity for its employees and officers or whether the corporation is willing to cooperate in the investigation of culpable individuals as outlined herein. Prosecutors should rarely negotiate away individual criminal liability in a corporate plea.

Rehabilitation, of course, requires that the corporation undertake to be law-abiding in the future. It is, therefore, appropriate to require the corporation, as a condition of probation, to implement a compliance program or to reform an existing one. As discussed above, prosecutors may consult with the appropriate state and federal agencies and components of the Justice Department to ensure that a proposed compliance program is adequate and meets industry standards and best practices. *See* USAM 9-28.800.

In plea agreements in which the corporation agrees to cooperate, the prosecutor should ensure that the cooperation is entirely truthful. To do so, the prosecutor may request that the corporation make appropriate disclosures of relevant factual information and documents, make employees and agents available for debriefing, file appropriate certified financial statements, agree to governmental or third-party audits, and take whatever other steps are necessary to ensure that the full scope of the corporate wrongdoing is disclosed and that the responsible personnel are identified and, if appropriate, prosecuted. *See generally* USAM 9-28.700. In taking such steps, Department prosecutors should recognize that attorney-client communications are often essential to a corporation's efforts to comply with complex regulatory and legal regimes, and that, as discussed at length above, cooperation is not measured by the waiver of attorney-client privilege and work product protection, but rather is measured by the disclosure of facts and other considerations identified herein such as making witnesses available for interviews and assisting in the interpretation of complex documents or business records.

These Principles provide only internal Department of Justice guidance. They are not intended to, do not, and may not be relied upon to create any rights, substantive or procedural, enforceable at law by any party in any matter civil or criminal. Nor are any limitations hereby placed on otherwise lawful litigative prerogatives of the Department of Justice.

[new August 2008]

APPENDIX 10

Morford Memorandum on Monitors

U.S. Department of Justice
Office of the Deputy Attorney General

The Deputy Attorney General

Washington, D.C. 20530
March 7, 2008

MEMORANDUM FOR HEADS OF DEPARTMENT COMPONENTS
UNITED STATES ATTORNEYS

FROM: Craig S. Morford

SUBJECT: Acting Deputy Attorney General Initial of Craig S.
                    Morford Selection and Use of Monitors in Deferred
                    Prosecution Agreements and Non-Prosecution Agree-
                    ments with Corporations[1]

I. INTRODUCTION

The Department of Justice's commitment to deterring and preventing corporate crime remains a high priority. The Principles of Federal Prosecution of Business Organizations set forth guidance to federal prosecutors regarding charges against corporations. A careful consideration of those principles and the facts in a given case may result in a decision to negotiate an agreement to resolve a criminal case against a corporation without a formal conviction—either a deferred prosecution agreement or a non-prosecution agreement.[2] As part of some negotiated corporate

---

1. As used in these Principles, the terms "corporate" and "corporation" refer to all types of business organizations, including partnerships, sole proprietorships, government entities, and unincorporated associations.

2. The terms "deferred prosecution agreement" and "non-prosecution agreement" have often been used loosely by prosecutors, defense counsel, courts and commentators. As the terms are used in these Principles, a deferred prosecution agreement is typically predicated upon the filing of a formal charging document by the government, and the agreement is filed with the appropriate court. In the non-prosecution agreement context, formal charges are not filed and the agreement is maintained by the parties rather than being filed with a court. Clear and consistent use of these terms will enable the Department to more effectively identify and share best practices and to track the use of such agreements. These Principles do not apply to plea agreements, which involve the formal conviction of a corporation in a court proceeding.

agreements, there have been provisions pertaining to an independent corporate monitor.[3] The corporation benefits from expertise in the area of corporate compliance from an independent third party. The corporation, its shareholders, employees and the public at large then benefit from reduced recidivism of corporate crime and the protection of the integrity of the marketplace.

The purpose of this memorandum is to present a series of principles for drafting provisions pertaining to the use of monitors in connection with deferred prosecution and non-prosecution agreements (hereafter referred to collectively as "agreements") with corporations.[4] Given the varying facts and circumstances of each case—where different industries, corporate size and structure, and other considerations may be at issue—any guidance regarding monitors must be practical and flexible. This guidance is limited to monitors, and does not apply to third parties, whatever their titles, retained to act as receivers, trustees, or perform other functions.

A monitor's primary responsibility is to assess and monitor a corporation's compliance with the terms of the agreement specifically designed to address and reduce the risk of recurrence of the corporation's misconduct, and not to further punitive goals. A monitor should only be used where appropriate given the facts and circumstances of a particular matter. For example, it may be appropriate to use a monitor where a company does not have an effective internal compliance program, or where it needs to establish necessary internal controls. Conversely, in a situation where a company has ceased operations in the area where the criminal misconduct occurred, a monitor may not be necessary.

In negotiating agreements with corporations, prosecutors should be mindful of both: (1) the potential benefits that employing a monitor may have for the corporation and the public, and (2) the cost of a monitor and its impact on the operations of a corporation. Prosecutors shall, at a minimum, notify the appropriate United States Attorney or Department Component Head prior to the execution of an agreement that includes a corporate monitor. The appropriate United States Attorney or Department Component Head shall, in turn, provide a copy of the agreement to the Assistant Attorney General for the Criminal Division at a reasonable time after it has been executed. The Assistant Attorney General for the Criminal Division shall maintain a record of all such agreements.

This memorandum does not address all provisions concerning monitors that have been included or could appropriately be included in agreements. Rather this memorandum sets forth nine basic principles in the areas of selection, scope of duties, and duration.

This memorandum provides only internal Department of Justice guidance. In addition, this memorandum applies only to criminal matters and does not apply to agencies other than the Department of Justice. It is not intended to, does not, and may not be relied upon to create any rights, substantive or procedural, enforceable at law by any party in any matter civil or criminal. Nor are any limitations hereby placed on otherwise lawful litigative prerogatives of the Department of Justice.

---

3.   Agreements use a variety of terms to describe the role referred to herein as "monitor," including consultants, experts, and others.

4.   In the case of deferred prosecution agreements filed with the court, these Principles must be applied with due regard for the appropriate role of the court and/or the probation office.

II. SELECTION

1. <u>Principle:</u> **Before beginning the process of selecting a monitor in connection with deferred prosecution agreements and non-prosecution agreements, the corporation and the Government should discuss the necessary qualifications for a monitor based on the facts and circumstances of the case. The monitor must be selected based on the merits. The selection process must, at a minimum, be designed to: (1) select a highly qualified and respected person or entity based on suitability for the assignment and all of the circumstances; (2) avoid potential and actual conflicts of interests; and (3) otherwise instill public confidence by implementing the steps set forth in this Principle.**

To avoid a conflict, first, Government attorneys who participate in the process of selecting a monitor shall be mindful of their obligation to comply with the conflict-of interest guidelines set forth in 18 U.S.C. § 208 and 5 C.F.R. Part 2635. Second, the Government shall create a standing or ad hoc committee in the Department component or office where the case originated to consider monitor candidates. United States Attorneys and Assistant Attorneys General may not make, accept, or veto the selection of monitor candidates unilaterally. Third, the Office of the Deputy Attorney General must approve the monitor. Fourth, the Government should decline to accept a monitor if he or she has an interest in, or relationship with, the corporation or its employees, officers or directors that would cause a reasonable person to question the monitor's impartiality. Finally, the Government should obtain a commitment from the corporation that it will not employ or be affiliated with the monitor for a period of not less than one year from the date the monitorship is terminated.

<u>Comment:</u> Because a monitor's role may vary based on the facts of each case and the entity involved, there is no one method of selection that should necessarily be used in every instance. For example, the corporation may select a monitor candidate, with the Government reserving the right to veto the proposed choice if the monitor is unacceptable. In other cases, the facts may require the Government to play a greater role in selecting the monitor. Whatever method is used, the Government should determine what selection process is most effective as early in the negotiations as possible, and endeavor to ensure that the process is designed to produce a high-quality and conflict-free monitor and to instill public confidence. If the Government determines that participation in the selection process by any Government personnel creates, or appears to create, a potential or actual conflict in violation of 18 U.S.C. § 208 and 5 C.F.R. Part 2635, the Government must proceed as in other matters where recusal issues arise. In all cases, the Government must submit the proposed monitor to the Office of the Deputy Attorney General for review and approval before the monitorship is established.

Ordinarily, the Government and the corporation should discuss what role the monitor will play and what qualities, expertise, and skills the monitor should have. While attorneys, including but not limited to former Government attorneys, may have certain skills that qualify them to function effectively as a monitor, other individuals, such as accountants, technical or scientific experts, and compliance experts, may have skills that are more appropriate to the tasks contemplated in a given agreement.

Subsequent employment or retention of the monitor by the corporation after the monitorship period concludes may raise concerns about both the appearance of a conflict of interest and the effectiveness of the monitor during the monitorship, particularly with regard to the disclosure of possible new misconduct. Such employment includes both direct and indirect, or subcontracted, relationships.

Each United States Attorney's Office and Department component shall create a standing or ad hoc committee ("Committee") of prosecutors to consider the selection or veto, as appropriate, of monitor candidates. The Committee should, at a minimum, include the office ethics advisor, the Criminal Chief of the United States Attorney's Office or relevant Section Chief of the Department component, and at least one other experienced prosecutor.

Where practicable, the corporation, the Government, or both parties, depending on the selection process being used, should consider a pool of at least three qualified monitor candidates. Where the selection process calls for the corporation to choose the monitor at the outset, the corporation should submit its choice from among the pool of candidates to the Government. Where the selection process calls for the Government to play a greater role in selecting the monitor, the Government should, where practicable, identify at least three acceptable monitors from the pool of candidates, and the corporation shall choose from that list.

III. SCOPE OF DUTIES

A. Independence

2. Principle: A monitor is an independent third-party, not an employee or agent of the corporation or of the Government.

Comment: A monitor by definition is distinct and independent from the directors, officers, employees, and other representatives of the corporation. The monitor is not the corporation's attorney. Accordingly, the corporation may not seek to obtain or obtain legal advice from the monitor. Conversely, a monitor also is not an agent or employee of the Government.

While a monitor is independent both from the corporation and the Government, there should be open dialogue among the corporation, the Government and the monitor throughout the duration of the agreement.

B. Monitoring Compliance with the Agreement

3. Principle: A monitor's primary responsibility should be to assess and monitor a corporation's compliance with those terms of the agreement that are specifically designed to address and reduce the risk of recurrence of the corporation's misconduct, including, in most cases, evaluating (and where appropriate proposing) internal controls and corporate ethics and compliance programs.

Comment: At the corporate level, there may be a variety of causes of criminal misconduct, including but not limited to the failure of internal controls or ethics and compliance programs to prevent, detect, and respond to such misconduct. A monitor's primary role is to evaluate whether a corporation has both adopted and effectively implemented ethics and compliance programs to address and reduce the risk of recurrence of the corporation's misconduct. A well-designed ethics and compliance program that is not effectively implemented will fail to lower the risk of recidivism.

A monitor is not responsible to the corporation's shareholders. Therefore, from a corporate governance standpoint, responsibility for designing an ethics and compliance program that will prevent misconduct should remain with the corporation, subject to the monitor's input, evaluation and recommendations.

4.   Principle: In carrying out his or her duties, a monitor will often need to understand the full scope of the corporation's misconduct covered by the agreement, but the monitor's responsibilities should be no broader than necessary to address and reduce the risk of recurrence of the corporation's misconduct.

Comment: The scope of a monitor's duties should be tailored to the facts of each case to address and reduce the risk of recurrence of the corporation's misconduct. Among other things, focusing the monitor's duties on these tasks may serve to calibrate the expense of the monitorship to the failure that gave rise to the misconduct the agreement covers.

Neither the corporation nor the public benefits from employing a monitor whose role is too narrowly defined (and, therefore, prevents the monitor from effectively evaluating the reforms intended by the parties) or too broadly defined (and, therefore, results in the monitor engaging in activities that fail to facilitate the corporation's implementation of the reforms intended by the parties).

The monitor's mandate is not to investigate historical misconduct. Nevertheless, in appropriate circumstances, an understanding of historical misconduct may inform a monitor's evaluation of the effectiveness of the corporation's compliance with the agreement.

C.   Communications and Recommendations by the Monitor

5.   Principle: Communication among the Government, the corporation and the monitor is in the interest of all the parties. Depending on the facts and circumstances, it may be appropriate for the monitor to make periodic written reports to both the Government and the corporation.

Comment: A monitor generally works closely with a corporation and communicates with a corporation on a regular basis in the course of his or her duties. The monitor must also have the discretion to communicate with the Government as he or she deems appropriate. For example, a monitor should be free to discuss with the Government the progress of, as well as issues arising from, the drafting and implementation of an ethics and compliance program. Depending on the facts and circumstances, it may be appropriate for the monitor to make periodic written reports to both the Government and the corporation regarding, among other things: (1) the monitor's activities; (2) whether the corporation is complying with the terms of the agreement; and (3) any changes that are necessary to foster the corporation's compliance with the terms of the agreement.

6. Principle: If the corporation chooses not to adopt recommendations made by the monitor within a reasonable time, either the monitor or the corporation, or both, should report that fact to the Government, along with the corporation's reasons. The Government may consider this conduct when evaluating whether the corporation has fulfilled its obligations under the agreement.

Comment: The corporation and its officers and directors are ultimately responsible for the ethical and legal operations of the corporation. Therefore, the corporation should evaluate whether to adopt recommendations made by the monitor. If the corporation declines to adopt a recommendation by the monitor, the Government should consider both the monitor's recommendation and the corporation's reasons in determining whether the corporation is complying with the agreement. A flexible timetable should be established to ensure that both a monitor's recommendations and the corporation's decision to adopt or reject them are made well before the expiration of the agreement.

D. Reporting of Previously Undisclosed or New Misconduct

7. Principle: The agreement should clearly identify any types of previously undisclosed or new misconduct that the monitor will be required to report directly to the Government. The agreement should also provide that as to evidence of other such misconduct, the monitor will have the discretion to report this misconduct to the Government or the corporation or both.

Comment: As a general rule, timely and open communication between and among the corporation, the Government and the monitor regarding allegations of misconduct will facilitate the review of the misconduct and formulation of an appropriate response to it. The agreement may set forth certain types of previously undisclosed or new misconduct that the monitor will be required to report directly to the Government. Additionally, in some instances, the monitor should immediately report other such misconduct directly to the Government and not to the corporation. The presence of any of the following factors militates in favor of reporting such misconduct directly to the Government and not to the corporation, namely, where the misconduct: (1) poses a risk to public health or safety or the environment; (2) involves senior management of the corporation; (3) involves obstruction of justice; (4) involves criminal activity which the Government has the opportunity to investigate proactively and/or covertly; or (5) otherwise poses a substantial risk of harm. On the other hand, in instances where the allegations of such misconduct are not credible or involve actions of individuals outside the scope of the corporation's business, the monitor may decide, in the exercise of his or her discretion, that the allegations need not be reported directly to the Government.

IV. DURATION

8. Principle: **The duration of the agreement should be tailored to the problems that have been found to exist and the types of remedial measures needed for the monitor to satisfy his or her mandate.**

Comment: The following criteria should be considered when negotiating duration of the agreement (not necessarily in this order): (1) the nature and seriousness of the underlying misconduct; (2) the pervasiveness and duration of misconduct within the corporation, including the complicity or involvement of senior management; (3) the corporation's history of similar misconduct; (4) the nature of the corporate culture; (5) the scale and complexity of any remedial measures contemplated by the agreement, including the size of the entity or business unit at issue; and (6) the stage of design and implementation of remedial measures when the monitorship commences. It is reasonable to forecast that completing an assessment of more extensive and/or complex remedial measures will require a longer period of time than completing an assessment of less extensive and/or less complex ones. Similarly, it is reasonable to forecast that a monitor who is assigned responsibility to assess a compliance program that has not been designed or implemented may take longer to complete that assignment than one who is assigned responsibility to assess a compliance program that has already been designed and implemented.

9. Principle: **In most cases, an agreement should provide for an extension of the monitor provision(s) at the discretion of the Government in the event that the corporation has not successfully satisfied its obligations under the agreement. Conversely, in most cases, an agreement should provide for early termination if the corporation can demonstrate to the Government that there exists a change in circumstances sufficient to eliminate the need for a monitor.**

Comment: If the corporation has not satisfied its obligations under the terms of the agreement at the time the monitorship ends, the corresponding risk of recidivism will not have been reduced and an extension of the monitor provision(s) may be appropriate. On the other hand, there are a number of changes in circumstances that could justify early termination of an agreement. For example, if a corporation ceased operations in the area that was the subject of the agreement, a monitor may no longer be necessary. Similarly, if a corporation is purchased by or merges with another entity that has an effective ethics and compliance program, it may be prudent to terminate a monitorship.

APPENDIX 11

Report of Investigation Pursuant to Section 21(a) of the Securities Exchange Act of 1934 and Commission Statement on the Relationship of Cooperation to Agency Enforcement Decisions (Exchange Act Release No. 44969, Accounting and Auditing Enforcement Release No. 1470, October 23, 2001) ("Cooperation Statement") (*Seaboard* Opinion)

SECURITIES AND EXCHANGE COMMISSION

SECURITIES EXCHANGE ACT OF 1934
Release No. 44969 / October 23, 2001

ACCOUNTING AND AUDITING ENFORCEMENT
Release No. 1470 / October 23, 2001

Report of Investigation Pursuant to Section 21(a) of the Securities Exchange Act of 1934 and Commission Statement on the Relationship of Cooperation to Agency Enforcement Decisions

Today, we commence and settle a cease-and-desist proceeding against Gisela de Leon-Meredith, former controller of a public company's subsidiary.[1] Our order finds that Meredith caused the parent company's books and records to be inaccurate and its periodic reports misstated, and then covered up those facts.

We are not taking action against the parent company, given the nature of the conduct and the company's responses. Within a week of learning about the apparent misconduct, the company's internal auditors had conducted a preliminary review and had advised company management who, in turn, advised the Board's audit committee, that Meredith had caused the company's books and records to be inaccurate and its financial reports to be misstated. The full Board was advised and authorized the company to hire an outside law firm to conduct a thorough inquiry. Four days later, Meredith was dismissed, as were two other employees who, in the company's view, had inadequately supervised Meredith; a day later, the company disclosed publicly and to us that its financial statements would be restated. The price of the company's shares did not decline after the announcement or after the restatement was published. The company pledged and gave complete cooperation to our staff. It provided the staff with all information relevant to the underlying violations. Among other things, the company produced the details of its internal investigation, including notes and transcripts of interviews of Meredith and others; and it did not invoke the attorney-client privilege, work product protection or other privileges or protections with respect to any facts uncovered in the investigation.

The company also strengthened its financial reporting processes to address Meredith's conduct—developing a detailed closing process for the subsidiary's accounting personnel, consolidating subsidiary accounting functions under a parent company CPA, hiring three new CPAs for the accounting department responsible for preparing the subsidiary's financial statements, redesigning the subsidiary's minimum annual audit requirements, and requiring the parent company's controller to interview and approve all senior accounting personnel in its subsidiaries' reporting processes.

Our willingness to credit such behavior in deciding whether and how to take enforcement action benefits investors as well as our enforcement program. When businesses seek out, self-report and rectify illegal conduct, and otherwise cooperate with Commission staff, large expenditures of government and shareholder resources can be avoided and investors can benefit more promptly.[2] In setting forth the criteria listed below, we think a few caveats are in order:

First, the paramount issue in every enforcement judgment is, and must be, what best protects investors. There is no single, or constant, answer to that question. Self-policing, self-reporting, remediation and cooperation with law enforcement authorities, among other things, are unquestionably important in promoting investors' best interests. But, so too are vigorous enforcement and the imposition of appropriate sanctions where the law has been violated. Indeed, there may be circumstances where conduct is so egregious, and harm so great, that no amount of cooperation or other mitigating conduct can justify a decision not to bring any enforcement action at all. In the end, no set of criteria can, or should, be strictly applied in every situation to which they may be applicable.

Second, we are not adopting any rule or making any commitment or promise about any specific case; nor are we in any way limiting our broad discretion to evaluate every case individually, on its own particular facts and circumstances. Conversely, we are not conferring any "rights" on any person or entity. We seek only to convey an understanding of the factors that may influence our decisions.

Third, we do not limit ourselves to the criteria we discuss below. By definition, enforcement judgments are just that—judgments. Our failure to mention a specific criterion in one context does not preclude us from relying on that criterion in another. Further, the fact that a company has satisfied all the criteria we list below will not foreclose us from bringing enforcement proceedings that we believe are necessary or appropriate, for the benefit of investors.

In brief form, we set forth below some of the criteria we will consider in determining whether, and how much, to credit self-policing, self-reporting, remediation and cooperation—from the extraordinary step of taking no enforcement action to bringing reduced charges, seeking lighter sanctions, or including mitigating language in documents we use to announce and resolve enforcement actions.

1. What is the nature of the misconduct involved? Did it result from inadvertence, honest mistake, simple negligence, reckless or deliberate indifference to indicia of wrongful conduct, willful misconduct or unadorned venality? Were the company's auditors misled?

2. How did the misconduct arise? Is it the result of pressure placed on employees to achieve specific results, or a tone of lawlessness set by those in control of the company? What compliance procedures were in place to prevent the misconduct now uncovered? Why did those procedures fail to stop or inhibit the wrongful conduct?

3. Where in the organization did the misconduct occur? How high up in the chain of command was knowledge of, or participation in, the misconduct? Did senior personnel participate in, or turn a blind eye toward, obvious indicia of misconduct? How systemic was the behavior? Is it symptomatic of the way the entity does business, or was it isolated?

4. How long did the misconduct last? Was it a one-quarter, or one-time, event, or did it last several years? In the case of a public company, did the misconduct occur before the company went public? Did it facilitate the company's ability to go public?

5. How much harm has the misconduct inflicted upon investors and other corporate constituencies? Did the share price of the company's stock drop significantly upon its discovery and disclosure?

6. How was the misconduct detected and who uncovered it?

7. How long after discovery of the misconduct did it take to implement an effective response?

8. What steps did the company take upon learning of the misconduct? Did the company immediately stop the misconduct? Are persons responsible for any misconduct still with the company? If so, are they still in the same positions? Did the company promptly, completely and effectively disclose the existence of the misconduct to the public, to regulators and to self-regulators? Did the company cooperate completely with appropriate regulatory and law enforcement bodies? Did the company identify what additional related misconduct is likely to have occurred? Did the company take steps to identify the extent of damage to investors and other corporate constituencies? Did the company appropriately recompense those adversely affected by the conduct?

9. What processes did the company follow to resolve many of these issues and ferret out necessary information? Were the Audit Committee and the Board of Directors fully informed? If so, when?

10. Did the company commit to learn the truth, fully and expeditiously? Did it do a thorough review of the nature, extent, origins and consequences of the conduct and related behavior? Did management, the Board or committees consisting solely of outside directors oversee the review? Did company employees or outside persons perform the review? If outside persons, had they done other work for the company? Where the review was conducted by outside counsel, had management previously engaged such counsel? Were scope limitations placed on the review? If so, what were they?

11. Did the company promptly make available to our staff the results of its review and provide sufficient documentation reflecting its response to the situation? Did the company identify possible violative conduct and evidence with sufficient precision to facilitate prompt enforcement actions against those who violated the law? Did the company produce a thorough and probing written report detailing the findings of its review? Did the company voluntarily disclose information our staff did not directly request and otherwise might not have uncovered? Did the company ask its employees to cooperate with our staff and make all reasonable efforts to secure such cooperation?[3]

12. What assurances are there that the conduct is unlikely to recur? Did the company adopt and ensure enforcement of new and more effective internal controls and procedures designed to prevent a recurrence of the misconduct? Did the company provide our staff with sufficient information for it to evaluate the company's measures to correct the situation and ensure that the conduct does not recur?

13. Is the company the same company in which the misconduct occurred, or has it changed through a merger or bankruptcy reorganization?

We hope that this Report of Investigation and Commission Statement will further encourage self-policing efforts and will promote more self-reporting, remediation and cooperation with the Commission staff. We welcome the constructive input of all interested persons. We urge those who have contributions to make to direct them to our Division of Enforcement. The public can be confident that all such communications will be fairly evaluated not only by our staff, but also by us. We continue to reassess our enforcement approaches with the aim of maximizing the benefits of our program to investors and the marketplace.

By the Commission (Chairman Pitt, Commissioner Hunt, Commissioner Unger).

Footnotes:

1. In the Matter of Gisela de Leon-Meredith, Exchange Act Release No. 44970 (October 23, 2001).

2. We note that the federal securities laws and other legal requirements and guidance also promote and even require a certain measure of self-policing, self-reporting and remediation. Section 10A of the Securities Exchange Act of 1934, 15 U.S.C. § 78j-1 (requiring issuers and auditors to report certain illegal conduct to the Commission); In the Matter of W.R. Grace & Co., Exchange Act Release No. 39157 (Sept. 30, 1997) (emphasizing the affirmative responsibilities of corporate officers and directors to ensure that shareholders receive accurate and complete disclosure of information required by the proxy solicitation and periodic reporting provisions of the federal securities laws); In the Matter of Cooper Companies, Inc., Exchange Act Release No. 35082 (Dec. 12, 1994) (emphasizing responsibility of corporate directors in safeguarding the integrity of a company's public statements and the interests of investors when evidence of fraudulent conduct by corporate management comes to their attention); In the Matter of John Gutfreund, Exchange Act Release No. 31554 (Dec. 3, 1992) (sanctions imposed against supervisors at broker-dealer for failing promptly to bring misconduct to attention of the government). Federal Sentencing Guidelines § 8C2.5(f) & (g) (organization's "culpability score" decreases if organization has an effective program to prevent and detect violations of law or if organization reports offense to governmental authorities prior to imminent threat of disclosure or government investigation and within reasonably prompt time after becoming aware of the offense); New York Stock Exchange Rules 342.21 & 351(e) (members and member organizations required to review certain trades for compliance with rules against insider trading and manipulation, to conduct prompt internal investigations of any potentially violative trades, and to report the status and/or results of such internal investigations).

3. In some cases, the desire to provide information to the Commission staff may cause companies to consider choosing not to assert the attorney-client privilege, the work product protection and other privileges, protections and exemptions with respect to the Commission. The Commission recognizes that these privileges, protections and exemptions serve important social interests. In this regard, the Commission does not view a company's waiver of a privilege as an end in itself, but only as a means (where necessary) to provide relevant and sometimes critical information to the Commission staff. Thus, the Commission recently filed an amicus brief arguing that the provision of privileged information to the Commission staff pursuant to a confidentiality agreement did not necessarily waive the privilege as to third parties. Brief of SEC as Amicus Curiae, McKesson HBOC, Inc., No. 99-C-7980-3 (Ga. Ct. App. Filed May 13, 2001). Moreover, in certain circumstances, the Commission staff has agreed that a witness' production of privileged information would not constitute a subject matter waiver that would entitle the staff to receive further privileged information. http://www.sec.gov/litigation/investreport/34-44969.htm

APPENDIX 12

Chapter Eight Fine Primer: Determining the Appropriate Fine under the Organizational Guidelines (U.S. Sentencing Commission)

Chapter Eight Fine Primer:
Determining the Appropriate Fine
Under the Organizational Guidelines

Prepared by
the Office of General Counsel
U.S. Sentencing Commission

May 2014

TABLE OF CONTENTS

i

Chapter Eight Fine Primer:
Determining the Appropriate Fine
Under the Organizational Guidelines

Chapter Eight of the *Guidelines Manual* sets forth the guidelines and policy statements that are applicable when the convicted defendant is an organization and which provide the criteria by which organizations convicted of federal criminal offenses will be punished. These guidelines, which were initially promulgated by the U.S. Sentencing Commission in 1991, were developed after extensive consultation with industry representatives, private defense attorneys, federal judges, prosecutors, and federal probation officers. They are "designed so that the sanctions imposed upon organizations and their agents, taken together, will provide just punishment, adequate deterrence, and incentives for organizations to maintain internal mechanisms for preventing, detecting, and reporting criminal conduct." *See* USSG, Ch.8, intro. comment.

As noted in the Introductory Commentary, the Chapter Eight guidelines reflect a number of general principles relating to the sentencing of organizations. First, when the convicted defendant is an organization, the court must, whenever practicable, order the organization to remedy any harm caused by the offense. *See* USSG, Ch.8, intro. comment. The harm caused by the offense may be remedied through a restitution order, a remedial order, an order of probation requiring restitution or community service, or an order of notice to victims. *See* USSG, Ch.8, Pt.B, intro. comment. Second, the court determines the appropriate fine to be imposed on the organization. *See* USSG §8A1.2(b). If the organization operated primarily for a criminal purpose or primarily by criminal means, the sentencing court should set the fine sufficiently high to divest the organization of all its assets. *See* USSG, Ch.8, intro. comment.; USSG §8C1.1. For all other organizations, the sentencing court should base the fine range on the seriousness of the offense and the culpability of the organization. *See* USSG, Ch.8, intro. comment. Finally, the court may order probation for an organizational defendant when needed to ensure that another sanction will be fully implemented, or to ensure that steps will be taken within the organization to reduce the likelihood of further criminal conduct. *Id.*

This primer focuses exclusively on the second step noted above — the manner in which a sentencing court calculates the appropriate fine for an organizational defendant. This determination is made pursuant to Chapter Eight, Part C of the *Guidelines Manual*.

I.   **FINE CALCULATION FOR ORGANIZATION OPERATING PRIMARILY FOR CRIMINAL PURPOSE OR BY CRIMINAL MEANS (§8C1.1)**

As noted above, in calculating the fine, the sentencing court applies §8C1.1 if, upon consideration of the offense and history and characteristics of the organization, it determines that the organization operated primarily for a criminal purpose or primarily by criminal means. *See* USSG §§8A1.2(b)(1), 8C1.1. Examples of an organization operating primarily for a criminal purpose include a front for a scheme that was designed to commit fraud

1

or an organization established to participate in the illegal manufacture, importation, or distribution of a controlled substance. *See* USSG §8C1.1, comment. (backg'd.). Examples of an organization that operates primarily by criminal means include a hazardous waste disposal business that had no legitimate means of disposing of hazardous waste. *Id.*

In such a case, the fine is set at an amount, subject to the statutory maximum, sufficient to divest the organization of all its net assets. *See* USSG §8C1.1. "Net assets" means the assets remaining after payment of all legitimate claims against assets by known innocent bona fide creditors. *See* USSG §8C1.1, comment. (n.1). If the extent of the assets of the organization is unknown, the court is to impose the maximum fine authorized by statute, absent innocent bona fide creditors. *See* USSG §8C1.1, comment. (backg'd.). When §8C1.1 applies, Part C, Subpart 2, regarding determining the fine for all other organizations, and §8C3.4, regarding fines paid by owners of closely held organizations, do not apply. *See* USSG §8C1.1.

II.   FINE CALCULATION FOR ALL OTHER ORGANIZATIONS (§§8C2.1-8C2.10)

Sections 8C2.1 through 8C2.10 guide the court's determination of a fine range for those organizations that do not operate primarily for a criminal purpose or primarily by criminal means.

A.   Applicability of Fine Guidelines (§8C2.1)

The rules for calculating the fine range in §§8C2.2 through 8C2.9 are limited to specifically-enumerated offenses for which pecuniary loss or harm can be more readily quantified, such as fraud, theft, and tax offenses. *See* USSG §8C2.1. The applicable Chapter Two guidelines covered by §§8C2.2 through 8C2.9 are listed in §8C2.1(a). As discussed in more detail below, in organizational cases involving offenses referenced to the enumerated Chapter Two guideline sections, the fine calculation first requires computation of the applicable Chapter Two offense level. In addition, §§8C2.2 through 8C2.9 apply to offenses sentenced pursuant to §§2E1.1, 2X1.1, 2X2.1, 2X3.1 and 2X4.1, but only with respect to those cases in which the offense level for the underlying offense is determined under one of the guideline sections in the list at §8C2.1(a). *See* USSG §8C2.1(b). For example, if an organizational defendant is found guilty of aiding and abetting a fraud, the court is directed by §2X2.1 that the organization's offense level is the same level as that for the underlying offense, which in this case would be determined pursuant to §2B1.1, a guideline section listed at §8C2.1(a). Similarly, the application notes explain that the provisions of §§8C2.2 through 8C2.9 apply if the Chapter Two offense is not listed in §8C2.1, but the applicable guideline results in the determination of the offense level by use of a listed guideline. *See* USSG §8C2.1, comment. (n.2).

The organizational guidelines do not contain fine provisions for most offenses involving environmental pollution, food, drugs, agricultural and consumer products, civil/individual rights, administration of justice (*e.g.*, contempt, obstruction of justice, and perjury), or national defense. Those counts for which the applicable guideline is not listed in either §8C2.1(a) or (b) are fined pursuant to §8C2.10 (Determining the Fine for Other Counts), which is discussed below.

2

B.   Preliminary Determination of Inability to Pay Fine (§8C2.2)

The court need not make a complete determination of the guideline fine range in a case in which the organizational defendant lacks the ability to pay restitution or the minimum fine called for by §8C2.7(a). *See* USSG §8C2.2, comment. (backg'd.). Where it is readily ascertainable that the organization cannot and is not likely to become able to pay the restitution required under §8B1.1, a determination of the fine range is unnecessary since, pursuant to §8C3.3 (Reduction of Fine Based on Inability to Pay), no fine would be imposed. *See* USSG §8C2.2(a). Moreover, where it is readily ascertainable through a preliminary determination of the minimum of the guideline fine range that the organization cannot and is not likely to become able to pay such a minimum guideline fine, the court may use the preliminary determination and impose the fine that would result from the application of §8C3.3. *See* USSG §8C2.2(b).

C.   Offense Level (§8C2.3)

For those counts covered by the guideline sections listed at §8C1.1, the court first determines the total offense level by calculating the base offense level and any applicable enhancements contained in the applicable Chapter Two guideline. *See* USSG §8C2.3(a). Where there is more than one count, the court applies the same rules from Chapter 3, Part D (Multiple Counts) that are used for individual defendants to determine the combined offense level. *See* USSG §8C2.3(b).

In determining the offense level, the court must apply the provisions from §§1B1.2 through 1B1.8, but should not apply the adjustments in Chapter Three, Parts A (Victim-Related Adjustments), B (Role in the Offense), C (Obstruction), and E (Acceptance of Responsibility). *See* USSG §8C2.3, comment. (n.2).

D.   Base Fine (§8C2.4)

Under this section, the court determines the base fine in one of three ways: (1) by using the fine amount from the table set forth at §8C2.4(d) that corresponds to the offense level determined under §8C2.3[1]; (2) by using the pecuniary gain to the organization from the offense; or (3) by using the pecuniary loss caused by the organization, to the extent that such loss was caused intentionally, knowingly, or recklessly. *See* USSG §8C2.4(a)(1)-(3), comment. (backg'd.). Whichever method results in the greatest base fine amount is applied.

In relation to the three above methods, the guidelines provide two exceptions. First, if the applicable offense guideline in Chapter Two contains a special instruction for organizational fines, the court shall apply that special instruction. *See* USSG §8C2.4(b). For example, the

---

[1] The offense level fine table at §8C2.4(d) lays out the fine amount associated with each offense level, which, when combined with the multipliers derived from the culpability score in §8C2.5, results in the applicable guideline fine range. *See* USSG §§8C2.4(d), 8C2.5, 8C2.6.

sentencing guidelines for antitrust violations and most bribery and kickback offenses contain specific formulations for calculating fines for organizations. *See* USSG §§2B4.1(c); 2C1.1(d); 2R1.1(d). Second, to the extent that the calculation of either pecuniary gain or pecuniary loss would unduly complicate or prolong the sentencing process, the court shall not use the pecuniary gain or loss for the determination of the base fine. *See* USSG §8C2.4(c).

E.   Culpability Score (§8C2.5)

After calculating the base fine, the sentencing court must determine the organization's culpability score. The court starts with a culpability score of five points and thereafter adds or subtracts points for certain aggravating and mitigating factors. *See* USSG §8C2.5(a)-(g).

The guideline lists four aggravating factors that increase the culpability score. The first aggravating factor concerns high-level or substantial authority personnel in organizations of varying sizes who participate in, condone, or are willfully ignorant of criminal activity. *See* USSG §8C2.5(b)(1)-(5). The organization's culpability score is increased by between one and five points depending on the number of employees in the organization or unit of the organization and the involvement of individuals who are either within high-level personnel or substantial authority personnel. *Id.*

The commentary to the guidelines defines the terms "high-level personnel" and "substantial authority personnel." "High-level personnel" means individuals who have substantial control over the organization or who have a substantial role in the making of policy within the organization, such as directors, executive officers, individuals in charge of sales, administration, or finance, and individuals with substantial ownership interests. *See* USSG §8A1.2, comment. (n.3(B)). "Substantial authority personnel" means individuals who within the scope of their authority exercise a substantial measure of discretion in acting on behalf of an organization, such as plant managers, sales managers, individuals with authority to negotiate or set price levels, or individuals authorized to negotiate or approve significant contracts. *See* USSG §8A1.2, comment. (n.3(C)).

The second aggravating factor involves the organization's prior history of misconduct. *See* USSG §8C2.5(c). The court adds one or two points to the organization's culpability score if the organization committed the instant offense within a specified time after a criminal adjudication based on similar misconduct or a civil or administrative adjudication based on two or more separate instances of similar misconduct. *See* USSG §8C2.5(c)(1)-(2).

The third aggravating factor increases the culpability score by one or two points if the commission of the instant offense violated a judicial order or injunction, or the organization violated a condition of probation. *See* USSG §8C2.5(d)(1)-(2).

The fourth aggravating factor concerns obstruction of justice. Under this provision, if the organization willfully obstructed or impeded, attempted to obstruct or impede, or aided, abetted or encouraged obstruction of justice during the investigation, prosecution, or sentencing of the

4

instant offense, the court adds three points to the organization's culpability score. *See* USSG §8C2.5(e). Similarly, this three-point enhancement is also applicable if the organization knew of such obstruction or impedance or attempted obstruction or impedance and failed to take reasonable steps to prevent it. *Id.*

The guideline lists two mitigating factors that decrease the culpability score. The first allows the court to subtract three points from the organization's culpability score if the organization had an effective compliance and ethics program as defined in §8B2.1 in place at the time of the offense. *See* USSG §8C2.5(f)(1). This reduction should be denied, however, if the organization unreasonably delayed reporting the offense to the appropriate governmental authorities or under specified instances in which high-level or substantial authority personnel participated in, condoned, or were willfully ignorant of the offense. *See* USSG §8C2.5(f)(2), (f)(3). It should be noted, however, that the involvement of high-level or substantial authority personnel is not an absolute bar to this reduction. *See* USSG §8C2.5(f)(3)(B)-(C).

The second mitigating factor decreases the culpability score by five points if the organization self-reported the offense to the appropriate governmental authorities, fully cooperated in the investigation, and clearly demonstrated recognition and affirmative acceptance of responsibility for its conduct. *See* USSG §8C2.5(g)(1). If the organization did not self-report, but fully cooperated in the investigation, and accepted responsibility for its conduct, the culpability score is reduced by two points. *See* USSG §8C2.5(g)(2). Finally, if the organization did not self-report or cooperate, but clearly demonstrated recognition and affirmative acceptance of responsibility for its conduct, the culpability score is reduced by one point. *See* USSG §8C2.5(g)(3).

F.   Maximum and Minimum Multipliers (§8C2.6)

Once the court has determined the culpability score, the court looks to the table set forth in §8C2.6 to identify the minimum and maximum multipliers that correspond to that culpability score. *See* USSG §8C2.6. For instance, a culpability score of 10 or more results in a minimum multiplier of 2.00 and a maximum multiplier of 4.00, while a lower culpability score of 3 results in a minimum multiplier of 0.60 and a maximum multiplier of 1.20. *Id.* The maximum and minimum multipliers are then used to calculate the guideline fine range under §8C2.7. Note that a special instruction for a fine in §2R1.1 (Bid-Rigging, Price-Fixing or Market-Allocation Agreements Among Competitors) sets a floor for minimum and maximum multipliers in cases covered by that guideline. *See* USSG §8C2.6, comment. (n.1).

G.   Guideline Fine Range - Organization (§8C2.7)

The guideline fine range is then determined by multiplying the base fine calculated under §8C2.4 by both the minimum multiplier calculated under §8C2.6, which yields the minimum of the guideline fine range, and by the maximum multiplier calculated under §8C2.6, which yields the maximum of the guideline fine range. *See* USSG §8C2.7(a), (b). For example, if the base fine is $85,000 and the culpability score is 5, the base fine is multiplied by 1.00 to determine the minimum fine and by 2.00 to determine the maximum fine, resulting in a guideline fine range of $85,000 to $170,000.

H.   Determining the Fine Within the Range (Policy Statement) (§8C2.8)

The policy statement at §8C2.8(a) instructs the sentencing court that, in determining the appropriate fine, the court must consider certain factors under 18 U.S.C. §§ 3553(a) and 3572(a), as well as additional factors that the Commission concluded may be relevant in determining the appropriate fine in a particular case, such as any non-pecuniary loss caused or threatened by the offense and whether the organization failed to have an effective compliance and ethics program at the time of the offense. *See* USSG §8C2.8(a)(1)-(11); *see also id.*, comment. (backg'd.). In addition, §8C2.8(b) allows a court to consider the relative importance of any factor used to determine the fine range, so that a court is able to differentiate between cases that have the same offense level but differ in seriousness or between two cases with the same aggravating factors but where the factors vary in their intensity. *See* USSG §8C2.8(b); *see also id.*, comment. (n.7).

I.   Disgorgement (§8C2.9)

Once the court has determined the fine pursuant to §8C2.8, it must add to that fine any gain that the organization has made from the offense that has not and will not be paid as restitution or through any other remedial measure. *See* USSG §8C2.9. This section typically will apply in cases where, although the organization received gain from the offense, the offense did not result in harm to identifiable victims. *See* USSG §8C2.9, comment. (n.1). Examples include money laundering, obscenity, and regulatory reporting offenses. *Id.*

J.   Determining the Fine for Other Counts (§8C2.10)

The Commission has not promulgated guidelines for determining the fines for counts not included in §8C2.1, such as environmental pollution offenses. *See* USSG §8C2.10, comment. (backg'd.). For such counts, the court should determine an appropriate fine by applying the provisions of 18 U.S.C. §§ 3553 and 3572. *See* USSG §8C2.10. In a case that has a count or counts not covered by §8C1.2 in addition to a count or counts covered by that guideline, the court is to apply the fine guidelines for the count(s) covered by the guidelines and add any additional amount to the fine, as appropriate, for the count(s) not covered. *See* USSG §8C2.10, comment. (backg'd.).

III.   IMPLEMENTING THE SENTENCE OF A FINE (§§8C3.1-8C3.4)

A.   Imposing a Fine (§8C3.1)

Section 8C3.1 describes the interaction of the fine or fine range determined under the guidelines with the maximum fine allowed by statute and any minimum fine required by statute. *See* USSG §8C3.1, comment. (backg'd.). Where the minimum guideline fine is greater than the maximum fine authorized by statute, the sentencing court must impose the maximum fine authorized by statute. *See* USSG §8C3.1(b). Where the maximum guideline fine is less than a minimum fine required by statute, the sentencing court must import the minimum fine required by statute. *See* USSG §8C3.1(c).[2] When an organization is convicted of multiple counts, the maximum fine authorized may increase because the maximum fine for each count of conviction may be added together for an aggregated maximum authorized fine. *See* USSG §8C3.1, comment. (backg'd).

B.   Payment of a Fine - Organizations (§8C3.2)

For those organizations that operated primarily for a criminal purpose or primarily by criminal means, the sentencing court must order immediate payment of the fine. *See* USSG §8C3.2(a). In any other case, the court must order immediate payment unless it finds that the organization is financially unable to make immediate payment or that such payment would pose an undue burden on the organization. *See* USSG §8C3.2(b). In this case, the court shall require full payment at the earliest possible date, either by setting a date certain or by establishing an installment schedule. *See* USSG §8C3.2(b). In no event should the period provided for payment exceed five years. *See* USSG §8C3.2, comment. (n.1).

C.   Reduction of Fine Based on Inability to Pay (§8C3.3)

The court must reduce the fine below that otherwise required by the guidelines to the extent that imposition of such fine would impair the organization's ability to make restitution to its victims. *See* USSG §8C3.3(a). The court may impose a fine below that otherwise required if the court finds that the organization is not able and, even with the use of a reasonable installment schedule, is not likely to become able to pay the minimum fine required, provided that the reduction is not more than necessary to avoid substantially jeopardizing the continued viability of the organization. *See* USSG §8C3.3(b).

D.   Fines Paid by Owners of Closely Held Organizations (§8C3.4)

The sentencing court may offset the fine for a closely held organization when one or more individuals, each of whom owns at least a 5 percent interest in the organization, has been fined in a federal criminal proceeding for the same offense conduct. *See* USSG §8C3.4. An organization is closely held, regardless of its size, when relatively few individuals own it. *See* USSG §8C3.4, comment. (n.1.). The organizational fine is offset by an amount that reflects the percentage ownership interest of the sentenced individuals and the fine amount imposed on those individuals. *Id.* For example, in a case in which five individuals own an organization, each with a twenty percent interest, and three of the individuals are convicted and fined a total of $100,000,

---

[2] In this regard, it is worth noting that the Supreme Court recently held that *Apprendi*'s prohibition against the use of judge-found facts to increase penalties for a crime beyond the statutory maximum (*i.e.*, the maximum sentence a judge may impose solely on the basis of the facts reflected in the jury verdict or admitted by the defendant) applies to fines levied against a corporation. *See Southern Union Co. v. United States*, 567 U.S. __, 132 S.Ct. 2344 (June 21, 2012).

the fine imposed upon the organization can be offset by up to 60 percent of their combined fine amounts, *i.e.,* by $60,000. *Id.*

IV.   DEPARTURES FROM THE FINE RANGE (§§8C4.1-8C4.11)

Subpart 4 of Part C of Chapter 8 sets forth policy statements for both aggravating and mitigating factors that may not have been adequately taken into consideration in the guidelines for certain offenses. *See* USSG Ch.8, Pt.4, intro. comment. These factors include:

(1)   the organization's substantial assistance to the authorities in the investigation or prosecution of crimes committed by individuals not directly affiliated with the organization or by other individuals (§8C4.1);

(2)   the offense resulted in death or bodily injury, or involved the foreseeable risk of death or bodily injury (§8C4.2);

(3)   the offense constituted a threat to national security (§8C4.3);

(4)   the offense presented a threat to the environment (§8C4.4);

(5)   the offense presented a risk to the integrity or continued existence of private or public market (§8C4.5);

(6)   the organization, in connection with the offense, bribed or unlawfully gave a gratuity to a pubic official, or attempted or conspired to do the same (§8C4.6);

(7)   the organization is a public entity (§8C4.7);

(8)   the members or beneficiaries, other than shareholders, of the organization are direct victims of the offense (§8C4.8);

(9)   the organization has paid or has agreed to pay remedial costs that greatly exceed the gain the organization received from the offense (§8C4.9);

(10)   the organization's culpability score was reduced for having an effective compliance and ethics program, but it had implemented that program in response to a court order or administrative order, or the organization was required to have such a program, but did not (§8C4.10); and

(11)   the organization's culpability score is greater than 10 (§8C4.11).

APPENDIX 13

United States Sentencing Guidelines: Effective Compliance and Ethics Programs

CHAPTER 8—PART B—REMEDYING HARM FROM CRIMINAL CONDUCT, AND EFFECTIVE COMPLIANCE AND ETHICS PROGRAM

§8B2.1 EFFECTIVE COMPLIANCE AND ETHICS PROGRAM

(a) To have an effective compliance and ethics program, for purposes of subsection (f) of § 8C2.5 (Culpability Score) and subsection (c)(1) of §8D1.4 (Recommended Conditions of Probation—Organizations), an organization shall—

(1) exercise due diligence to prevent and detect criminal conduct; and

(2) otherwise promote an organizational culture that encourages ethical conduct and a commitment to compliance with the law.

Such compliance and ethics program shall be reasonably designed, implemented and enforced so that the program is generally effective in preventing and detecting criminal conduct. The failure to prevent or detect the instant offense does not necessarily mean that the program is not generally effective in preventing and detecting criminal conduct.

(b) Due diligence and the promotion of an organizational culture that encourages ethical conduct and a commitment to compliance with the law within the meaning of subsection (a) minimally require the following:

(1) The organization shall establish standards and procedures to prevent and detect criminal conduct.

(2) (A) The organization's governing authority shall be knowledgeable about the content and operation of the compliance and ethics program and shall exercise reasonable oversight with respect to the implementation and effectiveness of the compliance and ethics program.

(B) High-level personnel of the organization shall ensure that the organization has an effective compliance and ethics program, as described in this guideline. Specific individual(s) within high-level personnel shall be assigned overall responsibility for the compliance and ethics program.

(C) Specific individual(s) within the organization shall be delegated day-to-day operational responsibility for the compliance and ethics program. Individual(s) with operational responsibility shall report periodically to high-level personnel and, as appropriate, to the governing authority, or an appropriate subgroup of the governing authority, on the effectiveness of the compliance and ethics program. To carry out such operational responsibility, such individual(s) shall be given adequate resources, appropriate authority, and direct access to the governing authority or an appropriate subgroup of the governing authority.

(3) The organization shall use reasonable efforts not to include within the substantial authority personnel of the organization any individual whom the organization knew, or should have known through the exercise of due diligence, has engaged in illegal activities or other conduct inconsistent with an effective compliance and ethics program.

(4)   (A) The organization shall take reasonable steps to communicate periodically and in a practical manner its standards and procedures, and other aspects of the compliance and ethics program, to the individuals referred to in subdivision (B) by conducting effective training programs and otherwise disseminating information appropriate to such individuals' respective roles and responsibilities.

(B) The individuals referred to in subdivision (A) are the members of the governing authority, high-level personnel, substantial authority personnel, the organization's employees, and, as appropriate, the organization's agents.

(5) The organization shall take reasonable steps—

(A) to ensure that the organization's compliance and ethics program is followed, including monitoring and auditing to detect criminal conduct.

(B) to evaluate periodically the effectiveness of the organization's compliance and ethics program; and

(C) to have and publicize a system, which may include mechanisms that allow for anonymity or confidentiality, whereby the organization's employees and agents may report or seek guidance regarding potential or actual criminal conduct without fear of retaliation.

(6) The organization's compliance and ethics programs shall be promoted and enforced consistently throughout the organization through (A) appropriate incentives to perform in accordance with the compliance and ethics program; and (B) appropriate disciplinary measures for engaging in criminal conduct and for failing to take reasonable steps to prevent or detect criminal conduct.

(7) After criminal conduct has been detected, the organization shall take reasonable steps to respond appropriately to the criminal conduct and to prevent further similar criminal conduct, including making any necessary modifications to the organization's compliance and ethics program.

(c) In implementing subsection (b), the organization shall periodically assess the risk of criminal conduct and shall take appropriate steps to design, implement or modify each requirement set forth in subsection (B) to reduce the risk of criminal conduct identified through this process.

COMMENTARY

Application Notes:

1. *Definitions*—For purposes of this guideline:
"Compliance and ethics program" means a program designed to prevent and detect criminal conduct.

"Governing authority" means the (A) Board of Directors; or (B) if the organization does not have a Board of Directors, the highest-level governing body of the organization.

"High-level personnel of the organization" and "substantial authority personnel" have the meaning given those terms in the Commentary to § 8A1.2 (Application Instructions—Organizations).

"Standard and procedures" means standards of conduct and internal controls that are reasonably capable of reducing the likelihood of criminal conduct.

2. *Factors to Consider in Meeting Requirements of this Guideline—*

   (A) *In General*—Each of the requirements set forth in this guideline shall be met by an organization; however, in determining what specific actions are necessary to meet those requirements, factors that shall be considered include: (i) applicable industry practice or the standards called for by any applicable governmental regulation; (ii) the size of the organization; and (iii) similar misconduct.

   (B) *Applicable Governmental Regulation and Industry Practice*—An organization's failure to incorporate and follow applicable industry practice or the standards called for by any applicable governmental regulation weighs against a finding of an effective compliance and ethics program.

   (C) *The Size of the Organization—*

      (i) *In General*—The formality and scope of actions that an organization shall take to meet the requirements of this guideline, including the necessary features of the organization's standards and procedures, depend on the size of the organization.

(ii) *Large Organizations*—A large organization generally shall devote more formal operations and greater resources in meeting the requirements of this guideline than shall a small organization. As appropriate, a large organization should encourage small organizations (especially those that have, or seek to have, a business relationship with the large organization) to implement effective compliance and ethics programs.

(iii) *Small Organizations*—In meeting the requirements of this guideline, small organizations shall demonstrate the same degree of commitment to ethical conduct and compliance with the law as large organizations. However, a small organization may meet the requirements of this guideline with less formality and fewer resources than would be expected of large organizations. In appropriate circumstances, reliance on existing resources and simple systems can demonstrate a degree of commitment that, for a large organization, would only be demonstrated through more formally planned and implemented systems.

Examples of the informality and use of fewer resources with which a small organization may meet the requirements of this guideline include the following: (I) the governing authority's discharge of its responsibility for oversight of the compliance and ethics program by directly managing the organization's compliance and ethics efforts; (II) training employees through informal staff meetings, and monitoring through regular "walk arounds" or continuous observation while managing the organization; (III) using available personnel, rather than employing separate staff, to carry out the compliance and ethics program; and (IV) modeling its own compliance and ethics program on existing, well-regarded compliance and ethics programs and best practices of other similar organizations.

(D) *Recurrence of Similar Misconduct*—Recurrence of similar misconduct creates doubt regarding whether the organization took reasonable steps to meet the requirements of this guideline. For purposes of this subdivision, "similar misconduct" has the meaning given that term in the Commentary to § 8A1.2 (Application Instructions – Organizations).

3. *Application of Subsection (b)(2)*—High-level personnel and substantial authority personnel of the organization shall be knowledgeable about the content and operation of the compliance and ethics program, shall perform their assigned duties consistent with the exercise of due diligence, and shall promote an organizational culture that encourages ethical conduct and a commitment to compliance with the law.

If the specific individual(s) assigned overall responsibility for the compliance and ethics program does not have day-to-day operational responsibility for the program, then the individual(s) with day-to-day operational responsibility for the program typically should, no less than annually, give the governing authority or an appropriate subgroup thereof information on the implementation and effectiveness of the compliance and ethics program.

4. *Application of Subsection (b)(3)—*

   (A) *Consistency with Other Law*—Nothing in subsection (b)(3) is intended to require conduct inconsistent with any Federal, State or local law, including any law governing employment or hiring practices.

   (B) *Implementation*—In implementing subsection (b)(3), the organization shall hire and promote individuals so as to ensure that all individuals within the high-level personnel and substantial authority personnel of the organization will perform their assigned duties in a manner consistent with the exercise of due diligence and the promotion of an organizational culture that encourages ethical conduct and a commitment to compliance with the law under subsection (a). With respect to the hiring or promotion of such individuals, an organization shall consider the relatedness of the individual's illegal activities and other misconduct (i.e., other conduct inconsistent with an effective compliance and ethics program) to the specific responsibilities the individual is anticipated to be assigned and other factors such as: (i) the recency of the individual's illegal activities and other misconduct; and (ii) whether the individual has engaged in other such illegal activities and other such misconduct.

5. *Application of Subsection(b)(6)*—Adequate discipline of individuals responsible for an offense is a necessary component of enforcement; however, the form of discipline that will be appropriate will be case specific.

6. *Application of Subsection (c)*—To meet the requirements of subsection (c), an organization shall:

   (A) Assess periodically the risk that criminal conduct will occur, including assessing the following:

   (i)   The nature and seriousness of such criminal conduct.

   (ii) The likelihood that certain criminal conduct may occur because of the nature of the organization's business. If, because of the nature of an organization's business, there is a substantial risk that certain types of criminal conduct may occur, the organization shall take reasonable steps to prevent and detect that type of criminal conduct. For example, an organization that, due to the nature of its business, employs sales personnel who have flexibility to set prices shall establish standards and procedures designed to prevent and detect price-fixing. An organization that, due to the nature of its business, employs sales personnel who have flexibility to represent the material characteristics of a product shall establish standards and procedures designed to prevent and detect fraud.

   (iii) The prior history of the organization. The prior history of an organization may indicate types of criminal conduct that it shall take actions to prevent and detect.

(B) Prioritize periodically, as appropriate, the actions taken pursuant to any requirement set forth in subsection (b), in order to focus on preventing and detecting the criminal conduct identified under subdivision (A) of this note as most serious, and most likely, to occur.

(C) Modify, as appropriate, the actions taken pursuant to any requirement set forth in subsection (b) to reduce the risk of criminal conduct identified under subdivision (A) of this note as most serious, and most likely, to occur.

Background: This section sets forth the requirements for an effective compliance and ethics program. This section responds to section 805(a)(2)(5) of the Sarbanes-Oxley Act of 2002, Public Law 107-204, which directed the Commission to review and amend, as appropriate, the guidelines and related policy statements to ensure that the guidelines that apply to organizations in this chapter "are sufficient to deter and punish organizational criminal misconduct."

The requirements set forth in this guideline are intended to achieve reasonable prevention and detection of criminal conduct for which the organization would be vicariously liable. The prior diligence of an organization in seeking to prevent and detect criminal conduct has a direct bearing on the appropriate penalties and probation terms for the organization if it is convicted and sentenced for a criminal offense.

APPENDIX 14

SEC Policy Statement Concerning Cooperation by Individuals in Its Investigations and Related Enforcement Actions

17 C.F.R. § 200.12 (2010)

Title 17: Commodity and Securities Exchanges
Part 202—Informal and Other Procedures

202.12 Policy statement concerning cooperation by individuals in its investigations and related enforcement actions.

Cooperation by individuals and entities in the Commission's investigations and related enforcement actions can contribute significantly to the success of the agency's mission. Cooperation can enhance the Commission's ability to detect violations of the federal securities laws, increase the effectiveness and efficiency of the Commission's investigations, and provide important evidence for the Commission's enforcement actions. There is a wide spectrum of tools available to the Commission and its staff for facilitating and rewarding cooperation by individuals, ranging from taking no enforcement action to pursuing reduced charges and sanctions in connection with enforcement actions. As with any cooperation program, there exists some tension between the objectives of holding individuals fully accountable for their misconduct and providing incentives for individuals to cooperate with law enforcement authorities. This policy statement sets forth the analytical framework employed by the Commission and its staff for resolving this tension in a manner that ensures that potential cooperation arrangements maximize the Commission's law enforcement interests. Although the evaluation of cooperation requires a case-by-case analysis of the specific circumstances presented, as described in greater detail below, the Commission's general approach is to determine whether, how much, and in what manner to credit cooperation by individuals by evaluating four considerations: the assistance provided by the cooperating individual in the Commission's investigation or related enforcement actions ("Investigation"); the importance of the underlying matter in which the individual cooperated; the societal interest in ensuring that the cooperating individual is held accountable for his or her misconduct; and the appropriateness of cooperation credit based upon the profile of the cooperating individual. In the end, the goal of the Commission's analysis is to protect the investing public by determining whether the public interest in facilitating and rewarding an individual's cooperation in order to advance the Commission's law enforcement interests justifies the credit awarded to the individual for his or her cooperation.

(a) *Assistance provided by the individual.* The Commission assesses the assistance provided by the cooperating individual in the Investigation by considering, among other things:

(1) The value of the individual's cooperation to the Investigation including, but not limited to:

(i) Whether the individual's cooperation resulted in substantial assistance to the Investigation;

(ii) The timeliness of the individual's cooperation, including whether the individual was first to report the misconduct to the Commission or to offer his or her cooperation in the Investigation, and whether the cooperation was provided before he or she had any knowledge of a pending investigation or related action;

(iii) Whether the Investigation was initiated based on information or other cooperation provided by the individual;

(iv) The quality of cooperation provided by the individual, including whether the cooperation was truthful, complete, and reliable; and

(v) The time and resources conserved as a result of the individual's cooperation in the Investigation.

(2) The nature of the individual's cooperation in the Investigation including, but not limited to:

(i) Whether the individual's cooperation was voluntary or required by the terms of an agreement with another law enforcement or regulatory organization;

(ii) The types of assistance the individual provided to the Commission;

(iii) Whether the individual provided non-privileged information, which information was not requested by the staff or otherwise might not have been discovered;

(iv) Whether the individual encouraged or authorized others to assist the staff who might not have otherwise participated in the Investigation; and

(v) Any unique circumstances in which the individual provided the cooperation.

(b) *Importance of the underlying matter.* The Commission assesses the importance of the Investigation in which the individual cooperated by considering, among other things:

(1) The character of the Investigation including, but not limited to:

(i) Whether the subject matter of the Investigation is a Commission priority;

(ii) The type of securities violations;

(iii) The age and duration of the misconduct;

(iv) The number of violations; and

(v) The isolated or repetitive nature of the violations.

(2) The dangers to investors or others presented by the underlying violations involved in the Investigation including, but not limited to:

(i) The amount of harm or potential harm caused by the underlying violations;

(ii) The type of harm resulting from or threatened by the underlying violations; and

(iii) The number of individuals or entities harmed.[1]

(c) *Interest in holding the individual accountable.* The Commission assesses the societal interest in holding the cooperating individual fully accountable for his or her misconduct by considering, among other things:

(1) The severity of the individual's misconduct assessed by the nature of the violations and in the context of the individual's knowledge, education, training, experience, and position of responsibility at the time the violations occurred;

(2) The culpability of the individual, including, but not limited to, whether the individual acted with scienter, both generally and in relation to others who participated in the misconduct;

(3) The degree to which the individual tolerated illegal activity including, but not limited to, whether he or she took steps to prevent the violations from occurring or continuing, such as notifying the Commission or other appropriate law enforcement agency of the misconduct or, in the case of a violation involving a business organization, by notifying members of management not involved in the misconduct, the board of directors or the equivalent body not involved in the misconduct, or the auditors of such business organization of the misconduct;

(4) The efforts undertaken by the individual to remediate the harm caused by the violations including, but not limited to, whether he or she paid or agreed to pay disgorgement to injured investors and other victims or assisted these victims and the authorities in the recovery of the fruits and instrumentalities of the violations; and

(5) The sanctions imposed on the individual by other federal or state authorities and industry organizations for the violations involved in the Investigation.

(d) *Profile of the individual.* The Commission assesses whether, how much, and in what manner it is in the public interest to award credit for cooperation, in part, based upon the cooperating individual's personal and professional profile by considering, among other things:

(1) The individual's history of lawfulness, including complying with securities laws or regulations;

(2) The degree to which the individual has demonstrated an acceptance of responsibility for his or her past misconduct; and

(3) The degree to which the individual will have an opportunity to commit future violations of the federal securities laws in light of his or her

occupation—including, but not limited to, whether he or she serves as:
A licensed individual, such as an attorney or accountant; an associated
person of a regulated entity, such as a broker or dealer; a fiduciary
for other individuals or entities regarding financial matters; an officer or director of public companies; or a member of senior management—together with any existing or proposed safeguards based upon
the individual's particular circumstances.

Note to §202.12: Before the Commission evaluates an individual's cooperation,
it analyzes the unique facts and circumstances of the case. The above principles
are not listed in order of importance nor are they intended to be all-inclusive or
to require a specific determination in any particular case. Furthermore, depending
upon the facts and circumstances of each case, some of the principles may not be
applicable or may deserve greater weight than others. Finally, neither this statement, nor the principles set forth herein creates or recognizes any legally enforceable rights for any person.

[75 FR 3123, Jan. 19, 2010]

NOTE

1. Cooperation in Investigations that involve priority matters or serious, ongoing, or widespread violations will be viewed more favorably.

APPENDIX 15

A Proposal for a United States Department of Justice Foreign Corrupt Practices Act Leniency Policy[1]

Robert W. Tarun and Peter P. Tomczak
Excerpted from a law review article first published in 47 Am. Crim. L. Rev 153 (2010)

1. LENIENCY BEFORE AN INVESTIGATION HAS BEGUN—PART A

Leniency (*i.e.*, non-prosecution) shall be granted to a corporation and its affiliates, and certain corporate employees and agents, reporting improper payment(s) to a foreign official before an investigation has begun, if the following eight conditions are met:

  (a) At the time the corporation comes forward and reports the improper payment activity, the Fraud Section has not received credible information from any other source about the improper payment activity being reporting by the corporation;

  (b) The corporation elects within sixty (60) days after receiving and promptly verifying preliminary allegations of improper payments to conduct a thorough internal investigation, to disclose fully all material underlying facts and the results of the investigation to the DOJ and/or SEC, and to fully cooperate with the agency(ies);

  (c) The corporation, upon its discovery of the improper payment activity being reported, takes steps to reasonably investigate and, thereafter, take prompt and effective action to terminate the activity;

  (d) In reporting improper payment activity, the corporation with candor and completeness discloses all material underlying facts and provides full, continuing and complete cooperation to the Fraud Section throughout the investigation;

  (e) The confession of improper payment activity is truly a corporate act, as opposed to isolated confessions of individual executives or employees;

  (f) If possible, the corporation makes restitution to injured parties—depending on whether the corporation was active or passive and whether the host or foreign country prosecutes the officials who participated in the acts of bribery;

    (g)   The corporation has not been named in an FCPA enforcement proceeding, including a deferred prosecution agreement or a non-prosecution agreement, in ten (10) years; and

    (h)   Corporate employees or agents who are not leaders or originators of bribery activity, who fully disclose improper payment activity to and cooperate fully with the corporation and the Fraud Section and who have not received any compensation or other benefits arising from or related to the improper activity from any person or entity other than the corporation shall not be prosecuted.

2. ALTERNATIVE REQUIREMENTS FOR FCPA LENIENCY—PART B

If a corporation comes forward to report improper payment activity to a foreign official and does not meet all eight of the conditions set out in Part A, above, then the corporation or its affiliates, whether it or they come forward before or after an investigation has begun, may be granted leniency (*i.e.*, non-prosecution) if the following seven conditions are met:

    (a)   The corporation elects within sixty (60) days after receiving and promptly verifying preliminary allegations of improper payments to conduct a thorough internal investigation, to disclose fully all material underlying facts and the results of the investigation to the DOJ and/or SEC, and to fully cooperate with the agency(ies);

    (b)   The Fraud Section, at the time the corporation comes forward, does not yet have evidence against the corporation that is likely to result in a sustainable conviction;

    (c)   The corporation, upon its discovery of the improper payment activity being reported, takes prompt and effective action to terminate the activity;

    (d)   In reporting improper payment activity, the corporation fully discloses all material underlying facts and provides full, continuing and complete cooperation that assists the Fraud Section in its investigation;

    (e)   The confession of improper payment activity is truly a corporate act, as opposed to isolated confessions of individual executives or officials;

    (f)   If possible, the corporation agrees to make restitution to injured parties—depending on whether the corporation was active or passive and whether the host or foreign country prosecutes the corporate officials who participated in the acts of bribery; and

    (g)   The Fraud Section determines the granting leniency would not be unfair to others, considering the nature of the illegal activity, the confessing corporation's role in it, and when the corporation comes forward.

In applying condition (g), the primary considerations shall be: (i) how soon the corporation comes forward after receiving and verifying preliminary allegations of improper payments; (ii) whether the corporation originated the improper payment activity or was the leader in, or originator of, the activity; and (iii) any FCPA enforcement history. The burden of satisfying condition (g) shall be low if the corporation comes forward when the Fraud Section has just begun an investigation into the improper payment activity, increasing as the Fraud Section approaches obtaining credible evidence that is likely to result in a sustainable conviction.

3. FCPA LENIENCY FOR CORPORATE DIRECTORS, OFFICERS, AND EMPLOYEES

The DOJ recognizes that the prosecution of individuals serves an important function in deterring other corporate employees and agents from engaging in improper payment activities. If a corporation qualifies for leniency under Part A, above, then directors, officers, and employees of the corporation and its affiliates who admit their involvement in the improper payment activity as part of the corporation confession,[2] other than the parent corporation's chief executive officer, chief financial officer, chief legal officer, and chief compliance officer who were leaders in or originators of, or directly participated in or condoned, the improper payment activity, will receive leniency, in the form of not being charged criminally for the illegal activity. If a corporation does not qualify for leniency under Part A, above, then only those directors, officers, and employees who come forward promptly, and not to include the parent corporation's chief executive official, chief financial officer, chief legal officer and chief compliance officer of the corporation who are leaders in or originators of, or directly participated in or condoned, the improper payment activity, will be considered for immunity from criminal prosecution on the same basis as if they had approached the Fraud Section individually.

4. RIGOROUS FCPA COMPLIANCE PROGRAM AND INTERNAL CONTROLS

In order to promote rigorous FCPA compliance programs and internal control systems, which are essential to the long-term eradication of international corporate corruption, the Fraud Section will reward corporations that have adopted and implemented, at the time of the improper payment activities, the following: (a) a system of internal accounting controls designed to ensure that the company makes and keeps fair and accurate books, records and accounts; and (b) a "rigorous" anti-corruption compliance program, with policies and procedures designed to detect and deter violations of the FCPA and other applicable anti-corruption laws. For purposes of the anti-bribery leniency policy, a rigorous anti-corruption compliance program must be comprised of at least the following elements:[3]

1. A clearly articulated, written corporate policy against violations of the FCPA and other applicable anti-corruption laws.
2. A system of financial and accounting procedures, including a system of internal accounting controls, designed to ensure the maintenance of fair and accurate books, records and accounts.
3. Promulgation of compliance policies and procedures designed to reduce the prospect of violations of FCPA, other applicable anti-corruption laws and the corporate compliance code. These policies and procedures shall apply to all directors, officers and employees and, where necessary and appropriate, outside parties acting on behalf of the corporation in foreign

jurisdictions, including agents, consultants, representatives, distributors, teaming partners and joint venture partners (collectively referred to as "outside agents and business partners").

4. The assignment of responsibility to one or more senior corporate officers for the implementation and oversight of compliance with policies, standards and procedures regarding the FCPA and other applicable anti-corruption laws. Such corporate official(s) shall have the authority to report matters directly to the corporation's Board of Directors, its Audit Committee, QLCC or corporate body charged with equivalent responsibilities. For corporations with 250 or more employees, agents or business partners in a geographic region (e.g., Asia Pacific, Europe, Middle East, Africa), there shall be one or more regional corporate officials responsible for the implementation and oversight of compliance with the same policies, standards and procedures in each region.

5. Mechanisms designed to ensure that the code of conduct and compliance policies and procedures of the corporation regarding the FCPA and other applicable anti-corruption laws are effectively communicated to all directors, officers and employees and, where necessary and appropriate, outside agents and business partners. These mechanisms shall include at least the following: (A) live anti-corruption training at least every 18 months for all directors and all employees, agents and business partners who interact with government officials, directly or indirectly; (B) annual certifications by all directors, employees, agents and business partners, attesting to their understanding and compliance with the corporation's anti-corruption program; and (C) quarterly reports by compliance officials to the corporation's Board of Directors, its Audit Committee or the equivalent.

6. An effective internal corporate system for reporting suspected criminal conduct and/or violations of the compliance policies, standards and procedures regarding the FCPA and other applicable anti-corruption laws for directors, officers, employees, and outside agents and business partners.

7. Appropriate internal corporate disciplinary procedures to address at least the following: violations of the FCPA, other applicable anti-corruption laws or a corporation's code of conduct by directors, officers, employees, and outside agents and business partners.

8. Appropriate due diligence requirements pertaining to the retention and oversight of agents and business partners.

9. Appropriate due diligence requirements pertaining to the acquisition of and merger with other corporations.

10. Standard provisions in agreements, contracts, and renewals thereof with all outside agents and business partners which are designed to prevent violations of the FCPA and other applicable anti-corruption laws, which provisions include: (A) anti-corruption representations and undertakings relating to compliance with the FCPA and other applicable anti-corruption laws; (B) rights to conduct audits of the books and records of the agent or business partner to ensure compliance with the foregoing; and (C) rights to terminate an outside agent or business partner as a result of any violation of anti-corruption laws, and regulations or representations and undertakings related to such matters.

11. An internal audit program specifically designed to address the FCPA and corruption risks of the corporation and its affiliates.

12. Every two years, testing of the code of conduct and compliance policies and procedures designed to evaluate their effectiveness in detecting and reducing violations of the anti-corruption laws and the corporation's internal controls system.

13. The burden shall be on a corporation seeking a rigorous FCPA compliance program discount to establish a contemporaneous record of each of the above elements, *e.g.*, annual teaming partner certifications, director training PowerPoints and sign-in sheets. The fact that a corporation has uncovered multiple violations of anti-corruption laws shall not, by itself, mean that its code of conduct and compliance policies and procedures were not rigorous, or that its internal controls were inadequate, and therefore it is ineligible for a rigorous FCPA compliance program discount. However, the longer, more far reaching and systemic the misconduct, the more likely a corporation cannot meet its burden of establishing with written documentation a contemporaneous rigorous FCPA or other anti-corruption compliance program.

14. All new hires or new employees as a result of a merger or acquisition shall receive the FCPA or anti-corruption training described in Element 5 above within six months of the date of their new employment. If the individuals identified as having violated FCPA or anti-corruption laws have been employed by the corporation or any of its affiliates six months or longer without having received the type of FCPA or anti-corruption training described in Element 5 above, or without having executed the above-referenced certifications, there shall be a rebuttable presumption that the corporation does not qualify for a rigorous FCPA compliance program discount.

5. COOPERATION AND COMPLIANCE PROGRAM DISCOUNTS, THIRD-PARTY ASSISTANCE, CALCULATION OF FINES, UPWARD DEPARTURES, AND DEBARMENT AND SUSPENSION UNDER FCPA LENIENCY POLICY

a. Cooperation Discounts

A corporation qualifying for leniency before an investigation has begun (Part A) shall be eligible for a 40% cooperation discount off the low-end or minimum of the fine range under the U.S. Sentencing Guidelines.

A corporation qualifying for leniency after an investigation has begun (Part B) may be eligible for a 20% cooperation discount off the low end or minimum of the fine range under the U.S. Sentencing Guidelines.

b. Rigorous FCPA Compliance Program Discount

A corporation shall be eligible for an additional 20% compliance program discount if it had in place at the time of the improper payment activity(ies) a rigorous FCPA compliance program satisfying the criteria set forth in Section 4.

c. Third-Party Investigation and Prosecution Assistance Discount

A corporation qualifying for leniency under Part A or Part B shall be eligible for an additional 20% cooperation discount if it provides information leading to the investigation and prosecution of another company, or its officers or employees.

d. Calculation of Fines

The calculation of any DOJ fine shall be based on an analysis of bribes and/or transactions in the territory of the United States or with a territorial connection to the United States.

   The combined discounted DOJ fine under Part A or Part B leniency, the Rigorous FCPA Compliance Program Discount, and/or the Third Party Investigation and Prosecution Assistance Discount, shall represent the total fine payable to the United States government, that is, to the DOJ and SEC.[4] Absent exceptional circumstances, the total fine shall be split evenly between the DOJ and SEC.

e. Investigation and Termination Plus

In the event of a conviction, the DOJ shall recommend a sentencing a 10% upward departure from the maximum Sentencing Guideline fine for a corporation whose parent corporation's chief executive officer, chief financial officer, chief legal officer or chief compliance officer was in receipt of credible allegations of the improper payment activity, and failed to conduct a prompt and reasonable investigation using qualified and experienced counsel.[5]

   In the event of a conviction, the DOJ shall recommend at sentencing an additional 10% upward departure from the maximum Sentencing Guideline fine for a corporation whose parent corporation's chief executive officer, chief financial officer, chief legal officer or chief compliance officer was in receipt of credible allegations of improper payment activity, and failed to implement effective remedial measures, including immediate termination of the improper payment activity.

f. Debarment and Suspension by United States and Foreign Governments

The DOJ shall assist a corporation qualifying for leniency under Part A or Part B wherever possible to avoid suspension and debarment as a U.S. or foreign government contractor unless there is evidence sustainable to obtain a conviction that the chief executive officer, chief financial officer, chief legal officer or chief compliance officer of the parent corporation knowingly participated in or approved improper payment activity with foreign officials.

   The Fraud Section of the DOJ and the FCPA unit of the SEC shall work with foreign law enforcement authorities to promote and establish similar leniency policies offering investigation, disclosure, cooperation, third party assistance and compliance program discounts to apply in determining foreign fines or penalties. A foreign law enforcement agency may not recover a fine for which the United States has asserted or intends to assert a fine claiming a territorial connection to the United States. If a foreign government does so, a United States corporation[6] shall be entitled to a credit, set off or refund from the DOJ or SEC fine for any related fine paid to a foreign government. The refusal of a foreign government to prosecute corrupt officials for which evidence sustainable to obtain a conviction exists shall be considered an additional leniency factor in assessing the appropriate fine against a United States corporation, or a foreign subsidiary of same.

NOTES:

1. This Proposal was originally published in the 25th anniversary issue of the AMERICAN CRIMINAL LAW REVIEW (47 AM. CRIM. L. REV. 153) (Spring 2010) and is republished with the permission of the American Criminal Law Review.
2. Such admission by such directors, officers and employees of the corporation must be made with candor and completeness, and they must continue to assist the Fraud Section throughout the investigation.
3. Many of the twelve elements are adopted in whole or in part from remedial compliance program requirements outlined in FCPA resolutions. *See, e.g.,* Deferred Prosecution Agreement, *United States v. Daimler AG*, 1:10-CR-00063-RJL, at 90-93 (D.D.C. Mar. 24, 2010) (Attachment C, Corporate Compliance Program).
4. The proposed leniency policy would not bar private litigants from seeking monetary relief; cooperating corporations would be barred from denying the essential bribery claims (though these corporations would be free to contest jurisdiction and damages).
5. Among other things, such FCPA counsel should be sufficiently independent and disinterested in order to exercise his or her own independent, professional judgment, Qualified and experienced FCPA counsel need not necessarily be counsel outside of the corporation.
6. For purposes of this Paragraph, a "United States corporation" shall mean any business entity headquartered in or formed under the laws of any jurisdiction or instrumentality of the United States.

Final Whistleblower Rules Pursuant to Section 922 of the Dodd-Frank Wall Street Reform and Consumer Protection Act (May 25, 2011)

Federal Register / Vol. 76, No. 113 / Monday, June 13, 2011 / Rules and Regulations   34363

240.21F-7   Confidentiality of submissions.
240.21F-8   Eligibility.
240.21F-9   Procedures for submitting original information.
240.21F-10   Procedures for making a claim for a whistleblower award in SEC actions that result in monetary sanctions in excess of $1,000,000
240.21F-11   Procedures for determining awards based upon a related action.
240.21F-12   Materials that may be used as the basis for an award determination and that may comprise the record on appeal.
240.21F-13   Appeals.
240.21F-14   Procedures applicable to the payment of awards.
240.21F-15   No amnesty.
240.21F-16   Awards to whistleblowers who engage in culpable conduct.
240.21F-17   Staff communications with individuals reporting possible securities law violations.

*   *   *   *   *

§ 240.21F–1   General.

Section 21F of the Securities Exchange Act of 1934 ("Exchange Act") (15 U.S.C. 78u-6), entitled "Securities Whistleblower Incentives and Protection," requires the Securities and Exchange Commission ("Commission") to pay awards, subject to certain limitations and conditions, to whistleblowers who provide the Commission with original information about violations of the Federal securities laws. These rules describe the whistleblower program that the Commission has established to implement the provisions of Section 21F, and explain the procedures you will need to follow in order to be eligible for an award. You should read these procedures carefully because the failure to take certain required steps within the time frames described in these rules may disqualify you from receiving an award for which you otherwise may be eligible. Unless expressly provided for in these rules, no person is authorized to make any offer or promise, or otherwise to bind the Commission with respect to the payment of any award or the amount thereof. The Securities and Exchange Commission's Office of the Whistleblower administers our whistleblower program. Questions about the program or these rules should be directed to the SEC Office of the Whistleblower, 100 F Street, NE., Washington, DC 20549–5631.

§ 240.21F–2   Whistleblower status and retaliation protection.

(a) *Definition of a whistleblower.* (1) You are a whistleblower if, alone or jointly with others, you provide the Commission with information pursuant to the procedures set forth in § 240.21F–9(a) of this chapter, and the information

relates to a possible violation of the Federal securities laws (including any rules or regulations thereunder) that has occurred, is ongoing, or is about to occur. A whistleblower must be an individual. A company or another entity is not eligible to be a whistleblower.

(2) To be eligible for an award, you must submit original information to the Commission in accordance with the procedures and conditions described in §§ 240.21F–4, 240.21F–8, and 240.21F–9 of this chapter.

(b) Prohibition against retaliation: (1) For purposes of the anti-retaliation protections afforded by Section 21F(h)(1) of the Exchange Act (15 U.S.C. 78u-6(h)(1)), you are a whistleblower if:

(i) You possess a reasonable belief that the information you are providing relates to a possible securities law violation (or, where applicable, to a possible violation of the provisions set forth in 18 U.S.C. 1514A(a)) that has occurred, is ongoing, or is about to occur, and;

(ii) You provide that information in a manner described in Section 21F(h)(1)(A) of the Exchange Act (15 U.S.C. 78u-6(h)(1)(A)).

(iii) The anti-retaliation protections apply whether or not you satisfy the requirements, procedures and conditions to qualify for an award.

(2) Section 21F(h)(1) of the Exchange Act (15 U.S.C. 78u-6(h)(1)), including any rules promulgated thereunder, shall be enforceable in an action or proceeding brought by the Commission.

§ 240.21F–3   Payment of awards.

(a) *Commission actions:* Subject to the eligibility requirements described in §§ 240.21F–2, 240.21F–8, and 240.21F–16 of this chapter, the Commission will pay an award or awards to one or more whistleblowers who:

(1) Voluntarily provide the Commission
(2) With original information
(3) That leads to the successful enforcement by the Commission of a Federal court or administrative action
(4) In which the Commission obtains monetary sanctions totaling more than $1,000,000.

Note to paragraph (a): The terms *voluntarily, original information, leads to successful enforcement, action,* and *monetary sanctions* are defined in § 240.21F–4 of this chapter.

(b) *Related actions:* The Commission will also pay an award based on amounts collected in certain related actions.

(1) A *related action* is a judicial or administrative action that is brought by:
(i) The Attorney General of the United States;

PART 240—GENERAL RULES AND REGULATIONS, SECURITIES EXCHANGE ACT OF 1934

■ 1. The authority citation for part 240 is amended by adding the following citation in numerical order to read as follows:

Authority: 15 U.S.C. 77c, 77d, 77g, 77j, 77s, 77z-2, 77z-3, 77eee, 77ggg, 77nnn, 77sss, 77ttt, 78c, 78d, 78e, 78f, 78g, 78-i, 78j, 78j-1, 78k, 78k-1, 78*l*, 78m, 78n, 78n-1, 78o, 78o-4, 78p, 78q, 78s, 78u-5, 78w, 78x, 78*ll*, 78mm, 80a-20, 80a-23, 80a-29, 80a-37, 80b-3, 80b-4, 80b-11, and 7201 *et seq.*; 18 U.S.C. 1350; and 12 U.S.C. 5221(e)(3), unless otherwise noted.

*   *   *   *   *

Section 240.21F is also issued under Pub. L. 111–203, § 922(a), 124 Stat. 1841 (2010).

*   *   *   *   *

■ 2. Add an undesignated center heading and §§ 240.21F–1 through § 240.21F–17 to read as follows:

Securities Whistleblower Incentives and Protections

Sec.
240.21F–1   General.
240.21F–2   Whistleblower status and retaliation protections.
240.21F–3   Payment of award.
240.21F–4   Other definitions.
240.21F–5   Amount of award.
240.21F–6   Criteria for determining amount of award.

---

[469] In advancing the argument, the commenter relies on *Aeronautical Repair Station Association* v. *Federal Aviation Administration,* 494 F.3d 161 (DC Cir. 2007). This case is inapposite, however, because there the agency's own rulemaking release expressly stated that the rule *imposed responsibilities directly* on certain small business contractors. The court reaffirmed its prior holdings that the Regulatory Flexibility Act limits its application to small entities "which will be subject to the proposed regulation—that is, those small entities to which the proposed rule will apply." *Id.* at 176 (emphasis and internal quotations omitted). *See also Cement Kiln Recycling Coal* v. *EPA,* 255 F.3d 855, 869 (DC Cir. 2001).

(ii) An appropriate regulatory authority;

(iii) A self-regulatory organization; or

(iv) A state attorney general in a criminal case, and is based on the same original information that the whistleblower voluntarily provided to the Commission, and that led the Commission to obtain monetary sanctions totaling more than $1,000,000.

Note to paragraph (b)(1): The terms *appropriate regulatory authority* and *self-regulatory organization* are defined in § 240.21F–4 of this chapter.

(2) In order for the Commission to make an award in connection with a related action, the Commission must determine that the same original information that the whistleblower gave to the Commission also led to the successful enforcement of the related action under the same criteria described in these rules for awards made in connection with Commission actions. The Commission may seek assistance and confirmation from the authority bringing the related action in making this determination. The Commission will deny an award in connection with the related action if:

(i) The Commission determines that the criteria for an award are not satisfied; or

(ii) The Commission is unable to make a determination because the Office of the Whistleblower could not obtain sufficient and reliable information that could be used as the basis for an award determination pursuant to § 240.21F–12(a) of this chapter. Additional procedures apply to the payment of awards in related actions. These procedures are described in §§ 240.21F–11 and 240.21F–14 of this chapter.

(3) The Commission will not make an award to you for a related action if you have already been granted an award by the Commodity Futures Trading Commission ("CFTC") for that same action pursuant to its whistleblower award program under Section 23 of the Commodity Exchange Act (7 U.S.C. 26). Similarly, if the CFTC has previously denied an award to you in a related action, you will be precluded from relitigating any issues before the Commission that the CFTC resolved against you as part of the award denial.

§ 240.21F–4   Other definitions.

(a) *Voluntary submission of information.* (1) Your submission of information is made *voluntarily* within the meaning of §§ 240.21F–1 through 240.21F–17 of this chapter if you provide your submission before a request, inquiry, or demand that relates to the subject matter of your submission

is directed to you or anyone representing you (such as an attorney):

(i) By the Commission;

(ii) In connection with an investigation, inspection, or examination by the Public Company Accounting Oversight Board, or any self-regulatory organization; or

(iii) In connection with an investigation by Congress, any other authority of the Federal government, or a state Attorney General or securities regulatory authority.

(2) If the Commission or any of these other authorities direct a request, inquiry, or demand as described in paragraph (a)(1) of this section to you or your representative first, your submission will not be considered voluntary, and you will not be eligible for an award, even if your response is not compelled by subpoena or other applicable law. However, your submission of information to the Commission will be considered voluntary if you voluntarily provided the same information to one of the other authorities identified above prior to receiving a request, inquiry, or demand from the Commission.

(3) In addition, your submission will not be considered voluntary if you are required to report your original information to the Commission as a result of a pre-existing legal duty, a contractual duty that is owed to the Commission or to one of the other authorities set forth in paragraph (a)(1) of this section, or a duty that arises out of a judicial or administrative order.

(b) *Original information.* (1) In order for your whistleblower submission to be considered *original information*, it must be:

(i) Derived from your independent knowledge or independent analysis;

(ii) Not already known to the Commission from any other source, unless you are the original source of the information;

(iii) Not exclusively derived from an allegation made in a judicial or administrative hearing, in a governmental report, hearing, audit, or investigation, or from the news media, unless you are a source of the information; and

(iv) Provided to the Commission for the first time after July 21, 2010 (the date of enactment of the *Dodd-Frank Wall Street Reform and Consumer Protection Act*).

(2) *Independent knowledge* means factual information in your possession that is not derived from publicly available sources. You may gain independent knowledge from your experiences, communications and

observations in your business or social interactions.

(3) *Independent analysis* means your own analysis, whether done alone or in combination with others. *Analysis* means your examination and evaluation of information that may be publicly available, but which reveals information that is not generally known or available to the public.

(4) The Commission will not consider information to be derived from your independent knowledge or independent analysis in any of the following circumstances:

(i) If you obtained the information through a communication that was subject to the attorney-client privilege, unless disclosure of that information would otherwise be permitted by an attorney pursuant to § 205.3(d)(2) of this chapter, the applicable state attorney conduct rules, or otherwise;

(ii) If you obtained the information in connection with the legal representation of a client on whose behalf you or your employer or firm are providing services, and you seek to use the information to make a whistleblower submission for your own benefit, unless disclosure would otherwise be permitted by an attorney pursuant to § 205.3(d)(2) of this chapter, the applicable state attorney conduct rules, or otherwise; or

(iii) In circumstances not covered by paragraphs (b)(4)(i) or (b)(4)(ii) of this section, if you obtained the information because you were:

(A) An officer, director, trustee, or partner of an entity and another person informed you of allegations of misconduct, or you learned the information in connection with the entity's processes for identifying, reporting, and addressing possible violations of law;

(B) An employee whose principal duties involve compliance or internal audit responsibilities, or you were employed by or otherwise associated with a firm retained to perform compliance or internal audit functions for an entity;

(C) Employed by or otherwise associated with a firm retained to conduct an inquiry or investigation into possible violations of law; or

(D) An employee of, or other person associated with, a public accounting firm, if you obtained the information through the performance of an engagement required of an independent public accountant under the Federal securities laws (other than an audit subject to § 240.21F–8(c)(4) of this chapter), and that information related to a violation by the engagement client or the client's directors, officers or other employees.

Federal Register / Vol. 76, No. 113 / Monday, June 13, 2011 / Rules and Regulations   **34365**

(iv) If you obtained the information by a means or in a manner that is determined by a United States court to violate applicable Federal or state criminal law; or

(v) Exceptions. Paragraph (b)(4)(iii) of this section shall not apply if:

(A) You have a reasonable basis to believe that disclosure of the information to the Commission is necessary to prevent the relevant entity from engaging in conduct that is likely to cause substantial injury to the financial interest or property of the entity or investors;

(B) You have a reasonable basis to believe that the relevant entity is engaging in conduct that will impede an investigation of the misconduct; or

(C) At least 120 days have elapsed since you provided the information to the relevant entity's audit committee, chief legal officer, chief compliance officer (or their equivalents), or your supervisor, or since you received the information, if you received it under circumstances indicating that the entity's audit committee, chief legal officer, chief compliance officer (or their equivalents), or your supervisor was already aware of the information.

(vi) If you obtained the information from a person who is subject to this section, unless the information is not excluded from that person's use pursuant to this section, or you are providing the Commission with information about possible violations involving that person.

(5) The Commission will consider you to be an *original source* of the same information that we obtain from another source if the information satisfies the definition of original information and the other source obtained the information from you or your representative. In order to be considered an original source of information that the Commission receives from Congress, any other authority of the Federal government, a state Attorney General or securities regulatory authority, any self-regulatory organization, or the Public Company Accounting Oversight Board, you must have voluntarily given such authorities the information within the meaning of these rules. You must establish your status as the original source of information to the Commission's satisfaction. In determining whether you are the original source of information, the Commission may seek assistance and confirmation from one of the other authorities described above, or from another entity (including your employer), in the event that you claim to be the original source of information

that an authority or another entity provided to the Commission.

(6) If the Commission already knows some information about a matter from other sources at the time you make your submission, and you are not an original source of that information under paragraph (b)(5) of this section, the Commission will consider you an original source of any information you provide that is derived from your independent knowledge or analysis and that materially adds to the information that the Commission already possesses.

(7) If you provide information to the Congress, any other authority of the Federal government, a state Attorney General or securities regulatory authority, any self-regulatory organization, or the Public Company Accounting Oversight Board, or to an entity's internal whistleblower, legal, or compliance procedures for reporting allegations of possible violations of law, and you, within 120 days, submit the same information to the Commission pursuant to § 240.21F–9 of this chapter, as you must do in order for you to be eligible to be considered for an award, then, for purposes of evaluating your claim to an award under §§ 240.21F–10 and 240.21F–11 of this chapter, the Commission will consider that you provided information as of the date of your original disclosure, report or submission to one of these other authorities or persons. You must establish the effective date of any prior disclosure, report, or submission, to the Commission's satisfaction. The Commission may seek assistance and confirmation from the other authority or person in making this determination.

(c) *Information that leads to successful enforcement.* The Commission will consider that you provided original information that led to the successful enforcement of a judicial or administrative action in any of the following circumstances:

(1) You gave the Commission original information that was sufficiently specific, credible, and timely to cause the staff to commence an examination, open an investigation, reopen an investigation that the Commission had closed, or to inquire concerning different conduct as part of a current examination or investigation, and the Commission brought a successful judicial or administrative action based in whole or in part on conduct that was the subject of your original information; or

(2) You gave the Commission original information about conduct that was already under examination or investigation by the Commission, the Congress, any other authority of the

Federal government, a state Attorney General or securities regulatory authority, any self-regulatory organization, or the PCAOB (except in cases where you were an original source of this information as defined in paragraph (b)(4) of this section), and your submission significantly contributed to the success of the action.

(3) You reported original information through an entity's internal whistleblower, legal, or compliance procedures for reporting allegations of possible violations of law before or at the same time you reported them to the Commission; the entity later provided your information to the Commission, or provided results of an audit or investigation initiated in whole or in part in response to information you reported to the entity; and the information the entity provided to the Commission satisfies either paragraph (c)(1) or (c)(2) of this section. Under this paragraph (c)(3), you must also submit the same information to the Commission in accordance with the procedures set forth in § 240.21F–9 within 120 days of providing it to the entity.

(d) An *action* generally means a single captioned judicial or administrative proceeding brought by the Commission. Notwithstanding the foregoing:

(1) For purposes of making an award under § 240.21F–10 of this chapter, the Commission will treat as a Commission action two or more administrative or judicial proceedings brought by the Commission if these proceedings arise out of the same nucleus of operative facts; or

(2) For purposes of determining the payment on an award under § 240.21F–14 of this chapter, the Commission will deem as part of the Commission action upon which the award was based any subsequent Commission proceeding that, individually, results in a monetary sanction of $1,000,000 or less, and that arises out of the same nucleus of operative facts.

(e) *Monetary sanctions* means any money, including penalties, disgorgement, and interest, ordered to be paid and any money deposited into a disgorgement fund or other fund pursuant to Section 308(b) of the Sarbanes-Oxley Act of 2002 (15 U.S.C. 7246(b)) as a result of a Commission action or a related action.

(f) *Appropriate regulatory agency* means the Commission, the Comptroller of the Currency, the Board of Governors of the Federal Reserve System, the Federal Deposit Insurance Corporation, the Office of Thrift Supervision, and any other agencies that may be defined as appropriate regulatory agencies under

34366   Federal Register / Vol. 76, No. 113 / Monday, June 13, 2011 / Rules and Regulations

Section 3(a)(34) of the Exchange Act (15 U.S.C. 78c(a)(34)).

(g) *Appropriate regulatory authority* means an appropriate regulatory agency other than the Commission.

(h) *Self-regulatory organization* means any national securities exchange, registered securities association, registered clearing agency, the Municipal Securities Rulemaking Board, and any other organizations that may be defined as self-regulatory organizations under Section 3(a)(26) of the Exchange Act (15 U.S.C. 78c(a)(26)).

§ 240.21F–5 Amount of award.

(a) The determination of the amount of an award is in the discretion of the Commission.

(b) If all of the conditions are met for a whistleblower award in connection with a Commission action or a related action, the Commission will then decide the percentage amount of the award applying the criteria set forth in § 240.21F–6 of this chapter and pursuant to the procedures set forth in §§ 240.21F–10 and 240.21F–11 of this chapter. The amount will be at least 10 percent and no more than 30 percent of the monetary sanctions that the Commission and the other authorities are able to collect. The percentage awarded in connection with a Commission action may differ from the percentage awarded in connection with a related action.

(c) If the Commission makes awards to more than one whistleblower in connection with the same action or related action, the Commission will determine an individual percentage award for each whistleblower, but in no event will the total amount awarded to all whistleblowers in the aggregate be less than 10 percent or greater than 30 percent of the amount the Commission or the other authorities collect.

§ 240.21F–6 Criteria for determining amount of award.

In exercising its discretion to determine the appropriate award percentage, the Commission may consider the following factors in relation to the unique facts and circumstances of each case, and may increase or decrease the award percentage based on its analysis of these factors. In the event that awards are determined for multiple whistleblowers in connection with an action, these factors will be used to determine the relative allocation of awards among the whistleblowers.

(a) *Factors that may increase the amount of a whistleblower's award.* In determining whether to increase the amount of an award, the Commission

will consider the following factors, which are not listed in order of importance.

(1) *Significance of the information provided by the whistleblower.* The Commission will assess the significance of the information provided by a whistleblower to the success of the Commission action or related action. In considering this factor, the Commission may take into account, among other things:

(i) The nature of the information provided by the whistleblower and how it related to the successful enforcement action, including whether the reliability and completeness of the information provided to the Commission by the whistleblower resulted in the conservation of Commission resources;

(ii) The degree to which the information provided by the whistleblower supported one or more successful claims brought in the Commission or related action.

(2) *Assistance provided by the whistleblower.* The Commission will assess the degree of assistance provided by the whistleblower and any legal representative of the whistleblower in the Commission action or related action. In considering this factor, the Commission may take into account, among other things:

(i) Whether the whistleblower provided ongoing, extensive, and timely cooperation and assistance by, for example, helping to explain complex transactions, interpreting key evidence, or identifying new and productive lines of inquiry;

(ii) The timeliness of the whistleblower's initial report to the Commission or to an internal compliance or reporting system of business organizations committing, or impacted by, the securities violations, where appropriate;

(iii) The resources conserved as a result of the whistleblower's assistance;

(iv) Whether the whistleblower appropriately encouraged or authorized others to assist the staff of the Commission who might otherwise not have participated in the investigation or related action;

(v) The efforts undertaken by the whistleblower to remediate the harm caused by the violations, including assisting the authorities in the recovery of the fruits and instrumentalities of the violations; and

(vi) Any unique hardships experienced by the whistleblower as a result of his or her reporting and assisting in the enforcement action.

(3) *Law enforcement interest.* The Commission will assess its programmatic interest in deterring

violations of the securities laws by making awards to whistleblowers who provide information that leads to the successful enforcement of such laws. In considering this factor, the Commission may take into account, among other things:

(i) The degree to which an award enhances the Commission's ability to enforce the Federal securities laws and protect investors; and

(ii) The degree to which an award encourages the submission of high quality information from whistleblowers by appropriately rewarding whistleblowers' submission of significant information and assistance, even in cases where the monetary sanctions available for collection are limited or potential monetary sanctions were reduced or eliminated by the Commission because an entity self-reported a securities violation following the whistleblower's related internal disclosure, report, or submission.

(iii) Whether the subject matter of the action is a Commission priority, whether the reported misconduct involves regulated entities or fiduciaries, whether the whistleblower exposed an industry-wide practice, the type and severity of the securities violations, the age and duration of misconduct, the number of violations, and the isolated, repetitive, or ongoing nature of the violations; and

(iv) The dangers to investors or others presented by the underlying violations involved in the enforcement action, including the amount of harm or potential harm caused by the underlying violations, the type of harm resulting from or threatened by the underlying violations, and the number of individuals or entities harmed.

(4) *Participation in internal compliance systems.* The Commission will assess whether, and the extent to which, the whistleblower and any legal representative of the whistleblower participated in internal compliance systems. In considering this factor, the Commission may take into account, among other things:

(i) Whether, and the extent to which, a whistleblower reported the possible securities violations through internal whistleblower, legal or compliance procedures before, or at the same time as, reporting them to the Commission; and

(ii) Whether, and the extent to which, a whistleblower assisted any internal investigation or inquiry concerning the reported securities violations.

(b) *Factors that may decrease the amount of a whistleblower's award.* In determining whether to decrease the amount of an award, the Commission

Federal Register / Vol. 76, No. 113 / Monday, June 13, 2011 / Rules and Regulations   34367

will consider the following factors, which are not listed in order of importance.

(1) *Culpability.* The Commission will assess the culpability or involvement of the whistleblower in matters associated with the Commission's action or related actions. In considering this factor, the Commission may take into account, among other things:

(i) The whistleblower's role in the securities violations;

(ii) The whistleblower's education, training, experience, and position of responsibility at the time the violations occurred;

(iii) Whether the whistleblower acted with scienter, both generally and in relation to others who participated in the violations;

(iv) Whether the whistleblower financially benefitted from the violations;

(v) Whether the whistleblower is a recidivist;

(vi) The egregiousness of the underlying fraud committed by the whistleblower; and

(vii) Whether the whistleblower knowingly interfered with the Commission's investigation of the violations or related enforcement actions.

(2) *Unreasonable reporting delay.* The Commission will assess whether the whistleblower unreasonably delayed reporting the securities violations. In considering this factor, the Commission may take into account, among other things:

(i) Whether the whistleblower was aware of the relevant facts but failed to take reasonable steps to report or prevent the violations from occurring or continuing;

(ii) Whether the whistleblower was aware of the relevant facts but only reported them after learning about a related inquiry, investigation, or enforcement action; and

(iii) Whether there was a legitimate reason for the whistleblower to delay reporting the violations.

(3) *Interference with internal compliance and reporting systems.* The Commission will assess, in cases where the whistleblower interacted with his or her entity's internal compliance or reporting system, whether the whistleblower undermined the integrity of such system. In considering this factor, the Commission will take into account whether there is evidence provided to the Commission that the whistleblower knowingly:

(i) Interfered with an entity's established legal, compliance, or audit procedures to prevent or delay detection of the reported securities violation;

(ii) Made any material false, fictitious, or fraudulent statements or representations that hindered an entity's efforts to detect, investigate, or remediate the reported securities violations; and

(iii) Provided any false writing or document knowing the writing or document contained any false, fictitious or fraudulent statements or entries that hindered an entity's efforts to detect, investigate, or remediate the reported securities violations.

§ 240.21F–7 Confidentiality of submissions.

(a) Section 21F(h)(2) of the Exchange Act (15 U.S.C. 78u–6(h)(2)) requires that the Commission not disclose information that could reasonably be expected to reveal the identity of a whistleblower, except that the Commission may disclose such information in the following circumstances:

(1) When disclosure is required to a defendant or respondent in connection with a Federal court or administrative action that the Commission files or in another public action or proceeding that is filed by an authority to which we provide the information, as described below;

(2) When the Commission determines that it is necessary to accomplish the purposes of the Exchange Act (15 U.S.C. 78a) and to protect investors, it may provide your information to the Department of Justice, an appropriate regulatory authority, a self regulatory organization, a state attorney general in connection with a criminal investigation, any appropriate state regulatory authority, the Public Company Accounting Oversight Board, or foreign securities and law enforcement authorities. Each of these entities other than foreign securities and law enforcement authorities is subject to the confidentiality requirements set forth in Section 21F(h) of the Exchange Act (15 U.S.C. 78u–6(h)). The Commission will determine what assurances of confidentiality it deems appropriate in providing such information to foreign securities and law enforcement authorities.

(3) The Commission may make disclosures in accordance with the Privacy Act of 1974 (5 U.S.C. 552a).

(b) You may submit information to the Commission anonymously. If you do so, however, you must also do the following:

(1) You must have an attorney represent you in connection with both your submission of information and your claim for an award, and your attorney's name and contact information

must be provided to the Commission at the time you submit your information;

(2) You and your attorney must follow the procedures set forth in § 240.21F–9 of this chapter for submitting original information anonymously; and

(3) Before the Commission will pay any award to you, you must disclose your identity to the Commission and your identity must be verified by the Commission as set forth in § 240.21F–10 of this chapter.

§ 240.21F–8 Eligibility.

(a) To be eligible for a whistleblower award, you must give the Commission information in the form and manner that the Commission requires. The procedures for submitting information and making a claim for an award are described in § 240.21F–9 through § 240.21F–11 of this chapter. You should read these procedures carefully because you need to follow them in order to be eligible for an award, except that the Commission may, in its sole discretion, waive any of these procedures based upon a showing of extraordinary circumstances.

(b) In addition to any forms required by these rules, the Commission may also require that you provide certain additional information. You may be required to:

(1) Provide explanations and other assistance in order that the staff may evaluate and use the information that you submitted;

(2) Provide all additional information in your possession that is related to the subject matter of your submission in a complete and truthful manner, through follow-up meetings, or in other forms that our staff may agree to;

(3) Provide testimony or other evidence acceptable to the staff relating to whether you are eligible, or otherwise satisfy any of the conditions, for an award; and

(4) Enter into a confidentiality agreement in a form acceptable to the Office of the Whistleblower, covering any non-public information that the Commission provides to you, and including a provision that a violation of the agreement may lead to your ineligibility to receive an award.

(c) You are not eligible to be considered for an award if you do not satisfy the requirements of paragraphs (a) and (b) of this section. In addition, you are not eligible if:

(1) You are, or were at the time you acquired the original information provided to the Commission, a member, officer, or employee of the Commission, the Department of Justice, an appropriate regulatory agency, a self-regulatory organization, the Public

Company Accounting Oversight Board, or any law enforcement organization;

(2) You are, or were at the time you acquired the original information provided to the Commission, a member, officer, or employee of a foreign government, any political subdivision, department, agency, or instrumentality of a foreign government, or any other foreign financial regulatory authority as that term is defined in Section 3(a)(52) of the Exchange Act (15 U.S.C. 78c(a)(52));

(3) You are convicted of a criminal violation that is related to the Commission action or to a related action (as defined in § 240.21F–4 of this chapter) for which you otherwise could receive an award;

(4) You obtained the original information that you gave the Commission through an audit of a company's financial statements, and making a whistleblower submission would be contrary to requirements of Section 10A of the Exchange Act (15 U.S.C. 78j–a).

(5) You are the spouse, parent, child, or sibling of a member or employee of the Commission, or you reside in the same household as a member or employee of the Commission;

(6) You acquired the original information you gave the Commission from a person:

(i) Who is subject to paragraph (c)(4) of this section, unless the information is not excluded from that person's use, or you are providing the Commission with information about possible violations involving that person; or

(ii) With the intent to evade any provision of these rules; or

(7) In your whistleblower submission, your other dealings with the Commission, or your dealings with another authority in connection with a related action, you knowingly and willfully make any false, fictitious, or fraudulent statement or representation, or use any false writing or document knowing that it contains any false, fictitious, or fraudulent statement or entry with intent to mislead or otherwise hinder the Commission or another authority.

§ 240.21F–9 Procedures for submitting original information.

(a) To be considered a whistleblower under Section 21F of the Exchange Act (15 U.S.C. 78u–6(h)), you must submit your information about a possible securities law violation by either of these methods:

(1) Online, through the Commission's Web site located at *http://www.sec.gov;* or

(2) By mailing or faxing a Form TCR (Tip, Complaint or Referral) (referenced in § 249.1800 of this chapter) to the SEC Office of the Whistleblower, 100 F Street NE., Washington, DC 20549–5631, Fax (703) 813–9322.

(b) Further, to be eligible for an award, you must declare under penalty of perjury at the time you submit your information pursuant to paragraph (a)(1) or (2) of this section that your information is true and correct to the best of your knowledge and belief.

(c) Notwithstanding paragraphs (a) and (b) of this section, if you are providing your original information to the Commission anonymously, then your attorney must submit your information on your behalf pursuant to the procedures specified in paragraph (a) of this section. Prior to your attorney's submission, you must provide your attorney with a completed Form TCR (referenced in § 249.1800 of this chapter) that you have signed under penalty of perjury. When your attorney makes her submission on your behalf, your attorney will be required to certify that he or she:

(1) Has verified your identity;

(2) Has reviewed your completed and signed Form TCR (referenced in § 249.1800 of this chapter) for completeness and accuracy and that the information contained therein is true, correct and complete to the best of the attorney's knowledge, information and belief;

(3) Has obtained your non-waivable consent to provide the Commission with your original completed and signed Form TCR (referenced in § 249.1800 of this chapter) in the event that the Commission requests it due to concerns that you may have knowingly and willfully made false, fictitious, or fraudulent statements or representations, or used any false writing or document knowing that the writing or document contains any false fictitious or fraudulent statement or entry; and

(4) Consents to be legally obligated to provide the signed Form TCR (referenced in § 249.1800 of this chapter) within seven (7) calendar days of receiving such request from the Commission.

(d) If you submitted original information in writing to the Commission after July 21, 2010 (the date of enactment of the Dodd-Frank Wall Street Reform and Consumer Protection Act) but before the effective date of these rules, your submission will be deemed to satisfy the requirements set forth in paragraphs (a) and (b) of this section. If you were an anonymous whistleblower, however, you must

provide your attorney with a completed and signed copy of Form TCR (referenced in § 249.1800 of this chapter) within 60 days of the effective date of these rules, your attorney must retain the signed form in his or her records, and you must provide of copy of the signed form to the Commission staff upon request by Commission staff prior to any payment of an award to you in connection with your submission. Notwithstanding the foregoing, you must follow the procedures and conditions for making a claim for a whistleblower award described in §§ 240.21F–10 and 240.21F–11 of this chapter.

§ 240.21F–10 Procedures for making a claim for a whistleblower award in SEC actions that result in monetary sanctions in excess of $1,000,000.

(a) Whenever a Commission action results in monetary sanctions totaling more than $1,000,000, the Office of the Whistleblower will cause to be published on the Commission's Web site a "Notice of Covered Action." Such Notice will be published subsequent to the entry of a final judgment or order that alone, or collectively with other judgments or orders previously entered in the Commission action, exceeds $1,000,000; or, in the absence of such judgment or order subsequent to the deposit of monetary sanctions exceeding $1,000,000 into a disgorgement or other fund pursuant to Section 308(b) of the Sarbanes-Oxley Act of 2002. A claimant will have ninety (90) days from the date of the Notice of Covered Action to file a claim for an award based on that action, or the claim will be barred.

(b) To file a claim for a whistleblower award, you must file Form WB–APP, *Application for Award for Original Information Provided Pursuant to Section 21F of the Securities Exchange Act of 1934* (referenced in § 249.1801 of this chapter). You must sign this form as the claimant and submit it to the Office of the Whistleblower by mail or fax. All claim forms, including any attachments, must be received by the Office of the Whistleblower within ninety (90) calendar days of the date of the Notice of Covered Action in order to be considered for an award.

(c) If you provided your original information to the Commission anonymously, you must disclose your identity on the Form WB–APP (referenced in § 249.1801 of this chapter), and your identity must be verified in a form and manner that is acceptable to the Office of the Whistleblower prior to the payment of any award.

(d) Once the time for filing any appeals of the Commission's judicial or administrative action has expired, or where an appeal has been filed, after all appeals in the action have been concluded, the staff designated by the Director of the Division of Enforcement ("Claims Review Staff") will evaluate all timely whistleblower award claims submitted on Form WB–APP (referenced in § 249.1801 of this chapter) in accordance with the criteria set forth in these rules. In connection with this process, the Office of the Whistleblower may require that you provide additional information relating to your eligibility for an award or satisfaction of any of the conditions for an award, as set forth in § 240.21F–(8)(b) of this chapter. Following that evaluation, the Office of the Whistleblower will send you a Preliminary Determination setting forth a preliminary assessment as to whether the claim should be allowed or denied and, if allowed, setting forth the proposed award percentage amount.

(e) You may contest the Preliminary Determination made by the Claims Review Staff by submitting a written response to the Office of the Whistleblower setting forth the grounds for your objection to either the denial of an award or the proposed amount of an award. The response must be in the form and manner that the Office of the Whistleblower shall require. You may also include documentation or other evidentiary support for the grounds advanced in your response.

(1) Before determining whether to contest a Preliminary Determination, you may:

(i) Within thirty (30) days of the date of the Preliminary Determination, request that the Office of the Whistleblower make available for your review the materials from among those set forth in § 240.21F–12(a) of this chapter that formed the basis of the Claims Review Staff's Preliminary Determination.

(ii) Within thirty (30) calendar days of the date of the Preliminary Determination, request a meeting with the Office of the Whistleblower; however, such meetings are not required and the office may in its sole discretion decline the request.

(2) If you decide to contest the Preliminary Determination, you must submit your written response and supporting materials within sixty (60) calendar days of the date of the Preliminary Determination, or if a request to review materials is made pursuant to paragraph (e)(1) of this section, then within sixty (60) calendar days of the Office of the Whistleblower

making those materials available for your review.

(f) If you fail to submit a timely response pursuant to paragraph (e) of this section, then the Preliminary Determination will become the Final Order of the Commission (except where the Preliminary Determination recommended an award, in which case the Preliminary Determination will be deemed a Proposed Final Determination for purposes of paragraph (h) of this section). Your failure to submit a timely response contesting a Preliminary Determination will constitute a failure to exhaust administrative remedies, and you will be prohibited from pursuing an appeal pursuant to § 240.21F–13 of this chapter.

(g) If you submit a timely response pursuant to paragraph (e) of this section, then the Claims Review Staff will consider the issues and grounds advanced in your response, along with any supporting documentation you provided, and will make its Proposed Final Determination.

(h) The Office of the Whistleblower will then notify the Commission of each Proposed Final Determination. Within thirty 30 days thereafter, any Commissioner may request that the Proposed Final Determination be reviewed by the Commission. If no Commissioner requests such a review within the 30-day period, then the Proposed Final Determination will become the Final Order of the Commission. In the event a Commissioner requests a review, the Commission will review the record that the staff relied upon in making its determinations, including your previous submissions to the Office of the Whistleblower, and issue its Final Order.

(i) The Office of the Whistleblower will provide you with the Final Order of the Commission.

§ 240.21F–11 Procedures for determining awards based upon a related action.

(a) If you are eligible to receive an award following a Commission action that results in monetary sanctions totaling more than $1,000,000, you also may be eligible to receive an award based on the monetary sanctions that are collected from a related action (as defined in § 240.21F–3 of this chapter).

(b) You must also use Form WB–APP (referenced in § 249.1801 of this chapter) to submit a claim for an award in a related action. You must sign this form as the claimant and submit it to the Office of the Whistleblower by mail or fax as follows:

(1) If a final order imposing monetary sanctions has been entered in a related

action at the time you submit your claim for an award in connection with a Commission action, you must submit your claim for an award in that related action on the same Form WB–APP (referenced in § 249.1801 of this chapter) that you use for the Commission action.

(2) If a final order imposing monetary sanctions in a related action has not been entered at the time you submit your claim for an award in connection with a Commission action, you must submit your claim on Form WB–APP (referenced in § 249.1801 of this chapter) within ninety (90) days of the issuance of a final order imposing sanctions in the related action.

(c) The Office of the Whistleblower may request additional information from you in connection with your claim for an award in a related action to demonstrate that you directly (or through the Commission) voluntarily provided the governmental agency, regulatory authority or self-regulatory organization the same original information that led to the Commission's successful covered action, and that this information led to the successful enforcement of the related action. The Office of the Whistleblower may, in its discretion, seek assistance and confirmation from the other agency in making this determination.

(d) Once the time for filing any appeals of the final judgment or order in a related action has expired, or if an appeal has been filed, after all appeals in the action have been concluded, the Claims Review Staff will evaluate all timely whistleblower award claims submitted on Form WB–APP (referenced in § 249.1801 of this chapter) in connection with the related action. The evaluation will be undertaken pursuant to the criteria set forth in these rules. In connection with this process, the Office of the Whistleblower may require that you provide additional information relating to your eligibility for an award or satisfaction of any of the conditions for an award, as set forth in § 240.21F–(8)(b) of this chapter. Following this evaluation, the Office of the Whistleblower will send you a Preliminary Determination setting forth a preliminary assessment as to whether the claim should be allowed or denied and, if allowed, setting forth the proposed award percentage amount.

(e) You may contest the Preliminary Determination made by the Claims Review Staff by submitting a written response to the Office of the Whistleblower setting forth the grounds for your objection to either the denial of an award or the proposed amount of an award. The response must be in the form and manner that the Office of the Whistleblower shall require. You may also include documentation or other evidentiary support for the grounds advanced in your response.

(1) Before determining whether to contest a Preliminary Determination, you may:

(i) Within thirty (30) days of the date of the Preliminary Determination, request that the Office of the Whistleblower make available for your review the materials from among those set forth in § 240.21F–12(a) of this chapter that formed the basis of the Claims Review Staff's Preliminary Determination.

(ii) Within thirty (30) days of the date of the Preliminary Determination, request a meeting with the Office of the Whistleblower; however, such meetings are not required and the office may in its sole discretion decline the request.

(2) If you decide to contest the Preliminary Determination, you must submit your written response and supporting materials within sixty (60) calendar days of the date of the Preliminary Determination, or if a request to review materials is made pursuant to paragraph (e)(1)(i) of this section, then within sixty (60) calendar days of the Office of the Whistleblower making those materials available for your review.

(f) If you fail to submit a timely response pursuant to paragraph (e) of this section, then the Preliminary Determination will become the Final Order of the Commission (except where the Preliminary Determination recommended an award, in which case the Preliminary Determination will be deemed a Proposed Final Determination for purposes of paragraph (h) of this section). Your failure to submit a timely response contesting a Preliminary Determination will constitute a failure to exhaust administrative remedies, and you will be prohibited from pursuing an appeal pursuant to § 240.21F–13 of this chapter.

(g) If you submit a timely response pursuant to paragraph (e) of this section, then the Claims Review Staff will consider the issues and grounds that you advanced in your response, along with any supporting documentation you provided, and will make its Proposed Final Determination.

(h) The Office of the Whistleblower will notify the Commission of each Proposed Final Determination. Within thirty 30 days thereafter, any Commissioner may request that the Proposed Final Determination be reviewed by the Commission. If no

Commissioner requests such a review within the 30-day period, then the Proposed Final Determination will become the Final Order of the Commission. In the event a Commissioner requests a review, the Commission will review the record that the staff relied upon in making its determinations, including your previous submissions to the Office of the Whistleblower, and issue its Final Order.

(i) The Office of the Whistleblower will provide you with the Final Order of the Commission.

§ 240.21F–12   Materials that may form the basis of an award determination and that may comprise the record on appeal.

(a) The following items constitute the materials that the Commission and the Claims Review Staff may rely upon to make an award determination pursuant to §§ 240.21F–10 and 240.21F–11 of this chapter:

(1) Any publicly available materials from the covered action or related action, including:

(i) The complaint, notice of hearing, answers and any amendments thereto;

(ii) The final judgment, consent order, or final administrative order;

(iii) Any transcripts of the proceedings, including any exhibits;

(iv) Any items that appear on the docket; and

(v) Any appellate decisions or orders.

(2) The whistleblower's Form TCR (referenced in § 249.1800 of this chapter), including attachments, and other related materials provided by the whistleblower to assist the Commission with the investigation or examination;

(3) The whistleblower's Form WB–APP (referenced in § 249.1800 of this chapter), including attachments, and any other filings or submissions from the whistleblower in support of the award application;

(4) Sworn declarations (including attachments) from the Commission staff regarding any matters relevant to the award determination;

(5) With respect to an award claim involving a related action, any statements or other information that the entity provides or identifies in connection with an award determination, provided the entity has authorized the Commission to share the information with the claimant. (Neither the Commission nor the Claims Review Staff may rely upon information that the entity has not authorized the Commission to share with the claimant); and

(6) Any other documents or materials including sworn declarations from third-parties that are received or

obtained by the Office of the Whistleblower to assist the Commission resolve the claimant's award application, including information related to the claimant's eligibility. (Neither the Commission nor the Claims Review Staff may rely upon information that the entity has not authorized the Commission to share with the claimant).

(b) These rules do not entitle claimants to obtain from the Commission any materials (including any pre-decisional or internal deliberative process materials that are prepared exclusively to assist the Commission in deciding the claim) other than those listed in paragraph (a) of this section. Moreover, the Office of the Whistleblower may make redactions as necessary to comply with any statutory restrictions, to protect the Commission's law enforcement and regulatory functions, and to comply with requests for confidential treatment from other law enforcement and regulatory authorities. The Office of the Whistleblower may also require you to sign a confidentiality agreement, as set forth in § 240.21F–(8)(b)(4) of this chapter, before providing these materials.

§ 240.21F–13   Appeals.

(a) Section 21F of the Exchange Act (15 U.S.C. 78u–6) commits determinations of whether, to whom, and in what amount to make awards to the Commission's discretion. A determination of whether or to whom to make an award may be appealed within 30 days after the Commission issues its final decision to the United States Court of Appeals for the District of Columbia Circuit, or to the circuit where the aggrieved person resides or has his principal place of business. Where the Commission makes an award based on the factors set forth in § 240.21F–6 of this chapter of not less than 10 percent and not more than 30 percent of the monetary sanctions collected in the Commission or related action, the Commission's determination regarding the amount of an award (including the allocation of an award as between multiple whistleblowers, and any factual findings, legal conclusions, policy judgments, or discretionary assessments involving the Commission's consideration of the factors in § 240.21F–6 of this chapter) is not appealable.

(b) The record on appeal shall consist of the Preliminary Determination, the Final Order of the Commission, and any other items from those set forth in § 240.21F–12(a) of this chapter that either the claimant or the Commission identifies for inclusion in the record.

The record on appeal shall not include any pre-decisional or internal deliberative process materials that are prepared exclusively to assist the Commission in deciding the claim (including the staff's Draft Final Determination in the event that the Commissioners reviewed the claim and issued the Final Order).

§ 240.21F–14 Procedures applicable to the payment of awards.

(a) Any award made pursuant to these rules will be paid from the Securities and Exchange Commission Investor Protection Fund (the "Fund").

(b) A recipient of a whistleblower award is entitled to payment on the award only to the extent that a monetary sanction is collected in the Commission action or in a related action upon which the award is based.

(c) Payment of a whistleblower award for a monetary sanction collected in a Commission action or related action shall be made following the later of:

(1) The date on which the monetary sanction is collected; or

(2) The completion of the appeals process for all whistleblower award claims arising from:

(i) The Notice of Covered Action, in the case of any payment of an award for a monetary sanction collected in a Commission action; or

(ii) The related action, in the case of any payment of an award for a monetary sanction collected in a related action.

(d) If there are insufficient amounts available in the Fund to pay the entire amount of an award payment within a reasonable period of time from the time for payment specified by paragraph (c) of this section, then subject to the following terms, the balance of the payment shall be paid when amounts become available in the Fund, as follows:

(1) Where multiple whistleblowers are owed payments from the Fund based on awards that do not arise from the same Notice of Covered Action (or related action), priority in making these payments will be determined based upon the date that the collections for which the whistleblowers are owed payments occurred. If two or more of these collections occur on the same date, those whistleblowers owed payments based on these collections will be paid on a pro rata basis until sufficient amounts become available in the Fund to pay their entire payments.

(2) Where multiple whistleblowers are owed payments from the Fund based on awards that arise from the same Notice of Covered Action (or related action), they will share the same payment priority and will be paid on a pro rata

basis until sufficient amounts become available in the Fund to pay their entire payments.

§ 240.21F–15 No amnesty.

The Securities Whistleblower Incentives and Protection provisions do not provide amnesty to individuals who provide information to the Commission. The fact that you may become a whistleblower and assist in Commission investigations and enforcement actions does not preclude the Commission from bringing an action against you based upon your own conduct in connection with violations of the Federal securities laws. If such an action is determined to be appropriate, however, the Commission will take your cooperation into consideration in accordance with its Policy Statement Concerning Cooperation by Individuals in Investigations and Related Enforcement Actions (17 CFR 202.12).

§ 240.21F–16 Awards to whistleblowers who engage in culpable conduct.

In determining whether the required $1,000,000 threshold has been satisfied (this threshold is further explained in § 240.21F–10 of this chapter) for purposes of making any award, the Commission will not take into account any monetary sanctions that the whistleblower is ordered to pay, or that are ordered against any entity whose liability is based substantially on conduct that the whistleblower directed, planned, or initiated. Similarly, if the Commission determines that a whistleblower is eligible for an award, any amounts that the whistleblower or such an entity pay in sanctions as a result of the action or related actions will not be included within the calculation of the amounts collected for purposes of making payments.

§ 240.21F–17 Staff communications with individuals reporting possible securities law violations.

(a) No person may take any action to impede an individual from communicating directly with the Commission staff about a possible securities law violation, including enforcing, or threatening to enforce, a confidentiality agreement (other than agreements dealing with information covered by § 240.21F–4(b)(4)(i) and § 240.21F–4(b)(4)(ii) of this chapter related to the legal representation of a client) with respect to such communications.

(b) If you are a director, officer, member, agent, or employee of an entity that has counsel, and you have initiated communication with the Commission relating to a possible securities law violation, the staff is authorized to

communicate directly with you regarding the possible securities law violation without seeking the consent of the entity's counsel.

PART 249—FORMS, SECURITIES EXCHANGE ACT OF 1934

■ 3. The authority citation for Part 249 is amended by adding the following citations in numerical order to read as follows:

> Authority: 15 U.S.C. 78a, *et seq.* and 7201 *et seq.;* and 18 U.S.C. 1350, unless otherwise noted.

*   *   *   *   *

Section 249.1800 is also issued under Public Law 111.203, § 922(a), 124 Stat 1841 (2010).

Section 249.1801 is also issued under Public Law 111.203, § 922(a), 124 Stat 1841 (2010).

*   *   *   *   *

■ 4. Add Subpart S to read as follows:

Subpart S—Whistleblower Forms

Sec.
249.1800   Form TCR, tip, complaint or referral.
249.1801   Form WB–APP, Application for award for original information submitted pursuant to Section 21F of the Securities Exchange Act of 1934.

§ 249.1800 Form TCR, tip, complaint or referral.

This form may be used by anyone wishing to provide the SEC with information concerning a violation of the Federal securities laws. The information provided may be disclosed to Federal, state, local, or foreign agencies responsible for investigating, prosecuting, enforcing, or implementing the Federal securities laws, rules, or regulations consistent with the confidentiality requirements set forth in Section 21F(h)(2) of the Exchange Act (15 U.S.C. 78u–6(h)(2)) and § 240.21F–7 of this chapter.

§ 249.1801 Form WB–APP, Application for award for original information submitted pursuant to Section 21F of the Securities Exchange Act of 1934.

This form must be used by persons making a claim for a whistleblower award in connection with information provided to the SEC or to another agency in a related action. The information provided will enable the Commission to determine your eligibility for payment of an award pursuant to Section 21F of the Securities Exchange Act of 1934 (15 U.S.C. 78u–6). This information may be disclosed to Federal, state, local, or foreign agencies responsible for investigating, prosecuting, enforcing, or implementing the Federal securities laws, rules, or regulations consistent with the confidentiality requirements set forth in Section 21F(h)(2) of the Exchange Act (15 U.S.C. 78u–6(h)(2))

and § 240.21F–7 of this chapter. Furnishing the information is voluntary, but a decision not to do so may result in you not being eligible for award consideration.

Note: The following Forms will not appear in the Code of Federal Regulations.

BILLING CODE 8011–01–P

SECURITIES AND EXCHANGE COMMISSION
Washington, DC 20549

FORM TCR
TIP, COMPLAINT OR REFERRAL

A.   INFORMATION ABOUT YOU

COMPLAINANT 1:

1. Last Name   First   M.I.

2. Street Address   Apartment/
                                                                                       Unit #

City   State/   ZIP/   Country
                               Province   Postal Code   Preferred
                                                                          method of
3. Telephone   Alt. Phone   E-mail Address   communication

4. Occupation

COMPLAINANT 2:

1. Last Name   First   M.I.

2. Street Address   Apartment/
                                                                                       Unit #

City   State/   ZIP/   Country
                               Province   Postal Code   Preferred
                                                                          method of
3. Telephone   Alt. Phone   E-mail Address   communication

4. Occupation

B.   ATTORNEY'S INFORMATION (If Applicable - See Instructions)

1. Attorney's Name

2. Firm Name

3. Street Address

City   State/   ZIP/   Country
                               Province   Postal Code

4. Telephone   Fax   E-mail Address

Federal Register / Vol. 76, No. 113 / Monday, June 13, 2011 / Rules and Regulations   34373

C.   TELL US ABOUT THE INDIVIDUAL OR ENTITY YOU HAVE A COMPLAINT AGAINST

INDIVIDUAL/ENTITY 1:   If an individual, specify profession:

1. Type: Individual   Entity   If an entity, specify type:

2. Name

3. Street Address   Apartment/
                                                                                     Unit #

City   State/   ZIP/
                                  Province   Postal Code   Country

4. Phone   E-mail Address   Internet address

INDIVIDUAL/ENTITY 2:   If an individual, specify profession:

1. Type: Individual   Entity   If an entity, specify type:

2. Name

3. Street Address   Apartment/
                                                                                     Unit #

City   State/   ZIP/
                                  Province   Postal Code   Country

4. Phone   E-mail Address   Internet Address

D.   TELL US ABOUT YOUR COMPLAINT

1. Occurrence Date (mm/dd/yyyy):   /   /   2. Nature of complaint:

3a. Has the complainant or counsel had any prior communication(s) with the SEC concerning this matter?   YES   NO

3b. If the answer to 3a is "Yes," name of SEC staff member with whom the complainant or counsel communicated

4a. Has the complainant or counsel provided the information to any other agency or organization, or has any other agency or organization requested the information or related information from you?

                                                                                     YES   NO

4b. If the answer to 4a is "Yes," please provide details. Use additional sheets if necessary.

4c. Name and contact information for point of contact at agency or organization, if known

34374   Federal Register/Vol. 76, No. 113/Monday, June 13, 2011/Rules and Regulations

5a. Does this complaint relate to an entity of which the complainant is or was an officer, director, counsel, employee, consultant or contractor?

YES   NO

5b. If the answer to question 5a is "yes," has the complainant reported this violation to his or her supervisor, compliance office, whistleblower hotline, ombudsman, or any other available mechanism at the entity for reporting violations?   YES   NO

5c. If the answer to question 5b is "yes," please provide details. Use additional sheets if necessary.

5d. Date on which the complainant took the action(s) described in question 5b (mm/dd/yyyy):   /   /

6a. Has the complainant taken any other action regarding your complaint?   YES   NO

6b. If the answer to question 6a is "yes," please provide details. Use additional sheets if necessary.

7a. Type of security or investment, if relevant

7c. Security/
Ticker Symbol or CUSIP no.

7b. Name of issuer or security, if relevant

8. State in detail all facts pertinent to the alleged violation. Explain why the complainant believes the acts described constitute a violation of the federal securities laws. Use additional sheets if necessary.

9. Describe all supporting materials in the complainant's possession and the availability and location of any additional supporting materials not in complainant's possession. Use additional sheets, if necessary.

Federal Register/Vol. 76, No. 113/Monday, June 13, 2011/Rules and Regulations   34375

10. Describe how and from whom the complainant obtained the information that supports this claim. If any information was obtained from an attorney or in a communication where an attorney was present, identify such information with as much particularity as possible. In addition, if any information was obtained from a public source, identify the source with as much particularity as possible. Attach additional sheets if necessary.

11. Identify with particularity any documents or other information in your submission that you believe could reasonably be expected to reveal your identity and explain the basis for your belief that your identity would be revealed if the documents were disclosed to a third party.

34376 Federal Register / Vol. 76, No. 113 / Monday, June 13, 2011 / Rules and Regulations

12. Provide any additional information you think may be relevant.

E. ELIGIBILITY REQUIREMENTS AND OTHER INFORMATION

1. Are you, or were you at the time you acquired the original information you are submitting to us, a member, officer or employee of the Department of Justice, the Securities and Exchange Commission, the Comptroller of the Currency, the Board of Governors of the Federal Reserve System, the Federal Deposit Insurance Corporation, the Office of Thrift Supervision; the Public Company Accounting Oversight Board; any law enforcement organization; or any national securities exchange, registered securities association, registered clearing agency, or the Municipal Securities Rulemaking Board?

YES   NO

2. Are you, or were you at the time you acquired the original information you are submitting to us, a member, officer or employee of a foreign government, any political subdivision, department, agency, or instrumentality of a foreign government, or any other foreign financial regulatory authority as that term is defined in Section 3(a)(52) of the Securities Exchange Act of 1934 (15 U.S.C. §78c(a)(52))?

YES   NO

3. Did you acquire the information being provided to us through the performance of an engagement required under the federal securities laws by an independent public accountant?

YES   NO

4. Are you providing this information pursuant to a cooperation agreement with the SEC or another agency or organization?

YES   NO

5. Are you a spouse, parent, child, or sibling of a member or employee of the SEC, or do you reside in the same household as a member or employee of the SEC?

YES   NO

6. Are you providing this information before you (or anyone representing you) received any request, inquiry or demand that relates to the subject matter of your submission (i) from the SEC, (ii) in connection with an investigation, inspection or examination by the Public Company Accounting Oversight Board, or any self-regulatory organization; or (iii) in connection with an investigation by the Congress, any other authority of the federal government, or a state Attorney General or securities regulatory authority?

YES   NO

7. Are you currently a subject or target of a criminal investigation, or have you been convicted of a criminal violation, in connection with the information you are submitting to the SEC?

YES   NO

8. Did you acquire the information being provided to us from any person described in questions E1 through E7?

YES   NO

9. Use this space to provide additional details relating to your responses to questions 1 through 8. Use additional sheets if necessary.

F. WHISTLEBLOWER'S DECLARATION

I declare under penalty of perjury under the laws of the United States that the information contained herein is true, correct and complete to the best of my knowledge, information and belief. I fully understand that I may be subject to prosecution and ineligible for a whistleblower award if, in my submission of information, my other dealings with the SEC, or my dealings with another authority in connection with a related action, I knowingly and willfully make any false, fictitious, or fraudulent statements or representations, or use any false writing or document knowing that the writing or document contains any false, fictitious, or fraudulent statement or entry.

Print name

Signature   Date

G. COUNSEL CERTIFICATION

I certify that I have reviewed this form for completeness and accuracy and that the information contained herein is true, correct and complete to the best of my knowledge, information and belief. I further certify that I have verified the identity of the whistleblower on whose behalf this form is being submitted by viewing the whistleblower's valid, unexpired government issued identification (e.g., driver's license, passport) and will retain an original, signed copy of this form, with Section F signed by the whistleblower, in my records. I further certify that I have obtained the whistleblower's non-waiveable consent to provide the Commission with his or her original signed Form TCR upon request in the event that the Commission requests it due to concerns that the whistleblower may have knowingly and willfully made false, fictitious, or fraudulent statements or representations, or used any false writing or document knowing that the writing or document contains any false fictitious or fraudulent statement or entry; and that I consent to be legally obligated to do so within 7 calendar days of receiving such a request from the Commission.

Signature   Date

BILLING CODE 8011-01-C

Privacy Act Statement

This notice is given under the Privacy Act of 1974. This form may be used by anyone wishing to provide the SEC with information concerning a possible violation of the federal securities laws. We are authorized to request information from you by various laws: Sections 19 and 20 of the Securities Act of 1933, Sections 21 and 21F of the Securities Exchange Act of 1934, Section 321 of the Trust Indenture Act of 1939, Section 42 of the Investment Company Act of 1940, Section 209 of the Investment Advisers Act of 1940 and Title 17 of the Code of Federal Regulations, Section 202.5.

Our principal purpose in requesting information is to gather facts in order to determine whether any person has violated, is violating, or is about to violate any provision of the federal securities laws or rules for which we have enforcement authority. Facts developed may, however, constitute violations of other laws or rules. Further, if you are submitting information for the SEC's whistleblower award program pursuant to Section 21F of the Securities Exchange Act of 1934 (Exchange Act), the information provided will be used in connection with our evaluation of your or your client's eligibility and other factors relevant to our determination of whether to pay an award to you or your client.

The information provided may be used by SEC personnel for purposes of investigating possible violations of, or to conduct investigations authorized by, the federal securities law; in

proceedings in which the federal securities laws are in issue or the SEC is a party; to coordinate law enforcement activities between the SEC and other federal, state, local or foreign law enforcement agencies, securities self regulatory organizations, and foreign securities authorities; and pursuant to other routine uses as described in SEC–42 "Enforcement Files."

Furnishing the information requested herein is voluntary. However, a decision not provide any of the requested information, or failure to provide complete information, may affect our evaluation of your submission. Further, if you are submitting this information for the SEC whistleblower program and you do not execute the Whistleblower Declaration or, if you are submitting information anonymously, identify the attorney representing you in this matter, you may not be considered for an award.

Questions concerning this form maybe directed to the SEC Office of the Whistleblower, 100 F Street, NE, Washington, DC 20549, Tel. (202) 551–4790, Fax (703) 813–9322.

Submission Procedures

• After manually completing this Form TCR, please send it by mail or delivery to the SEC Office of the Whistleblower, 100 F. Street, NE, Washington, DC 20549, or by facsimile to (703) 813–9322.

• You have the right to submit information anonymously. If you are submitting anonymously and you want to be considered for a whistleblower award, however, you must be represented by an attorney in this matter

and Section B of this form must be completed. Otherwise, you may, but are not required, to have an attorney. If you are not represented by an attorney in this matter, you may leave Section B blank.

• **If you are submitting information for the SEC's whistleblower award program, you must submit your information either using this Form TCR or electronically through the SEC's Electronic Data Collection System, available on the SEC web site at *www.sec.gov*.**

Instructions for Completing Form TCR:

Section A: Information about You

Questions 1–3: Please provide the following information about yourself:

• Last name, first name, and middle initial

• Complete address, including city, state and zip code

• Telephone number and, if available, an alternate number where you can be reached

• Your e-mail address (to facilitate communications, we strongly encourage you to provide your email address),

• Your preferred method of communication; and

• Your occupation

34378   Federal Register / Vol. 76, No. 113 / Monday, June 13, 2011 / Rules and Regulations

Section B: Information about Your Attorney. Complete this section only if you are represented by an attorney in this matter. You must be represented by an attorney, and this section must be completed, if you are submitting your information anonymously and you want to be considered for the SEC's whistleblower award program.

Questions 1–4: Provide the following information about the attorney representing you in this matter:
• Attorney's name
• Firm name
• Complete address, including city, state and zip code
• Telephone number and fax number, and
• E-mail address

Section C: Tell Us about the Individual and/or Entity You Have a Complaint Against. If your complaint relates to more than two individuals and/or entities, you may attach additional sheets.

Question 1: Choose one of the following that best describes the individual or entity to which your complaint relates:
• **For Individuals:** accountant, analyst, attorney, auditor, broker, compliance officer, employee, executive officer or director, financial planner, fund manager, investment advisor representative, stock promoter, trustee, unknown, or other (specify).
• **For Entity:** bank, broker-dealer, clearing agency, day trading firm, exchange, Financial Industry Regulatory Authority, insurance company, investment advisor, investment advisor representative, investment company, Individual Retirement Account or 401(k) custodian/administrator, market maker, municipal securities dealers, mutual fund, newsletter company/investment publication company, on-line trading firm, private fund company (including hedge fund, private equity fund, venture capital fund, or real estate fund), private/closely held company, publicly held company, transfer agent/paying agent/registrar, underwriter, unknown, or other (specify).

Questions 2–4: For each subject, provide the following information, if known:
• Full name
• Complete address, including city, state and zip code
• Telephone number,
• E-mail address, and
• Internet address, if applicable

Section D: Tell Us about Your Complaint

Question 1: State the date (mm/dd/yyyy) that the alleged conduct began.

Question 2: Choose the option that you believe best describes the nature of your complaint. If you are alleging more than one violation, please list all that you believe may apply. Use additional sheets if necessary.
• Theft/misappropriation (advance fee fraud; lost or stolen securities; hacking of account)
• Misrepresentation/omission (false/misleading marketing/sales literature; inaccurate, misleading or non-disclosure by Broker-Dealer, Investment Adviser and Associated Person; false/material misstatements in firm research that were basis of transaction)
• Offering fraud (Ponzi/pyramid scheme; other offering fraud)
• Registration violations (unregistered securities offering)
• Trading (after hours trading; algorithmic trading; front-running; insider trading, manipulation of securities/prices; market timing; inaccurate quotes/pricing information; program trading; short selling; trading suspensions; volatility)
• Fees/mark-ups/commissions (excessive or unnecessary administrative fees; excessive commissions or sales fees; failure to disclose fees; insufficient notice of change in fees; negotiated fee problems; excessive mark-ups/markdowns; excessive or otherwise improper spreads)
• Corporate disclosure/reporting/other issuer matter (audit; corporate governance; conflicts of interest by management; executive compensation; failure to notify shareholders of corporate events; false/misleading financial statements, offering documents, press releases, proxy materials; failure to file reports; financial fraud; Foreign Corrupt Practices Act violations; going private transactions; mergers and acquisitions; restrictive legends, including 144 issues; reverse stock splits; selective disclosure—Regulation FD, 17 CFR 243; shareholder proposals; stock options for employees; stock splits; tender offers)
• Sales and advisory practices (background information on past violations/integrity; breach of fiduciary duty/responsibility (IA); failure to disclose breakpoints; churning/excessive trading; cold calling; conflict of interest; abuse of authority in discretionary trading; failure to respond to investor; guarantee against loss/promise to buy back shares; high pressure sales techniques; instructions by client not followed; investment objectives not followed; margin; poor investment advice; Regulation E (Electronic Transfer Act); Regulation S–P, 17 CFR 248, (privacy issues);

solicitation methods (non-cold calling; seminars); suitability; unauthorized transactions)
• Operational (bond call; bond default; difficulty buying/selling securities; confirmations/statements; proxy materials/prospectus; delivery of funds/proceeds; dividend and interest problems; exchanges/switches of mutual funds with fund family; margin (illegal extension of margin credit, Regulation T restrictions, unauthorized margin transactions); online issues (trading system operation); settlement (including T+1 or T=3 concerns); stock certificates; spam; tax reporting problems; titling securities (difficulty titling ownership); trade execution.
• Customer accounts (abandoned or inactive accounts; account administration and processing; identity theft affecting account; IPOs: problems with IPO allocation or eligibility; inaccurate valuation of Net Asset Value; transfer of account)
• Comments/complaints about SEC, Self-Regulatory Organization, and Securities Investor Protection Corporation processes & programs (arbitration: bias by arbitrators/forum, failure to pay/comply with award, mandatory arbitration requirements, procedural problems or delays; SEC: complaints about enforcement actions, complaints about rulemaking, failure to act; Self-Regulatory Organization: failure to act; Investor Protection: inadequacy of laws or rules; SIPC: customer protection, proceedings and Broker-Dealer liquidations)
• Other (analyst complaints; market maker activities; employer/employee disputes; specify other).

Question 3a: State whether you or your counsel have had any prior communications with the SEC concerning this matter.

Question 3b: If the answer to question 3a is yes, provide the name of the SEC staff member with whom you or your counsel communicated.

Question 4a: Indicate whether you or your counsel have provided the information you are providing to the SEC to any other agency or organization.

Question 4b: If the answer to question 4a is yes, provide details.

Question 4c: Provide the name and contact information of the point of contact at the other agency or organization, if known.

Question 5a: Indicate whether your complaint relates to an entity of which you are, or were in the past, an officer, director, counsel, employee, consultant, or contractor.

Question 5b: If the answer to question 5a is yes, state whether you have reported this violation to your

Federal Register / Vol. 76, No. 113 / Monday, June 13, 2011 / Rules and Regulations   34379

supervisor, compliance office, whistleblower hotline, ombudsman, or any other available mechanism at the entity for reporting violations.

Question 5c: If the answer to question 5b is yes, provide details.

Question 5d: Provide the date on which you took the actions described in questions 5a and 5b.

Question 6a: Indicate whether you have taken any other action regarding your complaint, including whether you complained to the SEC, another regulator, a law enforcement agency, or any other agency or organization; initiated legal action, mediation or arbitration, or initiated any other action.

Question 6b: If you answered yes to question 6a, provide details, including the date on which you took the action(s) described, the name of the person or entity to whom you directed any report or complaint and contact information for the person or entity, if known, and the complete case name, case number, and forum of any legal action you have taken. Use additional sheets if necessary.

Question 7a: Choose from the following the option that you believe best describes the type of security or investment at issue, if applicable:

- 1031 exchanges
- 529 plans
- American Depositary Receipts
- Annuities (equity-indexed annuities, fixed annuities, variable annuities)
  - Asset-backed securities
  - Auction rate securities
  - Banking products (including credit cards)
  - Certificates of deposit (CDs)
  - Closed-end funds
  - Coins and precious metals (gold, silver, etc.)
  - Collateralized mortgage obligations (CMOs)
  - Commercial paper
  - Commodities (currency transactions, futures, stock index options)
  - Convertible securities
  - Debt (corporate, lower-rated or "junk", municipal)
  - Equities (exchange-traded, foreign, Over-the-Counter, unregistered, linked notes)
  - Exchange Traded Funds
  - Franchises or business ventures
  - Hedge funds
  - Insurance contracts (not annuities)
  - Money-market funds
  - Mortgage-backed securities (mortgages, reverse mortgages)
  - Mutual funds
  - Options (commodity options, index options)
  - Partnerships

- Preferred shares
- Prime bank securities/high yield programs
- Promissory notes
- Real estate (real estate investment trusts (REITs))
- Retirement plans (401(k), IRAs)
- Rights and warrants
- Structured note products
- Subprime issues
- Treasury securities
- U.S. government agency securities
- Unit investment trusts (UIT)
- Viaticals and life settlements
- Wrap accounts
- Separately Managed Accounts (SMAs)
  - Unknown
  - Other (specify)

Question 7b: Provide the name of the issuer or security, if applicable.

Question 7c: Provide the ticker symbol or CUSIP number of the security, if applicable.

Question 8: State in detail all the facts pertinent to the alleged violation. Explain why you believe the facts described constitute a violation of the federal securities laws. Attach additional sheets if necessary.

Question 9: Describe all supporting materials in your possession and the availability and location of additional supporting materials not in your possession. Attach additional sheets if necessary.

Question 10: Describe how you obtained the information that supports your allegation. If any information was obtained from an attorney or in a communication where an attorney was present, identify such information with as much particularity as possible. In addition, if any information was obtained from a public source, identify the source with as much particularity as possible. Attach additional sheets if necessary.

Question 11: You may use this space to identify any documents or other information in your submission that you believe could reasonably be expected to reveal your identity. Explain the basis for your belief that your identity would be revealed if the documents or information were disclosed to a third party.

Question 12: Provide any additional information you think may be relevant.

Section E: Eligibility Requirements

Question 1: State whether you are currently, or were at the time you acquired the original information that you are submitting to the SEC, a member, officer, or employee of the Department of Justice; the Securities and Exchange Commission; the Comptroller of the Currency, the Board

of Governors of the Federal Reserve System, the Federal Deposit Insurance Corporation, the Office of Thrift Supervision; the Public Company Accounting Oversight Board; any law enforcement organization; or any national securities exchange, registered securities association, registered clearing agency, the Municipal Securities Rulemaking Board

Question 2: State whether you are, or were you at the time you acquired the original information you are submitting to the SEC, a member, officer or employee of a foreign government, any political subdivision, department, agency, or instrumentality of a foreign government, or any other foreign financial regulatory authority as that term is defined in Section 3(a)(52) of the Securities Exchange Act of 1934.

- Section 3(a)(52) of the Exchange Act (15 U.S.C. § 78c(a)(52)) currently defines "foreign financial regulatory authority" as "any (A) foreign securities authority, (B) other governmental body or foreign equivalent of a self-regulatory organization empowered by a foreign government to administer or enforce its laws relating to the regulation of fiduciaries, trusts, commercial lending, insurance, trading in contracts of sale of a commodity for future delivery, or other instruments traded on or subject to the rules of a contract market, board of trade, or foreign equivalent, or other financial activities, or (C) membership organization a function of which is to regulate participation of its members in activities listed above."

Question 3: State whether you acquired the information you are providing to the SEC through the performance of an engagement required under the securities laws by an independent public accountant.

Question 4: State whether you are providing the information pursuant to a cooperation agreement with the SEC or with any other agency or organization.

Question 5: State whether you are a spouse, parent, child or sibling of a member or employee of the SEC, or whether you reside in the same household as a member or employee of the SEC.

Question 6: State whether you acquired the information you are providing to the SEC from any individual described in Question 1 through 5 of this Section.

Question 7: If you answered "yes" to questions 1 though 6, please provide details.

Question 8a: State whether you are providing the information you are submitting to the SEC before you (or anyone representing you) received any request, inquiry or demand that relates to the subject matter of your submission in connection with: (i) an investigation, inspection or examination by the SEC, the Public Company Accounting Oversight Board, or any self-regulatory organization; or (ii) an investigation by Congress, or any other authority of the federal government, or a state Attorney General or securities regulatory authority?

Question 8b: If you answered "no" to questions 8a, please provide details. Use additional sheets if necessary.

Question 9a: State whether you are the subject or target of a criminal investigation or have been convicted of a criminal violation in connection with the information you are submitting to the SEC.

Question 9b: If you answered "yes" to question 9a, please provide details,

including the name of the agency or organization that conducted the investigation or initiated the action against you, the name and telephone number of your point of contact at the agency or organization, if available and the investigation/case name and number, if applicable. Use additional sheets, if necessary.

SECTION F: Whistleblower's Declaration.

You must sign this Declaration if you are submitting this information pursuant to the SEC whistleblower program and wish to be considered for an award. If you are submitting your information anonymously, you must still sign this Declaration, and you must provide your attorney with the original of this signed form.

If you are *not* submitting your information pursuant to the SEC whistleblower program, you do not need to sign this Declaration.

SECTION G: COUNSEL CERTIFICATION

If you are submitting this information pursuant to the SEC whistleblower program and are doing so anonymously, your attorney *must* sign the Counsel Certification section.

If you are represented in this matter but you are *not* submitting your information pursuant to the SEC whistleblower program, your attorney does not need to sign the Counsel Certification Section.

BILLING CODE 8011–01–P

Federal Register/Vol. 76, No. 113/Monday, June 13, 2011/Rules and Regulations   **34381**

UNITED STATES
SECURITIES AND EXCHANGE COMMISSION
Washington, DC 20549

FORM WB-APP

APPLICATION FOR AWARD FOR ORIGINAL INFORMATION SUBMITTED
PURSUANT TO SECTION 21F OF THE SECURITIES EXCHANGE ACT OF 1934

A.   APPLICANT'S INFORMATION (REQUIRED FOR ALL SUBMISSIONS)

1. Last Name   First   M.I.   Social Security No.

2. Street Address   Apartment/Unit #

City   State/Province   ZIP Code   Country

3. Telephone   Alt. Phone   E-mail Address

B.   ATTORNEY'S INFORMATION (IF APPLICABLE – SEE INSTRUCTIONS)

1. Attorney's name

2. Firm Name

3. Street Address

City   State/Province   ZIP Code   Country

4. Telephone   Fax   E-mail Address

C.   TIP/COMPLAINT DETAILS

1. Manner in which original information was submitted to SEC: SEC website   Mail   Fax   Other

2a. Tip, Complaint or Referral number   2b. Date TCR referred to in 2a submitted to SEC   /   /

2c. Subject(s) of the Tip, Complaint or Referral:

D.   NOTICE OF COVERED ACTION

1. Date of Notice of Covered Action to which claim relates: /   /   2. Notice Number:

3a. Case Name   3b. Case Number

E.   CLAIMS PERTAINING TO RELATED ACTIONS

1. Name of agency or organization to which you provided your information

2. Name and contact information for point of contact at agency or organization, if known.

3a. Date you provided your information   /   /   3b. Date action filed by agency/organization   /   /

4a. Case Name   4b. Case number

F.   ELIGIBILITY REQUIREMENTS AND OTHER INFORMATION

1. Are you, or were you at the time you acquired the original information you submitted to us, a member, officer or employee of the Department of Justice, the Securities and Exchange Commission, the Comptroller of the Currency, the Board of Governors of the Federal Reserve System, the Federal Deposit Insurance Corporation, the Office of Thrift Supervision; the Public Company Accounting Oversight Board; any law enforcement organization; or any national securities exchange, registered securities association, registered clearing agency, the Municipal Securities Rulemaking Board?   YES   NO

34382   Federal Register / Vol. 76, No. 113 / Monday, June 13, 2011 / Rules and Regulations

2. Are you, or were you at the time you acquired the original information you submitted to us, a member, officer or employee of a foreign government, any political subdivision, department, agency, or instrumentality of a foreign government, or any other foreign financial regulatory authority as that term is defined in Section 3(a)(52) of the Securities Exchange Act of 1934 (15 U.S.C. §78c(a)(52))?   YES   NO

3. Did you obtain the information you are providing to us through the performance of an engagement required under the federal securities laws by an independent public accountant?   YES   NO

4. Did you provide the information identified in Section C above pursuant to a cooperation agreement with the SEC or another agency or organization?   YES   NO

5. Are you a spouse, parent, child, or sibling of a member or employee of the Commission, or do you reside in the same household as a member or employee of the Commission?   YES   NO

6. Did you acquire the information you are providing to us from any person described in questions F1 through F5?   YES   NO

7. If you answered "yes" to any of questions 1 through 6 above, please provide details. Use additional sheets if necessary.

8a. Did you provide the information identified in Section C above before you (or anyone representing you) received any request, inquiry or demand that relates to the subject matter of your submission (i) from the SEC, (ii) in connection with an investigation, inspection or examination by the Public Company Accounting Oversight Board, or any self-regulatory organization; or (iii) in connection with an investigation by the Congress, any other authority of the federal government, or a state Attorney General or securities regulatory authority?   YES   NO

8b. If you answered "yes" to question 8a, please provide details. Use additional sheets if necessary.

9a. Are you currently a subject or target of a criminal investigation, or have you been convicted of a criminal violation, in connection with the information upon which your application for an award is based?   YES   NO

9b. If you answered "Yes" to question 9a, please provide details. Use additional sheets if necessary.

G. ENTITLEMENT TO AWARD

Explain the basis for your belief that you are entitled to an award in connection with your submission of information to us, or to another agency in a related action. Provide any additional information you think may be relevant in light of the criteria for determining the amount of an award set forth in Rule 21F-6 under the Securities Exchange Act of 1934. Include any supporting documents in your possession or control, and attach additional sheets, if necessary.

H. DECLARATION

I declare under penalty of perjury under the laws of the United States that the information contained herein is true, correct and complete to the best of my knowledge, information and belief. I fully understand that I may be subject to prosecution and ineligible for a whistleblower award if, in my submission of information, my other dealings with the SEC, or my dealings with another authority in connection with a related action, I knowingly and willfully make any false, fictitious, or fraudulent statements or representations, or use any false writing or document knowing that the writing or document contains any false, fictitious, or fraudulent statement or entry.

Signature   Date

BILLING CODE 8011–01–C

Privacy Act Statement

This notice is given under the Privacy Act of 1974. We are authorized to request information from you by Section 21F of the Securities Exchange Act of 1934. Our principal purpose in requesting this information is to assist in our evaluation of your eligibility and other factors relevant to our determination of whether to pay a whistleblower award to you under Section 21F of the Exchange Act.

However, the information provided may be used by SEC personnel for purposes of investigating possible violations of, or to conduct investigations authorized by, the federal securities law; in proceedings in which the federal securities laws are in issue or the SEC is a party; to coordinate law enforcement activities between the SEC and other federal, state, local or foreign law enforcement agencies, securities self regulatory organizations, and foreign securities authorities; and pursuant to other routine uses as described in SEC–42 "Enforcement Files."

Furnishing this information is voluntary, but a decision not do so, or failure to provide complete information, may result in our denying a whistleblower award to you, or may affect our evaluation of the appropriate amount of an award. Further, if you are submitting this information for the SEC whistleblower program and you do not execute the Declaration, you may not be considered for an award.

Questions concerning this form may be directed to the SEC Office of the Whistleblower, 100 F Street, NE, Washington, DC 20549–5631, Tel. (202) 551–4790, Fax (703) 813–9322.

General

- This form should be used by persons making a claim for a whistleblower award in connection with information provided to the SEC or to another agency in a related action. In order to be deemed eligible for an award, you must meet all the requirements set forth in Section 21F of the Securities Exchange Act of 1934 and the rules thereunder.
- You must sign the Form WB–APP as the claimant. If you provided your information to the SEC anonymously, you must now disclose your identity on this form and your identity must be verified in a form and manner that is acceptable to the Office of the Whistleblower prior to the payment of any award.
  ○ If you are filing your claim in connection with information that you provided to the SEC, then your Form WB–APP, and any attachments thereto, **must be received by the SEC Office of the Whistleblower within sixty (60) days of the date of the Notice of Covered Action to which the claim relates.**
  ○ If you are filing your claim in connection with information you provided to another agency in a related action, then your Form WB–APP, and any attachments thereto, must be received by the SEC Office of the Whistleblower as follows:
- If a final order imposing monetary sanctions has been entered in a related action at the time you submit your claim for an award in connection with a Commission action, **you must submit your claim for an award in that related action on the same Form WB–APP that you use for the Commission action.**
- If a final order imposing monetary sanctions in a related action has not been entered at the time you submit your claim for an award in connection with a Commission action, **you must submit your claim on Form WB–APP within sixty (60) days of the issuance of**

a final order imposing sanctions in the related action.

- You must submit your Form WB–APP to us in one of the following two ways:
  ○ By mailing or delivering the signed form to the SEC Office of the Whistleblower, 100 F Street NE, Washington, DC 20549–5631; or
  ○ By faxing the signed form to (703) 813–9322.

Instructions for Completing Form WB–APP

Section A: Applicant's Information

Questions 1–3: Provide the following information about yourself:
- First and last name, and middle initial
- Complete address, including city, state and zip code
- Telephone number and, if available, an alternate number where you can be reached
- E-mail address

Section B: Attorney's Information. If you are represented by an attorney in this matter, provide the information requested. If you are not representing an attorney in this matter, leave this Section blank.

Questions 1–4: Provide the following information about the attorney representing you in this matter:
- Attorney's name
- Firm name
- Complete address, including city, state and zip code
- Telephone number and fax number, and
- E-mail address.

Section C: Tip/Complaint Details

Question 1: Indicate the manner in which your original information was submitted to the SEC.
Question 2a: Include the TCR (Tip, Complaint or Referral) number to which this claim relates.
Question 2b: Provide the date on which you submitted your information to the SEC.
Question 2c: Provide the name of the individual(s) or entity(s) to which your complaint related.

Section D: Notice of Covered Action

The process for making a claim for a whistleblower award begins with the publication of a "Notice of a Covered Action" on the Commission's Web site. This notice is published whenever a judicial or administrative action brought by the Commission results in the imposition of monetary sanctions exceeding $1,000,000. The Notice is published on the Commission's Web site subsequent to the entry of a final

judgment or order in the action that by itself, or collectively with other judgments or orders previously entered in the action, exceeds the $1,000,000 threshold.

Question 1: Provide the date of the Notice of Covered Action to which this claim relates.
Question 2: Provide the notice number of the Notice of Covered Action.
Question 3a: Provide the case name referenced in Notice of Covered Action.
Question 3b: Provide the case number referenced in Notice of Covered Action.

Section E: Claims Pertaining to Related Actions

Question 1: Provide the name of the agency or organization to which you provided your information.
Question 2: Provide the name and contact information for your point of contact at the agency or organization, if known.
Question 3a: Provide the date on which that you provided your information to the agency or organization referenced in question E1.
Question 3b: Provide the date on which the agency or organization referenced in question E1 filed the related action that was based upon the information you provided.
Question 4a: Provide the case name of the related action.
Question 4b: Provide the case number of the related action.

Section F: Eligibility Requirements

Question 1: State whether you are currently, or were at the time you acquired the original information that you submitted to the SEC a member, officer, or employee of the Department of Justice; the Securities and Exchange Commission; the Comptroller of the Currency; the Board of Governors of the Federal Reserve System, the Federal Deposit Insurance Corporation, the Office of Thrift Supervision; the Public Company Accounting Oversight Board; any law enforcement organization; or any national securities exchange, registered securities association, registered clearing agency, the Municipal Securities Rulemaking Board
Question 2: State whether you are, or were you at the time you acquired the original information you submitted to the SEC, a member, officer or employee of a foreign government, any political subdivision, department, agency, or instrumentality of a foreign government, or any other foreign financial regulatory authority as that term is defined in Section 3(a)(52) of the Securities Exchange Act of 1934.
- Section 3(a)(52) of the Exchange Act (15 U.S.C. § 78c(a)(52)) currently defines

"foreign financial regulatory authority" as "any (A) foreign securities authority, (B) other governmental body or foreign equivalent of a self-regulatory organization empowered by a foreign government to administer or enforce its laws relating to the regulation of fiduciaries, trusts, commercial lending, insurance, trading in contracts of sale of a commodity for future delivery, or other instruments traded on or subject to the rules of a contract market, board of trade, or foreign equivalent, or other financial activities, or (C) membership organization a function of which is to regulate participation of its members in activities listed above."

Question 3: Indicate whether you acquired the information you provided to the SEC through the performance of an engagement required under the securities laws by an independent public accountant.

Question 4: State whether you provided the information submitted to the SEC pursuant to a cooperation agreement with the SEC or with any other agency or organization.

Question 5: State whether you are a spouse, parent, child or sibling of a member or employee of the Commission, or whether you reside in the same household as a member or employee of the Commission.

Question 6: State whether you acquired the information you are providing to the SEC from any individual described in Question 1 through 5 of this Section.

Question 7: If you answered "yes" to questions 1 though 6, please provide details.

Question 8a: State whether you provided the information identified submitted to the SEC before you (or anyone representing you) received any request, inquiry or demand from the SEC, Congress, or any other federal, state or local authority, or any self regulatory organization, or the Public Company Accounting Oversight Board about a matter to which the information your submission was relevant.

Question 8b: If you answered "no" to questions 8a, please provide details. Use additional sheets if necessary.

Question 9a: State whether you are the subject or target of a criminal investigation or have been convicted of a criminal violation in connection with the information upon which your application for award is based.

Question 9b: If you answered "yes" to question 9a, please provide details, including the name of the agency or organization that conducted the investigation or initiated the action against you, the name and telephone number of your point of contact at the agency or organization, if available and the investigation/case name and number, if applicable. Use additional sheets, if necessary. If you previously provided this information on Form WB-DEC, you may leave this question blank, unless your response has changed since the time you submitted your Form WB-DEC.

Section G: Entitlement to Award

This section is optional. Use this section to explain the basis for your belief that you are entitled to an award in connection with your submission of information to us or to another agency in connection with a related action. Specifically address how you believe you voluntarily provided the Commission with original information that led to the successful enforcement of a judicial or administrative action filed by the Commission, or a related action.

Refer to Rules 21F–3 and 21F–4 under the Exchange Act for further information concerning the relevant award criteria. You may attach additional sheets, if necessary.

Rule 21F–6 under the Exchange Act provides that in determining the amount of an award, the Commission will evaluate the following factors: (a) the significance of the information provided by a whistleblower to the success of the Commission action or related action; (b) the degree of assistance provided by the whistleblower and any legal representative of the whistleblower in the Commission action or related action; (c) the programmatic interest of the Commission in deterring violations of the securities laws by making awards to whistleblowers who provide information that leads to the successful enforcement of such laws; and (d) whether the award otherwise enhances the Commission's ability to enforce the federal securities laws, protect investors, and encourage the submission of high quality information from whistleblowers. Address these factors in your response as well.

Additional information about the criteria the Commission may consider in determining the amount of an award is available on the Commission's Web site at *www.sec.gov/complaint/info_ whistleblowers.shtml.*

Section H: Declaration

This section must be signed by the claimant.

Dated: May 25, 2011.

By the Commission.

Elizabeth M. Murphy,

Secretary.

[FR Doc. 2011–13382 Filed 6–10–11; 8:45 am]

BILLING CODE 8011–01–P

U.K. Bribery Act Guidance (March 31, 2011)

THE BRIBERY ACT 2010

Guidance

about procedures which relevant commercial
organisations can put into place to prevent
persons associated with them from bribing
(section 9 of the Bribery Act 2010)

THE BRIBERY ACT 2010

Guidance

about procedures which relevant commercial organisations can put into place to prevent persons associated with them from bribing (section 9 of the Bribery Act 2010)

Foreword

Bribery blights lives. Its immediate victims include firms that lose out unfairly. The wider victims are government and society, undermined by a weakened rule of law and damaged social and economic development. At stake is the principle of free and fair competition, which stands diminished by each bribe offered or accepted.

Tackling this scourge is a priority for anyone who cares about the future of business, the developing world or international trade. That is why the entry into force of the Bribery Act on 1 July 2011 is an important step forward for both the UK and UK plc. In line with the Act's statutory requirements, I am publishing this guidance to help organisations understand the legislation and deal with the risks of bribery. My aim is that it offers clarity on how the law will operate.

Readers of this document will be aware that the Act creates offences of offering or receiving bribes, bribery of foreign public officials and of failure to prevent a bribe being paid on an organisation's behalf. These are certainly tough rules. But readers should understand too that they are directed at making life difficult for the mavericks responsible for corruption, not unduly burdening the vast majority of decent, law-abiding firms.

I have listened carefully to business representatives to ensure the Act is implemented in a workable way – especially for small firms that have limited resources. And, as I hope this guidance shows, combating the risks of bribery is largely about common sense, not burdensome procedures. The core principle it sets out is proportionality. It also offers case study examples that help illuminate the application of the Act. Rest assured – no one wants to stop firms getting to know their clients by taking them to events like Wimbledon or the Grand Prix. Separately, we are publishing non-statutory 'quick start' guidance. I encourage small businesses to turn to this for a concise introduction to how they can meet the requirements of the law.

Ultimately, the Bribery Act matters for Britain because our existing legislation is out of date. In updating our rules, I say to our international partners that the UK wants to play a leading role in stamping out corruption and supporting trade-led international development. But I would argue too that the Act is directly beneficial for business. That's because it creates clarity and a level playing field, helping to align trading nations around decent standards. It also establishes a statutory defence: organisations which have adequate procedures in place to prevent bribery are in a stronger position if isolated incidents have occurred in spite of their efforts.

Some have asked whether business can afford this legislation – especially at a time of economic recovery. But the choice is a false one. We don't have to decide between tackling corruption and supporting growth. Addressing bribery is good for business because it creates the conditions for free markets to flourish.

Everyone agrees bribery is wrong and that rules need reform. In implementing this Act, we are striking a blow for the rule of law and growth of trade. I commend this guidance to you as a helping hand in doing business competitively and fairly.

Kenneth Clarke
Secretary of State for Justice
March 2011

Contents

Introduction

1   The Bribery Act 2010 received Royal Assent on 8 April 2010. A full copy of the Act and its Explanatory Notes can be accessed at: www.opsi.gov.uk/acts/acts2010/ukpga_20100023_en_1 The Act creates a new offence under section 7 which can be committed by commercial organisations[1] which fail to prevent persons associated with them from committing bribery on their behalf. It is a full defence for an organisation to prove that despite a particular case of bribery it nevertheless had adequate procedures in place to prevent persons associated with it from bribing. Section 9 of the Act requires the Secretary of State to publish guidance about procedures which commercial organisations can put in place to prevent persons associated with them from bribing. This document sets out that guidance.

2   The Act extends to England & Wales, Scotland and Northern Ireland. This guidance is for use in all parts of the United Kingdom. In accordance with section 9(3) of the Act, the Scottish Ministers have been consulted regarding the content of this guidance. The Northern Ireland Assembly has also been consulted.

3   This guidance explains the policy behind section 7 and is intended to help commercial organisations of all sizes and sectors understand what sorts of procedures they can put in place to prevent bribery as mentioned in section 7(1).

4   The guidance is designed to be of general application and is formulated around six guiding principles, each followed by commentary and examples. The guidance is not prescriptive and is not a one-size-fits-all document. The question of whether an organisation had adequate procedures in place to prevent bribery in the context of a particular prosecution is a matter that can only be resolved by the courts taking into account the particular facts and circumstances of the case. The onus will remain on the organisation, in any case where it seeks to rely on the defence, to prove that it had adequate procedures in place to prevent bribery. However, departures from the suggested procedures contained within the guidance will not of itself give rise to a presumption that an organisation does not have adequate procedures.

5   If your organisation is small or medium sized the application of the principles is likely to suggest procedures that are different from those that may be right for a large multinational organisation. The guidance suggests certain procedures, but they may not all be applicable to your circumstances. Sometimes, you may have alternatives in place that are also adequate.

---

1   See paragraph 35 below on the definition of the phrase 'commercial organisation'.

6   As the principles make clear commercial organisations should adopt a risk-based approach to managing bribery risks. Procedures should be proportionate to the risks faced by an organisation. No policies or procedures are capable of detecting and preventing all bribery. A risk-based approach will, however, serve to focus the effort where it is needed and will have most impact. A risk-based approach recognises that the bribery threat to organisations varies across jurisdictions, business sectors, business partners and transactions.

7   The language used in this guidance reflects its non-prescriptive nature. The six principles are intended to be of general application and are therefore expressed in neutral but affirmative language. The commentary following each of the principles is expressed more broadly.

8   All terms used in this guidance have the same meaning as in the Bribery Act 2010. Any examples of particular types of conduct are provided for illustrative purposes only and do not constitute exhaustive lists of relevant conduct.

Government policy and Section 7 of the Bribery Act

9   Bribery undermines democracy and the rule of law and poses very serious threats to sustained economic progress in developing and emerging economies and to the proper operation of free markets more generally. The Bribery Act 2010 is intended to respond to these threats and to the extremely broad range of ways that bribery can be committed. It does this by providing robust offences, enhanced sentencing powers for the courts (raising the maximum sentence for bribery committed by an individual from 7 to 10 years imprisonment) and wide jurisdictional powers (see paragraphs 15 and 16 on page 9).

10   The Act contains two general offences covering the offering, promising or giving of a bribe (active bribery) and the requesting, agreeing to receive or accepting of a bribe (passive bribery) at sections 1 and 2 respectively. It also sets out two further offences which specifically address commercial bribery. Section 6 of the Act creates an offence relating to bribery of a foreign public official in order to obtain or retain business or an advantage in the conduct of business[2], and section 7 creates a new form of corporate liability for failing to prevent bribery on behalf of a commercial organisation. More detail about the sections 1, 6 and 7 offences is provided under the separate headings below.

11   The objective of the Act is not to bring the full force of the criminal law to bear upon well run commercial organisations that experience an isolated incident of bribery on their behalf. So in order to achieve an appropriate balance, section 7 provides a full defence. This is in recognition of the fact that no bribery prevention regime will be capable of preventing bribery at all times. However, the defence is also included in order to encourage commercial organisations to put procedures in place to prevent bribery by persons associated with them.

12   The application of bribery prevention procedures by commercial organisations is of significant interest to those investigating bribery and is relevant if an organisation wishes to report an incident of bribery to the prosecution authorities – for example to the Serious Fraud Office (SFO) which operates a policy in England and Wales and Northern Ireland of co-operation with commercial organisations that self-refer incidents of bribery (see 'Approach of the SFO to dealing with overseas corruption' on the SFO website). The commercial organisation's willingness to co-operate with an investigation under the Bribery Act and to make a full disclosure will also be taken into account in any decision as to whether it is appropriate to commence criminal proceedings.

---

2   Conduct amounting to bribery of a foreign public official could also be charged under section 1 of the Act. It will be for prosecutors to select the most appropriate charge.

13   In order to be liable under section 7 a commercial organisation must have failed to prevent conduct that would amount to the commission of an offence under sections 1 or 6, but it is irrelevant whether a person has been convicted of such an offence. Where the prosecution cannot prove beyond reasonable doubt that a sections 1 or 6 offence has been committed the section 7 offence will not be triggered.

14   The section 7 offence is in addition to, and does not displace, liability which might arise under sections 1 or 6 of the Act where the commercial organisation itself commits an offence by virtue of the common law 'identification' principle.[3]

Jurisdiction

15   Section 12 of the Act provides that the courts will have jurisdiction over the sections 1, 2[4] or 6 offences committed in the UK, but they will also have jurisdiction over offences committed outside the UK where the person committing them has a close connection with the UK by virtue of being a British national or ordinarily resident in the UK, a body incorporated in the UK or a Scottish partnership.

16   However, as regards section 7, the requirement of a close connection with the UK does not apply. Section 7(3) makes clear that a commercial organisation can be liable for conduct amounting to a section 1 or 6 offence on the part of a person who is neither a UK national or resident in the UK, nor a body incorporated or formed in the UK. In addition, section 12(5) provides that it does not matter whether the acts or omissions which form part of the section 7 offence take part in the UK or elsewhere. So, provided the organisation is incorporated or formed in the UK, or that the organisation carries on a business or part of a business in the UK (wherever in the world it may be incorporated or formed) then UK courts will have jurisdiction (see more on this at paragraphs 34 to 36).

---

3   See section 5 and Schedule 1 to the Interpretation Act 1978 which provides that the word 'person' where used in an Act includes bodies corporate and unincorporate. Note also the common law 'identification principle' as defined by cases such as Tesco Supermarkets v Nattrass [1972] AC 153 which provides that corporate liability arises only where the offence is committed by a natural person who is the directing mind or will of the organisation.
4   Although this particular offence is not relevant for the purposes of section 7.

Section 1:
Offences of bribing another person

17   Section 1 makes it an offence for a person ('P') to offer, promise or give a financial or other advantage to another person in one of two cases:

- **Case 1** applies where P intends the advantage to bring about the improper performance by another person of a relevant function or activity or to reward such improper performance.
- **Case 2** applies where P knows or believes that the acceptance of the advantage offered, promised or given in itself constitutes the improper performance of a relevant function or activity.

18   'Improper performance' is defined at sections 3, 4 and 5. In summary, this means performance which amounts to a breach of an expectation that a person will act in good faith, impartially, or in accordance with a position of trust. The offence applies to bribery relating to any function of a public nature, connected with a business, performed in the course of a person's employment or performed on behalf of a company or another body of persons. Therefore, bribery in both the public and private sectors is covered.

19   For the purposes of deciding whether a function or activity has been performed improperly the test of what is expected is a test of what a reasonable person in the UK would expect in relation to the performance of that function or activity. Where the performance of the function or activity is not subject to UK law (for example, it takes place in a country outside UK jurisdiction) then any local custom or practice must be disregarded – unless permitted or required by the written law applicable to that particular country. Written law means any written constitution, provision made by or under legislation applicable to the country concerned or any judicial decision evidenced in published written sources.

20   By way of illustration, in order to proceed with a case under section 1 based on an allegation that hospitality was intended as a bribe, the prosecution would need to show that the hospitality was intended to induce conduct that amounts to a breach of an expectation that a person will act in good faith, impartially, or in accordance with a position of trust. This would be judged by what a reasonable person in the UK thought. So, for example, an invitation to foreign clients to attend a Six Nations match at Twickenham as part of a public relations exercise designed to cement good relations or enhance knowledge in the organisation's field is extremely unlikely to engage section 1 as there is unlikely to be evidence of an intention to induce improper performance of a relevant function.

Section 6:
Bribery of a foreign public official

21   Section 6 creates a standalone offence of bribery of a foreign public official. The offence is committed where a person offers, promises or gives a financial or other advantage to a foreign public official with the intention of influencing the official in the performance of his or her official functions. The person offering, promising or giving the advantage must also intend to obtain or retain business or an advantage in the conduct of business by doing so. However, the offence is not committed where the official is permitted or required by the applicable written law to be influenced by the advantage.

22   A 'foreign public official' includes officials, whether elected or appointed, who hold a legislative, administrative or judicial position of any kind of a country or territory outside the UK. It also includes any person who performs public functions in any branch of the national, local or municipal government of such a country or territory or who exercises a public function for any public agency or public enterprise of such a country or territory, such as professionals working for public health agencies and officers exercising public functions in state-owned enterprises. Foreign public officials can also be an official or agent of a public international organisation, such as the UN or the World Bank.

23   Sections 1 and 6 may capture the same conduct but will do so in different ways. The policy that founds the offence at section 6 is the need to prohibit the influencing of decision making in the context of publicly funded business opportunities by the inducement of personal enrichment of foreign public officials or to others at the official's request, assent or acquiescence. Such activity is very likely to involve conduct which amounts to 'improper performance' of a relevant function or activity to which section 1 applies, but, unlike section 1, section 6 does not require proof of it or an intention to induce it. This is because the exact nature of the functions of persons regarded as foreign public officials is often very difficult to ascertain with any accuracy, and the securing of evidence will often be reliant on the co-operation of the state any such officials serve. To require the prosecution to rely entirely on section 1 would amount to a very significant deficiency in the ability of the legislation to address this particular mischief. That said, it is not the Government's intention to criminalise behaviour where no such mischief occurs, but merely to formulate the offence to take account of the evidential difficulties referred to above. In view of its wide scope, and its role in the new form of corporate liability at section 7, the Government offers the following further explanation of issues arising from the formulation of section 6.

Local law

24   For the purposes of section 6 prosecutors will be required to show not only that an 'advantage' was offered, promised or given to the official or to another person at the official's request, assent or acquiescence, but that the advantage was

one that the official was not permitted or required to be influenced by as determined by the written law applicable to the foreign official.

25   In seeking tenders for publicly funded contracts Governments often permit or require those tendering for the contract to offer, in addition to the principal tender, some kind of additional investment in the local economy or benefit to the local community. Such arrangements could in certain circumstances amount to a financial or other 'advantage' to a public official or to another person at the official's request, assent or acquiescence. Where, however, relevant 'written law' permits or requires the official to be influenced by such arrangements they will fall outside the scope of the offence. So, for example, where local planning law permits community investment or requires a foreign public official to minimise the cost of public procurement administration through cost sharing with contractors, a prospective contractor's offer of free training is very unlikely to engage section 6. In circumstances where the additional investment would amount to an advantage to a foreign public official and the local law is silent as to whether the official is permitted or required to be influenced by it, prosecutors will consider the public interest in prosecuting. This will provide an appropriate backstop in circumstances where the evidence suggests that the offer of additional investment is a legitimate part of a tender exercise.

Hospitality, promotional, and other business expenditure

26   Bona fide hospitality and promotional, or other business expenditure which seeks to improve the image of a commercial organisation, better to present products and services, or establish cordial relations, is recognised as an established and important part of doing business and it is not the intention of the Act to criminalise such behaviour. The Government does not intend for the Act to prohibit reasonable and proportionate hospitality and promotional or other similar business expenditure intended for these purposes. It is, however, clear that hospitality and promotional or other similar business expenditure can be employed as bribes.

27   In order to amount to a bribe under section 6 there must be an intention for a financial or other advantage to influence the official in his or her official role and thereby secure business or a business advantage. In this regard, it may be in some circumstances that hospitality or promotional expenditure in the form of travel and accommodation costs does not even amount to 'a financial or other advantage' to the relevant official because it is a cost that would otherwise be borne by the relevant foreign Government rather than the official him or herself.

28 Where the prosecution is able to establish a financial or other advantage has been offered, promised or given, it must then show that there is a sufficient connection between the advantage and the intention to influence and secure business or a business advantage. Where the prosecution cannot prove this to the requisite standard then no offence under section 6 will be committed. There may be direct evidence to support the existence of this connection and such evidence may indeed relate to relatively modest expenditure. In many cases, however, the question as to whether such a connection can be established will depend on the totality of the evidence which takes into account all of the surrounding circumstances. It would include matters such as the type and level of advantage offered, the manner and form in which the advantage is provided, and the level of influence the particular foreign public official has over awarding the business. In this circumstantial context, the more lavish the hospitality or the higher the expenditure in relation to travel, accommodation or other similar business expenditure provided to a foreign public official, then, generally, the greater the inference that it is intended to influence the official to grant business or a business advantage in return.

29 The standards or norms applying in a particular sector may also be relevant here. However, simply providing hospitality or promotional, or other similar business expenditure which is commensurate with such norms is not, of itself, evidence that no bribe was paid if there is other evidence to the contrary; particularly if the norms in question are extravagant.

30 Levels of expenditure will not, therefore, be the only consideration in determining whether a section 6 offence has been committed. But in the absence of any further evidence demonstrating the required connection, it is unlikely, for example, that incidental provision of a routine business courtesy will raise the inference that it was intended to have a direct impact on decision making, particularly where such hospitality is commensurate with the reasonable and proportionate norms for the particular industry; e.g. the provision of airport to hotel transfer services to facilitate an on-site visit, or dining and tickets to an event.

The Bribery Act 2010 – Guidance

31   Some further examples might be helpful. The provision by a UK mining company of reasonable travel and accommodation to allow foreign public officials to visit their distant mining operations so that those officials may be satisfied of the high standard and safety of the company's installations and operating systems are circumstances that fall outside the intended scope of the offence. Flights and accommodation to allow foreign public officials to meet with senior executives of a UK commercial organisation in New York as a matter of genuine mutual convenience, and some reasonable hospitality for the individual and his or her partner, such as fine dining and attendance at a baseball match are facts that are, in themselves, unlikely to raise the necessary inferences. However, if the choice of New York as the most convenient venue was in doubt because the organisation's senior executives could easily have seen the official with all the relevant documentation when they had visited the relevant country the previous week then the necessary inference might be raised. Similarly, supplementing information provided to a foreign public official on a commercial organisation's background, track record and expertise in providing private health care with an offer of ordinary travel and lodgings to enable a visit to a hospital run by the commercial organisation is unlikely to engage section 6. On the other hand, the provision by that same commercial organisation of a five-star holiday for the foreign public official which is unrelated to a demonstration of the organisation's services is, all things being equal, far more likely to raise the necessary inference.

32   It may be that, as a result of the introduction of the section 7 offence, commercial organisations will review their policies on hospitality and promotional or other similar business expenditure as part of the selection and implementation of bribery prevention procedures, so as to ensure that they are seen to be acting both competitively and fairly. It is, however, for individual organisations, or business representative bodies, to establish and disseminate appropriate standards for hospitality and promotional or other similar expenditure.

Section 7: Failure of commercial organisations to prevent bribery

33 A commercial organisation will be liable to prosecution if a person associated with it bribes another person intending to obtain or retain business or an advantage in the conduct of business for that organisation. As set out above, the commercial organisation will have a full defence if it can show that despite a particular case of bribery it nevertheless had adequate procedures in place to prevent persons associated with it from bribing. In accordance with established case law, the standard of proof which the commercial organisation would need to discharge in order to prove the defence, in the event it was prosecuted, is the balance of probabilities.

Commercial organisation

34 Only a 'relevant commercial organisation' can commit an offence under section 7 of the Bribery Act. A 'relevant commercial organisation' is defined at section 7(5) as a body or partnership incorporated or formed in the UK irrespective of where it carries on a business, or an incorporated body or partnership which carries on a business or part of a business in the UK irrespective of the place of incorporation or formation. The key concept here is that of an organisation which 'carries on a business'. The courts will be the final arbiter as to whether an organisation 'carries on a business' in the UK taking into account the particular facts in individual cases. However, the following paragraphs set out the Government's intention as regards the application of the phrase.

35 As regards bodies incorporated, or partnerships formed, in the UK, despite the fact that there are many ways in which a body corporate or a partnership can pursue business objectives, the Government expects that whether such a body or partnership can be said to be carrying on a business will be answered by applying a common sense approach. So long as the organisation in question is incorporated (by whatever means), or is a partnership, it does not matter if it pursues primarily charitable or educational aims or purely public functions. It will be caught if it engages in commercial activities, irrespective of the purpose for which profits are made.

36 As regards bodies incorporated, or partnerships formed, outside the United Kingdom, whether such bodies can properly be regarded as carrying on a business or part of a business 'in any part of the United Kingdom' will again be answered by applying a common sense approach. Where there is a particular dispute as to whether a business presence in the United Kingdom satisfies the test in the Act, the final arbiter, in any particular case, will be the courts as set out above. However, the Government anticipates that applying a common sense approach would mean that organisations that do not have a demonstrable business presence in the United Kingdom would not be caught. The Government would not expect, for example, the mere fact that a company's securities have been admitted to the UK Listing Authority's Official List and therefore admitted to trading on the

London Stock Exchange, in itself, to qualify that company as carrying on a business or part of a business in the UK and therefore falling within the definition of a 'relevant commercial organisation' for the purposes of section 7. Likewise, having a UK subsidiary will not, in itself, mean that a parent company is carrying on a business in the UK, since a subsidiary may act independently of its parent or other group companies.

Associated person

37   A commercial organisation is liable under section 7 if a person 'associated' with it bribes another person intending to obtain or retain business or a business advantage for the organisation. A person associated with a commercial organisation is defined at section 8 as a person who 'performs services' for or on behalf of the organisation. This person can be an individual or an incorporated or unincorporated body. Section 8 provides that the capacity in which a person performs services for or on behalf of the organisation does not matter, so employees (who are presumed to be performing services for their employer), agents and subsidiaries are included. Section 8(4), however, makes it clear that the question as to whether a person is performing services for an organisation is to be determined by reference to all the relevant circumstances and not merely by reference to the nature of the relationship between that person and the organisation. The concept of a person who 'performs services for or on behalf of' the organisation

is intended to give section 7 broad scope so as to embrace the whole range of persons connected to an organisation who might be capable of committing bribery on the organisation's behalf.

38   This broad scope means that contractors could be 'associated' persons to the extent that they are performing services for or on behalf of a commercial organisation. Also, where a supplier can properly be said to be performing services for a commercial organisation rather than simply acting as the seller of goods, it may also be an 'associated' person.

39   Where a supply chain involves several entities or a project is to be performed by a prime contractor with a series of sub-contractors, an organisation is likely only to exercise control over its relationship with its contractual counterparty. Indeed, the organisation may only know the identity of its contractual counterparty. It is likely that persons who contract with that counterparty will be performing services for the counterparty and not for other persons in the contractual chain. The principal way in which commercial organisations may decide to approach bribery risks which arise as a result of a supply chain is by employing the types of anti-bribery procedures referred to elsewhere in this guidance (e.g. risk-based due diligence and the use of anti-bribery terms and conditions) in the relationship with their contractual counterparty, and by requesting that counterparty to adopt a similar approach with the next party in the chain.

The Bribery Act 2010 - Guidance

40 As for joint ventures, these come in many different forms, sometimes operating through a separate legal entity, but at other times through contractual arrangements. In the case of a joint venture operating through a separate legal entity, a bribe paid by the joint venture entity may lead to liability for a member of the joint venture if the joint venture is performing services for the member and the bribe is paid with the intention of benefiting that member. However, the existence of a joint venture entity will not of itself mean that it is 'associated' with any of its members. A bribe paid on behalf of the joint venture entity by one of its employees or agents will therefore not trigger liability for members of the joint venture simply by virtue of them benefiting indirectly from the bribe through their investment in or ownership of the joint venture.

41 The situation will be different where the joint venture is conducted through a contractual arrangement. The degree of control that a participant has over that arrangement is likely to be one of the 'relevant circumstances' that would be taken into account in deciding whether a person who paid a bribe in the conduct of the joint venture business was 'performing services for or on behalf of' a participant in that arrangement. It may be, for example, that an employee of such a participant who has paid a bribe in order to benefit his employer is not to be regarded as a person 'associated' with all the other participants in the joint venture. Ordinarily, the employee of a participant will be presumed to be a person performing services for and on behalf of his employer. Likewise, an agent engaged by a participant in a contractual joint venture is likely to be regarded as a person associated with that participant in the absence of evidence that the agent is acting on behalf of the contractual joint venture as a whole.

42 Even if it can properly be said that an agent, a subsidiary, or another person acting for a member of a joint venture, was performing services for the organisation, an offence will be committed only if that agent, subsidiary or person intended to obtain or retain business or an advantage in the conduct of business for the organisation. The fact that an organisation benefits indirectly from a bribe is very unlikely, in itself, to amount to proof of the specific intention required by the offence. Without proof of the required intention, liability will not accrue through simple corporate ownership or investment, or through the payment of dividends or provision of loans by a subsidiary to its parent. So, for example, a bribe on behalf of a subsidiary by one of its employees or agents will not automatically involve liability on the part of its parent company, or any other subsidiaries of the parent company, if it cannot be shown the employee or agent intended to obtain or retain business or a business advantage for the parent company or other subsidiaries. This is so even though the parent company or subsidiaries may benefit indirectly from the bribe. By the same token, liability for a parent company could arise where a subsidiary is the 'person' which pays a bribe which it intends will result in the parent company obtaining or retaining business or vice versa.

43   The question of adequacy of bribery prevention procedures will depend in the final analysis on the facts of each case, including matters such as the level of control over the activities of the associated person and the degree of risk that requires mitigation. The scope of the definition at section 8 needs to be appreciated within this context. This point is developed in more detail under the six principles set out on pages 20 to 31.

Facilitation payments

44   Small bribes paid to facilitate routine Government action – otherwise called 'facilitation payments' – could trigger either the section 6 offence or, where there is an intention to induce improper conduct, including where the acceptance of such payments is itself improper, the section 1 offence and therefore potential liability under section 7.

45   As was the case under the old law, the Bribery Act does not (unlike US foreign bribery law) provide any exemption for such payments. The 2009 Recommendation of the Organisation for Economic Co-operation and Development[5] recognises the corrosive effect of facilitation payments and asks adhering countries to discourage

companies from making such payments. Exemptions in this context create artificial distinctions that are difficult to enforce, undermine corporate anti-bribery procedures, confuse anti-bribery communication with employees and other associated persons, perpetuate an existing 'culture' of bribery and have the potential to be abused.

46   The Government does, however, recognise the problems that commercial organisations face in some parts of the world and in certain sectors. The eradication of facilitation payments is recognised at the national and international level as a long term objective that will require economic and social progress and sustained commitment to the rule of law in those parts of the world where the problem is most prevalent. It will also require collaboration between international bodies, governments, the anti-bribery lobby, business representative bodies and sectoral organisations. Businesses themselves also have a role to play and the guidance below offers an indication of how the problem may be addressed through the selection of bribery prevention procedures by commercial organisations.

47   Issues relating to the prosecution of facilitation payments in England and Wales are referred to in the guidance of the Director of the Serious Fraud Office and the Director of Public Prosecutions.[6]

5   Recommendation of the Council for Further Combating Bribery of Foreign Public Officials in International Business Transactions.
6   Bribery Act 2010: Joint Prosecution Guidance of the Director of the Serious Fraud Office and the Director of Public Prosecutions.

Duress

48   It is recognised that there are circumstances in which individuals are left with no alternative but to make payments in order to protect against loss of life, limb or liberty. The common law defence of duress is very likely to be available in such circumstances.

Prosecutorial discretion

49   Whether to prosecute an offence under the Act is a matter for the prosecuting authorities. In deciding whether to proceed, prosecutors must first decide if there is a sufficiency of evidence, and, if so, whether a prosecution is in the public interest. If the evidential test has been met, prosecutors will consider the general public interest in ensuring that bribery is effectively dealt with. The more serious the offence, the more likely it is that a prosecution will be required in the public interest.

50   In cases where hospitality, promotional expenditure or facilitation payments do, on their face, trigger the provisions of the Act prosecutors will consider very carefully what is in the public interest before deciding whether to prosecute. The operation of prosecutorial discretion provides a degree of flexibility which is helpful to ensure the just and fair operation of the Act.

51   Factors that weigh for and against the public interest in prosecuting in England and Wales are referred to in the joint guidance of the Director of the Serious Fraud Office and the Director of Public Prosecutions referred to at paragraph 47.

The six principles

The Government considers that procedures put in place by commercial organisations wishing to prevent bribery being committed on their behalf should be informed by six principles. These are set out below. Commentary and guidance on what procedures the application of the principles may produce accompanies each principle.

These principles are not prescriptive. They are intended to be flexible and outcome focussed, allowing for the huge variety of circumstances that commercial organisations find themselves in. Small organisations will, for example, face different challenges to those faced by large multi-national enterprises. Accordingly, the detail of how organisations might apply these principles, taken as a whole, will vary, but the outcome should always be robust and effective anti-bribery procedures.

As set out in more detail below, bribery prevention procedures should be proportionate to risk. Although commercial organisations with entirely domestic operations may require bribery prevention procedures, we believe that as a general proposition they will face lower risks of bribery on their behalf by associated persons than the risks that operate in foreign markets. In any event procedures put in place to mitigate domestic bribery risks are likely to be similar if not the same as those designed to mitigate those associated with foreign markets.

A series of case studies based on hypothetical scenarios is provided at Appendix A. These are designed to illustrate the application of the principles for small, medium and large organisations.

Principle 1
Proportionate procedures

A commercial organisation's procedures to prevent bribery by persons associated with it are proportionate to the bribery risks it faces and to the nature, scale and complexity of the commercial organisation's activities. They are also clear, practical, accessible, effectively implemented and enforced.

Commentary

1.1   The term 'procedures' is used in this guidance to embrace both bribery prevention policies and the procedures which implement them. Policies articulate a commercial organisation's anti-bribery stance, show how it will be maintained and help to create an anti-bribery culture. They are therefore a necessary measure in the prevention of bribery, but they will not achieve that objective unless they are properly implemented. Further guidance on implementation is provided through principles 2 to 6.

1.2   Adequate bribery prevention procedures ought to be proportionate to the bribery risks that the organisation faces. An initial assessment of risk across the organisation is therefore a necessary first step. To a certain extent the level of risk will be linked to the size of the organisation and the nature and complexity of its business, but size will not be the only determining factor. Some small organisations can face quite significant risks, and will need more extensive procedures than their counterparts facing limited risks. However, small organisations are unlikely to need procedures that are as extensive as those of a large multi-national organisation. For example, a very small business may be able to rely heavily on periodic oral briefings to communicate its policies while a large one may need to rely on extensive written communication.

1.3   The level of risk that organisations face will also vary with the type and nature of the persons associated with it. For example, a commercial organisation that properly assesses that there is no risk of bribery on the part of one of its associated persons will accordingly require nothing in the way of procedures to prevent bribery in the context of that relationship. By the same token the bribery risks associated with reliance on a third party agent representing a commercial organisation in negotiations with foreign public officials may be assessed as significant and accordingly require much more in the way of procedures to mitigate those risks. Organisations are likely to need to select procedures to cover a broad range of risks but any consideration by a court in an individual case of the adequacy of procedures is likely necessarily to focus on those procedures designed to prevent bribery on the part of the associated person committing the offence in question.

1.4   Bribery prevention procedures may be stand alone or form part of wider guidance, for example on recruitment or on managing a tender process in public procurement. Whatever the chosen model, the procedures should seek to ensure there is a practical and realistic means of achieving the organisation's stated anti-bribery policy objectives across all of the organisation's functions.

1.5 The Government recognises that applying these procedures retrospectively to existing associated persons is more difficult, but this should be done over time, adopting a risk-based approach and with due allowance for what is practicable and the level of control over existing arrangements.

Procedures

1.6 Commercial organisations' bribery prevention policies are likely to include certain common elements. As an indicative and not exhaustive list, an organisation may wish to cover in its policies:

- **its commitment to bribery prevention** (see Principle 2)
- its general approach to mitigation of specific bribery risks, such as those arising from the conduct of intermediaries and agents, or those associated with hospitality and promotional expenditure, facilitation payments or political and charitable donations or contributions; (see Principle 3 on risk assessment)
- an overview of its strategy to implement its bribery prevention policies.

1.7 The procedures put in place to implement an organisation's bribery prevention policies should be designed to mitigate identified risks as well as to prevent deliberate unethical conduct on the part of associated persons. The following is an indicative and not exhaustive list of the topics that bribery prevention procedures might embrace depending on the particular risks faced:

- The involvement of the organisation's top-level management (see Principle 2).
- Risk assessment procedures (see Principle 3).
- Due diligence of existing or prospective associated persons (see Principle 4).
- The provision of gifts, hospitality and promotional expenditure; charitable and political donations; or demands for facilitation payments.
- Direct and indirect employment, including recruitment, terms and conditions, disciplinary action and remuneration.
- Governance of business relationships with all other associated persons including pre and post contractual agreements.
- Financial and commercial controls such as adequate bookkeeping, auditing and approval of expenditure.
- Transparency of transactions and disclosure of information.
- Decision making, such as delegation of authority procedures, separation of functions and the avoidance of conflicts of interest.
- Enforcement, detailing discipline processes and sanctions for breaches of the organisation's anti-bribery rules.
- The reporting of bribery including 'speak up' or 'whistle blowing' procedures.
- The detail of the process by which the organisation plans to implement its bribery prevention procedures, for example, how its policy will be applied to individual projects and to different parts of the organisation.
- The communication of the organisation's policies and procedures, and training in their application (see Principle 5).
- The monitoring, review and evaluation of bribery prevention procedures (see Principle 6).

The Bribery Act 2010 - Guidance

Principle 2
Top-level commitment

The top-level management of a commercial organisation (be it a board of directors, the owners or any other equivalent body or person) are committed to preventing bribery by persons associated with it. They foster a culture within the organisation in which bribery is never acceptable.

Commentary

2.1 Those at the top of an organisation are in the best position to foster a culture of integrity where bribery is unacceptable. The purpose of this principle is to encourage the involvement of top-level management in the determination of bribery prevention procedures. It is also to encourage top-level involvement in any key decision making relating to bribery risk where that is appropriate for the organisation's management structure.

Procedures

2.2 Whatever the size, structure or market of a commercial organisation, top-level management commitment to bribery prevention is likely to include (1) communication of the organisation's anti-bribery stance, and (2) an appropriate degree of involvement in developing bribery prevention procedures.

Internal and external communication of the commitment to zero tolerance to bribery

2.3 This could take a variety of forms. A formal statement appropriately communicated can be very effective in establishing an anti-bribery culture within an organisation. Communication might be tailored to different audiences. The statement would probably need to be drawn to people's attention on a periodic basis and could be generally available, for example on an organisation's intranet and/or internet site. Effective formal statements that demonstrate top level commitment are likely to include:

- a commitment to carry out business fairly, honestly and openly
- a commitment to zero tolerance towards bribery
- the consequences of breaching the policy for employees and managers
- for other associated persons the consequences of breaching contractual provisions relating to bribery prevention (this could include a reference to avoiding doing business with others who do not commit to doing business without bribery as a 'best practice' objective)
- articulation of the business benefits of rejecting bribery (reputational, customer and business partner confidence)
- reference to the range of bribery prevention procedures the commercial organisation has or is putting in place, including any protection and procedures for confidential reporting of bribery (whistle-blowing)
- key individuals and departments involved in the development and implementation of the organisation's bribery prevention procedures
- reference to the organisation's involvement in any collective action against bribery in, for example, the same business sector.

Top-level involvement in bribery prevention

2.4   Effective leadership in bribery prevention will take a variety of forms appropriate for and proportionate to the organisation's size, management structure and circumstances. In smaller organisations a proportionate response may require top-level managers to be personally involved in initiating, developing and implementing bribery prevention procedures and bribery critical decision making. In a large multi-national organisation the board should be responsible for setting bribery prevention policies, tasking management to design, operate and monitor bribery prevention procedures, and keeping these policies and procedures under regular review. But whatever the appropriate model, top-level engagement is likely to reflect the following elements:

- Selection and training of senior managers to lead anti-bribery work where appropriate.
- Leadership on key measures such as a code of conduct.
- Endorsement of all bribery prevention related publications.
- Leadership in awareness raising and encouraging transparent dialogue throughout the organisation so as to seek to ensure effective dissemination of anti-bribery policies and procedures to employees, subsidiaries, and associated persons, etc.

- Engagement with relevant associated persons and external bodies, such as sectoral organisations and the media, to help articulate the organisation's policies.
- Specific involvement in high profile and critical decision making where appropriate.
- Assurance of risk assessment.
- General oversight of breaches of procedures and the provision of feedback to the board or equivalent, where appropriate, on levels of compliance.

Principle 3
Risk Assessment

The commercial organisation assesses the nature and extent of its exposure to potential external and internal risks of bribery on its behalf by persons associated with it. The assessment is periodic, informed and documented.

Commentary

3.1 For many commercial organisations this principle will manifest itself as part of a more general risk assessment carried out in relation to business objectives. For others, its application may produce a more specific stand alone bribery risk assessment. The purpose of this principle is to promote the adoption of risk assessment procedures that are proportionate to the organisation's size and structure and to the nature, scale and location of its activities. But whatever approach is adopted the fuller the understanding of the bribery risks an organisation faces the more effective its efforts to prevent bribery are likely to be.

3.2 Some aspects of risk assessment involve procedures that fall within the generally accepted meaning of the term 'due diligence'. The role of due diligence as a risk mitigation tool is separately dealt with under Principle 4.

Procedures

3.3 Risk assessment procedures that enable the commercial organisation accurately to identify and prioritise the risks it faces will, whatever its size, activities, customers or markets, usually reflect a few basic characteristics. These are:

- Oversight of the risk assessment by top level management.
- Appropriate resourcing – this should reflect the scale of the organisation's business and the need to identify and prioritise all relevant risks.
- Identification of the internal and external information sources that will enable risk to be assessed and reviewed.
- Due diligence enquiries (see Principle 4).
- Accurate and appropriate documentation of the risk assessment and its conclusions.

3.4 As a commercial organisation's business evolves, so will the bribery risks it faces and hence so should its risk assessment. For example, the risk assessment that applies to a commercial organisation's domestic operations might not apply when it enters a new market in a part of the world in which it has not done business before (see Principle 6 for more on this).

The Bribery Act 2010 – Guidance

Commonly encountered risks

3.5 Commonly encountered external risks can be categorised into five broad groups – country, sectoral, transaction, business opportunity and business partnership:

- *Country risk:* this is evidenced by perceived high levels of corruption, an absence of effectively implemented anti-bribery legislation and a failure of the foreign government, media, local business community and civil society effectively to promote transparent procurement and investment policies.
- *Sectoral risk:* some sectors are higher risk than others. Higher risk sectors include the extractive industries and the large scale infrastructure sector.
- *Transaction risk:* certain types of transaction give rise to higher risks, for example, charitable or political contributions, licences and permits, and transactions relating to public procurement.
- *Business opportunity risk:* such risks might arise in high value projects or with projects involving many contractors or intermediaries; or with projects which are not apparently undertaken at market prices, or which do not have a clear legitimate objective.
- *Business partnership risk:* certain relationships may involve higher risk, for example, the use of intermediaries in transactions with foreign public officials; consortia or joint venture partners; and relationships with politically exposed persons where the proposed business relationship involves, or is linked to, a prominent public official.

3.6 An assessment of external bribery risks is intended to help decide how those risks can be mitigated by procedures governing the relevant operations or business relationships; but a bribery risk assessment should also examine the extent to which internal structures or procedures may themselves add to the level of risk. Commonly encountered internal factors may include:

- deficiencies in employee training, skills and knowledge
- bonus culture that rewards excessive risk taking
- lack of clarity in the organisation's policies on, and procedures for, hospitality and promotional expenditure, and political or charitable contributions
- lack of clear financial controls
- lack of a clear anti-bribery message from the top-level management.

Principle 4
Due diligence

The commercial organisation applies due diligence procedures, taking a proportionate and risk based approach, in respect of persons who perform or will perform services for or on behalf of the organisation, in order to mitigate identified bribery risks.

Commentary

4.1 Due diligence is firmly established as an element of corporate good governance and it is envisaged that due diligence related to bribery prevention will often form part of a wider due diligence framework. Due diligence procedures are both a form of bribery risk assessment (see Principle 3) and a means of mitigating a risk. By way of illustration, a commercial organisation may identify risks that as a general proposition attach to doing business in reliance upon local third party intermediaries. Due diligence of specific prospective third party intermediaries could significantly mitigate these risks. The significance of the role of due diligence in bribery risk mitigation justifies its inclusion here as a Principle in its own right.

4.2 The purpose of this Principle is to encourage commercial organisations to put in place due diligence procedures that adequately inform the application of proportionate measures designed to prevent persons associated with them from bribing on their behalf.

Procedures

4.3 As this guidance emphasises throughout, due diligence procedures should be proportionate to the identified risk. They can also be undertaken internally or by external consultants. A person 'associated' with a commercial organisation as set out at section 8 of the Bribery Act includes any person performing services for a commercial organisation. As explained at paragraphs 37 to 43 in the section 'Government Policy and section 7', the scope of this definition is broad and can embrace a wide range of business relationships. But the appropriate level of due diligence to prevent bribery will vary enormously depending on the risks arising from the particular relationship. So, for example, the appropriate level of due diligence required by a commercial organisation when contracting for the performance of information technology services may be low, to reflect low risks of bribery on its behalf. In contrast, an organisation that is selecting an intermediary to assist in establishing a business in foreign markets will typically require a much higher level of due diligence to mitigate the risks of bribery on its behalf.

4.4 Organisations will need to take considerable care in entering into certain business relationships, due to the particular circumstances in which the relationships come into existence. An example is where local law or convention dictates the use of local agents in circumstances where it may be difficult for a commercial organisation to extricate itself from a business relationship once established. The importance of thorough due diligence and risk mitigation prior to any commitment are paramount in such circumstances. Another relationship that carries particularly important due diligence implications is a merger of commercial organisations or an acquisition of one by another.

4.5 'Due diligence' for the purposes of Principle 4 should be conducted using a risk-based approach (as referred to on page 27). For example, in lower risk situations, commercial organisations may decide that there is no need to conduct much in the way of due diligence. In higher risk situations, due diligence may include conducting direct interrogative enquiries, indirect investigations, or general research on proposed associated persons. Appraisal and continued monitoring of recruited or engaged 'associated' persons may also be required, proportionate to the identified risks. Generally, more information is likely to be required from prospective and existing associated persons that are incorporated (e.g. companies) than from individuals. This is because on a basic level more individuals are likely to be involved in the performance of services by a company and the exact nature of the roles of such individuals or other connected bodies may not be immediately obvious. Accordingly, due diligence may involve direct requests for details on the background, expertise and business experience, of relevant individuals. This information can then be verified through research and the following up of references, etc.

4.6 A commercial organisation's employees are presumed to be persons 'associated' with the organisation for the purposes of the Bribery Act. The organisation may wish, therefore, to incorporate in its recruitment and human resources procedures an appropriate level of due diligence to mitigate the risks of bribery being undertaken by employees which is proportionate to the risk associated with the post in question. Due diligence is unlikely to be needed in relation to lower risk posts.

Principle 5
Communication (including training)

The commercial organisation seeks to ensure that its bribery prevention policies and procedures are embedded and understood throughout the organisation through internal and external communication, including training, that is proportionate to the risks it faces.

Commentary

5.1 Communication and training deters bribery by associated persons by enhancing awareness and understanding of a commercial organisation's procedures and to the organisation's commitment to their proper application. Making information available assists in more effective monitoring, evaluation and review of bribery prevention procedures. Training provides the knowledge and skills needed to employ the organisation's procedures and deal with any bribery related problems or issues that may arise.

Procedures
Communication

5.2 The content, language and tone of communications for internal consumption may vary from that for external use in response to the different relationship the audience has with the commercial organisation. The nature of communication will vary enormously between commercial organisations in accordance with the different bribery risks faced, the size of the organisation and the scale and nature of its activities.

5.3 Internal communications should convey the 'tone from the top' but are also likely to focus on the implementation of the organisation's policies and procedures and the implications for employees. Such communication includes policies on particular areas such as decision making, financial control, hospitality and promotional expenditure, facilitation payments, training, charitable and political donations and penalties for breach of rules and the articulation of management roles at different levels. Another important aspect of internal communications is the establishment of a secure, confidential and accessible means for internal or external parties to raise concerns about bribery on the part of associated persons, to provide suggestions for improvement of bribery prevention procedures and controls and for requesting advice. These so called 'speak up' procedures can amount to a very helpful management tool for commercial organisations with diverse operations that may be in many countries. If these procedures are to be effective there must be adequate protection for those reporting concerns.

5.4 External communication of bribery prevention policies through a statement or codes of conduct, for example, can reassure existing and prospective associated persons and can act as a deterrent to those intending to bribe on a commercial organisation's behalf. Such communications can include information on bribery prevention procedures and controls, sanctions, results of internal surveys, rules governing recruitment, procurement and tendering. A commercial organisation may consider it proportionate and appropriate to communicate its anti-bribery policies and commitment to them to a wider audience, such as other organisations in its sector and to sectoral organisations that would fall outside the scope of the range of its associated persons, or to the general public.

Training

5.5　Like all procedures training should be proportionate to risk but some training is likely to be effective in firmly establishing an anti-bribery culture whatever the level of risk. Training may take the form of education and awareness raising about the threats posed by bribery in general and in the sector or areas in which the organisation operates in particular, and the various ways it is being addressed.

5.6　General training could be mandatory for new employees or for agents (on a weighted risk basis) as part of an induction process, but it should also be tailored to the specific risks associated with specific posts. Consideration should also be given to tailoring training to the special needs of those involved in any 'speak up' procedures, and higher risk functions such as purchasing, contracting, distribution and marketing, and working in high risk countries. Effective training is continuous, and regularly monitored and evaluated.

5.7　It may be appropriate to require associated persons to undergo training. This will be particularly relevant for high risk associated persons. In any event, organisations may wish to encourage associated persons to adopt bribery prevention training.

5.8　Nowadays there are many different training formats available in addition to the traditional classroom or seminar formats, such as e-learning and other web-based tools. But whatever the format, the training ought to achieve its objective of ensuring that those participating in it develop a firm understanding of what the relevant policies and procedures mean in practice for them.

Principle 6
Monitoring and review

The commercial organisation monitors and reviews procedures designed to prevent bribery by persons associated with it and makes improvements where necessary.

Commentary

6.1 The bribery risks that a commercial organisation faces may change over time, as may the nature and scale of its activities, so the procedures required to mitigate those risks are also likely to change. Commercial organisations will therefore wish to consider how to monitor and evaluate the effectiveness of their bribery prevention procedures and adapt them where necessary. In addition to regular monitoring, an organisation might want to review its processes in response to other stimuli, for example governmental changes in countries in which they operate, an incident of bribery or negative press reports.

Procedures

6.2 There is a wide range of internal and external review mechanisms which commercial organisations could consider using. Systems set up to deter, detect and investigate bribery, and monitor the ethical quality of transactions, such as internal financial control mechanisms, will help provide insight into the effectiveness of procedures designed to prevent bribery. Staff surveys, questionnaires and feedback from training can also provide an important source of information on effectiveness and a means by which employees and other associated persons can inform continuing improvement of anti-bribery policies.

6.3 Organisations could also consider formal periodic reviews and reports for top-level management. Organisations could also draw on information on other organisations' practices, for example relevant trade bodies or regulators might highlight examples of good or bad practice in their publications.

6.4 In addition, organisations might wish to consider seeking some form of external verification or assurance of the effectiveness of anti-bribery procedures. Some organisations may be able to apply for certified compliance with one of the independently-verified anti-bribery standards maintained by industrial sector associations or multilateral bodies. However, such certification may not necessarily mean that a commercial organisation's bribery prevention procedures are 'adequate' for all purposes where an offence under section 7 of the Bribery Act could be charged.

Appendix A
Bribery Act 2010 case studies

Introduction

These case studies (which do not form part of the guidance issued under section 9 of the Act) look at how the application of the six principles might relate to a number of hypothetical scenarios commercial organisations may encounter. The Government believes that this illustrative context can assist commercial organisations in deciding what procedures to prevent persons associated with them from bribing on their behalf might be most suitable to their needs.

These case studies are illustrative. They are intended to complement the guidance. They do not replace or supersede any of the principles. The considerations set out below merely show in some circumstances how the principles can be applied, and should not be seen as standard setting, establishing any presumption, reflecting a minimum baseline of action or being appropriate for all organisations whatever their size. Accordingly, the considerations set out below are not:

- comprehensive of all considerations in all circumstances
- conclusive of adequate procedures
- conclusive of inadequate procedures if not all of the considerations are considered and/or applied.

All but one of these case studies focus on bribery risks associated with foreign markets. This is because bribery risks associated with foreign markets are generally higher than those associated with domestic markets. Accordingly case studies focussing on foreign markets are better suited as vehicles for the illustration of bribery prevention procedures.

Case study 1 – Principle 1
Facilitation payments

A medium sized company ('A') has acquired a new customer in a foreign country ('B') where it operates through its agent company ('C'). Its bribery risk assessment has identified facilitation payments as a significant problem in securing reliable importation into B and transport to its new customer's manufacturing locations. These sometimes take the form of 'inspection fees' required before B's import inspectors will issue a certificate of inspection and thereby facilitate the clearance of goods.

A could consider any or a combination of the following:

- Communication of its policy of non-payment of facilitation payments to C and its staff.
- Seeking advice on the law of B relating to certificates of inspection and fees for these to differentiate between properly payable fees and disguised requests for facilitation payments.
- Building realistic timescales into the planning of the project so that shipping, importation and delivery schedules allow where feasible for resisting and testing demands for facilitation payments.
- Requesting that C train its staff about resisting demands for facilitation payments and the relevant local law and provisions of the Bribery Act 2010.
- Proposing or including as part of any contractual arrangement certain procedures for C and its staff, which may include one or more of the following, if appropriate:
  - questioning of legitimacy of demands
  - requesting receipts and identification details of the official making the demand
  - requests to consult with superior officials
  - trying to avoid paying 'inspection fees' (if not properly due) in cash and directly to an official
  - informing those demanding payments that compliance with the demand may mean that A (and possibly C) will commit an offence under UK law
  - informing those demanding payments that it will be necessary for C to inform the UK embassy of the demand.
- Maintaining close liaison with C so as to keep abreast of any local developments that may provide solutions and encouraging C to develop its own strategies based on local knowledge.
- Use of any UK diplomatic channels or participation in locally active non-governmental organisations, so as to apply pressure on the authorities of B to take action to stop demands for facilitation payments.

Case study 2 – Principle 1
Proportionate Procedures

A small to medium sized installation company is operating entirely within the United Kingdom domestic market. It relies to varying degrees on independent consultants to facilitate business opportunities and to assist in the preparation of both pre-qualification submissions and formal tenders in seeking new business. Such consultants work on an arms-length-fee-plus-expenses basis. They are engaged by sales staff and selected because of their extensive network of business contacts and the specialist information they have. The reason for engaging them is to enhance the company's prospects of being included in tender and pre-qualification lists and of being selected as main or sub-contractors. The reliance on consultants and, in particular, difficulties in monitoring expenditure which sometimes involves cash transactions has been identified by the company as a source of medium to high risk of bribery being undertaken on the company's behalf.

In seeking to mitigate these risks the company could consider any or a combination of the following:

- Communication of a policy statement committing it to transparency and zero tolerance of bribery in pursuit of its business objectives. The statement could be communicated to the company's employees, known consultants and external contacts, such as sectoral bodies and local chambers of commerce.
- Firming up its due diligence before engaging consultants. This could include making enquiries through business contacts, local chambers of commerce, business associations, or internet searches and following up any business references and financial statements.
- Considering firming up the terms of the consultants' contracts so that they reflect a commitment to zero tolerance of bribery, set clear criteria for provision of bona fide hospitality on the company's behalf and define in detail the basis of remuneration, including expenses.
- Consider making consultants' contracts subject to periodic review and renewal.
- Drawing up key points guidance on preventing bribery for its sales staff and all other staff involved in bidding for business and when engaging consultants
- Periodically emphasising these policies and procedures at meetings – for example, this might form a standing item on meeting agendas every few months.
- Providing a confidential means for staff and external business contacts to air any suspicions of the use of bribery on the company's behalf.

Case study 3 – Principles 1 and 6
Joint venture

A medium sized company ('D') is interested in significant foreign mineral deposits. D proposes to enter into a joint venture with a local mining company ('E'). It is proposed that D and E would have an equal holding in the joint venture company ('DE'). D identifies the necessary interaction between DE and local public officials as a source of significant risks of bribery.

D could consider negotiating for the inclusion of any or a combination of the following bribery prevention procedures into the agreement setting up DE:

- Parity of representation on the board of DE.
- That DE put in place measures designed to ensure compliance with all applicable bribery and corruption laws. These measures might cover such issues as:
  - gifts and hospitality
  - agreed decision making rules
  - procurement
  - engagement of third parties, including due diligence requirements
  - conduct of relations with public officials
  - training for staff in high risk positions
  - record keeping and accounting.
- The establishment of an audit committee with at least one representative of each of D and E that has the power to view accounts and certain expenditure and prepare regular reports.

- Binding commitments by D and E to comply with all applicable bribery laws in relation to the operation of DE, with a breach by either D or E being a breach of the agreement between them. Where such a breach is a material breach this could lead to termination or other similarly significant consequences.

Case study 4 – Principles 1 and 5
Hospitality and Promotional expenditure

A firm of engineers ('F') maintains a programme of annual events providing entertainment, quality dining and attendance at various sporting occasions, as an expression of appreciation of its long association with its business partners. Private bodies and individuals are happy to meet their own travel and accommodation costs associated with attending these events. The costs of the travel and accommodation of any foreign public officials attending are, however, met by F.

F could consider any or a combination of the following:

- Conducting a bribery risk assessment relating to its dealings with business partners and foreign public officials and in particular the provision of hospitality and promotional expenditure.
- Publication of a policy statement committing it to transparent, proportionate, reasonable and bona fide hospitality and promotional expenditure.
- The issue of internal guidance on procedures that apply to the provision of hospitality and/or promotional expenditure providing:
  - that any procedures are designed to seek to ensure transparency and conformity with any relevant laws and codes applying to F
  - that any procedures are designed to seek to ensure transparency and conformity with the relevant laws and codes applying to foreign public officials
  - that any hospitality should reflect a desire to cement good relations and show appreciation, and that promotional expenditure should seek to improve the image of F as a commercial organisation, to better present its products or services, or establish cordial relations
  - that the recipient should not be given the impression that they are under an obligation to confer any business advantage or that the recipient's independence will be affected
  - criteria to be applied when deciding the appropriate levels of hospitality for both private and public business partners, clients, suppliers and foreign public officials and the type of hospitality that is appropriate in different sets of circumstances
  - that provision of hospitality for public officials be cleared with the relevant public body so that it is clear who and what the hospitality is for
  - for expenditure over certain limits, approval by an appropriately senior level of management may be a relevant consideration
  - accounting (book-keeping, orders, invoices, delivery notes, etc).
- Regular monitoring, review and evaluation of internal procedures and compliance with them.
- Appropriate training and supervision provided to staff.

Case study 5 – Principle 3
Assessing risks

A small specialist manufacturer is seeking to expand its business in one of several emerging markets, all of which offer comparable opportunities. It has no specialist risk assessment expertise and is unsure how to go about assessing the risks of entering a new market.

The small manufacturer could consider any or a combination of the following:

- Incorporating an assessment of bribery risk into research to identify the optimum market for expansion.
- Seeking advice from UK diplomatic services and government organisations such as UK Trade and Investment.
- Consulting general country assessments undertaken by local chambers of commerce, relevant non-governmental organisations and sectoral organisations.
- Seeking advice from industry representatives.
- Following up any general or specialist advice with further independent research.

Case study 6 – Principle 4
Due diligence of agents

A medium to large sized manufacturer of specialist equipment ('G') has an opportunity to enter an emerging market in a foreign country ('H') by way of a government contract to supply equipment to the state. Local convention requires any foreign commercial organisations to operate through a local agent. G is concerned to appoint a reputable agent and ensure that the risk of bribery being used to develop its business in the market is minimised.

G could consider any or a combination of the following:

- Compiling a suitable questionnaire for potential agents requiring for example, details of ownership if not an individual; CVs and references for those involved in performing the proposed service; details of any directorships held, existing partnerships and third party relationships and any relevant judicial or regulatory findings.
- Having a clear statement of the precise nature of the services offered, costs, commissions, fees and the preferred means of remuneration.
- Undertaking research, including internet searches, of the prospective agents and, if a corporate body, of every person identified as having a degree of control over its affairs.
- Making enquiries with the relevant authorities in H to verify the information received in response to the questionnaire.
- Following up references and clarifying any matters arising from the questionnaire or any other information received with the agents, arranging face to face meetings where appropriate.

- Requesting sight or evidence of any potential agent's own anti-bribery policies and, where a corporate body, reporting procedures and records.
- Being alert to key commercial questions such as:
  - Is the agent really required?
  - Does the agent have the required expertise?
  - Are they interacting with or closely connected to public officials?
  - Is what you are proposing to pay reasonable and commercial?
- Renewing due diligence enquiries on a periodic basis if an agent is appointed.

Case study 7 – Principle 5
Communicating and training

A small UK manufacturer of specialist equipment ('J') has engaged an individual as a local agent and adviser ('K') to assist with winning a contract and developing its business in a foreign country where the risk of bribery is assessed as high.

J could consider any or a combination of the following:

- Making employees of J engaged in bidding for business fully aware of J's anti-bribery statement, code of conduct and, where appropriate, that details of its anti-bribery policies are included in its tender.
- Including suitable contractual terms on bribery prevention measures in the agreement between J and K, for example: requiring K not to offer or pay bribes; giving J the ability to audit K's activities and expenditure; requiring K to report any requests for bribes by officials to J; and, in the event of suspicion arising as to K's activities, giving J the right to terminate the arrangement.
- Making employees of J fully aware of policies and procedures applying to relevant issues such as hospitality and facilitation payments, including all financial control mechanisms, sanctions for any breaches of the rules and instructions on how to report any suspicious conduct.
- Supplementing the information, where appropriate, with specially prepared training to J's staff involved with the foreign country.

Case study 8 – Principle 1, 4 and 6
Community benefits and charitable donations

A company ('L') exports a range of seed products to growers around the globe. Its representative travels to a foreign country ('M') to discuss with a local farming co-operative the possible supply of a new strain of wheat that is resistant to a disease which recently swept the region. In the meeting, the head of the co-operative tells L's representative about the problems which the relative unavailability of antiretroviral drugs cause locally in the face of a high HIV infection rate.

In a subsequent meeting with an official of M to discuss the approval of L's new wheat strain for import, the official suggests that L could pay for the necessary antiretroviral drugs and that this will be a very positive factor in the Government's consideration of the licence to import the new seed strain. In a further meeting, the same official states that L should donate money to a certain charity suggested by the official which, the official assures, will then take the necessary steps to purchase and distribute the drugs. L identifies this as raising potential bribery risks.

L could consider any or a combination of the following:

- Making reasonable efforts to conduct due diligence, including consultation with staff members and any business partners it has in country M in order to satisfy itself that the suggested arrangement is legitimate and in conformity with any relevant laws and codes applying to the foreign public official responsible for approving the product. It could do this by obtaining information on:

  - M's local law on community benefits as part of Government procurement and, if no particular local law, the official status and legitimacy of the suggested arrangement
  - the particular charity in question including its legal status, its reputation in M, and whether it has conducted similar projects, and
  - any connections the charity might have with the foreign official in question, if possible.

- Adopting an internal communication plan designed to ensure that any relationships with charitable organisations are conducted in a transparent and open manner and do not raise any expectation of the award of a contract or licence.

- Adopting company-wide policies and procedures about the selection of charitable projects or initiatives which are informed by appropriate risk assessments.

- Training and support for staff in implementing the relevant policies and procedures of communication which allow issues to be reported and compliance to be monitored.

- If charitable donations made in country M are routinely channelled through government officials or to others at the official's request, a red flag should be raised and L may seek to monitor the way its contributions are ultimately applied, or investigate alternative methods of donation such as official 'off-set' or 'community gain' arrangements with the government of M.

- Evaluation of its policies relating to charitable donations as part of its next periodic review of its anti-bribery procedures.

Case study 9 – Principle 4
Due diligence of agents

A small UK company ('N') relies on agents in country ('P') from which it imports local high quality perishable produce and to which it exports finished goods. The bribery risks it faces arise entirely as a result of its reliance on agents and their relationship with local businessmen and officials. N is offered a new business opportunity in P through a new agent ('Q'). An agreement with Q needs to be concluded quickly.

N could consider any or a combination of the following:

- Conducting due diligence and background checks on Q that are proportionate to the risk before engaging Q; which could include:
    - making enquiries through N's business contacts, local chambers of commerce or business associations, or internet searches
    - seeking business references and a financial statement from Q and reviewing Q's CV to ensure Q has suitable experience.
- Considering how best to structure the relationship with Q, including how Q should be remunerated for its services and how to seek to ensure Q's compliance with relevant laws and codes applying to foreign public officials.
- Making the contract with Q renewable annually or periodically.
- Travelling to P periodically to review the agency situation.

Case study 10 – Principle 2
Top level commitment

A small to medium sized component manufacturer is seeking contracts in markets abroad where there is a risk of bribery. As part of its preparation, a senior manager has devoted some time to participation in the development of a sector wide anti-bribery initiative.

The top level management of the manufacturer could consider any or a combination of the following:

- The making of a clear statement disseminated to its staff and key business partners of its commitment to carry out business fairly, honestly and openly, referencing its key bribery prevention procedures and its involvement in the sectoral initiative.
- Establishing a code of conduct that includes suitable anti-bribery provisions and making it accessible to staff and third parties on its website.
- Considering an internal launch of a code of conduct, with a message of commitment to it from senior management.
- Senior management emphasising among the workforce and other associated persons the importance of understanding and applying the code of conduct and the consequences of breaching the policy or contractual provisions relating to bribery prevention for employees and managers and external associated persons.
- Identifying someone of a suitable level of seniority to be a point-person for queries and issues relating to bribery risks.

Case study 11
Proportionate procedures

A small export company operates through agents in a number of different foreign countries. Having identified bribery risks associated with its reliance on agents it is considering developing proportionate and risk based bribery prevention procedures.

The company could consider any or a combination of the following:

- Using trade fairs and trade publications to communicate periodically its anti-bribery message and, where appropriate, some detail of its policies and procedures.
- Oral or written communication of its bribery prevention intentions to all of its agents.
- Adopting measures designed to address bribery on its behalf by associated persons, such as:
  - requesting relevant information and conducting background searches on the internet against information received
  - making sure references are in order and followed up
  - including anti-bribery commitments in any contract renewal
  - using existing internal arrangements such as periodic staff meetings to raise awareness of 'red flags' as regards agents' conduct, for example evasive answers to straightforward requests for information, overly elaborate payment arrangements involving further third parties, ad hoc or unusual requests for expense reimbursement not properly covered by accounting procedures.
- Making use of any external sources of information (UKTI, sectoral organisations) on bribery risks in particular markets and using the data to inform relationships with particular agents.
- Making sure staff have a confidential means to raise any concerns about bribery.

www.justice.gov.uk/guidance/bribery.htm

APPENDIX 18

Transparency International U.K. Anti-Bribery Due Diligence for Transactions

ANTI-BRIBERY
DUE DILIGENCE
FOR TRANSACTIONS

GUIDANCE FOR ANTI-BRIBERY
DUE DILIGENCE IN MERGERS,
ACQUISITIONS AND INVESTMENTS

SUPPORTED BY: Kroll Advisory Solutions

Transparency International (TI) is the world's leading non-governmental anti-corruption organisation. With more than 90 Chapters worldwide, TI has extensive global expertise and understanding of corruption.

Transparency International UK (TI-UK) is the UK chapter of TI. We raise awareness about corruption; advocate legal and regulatory reform at national and international levels; design practical tools for institutions, individuals and companies wishing to combat corruption; and act as a leading centre of anti-corruption expertise in the UK.

Acknowledgements

Transparency International UK is grateful to those individuals, companies and professionals who have assisted us in the course of this project. We would like to thank all those companies that have been involved in the development of the Transparency International tools on which it is based. The first draft of this document was published for public consultation in July 2011, and the final version has benefited greatly from the expertise and experience of those who engaged in the consultation process. The lead author of this document has been Peter Wilkinson.

We are particularly grateful to the following for their generous and expert advice: Jason Wright and Stefano Demichelis of Kroll Advisory Solutions; Jeremy Carver; Tony Parton of PwC; Randal Barker, Chris Vaughan and Benedict O'Halloran on behalf of the GC 100; Julian Glass on behalf of FTI Consulting; , William Jacobson of Weatherford International; and Michael Hershman of the Fairfax Group.

This publication has been kindly supported by Kroll Advisory Solutions [www.krolladvisory.com] a global leader in risk mitigation and response.

Lead Author: Peter Wilkinson
Editor: Robert Barrington, Transparency International UK
Adviser: Chandrashekhar Krishnan, Transparency International UK
Publisher: Transparency International UK

Published May 2012
ISBN 978-0-9569445-7-3

CONTENTS

TEN GOOD PRACTICE PRINCIPLES
FOR ANTI-BRIBERY DUE DILIGENCE
IN MERGERS, ACQUISITIONS AND INVESTMENTS

Internal policies and procedures

1. The purchaser (or investor)[1] has a public anti-bribery policy.

   Comment: *This will provide a reference point for the due diligence approach and also specific protection for the due diligence process - for example, in helping to ensure that no bribe should be made to obtain information or speed up the transaction, either directly or through a third party.*

2. The purchaser ensures it has an adequate anti-bribery programme that is compatible with the Business Principles for Countering Bribery or an equivalent international code or standard.

Due diligence – pre acquisition

3. Anti-bribery due diligence is considered on a proportionate basis for all investments.

   Comment: *This includes M&A transactions, acquisitions of businesses, private equity investments and other forms of investment.*

4. The level of anti-bribery due diligence for the transaction is commensurate with the bribery risks.

   Comment: *The level of bribery risk should be determined at the start of the process. This will be to ensure that the due diligence is conducted with sufficient depth and resources to be undertaken effectively.*

5. Anti-bribery due diligence starts sufficiently early in the due diligence process to allow adequate due diligence to be carried out and for the findings to influence the outcome of the negotiations or stimulate further review if necessary.

6. The partners or board provide commitment and oversight to the due diligence reviews.

   Comment: *The findings of anti-bribery due diligence should be properly examined and understood at the highest level of decision-making during the transaction, for example at the level of the board or investment committee.*

7. Information gained during the anti-bribery due diligence is passed on efficiently and effectively to the company's management once the investment has been made.

   Comment: *For example, information about the adequacy of the anti-corruption procedures in the target company should be used to initiate remedial action.*

Due diligence – post acquisition

8. The purchaser starts to conduct due diligence on a proportionate basis immediately after purchase to determine if there is any current bribery and if so, takes immediate remedial action.

   Comment: *Gathering sufficiently detailed information is one of the challenges of anti-bribery due diligence. Where this has not been possible pre-closure, a full due diligence should be carried out within a set time period post-completion.*

9. The purchaser ensures that the target has or adopts an adequate anti-bribery programme equivalent to its own.

10. Bribery detected through due diligence is reported to the authorities.

    Comment: *This principle is based on the presumption that bribery discovered during due diligence should be reported to the authorities. Purchasers may use their discretion, bearing in mind factors such as proportionality in reporting, the deal timetable and their own legal obligations, but it is in their interest to report to authorities as in this way they can discuss the issue and establish how the bribery could affect the deal.*

---

1. *Hereafter referred to as 'the purchaser'*

1

1.   INTRODUCTION

This guidance relates to mergers and acquisitions (M&A), private equity investments and other forms of investment. The definitions used in this guidance are:

Transaction: merger, acquisition or investment
Target: a company that is a target for merger acquisition or investment
Purchaser: the company making a merger, acquisition or investment of any size

Purpose of this guidance

Anti-bribery due diligence can help purchasers to manage their investment risk in transactions more effectively. However, it is often not undertaken, neglected, or allocated insufficient time and resources. A recent survey found that:

"Despite the many recent examples of the perils of ignoring the fraud and corruption dimension of these assessments, a fifth of companies still do not consider it as part of M&A due diligence, and a quarter never consider it in a post-acquisition review."[2]

This guidance is intended to provide a practical tool for companies on undertaking anti-bribery due diligence in the course of mergers, acquisitions and investment. It reflects the approach for corporate anti-bribery programmes set out in the Business Principles for Countering Bribery[3], which is an anti-bribery code widely recognised as an international benchmark for good practice, and developed in close consultation with companies and other stakeholders. This guidance is provided in the context of three overarching considerations:

A good practice approach is the most effective means for companies to manage bribery risks across multiple jurisdictions and in a changing legal and enforcement environment

- Anti-bribery due diligence should be applied to all investments but on a risk-based approach, with the level of due diligence being proportionate to the investment and the perceived likelihood of risk of bribery.
- In many cases the necessary information for due diligence may not be accessible, such as in acquisition of public companies, hostile take-overs, auctions or minority investments. This does not obviate the need for anti-bribery due diligence, but has an effect on the timing – i.e., it may need to be undertaken post-closure.
- A good practice approach characterises ethical and responsible businesses, but is also the most effective means for companies to manage bribery risks across multiple jurisdictions and in a changing legal and enforcement environment.

There are three intended audiences for this guidance:

- Companies that are considering or are undertaking a merger, acquisition or investment (hereafter referred to as a transaction);
- Companies that may be subject to due diligence, as companies positioning themselves to be acquired must also prepare themselves to be ready to meet the standards required in anti-bribery due diligence; and
- Professional firms and advisers that are involved in transactions and related due diligence.

---

2. *Driving ethical growth – new markets, new challenges, 11th Global Fraud Survey, Ernst & Young, 2011*

3. *www.transparency.org*

2

The broad principles and approaches to anti-bribery due diligence apply both to M&A transactions and private equity investments, and this guidance is therefore written for both audiences. However, the type of transaction and the size of the stake will clearly have an effect on the purchaser's ability and resources to undertake due diligence, its assessment of investment risks accruing from bribery, and its ability to access and influence the target company.

This guidance provides a generic framework for applying due diligence, but purchasers will need to decide in each case what level of due diligence is appropriate. Some targets will be judged to present low risks and to require lower levels of due diligence whereas others will have higher risks. The size of investment should not be a determining factor as small investments can carry disproportionate risks; and moreover the material risks attached to bribery may not necessarily reflect the size of the bribe.

A good practice approach is that the level of due diligence is proportionate to the bribery risks; however, the effectiveness of a risk-based approach depends on an adequate understanding of the risks, which may easily be overlooked due to factors such as pressure of time, poor quality information or members of the deal team being insufficiently experienced. A proper assessment of what is proportionate can only be made if the risks are properly understood. This in itself will require an early-stage allocation of resources and a genuine commitment to make an effective assessment.

> **What to look for in anti-bribery due diligence**
>
> - Has bribery taken place historically?
> - Is it possible or likely that bribery is currently taking place?
> - If so, how widespread is it likely to be?
> - What is the commitment of the board and top management of the target to countering bribery?
> - Does the target have in place an adequate anti-bribery programme to prevent bribery?
> - What would the likely impact be if bribery, historical or current, were discovered after the transaction had completed?

A changing environment

Deal-making can take place across multiple jurisdictions, and purchasers are faced with a changing legislative environment exemplified by the UK Bribery Act 2010 and new anti-bribery laws in Russia and China. Increasing enforcement in several jurisdictions, and most notably of the FCPA in the United States, presents heightened risks of criminal and civil penalties for individuals and companies. In 2010, companies settling FCPA-related charges in 2010 paid a record $1.8 billion in financial penalties to the DOJ and SEC compared to $641 million in 2009 and $890 million in 2008.

Almost 50% of US corruption-related prosecutions in 2007 were connected to M&A transactions.

In addition to legislation, there are changing expectations by stakeholders including governments, regulators, institutional investors, consumers, the media and civil society. Growing demands for integrity, responsibility, accountability and transparency are transforming the environment for purchasers and investors.

The UK's Serious Fraud Office (SFO) has made several statements about the responsibilities and liabilities of private equity and institutional investors – for example, in January 2012 it said: "Shareholders and investors in companies are obliged to satisfy themselves with the business practices of the companies they invest in…. It is particularly so for institutional investors who

3

have the knowledge and expertise to do it. The SFO intends to use the civil recovery process to pursue investors who have benefitted from illegal activity. Where issues arise, we will be much less sympathetic to institutional investors whose due diligence has clearly been lax in this respect."[4]

Deal flows are also changing, with M&A activity and private equity investments increasingly taking place in emerging markets where corruption is known to be prevalent. In the other direction, companies from the emerging nations are ever more active in purchases of companies from developed countries and must beware the attention of regulators. Companies positioning themselves to be acquired must also prepare themselves to be ready to meet the standards required in anti-bribery due diligence.

Companies positioning themselves to be acquired must also prepare themselves to be ready to meet the standards required in anti-bribery due diligence

Challenges of anti-bribery due diligence

Combined with the higher expectations being placed on purchasers with regard to due diligence, there are also significant challenges in carrying out due diligence.

One such limitation in carrying out due diligence is that information is often just not available as the target, even in a friendly acquisition, may be reluctant to provide or not have sufficient information or if a public company, there may be restrictions on what can be provided. Where there is a hostile acquisition or purchase through an auction, the purchaser may not be able to gain access to all necessary information. In such circumstances, the purchaser will have to rely on the limited available information before acquisition, judge whether to proceed and then carry out immediate and thorough due diligence after the acquisition is completed.

Other challenges may include time pressure, lack of senior management support and insufficient expertise in the deal team. A further pressure in some transactions may be because of a flawed assessment of cost: senior managers who do not understand the risks adequately may be reluctant to commit human and financial resources to an area that they may view as relatively unimportant.

Proceeding cautiously if bribery is suspected

In the event that due diligence identifies evidence of past or current bribery, this does not necessarily mean that the purchase should be aborted. Indeed, there can be a net benefit if a company with an anti-bribery culture takes over a company with a less rigorous approach. The prospective purchaser may be able to agree with the enforcement authorities a grace period, following acquisition, during which agreed mitigation steps are carried out.

---

4. *SFO press release of 13 January 2012 – 'Shareholder agrees civil recovery by SFO in Mabey & Johnson'*

4

2. INVESTMENT RISK AND THE ROLE OF ANTI-BRIBERY DUE DILIGENCE

The Purchaser's board members, senior management and investment committees should seek to develop a full understanding of bribery risks related to target companies during transactions in order to understand the **investment risk**. The nature of the investment risk from bribery falls into four broad areas:

- Financial: the financial data may be distorted or falsified, e.g., the target's sales figures may be inflated by contracts obtained through bribe-paying;
- Legal: there may be inheritance of legal risks e.g., the purchaser may incur liability, leading to fines and regulatory action;
- Reputational: for example, the purchaser may find that, owing to publicity surrounding a poor acquisition, it is regarded as a less favourable partner or investment vehicle by others, including institutional investors; and
- Ethical: purchasing companies, or acquiring individuals within those companies, that are willing to engage in bribery, risks infecting the ethical culture of the purchaser and having a deleterious effect on the organisation. A corrupt target may introduce dishonesty and corruption to the purchaser's own activities.

Bribery risk is a general term used to describe the likelihood that bribery has been, or continues to be, present in any aspect of a target's business practices. The due diligence process is designed to discover, or determine the likelihood of, both current and historical bribery in the target company. The due diligence may reveal this either during the transaction or post-closure.

There is a distinction between *inherent bribery risk* and *residual bribery risk*. Inherent risk exists in all geographies, all sectors and all transactions, but to a degree that varies according to factors such as the frequency with which bribes are typically paid in a particular country, sector or type of transaction. The residual bribery risk is the remaining risk after steps have been taken to mitigate the inherent risk. What is important, therefore, is to identify the inherent risks within the business being acquired and to understand what, if anything, the target does to minimise and manage the risks. The residual bribery risk is ultimately the key matter for the acquirer to consider.

While it is likely that much anti-bribery due diligence will be driven by compliance with legal obligations, it is important to recognise that taking a good practice approach is the best way to counter the risks of legal liabilities and the financial and reputational damage that may come from purchasing or investing in a company associated with bribery. Following good practice should also help companies to be compliant with the provisions of anti-bribery legislation in the multiple jurisdictions in which they operate including the UK Bribery Act and US Foreign Corrupt Practices Act (FCPA).

There are typically additional benefits of conducting anti-bribery due diligence over and above the direct benefits of bribery risk management:

- Management quality indicator: purchasers and investors, when conducting evaluation, should assess the positive qualities of the target including the excellence of management and its systems. Evidence from due diligence of a good practice and effective anti-bribery programme is an indicator of management quality;

> The due diligence process is designed to discover, or determine the likelihood of, both current and historical bribery in the target company

- Mitigation benefit: evidence of good practice due diligence could form part of a plea for mitigation in the event of a post-completion bribery incident or investigation of the target by the authorities;
- Reputational gain: a purchaser or investor may enhance its reputation with the target, regulators or its own investors if it shows integrity, responsibility and thoroughness during diligence; and
- Meeting investor expectations: a purchaser's or investor's limited partners and investors may seek assurances that purchasers or investors are addressing Environmental, Social and Governance risks, including bribery, during transactions.

Potential consequences of bribery in a target company

Investments made in companies that have committed or are at continuing risk from bribery are more risky investments for a number of reasons:

- The target or purchaser may face criminal, civil and financial sanctions
- Corrupt partners are unreliable and may be involved with or obligated to dubious entities and people
- Deals are at great risk of collapse
- Market value may be distorted
- Associates of the target may make a purchaser liable to investigation and prosecution
- A corrupt target may introduce dishonesty and corruption to the purchaser's own activities.

The consequences of bribery in a target company can include:

- **Diminished asset value and returns**
- Reduced investment and portfolio valuations
- Acquisition of an overvalued asset

- **Investigations and convictions**
- Criminal, civil and financial proceedings against the company
- Stringent settlement agreements
- Appointment of court monitors
- Diversion of management and board time
- Extensive professional fees

- **Business instability**
- Aborted deals
- Reputational damage and media attention
- Acquired business proves dysfunctional
- Diminished exit opportunities
- Debarment from government contracts
- Director disqualification
- Regulatory authority restrictions
- Employee de-motivation
- Loss of key people in investee companies if they are involved in bribery or convicted of an offence

- **Liability of directors, partners and officials**
- Criminal and civil penalties
- Debarment from office
- Professional damage

- **Media attention**

6

3.   THE DUE DILIGENCE PROCESS

This section outlines how anti-bribery due diligence can be integrated into standard due diligence procedures during M&A or investment activity.

SIGNPOST

Care should be taken that bribery does not take place during the investment or acquisition process itself. Such transactions can be particularly vulnerable to bribery owing to factors such as tight deadlines, the desire to obtain information, use of third parties and intermediaries, interaction with public officials over licensing, or attempts by third parties to gain access to insider information.

3.1   THE AIMS OF DUE DILIGENCE

The core aims of anti-bribery due diligence are:
- Assuring that the business to be acquired is sound and not distorted by bribery, and its apparent business value is not a product of bribery; this will include:
  - Identifying the inherent risks of bribery for the target based on indicators such as countries of operation and markets;
  - Assessing those risks particular to the target including organisational structure, integrity of the board, key managers and shareholders, and use of third parties, such as agents;
  - Assessing the adequacy of the target's anti-bribery programme with particular attention paid to risks identified in the due diligence, and thereby assessing its residual risks;
- Identifying early in the due diligence process, any bribery exposure that could cause the deal to be aborted or modified – it is better to do so earlier than later;
- Checking there will not be potential successor risks or inherited liability from bribery with resultant criminal and/or civil penalties, loss in business value and other consequences;
- Providing a basis for mitigating penalties in the event of a bribery violation by showing there was adequate due diligence;
- Providing a basis for monitoring the target once acquired to ensure the quality and effectiveness of its anti-bribery programme.

3.2   ORGANISING THE PURCHASER FOR DUE DILIGENCE

3.2.1 Due diligence policies and procedures
Anti-bribery due diligence is most effective when the purchaser itself has in place an anti-bribery programme, of which due diligence is a part. As part of its own anti-bribery programme, the purchaser should therefore establish risk-based policies and procedures for due diligence and draw on experience to improve the process.

3.2.2 Tone from the top
The 'tone from the top' is important as the starting point for effective anti-bribery due diligence. Without a commitment to anti-bribery standards, the purchaser will be sending mixed messages to those engaged in due diligence, probably leading to lack of rigour in the process. Similarly, mixed or weak messages may be sent to professional advisers and targets. Once a target has

Anti-bribery due diligence is most effective when the purchaser itself has in place an anti-bribery programme, of which due diligence is a part

been identified for potential purchase or investment, before starting the due diligence process, senior management should make a high-level review of the target and the potential bribery risks. The tone from the senior management should set the context for the due diligence process and ensure that the required attention and support is given to the process and allocate appropriate resources.

3.2.3 Internal team

Effective due diligence requires responsibilities and reporting lines to be clearly assigned, with good communication and coordination built into the process from the start. An individual should be appointed within the due diligence team with specific responsibility for anti-bribery due diligence. Depending on the nature of the target and transaction, this may require a supporting team of internal and external anti-bribery experts and others in relevant positions. The roles for those involved in due diligence will depend on the size of the purchaser and the scale and circumstances of the target.

The shortcomings of a target organisation's anti-bribery compliance framework often lie in the implementation of the programme rather than the design of policies and procedures. The expertise required to lead the due diligence should therefore require someone with good practical knowledge and experience of the effective implementation of anti bribery programmes, and knowledge of how bribes are and can be perpetrated.

The purchaser should define how the anti-bribery due diligence team will communicate and coordinate and designate responsibilities for sign-offs by management, the investment or portfolio management committee, partners or the board.

3.2.4 External advisers

Although some companies have in-house resources, in certain transactions the purchaser may rely heavily on external advisers in carrying out due diligence – these can include legal, accounting and other forensic outside advisers that offer specialist anti-corruption services. Legal advisers will wish to ensure that their report is legally privileged. A legal due diligence and an anti-corruption due diligence report can be combined or may sit separately. Where the purchaser uses external resources to assist with this aspect, it is essential that it ensures it engages ethical third parties, and that the purchaser has control over the activities carried out on its behalf.

3.2.5 Internal approvals

The board or partners of the purchaser would typically be responsible for the approval of the investment to proceed, directly or by delegation. As such, they will be responsible ultimately for ensuring that their own company has implemented adequate anti-bribery due diligence procedures during the transaction. They should receive the investment and due diligence reports and will need to review these carefully and question management as necessary to check that due diligence has been carried out to a proper extent in assessing bribery risks.

3.3 INTEGRATING ANTI-BRIBERY DUE DILIGENCE INTO THE PROCESS

Anti-bribery due diligence needs to be integrated from the start in the process to run alongside legal, financial and other due diligence. Effective integration and coordination will depend on a tone from the top of the organisation that makes clear the importance of anti-bribery due diligence. Coordination is necessary throughout the due diligence process so that the teams and advisers share knowledge and work closely together, leading to a greater probability of risks being identified and avoiding work being duplicated or omitted. Each function will have its own check-lists and research results and these should be aligned and shared.

Anti-bribery due diligence needs to be integrated from the start in the process to run alongside legal, financial and other due diligence. Effective integration and coordination will depend on a tone from the top of the organisation that makes clear the importance of anti-bribery due diligence

8

A due diligence process that follows a model template (which in practice rarely occurs) comprises six stages from the initiation of the idea to purchase to post-completion monitoring of the investment. The level of information obtained from the target is likely to influence the timing of the purchaser's ability to undertake anti-bribery due diligence. In the pre-signing period the purchaser must rely on the willingness of the target to provide access and even where there is a good relationship, there may still be constraints on what is provided. The opportunity to obtain information may increase at the signing of agreements and before closure of the deal but even then disclosures agreed as part of the signing may be limited having been negotiated at a competitive stage.

It is only after closure that the purchaser will have full access and in the event that bribery issues are discovered at this stage will need immediate resolution and may involve discussion with the authorities. Thus, however undesirable, due diligence on acquisitions must often be made on the basis of incomplete information and effective risk assessment and mitigation will rely heavily on the post-acquisition due diligence.

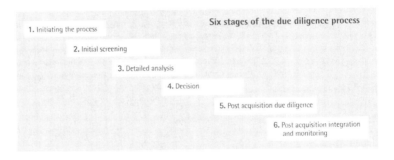

Six stages of the due diligence process

1. Initiating the process
2. Initial screening
3. Detailed analysis
4. Decision
5. Post acquisition due diligence
6. Post acquisition integration and monitoring

STAGE 1: INITIATING THE PROCESS

The process begins with a review by management to establish the scope and depth of the due diligence. Research, data collection and evaluation start at the second stage and continue throughout the stages until preparation of the report for approval.

Senior management will need to consider the likelihood of obtaining the necessary information and what should be the approach in such a case. Even if there is cooperation from the target, there may be constraints on what is provided, for example due to takeover regulations. The due diligence process may also be limited by the practicalities of gaining access to management and records. Therefore, where pre-closure due diligence is limited, post-acquisition anti-corruption due diligence is critical as this will enable the purchaser to review to a necessary scope and depth.

SIGNPOST

Make sure that anti-bribery due diligence starts at the beginning of the due diligence process; often it is left until the late stages which can have severe consequences – for example, a significant bribery issue may be discovered that endangers the investment or pressure to complete may lead to cutting corners.

Initial actions once the due diligence process is initiated

1. A manager is appointed to lead the anti-bribery component of the overall due diligence process. The manager should have the necessary expertise in finance and business case evaluation as well as practical experience of anti-bribery programmes ands will, if appropriate, put together a team of internal and external experts.
2. The anti-bribery due diligence team make an initial assessment of the target's bribery risks in order to make the case about what resources will be needed and what level of due diligence will be proportionate to the apparent risks.
3. The acquisition team communicates the launch of the project to the relevant internal teams and external advisers along with the expectation that they will cooperate in the anti-bribery due diligence.
4. At the initial meetings held with the internal teams and advisers, the anti-bribery component of the due diligence is given proper consideration alongside other aspects of due diligence. The initial meetings should include a cross-functional meeting.
5. A timetable with milestones is developed - the time allocated for completion will vary widely with each situation but adequate time should be allocated to the anti-bribery due diligence.
6. The information needed for anti-bribery due diligence is scoped and prioritised. This will mean making judgements on what is vital and what is 'nice to have', by striking a balance between the time schedule, resources available for due diligence, the target's willingness to undergo detailed scrutiny, and the need to ensure that issues are not overlooked.
7. A decision is made on the period to be reviewed for the anti-bribery due diligence. No absolute guidance can be given on the period but the purchaser will take into account among others, relevant statutes of limitation and the nature of the target's business e.g. the due diligence would look back further in a business engaged in major construction contracts than a retail business. A typical period for review might be three to five years.

STAGE 2: INITIAL SCREENING

SIGNPOST

Don't rely upon someone else's due diligence work. Risk approaches and risk circumstances are never the same. Each transaction is a fresh start.

This phase comprises initial external screening and first discussions will also be held with the target to:

- Understand its anti-bribery approach and programme and willingness to share information.
- Assess the commitment of the target's board and leadership to integrity and the target's anti-bribery programme.
- Identify any apparent significant exposures or risks related to bribery and discuss these with the management of the target.
- If the risks are high and remediation does not seem an option, this may lead to the proposed investment being dropped at this first stage before deeper due diligence is undertaken.

Factors related to corruption risk that can contribute to a decision not to proceed can include:

- Current investigations by the authorities involving the target;
- Lax management;
- Poor internal controls when operating in countries and sectors with high risks of corruption;
- Dependence on key associated persons known to be of poor or questionable integrity.

10

The acquisition team may carry out this phase through internal resources or by appointing an external adviser such as a legal firm, forensic accountant or a risk consultancy that specialises in anti-corruption work. The work can include asking the external advisers to undertake discreet checks on local and sector sources to determine if there are any potential bribery issues related to the target.

SIGNPOST

For an initial screening, the target can be sent an anti-corruption questionnaire in which it is asked to answer relevant questions e.g., where the company does business, its use of intermediaries, government officials

STAGE 3: DETAILED ANALYSIS

At this stage the detailed review is carried out, to a degree that is proportionate with the bribery risks. If an M&A, the parties, unless it is a hostile bid, would have agreed in principle that a deal should be pursued. This may be formalised in a term sheet where a preliminary understanding of the terms of the deal will have been reached, but before the signing of a binding contract. Much of the detailed examination will be done remotely online and by telephone with access to a virtual data room. Additionally, in some instances there will be the wish or necessity to visit countries of operation or the physical data room. It is likely that there will be restrictions on access to the target's information and data unless concerns or issues are identified which demand that full information be supplied.

As this stage may involve substantial detailed and specialist examination of the target, consideration may be given to appointing appropriate experts specialising in anti-bribery investigation and relevant legislation including the UK Bribery Act and the US FCPA. In certain transactions it is common for some or all of these activities to be carried out by the purchaser's external advisors.

The detailed review is carried out to a degree that is proportionate with the bribery risks

SIGNPOST

Much can be learnt from assessing the target's tone from the top. For example, determining whether bribery risks and the anti-bribery programme are on the agendas of board meetings; the extent of involvement of those at the very top of the organisation in anti-bribery training and communications, and actions taken by senior management when integrity and bribery issues are identified.

This stage commences with a request for detailed information from the management of the target, to be considered by the purchaser.

The stage concludes with preparation of an anti-bribery due diligence report for the deal or portfolio management team to consider alongside other due diligence (e.g., legal and financial etc). The report would be produced by the support functions, who might typically include the legal counsel, finance department, compliance officer, internal anti-corruption experts, and any other relevant functions such as corporate affairs, as well as external advisers.

As in stage 2, if risks are identified, the purchaser will explore how such risks could be mitigated. Certain risks, such as historical bribery, may require discussion with the authorities. If the risks cannot be mitigated and it is concluded that they are unacceptable the proposal may be dropped at this stage.

A thorough review will typically cover the activities listed below:

- *Detailed review of the target's markets and competitors'* activities to help form an assessment of whether bribery is a known or likely factor.
- *Corporate intelligence and background checks* undertaken on the target's business and key owners/directors and management.
- *The target's anti-bribery programme* examined in detail to assess its adequacy and any risks of bribery.
- *Assessing the tone from the top of the target company,* for example through using interviews with senior managers and directors to discuss the target's anti bribery programme, issues and risks.
- *Interviewing management representatives in key functions that represent bribery risks* (such as sales directors in certain markets). This will also involve assessing their openness to post-acquisition improvement in the target's anti-bribery programme as part of the integration process.
- *External interviews and site visits.* In addition to internal sources within the target, external sources will be interviewed including obtaining informal comments from actors within the relevant sectors and countries, such as customers, suppliers, industry experts, regulatory authorities, business associations, embassy officials, NGOs.
- *Walk-through tests,* carried out to confirm that policies and procedures are effectively implemented.
- *Review of data* provided by the target company – this will usually be located in a data room.
- *Detailed financial review* is a key aspect of the due diligence, and is outlined in the box below.

Due diligence financial review

A key part of the anti bribery due diligence is to address the veracity of financial transactions and it would be expected to cover the following:

- Understand the financial processes of the target In order to identify the data to be requested and be able to know that data provided is complete – the review team must be able to understand and navigate through the target's financial systems, as well as being able to understand the target's technology platform.
- Check that the financial system and finance function have appropriate controls, e.g., segregation of duties.
- Carry out extraction, and reconciliation, of accounting data together with careful analysis of the supporting documentation.
- Review of financial transactions should start with the audited accounts where these are available and a detailed listing of transactions that formed those accounts (together these are termed the 'ledger') – it will be important to ensure these accounts are reconciled for the review team to be assured that it has been given the correct information.
- Detailed scrutiny of books and records including electronic data and analysis of accounts in sufficient detail to be able to examine line entries which could be problematic, for example:
  - Expense transactions are recorded in a way that enables the substance of the transaction to be identified, including nature of product or service, price, provider and beneficiary of payments;
  - Sales transactions are recorded in such a way that the substance of the transaction can be identified, including the goods or services sold, the customer, the payor and the price;
  - Underlying records are available for inspection and able to be linked to specific transactions.
- The target should be expected to provide all supporting documentation to transactions including, where relevant, emails.
- Use of forensic software can help in identifying transactions for close scrutiny.
- Analytical tests on data and then examination of samples (this includes a review of supporting documentation) of:
  a. High risk payments to distributors, subcontractors, and/or consultants.
  b. High risk transactions paid for using cash.
  c. Payments for high risk expense types (includes visas, customs, taxes, government certificates, licences, bonuses, commissions, gifts, entertainment, travel, donations, marketing).
  d. Employee expense reports for high risk transactions.
  e. High risk revenue side transactions including price setting, discounts, credit notes and free of charge goods.

12

> **SIGNPOST**
>
> When carrying out financial analysis, the review team should first understand the financial processes of the target in order to identify the data to be requested and to then know that the data provided is complete.

STAGE 4: DECISION

The portfolio management or M&A team will prepare a proposal for the purchase or investment for review by the acquisition committee or equivalent body. The proposal will include a review of the due diligence findings related to bribery, any identified issues and how these could be mitigated, including discussions with the relevant authorities. Where the bribery risk is judged to be high, the purchaser must decide whether or not it should withdraw from the planned investment.

However, even when the bribery risk is considered high, there is an option to proceed and this might typically involve:

- Discussing with the management of the target how its anti-bribery programme could be brought to the required adequate level, risks remediated, contracts potentially renegotiated and re-tendered, and how any corrupt employees and associates would be removed from the target;
- Discussing the bribery concerns with the relevant legal authorities with a view to obtaining an opinion on whether proposed remedial actions would be satisfactory and that the purchaser would not be liable to criminal charges and sanctions.

If satisfactory assurances are obtained, the investment committee or executive review body can make its decision and the proposal will then proceed to the partners or board for approval.

> **SIGNPOST**
>
> In the UK, the SFO has advised that it encourages purchasers which discover problems in the course of M&A due diligence to talk to the SFO about what they propose to do if the acquisition goes ahead. The SFO states that it wants to be in a position to give assurance about the approach of the SFO if the company does carry out the programme of work for anti-bribery.

STAGE 5: POST-ACQUISITION DUE DILIGENCE

Due diligence continues after the investment is completed and will be critical and urgent if access to information has been restricted or denied in the pre-purchase phases as may often be the case.

If insufficient information was obtained to undertake a satisfactory due diligence pre-closure, this should be initiated as soon as the transaction completes. In such circumstances, the stages of due diligence outlined above should be taken post-completion with a clearly-defined timetable.

Remedial action will be needed if bribery risks are identified and it will be necessary to report suspected bribery promptly to the authorities. If the purchaser identifies any bribery issues quickly after acquisition and commits to full cooperation with the authorities, this could assist in reaching a settlement.

SIGNPOST

Companies can be especially vulnerable to side-lining anti-bribery issues in the post-acquisition integration. With many other issues to consider and the handover from a deal team to an integration team, anti-bribery due diligence and integration can easily be neglected. However, good practice is for it to form part of a post-completion phase such as a ninety-day plan.

STAGE 6: POST-ACQUISITION INTEGRATION AND MONITORING

At the same time as post-acquisition due diligence is being carried out, integration starts to bring the acquired company in line with the purchaser's anti-bribery programme. The post-acquisition due diligence will contribute to this by establishing any inadequacies in the acquired company's anti-bribery programme.

Depending on the size and nature of the purchased business, the post-acquisition due diligence and integration process can take a considerable time, possibly up to twenty-four months, as the revised anti-bribery programme will have to be amended or designed and then rolled out across the business operations of the acquired company.

When the integration process is complete, the acquired company or investment should be monitored as part of the purchaser's anti-bribery programme.

14

4.   CHECKLIST

This section provides a checklist of indicators as an aid to due diligence (referred to in the checklist as DD). The checklist is a general guide; it cannot be comprehensive as the scope and depth of due diligence will be determined by the purchaser's risk approach and the particular circumstances and risks of the target. Each M&A and acquisition will present unique circumstances.

It is stressed that the checklist should not be used as a 'tick-box approach' for due diligence but as an aid to prompt thinking about the areas to be considered during due diligence. Due diligence often involves subjective decisions based on qualitative information. Being able to tick every box will not in itself demonstrate that the due diligence is comprehensive in scope or carried out adequately. The purchaser should use this guidance as a starting point and through experience build on this and tailor it as a tool for use in due diligence on acquisitions and investments.

	Bribery due diligence process	Reviewed	Yet to be completed	Comment reference no.	Evidence reference no.
1	Is the bribery DD integrated into the DD process from the start?				
2	Have milestones been set for the bribery DD?				
3	Is the timetable adequate for effective anti-bribery DD?				
4	Have the deal and DD teams been trained in their company's anti-bribery programme including the significance of relevant legislation?				
5	Have the deal and DD teams been trained in anti-bribery DD?				
6	Is there a process implemented for co-ordination across functions?				
7	Has legal privilege been established with use of general counsel and external legal advisers?				
8	Is there a process for dealing with any bribery discovered during the DD?				
9	Is the person responsible for anti-bribery due diligence at a sufficiently senior level to influence the transaction's decision-makers?				

Inherent risks: geographical and sector

A target such as an extractives company operating in countries where corruption is prevalent will present higher risks than one operating only in developed countries in lower risk sectors. Some sectors such as construction and engineering, defence and healthcare, are known to have higher risks than others. However, companies that operate in difficult countries or sectors are more likely to have developed advanced anti-bribery programmes to mitigate the higher risks.

There are a number of resources that can be referred to in mapping geographical and sector risks. Transparency International provides surveys of aspects of corruption, notably the Corruption Perceptions Index which can be consulted for evaluation of corruption risks in the countries and business sectors in which the company is doing business.[5] A risk map can be useful in developing a picture of the target organisation's vulnerability – this will score countries, sectors and other risk areas.

---

5. *Surveys and risk-mapping resources include the Corruption Perceptions Index; the Bribe Payers Index; the Global Corruption Barometer; and National Integrity Studies. These can be downloaded from www.transparency.org*

Geographical and sector risks		Reviewed	Yet to be completed	Comment reference no.	Evidence reference no.
10	Is the target dependent on operations in countries where corruption is prevalent?				
11	Does the target operate in sectors known to be prone to high risk of bribery?				
12	Are competitors suspected to be actively using bribery in the target's markets?				

Business model risks

The organisational structure of the target and its business model should be reviewed as these may present inherent risks of bribery.

The target may be heavily decentralised, creating the risk of inconsistency in carrying through an anti-bribery programme across its operations. It may allow subsidiaries to adopt anti-bribery programmes to varying standards of practice.

There can be risks where the target is dependent on the award of large public or private sector contracts such as construction or critical licenses such as in telecommunications or the health sectors. It should be noted that bribery scandals have also occurred related to large public contracts in developed countries. If a market includes competitors that are actively bribing to win contracts this will be a risk both from the pressure on employees and intermediaries to make bribes and the imbalance it creates in the sector when contracts are not won on merit. The risks on large contracts or obtaining of licenses will also depend on the use agents and other intermediaries which are common areas of risk.

Where critical functions such as property, facilities, purchasing and contracts and accounting are outsourced, it will require greater attention to ensure the anti-bribery programme is embedded in their activities.

Business model risks		Reviewed	Yet to be completed	Comment reference no.	Evidence reference no.
13	Does the organisational structure of the target foster an effective anti-bribery programme or present risks?				
14	Is the target dependent on large contracts or critical licenses?				
15	Does the target implement an adequate anti-bribery programme in its subsidiaries?				
16	Is the target reliant on agents or other intermediaries?				
17	Has the target been assessed for its exposure to use of intermediaries that operate in countries and sectors prone to corruption risks?				
18	Does it have policies and effective systems to counter risks related to intermediaries?				
19	Does the target require contractual anti-bribery standards of its suppliers?				
20	Does the target's organisational structure present bribery risks – e.g. diversified structure?				
21	Is the target reliant on outsourcing and if so do the contracted outsourcers show evidence of commitment and effective implementation of the target's anti-bribery programme?				

Legislative footprint

While the UK Bribery Act and FCPA are important pieces of legislation, and are referred to in this guidance and the Annex, the purchaser should ensure that the target meets all relevant regulatory requirements in order to provide appropriate protection.

	Legislative footprint	Reviewed	Yet to be completed	Comment reference no.	Evidence reference no.
22	Is the target subject to the UK Bribery Act and/or the US FCPA?				
23	Are there equivalent laws from other jurisdictions that are relevant?				

Organisational

The purchaser should look for evidence that the target has an anti-bribery culture that is fully integrated into the corporate culture. This can be deduced, for example, by examining the commitment of the target's board and top management to integrity, both in embedding integrity in the target and to their personal integrity, measures of communication and training of employees and results of surveys of employee and supplier attitudes. There should be research to determine if there are any corruption allegations or incidents related to main shareholders and investors, directors and senior management of the target. Activism by shareholders and investors in requiring a culture of anti-corruption in the target will be a positive factor. There may be structural characteristics of the organisation that foster anti-corruption or conversely, present risk that the anti-bribery programme is poorly communicated and overseen.

	Organisational	Reviewed	Yet to be completed	Comment reference no.	Evidence reference no.
24	Does the target's board and leadership show commitment to embedding anti-bribery in their company?				
25	Does the target exhibit a culture of commitment to ethical business conduct? (Use evidence such as results of employee surveys)				
26	Has the senior management of the target carried out an assessment of bribery risk in the business?				
27	Have there been any corruption allegations or convictions related to members of the target's board or management?				
28	Have the main shareholders or investors in the target had a history of activism related to the integrity of the target?				
29	Have there been any corruption allegations or convictions related to the main shareholders or investors in the target?				
30	Does the target have an active audit committee that oversees anti-corruption effectively?				

---

6. *Guidance to the UK Bribery Act 2010 and good practice for corporate anti-bribery programmes – available from* http://www.transparency.org.uk/working-with-companies/adequate-procedures

7. *The terminology 'Foreign Public Official' or FPO is commonly used, although bribery of domestic officials is also illegal in most jurisdictions*

Anti-bribery Programme

The due diligence must establish the adequacy of the target's anti-bribery programme. Any deficiencies will present risks. External anti-bribery advisers can be used to assess the adequacy of the programme.

Anti-bribery Programme		Reviewed	Yet to be completed	Comment reference no.	Evidence reference no.
31	Does the target have an anti-bribery programme that matches that recommended by Transparency International UK?[6]				
32	Is the anti-bribery programme based on an adequate risk-based approach?				
33	Is the anti-bribery programme implemented and effective?				

Key bribery risks

There are high risk areas that should be singled out for review and these are listed below.

Key bribery risks		Reviewed	Yet to be completed	Comment reference no.	Evidence reference no.
34	Has the target been assessed for its exposure to risk of paying large bribes in public contracts or to kickbacks?				
35	Has the target been assessed for risks attached to hospitality and gifts?				
36	Has the target been assessed for risks attached to travel expenses?				
37	Has the target been assessed for risks attached to political contributions?				
38	Has the target been assessed for risks attached to charitable donations and sponsorships?				
39	Has the target been assessed for risks attached to facilitation payments?				

(Foreign) public officials (FPOs)[7]		Reviewed	Yet to be completed	Comment reference no.	Evidence reference no.
40	Is there an implemented policy and process for identifying and managing situations where FPOs are associated with intermediaries, customers and prospects?				
41	Have any FPOs been identified that are associated with intermediaries, customers and prospects?				
42	Is there an implemented policy and process for identifying and managing situations where FPOs are associated with intermediaries, customers and prospects?				
43	Have any FPOs been identified that present particular risk?				
44	Is there evidence or suspicion that subsidiaries or intermediaries are being used to disguise or channel corrupt payments to FPOs or others?				

Financial and ledger analysis[8]	Reviewed	Yet to be completed	Comment reference no.	Evidence reference no.
45	Have the financial tests listed on page 11 been carried out?				
46	Are the beneficiaries of banking payments clearly identifiable?				
47	Is there evidence of payments being made to intermediaries in countries different to where the intermediary is located and if so are the payments valid?				
48	Is there evidence of regular orders being placed in batches just below the approval level?				
49	Are payments rounded, especially in currencies with large denominations?				
50	Are suppliers appointed for valid reasons?				
51	Is there evidence of suppliers created for bribery e.g. just appointed for the transaction, no VAT registration?				
52	Is there evidence of special purpose vehicles created to act as channels for bribery?				

Incidents

The history of any incidents of bribery related to the target needs to known. This information will be obtained from a schedule provided by the target and review by forensic advisers.

Incidents	Reviewed	Yet to be completed	Comment reference no.	Evidence reference no.
53	Has a schedule and description been provided of pending or threatened government, regulatory or administrative proceedings, inquiries or investigations or litigation related to bribery and other corruption?				
54	Has the target provided a schedule of any internal investigations over the past five years into bribery allegations?				
55	Has the target been involved in any bribery incidents or investigations not reported by the target?				
56	Has the target sanctioned any employees or directors in the past five years for violations related to bribery?				
57	Has the target sanctioned any business partners in the past five years for violations related to bribery?				
58	Is there an implemented policy and process for reporting bribery when discovered during due diligence?				

Audit reports	Reviewed	Yet to be completed	Comment reference no.	Evidence reference no.
59	Has the target provided any reviews, reports or audits, internal and external, carried out on the implementation of its anti-bribery programme?				

---

8. *In certain transactions, for example with a high-risk target where there is a strong likelihood of bribery, the financial and ledger analysis will be a particularly important part of the process. In such cases, a deep-dive ledger analysis would comprise a fuller range of indicators than is listed here*

ANNEX I:
THE LEGAL CONTEXT

A.1 INTRODUCTION

This section aims to assist purchasers and investors in understanding the implications for transactional due diligence of the legal context, including the UK Bribery Act 2010 ('the Bribery Act') and the US Foreign Corrupt Practices Act (FCPA). It compares the provisions of the Bribery Act with enforcement theories already established in this area under the FCPA. Although the focus of this section is the Bribery Act and the FCPA, each jurisdiction will have its own variants of the legal environment and enforcement scenarios outlined in this section.

While it is likely that much anti-bribery due diligence will be driven by legal obligations, it is important to recognise that taking a good practice approach will be the best way to avoid both legal liabilities and the potential financial and reputational damage that may come from investing in or purchasing a company associated with bribery.

A.2 UK BRIBERY ACT

For the first time, the proper conduct of transactional due diligence will be considered necessary as part of a company's response to UK anti-bribery law. The mergers and acquisitions process now requires adequate due diligence in order to avoid Bribery Act liability. The legal requirements for due diligence for minority investors under the Bribery Act are less clear although there is greater clarity over their liabilities under the FCPA.

A.2.1 Current corruption by the target company

The Bribery Act creates four new offences of bribery. Paying a bribe, receiving a bribe and bribing a foreign public official are the 'principal' offences. The fourth offence is of failure by a commercial organisation to prevent bribery (the 'failure to prevent bribery offence').

It is too soon to know how the Bribery Act will be interpreted and enforced. However a preliminary analysis of the Bribery Act suggests that there is likely to be liability related to failures in due diligence for the purchaser when there is current or continuing bribery by an acquired company[9]. Enforcement action could be based upon the following scenarios:

a) Pre-closing due diligence is performed and current or continuing bribery is not identified and the diligence was inadequate. Following completion of the transaction the bribery continues and is undertaken by an associated person, e.g., an employee of the acquired company.

b) Bribery risks are identified in pre-closing due diligence but there is a failure to follow up adequately the risks identified during integration and/or through normal post-closing procedures. Bribery, that should have been uncovered through a proper follow up of the risks revealed in the due diligence, continues, and is undertaken by an associated person, e.g., an employee of the acquired company.

---

9. Ministry of Justice Guidance issued on 30 March 2011 (MoJ Guidance) para 42

A.2.2 Liability for a principal offence in a transaction

As a generality, liability for a principal offence arises where the purchaser knowingly joins with, encourages or turns a blind eye to (by way of consent or connivance) the bribery activities of the target and its employees or associated persons.

The purchaser will commit a principal bribery offence in cases where the diligence process has revealed bribery by the target and where the purchaser continues with the bribery or allows it to continue post-acquisition.

Equally, if the purchasing company knows of continuing bribery and deliberately fails to conduct diligence so that the deal completes, this conduct could be viewed as criminal intent to participate in continuing corruption.

A.2.3 Liability for the failure to prevent a bribery offence

A failure by a purchaser to discover continuing corruption will not make a person or company liable for a principal bribery offence. However, if the undiscovered bribery continues post-acquisition, and is subsequently discovered, the company may be guilty of the 'failure to prevent' offence.

This liability might be reinforced if poor anti-bribery due diligence was carried out. The Bribery Act provides a defence if an entity can demonstrate that it had established 'adequate procedures' to prevent bribery by associated persons, and it is likely that effective anti-bribery due diligence during M&A transactions would be viewed as an 'adequate procedure'.

Indeed, the Ministry of Justice (MoJ) Guidance references the requirement to carry out thorough due diligence in the mergers and acquisitions context[10], although little specific attention has been given to the basis of criminal liability in this context either in the MoJ Guidance or in authoritative public statements from the SFO.

A.2.4 Historic bribery by the target company

Concluded or 'historic' conduct, regardless of whether undiscovered or not revealed in the due diligence process, probably would not create liability in respect of the principal offences of the Bribery Act or the 'failure to prevent' offence.

This appears to be the case principally because it is only from the date of closing that the target becomes factually 'associated' with the purchaser. At the time the offences were committed by the target, it was not associated with the purchaser.

Further the purpose of the conduct would, in all likelihood, have been for the benefit of the target, not for the purchaser. Consequently it seems unlikely that the SFO would be able to bring an enforcement action for failure to prevent bribery based on the historic and concluded conduct of the target. However, the individuals involved in the bribery would be still liable to prosecution, which might well impact on the purchaser.

Moreover, where the purchaser benefits from historic corruption or purchases an asset tainted by corruption, it may have liability under the Proceeds of Crime Act 2002 (POCA). Historic bribery is likely to create an inherited liability for the purchaser under the FCPA in the US.

---

10. *MoJ Guidance para 4.4*

A.2.5 Bribery may trigger liability under other UK laws

Bribery can also be investigated and prosecuted under a variety of UK laws. Bribery investigations sometimes begin as money laundering allegations, and penalties can be secured under laws other than those specific to bribery offences such as the POCA in the UK.

For example, where a merger or acquisition results in the purchase of a target that either historically or currently is involved in bribery or, where a merger or acquisition is primarily the acquisition of an asset which itself has been obtained by bribery or other illegality, there is likely to be a benefit to the acquiring company. Going forward, there is also likely to be a revenue stream from the target or asset that accrues to the purchaser. In short the purchaser may acquire 'criminal property' and risk committing a money laundering offence under POCA, which can bring associated reporting obligations.

Cases have also been brought in relation to 'books and records offences' which, in the UK, are essentially charges brought under the Company's Act 1985 for failure to keep adequate accounting records.

A.3 US LAW AND ENFORCEMENT

The US Department of Justice (DOJ) has penalised companies for their failure to conduct transactional due diligence adequately in numerous enforcement actions and settlements under the FCPA. These enforcement actions and settlements provide a basis for understanding when the DOJ will bring an enforcement action and the legal basis for it. Additionally the DOJ has also provided guidance to companies through its Opinion Release Procedure, most notably in relation to Halliburton's proposed purchase of a UK-based company.[11]

The FCPA prohibits payments to foreign officials, foreign political parties or officials, or candidates for foreign political office in order to obtain, retain, or direct business.[12] The FCPA also requires issuers to maintain accurate books and records and a system of internal accounting controls. In the case of foreign corporations, the FCPA applies to issuers, or foreign companies that register securities on a U.S. securities exchange. If a foreign corporation is not an issuer, there must be some other connection to the US for jurisdiction to be implicated.

FCPA due diligence is now a standard component of a merger or acquisition, in part because the DOJ has taken a number of enforcement actions based on due diligence failures pre- or post-closing and/or the purchasers' failures to monitor compliance properly in the post-closing integration phase.

A.3.1 FCPA enforcement and successor liability

Enforcement actions have been based on two prosecutorial theories:

- First, that undiscovered pre-acquisition bribery conduct is inherited by the successor entity;
- Secondly, the purchaser also accrues failures subsequently to address bribery risks that are identified in the diligence process post-dating the closure of the transaction.

FCPA due diligence is now a standard component of a merger or acquisition, in part because the DOJ has taken a number of enforcement actions based on due diligence failures

11. *Opinion Release 08-02. See 15 U.S.C.A. §§ 78dd-1(a); 78dd-2(a); 78dd-3(a)*
12. *See 15 U.S.C. § 78m(b)*

22

US regulators approach successor liability under the FCPA for pre-transaction conduct by seeking to impose liability for knowingly purchasing or investing in circumstances where there is corrupt activity by the counterparty.[13]

> In 2009, the DOJ secured a conviction against investor Frederick Bourke in a related criminal trial for conspiring to violate the FCPA in relation to an $8 million investment by Bourke in a consortium which was seeking to invest in the privatisation of the State Oil Company of the Azerbaijan Republic (SOCAR).
>
> The DOJ successfully pursued the theory that Bourke had actual knowledge, or should have known – and was wilfully blind in not knowing - that the investment consortium provided improper gifts and payments to Azeri government officials in order to increase the likelihood that the privatisation would occur.
>
> At trial, the DOJ focused on Bourke's failure to conduct due diligence, failure to engage an experienced law firm to conduct any such due diligence on his behalf and that he ignored 'red flags' that would have alerted him to the corrupt nature of the investment.[14] The case continues on appeal and the eventual outcome is far from certain. However, it illustrates a potential approach the DOJ may take towards investors.

A.3.2 The role of anti-bribery due diligence in reducing FCPA-related risk

In a series of Opinion Procedure Releases, the DOJ has suggested that companies can minimise liability or insulate themselves from liability for unlawful payments made by foreign entities they are seeking to acquire by performing adequate due diligence prior to acquisition, disclosing any pre-acquisition misconduct to the government, and implementing effective compliance procedures to avoid further unlawful activity by the acquired entities.[15]

The DOJ and the Securities & Exchange Commission (SEC) generally take the position that 'red flags' identified during the due diligence must be fully investigated to determine whether a corrupt payment in fact occurred.

The unstated premise of these Opinion Procedure Releases is that a company that does not engage in adequate diligence and promptly disclose pre-acquisition misconduct by the entity that is to be acquired might face enforcement action for FCPA violations that occurred before the close of the transaction.

A.3.3 FCPA and liability for historical bribery

The DOJ and the SEC have taken the position that liability can attach for pre-acquisition conduct and have brought enforcement actions consistent with this approach. It is worth noting, however, that in these cases it seemed the illicit payments by the target continued past the closing date of

The DOJ and the SEC have taken the position that liability can attach for pre-acquisition conduct and have brought enforcement actions consistent with this approach

---

13. *U.S. Announces Settlement with Hedge Fund Omega Advisors, Inc. in Connection with Omega's Investment in Privatization Program in Azerbaijan*, Dep't of Justice Press Release No. 07-172, July 6, 2007, http://www.justice.gov/criminal/fraud/fcpa/cases/docs/07-06-07omega-settlement.pdf

14. *Connecticut Investor Found Guilty in Massive Scheme to Bribe Senior Government Officials in the Republic of Azerbaijan*, Dep't of Justice Press Release No. 09-667, July 9, 1020, http://www.justice.gov/criminal/fraud/fcpa/cases/docs/07-10-09bourke-verdict-sdny.pdf

15. U.S.C.A. §§ 78dd-1(a); 78dd-2(a); 78dd-3(a)

the transaction, and the government sought to charge the parent company for all the pre- and post-acquisition misconduct collectively. Whether the DOJ would bring an enforcement action for solely pre-acquisition conduct, and whether a court would uphold such a prosecution if challenged, are both open questions.

However, as the DOJ's recent Opinion Procedure Releases make clear, if a company undertakes sufficient due diligence in advance of the transaction and discloses any unlawful payments uncovered as a part of that investigation, it may be able to protect itself from prosecution. With respect to liability for unlawful activity occurring post-transaction, the DOJ has made clear that 'an acquiring company may be held liable as a matter of law for any unlawful payments made by an acquired company or its personnel after the date of acquisition.'[16]

Indeed, in recent years both the DOJ and the SEC have brought enforcement actions under the FCPA against parent companies for unlawful payments made by their newly-acquired subsidiaries, even though the bribes were made only shortly after the acquisition was completed. When charging violations of the FCPA under these circumstances, the DOJ and SEC have highlighted the failure of the acquiring company to perform adequate due diligence in advance of the transaction in order to uncover corrupt payments, or the failure of the company to take corrective action when diligence suggests the possibility that unlawful payments have been made in the past.[17]

A.4 ADDITIONAL CONSIDERATIONS FOR PRIVATE EQUITY INVESTMENT

There may be additional legal concerns for private equity companies in relation to the Bribery Act, over and above those encountered in M&A activity. For example, where senior officers of a private equity company participate or consent to or connive with the investment target or portfolio company there is potential liability for a principal bribery offence. Under the FCPA, the DOJ may develop an enforcement action based upon a knowing or reckless failure to diligence – whether it be in the majority or minority investment context.

Under the Bribery Act, one area of uncertainty is whether a private equity firm or a passive investor can be liable for their failure to conduct effective diligence over the actions of the target or portfolio company either during the investment or, in the case of private equity, during the management phase. Irrespective of this, it is good practice for private equity companies to undertake effective anti-bribery due diligence.

Often, but not always, the investment target or portfolio company does not perform services 'for or on behalf' of the investor or private equity firm and consequently they cannot be associates. However it is likely that the SFO will want to investigate where they consider the relationship is one where there is sufficient control over the associate and sufficient benefit to the investor or private equity firm. It is likely that the SFO will seek to penetrate corporate structures designed to frustrate the purposes of the legislation. Importantly in that respect, the Bribery Act defines an associate broadly, 'irrespective of capacity' and by reference to 'all the circumstances and not merely by reference to the nature of the relationship between the associated person and the commercial organisation.'[18]

Consequently, where the investor or the private equity firm in fact exercises strong control over

---

16. *DOJ Opinion Procedure Release No. 08-02 (June 13, 2008)*

17. *See, e.g., SEC Brings Settled Charges Against Tyco International Ltd. Alleging Billion Dollar Accounting Fraud, SEC Litigation Release No. 19657, Accounting & Auditing Enforcement Release No. 2414 (Apr. 17, 2006), http://www.sec.gov/litigation/litreleases/2006/lr19657.htm*

18. *Section 8(3)*

24

the portfolio company – it is possible that the SFO might develop enforcement actions. These could be based upon their being 'associates' for the purposes of the Bribery Act if the portfolio company bribes another person for the benefit or business advantage of the investor or private equity firm.

Furthermore, the recent use in the Mabey & Johnson case by the SFO of the Proceeds of Crime Act 2002 (POCA) to confiscate from a parent/holding company the dividends relating to corrupt transactions creates an additional precedent that is highly relevant to private equity investors.[19]

A.5 DUE DILIGENCE OBLIGATIONS FOR MINORITY INVESTMENTS

While the Bribery Act and FCPA create a clear legal rationale to perform due diligence in an acquisition or where the purchaser takes a majority or controlling investment, the point at which a minority investment become too small to warrant full due diligence remains an open question. Likewise, the legal risk to a minority investor or private equity firm in a non-controlling investment relationship is unclear. There is not an exact correlation between size of stake and the possible legal risks. In some cases, even taking a small stake in a corrupt company where the investor knew or where it could be inferred that it knew that the company was engaged in bribery could lead to a legal liability whether under the Bribery Act or when the private equity firm suspects bribery and fails to report its suspicion under POCA.

The investor must therefore judge the level of due diligence taking into account various factors. These will include the value of the investment, the percentage of ownership, the degree of influence over the target, the risks attached to the target such as markets and sectors, the reputational risk, the legal risk and the risk appetite. Each situation will depend on its own precise circumstances.

In the UK, there has to date been limited regulatory guidance on these questions. However, in response to questions over private equity, the Director of the SFO has stated:

"[One] issue ... is your responsibility if any of the companies that you own pays bribes. You might at first think that this is nothing to do with you as the owners of the company. It might be that as portfolio owners you are not committing an offence of failing to prevent bribery. But it does not end there... we will be looking at money laundering in order to see what money has been laundered as a result of the criminal conduct and to whom it has gone. It may be indeed that the owners have some knowledge of the contract that was obtained through bribery. We will be thinking about money laundering."[20]

A.6 REPORTING OBLIGATIONS

The presumption of this guidance is that, as good practice, any incidence of bribery discovered during due diligence should be reported to the appropriate authorities. Purchasers may use their discretion, bearing in mind factors such as proportionality in reporting, the deal timetable and their own legal obligations, but it is in their interest to report to authorities as in this way they can discuss the issue and establish how the bribery could affect the deal.

Reporting obligations vary by jurisdiction. In the UK, for example, reporting is mandatory in the

---

19. http://www.sfo.gov.uk/press-room/latest-press-releases/press-releases-2012/
shareholder-agrees-civil-recovery-by-sfo-in-mabey--johnson.aspx
20. Speech of 21 June 2011

money laundering context but discretionary when corruption is discovered. It is legally required in many jurisdictions, and professional advisors are often subject to separate regulations that may require them to report criminal behaviour. In the UK, for example, when a corrupt scheme is discovered, there may be a legal obligation to make a Suspicious Activity Report (SAR) to SOCA, and corruption-based SARs are automatically flagged to the SFO. There are enhanced requirements under POCA for firms involved in the regulated sector.

If a purchaser or investor subject to the FCPA discovers bribery or bribery indicators in a target, there are advantages in reporting the issues raised by due diligence to the DOJ and this may be done jointly with the target. At this point the purchaser or investor may decide not to proceed with the transaction but it could wait to see if the target can reach a settlement with the DOJ to clear the way for the M&A or investment to go ahead with no risk of successor liability.

In the UK, the SFO has stated that it is sympathetic to situations where a purchaser or investor reports that it has discovered corruption as part of due diligence[21] and that, in certain circumstances, it will take no action if the purchaser is committed to anti-bribery remedial actions.

It is unclear whether that stance is dependent upon the purchaser disclosing the corruption prior to closing. The Director of the SFO has stated with regard to private equity investments:

"What we encourage companies to do in those circumstances is to come to us as soon as they can after the acquisition in order to talk to us about the issues that they are finding...We would therefore be sympathetic if a company came to us and said that it had recently taken over another company and that there were a number of issues concerning corruption that had been identified. In those circumstances I can see little benefit in an SFO investigation at the corporate level...I would want the company to tell us about what it has found and about how it is proposing to deal with this. I would want to be satisfied that this is a genuine commitment and I would like to be kept informed from time to time about progress. In these circumstances I would want to let the company get on and do whatever was needed in these circumstances."[22]

It should also be noted that the SFO has sent out clear signals that senior individuals who decide not to report on-going bribery are potentially taking on personal liability. In a speech of November 2011 the Director of the SFO stated:

"The last feature of the Bribery Act that I want to draw attention to concerns the liability of senior officers of a corporation. There is a new offence that is committed by a senior officer with a UK connection who consents to or connives in bribery. You may be or you may know people who are senior officers such as Executive or Non Executive Directors of UK or foreign corporations and who have a UK connection. If you or they know about bribery and decide to do nothing about it, then you or they have connived in bribery. An offence under the Bribery Act has been committed. I tell Executives to be very careful not to turn a corporate criminal issue into a personal criminal issue. It is avoidable."

Senior individuals who decide not to report on-going bribery are potentially taking on personal liability

21. *Approach of the Serious Fraud Office to dealing with Overseas Corruption (2009) paragraphs 17–20*
22. *Speech of June 21 2011 - see http://www.SFO.gov.uk/about-us/our-views/director's-speeches/speeches-2011/private-equity-and-the-uk-bribery-act,-hosted-by-debevoise--plimpton-llp.aspx*

ANNEX II: DEFINITIONS

Agent: a representative who normally has authority to make commitments on behalf of the principal represented. The term 'representative' is being used more frequently since agent can imply more than intended and in some countries 'agent' implies power of attorney.

AML: anti-money laundering.

Anti-bribery programme:[23] the whole of a company's anti-bribery efforts including values, code of conduct, detailed policies and procedures, risk management, internal and external communication, training and guidance, internal controls, oversight, monitoring and assurance.

Business Principles for Countering Bribery: a good practice model for corporate anti-bribery policies and programmes developed through a multi-stakeholder process initiated and led by Transparency International.

Closing: the final event to complete the investment, at which time all the legal documents are signed and the funds are transferred.

Data room: physical rooms or online virtual sites used to store confidential data for disclosure to potential purchasers for the due diligence process.

Department of Justice (DOJ), USA: the central agency for enforcement of US federal laws.

Due diligence: also termed transactional due diligence, the process of investigation and evaluation of a business before making an investment or acquiring a company – in the case of anti-bribery this will be to assess any successor liability risks for past or current bribery, the adequateness of the target's anti-bribery programme and the inherent risks of bribery related to the target including its market sectors and the countries in which it operates.

Foreign Corrupt Practices Act 1977 (FCPA): a United States federal law (15 U.S.C. §§ 78dd-1, et seq.) generally prohibiting US companies and citizens and foreign companies listed on a US stock exchange from bribing foreign public officials to obtain or retain business. The FCPA also requires 'issuers' (any company including foreign companies) with securities traded on a US exchange to file periodic reports with the Securities and Exchange Commission to keep books and records that accurately reflect business transactions and to maintain effective internal controls.

Foreign Public Official (FPO): as defined in the Bribery Act, an individual who holds a legislative, administrative or judicial position of any kind, exercises a public function for or on behalf of a country or territory outside the UK or for any public agency or public company of that country or territory, or is an official or agent of a public international organisation. Unlike the FCPA, under the Bribery Act the term FPO does not include foreign political parties or candidates for foreign political office.

General partner: a partner who takes part in the daily operations of the partnership and is personally responsible for the liabilities of the partnership – see also, limited partner.

---

23. Business Principles for Countering Bribery, 2009 edition, page 6

Limited partner: a partner in a partnership who in the case of a private equity firm provides investment funds and has a share of ownership but takes no part in managing the partnership. A limited partner (LP) is not liable for any amount greater than the original investment in the partnership. The general partners pay the LPs a return on their investment that will be defined in a partnership agreement – see also, general partner.

Ministry of Justice, UK (MoJ): the UK government ministry responsible for the Bribery Act and its accompanying Guidance.

Politically Exposed Person (PEP): a person who has been entrusted with a prominent public function, is a senior political, or is closely related to such persons. By virtue of a public position and the influence it holds, and the provisions of anti-bribery acts related to FPOs, a PEP may present a higher risk related to bribery.

Portfolio company: a company in which a private equity firm invests – the portfolio comprises all the companies in which the firm invests.

Private equity firm[24]: a firm authorised that is managing or advising funds that either own or control one or more companies or have a designated capability to engage in such investment activity in the future where the company or companies are covered by the enhanced reporting guidelines for portfolio companies.

Purchaser: the investing entity – this could be a company making an acquisition or a merger, or a private equity form carrying out a portfolio investment.

Securities and Exchange Commission (SEC): the SEC is an independent United States agency which holds primary responsibility for enforcing the federal securities laws and regulating the securities industry, the nation's stock and options exchanges, and other electronic securities markets in the United States.

Serious Fraud Office (SFO): the SFO is an independent UK Government department which investigates and prosecutes serious or complex fraud, and corruption. It is part of the UK criminal justice system with jurisdiction in England, Wales and Northern Ireland but not in Scotland, the Isle of Man or the Channel Islands.

SOCA: Serious & Organised Crime Agency, UK

Target: the entity being considered for investment or acquisition.

---

24. Definition based on that given in the 2007 Walker Report

Transparency International UK

32–36 Loman Street

London SE1 0EH

Tel: 020 7922 7906

Fax: 020 7922 7907

info@transparency.org.uk

www.transparency.org.uk

Table of Cases

Index

Sigelman, Joseph, 593–594
Signer, Stephan, 548–552
Smith, Leo Winston, 453, 629 n.207
Smith & Nephew, Inc., 341, 554–555
Smith & Ouzman Ltd., 81, 645
Smith & Wesson Holding Corp., 341,
    415–417
Snamprogetti B.V., 338, 339, 340,
    502–504
sovereign wealth funds, 16–17
Spiller, Jonathan M., 490
Sporkin, Stanley, 21
sporting events, 179, 205–207
Srinivasan, Chandramowli, 366–367
SSI International Far East Ltd., 437–438
Stanley, Albert "Jack," 463–464, 475,
    501, 503
Statoil ASA, 436–437
statute of limitations, 28, 29–32, 227, 293
Steffen, Herbert, 60–61, 548–552
Steph, Jason Edward, 446–447
Stone v. Ritter, 94–96
Straub, Elek, 59–60
Stryker, 214, 414–415
subagents, subcontractors, and
    subdistributors, 153
subsidiaries, foreign, 20, 23, 65, 99–105,
    340, 668–669
successor liability, 83, 133, 137,
    155–160, 344
Sunderalingam, Periyasamy, 600–602
Syncor Taiwan, Inc., 2, 424–425

T
Technip S.A., 338, 339, 340, 500–502
Telecommunications D'Haiti S.A.M.
    (Teleco), 13
telecommunications industry, 4, 12, 13,
    26, 59–60, 144
Tenaris, S.A., 228–229, 307, 388–390
termination
    of joint ventures, 172
    of third-party contracts, 150–151
Terra Communications Comp, 12–13
territorial jurisdiction, 58–63
Tesco Supermarkets Ltd. v. Nattrass, 652, 683
Tesler, Jeffrey, 81, 473–475, 501, 503

Textron, Inc., 364–365
third parties
    agents as (*see* agents)
    annual certification of, 99, 149
    antibribery provisions on use of, 12,
        20, 58, 65
    audits of, 99, 119
    bank records of, 267–268
    compensation of, 135–136, 150
    compliance programs for, 99, 109,
        112–113, 153
    contracts with, 99, 113, 134,
        148–151, 153
    corporate disparagement by,
        268–269
    data protection restrictions for, 236
    dispute resolution with, 151
    distributors and resellers as, 25, 99,
        151–153
    due diligence on, 26, 134, 146–148, 152,
        174–175, 659
    enforcement investigations of, 345
    foreign official relationship to, 136
    interviews of, 243
    jurisdiction including, 58, 64–65
    liability for, 146, 152, 153
    penalties for violations by, 28–29
    red flags with, 135–136
    severance agreements with, 151
    subagents, subcontractors, and
        subdistributors as, 153
    termination of agreements with,
        150–151
    transactions with (*see* transactions)
    U.K. Bribery provisions on use of,
        646–647, 651–652, 659, 668–669,
        736
Thomsen, Linda, 271
Tidewater Marine International, Inc.,
    338, 521–523
Tillery, J. Kenneth, 446–447
Timms, Stephen, 187, 193–194, 203,
    418–420
Titan Corporation, 133, 209, 214, 344,
    430–431
Tolleson, Lee Allen, 489
Total, S.A., 338, 339, 340, 581–582

About the Author

Robert W. Tarun (robert.tarun@bakermckenzie.com) is a partner at Baker & McKenzie, LLP, in its San Francisco and Chicago offices. He has handled more than 100 sensitive internal investigations in the United States and in over 50 foreign countries. He regularly counsels public companies on Foreign Corrupt Practices Act, corporate governance, criminal antitrust, and other white-collar criminal matters. He has conducted anti-bribery training for multinational corporations on five continents. Mr. Tarun represents and defends U.S. and non-U.S. corporations and executives in federal grand jury investigations, in Securities and Exchange Commission proceedings, and in trials across the country involving conspiracy, criminal antitrust (price fixing, bid rigging, criminal environmental matters, and market allocation), export violations, financial fraud, FCPA charges, health care fraud, import violations, mail and wire fraud, securities fraud (accounting, insider trading, and revenue recognition), and tax fraud (U.S. and offshore) matters. He also represents corporations and executives in commercial litigation matters. He has tried over 50 federal jury trials across the country.

Mr. Tarun has represented multinational companies, boards of directors, audit committees and special committees, and executives in sensitive matters and foreign operations in over 50 jurisdictions, including Algeria, Australia, Bangladesh, Belgium, Bermuda, Bolivia, Brazil, Bulgaria, Canada, Chile, China, Colombia, Czech Republic, Ecuador, France, Germany, Gibraltar, Greece, Hong Kong, India, Indonesia, Ireland, Italy, Jamaica, Japan, Jordan, Lebanon, Libya, Lichtenstein, Macau, Mexico, Netherlands, Nigeria, Oman, Panama, Paraguay, Peru, Poland, Portugal, Romania, Russia, Qatar, Saudi Arabia, Singapore, South Korea, Spain, Switzerland, Syria, Taiwan, Turkey, Turks & Caicos, United Arab Emirates, United Kingdom, and Uruguay.

Mr. Tarun served as a federal prosecutor for 10 years in Chicago, where he was Deputy Chief of the Criminal Receiving and Appellate Division from 1979 to 1982 and the Executive Assistant U.S. Attorney from 1982 to 1985. In 1993 he co-authored and has since annually updated the treatise CORPORATE INTERNAL INVESTIGATIONS (Law Journal Press, 1993–2015). In 2010 he authored THE FOREIGN CORRUPT PRACTICES ACT HANDBOOK: A PRACTICAL GUIDE FOR MULTINATIONAL GENERAL COUNSEL, TRANSACTIONAL LAWYERS AND WHITE COLLAR CRIMINAL PRACTITIONERS, 4th edition (ABA, 2015). In 2010, he, along with Peter P. Tomczak, wrote the introductory essay for the 25th Anniversary White Collar Crime Survey—*A Proposal for a United States Department of Justice Foreign Corrupt Practices Act Leniency Policy*, 47 AM. CRIM. L. REV. 153 (Spring 2010).

In 1992 Mr. Tarun was inducted into the American College of Trial Lawyers, chaired its Federal Criminal Procedure Committee from 1999 to 2002, and served on its Board of Regents from 2003 to 2008. He drafted its *Report on the Proposed*

Codification of Disclosure of Favorable Information Under Federal Rules of Criminal Procedures 11 and 16, 41 AM. CRIM. L. REV. 93 (Winter 2003), and served as the Regent Liaison for its report *Recommended Practices for Companies and Their Counsel in Conducting Internal Investigations*, 46 AM. CRIM. L. REV. 73 (Winter 2009).

Mr. Tarun is a graduate of Stanford University (BA), DePaul University (JD), and the University of Chicago (MBA). From 2000 to 2005 he taught White Collar Criminal Practice as a Lecturer-in-Law at the University of Chicago Law School. He has served on the planning committee, has chaired, or has been a regular panelist at the annual American Bar Association National Institute on White Collar Crime, the American Bar Association and American Conference Institute Foreign Corrupt Practices Act programs, and the ABA/IBA International Cartel Workshops. He is a founder of the Wong Sun Society of San Francisco (1992).

Mr. Tarun has been listed in *Best Lawyers in America* (Commercial Litigation and White Collar Criminal Defense), Chambers USA *America's Leading Business Lawyers* (Foreign Corrupt Practices Act and White Collar Criminal Defense), *The International Who's Who of Business Lawyers—Business Crime Defense, Who's Who Legal Investigations, The 100 Top Lawyers in Illinois, Who's Who Legal Illinois Leading Business Lawyers*, and *Who's Who Legal California Leading Business Lawyers*. In 2009 the Ethisphere Institute, a leading independent think tank, named Mr. Tarun to its first annual Top Guns List, a national list of 15 white-collar criminal attorneys who are leaders in assisting corporations in effectively handling corporate compliance issues. He was the only lawyer west of Washington, D.C., so recognized. In 2012 he was appointed the independent corporate monitor for AU Optronics Corporation and AU Optronics America, corporate defendants in the Liquid Crystal Display (LCD) industry price fixing prosecution of *United States v. AU Optronics Corp.*, No. CR 09-0110 (N.D. Cal. Sept. 20, 2012). He is the first monitor ever appointed in a criminal antitrust case. Mr. Tarun is admitted to practice before the California and Illinois bars, numerous federal circuit courts of appeals, and the U.S. Supreme Court.